THE MEANING OF DIFFERENCE

American Constructions of Race and Ethnicity, Sex and Gender, Social Class, Sexuality, and Disability

A Text/Reader

Seventh Edition

Karen E. Rosenblum

George Mason University

Toni-Michelle C. Travis

George Mason University

THE MEANING OF DIFFERENCE: AMERICAN CONSTRUCTIONS OF RACE AND ETHNICITY, SEX AND GENDER, SOCIAL CLASS, SEXUALITY, AND DISABILITY, SEVENTH EDITION

Published by McGraw-Hill Education, 2 Penn Plaza, New York, NY 10121. Copyright © 2016 by McGraw-Hill Education. All rights reserved. Printed in the United States of America. Previous editions © 2012, 2008, and 2006. No part of this publication may be reproduced or distributed in any form or by any means, or stored in a database or retrieval system, without the prior written consent of McGraw-Hill Education, including, but not limited to, in any network or other electronic storage or transmission, or broadcast for distance learning.

Some ancillaries, including electronic and print components, may not be available to customers outside the United States.

This book is printed on acid-free paper.

1 2 3 4 5 6 7 8 9 0 DOC/DOC 1 0 9 8 7 6 5

ISBN 978-0-07-802702-4
MHID 0-07-802702-0

Senior Vice President, Products & Markets: *Kurt L. Strand*
Vice President, General Manager, Products & Markets: *Michael Ryan*
Vice President, Content Design & Delivery: *Kimberly Meriwether David*
Managing Director: *Gina Boedeker*
Brand Manager: *Courtney Austermehle*
Director, Product Development: *Meghan Campbell*
Product Developer: *Jamie Daron*
Marketing Manager: *Alexandra Schultz*
Director, Content Design & Delivery: *Terri Schiesl*
Program Manager: *Faye M. Herrig*
Content Project Managers: *Kelly Hart, Danielle Clement, Judi David*
Buyer: *Susan K. Culbertson*
Design: *Studio Montage, St. Louis, MO*
Cover Image: *© James Brey/Getty Images/RF*
Compositor: *Lumina Datamatics, Inc.*
Typeface: *10/12 Times Roman*
Printer: *R. R. Donnelley*

All credits appearing on page or at the end of the book are considered to be an extension of the copyright page.

Library of Congress Cataloging-in-Publication Data

Rosenblum, Karen Elaine.
The meaning of difference: American constructions of race and ethnicity, sex and gender, social class, sexuality, and disability / Karen E. Rosenblum, George Mason University, Toni-Michelle C. Travis, George Mason University.—Seventh Edition.
    pages cm
  Includes bibliographical references and index.
  ISBN 978-0-07-802702-4 (pbk.)—ISBN 0-07-802702-0 1. United States—Social conditions—1980- 2. Cultural pluralism—United States. I. Travis, Toni-Michelle, II. Title.
  HN59.2.R667 2015
  306.0973—dc23   2014036324

The Internet addresses listed in the text were accurate at the time of publication. The inclusion of a website does not indicate an endorsement by the authors or McGraw-Hill Education, and McGraw-Hill Education does not guarantee the accuracy of the information presented at these sites.

www.mhhe.com

ABOUT THE AUTHORS

KAREN E. ROSENBLUM is a professor of sociology at George Mason University in Fairfax, Virginia. She has served as the university's vice president for university life, was the founding director of its women's studies program, and was a Fulbright Lecturer in Japan and South Korea. Professor Rosenblum received her PhD in sociology from the University of Colorado, Boulder. Her areas of research and teaching include sex and gender, language, and deviance.

TONI-MICHELLE C. TRAVIS is a professor of government and politics at George Mason University in Fairfax, Virginia. Travis received her PhD in political science from the University of Chicago. Her areas of research and teaching include race and gender dimensions of political participation, Virginia politics, and American government. She is a former chair of the African American Studies program and has served as the president of the National Capital Area Political Science Association and the Women's Caucus of the American Political Science Association. In addition, Professor Travis has been a fellow at the Rothermere American Institute, Oxford University. A political analyst, she is a frequent commentator on Virginia and national politics.

CONTENTS

Preface   *xi*

SECTION I—**CONSTRUCTING CATEGORIES OF DIFFERENCE**

FRAMEWORK ESSAY   **2**

WHAT IS RACE? WHAT IS ETHNICITY?

1. "Race" and the Construction of Human Identity
   Audrey Smedley   51

2. Who Is Black? One Nation's Definition
   F. James Davis   61

3. The Evolution of Identity
   The Washington Post   70

Personal Account: A Loaded Vacation
Niah Grimes   71

4. Real Indians: Identity and the Survival of Native America
   Eva Marie Garroutte   71

5. An Interlocking Panethnicity: The Negotiation of Multiple Identities among
   Asian American Social Movement Leaders
   Dana Y. Nakano   80

Personal Account: I Thought My Race Was Invisible
Sherri H. Pereira   89

6. Latino Racial Choices: The Effects of Skin Colour and
   Discrimination on Latinos' and Latinas' Racial Self-Identifications
   Tanya Golash-Boza and William Darity, Jr.   89

v

7. Whiteness as an "Unmarked" Cultural Category
Ruth Frankenberg   101

8. Plus ça Change . . . ? Multiraciality and the Dynamics of
Race Relations in the United States
Frank D. Bean and Jennifer Lee   107

Personal Account: The Price of Nonconformity
Julia Morgenstern   114

Personal Account: Basketball
Andrea M. Busch   115

WHAT IS SEX? WHAT IS GENDER?

9. The Olympic Struggle over Sex
Alice Dreger   115

10. All Together Now: Intersex Infants and IGM
Riki Wilchins   117

11. Delusions of Gender: How Our Minds, Society,
and Neurosexism Create Difference
Cordelia Fine   123

WHAT IS SOCIAL CLASS?

12. What's Class Got to Do with It?
Michael Zweig   127

13. The Silver Spoon: Inheritance and the Staggered Start
Stephen J. McNamee and Robert K. Miller Jr.   131

Personal Account: I Am a Pakistani Woman
Hoorie I. Siddique   135

14. The Great Divergence: America's Growing Inequality
Crisis and What We Can Do about It
Timothy Noah   137

WHAT IS SEXUALITY?

15. Sexual Fluidity: Understanding Women's Love and Desire
Lisa M. Diamond   142

16. The Biology of the Homosexual
Roger N. Lancaster   147

17. The Heterosexual Questionnaire
Martin Rochlin   158

WHAT IS DISABILITY?

18. Disability Definitions: The Politics of Meaning
Michael Oliver   159

Personal Account: Invisibly Disabled
Heather L. Shaw   163

19. What Wounds Enable: The Politics of Disability and Violence
   in Chicago
   Laurence Ralph   163

20. Ethnicity, Ethics, and the Deaf-World
   Harlan Lane   176

SECTION II—EXPERIENCING DIFFERENCE

FRAMEWORK ESSAY   **194**

RACE AND ETHNICITY

21. Formulating Identity in a Globalized World
   Carola Suárez-Orozco   225

Personal Account: Hair
Sarah Faragalla   236

Personal Account: The Americanization of a Reluctant Vietnamese-American
Hoai Huong Tran   239

22. Latinos and the U.S. Race Structure
   Clara E. Rodríguez   242

23. Everybody's Ethnic Enigma
   Jelita McLeod   248

Personal Account: My Strategies
Eric Jackson   249

24. From Friendly Foreigner to Enemy Race
   John Tehranian   251

Personal Account: Master Status: Pride and Danger
Sumaya Al-Hajebi   258

SEX AND GENDER

25. The Privilege of Teaching about Privilege
   Michael A. Messner   261

26. Proving Manhood
   Timothy Beneke   267

Personal Account: Just Something You Did as a Man
Francisco Hernandez   271

27. "I'm Not a Feminist, But . . .": Popular Myths about Feminism
   Penny A. Weiss   272

SEXUALITY

28. Dude, You're a Fag: Adolescent Male Homophobia
   C. J. Pascoe   277

29. Gendered Sexuality in Young Adulthood: Double Binds and
Flawed Options
Laura Hamilton and Elizabeth A. Armstrong   287
Personal Account: Living Invisibly
Tara S. Ellison   297

30. Sexual Orientation and Sex in Women's Lives: Conceptual and
Methodological Issues
Esther D. Rothblum   297

SOCIAL CLASS

31. Cause of Death: Inequality
Alejandro Reuss   303

32. Why Are Droves of Unqualified, Unprepared Kids Getting into
Our Top Colleges? Because Their Dads Are Alumni
John Larew   307
Personal Account: That Moment of Visibility
Rose B. Pascarell   312

33. The Myth of the "Culture of Poverty"
Paul Gorski   313

DISABILITY

34. Public Transit
John Hockenberry   317

35. "Can You See the Rainbow?" The Roots of Denial
Sally French   325

36. Not Blind Enough: Living in the Borderland Called Legal Blindness
Beth Omansky   331
Personal Account: A Time I Didn't Feel Normal
Heather Callender   337

SECTION III—THE MEANING OF DIFFERENCE

FRAMEWORK ESSAY   340

RACE AND ETHNICITY

37. Fourteen Key Supreme Court Cases and the Civil War Amendments   359

38. Blink in Black and White
Malcolm Gladwell   390
Personal Account: Just Like My Mama Said
Anthony McNeill   395

39. Safe Haven in America? Thirty Years after the Refugee Act of 1980
David W. Haines   395

40. Hispanics Are Forgotten in Civil Rights History
Nicholas Dauphine   398

41. Balancing Identities: Undocumented Immigrant Asian American
Students and the Model Minority Myth
Tracy Poon Tambascia, Jonathan Wang, Breanne Tcheng,
and Viet T. Bui   399
Personal Account: Let Me Work for It!
Isabelle Nguyen   402

42. Segregated Housing, Segregated Schools
Richard Rothstein   403

SEX AND GENDER

43. Many Faces of Gender Inequality
Amartya Sen   405
Personal Account: He Hit Her
Tim Norton   410

44. The Not-So-Pink Ivory Tower
Ann Mullen   411

45. The Gender Revolution: Uneven and Stalled
Paula England   415

SEXUALITY

46. Sex Education and the Promotion of Heteronormativity
Tanya McNeill   424
Personal Account: Learning My Own Privilege
Mireille M. Cecil   432

47. Gaga Relations: The End of Marriage
J. Jack Halberstam   432

48. Queers without Money: They Are Everywhere. But We Refuse
to See Them
Amber Hollibaugh   439

SOCIAL CLASS

49. Rethinking American Poverty
Mark R. Rank   443

50. Tearing Down the Gates: Confronting the Class Divide
in American Education
Peter Sacks   447

51. Wealth Stripping: Why It Costs So Much to Be Poor
James H. Carr   452

DISABILITY

52. Disability Trouble
    Bradley A. Areheart   456

53. Learning Disabilities: The Social Construction of a Special
    Education Category
    Christine E. Sleeter   468

54. (Re)Creating a World in Seven Days: Place, Disability, and Salvation
    in *Extreme Makeover: Home Edition*
    Emily Askew   473

SECTION IV—**BRIDGING DIFFERENCES**

FRAMEWORK ESSAY   **482**

55. Adolescent Masculinity in an Age of Decreased Homohysteria
    Eric Anderson   492

56. What Can We Do? Becoming Part of the Solution
    Allan G. Johnson   502
Personal Account: Parents' Underestimated Love
Octavio N. Espinal   506

57. In Defense of Rich Kids
    William Upski Wimsatt   507
Personal Account: Where Are You From?
C.C.   511

58. Uprooting Racism: How White People Can Work for Racial Justice
    Paul Kivel   511

Credits   *C-1*

Index   *I-1*

PREFACE

The Meaning of Difference is an effort to understand how difference is constructed in contemporary American culture: How do categories of people come to be seen as "different"? How does being different affect people's lives? What does difference mean at the level of the individual, social institution, or society? What difference does "difference" make? What is *shared* across the most significant categories of difference in America—race, sex/gender, sexual orientation, social class, and disability? What can be learned from their commonalities? That *The Meaning of Difference* is now in its seventh edition makes us hopeful that this comparative approach can be useful in understanding American conceptions and constructions of difference.

ORGANIZATION AND CONCEPTUAL FRAMEWORK

The Meaning of Difference is divided into four sections. Each section includes an opening Framework Essay and a set of readings, with the Framework Essay providing the conceptual structure by which to understand the readings. Thus, the Framework Essays are not simply introductions to the readings; they are the "text" portion of this text/reader.

The first section's Framework Essay and readings describe how categories of difference are *created;* the second considers the *experience* of difference; the third examines the *meanings* that are assigned to difference, focusing especially on education, ideology, law, and public policy; and the fourth describes what people can do to *challenge and change these constructions* of difference.

Each of the readings included in the volume has been selected by virtue of its applicability to multiple categories of difference. For example, F. James Davis's conclusions about the construction of race (Reading 2) could be applied to a discussion of sexual identity or disability. How much of "x" does it take to locate someone as gay or straight, disabled or nondisabled, Middle-Eastern or American? Carola Suárez-Orozco's discussion of identity formation in a globalized world (Reading 21) can be applied toward an understanding of racial identity formation and even to the formation of identities tied to sexuality. Similarly, Michael Oliver's rendering of an alternative Survey of Disabled Adults (Reading 18)—which parallels Martin Rochlin's classic Heterosexual Questionnaire (Reading 17)— serves as an example of the insights that can be gained by a change of perspective. In all, our aim has been to select readings that help identify both what is unique and what is shared across our experiences of difference.

DISTINGUISHING FEATURES

Five features make *The Meaning of Difference* distinctive:

- First, it offers a conceptual framework by which to understand the commonalities among these categories of difference. This encompassing conceptual approach makes *The Meaning of Difference* unique.
- Second, no other book provides an accessible and historically grounded discussion of the Supreme Court decisions critical to the structuring of these categorical differences.
- Third, *The Meaning of Difference* has been designed with an eye toward the pedagogic difficulties that often accompany this subject matter. In our experience, when the topics of race, sex and gender, social class, sexual orientation, and disability are treated *simultaneously*, as they are here, no one group can be easily cast as victim or victimizer.
- Fourth, no other volume includes a detailed discussion and set of readings on how to challenge and change the constructions of difference.
- Finally, *The Meaning of Difference* is the first book of its kind to incorporate disability as a master status functioning in ways analogous to the operation of race and ethnicity, sex and gender, sexual orientation, and social class.

HIGHLIGHTS FROM THE SEVENTH EDITION

This edition includes twenty-seven new readings, one new personal account, and, in Reading 37, a discussion of two important new Supreme Court Cases: *U.S. v. Windsor* (2013), which established federal recognition of the rights of married same-sex couples and *Schuette v. Coalition to Defend Affirmative Action, Integration and Immigration Rights and Fight for Equality By Any Means Necessary (BAMN)* (2013), in which the Court upheld an amendment to the Michigan state constitution banning affirmative action in public employment, education, or contracting.

New to this volume are several readings that focus on education as a key site for the construction of difference and inequality. Paul Gorski considers how the myth of the culture of poverty affects teachers; Tracy Poon Tambascia, Jonathan Wang, Breanne Tcheng, and Viet T. Bui reflect on the impact of the model minority myth on undocumented immigrant Asian American university students; Tanya McNeill details the promotion of heterosexual monogamy in the policies of public schools; Peter Sacks describes the processes by which, over the last thirty years, American higher education has come to exclude poor and working-class students; and Christine Sleeter places the emergence of the idea of learning disability in the context of the educational reforms of the 1960s and 1970s. In combination with John Larew's timeless article on legacy admissions at elite universities and coverage of several Supreme Court cases about affirmative action in higher education, we believe the volume now allows faculty the opportunity for concentrated focus on education should they choose that.

Several readings new to this edition focus on the dramatic increase of economic inequality in the United States and the still-unfolding outcomes of the Great Recession. In "The Great Divergence," Timothy Noah describes the nature and extent of U.S. inequality; in "Wealth Stripping," James Carr details the effect of predatory "alternative" lending such as pay-day and auto-title loans; in "Rethinking American Poverty," Mark Rank considers the structural factors that shape relatively high rates of American poverty; and in "(Re)Creating a World in Seven Days," Emily Askew analyzes the messages about social class and disability embedded in ABC's hit television show *Extreme Makeover: Home Edition*.

In addition to the inclusion of new readings, we have, as always, concentrated on updating the Framework Essays, as these are the "text" portion of this text/reader. We aim for essays that offer a conceptual structure for thinking about (and teaching) this material, but in this edition in particular we thought of the essays as a place in which to grapple with how, increasingly, American constructions of difference appear to be *both* fluid and stable.

To highlight some of the changes in this edition, the first framework essay now considers the effects of our 21st century mapping of the human genome—an accomplishment that many predicted would be the death knell of the idea of race. What we see instead is that race is surprisingly resilient in both popular opinion and science, albeit now framed and profitably marketed as "geographic ancestry." In contrast to this persistence, however, the essay also examines the ways that ideas about race have broadened, especially as revealed by the use of multi-racial self-identifications. As discussed in this essay, increased breadth and fluidity also appears to characterize gender and sexuality categorizations, for example in the increased visibility and acceptance of those who identify as transgender and the emergence of bisexuality as a viable scientific and self-identification category.

In this edition, the second Framework Essay gives special attention to the idea of intersectionality, that is, the *interaction* of stigmatized statuses. Long a topic in women's studies scholarship, we have tried to make this complicated idea more accessible to students while also showing the practical consequences of acknowledging, or failing to acknowledge, intersectionality. Updates to the third Framework Essay have included the topics of intermarriage and residential segregation. The readings in the third section—focused on education, ideology, law, and public policy—are now organized into the master-status subsections used throughout the book.

Several readings from the previous edition have been retained not only because of their wide popularity among students and faculty, but also because they are classics in the field. Included in this category are F. James Davis's "Who Is Black? One Nation's Definition"; Ruth Frankenberg's "Whiteness as an 'Unmarked' Cultural Category"; Michael Oliver's "Disability Definitions"; Sally French's "Can You See the Rainbow?"; John Hockenberry's "Public Transit"; C. J. Pascoe's "Dude You're a Fag"; and Malcolm Gladwell's "Blink in Black and White." We also believe several readings new to this edition will become classics: Cordelia Fine's "Delusions of Gender"; Lisa Diamond's "Sexual Fluidity"; Laurence Ralph's "What Wounds Enable"; David Haines's "Safe Haven in America?"; Amartya Sen's "The Many Faces of Gender Inequality"; and Eric Anderson's "Adolescent Masculinity in an Age of Decreased Homohysteria" all have this potential.

SUPPLEMENTS

Instructor's Manual/Test Bank

An Instructor's Manual and Test Bank accompany this volume. In this edition, we have added a special section of advice on how to teach this material. Instructors can access this password-protected material on the website that accompanies the seventh edition of *The Meaning of Difference* at www.mhhe.com/rosenblum7e.

ACKNOWLEDGMENTS

Many colleagues and friends have helped us clarify the ideas we present here. David Haines has been unfailing in his willingness to help Karen think through conceptual, technical, and ethical dilemmas. She could not imagine a colleague more supportive or wise. Theodore W. Travis provided insight on Supreme Court decisions, their relationship to social values, and their impact on American society. Since this project first emerged, Victoria Rader has been generous in sharing her knowledge as a teacher and writer. Her wisdom especially guided our development of the "Bridging Differences" section. We are also grateful to our colleague and friend Beth Omansky for helping us understand the critical relationship of disability to our work. As a friend and friendly editor, none could be better than Sheila Barrows. Finally, we owe thanks to our students at George Mason University for sharing their experiences with us.

For this edition, we again convey our appreciation to Joan Lester and the Equity Institute of Emeryville, California, for their understanding of the progress that can be made through a holistic analysis.

Jamie Daron of McGraw-Hill and Melanie Lewis of ansrsource shepherded this volume to completion. Fred Courtright's work on acquiring permissions was especially appreciated. As in previous editions, McGraw-Hill proved itself committed to a thorough review process by putting together a panel of accomplished scholars with broad teaching expertise. All offered detailed and insightful critiques, and we are much in their debt:

Naomi Greyser, University of Iowa
Shepherd M. Jenks, Jr., Central New Mexico Community College
Earnest Perry, University of Missouri
Gloria L. Rowe, Cincinnati State Technical and Community College.

Karen Rosenblum
Toni-Michelle Travis
George Mason University

CONSTRUCTING CATEGORIES OF DIFFERENCE

FRAMEWORK ESSAY

In this book we consider how *difference* is constructed in contemporary American society. We explore how categories of people are seen as significantly different from one another and how people's lives are affected by these conceptions of difference. The four sections of the book are organized around what we consider to be the key questions about difference: how it is constructed, how it is experienced by individuals, how meaning is attributed to difference, and how differences can be bridged.

We believe that race, sex, social class, sexuality, and disability are currently the primary axes of difference in American society—they are also what social scientists would call *master statuses*. In common usage, the term *status* means prestige or esteem. But for social scientists, the term *status* refers to positions in a social structure. In this sense, statuses are like empty slots (or positions) that individuals fill. The most obvious kinds of statuses are kinship, occupation, and age. At any time an individual occupies multiple statuses, including those of race, sex, social class, sexuality, and disability.

This latter set of statuses—the ones we focus on in this book—are significantly more powerful than most other social statuses. Social scientists refer to these as *master* statuses because they so profoundly affect a person's life: "in most or all social situations master status will overpower or dominate all other statuses. . . . Master status influences every other aspect of life, including personal identity."[1] These master statuses may be said to "frame" how people are seen by others— especially strangers—as well as how they see themselves and much of what they experience in the world.[2] This does not mean, however, that people always understand the impact of the master statuses or "frames" that they occupy. Indeed, much of this book is about recognizing that impact.

This text will explore similarities in the operation of these master statuses. Although there are certainly differences of history, experience, and impact, we believe that similar processes are at work when people "see" differences of color, sex and gender, social class, sexuality, and disability, and we believe that there are similarities in the consequences of these master statuses for individuals' lives. Nonetheless, there are risks in our focus on similarities across master statuses, not the least of which is the assumption that similarity is a better ground for social change than a recognition of difference.[3] Thus, our focus on similarities across master statuses is literally only one side of the story.

Racism, sexism, homophobia, and diversity have been pervasive topics for discussion in American society for at least the last fifty years. Although the substance of these conversations has changed in many ways—for example, the term *diversity* once flagged the need for equal opportunity but now functions more as a marketing tool—the intensity around most of these topics persists. Many Americans have strong opinions on these subjects, and that is probably also the case for readers of this text. Two perspectives—essentialism and constructionism—are core to this book and should help you understand your own reaction to the material.

The Essentialist and Constructionist Perspectives

The difference between the *constructionist* and *essentialist* perspectives is illustrated in the tale of the three umpires, first apparently told by social psychologist Hadley Cantril:

> Hadley Cantril relates the story of three baseball umpires discussing their profession. The first umpire said, "Some are balls and some are strikes, and I call them as they are." The second replied, "Some's balls and some's strikes, and I call 'em as I sees 'em." The third thought about it and said, "Some's balls and some's strikes, but they ain't nothing 'till I calls 'em."[4]

The first umpire in the story can be described as an essentialist. When he says, "I call them as they are," he assumes that balls and strikes exist in the world regardless of his perception of them. For this umpire, balls and strikes are easily identified, and he is merely a neutral observer; he "regards knowledge as objective and independent of mind, and himself as the impartial reporter of things 'as they are.'"[5]

Thus, the essentialist perspective presumes that items in a category all share some "essential" quality, their "ball-ness" or "strike-ness." For essentialists, *race, sex, sexual orientation, disability,* and *social class* identify significant, empirically verifiable differences among people. From the essentialist perspective, each of these exists apart from any social processes; they are objective categories of real differences among people.

The second umpire is somewhat removed from pure essentialism. His statement, "I call 'em as I sees 'em," conveys the belief that while an independent, objective reality exists, it is subject to interpretation. For him, the world contains balls and strikes, but individuals may have different perceptions about which is which.

The third umpire, who says "they ain't nothing 'till I calls 'em," is a constructionist. He operates from the belief that "conceptions such as 'strikes' and 'balls' have no meaning except that given them by the observer."[6] For this constructionist umpire, reality cannot be separated from the way a culture makes sense of it; strikes and balls do not exist until they are constructed through social processes. From this perspective, difference is created rather than intrinsic to a phenomenon. Social processes—such as those in political, legal, economic, scientific, and religious institutions—create differences, determine that some differences are more important than others, and assign particular meanings to those differences. From this perspective, the way a society defines difference among its members tells us more about that society than the people so classified. *The Meaning of Difference* operates from the constructionist perspective, since it examines how we have arrived at our race, sex, disability, sexuality, and social class categories.

Few of us have grown up as constructionists. More likely, we are essentialists who believe that master statuses such as race or sex entail clear-cut, unchanging, and in some way meaningful differences. Still, not everyone is an essentialist. Those who grew up in multiple racial or religious backgrounds are familiar with the ways in which identity is not clear-cut. They grow up understanding how definitions of self vary with the context; how others try to define one as belonging in a particular category; and how, in many ways, one's very presence calls prevailing classification systems into question. For example, the experience Jelita McLeod describes in Reading 23 of being asked "What are you?" is a common experience for multiracial people. Such experiences make evident the social constructedness of racial identity.

Most of us are unlikely to be exclusively essentialist or constructionist. As authors of this book, although we take the constructionist perspective, we have still relied on essentialist terms we find problematic. The irony of questioning the idea of race but still talking about "blacks," "whites," and "Asians," or of rejecting a dualistic approach to sexual identity while still using the terms *gay* and *straight,* has not escaped us. Indeed, we have sometimes used the currently favored essentialist phrase *sexual orientation* over the more constructionist *sexual preference* because *sexual preference* is an unfamiliar phrase to many people.[a]

Further, there is a serious risk that a text such as this falsely identifies people on the basis of *either* their sex, race, sexuality, disability, or social class, despite the fact that master statuses are not parts of a person that can be broken off from one another like the segments of a Tootsie Roll.[7] All of us are always *simultaneously* all of our master statuses, an idea encompassed by the concept of *intersectionality* (a topic to which we will return in the Framework Essay for Section II). While the readings in this section may make it seem as if these were separable statuses, they are not. Indeed, even the concept of master status could mislead us into thinking that there could be only one dominating status in one's life.

Both constructionism and essentialism can be found in the social sciences. Indeed, social science research routinely operates from essentialist assumptions: when researchers report the sex, race, or ethnicity of their interviewees or experimental subjects they are treating these categories as "real," that is, as existing independent of the researchers' classifications. Both perspectives also are evident in social movements, and those movements sometimes shift from one perspective to the other over time. For example, some feminists and most of those opposed to feminism hold the essentialist belief that women and men are inherently different. The constructionist view that sexual identity is chosen dominated the gay rights movement of the 1970s,[8] but today, the essentialist view that sexual identity is something one is born with appears to dominate. By contrast, some of those opposed to gay relationships now take the constructionist view that sexuality is chosen and could therefore be changed. In this case, language often signals which perspective is being used. For example, sexual *preference* conveys active, human decision making with the possibility of change (constructionism), while sexual *orientation* implies something fixed and inherent to a person (essentialism).

Americans are now about equally split between those who hold essentialist and constructionist views on homosexuality—40 percent of those who responded to a

---

[a]The term *sexual identity* seems now to be replacing *sexual orientation*. It could be used in either an essentialist or a constructionist way.

2012 Gallup Poll answered that being gay was something a person was born with, compared to 37 percent who said that being gay was the result of upbringing or other social factors. Thirty-five years ago those opinions were the reverse, with 56 percent saying sexuality was the result of upbringing or other environmental factors.[9] This shift toward a more essentialist view of sexuality began in the late 1990s, when, as Roger Lancaster describes in Reading 16, the media focused on the biological (i.e., essentialist) research on the origin of homosexuality, much of which has now been discredited. Later in this chapter we will describe what appears to be another change in attitudes about sexuality, which is a turn toward a constructionist approach, at least among college students.

This example from journalist Darryl Rist shows the appeal that essentialist explanations might have for gay rights activists:

> [Chris Yates's parents were] Pentecostal ministers who had tortured his adolescence with Christian cures for sexual perversity. Shock and aversion therapies under born-again doctors and gruesome exorcisms of sexual demons by spirit-filled preachers had culminated in a plan to have him castrated by a Mexican surgeon who touted the procedure as a way to make the boy, if not straight, at least sexless. Only then had the terrified son rebelled.
>
> Then, in the summer of 1991, the journal *Science* reported anatomical differences between the brains of homosexual and heterosexual men. . . . The euphoric media—those great purveyors of cultural myths—drove the story wildly. Every major paper in the country headlined the discovery smack on the front page. . . . Like many others, I suspect, Chris Yates's family saw in this newly reported sexual science a way out of its wrenching impasse. After years of virtual silence between them and their son, Chris's parents drove several hundred miles to visit him and ask for reconciliation. Whatever faded guilt they might have felt for the family's faulty genes was nothing next to the reassurance that neither by a perverse upbringing nor by his own iniquity was Chris or the family culpable for his urges and actions. "We could never have condoned this if you could do something to change it. But when we finally understood that you were *born* that way, we knew we'd been wrong. We had to ask your forgiveness."[10]

Understandably, those who are discriminated against would find essentialist orientations appealing, just as the expansiveness of constructionist approaches would be appealing in more tolerant eras. Still, either perspective can be used to justify discrimination, since people can be persecuted for the choices they make as well as for their genetic inheritance. As Lisa Diamond concludes in Reading 15, on a topic as politicized as sexuality, there are no "safe" scientific findings—any finding can be used for just about any purpose.

Our inclusion here of disability as a social construction may generate an intense reaction—many will want to argue that disability is about real physical, sensory, or cognitive differences, not social constructs. However, two factors are at work here. One involves *impairment,* that is, "the physical, cognitive, emotional or sensory condition within the person as diagnosed by medical professionals."[11] The second is "the loss or limitation of opportunities to take part in the normal life of the community on an equal level with others due to physical and social barriers."[12] This latter dimension, called *disability,* has been the emphasis of what is called the "social model" of disability, which contends that disability is created by social, political, and environmental obstacles—that is, that social processes such as discrimination or lack of access to corrective technologies turn impairments into disabilities.[13] This form of discrimination is sometimes called *ableism.* In the historic words of Britain's Union of the Physically Impaired against Segregation (UPIAS), one of the first disability liberation groups in the world and the first run by disabled people themselves:[14]

> It is society which disables physically impaired people. Disability is something imposed on top of our impairment by the way we are unnecessarily isolated and excluded from full participation in society. Disabled people are therefore an oppressed group in society.[15]

That perspective is reflected in the 2007 United Nations Convention on the Rights of Persons with Disabilities, which reads in part:

> [D]isability should be seen as the result of the interaction between a person and his or her environment. Disability is not something that resides in the individual as the result of some impairment. . . . Disability resides in the society, not in the person. [For example,] in a society where corrective lenses are available for someone with extreme myopia (nearsightedness), this person would *not* be considered to have a disability, however someone *with the same condition* in a society where corrective lenses were not available would be considered to have a disability, especially if the level of vision prevented the person from performing tasks expected of this person. . . .[16]

For example, John Hockenberry (Reading 34) describes how mass transit systems that are inaccessible to wheelchair users "disable" them by making it difficult or impossible to work, attend school, or be involved in social activities. Beyond architectural, educational, and occupational barriers, disability is also constructed through cultural stereotypes and everyday interactions in which difference is defined as undesirable. We once heard a student with spina bifida tell a story addressing this point: In her first day at elementary school, other students kept asking what was "wrong" with her. As she put it, she had always known she was different, but she hadn't thought she was "wrong."

Not only can disability be understood as the result of disabling environments and cultural stereotypes, the categories of impairment and disability are also themselves socially constructed through medical and legal processes. "[I]llness, disease, and disability are not 'givens' in nature . . . but rather *socially constructed* categories that emerge from the interpretive activities of people acting together in social situations."[17] Learning disabilities are an example of this process.

> Before the late 1800s when observers began to write about "word blindness," learning disability (whatever its name) did not exist, although the human variation to which it ambiguously refers did—sort of! People who today might be known as learning disabled may have formerly been known as "slow," "retarded," or "odd." But mostly they would not have been known as unusual at all. The learning difficulties experienced today by learning disabled youth have not been experienced by most youth throughout history. For example, most youth have not been asked to learn to read. Thus, they could not experience any reading difficulties, the most common learning disability. As we have expected youth to learn to read and have tried to teach them to do so, many youth have experienced difficulty. However, until the mid-1960s we typically did not understand those difficulties as the consequences of a learning disability.[18]

The social model of disability first emerged out of the disabled people's movement in the 1970s in opposition to the "medical model," which approached disability as a matter of individual deficiencies or defects, rather than societal responses. From the perspective of the medical model, individuals have problems that need to be treated by medical specialists; from that of the social model, individual problems are the result of social structures that need to be changed. Thus, for adherents of the social model, the important questions are about civil rights such as equal access. The survey questions posed by Mike Oliver in Reading 18 show how the world is perceived differently from these two perspectives. Still, as Laurence Ralph describes in Reading 19, the social model of disability becomes less relevant when we consider the numbers of young black and Hispanic men disabled by gun violence (second to car accidents, gunshot wounds are the most common source of disability in urban areas). Ralph describes the case of a group of Chicago ex-gang members, now paralyzed by spinal cord injuries from gunshots. Although the social model would argue that society has disabled these young men, the men themselves operate from the medical model—in their mission to save teenagers from a similar fate, they focus on the defects of their bodies.

Why have we spent so much time describing the essentialist and constructionist perspectives? Discussions about race, sex, disability, sexual identity, and social class generate great intensity, partly because they involve the clash of essentialist and constructionist assumptions. Essentialists are likely to view categories of people as "essentially" different in some important way; constructionists are likely to see these differences as socially created and arbitrary. An essentialist asks what causes people to be different; a constructionist asks about the origin and consequence of the categorization system itself. While arguments about the nature and cause of racism, sexism, homophobia, and poverty are disputes about power and justice, from the perspectives of essentialism and constructionism they are also disputes about the meaning of differences in color, sexuality, and social class.

In all of this, the constructionist approach has one clear advantage. From that perspective, one understands that all this talk has a profound significance. Such talk is not simply *about* difference; it is itself the *creation* of difference. In the sections that follow, we examine how categories of people are named, dichotomized, and stigmatized—all toward the construction of difference.

Naming

Difference is constructed first by naming categories of people. Therefore, constructionists pay special attention to the names people use to refer to themselves and others—the times at which new names are asserted, the negotiations that surround the use of particular names, and those occasions when people are grouped together or separated out.

Asserting a Name Both individuals and categories of people face similar issues in the assertion of a name. A change of name involves, to some extent, the claim of a new identity. For example, one of our colleagues no longer wanted to be called by her nickname because it had come to seem childish to her, so she asked people to use her "real" name instead. It took a few times to remind people that this was her new name, and with most that was adequate. One colleague, however, argued that he could not adapt to the new name; she would just have to tolerate his continued use of the nickname. This was a small but public battle about who had the power to name whom. Did she have the power to enforce her own naming, or did he have the power to name her despite her wishes? Eventually, she prevailed.

A more disquieting example was a young woman who wanted to keep her maiden name after she married. Her fiancé agreed with her decision, recognizing that he would be reluctant to give up his name were the tables turned. When his mother heard of this possibility, however, she was outraged. In her mind, a rejection of her family's name was a rejection of her family. She urged her son to reconsider getting married.

Thus, asserting a name can create social conflict. On both a personal and societal level, naming can involve the claim of a particular identity and the rejection of others' power to impose a name. For example, is one Native American, American Indian, or Sioux; African American or black; girl or woman; Asian, Asian American, Korean, or Korean American; gay or homosexual; Chicano, Mexican American, Mexican, Latino/a, or Hispanic? For instance,

> [j]ust who is Hispanic? The answer depends on whom you ask.
>
> The label was actually coined in the mid-1970s by federal bureaucrats working under President Richard M. Nixon. They came up with it in response to concerns that the government was wrongly applying "Chicano" to people who were not of Mexican descent, and otherwise misidentifying and underserving segments of the population by generally classifying those with ancestral ties to the Spanish cultural diaspora as either Chicano, Cuban, or Puerto Rican.
>
> Nearly three decades later, the debate continues to surround the term Hispanic and its definition. Although mainly applied to people from Latin American countries with linguistic and cultural ties to Spain, it also is used by the U.S. government to refer to Spaniards themselves, as well as people from Portuguese-speaking Brazil.[19]

Comedian Carlos Mencia (a Honduran-born American) captures this confusion in a story about talking to college students twenty years ago, but its substance applies just as easily today: "I said 'Latinos,' and they said, 'We're not Latin!' And then I said 'Chicano,' and they said, 'We're not of Mexican descent.' So I said 'I don't know what to say—Hispanic? And they said, 'There's no such country as Hispania!'"[20] As of 2011, 33 percent of Hispanic/Latinos preferred *Hispanic,* 14 percent preferred *Latino,* but 53 percent had no preference.[21]

Deciding what name to use for a category of people is not easy. It is unlikely that all members of the category use the same name; the name members use for one another may not be acceptable for outsiders to use; nor is it always advisable to ask what name a person prefers. We once saw an old friend become quite angry when asked whether he preferred the term *black* or *African American.* "Either one is fine with me," he replied, "*I* know what *I* am." To him, the question meant that he was being seen as a member of a category, not as an individual.

Because naming may involve a redefinition of self, an assertion of power, and a rejection of others' ability to impose an identity, social change movements often claim a new name, while opponents may express opposition by continuing to use the old name. For example, in the 1960s *black* emerged in opposition to *Negro* as the Black Power movement sought to distinguish itself from the Martin Luther King–led moderate wing of the civil rights movement. The term *Negro* had itself been put forward by influential leaders such as W. E. B. Du Bois and Booker T. Washington as a rejection of the term *colored* that had dominated the mid- to late 19th century: "[D]espite its association with racial epithets, 'Negro' was defined to stand for a new way of thinking about Blacks."[22] Similarly, in 1988, Ramona H. Edelin, president of the National Urban Coalition, proposed that *African American* be substituted for *black*.[b] Now both terms are used about equally. Among blacks who have a preference, Gallup polls suggest a gradual trend toward the label "African American." Still, "a clear majority of blacks say they don't care which label is used"[23] and some still prefer the term *Negro*. "The immediate reason the word *Negro* is on the [2010] Census is simple enough: in the 2000 Census, more than 56,000 people wrote in *Negro* to describe their identity—even though it was already on the form. Some people, it seems, still strongly identify with the term, which used to be a perfectly polite designation," but is now considered by many an insult.[24]

Each of these name changes—from *Negro* to *black* to *African American*—was first promoted by activists as a way to demonstrate their commitment to a new social order. A similar theme is reflected in the history of the terms *Chicano* and *Chicanismo*. Although the origin of the terms is unclear, the principle was the same. As reporter Ruben Salazar wrote in the 1960s, "a Chicano is a Mexican-American with a non-Anglo image of himself."[25] (*Anglo* is a colloquialism for *white* used in the southwestern and western United States.)

Similarly, the term *homosexual* was first coined in 1896 by a Hungarian physician hoping to decriminalize same-sex relations between men. It was incorporated into the medical and psychological literature of the time, which depicted nonprocreative sex as pathological. In the 1960s, activists rejected the pathological characterization along with the name associated with it, turning to the terms *gay*[c] and *lesbian* rather than *homosexual* (and using *gay* to refer to men, or both men and women). Later, the 1990s group Queer Nation transformed what had been a common epithet into a slogan—"We're here! We're queer! Get used to it!"

> Well, yes, "gay" is great. It has its place. . . . [But] using "queer" is a way of reminding us how we are perceived by the rest of the world. It's a way of telling ourselves we don't have to be witty and charming people who keep our lives discreet and marginalized in the straight world. . . . Queer, unlike gay, doesn't mean male. . . . Yeah, queer can be a rough word but it is also a sly and ironic weapon we can steal from the homophobe's hands and use against him.[26]

---

[b]Thus, one can find Black Studies, Afro-American Studies, and African American Studies programs in universities across the country.

[c]In the 17th century, *gay* became associated with an addiction to social dissipation and loose morality, and was used to refer to female prostitutes (e.g., *gay girl*). The term was apparently first used in reference to homosexuality in 1925 in Australia. "It may have been both the connotations of femininity and those of immorality that led American homosexuals to adopt the title 'gay' with some self-irony in the 1920s. The slogan 'Glad to Be Gay,' adopted by both female and male homosexuals, and the naming of the Gay Liberation Front, which was born from the Stonewall resistance riots following police raids on homosexual bars in New York in 1969, bear witness to a greater self-confidence."[27]

Now, all terms—*homosexual, gay and lesbian, gay* as including both women and men or just men, *queer,* and the acronyms GLBTQ (gay, lesbian, bisexual, transgender, and questioning) and LGBTQ—appear to be in common use. People who identify as asexual, that is, not experiencing sexual attraction, also appears to be a growing category, with the likelihood that the LGBTQ umbrella will someday expand to LGBTQA. While "queer" maintains some of its history as both pejorative and defiant, it was apparently acceptable enough to serve as the title of a popular reality show, *Queer Eye,* that aired from 2003 to 2007.

Just as each of these social movements has involved a public renaming that proclaims pride, the women's movement has asserted *woman* as a replacement for *girl.* A student who described a running feud with her roommate illustrates the significance of these terms. The student preferred the word *woman,* arguing that *girl,* when applied to females past adolescence, was insulting, almost as if one could never grow up. Her female roommate just as strongly preferred the term *girl* and regularly applied it to the females she knew. Each of them had such strong feelings on the matter that it was clear they would not last as roommates.

How could these two words destroy their relationship? It appears that English speakers use the terms *girl* and *woman* to refer to quite different qualities. *Woman* is understood to convey adulthood, power, and sexuality; *girl* connotes youth, powerlessness, and irresponsibility. (The same qualities of age, power, responsibility, and sexuality operate in the choice between *boy* and *man.*) The two roommates were asserting quite different places for themselves in the world. One claimed adulthood; the other saw herself as not having achieved that yet. This explanation is offered by many females: It is not so much that they like being *girls,* as that they value youth and/or do not yet feel justified in calling themselves women. But the effort to remain a "girl" can create its own inconsistencies. We once overheard a woman describe a friend as a "girl"—the friend was fifty and about to adopt a child.

It seems to us that college students now often refer to themselves as "girls" and "boys." Sociologist Michael Kimmel argues that the use of *boys,* but more importantly, *guys,* speaks to the development of a new age demographic for American males, specifically an extended period in which they are neither dependent (like boys) or responsible (like men). On the use of *woman,* some of our students have said that they avoid the word because it is associated with feminism, and they are right to conclude that it is. After all, it is called the *women's* movement, not the *girls'* movement! The name conveys an identity: "we cannot be girls anymore, we must be women." In a now classic essay, political philosopher Penny Weiss (Reading 27) "diagnoses" the phrase that has been used by women for at least the last fifty years: "I'm not a feminist, but. . . ."

In all, different categories of people may claim a wide range of names for themselves. A name may reflect the analysis and aspirations of a social movement, and it may be the battleground for competing conceptions of the world. The name invoked by movement activists may have no immediate bearing on the language used by people in the streets, or everyday language may come to be shaped by policymakers external to the social movement. Sometimes, a variety of names may be in use—each with a constituency that feels strongly that only some words are appropriate.

Of all the master statuses we are considering in this book, the naming of those with disabilities is perhaps the least settled. The term *handicapped,* which predominated in the period following World War II, shifted to *disabled* with the emergence of the disability rights movement in the 1970s. As we have seen, theorists from the British social model draw a distinction between *impairment,* referring to "the physical, cognitive, emotional or sensory condition within the person as diagnosed by medical professionals," and *disability,* which is reserved for the social processes that disable a person[28]—but the U.S. disability rights movement uses *disability* to cover both of these features. The style guide for the American Psychological Association urges a "people first" approach, as in "people with disabilities" rather than "disabled people," and "people first" terminology has been formally authorized by some state and local governments. By contrast, one of the founders of the British disability rights movement—Mike Oliver—argued that *disabled people* is ultimately more appropriate:

> It is sometimes argued, often by [nondisabled] professionals and some disabled people, that "people with disabilities" is the preferred term, for it asserts the value of the person first and the disability then becomes an appendage. This liberal and humanist view flies in the face of reality as it is experienced by disabled people themselves who argue that far from being an appendage, disability is an essential part of the self. In this view, it is nonsensical to talk about the person and the disability separately, and consequently, disabled people are demanding acceptance as they are, disabled people.[29]

In all, the names that we call ourselves and others are rarely a matter of indifference; they are often carefully chosen to reflect worldview and aspirations, and they can materially shape our lives.

Creating Categories of People   While individuals and groups may assert names for themselves, governments also have the power to categorize. The history of the race and ethnicity questions asked in the U.S. Census illustrates this process.

Every census since the first one in 1790 has included a question about race. By 1970, the options for race were *white, Negro or black, American Indian* (with a request to print the name of the enrolled or principal tribe), *Japanese, Chinese, Filipino, Hawaiian, Korean,* and *Other* with the option of specifying. The 1970 census began the practice of allowing the head of the household to identify the race of household members: before that, the census taker had made that decision. Thus, in 1970 the Census Bureau began treating race as primarily a matter of *self*-identification. Still, it was assumed that a person could only be a member of *one* racial group, so respondents were allowed only one option for each household member.

The 1970 census also posed the first ethnicity question, asking whether the individual was of Hispanic or non-Hispanic ancestry. (Ethnicity, which generally refers to national or cultural ancestry, is a subject we will return to shortly.) The Hispanic/non-Hispanic question was added at the recommendation of the Census Bureau's Hispanic Advisory Committee as a way to correct for the *differential undercount* of the Hispanic population. A differential undercount means that more people are undercounted in one category than in another; for example, the census yields a larger undercount of those who rent their homes than of those who own them. Undercounting primarily affects the data on low-income residents of inner cities. This is the case because the poor often move and are thus difficult to contact; are more likely to be illiterate or non-English speakers (there was no Spanish-language census form until 1990); and are more likely to be illegal immigrants afraid to respond to a government questionnaire. (The Constitution requires a count of *all the people* in the United States, not just those who are citizens or legal residents.) Because census data affect the distribution of billions of dollars of federal aid, undercounting has a significant impact. Apart from the apportionment of seats in the U.S. House of Representatives, the census helps "determine how more than $400 billion dollars of federal funding each year [will be] spent on infrastructure and services like hospitals, job training centers, schools, senior centers, bridges, tunnels and other-public works projects, and emergency services."[30]

Most important for our purposes, census data can be used to identify patterns of discrimination and support the enforcement of civil rights. Thus, to improve the collection of this data, in the 1970s the Commission on Civil Rights reviewed the race categorization practices of federal agencies, concluding that while "the designations do not refer strictly to race, color, national or ethnic origin," the categories were nonetheless what the general public understood to be *minority groups* who were subject to discrimination.[31]

This understanding of the meaning of "minority group" was part of a remarkable bipartisan consensus that characterized the decade following the 1964 Civil Rights Act.

> It was a bipartisan project, including from both parties liberals and conservatives. . . . In the signature minority rights policy, affirmative action, the federal government went beyond African Americans and declared that certain groups were indeed "minorities"—an undefined term embraced by policymakers, advocates, and activists alike—and needed new rights and programs for equal opportunity and full citizenship. In the parlance of the period, minorities were groups seen as "disadvantaged" but not defined by income or education. African Americans were the paradigmatic minority, but there were three other ethnoracial minorities: Latinos, Asian Americans, and American Indians. Immigrants, women, and the disabled of all ethnic groups were also included and won new rights during this revolutionary period.[32]

In this context, in 1977, the Office of Management and Budget (OMB) issued Statistical Directive No. 15, "Race and Ethnic Standards for Federal Statistics and Administrative Reporting," which established standard categories and definitions for all federal agencies, including the Bureau of the Census. Directive No. 15 defined four racial and one ethnic category: American Indian

➤ NOTE: Please answer BOTH Question 5 about Hispanic origin and Question 6 about race. For this census, Hispanic origins are not races.

5 Is this person of Hispanic, Latino, or Spanish origin?

☐ **No,** not of Hispanic, Latino, or Spanish origin

☐ Yes, Mexican, Mexican Am., Chicano

☐ Yes, Puerto Rican

☐ Yes, Cuban

☐ Yes, another Hispanic, Latino, or Spanish origin — *Print origin, for example, Argentinean, Colombian, Dominican, Nicaraguan, Salvadoran, Spaniard, and so on.* ↘

_____

6 What is this person's race? *Mark* ☒ *one or more boxes.*

☐ White

☐ Black, African Am., or Negro

☐ American Indian or Alaska Native — *Print name of enrolled or principal tribe.* ↘

_____

☐ Asian Indian   ☐ Japanese   ☐ Native Hawaiian
☐ Chinese   ☐ Korean   ☐ Guamanian or Chamorro
☐ Filipino   ☐ Vietnamese   ☐ Samoan
☐ Other Asian — *Print race, for example, Hmong, Laotian, Thai, Pakistani, Cambodian, and so on.* ↘   ☐ Other Pacific Islander — *Print race, for example, Fijian, Tongan, and so on.* ↘

_____

☐ Some other race — *Print race.* ↘

_____

FIGURE 1
Questions from the 2010 Census.
Source: U.S. Census Bureau, 2010 Census.

or Alaskan Native, Asian or Pacific Islander, Negro or Black, White, and Hispanic. "The questions [on the census] follow the categories required by the federal Office of Management and Budget for federal statistics."[33] Thus, the question about Hispanic origin remains the only ethnicity question on the decennial census. (A question asking respondents to identify their "ancestry or national origin" is, however, included in the Census Bureau's annual American Community Survey, which samples U.S. households). Reading 3, "The Evolution of Identity," shows how census questions on race and ethnicity changed between 1860 and 2000. Figure 1 shows the relevant questions in the 2010 census.

For our purposes, the most notable recent change in the census has been recognition that a person may identify himself or herself as being a member of more than one racial group, although the census did not include a category called *multiracial.* This change was one outcome of a comprehensive review and revision of OMB's Directive No. 15 that included public hearings, sample surveys of targeted populations, and collaboration among the more than thirty federal agencies that collect and use data on race and ethnicity. While this change was spurred by activists who identified themselves as multiracial, the Bureau's pretesting also indicated that less than 2 percent of respondents would mark more than one race for themselves, and thus the historical continuity with previous censuses would not be compromised. The Bureau's expectation was close to the mark for the 2000 census—2.4 percent of the population, 6.8 million people, marked two or more races for themselves. But by the 2010 census, that figure had risen to 2.9 percent, or 9 million people.[34]

One change that has not been made in the census, however, is the inclusion of an ethnic category called *Arab* or *Middle Eastern,* because public comment did not indicate agreement on a definition for this category. For census purposes, *white* "refers to a person having origins in any of the original peoples of Europe, the Middle East, or North Africa. It includes people who indicated their race(s)[on the Census] as "white" or reported entries such as Irish, German, Italian, Lebanese, Arab, Moroccan, or Caucasian."[35]

As in previous censuses, undercounting remains an important fiscal and political issue, given the disproportionate undercounting of people of color and the poor. Still, gay couples may well be the most undercounted population. Since the 1990 census, the form has provided *unmarried partner* as a possible answer to the question of how the people in the household are related to one another. The 2010 census showed 131,729 same-sex couples who identified as *spouses* (which is a rate of 2.3 same-sex spouses per 1,000 male/female spouses) and 514,735 same-sex couples who identified themselves as *unmarried partners* (a rate of 70 same-sex, unmarried partners for every 1,000 unmarried male/female partners).[36] Certainly the unmarried, same-sex partner category is a significant undercount, attributable to respondents' reluctance to report.

We end this phase of our discussion with three cautions. First, on a personal level, many of us find census categorizations objectionable. But as *citizens,* we still seek the benefits and protections of the laws and policies based on these data—and as citizens we share the goal of eliminating discriminatory practices. For example, in the case of racial discrimination,

[r]eliable racial data are crucial to enforcing our basic laws against intentional racial discrimination, which enjoy broad public support. For example, in order to demonstrate that an employer is engaging in a broad-based "pattern or practice" of discrimination in violation of the Civil Rights Act of 1964, a plaintiff must rely on statistical proof that goes beyond the plight of an individual employee. Supreme Court precedent in such cases requires plaintiffs to show a statistically significant disparity between the proportion of qualified minorities in the local labor market and the proportion within the employer's

work force. A disparity of more than two standard deviations creates a legal presumption that intentional discrimination is occurring, since a disparity of that magnitude almost never occurs by accident.

Demographic information, in other words, provides the "big picture" that places individual incidents in context. Voting rights cases require similar proof, as do many housing discrimination cases and suits challenging the discriminatory use of federal funds. Without reliable racial statistics, it would be virtually impossible for courts or agencies to detect institutional bias, and antidiscrimination laws would go unenforced. More fundamentally, we simply cannot know as a society how far we've come in conquering racial discrimination and inequality without accurate information about the health, progress and opportunities available to communities of different races.[37]

Second, we need to remember that although the census is a fairly direct count of how people classify themselves, many other "counts" are taking place that may not be consistent with census categorization. For example, a student who describes herself as of multiple race and ethnic ancestry will be considered "Hispanic" by the federal Department of Education if even one of those categories can be classed as that, but she will be classified as Asian and Hispanic by the National Center for Health Statistics. Her birth certificate may have no racial designation or an option for multiple designations; these designations may be assigned by her mother or by the attending nurse or doctor. In all, we cannot expect consistency across data collection instruments.[38]

Last, when considering official counts of the population, we must be careful not to assume that what is counted is real. Although census data contribute to the essentialist view that the world is populated by distinct, scientifically defined categories of people, this brief history demonstrates that not even those who collect the data make that assumption. As even the Census Bureau notes, "The concept of race as used by the Census Bureau reflects self-identification by people according to the race or races with which they most closely identify. These categories are socio-political constructs and should not be interpreted as being scientific or anthropological in nature. Furthermore, the race categories include both racial and national-origin groups."[39]

Aggregating and Disaggregating

The federal identification policies we have been describing collapse nonwhite Americans into three categories—American Indians, Blacks, and Asian or Pacific Islanders—and recognize one "ethnic group," that is, Hispanics. In effect, this process *aggregates* categories of people; that is, it combines, or "lumps together," different groups. For example, the ethnic category *Hispanic, Latino, or Spanish origin* includes 28 different census categories.[d] While census data distinguishes

---

[d]The Census Bureau's Hispanic or Latino origin categories are Mexican, Puerto Rican, Cuban, Dominican; Costa Rican, Guatemalan, Honduran, Nicaraguan, Panamanian, Salvadoran, and Other Central American; Argentinian, Bolivian, Chilean, Colombian, Ecuadorian, Paraguayan, Peruvian, Uruguayan, Venezuelan, and Other South American; and finally Other Hispanic or Latino, including Spaniard, Spanish, Spanish American, and All other Hispanic or Latino.[40]

many of these groups, in public discussion the more common reference is to "Hispanics and Latinos," which both aggregates all those categories and masks which groups predominate. (The Census Bureau's 2011 American Community Survey found that 65 percent of U.S. Hispanics identify themselves as of Mexican origin, 9 percent as of Puerto Rican origin, 4 percent as of Salvadoran origin, 4 percent as of Cuban origin, and 3 percent as of Dominican origin.)[41] On top of that, the category "Hispanic and Latino" is used to encompass recent immigrants, Puerto Ricans (who are U.S. citizens), and those from some of the earliest settlements in what is now the United States.

> The difficulty with determining who counts as Hispanic is that Hispanics do not appear to share any properties in common. Linguistic, racial, religious, political, territorial, cultural, economic, educational, social class, and genetic criteria fail to identify Hispanics in all places and times. . . .
>
> [Nonetheless], we are treated as a homogeneous group by European Americans and African Americans; and even though Hispanics do not in fact constitute a homogeneous group, we are easily contrasted with European Americans and African Americans because we do not share many of the features commonly associated with these groups.[42]

The groups that are lumped together in this aggregate have historically regarded one another as different, and thus in people's everyday lives the aggregate category is likely to *disaggregate,* or fragment, into its constituent national-origin elements. For example, a 2013 survey of adults found that "when describing their identity, more than half (54%) of Hispanics say they most often use the name of their ancestors' Hispanic origin (such as Mexican, Dominican, Salvadoran or Cuban)." Only 20 percent said they most often described themselves as "Hispanic" or "Latino." (Twenty-three percent reported most often describing themselves as "American.")[43] Not surprisingly, 69 percent of Latinos surveyed in the 2011 Census Bureau's American Community Survey said that they do not share a common culture with other Latinos.[44]

And how do "Hispanics" identify themselves by race? In 2011, census data showed that 36 percent identified themselves as white, 10 percent identified themselves as black, 26 percent identified themselves as some other race, and 25 percent identified their race as Hispanic/Latino.[45] Indeed, most of those who choose "some other race" on the Census are Latinos.[46] Nonetheless, as Tanya Golash-Boza and William Darity, Jr. write in Reading 6, the way that Latinos describe their race is changeable, because it is responsive to their skin color and experiences of discrimination, and—for those who are recent immigrants—also responsive to definitions of race in their home country. All of these factors interact, and not necessarily in predictable ways.

In the same way that many differences are masked by the terms *Latino* and *Hispanic,* the category *Asian Pacific American* or *Asian American* includes groups with different languages, cultures, and religions, and sometimes centuries of mutual hostility. Like *Hispanic/Latino,* the category *Asian American* is based more on geography than on any cultural, racial, linguistic, or religious commonalities. "Asian

Americans are those who come from a region of the world that *the rest of the world has defined as Asia.*"[47e]

Much the same can be said for the terms *Middle East* and *Middle Eastern.* As John Tehranian writes in Reading 24, the term *Middle East* emerged at the beginning of the 20th century as part of political strategies. As a region that encompasses multiple continents, languages, ethnic groups, and religions, "the term is riddled in ambiguity, sometimes encompassing the entire North African coast, from Morocco to Egypt and other parts of Africa, including the Sudan and Somalia, the former Soviet Caucasus Republics of Georgia, Azerbaijan, and Armenia, and occasionally Afghanistan, Pakistan, and Turkistan. The Middle East is therefore a malleable geopolitical construct of relatively recent vintage."

Aggregate classifications have also been promoted by social movements; terms such as *Latino* or *Asian American* were not simply the result of federal classifications. Student activists inspired by the Black Power and civil rights movements first proposed the terms. *Asian American, Hispanic, Middle Eastern,* and *Latino* are examples of *panethnic* terms, that is, classifications that span national-origin identities. Student activists inspired by the Black Power and civil rights movements supported (and sometimes initiated) these panethnic classifications as a way to highlight the experiences of discrimination that groups within each classification shared. Thus, panethnic terminology often signaled the development of bridging organizations and other forms of solidarity across groups.

The concept of panethnicity is useful at many levels, but unstable in practice. "The elites representing such groups find it advantageous to make political demands by using the numbers and resources panethnic formations can mobilize. The state, in turn, can more easily manage claims by recognizing and responding to large blocs as opposed to dealing with the specific claims of a plethora of ethnically defined interest groups."[50] At the same time, competition and historic antagonisms make such alliances unstable. "At times it is advantageous to be in a panethnic bloc, and at times it is desirable to mobilize along particular ethnic lines."[51]

The disability movement is similar to panethnic movements in that it has brought together people with all types of impairments. This approach was a

---

[e]In census classification, the category *Asian* includes Asian Indian, Chinese, Filipino, Japanese, Korean, Vietnamese; *Other Asian* includes Bangladeshi, Bhutanese, Burmese, Cambodian, Hmong, Indo-Chinese, Indonesian, Iwo Jiman, Laotian, Malaysian, Maldivian, Mongolian, Nepalese, Okinawan, Pakistani, Singaporean, Sri Lankan, Thai, and Taiwanese. The category *Pacific Islander* includes Native Hawaiian, Guamanian or Chamorro, Samoan; *Other Pacific Islander* includes Carolinian, Chuukese, Fijian, Kirabati, Kosraean, Mariana Islander, Marshallese, Melanesian, Micronesian, New Hebridian, Palauan, Papua New Guinean, Pohnpeian, Polynesian, Saipanese, Solomon Islander, Tahitian, Tokelauan, Tongan, and Yapese.[48]

In 1980, Asian Indians successfully lobbied to change their census classification from *white* to *Asian American* by reminding Congress that historically, immigrants from India had been classed as *Asian*. With other Asians, those from India had been barred from immigration by the 1917 Immigration Act, prohibited from becoming naturalized citizens until 1946, and denied the right to own land by 1920 Alien Land Law. Indeed, in 1923 the U.S. Supreme Court (in *U.S. v. Thind*) ruled that Asian Indians were nonwhite, and could therefore have their U.S. citizenship nullified.[49] Thus, for most of their history in the United States, Asian Indians had been classed as *Asian*.

historic "first," running counter both to the tradition of organizing around specific impairments and to the fact that the needs of people with different impairments are sometimes in conflict. For example, some of the curb cuts that make wheelchair access possible can make walking more difficult for blind people who need to be able to feel the edges of a sidewalk with their canes. The aggregating of disabled people that began with the disability rights movement was reinforced in the 1990 Americans with Disabilities Act (ADA).

The terms *Native American* and *African American* are also aggregate classifications, but in this case they are the result of conquest and enslavement.

> The "Indian," like the European, is an idea. The notion of "Indians" was invented to distinguish the indigenous peoples of the New World from Europeans. The "Indian" is the person on shore, outside of the boat. . . . There [were] hundreds of cultures, languages, ways of living in Native America. The place was a model of diversity at the time of Columbus's arrival. Yet Europeans did not see this diversity. They created the concept of the "Indian" to give what they did see some kind of unification, to make it a single entity they could deal with, because they could not cope with the reality of 400 different cultures.[52f]

Conquest made "American Indians" out of a multitude of tribes and nations that had been distinctive on linguistic, religious, and economic grounds. It was not only that Europeans had the unifying concept of *Indian* in mind—after all, they were sufficiently aware of cultural differences to generate an extensive body of specific treaties with individual tribes. It was also that conquest itself—encompassing as it did the appropriation of land, the forging and violation of treaties, and policies of forced relocation—structured the lives of Native Americans along common lines. Whereas contemporary Native Americans still identify themselves by tribal ancestry, rather than "Native American" or "American Indian," their shared experience of conquest also forged the common identity reflected in the collective name, *Native American.*

Similarly, the capture, purchase, and forced relocation of Africans, and their experience of forcibly being moved from place to place as personal property, created the category now called *African American.* This experience forged a single people out of a culturally diverse group; it produced an "oppositional racial consciousness," that is, a unity-in-opposition. "Just as the conquest created the 'native' where once there had been Pequot, Iroquois, or Tutelo, so too it created the 'black' where once there had been Asante or Ovimbundu, Yoruba or Bakongo."[53]

Even the categories of *gay and straight, male and female, people of color,* and *poor and middle class* are aggregations that presume a commonality by virtue of shared master status. For example, the category *gay and lesbian* assumes that sharing a sexual identity binds people together despite all the issues that

---

[f]The idea of *Europe* and the *European* is also a constructed, aggregate category. "Physically, Europe is not a continent. Where is the water separating Europe from Asia? It is culture that separates Europe from Asia. Western Europe roughly comprises the countries that in the Middle Ages were Latin Christendom, and Eastern Europe consists of those countries that in the Middle Ages were Eastern Orthodox Christendom. It was about A.D. 1257 when the Pope claimed hegemony over the secular emperors in Western Europe and formulated the idea that Europeans, Christians, were a unified ethnicity even though they spoke many different languages."[54]

might divide them as men and women, people of color, or people of different social classes. And, just as in the cases we have previously discussed, the formation of alliances between gays and lesbians will depend on the circumstances and specific issues.

Still, our analysis has so far ignored one category of people. From whose perspective do the categories of *Native American, Asian American, African American, Middle Eastern American, Arab American,* and *Latino/Hispanic* exist? Since "difference" is always "difference *from*," from whose perspective is "difference" determined? Who has the power to define "difference"? If "we" are in the boat looking at "them," who precisely are "we"?

Every perspective on the social world emerges from a particular vantage point, a particular social location. Ignoring who is in the boat treats that place as if it were just the view "anyone" would take. Historically, the people in the boat were European; at present, they are white Americans. As Ruth Frankenberg frames it in Reading 7, in the United States "whites are the nondefined definers of other people," "the unmarked marker of others' differentness." Failing to identify the "us" in the boat means that "white culture [becomes] the unspoken norm," a category that is powerful enough to define others while itself remaining invisible and unnamed.

Thus,

> [F]or most whites, most of the time, to think or speak about race is to think or speak about people of color, or perhaps, at times, to reflect on oneself (or other whites) in relation to people of color. But we tend not to think of ourselves or our racial cohort as racially distinctive. Whites' "consciousness" of whiteness is predominantly unconsciousness of whiteness.[55]

Because whites do not usually identify themselves by race, they do not easily understand the significance of racial identities.[56] In all, those with the most power in a society are best positioned to have their own identities left unnamed, thus masking their power.

The term *androcentrism* describes the world as seen from a male-centered perspective. For example, if we define a good employee as one who is willing to work extensive overtime, we are thinking from a male-centered perspective, since women's child-care responsibilities often preclude extra work commitments. We may also describe *Eurocentric* and *physicalist*[57] perspectives, that is, viewpoints that assume everyone is of European origin or physically agile. Similarly, the term *heteronormativity* turns our attention to the ways that heterosexuality is built into the assumptions and operation of all aspects of daily life, both sexual and nonsexual.[58] Heteronormativity is one of a set of terms that has emerged to describe individual- and societal-level treatment of homosexuality. In 1972, in *Society and the Healthy Homosexual,* psychologist George Weinberg offered the term *homophobia* to describe the aversion to homosexuals that he found among people at the time. As he said later, "It was a fear of homosexuals which seemed to be associated with a fear of contagion, a fear of reducing the things one fought for—home and family. . . . [I]t led to great brutality as fear always does."[59] The term was a watershed; it defined the problem as heterosexual intolerance, not homosexuality.

Weinberg was not thinking of homophobia in clinical terms,[60] for example, phobias are usually experienced as "unpleasant and dysfunctional," which is not the case with "homophobia." Nonetheless, the term is now pervasive and routinely identified as part of the triumvirate, "sexism, racism, and homophobia." One problem with that, however, is that homophobia focuses on individual prejudices rather than societal structures. Thus, in 1990, psychologist Gregory Herek offered the word *heterosexism* to describe "an ideological system that denies, denigrates, and stigmatizes any nonheterosexual form of behavior, identity, relationship or community."[61] A decade later, he suggested that the term *sexual prejudice* replace homophobia.[62]

The more recent concept of *heteronormativity* turns our attention to all the ways in which heterosexuality is presumed to be the natural, normal, and inevitable structure of society. It is the "view from the boat." First put forward by English professor Michael Warner, heteronormativity describes heterosexuality as akin to an "official national culture";[63] a "sense of rightness—embedded in things and not just in sex—is what we call heteronormativity."

> People are constantly encouraged to believe that heterosexual desire, dating, marriage, reproduction, childrearing, and home life are not only valuable to themselves, but the bedrock on which every other value in the world rests. Heterosexual desire and romance are thought to be the very core of humanity. It is the threshold of maturity that separates the men from the boys (though it is also projected onto all boys and girls). It is both nature and culture. It is the one thing celebrated in every film plot, every sitcom, every advertisement. It is the one thing to which every politician pays obeisance, couching every dispute over guns and butter as an effort to protect family, home, and children. What would a world look like in which all these links between sexuality and people's ideas were suddenly severed? Nonstandard sex has none of this normative richness, this built-in sense of connection to the meaningful life, the community of the human, the future of the world.[64]

> . . . [F]rom senior proms to conjugal rights in prison, from couples' discounts at hotels to the immediate immigration rights of foreign marital partners, from a nonchalant goodbye kiss at the airport to incessant male-female couples grinning down from billboards, to fairy tales with princes rescuing princesses. It is, indeed, difficult to find any aspect of modern life that does not include men desiring women and women desiring men as a premise, as necessary to being human as thinking and breathing.[65]

In all, naming androcentrism, Eurocentrism, physicalism, and heteronormativity helps us recognize them as particular social locations, like the other master statuses we have considered. Indeed, it is possible to argue that, no matter what their master statuses, all Americans operate from these particular biases because they are built into the basic fabric of our culture.

Dichotomizing

Many forces promote the construction of aggregate categories of people. Frequently, these aggregates emerge as *dichotomies.* Sociologists have argued that the creation of dichotomized categories is a regular feature of social life because it is a way to resolve life's routine problems, for example, allocating tasks by gender. More important, dichotomization inevitably yields categories that will be unequally valued and rewarded; in social life, the two parts of a dichotomy will never be "equal." Categorical inequalities emerge and persist because some benefit from them and because there is a societal cost to transitioning out of their use. Thus, inequality between categories of people becomes "durable" over interactions, time, space, and lifetimes. The extent of inequality between dichotomous pairs may vary, the grounds on which categories are established may differ, and the efforts directed at reducing such inequalities may change, but dichotomized categorical inequalities are likely a constant of social life.[66]

But to dichotomize is not only to divide something into two parts; it is also to see those parts as mutually exclusive and in opposition. Dichotomization encourages the sense that there are only two categories, that everyone fits easily in one or the other, and that the categories stand in opposition to each other. In contemporary American culture, we appear to treat the master statuses of race, sex, class, sexual identity, and disability as if each embodied "us" and "them"—as if for each master status, people could be easily sorted into two mutually exclusive, opposed groupings.[g]

Dichotomizing Race   Perhaps the clearest example of the historic and continuing dichotomization of race is provided by the "one-drop rule," which is described by F. James Davis in Reading 2. This "rule" became a law but now operates only as an informal social practice, holding that people with any traceable African heritage should classify themselves as *black*. President Barack Obama's identification of himself as African American on the 2010 census is consistent with this practice. The rule, which is unique to the United States and South Africa, grew out of the efforts of southern whites to enforce segregation after the Civil War, but over time came to be endorsed by *both* blacks and whites. Consistent with this practice, only about 4 percent of black Americans identify themselves as having ancestry from more than one race, even though a much larger percentage have Native American and/or white ancestry.[67]

While the one-drop rule applied to the identification of who was black, the three racial categories identified by the census throughout the 19th century—*White, Negro,* and *Indian*—were functionally collapsed into a white/nonwhite binary. For example, in 1854, the California Supreme Court in *People v. Hall* held that blacks, mulattos, Native Americans, and Chinese were "not white" and therefore could not testify for or against a white man in court. (Hall, a white man, had been convicted of killing a Chinese man on the testimony of one white and three Chinese witnesses; the Supreme Court overturned the conviction.) The same dichotomization can be seen in the Supreme Court's decision in *Plessy v. Ferguson* (1896) described in Reading 37.

At the insistence of the Mexican government, Mexican residents of the southwest territories ceded to the United States in the 1848 Treaty of Guadalupe Hidalgo were placed on the "white" side of the ledger, and accorded the political-legal status of "free white persons."[68] European immigrants such as the Irish were initially treated as nonwhite, and lobbied for their inclusion in American society on the basis of the white/nonwhite distinction.

---

[g]Springer and Deutsch (1981) coined the term *dichotomania* to describe the belief that there are male and female sides of the brain. We think that term also fits our discussion.

[Immigrants struggled to] equate whiteness with Americanism in order to turn arguments over immigration from the question of who was foreign to the question of who was white. . . .

Immigrants could not win on the question of who was foreign. . . . But if the issue somehow became defending "white man's jobs" or "white man's government" . . . [they] could gain space by deflecting debate from nativity, a hopeless issue, to race, an ambiguous one. . . . After the Civil War, the new-coming Irish would help lead the movement to bar the relatively established Chinese from California, with their agitation for a "white man's government," serving to make race, and not nativity, the center of the debate and to prove the Irish white.[69]

Thus, historically, *American* has meant *white,* as many contemporary Americans of Asian ancestry learn when they are complimented on their English—a compliment that presumes that someone who is Asian could not be a native-born American.[h] A story from the 1998 Winter Olympics illustrates the same point. At the conclusion of the figure skating competition, MSNBC posted a headline that read "American Beats Out Kwan for Women's Figure Skating Title." The reference was to Michelle Kwan, who won the silver medal, losing the gold to Tara Lapinsky. But both Kwan and Lapinsky are Americans. While Kwan's parents immigrated from Hong Kong, she was born and raised in the United States, is a U.S. citizen, and was a member of the U.S. team. The network attributed the mistake to overworked staff and apologized. But for Asian American activists, this was an example of how people of Asian descent have remained perpetual foreigners in American society.

African American novelist Toni Morrison would describe this as a story about "how *American* means *white*":

Deep within the word "American" is its association with race. To identify someone as South African is to say very little; we need the adjective "white" or "black" or "colored" to make our meaning clear. In this country it is quite the reverse. American means white, and Africanist people struggle to make the term applicable to themselves with . . . hyphen after hyphen after hyphen.[70]

Insofar as *American* means *white,* those who are not white are presumed to be recent arrivals and often told to go "back where they came from." Thus, we appear to operate within the dichotomized *racial* categories of *American/non-American*—these are racial categories, because they effectively mean *white/nonwhite.*

Yet it is possible that the "white/nonwhite dichotomy" is in the midst of an ironic transformation, into what Lee and Bean in Reading 8 characterize as a "black/nonblack" dichotomy. Unlike Latinos and Asian Americans who, with success, have come to be seen as similar to whites, African Americans are seen by whites as dissimilar no matter what their success, just as the children of black-white parentage are perceived by both blacks and whites as black. This black/

---

[h]Since the historic American ban on Asian immigration remained in place until 1965, it is the case that a high proportion of Asian Americans—about 75 percent—are foreign born (although the percentage who are foreign-born varies by national origin).[71]

nonblack dichotomy argues for an "African American exceptionalism" to the incorporation of minority groups into whiteness.

Defining Race and Ethnicity   But what exactly *is* race? First, we need to distinguish *race* from *ethnicity*. Social scientists define *ethnic groups* as categories of people who are distinctive on the basis of national origin or heritage, language, or cultural practices. "Members of an ethnic group hold a set of common memories that make them feel that their customs, culture, and outlook are distinctive."[72] Indeed, in Reading 20, Harlan Lane argues that there is a Deaf-World ethnic group distinct from those for whom deafness is a hearing impairment.

Thus, *ethnicity* is very much about the intensity of people's feelings, and these may be inconsistent, as well as, change over time. For example, being an Italian American in the 1920s involved much more intensity of feeling, interaction, and political organization than it does now, and being a Jew has become an ethnic, rather than a religious, identity for many. For others, such as Bosnian refugees, ethnic identity can involve a painful choice between religion and nationality—are they Bosnian, Bosnian Muslim, or Muslim, or do they reject ethnic identity altogether since "ethnic cleansing" made them refugees in the first place?[73]

Finally, even though ethnic identity is often more important to people than race, it can be obscured by race. For example, focusing only on race would hide the important differences between African Americans, Haitians, Somalis, Ethiopians, or Jamaicans—all black American ethnic groups. Similarly, Americans with Middle Eastern heritage (who are classified as *white* in the census) are often misdescribed as *Arabs,* which includes only those from Arabic-speaking countries. A scene in the movie *Crash* made this point: in vandalizing the store of an Iranian grocer, the looters left behind graffiti about "Arabs," but Iranians speak Farsi and do not consider themselves Arabic. In all, beneath panethnic terms such as *Middle Eastern, Arab American, Latino,* or *Asian American,* one will find strong ethnic attachments based on national origin or religion.

The term *race* first appeared in the Romance languages of Europe in the Middle Ages to refer to breeding stock. A race of horses described common ancestry and a distinctive appearance or behavior. *Race* appears to have been first applied to New World peoples by the Spanish in the 16th century. Later it was adopted by the English, again in reference to people of the New World, and it generally came to mean *people, nation,* or *variety.* By the late 18th century, "when scholars became more actively engaged in investigations, classifications, and definitions of human populations, the term *race* was elevated as the one major symbol and mode of human group differentiation employed extensively for non-European groups and even those in Europe who varied in some way from the subjective norm."[74]

Though elevated to the level of science, the concept of race continued to reflect its origins in animal breeding. Farmers and herders had used the concept to describe stock bred for particular qualities; scholars used it to suggest that human behaviors could also be inherited. "Unlike other terms for classifying people . . .

the term 'race' places emphasis on innateness, on the inbred nature of whatever is being judged."[75] Like animal breeders, scholars also presumed that appearance revealed something about potential behavior. Just as the selective breeding of animals entailed the ranking of stock by some criteria, scholarly use of the concept of race involved the ranking of humans. Differences in skin color, hair texture, and the shape of head, eyes, nose, lips, and body were developed into an elaborate hierarchy of merit and potential for "civilization."

As described by Audrey Smedley in Reading 1, the idea of race emerged among all the European colonial powers, although their conceptions of it varied. However, only the British in colonizing North America and South Africa constructed a system of rigid, exclusive racial categories and a social order *based on race*, a "racialized social structure."[76] "[S]kin color variations in many regions of the world and in many societies have been imbued with some degree of social value or significance, but color prejudice or preferences do not of themselves amount to a fully evolved racial worldview."[77]

This racialized social structure—which in the United States produced a race-based system of slavery and subsequently a race-based distribution of political, legal, and social rights—was a historical first. "Expansion, conquest, exploitation, and enslavement have characterized much of human history over the past five thousand years or so, but none of these events before the modern era resulted in the development of ideologies or social systems based on race."[78] Although differences of color had long been noted, societies had never before been built on those differences.

The sciences that emerged from this racialized social structure were also racialized; because scientists presumed that "race" involved more than just color, they sought the biological distinctivness of race categories. Their belief that they had found such differences followed from their flawed assumptions and research methods. By the early 20th century, anthropologists discovered that the physical features that had been used to distinguish the races such as height, stature, and head shape could be changed by environment and nutrition. Thus, the certainties about "race" and what it meant—at least in the sciences—began to be questioned.[79]

In effect, science was confronting a kind of "bottom line" about race: while there are many ways humans can be grouped, those do not correspond to traditional notions of race.

If our eyes could perceive more than the superficial, we might find race in chromosome 11: there lies the gene for hemoglobin. If you divide humankind by which of two forms of the gene each person has, then equatorial Africans, Italians and Greeks fall into the "sickle-cell race"; Swedes and South Africa's Xhosas (Nelson Mandela's ethnic group) are in the healthy hemoglobin race. Or do you prefer to group people by whether they have epicanthic eye folds, which produce the "Asian" eye? Then the !Kung San (Bushmen) belong with the Japanese and Chinese. . . . [D]epending on which traits you pick, you can form very surprising races. Take the scooped-out shape of the back of the front teeth, a standard "Asian" trait. Native Americans and Swedes have these shovel-shaped incisors, too, and so would fall in the same race. Is biochemistry better? Norwegians, Arabians, north Indians and the Fulani of northern Nigeria . . . fall into the "lactase race" (the lactase enzyme digests milk sugar). Everyone else—other Africans, Japanese, Native Americans—form the "lactase-deprived race" (their ancestors did not drink milk from cows or goats and hence never evolved the lactase gene). How about blood types, the familiar A, B, and O groups? Then Germans and New Guineans, populations that have the same percentages of each type, are in one race; Estonians and Japanese comprise a separate one for the same reason. . . . The dark skin of Somalis and Ghanaians, for instance, indicates that they evolved under the same selective force (a sunny climate). But that's all it shows. It does *not* show that they are any more closely related in the sense of sharing more genes than either is to Greeks. Calling Somalis and Ghanaians "black" therefore sheds no further light on their evolutionary history and implies—wrongly—that they are more closely related to each other than either is to some-one of a different "race."[80]

As one anthropologist has put it, "Classifying people by color is very much like classifying cars by color. Those in the same classification look alike . . . but the classification tells you nothing about the hidden details of construction or about how the cars or people will perform."[81]

By the late 1960s, a "no race" position came to be widely accepted in physical anthropology and human genetics. This perspective argues that "(1) Biological variability exists but this variability does not conform to the discrete packages labeled races. (2) So-called racial characteristics are not transmitted as complexes. (3) Races do not exist because isolation of groups has been infrequent; popula-tions have always interbred."[82] Yet while there is a kind of "commonsense" under-standing in the social sciences that race is a social construction, that recognition has not especially shaped the substance of social science research.

> [I]t will suffice to point out that virtually all scholars who write about "race and intelligence" assume that the "races" which they study are distinguished on the basis of biologically relevant criteria. So accepted is this fact that most scholars engaged in such research never consider it necessary to justify their assignment of individuals to this or that "race." . . . [Thus], the layman who reads the literature on race and racial groupings is justified in assuming that the existent typologies have been derived through the application of theories and methods current in disciplines concerned with the biological study of human variation. Since the scientific racial classifications which a layman finds in the literature are not too different from popular ones, he can be expected to feel justified in the maintenance of his views on race.[83]

The complexities of incorporating a "no race" position into social science research is highlighted by how the professional associations in anthropology and sociology treat the concept. In 1998, the American Anthropological Association (AAA) adopted an unambiguous "Statement on Race": "Racial beliefs constitute myths about the diversity in the human species and about the abilities and behavior of people homogenized into 'racial' categories." But for the American Sociological Association (ASA), that does not mean we should stop collecting data on race: its 2002 statement, "The Importance of Collecting Data and Doing Social Scientific Research on Race," urges the continued study of race as a *social* phenomenon because it affects major aspects of social life—including employment, housing, education, and health. The title of the ASA's press release on the topic reads, "Would 'Race' Disappear if the United States Officially Stopped Collecting Data on It?" Their answer to that is clearly "no"; anthropologists would certainly agree.

Still, the assumption that racial categories are biologically distinctive has not disappeared—indeed, it gathered strength with the mapping of the human genome at the beginning of the 21st century. Completion of the Human Genome Project was met with pronouncements that, finally, our notions of race could be put to rest since humans were found to share shared 99.9 percent of all genetic material. Yet attention quickly shifted to finding groupings within that genetic material and determining the significance of the 0.1 percent difference. (Because humans and chimpanzees share 98.7 percent of their genes, for example, that 0.1 percent difference could make a difference.)

By 2002, in a landmark article published in *Science,* "researchers announced that they had 'identified six main genetic clusters, five of which correspond to major geographic regions.'" *Although race was not mentioned,* the "major geographic regions" that matched the genetic clusters they discovered—Africa, Eurasia, East Asia, Oceania, and America—were quickly translated into traditional racial divisions."[84] Other research along this line followed, using similar sampling techniques and contributing to a burgeoning data set. Thus, as legal scholar Dorothy Roberts frames it, "geographic ancestry" emerged as a proxy for race.

Yet each decision in this research—sampling isolated (and thereby "pure") populations rather than regions like India where people are not easily classifiable, "cherry picking" population samples that fit preexisting conceptions of race rather than pursuing a random sample of the global population, deciding that the statistical analysis of a huge data set is best captured by a model of six rather than twenty geographic regions, as in the *Science* article—draws on preexisting conceptions of race.

> [R]emember, the number of genetic clusters is dictated by the computer user, not the computer program. . . . Rosenberg [lead author of the *Science* article] later revealed that his team also analyzed the data set using six to twenty clusters. . . . The larger number of clusters identified by the study could just as easily have been highlighted to demonstrate the difficulty of dividing human beings into genetic races. There is nothing in the team's findings to suggest that six clusters represent human population structure better than ten, or fifteen, or twenty.[85]

The six groupings mapped onto conventional notions of race—indigenous people from five continents plus one isolated group in Northern Pakistan. Instead of talking about race, we could talk about ancestry.

New marketing opportunities for "ancestry" flourish; each reinforces the idea of biological races. For example, many students in high school learn about DNA by sending a sample to a company that analyzes it for the geographic origins of the student's family (using the same questionable sampling and data sets described earlier). Because those geographic groupings are broken down into the continents we associate with race, it is not surprising that the results are read as being one's "racial" composition, as if there were "pure" racial groups and we are some mix of these ("I am 43 percent European, 26 percent Sub-Saharan African, and 31 percent East Asian," sounds very much like white, black, and Asian).

But many more lucrative opportunities exist in the realm of race-specific medications, the first of which was BiDil, a 2004 drug for heart disease and the first race-targeted medication approved by the FDA. (BiDil is a combination of two generic drugs and thus could be patented as something new.) If race were not "real," how could the drug be more effective for African Americans, as the manufacturer claimed? Actually, whether BiDil has a differential effect by race remains unknown. The first clinical trial of the drug found that a small subsample of African Americans did better than whites. On that basis, the drug went to a full-scale clinical trial, but only on self-identified African Americans; there was no comparison with other groups. Why not? Because the drug's manufacturer, NitroMed, "had a financial disincentive for finding that BiDil worked regardless of race—its patent (and market monopoly) applied only to its use by African American patients."[86] Ultimately, BiDil was neither especially prescribed nor used; NitroMed went out of business in 2009.[87]

Certainly, the search for "race"-based drugs continues. These efforts to find the biological distinctiveness of racial categories function much as earlier efforts did, that is, as a distraction from the *social* factors that affect the quality and length of people's lives.

> By looking at what's in the blood, [geneticists] avoid the messy stuff that happens when humans interact with each other. It's easier to look inside the body because genes, proteins, and SNP [single nucleotide polymorphisms] patterns are far more measurable than the complex dynamics of society. . . .
>
> When you're talking about genetic diseases, there's usually something in the environment that triggers their onset. Shouldn't we be talking about the trigger?
>
> Take the case of black men and prostate cancer. African-American males have twice the prostate cancer rate that whites do. Right now, the National Cancer Institute is searching for cancer genes among black men. They're not asking, How come black men in the Caribbean and in sub-Saharan Africa have much lower prostate cancer rates than all American men?
>
> A balanced approach might involve asking, Is there something in the American environment triggering these high rates? Is it diet, stress or what?[88]

The primary significance of race is as a *social* concept. We "see" race; we expect it to tell us something significant about a person, and we organize social policy, law, and the distribution of wealth, power, and prestige around it. From the essentialist position, race is assumed to exist independently of our perception of it; it is assumed to significantly distinguish one group of people from another. From the constructionist perspective, race exists because we have created it as a meaningful category of difference among people.

Race has been characterized as a biological fiction, but a social fact. Yet the strength of this fiction suggests that it functions like a contemporary folk story.

> Most Americans do not deduce that biological races exist from sound scientific evidence and reasoning. They are inculcated with this belief in the same way a child is raised in a religion. Children in the United States learn to divide all people into racial groups and come

to have faith in race as a self-evident truth, like a traditional creation story that explains how the world works.

According to folklorist Judith Neulander, for a folk story to persist it must contain "elements that can be modified without changing what the tale is about," enabling it "to dodge later discreditation" Science has been responsible for giving racial folklore its superficial plausibility by updating its definitions, measurements, and rationales without changing what the tale is about: once upon a time human beings all over the world were divided into large biological groups called races.

Believing in race can be compared to believing in astrology. People who have faith in astrology find constant confirmation that horoscope predictions are reliable and that astrological signs determine personality types.[89]

Dichotomizing Sexuality   Many similarities have existed in the construction of race and sexuality categories. First, historically both have been dichotomized— into black/white, white/nonwhite, or gay/straight—and individuals have been expected to fit easily into one category or the other. Scientists have also sought biological differences between gay and straight people just as they have looked for such differences between the "races." Usually the search has been for what causes same-sex attraction, rather than for what causes heterosexuality—the point made by Martin Rochlin's Heterosexual Questionnaire (Reading 17). But, as with investigations of race difference, the research is suspect here as well, because we are unlikely to find any biological structure or process that *all* gay people share but *no* straight people have. Still, as Roger Lancaster describes in Reading 16, the conviction that such differences must exist propels the search and leads to the popularization of questionable findings.

As with race, sexual identity appears more straightforward than it really is. Because sexuality encompasses physical, social, and emotional attraction, as well as fantasies, self-identity, and actual sexual behavior over a lifetime, determining one's sexual "identity" may require emphasizing one of these features over the others. Further, there is no necessary correspondence between identity and sexual behavior (which Esther Rothblum explores for women in Reading 30). Someone who self-identifies as gay is still likely to have had some heterosexual experience; someone who self-identifies as straight may have had some same-sex experience; and even those who have had *no* sexual experience may lay claim to being gay or straight. Identity is not always directly tied to behavior. Indeed, a person who self-identifies as gay may have had *more* heterosexual experience than someone who self-identifies as straight. Yet just as the system of racial classification asks people to pick *one* race, the sexual-identity system has so far required that all the different aspects of sexuality be distilled into one of two options.

For example, an acquaintance described the process by which he came to self-identify as gay. In high school and college he had dated and been sexually active with women, but his relationships with men had always been more important to him. He looked to men for emotional and social gratification, as well as for relief from the "gender games" he felt required to play with women. He had been engaged to be married, but when that ended, he spent his time exclusively with other men. Eventually, he established a sexual relationship with another man and came to identify himself as gay. His experience reflects the varied dimensions of sexuality and shows the resolution of those differences by choosing a single sexual identity.

Until recently, "gay" and "straight" would have been his only real options. Despite commonplace use of the term, bisexuality has rarely been taken seriously by sex researchers or those in the gay and lesbian communities, where bisexuality has been demeaned as a phase, a form of homophobia, or simple promiscuity. The possibility of male bisexuality has especially been discounted by self-identified gay men.

Describing "biphobia" and "bi erasure," a newly emerging movement of self-identified bisexuals has been supported by survey and sexuality research. In 2011, the Williams Institute, which specializes in LGBT research, reported on their review of eleven surveys, finding that "among adults who identify as L.G.B., bisexuals comprise a slight majority."[90] Indeed, one of the larger surveys the Williams Institute reviewed found that *more* American adults identified themselves as bisexual than as gay/lesbian (3.1 percent compared to 2.5 percent). Similarly, as population sampling and sexuality research methods have broadened, it has become possible to demonstrate patterns of arousal that are bisexual,[91] with one possibility that "what makes a bisexual person may be less about what they're strongly attracted to and more about what they're not averse to."[92] While sexual fluidity has long been seen as a characteristic of women but not men, even the author of one of our readings, Lisa Diamond, has revised her opinion. Five years after the publication of her 2009 book (from which our reading is taken), she presented a paper titled "I Was Wrong! Men are Pretty Darn Sexually Fluid, Too!"[93]

Why has bisexuality been so systematically "erased"? The convenience of dichotomous thinking, fear of prejudice (people who identify as straight appear to have more negative attitudes about those who are bisexual than about those who are gay or lesbian);[94] lack of visible bisexuals (only 28 percent of people who identify as bisexual say they are open about it);[95] and the very contentious debate about whether sexuality is fixed and innate or changeable, would all have contributed to the invisibility of bisexuality. Finally, people may simply want to reduce the complexity of their lives: "To come out as bisexual now would be like starting over in a way. My mom and dad would fall over. It was hard enough to convince them that I was gay."[96]

To return to our initial comparison of sexual identity and race, one last analogy bears discussion. Most Americans would not question the logic of this sentence: "Tom has been married for 30 years and has a dozen children, but I think he's *really* gay." In a real-life illustration of the same logic, a young man and woman were often seen kissing on our campus. When this became the subject of a class discussion, a suggestive ripple of laughter went through the room: Everyone "knew" that the young man was really gay.

How could they "know" that? For such conclusions to make sense, we must believe that someone could be gay irrespective of his or her actual behavior.

Just as it is possible in this culture for one to be "black" even if one looks "white," apparently one may be gay despite acting straight. Just as "black" can be established by any African heritage, "gay" is apparently established by displaying any behavior thought to be associated with gays, especially for men. Indeed, "gay" can be "established" by reputation alone, by a failure to demonstrate heterosexuality, or even by the demonstration of an overly aggressive heterosexuality. Therefore, "gay" can be assigned no matter what one does. In this sense, "gay" can function as an *essential identity,*[97] that is, an identity assigned to an individual *irrespective of his or her actual behavior,* as in "I know she's a genius even though she's flunking all her courses." Because no behavior can ever conclusively prove one is *not* gay, this label is an extremely effective mechanism of social control.

In all, several parallels exist between race and sexuality classifications. At least until recently, we have assumed there are a limited number of possibilities—usually two, but no more than three—and we have assumed individuals can easily fit into one option. We have treated both race and sexuality as encompassing populations that are internally homogeneous and profoundly dissimilar from each other. In both cases, this presumption of difference has prompted a wide-ranging search for the biological distinctiveness of the categories. Different races and sexualities have been judged superior and inferior to one another, and members of each category historically have been granted unequal legal and social rights. Finally, we have assumed that sexual orientation, like skin color, tells us something meaningful about a person.

You may notice we used the past tense in the previous paragraph. This is because it seems to us that the traditional race and sexuality systems are undergoing change, although probably not to the same extent. As with the increasing presence of people who identify as multiracial, bisexuality has emerged as a category around which people organize. The outstanding question, however, is whether bisexuality will emerge as a "third" option, or upend our notions of sexuality altogether. College students and perhaps young people generally appear to have an increasing desire to move away from gender and sexuality labels. Accompanying the increased visibility and acceptance of both gay and transgender people—and the conceptual system that understands these as separate decisions, one about sexuality and the other about sex—there is a case that youth especially are less inclined to sexuality/gender classifications and more open in their own sexual behavior. We are not sure how widespread this change is, but have included in the readings an article by Eric Anderson (Reading 55), who contends that we are now past the era of "homohysteria." Anderson's conclusions are at odds with other readings in this volume, but we think this speaks to the real lack of clarity about the future of American sexuality and gender systems. We turn now to the topic of dichotomies in gender.

Dichotomizing Sex and Gender   As is the case for sexuality, the meanings of the terms *sex* and *gender* have also become destabilized. Traditionally, research in the social sciences used *sex* to refer to females and males—that is, to chromosomal, hormonal, anatomical, and physiological differences—and *gender* to describe the socially constructed roles associated with each sex, that is, masculinity and femininity. Over the last thirty or so years, however, *gender* has come to be used in popular culture to encompass both biological differences and social behavior. For example, it has become common to see descriptions of male and female voting patterns as *gender* differences, rather than as *sex* differences. In this same period, many scholars in the humanities and social sciences began conceptualizing sex in ways similar to gender, that is, they came to the conclusion that biological sex, like masculinity and femininity, was socially created. Thus, the language of scholarship also turned toward *gender* and away from *sex*.

Like sexuality, even physiological/biological sex refers to a complex set of attributes that may sometimes be inconsistent with one another or with individuals' sense of their own identity. As Alice Dreger in Reading 9 describes, even those on the Olympic Committee who want to use a hormone-based system to identify the sex of athletes (rather than letting the athletes self-identify), understand that determining sex is very complicated. As Dreger writes, "There's no one magical gene, chromosome, hormone, or body part that can do for us the hard work of sharp division into male and female leagues." Ultimately, biological/physiological sex is the product of a *decision*.

But in day-to-day life, rather than recognize the complexity of sex, we have commonly assumed that there are two and only two sexes and that people can be easily classified as one or the other. Despite the popularity of the word *gender,* apart from scholars the language of gender has not signaled a move away from the idea of biological sex as fixed and dichotomous. Rather, just as with race and sexuality categories, people are assigned as male or female irrespective of inconsistent or ambiguous evidence. Indeed, as Riki Wilchins describes in Reading 10, we have tried to make bodies "at the margins" fit into our existing categories. Out of the imperative that there be consistency between the physical and the psychological, some people pursue sex change surgery to produce a body consistent with their self-identity. Others pursue psychotherapy to find a self-identity consistent with their body. In either case, it has made more sense to use surgery and/or therapy to create consistency than to accept inconsistency.

All of this now seems up for discussion. A move away from the idea of biological sex as unitary, binary, and fixed has been spurred by transgender activism, which encompasses people who live as a gender different from their birth assignment, who identify with neither of the currently available biological sexes, who feel themselves to be both genders simultaneously or sequentially, whose biological/physiological sex is inconsistent, who have undergone sex reassignment hormone treatment or surgery, and/or who cross dress occasionally or regularly.

Since the early 1990s when the term was coined, the category trans-gender has come to be understood as a collective category of identity which incorporates a diverse array of male- and female-bodied gender variant people who had previously been understood as distinct kinds of persons, including self-identified transexuals and transvestites. . . . In its collectivity, the capacity of transgender to incorporate all gender variance has become a powerful tool of activism and personal identification. And, even more remarkably, in the period since the early 1990s it has already become institutionalized in a vast range of contexts, from grassroots activism, social service provision, and individual identification, to journalistic accounts. . . . Most importantly, transgender identification is understood across these domains to be explicitly and fundamentally different in origin and being from homosexual identification. . . . In short, "transgender" has changed the terms by which U.S. Americans understand and differentiate between gendered and sexual variance.[98]

Although it is not yet "mainstream" to treat sex as neither fixed nor dichotomous, it is not marginal either. For example, in 2014 Facebook added an option that provided about fifty different terms people could use to identify their sex; advertisements run by luxury retailer Barneys New York featured transgender models; newspaper space was devoted to the experience of parents whose young children rejected gender binaries; and courts ruled on which bathrooms transgender elementary students may use. Perhaps most important, "transgender" (rather than transgender*ed*, which connotes directionality) has become a way to identify oneself. Intrinsic to that self-identification is movement beyond the simple gender/sex binary that has predominated until now.

Dichotomizing Class Any discussion of social class in the United States must begin with the understanding that Americans "almost never speak of themselves or their society in class terms. In other words, class is not a central category of cultural discourse in America."[99] Indeed, considering the time and attention Americans devote to sexual orientation, sex/gender, or race, it is hard not to conclude that discussion of social class is "the last taboo."[100] Because social class is so seldom discussed, the vocabulary for talking about it is not well developed.

> Class analyses . . . are not curricular themes covered in schools at the primary or secondary level and are seldom included in university-level courses. . . . Every major U.S. daily newspaper includes a separate business section, but none includes a separate "class" or even "labor" section. . . . Politicians typically avoid class-based rhetoric, especially the use of language and policy labels that might openly emphasize or reveal the conflicting economic and political interests of working-class versus privileged-class members. . . . [P]olitical candidates, especially presidential candidates, who violate what amounts to an unwritten rule against framing class inequalities as legitimate public policy issues, risk being accused of promoting divisive and disruptive "class warfare" by privileged-class-based mainstream media pundits. . . . Only two exceptions exist to the taboo on public discussions of class issues. First, it is acceptable to discuss the "middle class" and problems faced by this class. Because large numbers of Americans identify themselves as middle class, references to this group actually serve to disguise and mute class differences because the term is so inclusive. . . . The second exception to avoidance of class issues includes mass media glimpses into the lives of the privileged class, as well as tours of the excluded class. . . . The glamour of life at the top is routinely showcased on both conventional and tabloid style TV news magazines. . . . The grim realities of life-at-the-bottom experiences turn up most often on occasional PBS or cable TV documentaries. . . .[101]

Despite its relative invisibility, as Michael Zweig notes in Reading 12, social class operates in ways quite similar to race and sex. That is, just as American culture offers interpretations of what differences in color or sex mean, it also provides interpretations about what differences in income, wealth, or occupation might mean. As sociologists Perrucci and Wysong noted in the quote above, social class is also often dichotomized, usually into those called *poor* and those called *middle class.*

What is especially interesting about this language of "poor" and "middle class" is the degree to which it masks the real polarization of income in American society, which now can be described as between the rich and everyone else. As Timothy Noah writes in Reading 14, the share of total income going to the top earners increased steadily after the 1970s, while the share going to middle- and low-earners shrank. Social scientists have been aware of this change for some time; it is especially significant since it reverses the closing of the income gap that took place between the 1930s and 1970s. As Noah notes, no one would have expected an advanced industrial democracy to become *more* unequal over time. The growth of this gap seems to have been unaffected by the Great Recession of 2007 to 2009: from 2009 to 2011 the income of the top 1 percent of families grew by 11.2 percent, while the income of the bottom 99 percent shrunk by 0.4 percent.[102]

Thus, "In simple but stark terms, by the end of the twentieth century all of the declines in inequality achieved in the New and Fair Deals had been wiped out and the United States had unambiguously returned to levels of inequality not seen since the laissez-faire era of the 1920s."[103] Despite the recent Great Recession, the fleeting Occupy Wall Street movement of 2011, and the fact that the vast majority of Americans have been negatively affected by change in income distribution over the last thirty years, it still can be argued that class is not a central category of cultural discourse in America. How can this be the case?

Just as American culture offers interpretations of what differences in color or sex mean, it also provides interpretations about what differences in income, wealth, or occupation might mean. In the Framework Essay for Section III we will more thoroughly discuss the concept of *ideology*—culturally dominating beliefs which, though widely shared, reflect the experience of only a few—but ideology certainly helps understand why social class remains an underdeveloped concept in American culture.

For example, it is a commonplace American belief that social class reflects a person's merit rather than social or economic forces. Surveys show that over half of the American public believes "that lack of effort by the poor was the principal reason for poverty, or a reason at least equal to any that was beyond a person's control. . . . Popular majorities did not consider any other factor to be a very important cause of poverty—not low wages, or a scarcity of jobs, or discrimination, or even sickness."[104]

The belief that merit is rewarded—and, conversely, that the lack of merit is punished—stands as a uniquely American belief. As Noah writes, surveys consistently show that Americans—*more than people of any other country*—believe that people are rewarded for their intelligence, skill, and effort. The American attachment to this belief is particularly ironic, since, as Noah discusses, virtually every developed nation in the world has more income mobility than the United States.

That Americans could persist in a belief so detached from reality speaks to the power of ideology.

But Americans have not always thought this way. In the early part of the 20th century, those who were poor were more likely to be considered hardworking, economically productive, constrained by artificial barriers, and probably in the majority. Today, however, "many of the least well off are not regarded as productive in any respect"[105]; popular opinion and even social science research are more likely to explain social class standing in terms of individual attributes and values rather than economic changes or discrimination.[106] Although it is beyond the scope of this text, these ideologies changed in response to new economic assumptions and policies (generally called neoliberalism). Thus, while ideologies are embedded in social context, but they are not outside historical change.

This attribution of poverty and wealth to individual merit hides not only the complex reality of American social class, it is an essentialist myth that legitimates the dramatic and increasing inequality of American society.

Dichotomization and Disability   Our discussion of race, sexuality, sex and gender, and social class has emphasized that each of these categories encompasses a continuum of behavior and characteristics rather than a finite set of discrete or easily separated groupings. It has also stressed that difference is a social creation—that differences of color or sex, for example, have no meaning other than what is attributed to them.

Can the same be said about disability? It is often assumed that people are easily classed as disabled or nondisabled, but that is no more true in this case than it is for the other master statuses. Sociologist Irving Zola provided the classic critique of how our use of statistics contributes to this misconception.

> The way we report statistics vis-à-vis disability and disease is generally misleading. If we speak of ratio figures for a particular disease as 1 in 8, 1 in 14, etc., we perpetuate what Rene Dubos (1961) once called "The Mirage of Health." For these numbers convey that if 1 person in 10 does get a particular disease, that 9 out of 10 do not. This means, however, only that those 9 people do not get that particular disease. It does not mean that they are disease-free, nor are they likely to be so. . . .
>
> Similarly deceptive is the now-popular figure of "43 million people with a disability" . . . for it implies that there are over 200 million Americans without a disability. . . . But the metaphor of being but a banana-peel slip away from disability is inappropriate. The issue of disability for individuals . . . is not *whether* but *when*, not so much *which one* but *how many* and *in what combination.*[107]

Apart even from how we count the disabled, how do we determine the disability of any particular person, on any particular day? Zola describes his experience of being able to work longer hours than others on an assembly line because his torso was in a brace;[108] although he was "disabled," on the line he was also less disabled than others. This situation, where impairment is relative, is more the rule than the exception and thus undermines notions about fixed distinctions between disability and nondisability.

Constructing the "Other"

We have seen how the complexity of a population may be reduced to aggregates and then to a simplistic dichotomy. Aggregation assumes that those who share a master status are alike in "essential" ways. It ignores the multiple and conflicting statuses any individual inevitably occupies. Dichotomization especially promotes the image of a mythical *other* who is not at all like *us*. Whether in race, sex, sexuality, social class, or disability, dichotomization yields a vision of "them" as profoundly different. Ultimately, dichotomization results in stigmatizing those who are less powerful. It provides the grounds for whole categories of people to become the objects of contempt.

Constructing "Others" as Profoundly Different The expectation that "others" are profoundly different can be seen most clearly in the significance that has been attached to sex differences. In this case, biological differences between males and females have been the grounds from which to infer an extensive range of nonbiological differences. Women and men are assumed to differ from each other in behavior, perception, and personality, and such differences are used to argue for different legal, social, and economic roles and rights. The expectation that men and women are not at all alike is so widespread that we often talk about them as members of the "opposite" sex; indeed, it is not unusual to talk about the "war" between the sexes.

While this assumption of difference undergirds everyday life, few significant differences in behavior, personality, or even physical ability have been found between men and women of any age. Indeed, there are more differences *within* each sex than *between* the sexes. Psychologist Susan Basow illustrates this point in the following:

> The all-or-none categorizing of gender traits is misleading. People just are not so simple that they either possess all of a trait or none of it. This is even more true when trait dispositions for groups of people are examined. Part [a] of Figure 2 [next page] illustrates what such an all-or-none distribution of the trait "strength" would look like: all males would be strong, all females weak. The fact is, most psychological and physical traits are distributed according to the pattern shown in Part [b] of Figure 2 with most people possessing an average amount of that trait and fewer people having either very much or very little of that trait.
>
> To the extent that females and males may differ in the average amount of the trait they possess (which needs to be determined empirically), the distribution can be characterized by *overlapping normal curves,* as shown in Part [c] of Figure 2. Thus, although most men are stronger than most women, the shaded area indicates that some men are weaker than some women and vice versa. The amount of overlap of the curves generally is considerable. Another attribute related to overlapping normal curves is that differences within one group are usually greater than the differences between the two groups. Thus, more variation in strength occurs within a group of men than between the average male and the average female.[109]

The lack of difference between women and men is especially striking given the degree to which we are all socialized to produce such differences. Thus, while boys and girls, and men and women, are often treated differently as well as socialized to be different, this does not mean they inevitably *become* different. Yet, even

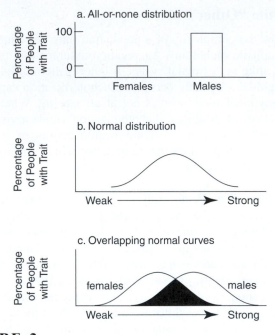

FIGURE 2
Three types of distribution for the trait "strength." (Basow, 1992:8; Figure 1)

though decades of research have confirmed few sex differences, the search for difference continues and some suggest it may even have been intensified by the failure to find many differences.

The same expectation that the "other" differs in personality or behavior emerges in race, class, and sexuality classifications. Race differences are expected to involve more than just differences of color, those who are "gay" or "straight" are expected to differ in more ways than just their sexual orientation, and social classes are expected to differ in more than their income. In each case, scientific research is often directed toward finding such differences.

Sanctioning Those Who Associate with the "Other" There are also similarities in the sanctions against those who cross race, sex, class, or sexual orientation boundaries. Parents sometimes disown children who marry outside of their racial or social class group, just as they often sever connections with children who are gay. Those who associate with the "other" are also in danger of being labeled a member of that category.

For example, during the Reconstruction period following the Civil War, the fear of invisible black ancestry was pervasive among southern whites, because that heritage would subject them to a restricted life based on *de jure* segregation. "Concern about people passing as white became so great that even behaving like blacks or willingly associating with them were often treated as more important than any proof of actual black ancestry."[110] Thus, southern whites who associated with blacks ran the risk of being defined as black.

A contemporary parallel can be found in gay/straight relations. Those who associate with gays and lesbians or defend gay rights are often presumed—by gays and straights alike—to be gay. Many men report that when they object to homophobic remarks, they simply become the target of them. Indeed, the prestige of young men in fraternities and other all-male groups often rests on a willingness to disparage women and gays.

Similarly, few contemporary reactions are as strongly negative as that against men who appear feminine. Because acting like a woman is so disparaged, boys learn at an early age to control their behavior or suffer public humiliation. This ridicule has its greatest effect on young men; the power and prestige usually available to older men reduces their susceptibility to such accusations. Young men must avoid a long list of behaviors for fear of being called feminine or gay: don't be too emotional, watch how you sit, don't move your hips when you walk, take long strides, don't put your hands on your hips, don't talk too much, don't let your voice show emotion, don't be too compliant or eager to please, and so on.

Because boys and men who exhibit such traits are often assumed to be gay, they become targets for verbal and physical abuse. In Reading 28, for example, C.J. Pascoe describes the ubiquity and function of the "fag trope" in an American high school:

> Fag talk and fag imitations serve as a discourse with which boys discipline themselves and each other through joking relationships. Any boy can temporarily become a fag in a given social space or interaction. This does not mean that boys who identify as or are perceived to be homosexual aren't subject to intense harassment. Many are. But becoming a fag has as much to do with failing at the masculine tasks of competence, heterosexual prowess, and strength or in any way revealing weakness or femininity, as it does with a sexual identity. This fluidity of the fag identity is what makes the specter of the fag such a powerful disciplinary mechanism. It is fluid enough that boys police their behaviors out of fear of having the fag identity permanently adhere. . . .

The popular linkage of effeminate behavior with gay sexuality is so strong that it may be the primary criterion most Americans use to decide who is gay: A "masculine" man must be straight; a "feminine" man must be gay. But gender and sexual orientation are *separate* phenomena. Knowing that someone is a masculine man or a feminine woman does not tell us what that person's sexual orientation is—indeed, our guesses are most likely to be "false negatives"; that is, we are most likely to falsely identify someone as straight. Because we do not know who among us is gay, we cannot accurately judge how gay people behave.

In the world of mutual "othering," being labeled one of "them" is a remarkably effective social control mechanism. Boys and men control their behavior so that they are not called gay. Members of racial and ethnic groups maintain distance from one another to avoid the criticism that might be leveled by members of their own and other groups. These social controls are effective because all parties continue to enforce them.

Stigma

The term *stigma* comes from ancient Greece, where it meant a "bodily sign designed to expose something unusual and bad about the moral status of [an individual]." Such signs were "cut or burnt into the body to advertise that the bearer was a slave, a criminal, or a blemished person, ritually polluted, to be avoided, especially in public places."[111] Stigmatized people are those "marked" as bad, unworthy, and polluted because of the category they belong to: for example, because of their disability, or their race, sex, sexuality, or social class category. The core assumption behind stigma is that internal merit is revealed through external features—for the Greeks, that a brand or a cut showed a person's lack of moral worth. This is not an unusual linkage. For example, physically attractive people are often assumed to possess a variety of positive attributes. We often assume that people who look good must *be* good.

Judgments of worth based on membership in certain categories have a self-fulfilling potential. Those who are judged superior by virtue of their membership in some category are given more opportunity to prove themselves; those who are judged less worthy by virtue of membership in a stigmatized category have difficulty establishing their merit no matter what they do. For example, social psychology experiments show that many whites perceive blacks as incompetent, regardless of evidence to the contrary: white subjects were "reluctant or unable to recognize that a black person is higher or equal in intelligence compared to themselves."[112] This would explain why many whites react negatively to affirmative action programs. If they cannot conceive of black applicants being *more* qualified than whites, they will see such programs as mandates to hire the less qualified.

Stigma involves objectification and devaluation. *Objectification* means treating people as if they were objects, members of a category rather than possessors of individual characteristics. In objectification, the "living, breathing, complex individual" ceases to be seen or valued.[113] In its extreme, those who are objectified are "viewed as having no other noteworthy status or identity. When that point is reached, a person becomes *nothing* but 'a delinquent,' 'a cripple,' 'a homosexual,' 'a black,' 'a woman.' The indefinite article 'a' underlines the depersonalized nature of such response."[114]

Examples of Stigmatized Master Statuses: Women, Poor People, and Disabled People   Sociologist Edwin Schur argues that because women are subject to both objectification and devaluation, they are discredited, that is, stigmatized. First, considering objectification, Schur argues that women are seen

> as all alike, and therefore substitutable for one another; as innately passive and objectlike; as easily ignored, dismissed, trivialized, treated as childlike, and even as a non-person; as having a social standing only through their attachments to men (or other non-stigmatized groups); and as a group which can be easily victimized through harassment, violence, and discrimination.[115]

Objectification occurs when women are thought of as generally indistinguishable from one another; for example, when someone says, "Let's get the woman's angle on this story." It also occurs when women are treated as nothing more than their body parts, for example, when young girls are assumed to be sexually promiscuous because they are big-breasted; they are nothing more than their cup size; they are objects.

The T-shirt designed for a 2012 fraternity party at Amherst College exemplifies both objectification and devaluation:

[W]hen a fraternity at self-described "elite" Amherst College in Massachusetts (not a big university in the South where we stereotypically assume these things occur) designed a T-shirt for their pig roast party of a pig smoking a cigar and watching a naked woman roast on a spit with the words ROASTING FAT ONES SINCE 1847, the guys didn't understand why that was such a problem. Here's Dana Bloger, a female student at Amherst, explaining why the T-shirt is a problem:

The woman on the shirt is depicted as an animal—or rather, as inferior to an animal, since she has not only replaced the pig on the spit but is being roasted by it. She is objectified as a literal piece of meat, whose thoughts, feelings, and humanity are rendered nonexistent and her consent therefore irrelevant. The hypersexualization of her body links violence with sex, thus perpetuating the notion that violence is sexy and sexuality violent. While I am not suggesting that this image would ever directly cause the infliction of violence on any individual woman, dehumanization is always the first step toward justifying such violence.[116]

African Americans, Latinos, Asian Americans, and gay/lesbian people are often similarly treated as indistinguishable from one another. Indeed, hate crimes have been defined by precisely this quality of interchangeability, such as an attack on *any* black family that moves into a neighborhood or the assault of *any* woman or man who looks gay. Hate crimes are also marked by excessive brutality and personal violence rather than property destruction—all of which indicate that the victims have been objectified.

Some members of stigmatized categories objectify themselves in the same ways that they are objectified by others. Thus, women may evaluate their own worth or the worth of other women in terms of physical appearance. In the process of self-objectification, a woman "joins the spectators of herself"; that is, she views herself as if from the outside, as if she were nothing more than what she looked like.[117] While young men are also objectified in terms of their bodies, over their lifetime they are likely to be objectified in terms of wealth and power.

There is a strong case that American women as a category continue to remain devalued, a conclusion drawn from the characteristics most frequently attributed to men and women. Research conducted over the last forty years has documented a remarkable consistency in those attributes. Both sexes are described as possessing valued qualities, but the characteristics attributed to men are more valued in the culture as a whole. For example, the female-valued characteristics include being talkative, gentle, religious, aware of the feelings of others, security oriented, and attentive to personal appearance. Male-valued traits include being aggressive, independent, unemotional, objective, dominant, active, competitive, logical, adventurous, and direct.[118i] (Remember that these attributes are only people's *beliefs* about sex differences.)

In many ways, the characteristics attributed to women are inconsistent with core American values. Although American culture values achievement, individualism, and action—all understood as male attributes—women are expected to subordinate their own desires for individual achievement to the needs of their family. Therefore, "women are asked to become the kind of people that this culture does not value."[120] Thus, it is more acceptable for women to display masculine traits, since these are culturally valued, than it is for men to display the less-valued feminine characteristics.

Much of what we have described about the stigmatization of women applies to people who are poor as well. Indeed, being poor is a much more obviously shameful status than being female. The category *poor* is intrinsically devalued. As Paul Gorski describes in Reading 33, it is presumed that there is little commendable to be said about people who are poor; "they" are primarily constructed as a "problem." Poor people are also objectified; they are described as "*the* poor," as if they were all alike, substitutable for and interchangeable with one another.

> Most of the writing about poor people, even by sympathetic observers, tells us that they are different, truly strangers in our midst: Poor people think, feel, and act in ways unlike middle-class Americans. . . .
>
> We can think about poor people as "them" or as "us." For the most part, Americans have talked about "them." Even in the language of social science, as well as in ordinary conversation and political rhetoric, poor people usually remain outsiders, strangers to be pitied or despised, helped or punished, ignored or studied, but rarely full citizens, members of a larger community on the same terms as the rest of us. They are . . . "those people," objects of curiosity, analysis, prurience, or compassion, not subjects who construct their own lives and history. Poor people seem cardboard cutouts, figures in single dimension, members of inferior categories, rarely complex, multifaceted, even contradictory in the manner of other persons.[121]

And, like women, those who are poor are not expected to display attributes valued in the culture as a whole.

Everything that we have described about stigma also applies directly to the experience of disabled people. The concept of stigma was initially developed by sociologist Erving Goffman with disabled people in mind, and there are so many ways that the term applies that it is difficult to select a single focus. From assumptions that one is pitiable, sick, unhappy, incompetent, dependent, childlike, unattractive,

---

[i]"Compared with White women, Black women are viewed as less passive, dependent, status conscious, emotional and concerned about their appearance. . . . Hispanic women tend to be viewed as more 'feminine' than White women in terms of submissiveness and dependence. . . . [A] similar stereotype holds for Asian women, but with the addition of exotic sexuality. . . . Native-American women typically are stereotyped as faceless . . . drudges without any personality. . . . Jewish women are stereotyped as either pushy, vain 'princesses' or overprotective, manipulative 'Jewish mothers' . . . working-class women are stereotyped as more hostile, confused, inconsiderate and irresponsible than middle-class women . . . and lesbians are stereotyped as possessing masculine traits."[119]

and sexually undesirable, to notions that disability is a punishment for sin, disabled people are cast as essentially unworthy.

In addition to the stigma, those who are disabled—like many others in stigmatized categories—must also manage the paternalism of those who are not disabled. Taken from the position of a father toward his children, paternalism is the automatic assumption of superiority.

> Paternalism is often subtle in that it casts the oppressor as benign, as protector. . . . Paternalism often must transform its subjects into children or people with childlike qualities. . . . Paternalism is experienced as the bystander grabs the arm of a blind person and, without asking, 'helps' the person across the street. . . . It is most of all, however, the assumption that people with disabilities are intrinsically inferior and unable to take responsibility for their own lives.[122]

For those of us outside the stigmatized group, a paternalistic attitude is dangerous because it keeps us from actually seeing the person in front of us: "A person who cannot see or is using a wheelchair for mobility may be a happy, prosperous, well-adjusted person, but most people encountering him or her immediately feel pity."[123]

Stereotypes About People in Stigmatized Master Statuses Finally, in an effort to capture the general features of what "we" say about "them," let us consider five common stereotypes about individuals in stigmatized master statuses.

First, they are presumed to lack the values the culture holds dear. Neither women nor those who are poor, disabled, gay, black, Asian American, or Latino are expected to be independent, unemotional, objective, dominant, active, competitive, logical, adventurous, or direct. Stigmatized people are presumed to lack precisely those values that nonstigmatized people are expected to possess.

Second, stigmatized people are likely to be seen as a problem. Certainly black, Latino, and Native American men and women, gay and lesbian people of all colors, white women, all disabled people, and people living in poverty are constructed as *having* problems and *being* problems. Often the implication is that they are also responsible for many of our national problems. While public celebrations often highlight the historic contributions of such groups to the culture, little in the public discourse lauds their current contributions. Indeed, those in stigmatized categories are often constructed as *nothing but a problem*, as if they did not exist apart from those problems. This was once illustrated by a black student who described her shock at hearing white students describe her middle-class neighborhood as a "ghetto."

Ironically, this depiction of stigmatized people as nothing but a problem is often accompanied by the trivialization of those problems. For example, there is a significant gap between black and white assessments of the persistence of race discrimination. The same gap holds in terms of the perception of sex discrimination:

> On the one hand, men and women largely agree that discrimination against women was much greater in the past compared to the present. . . . [On the other hand], men perceive the discrimination gap (the relative degrees of discrimination facing women versus men) to

be smaller at all time periods than women do. Moreover, men believe that there is now relatively little difference in the amount of discrimination facing men versus women.[124]

Similarly, despite the participation of thousands of people in annual Gay Pride marches throughout the country, images from the parades typically trivialize participants by focusing on the small number in drag or leather. Indeed, much of what is disparaged as "gay lifestyle" has been forged by gay and lesbian people who have been excluded from mainstream, heterosexual society. Finally, despite dramatic federal reductions in the cash assistance programs to poor people begun in 1994 under President Bill Clinton's pledge to "end welfare as we know it," stereotypes about poor people getting government "handouts" persist. In all, the problems that stigmatized categories of people create for those in privileged statuses are highlighted, while the problems they experience are discounted, especially those problems created by "us."

Third, people in stigmatized master statuses are often stereotyped as lacking self-control; they are characterized as being lustful, immoral, and carriers of disease.[125] Currently, such accusations hold center stage in the depiction of gay men, but historically such charges have been leveled at African American, Latino, and Asian American men (e.g., Chinese immigrants in the late 19th century). Poor women and women of color have been and continue to be depicted as promiscuous, while poor men and women are presumed to be morally irresponsible.

Fourth, people in stigmatized categories are often marked as having too much or too little intelligence, and in either case as tending to deception or criminality. Many stigmatized categories of people have been assumed to use their "excessive" intelligence to unfair advantage. This was historically the charge against Jews, and now appears to be a characterization of Asian Americans.

> [T]he educational achievement of Asian American students was, and continues to be, followed by a wave of reaction. The image of Asian Americans as diligent super-students has often kindled resentment in other students. Sometimes called "damned curve raisers," a term applied first to Jewish students at elite East Coast colleges during the 1920s and 1930s, Asian American students have increasingly found themselves taking the brunt of campus racial jokes.[126]

Fifth, people in stigmatized categories are depicted as both childlike and savagely brutal. Historically, characterizations of Native Americans, enslaved Africans, and Chinese immigrants reflected these conceptions. Currently, the same is true for the poor in their representation as both pervasively violent and irresponsible. A related depiction of women as both "virgins and whores" has been well documented in scholarship over time.

Perhaps because people in stigmatized master statuses are stereotyped as deviant, it appears that those who commit violence against them are less severely punished. For example, "most murders in the USA are intra-racial, that is, the alleged perpetrator and the victim are of the same race. . . . Yet of the 845 prisoners executed between 17 January 1977 and 10 April 2003, 53 percent were whites convicted of killing whites and 10 percent were blacks convicted of killing blacks."[127] Although a number of factors are operating here, one conclusion is that stigmatized minority victims are valued less than white victims. The same conclusion could be reached in terms of the punishment meted out to those accused of sexual assault. "Major offenses *against* women, which we *profess* to consider deviant, in practice have been responded to with much ambivalence."[128] Indeed, some have argued that one way to recognize a stigmatized category of people is that the violence directed at them is not treated seriously.

Overall, individuals in stigmatized master statuses are represented not only as physically distinctive but also as the antithesis of the culture's desired behaviors and attributes. Such characterizations serve to dismiss claims of discrimination and unfair treatment, affirming that those in stigmatized categories deserve such treatment, that they are themselves responsible for their plight. Indeed, many of these stereotypes are also applied to teenagers, whom the media depict as violent, reckless, hypersexed, ignorant, out of control, and the cause of society's problems.[129]

A Final Comment

It is disheartening to think of oneself as a member of a stigmatized group, just as it is disheartening to think of oneself as thoughtlessly perpetuating stigma. Still, there are at least two important points to bear in mind. First, the characteristics attributed to stigmatized groups are similar across a great variety of master statuses. They are not tied to the actual characteristics of any particular group; in a way, they are quite impersonal. Second, people who are stigmatized have often formed alliances with those who are not stigmatized to successfully lobby against these attributions.

As we said at the outset of this essay, our hope is to provide you with a framework by which to make sense of what sex, disability, race, social class, and sexuality mean in contemporary American society. Clearly, these categorizations are complex; they are tied to emotionally intense issues that are uniquely American; and they have consequences that are both mundane and dramatic. From naming, to aggregating, to dichotomizing, and ultimately to stigmatizing, difference has a meaning for us. The readings in Section I will explore the construction of these categorizations; the readings in Section II examine how we experience them; the readings in Section III address the meaning that is attributed to difference; and the readings in Section IV describe how we can bridge these differences.

KEY CONCEPTS

ableism Analogous to racism and sexism, a system of cultural, institutional, and individual discrimination against people with impairments. Disablism is the British term; disability oppression is synonymous. (page 6)

aggregate To combine or lump together (verb); something composed of different elements (noun). (pages 15)

-centrism or -centric Suffix meaning centered around, focused around, taking the perspective of. Thus,

androcentric means focused around or taking the perspective of men; **heterocentric** means taking the perspective of heterosexuals; and **Eurocentric** means having a European focus. (page 19)

constructionism The view that reality cannot be separated from the way a culture makes sense of it—that meaning is "constructed" through social, political, legal, scientific, and other practices. From this perspective, differences among people are created through social processes. (page 3)

dichotomize To divide into two parts and to see those parts as mutually exclusive. (page 20)

differential undercount In the census, undercounting more of one group than of another. (page 12)

disability The loss or limitation of opportunities to take part in the normal life of the community on an equal level with others because of physical and social barriers (page 3)

disaggregate To separate something into its constituent elements. (pages 16)

essential identity An identity that is treated as core to a person. Essential identities can be attributed to people even when they are inconsistent with actual behavior. (page 30)

essentialism The view that reality exists independently of our perception of it, that we perceive the meaning of the world rather than construct that meaning. From this perspective, there are real and important (essential) differences among categories of people. (page 3)

ethnic group, ethnicity Those who share a sense of being a "people," usually based on national origin, language, or religion. (page 23)

gender Masculinity and femininity; the acting out of the behaviors thought to be appropriate for a particular sex. (page 30)

heteronormativity All the beliefs, norms, and social structures that contribute to the presumption that heterosexuality is the natural, normal, and inevitable structure of society (page 19)

impairment Physical, cognitive, emotional, or sensory conditions within the person as diagnosed by medical professionals (page 5)

intersectionality Consideration of the ways that master statuses interact and mutually construct one another. (page 4)

master status A status that has a profound effect on one's life, that dominates or overwhelms the other statuses one occupies. (page 2)

objectification Treating people as if they were objects, as if they were nothing more than the attributes they display. (page 38)

Other A usage designed to refer to those considered profoundly unlike oneself. (page 11)

panethnic A classification that spans ethnic identities. (page 17)

race The conception that people can be classified into groups based on skin color, hair texture, shape of head, eyes, nose, and lips. (pages 3)

sex The categories of male and female. (page 3)

status A position in society. Individuals occupy multiple statuses simultaneously, such as occupational, kinship, and educational statuses. (page 2)

stigma An attribute for which someone is considered bad, unworthy, or deeply discredited. (pages 38)

transgender People who systematically ignore or violate gender expectations; sometimes includes people who are transsexual. (page 32)

NOTES

1. Scott and Marshall, 2009:452–53.
2. Ridgeway, 2011. Ridgeway argues that gender "framing," i.e., the processes by which behavior is interpreted through the "lens" of gender, accounts for the contemporary inability to fully eliminate inequalities between women and men.
3. For example see Janet Jacobsen, "Queers Are Like Jews, Aren't They? Analogy and Alliance Politics," in *Queer Theory and the Jewish Question* edited by Daniel Boyarin, Daniel Itzkovitz, and Ann Pellegrini. New York: Columbia University Press, 2003, 64–90; Tina Grillo and Stephanie M. Wildman. "Obscuring the Importance of Race: The Implication of Making Comparisons between Racism and Sexism or other Isms," in *Critical Race Feminism* edited by Adrien Katherine Wing. New York: NYU Press, 1997; Barbara F. Reskin, "Including Mechanisms in Our Models of Ascriptive Inequality," *American Sociological Review,* 2003, v. 68 Feb: 1–21.
4. Henshel and Silverman, 1975:26.
5. Pfuhl, 1986:5.
6. Ibid.
7. Spelman, 1988.
8. Faderman, 1991; Armstrong, 2002.
9. Saad, 2012.
10. Rist, 1992: 425–26.
11. Omansky, 2006:27.
12. Disabled People's International, 1982.
13. Barnes and Mercer, 2003; Oliver, 1990, 1996, 2009.
14. Hunt, 2001.
15. Union of Physically Impaired Against Segregation, 1973:4.
16. United Nations, 2007.
17. Schneider, 1988:65.
18. Higgins, 1992:53.
19. Schmidt, 2003.
20. Grigsby Bates, 2014.
21. Pew Research Hispanic Trends Project, 2013.

22. Smith, 1992:497–98.
23. Gallup, 2007.
24. Kiviat, 2010.
25. Shorris, 1992:101.
26. Queer Nation Manifesto, 1990.
27. Mills, 1989:102.
28. Omansky, 2006:27.
29. Oliver, 1990:xiii.
30. U.S. Census, 2010.
31. U.S. Commission on Civil Rights, 1973:39.
32. Skrentny, 2002:2.
33. U.S. Census, 2010.
34. U.S. Census, 2012.
35. Ibid.
36. Gates and Cook, nd.
37. Jenkins, 1999:15–16.
38. Saulny, 2011.
39. U.S. Bureau of the Census, 2010a.
40. U.S. Census Bureau, 2006–2008, American Community Survey.
41. Pew Research Hispanic Trends Project, 2013.
42. Gracia, 2000:204–5.
43. Lopez, 2013.
44. Pew Research Hispanic Trends Project, 2013.
45. Ibid.
46. Cohn, 2012.
47. Hu-Dehart, 1994.
48. U.S. Census Bureau, 2001.
49. Espiritu, 1992:124–25.
50. Omi, 1996:180.
51. Omi, 1996:181.
52. Mohawk, 1992:440.
53. Omi and Winant, 1994:66.
54. Mohawk, 1992:439–40.
55. Flagg, 1993:970.
56. Okizaki, 2000:483.
57. Russell, 1994.
58. Warner, 1993.
59. Herek, 2004:7.
60. Ibid.
61. Herek, 1990:316.
62. Herek, 2000.
63. Berlant and Warner, 1998:547.
64. Warner, 1999:47.
65. Dennis, 2004:383.
66. Tilly, 1999.
67. Lee and Bean, 2004.
68. Omi and Winant, 1994.
69. Roediger, 1994:189–90.
70. Morrison, 1992:47.
71. Pew Research Social and Demographic Trends, 2012.
72. Blauner, 1992.
73. Haines, 2007.
74. Smedley, 1993:39.
75. Ibid.
76. Omi and Winant, 1994.
77. Smedley, 1993:25.
78. Ibid.
79. Gould, 1981.
80. Begley, 1995:67, 68.
81. Cohen, 1998:12.
82. Lieberman, 1968:128.
83. Marshall, 1993:117, 121.
84. Roberts, 2011:59 Emphasis added.
85. Ibid., p. 60.
86. Ibid., p. 172.
87. Zuger, 2012.
88. Dreifus, 2005.
89. Roberts, 2011:78.
90. Gates, 2011.
91. Rosenthal, *et al,* 2011:112–115.
92. Denizet-Lewis, 2014.
93. Ibid.
94. Ibid.
95. Pew Research Center, 2013.
96. Denizet-Lewis, 2014.
97. Katz, 1975.
98. Valentine, 2007:80.
99. Ortner, 1991:169.
100. Perrucci and Wysong, 2008.
101. Perrucci and Wysong, 2008:48–50.
102. Saez, 2013.
103. Massey, 2007:35–6.
104. Schwarz and Volgy, 1992:11.
105. Arrow, Bowles, and Durlauf, 2000:x.
106. Kahlenberg, 1997; Mincey, 1994.
107. Zola, 1993:18.
108. Ibid.
109. Basow, 1992:8.
110. Davis, 1991:56.
111. Goffman, 1963:1.
112. Gaertner and Dovidio, 1986:75.
113. Allport, 1958:175.
114. Schur, 1984:30–1.
115. Ibid., 33.
116. Wiseman, 2013:20.
117. Berger, 1963:50.
118. Baron and Byrne, 2004; Sczesny *et al.,* 2008.
119. Basow, 1992:4.
120. Richardson, 1977:11.
121. Katz, 1989:6, 126.
122. Charlton, 2000:53.
123. Ibid., 55.
124. Bosson, Vandello, Michniewicz & Lenes, 2012:228–9.
125. Gilman, 1985, 1991.
126. Takagi, 1992:60
127. Amnesty International, 2003.
128. Schur, 1984:7.
129. Males, 1994.

REFERENCES

Allport, Gordon. 1958. *The Nature of Prejudice.* Garden City, NY: Doubleday Anchor.

Amnesty International. 2003. Death by Discrimination: The Continuing Role of Race in Capital Cases. (http://web.amnesty.org/library/print /ENGAMR510462003.) Retrieved November 2, 2010.

Armstrong, Elizabeth A. 2002. *Forging Gay Identities: Organizing Sexuality in San Francisco, 1950–1994.* Chicago: University of Chicago Press.

Arrow, Kenneth, Samuel Bowles, and Steven Durlauf. 2000. Introduction. *Meritocracy and Economic Inequality,* edited by Kenneth Arrow, Samuel Bowles, and Steven Durlauf, ix–xv. Princeton, NJ: Princeton University Press.

Barnes, Colin, and Geof Mercer. 2003. *Disability.* Cambridge, UK: Polity Press.

Baron, Robert A., and Donn Byrne. 2004. *Social Psychology.* Boston: Pearson.

Basow, Susan A. 1992. *Gender: Stereotypes and Roles.* 3d ed. Pacific Grove, CA: Brooks/Cole Publishing.

Begley, Sharon. 1995. Three Is Not Enough. *Newsweek,* February 13, 67–69.

Berger, Peter L. 1963. *Invitation to Sociology: A Humanistic Perspective.* Garden City, NY: Doubleday Anchor.

Berlant, Lauren, and Michael Warner. 1998. Sex in Public. *Critical Inquiry* 24(2): 547–66.

Blauner, Robert. 1992. Talking Past Each Other: Black and White Languages of Race. *The American Prospect,* 10.

Bosson, Jennifer K., Joseph A. Vandello, Kenneth S. Michniewicz, and Joshua Guy Lenes. 2012. American Men's and Women's Beliefs about Gender Discrimination: For Men, It's Not Quite a Zero Sum Game. *MCS: Masculinities and Social Change.* 1(3): 210–39.

Charlton, James. 2000. *Nothing about Us Without Us: Disability Oppression and Empowerment.* Los Angeles, CA: University of California Press.

Cohen, Mark Nathan. 1998. *Culture of Intolerance: Chauvinism, Class, and Racism in the United States.* New Haven, CT: Yale University Press.

Cohn, D'Vera. 2012. Census Bureau Considers Changing Its Race/Hispanic Questions, Pew Research, Social and Demographic Trends, August 7. Retrieved March 25, 2014. http://www.pewsocialtrends .org/2012/08/07/census-bureau-considers-changing -its-racehispanic-questions/

Davis, F. James. 1991. *Who Is Black? One Nation's Rule.* University Park, PA: Pennsylvania State University Press.

Denizet-Lewis, Benoit. 2014. The Scientific Quest to Prove Bisexuality Exists. *The New York Times Magazine.* March 20. Retrieved April 28, 2014. http://www.nytimes.com/2014/03/23/magazine/the-scientific-quest-to-prove-bisexuality-exists .html

Dennis, Jeffrey P. 2004. Heteronormativity. *Men and Masculinities: A Social, Cultural, and Historical Encyclopedia,* edited by Michael Kimmel and Amy Aronson, 382–83. Santa Barbara, CA: ABC-CLIO, Inc.

Disabled People's International. 1982. *Proceedings of the First World Congress.* Singapore: Disabled People's International.

Dreifus, Claudia. 2005. A Sociologist Confronts "The Messy Stuff": A Conversation with Troy Duster. *The New York Times,* Science Times, October 18.

Dubos, Rene. 1961. *Mirage of Health.* Garden City, NY: Anchor Books.

Espiritu, Yen Le. 1992. *Asian American Panethnicity: Bridging Institutions and Identities.* Philadelphia: Temple University Press.

Faderman, Lillian. 1991. *Odd Girls and Twilight Lovers: A History of Lesbian Life in Twentieth-Century America.* New York: Penguin Books.

Flagg, Barbara J. 1993. *"Was Blind, But Now I See": Race Consciousness and the Requirement of Discriminatory Intent.* 91 Mich. L. Rev., 953–71.

Gaertner, Samuel L., and John F. Dovidio. 1986. The Aversive Form of Racism. *Prejudice, Discrimination, and Racism,* edited by John F. Dovidio and Samuel L. Gaertner, 61–89. Orlando, FL: Academic Press.

Gallup, Inc. 2007. Black or African American? Retrieved May 26, 2010 (http://www.gallup.com /poll/28816/black-african-american.aspx).

Gallup, Inc. 2010. Americans' Acceptance of Gay Relations Crosses 50% Threshold. May 3–6. Retrieved June 23, 2010 (http://www.gallup.com /poll/135764/americans-acceptance-gay-relations-crosses-threshold.aspx).

Gallup Organization, Gallup Poll News Service. 2003. Q&A: Black-White Relations in the U.S.

Gates, Gary J., and Abigail Cook. Nd. United States Census Snapshot: 2010. The Williams Institute. Retrieved March 23, 2014. http://williamsinstitute.law.ucla.edu/wp-content/uploads/Census2010Snapshot-US-v2.pdf?r=1

Gates, Gary J. 2011. How Many People Are Lesbian, Gay, Bisexual, and Transgender? The Williams Institute, April. Retrieved April 4, 2014. http://williamsinstitute.law.ucla.edu/research/census-lgbt-demographics-studies/how-many-people-are-lesbian-gay-bisexual-and-transgender/.

Gilman, Sander. 1985. *Difference and Pathology: Stereotypes of Sexuality, Race, and Madness.* Ithaca, NY: Cornell University Press.

———. 1991. *The Jew's Body.* New York: Routledge.

Goffman, Erving. 1963. *Stigma: Notes on the Management of Spoiled Identity.* Englewood Cliffs, NJ: Prentice-Hall.

Gould, Stephen Jay. 1981. *The Mismeasure of Man.* New York: W. W. Norton.

Gracia, Jorge J. E. 2000. Affirmative Action for Hispanics? Yes and No. *Hispanics/Latinos in the United States: Ethnicity, Race, and Rights,* edited by Jorge J. E. Gracia and Pablo De Greiff, 201–222. New York: Routledge.

Grigsby Bates, Karen. 2014. "Hispanic" or "Latino"? Polls Say It Doesn't Matter—Usually, *National Public Radio,* Code Switch," January 21.

Haines, David W. 2007. Ethnicity's Shadows: Race, Religion, and Nationality as Alternative Identities among Recent United States Arrivals. *Identities: Global Studies in Culture and Power,* 14:1–28.

Henshel, Richard L., and Robert A. Silverman. 1975. *Perceptions in Criminology.* New York: Columbia University Press.

Herek, Gregory M. 1990. The Context of Anti-gay Violence: Notes on Cultural and Psychological Heterosexism. *Journal of Interpersonal Violence,* 5(3): 316–33.

——— 2000. The Psychology of Sexual Prejudice. *Current Directions in Psychological Science, 9*(1): 19–22.

——— 2004. Beyond "Homophobia": Thinking about Sexual Stigma and Prejudice in the Twenty-first Century. *Sexuality Research and Social Policy, 1*(2): 6–24.

Higgins, Paul C. 1992. *Making Disability: Exploring the Social Transformation of Human Variation.* Springfield, IL: Charles C. Thomas.

Hu-Dehart, Evelyn. 1994. Asian/Pacific American Issues in American Education. Presentation at the 7th Annual National Conference on Race and Ethnicity in American Higher Education, Atlanta, sponsored by The Southwest Center for Human Relations Studies, University of Oklahoma, College of Continuing Education.

Hunt, Judy. 2001. The Union of the Physically Impaired Against Segregation. Retrieved June 2, 2010 (http://www.labournet.net/other/0107/upias1.html).

Jenkins, Alan. 1999. See No Evil. *The Nation,* June 28: 15–19.

Kahlenberg, Richard D. 1997. *The Remedy: Class, Race, and Affirmative Action.* New York: Basic Books.

Katz, Jack. 1975. Essences as Moral Identities: Verifiability and Responsibility in Imputations of Deviance and Charisma. *American Journal of Sociology,* 80:1369–90.

Katz, Michael B. 1989. *The Undeserving Poor: From the War on Poverty to the War on Welfare.* New York: Pantheon Books.

Kiviat, Barbara. 2010. Should the Census Be Asking People if They Are Negro? *Time,* January 23. Retrieved May 28, 2010 (http://www.time.com/time/nation/article/0,8599,1955923,00.html).

Lee, Jennifer, and Frank D. Bean. 2004. America's Changing Color Lines: Immigration, Race/Ethnicity, and Multi-racial Identification. *Annual Review of Sociology,* 30: 221–242.

Lieberman, Leonard. 1968. A Debate over Race: A Study in the Sociology of Knowledge. *Phylon,* 29: 127–41.

Lopez, Mark Hugo. 2013. Hispanic Identity. Pew Research Hispanic Trends Project, October 22. Retrieved March 25, 2014. http://www.pewhispanic.org/2013/10/22/3-hispanic-identity/

Males, Mike. 1994. Bashing Youth: Media Myths about Teenagers. *Extra!* March/April 8–11.

Marshall, Gloria. 1993. Racial Classifications: Popular and Scientific. *The "Racial" Economy of Science: Toward a Democratic Future,* edited by Sandra Harding, 116–27. Bloomington, IN: Indiana University Press (Originally published 1968).

Massey, Douglas S. 2007. *Categorically Unequal: The American Stratification System.* New York: Russell Sage.

Mills, Jane. 1989. *Womanwords: A Dictionary of Words about Women.* New York: Henry Holt.

Mincey, Ronald B. 1994. *Confronting Poverty: Prescriptions for Change.* Cambridge: Harvard University Press.

Mohawk, John. 1992. Looking for Columbus: Thoughts on the Past, Present and Future of Humanity. *The State of Native America: Genocide, Colonization, and Resistance,* edited by M. Annette Jaimes, 439–44. Boston: South End Press.

Morrison, Toni. 1992. *Playing in the Dark.* New York: Vintage.

Office of Management and Budget. October 1997. *Revisions to the Standards for the Classification of Federal Data on Race and Ethnicity.* Washington, DC: U.S. Government Printing Office.

Okizaki, Carrie Lynn H. 2000. "What Are You?" Hapa-Girl and Multiracial Identity. 71 U. Colo. Law Review, 463–81.

Oliver, Michael. 1990. *The Politics of Disablement.* London: Macmillan.

———. 1996. *Understanding Disability.* New York: Palgrave.

———. 2009. *Understanding Disability: From Theory to Practice.* Second edition. London: Palgrave MacMillan.

Omansky, Beth. 2006. *Not Blind Enough: Living in the Borderland Called Legal Blindness.* Ph.D. Thesis, University of Queensland.

Omi, Michael. 1996. Racialization in the Post–Civil Rights Era. *Mapping Multiculturalism,* edited by A. Gordon and C. Newfield, 178–85. Minneapolis: University of Minnesota Press.

——— and Howard Winant. 1994. *Racial Formation in the United States.* New York: Routledge.

Ortner, Sherry B. 1991. Reading America. Preliminary Notes on Class and Culture. *Recapturing Anthropology: Working in the Present,* edited by Richard G. Fox, 163–89. Santa Fe, NM: School of American Research Press.

Perrucci, Robert, and Earl Wyson. 2008. *The New Class Society: Goodbye American Dream?* Third edition. Lanham, MD.: Rowman & Littlefield.

Pew Research Center. 2009. Between Two Worlds: How Young Latinos Come of Age in America. December 11. Retrieved December 11, 2009 (http://pewresearch.org/pubs/1438/young-latinos-coming-of-age-in-america).

Pew Research Social and Demographic Trends. 2012. The Rise of Asian Americans, June 12. [Updated April 4, 2013]. Retrieved March 28, 2014. http://www.pewsocialtrends.org/2012/06/19/the-rise-of-asian-americans/

Pew Research Hispanic Trends Project. 2013. Hispanic Population Trends, A Statistical Portrait of U.S. Hispanics Based on the U.S. Census Bureau's 2011 American Community Survey, February 13. Retrieved March 24, 2014. http://www.pewhispanic.org/2013/02/15/hispanic-population-trends/ph_13-01-23_ss_hispanics1/

Pew Research Center. June 13, 2013. A Survey of LGBT Americans: Attitudes, Experiences and Values in Changing Times. Retrieved April 3, 2014. http://www.pewsocialtrends.org/files/2013/06/SDT_LGBT-Americans_06-2013.pdf

Pfuhl, Erdwin H. 1986. *The Deviance Process.* 2nd ed. Belmont, CA: Wadsworth.

Queer Nation. Queer Nation Manifesto. 1990. Retrieved June 27, 2010. http://www.digenia.se/andras%20texter/THE%20QUEER%20NATION%20MANIFESTO.htm

Richardson, Laurel. 1977. *The Dynamics of Sex and Gender: A Sociological Perspective.* New York: Harper and Row.

———. 1988. *The Dynamics of Sex and Gender: A Sociological Perspective.* 3rd ed. New York: Harper and Row.

Ridgeway, Cecilia. 2011. *Framed by Gender: How Gender Inequality Persists in the Modern World.* New York: Oxford University Press.

Rist, Darrell Yates. 1992. Are Homosexuals Born That Way? *The Nation,* 255: 424–29.

Roberts, Dorothy. 2011. *Fatal Invention: How Science, Politics, and Big Business Re-create Race in the Twenty-First Century.* New York: The New Press.

Roediger, David. 1994. *Towards the Abolition of Whiteness.* London: Verso.

Rosenthal, A. M., D. Sylvia, A. Safron, and J. M. Bailey. 2011. Sexual Arousal Patterns of Bisexual Men Revisited. *Biological Psychology.* 881: 112–15. Retrieved April 4, 2014. http://www.thestranger.com/images/blogimages/2011/08/16/1313530258-rosenthal_et_al.pdf

Russell, Marta. 1994. Malcolm Teaches Us Too. *The Ragged Edge: The Disability Experience from the Pages of the First Fifteen Years of the Disability Rag,* edited by Barrett Shaw, 11–14. Louisville, KY: Avocado Press.

Saad Lydia. 2012. U.S. Acceptance of Gay/Lesbian Relations Is the New Normal. May 14, Gallup Politics. Retrieved March 19, 2014. http://www.gallup.com/poll/154634/acceptance-gay-lesbian-relations-new-normal.aspx

Saez, Emmanuel. January 23, 2013. Striking it Richer: The Evolution of Top Incomes in the United States. Updated with 2011 Estimates. Retrieved April 7, 2014. http://elsa.berkeley.edu/~saez/saez-UStopincomes-2010.pdf

Saulny, Susan. 2011. Race Remixed: In a Multiracial Nation, Many Ways to Tally. *The New York Times,* February 10. Retrieved April 28, 2014. http://query.nytimes.com/gst/fullpage.html?res=9E01E5DA1E3BF933A25751C0A9679D8B63

Schmidt, Peter. 2003. The Label "Hispanic" Irks Some, but Also Unites. *The Chronicle of Higher Education,* November 23, A9.

Schneider, Joseph W. 1988. Disability as Moral Experience: Epilepsy and Self in Routine Relationships. *Journal of Social Issues,* 44:63–78.

Schur, Edwin. 1984. *Labeling Women Deviant: Gender, Stigma, and Social Control.* New York: Random House.

Schwarz, John E., and Thomas J. Volgy. 1992. *The Forgotten Americans.* New York: W. W. Norton.

Scott, John, and Gordon Marshall. 2009. *Oxford Dictionary of Sociology.* Third edition revised. Oxford: Oxford University Press.

Sczesny, Sabine, Janine Bosak, Amanda B. Diekman, and Jean M. Twenge. 2008. Dynamics of Sex-Role Stereotypes. *Stereotype Dynamics: Language-based Approaches to the Formation, Maintenance, and Transformation of Stereotypes,* edited by Yoshihisa Kashima, Klaus Fiedler, and Peter Freytag, 135–61. New York: Taylor & Francis Group.

Shorris, Earl. 1992. *Latinos: A Biography of the People.* New York: W. W. Norton.

Skrentny, John D. 2002. *The Minority Rights Revolution.* Cambridge, MA: Harvard University Press.

Smedley, Audrey. 1993. *Race in North America: Origin and Evolution of a Worldview.* Boulder, CO: Westview Press.

Smith, Tom W. 1992. Changing Racial Labels: From "Colored" to "Negro" to "Black" to "African American." *Public Opinion Quarterly,* 56:496–514.

Spelman, Elizabeth. 1988. *Inessential Woman.* Boston: Beacon Press.

Springer, S. P., and G. Deutsch. 1981. *Left Brain, Right Brain.* San Francisco: Freeman.

Takagi, Dana Y. 1992. *The Retreat from Race: Asian-American Admission and Racial Politics.* New Brunswick, NJ: Rutgers University Press.

Tilly, Charles. 1999. *Durable Inequality.* Berkeley, CA: University of California Press.

Union of the Physically Impaired Against Segregation. 1976. Fundamental Principles of Disability. Retrieved June 2, 2010 (http://www.leeds.ac.uk/disability-studies/archiveuk/UPIAS/fundamental%20principles.pdf).

United Nations. 2007. Enable. Department of Economic and Social Affairs, Division for Social Policy and Development. Frequently Asked Questions: What is Disability and Who are Persons with Disabilities? Retrieved on June 3, 2010 (http://www.un.org/esa/socdev/enable/faqs.htm).

U.S. Census Bureau. 2001. *Census 2000 Summary File 2, Technical Documentation:* September 2001, SF2/01:G39–G41.

U.S. Census Bureau. 2010. The Whole Story: Real People, Real Questions, Real Answers. Retrieved May 29, 2010. http://2010.census.gov/2010census/about/whole.php

U.S. Census Bureau. 2012. The Two or More Races Population: 2010. Nicholas A. Jones and Jungmiwha Bullock. September. Retrieved March 23, 2014. http://www.census.gov/prod/cen2010/briefs/c2010br-13.pdf.

U.S. Census Bureau, American FactFinder. 2006–2008 data set. American Community Survey 3-Year Estimates, Hispanic or Latino Origin. Retrieved May 28, 2010. http://factfinder.census.gov/servlet/DTTable?_bm=y&-geo_id=01000US&-ds_name=ACS_2008_3YR_G00_&-mt_name=ACS_2008_3YR_G2000_B03001

Valentine, David. 2007. *Imagining Transgender: An Ethnography of a Category.* Durham, NC: Duke University Press.

Warner, Michael. 1999. *The Trouble with Normal: Sex, Politics, and the Ethics of Queer Life.* Cambridge, MA: Harvard University Press.

Weinberg, George. 1973. *Society and the Healthy Homosexual.* Garden City, NY: Anchor.

Wiseman, Rosalind. 2013. *Masterminds and Wingmen: Helping Our Boys Cope with Schoolyard Power, Locker-Room Tests, Girlfriends, and the New Rules of Boy World.* New York: Harmony Books.

Zola, Irving K. 1993. Disability Statistics, What We Count and What It Tells Us: A Personal and Political Analysis. *Journal of Disability Policy Studies,* 4: 10–37.

Zuger, Abigail. 2012. From Bang to Whimper: A Heart Drug's Story, *New York Times,* December 24.

WHAT IS RACE? WHAT IS ETHNICITY?

READING 1

"Race" and the Construction of Human Identity

Audrey Smedley

HISTORICAL CONSTRUCTIONS OF IDENTITY

Historical records, including the Old and New Testaments of the Bible, evince scenarios of inter-ethnic interaction that suggest some very different principles in operation throughout much of human history.[1] Ethnic groups have always existed in the sense that clusters of people living in demarcated areas develop lifestyles and language features that distinguish them from others and they perceive themselves as being separate societies with distinct social histories. Although some conflicts among different groups have been characteristic from the earliest recorded histories, hostilities were usually neither constant nor the basis on which long-term relationships were established.

One factor separates many in the contemporary world, at least some of our understandings of it, from earlier conceptions of human identity. That is that "ethnic" identity was not perceived as in-eluctably set in stone. Individuals and groups of individuals often moved to new areas or changed their identities by acquiring membership in a different group. People of the ancient world seemed to have understood that cultural characteristics were external and acquired forms of behavior, and that "barbarians" could learn to speak the language of the Romans or the Greeks and become participants in those cultures, and even citizens of these states. Languages were indeed avenues to

new social identities, and ethnic identity itself was fluid and malleable.

Until the rise of market capitalism, wage labor, the Protestant Ethic, private property, and possessive individualism, kinship connections also operated as major indices that gave all peoples a sense of who they were. Even in the technologically and politically most advanced societies of the ancient world such as in Rome, kinship was the important diacritic of connectedness to the social system. In all of the mostly patrilineal societies of the Middle East. Africa, and the Mediterranean, the normal person was identified by who his or her father was. The long list of names of who begat whom in the Old Testament (Book of Genesis) attests to the importance, especially at the tribal and chiefdom levels, of genealogical identity.

Another important diagnostic of identity was occupation. Whether one was a farmer, carpenter, fisherman, tanner, brass worker, herdsman, philosopher, government official, senator, poet, healer, warrior, or harlot, was significantly salient in the eyes of the ancient world to require the label. Occupations determined to some extent how people were viewed and treated, as well as underscored their contribution to the society.

Throughout much of the period of the early imperial states, numerous groups were in contact with one another, and individuals often traveled from one region to another as traders, warriors, craftsmen, travelers, geographers, teachers, and so forth. From one end of the Mediterranean to another, in spite of the lack of modern forms of transportation, many men and women were interacting in an inter-ethnic melange that included a wide range of cultures and peoples. From time to time, a conquest state would expand outward and incorporate some or most of this great variety. Populations did not necessarily lose any form of ethnic identity, but change was clearly understood as virtually inevitable as each society learned something new from the cultures of others. . . .

Audrey Smedley is professor emeritus of anthropology at Virginia Commonwealth University.

When Alexander conquered peoples and lands all the way to the Indus Valley in India, interacting with "civilized" populations, nomadic pastoralists, settled villagers, and a variety of hunting and fishing peoples, he exhorted his warriors to intermarry with the peoples they conquered in order to learn their languages and cultures. Garrisons of military men were stationed all over the Roman world, from Brittany to the Danube and the Black Sea, from Gibraltar to the Tigris/Euphrates valley and the Indian Ocean, and soldiers often took local women as wives. When the armies of the Moroccan king brought down the Songhai empire in 1591, his soldiers stayed on the Western Sudan frontier area and intermarried with the local people. Most of northern Africa, including Egypt of the Delta, has been periodically invaded and ruled by outsiders for the last three thousand years or so. Hittites and Hyksos from the mountainous areas of Turkey, Assyrians, Persians, Syrians, Phoenicians, Greeks, Babylonians, Romans, and various more recent Turkish and Arabian groups have settled in the towns of the coasts and interacted with the indigenous Berbers and other peoples like the Libyan groups, the Garamantes, the Carthaginians, Syngambrians, and many others. Less well known is the fact that both the Greeks and the Romans used mercenaries from inner Africa (Nubians, Ethiopians, Kushites, among others) in conflicts such as the Persian and Peloponnesian wars (Herodotus, in Godolphin 1942).[2]

Peoples of different cultures coexisted for the most part without strife, with alien segments often functioning in distinct roles in the larger cities. One-third of the population of Athens were foreigners as early as the Classical period, five hundred years before the Christian era (Boardman et al. 1986:222). And the city of Alexandria was (and still is) a heterogeneous, sophisticated, and complex community under the Greeks, Romans, Christians, and Arabs. Carthage was founded in North Africa by Phoenicians, but peoples from all over the Mediterranean world and other parts of Africa made their residence, or served as slaves, in this great trading city. Moreover, men and women of different ethnic groups intermarried frequently,

largely because marriage was often used as a political or economic strategy. Men gave their daughters and sisters to other men, the historians tell us, because they desired political and/or economic alliances with powerful and wealthy men, without regard to ethnic origins. Timotheus was the son of a Jewish mother and a Greek father. Samson married a Philistine woman; Moses married an Ethiopian woman; and many leaders, and lesser men, of the Greeks and Romans married women not from their own societies.

Different societies and localized segments of larger societies were known either by their ethnic name for themselves or by the region, town, or village of their origins. That identities of this type were fluid is indicated by the depictions of individual lives. Paul of Tarsus traveled and preached extensively throughout much of the known Mediterranean world during the early Christian era and encountered individuals of different ethnic backgrounds. He even identified himself as a Roman on occasion when it was useful to do so. There are other examples of individuals in ancient writings who changed their ethnic identities for personal or private reasons.

Scholars who have studied African societies, especially African history, have also been aware of the malleability of ethnic identity on that continent. New ethnic groups have emerged out of the colonial period, and individuals have been known to transform themselves according to their ethnic or religious milieus. One may be a Christian in one context, and a Muslim in another, with no sense of ambivalence or deception. I have encountered this phenomenon myself. Most Africans spoke several different languages, and this facilitated the molding of multiple ethnicities by providing immediate access to cultural knowledge. In situations of potential or real conflict, allegiances could be firmly established without denial of the extrinsic nature of social/ethnic identities (Connah 1987; Davidson 1991).

In addition to identities that are predicated on place of birth, membership in kin groups, or descent in the male or female line from known ancestors, language spoken, and lifestyle to which individuals have been conditioned, another feature critical to individual identity in the state systems was social position. Aristocrats seemed to have been recognized even beyond the boundaries of their immediate societies. And certain men were widely famed for their specialized skills or crafts that set them above others. Every society had its large body of commoners and usually a great number of slaves captured in war or traded in when this enterprise became a common regional feature. Slaves were usually outsiders, but slavery was not considered by law and custom a permanent condition as slaves could be manumitted, redeemed by kinspeople, or could purchase their own freedom (Smedley [1993]1999: ch. 6). While enslavement was considered an unfortunate circumstance and most slaves did the menial and onerous tasks of society, the roles of slaves varied widely. There are numerous examples of slaves rising to political power in the ancient states of the Mediterranean and in the Muslim world. Often they held positions as generals who led armies of conquest and were frequently rewarded for their successes. Whole slave dynasties like the Mamluks in Egypt reigned in various areas of the Muslim world (Hitti 1953).

With the appearance of the proselytizing universal religions, Christianity and later Islam, that became competitors with one another for the souls of all human groups, a new focus of identity was gradually and increasingly placed on membership in a religious community. During the Middle Ages of Europe, Christians and Muslims were competing not only for land and souls, but for political power and influence. And various sects that developed within each large religious community complicated matters by fostering internal dissension and even warfare *inter alia*. Whether one was Sunni or Shiite, Protestant or Catholic, was a critical determinant of one's identity locally and in the wider world. As with other aspects of ethnicity and ethnic differences, individuals often changed their religious affiliation under circumstances prompted by self-interest, or self-preservation, as in the case of the 300,000 or more Jews who were forced to convert to Catholicism in Medieval Spain during the Inquisition

(Castro 1971). Yet Christians, Jews, and Muslims had lived together in relative amity, and even intermarried, for several hundred years after the Muslim conquests and before the rise of the Christian kingdoms to challenge Muslim power.

What was absent from these different forms of human identity is what we today would perceive as classifications into "racial" groups, that is, the organization of all peoples into a limited number of unequal or ranked categories theoretically based on differences in their biophysical traits. There are no "racial" designations in the literature of the ancients and few references even to such human features as skin color. Frank Snowden has demonstrated that ever since at least the second millennium B.C. the peoples of the Mediterranean world have interacted with other groups having a variety of physical traits that differed from the Italians and Greeks. Artistic depictions of Africans of clear "negroid" features have been found, and numerous statues and paintings throughout the classical era show that physical variations in different populations were recognized and accurately depicted (Snowden 1983).

Except for indigenous Americans, members of all three of the large geographic areas that came to be categorized as "races" in the nineteenth and twentieth centuries (Mongoloid, Negroid, and Caucasoid) interacted in the ancient world. Chinese porcelain vases have been found widely distributed in the East African coastal trading cities, indicating trade between these peoples at least two thousand years old. The peoples of the Malagasy Republic represent a mixture of African and Asian (Indonesian) ancestry dating back several thousand years. Greek sailors sailed down the Red Sea into the Indian Ocean and met East Africans long before the Christian era. The peoples of the Mediterranean regularly traded with dark-skinned peoples of the upper Nile valley (and all those in between) northwest Africa, and the contrasting lighter-skinned peoples of Northern Europe. Various states of the Mediterranean called upon and used Ethiopian warriors as mercenaries in their armies, as we have seen. Some of the more desired slaves were very fair-skinned Slavs (from whom the term *slave* was derived) who were traded down the Danube by German tribesmen. Northern European slaves were shipped as far away as Egypt, Syria, Saudi Arabia, and the Muslim capital at Baghdad (Davis 1966).

What seems strange to us today is that the biological variations among human groups were not given significant social meaning. Only occasionally do ancient writers ever even remark on the physical characteristics of a given person or people. Herodotus, in discussing the habits, customs, and origins of different groups and noting variations in skin color, specifically tells us that this hardly matters. The Colchians are of Egyptian origin, he wrote, because they have black skins and wooly hair "which amounts to but little, since several other nations are so too."[3] Most writers explained such differences as due to natural environmental factors such as the hot sun causing people to be dark skinned. No structuring of inequality, whether social, moral, intellectual, cultural or otherwise, was associated with people *because of their skin color,* although all "barbarians" varied in some ways from the somatic norm of the Mediterranean world. But barbarians were not irredeemably so, and, as we have seen, nothing in the values of the public life denied the transformability of even the most backward of barbarians.

We in the contemporary Western world have often found it difficult to understand this phenomenon and assume that differences in skin color must have had some important meaning. Historians have tried to discover "racial" meanings in the literature of the ancients, assuming that these writers had the same attitudes and beliefs about human differences found in nineteenth- and twentieth-century North America. The reason for our myopia has to do with our deeply entrenched conditioning to the racial worldview (Smedley 1993, 1998). When "race" appeared in human history, it brought about a subtle but powerful transformation in the world's perceptions of human differences. It imposed social meanings on physical variations among human groups that served as the basis for the structuring of the total society. Since that time many people in the West have continued to link human identity to external physical features. We have been socialized to an ideology about the meaning of these differences based on a notion of heredity and permanence that was unknown in the ancient world and in the Middle Ages.

RACE: THE MODERN CONCEPTION OF HUMAN DIFFERENCES AND HUMAN IDENTITY

In the eighteenth century this new mode of structuring inequality in human societies evolved in the American colonies and soon was present throughout the overseas territories of the colonizing countries of Western Europe. "Race" was a form of social identification and stratification that was seemingly grounded in the physical differences of populations interacting with one another in the New World, but whose real meaning rested in social and political realities. The term *race* had been used to refer to humans occasionally since the sixteenth century in the English language but was rarely used to refer to populations in the slave trade. It was a mere classificatory term like *kind, type,* or even *breed,* or *stock,* and it had no clear meaning until the eighteenth century. During this time, the English began to have wider experiences with varied populations and gradually developed attitudes and beliefs that had not appeared before in Western history and which reflected a new kind of understanding and interpretation of human differences. Understanding the foundations of race ideology is critical to our analysis.

English settlers in North America failed to assimilate the peoples whom they conquered; indeed they generally kept them at great length and social distance from themselves (Morgan 1975; Nash 1982). Indigenous Indians were different in both cultural and biological features, but this was not the necessary and sufficient reason for the English habits and policies of separateness. They had had a long history of enmity with earlier peoples, especially the Irish, on their very borders and had generated out of their hostility with the Irish an image of "savagery" that became institutionalized as a major part of public consciousness about "the other." The policies and practices of the English in Ireland functioned to keep those Irish who refused to accept English domination segregated from themselves. Failing to even attempt an understanding of Irish customs and institutions, the English expressed an abiding contempt and hatred for both Irish culture and people that reached a crescendo during the sixteenth and seventeenth centuries when the English were also settling in the New World. It was an extreme form of ethnocentrism or ethnic chauvinism that some historians believe came close to being racial (Allen 1994; Canny 1973; Liggio 1976).

"Savagery" was an image about human differences that became deeply embedded in English life and thought and provided a foil against which they constructed their own identity as "civilized" Englishmen. They brought this image of what savagery was all about with them to the New World where it was soon imposed on the native populations when they, too, began to resist English encroachment. Savagery carried with it an enormous burden of negative and stereotypic characteristics grotesquely counterposed against the vision that the English had of themselves as a civilized people. Every new experience, along with a growing technological superiority, widened the differences and denigrated all other peoples who were not part of the civilized world. The concept of "civilized" polities in contrast to savagery and barbarism was beginning to take hold in much of Western Europe, and in this sense Englishmen were not much different from the rest of the Western world. But English notions of their own superiority were enhanced by their technological, material, and political successes, by their earlier successful split from the Catholic realm, by the early rise of merchant capitalism, the development of new forms of wealth, notions about individual freedom, property rights, and self-sufficiency, and by a growing sense of their own uniqueness even among other Europeans. This was summed up in the myth of Anglo-Saxonism (Horsman 1981).

"Race" emerged as a social classification that reflected this greatly expanded sense of human separateness and differences. Theodore Allen (1997) argues that the "invention" of the white race took place after an early, but unsuccessful, colonial revolt of servants and poor freedmen known as Bacon's Rebellion in 1676. Colonial leaders subsequently decided it would be useful to establish a division among the masses of poor to prevent their further collaboration against the governmental authorities. As African servants were vulnerable to policies that kept them in servitude indefinitely, and European servants had the protection of English law, colonial leaders developed a policy backed by new laws that separated African servants and freedmen from those of European background. Over the next half century, they passed numerous laws that provided resources and benefits to poor, white freedmen and other laws that restricted the rights of "Africans," "mulattoes," and "Indians."

Calling upon the model of the Chain of Being, and using natural differences in physical features, they created a new form of social identity. "Race" developed in the minds of some Europeans as a way to rationalize the conquest and brutal treatment of Native American populations, and especially the retention and perpetuation of slavery for imported Africans. As an ideology structuring social, economic, and political inequality, "race" contradicted developing trends in England and in Western European societies that promoted freedom, democracy, equality, and human rights. Europeans justified this attitude toward human differences by focusing on the physical features of the New World populations, magnifying and exaggerating their differences, and concluding that the Africans and Indians and their descendants were lesser forms of human beings, and that their inferiority was natural and/or God-given.

The creation of "race" and racial ideology imposed on the conquered and enslaved peoples an identity as the lowest status groups in society. Myths about their inferior moral, intellectual, and behavioral features had begun to develop and these facilitated proscription of any competition with Europeans. By the mid-eighteenth century, Negroes had been segregated from poor whites in the laws of most colonies and transformed into property as slaves in a state of permanent bondage.

Edmund Morgan (1975) also interpreted the actions of the early colonists in the process of establishing "racial" identities as stemming from the propertied colonists' fear of poor whites and possibly slaves engaging in rebellions together. Colonial leaders consciously formulated policies that would separate poor whites from Indians, blacks, and mulattoes and proceeded to provide the white poor, whom they had hitherto treated with contempt and hatred, with some privileges and special advantages.[4] In time, class divisions diminished in the minds of poor whites and they saw themselves as having something in common with the propertied class, symbolized by their light skins and common origins in Europe. With laws progressively continuing to reduce the rights of blacks and Indians, it was not long before the various European groups coalesced into a white "racial" category whose high-status identity gave them access to wealth, power, opportunity, and privilege.[5]

By the mid-nineteenth century virtually all Americans had been conditioned to this arbitrary ranking of the American peoples, and racial ideology had diffused around much of the world, including to the colonized peoples of the Third World and among Europeans themselves.

"RACE" AS IDENTITY

In the United States the biophysical features of different populations, which had become markers of social status, were internalized as sources of individual and group identities. After the Civil War, although slavery ended, race and racial ideology remained and were strengthened. African Americans particularly had to grapple with the reality of being defined as the lowest status group in American society and with the associated stereotyping that became increasingly part of the barriers to their integration into American society (Conrad 1969). And Native Americans had to try to reinvent their identities, whether in towns or isolated on remote reservations where traditional lifestyles were no

longer possible. American society had made "race" (and the physical features connected to it) equivalent to, and the dominant source of, human identity, superseding all other aspects of identity.

The problems that this has entailed, especially for the low-status "races," have been enormous, immensely complex, and almost intractable. Constant and unrelenting portrayals of their inferiority conditioned them to a self-imagery of being culturally backward, primitive, intellectually stunted, prone to violence, morally corrupt, undeserving of the benefits of civilization, insensitive to the finer arts, and (in the case of Africans) aesthetically ugly and animal-like. Because of the cultural imperative of race ideology, all Americans were compelled to the view that a racial status, symbolized by biophysical attributes, was the premier determinant of their identity. "Race" identity took priority over religion, ethnic origin, education and training, socioeconomic class, occupation, language, values, beliefs, morals, lifestyles, geographical location, and all other human attributes that hitherto provided all groups and individuals with a sense of who they were. The dilemma for the low-status races was, and still is, how to construct a positive identity for themselves in the light of the "racial" identity imposed on them by the dominant society.

In recent decades, one response to this dilemma on the part of some African Americans has been Afrocentrism (which is not the same as an older version of "Negritude" that black intellectuals had developed earlier in this century). And for some Indians a new form of "Nativism" has emerged, harkening back to a Native American lifestyle. Afrocentrism seeks to reidentify with the peoples and cultures of Africa and to elevate Africans to a position of esteem by emphasizing valuable aspects of African cultures. Some Afrocentrists also make assertions about the positive qualities of African people and seek to recognize and objectify Africanisms in the behavior of African-descended peoples who have been scattered all over the New World. Many assume or operate on the premise that all peoples who descended from Africans during the diaspora maintain certain behaviorisms that mark them off from other peoples. Their arguments seem similar to that of the biological determinists in the dominant society, but most would probably not go so far as to assert a genetic basis to certain "African"-originated behaviors. Those who take the position asserting a common African personality or behavior reflect the degree to which the ideology of "race" has been implanted in them. Like most Americans, they find it difficult to think beyond the racial world-view and draw upon the same strategies as white racists in claiming superior features for "African" people. At the same time, there are many Afrocentrists who are very conscious of the fact that theirs is a political position and that they are using the same biological arguments as racists, the people whom they theoretically oppose. They fail to realize that operating within the racial worldview, accepting its premises that biologically distinct races exist, each with unique cultural/behavioral features, and simply denying inferiority while asserting African superiority does nothing to change the racism in our society.

However, we also must understand that what Afrocentrism is really intended to do is to restore a sense of pride and dignity to ordinary African Americans, regardless of how whites and others regard their positions. By looking to the "real" Africa, studying her history, learning about and being involved in certain rituals and festivals that focus on African arts, dance, dress, music, and so on, some activists feel that they are engendering this pride and helping to remove the contempt and denigration that has accompanied our ideas about Africa in the past. They understand that for too long African Americans have been conditioned to the same negative beliefs about Africa and Africans as have whites and others and that there is a need to eliminate the self-deprecation and self-hatred that black Americans have experienced with regard to their African ancestry. . . .

THE NON-PROBLEM OF "MIXED-RACE" PEOPLE

One of the more tragic aspects of the racial world-view has been the seeming dilemma of people whose parents are identifiably of different "races."

Historically, "race" was grounded in the myth of biologically separate, exclusive, and distinct populations. No social ingredient in our race ideology allowed for an identity of "mixed-races." Indeed over the past century and a half, the American public was conditioned to the belief that "mixed-race" people (especially of black and white ancestry) were abnormal products of the unnatural mating of two species, besides being socially unacceptable in the normal scheme of things. The tragedy for "mixed" people is that powerful social lie, the assumption at the heart of "race," that a presumed biological essence is the basis of one's true identity. Identity is biology, racial ideology tells us, and it is permanent and immutable. The emphasis on and significance given to "race" precludes any possibility for establishing our premier identities on the basis of other characteristics. In this sense it may be argued that the myth of "race" has been a barrier to true human identities.

The unfortunate consequence of race ideology is that many of the people with this "mixed-race" background have also been conditioned to the belief in the biological salience of "race." Their efforts to establish a "Mixed-Race" category in the American census forms show a total misunderstanding of what "race" is all about, and this is, of course, a major part of the tragedy. Their arguments imply a feeling of having no identity at all because they do not exist formally (that is, socially) as a "biological" category.

The fact is that from the standpoint of biology, there have been "mixed" people in North America ever since Europeans first encountered indigenous Americans and the first Africans were brought to the English colonies in the 1620s. The average African American has about one-quarter of his or her genes from non-African (nonblack) ancestors, although most estimates are likely to be conservative (cf. Marks 1995; Reed 1969). There is a greater range of skin colors, hair textures, body sizes, nose shapes, and other physical features among black Americans than almost any other people identified as a distinct population. Virtually all of them could identify as of "mixed-race." But the physical markers of race status are always open to interpretation by others. "Race" as social status is in the eye of the beholder. "Mixed" people will still be treated as black if their phenotypes cause them to be so perceived by others. Insistence on being in a separate classification will not change that perception or the reaction of people to them.

What compounds and complicates matters is another lie that is one of the basic tenets, or constituent components, of the racial worldview: the myth that biology has some intrinsic connection to culture. Some advocates of a new "mixed-race" category have argued that they want to recognize the "culture" of their other parent. For example, in a black/white mixed marriage, a black parent presumably has "black" culture, and the white parent has "white" culture. These advocates fail to realize what anthropologists have long known, that there is no relationship between one's culture or lifestyle and one's genes or biological features. All native-born Americans share some basic cultural similarities, and the ancestors of modern African Americans have been "American" longer than the ancestors of most European Americans.[6] It is the ideological myths of the racial worldview that prevent us from seeing how very much alike culturally black and white Americans are. (This is not to suggest that there are not differences in the way blacks and whites experience our culture and lifestyle variations that reflect social-class differences and the isolation of inner-city populations.)

On the other hand, if one parent did come from a very different cultural background (e.g., recently emigrated from Asia), a child does not automatically have that culture because of the biology of the parent. Humans acquire culture; it is learned behavior. In order for Tiger Woods (a golfing star) to have Thai culture, he would have to *learn* the language and the elements of Thai culture. One can learn these without having a single gene from a Thai parent. Moreover, there is no reason why one should learn the cultures of ancestors merely because of some genetic or genealogical connections. None of us have the cultures of any of our ancestors two centuries ago because all cultures,

including American culture, have changed, some of them drastically, during that time. Cultures constantly change without any corresponding changes in biological features.

Americans should understand clearly that humans learn cultural features from one another all the time because that has been one of the most profound experiences of human, and especially American, history. What prevents us from understanding this is that component in the ideology of "race," as we have seen, that holds that each race has separate, biologically determined patterns of cultural behavior. The racial worldview, with its emphasis on assumptions of innateness and immutability, makes it possible to interpret all forms of human behavior as hereditary. In fact, it almost mandates such a perspective because of powerful forces within our culture that preserve and promote hereditarian ideas. The belief in racially determined cultural behavior, despite all evidence to the contrary, is perpetuated in American society by the popular media and as a part of folk wisdom about human differences. Witness the inordinate attention to and sales of Herrnstein and Murray's *The Bell Curve* (1994). This belief has been a necessary component of the ideology of "race," because it helps to perpetuate the notion that major differences between "races" exist.

People who consider themselves of "mixed race" and experience some form of psychic stress because they feel they have no identity in American society, perhaps more than most, need to have understanding of this history. . . .

TRANSCENDING THE RESTRICTIONS OF "RACIAL" IDENTITY

Today scholars are beginning to realize that "race" is nothing more and nothing less than a social invention. It has nothing to do with the intrinsic, or potential, qualities of the physically differing populations, but much to do with the allocation of power, privilege, and wealth among them. *This conceptual separation of actual physical variations within the species from the socially invented characterizations of them represents a major paradigm shift in how many scholars now think about the human experience.* Anthropologists and biologists no longer see "races" as discrete populations defined by blood-group patterns or "types" defined by averages of statistical measurements. Biophysical variations are seen as continuous and gradual, overlapping population boundaries, fluid, and subject to evolutionary changes. In like manner, scholars honestly examining the history of American attitudes toward human differences have concluded that "race" was a social invention of the eighteenth century that took advantage of the superficial physical differences among the American population and the social roles that these peoples played, and transposed these into a new form of social stratification. The symbols of race identity became the substance.

Recognizing the reality of the racial worldview and how it developed as a sociocultural reality requires a whole new way of looking at human diversity in all of its many forms. It means that (1) we can better recognize and comprehend accurately and objectively the natural causes of human physical variations around the world without attempting to homogenize people into limited "racial" categories; (2) we can liberate ourselves from the need to utilize physical differences in apprehending human identities; (3) freed from the myths of racial determinism, we can now improve our understanding of the true nature of culture and cultural differences and begin to view the processes of cultural change in a more accurate light; and (4) we can begin to understand the real nature of "race" as a social construct and to deal with the problems that racial identities have imposed on people.

For example, using this new perspective, we would be able to avoid the problems encountered when scholars examine the African Diaspora and attempt to determine which peoples are legitimately black products of this massive process of displacement. Several years ago, two Asian students who had recently immigrated to the United States came to me confidentially after class with a puzzle. They wanted to know why were people like Hazel O'Leary (just appointed as U.S. Secretary of Energy) and Thurgood Marshall, Justice of the United States Supreme Court, identified as "black" in American society when it was obvious that they were not. I explained some of the history of the idea of "race" and the interactions among peoples in the New World. I also pointed out that there is a great deal more to the identification of African Americans than similarities in physical traits, that in fact, biological variations have little to do with the social categories of race. Indeed the people of the African Diaspora are a biogenetically diverse category of people who have an identity derived from common experiences of exploitation and racism. It is far more accurate and more fruitful to scholarship, and possibly to the future of humankind, to define African American people by their sense of *community, consciousness,* and *commitment* than by some mystical "racial" essence. It is the Community into which they were born and reared, a Consciousness of the historical realities and shared experiences of their ancestors, and a Commitment to the perspectives of their "blackness" and to the diminishing of racism that is critical to the identities of the Thurgood Marshalls and Hazel O'Learys of our society. The social categories of "race" have always encompassed more than mere physical similarities and differences. Theodore Allen tells us in the acknowledgements to his two-volume excoriation of white racism that he has learned to say, "I am not white" (1994).

Even without all of the intermixtures of peoples, some Americans have already experienced a high level of uncertainty about the "racial" status of individuals with whom they have had some interaction. Many peoples in the world, from Morocco to the Persian Gulf, to the islands in the South Pacific Ocean, have physical features that cause them to be "mistaken" for black Americans. In that broad band of the earth called the tropics we find indigenous peoples with tan to brown to dark brown skins, and hair that may be frizzly, kinky, curly, or straight. As more and more of these peoples either travel to the United States or are encountered by Americans on missions abroad, Americans must deal with their perceptions of these peoples. Some time ago, in the space of about eight months, I met a Samoan, a person from the New Guinea area, and a number of Arabs who in the course of conversations have indicated that they have been "mistaken" for blacks.[7] Many peoples from the southern regions of Saudi Arabia look very much like their neighboring Africans across the Red Sea, having evolved in the same climate and latitude (and having intermingled over eons of time). To try to maintain racial categories based on physical features in the face of the real world of human biological diversity, I suspect, will be increasingly difficult.

There is another option, one that we have not yet claimed in the establishing and referencing of our human identities. We cannot ignore the fact that since the fifteenth century, what has happened in the Americas, and to varying degrees in many parts of the Third World, has been the fusion of genetic materials from all of the great continents. So-called "racial" mixture has occurred extensively in Latin America, and to a lesser extent in North America, so that most people are descendants of ancestors from Europe, Africa, and the Americas, and in many places like the Caribbean, from Asia also (Graham 1990: Morner 1967). Throughout the colonial world, complex genetic mixtures among various peoples have taken place; and increasingly Europeans at home are participants in, and products of, new genetic combinations with individuals absorbed into their societies from distant lands.

In addition to the increasing genetic heterogeneity of individuals and groups, there is the obvious fact that cultural features have traveled all over the world independently of the spread of genetic material. In the midst of the Sahara desert, signs proclaim "Coca-Cola," everyone from the Siberian tundra to the Melanesian forests wears "jeans," African clothing and designs are found from Paris to Sydney, Australia, and Americans eat more pizzas and tacos (burritos, tortillas, etc.) than almost any other people outside of Italy and Mexico. White boys wear dreadlocks, and Chinese and other Asian, and increasingly African, ethnic restaurants are found around the world. Fast foods, music, dance, dress, Hollywood films, whole industrial complexes (including the world of computers), and a wide range of political, religious, and social beliefs have diffused around the world. Few cultures have not experienced the impact of such massive infusion of new traits.

The peoples who have resulted from all this continuous blending of genetic features and cultural traits are truly "universal" human beings, regardless of what languages they speak or cultures they participate in. The concept of "universal" human beings might very well in time obviate racial categories (but not ethnic identities) and may help to bring about the elimination of all such designations. Many persons will come to recognize themselves as "universal" human beings, and there should be perhaps an early census category that proclaims this reality. What anthropologists must do is to make sure that the ideas of "ethnicity" and "ethnic identity" do not become perceived as hereditary, permanent, and unalterable, but remain fluid forms of identity that will make us all "multicultural."

DISCUSSION QUESTIONS

1. Why was the social classification of race invented?
2. Is Afrocentrism a response to racism?

NOTES

1. Reference materials for this section were taken largely from the following: Boardman et al. (1986), Godolphin (1942), and Snowden (1983). But I have read widely in ancient history and am aware that such materials are not generally considered part of the anthropological repertoire. We need to realize that historical materials are widely available to all, and we should encourage students to avail themselves of them, especially since American students have been shown to be woefully ignorant of history and geography.
2. Herodotus lists more than two dozen different nations that fought on the different sides in the Persian wars: Arabians, Ethiopians, Armenians, Thracians, Libyans, and many others.
3. The Persian Wars, Book II, p. 130, in Godolphin (1942).

4. Morgan claims that the Virginia Assembly "deliberately did what it could to foster the contempt of whites for blacks and Indians" (1975:331).

5. For insightful analysis of this process, see also Allen (1994, 1997).

6. Bohannan and Curtin (1995:13) have observed that half the ancestors of African Americans were already here in the United States by 1780 while the median date for the arrival of European ancestors was "remarkably late, 1890s." We need more of this kind of honesty in recognizing historical realities on the part of scholars in all disciplines.

7. See Morsy (1994). When Arabs began to migrate to the Detroit area several generations ago, many were frequently mistaken for blacks. This became an acute problem in the area around Dearborn, Michigan, where many of them settled. There had long been a law in Dearborn that prohibited blacks from being in the city after sundown. The Dearborn police, among others, were often very confused.

REFERENCES

Allen, Theodore W. [1994]1997 *The Invention of the White Race,* vols. 1 and 2, London: Verso.

Boardman, John, J. Griffin, and O. Murray, eds. 1986 *The Oxford History of the Classical World.* Oxford: Oxford University Press.

Canny, Nicholas P. 1973 The Ideology of English Colonialization: From Ireland to America. *William and Mary Quarterly* (3rd ser.) 30:575–598.

Castro, Americo 1971 *The Spaniards.* Berkeley: University of California Press.

Connah, Graham 1987 *African Civilizations.* New York: Cambridge University Press.

Conrad, Earl 1969 *The Invention of the Negro.* New York: Paul S. Erikson.

Davidson, Basil 1991 *African Civilization Revisited.* Trenton, NJ: African World Press.

Davis, David Brion 1966 *The Problem of Slavery in Western Culture.* Middlesex, England: Penguin.

Godolphin, Francis R. B., ed. 1942 *The Greek Historians,* vols. 1 and 2. New York: Random House.

Graham, Richard, ed. 1990 *The Idea of Race in Latin America, 1870–1940.* Austin: University of Texas Press.

Hitti, Phillip 1953 *History of the Arabs.* London: Macmillan Publishing Co.

Horsman, Reginald 1981 *Race and Manifest Destiny.* Cambridge, MA: Harvard University Press.

Liggio, Leonard P. 1976 English Origins of Early American Racism. *Radical History Review* 3(1):1–26.

Marks, Jonathan 1995 *Human Biodiversity: Genes, Race, and History.* New York: Aldine de Gruyter.

Morgan, Edmund S. 1975 *American Slavery: American Freedom.* New York: W. W. Norton and Co.

Mörner, Magnus 1967 *Race Mixture in the History of Latin America.* Boston: Little, Brown.

Morsy, Soheir 1994 Beyond the Honorary "White" Classification of Egyptians: Societal Identity in Historical Context. In *Race.* S. Gregory and R. Sanjek, eds. Pp. 175–198. New Brunswick, NJ: Rutgers University Press.

Nash, Gary 1982 *Red, White, and Black: The Peoples of Early America.* Englewood Cliffs, NJ: Prentice Hall.

Reed, T.E. 1969 Caucasian Genes in American Negroes. *Science* 165 (3,895): 762–768.

Smedley, Audrey [1993]1999 *Race in North America: Origin and Evolution of a Worldview.* 2nd edition, revised and enlarged. Boulder, CO: Westview Press.

Snowden, Frank M., Jr. 1983 *Before Color Prejudice.* Revised edition. Cambridge, MA: Harvard University Press.

READING 2

Who Is Black? One Nation's Definition

F. James Davis

In a taped interview conducted by a blind, black anthropologist, a black man nearly ninety years old said: "Now you must understand that this is just a name we have. I am not black and you are not black either, if you go by the evidence of your eyes. . . . Anyway, black people are all colors. White people don't look all the same way, but there are more different kinds of us than there are of them. Then too, there is a certain stage [at] which you cannot tell who is white and who is black. Many of the people I see who are thought of as black could just as well be white in their appearance. Many of the white people I see are black as far as I can tell by the way they look. Now, that's it for looks. Looks don't mean much. The things that makes us different is how we think. What we believe is important, the ways we look at life" (Gwaltney, 1980:96).

How does a person get defined as a black, both socially and legally, in the United States? What is

F. James Davis (1920–2012) was professor emeritus of sociology at Illinois State University.

the nation's rule for who is black, and how did it come to be? And so what? Don't we all know who is black, and isn't the most important issue what opportunities the group has? Let us start with some experiences of three well-known American blacks—actress and beauty pageant winner Vanessa Williams, U.S. Representative Adam Clayton Powell, Jr., and entertainer Lena Horne.

For three decades after the first Miss America Pageant in 1921, black women were barred from competing. The first black winner was Vanessa Williams of Millwood, New York, crowned Miss America in 1984. In the same year the first runner-up—Suzette Charles of Mays Landing, New Jersey—was also black. The viewing public was charmed by the television images and magazine pictures of the beautiful and musically talented Williams, but many people were also puzzled. Why was she being called black when she appeared to be white? Suzette Charles, whose ancestry appeared to be more European than African, at least looked like many of the "lighter blacks." Notoriety followed when Vanessa Williams resigned because of the impending publication of some nude photographs of her taken before the pageant, and Suzette Charles became Miss America for the balance of 1984. Beyond the troubling question of whether these young women could have won if they had looked "more black," the publicity dramatized the nation's definition of a black person.

Some blacks complained that the Rev. Adam Clayton Powell, Jr., was so light that he was a stranger in their midst. In the words of Roi Ottley, "He was white to all appearances, having blue eyes, an aquiline nose, and light, almost blond, hair" (1943:220), yet he became a bold, effective black leader—first as minister of the Abyssinian Baptist Church of Harlem, then as a New York city councilman, and finally as a U.S. congressman from the state of New York. Early in his activist career he led 6,000 blacks in a march on New York City Hall. He used his power in Congress to fight for civil rights legislation and other black causes. In 1966, in Washington, D.C., he convened the first black power conference.

In his autobiography, Powell recounts some experiences with racial classification in his youth that left a lasting impression on him. During Powell's freshman year at Colgate University, his roommate did not know that he was a black until his father, Adam Clayton Powell, Sr., was invited to give a chapel talk on Negro rights and problems, after which the roommate announced that because Adam was a Negro they could no longer be roommates or friends.

Another experience that affected Powell deeply occurred one summer during his Colgate years. He was working as a bellhop at a summer resort in Manchester, Vermont, when Abraham Lincoln's aging son Robert was a guest there. Robert Lincoln disliked blacks so much that he refused to let them wait on him or touch his luggage, car, or any of his possessions. Blacks who did got their knuckles whacked with his cane. To the great amusement of the other bellhops, Lincoln took young Powell for a white man and accepted his services (Powell, 1971:31–33).

Lena Horne's parents were both very light in color and came from black upper-middle-class families in Brooklyn (Horne and Schickel, 1965; Buckley, 1986). Lena lived with her father's parents until she was about seven years old. Her grandfather was very light and blue-eyed. Her fair-skinned grandmother was the daughter of a slave woman and her white owner, from the family of John C. Calhoun, well-known defender of slavery. One of her father's great-grandmothers was a Blackfoot Indian, to whom Lena Horne has attributed her somewhat coppery skin color. One of her mother's grandmothers was a French-speaking black woman from Senegal and never a slave. Her mother's father was a "Portuguese Negro," and two women in his family had passed as white and become entertainers.

Lena Horne's parents had separated, and when she was seven her entertainer mother began placing her in a succession of homes in different states. Her favorite place was in the home of her Uncle Frank, her father's brother, a red-haired, blue-eyed teacher in a black school in Georgia. The black children in that community asked her why she was so light and called her a "yellow bastard." She learned that when satisfactory evidence of respectable black parents is lacking, being light-skinned implies illegitimacy and having an underclass white parent and is thus a disgrace in the black community. When her mother married a white Cuban, Lena also learned that blacks can be very hostile to the white spouse, especially when the "black" mate is very light. At this time she began to blame the confused color line for her childhood troubles. She later endured much hostility from blacks and whites alike when her own second marriage, to white composer-arranger Lennie Hayton, was finally made public in 1950 after three years of keeping it secret.

Early in Lena Horne's career there were complaints that she did not fit the desired image of a black entertainer for white audiences, either physically or in her style. She sang white love songs, not the blues. Noting her brunette-white beauty, one white agent tried to get her to take a Spanish name, learn some Spanish songs, and pass as a Latin white, but she had learned to have a horror of passing and never considered it, although Hollywood blacks accused her of trying to pass after she played her first bit part in a film. After she failed her first screen test because she looked like a white girl trying to play black-face, the directors tried making her up with a shade called "Light Egyptian" to make her look darker. The whole procedure embarrassed and hurt her deeply. . . .

Other light mulatto entertainers have also had painful experiences because of their light skin and other caucasoid features. Starting an acting career is never easy, but actress Jane White's difficulties in the 1940s were compounded by her lightness. Her father was NAACP leader Walter White. Even with dark makeup on her ivory skin, she did not look like a black person on the stage, but she was not allowed to try out for white roles because blacks were barred from playing them. When she auditioned for the part of a young girl from India, the director was enthusiastic, although her skin color was too light, but higher management decreed that it was unthinkable for a Negro to play the part of an Asian Indian (White, 1948:338). Only after great perseverance did Jane White make her debut as the educated mulatto maid Nonnie in the stage version of Lillian Smith's *Strange Fruit* (1944). . . .

THE ONE-DROP RULE DEFINED

As the above cases illustrate, to be considered black in the United States not even half of one's ancestry must be African black. But will one-fourth do, or one-eighth, or less? The nation's answer to the question "Who is black?" has long been that a black is any person with *any* known African black ancestry (Myrdal, 1944:113–18; Berry and Tischler, 1978:97–98; Williamson, 1980:1–2). This definition reflects the long experience with slavery and later with Jim Crow segregation. In the South it became known as the "one-drop rule," meaning that a single drop of "black blood" makes a person a black. It is also known as the "one black ancestor rule," some courts have called it the "traceable amount rule," and anthropologists call it the "hypo-descent rule," meaning that racially mixed persons are assigned the status of the subordinate group (Harris, 1964:56). This definition emerged from the American South to become the nation's definition, generally accepted by whites and blacks alike (Bahr, Chadwick, and Stauss, 1979:27–28). Blacks had no other choice. This American cultural definition of blacks is taken for granted as readily by judges, affirmative action officers, and black protesters as it is by Ku Klux Klansmen.

Let us not be confused by terminology. At present the usual statement of the one-drop rule is in terms of "black blood" or black ancestry, while not so long ago it referred to "Negro blood" or ancestry. The term "black" rapidly replaced "Negro" in general usage in the United States as the black power movement peaked at the end of the 1960s, but the black and Negro populations are the same. The term "black" is used [here] for persons with any black African lineage, not just for unmixed members of populations from sub-Saharan Africa. The term "Negro," which is used in certain historical contexts, means the same thing. Terms such as "African black," "unmixed Negro," and "all black" are used here to refer to unmixed blacks descended from African populations.

We must also pay attention to the terms "mulatto" and "colored." The term "mulatto" was originally used to mean the offspring of a "pure African Negro" and a "pure white." Although the root meaning of mulatto, in Spanish, is "hybrid," "mulatto" came to include the children of unions between whites and so-called "mixed Negroes." For example, Booker T. Washington and Frederick Douglass, with slave mothers and white fathers, were referred to as mulattoes (Bennett, 1962:255). To whatever extent their mothers were part white, these men were more than half white. Douglass was evidently part Indian as well, and he looked it (Preston, 1980:9–10). Washington had reddish hair and gray eyes. At the time of the American Revolution, many of the founding fathers had some very light slaves, including some who appeared to be white. The term "colored" seemed for a time to refer only to mulattoes, especially lighter ones, but later it became a euphemism for darker Negroes, even including unmixed blacks. With widespread racial mixture, "Negro" came to mean any slave or descendant of a slave, no matter how much mixed. Eventually in the United States, the terms mulatto, colored, Negro, black, and African American all came to mean people with any known black African ancestry. Mulattoes are racially mixed, to whatever degree, while the terms black, Negro, African American, and colored include both mulattoes and unmixed blacks. These terms have quite different meanings in other countries.

Whites in the United States need some help envisioning the American black experience with ancestral fractions. At the beginning of miscegenation between two populations presumed to be racially pure, quadroons appear in the second generation of continuing mixing with whites, and octoroons in the third. A quadroon is one-fourth African black and thus easily classed as black in the United States, yet three of this person's four grandparents are white. An octoroon has seven white great-grandparents out of eight and usually looks white or almost so. Most parents of black American children in recent decades have themselves been racially mixed, but often the fractions get complicated because the earlier details of the mixing were obscured generations ago. Like so many white Americans, black people are forced to speculate about some of the fractions—one-eighth this, three-sixteenths that, and so on. . . .

PLESSY, PHIPPS, AND OTHER CHALLENGES IN THE COURTS

Homer Plessy was the plaintiff in the 1896 precedent-setting "separate-but-equal" case of *Plessy v. Ferguson* (163 U.S. 537). This case challenged the Jim Crow statute that required racially segregated seating on trains in interstate commerce in the state of Louisiana. The U.S. Supreme Court quickly dispensed with Plessy's contention that because he was only one-eighth Negro and could pass as white he was entitled to ride in the seats reserved for whites. Without ruling directly on the definition of a Negro, the Supreme Court briefly took what is called "judicial notice" of what it assumed to be common knowledge: that a Negro or black is any person with any black ancestry. (Judges often take explicit "judicial notice" not only of scientific or scholarly conclusions, or of opinion surveys or other systematic investigations, but also of something they just assume to be so, including customary practices or common knowledge.) This has consistently been the ruling in the federal courts, and often when the black ancestry was even less than one-eighth. The federal courts have thus taken judicial notice of the customary boundary between two sociocultural groups that differ, on the average, in physical traits, not between two discrete genetic categories. In the absence of proof of a specific black ancestor, merely being known as a black in the community has usually been accepted by the courts as evidence of black ancestry. The separate-but-equal doctrine established in the Plessy case is no longer the law, as a result of the judicial and legislative successes of the civil rights movement, but the nation's legal definition of who is black remains unchanged.

State courts have generally upheld the one-drop rule. For instance, in a 1948 Mississippi case a young man, Davis Knight, was sentenced to five years in jail for violating the antimiscegenation statute. Less than one-sixteenth black, Knight said he was not aware that he had any black lineage, but the state proved his great-grandmother was a slave girl. In some states the operating definition of black has been limited by statute to particular fractions, yet the social definition—the one-drop rule—has generally prevailed in case of doubt. Mississippi, Missouri, and five other states have had the criterion of one-eighth. Virginia changed from one-fourth to one-eighth in 1910, then in 1930 forbade white intermarriage with a person with any black ancestry. Persons in Virginia who are one-fourth or more Indian and less than one-sixteenth African black are defined as Indians while on the reservation but as blacks when they leave (Berry, 1965:26). While some states have had general race classification statutes, at least for a time, others have legislated a definition of black only for particular purposes, such as marriage or education. In a few states there have even been varying definitions for different situations (Mangum, 1940:38–48). All states require a designation of race on birth certificates, but there are no clear guidelines to help physicians and midwives do the classifying.

Louisiana's latest race classification statute became highly controversial and was finally repealed in 1983 (Trillin, 1986:77). Until 1970, a Louisiana statute had embraced the one-drop rule, defining a Negro as anyone with a "trace of black ancestry." This law was challenged in court a number of times from the 1920s on, including an unsuccessful attempt in 1957 by boxer Ralph Dupas, who asked to be declared white so that a law banning "interracial sports" (since repealed) would not prevent him from boxing in the state. In 1970 a lawsuit was brought on behalf of a child whose ancestry was allegedly only one two-hundred-fifty-sixth black, and the legislature revised its law. The 1970 Louisiana statute defined a black as someone whose ancestry is more than one thirty-second black (La. Rev. Stat. 42:267). Adverse publicity about this law was

widely disseminated during the Phipps trial in 1983 (discussed below), filed as *Jane Doe v. State of Louisiana*. This case was decided in a district court in May 1983, and in June the legislature abolished its one thirty-second statute and gave parents the right to designate the race of newborns, and even to change classifications on birth certificates if they can prove the child is white by a "preponderance of the evidence." However, the new statute in 1983 did not abolish the "traceable amount rule" (the one-drop rule), as demonstrated by the outcomes when the Phipps decision was appealed to higher courts in 1985 and 1986.

The history in the Phipps (Jane Doe) case goes as far back as 1770, when a French planter named Jean Gregoire Guillory took his wife's slave, Margarita, as his mistress (Model, 1983:3–4). More than two centuries and two decades later, their great-great-great-great-granddaughter, Susie Guillory Phipps, asked the Louisiana courts to change the classification on her deceased parents' birth certificates to "white" so she and her brothers and sisters could be designated white. They all looked white, and some were blue-eyed blonds. Mrs. Susie Phipps had been denied a passport because she had checked "white" on her application although her birth certificate designated her race as "colored." This designation was based on information supplied by a midwife, who presumably relied on the parents or on the family's status in the community. Mrs. Phipps claimed that this classification came as a shock, since she had always thought she was white, had lived as white, and had twice married as white. Some of her relatives, however, gave depositions saying they considered themselves "colored," and the lawyers for the state claimed to have proof that Mrs. Phipps is three thirty-seconds black (Trillin, 1986:62–63, 71–74). That was more than enough "blackness" for the district court in 1983 to declare her parents, and thus Mrs. Phipps and her siblings, to be legally black.

In October and again in December 1985, the state's Fourth Circuit Court of Appeals upheld the district court's decision, saying that no one can change the racial designation of his or her parents or anyone else's (479 So. 2d 369). Said the majority of the court in its opinion: "That appellants might today describe themselves as white does not prove error in a document which designates their parents as colored" (479 So. 2d 371). Of course, if the parents' designation as "colored" cannot be disturbed, their descendants must be defined as black by the "traceable amount rule." The court also concluded that the preponderance of the evidence clearly showed that the Guillory parents were "colored." Although noting expert testimony to the effect that the race of an individual cannot be determined with scientific accuracy, the court said the law of racial designation is not based on science, that "individual race designations are purely social and cultural perceptions and the evidence conclusively proves those subjective perspectives were correctly recorded at the time the appellants' birth certificates were recorded" (479 So. 2d 372). At the rehearing in December 1985, the appellate court also affirmed the necessity of designating race on birth certificates for public health, affirmative action, and other important public programs and held that equal protection of the law has not been denied so long as the designation is treated as confidential.

When this case was appealed to the Louisiana Supreme Court in 1986, that court declined to review the decision, saying only that the court "concurs in the denial for the reasons assigned by the court of appeals on rehearing" (485 So. 2d 60). In December 1986 the U.S. Supreme Court was equally brief in stating its reason for refusing to review the decision: "The appeal is dismissed for want of a substantial federal question" (107 Sup. Ct. Reporter, interim ed. 638). Thus, both the final court of appeals in Louisiana and the highest court of the United States saw no reason to disturb the application of the one-drop rule in the lawsuit brought by Susie Guillory Phipps and her siblings.

CENSUS ENUMERATION OF BLACKS

When the U.S. Bureau of the Census enumerates blacks (always counted as Negroes until 1980), it does not use a scientific definition, but rather the one accepted by the general public and by the courts. The Census Bureau counts what the nation wants counted. Although various operational instructions have been tried, the definition of black used by the Census Bureau has been the nation's cultural and legal definition: all persons with any known black ancestry. Other nations define and count blacks differently, so international comparisons of census data on blacks can be extremely misleading. For example, Latin American countries generally count as black only unmixed African blacks, those only slightly mixed, and the very poorest mulattoes. If they used the U.S. definition, they would count far more blacks than they do, and if Americans used their definition, millions in the black community in the United States would be counted either as white or as "coloreds" of different descriptions, not as black.

Instructions to our census enumerators in 1840, 1850, and 1860 provided "mulatto" as a category but did not define the term. In 1870 and 1880, mulattoes were officially defined to include "quadroons, octoroons, and all persons having any perceptible trace of African blood." In 1890 enumerators were told to record the *exact* proportion of the "African blood," again relying on visibility. In 1900 the Census Bureau specified that "pure Negroes" be counted separately from mulattoes, the latter to mean "all persons with some trace of black blood." In 1920 the mulatto category was dropped, and black was defined to mean any person with any black ancestry, as it has been ever since.

In 1960 the practice of self-definition began, with the head of household indicating the race of its members. This did not seem to introduce any noticeable fluctuation in the number of blacks, thus indicating that black Americans generally apply the one-drop rule to themselves. One exception is that Spanish-speaking Americans who have black ancestry but were considered white, or some designation other than black, in their place of origin generally reject the one-drop rule if they can. American Indians with some black ancestry also generally try to avoid the rule, but those who leave the reservation are often treated as black. At any rate, the 1980 census count showed that self-designated blacks made up about 12 percent of the population of the United States.

No other ethnic population in the nation, including those with visibly non-caucasoid features, is defined and counted according to a one-drop rule. For example, persons whose ancestry is one-fourth or less American Indian are not generally defined as Indian unless they want to be, and they are considered assimilating Americans who may even be proud of having some Indian ancestry. The same implicit rule appears to apply to Japanese Americans, Filipinos, or other peoples from East Asian nations and also to Mexican Americans who have Central American Indian ancestry, as a large majority do. For instance, a person whose ancestry is one-eighth Chinese is not defined as just Chinese, or East Asian, or a member of the mongoloid race. The United States certainly does not apply a one-drop rule to its white ethnic populations either, which include both national and religious groups. Ethnicity has often been confused with racial biology and not just in Nazi Germany. Americans do not insist that an American with a small fraction of Polish ancestry be classified as a Pole, or that someone with a single remote Greek ancestor be designated Greek, or that someone with any trace of Jewish lineage is a Jew and nothing else.

It is interesting that, in *The Passing of the Great Race* (1916), Madison Grant maintained that the one-drop rule should be applied not only to blacks but also to all the other ethnic groups he considered biologically inferior "races," such as Hindus, Asians in general, Jews, Italians, and other Southern and Eastern European peoples. Grant's book went through four editions, and he and others succeeded in getting Congress to pass the national origins quota laws of the early 1920s. This racist quota legislation sharply curtailed immigration from everywhere in the world except Northern and Western Europe and the Western Hemisphere, until it was repealed in 1965. Grant and other believers in the racial superiority of their own group have confused

race with ethnicity. They consider miscegenation with any "inferior" people to be the ultimate danger to the survival of their own group and have often seen the one-drop rule as a crucial component in their line of defense. Americans in general, however, while finding other ways to discriminate against immigrant groups, have rejected the application of the drastic one-drop rule to all groups but blacks.

UNIQUENESS OF THE ONE-DROP RULE

Not only does the one-drop rule apply to no other group than American blacks, but apparently the rule is unique in that it is found only in the United States and not in any other nation in the world. In fact, definitions of who is black vary quite sharply from country to country, and for this reason people in other countries often express consternation about our definition. James Baldwin relates a revealing incident that occurred in 1956 at the Conference of Negro-African Writers and Artists held in Paris. The head of the delegation of writers and artists from the United States was John Davis. The French chairperson introduced Davis and then asked him why he considered himself Negro, since he certainly did not look like one. Baldwin wrote, "He *is* a Negro, of course, from the remarkable legal point of view which obtains in the United States, but more importantly, as he tried to make clear to his interlocutor, he was a Negro by choice and by depth of involvement—by experience, in fact" (1962:19).

The phenomenon known as "passing as white" is difficult to explain in other countries or to foreign students. Typical questions are: "Shouldn't Americans say that a person who is passing as white is white, or nearly all white, and has previously been passing as black?" or "To be consistent, shouldn't you say that someone who is one-eighth white is passing as black?" or "Why is there so much concern, since the so-called blacks who pass take so little negroid ancestry with them?" Those who ask such questions need to realize that "passing" is so much more a social phenomenon than a biological one, reflecting the nation's unique definition of what makes a person black. The concept of "passing" rests on the one-drop rule and on folk beliefs about race and miscegenation, not on biological or historical fact.

The black experience with passing as white in the United States contrasts with the experience of other ethnic minorities that have features that are clearly non-caucasoid. The concept of passing applies only to blacks—consistent with the nation's unique definition of the group. A person who is one-fourth or less American Indian or Korean or Filipino is not regarded as passing if he or she intermarries and joins fully the life of the dominant community, so the minority ancestry need not be hidden. It is often suggested that the key reason for this is that the physical differences between these other groups and whites are less pronounced than the physical differences between African blacks and whites, and therefore are less threatening to whites. However, keep in mind that the one-drop rule and anxiety about passing originated during slavery and later received powerful reinforcement under the Jim Crow system.

For the physically visible groups other than blacks, miscegenation promotes assimilation, despite barriers of prejudice and discrimination during two or more generations of racial mixing. As noted above, when ancestry in one of these racial minority groups does not exceed one-fourth, a person is not defined solely as a member of that group. Masses of white European immigrants have climbed the class ladder not only through education but also with the help of close personal relationships in the dominant community, intermarriage, and ultimately full cultural and social assimilation. Young people tend to marry people they meet in the same informal social circles (Gordon, 1964:70–81). For visibly non-caucasoid minorities other than blacks in the United States, this entire route to full assimilation is slow but possible.

For all persons of any known black lineage, however, assimilation is blocked and is not promoted by miscegenation. Barriers to full opportunity and participation for blacks are still formidable, and a fractionally black person cannot escape these obstacles without passing as white and cutting off all ties to the black family and community. The pain of this separation, and condemnation by the black family and community, are major reasons why many or most of those who could pass as white choose not to. Loss of security within the minority community, and fear and distrust of the white world are also factors.

It should now be apparent that the definition of a black person as one with any trace at all of black African ancestry is inextricably woven into the history of the United States. It incorporates beliefs once used to justify slavery and later used to buttress the castelike Jim Crow system of segregation. Developed in the South, the definition of "Negro" (now black) spread and became the nation's social and legal definition. Because blacks are defined according to the one-drop rule, they are a socially constructed category in which there is wide variation in racial traits and therefore not a race group in the scientific sense. However, because that category has a definite status position in the society it has become a self-conscious social group with an ethnic identity.

The one-drop rule has long been taken for granted throughout the United States by whites and blacks alike, and the federal courts have taken "judicial notice" of it as being a matter of common knowledge. State courts have generally upheld the one-drop rule, but some have limited the definition to one thirty-second or one-sixteenth or one-eighth black ancestry, or made other limited exceptions for persons with both Indian and black ancestry. Most Americans seem unaware that this definition of blacks is extremely unusual in other countries, perhaps even unique to the United States, and that Americans define no other minority group in a similar way. . . .

DISCUSSION QUESTIONS

1. Is black a color category or a status?
2. Do you think passing still occurs?

REFERENCES

Bahr, Howard M., Bruce A. Chadwick, and Joseph H. Stauss. 1979. *American Ethnicity.* Lexington, MA: D.C. Heath & Co.

Baldwin, James. 1962. *Nobody Knows My Name.* New York: Dell Publishing Co.

Bennett, Lerone, Jr. 1962. *Before the Mayflower: A History of the Negro in America 1619–1962.* Chicago: Johnson Publishing Co.

Berry, Brewton. 1965. *Race and Ethnic Relations.* 3rd ed. Boston: Houghton Mifflin Co.

Berry, Brewton, and Henry L. Tischler. 1978. *Race and Ethnic Relations.* 4th ed. Boston: Houghton Mifflin Co.

Buckley, Gail Lumet. 1986. *The Hornes: An American Family.* New York: Alfred A. Knopf.

Gordon, Milton M. 1964. *Assimilation in American Life.* New York: Oxford University Press.

Grant, Madison. 1916. *The Passing of the Great Race.* New York: Scribner.

Gwaltney, John Langston. 1980. *Drylongso: A Self-Portrait of Black America.* New York: Vintage Books.

Harris, Melvin. 1964. *Patterns of Race in the Americas.* New York: W. W. Norton.

Horne, Lena, and Richard Schickel. 1965. *Lena.* Garden City, NY: Doubleday & Co.

Mangum, Charles Staples, Jr. 1940. *The Legal Status of the Negro in the United States.* Chapel Hill: University of North Carolina Press.

Model, F. Peter, ed. 1983. "Apartheid in the Bayou." *Perspectives: The Civil Rights Quarterly 15* (Winter–Spring), 3–4.

Myrdal, Gunnar, assisted by Richard Sterner and Arnold M. Rose. 1944. *An American Dilemma.* New York: Harper & Bros.

Ottley, Roi. 1943. *New World A-Coming.* Cleveland: World Publishing Co.

Powell, Adam Clayton, Jr. 1971. *Adam by Adam: The Autobiography of Adam Clayton Powell, Jr.* New York: Dial Press.

Preston, Dickson J. 1980. *Young Frederick Douglass: The Maryland Years.* Baltimore: Johns Hopkins University Press.

Trillin, Calvin. 1986. "American Chronicles: Black or White." *New Yorker,* April 14, 1986, pp. 62–78.

White, Walter. 1948. *A Man Called White: The Autobiography of Walter White.* New York: Viking Press.

Williamson, Joel. 1980. *New People: Miscegenation and Mulattoes in the United States.* New York: The Free Press.

READING 3

The Evolution of Identity

The Washington Post

Decade to decade, the U.S. census has changed its classifications of race and ethnicity. Partially, this reflects the growing diversity of the country. It also reveals the nation's evolving politics and social mores. When the first census was taken in 1790, enumerators classified free residents as white or "other," while slaves were counted separately. By 1860, residents were classified as white, black, or mulatto. Hispanic origin first became a category in 1970. Here are the categories used in the decennial counts from 1860 to 2000, as presented by AmeriStat (www.ameristat.org).

1860	1870	1880	1890[1]	1900[2]	1910	1920	1930	1940	1950	1960	1970	1980	1990	2000
White	White	White	White	White	White	White	White	White	White	White	White	White	White	White
Black	Black	Black	Black	Black (Negro descent)	Black	Black	Black	Black	Negro	Negro	Negro or Black	Black or Negro	Black or Negro	Black, African American or Negro
Mulatto	Mulatto	Mulatto	Mulatto		Mulatto	Mulatto								
			Quadroon											
			Octoroon											
	Chinese	Chinese	Chinese	Chinese	Chinese	Chinese	Chinese	Chinese	Chinese	Chinese	Chinese	Chinese	Chinese	Chinese
	Indian	Indian	Indian	Indian	Indian	Indian	Indian	Indian	Amer. Indian	Amer. Indian	Indian (Amer.)	Indian	Indian (Amer.)	Amer. Indian or Alaska Native
			Japanese	Japanese	Japanese	Japanese	Japanese	Japanese	Japanese	Japanese	Japanese	Japanese	Japanese	Japanese
						Filipino	Filipino	Filipino	Filipino	Filipino	Filipino	Filipino	Filipino	Filipino
						Hindu	Hindu	Hindu						
						Korean	Korean	Korean			Korean	Korean	Korean	Korean
							Mexican							
												Asian Indian	Asian Indian	Asian Indian
										Aleut		Aleut	Aleut	
										Eskimo		Eskimo	Eskimo	
										Hawaiian	Hawaiian	Hawaiian	Hawaiian	Native Hawaiian
										Part Hawaiian				
												Vietnamese	Vietnamese	Vietnamese
												Guamanian	Guamanian	Guamanian or Chamorro
												Samoan	Samoan	Samoan
													Other Asian	**Other Asian**
													Pacific Islander	**Other Pacific Islander**
					Other	Other	Other	Other	Other	Other	Other	Other	Other race	Some other race

ETHNICITY

1970	1980	1990	2000
Mexican	Mexican, Mexican Amer., **Chicano**	Mexican, Mexican Amer., Chicano	Mexican, Mexican Amer., Chicano
Puerto Rican	Puerto Rican	Puerto Rican	Puerto Rican
Central/So. American			
Cuban	Cuban	Cuban	Cuban
Other Spanish	Other Spanish/Hispanic	Other Spanish/Hispanic	Other Spanish/Hispanic/Latino
(None of these)	Not Spanish/Hispanic	Not Spanish/Hispanic	Not Spanish/Hispanic/Latino

1 In 1890, mulatto was defined as a person who was three-eighths to five-eighths black. A quadroon was one-quarter black and an octoroon one-eighth black.

2 American Indians have been asked to specify their tribe since the 1900 Census.

Bold letters indicate first usage since 1860.

NOTE: Before the 1970 Census, enumerators wrote in the race of individuals using the designated categories. In subsequent censuses, respondents or enumerators filled in circles next to the categories with which the respondent identified. Also beginning with the 1970 Census, people choosing American Indian, other Asian, other race, or for the Hispanic question, other Hispanic categories, were asked to write in a specific tribe or group. Hispanic ethnicity was asked of a sample of Americans in 1970 and of all Americans beginning with the 1980 Census. The 2000 Census allowed Americans to select more than one race.

Sources: AmeriStat, "200 Years of U.S. Census Taking: Population and Housing Questions 1790–1990;" U.S. Census Bureau. FROM: *The Washington Post*, Federal Page, August 13, 2001.

PERSONAL ACCOUNT

A Loaded Vacation

Every summer since I can remember, I go on vacation with my aunt and uncle. Last summer, my aunt took my cousin, brother, and me to Florida. My aunt grew up in Maryland along with my mother. She was college educated and until recently worked in corporate America. Now she owns her own daycare center.

I rarely thought about how my background was different from my aunt's until one night in Florida. We were all in the hotel suite when she asked me about my plans for the future and what I wanted to do with my degree, since I was entering college in the fall. I told her I wanted to be a lawyer. She told me that was going to be a hard goal to reach for a black female, but then again she said that I wasn't really black. I didn't understand. She went on to say that if I make it anywhere in life, it would be because I talk white. She said, "Just remember that, even though everything about you is white—your clothes, the way you talk, your friends—doesn't mean when they look at you they don't still see black."

I didn't know what to say. I sat there silently taking it all in. Was this the same aunt I'd known all my life? She told my brother that anything he accomplished would be due to his skin complexion, and that if he had been dark skinned "he wouldn't have a shot in hell, because white people determine how far we get in life." This went against everything I believed. I said, "What about my high

GPA and the fact that I'm intelligent? That means nothing?" She said, "Exactly. Even with all of that, you'll only go as far as they let you."

After she finished ranting about how far we would go in life, she went on to say that we were foolish for having so many white friends, because white people were the devil. At that point I had to speak up. I told her that I've never had a problem with any of my white friends and that she shouldn't talk about people she's never met. She replied by saying, "All white people are the same. Some are just closet racists." I said that my best friend Monica is white. How could she be my best friend if she was racist? My aunt said, "She may be your friend now, but if the two of you got into any trouble she would throw you right under the bus." The conversation ended with her telling me how naive I was, and that one day I would learn the truth.

That day came, and soon. A few months after that dreadful vacation Monica and I got into trouble. Monica was only 17, whereas I was 18. Because of my age, I would not be let off with a phone call home. Monica took the blame and covered for me. Thanks to her, I don't have a criminal record. I thought about calling my aunt to tell her how wrong she had been, but I decided that there was no point in arguing. I knew the truth.

Niah Grimes

READING 4

Real Indians: Identity and the Survival of Native America

Eva Marie Garroutte

The most common tribal requirement for determining citizenship concerns "blood quantum," or degree of Indian ancestry. . . . About two-thirds of all federally recognized tribes of the coterminous

Eva Marie Garroutte is a professor of sociology at Boston College.

United States specify a minimum blood quantum in their legal citizenship criteria, with one-quarter blood degree being the most frequent minimum requirement.[1] (In the simplest instance, an individual has a one-quarter blood quantum if any one of her four grandparents is of exclusively Indian ancestry and the other three are non-Indian.) The remaining one-third of Indian tribes specify *no* minimum blood quantum. They often simply require that any new enrollee be a lineal (direct) descendant of another tribal member. . . .

Legal definitions of tribal membership regulate the rights to vote in tribal elections, to hold tribal office, and generally to participate in the political, and sometimes also the cultural, life of the tribe.

One's ability to satisfy legal definitions of identification may also determine one's right to share in certain tribal revenues (such as income generated by tribally controlled businesses). Perhaps most significantly, it may determine the right to live on a reservation or to inherit land interests there.

The tribes' power to determine citizenship allows them to delimit the distribution of certain important resources, such as reservation land, tribal monies, and political privileges. But this is hardly the end of the story of legal definitions of identity. The federal government has many purposes for which it, too, must distinguish Indians from non-Indians, and it uses its own, separate legal definition for doing so. More precisely, it uses a whole array of legal definitions. Since the U.S. Constitution uses the word "Indian" in two places but defines it nowhere, Congress has made its own definitions on an ad hoc basis.[2] A 1978 congressional survey discovered no less than *thirty-three* separate definitions of Indians in use in different pieces of federal legislation.[3] These may or may not correspond with those any given tribe uses to determine its citizenship.

Most federal legal definitions of Indian identity specify a minimum blood quantum—frequently one-quarter but sometimes one-half—but others do not. Some require or accept tribal citizenship as a criterion of federal identification, and others do not. Some require reservation residency, or ownership of land held in trust by the government, and others do not. Other laws affecting Indians specify *no* definition of identity, such that the courts must determine to whom the laws apply.[4] Because of these wide variations in legal identity definitions and their frequent departure from the various tribal ones, many individuals who are recognized by their tribes as citizens are nevertheless considered non-Indian for some or all federal purposes. The converse can be true as well.[5]

There are a variety of contexts in which one or more federal legal definitions of identity become important. The matter of economic resource distribution—access to various social services, monetary awards, and opportunities—probably comes immediately to the minds of many readers. The legal situation of Indian people, and its attendant opportunities and responsibilities, are the result of historic negotiations between tribes and the federal government. In these, the government agreed to compensate tribes in various ways for the large amounts of land and other resources that the tribes had surrendered, often by force.[6] Benefits available to those who can satisfy federal definitions of Indian identity are administered through a variety of agencies, including the Bureau of Indian Affairs, the Indian Health Service, the Department of Agriculture, the Office of Elementary and Secondary Education, and the Department of Labor, to name a few.[7]

Legal definitions also affect specific economic rights deriving from treaties or agreements that some (not all) tribes made with the federal government. These may include such rights as the use of particular geographic areas for hunting, harvesting, fishing, or trapping. Those legally defined as Indians are also sometimes exempted from certain requirements related to state licensure and state (but not federal) income and property taxation.[8] . . .

"IF HE GETS A NOSEBLEED, HE'LL TURN INTO A WHITE MAN"

North American Indians who successfully negotiate the rigors of legal definitions of identity at the federal level can achieve what some consider the dubious distinction of being a "card-carrying Indian." That is, their federal government can issue them a laminated document (in the United States, a CDIB; in Canada an Indian status card) that certifies them as possessing a certain "degree of Indian blood."

. . . Canadian-born country music singer Shania Twain has what it takes to be a card-carrying Indian: she is formally recognized as an Anishnabe (Ojibwe) Indian with band membership in the Temagami Bear Island First Nation (Ontario, Canada). More specifically, she is legally on record as possessing one-half degree Indian blood. Given this information, one might conclude that Twain's identity as an Indian person is more or less unassailable. It's not.

Controversy has engulfed this celebrity because of an anonymous phone call to a Canadian newspaper a few years ago that led to the disclosure of another name by which Shania was once known: Eileen Regina Edwards. Eileen/Shania was adopted by a stepfather in early childhood and took the surname of Twain at that time. So far well and good—except for one thing. Both sides of her *biological* family describe themselves not as Indian but as white. It is only Jerry Twain, her late stepfather, who was Indian.

As the adopted child of an Anishnabe man, Shania Twain occupies an unusual status. Though the U.S. government allows for the assignment of blood quantum only to biological descendants of Indian people, Canada allows for the naturalization of non-Native children through adoption.[9] Although Twain has stated that her white mother (now deceased) had told her, in childhood, that her biological father (also deceased) had some Indian heritage, his family denies the suggestion entirely. They say they are French and Irish. Ms. Twain explains: "I don't know how much Indian blood I actually have in me, but as the adopted daughter of my father Jerry, I became legally registered as 50-percent North American Indian. Being raised by a full-blooded Indian and being part of his family and their culture from such a young age is all I've ever known. That heritage is in my heart and my soul, and I'm proud of it."[10]

Twain has been sharply criticized, in both the United States and Canada, for not making the full details of her racial background clearer, especially to awards-granting agencies such as the First Americans in the Arts (FAITA), which honored her in February 1996 as a Native performer. FAITA itself has made no such complaint. The group states that it is satisfied that "Ms. Twain has not intentionally misrepresented herself." And more importantly, her adopted family defends her. An aunt observes: "She was raised by us. She was accepted by our band. If my brother were alive, he'd be very upset. He raised her as his own daughter. My parents, her grandparents, took her into the bush and taught her the [Native] traditions."[11]

Twain's case shows with uncommon clarity that legal and biological definitions are conceptually distinct. . . .

In their modern American construction, at least, biological definitions of identity assume the centrality of an individual's genetic relationship to other tribal members. Not just any degree of relationship will do, however. Typically, the degree of closeness is also important. And this is the starting point for much of the controversy that swirls around issues of biological Indianness. . . .

Sociologist Eugeen Roosens summarizes such common conceptions about the importance of blood quantum for determining Indian identity:

> There is . . . [a] principle about which the whites and the Indians are in agreement. . . . People with more Indian blood . . . also have more rights to inherit what their ancestors, the former Indians, have left behind. In addition, full blood Indians are more authentic than half-breeds. By *being* pure, they have more right to respect. They *are,* in all aspects of their being, more *integral.*[12]

Biological ancestry can take on such tremendous significance in tribal contexts that it overwhelms all other considerations of identity, especially when it is constructed as "pure." As Cherokee legal scholar G. William Rice points out, "Most [people] would recognize the full-blood Indian who was enrolled in a federally recognized tribe as an Indian, even if the individual was adopted at birth by a non-Indian family and had never set foot in Indian country nor met another Indian."[13] Mixed-race individuals, by contrast, find their identity claims considerably complicated. Even if such an individual can demonstrate conclusively that he has *some* Native ancestry, the question will still be raised: Is the *amount* of ancestry he possesses "enough"? Is his "Indian blood" sufficient to distinguish him from the mixed-blood individual spotlighted by an old quip: "If he got a nosebleed, he'd turn into a white man"?

Members of various tribes complain of factionalism between these two major groups—full bloods and mixed bloods—and they suggest that the division arose historically because of mixed bloods' greater access to the social resources of the dominant society and their enhanced ability to impose values and ideas upon others.[14] As Julie M., a citizen of the United Keetowah Band of Cherokee Indians, says: "For the Cherokee people, there's been this mixed blood/full blood kind of dynamic going from before the removal [in 1838, also known as the Trail of Tears]. . . . It's kind of like us-and-them. . . . It's almost been like a *war* in some cases. . . . It's a 'who's-really-going-to-be-in-control-of-the-tribe?' kind of thing." Many historians have similarly found it logical that political allegiances would tend to shift for those Indian people who formed alliances, through intermarriage, with members of the dominant society, and that this has made the division between full bloods and mixed bloods politically important.[15]

Modern biological definitions of identity, however, are much more complicated than this historical explanation can account for. This complexity did not originate in the ideas and experiences of Indian tribes. Instead, they closely reflect nineteenth- and early-twentieth-century theories of race introduced by Euro-Americans. These theories (of which there were a great many) viewed biology as definitive, but they did not distinguish it from culture. Thus, blood became quite literally the vehicle for the transmission of cultural characteristics. "'Half-breeds' by this logic could be expected to behave in 'half-civilized,' i.e., partially assimilated, ways while retaining one half of their traditional culture, accounting for their marginal status in both societies."[16]

These turn-of-the-century theories of race found a very precise way to talk about *amount* of ancestry in the idea of blood quantum, or degree of blood. The notion of blood quantum as a standard of Indianness emerged with force in the nineteenth century. Its most significant early usage as a standard of identification was in the General Allotment (Dawes) Act of 1887, which led to the creation of the Dawes Rolls [the "base roll" or written record of tribal membership in a specific year]. It has been part of the popular—and legal and academic—lore about Indians ever since.

Given this standard of identification, full bloods tend to be seen as the "really real," the quintessential Indians, while others are viewed as Indians in diminishing degrees. The original, stated intention of blood quantum distinctions was to determine the point at which the various responsibilities of the dominant society to Indian peoples ended. The ultimate and explicit federal intention was to use the blood quantum standard as a means to liquidate tribal lands and to eliminate government trust responsibility to tribes, along with entitlement programs, treaty rights, and reservations. Through intermarriage and application of a biological definition of identity Indians would eventually become citizens indistinguishable from all other citizens.[17]

Degree of blood is calculated, with reference to biological definitions, on the basis of the immediacy of one's genetic relationship to those whose bloodlines are (supposedly) unmixed. As in the case with legal definitions, the initial calculation for most tribes' biological definitions begins with a base roll, a listing of tribal membership and blood quanta in some particular year. These base rolls make possible very elaborate definitions of identity. For instance, they allow one to reckon that the offspring of, say, a full-blood Navajo mother and a white father is one-half Navajo. If that half-Navajo child, in turn, produces children with a Hopi person of one-quarter blood degree, those progeny will be judged one-quarter Navajo and one-eighth Hopi. Alternatively, they can be said to have three-eighths general Indian blood.

As even this rather simple example shows, over time such calculations can become infinitesimally precise, with people's ancestry being parsed into so many thirty-seconds, sixty-fourths, one-hundred-twenty-eighths, and so on. . . .

For those of us who have grown up and lived with the peculiar precision of calculating blood quantum, it sometimes requires a perspective less influenced by the vagaries of American history to remind us just how far from common sense the concepts underlying biological definitions of identity are. I recall responding to an inquiry from a Southeast Asian friend about what blood quantum was and how it was calculated. In mid-explanation, I noticed his expression of complete amazement. "That's the dumbest thing I ever heard," he burst out. "Who ever thought of *that*?"

The logic that underlies the biological definition of racial identity becomes even more curious and complicated when one considers the striking difference in the way that American definitions assign individuals to the racial category of "Indian," as opposed to the racial category "black." As a variety of researchers have observed, social attributions of black identity have focused (at least since the end of the Civil War) on the "one-drop rule," or rule of hypodescent.[18] . . .

Far from being held to a one-drop rule, Indians are generally required—both by law and by popular opinion—to establish rather *high* blood quanta in order for their claims to racial identity to be accepted as meaningful, the individual's own opinion notwithstanding. Although people must have only the slightest trace of "black blood" to be *forced* into the category "African American," modern American Indians must (1) formally produce (2) strong evidence of (3) often rather substantial amounts of "Indian blood" to be *allowed* entry into the corresponding racial category. The regnant biological definitions applied to Indians are simply quite different than those that have applied (and continue to apply) to blacks. Modern Americans, as Native American Studies professor Jack Forbes (Powhatan/Lenape/Saponi) puts the matter, "are *always finding 'blacks'* (even if they look rather un-African), and . . . *are always losing 'Indians.'*"[19]

BIOLOGICAL DEFINITIONS: CONTEXTS AND CONSEQUENCES

Biological definitions of Indian identity operate, in short, in some curious and inconsistent ways. They are nevertheless significant in a variety of contexts. And they have clear relationships, both direct and indirect, to legal definitions. The federal government has historically used a minimum blood quantum standard to determine who was eligible to receive treaty rights, or to sell property and manage his or her own financial affairs.[20] Blood quantum is *one* of the criteria that determines eligibility for citizenship in many tribes; it therefore indirectly influences the claimant's relationship to the same kinds of rights, privileges, and responsibilities that legal definitions allow.[21]

But biological definitions of identity affect personal interactions as well as governmental decisions. Indian people with high blood quanta frequently have recognizable physical characteristics. As Cherokee Nation principal tribal chief Chad Smith observes, some people are easily recognizable as Indians because they pass "a brown paper bag test," meaning that their skin is "darker than a #10 paper sack." It is these individuals who are often most closely associated with negative racial stereotypes in the larger society. Native American Studies professor Devon Mihesuah makes a point about Indian women that is really applicable to either gender: "Appearance is the most visible aspect of one's race; it determines how Indian women define themselves and how others define and treat them. Their appearance, whether Caucasian, Indian, African, or mixed, either limits or broadens Indian women's choices of ethnic identity and ability to interact with non-Indians and other Indians."[22]

Every day, identifiably Indian people are turned away from restaurants, refused the use of public rest rooms, ranked as unintelligent by the education system, and categorized by the personnel of medical, social service, and other vital public agencies as "problems"—all strictly on the basis of their appearance. As Keetoowah Band Cherokee full-blood Donald G. notes, a recognizably Indian appearance can be a serious detriment to one's professional and personal aspirations: "It seems the darker you are, the less important you are, in some ways, to the employer. . . . To some, it would be discouraging. But I am four-fourths [i.e., full-blood] Cherokee, and it doesn't matter what someone says about me. . . . I feel for the person who doesn't like my skin color, you know?"

There are circumstances, however, in which it is difficult for the victims of negative racial stereotyping to maintain an attitude as philosophical as this.

In one interview, a Mohawk friend, June L., illustrated the potential consequences of public judgments based on skin color. She reminded me of a terrifying episode that had once unfolded while I was visiting at her house. Our conversation was interrupted by a phone call informing this mother of five that her college-student son, who had spent the summer day working on a roof, had suddenly become ill while driving home. Feeling faint, he had pulled up to a local convenience store and made his way inside, asking for a drink of water. The clerk refused. Dangerously dehydrated, the young man collapsed on the floor from sunstroke. "The worst thing about it," June recalled, "was that I have to keep wondering: What was the reason for that? Did that clerk refuse to help my son because she was just a mean person? Or was it because she saw him stumble into the store and thought, 'Well, it's just some drunken Indian'?" Anxiety about social judgments of this kind are a fact of daily life for parents of children whose physical appearance makes their Indian ancestry clearly evident.

At the same time, June's remarks showed the opposite side to the coin of physical appearance. In some contexts, not conforming to the usual notions of "what Indians look like" can also be a liability:

> My aunt was assistant dean at a large Ivy League university. One day she called me on the phone. She had one scholarship to give out to an Indian student. One of the students being considered was blonde-haired and blue-eyed. The other one was black-haired and dark-skinned, and she looked Indian. The blonde girl's grades were a little better. My aunt didn't know what to do. She said to me, "Both these girls are tribal members. Both of them are qualified [for the scholarship]. They're sitting outside my office. What would *you* do?" I told her that, as an Indian person, there was only one thing I *could* say. Which was to give the money to the one with the dark skin. As Indian people, we *do* want to have Indian people that *look* like they're Indian to represent us.

Readers may be surprised by such a candid statement. But June's pragmatic reasoning takes account of certain historical realities. As she explained further, "We like people to *know* who's doing those accomplishments, like getting scholarships. We want them to know this is an Indian person doing this. Because I come from a background where if you looked Indian, you were put in special education because the schools said you couldn't learn. And it wasn't true. We need Indian people today who look Indian to show everyone the things we can do."

A physical appearance that is judged insufficiently "Indian" can also act as a barrier to participation in certain cultural activities. Bill T., a Wichita and Seneca minister in his mid-fifties, recalls that, in his youth, he witnessed light-skinned individuals who attempted to participate in powwow dances being evicted from the arena. "That kind of thing is still happening today," he added sadly, and other respondents readily confirmed this observation. A more unusual instance of the relevance of physical appearance to cultural participation was volunteered by Frank D., a Hopi respondent. His tribe's ceremonial dances feature the appearance of powerful spirit beings called kachinas, which are embodied by masked Hopi men. Ideally, the everyday, human identity of the dancers remains unknown to observers. Frank commented on the subject of tribal members whose skin tone is noticeably either lighter or darker than the norm:

Frank D.: Say, for instance, if a Hopi marries a black person . . . [and] you get a male child . . . it's gonna be darker skinned. It might even be black. A black kachina just wouldn't fit out here [at Hopi]. You see, everybody'd know who it is. He'd be very visible [in the ceremonial dances]. . . . It'd be very hard on that individual. Kids don't work the other way, too—if they're real light. . . . Kachinas gotta be *brown.*

Author: So there are certain ceremonial roles that people could not fill because of their appearance?

Frank D.: Well, they *could,* but it would be awful tough. A lot of these [ceremonial] things are done with secrecy. No one knows who the kachinas are. Or at least, the kids don't. And then, say you get somebody who really stands out, then everybody knows who that [dancer] is, and it's not good. For the ceremony—because everybody knows who that person is. And so the kids will start asking questions—"How come that kachina's so dark, so black?" or "How come that kachina's white?" They start asking questions and it's really hard. So I think, if you're thinking about kids, it's really better if kachinas are brown.

Finally, the physical appearance borne by mixed bloods may not only create barriers to tribal cultural participation; it may also offer an occasion for outrightly shaming them. Cornelia S. remembers her days at the Eufala Indian School:

> You *had* to be Indian to be [allowed admission] there. . . . But . . . if [certain students] . . . didn't look as Indian as we did, or if they looked like they were white, they were kind of looked down upon, like treated differently because [people would say] "oh, that's just a white person." . . . They just [would] tease 'em and stuff. Say "oh, whatcha doin' white boy" or "white girl"—just stuff like that.

Nor is the social disapproval of light-skinned mixed bloods strictly the stuff of schoolyard teasing. The same respondent added that even adults confront questions of blood quantum with dead seriousness:

> Us Indians, whenever we see someone else who is saying that they're Indian . . . or trying to be around us Indians, and act like us, and they don't look like they're Indian and we know that they're not as much Indian as *we* are, yeah, we look at them like they're not Indian and, ya know, don't really like why they're acting like that. . . . But you know, I'm not *that* far off . . . into judging other people and what color [they are].

The late author Michael Dorris, a member of the Modoc tribe (California), has written that humiliations related to his appearance were part of his daily experience. He describes (in his account of his family's struggle with his son's fetal alcohol syndrome, *The Broken Cord*) an encounter with a hospital admissions staff, to whom he had just identified himself and his son as Indians. "They surveyed my appearance with curiosity. It was an expression I recognized, a reaction, familiar to most people of mixed-blood ancestry, that said, 'You don't *look* like an Indian.' No matter how often it happened, no matter how frequently I was blamed by strangers for not resembling their image of some Hollywood Sitting Bull, I was still defensive and vulnerable. 'I'm part Indian,' I explained."[23]

Even his tragic death has not safeguarded Dorris from insinuations about inadequate blood quantum. Shortly after his 1997 suicide, a story on his life and death in *New York* magazine reported that the author's fair complexion had always caused some observers to wonder about his racial identity and archly repeated a rumor: "It is said he . . . [eventually] discovered tanning booths."[24]

In short, many Indian people, both individually and collectively, continue to embrace the assumption that close biological connections to other Indian people—and the distinctive physical appearance that may accompany those connections—imply a stronger claim on identity than do more distant ones. As Potawatomi scholar of Native American Studies Terry Wilson summarizes, "Few, if any, Native Americans, regardless of upbringing in rural, reservation, or urban setting, ignore their own and other Indians' blood quantum in everyday life. Those whose physical appearances render their Indian identities suspect are subject to suspicious scrutiny until precise cultural explanations, especially blood quantum, are offered or discovered."[25]

DISCUSSION QUESTIONS

1. As Garroutte describes them, what are the various ways that one might be defined as a "real" Indian? When might these different definitions of "Indianness" conflict?

2. Thinking about June's description of her son being refused a drink of water and her advice about who should receive the Indian scholarship, do you see any consistencies or inconsistencies in her approach?

NOTES

1. Thornton surveyed 302 of the 317 tribes in the lower forty-eight states that enjoyed federal acknowledgment in 1997. He found that 204 tribes had some minimum blood quantum requirement, while the remaining 98 had

none. Russell Thornton, "Tribal Membership Requirements and the Demography of 'Old' and 'New' Native Americans," *Population Research and Policy Review* 16 (1997): 37.

2. The two mentions of "Indians" in the Constitution appear in passages regarding the regulation of commerce and the taking of a federal census. The word "tribe" also appears once in the Constitution, in the Commerce Clause.

3. Sharon O'Brien, "Tribes and Indians: With Whom Does the United States Maintain a Relationship?" *Notre Dame Law Review* 66 (1991): 1481.

4. One particularly important law that provides no definition of "Indian" is the Major Crimes Act of 1885 (23 Stat. 385, U.S.C. Sec. 1153). It subjects reservation Indians to federal prosecution for certain offenses for which non-Indians would face only state prosecution.

5. For a detailed discussion of legal cases bearing on the definition of "Indian," see Felix S. Cohen, *Handbook of Federal Indian Law* (Charlottesville, Va.: Michie/Bobbs-Merrill, 1982).

6. Wilcomb E. Washburn, *Red Man's Land/White Man's Law: A Study of the Past and Present States of the American Indian* (New York: Charles Scribner's Sons, 1971).

7. These agencies administer resources and programs in areas such as education, health, social services, tribal governance and administration, law enforcement, nutrition, resource management, tribal economic development, employment, and the like. The most recently published source describing various programs and the requirements for participation is Roger Walk, *Federal Assistance to Native Americans: A Report Prepared for the Senate Select Committee on Indian Affairs of the US Senate* (Washington, D.C.: Government Printing Office, 1991). In fiscal year 2001, recognized tribes and their members had access to approximately four billion dollars of federal funding for various social programs. U.S. Government Accounting Office, *Indian Issues: Improvements Needed in Tribal Recognition Process,* Report to Congressional Requesters, Washington D.C.: Government Printing Office, November 2001.

8. Non-Indian students in my classes sometimes tell me that Indians also regularly receive such windfalls as free cars and monthly checks from the government strictly because of their race. It is my sad duty to puncture this fantasy; there is no truth in it. The common belief that Indians receive "free money" from the government probably stems from the fact that the government holds land in trust for certain tribes. As part of its trust responsibility, it may then lease that land, collect the revenue, and distribute it to the tribal members. Thus, some Indians do receive government checks, but these do not represent some kind of manna from heaven; they are simply the profits derived from lands which they own. For

details on the special, political-economic relationship of Indians to the federal government in relation to taxation and licensure, see Gary D. Sandefur, "Economic Development and Employment Opportunities for American Indians," in *American Indians: Social Justice and Public Policy,* ed. Donald E. Green and Thomas V. Tonneson, Ethnicity and Public Policy Series, vol. 9 (Milwaukee: University of Wisconsin System Institute on Race and Ethnicity, 1991), 208–22.

9. Aside from the issue of adopted children, the legal requirements for establishing legal status as Indian in Canada have been even more complicated and peculiar than the U.S. ones, and the tensions related to them even more severe. Until 1985, a Canadian Indian woman who married a legally non-Indian man lost her legal status as an Indian, and her children (who might have a blood quantum of one-half) could never be recognized as Indian under Canadian law. A non-Indian woman who married an Indian man, however, gained Indian status for herself and her children. Men could neither gain nor lose Indian status through marriage. When a 1985 bill amended the Indian Act, which governed such matters, the issue of "real Indianness" came to a head. Many Canadian Indian women and children sought and received Indian legal status, but when they attempted to return to the reservations, they often got a chilly welcome from Indian communities already overburdened with financial obligations to their existing population. Like their American counterparts, Canadian Indian bands continue to struggle with the issue of how to conceive the boundaries of their membership. For a good discussion of Canadian Indian identification policies, see Eugeen Roosens, *Creating Ethnicity: The Process of Ethnogenesis* (Newbury Park, Calif.: Sage, 1989).

10. Shania Twain quoted in Jackie Bissley, "Country Star Shania Twain's Candor Is Challenged," *Indian Country Today,* 9–16 April 1996.

11. Quoted in Jackie Bissley, "Country Singer Says Stories Robbing Her of Her Native Roots," *Indian Country Today,* 16–23 April 1996. Even Twain's unusual situation does not exhaust the intricate aspects of the Canadian legal system as it struggles with matters of Indian identity. Roosens describes other fine points of Indian identity in force north of the border over a period of several decades:

Since 1951, to be registered as an Indian one has to be the legitimate child of an Indian father. The ethnic origin of the mother is irrelevant. . . . Furthermore, if the grandmother on the Indian side of a mixed marriage (the father's mother) is a non-Indian by descent, then the grandchild loses his or her status at the age of 21. Thus, one can be officially born an Indian and lose this status at the age of maturity. (Roosens, *Creating Ethnicity,* 24)

12. Roosens, *Creating Ethnicity,* 41–42. Roosens is discussing the situation of Canadian Indians, but the same remarks apply to American Indians.

13. G. William Rice, "There and Back Again—An Indian Hobbit's Holiday: Indians Teaching Indian Law," *New Mexico Law Review* 26, no. 2 (1996): 176.

14. Melissa L. Meyer, "American Indian Blood Quantum Requirements: Blood Is Thicker than Family," in *Over the Edge: Remapping the American West,* ed. Valerie J. Matsumoto and Blake Allmendiger (Berkeley: University of California Press, 1999).

15. Historians such as Grace Steele Woodward and Marion Starkey have made this argument. But see also Julia Coates, "None of Us Is Supposed to Be Here" (Ph.D. diss., University of New Mexico, 2002) for a revisionist understanding of Cherokee history.

16. C. Matthew Snipp, "Who Are American Indians? Some Observations about the Perils and Pitfalls of Data for Race and Ethnicity," *Population Research and Policy Review* 5 (1986): 249. For excellent and intriguing discussions of the evolution of ideas about blood relationships among European and Euro-American peoples over several centuries, and transference of these ideas into American Indian tribal populations, see Meyer, "Blood Quantum Requirements," and Circe Sturm, *Blood Politics: Race, Culture, and Identity in the Cherokee Nation of Oklahoma* (Berkeley: University of California Press, 2002). See further Peggy Pascoe, "Miscegenation Law, Court Cases, and Ideologies of 'race' in Twentieth Century America," *Journal of American History* 83, no. 1 (June 1996): 44–69. For the processes by which some of these theories were rejected by scientists, see Elazar Barkan, *Retreat of Scientific Racism: Changing Concepts of Race in Britain and the United States between the World Wars* (Cambridge: Cambridge University Press, 1992).

17. Thomas Biolsi, "The Birth of the Reservation: Making the Modern Individual among the Lakota," *American Ethnologist* 22, no. 1 (February 1995): 28–49; Patrick Limerick, *The Legacy of Conquest: The Unbroken Past of the American West* (New York: W. W. Norton, 1988).

18. Naomi Zack, "Mixed Black and White Race and Public Policy," *Hypatia* 10, 1 (1995): 120–32; Ariela J. Gross, "Litigating Whiteness: Trials of Racial Determination in the Nineteenth-Century South," *Yale Law Journal* 108 (1998): 109–88.

19. Jack D. Forbes, "The Manipulation of Race, Caste, and Identity: Classifying AfroAmericans, Native Americans and Red-Black People," *Journal of Ethnic Studies* 17, no. 4 (1990): 24; original emphasis. Indians are "lost," in Forbes' sense, both to black *and* to white racial classifications, but at differing rates. Popular conventions of racial classification in America tend to prevent individuals with any discernible black ancestry from identifying themselves as Indians. As an interview respondent quoted by anthropologist Circe Sturm observes, "This is America, where being to any degree Black is the same thing as being to any degree pregnant." Sturm, *Blood Politics,* 188.

By contrast, individuals with discernible white ancestry are *sometimes* allowed by others to identify as Indian. In their case the legitimacy of their assertion is likely to be evaluated with reference to the *amount* of white ancestry, and with beliefs about whether that amount is enough to merely *dilute* or to entirely *compromise* Indian identity. Other factors, such as culture and upbringing, may also be taken into account. People of partial white ancestry, in other words, are typically somewhat more free (although not entirely free) to negotiate a legitimate identity as Indian than are people of partial black ancestry.

20. For further details on the historical impact of blood quantum on individuals' legal rights, see Felix S. Cohen, *Cohen's Handbook of Federal Indian Law* (Charlottesville, Va.: Michie/Bobbs-Merrill, 1982).

21. For a listing of the blood quantum requirements that different tribes require for tribal citizenship, see Edgar Lister, "Tribal Membership Rates and Requirements," unpublished table (Washington, D.C.: Indian Health Service, 1987). An edited version of the table appears in C. Matthew Snipp, *American Indians: The First of This Land* (New York: Russell Sage Foundation, 1989), appendix.

22. Devon A. Mihesuah, "Commonality of Difference: American Indian Women and History," in *Natives and Academics: Researching and Writing about American Indians,* ed. Devon A. Mihesuah (Lincoln: University of Nebraska Press, 1998), 42. For a fascinating and detailed discussion of the significance of appearance among contemporary Cherokees in Oklahoma, see Sturm, *Blood Politics,* 108–15.

23. Michael Dorris, *The Broken Cord* (New York: Harper Perennial, 1990), 22.

24. Eric Konigsberg, "Michael Dorris's Troubled Sleep," *New York Magazine,* 16 June 1997, 33. For a related article, see Jerry Reynolds, "Indian Writers: The Good, the Bad, and the Could Be, Part 2: Indian Writers: Real or Imagined," *Indian Country Today,* 15 September 1993.

25. Terry P. Wilson, "Blood Quantum: Native American Mixed Bloods," in *Racially Mixed People in America,* ed. Maria P. P. Root (Newbury Park, Calif.: Sage, 1992), 109.

READING 5

An Interlocking Panethnicity: The Negotiation of Multiple Identities among Asian American Social Movement Leaders

Dana Y. Nakano

> *Compromise bills—Down down!*
> *Immigrant rights—Ho yea! (Chinese)*
> *[or] Immigrant rights—Phai day! (Vietnamese)*
> *[or] Immigrant rights—Zindabhad! (Punjabi)*
>
> *Employer sanctions—Down down!*
> *Workers rights—Mabuhay! (Tagalog)*
>
> *Guest worker slavery—Down down!*
> *Immigrant rights—Mansei! (Korean)*

In the early afternoon of an April Sunday in 2006, the Asian Pacific Islander (API) contingent marched down San Francisco's Market Street proudly chanting their rallying call.[1] These API activists advanced in solidarity within a multicolor sea of signs and people stretching multiple city blocks in support of immigrant rights. Numbering in the hundreds, the Asian American protestors came together from a diverse array of ethnic backgrounds advancing to the beat of Korean drums. The opening chant is a tactic leaders of the API contingent utilized to highlight both the collective investment of Asian Americans in immigration reform debates contemporaneously occurring on the floor of the United States Senate and the diversity within the Asian American population. The inclusion of multiple ethnic voices is evidence of panethnic solidarity among discrete Asian American communities. This solidarity is further underscored by how the chant is recited. The whole contingent shouts the same cry in unison, not just in an individual's own ethnic language. There are Filipino Americans shouting in

Dana Y. Nakano is a graduate student in sociology at the University of California, Irvine.

Punjabi; Japanese Americans shouting in Chinese; Korean Americans shouting in Vietnamese.

As a panethnic mobilization, the API contingent and its linguistically diverse chant run counter to sociological understandings where panethnicity is conceptualized as largely subsuming and replacing single-ethnic identifications and orientations depending on context (Espiritu 1992; Itzigsohn and Dore-Cabral 2000; Vo 2004; Waters 1999). To the contrary, the multiple languages within this chant exemplify a broader and persistent ethnic diversity exercised within panethnic spaces. As such, the rally's API contingent raises questions about the relationship between single-ethnic and panethnic identities and the coexistence of solidarity and diversity within a cohesive social movement. . . .

Espiritu (1992:14), in her seminal study, defines Asian American panethnicity as "the development of bridging organizations and solidarities among several ethnic and immigrant groups of Asian ancestry." While Asian American panethnicity originated through the racial lumping of all Asian ethnicities by outsiders, panethnicity has become a political resource for insiders (Espiritu 1992). Scholarship on identity work within panethnic Asian American contexts describes the outcomes of such negotiations in two ways: (1) panethnic identity subsuming single-ethnic identification, and (2) panethnic and single-ethnic identities coexist but are situationally exercised depending on context. The first potential outcome places multiple identities within a salience hierarchy. One identity is privileged above all others. This rank ordering of identity is applicable to many of the descriptions of the earliest incarnations of Asian American panethnic identity. In the late 1960s, activists sought to construct a monolithic, politicized Asian American collective consciousness that required a relinquishing of single-ethnic orientations, as well as feminist and class identities (Liu, Geron, and Lai 2008; Louie and Omatsu 2006; Maeda 2009; Umemoto 1989; Wei 1993). From this perspective, single-ethnic and panethnic identities are reconciled by muting single-ethnic consciousness in favor of a panethnic Asian American orientation.

In contrast to the findings supporting a salience hierarchy, studies of contemporary panethnic Asian American organizing have largely found a situational exercise of panethnic versus single-ethnic identity (Espiritu 1992; Kibria 2002; Vo 2004). These scholars assert panethnic and single-ethnic identities are utilized singularly, strategically, and instrumentally according to specific contexts. For example, Espiritu (1992) demonstrates how depending on social, economic, or political situations, individuals may mobilize themselves along single-ethnic or panethnic lines. Vo (2004:225) posits "individuals may have multiple ethnic identities, but these identities are salient according to constantly shifting circumstances." In Vo's study, respondents were often involved in both panethnic- and single-ethnic–focused organizations. Within single-ethnic contexts such as single-ethnically focused organizations or personal ethnic networks, respondents chose to deploy their single-ethnicity as their primary identification. However, when working in panethnic organizations, Vo's respondents spoke of more freely exercising a panethnic Asian American identity over single-ethnic identification.

For Espiritu and Vo, both single-ethnic and panethnic identities exist as discrete identities and are separately exercised at different times and in different situations. While this interpretation speaks to the continued presence of single-ethnic orientations within the API contingent at the April 2006 march, the framework is less apt to explain the *simultaneous* display of panethnic solidarity and single-ethnic diversity within the chant and mobilization. Rather than viewing single-ethnicity and panethnicity as situational and separate, I look toward the possibility of continuous interplay between single-ethnic and panethnic identities. . . . [This] study explores the inner workings of single-ethnic and panethnic coexistence, examining the ways individual leaders negotiate an interlocking relationship between single-ethnic and panethnic identities within their respective organizations. . . .

The concept of interlocking identities, structures, or categories is strongly related to the concept of intersectionality (Anthias 1998; Collins 2005; Crenshaw 1991). Anthias (1998) describes intersectionality in identity as a series of different layers of self and imposed definitions that can be worn in different orders at different times. Rather than only the top layer as a situational understanding of identity would predict, the *sum of all* layers positions each individual, or group, in the social order (Anthias 1998). In this way, an individual or group may be at once Asian American, Chinese American, female, and working class. Similar to the idea of situational identity, an individual may differentially exercise and emphasize one identity under different circumstances. However, this ability to shift identities does not detract from the fact that this individual or group is still defined by and draws from all facets of identity across all situations.

Glenn (2002) pushes the concept of intersectionality further and introduces the concept of interlocking systems of oppression to describe the experiences of women of color that are starkly different than both white women and men of color (also see Collins 2005; Crenshaw 1991). Glenn (2002:7) focuses on the notion of interlockedness in her assertion that race and gender are not experienced as "separate or additive" but, rather, are "simultaneous and linked." Women of color experience both race and gender simultaneously. Race and gender are viewed as relational categories: "they are positioned and therefore gain meaning in relation to each other" (Glenn 2002:13). Gender affects the way racial identity is conceptualized and vice versa: "gender is racialized and race is gendered" (Glenn 2002:7). Understanding single-ethnic and panethnic identities as relational and interlocking acknowledges the dynamic and shifting understandings of both identities vis-à-vis one another. As will be demonstrated in this study, understandings of what it means to be Filipino American, Indian American, or Chinese American are informed by a panethnic Asian American identity and how each distinct single-ethnic identity fits under this broad umbrella category. Panethnic Asian American identity is fundamentally shaped by the varied single-ethnic groups and identities that it claims to represent. . . .

I locate my study in the greater San Francisco Bay Area, a particularly apt site. The Bay Area boasts the three continental United States metropolitan areas with the highest percentage of Asian American residents: Fremont, 39.8 percent; San Francisco, 32.6 percent; and San Jose, 28.8 percent (U.S. Census Bureau n.d.a). The Bay Area is also home to a long Asian American political history including the Third World Liberation Front and the creation of a radical and progressive Asian American politics in the late 1960s (Maeda 2009). The specificities of the Bay Area region speak to the need to analyze racial identity formations in local or regional terms (Pulido 2006; Rumbaut 2009; Vo 2004).[2]

As this project is particularly interested in the identity work conducted by organizational leaders and how identity affects organizational processes and practices, I draw on data from in-depth, semistructured interviews [conducted in 2006] with contemporary leaders of Asian American social movement organizations.

My interview respondents pointed to the synergy of two social and historical factors in creating the need for an interlocking panethnicity: (1) the shifting demographics of an increasingly diverse Asian American population and (2) the institutionalization of panethnicity within organizations stemming from the Asian American Movement of the 1960s and 1970s.

DEMOGRAPHY AND ASIAN AMERICAN DIVERSITY

The story of Asian America is one of increasing diversity. When Yuji Ichioka coined the term "Asian American" during the 1960s, the U.S. Census only recorded three distinct Asian American ethnic groups: Chinese, Japanese, and Filipino. By the 1970 Census, only four ethnic groups were enumerated. While the Census may not accurately portray the existence of smaller, and hence uncounted, populations of other ethnic groups, it provides a sense of visibility for various ethnic groups during each Census period. As the effects of the Immigration

and Nationality Act of 1965, the legitimate reopening of immigration from Asia, began to impact the population, the number of ethnic categories began to show growth. The count of enumerated Asian racial subgroup categories grew slowly at first to seven in 1980, then rapidly to eighteen in 1990, and reached twenty-two by the 2010 Census (Ruggles et al. 2008; U.S. Census Bureau n.d.c).

Over the same time period, the Asian American population in the San Francisco Bay Area and across the nation also increased its diversity in terms of income, place of residence, political orientation, educational attainment, as well as nativity. In 1960, the majority of Asian Americans were native-born. Beginning with the 1970 Census, the predominant nativity began to shift, with Filipino Americans becoming a majority foreign-born population. By 1980, Asian Americans as a whole became a majority foreign-born racial group and all single-ethnic groups, with the exception of Japanese Americans, were also predominantly foreign-born. This pattern continues into the present day (Ruggles et al. 2008).

The number of ethnic groups and the size of each group grew tremendously over the second half of the twentieth century. Leaders of contemporary panethnic organizations mobilize an Asian American community that must negotiate more differences than their predecessors in creating and maintaining a cohesive panethnic collective identity. If distinct single-ethnic Asian American communities have such disparate needs and issues and their individual populations have grown, one must ask why panethnic organizations continue to exist. As communities reach critical mass, why not advocate for themselves and organize around single-ethnic identities? The answer to this question is two-fold: First, while the Asian American population has seen increases, they remain a numerical minority in the 2010 U.S. Census. The Asian American population accounted for less than 6 percent of the total U.S. population and 15 percent of California. In the San Francisco Bay Area, Asian Americans constitute a much higher percentage, 32, but remain a minority population. Furthermore, no single-ethnic community accounted for more than 12 percent of the total Bay Area population (U.S. Census Bureau n.d.c). Panethnicity continues to provide a competitive advantage in the modern democratic state where there is power in numbers (Espiritu 1992). Second, even if certain single-ethnic groups reached critical mass in the Bay Area, there remains a need to maintain a panethnic orientation when building coalitions with organizations in other regions that continue to rely on panethnic formations due to smaller Asian American populations. In addition, the panethnic label continues to provide political recognition via an institutionally recognized racial category: Asian American (Espiritu 1992).

PANETHNICITY AS ORGANIZATIONAL INSTITUTION

Looking at historical trajectories, Espiritu (1992) argues that among the early reasons Asian Americans across diverse ethnic groups came together in panethnic groupings was to secure government funding that favors multiethnic programs and impacts the highest number of people possible. Many of these organizations have been in existence for more than 20 years and have maintained panethnic orientations due to their organizational legacy and funding realities. Speaking more specifically to the institutionalization and reproduction of panethnicity, some organizations in this study began as single-ethnic organizations but have shifted toward panethnic missions in large part due to the need to attract public and private funds. In favoring multiethnic programs, government agencies have helped to institutionalize panethnic organizing and identity among Asian Americans. As organizations have structured themselves and their missions in accordance with continuing panethnically oriented funding and service guidelines, they continue to promote panethnic Asian American identity (Espiritu 1992). Such panethnic institutionalization is evident in the organizations represented in this study.

The increased diversity of the Asian American population from 1960 to the present day, particularly in terms of ethnicity, nativity, and class, serves as a causal factor for increased awareness of specific issues of single-ethnic communities. This increased demographic diversity impacts organizations directly through a diversification of organizational clients, members, staff, and leadership, forcing organizations to reconcile single-ethnic differences under a reimagined panethnic collectivity. The maintenance of panethnic identity within these organizations is bolstered by the continued minority status, even in the San Francisco Bay Area, and common racialized experiences of Asian Americans. Panethnic orientations also continue within Asian American activism due to the legacy of panethnic organizing reaching back to the 1960s Asian American Movement. The preexisting panethnic organizational forms serve as a model for contemporary Asian American activism, dictating coalitional efforts among single-ethnic communities, but not the form those efforts take. As such, panethnicity is still seen as an effective mobilizing strategy and organizational form, but only if it takes into account the diverse perspectives and issues facing distinct single-ethnic communities. . . .

RECONCEPTUALIZING PANETHNICITY AS INTERLOCKING

The Asian American Movement, largely taking place in the early 1970s, sought to expose the common racialized experience of American peoples of Asian ancestry and create greater solidarity among Asian ethnic groups. Wei (1993:272) claims the identity emerging from the Asian American Movement "transcended the communal and cultural limits of particular Asian ethnic groups to identity with the past experiences, present circumstances, and future aspirations" of an Asian American collectivity. Panethnic Asian American identity is described as "overcoming the separate ethnic nationalism that originally divided them" (Wei 1993:272). In present-day San Francisco, I observe a contrasting panethnicity that does not act independently or in place of single-ethnic identity and mobilization.

Rather, panethnic orientations intersect and take into consideration the diverse single-ethnic experiences that exist within the population. Borrowing from Glenn's framework, panethnicity and single-ethnicity are interlocking structures—simultaneous and mutually affecting (Glenn 2002).

All leaders [I interviewed] shared a strong commitment to panethnic coalitions and noted their necessity and effectiveness. As stated by Eleanor, a Chinese American leader:

> I think it's necessary that we band together. I think we always have to, bottom line, we have to unite in order to disunite. . . . We have to unite as Asian Americans in order to distinguish ourselves from one another.

Similar to the intentions and strategies leveraged by Asian American activists in the 1960s and 1970s, Eleanor and other contemporary leaders see panethnic organizing as an important way to garner political power and visibility with greater numbers. However, Eleanor's statement also demonstrates that panethnicity is not viewed as an end, but rather as a means for increased recognition and social justice. The expanded notoriety gained through panethnic organizing can serve as a platform for single-ethnic concerns. If panethnic organizing is important for single-ethnic communities to have their claims heard and acted upon in an overcrowded political field, joining panethnic coalitions and organizations cannot erase or override single-ethnic identity. Rather, leaders in this study note that single-ethnic identities must be voiced and present in panethnic spaces.

Respondents lament and actively work to deconstruct the monolithic perception of, what Wendy named, an "Asian American mainstream." Wendy, a 36-year-old Asian American leader of mixed heritage, continued by posing a question that seemed to weigh heavy on the minds of leaders within this study's sample: "How do we maintain our specific heritages and identities at the same time that we stand together as an Asian American community?"

Despite their diverse backgrounds, participating leaders hold strikingly similar views on the contemporary state of Asian American panethnicity. Leaders felt that significant progress had been made in recognizing the importance of single-ethnic identities within the broader panethnic movement. Calvin, for instance, shared:

> I think it's evolved to the point where an Asian American identity can encompass people who identify more as their own ethnic group. Whereas, maybe 20 years ago . . . there was more of this tension "Hey, give up being *Chinese,* you should say you're *Asian* so we can have more people power as *Asians.*" I think the movement has gotten to this point where people can identify primarily as a Vietnamese refugee but also consider themselves part of the movement. (emphasis added) . . .

MECHANISMS AND PRACTICES OF INTERLOCKING PANETHNICITY

. . . Understanding the reconceptualizations of an interlocking panethnicity, I now turn to the mechanisms and practices of this new panethnic orientation within the organizations in this study. Leaders demonstrate the interlocking nature of single-ethnicity and panethnicity in the philosophy and practices within their respective organizations. In discussing how panethnicity is constructed as a cohesive collective identity in the presence of distinct single-ethnic identifications, leaders spoke of the mechanism of an interlocking panethnicity in five ways: (1) encouraging maintenance of single-ethnic identities, (2) accounting for linguistic and cultural diversity, (3) coming to terms with ethnic and class privilege, (4) leveraging resources for the panethnic good, and (5) building collaborative and deliberative organizational frameworks and processes. These practices demonstrate the difficult identity work undertaken by leaders and the organizational effect of a reconceptualized panethnic identity.

Modeling Single-Ethnic Identity Narration

. . . Leaders in this study speak of a panethnic identity that encourages the maintenance of single-ethnicity as integral to the ultimate success of the movement. They see a need for diverse representation of single-ethnic organizations within the Asian American organizational field and within panethnic organizations themselves. Maintained single-ethnic identity is demonstrated within organizations as leaders discussed the strategic importance of "self" representation of single-ethnic community interests in leadership and decision-making processes of panethnic organizations. Leaders lead by example by maintaining their own single-ethnic identity and encourage members to speak from the experience of their particular ethnic communities. The maintenance of single-ethnic identity among leaders is particularly salient as they discussed whom they feel they represent within their leadership capacity. While all study participants hold leadership positions that engage in panethnic mobilization in some form, they conceptualize their ability to truly represent in very narrow terms. "A more progressive Vietnamese community," "Chinatown woman activists," "a hapa, biracial experience," "Filipino privileged people;" and "an East Oakland, working class, immigrant, woman experience" are some examples of this specificity. [Two respondents], Briana and Edwin, further explain the reason for such specificity:

> I don't know that I feel I am representing any one mass community because it is extremely diverse and has a lot of different complexities and complications to it. . . . I feel like I am representing part of the divisions. (Briana, Indian American)
>
> I hope I represent Asian Americans generally, but I think I represent other East Asian people better than other Asian Americans. Particularly, like South Asians, because I just don't know that much about their culture. (Edwin, Chinese American)

Leaders feel they are only able to represent their own personal ethnic experience as they feel ill equipped to fully and accurately represent the needs and concerns of other single-ethnic communities. Representation is understood as fundamentally tied to a lived experience. Single-ethnic identities can only be truly represented by individuals who come from particular communities. In order to build panethnic organizations that are truly representative of diverse Asian American populations, leaders often spoke of the intentional invitations to and recruitment of potential leaders from underrepresented single-ethnic communities.

Accounting for Linguistic and Cultural Diversity

Maintenance of interlocking single-ethnic identities and orientations in panethnic organizing are also important in instrumental terms. . . .

Cultural and language capacities are particularly important for Asian American community mobilizations, as over 37 percent of the Asian American population in the four-county San Francisco Bay Area is classified as limited English proficient (LEP).[3] Furthermore, Asian Americans remain a predominantly foreign-born population, approximately 70 percent in the four-county region (U.S. Census Bureau n.d.a). Language and cultural competencies provided by single-ethnically oriented individuals, then, are instrumentally important and must be maintained within panethnic organizations to effectively outreach to and mobilize the large LEP and foreign-born segments of the Asian American population. Tristan, a Hapa American, offers a more concrete description of a mechanism used to address the linguistic and cultural diversity of the Asian American population:

> A Filipino TV station came and covered the press conference, which was great, and we actually did have somebody who spoke Tagalog, but we don't always and there are certainly other languages that we just don't have represented. And we really try to invite the API press to these events and many of them cover it in English and the article they produce may be in another language. But many of them want to interview

somebody in the language they are ultimately going to write in. That is a big thing on our to-do list.

For Tristan, having linguistic and cultural diversity represented within his organization and at organizational events is important for the dissemination of information to a broader Asian American public.

Aside from communicative importance, a culturally and linguistically competent staff is also central to a panethnic organization's ability to provide direct services to diverse Asian American communities that continue to speak ethnic-specific languages and practice ethnic-specific cultures. As discussed earlier, demographic shifts in the Asian American population have had a direct impact on organizations by increasing the diversity of clients served by various organizations as well as the members and leaders who make up the organization itself. As organizational clients have increased in ethnic diversity, organizational leadership has been forced to grapple with how to provide services to largely immigrant communities with distinct languages and cultures. . . .

Coming to Terms with Privilege

. . . The experiences of a perceived homogenous Asian American population are generally categorized within the model minority paradigm and therefore lay outside the boundary to "legitimate" oppression. Asian American organizations may champion the issues of less privileged segments of the Asian American population in order to increase political relevance.[4] When promoting panethnic Asian American agendas externally, the issues of these marginalized Asian Americans take center stage. This agenda shift, however, is not always accompanied by an equal shift in ethnic make-up of decision-makers and visible leadership. While placing marginalized Asian American concerns at the forefront of a public panethnic agenda is empowering and may achieve gains for a marginalized segment of the population, it also serves to obscure the ethnic privileges and power positions held by Japanese and Chinese Americans within many panethnic mobilizations. The power

structure and privilege within the panethnic community is left intact. In their quest for racial equality, Asian American organizations may replicate the system of oppression they seek to dismantle; marginalized Asian American ethnic groups may remain powerless to assert their own issues into panethnic agendas. . . .

Leveraging Human and Social Capital for the Panethnic Good

Leaders who hold privileged social positions due to their ethnic or class background can also leverage their elevated human and social capital for the benefit of less privileged segments of the Asian American population and Asian Americans as a whole. [One respondent] spoke of an organizational process of open dialogue, whereby individuals learn from those of other ethnic backgrounds and incorporate an understanding of the issues that affect less visible and less privileged Asian Americans. Importantly, individuals from marginalized Asian American communities are the ones who speak, teach, and lead on these less familiar struggles. East Asian Americans are confronted with the realities of other Asian American ethnic groups within the panethnic formation, which forces them to recognize their own privileged position and alters their engagement with the organization.

In the process of deconstructing divisive hierarchies of privilege, leaders leverage organizational resources from across the panethnic spectrum to uplift other less privileged segments of the Asian American community. Ryan, for example, leads a sizable and longstanding organization with roots in the Japanese American community. Across its history, Ryan's organization has been able to accrue many resources, capacities, and connections that are unavailable to more recently arrived ethnic communities and recently formed organizations. Rather than hoard such resources, Ryan expresses a philosophy of sharing and empowerment:

> Over time the organization has grown, its capacity has increased and the bottom line is [we work with other

communities] because we can . . . and, in actuality, we want to. We have been fortunate as an organization to be able to evolve to do many things. I take a lot of pride in the fact that there is a Japanese American youth organization in this country that can serve everybody.

. . . The skills and resources brought to organizations by different leaders vary widely from accounting skills and public speaking to network connections and fundraising. The demographics of the leaders participating in this study show that all inhabit a privileged social class position, which is often accompanied by greater social and cultural capital. Leaders in this study, regardless of ethnicity, are highly conscious of their privileged positions within their organizations, within the community, and oftentimes within society at large. A frequent assertion by study participants was an earnest interest in using their privileged, educated positions, and the access to information and networks that comes with it, for the betterment of the panethnic community as a whole. In particular, leaders wished to be a conduit of information and access point for segments of the community that largely do not have a voice. Privilege is not used as a tool of domination over the lower rungs of the class hierarchy, but rather a means to uplift, educate, and empower the broadest segment of the community possible.

Collaborative Frameworks and Privileging Marginalized Voices

In addition to acknowledging privilege and leveraging the resources of privilege for a broader panethnic community, leaders also foster collaborative processes within their respective organizations to give voice to the diversity within the Asian American population. Such practices also stem from the nonprofit orientation of the Asian American social movement organizations in this study. Nonprofit organizations often utilize nonhierarchical structures and decision-making processes due to their service and advocacy-oriented missions (DiMaggio and Anheier 1990). However, Asian American social movement organization leaders espouse an approach to the recognition of privilege and flattening

of hierarchies that is explicitly racialized. According to leaders in this study, fostering collaboration, open dialogue, and participation among distinct single-ethnic communities are fundamental to the success of panethnic Asian American collective action. Leaders frequently discussed the need to create an open atmosphere within their organizations in order to foster collaboration among members. . . .

CONCLUSION

Taken together, the evidence drawn from my interviews with organizational leaders shows that single-ethnicities persist in panethnic mobilizations and that this continued presence has mutual effects on both single-ethnic and panethnic identities. Building upon the works of panethnicity scholars Espiritu and Vo, this study demonstrates that exercise of single-ethnic and panethnic identities are not simply driven by situations and contexts that favor one identity over the other. Rather, single-ethnic and panethnic identities are "both simultaneous and linked," informing and altering one another (Glenn 2002:7). It follows that panethnic identity, in its contemporary form, may be better understood as interlocking with single-ethnic identity, rather than within a salience hierarchy or being situationally determined. The identity negotiations that take place lead to the coexistence and mutual effect of multiple identities within a single movement. . . .

DISCUSSION QUESTIONS

1. What are ways to measure panethnic solidarity?
2. What are some of the problems of maintaining single-ethnic identity when the larger goal is panethnicity?
3. What are some of the mechanisms for creating an interlocking panethnicity?

NOTES

1. For the majority of this article, I speak specifically about the panethnic *Asian American* community, rather than *API*. This is a conscious effort not to tokenize the Pacific Islander experience in my analysis. This is not to say that Pacific Islanders should not be included in panethnic

Asian American formations. Rather, I nod at the limitations of my sample, which only includes one Pacific Islander–identified respondent. She is ethnically mixed (Filipino, Chamorro, and Samoan) and is treated as a person of mixed race. References to API are maintained only in reference to the April 2006 rally and the nomenclature explicitly used by interview respondents.

2. While the San Francisco metropolitan area is an apt site for a study of progressive race-based movement identities, it also produces some biases. A potentially skewed conception of panethnic identity may arise as leaders attempt to mobilize in the generally progressive political environment of San Francisco. Additionally, the deep history of panethnic organizing associated with the Bay Area may create a more easily mobilized base and heightened consciousness in the community. Lastly, the high percentages of Asian Americans in the greater San Francisco Bay Area may also influence panethnic identity formations and mobilization efforts.

3. LEP is defined as individuals who speak a language other than English and have self-rated their proficiency in English as less than "very well." All LEP and nativity data are derived from the American Community Survey 2010 five-year Aggregate dataset accessed through American Factfinder.

4. This is not to say that Chinese or Japanese Americans do not have legitimate grievances deserving of attention. Rather, the social position of Southeast Asian Americans is more justifiable within the normative discourse of racial inequalities.

REFERENCES

Anthias, Floya. 1998. "Rethinking Social Divisions: Some Notes Towards a Theoretical Framework." *Sociological Review* 46:506–35.

Collins, Patricia Hill. 2005. "Black Feminist Thought." Pp. 404–20 in *Theories of Race and Racism,* edited by L. Back and J. Solomos. New York: Routeledge.

Crenshaw, Kimberle. 1991. "Mapping the Margins: Intersectionality, Identity Politics, and Violence against Women of Color." *Stanford Law Review* 43:1241–99.

DiMaggio, Paul J. and Helmut K. Anheier. 1990. "The Sociology of Nonprofit Organizations and Sectors." *Annual Review of Sociology* 16:137–59.

Espiritu, Yen Le. 1992. *Asian American Panethnicity: Bridging Institutions and Identities.* Philadelphia: Temple University Press.

Glenn, Evelyn Nakano. 2002. *Unequal Freedom: How Race and Gender Shaped American Citizenship and Labor.* Cambridge, MA: Harvard University Press.

Itzigsohn, Jose and Carlos Dore-Cabral. 2000. "Competing Identities? Race, Ethnicity and Panethnicity among Dominicans in the United States." *Sociological Forum* 15:225–47.

Kibria, Nazli. 2002. *Becoming Asian American: Second-Generation Chinese and Korean American Identities.* Baltimore: Johns Hopkins University Press.

Liu, Michael, Kim Geron, and Traci Lai. 2008. *The Snake Dance of Asian American Activism: Community, Vision, and Power.* Lanham, MD: Lexington Books.

Louie, Steve and Glenn Omatsu. 2006. *Asian Americans: The Movement and the Moment.* Los Angeles: UCLA Asian American Studies Center Press.

Maeda, Daryl J. 2009. *Chains of Babylon: The Rise of Asian America.* Minneapolis: University of Minnesota Press.

Pulido, Laura. 2006. *Black, Brown, Yellow and Left: Radical Activism in Los Angeles.* Berkeley: University of California Press.

Ruggles, Steven, Matthew Sobek, Trent Alexander, Catherine A. Fitch, Ronald Goeken, Patricia Kelly Hall, Miriam King, and Chad Ronnander. 2008. "Integrated Public Use Microdata Series: Version 4.0 [machine-readable database]." Minnesota Population Center [producer and distributor].

Rumbaut, Rubén G. 2009. "Pigments of Our Imagination: On the Racialization and Racial Identities of 'Hispanics' and 'Latinos.'" Pp. 15–36 in *How the U.S. Racializes Latinos: White Hegemony and Its Consequences,* edited by J. A. Cobas, J. Duany, and J. R. Feagin. Boulder, CO: Paradigm Publishers.

U.S. Census Bureau. n.d.a. American Community Survey, 2010 American Community Survey Five-year Estimates; generated by Dana Y. Nakano; using American FactFinder (February 15, 2012).

———. n.d.b. Census 2000, Summary File 1; generated by Dana Y. Nakano; using American FactFinder (February 15, 2012).

———. n.d.c. Census 2010, Summary File 1; generated by Dana Y. Nakano; using American FactFinder (February 15, 2012).

Umemoto, Karen. 1989. "'On Strike!' San Francisco States College, 1968–69: The Role of Asian American Students." *Amerasia* 15:3–41.

Vo, Linda Trinh. 2000. "Performing Ethnography in Asian American Communities: Beyond the Insider-Versus-Outsider Perspective." Pp. 17–37 in *Cultural Compass: Ethnographic Explorations of Asian America,* edited by M. F. Manalansan IV. Philadelphia: Temple University Press.

———. 2004. *Mobilizing an Asian American Community.* Philadelphia: Temple University Press.

Waters, Mary C. 1999. *Black Identities: West Indian Immigrant Dreams and American Realities.* Cambridge, MA: Harvard University Press.

Wei, William. 1993. *The Asian American Movement.* Philadelphia, PA: Temple University Press.

PERSONAL ACCOUNT

I Thought My Race Was Invisible

In a conversation with a close friend, I noticed that I am, to her, a representative of my entire racial category. To put things in perspective, my friend Janet and I have been friends for eight years. During this period, it has come up that I am a third-generation Japanese-American who has no ties to being Japanese other than a couple of sushi dishes I learned how to make from my grandmother. Nonetheless, whenever a question regarding "Asians" comes up, she comes to me as if I can provide the definitive answer to every Asian mystery.

Yesterday Janet asked me if there is a cultural reason why Asians "always drive so slow." Not having noticed that Asians drive slowly (in fact, I have noticed a number of Asians who actually exceed the speed limit), I commented that perhaps they are law-abiding citizens. She said that must explain it: "They are used to following the law." I thought, "Am I one of 'they'?" but didn't comment further. Before we switched subjects, she noted that she "knew there had to be a cultural reason" for their driving.

Janet then told me about a Vietnamese woman at the Hair Cuttery who cut her husband's hair. As is normal, her husband talked to the woman as she worked on his hair; he asked her what she did before working at the Hair Cuttery. She said that she used to work in the fields in California (i.e., she was a field hand). Janet told me of the healthy respect that she and her husband had for a woman who worked in the fields, put herself through cosmetology school, moved East, and became a professional hairstylist. She commented that "Blacks" should follow her example and work instead of complaining of their lot in life.

This conversation was interesting and a bit startling. Janet is a good friend who shares many interests with me. What I realized from this conversation, and in remembering others that were similar, is that she feels that I am a representative of the whole Asian race. Not only is this unrealistic, but it is surprising that she would imagine I could answer for my race given my lack of real cultural exposure. In relaying the story of the Vietnamese woman, I had a sense that she was complimenting me, and my race, for the industriousness "we" demonstrate. It seems to me that she approved of the "typically" Asian way of working (quietly, so as not to insult or offend), even though this woman was probably underpaid and overworked in her field hand job. While she approved of her reticence, Janet did not approve of "Black" complaints.

I realize that to Janet, I will always be Asian. I had not really thought about it before, but I never think of Janet as White; her race is invisible to me. I had thought that my race was invisible too; however, I realize now that I will always be the "marked" friend. This saddens me a bit, but I accept it with the knowledge that she is a close friend. Nonetheless, it is unfortunate to think that even between friends, race is an issue.

Sherri H. Pereira

READING 6

Latino Racial Choices: The Effects of Skin Colour and Discrimination on Latinos' and Latinas' Racial Self-Identifications

Tanya Golash-Boza and William Darity, Jr

If you had a choice of colors, which one would you choose, my brother? (Curtis Mayfield)

Tanya Golash-Boza is a professor of sociology at the University of California, Merced. William Darity, Jr is a professor of public policy, African and African American Studies, and economics at Duke University.

INTRODUCTION

On 19 June 2003, an article in *USA Today* proclaimed that 'Hispanics outnumber[ed] blacks as the largest minority group in the USA'.[1] A few months later, the US Census undertook a project to predict what the US's racial make-up would be in 2050. The authors of this project, funded by the Minority Business Development Agency of the US Department of Commerce, predicted that non-Hispanic whites will constitute only 53 per cent of the US population in 2050, while Hispanic whites will make up 22 per cent of the total population, Hispanic blacks 2 per cent and non-Hispanic blacks 13 per cent.[2]

These predictions are based on the problematic assumption that current patterns of racial and ethnic identification can be used to predict future identification patterns without taking into account the possibility that Hispanics' racial and ethnic identifications can and do change. Notably, the authors of the Census project seem to expect the ethnic and racial identification patterns of Hispanics to remain unchanged for the next fifty years. This mode of thinking runs contrary to the assimilation canon – most theorists who study assimilation agree that ethnic identifications can be expected to change (see Alba and Nee (1997) for a discussion of the assimilation canon and its merits). In addition, recent works by Harris and Sim (2002) and Brown, Hitlin and Elder (2006) suggest that racial self-identifications can also be expected to change. This paper takes on the question of what the future face of the US will look like by developing a theoretical framework that takes into account the viability of racial and ethnic identifiers for Latinos and Latinas in the US.

. . . In this article, we address the changing structure of the US racial hierarchy, but also argue that it is important to consider the factors that influence how individual Latinos/as self-identify in order better to predict how Latinos/as will identify in the future.

Before continuing, we should clarify the distinction between Hispanic as a racial category and Hispanic as an ethnic category. On the 2000 US Census, there were separate questions for race and ancestry. The race question was not open-ended. Respondents had to choose one or more of the following categories as their race: American Indian or Alaska Native; Asian; Black or African American; Native Hawaiian or Other Pacific Islander; and White. In addition, there was the option of selecting 'other'. Ethnicity was a separate question, in which there were two minimum categories: 'Hispanic or Latino' and 'Not Hispanic or Latino'. Respondents were asked to choose between: 'NO, I am not Hispanic/Latino/Spanish'; 'YES, Mexican'; 'YES, Cuban'; 'YES, Puerto Rican'; and 'YES, other'. People who ethnically self-identified as Hispanic or Latino also could self-identify with any of the racial categories, and respondents were asked explicitly

to answer both the race and ethnicity questions. For this reason, data from the Census allow social scientists to talk about white Hispanics versus black Hispanics or to speculate on what it means for a Hispanic to choose 'other' for his or her race.

Although the US Census considers 'Hispanic' to be an ethnic identifier, this category differs in important ways from other ethnic identifiers such as Italian-American or Irish-American. If Hispanic were 'merely' an ethnic identifier, we would not expect for it to persist at the individual level for the next two generations, or at least would expect that it would dissipate to some extent. Thus, despite evidence that ethnic identifiers have generally become less salient over the course of generations, the current predictions about the future demographics of the US expect the children of Hispanics also to be Hispanics.

Most social scientists expect the category 'Hispanic' to persist because it is a racialized ethnic label. (Notably, those who expect it to disappear, such as Yancey (2003), treat Hispanic as an ethnic label.) However, we take the position that Hispanic is a racialized ethnic label because it is used and applied in a very similar way to other racial labels in the US – on the basis of physical appearance. In daily interactions, people in the US do not label people as Hispanic based on their ancestry, as it would be difficult to conduct genealogical analyses of people whom we encounter on a daily basis. We do, however, react to symbolic markers of ancestry, such as phenotype, accent and other cultural codes, thereby racializing the category 'Hispanic'. To the extent that we, in the United States, associate Latin American ancestry with a particular somatic image, we give racial meaning to Latin American ancestry, and treat people who fit that somatic norm, not as whites or blacks, but as Hispanics.

The US Census uses a definition of Hispanic that includes all people whose origin can be traced to Mexico, Puerto Rico, Cuba or Central or South America. Given the great diversity of people from this area, combined with the social practice of associating a particular somatic norm image with Hispanicity in the US, we can expect some Latin

Americans and their descendants not to self-identify as Hispanic. Specifically, we can expect those Census-defined Hispanics who do not fit this somatic norm image to be less likely to self-identify as Hispanic. We can further speculate that the children of this group of people who do not fit this somatic norm image will be even less likely to self-identify as Hispanic, as their relative lack of ethnic *and* racial identifiers render them even less likely to be identified as Hispanic in daily interactions. As such, some persons of Hispanic descent could potentially opt out of the Latino category and become non-Hispanic blacks or whites, while others could disassociate themselves from both labels, black and white, and adopt 'Hispanic' or 'Latino' as their racial identification. The possibility of such a change in racial and ethnic identification patterns renders predictions based on projected immigration patterns and birth rates less useful. It means further that social scientists need to consider how Latinos/as racially self-identify and what factors affect those choices.

Social scientists who have considered Latinos' and Latinas' racial self-identification do not agree as to how Latinos/as' racial identifications work presently or will work in the future. Clara Rodríguez (2000) tells us that Latinos/as' racial identifications are fluid and contextual; Yancey (2003) predicts that the majority of Latinos/as will become white; Bonilla-Silva (2004) predicts that the majority will join the 'collective black' and Haney López (2005) argues that some identify racially as white, others as black and others as Latino or Latina. Without understanding the processes that underlie racial identification for Hispanics, our predictions and calculations about the future racial make-up of the United States hold very little water.

Despite the numerous implications of Hispanics actually becoming the 'nation's largest minority', social scientists have done remarkably little research on patterns of racial identification among Latinos/as in the United States. Current research indicates that racial and ethnic self-identifiers are fluid, and can vary over the course of one's life, or even the course of one's day (Rodríguez 2000).

Studies by Eschbach and Gomez (1998) and Brown, Hitlin and Elder (2006) demonstrate that Hispanics are quite likely to change their racial and ethnic self-identifications from one survey to the next. Predictions about the future racial make-up of the US are based on self-reports of race and ethnicity, yet often do not take into account the fluid nature of these identifiers. In addition, it is not only important to describe racial fluidity as these studies have done, but to develop a theoretical framework that explains and potentially predicts Latinos' racial choices in order to predict what the future face of America will look like. . . .

. . . We find convincing the arguments that the racial structure is changing in the United States, and that Hispanic is emerging as a racial category but, in this paper, ask the question: what factors influence how people currently defined as Hispanic racially self-identify on surveys? Knowing what factors currently influence racial self-identifications will provide us with tools to better predict how people will self-identify in the future.

THEORETICAL FRAMEWORK: RACIAL IDENTIFICATIONS IN LATIN AMERICA AND THE U.S.

Before we can answer this question, it will be useful briefly to review the evidence that indicates that racial self-identifications are subject to change, specifically among Latin Americans. One reason for this is that processes of racial categorization and identification in Latin America do not parallel those of the United States (Rodríguez 1994; Duany 2005). Scholars are not in full agreement on exactly how these systems differ, yet it is worthwhile to set forth some claims. First of all, 'Latino' and 'Hispanic' are not common racial or ethnic descriptors in Latin America. (This claim is perhaps the most widely accepted.) Second, people of African or indigenous descent in Latin America are more likely to self-identify as white than similar people in the US (Wade 1997: 14, 38). Third, the use of terminology for mixed categories such as mulatto (white/black) or *mestizo* (white/Indian) or *zambo* (black/Indian) is more prevalent in Latin America than in the US, although the use of an array of mixed categories was also common in the US until the 1920s (Skidmore 1993; Duany 2005). Fourth, people of African descent are less likely to self-identify as black in Latin America than in the US (Cruz-Jansen 2001; Darity, Dietrich, and Hamilton 2005; Wade 1993). Finally, many studies have shown that in Latin America one's racial status is determined, in part, by one's social status. This means that people of higher economic or class status tend to classify themselves as whiter than their counterparts in lower strata, regardless of actual physical characteristics. In Brazil, for example, non-whites may change their racial identification to a whiter classification as they move up the class hierarchy (Lovell and Wood 1998). Notably, Telles (2004) and Wade (1993) point out that this ability to whiten is limited to people who hold a racially ambiguous status.

The reality of a distinct racialized social structure in Latin America has consequences for the racial self-identifications of immigrants from Latin America who reside in the US. Since these immigrants encounter a different system of racial classifications in the US, their racial self-identifications may change as they adapt to the US. For example, this distinct system of racial classification means that, in Latin America, there are people who self-identify as white who may not be seen as white in the United States. In addition, there are people who could begin to self-identify as black in the US that may not have considered themselves to be black in Latin America. Thus, some Latin American immigrants to the United States are likely to self-identify racially as something other than how they identified in their country of origin. For Dominicans in particular, Itzigshon, Giorguli and Vasquez (2005, p. 51) found that Dominican immigrants 'confront a racial classification system that classifies many of them as black' despite the fact that many of these Dominicans do not perceive themselves to be black.

As Latin American immigrants acculturate to the United States, it is conceivable that they would be influenced by the US system of racial classification and may even begin to adapt to it. Lee and Bean posit that 'changes in ethnic and racial boundaries are a fundamental part of the immigration incorporation experience' (2004, p. 226). One way this could play out is that a person who considered herself to be 'white' in Peru may initially identify as 'white' in the US. However, if she is not seen as white in the US but as Latina, she may begin to self-identify as a Latina. Alternatively, she may resist these categorizations and insist on her whiteness. It is also reasonable to suggest that this hypothetical Peruvian immigrant would be able to pass for white if she had the financial and educational resources to downplay her ethnic origins. She also may be able to marry a white American and pass their collective whiteness on to their children. In another scenario, she may not be able to be classified as white, but her US-born children may be. At the other end of the spectrum, Bailey (2001) found that second-generation Dominicans use their knowledge of the Spanish language to ward off categorization as black. Given the rapid loss of Spanish language use and ability across generations, it is unlikely that their children will have the option of using Spanish to avoid being categorized as black. Will these third- (and later-) generation Dominican-Americans continue to identify as Hispanics, as black Hispanics, or will they consider themselves to be simply African-Americans? How likely are the descendants of immigrants from Peru to self-identify as Hispanic after they have been in the US for several generations?

It is important to point out that not only immigrants from Latin America might change their racial classifications, but also Latinos/as who are born in the US. The racial self-identifications of second- and third-generation immigrants from Latin America may also change over the course of their lives. As families move out of or into ethnic enclaves, as students attend university, and as people join political movements, it is reasonable to suggest that their racial or ethnic self-identifications may change. We currently consider Hispanics to be those people who identify as such on the US Census and other national surveys. In addition, social scientists make predictions about the future ethnic and racial make-up of the US on the basis of these self-reported data. However, we have very little information on the viability of the category 'Hispanic' and on what factors affect Hispanics' decision to self-identify as such on surveys.

This paper is grounded in the theoretical work on assimilation in the US. Whereas assimilation traditionally meant that immigrants would become part of the Anglo-Saxon core in the US, thereby abandoning their ethnic affiliations, recent work on assimilation has contested this idea, and put forth the notion that there is more than one path of assimilation. Rumbaut and Portes (2001) and Zhou (1997), for example, argue that, while some immigrants will embark on the traditional path of assimilation towards the Anglo-Saxon core, others will retain some of their traditional values and practices through selective acculturation, and still others will experience downward assimilation and identify with the experiences of non-whites in the US. This paper builds on this work by highlighting the importance of racialization for the process of assimilation. We question the extent to which individuals who are non-white, even if they have the necessary accoutrements of middle-class status, can and will assimilate to the Anglo-Saxon core. . . .

WHAT ARE LATINOS' AND LATINAS' RACIAL CHOICES?

Our current understandings of Latinos/as' racial identifications are largely based on two sources of data – ethnographic and interview-based studies, and small-scale statistical analyses of Puerto Rican and Dominican racial identifications. Clara Rodríguez (2000) found, in her interview-based study of Latinos/as in New York, that some of her interviewees found themselves subject to external pressure to self-identify as 'white' or 'black', and that many of them recognized their whiteness or blackness in this context but insisted that they were also Latino. Her case studies demonstrate that many Latinos/as racially identify as white, black or other, but culturally identify as Latinos/as or with their national origin. Landale and Oropesa (2002), in their study of

Puerto Rican women, found that about 30 per cent of their Puerto Rican female respondents on the US mainland racially identified as Hispanic or Latina, as compared to only about 10 per cent of their Puerto Rican female respondents on the island. Surprisingly, the island women were more likely to choose 'white' or 'black' as a racial identifier than the mainland women. Their results indicate that some Puerto Ricans may be adopting 'Latino' or 'Hispanic' as a racial identification in the US, even if they racially identified as 'white' or 'black' on the island. This is also in line with Duany's (2005, p. 182) argument that Puerto Ricans respond that their race is neither white nor black, but 'other', because 'other' seems to be increasingly used as a racialized synonym for Hispanic. Itzigsohn, Giorguli and Vasquez (2005) found that 21 per cent of the first-generation Dominicans in their New York City-based study self-identified racially as Hispanics and that 5 per cent self-identified as blacks. However, they also found that 29 per cent thought that others would racially identify them as Hispanic and that 35 per cent thought that others would identify them as black. These studies indicate that many Dominicans and Puerto Ricans in the US understand 'Hispanic' as a racialized category that fits into the US racial hierarchy somewhere between white and black. What these studies do not provide us with is an understanding of what factors affect the decisions of that segment of the population that is defined by the US Census as being ethnically Hispanic to self-identify racially as white, black or 'other'.

While Hispanic/Latino is in many ways an ethnic category, we cannot ignore Latinas/os' and non-Latinas/os' perception of the category as a racial identifier. For example, in the 1989 Latino National Political Survey (de la Garza et al. 1992), 18 per cent of the 2807 respondents reported their race to be Latino, Hispanic or their respective national origin. In addition, 46 per cent of the respondents to the 2002 National Latino Survey reported their race to be Hispanic or Latino, and not white or black. This large increase over the course of twelve years is in part indicative of the different survey measures, but is also in part due to the changing racial structure in the US, where 'Latino' is emerging as a racialized category. For example, in February 2006, when there were riots inside a prison near Los Angeles, the African-American and Latino prisoners formulated a written request to separate the inmates by 'race' to avoid more mayhem. In this case, the Latinos/as and blacks involved in those riots saw 'Latino' as a racial category that does not include African-Americans. . . .

In this paper, we will consider three hypotheses that could explain Latinos' racial choices and that could be useful for predicting future demographic trends. Subsequently, we will test each of these hypotheses using two national datasets – the 1989 Latino National Political Survey and the Pew Hispanic Center/Kaiser Family Foundation 2002 National Survey of Latinos. Finally, we will make a case for incorporating ideas of racialization into understanding Latinos' and Latinas' current and future racial choices.

Hypothesis 1 – the social whitening hypothesis: Hispanics with higher incomes and higher levels of education are more likely to choose 'white' for their race, and less likely to choose 'black'.

The first hypothesis is that Latinos/as of higher class statuses are more likely to self-identify as white. This hypothesis derives from social whitening arguments made by some scholars who study Latin America. (For a full discussion of social whitening in Latin America, see Nutini 1997; Wade 1997; Wright 1990; Whitten and Torres 1998; Telles 2004; Twine 1998.) According to these scholars, social class plays an important role in racial identification in Latin America. Some of these scholars argue that social class trumps skin colour insofar as a dark-skinned person can self-identify as white if he or she is of high class standing. Others, such as Telles (2004) and Wade (1993), argue that only people who are racially ambiguous are able to experience social whitening, while people who are clearly black, such as the Brazilian soccer player Pele, will be identified as black, no matter their class standing. It will be useful to understand whether or not this process carries over to the United States. In the US context, this would mean that Latinos/as who have

higher educational levels and higher incomes are more likely to identify as white, especially those who do not have very dark skin. This would also serve as an indication of Latinos/as' resistance to US racial categorizations, which are not based on social characteristics such as income or education.

Hypothesis 2 – identificational assimilation hypothesis: Hispanics who are more assimilated are more likely to self-identify as 'white'.

The second hypothesis invokes assimilation as a central theme. Early theorists of assimilation such as Gordon (1964) and Park (1950) argued that, over the course of generations, immigrants eventually would lose their ethnic ties and fold into the American melting pot. An outcome of this process, identificational assimilation, means that the immigrant no longer considers himself to be an Italian-American, an Irish-American or a Mexican-American, but an American. This unmarked identity as 'American' could be interpreted as becoming 'white', since the unmarked requisite precludes the entry of African-Americans or Asian-Americans into this category. For example, Feagin (2000) argues that the unhyphenated 'American' label refers to those people in the US who have the luxury of acting as if they do not have a racial or ethnic status. This category of people thus includes only white Americans.

According to the traditional model, assimilation involves upward socioeconomic mobility, residential integration and intermarriage (Hirschman 2001). In order to determine whether or not the identificational assimilation hypothesis works in the case of Latino-Americans, it will be necessary to determine whether Latinos/as who have been in the US longer, have intermarried with whites and speak English are more likely to self-identify as white than Latinos/as who are less acculturated. This analysis also will allow us to examine the argument made by Yancey (2003) that nearly all Latino Americans will eventually adopt a white racial identity. On the basis of his finding that Latinos/as are likely to have opinions on racialized matters that are more similar to European Americans than to African Americans and previous evidence that some

Latinos/as are assimilating residentially and maritally, Yancey contends that Hispanic Americans will eventually adopt a white racial identity. Nevertheless, Yancey's analyses do not take generational status into account, thereby weakening his ability to predict future trends. The analyses presented in this paper allow us to test this prediction more directly.

Hypothesis 3 – racialized assimilation hypothesis: Hispanics who have lighter skin and who have not experienced discrimination are more likely to self-identify as white, while Hispanics with darker skin and who have experienced discrimination are more likely to self-identify as black or Hispanic.

The third hypothesis draws on recent studies that have highlighted the dynamic relationship between external racial categorization and racial self-identification, as well as on studies of assimilation. Henry and Bankston (2001) argue that ethnic self-identification is affected by outsiders' ethnic designations. Specifically for Latinos/as, Clara Rodríguez (2000: 140–1) found that dark-skinned Dominicans in New York recognize a racial categorization as black, while Ginetta Candelario (2001) reported that the majority of Dominicans in the predominantly black city of Washington, DC, racially identified themselves as black. Steven Ropp (2000, p. 24) tells us that Asian Latinos/as are categorized as Asian in daily interactions. These findings indicate that Latinos/as experience a diverse array of experiences of racial categorization in the US. Some people who fit the Census's definition of Hispanic/Latino are racially categorized in everyday interactions as black, others as white, others as Asian and still others as Hispanic.

Scholars of race in Latin America and the US are not in full agreement about the extent to which racial categories differ in the US and in Latin America. However, we can say with certainty that, at the very least, there is one fundamental difference between Latin America and the US, and that is that the categories 'Latino' and 'Hispanic' are not commonly used in Latin America, while they are in the US. The racialized assimilation hypothesis entails that that some Latinos/as will be racialized as Latinos/as

in the US, while others will not, and that those that belong to the former group are more likely to self-identify as Latinos/as and, in this fashion, to assimilate into the Latino category. This hypothesis draws on Nagel's (1994) argument that categorizations are dialectically related to identifications, meaning that they are both subject to change, and that they affect one another. In light of this and other research, it is reasonable to suggest that Latinos/as' racial self-identifications will be affected by external categorizations.

How do we know how Latinos/as are racially classified by people in the US? We suggest that Latinos/as are categorized in the same way as non-Latinos/as, on the basis of their skin colour. Brown, Dane and Durham conducted a series of interviews to find out what features people use to determine race. They found that '[s]kin color was rated the most important feature, followed by hair, eyes, nose, mouth, cheeks, eyebrows, forehead, and ears' (1998, p. 298). In one of the datasets we will be using, we fortunately have a measure of skin colour, which is the feature that people in the US are most likely to use to determine another person's race. Thus, to test this hypothesis, we will consider the relationship between skin colour and racial self-identification among Latinos/as. While we cannot use skin colour alone to predict how Latinos/as are categorized racially in the US, it is reasonable to suggest that skin colour is one of many indicators that affects racial categorization in the US.

We can predict that skin colour will affect racial categorization and thus identification. However, we can also use experiences of discrimination in our analyses because categorization is a necessary condition for discrimination. In order to discriminate against a person based on one's pre-conceived notions about their group, it is first necessary to categorize them as a member of that group. As such, if a respondent reports experiences of racial discrimination, we can conclude that he or she has been categorized as a member of a racial group. We assume that this discrimination would be based on the respondent being non-white, since whites are much less likely to experience racial discrimination than non-whites. As such, Latinos/as who are perceived by others to be white are less likely to be victims of racial discrimination than those who are perceived by others to be non-whites. In this sense, racial discrimination can be used as a proxy for non-whiteness. Of course, Latinos/as who are perceived to be white may have more access to white spaces and thus may witness more subtle forms of discrimination against other Latinos/as. Nevertheless, they would be less likely to experience racial discrimination themselves.

DATA AND METHODS

For the analyses, we use two datasets—the 1989 Latino National Political Survey (LNPS) and the Pew Hispanic Center/Kaiser Family Foundation 2002 National Survey of Latinos (NSL). We chose the LNPS (1989) because of its inclusion of measures of skin colour and NSL (2002) because of its recency and its extensive questions pertaining to discrimination. The similarities in these two datasets strengthen our claims, while the differences allow us to put some of our claims into perspective. Both of these datasets are unique insofar as they are nationally representative samplings of the English- and Spanish-speaking Latino populations, in contrast with studies such as the General Social Survey which include only English-speaking adults.

1989 LATINO NATIONAL POLITICAL SURVEY

The LNPS is a representative national sample of the three largest Latino groups in the USA – Mexicans, Cubans and Puerto Ricans. The LNPS includes 2,807 respondents, and the interviews were conducted between 1989 and 1990. This dataset is particularly well suited to addressing the questions posed in this paper because of the broad sample of Latinos/as from all over the country and because of the different generational statuses included. In addition to the representative sample population of

the LNPS, we were also interested in the unique data on interviewer-coded skin colour.

The LNPS was conducted in forty standard metropolitan statistical areas, and was representative of 91 per cent of the Mexican, Puerto Rican and Cuban populations in the United States. All respondents were at least 18 years of age, and had at least one parent solely of Mexican, Cuban or Puerto Rican ancestry, or at least any two grandparents of solely Mexican, Cuban or Puerto Rican ancestry. The response rate was 74 per cent. . . .

Respondents to the LNPS survey were asked if they consider themselves to be white, black or something else, and were asked to specify if they considered themselves neither white nor black. . . . A substantial majority of respondents chose to self-identify racially as white. About 2 per cent – only fifty-two respondents – chose to classify themselves as black. The remainder typically chose colour-oriented labels intermediate between black and white or national group labels, either collective labels like 'Latino' or country-specific labels (e.g. '*Mi raza es Puertorriqueña*'). In what follows, we will collapse the latter responses into a single category, 'other', separate from white or black. Using these three categories, 62 per cent of respondents in the LNPS said they are racially white, 2 per cent said they are black and 36 per cent chose another category, neither black nor white. The numbers do suggest that Latinos/as in this sample were not following the dictates of a 'one-drop rule' or notions of hypodescent with respect to black self-identification, since it is clearly the case that more than 2 per cent of the Cubans, Puerto Ricans and Mexicans in the US have some African ancestry. According to the conservative estimates included in the 1992 NACLA *Report on the Americas,* in Mexico, the African-descended population is between 1 and 10 per cent; in Puerto Rico, it is between 23 and 70 per cent; and in Cuba it is between 34 and 62 per cent (Oveido 1992). We do not have these sorts of data for the Latin American population that resides in the United States, but we are comfortable in assuming that it is much more than 2 per cent. In any case, the fact that we do not have these data points to the need for better measures of the racial composition of the Hispanic population in the US.

[Next] we examine how the interviewers' grading of individual skin shade corresponded to the individual's self-reported race. A slight majority of participants in the survey were graded as having a medium skin shade out of the five categories used by the interviewers ('very dark', 'dark', 'medium', 'light', 'very light') closely followed by those graded as having a light skin shade. Comparable numbers were placed in the dark and very light categories. The smallest number of respondents (fifty-nine) was rated as having a very dark skin tone.

[Individuals self-reported race, however, demonstrates a] general Latino preference in 1989 to be identified as white. (See Darity, Hamilton and Dietrich (2002) for a related discussion in the context of labour market discrimination.) While most of the very dark and dark respondents chose a racial category other than black or white, more than one-third [of those] chose to self-identify as white. The majority of respondents identified as having a medium skin shade by the interviewers self-reported their race as white. In the two lightest categories, about 80 per cent of the respondents said they were white, largely eschewing the 'other' categories, never mind the black category. As skin shade lightens, more and more respondents chose white as their race, but significant proportions of darker-skinned respondents did so as well.

. . . The preference for racial self-identification as white among Latinos/as attenuates somewhat the longer a person is in the USA. The proportion of Latinos/as self-identifying as white falls with each generation more distant from immigration. This contrasts with Yancey's (2003) prediction that most Latinos/as will become white. Note, however, in this survey, there is no evidence of an increasing preference for a black racial identity. If anything, black Latinos/as continue to disappear based upon self-reported race, just as they have disappeared

historically in national data in Latin American countries (Andrews 2004). The second and third generations shift more and more towards self-classifications separate from white or black. In particular, they demonstrate a growing preference for the collective national labels as ethnic classifiers, Latino or Hispanic . . .

2002 NATIONAL SURVEY OF LATINOS

The 2002 National Survey of Latinos/as is a representative sample of the Hispanic population in 2002. This survey was conducted by telephone between 4 April 2002 and 11 June 2002 among a nationally representative sample of 4,213 adults 18 years and older, including 2,929 Latinos/as and 1,284 non-Latinos. We chose this sample because of its relative recency and its similarity to the 1989 LNPS survey. . . .

Respondents to the National Survey of Latinos were asked: 'What race do you consider yourself to be? White, Black or African-American, Asian, or some other race?' and were given the opportunity to specify their race if they did not consider themselves to be white, black or Asian. In response to this question, more respondents identified as Hispanic (1,175) than as white (1,022). Only 157 identified as black, 20 as Asian and 527 as something else. It is important to note that Latinos/as' racial self-identification as 'Hispanic' as opposed to white indicates that the respondents see Hispanic as a racial categorization, similar to white or black. In contrast to the 1989 LNPS study, the 2002 NLS survey reveals a moderately declining preference for the black and Hispanic labels across generations. It is particularly noteworthy that the preference for the 'other' label increases from the first to the second generation, as one would expect first-generation respondents to be the least accepting of US racial classifications. The second generation turns out to be the least likely to self-identify as 'white' and the most likely to self-identify as 'Hispanic'. . . .

DISCUSSION OF FINDINGS

[Our analysis provides] mixed evidence for the social whitening hypothesis. Respondents to the NLS who had a family income over $50,000 are less likely to self-identify as black or Hispanic, and more likely to identify as white, and Hispanics with some college or who have graduated from college are more likely to self-identify as white than as Hispanic. This seems to support the social whitening argument, the idea that Hispanics with more money and education are more likely to self-identify as white. However, these same coefficients are not significant in the analyses using the LNPS data. And, when we control for skin colour in the comparison model, we see that Hispanics whose household incomes were between $20,000 and $34,999 were more likely to self-identify racially as 'other' than as white in the LNPS survey.

One way to understand the differences in the findings between these two datasets is that the 2002 National Latino Survey does not include a variable for skin colour. As such, it is possible that Hispanics who earn more money are in fact lighter skinned in the US. This is a possibility given the strong relationship between social class and skin colour in Latin America (Rodríguez 2000). . . .

There is also mixed evidence for the identificational assimilation hypothesis. . . . [Our data] indicate that Hispanics who have been in the US for longer prefer to adopt a Hispanic identity. Nevertheless, English-dominant Hispanics and those who have an 'other' (perhaps black) spouse prefer to self-identify as 'black'. Additionally, English-speaking respondents are more likely to self-identify as other than as white. These findings do not support the hypothesis that assimilation leads to self-identification as white. Overall, these data do not demonstrate a trend towards whiteness among Hispanics who have structurally or linguistically assimilated into the United States. . . .

There is the most consistent evidence in favour of the racialization hypothesis. . . . [D]arker-skinned Hispanics are consistently more likely to self-identify as 'black' or 'other' than as 'white' net of all other variables. Notably, when comparing relatively dark-skinned Latinos/as to lighter-skinned Latinos/as, very dark-skinned Latinos/as were 256 times more likely to self-identify as 'black', dark-skinned respondents were 48 times more likely to self-identify as 'black' and medium-skinned respondents were 5.4 times more likely to self identify as 'black' than as 'white'. . . . [R]espondents who have experienced discrimination are significantly more likely to self-identify as 'black', 'other' or 'Hispanic' and less likely to self-identify as 'white'. Both sets of [data] confirm the hypothesis that Hispanics who experience discrimination* are less likely to self-identify as white than those who do not. We also can confirm the hypothesis that, net of all other factors, Hispanics with darker skin shades are less likely to self-identify as white than Hispanics of lighter hues. The finding that self-identification as Hispanic is related to experiences of discrimination in the US points to the politicization of this term and the growing understanding of the term as a racialized label. . . .

CONCLUSION

Skin shade clearly influences choice of racial category among Latinos/as, but this is complicated by the fact that so few respondents to the LNPS 1989 survey chose the black category and a significant share of darker respondents chose the white category. Lighter complexioned Latinos/as simply would not choose black as their racial category, but darker complexioned Latinos/as often would choose white as their racial category. This is reflective of a general Latino preference for whiteness. Nevertheless, the results from both survey analyses do show that darker skin, experiences of discrimination, lower incomes and limited Spanish ability all increase the likelihood that Latinos/as will self-identify as 'black' when given a choice to do so. Latinos/as who report

---

*Respondents in both surveys were asked about experiences of discrimination.

having experienced discrimination on the basis of their racial or ethnic background are unlikely to self-identify as white. In the NLS 2002 survey, 61 per cent of the respondents reported that they had experienced discrimination on the basis of their race or ethnicity. They were made to feel not white, and thus were less likely to self-identify as white during the telephone survey. The NLS data also demonstrate that the experience of non-whiteness is not uniform. Some of those Latinas/os who reported discrimination self-identified as black, others as Hispanic and still others as 'other'.

In sum, these analyses indicate that Hispanics' experiences in the US are likely to affect their racial choices. This process of learning to adapt to the US racial system could be called *racialized assimilation*. A concept of racialized assimilation takes into account the overwhelming importance that skin colour has in shaping our interactions with others. Just as our racial status can be used to predict where we live, who we will marry and our life expectancy, how immigrants are racially categorized by others will heavily influence their path of assimilation. . . .

The finding that skin colour and experiences of discrimination affect racial identifications among Hispanics is evidence that Hispanics do not all experience the same process of racialization in the United States. As a consequence, predictions about the future racial make-up of the United States cannot rely on predictions based solely on whom researchers identify as Hispanic today. These studies must also take into account the fact that some Hispanics will become white, others black, and not all are likely to continue to identify as Hispanic. . . .

DISCUSSION QUESTIONS

1. What impact does discrimination have on choosing a racial category?
2. What problems might develop if each generation of Latino/a immigrants chooses to identify with a different label?
3. Do you think that money will ever be more important than skin color in the United States? Why or why not?

NOTES

1. http://www.usatoday.com/news/nation/census/2003-06-18-Census_x.htm (accessed April 2005).
2. http://www.mbda.gov/documents/mbdacolor.pdf (accessed 13 April 2005).

REFERENCES

ALBA, RICHARD and VICTOR NEE 1997 'Rethinking Assimilation Theory for a New Era of Immigration', *International Migration Review,* vol. 31, pp. 826–74

ANDREWS, GEORGE REID 2004 *Afro-Latin America, 1800–2000,* New York: Oxford University Press

BAILEY, BENJAMIN 2001 'Dominican-American Ethnic/Racial Identities and United States Social Categories', *International Migration Review,* vol. 35, no. 3, pp. 677–708

BONILLA-SILVA, EDUARDO 2004 'From Bi-Racial to Tri-Racial: Towards a New System of Racial Stratification in the USA', *Ethnic and Racial Studies,* vol. 27, pp. 931–50

BROWN, J. S., HITLIN, S. and ELDER, G. H. JR 2006 'The Greater Complexity of Lived Race: An Extension of Harris and Sim', *Social Science Quarterly,* vol. 87, pp. 411–31

BROWN, T. D., DANE, F. C. and DURHAM, M. D. 1998 'Perception of Race and Ethnicity', *Journal of Social Behavior and Personality,* vol. 13, no. 2

CANDELARIO, GINETTA E. B. 2001 '"Black Behind the Ears" – and Up Front Too? Dominicans in the Black Mosaic', *The Public Historian,* vol. 23, no. 4, pp. 55–72

CRUZ-JANZEN, MARTA I. 2001 'Latinegras: Desired Women – Undesirable Mothers, Daughters, Sisters, and Wives', *Frontiers,* vol. 22, pp. 168–83

DARITY, WILLIAM, HAMILTON, DARRICK and DIETRICH, JASON 2002 'Passing on Blackness: Latinos, Race, and Earnings in the USA', *Applied Economics Letters,* vol. 9, no. 13, pp. 847–53

DARITY, WILLIAM, DIETRICH, JASON and HAMILTON, DARRICK 2005 'Bleach in the Rainbow: Latin Ethnicity and Preference for Whiteness', *Transforming Anthropology,* vol. 13, no. 2

DE LA GARZA, RODOLFO, FALCON, ANGELO, GARCIA, F. CHRIS and GARCIA, JOHN A. 1992 *Latino National Political Survey, 1989–1990 Computer file,* 3rd ICPSR version, producer: Philadelphia, PA: Temple University, Institute for Social Research; distributor: Ann Arbor, MI: Inter-university Consortium for Political and Social Research, 1998

DUANY, JORGE. 2005. 'Neither White nor Black: The Representation of Racial Identity among Puerto Ricans on the Island and in the US Mainland', in Anani Dzidzienyo and Suzanne Oboler (eds), *Neither Enemies nor Friends: Latinos, Blacks, Afro-Latinos,* New York: Palgrave Macmillan, pp. 173–88

ESCHBACH, KARL and GOMEZ, CHRISTINA 1998 'Choosing Hispanic Identity: Ethnic Identity Switching among Respondents to High School and Beyond', *Social Science Quarterly,* vol. 79, no. 1, p. 74

FEAGIN, JOE 2000 *Racist America: Roots, Current Realities, and Future Reparations,* New York: Routledge

FORMAN, TYRONE, GOAR, CARLA and LEWIS, AMANDA E. 2002 'Neither Black nor White? An Empirical Test of the Latin Americanization Thesis', *Race and Society,* vol. 5, pp. 65–84

GOLASH-BOZA, TANYA 2006 'Dropping the Hyphen? Becoming Latino(a)-American through Racialized Assimilation', *Social Forces,* vol. 85, p. 1

GORDON, MILTON M. 1964 *Assimilation in American Life,* New York: Oxford University Press

HANEY-LÓPEZ, IAN 2005 'Race on the 2010 Census: Hispanics and the Shrinking White Majority', *Daedalus,* Winter

HARRIS, DAVID R. and SIM, JEREMIAH JOSEPH 2002 'Who Is Multiracial? Assessing the Complexity of Lived Race', *American Sociological Review,* vol. 67, no. 614

HENRY, JACQUES and BANKSTON, CARL L. III 2001 L, *Ethnic and Racial Studies,* vol. 24, pp. 1020–45

HIRSCHMAN, CHARLES 2001 The Educational Enrollment of Immigrant Youth: A Test of the Segmented-Assimilation Hypothesis', *Demography,* vol. 38, pp. 317–36

ITZIGSOHN, JOSÉ, GIORGULI, SILVIA and VASQUEZ, OBED 2005 'Immigrant Incorporation and Racial Identity: Racial Self-Identification among Dominican Immigrants', *Ethnic and Racial Studies,* vol. 28, no. 1, pp. 50–78

LANDALE, N. S. and OROPESA, R. S. 2002 'White, Black or Puerto Rican? Racial Self-Identification among Mainland and Island Puerto Ricans', *Social Forces,* vol. 81, pp. 231–54

LEE, JENNIFER and BEAN, FRANK D. 2004 'America's Changing Color Lines: Immigration, Race/Ethnicity and Multiracial Identification', *Annual Review of Sociology,* vol. 30

LOVELL, PEGGY A. and WOOD, CHARLES H. 1998 'Skin Color, Racial Identity and Life Chances in Brazil', *Latin American Perspectives,* vol. 25, no. 3, pp. 90–109

NAGEL, JOANE. 1994 'Constructing Ethnicity: Creating and Recreating Ethnic Identity and Culture', *Social Problems,* vol. 41, no. 1

NUTINI, HUGO G. 1997 'Class and Ethnicity in Mexico: Somatic and Racial Considerations', *Ethnology,* vol. 36, no. 3, pp. 227–38

OVEIDO, R. M. 1992 'Are We or Aren't We?', *NACLA Report on the Americas: The Black Americas 1492–1992,* vol. 25, no. 4, p. 19. North American Congress on Latin America

PARK, ROBERT EZRA 1950 *Race and Culture,* Glencoe. IL: The Free Press

RODRíGUEZ, CLARA 1994 'Challenging Racial Hegemony: Puerto Ricans in the United States', in Steven Gregory and Roger Sanjek (eds), *Race,* New Brunswick, NJ: Rutgers University Press

——— 2000 *Changing Race: Latinos, the Census, and the History of Ethnicity in the United States,* New York: New York University Press

ROPP, STEVEN MASAMI 2000 'Secondary Migration and the Politics of Identity for Asian Latinos in Los Angeles', *JAAS,* pp. 219–29

RUMBAUT, RUBÉN and PORTES, ALEJANDRO (eds) 2001 *Ethnicities: Children of Immigrants in America,* Berkeley, CA: University of California Press

SKIDMORE, THOMAS 1993 'Bi-racial USA vs Multiracial Brazil: Is the Contrast Still Valid?', *Journal of Latin American Studies,* vol. 25, pp. 373–86

TELLES, EDWARD 2004 *Race in another America: The Significance of Skin Color in Brazil,* Princeton, NJ: Princeton University Press

TWINE, FRANCE 1998 *Racism in a Racial Democracy: The Maintenance of White Supremacy in Brazil,* New Brunswick, NJ: Rutgers University Press

WADE, PETER 1993 *Blackness and Race Mixture: The Dynamics of Race Mixture in Colombia,* Baltimore, MD: Johns Hopkins University Press

——— 1997 *Race and Ethnicity in Latin America,* Chicago, IL: Pluto Press

WHITTEN, NORMAN and TORRES, ARLENE 1998 'To Forge the Future in the Fires of the Past: An Interpretive Essay on Racism, Domination, Resistance and Liberation', in Norman Whitten and Arlene Torres (eds) *Blackness in Latin America and the Caribbean,* Vol. 1. Bloomington, IN: Indiana University Press

WRIGHT, WINTHROP 1990 *Café con Leche: Race, Class. and National Image in Venezuela,* Austin, TX: University of Texas Press

YANCEY, GEORGE 2003 *Who is White? Latinos, Asians, and the New Black/Nonblack Divide,* Boulder, CO: Lynne Rienner

ZHOU, MIN 1997 'Growing up American: The Challenge Confronting Immigrant Children and Children of Immigrants', *Annual Review of Sociology,* vol. 23, pp. 63–95

READING 7

Whiteness as an "Unmarked" Cultural Category

Ruth Frankenberg

America's supposed to be the melting pot. I know that I've got a huge number of nationalities in my blood, but how do I—what do I call myself? And hating this country as I do, I don't like to say I'm an American. Even though it is what I am. I hate identifying myself as only an American, because I have so much objections to Americans' place in the world. I don't know how I felt about that when I was growing up, but I never—I didn't like to pledge allegiance to the flag. . . . Still, at this point in my life, I wonder what it is that somebody with all this melting pot blood can call their own. . . .

Especially growing up in the sixties, when people *did* say "I'm proud to be Black," "I'm proud to be Hispanic," you know, and it became very popular to be proud of your ethnicity. And even feminists, you know, you could say, "I'm a woman," and be proud of it. But there's still a majority of the country that can't say they are proud of anything!

Suzie Roberts's words powerfully illustrate the key themes . . . that stirred the women I interviewed* as they examined their own identities: what had formed them, what they counted as (their own or others') cultural practice(s), and what constituted identities of which they could be proud. This [discussion] explores perceptions of whiteness as a location of culture and identity, focusing mainly on white feminist . . . women's views and contrasting their voices with those of more politically conservative women. . . .

[M]any of the women I interviewed, including even some of the conservative ones, appeared to

be self-conscious about white power and racial inequality. In part because of their sense of the links and parallels between white racial dominance in the United States and U.S. domination on a global scale, there was a complex interweaving of questions about race and nation—whiteness and Americanness—in these women's thoughts about white culture. Similarly, conceptions of racial, national, and cultural belonging frequently leaked into one another.

On the one hand, then, these women's views of white culture seemed to be distinctively modern. But at the same time, their words drew on much earlier historical moments and participated in long-established modes of cultural description. In the broadest sense, Western colonial discourses on the white self, the nonwhite Other, and the white Other too, were very much in evidence. These discourses produced dualistic conceptualizations of whiteness versus other cultural forms. The women thus often spoke about culture in ways that reworked, and yet remained tied to, "older" forms of racism.

For a significant number of young white women, being white felt like being cultureless. Cathy Thomas, in the following description of whiteness, raised many of the themes alluded to by other feminist and race-cognizant women. She described what she saw as a lack of form and substance:

> . . . the formlessness of being white. Now if I was a middle western girl, or a New Yorker, if I had a fixed regional identity that was something palpable, then I'd be a white New Yorker, no doubt, but I'd still be a New Yorker. . . . Being a Californian, I'm sure it has its hallmarks, but to me they were invisible. . . . If I had an ethnic base to identify from, if I was even Irish American, that would have been something formed, if I was a working-class woman, that would have been something formed. But to be a Heinz 57 American, a white, class-confused American, land of the Kleenex type American, is so formless in and of itself. It only takes shape in relation to other people.

Whiteness as a cultural space is represented here as amorphous and indescribable, in contrast with a range of other identities marked by race, ethnicity, region, and class. Further, white culture is viewed

---

Ruth Frankenberg (1957–2007) was a professor of American studies at the University of California, Davis. Her work helped define the field of whiteness studies.

*Between 1984 and 1986 Ruth Frankenberg interviewed 30 white women, diverse in age, class, region of origin, sexuality, family situation and political orientation, all living in California at the time of the interviews.

here as "bad" culture. In fact, the extent to which identities can be named seems to show an inverse relationship to power in the U.S. social structure. The elisions, parallels, and differences between characterizations of white people, Americans, people of color, and so-called white ethnic groups will be explored [here].

Cathy's own cultural positioning seemed to her impossible to grasp, shapeless and unnameable. It was easier to know others and to know, with certainty, what one was *not*. Providing a clue to one of the mechanisms operating here is the fact that, while Cathy viewed New Yorkers and midwesterners as having a cultural shape or identity, women from the East Coast and the Midwest also described or mourned their own seeming lack of culture. The self, where it is part of a dominant cultural group, does not have to name itself. In this regard, Chris Patterson hit the nail on the head, linking the power of white culture with the privilege not to be named:

> I'm probably at the stage where I'm beginning to see that you can come up with a definition of white. Before, I didn't know that you could turn it around and say, "Well what *does* white mean?" One thing is, it's taken for granted. . . . [To be white means to] have some sort of advantage or privilege, even if it's something as simple as not having a definition.

The notion of "turning it around" indicates Chris's realization that, most often, whites are the nondefined definers of other people. Or, to put it another way, whiteness comes to be an unmarked or neutral category, whereas other cultures are specifically marked "cultural."

Many of the women shared the habit of turning to elements of white culture as the unspoken norm. This assumption of a white norm was so prevalent that even Sandy Alvarez and Louise Glebocki, who were acutely aware of racial inequality as well as being members of racially mixed families, referred to "Mexican" music versus "regular" music, and regular meant "white."

Similarly, discussions of race difference and cultural diversity at times revealed a view in which people of color actually embodied difference and whites stood for sameness. Hence, Margaret Phillips said of her Jamaican daughter-in-law that: "She *really* comes with diversity." In spite of its brevity, and because of its curious structure, this short statement says a great deal. It implicitly designates whiteness as norm, and Jamaicans as having or bearing with them "differentness." At the risk of being crass, one might say that in this view, diversity is to the daughter-in-law as "the works" is to a hamburger—added on, adding color and flavor, but not exactly essential. Whiteness, seen by many of these women as boring, but nonetheless definitive, could also follow this analogy. This mode of thinking about "difference" expresses clearly the double-edged sword of a color- and power-evasive repertoire, apparently valorizing cultural difference but doing so in a way that leaves racial and cultural hierarchies intact.

For a seemingly formless entity, then, white culture had a great deal of power, difficult to dislodge from its place in white consciousness as a point of reference for the measuring of others. Whiteness served simultaneously to eclipse and marginalize others (two modes of making the other inessential). Helen Standish's description of her growing-up years in a small New England town captured these processes well. Since the community was all white, the differences at issue were differences between whites. (This also enables an assessment of the links between white and non-white "marked" cultures.) Asked about her own cultural identity, Helen explained that "it didn't seem like a culture because everyone else was the same." She had, however, previously mentioned Italian Americans in the town, so I asked about their status. She responded as follows, adopting at first the voice of childhood:

> They are different, but I'm the same as everybody else. They speak Italian, but everybody else in the U.S. speaks English. They eat strange, different food, but I eat the same kind of food as everybody else in the U.S. . . . The way I was brought up was to think that everybody who was the same as me were "Americans," and the other people were of "such and such descent."

Viewing the Italian Americans as different and oneself as "same" serves, first, to marginalize, to push from the center, the former group. At the same time, claiming to be the same as everyone else makes other cultural groups invisible or eclipses them. Finally, there is a marginalizing of all those who are not like Helen's own family, leaving a residual, core or normative group who are the true Americans. The category of "American" represents simultaneously the normative and the residual, the dominant culture and a nonculture.

Although Helen talked here about whites, it is safe to guess that people of color would not have counted among the "same" group but among the communities of "such and such descent" (Mexican American, for example). Whites, within this discursive repertoire, became conceptually the real Americans, and only certain kinds of whites actually qualified. Whiteness and Americanness both stood as normative and exclusive categories in relation to which other cultures were identified and marginalized. And this clarifies that there are two kinds of whites, just as there are two kinds of Americans: those who are truly or only white, and those who are white but also something more—or is it something less?

In sum, whiteness often stood as an unmarked marker of others' differentness—whiteness not so much void or formlessness as norm. I associate this construction with colonialism and with the more recent assymetrical dualisms of liberal humanist views of culture, race, and identity. For the most part, this construction views nonwhite cultures as lesser, deviant, or pathological. However, another trajectory has been the inverse: conceptualizations of the cultures of peoples of color as somehow better than the dominant culture, perhaps more natural or more spiritual. These are positive evaluations of a sort, but they are equally dualistic. Many of the women I interviewed saw white culture as less appealing and found the cultures of the "different" people more interesting. As Helen Standish put it:

> [We had] Wonder bread, white bread. I'm more interested in, you know, "What's a bagel?" in other people's cultures rather than my own.

The claim that whiteness lacks form and content says more about the definitions of culture being used than it does about the content of whiteness. However, I would suggest that in describing themselves as cultureless these women are in fact identifying specific kinds of unwanted absences or presences in their own culture(s) as a generalized lack or nonexistence. It thus becomes important to look at what they *did* say about the cultural content of whiteness.

Descriptions of the content of white culture were thin, to say the least. But despite the paucity of signifiers, there was a great deal of consistency across the narratives. First, there was naming based on color, the linking of white culture with white objects—the clichéd white bread and mayonnaise, for example. Freida Kazen's identification of whiteness as "bland," together with Helen Standish's "blah," also signified paleness or neutrality. The images connote several things—color itself (although exaggerated, and besides, bagels are usually white inside, too), lack of vitality (Wonder bread is highly processed), and homogeneity. However, these images are perched on a slippery slope, at once suggesting "white" identified as a color (though an unappealing one) and as an absence of color, that is, white as the unmarked marker.

Whiteness was often signified in these narratives by commodities and brands: Wonder bread, Kleenex, Heinz 57. In this identification whiteness came to be seen as spoiled by capitalism, and as being linked with capitalism in a way that other cultures supposedly are not. Another set of signifiers that constructed whiteness as uniquely tainted by capitalism had to do with the "modern condition": Dot Humphrey described white neighborhoods as "more privatized," and Cathy Thomas used "alienated" to describe her cultural condition. Clare Traverso added to this theme, mourning her own feeling of lack of identity, in contrast with images of her husband's Italian American background (and here, Clare is again talking about perceived differences between whites):

> Food, old country, mama. Stories about a grandmother who can't speak English. . . . Candles, adobe houses, arts, music. [It] has emotion, feeling, belongingness that to me is unique.

In linking whiteness to capitalism and viewing nonwhite cultures as untainted by it, these women were again drawing on a colonial discourse in which progress and industrialization were seen as synonymous with Westernization, while the rest of the world is seen as caught up in tradition and "culture." In addition, one can identify, in white women's mourning over whiteness, elements of what Raymond Williams has called "pastoralism," or nostalgia for a golden era now gone by (but in fact, says Williams, one that never existed).[1]

The image of whiteness as corrupted and impoverished by capitalism is but one of a series of ways in which white culture was seen as impure or tainted. White culture was also seen as tainted by its relationship to power. For example, Clare Traverso clearly counterposed white culture and white power, finding it difficult to value the former because of the overwhelming weight of the latter:

> The good things about whites are to do with folk arts, music. Because other things have power associated with them.

For many race-cognizant white women, white culture was also made impure by its very efforts to maintain race purity. Dot Humphrey, for example, characterized white neighborhoods as places in which people were segregated by choice. For her, this was a good reason to avoid living in them.

The link between whiteness and domination, however, was frequently made in ways that both artificially isolated culture from other factors and obscured economics. For at times, the traits the women envied in Other cultures were in fact at least in part the product of poverty or other dimensions of oppression. Lack of money, for example, often means lack of privacy or space, and it can be valorized as "more street life, less alienation." Cathy Thomas's notion of Chicanas' relationship to the kitchen ("the hearth of the home") as a cultural "good" might be an idealized one that disregards the reality of intensive labor.

Another link between class and culture emerged in Louise Glebocki's reference to the working-class Chicanos she met as a child as less pretentious,

"closer to the truth," more "down to earth." And Marjorie Hoffman spoke of the "earthy humor" of Black people, which she interpreted as, in the words of Langston Hughes, a means of "laughing to keep from crying." On the one hand, as has been pointed out especially by Black scholars and activists, the positions of people of color at the bottom of a social and economic hierarchy create the potential for a critique of the system as a whole and consciousness of the need to resist.[2] From the standpoint of race privilege, the system of racism is thus made structurally invisible. On the other hand, descriptions of this kind leave in place a troubling dichotomy that can be appropriated as easily by the right as by the left. For example, there is an inadvertent affinity between the image of Black people as "earthy" and the conservative racist view that African American culture leaves African American people ill equipped for advancement in the modern age. Here, echoing essentialist racism, both Chicanos and African Americans are placed on the borders of "nature" and "culture."

By the same token, often what was criticized as "white" was as much the product of middle-class status as of whiteness as such. Louise Glebocki's image of her fate had she married a white man was an image of a white-collar, nuclear family:

> Him saying, "I'm home, dear," and me with an apron on—ugh!

The intersections of class, race, and culture were obscured in other ways. Patricia Bowen was angry with some of her white feminist friends who, she felt, embraced as "cultural" certain aspects of African American, Chicano, and Native American cultures (including, for example, artwork or dance performances) but would reject as "tacky" (her term) those aspects of daily life that communities of color shared with working-class whites, such as the stores and supermarkets of poor neighborhoods. This, she felt, was tantamount to a selective expansion of middle-class aesthetic horizons, but not to true antiracism or to comprehension of the cultures of people of color. Having herself grown up in a white working-class family, Pat also felt that middle-class white feminists were able to use selective engagement to avoid addressing their class privilege.

I have already indicated some of the problems inherent in this kind of conceptualization, suggesting that it tends to keep in place dichotomous constructions of "white" versus Other cultures, to separate "culture" from other dimensions of daily life, and to reify or strip of history *all* cultural forms. There are, then, a range of issues that need to be disentangled if we are to understand the location of "whiteness" in the terrain of culture. It is, I believe, useful to approach this question by means of a reconceptualization of the concept of culture itself. A culture, in the sense of the set of rules and practices by means of which a group organizes itself and its values, manners, and worldview—in other words, culture as "a field articulating the lifeworld of subjects . . . and the structures created by human activity"[3]—is an indispensable precondition to any individual's existence in the world. It is nonsensical in terms of this kind of definition to suggest that anyone could actually have "no culture." But this is not, as I have suggested, the mode of thinking about culture that these women are employing.

Whiteness emerges here as inextricably tied to domination partly as an effect of a discursive "draining process" applied to both whiteness and Americanness. In this process, any cultural practice engaged in by a white person that is not identical to the dominant culture is automatically counted as either "not really white"—and, for that matter, not really American, either—(but rather of such and such descent), or as "not really cultural" (but rather "economic"). There is a slipperiness to whiteness here: it shifts from "no culture" to "normal culture" to "bad culture" and back again. Simultaneously, a range of marginal or, in Trinh T. Minh-ha's terminology, "bounded" cultures are generated. These are viewed as enviable spaces, separate and untainted by relations of dominance or by linkage to other structures or systems. By contrast, whiteness is conceived as axiomatically tied to dominance, to economics, to political structures. In this process,

both whiteness and nonwhiteness are reified, made into objects rather than processes, and robbed of historical context and human agency. As long as the discussion remains couched in these terms, a critique of whiteness remains a double-edged sword: for one thing, whiteness remains normative because there is no way to name the cultural practices associated with it *as* cultural. Moreover, as I have suggested, whether whiteness is viewed as artificial and dominating (and therefore "bad") or civilized (and therefore "good"), whiteness and all varieties of nonwhiteness continue to be viewed as ontologically different from one another.

A genuine sadness and frustration about the meaning of whiteness at this moment in history motivated these women to decry white culture. It becomes important, then, to recognize the grains of truth in their views of white culture. It is important to acknowledge their anger and frustration about the meaning of whiteness as we reach toward a politicized analysis of culture that is freer of colonial and pastoral legacies.

The terms "white" and "American" as these women used them signified domination in international and domestic terms. This link is both accurate and inaccurate. While it is true that, by and large, those in power in the United States are white, it is also true that not all those who are white are in power. Nor is the axiomatic linkage between Americanness and power accurate, because not all Americans have the same access to power. At the same time, the link between whiteness, Americanness, and power *are* accurate because, as we have seen, the terms "white" and "American" both function discursively to exclude people from normativity—including white people "of such and such descent." But here we need to distinguish between the fates of people of color and those of white people. Notwithstanding a complicated history, the boundaries of Americanness and whiteness have been much more fluid for "white ethnic" groups than for people of color.

There have been border skirmishes over the meaning of whiteness and Americanness since the inception of those terms. For white people, however, those skirmishes have been resolved through processes of assimilation, not exclusion. The late nineteenth and early twentieth centuries in the United States saw a systematic push toward the cultural homogenization of whites carried out through social reform movements and the schools. This push took place alongside the expansion of industrial capitalism, giving rise to the sense that whiteness signifies the production and consumption of commodities under capitalism.[4] But recognition of this history should not be translated into an assertion that whites were stripped of culture (for to do that would be to continue to adhere to a colonial view of "culture"). Instead one must argue that certain cultural practices replaced others. Were one to undertake a history of this "generic" white culture, it would fragment into a thousand tributary elements, culturally specific religious observances, and class survival mechanisms as well as mass-produced commodities and mass media.

There are a number of dangers inherent in continuing to view white culture as no culture. Whiteness appeared in the narratives to function as both norm or core, that against which everything else is measured, and as residue, that which is left after everything else has been named. A far-reaching danger of whiteness coded as "no culture" is that it leaves in place whiteness as defining a set of normative cultural practices against which all are measured and into which all are expected to fit. This normativity has underwritten oppression from the beginning of colonial expansion and has had impact in multiple ways: from the American pioneers' assumption of a norm of private property used to justify appropriation of land that within their worldview did not have an owner, and the ideological construction of nations like Britain as white,[5] to Western feminism's Eurocentric shaping of its movements and institutions. It is important for white feminists not to continue to participate in these processes.

And if whiteness has a history, so do the cultures of people of color, which are worked on, crafted, and created, rather than just "there." For peoples of color in the United States, this work has gone on as much in the context of relationships to imperialism and capitalism as has the production of whiteness, though it has been premised on exclusion and resistance to exclusion more than on assimilation. Although not always or only forged in resistance, the visibility and recognition of the cultures of U.S. peoples of color in recent times *is* the product of individual and collective struggle. Only a short time has elapsed since those struggles made possible the introduction into public discourse of celebration and valorization of their cultural forms. In short, it is important not to reify any culture by failing to acknowledge its createdness, and not to view it as always having been there in unchanging form.

Rather than feeling "cultureless," white women need to become conscious of the histories and specificities of our cultural positions, and of the political, economic, and creative fusions that form all cultures. The purpose of such an exercise is not, of course, to reinvert the dualisms and valorize whiteness so much as to develop a clearer sense of where and who we are.

DISCUSSION QUESTIONS

1. Why is whiteness considered to be lacking diversity?
2. How would you describe the cultural content of whiteness?

NOTES

1. Raymond Williams, *The Country and the City* (New York: Oxford University Press, 1978).
2. The classic statement of this position is W. E. B. Du Bois's concept of the "double consciousness" of Americans of African descent. Two recent feminist statements of similar positions are Patricia Hill Collins, *Black Feminist Thought: Knowledge, Consciousness, and the Politics of Empowerment* (Boston: Unwin Hyman, 1990); and Aida Hurtado, "Relating to Privilege: Seduction and Rejection in the Subordination of White Women and Women of Color," *Signs* 14, no. 4:833–55.
3. Paul Gilroy, *There Ain't No Black in the Union Jack*. London: Hutchinson, 1987.
4. See, for example, Winthrop Talbot, ed., *Americanization* (New York: H. W. Wilson, 1917), esp. Sophonisba P. Breckinridge, "The Immigrant Family," 251–52, Olivia

Howard Dunbar, "Teaching the Immigrant Woman," 252–56, and North American Civic League for Immigrants, "Domestic Education among Immigrants," 256–58; and Kathie Friedman Kasaba, "'To Become a Person': The Experience of Gender, Ethnicity and Work in the Lives of Immigrant Women, New York City, 1870–1940," doctoral dissertation, Department of Sociology, State University of New York, Binghamton, 1991. I am indebted to Katie Friedman Kasaba for these references and for her discussions with me about working-class European immigrants to the United States at the turn of this century.

5. Gilroy, *There Ain't No Black in the Union Jack.*

READING 8

Plus ça Change . . . ? Multiraciality and the Dynamics of Race Relations in the United States

Frank D. Bean and Jennifer Lee

. . . The issue of race has long cast a shadow on the founding mythology of the United States. Well after the end of the Civil War, the country coped with the contradiction between immigration and race by compartmentalizing depictions of immigrant and slavery experiences, at least at an intellectual level. Historians tended to embed discussions of immigration in narratives about the frontier and industrialization, while confining slavery to the history of the South (Davis, 1998). If race was a problem, scholars viewed it as a regional issue, not one pertaining to the country as a whole. This convenient (and patronizing) approach appeared to come to an end during the 1960s, when the geostrategic exigencies of the Cold War, and the not-easily ignored claims for equal opportunity of post–World War II Black veterans, culminated in 1965 in two landmark pieces of legislation: the Civil Rights Act making discrimination against Blacks illegal; and the Hart-Celler Act abolishing

Frank D. Bean is a professor of sociology at the University of California, Irvine.

Jennifer Lee is a professor of sociology at the University of California, Irvine.

national origin quotas as bases for immigrant admissions (Bean & Bell-Rose, 1999; Reimers, 1992). Many scholars thought the former would quickly lead to full incorporation of Blacks into American society (Glazer, 1997), whereas others generally expected the latter not to generate much in the way of new immigration, but rather simply to remove the embarrassment of the country's discriminatory admissions policies (Reimers, 1998). What both shared at the time was that each seemed to offer the prospect of improving racial/ethnic relations in the United States.

Neither, however, turned out as anticipated. Blacks did not quickly become economically incorporated and millions of new non-White immigrants unexpectedly came to the country (Bean & Stevens, 2003). But as post–World War II economic prosperity created new job opportunities and its expanding cities brought persons from different backgrounds increasingly into contact with one another (Fischer & Hout, 2006), religious and ethnic group intermarriage flourished (Pagnini & Morgan, 1990). The politics of racial identity eventually gained new, if controversial, traction, leading to heightened awareness that tangible benefits could accrue to those with official minority status (Skrentny, 2002). Partly as a result of affirmative action and other policies, new movements sprang up at the end of the century advocating that the offspring of mixed-race relationships should be allowed to self-identify as belonging to more than one racial group in government surveys (Renn, 2009; Rockquemore, Brunsma, & Delgado, 2009). At first glance, such changes would seem to portend salutary effects for race relations in the United States. Not only are relatively more mixed-marital unions now occurring than previously, but the offspring of such unions are able to acknowledge their mixed-race backgrounds if they wish. The old strictures of race appear to be melting away. . . .

The extent to which the color line has changed in recent decades, particularly as a consequence of recent non-White immigration, carries major analytical significance for research on multiraciality and multiracial identification. If the color line is roughly the same for Latinos and Asians as it is for Blacks, then studies of multiracial contextual and individual manifestations need worry little about what kinds of multiracial combinations they examine. What holds true for Black–White multiracial pairings and individuals would seem likely to apply to other multiracials as well. However, if one racial category were found to carry considerably stronger salience than another, the dynamics could be different. For example, if Black–White marriages and individuals confront greater stigmatization than Asian-White or Latino-White ones, then the individual and social dynamics of multiraciality would be likely to vary across groups and combinations. In some ways, this is an obvious point, but it bears repeating, not only because it carries theoretical significance, but also because the Black–White divide has so hauntingly preoccupied the history of the United States that we often transfer ideas about Black–White dynamics to the cases of other racial/ethnic minority groups, often without careful consideration of whether these apply. . . .

HYPOTHETICAL NEW MODELS OF THE U.S. COLOR LINE

Given that today's immigrant newcomers from Latin America and Asia are neither Black nor White, the traditional Black–White model of race relations may inaccurately depict the character of race/ethnic relations for Asians and Latinos as compared to Blacks. Consequently, an important research issue in U.S. race/ethnic relations is: Are the experiences of America's newest non-White immigrant groups tracking those of their European predecessors, or are these groups becoming racialized minorities who see their experiences as more akin to those of African Americans than to earlier immigrants? In other words, do Asians and Latinos, particularly the later-generation members of these groups, more closely resemble Whites or Blacks in the United States at this point in time? An answer to this question can help to reveal whether the Black–White color line of the past is evolving into some sort of other pattern—the three major possibilities

for which are a White/non-White divide, a new triracial hierarchy, or a Black/non-Black divide. If, as W. E. Du Bois said, "the problem of the twentieth century (was) that of the (Black–White) color line," the question of the 21st century is: Where is the color line now drawn? Below we consider the nature and contemporary relevance of these three alternative models of today's color line(s) that scholars have articulated.

The Hypothesis of a White/Non-White Divide

Many observers think a White/non-White divide is emerging. For one thing, such a divide has been legally enforced throughout the history of the United States, well into the 20th century. In 1924, for example, the state of Virginia passed a Racial Integrity Law that created two distinct racial categories: "pure" White and all others. The statute defined a "White" person as one with "no trace whatsoever of blood other than Caucasian," and emerged to legally ban intermarriage between Whites and other races. While Blacks were clearly non-White under the legislation, Asians and Latinos also fell on the non-White side of the strict binary divide. The statute reflected the Supreme Court rulings of *Takao Ozawa v. United States* (1922) and *United States v. Bhagat Singh Thind* (1923), in which persons of Asian origin were not only classified as non-White but also considered ineligible for U.S. citizenship. In the first case, Takao Ozawa (a Japanese citizen of the United States) filed for U.S. citizenship under the Naturalization Act of June 29, 1906, which allowed Whites and persons of African descent or African nativity to naturalize. Rather than challenging the constitutionality of the racial restrictions to U.S. citizenship, Ozawa argued his skin color made him a "White person" and that Japanese persons should be classified as "White." The Supreme Court ruled that only Caucasians were White, and because the Japanese were not of the Caucasian race, could not be deemed White, but rather were members of an "unassimilable race," lacking provisions standing under the Naturalization Act.

Three months later, in *United States v. Bhagat Singh Thind* (1923), the Supreme Court handed down a similar ruling, denying citizenship to a man of Asian-Indian origin. The court ruled that Bhagat Singh Thind, a native of India, could not be a naturalized citizen despite the fact that anthropologists had defined members of the Indian subcontinent as members of the Caucasian race. In his case, while the court did not dispute that Thind was a Caucasian, they ruled that not all Caucasians were White. According to the Supreme Court, while Thind may have been Caucasian, he was not a "White person" as "used in common speech, to be interpreted in accordance with the understanding of the common man." While Takao Ozawa was denied citizenship because he was not of the Caucasian race, and therefore not White, Bhagat Singh Thind was denied citizenship because he was not White according to the common understanding of Whiteness, even though the court conceded he was Caucasian. The rulings reflected the idea that persons of Asian origin were not only a distinct racial or color category from Whites, but were also considered "unassimilable."

Administrative policies adopted in the latter half of the 1960s following the Civil Rights Movement reinforced the idea of a White/non-White demarcation. Most prominently, affirmative action policies were extended to minority groups who were perceived as "analogous to Blacks" with respect to physical distinctiveness and to having "suffered enough" to be similarly categorized (Skrentny, 2002). According to these criteria, Latinos, Native Americans, and Asians became eligible for affirmative action programs while disadvantaged White ethnics did not. One potential unintended consequence of such policies was that Asians and especially Latinos may have become perceived and labeled as racialized minorities who were more akin to Blacks than to Whites. In essence, many affirmative action policies placed Asians and Latinos on the non-White side of the divide, firmly establishing a delineation between Whites and non-Whites.

Further cementing the divide was the introduction of the label "people of color," which gained momentum and popularity in the late 1980s (Hollinger, 2005). Such omnibus terms combine all non-White groups on the basis of presumed racialized minority status, thus connoting that the individuals to which they refer share a similar subordinate status vis-à-vis Whites. By homogenizing (and thus reifying the experiences of all non-White groups), the "people of color" rubric indicates the boundaries among non-White groups are less distinct and salient than the boundary separating Whites from non-Whites. Accordingly, a White/non-White model of racial/ethnic relations would envision Asians and Latinos falling closer to Blacks than to Whites in their experiences in the United States, suggesting that extent of multiraciality and multiracial identification should be similar for Asians, Latinos, and Blacks.

The Hypothesis of a Triracial Hierarchy

Other social scientists propose still another possibility—a triracial stratification system similar to that of many Latin American and Caribbean countries. In the United States, this has been viewed as consisting of Whites, honorary Whites, and collective Blacks (Bonilla-Silva, 2004a, b). Included in the "White" category would be Whites, assimilated White Latinos, some multiracials, assimilated Native Americans, and a few Asian-origin people. "Honorary Whites" would include light-skinned Latinos, Japanese Americans, Korean Americans, Chinese Americans, Asian Indians, Middle Eastern Americans, and most multiracials. Finally, the "collective Black" category would include Blacks, Filipinos, Vietnamese, Hmong, Laotians, dark-skinned Latinos, West Indian and African immigrants, and reservation-bound Native Americans.

Because many of today's new immigrants hail from Latin America and the Caribbean, Bonilla-Silva argued that a more complex triracial order will emerge given what he terms the "darkening" of the United States. In his view, a triracial order would also serve to help maintain "White supremacy" by creating an intermediate racial group to buffer racial conflict (Bonilla-Silva, 2004b, p. 5). While a few new immigrants might fall into the honorary White strata and may even eventually become White, the majority would incorporate into the collective Black strata, including most Latino immigrants who he labels as "racial others" whose experiences with race are seen as similar to those of Blacks. In this regard, the triracial model differs fundamentally from the Black/non-Black divide because Bonilla-Silva posits that Latinos are racialized in a manner similar to African Americans, and therefore fall on the Black side of the divide.

While some research evidence seems to support the Latin Americanization thesis, it has not gone without criticism. For instance, Murguia and Saenz (2004) argued that a three-tier system predated substantial Latin American immigration to the United States. Other social scientists contest the uniform characterization of Latinos as a monolithic group (Forman, Goar, & Lewis, 2004; Murguia & Saenz, 2004). For instance, examining Latinos' social attitudes toward other racial/ethnic groups, Forman et al. (2004) found that Latinos fall into different segments of the triracial hierarchy depending on national origin. For instance, Puerto Ricans differ from Mexicans in their expressed feelings toward Blacks, with the former group demonstrating more positive attitudes if they show darker skin color. Mexicans, however, are much more uniform in their feelings toward Blacks and express attitudes that are closer to non-Hispanic Whites than to non-Hispanic Blacks, perhaps as a result of the history of racial mixing in Mexico, which involved very few Africans, unlike the history of mixing in Puerto Rico (Forman et al., 2004). In any case, regardless of skin color, Latinos overall fall closer to non-Hispanic Whites in their attitudes toward Blacks than to non-Hispanic Blacks. Such results suggest considerable variation in the racialization experiences of Latinos in the United States. Contrary to the Latin Americanization thesis, many Latinos, especially Mexicans, do not appear to see themselves as falling into the collective Black category. However, if the Latin Americanization hypothesis holds and a triracial hierarchy is forming, similar patterns

of and experiences with multiraciality identification should occur among Blacks and Latinos because both are "racial others," whereas differences would exist between these two groups and Asians.

The Hypothesis of a Black/Non-Black Divide

In the 1990s, a number of other social scientists began to argue that a new racial structure was emerging that differed from a Black–White, a White/non-White or a triracial hierarchy. They suggested a new binary color line—a Black/non-Black divide—that highlighted the continuing and unique separation of Blacks, not only from Whites but also from other non-White racial/ethnic groups (Alba, 1990; Gans, 1999; Gitlin, 1995). The concept of the Black/non-Black divide surfaced in conjunction with a scholarship documenting the processes by which previously "non-White" immigrant ethnic groups such as the Irish, Italians, and Eastern European Jews became "White" (Alba, 1985, 1990; Brodkin, 1998; Gerstle, 1999; Ignatiev, 1995; Jacobson, 1998; Roediger, 1991). For example, Ignatiev (1995) detailed how Irish immigrants—once referred to as "White Negroes" by the country's Anglo-Saxons—became "White" by shifting their political alliances, achieving economic mobility, and adopting deliberate and extreme measures to distance themselves from African Americans. With economic mobility also came a decoupling of the conflation of national origin differences and "racial" differences, further contributing to the development of the idea that for Irish immigrants (and other European immigrants) race was an achieved rather than an ascribed status (Alba, 1990; Haney-Lopez, 1996; Perlmann & Waldinger, 1997; Waters, 1990). In other words, as economic and cultural differences diminished and eventually faded between White and non-White immigrants groups, the Irish, Italians, and Eastern European Jews became racially reconstructed as White.

Other scholars noted that European immigrants were not the only ones to have changed their status from non-White to White. Asian ethnic immigrant groups such as the Chinese and the Japanese also managed to transform their racial status from "almost Black" to "almost White." Loewen (1971), for example, documents how Chinese immigrants in the Mississippi Delta consciously strove to modify their lowly racial status through economic mobility, the emulation of the cultural practices and institutions of Whites, the intentional distancing of themselves from Blacks, and the rejection of fellow ethnics who married Blacks and any Chinese-Black multiracial children they bore. By adopting the anti-Black sentiment embraced by Mississippi Whites and by closely following White moral codes, the Chinese accepted rather than challenged the existing racial hierarchy and essentially were able to cross the Black–White color line. Spickard (1989) noted a similar process of change among Japanese Americans who, at the beginning of the 20th century, were consigned with Blacks to the bottom of the racial hierarchy, but whose status rose dramatically just three quarters of a century later. Today, so extreme is the shift in America's racial hierarchy that Asians, now donning titles of "model minority" and "honorary Whites," have become groups against which other non-White groups are often judged and compared—a far cry from the derisive designation "yellow horde" that once described Asian immigrants at the turn of the twentieth century (Gans, 2005; Zhou, 2004).

While a number of immigrant groups have changed their status from non-White to White, African Americans have not been able to do the same. Gans (2005, pp. 19–20) referred to this as the pattern of "African American exceptionalism." He elaborates, "The only population whose racial features are not automatically perceived differently with upward mobility are African Americans: Those who are affluent and well educated remain as visibly Black to Whites as before." Warren and Twine (1997, p. 208) argued this is because the construction of "Whiteness" depends on the perceived existence of "Blackness." They note:

[B]ecause Blacks represent the "other" against which Whiteness is constructed, the back-door to Whiteness is open to non-Blacks. Slipping through the opening is, then, a tactical matter for non-Blacks of conforming to White standards, of distancing themselves from *Blackness*, and of reproducing anti-Black ideas and sentiments.

Others like Guinier and Torres (2002) also suggested that throughout the history of the United States, Blacks have served a critical role in the construction and expansion of Whiteness by serving as the definition of what White is not. Given the rigidity of the boundary surrounding blacks, some social scientists argue that a Black/non-Black divide is emerging, in which Asians and Latinos fall on the non-Black side of the divide. Consequently, a Black/non-Black model of racial/ethnic relations would entail Asians and Latinos falling closer to Whites than to Blacks in their experiences in the United States, suggesting that extent of multiraciality and multiracial identification should be similar for Asians and Latinos, but dissimilar to Blacks.

Research Findings Relevant to the Models of the Color Line

Recent research evidence suggests that Whiteness has continued to expand to incorporate new immigrant groups with Asians and Latinos now appearing to "blend" more easily with Whites than with Blacks (Gallagher, 2004; Gerstle, 1999; Warren & Twine, 1997). Furthermore, Gallagher (2004) argued that many Whites view Asians and Latinos as more culturally similar to them than to Blacks, and posits that the United States is currently undergoing a process of "racial redistricting," allowing Asians and Latinos (especially multiracials) to "glide easily" into the White category. Twine's research on multiracial identification reinforces this point; she found that the children of Black intermarriages are usually perceived by others as Black (Twine, 1996). By contrast, the children of Asian and Latino intermarriages are not similarly perceived monoracially as Asian or Latino. Studies of Asian-White multiracial youth show that they are equally likely to select White or Asian as the single category that best describes their racial background, pointing to the latitude such adolescents have in designating their own racial/ethnic heritage (Harris & Sim, 2002; Saenz, Hwang, Aguirre, & Anderson, 1995; Xie & Goyette, 1997). Similarly, multiethnic Mexican Americans exercise a great deal of choice in how they identify (Jiménez, 2004).

Other empirical studies of multiracial identification also report results relevant to the question of the nature of America's color lines today. Lee and Bean (2007) found that both census data and qualitative subjective interviews indicate that group boundaries appear to be fading more rapidly for Latinos and Asians than for Blacks, signaling that today's new non-Whites are not strongly assimilating as racialized minorities who see their experiences with race as akin to those of Blacks, as would be predicted by the White/non-White model. Moreover, these researchers argue that a triracial hierarchy model that would place Latinos and most new immigrants into the "collective Black" category and label them as "racial others" does not appear to characterize accurately the racialization process of America's non-White newcomers. Instead, both multiraciality and multiracial identification among Latinos and Asians appear consistent with hypotheses that place them closer to Whites than to Blacks. Moreover, that racial and ethnic affiliations and identities are much less matters of choice for multiracial Blacks indicate that Black remains a more salient racial category than others. The lower rate of Black multiracial reporting in census data and the racial constraints that many multiracial Blacks experience suggest that Blackness continues to constitute a fundamental racial construction in American society. Hence, it is not simply that race matters, but more specifically, that Black race matters, providing support for the African-American exceptionalism thesis. Such patterns strongly suggest that a Black/non-Black divide is taking shape, one in which Asians and Latinos fall closer to Whites to Blacks (Gans, 1999, 2005; Glazer, 1997; Lee & Bean, 2007; Quillian & Campbell, 2003; Sears, 2003; Sears, Fu, Henry, & Bui, 2003; Sears & Savalei, 2006; Waters, 1999; Yancey, 2003).

IMPLICATIONS

A pattern involving fading color lines for Asians and Latinos implies improvements in U.S. race relations. However, it also forebodes dangers. For one thing, it invites misinterpretation about progress in Black–White relations in the United States. Because boundaries are loosening for some non-White groups, many observers might erroneously conclude that race is declining in significance for all groups, and moreover, that race relations are improving at the same pace for all racial/ethnic minorities. However, the results of the research discussed above suggest that the social construction of race is more consequential for Blacks than for Asians and Latinos. Not accounting for this difference in research and the formulation of public policy could easily lead the endorsement of a flawed logic claiming that if race does not impede the process of incorporation for Asians and Latinos, then it must not matter much for Blacks either. Not only is this line of reasoning incorrect, it also risks fostering support for so-called "colorblind" policies that fail to recognize that race and the color line have different consequences for different minority groups (Brown et al., 2003; Loury, 2002). . . .

DISCUSSION QUESTIONS

1. What criteria do you use to define black?
2. What criteria do you use to define white?
3. If there is a third category, who can move from that category to white? Why?

REFERENCES

Alba, R. (1985). *Italian Americans: Into the twilight of ethnicity.* Englewood Cliffs, NJ: Prentice Hall.

Alba, R. (1990). *Ethnic identity: The transformation of White America.* New Haven, CT: Yale University Press.

Bean, F. D., & Beli-Rose, S. (1999). *Immigration and opportunity: Race, ethnicity and employment in the United States.* New York: Russell Sage.

Bean, F. D., & Stevens, G. (2003). *America's newcomers and the dynamics of diversity.* New York: Russell Sage Foundation.

Bonilla-Silva, E. (2004a). From bi-racial to tri-racial. *Ethnic and Racial Studies, 27,* 931–950.

Bonilla-Silva, E. (2004b). We are all Americans. *Race and Society, 5,* 3–16.

Brodkin, K. (1998). *How Jews became White folks, and what that says about race in America.* New Brunswick, NJ: Rutgers University Press.

Brown, M. K., Carnoy, M., Currie, E., Dusler, T., Oppenheimer, D. B., Shultz, M. M., & Wellman, D. (2003). *Whitewashing race: The myth of a color-blind society.* Berkeley: University of California Press.

Davis, D. B. (1998). A big business. *New York Review of Books, 45,* 50–53.

W. E. B. (1935). *Black reconstruction in America.* New York: Harcourt, Brace.

Fischer, C. S., & Hout, M. (2006). *Century of difference: How America changed in the last one hundred years,* New York: Russell Sage Foundation.

Forman, T., Goar, C., & Lewis, A. E. (2004). Neither black nor white? *Race and Society, 5,* 65–84.

Gallagher, C. A. (2004). Racial redistricting: Expanding the boundaries of whiteness. In H. M. Dalmage (Ed.), *The Politics of multiracialism: Challenging racial thinking* (pp. 59–76). Albany: State University of New York Press.

Gans, H. J. (1999). The possibility of a new racial hierarchy in the twenty-first century United States. In M. Lamont (Ed.), *The cultural territories of race: Black and white boundaries* (pp. 371–390). Chicago and New York: University of Chicago Press and Russell Sage Foundation.

Gans, H. J. (2005). Race as class. *Contexts, 4,* 17–21.

Gerstle, G. (1999). Liberty, coercion, and the making of Americans. In C. Hirschman, J. DeWind, & P. Kasinitz (Eds.), *The handbook of international migration* (pp. 275–293). New York: Russell Sage Foundation.

Gitlin, T. (1995). *The twilight of common dreams.* New York: Metropolitan.

Glazer, N. (1997). *We are all multiculturalists now.* Cambridge, MA: Harvard University Press.

Guinier, L., & Torres, G. (2002). *The miner's canary.* Cambridge, MA: Harvard University Press.

Haney-Lopez, I. (1996). *White by law: The legal construction of race.* New York: New York University Press.

Harris, D. R., & Sim. J. J. (2002). Who is multiracial? Assessing the complexity of lived race. *American Sociological Review, 67,* 614–627.

Hollinger, D. A. (2005). The one-drop rule and the one-hate rule. *Daedalus, 134,* 18–28.

Ignatiev, N. (1995). *How the Irish became White.* New York: Routledge.

Jacobson, M. F. (1998). *Whiteness of a different color: European immigrants and the alchemy of race.* Cambridge, MA: Harvard University Press.

Jiménez, T. (2004). Negotiating ethnic boundaries. *Ethnicities, 4,* 75–97.

Lee, J., & Bean, F. D. (2007). Reinventing the color line: Immigration and America's new racial/ethnic divide. *Social Forces, 86,* 561–586.

Loewen, J. (1971). *The Mississippi Chinese: Between black and white.* Cambridge, MA: Harvard University Press.

Loury, G. C. (2002). *The anatomy of racial inequality.* Cambridge, MA: Harvard University Press.

Murguia, E., & Saenz, R. (2004). An analysis of the Latinamericanization of race in the United States. *Race and Society, 5,* 85–101.

Pagnini, D. L., & Morgan, S. P. (1990). Intermarriage and social distance among U.S. immigrants at the turn of the century. *American Journal of Sociology, 96,* 405–432.

Perlmann, J., & Waldinger, R. (1997). Second generation decline? Children of immigrants, past and present—a reconsideration. *International Migration Review, 31,* 893–922.

Quillian, L., & Campbell, M. (2003). Beyond black and white. *American Sociological Review, 68,* 540–566.

Reimers, C. W. (1998). Unskilled immigration and changes in the wage distributions of black, Mexican American, and non-Hispanic White male dropouts. In D. S. Hamermesh & F. D. Bean (Eds.), *Help or hindrance? The economic implications of immigration for African Americans* (pp. 107–148). New York: Russell Sage Foundation.

Reimers, D. M. (1992). *Still the golden door: The third world comes to America.* New York: Columbia University Press.

Renn, K. A. (2009). Educational policy, politics, and mixed heritage students in the United States. *Journal of Social Issues, 65*(1), 163–181.

Rockquemore, K. A., Brunsma, D. L., & Delgado, D. J. (2009). Racing to theory or re-theorizing race? Understanding the struggle to build a multiracial identity theory. *Journal of Social Issues, 65*(1), 13–34.

Roediger, D. (1991). *The wages of whiteness.* New York: Verso.

Saenz, R., Hwang, S., Aguirre, B. E., & Anderson, R. N. (1995). Persistence and change in Asian identity among children of intermarried couples. *Sociological Perspectives, 38,* 175–194.

Sears, D. O. (2003). Black-White conflict. In D. Halle (Ed.), *New York & Los Angeles* (pp. 367–389). Chicago: University of Chicago Press.

Sears, D. O., Fu, M., Henry, P. J., & Bui, K. (2003). The origins and persistence of ethnic identity among the 'new immigrant' groups. *Social Psychology Quarterly, 66,* 419–437.

Sears, D. O., & Savalei, V. (2006). The political color line in America: Many "peoples of color" or Black exceptionalism? *Political Psychology, 27,* 895–924.

Skrentny, J. D. (2002). *The minority rights revolution.* Cambridge, MA: Harvard University Press.

Spickard, P. R. (1989). *Mixed blood: Intermarriage and ethnic identity in twentieth-century America.* Madison: University of Wisconsin Press.

Twine, F. W. (1996). Brown-skinned White girls. *Gender, Place, and Culture,* 3, 205–224.

Warren, J. W., & Twine, F. W. (1997). White Americans, the new minority? *Journal of Black Studies,* 28, 200–218.

Waters, M. C. (1990). *Ethnic options: choosing identities in America.* Berkeley: University of California Press.

Waters, M. C. (1999). *Black identities: West Indian immigrant dreams and American realities.* New York and Cambridge, MA: Russell Sage Foundation and Harvard University Press.

Xie, Y., & Goyette, K. (1997). The racial identification of biracial children with one Asian parent: Evidence from the 1990 census. *Social Forces, 76,* 547–570.

Yancey, G. (2003). *Who is White?* Boulder, CO: Lynne Rienner.

Zhou, M. (2004). Are Asian Americans becoming "White"? *Contexts, 3,* 29–37.

PERSONAL ACCOUNT

The Price of Nonconformity

I moved to the United States from Germany three years ago, and moved in with my American cousin and her family, which consists of her husband (who is Iranian) and two children, a boy and a girl. Things were going fine in the beginning, but then after three months I met my boyfriend and everything changed. Tony and I had been dating for about three weeks when I told my cousin I was seeing someone. She didn't seem to mind and just asked me to bring him over one night so she could meet him. A couple of days later, Tony stopped by the house to pick me up for dinner. We waited for my cousin to come home from her job, so they could be introduced. I will never forget the look on her face when she walked in the door and saw that Tony is black. Even though she contained herself quickly, it was obvious that she did not approve of this interracial relationship. For the next two months, she tried to keep me away from him by imposing curfews (I was 21 at the time), not allowing me to take the car, prohibiting him from coming into the house, ignoring him when he picked me up, and not talking to me when I was at home. All of this happened without her ever having to say that she didn't like him because he is black and I am white. But when all of her attempts to separate us failed, she had a talk with me that I will never forget.

She told me that I had no idea what I was getting myself into, and that a relationship between a black man and a white woman was unacceptable. Since we were from two different cultures—black vs. white—it would never work; our friends, family, and society would not accept it. Tony would never fit into my "white" life, and I would never fit into his "black" life. My friends would eventually turn away from me because I am with him, and also because the differences between my friends—who she assumed all to be white—and Tony would be insurmountable. Moreover, she was outraged that I would even consider having a black man's children. She said that my children would always be stigmatized as black children. They would suffer from prejudice and discrimination, and I was a terrible person for choosing that life for them.

So in the end, she gave me the choice of ending the relationship with Tony, or moving out. She said she could not allow such behavior in her house, since I was supposed to be a role model for her eleven-year-old daughter. She did not want her daughter to follow in my footsteps. Since I don't respond well to ultimatums, especially when they are as ridiculous and racist as this one, I packed my stuff and moved out shortly after this conversation.

Julia Morgenstern

PERSONAL ACCOUNT

Basketball

I frequently watch my boyfriend play basketball at an outdoor court with many other males in pick-up games. One time when I was there, there was a new face among the others waiting to play—a female face, and she was not sitting with the rest of the women who were watching. She was dressed and ready to play. I had never seen her in all the time I'd been there before, nor had I ever seen another woman there try to play.

For several games, she did not play. The guys formed teams and she was not asked to join. It was almost like there was a purposeful avoidance of her, with no one even acknowledging that she was there. Finally, she made a noticeable effort, and with some reluctance she was included in the next team waiting to play the winner of the current game. There were whispers and snickers among the guys, and I think it had a lot to do with the perception that she was challenging their masculinity. A "girl" was intruding into their area. My guess is that they were also somewhat nervous about the fact that she really might be good and embarrass some of them.

Anyway, the first couple of times up and down the court she was not given the ball despite the fact that she was wide open. The other guys on the team forced bad shots and tried super hard in what seemed like an effort to prove that she was not needed. The guy who was supposed to guard her on defense really didn't pay her much attention, and that same guy who she was guarding at the other end made sure he drove around her and scored on two occasions.

Finally, one time down the court she called for the ball and sank a shot from at least 16 feet. A huge feeling of relief and satisfaction came over me. Being a basketball player myself, I figured she was probably good or would not be there in the *first* place, but being a woman I was also happy to see her first shot go in. I found out later she had played basketball for a university and she had a great outside shot.

Even after she made one more shot off a rebound that ended up in her hands, she was not given the ball again. I suppose after some of the loud comments from some of the guys on the sidelines, that she was beating the male players out there, she wasn't going to get the ball again. I was kind of shocked that she wasn't *more* accepted even after she showed she was talented. I haven't seen her there since.

Andrea M. Busch

WHAT IS SEX? WHAT IS GENDER?

READING 9

The Olympic Struggle over Sex

Alice Dreger

What is sport ultimately for? That fundamental philosophical question lies behind the debate over what to do with women athletes who were raised as girls but whose bodies seem to be unusually masculine. And in that debate, two clear philosophical camps have emerged.

One camp, led by the International Olympic Committee (IOC), believes the line imposed between putative male and putative female athletes must be biological. These folks—let's call them the Anatomists—fully admit that sex is really complicated. They acknowledge there's no one magical gene, chromosome, hormone, or body part that can do for us the hard work of sharp division into male and female leagues. Says the IOC in its latest declaration on the problem: "Human biology [. . .] allows for forms of intermediate levels between the conventional categories of male and female, sometimes referred to as intersex."

Alice Dreger is a professor of clinical medical humanities and bioethics in the Feinberg School of Medicine at Northwestern University.

But the Anatomists still think we should base our sex division in sports on some sort of biological feature, even if it means we have to just pick one. They point out that sports require us to create all sorts of rules that aren't simply natural and self-evident, so why not do it here, too?

And so, the IOC . . . decided that, for the London Olympic Games, the rule of sex [would] be based on something called "functional androgens" (or "functional testosterone"). This means that an athlete who was raised a girl and identifies as a woman will be allowed to play as a woman so long as the IOC does not discover that her body makes and responds to high levels of androgens. Androgens, of which testosterone is one type, naturally occur in both male and female bodies, but higher production usually means more male-typical development.

Notice that the IOC won't just be looking at how much androgens a woman's body *makes,* but also how much her cells *respond.* This is because some women are born with testes that make a lot of testosterone, but they lack androgen-sensitive receptors, so the androgens have little-to-no effect on their cells. This condition is called complete Androgen Insensitivity Syndrome. Those who have it—women like Spanish hurdler Maria Patino—develop essentially as girls and women.

The new IOC policy isn't meant to pick out these women. The athletes who *are* targeted by this policy on "female hyperandrogenism" include women born with conditions that can result in masculinization—conditions including *partial* Androgen Insensitivity Syndrome and Congenital Adrenal Hyperplasia.

This hormone-honing approach to sex divisions in sports appalls the other camp, whom we might call the Identifiers. The Identifiers, led mostly by outsiders, believe the line between men and women athletes ought to be based in self-identity. The Identifiers take the messiness of sex development as a reason to give up on biology as the way to distinguish athletes by sex. They argue that, since the borders between sex categories are naturally open, we should not attempt to police them. Instead, we ought to go simply with an athlete's self-identity as

man or woman (only requiring, perhaps, that it be confirmed by her or his legal status).

Make no mistake: there are problems with the new IOC biologically-oriented policy. For one, the policy doesn't actually specify what *is* the permissible level of functional testosterone for women athletes. As a result, there is no way for a woman to get herself tested in private, in advance of the games, to see if she should avoid the possibility of being plucked out of play for a sex crime, so to speak. It also seems odd that apparently the committee isn't going to decide a level until they get a case. That's like writing a criminal law after you've arrested a suspect.

The new policy gives away another problem in its title: "IOC Regulations on *Female* Hyperandrogenism." Why specify "female"? Because the IOC is allowing male athletes to play with conditions that cause *them* to be hyperandrogenized—sometimes the very same conditions for which women will be disqualified! The result is that a woman's supposed disease is accepted by the IOC as a man's natural advantage. This hardly seems like a fair way to treat a lady, unless your goal is to keep her down.

Third, the policy appears to be out of whack with another IOC policy known as "the Stockholm Consensus," designed for dealing with male-to-female transsexual athletes. That policy requires transgender women—women who were raised as boys—to medically squash their androgen levels way down, seemingly well below where the policy on "female hyperandrogenism" would likely allow intersex women raised as girls to still play.

And whereas the female hyperandrogenism policy hints that a women with one of the "problem" intersex conditions might be chucked out if her medical records indicate she's benefitted from a lifetime of male-typical functional androgens, the Stockholm Consensus allows transgender women with those same lifetime androgen histories to play, so long as they have endocrinologically obeyed the IOC's rules for their womanhood for the previous couple of years.

In spite of these problems with the new IOC policy, and even though I fully support the right of any individual to self-identify socially as any gender she or he wishes, I find myself sympathetic to the Anatomists' philosophy in this case. Here's why:

Our history of liberal democracy demonstrates a grand trend with regard to the relationship between anatomy and identity, and that is the trend *away* from using anatomy to draw distinctions in identities where social and political rights are concerned. The Founding Fathers started this trend by challenging the idea that power must derive from bloodline. The women's rights movement, the civil rights movement, the disability rights movement—all have successfully dismantled the idea that anatomical difference should mean some people are treated as more worthy of rights and resources than others. As Drs. King and Seuss taught us, in a just and rational world, having a star on your belly doesn't make you special.

Sport has been used as one way to push this liberalizing agenda—with Title IX and major league racial integration standing as two good examples of the push. The Identifiers are now trying to do the same thing in the debate on sex testing, and in doing so, are making what might be the most extreme version of the anti-anatomy argument: we should not bother thinking about sex anatomy *at all,* and just let anyone who says she's a woman play as a woman.

But maybe here we've finally hit the limit of using sport for this kind of social agenda. I mean, sure, we could do it—we could force sport to keep being the Joan of Arc of liberal democracy, and so we could decide common biological sex differences don't matter to gender divisions in sports. But if we do this, in the process we may be neutering sport itself.

Because at the end of the day, no matter how little we think anatomy should matter to one's social and political rights, surely we can't pretend biology doesn't matter in sports. Surely there's a reason we don't let adults play in the t-ball leagues, and a reason most women athletes want their own leagues.

And much as the IOC might try to make it sound like the Olympic Games represent the ultimate peace-and-justice movement on Earth, we're not actually talking about law and justice. We're talking about *games*—games that have, as their necessary condition, bodies with bodily differences.

So, much as I am drawn, as a good political progressive, to the position of the Identifiers who want to just let athletes self-declare genders, and as frustrated as I am that the IOC still doesn't have an adequately clear policy on intersex—nor one consistent with its policy on transsexualism—part of me feels like we have to admit that the Anatomists are acting more true to the game.

Does that make me a traitor to progressivism—acknowledging that people have some biological differences, such that some people have natural advantages or disadvantages in some realms of life? I don't think so. I know the Identifiers seem to fear that if we acknowledge any average differences between males and females, progress in women's rights and transgender rights will collapse. But I think we are actually mature enough, as a species, to know what is a game, and what is not.

DISCUSSION QUESTIONS

1. Which side of the Anatomist/Identifier debate do you find yourself most sympathetic to?
2. Which side do you think should prevail in Olympic competitions or other sports competitions?
3. Do Olympic Committee determinations about sex have any bearing beyond the Games?

READING 10

All Together Now: Intersex Infants and IGM

Riki Wilchins

"There is nothing abstract about the power that sciences and theories have to act materially and actually upon our bodies and our minds, even if the discourse

Riki Wilchins is the founding executive director of the Gender Public Advocacy Coalition.

that produces it is abstract. It is one of the forms of domination, its very expression."

Monique Wittig, *The Straight Mind*

BODIES AT THE MARGINS

As Foucault once pointed out, the effects of discursive power are hard to see once a discourse is in place. Once we *see* gay, black, female, or transgender people, it's hard to imagine that they weren't always there. We imagine the cultural discourse about them just popped up in response; rather, it was the discourse that created such identities in the first place.

To clearly see discursive power at work, we need bodies at society's margins. Margins are margins because that's where the discourse begins to fray, where whatever paradigm we're in starts to lose its explanatory power and all those inconvenient exceptions begin to cause problems.

We can see the marginalization of such bodies as evidence of their unimportance. Or we can see their marginalization as important evidence of the model's imperfection and begin to admit how the operations of language, knowledge, and truth have shaped our consciousness.

Once we might have turned to women, gays, transgender people, or even racial minorities for this kind of understanding. But as each of these groups has won greater or lesser degrees of social legitimacy, it has become necessary to look a little further out to find a really marginal, inconvenient body. We need a body that is still off the grid of cultural intelligibility, one that hasn't "set" yet into a socially recognized identity. What we need, of course, is a *herm*.

Cheryl Chase is a "true hermaphrodite." This is a very rare thing, since most intersex people are "only" pseudo-hermaphrodites.

When most people hear the word *hermaphrodite,* they're apt to think of a person born with "both sets of genitals," although this is actually impossible. *Hermaphrodite* is actually an archaic medical term, and the correct term is *intersex*.

According to Brown University medical researcher Dr. Anne Fausto-Sterling, one in every 2,000 births is intersex. As intersex activists say, these are children born with unexpected genitals, which is to say their genitals are perhaps worse, maybe better, or at least every bit as good as yours and mine (well, *yours* anyway).

Cheryl founded the Intersex Society of North America (ISNA), a national intersex advocacy group, and cofounded (with me) Hermaphrodites With Attitude—an intersex protest group, in itself a pretty rare thing. I just call her the Head Herm.

CONSTRUCTING CHERYL

"Cheryl" was born as "Charlie," a fairly happy, well-adjusted little boy. His doctor, however, was not as happy or well-adjusted.

For one thing, it must be admitted that Charlie had a pretty small penis. For another, Charlie had "ovaries" that contained both testicular and ovarian tissue.

Language is again a crucial issue here, especially at the margins, where labeling is the first discursive act that determines how a thing is seen and understood. For instance, if a boy has an ovary, is it still an ovary, especially if it also contains significant amounts of testicular tissue, as Cheryl's did? Medicine gives us no nonbinary options here, although the term *gonad* would do nicely enough.

Charlie was a year and a half old when—after tests, consultations, and diagnostic conferences— doctors decided that Charlie was actually a Cheryl. This meant his small penis was actually an abnormally large clitoris. So they cut it off.

Following the treatment protocols for a diagnosis of intersexuality, all evidence of Charlie's existence was hidden. Boy's clothes and toys were thrown out and replaced with girl's clothes and toys. Out blue, in pink.

Cheryl/Charlie's parents were warned to lie to her if he ever asked about her history, because the truth—intersexuality and surgery—would permanently traumatize the child. Doctors feared that acknowledging a history of intersexuality would undermine the sense of gender identity they had created in the child through secrecy and surgery.

Charlie had become Cheryl, but at an enormous price. The operation had removed a lot what the doctors thought was Charlie, but it also removed most of his erotic sensation, and along with it baby Cheryl's future ability to have an orgasm.

THE ABC'S OF IGM

"Intersexuality is a psychiatric emergency on the part of the doctors and parents, who treat it by cutting into the body of the infant, even though the adults—as the ones in distress—are the real patients."

Cheryl Chase

"The Academy is deeply concerned about the *emotional, cognitive, and body image* development of intersexuals, and believes that successful early genital surgery minimizes these issues."

Press Release on IGM from the American Academy of Pediatricians (emphasis added)

"Knowledge is not made for understanding; it is made for cutting."

Michel Foucault, *Language, Counter-Memory*

The surgical procedure Cheryl underwent is sometimes referred to as intersex genital mutilation. IGM refers to cosmetic genital cutting that is performed solely to make intersex infants resemble normal males and females. The definition of IGM does not include the small fraction of surgeries that are preformed to cure functional abnormalities, urinary obstructions, recurring infection, and so on.

It was not until the 1950s that IGM became a common pediatric practice. Prior to that, unless infants were born with genital deformities that caused ongoing pain or endangered their health, they were left alone. Today, according to Fausto-Sterling, about 1,000 infants are surgically altered for cosmetic reasons each year in U.S. hospitals, or about five every day.

Advocacy organizations like ISNA and Gender-PAC do not advocate raising intersex children without a sex, which is a social impossibility anyway, at least right now. They do advocate forgoing permanent genital alteration of infants for strictly cosmetic reasons until they have grown old enough to participate in life-altering decisions about their own bodies and sexual health, and to offer informed consent.

LANGUAGE AS THE REAL

A pediatric nurse in one of my presentations complained, "But you don't mention all these tests we run to find out the infant's real sex." The discourse on intersex infants is concerned with discovering what binary sex they "really" are, so we can "fix" them properly. The possibility that intersex infants' sex might not be immediately available to us, that they might not have the sort of binary sex the doctors are so anxious to locate and assign, just doesn't register. Neither does the possibility that intersex bodies have nothing to tell us, or that these infants are whatever sex they are because that nonbinary outcome appears to the medical community (and indeed to most of society) as a logical impossibility.

As Cheryl notes, intersex is the sex that doesn't exist. First because it's always another sex "underneath" and, second, because as soon as it appears, we erase it. Whatever sex we "discover" in intersex infants' bodies is highly dependent upon what markers we choose—hormones, genitals, overall body structure, chromosomes, and gonads—and how we prioritize them.

Words are real; bodies are not.

There is no pretext of transparency here: We don't fit the words to the bodies; instead, it is the bodies that must fit the words. The only language we have for herm-bodies is directed toward pathologizing—and thereby delegitimating—them.

Nor can we raise the usual argument—"It's Nature's way"—when Sex is questioned. Clearly, Nature has other things in mind, even if we don't.

In this vein, I once tried to help a network producer who was searching for an intersex person to interview. He was interested only in one who had been surgically misassigned the "wrong sex." Our conversation went like this:

Producer: We're looking for someone whose sex was misassigned and who was then raised as the wrong sex, like John/Joan.

Me: How do we know if it was the wrong sex?

Producer: If they were really male but assigned female, or really female but assigned male.

Me: Okay. But what if they were really intersex?

Producer: Right. I get your point. But we're looking for someone who was misassigned.

Me: But if they're really intersex, then any assignment would be a misassignment.

Producer: Right. I get your point. Really.

Me: Why don't you interview Cheryl Chase? She/he's well known and very articulate.

Producer: Cheryl was misassigned?

Me: Yes. She/he was raised as a boy, then they decided she/he was a girl.

Producer: So she's really male?

Me: No, she/he's really Cheryl.

Producer: Right. I get it. I really do. But she's really a girl, right?

Me: Well, to me she/he looks like a woman, but do you mean hair, hormones, chromosomes, or genitals?

Producer: You know. Her *real* sex.

Me: Cheryl's real sex is intersex.

Producer: Uh-huh. I get it, honest. But can you give me an intersex person who was misassigned?

DISCOURSE: A PRACTICE WITH EFFECTS

Cheryl/Charlie had no say in what was done to him/her, nor had she/he complained that anything was wrong with him/her. The doctors and nurses involved were not spiteful or intolerant. On the contrary, they were dedicated healers, trained in pediatrics and deeply committed to Cheryl/Charlie's

well-being. IGM is always considered compassionate surgery. Everything was done for his/her "own good."

Cheryl's mutilation did not result from the top-down power held by big institutions. Unlike that reliable villain, the State, the power involved was not that of repression and negation, so common when sex is involved. In fact, the discourse of Sex where Cheryl was involved did not *restrain* her Sex, but rather interpreted it, compelled it, and *demanded* it.

Her transformation from Charlie to Cheryl was carried out in a micro-politics of power: small, impersonal judgments and practices that involved myriad individuals, power that was held by no one in particular but exercised by practically everyone—except, of course, Charlie.

The power involved was productive, using language and meaning to interpret her genitals as defective, to produce her body as intersexed, and to require that she be understood through a lens of normal male and normal female. Through a series of silences and erasures, it socially produced a new person, one with a new name, history, wardrobe, bedroom decor, and toys.

This is not the familiar "big stick" approach to power that requires policemen, courts, and legislatures. That is something we are familiar with; at least it is something we know how to fight. The power that attached itself to Charlie's body is a different kind of power entirely, one we have little experience in dealing with, let alone have strategies to counter.

The Science involved in Charlie's surgery was also of a different order than we are accustomed to. That Science is logical, objective, and impartial. But the Science that has attached itself to herm-bodies is not disinterested at all, but rather interested in the most urgent way with preserving the universality of Sex and with defending society's interest in reproduction. In fact, one of IGM's basic rules is that any infant who might one day be able to become pregnant as an adult must be made into a female.

This kind of Science is characterized by a deliberate nonknowing, by its refusal to recognize the most obvious facts of the infant bodies before it. It is remarkable for its sturdy denial of any facts or interpretations that might contradict its own intentions.

THE SCIENCE OF SEX: PARTIAL, PASSIONATE, POLITICAL

Medical theories of Sex, like so much of theory, are concerned with the resolution and management of difference. Intersex infants represent one of society's most anxious fears—the multiplicity of Sex, the pinging under the binary hood, a noise in the engine of reproduction that must be located and silenced.

This kind of Science is not limited to bodies. Its psychiatric counterpart is called Gender Identity Disorder, or GID. GID does for insubordinate genders what IGM does for insubordinate genitals.

In GID, noncomplaining children as young as 3 and as old as 18 are made to undergo treatment that includes behavioral modification, confinement to psychiatric wards, and psychotropic medication, all because they transcend binary gender norms and/or cross-gender identify. These treatment measures are intended to help the child fit back into a defined gender role.

In many cases the psychiatrists who treat GID believe that norm-transcending "sissy boys" and "tomboy girls" are more likely to grow up to be gay, and GID treatment is designed to prevent homosexuality in adults. Yet gay activists largely ignore GID because they represent gay and lesbian Americans, and a 3-year-old doesn't have that kind of identity yet.

Of course the effort to regulate gender in children is not limited to those "at the margins." We have a host of social practices designed to masculinize boys and feminize girls that start at birth. For instance, infants who cry are more likely to be described as angry by adults who think they are boys, sad if they think they are girls. Caregivers are more likely to stroke and caress babies if they think they are girls and to bounce them if they think they are boys.

Up until a few years ago, the U.S. government was funding research into the best treatments for norm-transcending kids. Tax dollars were appropriated to pay for a new sort of knowledge manipulation: the prevention of "sissy boys." This has helped fuel a new counterscience devoted to providing biological basis for homosexuality. Our power *over* such bodies is enabled by the kinds of knowledge we create *about* them.

By asserting that the knowledge and language we create is transparent and objective, we confer enormous authority to it. We insulate it from criticism and deny its political origins; we justify excesses that might otherwise be unthinkable. At the margins, Science no longer asks but tells. Nature no longer speaks the truth, but is spoken to. Here, where our narrative of Sex breaks down, Knowledge finally bares its teeth.

IS IDENTITY POLITICS PERMANENTLY TROUBLED?

Cheryl can be understood as a genitally mutilated female, a genitally mutilated male, a transgender individual, an intersex individual, a man who sleeps with women, a woman who sleeps with women, or even a man with a vagina. This proved to be a real obstacle when Cheryl dealt with identity-based groups.

When we approached the board of a national women's organization for help, the organization's representatives responded that IGM was a terrible practice, and someone should stop it. But why, they wanted to know, was IGM a women's issue?

We pointed out that the overwhelming majority of infants diagnosed as "intersex" are otherwise unremarkable children whose clitorises happen to be larger than two standard deviations from the mean—an arbitrary measure equal to about three eighths of an inch. It turns out birth sex is like a menu. If your organ is less than three eighths of an inch long, it's a clitoris and you're a baby girl. If it's longer than an inch, it's a penis and you're a baby boy.

It is a startling example of the power of language, knowledge, and science to create bodies to realize that, if pediatricians agreed to increase this rule to, say, three standard deviations from the mean, thousands of intersex infants would be instantly "cured."

On the other hand, if they decided to decrease it to one-and-a half standard deviations, one third to half of the female readers of this book would suddenly find themselves intersexed, and therefore candidates for genital surgery.

But if it's in between, you're a baby herm: The organ is an enlarged clit, and it gets cut off. The pediatrician will apologetically explain to your parents that you were born genitally "deformed," but—through the miracle of modern Science—they can make you into a "normal little girl."

Of course, this never happens in reverse. No pediatrician will ever apologetically explain to your parents that, "I'm afraid your son's penis is going to be too big, maybe eight or nine inches long. No one will ever be attracted to him but homosexuals and oversexed women. If we operate quickly we can save him."

To help board members of the women's organization to understand, I showed them how to make a diagnosis. Holding up a thumb and forefinger about a quarter inch apart, I said, "female." Moving them about three-eighths of an inch apart, I said "intersex." I repeated this finger movement from "female" to "intersexed" over and over until heads began to nod.

Since many intersex infants were "really" women, this made IGM a women's issue. The board members even accepted Cheryl—a true hermaphrodite if ever there was one—as a woman.

Unfortunately, several board members insisted that since they were a women's group, I had to articulate everything in terms of "intersex" girls, a term with no meaning that contradicted everything I was trying to tell them.

Flushed with success, I asked a gathering of national gay organizations for their support on IGM, too. After what I thought was an impassioned presentation, they all agreed that IGM was a terrible practice and someone should stop it. But why, they wanted to know, was IGM a gay and lesbian issue? I pointed out that many intersex infants are heterosexualized as infants, surgically altered simply to ensure their bodies can accommodate a penis during intercourse.

Even worse, some doctors perform IGM out of the antique fear that girls with large clits (which no man likes) will repel potential husbands (which every woman needs), interfere with penetration (which every woman enjoys), and increase their chance of growing up to be masculinized lesbian women (which practically no woman wants to be). IGM was no longer an intersex issue or even a women's issue; it had become a gay issue.

I decided to cap my success by addressing a meeting of transgender organizations. Gender-queerness was their beat. This would be a walk in the park. And it was. They understood IGM right away. It was, they all agreed, a terrible practice, that someone should stop. But why, they wanted to know, was IGM a transgender issue?

Soft-pedaling Cheryl's identities as intersex, female, or lesbian, I focused like a laser on gender stereotypes. I pointed out that Cheryl had changed from one sex to another: She was transgender. Even more, IGM was a tell-tale example of enforcing exactly the kind of rigid, narrow, outdated gender stereotypes that hurt transgender people. In addition, a significant minority of transsexuals have some sort of organ development (such as hormonal imbalances and small or partial gonads) that could easily have gotten them diagnosed as intersex.

After extended discussion, IGM became a transgender issue.

Of course, none of these groups was ill intentioned or predisposed toward excluding intersex issues and IGM. They were all progressive, committed, and compassionate. Yet if national feminist groups even suspected that doctors performed clitoridectomies on thousands of baby girls each year, they would try to shut down hospitals across the country. If gay rights activists suspected that doctors were using hormones and surgery to erase thousands of potential lesbians each year, queer activists would be demonstrating in the halls of hospitals and lobbying in the halls of Congress.

But none of these scenarios have happened, all because an arbitrary definition means that these infants aren't female or possibly lesbian or even transgender. They're this other thing called intersex, which is not an issue for women or gays or transgender people; it's a medical issue. Presented with an enormously damaging and barbaric practice that harms thousands of kids, no group was able to embrace IGM as an issue. The rules of identity meant that intersex infants—the noise in the system—didn't fit. . . .

DISCUSSIONS QUESTIONS

1. What are particular words, phrases, and concepts that especially contribute to the "need" for genital surgery?
2. Would you agree that the genital surgeries Wilchins describes are for cosmetic reasons?

READING 11

Delusions of Gender: How Our Minds, Society, and Neurosexism Create Difference

Cordelia Fine

If you're ever feeling bored and aimless in a shopping mall, try this experiment. Visit ten children's clothing stores, and each time approach a salesperson saying that you are looking for a present for a newborn. Count how many times you are asked, "Is it a boy or a girl?" You are likely to have a 100 percent hit rate if you try this one spare afternoon. It is so ubiquitous now to dress and accessorize boys and girls differently, from birth, that it is easy to forget to wonder why we do this or to ask what children themselves might make of

Cordelia Fine, professor at the University of Melbourne, is an academic psychologist and writer.

this rigidly adhered-to code. And it is a rigid code. I recently stood in a clothing store, paralyzed with indecision as I deliberated which sleeper to choose for a friend's new baby girl. The cutest one had little honking cars on it. Yet even though my friend lives in England, rather than Saudi Arabia, I just couldn't choose it. I knew that if my friend ever did put her baby in that sleeper (rather than just toss it in the Goodwill pile thinking, The sooner Cordelia finishes that book on gender the better . . .), she would spend the rest of the day correcting strangers who congratulated her on her beautiful baby boy.

And well before dinnertime she would have learned that you can dress babies in clothing intended for the other sex or you can avoid being looked at as if you were insane, but you cannot do both. And yet this dress code for young children, despite being so strict, is a relatively recent phenomenon. Until the end of the nineteenth century, even five-year-old children were being dressed in more-or-less unisex white dresses, according to sociologist Jo Paoletti. The introduction of colored fabrics for young children's clothing marked the beginning of the move toward our current pink-blue labeling of gender, but it took nearly half a century for the rules to settle into place. For a time, pink was preferred for boys, because it was "a decided and stronger" color, a close relative to red, symbolizing "zeal and courage." Blue, being "more delicate and dainty" and "symbolic of faith and constancy" was reserved for girls. Only toward the middle of the twentieth century did existing practices become fixed.[1]

Yet so thoroughly have these preferences become ingrained that psychologists and journalists now speculate on the genetic and evolutionary origins of gendered color preferences that are little more than fifty years old.[2] For example, a few years ago an article in an Australian newspaper discussed the origins of the pink princess phenomenon. After trotting out the ubiquitous anecdote about the mother who tried and failed to steer her young daughter away from the pink universe, the journalist writes that the mother's failure "suggests her daughter was perhaps genetically wired that way" and asks, "is there a pink princess gene that suddenly blossoms when little girls turn two?" Just in case we mistake for a joke the idea that evolution might have weeded out toddlers uninterested in tiaras and pink tulle, the journalist then turns to prominent child psychologist Dr. Michael Carr-Gregg for further insight into the biological basis of princess mania: "The reason why girls like pink is that their brains are structured completely differently to boys," he sagely informs us. "Part of the brain that processes emotion and part of the brain that processes language is one and the same in girls but is completely different in boys." (Now where have we heard that before?) "This explains so much—you can give a girl a truck and she'll cuddle it. You can give a boy a Barbie doll and he'll rip its head off."[3]

But what is also overlooked is *why,* according to Paoletti, children's fashions began to change. Dresses for boys older than two years old began to fall out of favor toward the end of the nineteenth century. This was not mere whim, but seemed to be in response to concerns that masculinity and femininity might not, after all, inevitably unfurl from deep biological roots. At the same time that girls were being extended more parental license to be physically active, child psychologists were warning that "gender distinctions could be taught and must be." Some pants, please, for the boys. After the turn of the century, psychologists became more aware of just how sensitive even infants are to their environments. As a result, "[t]he same forces that had altered the clothing styles of preschoolers—anxiety about shifting gender roles and the emerging belief that gender could be taught—also transformed infantswear."[4]

In other words, color-coding for boys and girls once quite openly served the purpose of helping young children learn gender distinctions. Today, the original objective behind the convention has been forgotten. Yet it continues to accomplish exactly that, together with other habits we have that also draw children's attention to gender, as a number of developmental psychologists have insightfully argued.[5]

Imagine, for a moment, that we could tell at birth (or even before) whether a child was left-handed or right-handed. By convention, the parents of left-handed babies dress them in pink clothes, wrap them in pink blankets, and decorate their rooms with pink hues. The left-handed baby's bottle, bibs, and pacifiers—and later, cups, plates, and utensils, lunch box, and backpack—are often pink or purple with motifs such as butterflies, flowers, and fairies. Parents tend to let the hair of left-handers grow long, and while it is still short in babyhood a barrette or bow (often pink) serves as a stand-in. Right-handed babies, by contrast, are never dressed in pink; nor do they ever have pink accessories or toys. Although blue is a popular color for right-handed babies, as they get older any color, excluding pink or purple, is acceptable. Clothing and other items for right-handed babies and children commonly portray vehicles, sporting equipment, and space rockets; never butterflies, flowers, or fairies. The hair of right-handers is usually kept short and is never prettified with accessories.

Nor do parents just segregate left- and right-handers symbolically, with color and motif, in our imaginary world. They also distinguish between them verbally. "Come on, left-handers!" cries out the mother of two left-handed children in the park. "Time to go home." Or they might say, "Well, go and ask that right-hander if you can have a turn on the swing now." At playgroup, children overhear comments like, "Left-handers love drawing, don't they," and "Are you hoping for a right-hander this time?" to a pregnant mother. At preschool, the teacher greets them with a cheery, "Good morning, left-handers and right-handers." In the supermarket, a father says proudly in response to a polite enquiry, "I've got three children altogether: one left-hander and two right-handers."

And finally, although left-handers and right-handers happily live together in homes and communities, children can't help but notice that elsewhere they are often physically segregated. The people who care for them—primary caregivers, child care workers, and kindergarten teachers, for example—are almost all left-handed, while building sites and garbage trucks are peopled by right-handers. Public restrooms, sports teams, many adult friendships, and even some schools, are segregated by handedness.

You get the idea.

It's not hard to imagine that, in such a society, even very young children would soon learn that there are two categories of people—right-handers and left-handers—and would quickly become proficient in using markers like clothing and hairstyle to distinguish between the two kinds of children and adults. But also, it seems more than likely that children would also come to think that there must be something fundamentally important about whether one is a right-hander or a left-hander, since so much fuss and emphasis is put on the distinction. Children will, one would imagine, want to know what it means to be someone of a particular handedness and to learn what sets apart a child of one handedness from those with a preference for the other hand.

We tag gender in exactly these ways, all of the time. Anyone who spends time around children will know how rare it is to come across a baby or child whose sex is not labeled by clothing, hairstyle, or accessories. Anyone with ears can hear how adults constantly label gender with words: *he, she, man, woman, boy, girl,* and so on. And we do this even when we don't have to. Mothers reading picture books, for instance, choose to refer to storybook characters by gender labels (like *woman*) twice as often as they choose nongendered alternatives (like *teacher* or *person*).[6] Just as if adults were always referring to people as left-handers or right-handers (or Anglos and Latinos, or Jews and Catholics), this also helps to draw attention to gender as an important way of dividing up the social world into categories.

This tagging of gender—especially different conventions for male and female dress, hairstyle, accessories, and use of makeup—may well help children to learn how to divvy up the people around them by sex. We've seen that babies as young as three to four months old can discriminate between males and females. At just ten months old, babies

have developed the ability to make mental notes regarding what goes along with being male or female: they will look longer, in surprise, at a picture of a man with an object that was previously only paired with women, and vice versa.[7] This means that children are well-placed, early on, to start learning the gender ropes. As they approach their second birthday, children are already starting to pick up the rudiments of gender stereotyping. There's some tentative evidence that they know for whom fire hats, dolls, makeup, and so on are intended before their second birthday.[8] And at around this time, children start to use gender labels themselves and are able to say to which sex they themselves belong.[9]

It's at this critical point in their toddler years that children lose their status as objective observers. It is hard to merely dispassionately note what is for boys and what is for girls once you realize that you are a boy (or a girl) yourself. Once children have personally relevant boxes in which to file what they learn (labeled "Me" versus "Not Me"), this adds an extra oomph to the drive to solve the mysteries of gender.[10] Developmental psychologists Carol Martin and Diane Ruble suggest that children become "gender detectives," in search of clues as to the implications of belonging to the male or female tribe.[11] Nor do they wait for formal instruction. The academic literature is scattered with anecdotal reports of preschoolers' amusingly flawed scientific accounts of gender difference:

> [O]ne child believed that men drank tea and women drank coffee, because that was the way it was in his house. He was thus perplexed when a male visitor requested coffee. Another child, dangling his legs with his father in a very cold lake, announced "only boys like cold water, right Dad?" Such examples suggest that children are actively seeking and "chewing" on information about gender, rather than passively absorbing it from the environment.[12]

In fact, young children are so eager to carve up the world into what is female and what is male that Martin and Ruble have reported finding it difficult to create stimuli for their studies that children see as gender neutral, "because children appear to seize on any element that may implicate a gender norm so that they may categorize it as male or female."[13] For instance, when creating characters from outer space for children, it proved difficult to find colors and shapes that didn't signify gender. Even something as subtle as the shape of the head could indicate gender in the eyes of the children: aliens with triangular heads, for example, were seen as male.[14] (Later, we'll see why.) And experimental studies bear out children's propensity to jump to Men Are from Mars, Women Are from Venus-style conclusions on rather flimsy evidence. Asked to rate the appeal of a gender-neutral toy (which girls and boys on average like the same amount), boys assume that only other boys will like what they themselves like; ditto for girls.[15]

It's hardly surprising that children take on the unofficial occupation of gender detective. They are born into a world in which gender is continually emphasized through conventions of dress, appearance, language, color, segregation, and symbols. Everything around the child indicates that whether one is male or female is a matter of great importance. At the same time . . . the information we provide to children, through our social structure and media, about what gender means—what goes with being male or female—still follows fairly old-fashioned guidelines.

DISCUSSION QUESTIONS

1. Fine describes the historical change in fashion that followed anxiety about shifting gender roles. Are there contemporary equivalents?
2. Do you think the emphasis on gender difference in clothing for children is diminishing?
3. How do you assess Fine's comparison of gender with being left- or right-handed?

NOTES

1. "What color for your baby?" *Parents'* 14, no. 3 (March 1939), p. 98. Quoted in (Paoletti, 1997), p. 32.
2. (Hurlbert & Ling, 2007; Alexander, 2003).
3. (Lawson, 2007). Quotations from paras. 4, 5, 8, 8, and 10, respectively.
4. (Paoletti, 1997), pp. 30 and 31.

5. The salience of gender in the social world, and the active role played by the child in gender development that the salience and importance of gender motivates, has been highlighted by a number of researchers, for example (Arthur et al., 2008; Bem, 1983; Bigler & Liben, 2007; Martin & Halverson, 1981). The material that follows all draws on the insights of Gender Schema Theory and especially Developmental Intergroup Theory.
6. (Gelman, Taylor, & Naguyen, 2004).
7. (Levy & Haaf, 1994).
8. For example (Serbin, Poulin-Dubois, & Eichstedt, 2002), also (Poulin-Dubois et al., 2002), who found that knowledge was seen earlier in girls than in boys.
9. (Zosuls et al., 2009).
10. (Martin, Ruble, & Szkrybalo, 2002; Martin & Halverson, 1981).
11. (Martin & Ruble, 2004), p. 67.
12. (Ruble, Lurye, & Zosuls, 2008), p. 2.
13. (Martin & Ruble, 2004), p. 68.
14. Carol Martin, personal communication, September 9, 2009.
15. (Martin, Eisenbud, & Rose, 1995).

BIBLIOGRAPHY

Arthur, A. E., Bigler, R. S., Liben, L. S., Gelman, S. A., & Ruble, D. N. (2008). Gender stereotyping and prejudice in young children: A developmental intergroup perspective. In S. R. Levy & M. Killen (eds.), *Intergroup attitudes and relations in childhood through adulthood* (pp. 66–86). Oxford: Oxford University Press.

Bem, S. L. (1983). Gender schema theory and its implications for child development: Raising gender-aschematic children in a gender-schematic society. *SIGNS: Journal of Women in Culture & Society,* 8(4), 598–616.

Bigler, R. S., & Liben, L. S. (2007). Developmental intergroup theory: Explaining and reducing children's social stereotyping and prejudice. *Current Directions in Psychological Science,* 16(3), 162–166.

Fine, Cordelia (2011-08-08). *Delusions of Gender: How Our Minds, Society, and Neurosexism Create Difference.* Norton. Kindle Edition.

Gelman, S. A., Taylor, M. G., & Naguyen, S. P. (2004). III. How children and mothers express gender essentialism. *Monographs of the Society for Research in Child Development,* 69(1), 33–63.

Hurlbert, A. C., & Ling, Y. (2007). Biological components of sex differences in color preference. *Current Biology,* 17(16), R623–R625.

Lawson, A. (2007, May 23). The princess gene. *The Age,* 18.

Levy, G. D., & Haaf, R. A. (1994). Detection of gender-related categories by 10-month-old infants. *Infant Behavior & Development,* 17(4), 457–459.

Martin, C. L., Eisenbud, L., & Rose, H. (1995). Children's gender-based reasoning about toys. *Child Development,* 66(5), 1453–1471.

Martin, C. L., & Halverson, C. F. (1981). A schematic processing model of sex typing and stereotyping in children. *Child Development,* 52, 1119–1134.

Martin, C. L., & Ruble, D. (2004). Children's search for gender cues: Cognitive perspectives on gender development. *Current Directions in Psychological Science,* 13(2), 67–70.

Martin, C.L., Ruble, D. N., & Szkrybalo, J. (2002). Cognitive theories of early gender development. *Psychological Bulletin,* 128(6), 903–933.

Paoletti, J. B. (1997). The gendering of infants' and toddlers' clothing in America. In K. Martinez & K. L. Ames (eds.), *The material culture of gender: The gender of material culture* (pp. 27–35). Hanover, NH, and London: University Press of New England.

Poulin-Dubois, D., Serbin, L. A., Eichstedt, J. A., Sen, M. G., & Beissel, C. F. (2002). Men don't put on make-up: Toddlers' knowledge of the gender stereotyping of household activities. *Social Development,* 11(2), 166–181.

Ruble, D., Lurye, L., & Zosuls, K. (2008). Pink frilly dresses (PFD) and early gender identity [Electronic Version]. Princeton Report on Knowledge. http://www.princeton.edu/prok/issues/2-2/pink_frilly.xml. Accessed on April 23, 2008.

Serbin, L. A., Poulin-Dubois, D., & Eichstedt, J. A. (2002). Infants' responses to gender-inconsistent events. *Infancy,* 3(4), 531–542.

Zosuls, K. M., Ruble, D. N., Tamis-LeMonda, C. S., Shrout, P. E., Bornstein, M. H., & Greulich, F. K. (2009). The acquisition of gender labels in infancy: Implications for sex-typed play. *Developmental Psychology,* 45(3), 688–701.

WHAT IS SOCIAL CLASS?

READING 12

What's Class Got to Do with It?

Michael Zweig

Whether in regard to the economy or issues of war and peace, class is central to our everyday lives. Yet class has not been as visible as race or gender, not nearly as much a part of our conversations and sense of ourselves as these and other "identities." We are of course all individuals, but our individuality and personal life chances are shaped—limited or enhanced—by the economic and social class in which we have grown up and in which we exist as adults.

Even though "class" is an abstract category of social analysis, class is real. Since social abstractions can seem far removed from real life, it may help to consider two other abstractions that have important consequences for flesh-and-blood individuals: race and gender. Suppose you knew there

Michael Zweig is a professor of economics at the State University of New York, Stony Brook.

were men and women because you could see the difference, but you didn't know about the socially constructed concept of "gender." You would be missing something vitally important about the people you see. You would have only a surface appreciation of their lives. If, based only on direct observation of skin color, you knew there were white people and black people, but you didn't know about "race" in modern society, you would be ignorant of one of the most important determinants of the experience of those white and black people. Gender and race are abstractions, yet they are powerful, concrete influences in everyone's lives. They carry significant meaning despite wide differences in experience within the populations of men, women, whites, blacks.

Similarly, suppose that based on your observation of work sites and labor markets you knew there were workers and employers, but you didn't recognize the existence of class. You would be blind to a most important characteristic of the individual workers and employers you were observing, something that has tremendous influence in their lives. Despite the wide variety of experiences and identities among individual workers, capitalists, and middle class people, it still makes sense to acknowledge the existence and importance of class in modern society. In fact, without a class analysis we would have only the most superficial knowledge of our own lives and the experiences of others we observe in economic and political activity. . . .

When people in the United States talk about class, it is often in ways that hide its most important parts. We tend to think about class in terms of income, or the lifestyles that income can buy. . . . [But class can be better understood] as mainly a question of economic and political power. . . . Power doesn't exist alone within an individual or a group. Power exists as a relationship between and among different people or groups. This means that we cannot talk about one class of people alone, without looking at relationships between that class and others.

The working class is made up of people who, when they go to work or when they act as citizens, have comparatively little power or authority. They are the people who do their jobs under more or less close supervision, who have little control over the pace or the content of their work, who aren't the boss of anyone. They are blue-collar people like construction and factory workers, and white-collar workers like bank tellers and writers of routine computer code. They work to produce and distribute goods, or in service industries or government agencies. They are skilled and unskilled, engaged in over five hundred different occupations tracked by the U.S. Department of Labor: agricultural laborers, baggage handlers, cashiers, flight attendants, home health care aides, machinists, secretaries, short order cooks, sound technicians, truck drivers. In the United States, working class people are by far the majority of the population. Over eighty-eight million people were in working class occupations in 2002, comprising 62 percent of the labor force.[1]

On the other side of the basic power relation in a capitalist society is the capitalist class, those most senior executives who direct and control the corporations that employ the private-sector working class. These are the "captains of industry" and

finance, CEOs, chief financial officers, chief operating officers, members of boards of directors, those whose decisions dominate the workplace and the economy, and whose economic power often translates into dominant power in the realms of politics, culture, the media, and even religion. Capitalists comprise about 2 percent of the U.S. labor force.

There are big differences among capitalists in the degree of power they wield, particularly in the geographic extent of that power. The CEO of a business employing one hundred people in a city of fifty thousand might well be an important figure on the local scene, but not necessarily in state or regional affairs. On the national scale, power is principally in the hands of those who control the largest corporations, those employing over five hundred people. Of the over twenty-one million business enterprises in the United States, only sixteen thousand employ that many. They are controlled by around two hundred thousand people, fewer than two-tenths of 1 percent of the labor force.

Even among the powerful, power is concentrated at the top. It's one thing to control a single large corporation, another to sit on multiple corporate boards and be in a position to coordinate strategies across corporations. In fact, if we count only those people who sit on multiple boards, so-called interlocking directors, they could all fit into Yankee Stadium. They and the top political leaders in all branches of the federal government constitute a U.S. "ruling class" at the pinnacle of national power.

Capitalists are rich, of course. But when vice-president Dick Cheney invited a select few to help him formulate the country's energy policy shortly after the new Bush administration came into office in 2001, he didn't invite "rich people." He invited people who were leaders in the energy industry, capitalists. The fact that they were also rich was incidental. Capitalists are rich people who control far more than their personal wealth. They control the wealth of the nation, concentrated as it is in the largest few thousand corporations. There is no lobby in Washington representing "rich people." Lobbyists represent various industries or associations of industries that sometimes coordinate their efforts on behalf of industry in general. They represent the interests that capitalists bring to legislative and regulatory matters.

Something similar operates for the working class. Over thirteen million people are in unions in the United States. Most of these unions—like the United Auto Workers (UAW); the American Federation of State, County, and Municipal Employees (AFSCME); the Carpenters; and the International Brotherhood of Teamsters (IBT)—maintain offices in Washington and in major and even smaller cities where their members work. In addition to engaging in collective bargaining at the workplace, these unions lobby for their members and occasionally coordinate their efforts to lobby for broader working class interests. Sixty-eight unions have joined under the umbrella of the American Federation of Labor, Congress of Industrial Organizations (AFL-CIO) to pool resources and try to advance the interests of working people in general. These organizations represent workers, not "the poor" or "middle-income people," even though some workers are poor and some have an income equal to that of some in the middle class.[2]

In between the capitalist and the working classes is the middle class. The "middle class" gets a lot of attention in the media and political commentary in the United States, but this term is almost always used to describe people in the middle of the income distribution. People sometimes talk about "middle class workers," referring to people who work for a wage but live comfortable if modest lives. Especially in goods-producing industries, unionized workers have been able to win wages that allow home ownership, paid vacations, nice cars, home entertainment centers, and other consumer amenities.

When class is understood in terms of income or lifestyle, these workers are sometimes called "middle class." Even leaders of the workers' unions use the term to emphasize the gains unions have been able to win for working people. "Middle class workers" are supposed to be "most people," those with stable jobs and solid values based in the work ethic, as opposed to poor people—those on welfare or the "underclass"—on one side, and "the rich" on the other. When people think about classes in terms of "rich, middle, and poor," almost everyone ends up in the middle.

Understanding class in terms of power throws a different light on the subject. In this view, middle class people are in the middle of the power grid that has workers and capitalists at its poles. The middle class includes professional people like doctors, lawyers, accountants, and university professors. Most people in the "professional middle class" are not self-employed. They work for private companies or public agencies, receive salaries, and answer to supervisors. In these ways they are like workers.

But if we compare professional middle class people with well-paid workers, we see important differences. A unionized auto assembly worker doing a lot of overtime makes enough money to live the lifestyle of a "middle class worker," even more money than some professors or lawyers. But a well-paid unionized machinist or electrician or auto-worker is still part of the working class. Professors and lawyers have a degree of autonomy and control at work that autoworkers don't have. The difference is a question of class.

It is also misleading to equate the working class as a whole with its best-paid unionized members. Only 9 percent of private sector workers belong to unions, and millions of them are low-paid service employees. The relatively well-paid manufacturing industries are not typical of American business, and they are shrinking as a proportion of the total economy.

The middle class also includes supervisors in the business world, ranging from line foremen to senior managers below the top decision-making executives. As with the professional middle class, some people in the supervisory middle class are close to working people in income and lifestyle. We see this mostly at the lower levels of supervision, as with line foremen or other first-level supervisors. They often are promoted from the ranks of workers, continue to live in working class areas, and socialize with working class friends. But a foreman is not a worker when it comes to the power grid. The foreman is on the floor to represent the owner, to execute orders in the management chain of command. The foreman is in the middle—between the workers and the owners. When a worker becomes a supervisor, he or she enters the middle class. But just as the well-paid "middle class worker" is atypical, so "working class bosses" make up a small fraction of supervisory and managerial personnel in the U.S. economy.

We see something similar with small business owners, the third component of the middle class. Some come out of the working class and continue to have personal and cultural ties to their roots. But these connections do not change the fact that workers aspire to have their own business to escape the regimentation of working class jobs, seeking instead the freedom to "be my own boss." That freedom, regardless of how much it might be limited by competitive pressures in the marketplace and how many hours the owner must work to make a go of it, puts the small business owner in a different class from workers.

At the other end of the business scale, senior managers and high-level corporate attorneys and accountants share quite a bit with the capitalists they serve. They have considerable authority, make a lot of money, and revolve in the same social circles. But they are not the final decision makers. They are at a qualitatively different level in the power grid from those they serve, who pay them well for their service but retain ultimate authority. They, too, are in the middle class.

In all three sections of the middle class—professionals, supervisors, and small business owners—there are fuzzy borders with the working class and with the capitalists. Yet the differences in power, independence, and life circumstances among these classes support the idea of a separate middle class. The middle class is about 36 percent of the labor force in the United States—sizable, but far from the majority, far from the "typical" American.

Like the working class and the capitalists, the middle class is represented in the political process by professional associations and small business groups. There is no "middle-income" lobby, but there are, for example, the Trial Lawyers Association, the American Medical Association, the American Association of University Professors, the National Association of Realtors.

Clearly, classes are not monolithic collections of socially identical people. We have seen that each class contains quite a bit of variation. Rather than sharp dividing lines, the borders between them are porous and ambiguous—important areas to study and better understand. Also, beyond the differences in occupations and relative power within classes, which lead to differences in incomes, wealth, and lifestyles, each class contains men and women of every race, nationality, and creed. Yet, despite these rich internal variations and ambiguous borders, a qualitative difference remains between the life experience of the working class compared with that of the professional and managerial middle class, to say nothing of differences both of these have with the capitalists.

DISCUSSION QUESTIONS

1. How is social class like and also different from race, sex, gender, and sexual orientation?
2. Would you agree with Zweig that "without a class analysis, we would have only the most superficial knowledge of our own lives and the experience of others"?

NOTES

1. For a detailed discussion of the class composition of the United States, on which these and the following findings are based, see Michael Zweig, *The Working Class Majority: America's Best Kept Secret* (Ithaca, NY: Cornell University Press, 2000), chap. 1.
2. Some middle class people are represented by unions, such as university professors in the American Federation of Teachers (AFT) and legal aid attorneys in the UAW. Most union members are in the working class.

READING 13

The Silver Spoon: Inheritance and the Staggered Start

Stephen J. McNamee and Robert K. Miller Jr.

To heir is human.

—Jeffrey P. Rosenfeld, *Legacy of Aging*

A common metaphor for the competition to get ahead in life is the foot race. The imagery is that the fastest runner—presumably the most meritorious—will be the one to break the tape at the finish line. But in terms of economic competition, the race is rigged. If we think of money as a measure of who gets how much of what there is to get, the race to get ahead does not start anew with each generation. Instead, it is more like a relay race in which we inherit a starting point from our parents. The baton is passed, and for a while, both parents and children run together. When the exchange is complete, the children are on their own as they position themselves for the next exchange to the next generation. Although each new runner may gain or lose ground in the competition, each new runner inherits an initial starting point in the race.

In this intergenerational relay race, children born to wealthy parents start at or near the finish line, while children born into poverty start behind everyone else. Those who are born close to the finish line need no merit to get ahead. They already are ahead. The poorest of the poor, however, need to traverse the entire distance to get to the finish line on the basis of merit alone. In this sense, meritocracy applies strictly only to the poorest of the poor; everyone else has at least some advantage of inheritance that places him or her ahead at the start of the race.

In comparing the effects of inheritance and individual merit on life outcomes, the effects of inheritance come first, *followed by* the effects of individual merit—not the other way around. Figure 1 depicts the intergenerational relay race to get ahead.

Stephen J. McNamee is a professor of sociology at the University of North Carolina, Wilmington. Robert K. Miller, Jr. is a professor of sociology at the University of North Carolina, Wilmington.

FIGURE 1

The intergenerational race to get ahead. Note: solid lines are effects of inheritance; dashed lines are potential effects of merit.

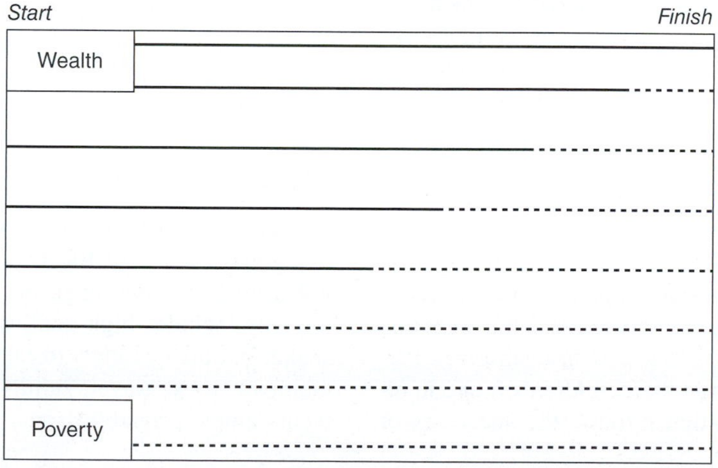

The solid lines represent the effects of inheritance on economic outcomes. The dotted lines represent the potential effects of merit. The "distance" each person needs to reach the finish line on the basis of merit depends on how far from the finish line each person starts the race in the first place.

It is important to point out that equivalent amounts of merit do not lead to equivalent end results. If each dash represents one "unit" of merit, a person born poor who advances one unit on the basis of individual merit over a lifetime ends up at the end of her life one unit ahead of where she started but still at or close to poverty. A person who begins life one unit short of the top can ascend to the top based on an equivalent one unit of merit. Each person is equally meritorious, but his or her end position in the race to get ahead is very different.

Heirs to large fortunes in the world start life at or near the finish line. Barring the unlikely possibility of parental disinheritance, there is virtually no realistic scenario in which they end up destitute—regardless of the extent of their innate talent or individual motivation. Their future is financially secure. They will grow up having the best of everything and having every opportunity money can buy.

Most parents want the best for their children. As a result, most parents try to do everything they can to secure their children's futures. Indeed, that parental desire to provide advantages for children may even have biological origins. Under the "inclusive fitness-maximizing" theory of selection, for instance, beneficiaries are favored in inheritance according to their biological relatedness and reproductive value. Unsurprisingly, research shows that benefactors are much more likely to bequeath estates to surviving spouses and children than to unrelated individuals or institutions (Schwartz 1996; Willenbacher 2003). In a form of what might be called "reverse inheritance," parents may invest in children to secure their own futures in the event that they become unable to take care of themselves. Parents may also invest in their children's future to realize vicarious prestige through the successes of their children, which may, in turn, be seen as a validation of their own genetic endowments or child-rearing skills.

Regardless of the source of parental motivation, most parents clearly wish to secure children's futures. To the extent that parents are successful in passing on advantages to children, meritocracy does not operate as the basis for who ends up with what. Despite the ideology of meritocracy, the reality in America, as elsewhere, is inheritance first and merit second. . . .

THE CUMULATIVE ADVANTAGES OF WEALTH INHERITANCE

Inheritance is more than bulk estates bequeathed to descendants; more broadly defined, it refers to the total impact of initial social-class placement at birth on future life outcomes. Therefore, it is not just the superwealthy who are in a position to pass advantages on to children. Advantages are passed on, in varying degrees, to all of those from relatively privileged backgrounds. Even minor initial advantages may accumulate during the life course. In this way, existing inequalities are reinforced and extended across generations. As Harvard economist John Kenneth Galbraith put it in the opening sentence of his well-known book *The Affluent Society,* "Wealth is not without its advantages and the case to the contrary, although it has often been made, has never proved widely persuasive" (1958, 13). Specifically, the cumulative advantages of wealth inheritance include the following.

Childhood Quality of Life

Children of the privileged enjoy a high standard of living and quality of life regardless of their individual merit or lack of it. For the privileged, this not only includes high-quality food, clothing, and shelter but also extends to luxuries such as entertainment, toys, travel, family vacations, enrichment camps, private lessons, and a host of other indulgences that wealthy parents and even middle-class parents bestow on their children (Lareau 2003). Children do not earn a privileged lifestyle; they inherit and benefit from it long before their parents are deceased.

Knowing with Which Fork to Eat

Cultural capital refers to what one needs to know to function as a member of the various groups to which one belongs. All groups have norms, values, beliefs, ways of life, and codes of conduct that identify the group and define its boundaries. The culture of the group separates insiders from outsiders. Knowing and binding by these cultural codes of conduct is required to maintain one's status as a member in good standing within the group. By growing up in privilege, children of the elite are socialized into elite ways of life. This kind of cultural capital has commonly been referred to as "breeding," "refinement," "social grace," "savoir faire," or simply "class" (meaning upper class). Although less pronounced and rigid than in the past, these distinctions persist into the present. In addition to cultivated tastes in art and music ("highbrow" culture), cultural capital includes, but is not limited to, interpersonal styles and demeanor, manners and etiquette, and vocabulary. Those from more humble backgrounds who aspire to become elites must acquire the cultural cachet to be accepted in elite circle, and this is no easy task. Those born to it, however, have the advantage of acquiring it "naturally" through inheritance, a kind of social osmosis that takes place through childhood socialization (Lareau 2003).

Having Friends in High Places

Everybody knows somebody else. Social capital refers to the "value" of whom you know. For the most part, privileged people know other privileged people, and poor people know other poor people. Another nonmerit advantage inherited by children of the wealthy is a network of connections to people of power and influence. These are not connections that children of the rich shrewdly foster or cultivate on their own. The children of the wealthy travel in high-powered social circles. These connections provide access to power, information, and other resources. The difference between rich and poor is not in knowing people; it is in knowing people in positions of power and influence who can do things for you.

Early Withdrawals on the Family Estate

Children of the privileged do not have to wait until their parents die to inherit assets from them. Inter vivos transfers of funds and "gifts" from parents to children can be substantial, and there is strong evidence suggesting that such transfers account for a greater proportion of intergenerational transfers than lump-sum estates at death (Gale and Scholz 1994). Inter vivos gifts to children provide a means of legally avoiding or reducing estate taxes. In this way, parents can "spend down" their estates during their lives to avoid estate and inheritance taxes upon their deaths. Furthermore, in 2001 the federal government enacted legislation that is scheduled to ultimately phase out the federal estate tax. Many individual states have also reduced or eliminated inheritance taxes. The impact of these changes in tax law on intergenerational transfers is at this point unclear. If tax advantages were the only reasons for inter vivos transfers, we might expect parents to slow down the pace of inter vivos transfers. But it is unlikely that the flow of such transfers will be abruptly curtailed because they serve other functions. Besides tax avoidance, parents also provide inter vivos transfers to children to advance their children's current and future economic interests, especially at critical or milestone stages of the life cycle. These milestone events include going to college, getting married, buying a house, and having children. At each event, there may be a substantial infusion of parental capital—in essence an early withdrawal on the parental estate. One of the most common forms of inter vivos gifts is payment for children's education. A few generations ago, children may have inherited the family farm or the family business. With the rise of the modern corporation and the decline of family farms and businesses, inheritance increasingly takes on more fungible or liquid forms, including cash transfers. Indeed, for many middle-class Americans, education has replaced tangible assets as the primary form by which advantage is passed on between generations.

What Goes Up Doesn't Usually Come Down

If America were truly a meritocracy, we would expect fairly equal amounts of both upward and downward mobility. Mobility studies, however, consistently show much higher rates of upward than downward mobility. There are two key reasons for this. First, most mobility that people have experienced in American in the past century, particularly occupational mobility, was due to industrial expansion and the rise of the general standard of living in society as a whole. Sociologists refer to this type of mobility as "structural mobility," which has more to do with changes in the organization of society than with the merit of individuals. A second reason why upward mobility is more prevalent than downward mobility is that parents and extended family networks insulate children from downward mobility. That is, parents frequently "bail out," or "rescue," their adult children in the event of life crises such as sickness, unemployment, divorce, or other setbacks that might otherwise propel adult children into a downward spiral. In addition to these external circumstances, parents also rescue children from their own failures and weaknesses, including self-destructive behaviors. Parental rescue as a form of inter vivos transfer is not a generally acknowledged or well-studied benefit of inheritance. Indirect evidence of parental rescue may be found in the recent increase in the number of "boomerang" children, adult children who leave

home only to return later to live with parents. Social scientists report that 34 percent of young adults are now moving back in with their parents during their twenties (*Contexts* 2008). The reasons for adult children returning to live at home are usually financial: adult children may be between jobs, between marriages, or without other viable means of self-support. Such living arrangements are likely to increase during periods of high unemployment, which in early 2009 topped 8 percent of the civilian labor force.

If America operated as a "true" merit system, people would advance solely on the basis of merit and fail when they lacked merit. In many cases however, family resources prevent, or at least reduce, "skidding" among adult children. One of the authors of this book recalls that when he left home as an adult, his parents took him aside and told him that no matter how bad things became for him out there in the world, if he could get to a phone, they would wire him money to come home. This was his insurance against destitution. Fortunately, he has not yet had to take his parents up on their offer, but neither has he forgotten it. Without always being articulated, the point is that this informal familial insurance against downward mobility is available in varying degrees, to all except the poorest of the poor, who simply have resources to provide.

Live Long and Prosper

From womb to tomb, the more affluent one is, the less the risk of injury, illness, and death (Budrys 2003; Cockerham 2000; National Center for Health Statistics 2007; Wermuth 2003). Among the many nonmerit advantages inherited by those from privileged backgrounds is higher life expectancy at birth and a greater chance of better health throughout life. There are several possible reasons for the strong and persistent relationship between socioeconomic status and health. Beginning with fetal development and extending through childhood, increasing evidence points to the

PERSONAL ACCOUNT

I Am a Pakistani Woman

I am a Pakistani woman, raised in the U.S. and Canada, and often at odds with the Western standard of beauty.

As a child in Nova Scotia and later growing up in New York and Indiana, I was proud of my uniqueness. On traditional Pakistani and Muslim holidays, I got to wear bright, fun clothes from my country and colorful jewelry. I had a whole rich tradition of my own to celebrate in addition to Christmas and Easter. However, as I started school, I somehow came to realize that being different wasn't so great—that in other people's viewpoint, I looked strange and acted funny. I learned the importance of fitting in and behaving like the other girls. This involved dressing well, giggling a lot, and having a superior, but flirtatious attitude toward boys. I was very outgoing and had very good grades, so outwardly I was able to "assimilate" with some success. But my sister, who was quiet and reticent, often took the brunt of other children's cruelty. I realize how proud and ashamed I was of my heritage when I look at my relationship with my family.

A lesson I learned early on in the U.S. was that being beautiful took a lot of money. It is painful, as an adult, for me to consider the inexorable, never-ending pressure that my father was under to embody the dominant, middle-class cultural expressions of masculinity, as in success at one's job, making a big salary, and owning status symbols. I resented him so much then for being a poor, untenured professor and freelance writer. I wanted designer clothes, dining out at nice restaurants, and a big allowance. Instead, I had a deeply spiritual thinker, writer, and theologian for a dad. I love(d) him and am so very grateful for what he's taught me, but as a child I didn't think of him as a success.

The prettiest girls in school all had a seemingly endless array of outfits, lots of makeup and perfume, and everything by the "right" designers. I hated my mom for making many of my clothes and buying things on sale (and my mom was a great seamstress). I felt a sense of hopelessness that I could never have the resources or opportunities necessary to compete, to be beautiful.

Instead I found safety in conformity. When I was in high school, the WASPy, preppy look was hot; it represented the epitome of success and privilege in America. I worked hard to purchase a wardrobe of clothes with a polo-horse insignia, by many hours at an after-school job. I tried to hide my exotic look behind Khakis, boat shoes, hair barrettes, and pearl studs. There was comfort in conformity. I saw the class "sex symbol" denigrated for wearing tight dresses and having a very well-developed body for a sixteen-year-old, and the more unique dressers dismissed as frivolous, trendy, and more than a little eccentric. You couldn't be too pretty, too ugly, too different—you had to just blend in.

Though I did it well, I perpetually felt like an imposter. This rigidly controlled, well-dressed preppy going through school with good grades in advanced placement classes in no way represented what I felt to be my true essence.

Hoorie I. Siddique

effects of "the long reach of early childhood" on adult health (Smith 1999). Prenatal deprivations, more common among the poor, for instance, are associated with later life conditions such as retardation, coronary heart disease, stroke, diabetes and hypertension. Poverty in early childhood is also associated with increased risk of adult diseases. This may be due in part to higher stress levels among the poor. There is also evidence that cumulative wear and tear on the body over time occurs under conditions of repeated high stress.

Another reason for the health-wealth connection is that the rich have greater access to quality health care. In America, access to quality health care is still largely for sale to the highest bidder. Under these conditions, prevention and intervention are more widely available to the more affluent. Finally, not only does lack of income lead to poor health, but poor health leads to reduced earnings. That is, if someone is sick or injured, he or she may not be able to work or may have limited earning power.

Overall, the less affluent are at a health disadvantage due to higher exposure to a variety of unhealthy living conditions. As medical sociologist William Cockerham points out,

> Persons living in poverty and reduced socioeconomic circumstances have greater exposure to physical (crowding, poor sanitation, extreme temperatures), chemical and biochemical (diet, pollution, smoking, alcohol, and drug abuse), biological (bacteria, viruses) and psychological (stress) risk factors that produce ill health than more affluent individuals. (1998, 55).

Part of the exposure to health hazards is occupational. According to the Department of Labor, those in the following occupations (listed in order of risk) have the greatest likelihood of being killed on the job: fishers, timber cutters, airplane pilots, structural metal workers, taxicab drivers, construction laborers, roofers, electric power installers, truck drivers, and farm workers. With the exception of airline pilot, all the jobs listed are working-class jobs. Since a person's occupation is strongly affected by family background, the prospects for generally higher occupational health risks are in this sense at least indirectly inherited. Finally, although homicides constitute only a small proportion of all causes of death, it is worth noting that the less affluent are at higher risk for being victims of violent crime, including homicide.

Some additional risk factors are related to individual behaviors, especially smoking, drinking, and drug abuse—all of which are more common among the less affluent. Evidence suggests that these behaviors, while contributing to poorer health among the less affluent, are responsible for only one-third of the "wealth-health gradient" (Smith 1999, 157). These behaviors are also associated with higher psychological as well as physical stress. Indeed, the less affluent are not just at greater risk for physical ailments; research has shown that the less affluent are at significantly higher risk for mental illness as well (Cockerham 2000; Feagin and McKinney 2003). Intriguing new evidence suggests that, apart from material deprivations, part of the link between wealth and health may be related to the psychological stress of relative deprivation, that is, the stress of being at the bottom end of an unequal social pecking order, especially when the dominant ideology attributes being at the bottom to individual deficiencies.

Despite the adage that "money can't buy happiness," social science research has consistently shown that happiness and subjective well-being tend to be related to the amount of income and wealth people possess (Frey and Stutzer 2002; Frank 2007a; Schnittker 2008). This research shows that people living in wealthier (and more democratic) countries tend to be happier and that rates of happiness are sensitive to overall rates of unemployment and inflation. In general, poor people are less happy than others, although increments that exceed average amounts of income only slightly increase levels of happiness. That is, beyond relatively low thresholds, additional increments of income and wealth are not likely to result in additional increments of happiness. Although money may not *guarantee* a long, happy, and healthy life, a fair assessment is that it aids and abets it. . . .

SUMMARY

The United States has high levels of both income and wealth inequality. In terms of the distribution of income and wealth, America is clearly not a middle-class society. Income and especially wealth are not evenly distributed, with a relatively small number of well-off families at one end and a small number of poor families much worse off at the other. Instead, the overall picture is one in which the bulk of the available wealth is concentrated in a narrow range at the very top of the system. In short, the distribution of economic resources in society is not symmetrical and certainly not bell-shaped: the poor who have the least greatly outnumber the rich who have the most. Moreover, in recent decades, by all measures, the rich are getting richer, and the gap between the very rich and everyone else has appreciably increased.

The greater the amount of economic inequality in society, the more difficult it is to move up within the system on the basis of individual merit alone. Indeed, the most important factor in terms of where people will end up in the economic pecking order of society is where they started in the first place. Economic inequality has tremendous inertial force across generations. Instead of a race to get ahead that begins anew with each generation, the race is in reality a relay race in which children inherit different starting points from parents. Inheritance, broadly defined as one's initial starting point in life based on parental position, includes a set of cumulative non-merit advantages for all except the poorest of the poor. These include enhanced childhood standard of living, differential access to cultural capital, differential access to social networks of power and influence, infusion of parental capital while parents are still alive, greater health and life expectancy, and the inheritance of bulk estates when parents die. . . .

DISCUSSION QUESTIONS

1. On what grounds do McNamee and Miller conclude that America is not a middle-class society? Is their conclusion supportable?
2. In what ways does America function as a meritocracy and in what ways does it not?

REFERENCES

Budrys, Grace. 2003. *Unequal Health: How Inequality Contributes to Health or Illness.* Lanham, MD: Rowman & Littlefield.

Cockerham, William. 1998. *Medical Sociology.* 7th ed. Upper Saddle River, NJ: Prentice Hall.

Feagin, Joe. R., and Mary D. McKinney. 2003. *The Many Costs of Racism.* Lanham, MD: Rowman & Littlefield.

Frey, Bruno S., and Alois Stutzer. 2002. *Happiness and Economics: How the Economy and Institutions Affect Well-being.* Princeton, NJ: Princeton University Press.

Galbraith, John Kenneth. 1958. *The Affluent Society.* New York: Mentor Press.

Gale, William G., and John Karl Scholz. 1994. "Intergenerational Transfers and the Accumulation of Wealth." *Journal of Economic Perspectives* 8: 145–60.

Lareau, Annette. 2003. *Unequal Childhood: Class, Race, and Family Life.* Berkeley: University of California Press.

National Center for Health Statistics. 2007. *Health, United States, 2007, with Chart-book on Trends in the Health of Americans.* Hyattsville, MD: National Center for Health Statistics, U.S. Department of Health and Human Services.

Smith, James P. 1999. "Healthy Bodies and Thick Wallets: The Dual Relation between Health and Economic Status." *Journal of Economic Perspectives* 13: 145–66.

Wermuth, Laurie. 2003. *Global Inequality and Human Needs: Health and Illness in an Increasingly Unequal World.* Boston: Allyn Bacon.

READING 14

The Great Divergence: America's Growing Inequality Crisis and What We Can Do about It

Timothy Noah

During the past thirty-three years the difference in America between being rich and being middle class became much more pronounced. People with high incomes consumed an ever-larger share of the nation's total income, while people in the middle saw their share shrink. For most of this time the phenomenon attracted little attention from the general public and the press because it occurred in increments over one third of a century. During the previous five decades—from the early 1930s through most of the 1970s—the precise opposite had occurred. The share of the nation's income that went to the wealthy had either shrunk or remained stable. At the first signs, during the early 1980s, that this was no longer happening, economists figured they were witnessing a fluke, an inexplicable but temporary phenomenon, or perhaps an artifact of faulty statistics. But they weren't. A democratization of

_____

Timothy Noah is a journalist and author.

incomes that Americans had long taken for granted as a happy fact of modern life was reversing itself. Eventually it was the steady growth in income inequality that Americans took for granted. The divergent fortunes of the rich and the middle class became such a fact of everyday life that people seldom noticed it, except perhaps to observe now and then with a shrug that life was unfair. . . .

. . . As late as 1979, the prevailing view among economists was that incomes in any advanced industrial democracy would inevitably become more equal or remain stable in their distribution. They certainly wouldn't become more unequal. That sorry fate was reserved for societies at an earlier stage of development or where the dictatorial powers of the state preserved privilege for the few at the expense of the many. In civilized, mature, and free nations, the gaps between rich, middle class, and poor did not increase.

That seemed the logical lesson to draw from U.S. history. The country's transformation from an agrarian society to an industrial one during the late nineteenth and early twentieth centuries had created a period of extreme economic inequality—one whose ramifications can still be glimpsed by, say, pairing a visit to George Vanderbilt's 125,000-acre Biltmore Estate in Ashville, North Carolina, with a trip to the Tenement Museum on Manhattan's Lower East Side. But from the early 1930s through the early 1970s, incomes became more equal, and remained so, while the industrial economy lost none of its rude vitality. As the 1970s progressed, that vitality diminished, but income distribution remained unchanged. "As measured in the official data," the Princeton economist Alan Blinder wrote in 1980, "income inequality was just about the same in 1977 . . . as it was in 1947."[1] What Blinder couldn't know (because he didn't have more recent data) was that this was already beginning to change. Starting in 1979, incomes once again began to grow unequal. When the economy recovered in 1983, incomes grew even more unequal. They have continued growing more unequal to this day.

The United States is not the only advanced industrialized democracy where incomes have become more unequal in recent decades. The trend is global. A 2008 report by the Organisation for Economic Co-operation and Development, which represents thirty-four market-oriented democracies, concluded that since the mid-1980s, income inequality had increased in two thirds of the twenty-four OECD countries for which data were available, which included most of the world's leading industrial democracies.[2] But the level and growth rate of income inequality in the United States has been particularly extreme.

There are various ways to measure income distribution, and by all of them the United States ranks at or near the bottom in terms of equality. The most common measure, the Gini coefficient, is named for an Italian statistician named Corrado Gini (1884–1965).[3] It measures distribution—of income or anything else—on a scale that goes from 0 to 1. Let's imagine, for instance, that we had fifty marbles to distribute among fifty children. Perfect equality of distribution would be if each child got one marble. The Gini coefficient would then be 0. Perfect inequality of distribution would be if one especially pushy child ended up with all fifty marbles. The Gini coefficient would then be 1.[4] As of 2005, the United States' Gini coefficient was 0.38, which on the income-equality scale ranked this country twenty-seventh of the thirty OECD nations for which data were available. The only countries with more unequal income distribution were Portugal (0.42), Turkey (0.43), and Mexico (0.47). . . . When you calculated the percentage of national income that went to the top 1 percent, the United States was the undisputed champion. Its measured income distribution was more unequal than that of any other OECD nation.[5] As of 2007 (i.e., right before the 2008 financial crisis), America's richest 1 percent possessed nearly 24 percent of the nation's pretax income, a statistic that gave new meaning to the expression "Can you spare a quarter?" (I include capital gains as part of income, and will do so whenever possible throughout this book.) In 2008, the last year for which data are available, the recession drove the richest 1 percent's income share down to 21 percent.[6] To judge from Wall Street's record bonuses and corporate America's surging profitability in the years following the 2008 financial crisis, income share for the top 1 percent will resume its upward climb momentarily, if it hasn't already. We already know from census data that in 2010 income share for the bottom 40 percent fell and that the poverty rate climbed to its highest point in nearly two decades.[7]

In addition to having an unusually high *level* of income inequality, the United States has seen income inequality increase at a much faster *rate* than most other countries. Among the twenty-four OECD countries for which Gini-coefficient change can be measured from the mid-1980s to the mid-aughts, only Finland, Portugal, and New Zealand experienced a faster growth rate in income inequality. Of these, only Portugal ended up with a Gini rating worse than the United States'. Another important point of comparison is that some OECD countries saw income inequality decline during this period. France, Greece, Ireland, Spain, and Turkey all saw their Gini ratings go *down* (though the OECD report's data for Ireland and Spain didn't extend beyond 2000). That proves it is not woven into the laws of economics that an advanced industrial democracy must, during the present epoch, see its income-inequality level fall, or even stay the same. Some of these countries are becoming more economically egalitarian, not less, just as the United States did for much of the twentieth century.[8]

Many changes in the global economy are making incomes less equal in many countries outside the United States, but the income-inequality trend of the past three decades has been unusually fierce here in the world's richest nation. Americans usually invoke the term "American exceptionalism" to describe what it is that makes our country so much more blessed than all others. But American exceptionalism can also describe ingrained aspects of our country's economy, or government, or character, that put us at a disadvantage on the world stage. Income inequality is one of the more notable ways that the United States differs, in ways we can only regret, even from nations that resemble us more than they do not. . . .

Upward mobility is America's creed. Circumstances at the bottom might be hard, but a plucky young bootblack with his eye on the main chance can rise in the world through hard work. Americans believe this more fervently than do citizens of other advanced industrial democracies. But the limited data we have show that we demonstrate it less than most of those other countries do. The United States today is no longer, by international standards, a land notably rich in opportunities to move up the income ladder.

A survey of twenty-seven nations conducted from 1998 to 2001 asked participants whether they agreed with the statement "People are rewarded for intelligence and skill." The country with the highest proportion answering in the affirmative was the United States (69 percent), compared to a median among all countries of about 40 percent. Similarly, more than 60 percent of Americans agreed that "people get rewarded for their effort," compared to an international median of less than 40 percent. When participants were asked whether coming from a wealthy family was "essential" or "very important" to getting ahead, the percentage of American affirmatives was much lower than the international median: 19 percent versus 28 percent.[9]

The nonprofit Pew Charitable Trusts sponsored a U.S. poll on income mobility in March 2009, when the country was enduring the worst recession since the Great Depression. Thirty-nine percent of the respondents agreed with the statement that it was common for someone in the United States to start out poor and become rich. A poll taken six years before by the Gallup organization found that 31 percent of Americans expected to get rich themselves before they die, with "rich" defined by respondents (according to the median) as an income of $120,000 per year (roughly in the top 10 percent). Among those age eighteen to twenty-nine, 51 percent expected to get rich.[10]

Economic reality does not match these expectations. Only 6 percent of Americans born at the bottom of the heap (defined as the lowest fifth in income distribution, i.e., those whose family incomes go up to about $25,000) ever make it in adulthood to the top (defined as the highest fifth in income distribution, i.e., those whose family incomes are above $100,000).[11] The most striking finding about upward mobility in contemporary America concerns the relationship between who your parents are and how much money you can expect to make. Parentage is a greater determinant of a man's future earnings than it is of his height and weight.[12] Height and weight are influenced by the genes passed from parents to children. Future earnings are not. But you wouldn't know that from available data on economic mobility in the United States. . . .

To summarize the society-wide trend: Upward mobility in the United States is not as brisk as economists once believed it was. There's some evidence that it has slowed since the 1970s. Certainly it hasn't accelerated. Now let's look at how the United States stacks up against traditionally class-bound

nations of western Europe—what we once called the Old World.

Short answer: very poorly. A 2007 study by the Organisation for Economic Co-operation and Development combined a number of previous estimates and found income heritability to be greater (and economic mobility therefore lower) in the United States than in Demark, Australia, Norway, Finland, Canada, Sweden, Germany, Spain, and France. Italy was a little bit less mobile than the United States, and the United Kingdom brought up the rear. This ranking was based on a somewhat conservative U.S. estimate of 47 percent income heritability;[13] Mazumder of the Chicago Fed . . . puts it at 50 to 60 percent which would rank the United States either tied with the United Kingdom for last place or dead last *after* the United Kingdom. *Almost (arguably every) comparably developed nation for which we have data offers greater income mobility than the United States.* A common American criticism of the

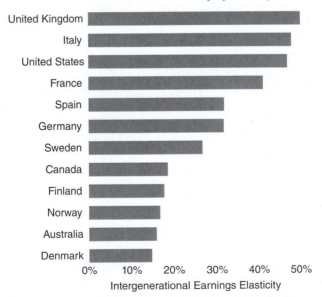

Income Heritability by Country

Source: Anna Cristina D'Addio, "Intergenerational Transmission of Disadvantage: Mobility or Immobility Across Generations? A Review of the Evidence for OECD Countries," *Social, Employment, and Migration Working Paper 52* (Paris: OECD, 2007), 33.

"socialist" countries of western and particularly northern Europe is that by providing guaranteed health care and a social safety net for the poor and unemployed that is more comprehensive than the one in the United States, these nations diminish their economies' ability to create economic opportunity. That argument is refuted by the evidence presented here that western and northern European countries provide, in fact, *greater opportunity* than the United States to move up the economic ladder. . . .

DISCUSSION QUESTIONS

1. How do you explain the strength and persistence of Americans' belief in the possibility of their upward mobility? Do you think this has changed in recent times?

2. How do you assess your own chances for upward mobility?

NOTES

1. Alan Blinder, "The Level and Distribution of Economic Well-Being," Working Paper 488 (Cambridge, MA: National Bureau of Economic Research, 1980).

2. *Growing Unequal? Income Distribution and Poverty in OECD Countries* (Paris: Organisation for Economic Co-operation and Development, 2008), 27.

3. I would be remiss if I failed to note here the awkward debt that the science of income and wealth distribution owes to Italian fascism. Gini was president of Italy's Central Institute of Statistics under Benito Mussolini. Another pioneer in the field was the French-Italian Vilfredo Pareto (1848– 1923), inventor of an alternative measure called the Pareto distribution. Pareto was a dedicated Fascist who harbored truly repellant beliefs, but Gini appears to have been much less interested in politics than in statistics. Il Duce was an enthusiastic student of statistical science, presumably in the service of measuring whether the trains were in fact running on time (and other less praiseworthy efficiencies). The fascism connection is a ripe opportunity for right-wing demagogues to condemn all discussion of income distribution—one that, unaccountably, was never seized in the journalist Jonah Goldberg's 2007 tome, *Liberal Fascism: The Secret History of the American Left, from Mussolini to the Politics of Meaning*. But math is math, and Pareto's and, especially, Gini's statistical work have withstood the test of time.

4. The Gini coefficient is derived from the Lorenz curve, a graphic representation of income distribution named for an American economist named Max Otto Lorenz (1876–1959). The Lorenz curve plots cumulative percentage population share (x-axis) against cumulative percentage income share (y-axis). Perfect equality is when every population share matches every income share. This hypothetical distribution is represented by a straight line extending at a forty-five-degree angle. Actual real-world distribution, which is always unequal to some degree, is represented by a line that curves underneath the forty-five-degree line. Imagine the two lines as representing a bow that you would use to shoot an arrow (only forget the arrow and forget pulling the string, which must remain a straight line). The lower the real-world distribution dips—the more curved the bow is—the more unequal the distribution. The Gini coefficient is derived by calculating the area inside the bow and then dividing that by the sum of the area inside the bow plus the area below the bow.

5. *Growing Unequal?*, 25, 32, 51– 52.

6. Facundo Alvaredo, Tony Atkinson, Thomas Piketty, and Emmanuel Saez, "The World Top Incomes Database," http://g-mond.parisschoolofeconomics.eu/topincomes/.

7. *Income, Poverty, and Health Insurance Coverage in the United States: 2010* (Washington: U.S. Census Bureau, 2011), 10, 14.

8. *Growing Unequal?*, 27, 51. Finland's very low Gini rating (0.27) ranks it the seventh most income-equal nation in the OECD, while New Zealand's very high Gini coefficient (0.34) ranks it a mere four places above the United States' dismal twenty-seventh out of thirty. Portugal's disturbingly high level of income inequality and high rate of increase in income inequality, which exceed those in the United States, appear to result largely from the fact that nearly 78 percent of its households are headed by people who lack a high school degree. By European standards, that's an extraordinarily low high school graduation rate. But even in poorly educated Portugal, the top 1 percent's income share is just a little more than half what it is in the United States. To achieve American-style income inequality, you need lots of poor people, which Portugal has, and lots of rich people, which it lacks.

9. 1999 Social Inequality III survey, International Social Survey Program. Quoted in Julia B. Isaacs, Isabel V. Sawhill, and Ron Haskins, *Getting Ahead or Losing Ground: Economic Mobility in America* (Washington: Brookings Institution, 2008), 37. Scott Winship, an economic studies fellow at Brookings's Center on Children and Families, informs me that the question about whether coming from a wealthy family was "essential"

or "very important" to getting ahead was asked once again in the 2009 Social Inequality IV survey. This time the international median was an even higher 32 percent. But the countries polled in 2009 were different from those polled in 1999, and in 2009 the United States wasn't polled on this question at all.

10. Greenberg Quinlan Rosner poll for Pew Charitable Trusts Economic Mobility Project, Mar. 12, 2009, at http://www.pewtrusts.org/uploadedFiles/wwwpewtrustsorg/Reports/Economic_Mobility/EMP%202009%20Survey%20on%20Economic%20Mobility%20FOR%20PRINT%203.12.09.pdf; Gallup poll, "Half of Young People Expect to Strike It Rich," Mar. 11, 2003, at http://www.gallup.com/poll/7981/half-young-people-expect-strike-rich.aspx; and Thomas A. DiPrete, "Is This a Great Country? Upward Mobility and the Chance for

Riches in Contemporary America," Nov. 28, 2005, at http://www.ssc.wisc.edu/soc/faculty/docs/diprete/richesl12805.pdf.

11. Isaacs et al., *Getting Ahead*, 19.

12. Bhashkar Mazumder, "Sibling Similarities, Differences and Economic Inequality," *Working Paper 2004–13* (Chicago: Federal Reserve Bank, 2004), 23.

13. Anna Cristina d'Addio, "Intergenerational Transmission of Disadvantage: Mobility or Immobility Across Generations? A Review of the Evidence for OECD Countries," *OECD Social, Employment and Migration Working Papers 52* (Paris: OECD, 2007), 33; and Miles Corak, "Do Poor Children Become Poor Adults? Lessons from a Cross Country Comparison of Generational Earnings Mobility," *Discussion Paper No. 1993* (Bonn: Institute for the Study of Labor [IZA], 2006), 53, 63.

WHAT IS SEXUALITY?

READING 15

Sexual Fluidity: Understanding Women's Love and Desire

Lisa M. Diamond

In 1997, the actress Anne Heche began a widely publicized romantic relationship with the openly lesbian comedian Ellen DeGeneres after having had no prior same-sex attractions or relationships. The relationship with DeGeneres ended after two years, and Heche went on to marry a man. The actress Cynthia Nixon of the HBO series *Sex and the City* developed a serious relationship with a woman in 2004 after ending a fifteen-year relationship with a man. Julie Cypher left a heterosexual marriage for the musician Melissa Etheridge in 1988. After twelve years together, the pair separated and Cypher—like Heche—has returned to heterosexual relationships. In other cases, longtime lesbians have unexpectedly initiated relationships with

men, sometimes after decades of exclusively same-sex ties (examples include the feminist folk singer Holly Near, the activist and writer Jan Clausen, and Deborah Sundahl, a founding editor of the lesbian magazine *On Our Backs*). What's going on? Are these women confused? Were they just going through a phase before, or are they in one now?

Consider, too, the growing number of popular terms that have been coined to describe women with changing patterns of same-sex and other-sex behavior, such as "heteroflexibility," "has-bian," and "LUG—lesbian until graduation."[1] This new lexicon has been matched by increasing media depictions of women who pursue sexual contact that runs counter to their avowed sexual orientation, ranging from the much-ballyhooed kiss between Madonna and Britney Spears at the MTV Video Music Awards to films such as *Kissing Jessica Stein* and *Chasing Amy,* which depicts a lesbian becoming involved with a man, contrary to the more widespread depictions of heterosexual women becoming involved in same-sex relationships. The reason such cases are so perplexing is that they flatly contradict prevailing assumptions about sexual orientation. These assumptions hold that an individual's sexual predisposition for the same sex or the other sex is an

Lisa Diamond is a professor of psychology at the University of Utah.

early-developing and stable trait that has a consistent effect on that person's attractions, fantasies, and romantic feelings over the lifespan. What few people realize, however, is that these assumptions are based primarily on men's experiences because most research on sexual orientation has been conducted on men.[2] Although this model of sexual orientation describes men fairly accurately, it does not always apply so well to women.

Historically, women who deviated from this model by reporting shifts in their sexuality over time—heterosexual women falling in love with female friends, lesbian women periodically dating men—were presumed few in number and exceptional in nature. In other words, they were just inconvenient noise cluttering up the real data on sexual orientation. Yet as research on female sexuality has increased over the years, these "exceptional" cases now appear to be more common than previously thought. In short, the current conventional wisdom about the nature and development of sexual orientation provides an incomplete picture of women's experiences. Researchers now openly acknowledge that despite significant advances in the science of sexuality over the past twenty years, "female sexual orientation is, for the time being, poorly understood."[3]

This situation is now changing. As scientists have begun investigating female and male sexual orientation as distinct phenomena instead of two sides of the same coin, consensus is gradually building on why women appear so different from men. Specifically, we have found that one of the fundamental, defining features of female sexual orientation is its fluidity. We are now on the brink of a revolutionary new understanding of female sexuality that has profound scientific and social implications.

Sexual fluidity, quite simply, means situation-dependent flexibility in women's sexual responsiveness. This flexibility makes it possible for some women to experience desires for either men or women under certain circumstances, regardless of their overall sexual orientation. In other words, though women—like men—appear to be born with distinct sexual orientations, these orientations do not provide the last word on their sexual attractions

and experiences. Instead, women of all orientations may experience variation in their erotic and affectional feelings as they encounter different situations, relationships, and life stages. This is why a woman like Anne Heche can suddenly find herself falling madly in love with Ellen DeGeneres after an exclusively heterosexual past, and why a longtime lesbian can experience her very first other-sex attractions in her late forties.

The notion of sexual fluidity is not a new one. Rather, evidence for this phenomenon has circulated in the scientific literature for decades, though it has tended to be "submerged in the data rather than explicitly theorized." . . . [4]

I am well aware that the notion of sexual fluidity is potentially controversial and susceptible to politically motivated distortions.[5] For that reason, I would like to address some of the most common misconceptions at the outset:

Does fluidity mean that all women are bisexual? No. Just as women have different sexual orientations, they have different degrees of sexual fluidity. Some women will experience relatively stable patterns of love and desire throughout their lives, while others will not. Currently, we simply do not know how many women fall into each group because a number of different factors determine whether a woman's capacity for sexual fluidity will actually manifest itself.

Does fluidity mean that there is no such thing as sexual orientation? No. Fluidity can be thought of as an additional component of a woman's sexuality that operates in concert with sexual orientation to influence how her attractions, fantasies, behaviors, and affections are experienced and expressed over the life course. Fluidity implies not that women's desires are endlessly variable but that some women are capable of a wider variety of erotic feelings and experiences than would be predicted on the basis of their self-described sexual orientation alone.

Does sexual fluidity mean that sexual orientation can be changed? No. It simply means that a woman's sexual orientation is not the only factor determining her attractions. A predominantly heterosexual woman might, at some point in time, become attracted to a woman, just as a predominantly lesbian woman might at some point become attracted to a man. Despite these experiences, the women's overall orientation remains the same.

Does fluidity mean that sexual orientation is a matter of choice? No. Even when women undergo significant shifts in their patterns of erotic response, they typically report that such changes are unexpected and beyond their control. In some cases they actively resist these changes, to no avail. This finding is consistent with the extensive evidence . . . showing that efforts to change sexual orientation through "reparative therapy" simply do not work.[6]

Does fluidity mean that sexual orientation is due to "nurture" instead of "nature"? No. In fact, sexual fluidity sheds no light on this question, since it deals with the expression of same-sex and other-sex attractions rather than with their causes. Questions of causation typically receive the most debate and attention, but questions about expression are equally important. Nonetheless, fluidity raises important questions about how we think about biological versus cultural influences on sexuality, and it highlights the need for more integrative models.

Couldn't all individuals be characterized as fluid? Perhaps, though women appear to be more fluid than men. Certainly, few researchers would argue that sexual orientation is the sole factor determining each and every instance of sexual desire and behavior. Human sexual responses have been shown to be somewhat flexible, and thus any individual should be capable of experiencing desires that run counter to his or her overall sexual orientation.[7] For example, many men from different cultures and times have been shown to periodically pursue sexual behaviors that are atypical of their overall pattern of desire.[8] But in general, the degree of fluidity in women appears substantially greater than in men, though we do not yet have enough data to fully evaluate this possibility. . . .

KEY TERMS AND CONCEPTS

. . . I use the term "sexual orientation" to mean a consistent, enduring pattern of sexual desire for individuals of the same sex, the other sex, or both sexes, regardless of whether this pattern of desire is manifested in sexual behavior. A woman can have a lesbian orientation but never have a same-sex relationship, just as she can have a heterosexual orientation and still pursue multiple same-sex affairs. Most scientists consider desire, not behavior, the marker of sexual orientation. "Sexual identity" refers to a culturally organized conception of the self, usually "lesbian/gay," "bisexual," or "heterosexual." As with sexual orientation, we cannot presume that these identities correspond to particular patterns of behavior. Nor can we presume that they correspond to particular patterns of desire. Because sexual identities represent self-concepts, they depend on individuals' own notions about the most important aspects of their sexual selves. These notions, as we will see, can vary quite a bit from individual to individual. Moreover, some people—particularly women—reject conventional lesbian/gay/bisexual identity labels in favor of alternative labels such as "queer," "questioning," or "pansexual." Others reject all identity labels in order to make room for a broad range of sexual possibilities, as well as to acknowledge the fact that all labels are somewhat arbitrary.[9] I devote substantial attention to this issue later in the book, as it is directly related to the phenomenon of fluidity.

Global terms like "homosexuality" or "lesbianism" imply that same-sex desires, behaviors, and identities cluster together as part of an overall syndrome. But again, this is not always true. For this reason I find such terms to be potentially misleading. Instead, I use the term "same-sex sexuality" to refer to all experiences of same-sex desire, romantic affection, fantasy, or behavior. A person might experience one and only one form of same-sex sexuality (like same-sex attractions), or perhaps several (such as same-sex attraction and a lesbian identity), but I do not assume that any of these experiences necessarily cluster together. Correspondingly, I use the term "other-sex sexuality" to refer to all aspects of other-sex desire, romantic affection, fantasy, or behavior (readers will be more familiar with the phrase "opposite-sex," but researchers have increasingly gravitated toward "other-sex" because it is more scientifically accurate. The two sexes are certainly different from each other, but they are by no means opposites). Terms like "lesbian" and "bisexual" are also problematic. Do they refer to an individual's sexual orientation, sexual identity, or sexual behavior? To avoid confusion, I always pair these terms with the words "orientation" and "identity." Hence a "lesbian sexual orientation" can be taken to mean a pattern of near-exclusive desire for the same sex, even if a woman does not call herself a lesbian. A "lesbian sexual identity," in contrast, refers to a woman's self-description and self-presentation. Thus she might have a bisexual orientation but a lesbian identity (or vice versa).

When referring to desires and behavior, I use the descriptors "same-sex" and "other-sex." I refer to attractions and behaviors pursued with both sexes (either concurrently or sequentially) as "nonexclusive." If being 100 percent attracted to one sex means that you are exclusively attracted, then all other patterns of attraction are nonexclusive. I use this term rather than "bisexual," which has a wide range of different definitions across cultures and communities, making it potentially confusing. Of course, "nonexclusive" comes with its own problems. Because the term "exclusive" is often used to describe monogamous sexual relationships, "nonexclusivity" could be misinterpreted as sexual infidelity. This is not what I mean! I use "nonexclusive" simply to refer to the capacity to experience both same-sex and other-sex desires and behaviors, though not necessarily at the same point in time. Someone with nonexclusive attractions might have experienced only other-sex attractions up until adolescence, and then only same-sex attractions thereafter. Someone else might experience desires for both women and men concurrently. All that matters is that for that person, both types of desire are possible, in contrast to someone who has always been exclusively attracted to one sex or the other.

Finally, when speaking in the most general sense about individuals who have any experience with same-sex sexuality, at the level of orientation, desire, behavior, or identity, I use the term "sexual minority." This term captures the fact that regardless of a person's identity or orientation, any experience with same-sex sexuality—from fantasy to unrequited love to sexual behavior—violates societal norms prescribing exclusive heterosexuality, thereby making that person a sexual minority.

WHY IT MATTERS

The writer Minnie Bruce Pratt, reflecting on the confusion she experienced when she first discovered her capacity for same-sex sexuality, recalled being aware that such an abrupt change seemed impossible and incongruous:

> I didn't feel "different," but was I? (From whom?) Had I changed? (From what?) Was I heterosexual in adolescence only to become lesbian in my late twenties? Was I lesbian always but coerced into heterosexuality? Was I a less authentic lesbian than my friends who had "always known" that they were sexually and affectionally attracted to other women? What kind of woman was a lesbian woman?[10]

Pratt perfectly captures the conundrum created by sexual fluidity. Because our culture believes that all individuals are, unequivocally, one sexual type or the other (such that a lesbian must have "always known" of her essential lesbian nature), women with more complex and variable patterns of sexual experience are inherently suspect. No wonder Pratt felt "inauthentic" when comparing herself with the cultural prototype of lesbianism as uniformly stable, early developing, and exclusive.

Yet it is this rigid prototype that is inauthentic, not experiences like Pratt's. Greater appreciation and awareness of sexual fluidity are critical not only for building more accurate models of sexuality but also for communicating to women—young and old, lesbian and heterosexual, married and single—that flexible, changing patterns of sexual response are normal rather than deviant, and that they can occur in any woman at any stage of life. This information needs to be integrated into the numerous educational and therapeutic programs aimed at providing support and acceptance for individuals coming to grips with their same-sex desires. If such programs cling to rigid models of sexual orientation that inadequately represent the enormous variability in female sexuality, women may end up feeling doubly deviant, their experiences reflecting neither mainstream societal expectations nor perceived norms of "typical" gay experience. We must refashion science and public outreach to better represent women's experiences.

But this brings its own challenges. Almost every time I present my research publicly, someone raises their hand and asks, "Isn't the idea of fluidity dangerous? Couldn't it feed right into antigay arguments that sexual orientation can—and should—be changed?" Let me be clear: fluidity does not, in fact, imply that sexual orientation can be intentionally changed. But I know from experience that some people will nonetheless manipulate and misuse the concept of fluidity, despite my best efforts to debunk such distortions. Yet the solution to this danger is not to brush fluidity under the rug and stick to outdated, overly simplistic models of sexuality. Such an approach offers no real protection against political distortion: the truth is that any scientific data on sexual orientation can be—and pretty much have been—appropriated to advance particular worldviews. If scientists discovered tomorrow that same-sex sexuality was 100 percent genetically determined, some people would say, "Aha, this proves that homosexuality is normal, natural, and deserving of social acceptance and full legal status!" Others would say, "Aha, this proves that homosexuality is a dangerous genetic disorder that can be screened for, corrected, and eliminated!" In short, there are no "safe" scientific findings—all models of sexuality are dangerous in the present political climate. The only way to guard against the misuse of scientific findings is to present them as accurately and completely as possible, making explicit the conclusions that they do and do not support. . . .

The well-being of all women will be improved through a more accurate, comprehensive understanding of female sexuality in all its diverse and fluid manifestations. In short, women like Anne Heche, Cynthia Nixon, Julie Cypher, and Holly Near are not "noise in the data" on sexual orientation. Rather, they are the data with something important to tell us about the nature of female sexuality.

Any model of female sexual orientation that fails to account for their experiences is no model at all.

DISCUSSION QUESTIONS

1. How does Diamond define sexual fluidity?
2. Do Americans now generally assume that women's sexuality is fluid? How prevalent is the assumption of sexual fluidity?
3. Why is the idea of sexual fluidity controversial?

NOTES

1. Reviewed in Diamond, 2003b.
2. Reviewed in Mustanski, Chivers, and Bailey, 2002. Also see Blackwood and Wieringa, 2003, for an anthropological perspective on the invisibility of female same-sex sexuality.
3. Rahman and Wilson, 2003, p. 1371.
4. Kitzinger and Wilkinson, 1995, p. 95.
5. For perspectives on these issues see Brookey, 2000; Gonsiorek, 2004; Stein, 1994; Tygart, 2000.
6. Drescher, 2002.
7. Bancroft, 1989; Cass, 1990; Money, 1988.
8. Gagnon and Simon, 1968; Garland, Morgan, and Beer, 2005; Herdt, 1984; Laumann et al., 1994; Murray, 2000.
9. See Diamond, 2003a, 2005c; Hollander, 2000; Rust, 2003.
10. Pratt, 1995, p. 11.

REFERENCES

Bancroft, J. H. (1989). Sexual desire and the brain. *Sexual and Marital Therapy,* 3, 11–27.

Blackwood, E., and S. E. Wieringa. (2003). Sapphic shadows: Challenging the silence in the study of sexuality. In L. D. Garnets and D. C. Kimmel, eds., *Psychological perspectives on lesbian, gay, and bisexual experiences,* 2nd ed. (pp. 410–434). New York: Columbia University Press.

Brookey, R. A. (2000). Saints or sinners: Sociobiological theories of male homosexuality. *International Journal of Sexuality and Gender Studies,* 5, 37–58.

Cass, V. (1990). The implications of homosexual identity formation for the Kinsey model and scale of sexual preference. In D. P. McWhirter, S. A. Sanders, and J. M. Reinisch, eds., *Homosexuality/heterosexuality: Concepts of sexual orientation* (pp. 239–266). New York: Oxford University Press.

Diamond, L.M. (2003a). Was it a phase? Young women's relinquishment of lesbian/bisexual identities over a five-year period. *Journal of Personality and Social Psychology,* 84, 352–364.

———. (2003b). What does sexual orientation orient? A biobehavioral model distinguishing romantic love and sexual desire. *Psychological Review,* 110, 173–192.

———. (2005). What we got wrong about sexual identity development: Unexpected findings from a longitudinal study of young women. In A. Omoto and H. Kurtzman, eds., *Sexual orientation and mental health: Examining identity and development in lesbian, gay, and bisexual people* (pp. 73–94). Washington, D.C.: American Psychological Association Press.

——— Gonsiorek, J. C. (2004). Reflections from the conversion therapy battlefield. *Counseling Psychologist,* 32, 750–759.

Drescher, J. (2002). Sexual conversion ("reparative") therapies: History and update. In B. E. Jones and M. J. Hill, eds., *Mental health issues in lesbian, gay, bisexual, and transgender communities* (pp. 71–91). Arlington, VA: American Psychiatric Publishing.

Gagnon, J. H., and W. Simon. (1968). The social meaning of prison homosexuality. *Federal Probation,* 32, 28–29.

Garland, J. T., R. D. Morgan, and A. M. Beer. (2005). Impact of time in prison and security level on inmates' sexual attitude, behavior, and identity. *Psychological Services,* 2, 151–162.

Herdt, G. (1984). *Ritualized homosexuality in Melanesia.* Berkeley, CA: University of California Press.

Hollander, G. (2000). Questioning youths: Challenges to working with youths forming identities. *School Psychology Review,* 29, 173–179.

Kitzinger, C., and S. Wilkinson. (1995). Transitions from heterosexuality to lesbianism: The discursive production of lesbian identities. *Developmental Psychology,* 31, 95–104.

Laumann, E. O., J. H. Gagnon, R. T. Michael, and F. Michaels. (1994). *The social organization of sexuality: Sexual practices in the United States.* Chicago: University of Chicago Press.

Money, J. (1988). *Gay, straight, and in-between: The sexology of erotic orientation.* New York: Oxford University Press.

Murray, S. O. (2000). *Homosexualities.* Chicago: University of Chicago Press.

Mustanski, B. S., M. L. Chivers, and J. M. Bailey. (2002). A critical review of recent biological research on human sexual orientation. *Annual Review of* Sex *Research,* 13, 89–140.

Pratt, M. B. (1995). *S/he.* Ithaca, NY: Firebrand Books.

Rahman, Q., and G. D. Wilson. (2003). Born gay? The psychobiology of human sexual orientation. *Personality and Individual Differences,* 34, 1337–1382.

Rust, P.C.R. (2003). Finding a sexual identity and community: Therapeutic implications and cultural assumptions in scientific models of coming out. In L. D. Garnets and D. C. Kimmel, eds., *Psychological perspectives on lesbian, gay, and bisexual experiences,* 2nd ed. (pp. 227–269). New York: Columbia University Press.

Stein, E. (1994). The relevance of scientific research about sexual orientation to lesbian and gay rights. *Journal of Homosexuality,* 27, 269–308.

Tygart, C. E. (2000). Genetic causation attribution and public support of gay rights. *International Journal of Public Opinion Research,* 12, 259–275.

READING 16

The Biology of the Homosexual

Roger N. Lancaster

Three studies, published close on each other's heels in the early 1990s, have been widely ballyhooed in the mass media as establishing the "organic seat," the "hormonal link," and the "genetic cause" of homosexual desire and gay identity: Simon LeVay's "gay brain" research, Michael J. Bailey and Richard Pillard's "gay twins" survey, and Dean Hamer's "gay gene" study. Major design flaws, problems with the definition and operationalization of terms, and alternative interpretations of the data were lost in the din of blaring headlines: "First Evidence of a Biological Cause for Homosexuality," "Genes Tied to Sexual Orientation; Study of Gay Men Bolsters Theory," "Study Shows Homosexuality Is Innate," "Genes Linked to Being Gay," "Report Suggests Homosexuality Is Linked to Genes," "Study Provides New Evidence of a 'Gay Gene'" . . .[1]

THE INTERSEXED HYPOTHALAMUS

Simon LeVay's much-cited "gay brain" study was published, with much fanfare, in 1991. The journal *Science* set the tone for press reportage, vigorously spinning LeVay's study to the media under its own press-release headline: "THE HOMOSEXUAL BRAIN: BIOLOGICAL BASIS FOR SEXUAL ORIENTATION?"[2]

Roger N. Lancaster is a professor of anthropology and cultural studies at George Mason University.

LeVay found that the third interstitial nucleus of the hypothalamus (a neural structure at the base of the brain) is, on the average, smaller in gay men and straight women than in straight men.[3] (In theory, lesbians' hypothalami would resemble those of straight men—in other words, where gay men show a "feminized" pattern, lesbians would show a "masculinized" effect.) . . . The hypothalamus affects certain endocrine functions and is thought to influence "basic urges" such as hunger, thirst, and sexual arousal. . . .

The results of LeVay's research were widely disseminated in mass-media outlets, but LeVay's data are less impressive than the public was led to believe, and his study is plagued with methodological problems. LeVay's study examined the hypothalami of forty-one cadavers. While living, nineteen of the subjects were described in hospital records as "homosexual" (a figure that includes one "bisexual"). We do not actually know for how long, or with what degree of consistency, or for that matter even *whether* the "homosexual" subjects described themselves as gay. We know only what someone saw fit to observe (speculate?) in their hospital records. We also do not know how the other subjects described themselves when they were alive, nor do we know *anything* about *anyone's* sexual fantasies or sexual histories, but for purposes of LeVay's study, the sixteen other male subjects are presumed to have been "heterosexual," and all six women subjects are presumed to have been "heterosexual." Many critics have commented on the vagueness—indeed, the capriciousness—of the labels and classifications employed by LeVay.

Needless to say, important aspects of LeVay's research were not always given due weight in science journalism. Note, for instance, that the much-reported difference between "gay" and "straight" men in LeVay's sample is a statistical average, not an absolute difference. Individual measurements overlap: Some of the men in the "gay" sample had larger hypothalami than most of the men in the "straight" sample. Since many individuals did not fit the "average" picture, one could not thus predict who was what simply by looking at his hypothalamus. Such results in such a small sample mean that the resulting numbers lie close to the statistical margin of error—and that the reclassification of a small number of brains in the study would render LeVay's findings statistically insignificant.[4]

To make matters more complicated, LeVay talks as though identifying, delineating, and measuring the third interstitial nucleus were a simple matter. This is not the case.[5] The nucleus LeVay measured is a tiny structure by no means clearly differentiated from the similar neural tissue surrounding it. The fact that LeVay, rather than a colleague, performed the measurements, coupled with the absence of a "blind rater" to confirm his measurements independently, departs from the usual standards in research of this sort and does nothing to lend credibility to the findings.[6]

Worse yet, *all* of the "homosexual" men in LeVay's sample died from AIDS-related illnesses. Both AIDS and HIV medical treatments are known to affect a variety of brain structures. LeVay's inclusion of six (again, presumably) "heterosexual" men who died from AIDS scarcely addresses this problem.[7] Nor does the subsequent examination of the brain of one gay man who died from causes other than AIDS.[8]

In serious publications, LeVay rightly acknowledges that his results are open to a variety of interpretations. For instance, even if his results held—and to date his findings have not been replicated by a single subsequent study—it is by no means clear whether LeVay's average difference would measure biological "cause" or sociological "effect." As LeVay himself puts it, "It is not possible, purely on the basis of my observations, to say whether the structural differences were present at birth, and latter influenced the men to become gay or straight, or whether they arose in adult life, perhaps as a result of the men's sexual behavior."[9] It is also not possible to say whether the average structural differences have anything to do with sexual object choice per se or with other aspects of life associated with sexual object choice. Certainly, extended anxieties, social stress, the experience of inequality, sexual activity and inactivity, and various other cumulative life experiences affect organic processes, brain structures, and hormonal systems in human beings. . . .

LeVay has made far less cautious claims in public discussions of his study. LeVay's interpretation of his results, aggressively forwarded in a variety of media, is in no small part driven by his personal conviction that he was "born gay" and from his belief that the innatist scenario advances the social interests of gays and lesbians. LeVay thus favors a biologically reductive argument: The hypothalamus is the "seat" of sexual desire, and sexual object choice (or preference, or orientation) is physically *there,* in the third interstitial nucleus. As LeVay told *Newsweek,* "I felt if I didn't find any [differences between gay and straight men's hypothalami], I would give up a scientific career altogether."[10]. . .

BROTHERHOOD

Only months later the same year LeVay's study appeared, Michael Bailey and Richard Pillard published the results of a survey they conducted among gay men and their brothers.[11] The researchers recruited respondents by placing ads in gay newspapers across the Midwest and Southwest, ultimately gathering information on 56 pairs of identical (monozygotic) twins, 54 pairs of fraternal (dizygotic) twins, 142 non-twin brothers, and 57 pairs of adoptive brothers. They found that the "concordance rate" of homosexual self-identification—that is, the percentage of pairs in which both brothers called themselves gay—was highest for identical twins (52 percent), next highest for fraternal twins (22 percent), and lowest for non-twin and adoptive brothers (roughly 10 percent each).

Once again, methodological concerns and alternative interpretations were ignored or brushed aside. And once again, headlines trumpeted "mounting evidence" of a genetic basis for homosexuality.

How one interprets this data is largely a matter of the perspective one takes. As Ruth Hubbard and Elijah Wald dryly observe: "The fact that fraternal twins of gay men were roughly twice as likely to be gay as other biological brothers shows that environmental factors are involved, since fraternal twins are no more similar biologically than are other biological brothers."[12] Indeed, genetically unrelated adoptive brothers show the same concordance rate as

blood brothers, which would further seem to falsify the genetic hypothesis. And by definition, the monozygotic twins are genetically identical—yet *only half* of the pairs were sexually concordant. Given the conditions and assumptions of Bailey and Pillard's study, this figure could be viewed as surprisingly high or as revealingly low. It could even indicate that sexual orientation has *no* genetic basis whatsoever.

This is because twin studies normally use pairs of identical twins who were separated at birth. Such studies thus attempt to view the development of genetically identical individuals in (supposedly) different environments.[13] Since the identical twins in Bailey and Pillard's study in fact *shared* a family environment, it is a non sequitur to claim that the comparatively high (although theoretically low?) degree of concordance is genetically caused. It might just as easily result from the fact that the two occupy the same environment. As Hubbard and Wald put it: "If being a fraternal twin exerts an environmental influence, it does not seem surprising that this should be even truer for identical twins, who the world thinks of as 'the same' and treats accordingly, and who often share those feelings of sameness."[14] Gilbert Zicklin goes even further: "The intensely shared life of identical twins, including the phenomena of identification, mirroring, and imitation, might plausibly constitute fertile ground for the development of same-sex erotics."[15] Zicklin's suggestion is at least as plausible as the invocation of "genetic causation" to explain the 52 percent of identical-twin pairs who were concordant and "environmental factors" to account for the 48 percent who were discordant, an accounting that in no way follows from the data, but that dominated media presentations of the topic.

Consider the extraordinary anecdote related in *Newsweek*'s 1992 cover story, "Born or Bred: The Origins of Homosexuality."

> Until the age of twenty-eight, Doug Barnett (not his real name) was a practicing heterosexual. He was vaguely attracted to men, but with nurturing parents, a lively interest in sports and appropriate relations with women, he had little reason to question his proclivities. Then an astonishing thing happened: his

identical twin brother "came out" to him, revealing he was gay. Barnett, who believed sexual orientation is genetic, was bewildered. He recalls thinking, "If this is inherited and we're identical twins—what's going on here?" To find out, he thought he should try sex with men. When he did, he says, "The bells went off, for the first time. Those homosexual encounters were more fulfilling." A year later both twins told their parents they were gay.[16]

The author of the *Newsweek* piece relates this tale as evidence of a fixed, clear-cut, and genetic basis for sexual orientation.[17] That is, no doubt, what the protagonist, "Doug Barnett," himself believes. But the tale could be read just as easily as a demonstration of the flux, ambiguity, and capriciousness—indeed, the *suggestibility*—of sexual desire. The subject's description of his life as a "practicing heterosexual" is in no sense unusual. In various surveys, beginning with the Kinsey study, large percentages of men whose sexual activity is predominately or exclusively heterosexual agree, in principle, that everyone experiences "vague feelings" of "occasional attraction" toward members of their own sex.[18] Such findings are conveniently forgotten in the current rush to geneticize and typologize desire. The *Newsweek* anecdote could be understood as a particularly sharp example of the "twinning" behavior Zicklin invokes. Indeed, if taken seriously, it could even be understood from a constructionist perspective—why not?—as a gauge of the social force of reductionist theories in shaping personal life and identity formation.

In the end, even if we take Bailey and Pillard's figures as reliable ones, we simply do not know which had more of an effect on the identical twins' sexuality, shared genes or a shared environment, and we cannot even be sure whether we are monitoring a genetic tendency through degrees of sibling relatedness, a social tendency for twins—especially identical twins—to be alike, to mimic mirror, and "twin" each other, or even a homoerotic tendency among identical twins.

So far, all of these interpretations lie within the realm of a generous reading of Bailey and Pillard's

study—that is, within the assumption that their results are meaningful, that their numbers actually reflect real trends among siblings. But this is not necessarily the case.

The authors' sampling procedure almost guarantees a certain skewing. It is based on the self-selection of volunteers recruited through gay newspapers, rather than on a random sample of the general population. Given the stated aims of the study, which are clear enough in the ad, and given the cultural and political background of the question, which includes the active promotion of "innatist" scenarios in most gay newspapers, it is altogether possible that those who were most motivated to participate were those who already believed that sexual orientation is genetically determined. And it is altogether conceivable that those most likely to respond to the ad—to nominate themselves for study—would be concordant sets of identical twins.

These are not minor problems. They fatally undermine the study's reliability. As Zicklin elaborates:

> The overrepresentation of concordant MZ [monozygotic, identical] twins is quite possible, since gay MZ twins are likely to be more interested in studies that highlight the special meaning of close biological connections, and they might also have less trepidation about participating since there is a greater likelihood that they would be "out" with one another than would any other pair of male siblings. Conversely, some twins who perceive themselves as discordant on sexual orientation may be motivated to avoid studies wherein this difference may be revealed. Thus Bailey and Pillard have a double problem: they attract the kind of twins who fit their hypothesis and deter the ones who might weaken it.[19]

Bailey and Pillard skirt the usual standards of twin studies, sampling procedures, and logical deduction. Again, only those already committed to the notion that homosexuals have biologically marked bodies would be swayed by this kind of evidence.

THE "GAY GENE"

The 1993 study by Dean Hamer and his associates is usually praised for being the most serious, sophisticated, and careful of the three major studies purporting to substantiate a link between genes and male homosexuality.

Hamer's research team recruited an original group of 76 gay men for a pedigree study. (A "pedigree study" is an attempt to determine how a trait is distributed among members of a kin group.) One or more relatives from 26 of these men's families were also interviewed, for a total of 122 participants. Hamer's team found elevated levels of homosexuality among gay men's maternal uncles and among their maternal cousins, linked by aunts, as compared to their paternally linked relatives. Hypothesizing transmission of a homosexual gene through the X chromosome, the researchers then recruited 38 pairs of gay brothers for a second pedigree study. These pairs of gay brothers were specifically culled from families without known lesbians or paternally linked homosexuals in order to eliminate subjects likely to display "nonmaternal" routes of "transmission." The second pedigree study found a somewhat more pronounced maternal pattern. Finally, the Hamer team performed DNA linkage analysis on the 38 pairs of gay brothers from the second pedigree study, plus two pairs of gay brothers from the first study. Hamer et al. reported that 33 of 40 pairs (or 82 percent) shared a DNA marker, Xq28, located on the tip of the X chromosome. (The term "DNA marker" denotes a strip of DNA that is usually transmitted "whole" from parent to offspring; it thus allows geneticists to work with units of a few million base pairs of DNA, rather than trying to sort out individual genes from among several billion base pairs. Xq28, as the authors note, is large enough to contain several hundred genes.)[20] Hamer et al. conclude: "We have now produced evidence that one form of male homosexuality is preferentially transmitted through the maternal side and is genetically linked to chromosomal region Xq28." The authors suggest that a thorough mapping of the region will eventually yield a gene involved in homosexual expression, but they also suggest that more than one gene might contribute to sexual orientation, and that environmental factors also play a role.[21]

("Hey, Mom, Thanks for the Genes!" is the message that with minor variations appeared on gay T-shirts across the country—a line that proved even more popular than the camp come-on "How Big Is Your Hypothalamus?")

In his scientific (as opposed to journalistic or popularizing) publications, Hamer has been careful to avoid extreme variants of biological determinist arguments. Indeed, Hamer himself often points out that a "link" is not the same as a "cause." He distinguishes between "genetic influences" and "genetic destiny," and even while in search of a "gay gene," he often puts the term inside eyebrow-raising quotation marks.[22] Still, there is something less than fully congruous about searching for a "gay gene" while claiming that one does not exist, and the problems with Hamer's study are quite serious.

The pedigree studies invite certain preliminary observations. First, not all of the families in Hamer's samples exhibit the "maternal pattern" highlighted in the subsequent genetic study of gay brothers. The results suggest a "significant" but not dramatic elevation of homosexuality among the maternally linked relatives of gay men.

Next, some of the raw numbers supporting the idea of a maternal linkage are in fact quite low. In the first pedigree study, 7 of 96 gay men (7.3 percent) reported having a gay maternal uncle, as opposed to only 2 of 119 (1.7 percent) who reported a gay paternal uncle. But there is little difference between the 4 of 52 (7.7 percent) who reported a gay maternal cousin on their aunt's side and the 3 of 56 (5.4 percent) who reported a gay paternal cousin on their uncle's side.

In consequence, the difference between rates of homosexuality among maternal and paternal kin is statistically significant *only* if one assumes a (relatively low) 2 percent "base rate" of male homosexuality. As Edward Stein and others have pointed out, the difference becomes statistically insignificant if one assumes a (more plausible) base rate of 4 percent.[23]

Finally, given such small raw numbers, Hamer's pedigree analysis is open to charges that it fails to account for even the most obvious relevant effects of gender and family relations in American society. Women—mothers—play a much greater role than men in negotiating and cementing family ties, a tendency that is well established in the sociological and anthropological literature.[24] As a result, Americans tend to be closer to and to know more about their maternal relatives than their paternal ones. This sociological effect is likely to be even more pronounced in the case of gay men than in society at large. Given the role of fathers in perpetuating cultural expectations of masculinity, given the cultural anxieties that a gay son reflects upon his father, and given the nature of the idealized maternal role (nurturing caregiver), it is certainly conceivable that on the average, gay men tend to be closer to their mothers and to know more about their maternal, consanguineal kin than they are to their fathers, about whose blood relations they know correspondingly less.[25]

Hamer's team did attempt to apply a reasonable check on information provided by the gay men. They also interviewed at least one relative each for twenty-six participants (for a total of forty-six relatives interviewed). On this basis, Hamer concluded that the information provided by the seventy-six total participants was reliable. One might suggest, instead, that the claims were merely *consistent*: that one relative tended to think pretty much what another relative thought. Since extensive networks of the gay men's relatives were not systematically interviewed, either or both of the above sociological factors could fully account for the maternally skewed results of Hamer's pedigree study.[26]

At this point in a review of Hamer's study, it is usually conceded: "Yes, but Hamer's group nonetheless found *something*—a genetic marker—shared by gay brothers, and that is in itself significant." And after all, Hamer's group claims only to have established a genetic link for "one form" of male homosexuality—presumably the kind genetically transmitted along maternal lines. Still, there is considerably less significance here than one could glean from media reports, which took Hamer's study as the charmed third to seal the argument.

It is important to specify first what has *not* been shown by Hamer's group. First, no "gay gene" has been identified. Nor can we safely conclude that one is there, in Xq28, like a needle in the proverbial haystack, awaiting discovery. All kinds of traits "run in families" without having a genetic basis. And because human populations are quite variable, when a trait "runs in families,'" a "DNA sequence that is a marker for a particular trait in one family may not be associated with that trait in another."[27] The complexity of the relationships between genes, heredity, and even relatively simple phenotypic and behavioral characteristics has frustrated the search for genes "for" all manner of things that would appear far more straightforward than sexual desire.

There also is no genetic on/off switch for homosexuality. Even after a deliberate screening and selection process designed to produce a "maternal pattern" of "linkages," if not "transmission," not all the pairs of gay brothers whose X chromosomes were examined shared DNA markers for Xq28. A subsequent study by the Hamer group reported a somewhat lower percentage of Xq28 concordance among gay brothers.[28] Even a generous interpretation of these results along the lines laid out by the authors clearly does not indicate a simple or direct genetic "cause" for homosexuality.

There is no conceivable genetic "test" for homosexuality. Specifically, it has been reported that a percentage of pairs of self-identified gay brothers, culled from certain highly selected samples, share a genetic marker. Note that this selectively culled group of gay brothers share that marker *with each other,* not with unrelated gay men. Thus, even if Hamer's results hold, no one can take a blood sample and look at this genetic marker to determine whether a person is gay or straight.

Finally, in larger terms, the search for an "organic seat" or "biological cause" of homosexuality remains an undemonstrated conceit—a mishmash of selective citation from the animal kingdom and speculative parallels to poorly understood human processes. Although various commentators have speculated that some gene in Xq28 *might* play a role in sexual orientation by way of neurohormonal links with the hypothalamus, no one has specified exactly how this might happen, much less tested a coherent hypothesis. In view of the aforementioned problems with LeVay's hypothalamus work, it is unlikely that they will. . . .

The questions raised about the reliability of Hamer's pedigree studies are crucial. Because the pedigree study is based on such poor design for sociological research, the likelihood is increased that the Xq28 concordance rates are the equivalent of "false positive" readings, results that appear to be significant but that are not replicated in subsequent research. (This kind of result happens all the time, even in unimpeachable, well-designed research.)

Notably, the Hamer group did not try to determine how many *nongay brothers* share this region of the chromosome with their gay brothers, much less whether pairs of straight brothers exhibit high rates of Xq28 concordance among themselves. This is not a trivial matter, because unless we know the Xq28 concordance rates for gay men with their heterosexual brothers, we have no way of interpreting the meaning of the 82 percent rate among gay brothers reported in the first study or the 67 percent rate reported in the Hamer group's follow-up study. Hamer's conclusions—that the gay men received a maternal chromosome for homosexuality and that Xq28 is *a* (or even *the*) genetic site involved in sexual orientation—depend on a viable control group that has never been established. The absence of such a control group renders *Hamer's* first *study's* results virtually meaningless.

The follow-up study, which found a lower rate of Xq28 consonance between gay brothers, did report a *very* small sample of eleven families in which two gay brothers shared the Xq28 marker and also had a nongay brother. It is reported that nine of the nongay brothers did not share the marker with their two gay brothers and that two did—but these numbers are very small indeed, scarcely adequate for a viable control group.

Perhaps most significantly, the Xq28 concordance rate for gay brothers fell from 83 percent in the first study to 67 percent in the second study. As Jonathan Marks makes clear in his discussion of

inflated claims in the field of "behavioral genetics," the design of Hamer's study makes it extremely sensitive to a small number of families matching or not. The real question is not "Is there a gene for homosexuality?" but rather, "Is the 82 percent concordance result sufficiently different from the 50 percent rate that would occur by chance to be meaningful?" The concordance rate in the second study lies considerably closer to the 50 percent rate that would presumably occur in a DNA linkage analysis of pairs of brothers chosen entirely at random.[29]

More significant than any technical problems with Hamer's research design, however, are fundamental problems with the conception of the research and with the untested and untestable assumptions embedded therein. As is frequently the case with such research, the Hamer study implicitly understands phenotype (the aggregate physical and behavioral characteristics of an organism, usually understood as the product of a dynamic interaction between genes and environment) as the more or less direct expression of genotype (the state of the organism's genes, or the inherited genetic "givens" that are brought to the interaction), thus demoting "environmental" factors to an order of secondary importance. Whereas genes "for" this or that trait are conceived as playing a stable and "active" role in constructing the person, the environment serves as a backdrop and plays an essentially "passive" role, either speeding along the pre-given results or posing obstacles for the normal course of their expression.

This conception has the effect of obscuring the peculiar environment established by the study itself. Note the selection process that produced the sib-pair sample: There are always two gay brothers, maternally linked to other homosexual kin. We do not know how to compare this very specific sample with gay men who do *not* have gay brothers or other gay kin. This is no minor quibble, for the sampling procedure makes it impossible to distinguish environmental and social factors from genetic ones. There might well be major *social* differences between the development and experience of sexuality where a gay sibling is present, as opposed to sexual development and experience in other kinds of settings. Hamer has presumably accounted for this objection by claiming that he has identified "one form" of male homosexuality—presumably the kind genetically "transmitted" from mother to son. But this does not necessarily follow, and there are no compelling grounds for concluding it, unless one assumes that Xq28 in fact hides a "gay gene," which has not been demonstrated.

An alternative hypothesis, then: If older and successfully homosexual relatives serve as role models, fostering a sense of esteem for the homosexual feelings of younger relatives during crucial periods, then the "trait" in question might actually be "transmitted" *socially,* from uncle to nephew, from cousin to cousin, from brother to brother. . . . And the "form" of homosexuality identified here might mean only that there is an environmental difference—in that having a gay brother constitutes a different environment than not having a gay brother.

In this context, consider the most generous possible reading of Hamer's results, on their own terms—including the assumption that there must be some kind of "linkage" between genes and sexual object choice. Even assuming that Hamer's data, in toto, are reliable, there is no way of specifying exactly *what* is shared by gay brothers in Xq28: some gene *directly* related to sexuality and sexual orientation? Or some gene that has nothing to do with sexuality *directly,* but that can become linked, *indirectly* and under certain circumstances, to sexuality? In other words, the question of cause versus effect—indeed, of multiple causes and effects—has not been settled. Are consonant sibling pairs simply expressing a genetic predisposition toward homosexuality? Or are they being subtly socialized into homosexuality based on some other characteristic or set of traits? Or are they indirectly prodded toward the resolution of various conflicts through a homosexual outcome? Or even, yet again: Are they discovering and/or coming to emphasize a homosexual potential by way of some other characteristic, or by way of some other affinity with close kin?

Media reportage of genetic research like Hamer's invariably traffics in over-simplified, folkloric understandings of genetics and heritability. Headlines tell us that biologists have unearthed the "roots" of sexual orientation, or that geneticists have identified the gene "for" thrill seeking or a love of novelty. . . .[30] Such reportage, directed at the lay public, inevitably glosses complex technical questions. But it is not always clear that the research itself, considered apart from its splashy publicity, maintains a properly scientific approach to the question of heritability or the role of genetics in biological processes.

In the vernacular, heredity denotes what is "given," what is "in" the "blood": It is the part of human variation that is "caused" by genetic "nature," rather than by environmental "nurture." The folk conception of heredity also implies "immutability": The leopard cannot change his spots, and short of wearing colored contact lenses, human beings cannot change the color of their eyes.[31]

The biological conception of heritability is more precise and less deterministic. In biological terms, heritability is a measure of the likelihood that a trait present in one generation will recur in subsequent generations sharing a common gene pool in the same environment. Expressed as an equation, heredity includes both a numerator and a denominator. Richard Lewontin, Steven Rose, and Leon Kamin give that equation this way:

$$\text{Heritability} = H = \frac{\text{genetic variance}}{\text{genetic variance} + \text{environmental variance}}$$

where "genetic variance" refers to "the average performance of different genotypes" and "environmental variance" refers to the "variation among individuals of the same genotype."[32]

Two important qualifications follow from this formula. First, scientists attempting to determine the heritability of a trait assess average genetic variation. They do not measure genetic "causes." Second, environmental variation is part of the denominator—a basic point that is often forgotten in genetic research on complex human behaviors.

Note what limited arguments a properly biological conception of heritability and genetic factors actually permits. To say that a trait is "highly heritable"—that a high percentage of phenotypic variation is correlated to genetic variance—does not preclude saying that the trait also responds dramatically to environmental conditions. For example, if we say that height among a group of human beings has a heritability factor of about .9, or 90 percent, what this implies is that children in that group tend to be about the same height as their parents, all other things being equal.[33] But height also responds, impressively, to environmental factors, especially to childhood nutrition. Drought in the Sahel and famine in North Korea produce children whose height is substantially less than that of their parents, as is their body weight, among other things. In much of Asia, a shift away from traditional rice-and-fish staples to a cuisine more closely resembling the Western diet, with its emphasis on red meat, has dramatically raised the average height—along with body weight, average cholesterol levels, cardiovascular ailments, and the like. Heritability, then—even an extremely high measure of heritability—does not imply inevitability, immutability, or even genetic "causation." To say that a trait is "highly heritable" for a given population means only that the trait in question recurs at a certain rate among genetically related kin reproducing in a shared and relatively stable environment. It also implies a number of very substantial contingency clauses. If the environment changes, whether by accident, by migration, or as a result of changes introduced by the activity of the population itself, then the trait in question could also change dramatically.

To make matters yet more complicated, the heritability of a given trait can vary from group to group and place to place: "Some populations may have a lot of genetic variance for a character[istic], some only a little. Some environments are more variable than others."[34] For certain complex traits correlated to polygenic factors, environmental changes could signal the appearance of the trait in families where it was previously absent—or its elimination from lines where it had previously occurred. Finally, some simple, highly heritable traits in some species respond

dramatically to changes in the environment—but not in any linear or straightforward way.[35] Famous experiments by Jens Clausen, David Keck, and William Heisey elegantly illustrate this principle.[36] The scientists took three clippings each from several different individual plants of the species *Achillea millefolium*. Such clippings will produce "clone" plants genetically identical to their parent plant and to each other. The scientists planted the clippings from each of the different plants in three different environments to observe how they grew under different conditions: one each at low, medium, and high elevations. The genetically identical plants grew to different heights at different elevations, but some were "tall" at low elevations, "short" at medium elevations, and "tall" again at high elevations. Others exhibited the opposite relationship: "short," "tall," and "short" from low to high elevation. Some showed a wide range of variation in different climates, others a narrow range. Although it was clear that the plants' heights were affected by elevation, it proved impossible to predict just how individuals would actually respond to different environments.[37]

Let us imagine, then, that homosexuality *has* a heritability factor, and that Hamer and his team are on to something. Even if one takes the Hamer results at face value—and I have tried to indicate some of what might be wrong with the research itself—and even if the findings withstand subsequent restudies, which is already very doubtful, the correlation of some form of sexual variation with some kind of genetic variation has many fewer implications than the lay public (or for that matter much of the science establishment) seems to think. Even a relatively high correlation—a high heritability factor (the worst-case scenario for partisans of a constructionist perspective)—could not preclude dramatic or unpredictable environmental effects on sexual orientation. Nor could it preclude the possibility that, under other circumstances, the "trait" in question could manifest itself differently or among altogether different kin groups.

Genetic research like Hamer's almost never announces itself with anything resembling the range of caveats appropriate for properly restrained biogenetic research. More often than not, it lapses into an essentially folkloric understanding of heritability; the search for "the" "gay" "gene," the confusion of "genetic correlation" with "genetic causation." That is because biologists, as a group, tend to be committed to an ideology of biological reductionism, with its reification of practices into things, even when such reduction runs contrary to their own best methods.[38] They also tend to reject the notion that science cannot answer every question.[39]

Readers will no doubt see where I stand. I do not believe that homosexuality is really susceptible to even "good" biological research. As a complex, meaningful, and motivated human activity, same-sex desire is simply not comparable to questions like eye color, hair color, or height. I am not even convinced that "desire" can be definitively identified, isolated from other human feelings, objectively classified, gauged, or compared. For how are we to measure the "occurrence" (or non-occurrence) of a "trait" that is itself relational, subtle, and subject to varied modalities and modulations? And how are we to measure environmental constancy across generations on a subject defined by contestation, volatility, and change?

DISCUSSION QUESTIONS

1. What are some of the flaws Lancaster identifies in this research on sexuality?
2. Should one study sexuality in the same way that one studies genetic traits such as eye or hair color?

NOTES

1. Thomas H. Maugh II and Nora Zamichow, *Los Angeles Times,* August 30, 1991. Malcolm Gladwell, *Washington Post,* December 17, 1991. Jamie Talan, *Newsday,* December 9, 1991. Kim Painter, *USA Today,* December 17, 1991. Natalie Angier, *New York Times,* July 16, 1993. Curt Suplee, *Washington Post,* October 31, 1995.
2. Anne Fausto-Sterling, *Myths of Gender: Biological Theories about Women and Men,* rev. ed. (1985; New York: Basic Books, 1992), 257.
3. Simon LeVay, "A Difference in Hypothalamic Structure between Heterosexual and Homosexual Men," *Science* 253 (1991): 1034–37.

4. See Edward Stein's calculations in *The Mismeasure of Desire: The Science, Theory, and Ethics of Sexual Orientation* (Oxford: Oxford University Press, 1999), 200–201.
5. Gail Vines, *Raging Hormones: Do They Rule Our Lives?* (Berkeley: University of California Press, 1994), 112. John Maddox, "Is Homosexuality Hardwired?" *Nature* 353 (1991): 13.
6. Gilbert Zicklin, "Media, Science, and Sexual Ideology: The Promotion of Sexual Stability," in *A Queer World: The Center for Lesbian and Gay Studies Reader,* ed. Martin Duberman (New York: New York University Press; 1997), 383.
7. See Simon LeVay, *The Sexual Brain* (Cambridge, Mass.: MIT Press, 1993), 121–22. William Byne, "LeVay's Thesis Reconsidered," in *A Queer World,* 325, and Stein, *The Mismeasure of Desire,* 201.
8. Stein, *The Mismeasure of Desire,* 210. Simon LeVay and Dean Hamer, "Evidence for a Biological Influence in Male Homosexuality," *Scientific American* 270 (May 1994): 44–49.
9. LeVay, *The Sexual Brain,* 122.
10. David Gelman with Donna Foote, Todd Barrett, and Mary Talbot, "Born or Bred?" *Newsweek,* February 24, 1992, 49. See also Ruth Hubbard and Elijah Wald, *Exploding the Gene Myth: How Genetic Information Is Produced and Manipulated by Scientists, Physicians, Employers, Insurance Companies, Educators, and Law Enforcers* (Boston: Beacon, 1993), 97–98.
11. Michael J. Bailey and Richard Pillard, "A Genetic Study of Male Sexual Orientation," *Archives of General Psychiatry* 48 (1991): 1089–96. See also Michael J. Bailey and Richard Pillard, "Are Some People Born Gay?" *New York Times,* December 17, 1991.
12. Hubbard and Wald, *Exploding the Gene Myth,* 97.
13. Actually, adoption procedures tend to select for relatively homogeneous, middle-class environments, even for twins separated at birth. And it turns out that many twins called "separated at birth" were not really so separated after all. Many such twins are actually reared by different sets of relatives in the same town.
14. Hubbard and Wald, *Exploding the Gene Myth,* 97.
15. Zicklin, "Media, Science, and Ideology," 385.
16. David Gelman et al., "Born or Bred: The Origins of Homosexuality," *Newsweek,* February 24, 1992, 46.
17. I leave aside here a discussion of all those terms that give away more than they need divulge of the author's presuppositions, for example, "nurturing" parents, a "lively interest" in sports, and "appropriate relations with women."
18. See the section entitled "Homosexual Outlet" in Alfred C. Kinsey et al., *Sexual Behavior in the Human Male* (Philadelphia: W. B. Saunders, 1948), 610–66.
19. Zicklin, "Media, Science, and Sexual Ideology," 384.

20. See Dean Hamer and Peter Copeland, *The Science of Desire: The Search for the Gay Gene and the Biology of Behavior* (New York: Simon and Schuster, 1994), 21.

21. Dean Hamer, Stella Hu, Victoria Magnuson, Nan Hu, and Angela Pattatucci, "A Linkage between DNA Markers on the X Chromosome and Male Sexual Orientation," *Science* 261 (1993): 321–27.

22. Hamer and Copeland, *The Science of Desire,* 203–4, 17–38.

23. Stein, *The Mismeasure of Desire,* 217. Neil Risch, E. Squires-Wheeler, and B. J. B. Keats, "Male Sexual Orientation and Genetic Evidence," *Science 262* (December 24, 1993): 2063–65.

24. On the matrilateral skewing of American and English kinship systems, especially but not exclusively patterns of kinship in the lower classes, see David M. Schneider and Raymond T. Smith, *Class Differences in American Kinship* (1973; Ann Arbor: University of Michigan Press, 1978), 9, 40–43, 53–55. On the significance of maternal kin work, see Micaela di Leonardo, "The Female World of Cards and Holidays: Women, Families, and the Work of Kinship," *Signs* 12, no. 3 (1987): 440–53.

25. See Zicklin, "Media, Science, and Sexual Ideology," 385.

26. In *The Science of Desire* and in response to Hamer's critics, Hamer and Copeland report that the Hamer team *did* attempt other checks: the first was to ponder the distribution of *lesbian* relatives of the gay male subjects. Theoretically, if the maternal links simply reflected better knowledge of one's maternal kin, then there ought to also be elevated reportage of lesbianism along maternal lines. Hamer and Copeland report that the research team found no such pattern. The second check was to review lesbian informants' reportage of *gay male* relatives from a separate study. The authors report that there was no significant difference between maternal and paternal links for lesbian subjects (103–4). Of course, these "checks" assume that communication about relatives' sex lives occurs in a transparent environment unaffected by either sexual intolerance or gender inequalities—that talk about sex is uninflected by different maternal as opposed to paternal (and male as opposed to female, or mother-son, as opposed to mother-daughter, etc.) strategies of revelation and concealment. . . . It is by no means unthinkable that such factors could differentially distribute family knowledge about gays and lesbians. As Edward Stein demonstrates in *The Mismeasure of Desire* (218), it remains altogether plausible that the elevated maternal pattern of homosexuality reported by gay subjects is a *strictly* sociological effect, derived from partial knowledges, selectively revealed and asymmetrically conveyed.

27. Hubbard and Wald, *Exploding the Gene Myth,* 75.

28. Stella Hu, Angela Pattatucci, C. Patterson, L. Li, D.W. Fulker, S. S. Cherny, L. Kruglak, and Dean Hamer, "Linkage between Sexual Orientation and Chromosome Xq28 in Males but Not in Females," *Nature Genetics* 11, no. 3 (1995): 248–56.

29. Jonathan Marks, "Behavioral Genetics," chapter 5 in *What It Means to Be 98 Percent Chimpanzee* (Berkeley: University of California Press, 2002).

30. Natalie Angier, "Variant Gene Tied to a Love of New Thrills," *New York Times*, January 2, 1996. See Angier's follow-up story later the same year, which reports a failure to replicate the original studies: "Maybe It's Not a Gene behind a Person's Thrill-Seeking Ways," *New York Times,* November 1, 1996.

31. Although the shorthand that refers to genetic "causes" is appealing when simple Mendelian traits such as eye color are under discussion, the idea of a genetic "cause" founders when polygenic traits are in question. Simple Mendelian traits account for only a small percentage of human traits. See Hubbard and Wald's discussion in *Exploding the Gene Myth,* 40–42.

32. R. C. Lewontin, Steven Rose, and Leon J. Kamin, *Not in Our Genes: Biology, Ideology, and Human Nature* (New York: Pantheon, 1984), 97.

33. To be more precise, it means that 90 percent of the variance in height for a population is accounted for by genetic variance. See Lewontin, Rose, and Kamin, *Not in Our Genes,* 97.

34. Ibid.

35. This important point is meticulously illustrated by Richard Lewontin, from whom I draw the following example, in *The Triple Helix: Gene, Organism, and Environment* (Cambridge, Mass.: Harvard University Press, 2000), 20–24.

36. Jens Clausen, David Keck, and William Heisey, *Experimental Studies on the Nature of Species, Vol. 3: Environmental Responses of Climatic Races of Achillea,* Carnegie Institution of Washington Publication 581 (1958), 1–129.

37. I leave aside certain well-known paradoxes of the scientific approach to heritability. Since heritability is a measure of *variance*, certain traits that are absolutely genetic show no variation—hence, zero heritability. (Imagine a population in which everyone has brown eyes.) Correlatively, if certain other traits "run in families" (because of where the families live) or are *socially* attached to a genetic trait (like skin color), they display high heritability, despite having plainly environmental origins. See Edward Stein's discussion in *The Mismeasure of Desire,* 142–44.

38. See Richard Lewontin's short masterpiece of science criticism, *Biology as Ideology: The Doctrine of DNA* (New York: HarperPerennial, 1992).

39. See John Horgan, *The End of Science: Facing the Limits of Knowledge in the Twilight of the Scientific Age* (Reading, Mass.: Addison-Wesley, 1996), and *The Undiscovered Mind—How the Human Mind Defies Replication, Medication, and Explanation* (New York: The Free Press, 1999).

READING 17

The Heterosexual Questionnaire

Martin Rochlin

This Heterosexual Questionnaire reverses the questions that are very often asked of gays and lesbians by straight people. By having to answer this type of question, the heterosexual person will get some intellectual and emotional insight into how oppressive and discriminatory a "straight" frame of reference can be to lesbians and gays.

1. What do you think caused your heterosexuality?
2. When and how did you first decide you were a heterosexual?
3. Is it possible that your heterosexuality is just a phase you may grow out of?
4. Is it possible that your heterosexuality stems from a neurotic fear of others of the same sex?
5. If you've never slept with a person of the same sex, is it possible that all you need is a good gay lover?
6. To whom have you disclosed your heterosexual tendencies?
7. Why do you heterosexuals feel compelled to seduce others into your lifestyle?

8. Why do you insist on flaunting your heterosexuality? Can't you just be what you are and keep it quiet?
9. Would you want your children to be heterosexual, knowing the problem they'd face?
10. A disproportionate majority of child molesters are heterosexuals. Do you consider it safe to expose your children to heterosexual teachers?
11. Even with all the societal support marriage receives, the divorce rate is spiraling. Why are there so few stable relationships among heterosexuals?
12. Why do heterosexuals place so much emphasis on sex?
13. Considering the menace of overpopulation, how could the human race survive if everyone were heterosexual like you?
14. Could you trust a heterosexual therapist to be objective? Don't you fear that the therapist might be inclined to influence you in the direction of his or her own leanings?
15. How can you become a whole person if you limit yourself to compulsive, exclusive heterosexuality and fail to develop your natural, healthy homosexual potential?
16. There seem to be very few happy heterosexuals. Techniques have been developed that might enable you to change if you really want to. Have you considered trying aversion therapy?

DISCUSSION QUESTIONS

1. What is your reaction to the Heterosexual Questionnaire?
2. What are the assumptions behind these questions?

Martin Rochlin (1928–2003) was one of the founders of the Association of Gay Psychologists and a leader in the campaign that led to removing homosexuality from the list of mental disorders in the *Diagnostic and Statistical Manual of Mental Disorders*.

WHAT IS DISABILITY?

Disability Definitions: The Politics of Meaning

Michael Oliver

THE IMPORTANCE OF DEFINITIONS

The social world differs from the natural world in (at least) one fundamental respect; that is, human beings give meanings to objects in the social world and subsequently orient their behavior towards these objects in terms of the meanings given to them. W. I. Thomas (1966) succinctly puts it thus: "if men define situations as real, they are real in their consequences." As far as disability is concerned, if it is seen as a tragedy, then disabled people will be treated as if they are the victims of some tragic happening or circumstance. This treatment will occur not just in everyday interactions but will also be translated into social policies which will attempt to compensate these victims for the tragedies that have befallen them.

Alternatively, it logically follows that if disability is defined as social oppression, then disabled people will be seen as the collective victims of an uncaring or unknowing society rather than as individual victims of circumstance. Such a view will be translated into social policies geared towards alleviating oppression rather than compensating individuals. It almost goes without saying that at present, the individual and tragic view of disability dominates both social interactions and social policies.

A second reason why definitions are important historically centres on the need to identify and classify the growing numbers of the urban poor in modern industrial societies. In this process of identification and classification, disability has always been an important category, in that it offers a legitimate social status to those who can be defined as unable to work as opposed to those who may be classified as unwilling to do so (Stone, 1985). Throughout the twentieth century this process has become ever more sophisticated, requiring access to expert knowledge, usually residing in the ever-burgeoning medical and paramedical professions. Hence the simple dichotomy of the nineteenth century has given way to a whole new range of definitions based upon clinical criteria or functional limitation.

A third reason why definitions are important stems from what might be called "the politics of minority groups." From the 1950s onwards, though earlier in the case of alcoholics, there was a growing realisation that if particular social problems were to be resolved, or at least ameliorated, then nothing more or less than a fundamental redefinition of the problem was necessary. Thus a number of groups including women, black people and homosexuals, set about challenging the prevailing definitions of what constituted these problems by attacking the sexist and racist biases in the language used to underpin these dominant definitions. They did this by creating, substituting or taking over terminology to provide more positive imagery (e.g., gay is good, black is beautiful, etc.). Disabled people too have realised that dominant definitions of disability pose problems for individual and group identity and have begun to challenge the use of disablist language. Whether it be offensive (cripple, spastic, mongol, etc.) or merely depersonalising (the handicapped, the blind, the deaf, and so on), such terminology has been attacked, and organisations of disabled people have fostered a growing group consciousness and identity.

There is one final reason why this issue of definitions is important. From the late fifties onwards there was an upswing in the economy and an increasing concern to provide more services for

---

Michael Oliver is professor emeritus of disability studies at the University of Greenwich in the United Kingdom.

disabled people out of an ever-growing national cake. But clearly, no government (of whatever persuasion) was going to commit itself to a whole range of services without some idea of what the financial consequences of such a commitment might be. Thus, after some pilot work, the Office of Population Censuses and Surveys (OPCS) was commissioned in the late sixties to carry out a national survey in Britain which was published in 1971 (Harris, 1971). Subsequent work in the international context (Wood, 1981) and more recently a further survey in this country, which has recently been published (Martin, Meltzer and Elliot, 1988), built on and extended this work. However, this work has proceeded isolated from the direct experience of disability as experienced by disabled people themselves, and this has led to a number of wide-ranging and fundamental criticisms of it. . . .

THE POLITICS OF MEANING

It could be argued that in polarising the tragic and oppressive views of disability, a conflict is being created where none necessarily exists. Disability has both individual and social dimensions and that is what official definitions from Harris (1971) through to WHO [World Health Organization] (Wood, 1981) have sought to recognize and to operationalize. The problem with this, is that these schemes, while acknowledging that there are social dimensions to disability, do not see disability as arising from social causes. . . .

This view of disability can and does have oppressive consequences for disabled people and can be quite clearly shown in the methodology adopted by the OPCS survey in Britain (Martin et al., 1988). [Table 1 presents] a list of questions drawn from the face-to-face interview schedule of this survey.

These questions clearly ultimately reduce the problems that disabled people face to their own personal inadequacies or functional limitations. It would have been perfectly possible to reformulate these questions to locate the ultimate causes of disability as within the physical and social environments [as they are in Table 2].

TABLE 1

SURVEY OF DISABLED ADULTS—OPCS, 1986

Can you tell me what is wrong with you?

What complaint causes your difficulty in holding, gripping or turning things?

Are your difficulties in understanding people mainly due to a hearing problem?

Do you have a scar, blemish or deformity which limits your daily activities?

Have you attended a special school because of a long-term health problem or disability?

Does your health problem/disability mean that you need to live with relatives or someone else who can help look after you?

Did you move here because of your health problem/ disability?

How difficult is it for you to get about your immediate neighborhood on your own?

Does your health problem/disability prevent you from going out as often or as far as you would like?

Does your health problem/disability make it difficult for you to travel by bus?

Does your health problem/disability affect your work in any way at present?

This reformulation is not only about methodology or semantics, it is also about oppression. In order to understand this, it is necessary to understand that, according to OPCS's own figures, 2231 disabled people were given face-to-face interviews (Martin et al., 1988, Table 5.2). In these interviews, the interviewer visits the disabled person at home and asks many structured questions in a structured way. It is in the nature of the interview process that the interviewer presents as expert and the disabled person as an isolated individual inexperienced in research, and thus unable to reformulate the questions in a more appropriate way. It is hardly surprising that, given the nature of the questions and their direction that, by the end of the interview, the disabled person has come to believe that his or her problems are caused by their own health/disability problems rather than by the organization of society. It is in this sense that the process of the interview is oppressive, reinforcing onto isolated, individual disabled people the idea that the problems they experience in everyday living are a direct result of their own personal inadequacies or functional limitations. . . .

TABLE 2

ALTERNATIVE QUESTIONS

Can you tell me what is wrong with society?

What defects in the design of everyday equipment like jars, bottles and tins causes you difficulty in holding, gripping or turning them?

Are your difficulties in understanding people mainly due to their inabilities to communicate with you?

Do other people's reactions to any scar, blemish or deformity you may have, limit your daily activities?

Have you attended a special school because of your education authority's policy of sending people with your health problem or disability to such places?

Are community services so poor that you need to rely on relatives or someone else to provide you with the right level of personal assistance?

What inadequacies in your housing caused you to move here?

What are the environmental constraints which make it difficult for you to get about in your immediate neighborhood?

Are there any transport or financial problems which prevent you from going out as often or as far as you would like?

Do poorly designed buses make it difficult for someone with your health problem/disability to use them?

Do you have problems at work because of the physical environment or the attitudes of others?

IMPAIRMENT: A STRUCTURED ACCOUNT

Recently it has been estimated that there are some 500 million severely impaired people in the world today, approximately one in ten of the population (Shirley, 1983). These impairments are not randomly distributed throughout the world but are culturally produced.

> The societies men live in determine their chances of health, sickness and death. To the extent that they have the means to master their economic and social environments, they have the means to determine their life chances. (Susser and Watson, 1971, p. 45)

Hence in some countries impairments are likely to stem from infectious diseases, poverty, ignorance and the failure to ensure that existing medical treatments reach the population at risk (Shirley,

1983). In others, impairments resulting from infectious diseases are declining, only to be replaced by those stemming from the aging of the population, accidents at work, on the road or in the home, the very success of some medical technologies in ensuring the survival of some severely impaired children and adults and so on (Taylor, 1977). To put the matter simply, impairments such as blindness and deafness are likely to be more common in the Third World, whereas heart conditions, spina bifida, spinal injuries and so on, are likely to be more common in industrial societies.

Again, the distribution of these impairments is not a matter of chance, either across different societies or within a single society, for

> Social and economic forces cause disorder directly; they redistribute the proportion of people at high or low risk of being affected; and they create new pathways for the transmission of disorders of all kinds through travel, migration and the rapid diffusion of information and behaviour by the mass communication media. Finally, social forces affect the conceptualisation, recognition and visibility of disorders. A disorder in one place and at one time is not seen as such in another; these social perceptions and definitions influence both the provision of care, the demands of those being cared for, and the size of any count of health needs. (Susser and Watson, 1971, p. 35)

Social class is an important factor here both in terms of the causes of impairments or what Doyal (1979) calls degenerative diseases, and in terms of outcomes, what Le Grand (1978) refers to as long-standing illnesses.

Just as we know that poverty is not randomly distributed internationally or nationally (Cole and Miles, 1984; Townsend, 1979), neither is impairment, for in the Third World at least

> Not only does disability usually guarantee the poverty of the victim but, most importantly, poverty is itself a major cause of disability. (Doyal, 1983, p. 7)

There is a similar relation in the industrial countries. . . . Hence, if poverty is not randomly distributed and there is an intrinsic link between poverty and impairment, then neither is impairment randomly distributed.

Even a structured account of impairment cannot, however, be reduced to counting the numbers of impaired people in any one country, locality, class or social group, for

> Beliefs about sickness, the behaviours exhibited by sick persons, and the ways in which sick persons are responded to by family and practitioners are all aspects of social reality. They, like the health care system itself, are cultural constructions, shaped distinctly in different societies and in different social structural settings within those societies. (Kleinman, 1980, p. 38)

The discovery of an isolated tribe in West Africa where many of the population were born with only two toes illustrates this point, for this made no difference to those with only two toes or indeed the rest of the population (Barrett and McCann, 1979). Such differences would be regarded as pathological in our society, and the people so afflicted subjected to medical intervention.

In discussing impairment, it was not intended to provide a comprehensive discussion of the nature of impairment but to show that it occurs in a structured way. However

> such a view does not deny the significance of germs, genes and trauma, but rather points out that their effects are only ever apparent in a real social and historical context, whose nature is determined by a complex interaction of material and nonmaterial factors. (Abberley, 1987, p. 12)

This account of impairment challenges the notion underpinning personal tragedy theory, that impairments are events happening to unfortunate individuals. . . .

DISCUSSION QUESTIONS

1. Can you list some words that have changed meaning over time?
2. Why must minority groups continue to challenge definitions?

REFERENCES

Abberley, P. (1987). "The Concept of Oppression and the Development of a Social Theory of Disability," *Disability, Handicap and Society,* Vol. 2, no. 1, 5–19.

Barrett, D., and McCann, E. (1979). "Discovered: Two Toed Man," *Sunday Times Colour Supplement,* n.d.

Cole, S., and Miles, I. (1984). *Worlds Apart* (Brighton: Wheatsheaf).

Doyal, L. (1979). *The Political Economy of Health* (London: Pluto Press).

Doyal L. (1983). "The Crippling Effects of Underdevelopment" in Shirley, O. (ed.).

Harris, A. (1971). *Handicapped and Impaired in Great Britain* (London: HMSO).

Le Grand, J. (1978). "The Distribution of Public Expenditure: the Case of Health Care," *Economica,* Vol. 45.

Martin, J., Meltzer, H., and Elliot, D. (1988). *The Prevalence of Disability Amongst Adults* (London: HMSO).

Shirley, O. (ed.) (1983). *A Cry for Health*: *Poverty and Disability in the Third World* (Frome: Third World Group and ARHTAG).

Stone, D. (1985). *The Disabled State* (London: Macmillan).

Susser, M., and Watson, W. (2nd ed.) (1971). *Sociology in Medicine* (London: Oxford University Press).

Taylor, D. (1977). *Physical Impairment—Social Handicap* (London: Office of Health Economics).

Thomas, W. I. (1966). In Janowitz, M. (ed.), *Organization and Social Personality*: *Selected Papers* (Chicago: University of Chicago Press).

Townsend, P. (1979). *Poverty in the United Kingdom* (Harmondsworth: Penguin).

Wood, P. (1981). *International Classification of Impairments, Disabilities and Handicaps* (Geneva: World Health Organization).

PERSONAL ACCOUNT

Invisibly Disabled

I am a disabled individual. I am an invisibly disabled person, which makes me not disabled enough. My earliest memories are of being in pain. Unfortunately, when those around me could not see my pain and, when doctors could not diagnose my pain, it was decided for me that my pain did not exist. If someone grabbed my arm and it was not "that hard," I learned I was not supposed to say it hurt, because it didn't *really* hurt—at least not them. This is when I began to put my disabilities in the closet.

I was 17 years old when I went to a rheumatologist about my medical problems. I heard the words, "Well, I am sorry to tell you this, but your daughter has fibromyalgia." I smiled with relief to finally find out what it was that was causing my problems. "Great, so . . . how do we fix it?" I asked. The look on his face was serious and almost sad as he told me, "Well, there is no cure. What I mean is we can treat some of the symptoms." That is when it hit me; I would be in pain for the rest of my life. The medications I have had to take since I was 17 have caused their own medical conditions. When I was 19, my rheumatologist realized I had rheumatoid arthritis as well, and when I was 22, I began showing the signs of what I would later find out is myoclonic epilepsy. At the age of 27, I experienced a full seizure; my body was flipping around like a fish out of water on the floor. The only time I ever remember being so scared was waking up as a child not being able to feel my legs.

With all that I am because of, in spite of, and thanks to my disabilities, I continue to try to keep them to myself and people close to me. Making my disabilities visible to someone is a choice I do not make lightly, or very often. From experience, I know they will make certain judgments about me and/or view me differently. Most of all, I fear people not believing me. It takes most people a long time to believe I am in pain at all, and explaining that I have had a lifetime of masking my pain is always a pointless endeavor.

I find myself using phrases like "I'm all right" and "Don't worry about me" because worrying about me will do no good, and I am all right—I am not completely helpless on the ground and unable to move, not yet anyway. As long as others are seeing me as able, I feel and act more able. It makes it more of a reality to some extent. Every time I see someone who is physically disabled treated poorly because of their disability, I take it personally. I see my own future and become angry, because I know they would not treat me that way since they view me as able . . . for now.

Heather L. Shaw

READING 19

What Wounds Enable: The Politics of Disability and Violence in Chicago

Laurence Ralph

We're in Kemo's garage. I sit near a pile of DVD players, cell phones, car stereos, laptops, and Internet routers.[1]

_____

Laurence Ralph is a professor of anthropology and African and African American Studies at Harvard University.

"When wintertime hits, and it's hard to get people to stand on the corner, he goes all bootleg and starts selling everything," Justin mutters.

Justin's back faces me. He's gripping the armrests of his wheelchair, raising his body up and down—slow, fluid movements—his triceps bulge and his breath labors as he finishes his third set of inverted push-ups. He catches me in his peripheral vision, studying the latest contraband from a rusted foldout chair. This "hot" merchandise means it's cold outside, as confirmed by the draft that stings us from the side door someone has left ajar. Kemo closes it when he arrives.

"What's Urkel doin' here?" Kemo says as he enters.

"I told you, he's helping out with the forum. He's here to take notes," Justin says.

"I don't want you guys mentioning any gang leaders or any sets by name," he says, looking back and forth between the two of us. "No blocks, no streets, nothing like that. I don't know who's gonna be around, you know."[2]

"Nah, I don't do that," Justin replies. "That's not the point of what I do."

"Well, that's good . . . that's good, then." Kemo seems pleased.

"But, I *am* going to talk about the consequences," Justin continues. "You know, the consequences of gang banging. I *am* going to talk about what happened to me, and how it's affected my life."

"I ain't got no problem with that," Kemo says with a smirk. "But, good luck getting them to listen. I'll do my part. I'll get them there. Then they're all yours."

Why would a paralyzed, ex-gang member-turned-activist team up with a gang leader to organize a community forum on violence? What can this event teach us about the concept of disability? And what can this event show us about the seemingly contradictory ways that people disempower themselves in order to empower others?

In 2009 the rate of violent crime in Chicago was almost double that of New York City and Los Angeles. Among the nation's 10 largest cities, only Philadelphia had higher rates of murder and violent crime than Chicago.[3] What is more, during the 2008–2009 academic year, a record number of public school students (38) were murdered. The enormity of these numbers naturally focuses our attention on murder and death. Such a focus, however, limits our understanding of urban violence. Unacknowledged in these disheartening statistics is a more complex reality: most victims of gun violence do not die. While the most common cause of violence in urban areas is gun violence, a victim of a gunshot wound is four times more likely to end up disabled than killed. Though guns are no doubt deadly, equally important is that gunshot injuries constitute the second most common cause of disability in urban areas overall (only paralysis as a

result of car crashes is more common). And for our purposes, we must note that gun violence is the *primary* cause of disability among Hispanics and blacks; these two populations, in turn, make up the majority of gang members in Chicago.

This paper is about what injury allows us to see about the diversity among disabled populations. My argument is that, while admirable, the focus on assuaging social difference within the disability right's movement has served to obscure key distinctions within disabled communities along the axes of race and socioeconomic status. While the larger community of disabled activists in Chicago tends to use the social model of disability, in which there is multiple ways to view ability and physical capacities are not devalued, disabled ex-gang members rely on a medical model of disability that highlights physical differences rather than seeking to diminish them. I contend that the reliance on the medical model is one (of many) demonstrations of the severity of circumstances for these disabled, African American ex-gang members.

I demonstrate this point by discussing how notions of debt and obligation surface as critical components of gang sociality. When it comes to the familiar sequence (wherein a gang member shoots an affiliate of a rival gang, and in response, members of the rival gang retaliate) death and injury can be thought of as forms of debt exchange. I show that it is precisely because social relations between gang members are so often solidified through violence that expressive communication by a disabled gang member (which transmits knowledge about the streets and about injury) can be strategically deployed to disrupt a cycle of vengeance. Since the audience now owes it to the disabled affiliate who sacrificed his life, to change theirs, *wounds* become the precondition that *enable* social transformation.

RACE AND THE DISCOURSE OF DISABILITY

Social scientists interested in race and urban America have long pointed out the underbelly of American exceptionalism. The "land of promise" celebrated in the Constitution of the United States, they argue, has a flipside, which is the construction of the "defective" black subject.[4] Whether in the 1890s, when anthropologists measured the skulls of African descendants to show that behaviors and abilities corresponded to different racial groups, or more recently when scholars and government agencies suggested that the socioeconomic plight of urban blacks was associated with degenerate cultural values, notions of the defective body, born in the 19th century, continue to shape the 21st.[5]

The nascent literature on disability can thus serve as a point of intervention—a way to examine the relationship between biology and culture without invoking ideas of innate dysfunction—since scholars in this field have been attentive to bodily injury, yet have also advanced a "social model" of illness.[6] As these scholars have viewed disability as an institutionalized source of oppression, comparable to inequalities based on race, gender, and sexual orientation, they have argued that it is not an individual's actual "impairments" which construct disability as a subordinate social status and devalued life experience but socially imposed barriers (anything from inaccessible buildings, to limited modes of transportation and communication, to prejudicial attitudes).[7] This "social model," not surprisingly, is a radical step away from the medical model of illness, which has dominated Western thinking since the early 1900s, and which views disabilities and diseases as physical conditions that reduce a person's quality of life, and thus pose clear disadvantages to that person. In this way, the medical model echoes the 19th century notion of the black defective body. It is important to point out that advocates of disability rights have long rejected the medical model of disability, and instead emphasize a rights-based model that "emphasizes people's personal adjustment to impairment and their adaptation to a medical-rehabilitative regimen of treatment."[8]

The medical model is often presumed to silence a disabled person's voice . . . because a core expectation of being disabled is surrendering oneself to the care of a physician. The act of telling one's own story is therefore an act of empowerment. In *Crip Theory,* Robert McRuer brilliantly demonstrates how, by turning a story of suffering into testimony, disabled activists who "come out crip," endow the pejorative slur "crippled" with a positive valence. In a similar vein, . . . the wounded storyteller's disavowal of medical experience is the basis by which he voices his own experience of suffering. The notion that a person should embrace his own wounded body as an act of empowerment has been greatly influenced by the Americans with Disabilities Act of 1990. The Act makes discrimination based on disability illegal, but just as importantly, it has made acceptable the idea that people with disabilities face systemic societal barriers that impact their worldview and the ways in which they navigate their social environment.

Though the ADA has made great strides in providing resources for disabled people, one unintended consequence has been that in the process of leveling the playing field, both scholars of bodily impairment and the public have glossed over the ways race operates within disabled communities.[9] My time in Eastwood reveals the perils of such an omission. Justin's wheelchair-bound life, and the way he uses his disability, as we'll see, would be nearly unrecognizable—not to mention incomprehensible—to, for example, a well-off, white, middle-aged, suburban polio survivor.

. . . I aim to pinpoint how disabled populations have always had to highlight their differences in order to advocate for themselves, typically in ways that are politically strategic and reflective of their marginalized status. I ask: how, within a model of disability rights, do we account for the fact that, depending on the way a disability was acquired, what caused it, and the factors that might stop others from becoming similarly hurt, disabled people may choose to define themselves in terms of their defectiveness?

. . . The success of the disability rights movement has created the impression that the medical model is harmful, an outmoded relic of a discriminatory past, but the efforts of these disabled ex-gang members suggests that perhaps the disability rights movement has eschewed the medical model all too soon. Although these ex-gang members in Chicago face criticism from the wider disability rights community for highlighting variations in social difference (between "the normals" and the stigmatized, the paralyzed and the able-bodied) they feel that they must do so—since, as they put it, their wounds *enable* them to saves lives. Though I focus on the anti-gang forums hosted by disabled ex-gang members, rather than their positionality within the larger disability rights movement, both these forums, and the tenuous subject position of the people who run them, highlight the ways in which disabled communities are stratified along the lines of race, masculinity, and socioeconomic status.[10] It is the interplay of these culturally constructed identities that map the contours of oppression that African Americans face, allowing us to see the extent to which violence becomes both a gang and community-defining feature.[11]

GANG GEOGRAPHIES OF COMMERCE

Days after Justin and I met with Kemo, I see him again. Only this time, instead of a garage, he is holding court in an abandoned lot. A group of 8 teenage boys sit on the rubbled, glass-strewn ground at his feet. The leader of the local gang set waves his arms, punctures his words with stares. As he scolds the small group for failing to police their neighborhood, Kemo looks like an urban griot.

"You know what? Y'all lack discipline," he says. "That's why you got the Bandits comin' in here shooting up the place." Kemo is referring to a rival gang set, whose members recently infiltrated his territory, injuring two people. Pete, an affiliate who was shot in the leg during that incident, sits next to Kemo. The cane he will use for the rest of his life lies between them. After Kemo praises Pete for his bravery, and announces to the group that he is one of the few among them who has "what it takes" to be a gang leader, he reaches for Pete's curved handle cane and drags the rubber tip through the dirt, sketching the boundaries of their block. X's mark the places he predicts rival gangs will attempt to invade. Then he draws a series of arrows that surround the Xs. These are the routes gang members should travel to safeguard their domain.

"Y'all gotta protect your turf," Kemo barks: "*That's* the most important thing."

Kemo's depiction of his commercial strategy literally relies on a marker of disability—the cane. In other words, the cane is the tool Kemo uses to explain to his foot soldiers how they are going to maintain economic control; the cane is simultaneously a reminder of the consequences of that task. . . .

Since the 1920s, the term "gang" has been used to describe all kinds of collectives, from groups of well-dressed mobsters to petty criminals and juvenile delinquents—everything from substitute family units to religious groups and entrepreneurial drug-dealing cartels.[12] Perhaps the only thing that has remained consistent about gangs in nearly a century of research is their characterization as an internal Other from the vantage point of the law—a group that lives amongst us but does not abide by our "normal" rules.[13]

As we saw through Kemo's inscription in the dirt, the interplay between wounding and enabling surfaces in the ways in which gang cultures have been said to emerge out of the rationalities and strategies of protecting "turf"—i.e. territory, property, access—as a means to accrue good standing in a society in which people are frequently excluded from participation in the American polity.[14] On the face of it, the violent event associated with injury allows the disabled gang member to rise in social stature and moral standing, similar to the war veteran in contemporary American society. And like the war veteran in contemporary society, the rhetorical effect of this patriotism stands in sharp relief to reality. Unlike the gang member who has been labeled as a police informant (or "snitch"), disabled gang members in Eastwood are not given a "dishonorable discharge"—rather, they are released from service. An "honorable discharge" would be the appropriate analogy here. Of course, some disabled gang members will prefer to resume their activities, and in such cases, they are not so much willfully ignored as forgotten about, marginalized, or neglected. Hence, in contrast to members who die in gang wars and become martyrs—those bygone affiliates often emblematized on graffiti'd R.I.P. t-shirts—the disabled gang member, who cannot contribute to the organization in the way that is most valued (that is, as a street-corner drug dealer) becomes like the presumably honored war veteran who begs for change by day, and is tucked beneath a highway underpass by night.

As disability can signal honor and ignominy at the same time, wounding as it pertains to disabled bodies should be read as a commentary on enabling—whether this is the enabling of gang entrepreneurship and the forms of violence associated with it or, as we will see, the enabling of initiatives to stop violence. Likewise, *enabling* should be read as a commentary on *wounding*—whether this is the injury that stems from the drug trade, or the criminalization of black urbanites, which make them prone to debilitation. Hence, if this analysis of wounding is to be read with a negative moral valence, it is not because the notion of disability itself should be devalued. Rather, the disabled subject signals the ways in which the intersection of race and socioeconomics funnels risk of morbidity, unemployment, incarceration and mortality rates towards young urban residents in Chicago, who are far more likely than most of those who will read this article to fall victim to a stray bullet in the midst of drug-related gang warfare.

IN MY SHOES

In the aftermath of 2009's record number of shootings of public school students, community forums on violence became commonplace in Eastwood, the west side neighbourhood. . . . These forums were typically sponsored by non-profit organizations, schools, or churches and coordinated by adults who—though well intentioned by all accounts—had only a tangential relationship to the troubled youths they were targeting. . . .

Justin had attended many such forums over the past year, but had not seen many young men at any of them, so he worried about their efficacy: "I don't know man," he says to me one day, as we put away basketballs in the after-school program where he works and I volunteer, "It's like they're preaching to the choir. The guys who *really* need to be there, them boys who *really* need to hear those stories, they're out on the street."

Justin, however, has a solution: sessions offered by a very different group of men, forums which differed from the approaches of what he refers to as the "out-of-touch" gang-prevention programs. And, even though Justin himself does not organize these forums, he identifies with the people who do. The men who Justin is speaking of are in their early to mid-twenties—young enough to relate. Many of them still communicate with members of the Divine Knights, so they do not underestimate the gang's influence in the lives of young people. Plus, their very presence makes the consequences of gang life salient for everyone who attends their events—these men are all in wheelchairs. This group of paralyzed ex-gang members first met at Eastwood Hospital. Across the last five years, they participated in a rehabilitation program that teaches people suffering from spinal cord injuries how to adapt to their new lives. After finishing the program, a few of these men petitioned the hospital to sponsor the next step in their work: with the "In My Shoes" program, these former gang affiliates—themselves the victims of gun violence—travel to schools to discuss what it feels like to have your life permanently altered by a disability.

One day I accompany Justin to Jackson High, where the school administrators decide to dedicate the bulk of the day to violence prevention programming . . .

I watch with the boisterous crowd as four ex-affiliates form a semi-circle on the stage of the school's auditorium . . .

"Welcome to the 'In My Shoes' program," the leader of the group, Darius, starts.

"What we are is a violence prevention program. We're a little different from other programs. Like, we're not here to scare you or anything like that. We're basically here to educate you about the consequences of drug activities and gang life. As you can see, all of us here have wheelchairs," he continues. "And the reason we have wheelchairs is because we were out in the streets gang banging, selling drugs. We got shot, and ultimately we got paralyzed. So what we're gonna do today is tell you what happens to your body when you have a spinal cord injury."

The "In My Shoes" speakers have two primary goals in a situation like this. First, they try to counteract the foundational belief that perpetuating violence unifies the gang. Next, they argue that when the gang is no longer around, gunshot victims have to care for themselves.

"There's two types of spinal cord injuries," Darius begins, "there's a paraplegic and a quadriplegic. *Par-* meaning two: it means two of your limbs are affected. I'm a paraplegic. I'm paralyzed from the waist down. A quadriplegic is paralyzed from the neck down."

"See, the thing about the spine," he adds, "is that it's one of the few parts of your body that doesn't heal for itself. You know how if you break your arm or you get a cut, your body naturally heals itself, right? Well, when you have a spinal cord injury or a brain injury, that's permanent because there ain't no medicine or no doctor in the world that can fix that."

With a few sentences, Darius establishes his authority through medical expertise. The teenagers in the audience still fidget, hesitant to look directly at the injured bodies on stage. Then he tells the crowd how much his life has changed since he has become paralyzed.

"Aside from your movement, one of the first things that gets affected is your bladder. Y'all know when you gotta use the washroom, you get that feeling, right? Well when you're in a situation like ours, you no longer get that sensation. So what happens is that you gotta be on the clock. You know every four-to-six hours, you have to manually extract the urine. And that's done with one of these. This right here is a catheter."

He holds up a cloudy plastic bag, which is met with a collective groan from the crowd. Then he

places his thumb and index finger a couple of inches apart: "For males it'll probably go about *tha-a-a-t* deep inside the pee hole before it starts draining."

The group of adolescents erupt in a deafening chorus of gags and grimaces—this, at the mere thought of using a device in service of something which seems so natural.

"And this gotta be done every four-to-six hours for the rest of your life. Cause what can happen is, either you're gonna pee all over yourself . . . and you can imagine you're on the corner chillin' and all of a sudden: You're wet."

More groans. Now laughter. Nervous, embarrassed laughter. I worry that the kids in the audience are actually making fun of Darius. Some boys point at the catheter. But Darius waits out the snickers; he smiles with the kids, willing to indulge their nervousness, willing to play the role of the hapless, disabled person.

"Or it can stay in your system," Darius continues as the tittering from the crowd dies down. "And, basically, urine is just waste. So if it stays in your system, you can get sick, catch infections from it, and ultimately be hospitalized. What I'ma do is pass this around so you can check it out. It ain't never been used or nothing like that."

The crowd laughs in relief.

After Darius describes how the most prominent biological feature of manhood is transformed from the penetrat*or* to that which is penetrat*ed*, another activist, Aaron, begins to speak.

"One of the most important things that you have to look out for is the health of your skin, cause it can also get infected. Y'all know when you've been sitting down for a long time, how your butt starts to hurt and you get a little uncomfortable. You know, you gotta fidget a little bit. Well in a situation like ours, we can't feel our butts. So what we have to do is, we have to be constantly lifting off our chairs, doing 'pressure reliefs.' So you'll see me every once and a while do this—" he grabs the armrests of his chair and lifts his body above it, holding himself in an inverted push-up.

"'Cause what could happen is, I can develop a 'pressure sore'—also known as a 'bedsore,' or a 'ubiquitous ulcer.' That's when the bone starts digging through the skin. It starts off as a little pimple; but this is one pimple you don't wanna pop, 'cause you could make it worse."

"The thing about these pressure sores is that I can get one in a matter of hours. If I was to sit down in one of those chairs for two or three hours," Darius says, gesturing towards the wooden seats in the crowd, "I could develop a pressure sore."

"The problem is gettin' *rid* of one," Aaron intervenes. "To get rid of one could take anywhere from two months to a year. And the only way to heal it is to stay off it. *Bed rest.* So you can imagine if it's the summer. Summer just kicked off, and I got a pressure sore—now I gotta stay in bed to heal it."

"And what a lot of people don't know," Oscar says, taking the reigns, "is that Christopher Reeves, you know the actor that played Superman; he actually passed away from one of these. He caught a pressure sore, it got infected, and it got into his blood. And you know how blood is constantly traveling through your body? Well, it hit his heart, and he had a heart attack. What I try to tell people is that this is Christopher Reeves: this is *Superman.* He had *Superman money.* And he couldn't prevent one of these? What's gonna happen to one of us from the 'hood? We don't got that kind of money. We don't have that kind of around-the-clock care."

Here, Oscar's reference to Superman does not merely underscore the gulf in access to medical resources between a world-renowned actor and a poor person of color. He highlights another register of wounding: the fact that no one is actually fast enough to dodge a speeding bullet. Even Superman can die from a pimple.

The "In My Shoes" presentation at Jackson High resonates with Arthur and Joan Kleinman's insights about the stakes of telling stories through wounded bodies.[15] They argue that illness stories transcend the bodies of the ill. It is not merely that culture "infolds" into the body through differing ways to define disease, or varying access to, and attitudes towards, healthcare. Our bodily processes also "outfold" into social space, giving shape and meaning to the society in which we live. Borrowing from the Kleinmans, I want to suggest that the stories of these disabled, ex-gang members are not just about the interpersonal affects of disability. These stories outfold as well, inviting "at risk" teenage, black males to recognize themselves in them.[16] By speaking about what it is like to be disabled former gang members signal the mutual constitution between wounding and enabling as a means to respond to the gang's far-reaching influence in Eastwood.

. . . The men at Jackson High show no anger or resentment towards the medical establishment. To the contrary, disabled ex-gang members build their narratives out of the medical model of disability, in order to emphasize the biological reality of their now "broken" body. They do so to amplify the magnitude of urban violence. For members of racial groups who are prone to debilitation through gun violence, highlighting one's body as broken is a political act. The members of "In My Shoes," like Justin and every other disabled ex-gang member I have met, speak about the best ways to craft their stories; they borrow narrative techniques from each other; they rehearse, constantly. They learn by hearing themselves tell their own stories, absorbing each others' reactions, and experiencing their stories being shared.[17] On this day, for example, one of the disabled ex-gang members, Sam, did not speak at all. He listened and watched, still honing his own illness narrative in preparation for the next school assembly when, perhaps, he will feel ready to testify. In this way, the "In My Shoes" speakers draw on presuppositions of illness that enable collectively salient descriptions of disability. Crafting their paralysis as undesirable and preventable is crucial since it helps excavate an altered vision of a world, already radically transformed by violence. Disabled ex-gang members hope that by seeing the world through their eyes—the eyes of the injured—these inner city students will come to see the effects of violence more clearly.

INJURIOUS DEBTS AND ENABLING OBLIGATIONS

A couple of days after the assembly I run into Marcus, a neighbor whom I haven't seen on the block in a while. He is a senior at Jackson High; I ask him what he thought about "In My Shoes."

Marcus invites me into his house; his mother is cooking dinner and asks if I want to stay. Marcus and I sit at the dining room table while she prepares food in the adjoining kitchen. He tells me about how the assembly has altered his perspective on gang life.

"Yeah," Marcus begins, "it was real deep to hear them speak, 'cause my mom kept telling me that my associations will lead me to one day, God forbid, be in the same predicament. And my heart was beating like 100 miles an hour, 'cause I could just see myself in the position they're in."

"Most of the people I hang out with are gang bangers," he explains. "And I was the type that always wanted to do right, but did wrong. I didn't want my brothers and them fighting, but I was right there in front—fighting everybody. But it's kinda like . . . over here . . . in this area . . . in the school I go to . . . thinking about *tomorrow* is the last thing you wanna do. Cause you wanna live through *today.*"

Marcus' statement is meant to set the backdrop for life in Eastwood, where gangs are commonly imagined as stand-in family units, where even a teenager who opts not to join the Divine Knights will be cognizant of who belongs to which set, and the jurisdictions of each, where young people are well aware that although most of the gang sets in their neighborhood fall under the Divine Knights umbrella, two factions can inspire violence at any given moment, becoming de facto rivals.[18] It is for this reason, at least in part, that a gang's legacy is heightened even as the immediacy of "tomorrow" is diminished.

"You know how it is," Marcus says. "We got all the rival gangs. I actually got pulled outta my last high school 'cause me and my friends got into it with some Bandits. My momma feared for my life. And I noticed when she took me out of school that

most of the fights I was getting into wasn't because of me, or something I did. It was because of my friends. That's why when the paralyzed speakers came to my new school, it was kinda like a privilege because before I didn't think it was real."

"But two of my friends just died over the past three weeks now," he continues. "And one of my cousin's friends, he died also. I know you heard about the fifteen-year-old boy that was found in the dumpster. *That* was *him.*"

Marcus takes a sip from a glass of water and looks out of the window. I think about what he has just told me. The notion that he does not start most of the fights in which he is engaged could be read as a convenient excuse (especially with his mother within earshot). But even so, the stakes of the peer pressure that he describes are painfully high in a context in which teenagers are regularly murdered and debilitated. Trade in injury is so common that even a hospital bed doesn't necessarily occasion a person to orient his life away from the gang. It may simply lead him to seek revenge.

"I got jumped on a while back. I got put in the hospital—in the trauma center. She'll tell you," Marcus says, gesturing towards his mother. "When my momma came in there I was talking to the doctor like: 'So, umm . . . What's up? What's your son's name? Can I play video games?' I was having fun—not knowing that something could've seriously been wrong with me. When my friends came I was jumping on the bed like, 'Yeah, man, they ain't do *nothing* to me! They ain't do *nothing* to me!'"

"I wanted revenge. I didn't think nothing really bad could happen. I even put the hospital band—the one that was on my arm—I put it around my neck and I wore it as a chain, like a trophy. My momma said that scared her. She told me that I could be dead, 'cause I blacked out for a second while I was fighting. In the meantime, I ain't really know what was happening."

"After I got out of the hospital, the next day, my friends came to my house. They were like, 'Man, what up? What you gonna do?'"

"Inside my head I'm like, 'Do I really want to go with them, or do I wanna listen to my momma?'"

For the next several minutes, Marcus describes arguing with his friends about his decision not to retaliate, and their response that he would look "weak" if he didn't. It wasn't just his reputation that was on the line, they argued, but that of the whole set. Still, Marcus insists that he remained adamant about resisting the temptation to strike back.

"The point is," Marcus says, "instead of listening to my friends, I listened to what my momma said. And they were looking at me like, 'Dang man, what's wrong with you? Why you actin' like this?'"

He pauses, takes another sip of water. His mother has stopped preparing dinner; I can't tell if she is paying attention.

"So I know how hard it is to get up on stage and do what they did. I saw one of the speakers, Darius, the other day and I told him. I said, 'I take my hat off to y'all. For y'all to come to my school and have the courage to say that in front of everybody, that means a lot. So I thank y'all, man, for real.'"

Marcus' insights allude to the fact that in Eastwood the obligation to seek vengeance is frequently anticipated, and its fulfillment relentlessly planned. Here, vengeance is an enduring ritual of exchange. Still, it is critical to note that in a context in which the Divine Knights cultivate feuds over territory and economic control, violence does not merely wound. More importantly, as we will see, it can enable. The fact that my conversation with Marcus takes place in his mother's house highlights the similarities between their familial bond and a kind of gang sociality in which members habitually express social obligations in an idiom of kinship. Here, the dichotomy between the Divine Knights' imagined community and physical debility does not merely surface through wounds, or the bodily pain that Marcus endures on behalf of his gang. It is also evidenced through the invocation of his mother who, he says, steers him away from gang affiliation.[19] But despite Marcus' discussion of his choice to stay in the house rather than enact revenge in the streets (to listen to "what my momma said"), one should not read my conversation with this teenage gang member as a story of redemption, primarily.

. . . In the days after Marcus' beating, as he chooses to listen to his mother, a curious thing happens. He leaves school and comes home. He doesn't dawdle on the corner. He stays inside. His friends stop talking to him. He gets dirty looks. At one point the leader of his local set even visits him at home, and says he has turned his back on his friends and his community. In other words, he is viewed by other affiliates as abandoning the gang. The crucial point here is that in refusing to retaliate, by being willing to look "weak," by extracting himself from social activities outside of his home, Marcus forgoes the opportunity to cultivate bonds with his brethren; and it is primarily because he withdraws from a system in which injury is often proposed as a means for debt settlement, that he is viewed as a deserter.

CASHING IN

Intimately felt obligations have an immeasurable impact on the ways in which a teenager like Marcus navigates his social world. But this sense of indebtedness does not always have to wound. It is because Justin knows intuitively that the most significant aspect of gang rivalry is its ability to maintain relationships between affiliates, that he brings a gang leader to the negotiating table to talk about the crippling violence that the gang set he commands has become known for. By rechanneling gang notions of reciprocity—and in the process allowing his wounds to enable peace, rather than violence—Justin frames his community forum as a harmonious way to settle debts between gang members.

In the winter of 2008, Justin decides that he wants the "In My Shoes" program to sponsor a community forum on violence. Even though he is not one of the speakers, he appreciates their approach. But, when he brings his proposal to the administrators at Eastwood Hospital, they decline. . . . As he seeks financial support, one of the first people to contact him is Kemo, on behalf of the Divine Knights. He pledges to donate funds for the purchase of food and promises to make the event a mandatory meeting for his constituency.

Even though I know Justin and Kemo's relationship dates back 17 years, when the two of them were budding gang bangers, I am initially taken aback when I hear that Kemo, a gang leader, is contributing to the forum that will talk about the hazards of gang life.

One day I ask about the gang leader's motivation: "So, Kemo is actually telling his crew to go to the forum?" I question. "How did you convince him to do that?"

"I mean, Kemo don't want the killings either," Justin replies. "You gotta remember: some of those boys are his cousins, and the little brothers of people we grew up with. Besides Kemo *owes me* and now I'm cashin' in."

On the brisk Saturday morning of May 10, 2009—three days after the 36th killing of a Chicago public school student—Kemo delivers. He personally drops off an Escalade full of young gang members at the House of Worship for Justin's violence forum. Kemo and some of the leaders from the other neighborhood gang sets linger outside of the church while the members of their respective constituencies file in. . . . Justin is seated in his wheelchair. He quickly grabs the crowd's attention by describing how he got "plugged" into the gang.

"I was raised right here in Eastwood," Justin begins after introducing himself. "And just like today, there was a lot of violence when I was growing up. It was real bad over here."

"You know, Eastwood is not that big of a community," he continues, "but when I was coming up, there was a lot of different gang sets; and they were all at war. To make matters worse, there was only one high school in the entire area. So everybody within those gang boundaries had to attend *that* high school. Being that the school was within a particular gang's territory, it was pretty rough. I remember in the ninth grade—before I was even in the gang—I would get frustrated because I had to cross rival territories to get to school. I was getting chased, beat up, and robbed constantly. Sometimes the people from my block would stick up for me. . . What would happen was, members of the rival gangs would see me with the boys from my block

and would assume I was in the same gang. So now they started treating me like opposition. It got to the point where I was already marked as a gang member, so I just decided to join the gang." . . .

"I joined up, and I never really thought twice about it. It seemed like I was where I should be because a lot of my friends, my cousins, and my uncles—even my grandfather—they were all involved in the gang. So it wasn't nothing new to me. But after awhile I started going to school less and less, and I was surrounded by violence more and more. I saw close family members and good friends die. I thought, 'If my friends and my family, they all died for the gang, then why not me? What makes me better than them?' I started telling myself, 'Man, I'm willing to die for this.'"

"At the time, I needed that mentality because I started dealing drugs. My two closest friends were becoming gang leaders and big-time drug dealers. They were the ones giving the product to everyone in my neighborhood. One day, there was a meeting with the high-ranking gang officials and the guy who was supplying both of them said that they would have to consolidate their gang sets. He said they could play Rock, Paper, Scissors, for all he cared, but someone had to step up, and someone had to fall back. It had to be done, he said. So my two boys decided to set up a meeting."

"It was January 3, 2000," Justin continues after taking a deep breath, "That day, the friend who I worked for picked me up and told me what they decided. They were gonna do it like the old-timers: meet and fight, one-on-one. Whoever won the fight would get the neighborhood drug market. The other person would be the right-hand man, and make his crew fall in line. They would even shake hands afterwards."

"They decided to fight in an abandoned lot. No one was there when we arrived, so me and my boy got out and waited for my other friend to show."

"After a couple minutes, a car came down the street. I made eye contact with the driver, but didn't recognize him. The car kept going. When it reached the dead end, it circled back around. It was creeping up slowly, so my boy said 'Let's get outta here.' But by the time we got back inside, the car was right beside us. I looked up and the person in the passenger seat had pulled out a pistol."

"*Tink . . . Tink . . . t-t-tink. Tink. Tink.* That's all I heard. I saw flashes. My boy said, '*Pull off. Pull off,*' so I started driving. But I was already hit, so I lost control of the vehicle. Eventually, I crashed. That's when I noticed that I was bleeding from my shoulder and my thigh. I started screaming: '*I got shot. I got shot.*' Next thing you know, I hear the car door slam shut. Just then I realized: one of my friends had left me, and my other friend wanted me dead.'" . . .

During this brief lull, I recall how weeks ago he told me that Kemo "owes" him because they were together when he was shot. It hadn't registered before now: Kemo had been in the car with Justin. His words now resonate with what I already knew about his shooting. Another affiliate, Eric, once told me that Kemo wanted badly to retaliate against the person who shot Justin, but he forbade it. As Justin had made a commitment to God to turn his life around on what he thought was his deathbed, the most he allowed Kemo to do was to confront the perpetrator, tell him to leave the neighborhood, and warn him to never come back. Because Kemo hoped that one day Justin would change his mind and permit revenge, the gang never informed the police about the shooter. The assailant escaped without sanction. As I reflect on these circumstances, Kemo's commitment to the forum makes all the more sense—as does Justin's willingness, to accept his help.

"I just got out of the car and started running," Justin continues. "I cut through an alleyway and stopped at the first house I saw. I knocked on the door. Then I knocked harder."

"All of a sudden the porch lit up. I got excited at first, but then I realized that the light wasn't coming from inside of the house. Headlights were beaming on the door from behind me. The car from before was approaching fast."

"Someone got out and started running towards me with a gun so I hopped over the porch railing. I almost reached the back of the house when I heard a shot go off—*BANG.*"

"I just remember falling to the ground. I wasn't in pain or anything like that. I was in shock. All I knew is that my legs wouldn't work. I was trying and trying, but I couldn't move my legs. I couldn't get up. I just couldn't. I laid my head on the grass, and that's when I heard footsteps running away and a car screeching off."

"I started yelling: '*Help, Help.*' I was screaming my boys' names. '*Help.*' One-by-one, I screamed by cousins' names and all the people that I was willing to die for: '*Help.*'"

"Then all of sudden I saw this lady look out her window. I sat up and called out to her, the best I could. I said, 'I've been shot. I've been shot. Please, ma'am, help me. I've been shot.'"

"While I was waiting to see if she would come out I tried to get up. I grabbed the storm drain and lifted my upper body. I remember looking at my legs and they were dangling. They were dead. When I saw that, I fell back down."

"The lady came out with a cell phone and called the ambulance. If it wasn't for her, who knows if I'd be here today. She waited with me and tried to comfort me: 'Everything's gonna be *alright,*' she said. '*Don't worry,* everything's gonna be *alright.*'"

"As she's telling me this, I see her eyes watering. Tears are coming down her face. And I just remember thinking, like, 'man, I don't wanna die.' I remember thinking that in my head. All my life I told myself that, I'm willing to die for this. I was willing to get shot. I didn't care. But, when I was lying there. I was scared to die. I didn't want to die. I don't know why, but *I didn't want to die.*"

Justin ends his story with a somber description of the day the doctor informs him that he will "never walk again." As he begins to recount his early days in a wheelchair, what strikes me most is how Justin felt abandoned. The pain of Kemo running from their car, and his recitation of the names of his gang brethren while lying in the woman's yard, seem to eclipse even the pain of the bullets lodged in his body.

. . . Today, Justin's inability to feel—the physical and psychological wounds of paralysis—enables him to elicit rare shades of empathy and sorrow from otherwise unshakeable young gang members. Days prior to the event, I overheard Kemo telling young affiliates of how Justin sacrificed his body so that he could flee in a gun battle. It is for this reason that Justin should be respected, the gang leader said. Watching them now, I hope they understand: not only did Justin sacrifice himself. But after doing so, he forgave the debt that was owed to him and transformed it into a communal project to stop the killings. This sacrifice, Justin hopes, will help youngsters like Marcus break free from the obligations that gang life is built upon.

WOUNDS THAT ENABLE

While traveling to local high schools and talking to "at risk" youth, disabled ex-gang members are willing to insist on the defectiveness of their bodies in order to highlight the burden that violence creates in communities like Eastwood. Their methods contrast sharply with the aims of the disability rights movement, in which constructing physical difference as an inferior identity is routinely and unequivocally criticized. This incongruity suggests that paralyzed ex-gang members and the larger world of disabled activists are not fully visible to each other. The disconnection also points to the fact that the disability rights movement and the field of disability studies have generally been silent about the ways in which race and socioeconomic status intersect. The success of the disability rights movement has created the impression that the medical model of disability breeds pity. My examination, however, reveals another more complex possibility. The sympathy, disgust, fear, and perhaps even the relief at being able-bodied, are all indicative of disabled, ex-gang members' approach to anti-violence. They essentially disempower themselves in order to empower others. Their efforts show that a medical model of disability does not always muffle the voices of the injured, but can demonstrate the scale of the social problems that African Americans growing up in violent neighbourhoods face.

Justin and Kemo, the organizers of the forum, attempt to address gang violence by establishing meaningful bonds between members, a bond that mirrors the sense of debt and obligation intrinsic to

their own lifelong friendship. . . . Young gang members from rival gang sets are supposed to use Justin's life story as a conduit through which to become more peaceful. Debilitated gang members' stories of catheters and enemas, pressure sores and bed rest, stories of their mothers warning them about their associations, illuminate an invisible aspect of gang sociality: disability is a distinct, though often frequently invisible, reality.

Unlike many researchers, gang members themselves acknowledge the fact of disability, and even place paralyzed members on a pedestal in gang lore. Disabled ex-gang members like Justin, however, counter the prominent belief that by sacrificing yourself for the gang you'll become a martyr or time-honored veteran. It is critical that their method of exposing this myth is by fixing themselves as inhabitants of imprisoned bodies—as a disabled gang member, Tony, reminded us in yet another Eastwood forum:

> "They say when you gang bang. . . when you drug deal, the outcomes are either death or jail. You never hear about the wheelchair. I ain't know this was an option. And if you think about it, it's a little bit of both worlds cause half of my body's dead. Literally. From the waist down, I can't feel it. I can't move it. I can't do nothing with it. The rest of it's confined to this wheelchair. This is my prison for the choices I've made."

This "imprisoned" body, I would add to Tony's statement, should not be dismissed as an outmoded and narrow-minded conception of disability. Rather, Tony is calling attention to his immobility to make the argument that the violence to which his body bears witness can and should be prevented.

DISCUSSION QUESTIONS

1. Was it a surprise to you to learn that disability resulting from a gunshot wound is so common in urban areas? Why do you think this is not a well-known fact?

2. Why might the disabled activists in Chicago prefer the medical model of disability, rather than the social model?

3. How effective do you think these anti-gang forums are?

NOTES

1. In accordance with the Internal Review Board protocol for the University of Chicago (my institutional affiliation on when this research was conducted) I have changed the names of people (i.e. "Justin and Kemo"), gangs (i.e. "The Divine Knights"), institutions (i.e. "Eastwood Hospital") and specific neighborhoods (i.e. "Eastwood") throughout this study.

2. The Divine Knight gang is split into segments, referred to by gang members as "sets." There are currently eight gang sets of the Divine Knight gang dispersed throughout Chicago. These sub-groups are overwhelmingly male and African American. Of this membership, crews of 4 to 6 members serve as "foot soldiers," responsible for street level dealing in open-air markets. Approximately 8–10 members fulfill other drug-related duties (i.e., runners, muscle, treasurers) (c.f. Levitt and Venkatesh 2000). The rest of the affiliates may or may not have an explicit connection to the gang's drug distribution network. For them, the gang is primarily a social group.
Levitt, Steven D., and Sudhir Alladi Venkatesh. 2000. "An Economic Analysis of a Drug-Selling Gang's Finances[*]." Quarterly Journal of Economics 115 (3): 755–789.

3. These statistics are from the Annual Crime Statistics released by the Federal Bureau of Investigation in May 2010.

4. See Muhammad, Khalil Gibran. 2010. *The Condemnation of Blackness: Race, Crime, and the Making of Modern Urban America.* Cambridge, Mass: Harvard University Press. See also Parenti, Christian. 1999. *Lockdown America: Police and Prisons in the Age of Crisis.* London: Verso.

5. For an early critique of biologically based theories of innate dysfunction, see: Boas, Franz. 1910. *Changes in Bodily Form of Descendants of Immigrants.* Washington, D.C.: United States Immigration Commission. For a prominent example of a "culture of poverty" thesis, see: Moynihan, Daniel Patrick. 1965. *The Negro Family: The Case for National Action.* Washington, D.C.: Office of Policy Planning and Research, U.S. Department of Labor.

6. Linton, Simi. 1998. *Claiming Disability: Knowledge and Identity.* New York: New York University Press.

7. Berger, Ronald and Melvin Juette. 2008. *Wheelchair Warrior: Gangs, Disability, and Basketball.* Philadelphia: Temple University Press.
See also Siebers, Tobin Anthony 2008. *Disability Theory.* Ann Arbor: University of Michigan Press.

8. Berger and Juette 2008: 10.

9. For a similar critique see Garland-Thomson, Rosemarie. 2009. *Staring: How We Look.* New York: Oxford University Press.

10. See Jain, Sarah S. 1999. "The Prosthetic Imagination: Enabling and Disabling the Prosthesis Trope." *Science, Technology & Human Values* 24, no. 1 (Winter 1999): 31-54. Here, I borrow from Jain (1999) who similarly views disabled bodies or bodies "dubbed as not fully whole" through these "richly intertwined (and ultimately inseparable) axes of identity." Only instead of socioeconomic status, Jain's focus on prostheses draws her to "another category that considers identity as correlate to technology" (32).

11. See Crenshaw, Kimberlé, ed. 1995. *Critical Race Theory.* New York: New Press.
See also Lorde, Audre. 1984. *Sister Outsider: Essays and Speeches.* Crossing Press Feminist Series. Trumansburg, NY: Crossing Press.

12. For the gang as mobsters see: Adler, Jeffrey S. 2006. *First in Violence, Deepest in Dirt: Homicide in Chicago, 1875–1920.* Cambridge, Mass: Harvard University Press. Asbury, Herbert. [1940] 2002. *The Gangs of Chicago: An Informal History of the Chicago Underworld.* New York: Thunder Mouth Press. For the gang as petty criminals and juvenile delinquents see: Thrasher, Frederic Milton. 1926 [1963]. *The Gang: A Study of 1,313 Gangs in Chicago.* Abridged ed. Chicago: University of Chicago Press. For the gang as substitute family units see: Decker, Scott H. and Barrik van Winkle. 1996. *Life in the Gang: Family, Friends, and Violence.* 1st ed.Cambridge University Press. For the gang as religious groups see: Brotherton, David. 2004. *The Almighty Latin King and Queen Nation Street Politics and the Transformation of a New York City Gang.* New York: Columbia University Press. For the gang as entrepreneurial drug-dealing cartels see: Venkatesh, Sudhir Alladi. 2006. *Off the Books: The Underground Economy of the Urban Poor.* Cambridge, Mass: Harvard University Press.

13. Thrasher 1926, Klein 1995, Hayden 2004, Venkatesh 2006.

14. Venkatesh 2006.

15. Kleinman, Arthur and Joan Kleinman, "How Bodies Remember: Social Memory and Bodily Experience of Criticism, Resistance, and Delegitimation Following China's Cultural Revolution," *New Literary History* 25 (1994): 710–711.

16. Frank, Arthur W. 1995. *The Wounded Storyteller: Body, Illness, and Ethics.* 1st ed. Chicago: University of Chicago Press, 50.

17. Frank 1995: 1.

18. Decker and Winkle 1996. For the geography of gang territories, see: Jankowski, Martin Sanchez. 1991. *Islands in the Street: Gangs and American Urban Society.* Berkeley: University of California Press. For violence as related to gang rivalries, see: Levitt and Venkatesh 2000. "An Economic Analysis of a Drug-Selling Gang's

Finances." *Quarterly Journal of Economics* 115, no. 3: 755–789.

19. Though not a central concern of this paper, I use Marcus' description of his neighborhood, and the recollections of his mother's warnings, to gesture towards the fact that it is one's family members-oftentimes, those who condemn gang lite the most-who become the primary caretakers for black urban youth who are disabled (Devlieger et al. 2007). Devlieger, Patrick J., Gary L. Albrecht, and Miram Hertz. 2007. The production of disabilty culture among young African-American men. *Social Science & Medicine* 64, no. 9 (May): 1948–1959.

READING 20

Ethnicity, Ethics, and the Deaf-World

Harlan Lane

It has become widely known that there is a Deaf-World in the United States, as in other nations, citizens whose primary language is American Sign Language (ASL) and who identify as members of that minority culture. The size of the population is not known, but estimates generally range from half a million to a million members (Schein, 1989). The English terms *deaf* and *hearing impaired* are commonly used to designate a much larger and more heterogeneous group than the members of the Deaf-World. Most of the 20 million Americans (Binnie, 1994) who are in this larger group had conventional schooling and became deaf after acculturation to hearing society; they communicate primarily in English or one of the spoken minority languages; they generally do not have Deaf spouses; they do not identify themselves as members of the Deaf-World or use its language, participate in its organizations, profess its values, or behave in accord with its mores; rather, they consider themselves hearing people with a disability. Something similar is true of most nations: There is a Deaf-World, a relatively

Harlan Lane is a professor of psychology at Northeastern University.

small group of visual people (Bahan, 2004; Padden & Humphries, 1988) who use a natural visual-gestural language and who are often confused with the larger group who view themselves as hearing impaired and use a spoken language in its spoken or written form. To acknowledge this contrast, often signaled in the scholarly literature by capital-D *Deaf* versus small-d *deaf*, is not to deny that there is a gray area between the two; for example, some hard-of-hearing people are active in the American Deaf-World; others are not. Oral deaf adults and late-deafened adults usually consider that they have a hearing impairment and do not self-identify as members of the Deaf-World.

This article is concerned exclusively with the smaller group, the Deaf-World. It aims to show that the Deaf-World qualifies as an ethnic group, and that an unsuitable construction of the Deaf-World as a disability group has led to programs of the majority that aim to discourage Deaf children from participating in the Deaf-World (programs such as oral education and cochlear implant surgery) and that aim to reduce the number of Deaf births, programs that are unethical from an ethnic group perspective. In other words, this article makes the case that our ethical standards for the majority's treatment of Deaf people depend, not surprisingly, on whether our representation of the Deaf-World is that of a disability group on the one hand or an ethnic group on the other.

THE DEAF-WORLD IS AN ETHNIC GROUP

Internal Properties

Table 1 shows the criteria that have been advanced by social scientists for characterizing a social group as an ethnic group.

Collective Name

The members of this group have a collective name in their manual-visual language by which they refer to themselves. We refer to them by that name in adopting the English gloss of their compound sign: the *Deaf-World*.

TABLE 1
PROPERTIES OF ETHNIC GROUPS: DISTINCT

Collective name	Customs
Feeling of community	Social structure
Norms for behavior	Language
Values	Art forms
Knowledge	History
Kinship	

Feeling of Community

Self-recognition, and recognition by others, is a central feature of ethnicity (Barth, 1969; A. D. Smith, 1986). Americans in the Deaf-World do indeed feel a strong identification with that world and show great loyalty to it. This is not surprising: The Deaf-World offers many Deaf Americans what they could not find at home: easy communication, a positive identity a surrogate family. The Deaf-World has the highest rate of endogamous marriages of any ethnic group—an estimated 90% (Schein, 1989).

Norms for Behavior

In Deaf culture, there are norms for relating to the Deaf-World: for decision making, consensus is the rule, not individual initiative; for managing information; for constructing discourse; for gaining status; for managing indebtedness; and many more such rules. Cultural rules are not honored all the time by everyone any more than are linguistic rules. Such rules tell what you must know as a member of a particular linguistic and cultural group; what one actually does or says depends on a host of intervening factors, including other rules that have priority.

Distinct Values

The underlying values of an ethnic group can often be inferred from cultural norms. A value that appears to be fundamental in the Deaf-World is allegiance to the culture, which is expressed in prizing one's relation to the Deaf-World, in endogamous marriage, in gaining status by enhancing the group and acknowledging its contributions, in the giving of culturally related names, in consensual decision making, in defining oneself in relation to the culture, in distributed indebtedness, in the priority given to evidence that arises from experience as a member of the culture, in treasuring the language of the Deaf-World, and in promoting among Deaf people dissemination of culturally salient information (cf., Lane, 2004a; Mindess, 1999; T. Smith, 1997).

Knowledge

Deaf people have culture-specific knowledge, such as who their leaders are (and their characteristics); the concerns of rank-and-file members of the Deaf-World; important events in Deaf history; how to manage trying situations with hearing people. Knowing when and with whom to use ASL and when to use English- marked varieties of sign language is an important part of being recognized as Deaf (Johnson & Erting, 1989).

Customs

The Deaf-World has its own ways of doing introductions and departures, of taking turns in a conversation, of speaking frankly and of speaking politely; it has its own taboos.

Social Structure

There are numerous organizations in the American Deaf-World: athletic, social, political, literary, religious, fraternal, and many more (Lane, Hoffmeister, & Bahan, 1996). As with many ethnic minorities, there are charismatic leaders who are felt to embody the unique characteristics of the whole ethnic group (A. D. Smith, 1986).

Language

"The mother tongue is an aspect of the soul of a people. It is their achievement par excellence. Language is the surest way for individuals to safeguard or recover the authenticity they inherited from their ancestors as well as to hand it on to generations yet unborn" (Fishman, 1989, p. 276). Competence in ASL is a hallmark of Deaf ethnicity in the United States and some other parts of North America. A language not based on sound is the primary element that sharply demarcates the Deaf-World from the engulfing hearing society.

The Arts

First, the language arts: ASL narratives, storytelling, oratory, humor, tall tales, word play, pantomime, and poetry. Theatre arts and the visual arts also address Deaf culture and experience.

History

Ethnic groups construct rootedness, with forms of expression that include history, territory and genealogy. The Deaf-World has a rich history recounted in stories, books, films, and the like. Members of the Deaf-World have a particular interest in their history for "[T]he past is a resource in the collective quest for meaning [and ethnic identity]" (Nagel, 1994, p. 163). A sense of common history unites successive generations (Fishman, 1982, 1989; A. D. Smith, 1986).

Kinship

Many ethnic groups have a belief in the land of their ancestors. However, "territory is relevant not because it is actually possessed but because of an alleged and felt connection. The land of dreams is far more significant than any actual terrain" (A. D. Smith, 1986, p. 34). Land that the Deaf-World in the United States has traditionally felt an attachment to includes the residential schools; Deaf travel is often planned around visits to some of those schools. There is a Deaf utopian vision of "a land of our own" expressed in folk tales, novels, journalism, theater, and political discussions (Bullard, 1986; Lane, 1984; Levesque, 1994; Van Cleve & Crouch, 1989; Winzer, 1986). Deaf-Worlds are to be found around the globe, and when Deaf members from two different cultures meet, they feel a strong bond although they share no common territory and are limited in their ability to communicate with one another. In this, they are like Diaspora groups, such as the Jews. And, like the Diaspora ethnic minorities worldwide, prejudice and discrimination in the host society encourage them to cultivate their ethnicity to maintain their dignity despite social marginalization.

Some scholars maintain that the core of ethnicity lies in the cultural properties we have examined, so kinship is not necessary for the Deaf-World or any other group to qualify as an ethnic group (Barth, 1969; Petersen, 1980; Schneider, 1972; Sollors, 2001). Others say kinship should be taken in its social meaning as "those to whom we owe primary solidarity" (Schneider, 1969). "*Ethnie* embody the sense of being a large unique family; the members feel knit to one another and so committed to the cultural heritage, which is the family's inheritance" (A. D. Smith, 1986, p. 49). What is involved is a sense of tribal belonging, not necessarily genetic and blood ties. Certainly, there is a strong sense of solidarity in the Deaf-World; the metaphor of family goes far in characterizing many Deaf-World norms and practices.

What kinship is really about, other scholars contend, is a link to the past; it is about "intergenerational continuity" (Fishman, 1989). The Deaf-World does pass its norms, knowledge, language, and values from one generation to the next: first through socialization of the child by Deaf adults (parent or other) and second through peer socialization. Here, however, there is a significant difference from other ethnic groups: For many Deaf children, socialization into Deaf culture starts late, usually when the Deaf child meets other Deaf children in school (Johnson & Erting, 1989). Members of the Deaf-World have a great handicap and a great advantage when it comes to intergenerational continuity. The handicap is that their hearing parents usually have a different ethnocultural identity that, lacking a shared language, they cannot pass on to their children. Moreover, they commonly do not advocate in the schools, community, courts, and so on for their Deaf child's primary language. Minority languages without parental and community support are normally endangered. The great advantage of the Deaf-World lies in the fact that there will always be intergenerational continuity for sign language because there will always be visual people who take possession of that language in preference to any other and with it the wisdom and values of generations of Deaf people before them. (Although one can imagine an intervention in the future that would provide high-fidelity hearing to Deaf children and thus threaten intergenerational continuity, it seems likely that most countries will not be able to afford it, and that most Deaf parents will continue to refuse such interventions with their Deaf children.)

When we think of kinship, yet other scholars maintain, what is at stake is common ancestors, what Joshua Fishman (1977) termed paternity—real or putative biological connections across generations. Johnson and Erting (1989) suggested that what is primary in this biological criterion for kinship is not genealogy but biological resemblance across generations. In that case, members of the Deaf-World are kin because Deaf people resemble one another biologically in their reliance on vision for language and for much else (Johnson & Erting, 1989). To some extent, like the members of many other ethnic groups, Deaf people come by their biological resemblance through heredity more often than not. The estimate commonly cited is 50% of all people born deaf with little or no usable hearing are so for hereditary reasons (Reardon et al., 1992). However, another 20% are Deaf for reasons unknown; many of those may be hereditarily Deaf people not aware of the role of their ancestry (S. Smith, 1995).

To summarize in the words of social scientist Arthur Smith

> By involving a collective name, by the use of symbolic images of community, by the generation of stereotypes of the community and its foes, by the ritual performance and rehearsal of ceremonies, by the communal recitation of past deeds and ancient hero's exploits, men and women partake of a collectivity and its historic fate which transcend their individual existences. (A. D. Smith, 1986, p. 46)

Many scholars in the field of ethnicity believe that these "internal" properties of the ethnic group just reviewed must also be accompanied by an "external" property a boundary separating the minority from other ethnicities, in particular, the majority ethnicity (Barth, 1969). Does the Deaf-World in the United States occupy its own ecological niche? Does it look to itself for the satisfaction of certain needs, while looking to the larger society for the satisfaction of other needs—and conversely?

Ethnic Boundaries

Table 2 shows, at the left, activities that are primarily conducted by Deaf people for Deaf people in the Deaf-World in the United States; at the right, activities in the hearing world that impact Deaf people; and in the middle, areas of overlap. The more Deaf people celebrate their language and culture, the more they affirm their distinct identity, the more they reinforce the boundary delineating them from the hearing world. Language comes first for it always plays a powerful role in maintaining ethnic boundaries, but especially so in the case of Deaf people because bearing people are rarely fluent in visual language and members of the Deaf-World are rarely fluent in spoken language. Next, Deaf-World social activities are

TABLE 2

DEAF-WORLD—HEARING WORLD BOUNDARIES

Deaf-World	Overlap	Hearing world
Sign language	Interpreter services	Spoken language
Social activities	Religious services	Law enforcement
Sign language teaching	Consumer goods and services	Employment (not Deaf related)
Political activities	Deaf history	Military services
Athletics	Deaf education	Garbage collection
Arts and leisure	Deaf service agencies	Medical care
Finding employment		Banking
Publishing		Transportation

organized and conducted by Deaf people with little or no hearing involvement. On the other hand, law enforcement is a hearing world activity. Religious services overlap the Deaf and hearing worlds; there are missions to the Deaf, Deaf pastors, and signed services, but the operation of the house of worship is generally in hearing hands. All in all, the Deaf-World keeps to itself for many of its activities; it collaborates in a few with the hearing world; and it leaves the really broad responsibilities such as law enforcement to the larger society; in this, it is like other ethnic groups, such as Hispanic Americans.

This brief survey is intended to show that the Deaf-World in the United States today meets the criteria put forth for ethnic groups (also see Erting, 1978, 1982; Johnson & Erting, 1979, 1982, 1984, 1989; Markowicz & Woodward, 1978; Padden & Markowicz, 1976). Classifying the Deaf-World as an *ethnic group* should encourage those who are concerned with Deaf people to do appropriate things: learn their language, defend their heritage against more powerful groups, study their ethnic history; and so on. In this light, the Deaf-World should enjoy the rights and protections accorded other ethnic groups under international law and treaties, such as the United Nations Declaration of the Rights of Persons Belonging to National or Ethnic, Religious and Linguistic Minorities (United Nations, 2003a).

REASONS ADVANCED TO VIEW THE DEAF-WORLD AS A DISABILITY GROUP

Is it also appropriate to label the Deaf-World a disability group? We do not ask whether Deaf people in fact have a disability because it is not a matter of fact: Disability, like ethnicity, is a social construct, not a fact of life, although it is a property of such constructs that they appear misleadingly to be a fact of life. For example, the social problem of alcoholism evidently consists of this: Many Americans suffer from alcoholism; there are specially trained people to help them (alcoholism counselors, psychologists, psychiatrists, and others) and special facilities to care for them, such as detox centers. However, this understanding of alcoholism dates from the latter half of the 20th century. In the first half, the temperance movement branded excessive drinking as voluntary, and the movement promoted not treatment but prohibition. With the shift in the construction of alcoholism from illegal (and immoral) behavior to illness, the need was for medical research and treatment, halfway houses, hospital wards, outpatient clinics, and specialized hospitals (Gusfield, 1982).

Homosexuality went from moral flaw, to crime, to treatable disability, to a minority group seeking civil rights (Conrad & Schneider, 1980). Shortness came to be seen as a disability of childhood, not a normal variation, when growth enzyme was discovered, not before (Downie et al., 1996; Werth, 1991). Mild mental retardation came to be seen as a disability, not merely normal human variation in intellect, with the arrival of the IQ test (Gelb, 1987). In societies in which sign language use is mostly restricted to Deaf people, hearing people commonly see being Deaf as a serious problem requiring professional intervention; but in societies in which sign language use is widespread because of a substantial Deaf population—on Martha's Vineyard and Bali, for example—being Deaf is simply seen as a trait, not a disability (Lane, Pillard, & French, 2000).

The case of the forest dwellers of Central Africa is instructive. Their short stature, some 4.5 feet on average, allows them modest caloric requirements, easy and rapid passage through dense jungle cover in search of game, and construction of small huts rapidly disassembled and reassembled for self-defense and hunting. The Bantu villagers, formerly herdsmen, now farmers, have contempt for the pygmies because of their puny size, and they in turn have contempt for the villagers who are "clumsy as elephants" in the forest, much too tall to move swiftly and silently; they "do not know how to walk" (Turnbull, 1962, p. 79). Each group considers the other handicapped by their physical size. Each fails to appreciate how physical makeup, culture, and environment are intertwined.

Despite all this evidence that disability is constructed in a given society at a given time, many writers addressing ethics and Deaf people, apparently unaware of disability studies and medical anthropology, simply adopt the naïve materialist view when it comes to disability: "Almost by definition deaf persons . . . have a disability" (Gonsoulin, 2001, p. 554). "I maintain that the inability to hear is a deficit, a disability, a lack of perfect health" (D. S. Davis, 1997, p. 254). And, their ethical conclusions turn on this postulate. We understand, however, that disability is a label that can be applied with more or with less aptness to a particular group. That application is not a matter of chance, even less is it foreordained; it is powerfully influenced by the "technologies of normalization" (Foucault, 1980, p. 21) that exist to mitigate what is seen as a disability for they have a great stake in retaining that conception of the group. In the next section, arguments that have been made for including members of the Deaf-World among disability groups are examined critically.

Oppression from Deaf Bodies

Advocates of classifying Deaf people with disability groups claim that Deaf people have this in common with people who avowedly have disabilities: They are discriminated against because general social customs do not accommodate their bodies. Deaf people are indeed discriminated against in school, on the job, and in gaining access, but it is much more their language that is the target of discrimination than their bodies: "The major impact of deafness is on communication" (Baynton, 2000, p. 391). Thus, the Deaf are more like oppressed language minorities than oppressed disability groups. Like many Hispanic Americans, for example, many Deaf people have difficulty learning in school because the teacher cannot communicate with them fluently; they have difficulty getting a

job when the job requires good English; they miss out on important information because it has not been provided in their language.

Still, say the Deaf-are-disabled advocates, why not acknowledge the many things that physically different people share by using a common label (Baynton, 2002). After all, some disability activists make a claim for disability culture, just as there is a Deaf culture; many oppose mainstreaming, as do many Deaf activists. Both groups pay the price of social stigma, and stigmatized groups—among them disabled people, blacks, women, gays, and the Deaf—are often claimed to be biologically inferior. Moreover, both the Deaf-World and disability groups struggle with the troubled-persons industries for control of their destiny (Gusfield, 1984). Both endeavor to promote their construction of their identity in competition with the efforts of professionals to promote *their* constructions (Finkelstein, 1981). Finally, because there are great differences among disability groups, accommodating one more with its unique issues need not be a problem.

At one level, oppressed minorities do indeed share important traits and a common struggle for the defense and valuing of their diversity. At that level, disabled people, blacks, women, gays, the Deaf, and other language minorities can inform and reinforce one another's efforts. They can promote an understanding of the value of diversity, learn successful strategies from one another, and use their combined numbers to urge government in the right directions. At another level, however, many practical truths apply only to individual minorities, with their own makeup, demographics, histories, and cultures. To minimize that diversity with the same global representation would undermine the most cherished goal of each group: to be respected and valued for its difference. After all, beyond being stigmatized because of their physical difference, what, practically speaking, do the Deaf have in common with gays, women, blacks, Little People, and people with mobility impairment, for example? Deaf people have been subject to the globalizing disability label, and it has widely led to the wrong questions and the wrong answers, which are considered later in this article under reasons to reject it. This is the pragmatic answer to disability scholar Lennard Davis's proposal that Deaf people abandon the category of ethnicity in favor of a coalition with gays, hearing children with Deaf parents, and people with disabilities (L. Davis, 2002): Their agendas are utterly different.

The Shared Struggle for Rights

Another argument advanced for Deaf people to embrace the disability label is that it might assist them in gaining more of their rights (Baynton, 2002). For example, interpreters are not normally provided in the classroom for members of ethnic groups; Deaf people have them in many places under a disability umbrella. However, much that is important to Deaf people has come through an understanding of the Deaf-World as an ethnic group. Let us cite the burgeoning of ASL in high schools and colleges in the United States and the increasing acceptance of ASL classes in fulfillment of the foreign language and culture requirement; the mushrooming of scholarship in the last 40 years concerning Deaf ethnicity—history, arts, social structure, culture, and language; the flourishing of the interpreting profession; the development of the discipline of Deaf studies; bilingual bicultural Deaf education; the growing community of nations that formally recognize their national sign language. All these gains reflect an understanding of the Deaf as an ethnic group.

Although the disability label seems inappropriate for the Deaf-World, its members have not aggressively promoted governmental understanding of its ethnicity and of the poor fit of the disability label. As a result, the majority's accommodation of the Deaf has come under a disability label, and Deaf people must in effect subscribe to that label to gain their rights in access to information, in education, and in other areas. This is the Deaf dilemma: retain some important rights as members of their society at the expense of being mischaracterized by

that society and government or surrender some of those rights in the hope of gradually undermining that misconstruction. This dilemma is reminiscent of similarly oppressive choices offered to other minority groups: for gays to embrace the disability label and be spared classification as a criminal and entry into the army; for women to conform to the masculine idea of the feminine ideal and gain men's support and approval.

In principle, it should be possible for members of the Deaf-World in the United States to base their demand for language access on existing legislation and court rulings protecting language minorities. For example, in the field of education, the U.S. Congress has passed two types of statutes to remedy the disadvantage experienced by language-minority students who cannot communicate freely in the classroom by using their primary language: the Bilingual Education Act (P.L. 89–10, Title VII, 1965), which provides funding for a variety of programs promoting the use of minority languages in the schools, and civil rights statutes (P.L. 88–352, Title VI, 1964; P.L. 93–380, 1974), which impose an affirmative duty on the schools to give children who speak a minority language an equal educational opportunity by lowering the English language barriers. The provision of language rights in Deaf education should bring with it appropriate school curricula and materials, teachers who are ethnic models, interpreters, real television access through sign language, and video-telephone communication. But, in practice that would require that the public come to understand the Deaf-World as the Deaf-World understands itself. Until this happens, the Deaf-World can expect scant support from other ethnic groups.

Among the obstacles to a change from the disability to the ethnic construction of Deaf people are the numerous professional organizations predicated on the disability construction and who wish to own the problem of Deaf children. "To 'own' a social problem is to possess the authority to name that social condition a problem and to suggest what might be done about it" (Gusfield, 1989, p. 433). Consider just two of the many organizations that have Deaf children as clients. The American Academy of Otolaryngology, with over 10,000 members, has registered two paid lobbyists in Washington; the American Speech-Language-Hearing Association, with 115,925 members, has three (http://sopr.senate.gov). Members of these organizations collaborate with government officials in approving treatments, in drawing up legislation, and in evaluating proposed research and training activities. The Deaf-World has none of these advantages in seeking to promote an ethnic understanding of being Deaf.

FOUR REASONS TO REJECT THE DISABILITY LABEL

It "Doesn't Compute"

The overwhelming reason to reject the view of culturally Deaf people as members of a disability group concerns how Deaf people see themselves. People who have grown up Deaf and have become integrated into Deaf culture are naturally aware of their biological difference, but they do not, as a rule, see in that difference a reason to consider them members of a disability group. This is a very strong argument for rejecting the disability label because there is no higher authority on how a group should be regarded than the members of the group themselves. Some writers, convinced that the Deaf have a disability and baffled by their refusal to acknowledge it, conclude that Deaf people are simply denying the truth of their disability to avoid stigma (Baynton, 2002; Finkelstein, 1991; Gonsoulin, 2001). But, many people have, like the Deaf, physical differences that are not accommodated (Zola, 1993)—relatively short and tall people, for example—and they also deny they have a disability. Surely, in doing so they are not simply trying to avoid stigma. The gender preferences of gay men and women were at one time viewed as an expression of mental illness. In rejecting that disability categorization, the gay rights movement was not simply trying to avoid a stigma; it was trying instead to promote a new representation of gay men and women that would be better for them,

their families, and the wider society (Conrad & Schneider, 1980).

When Gallaudet University's president, I. King Jordan, was asked on the television program *Sixty Minutes* if he would like to be hearing, he replied: "That's almost like asking a black person if he would rather be white . . . I don't think of myself as missing something or as incomplete. . . . It's a common fallacy if you don't know Deaf people or Deaf issues. You think it's a limitation" (Fine & Fine, 1990). Deaf scholars like I. King Jordan, Tom Humphries, and MJ Bienvenu in the United States and Paddy Ladd in England are not rejecting the disability label because they want to avoid stigma associated with disability (Ladd, 2003). That would be to give them little credit. Rather, they are rejecting it because, as Tom Humphries has said so well, "It doesn't compute" (1993, pp. 6, 14). In ASL, the sign with a semantic field that most overlaps that of the English "disability" can be glossed in English LIMP-BLIND-ETC. I have asked numerous Deaf informants to give me examples from that category: They have responded by citing people in wheelchairs, blind people, mentally retarded people, and people with cerebral palsy, among others, but no informant has ever listed Deaf, and all reject it as an example of a disability group when asked.

Further examples of how the disability label does not compute come from Deaf preferences in marriage and childbearing. Like the members of many ethnic groups, culturally Deaf people prefer to socialize with and to marry other members of their cultural group; as noted, the Deaf have one of the highest endogamous marriage rates of any ethnic group (Schein, 1989). When it comes to Deaf preferences in childbearing, there are no hard statistics, but in interviews with the press and with me, Deaf parents have expressed a wish for children like themselves—much as all parents do who do not see themselves as disabled. "I want my daughter to be like me, to be Deaf," one expectant Deaf mother declared in an interview with the *Boston Globe*. She explained that she came from a large Deaf family, all of whom had hoped that her baby would be born Deaf (Saltus, 1989; also see

Mills, 2002). Other expectant Deaf parents reportedly say it will be fine either way, Deaf or hearing. These views contrast sharply with the tendency of disability groups. A study of blind people, for example, reported that they tend to shun the company of other blind people, associate with each other only when there are specific reasons for doing so, seek sighted mates, and do not wish to transmit their blindness to their children (Deshen, 1992). Leaders of the disability rights movement call for ambivalence: They want their physical difference valued, as a part of who they are; at the same time, they do not wish to see more children and adults with disabilities in the world (Abberley, 1987; Lane, 1995).

We should not be surprised that Deaf people want Deaf spouses, welcome Deaf children, and prefer to be together with other culturally Deaf people—in clubs, in school, at work if possible, in leisure activities, in political action, in sports, and so on—in short, they see being Deaf as an inherent good. Do not ethnic groups characteristically value their physical difference, from the pygmies of the Iturbi forest in Central Africa to the tall pale inhabitants of, say, Finland? Of course they do, so it is perfectly expected that culturally Deaf people positively value the Deaf difference and that hearing folks find in their own cultures a preference for hearing bodies, despite their poorer performance on some visual processing tasks compared to the Deaf (Lane, 2004a).

Thus, embracing the disability label in hopes it might assist Deaf people in gaining more of their rights is fundamentally flawed because Deaf people do not believe it. For Deaf people to surrender anyway to how others define them is to misrepresent themselves, and that is the first reason to reject the disability label.

Greater Risk for the Deaf Child

There are many penalties for misrepresenting, for allowing the disability label. An important penalty concerns the risk to the Deaf child. It appears that children are at greater medical and surgical risk

when their bodies differ from their parents in important ways that age alone does not explain. Parents want children like themselves, and if they are significantly unlike, they will listen to the doctors who say they can reduce or eliminate the difference, sometimes harming the child in the process. It is very tempting to locate the source of the social stigma with the child rather than the society; after all, the child is right there and much more manageable than an entire society. Moreover, the technologies of normalization are knocking at the door. However, the medicalization of difference deflects us from the real issue, which is the stigmatizing of difference in our society. When children who have undergone surgical normalizing become adults, many decry what was done to them as children.

For example, it has been the practice in the United States to operate on children with ambiguous genitalia, most often carving a vagina in male children because the surgical methods are not available to create a suitable penis. Once grown to adulthood, these and other intersexuals have been campaigning to dissuade urologists from continuing to perform this maiming surgery on children (Dreger, 1998). Little People, when their parents are not dwarfs, are frequently subjected as children to bone-breaking surgery for limb lengthening. It is painful, it is risky, and it is incapacitating. At best, it places the child in a no-man's land, neither short as a dwarf nor average size, and most adult dwarfs are utterly opposed to the surgery (Kennedy, 2003). There are many more victims of the medical-surgical imperative. One thinks of the horrors visited on the mentally ill, like frontal lobotomy (Valenstein, 1986), and those visited on homosexuals, such as deconditioning (Conrad & Schneider, 1980). Not all medical intervention in social issues is bad, of course; sometimes, it serves us well, and it derives great prestige from doing so. That is just why it overreaches at times and why we have to be wary of its abuse.

Cochlear Implant Surgery. Now to label the Deaf child as having a disability places that child at risk for interventions like cochlear implant surgery. Cochlear implant surgery lasts about 3.5 hours under general anesthesia and requires hospitalization from 2 to 4 days. A broad, crescent-shaped incision is made behind the operated ear, and the skin flap is elevated. A piece of temporalis muscle is removed. A depression is drilled in the skull and reamed to make a seat for the internal electrical coil of the cochlear implant. A section of the mastoid bone is removed to expose the middle ear cavity. Further drilling exposes the membrane of the round window on the inner ear. Observing the procedure under a microscope, the surgeon pierces the membrane. A wire about 18mm long is pushed through the opening. The wire seeks its own path as it moves around and up the coiled inner ear. The microstructure of the inner ear is destroyed; if there was any residual hearing in the ear, it is likely destroyed as well. The auditory nerve itself is unlikely to be damaged, however, and the implant stimulates the auditory nerve directly. The internal coil is then sutured into place. Finally, the skin is sewn back over the coil.

Clear Risks. The surgery and general anesthesia entail medical and surgical risks. The incidence of bacterial meningitis in implanted children is 30 times higher than in age-matched unimplanted children (Daneshi et al., 2000; Reefhuis et al., 2003). Other risks include anesthesia risk (Svirsky, Teoh, & Neuburger, 2004); loss of vestibular function (Huygen et al., 1995); cerebrospinal fluid leak (Reefhuis et al., 2003); facial nerve stimulation and injury (Kelsall et al., 1997); and damage to the carotid artery (Gastman et al., 2002). The surgery can have fatal consequences (Jalbert, 2003). Nine of ten candidates for pediatric implant surgery, those with no or little usable hearing, were born Deaf (Allen, Rawlings & Remington, 1994; Center for Assessment, 1992). Such children rarely receive the main benefit sought: fluency in a spoken language (Lane & Bahan, 1998). Compounding the harm, special educators who work with the surgical team commonly urge oral educational programs on the parents and discourage sign language use (Tye-Murray, 1992). If implanted children are unable to learn spoken English and are prevented from mastering ASL, they will remain languageless for many years. Developmental milestones for signed languages are similar to those for spoken languages, and the later the acquisition of ASL, the poorer its mastery on the average (Mayberry & Eichen, 1991; Newport, 1990; Petitto, 1993). It is inexcusable to leave a child without fluent language for years on end. Medicine is coming to realize that it is the overall quality of life of the person and not just the concerned organ that must be considered (Reisenberg & Glass, 1989).

Dubious Benefits. Advocates for childhood implantation acknowledge that "implants do not restore normal hearing," and that, after the operation, "long-term habilitation continues to be essential" (Balkany et al., 2002, p. 356). According to a recent report, 59% of implanted children are judged by their parents to be behind their hearing peers in reading, and 37% are behind in math (Christiansen & Leigh, 2004). It seems unlikely these children will be full-fledged members of the hearing world (Lane, 1999; Lane & Bahan, 1998). We know that early acquisition of ASL facilitates later mastery of English (Padden & Ramsey, 2000; Strong & Prinz, 1997). This linguistic intervention might deliver greater English mastery than implant surgery; the comparison study has not been done. On the contrary, every study that has compared the performance of children with cochlear implants to an unimplanted control group employed controls that apparently had not mastered any language (see, for example, the literature review in Geers, Nicholas, & Sedey, 2003). . . .

If medical and surgical procedures used with children who are Deaf, or intersexuals, or dwarfs required informed consent from adults *like* the child, they would almost never take place. And, when the parents are like the child, in fact they rarely take place. . . .

Survival Risk for the Deaf-World

A third argument against the disability label for the Deaf-World concerns the risk to the Deaf-World as a whole if that representation prevails. A majority of people in the Deaf-World have inherited their ethnicity. Deaf inheritance and a failure to understand the ethnic status of culturally Deaf people have historically and at present placed the Deaf-World in jeopardy of ethnocide and even genocide. Despite surgical and medical experiments on large numbers of Deaf children in the 19th century, medicine made no inroads against the Deaf-World as a whole. However, developments in biology in the late 19th century gave rise to the eugenics movement, which sought to improve the race and eliminate the Deaf-World, among other groups considered undesirable, by selective breeding. From the point of view of the variety of humankind favored by selective breeding, the practice is eugenic; from the point of view of the varieties disfavored, it is genocidal.

The most famous advocate of regulating Deaf marriage to reduce Deaf childbirth was one of the founders of oral education in America, Alexander Graham Bell, who devoted his great wealth and prestige to these eugenic measures (Lane, 1984). When the American Breeders Association created a section on eugenics "to emphasize the value of superior blood and the menace to society of inferior blood," Bell agreed to serve. He engaged the issue of eugenics and the Deaf population beginning in the 1880s. Sign language and residential schools were creating a Deaf community, he warned, in which Deaf people intermarried and reproduced, a situation fraught with danger to the rest of society. He sounded the alarm in his *Memoir Upon the Formation of a Deaf Variety of the Human Race,* presented to the National Academy of Sciences in 1883. Because there are familial patterns of deafness, Bell wrote, "It is to be feared that the intermarriage of such persons would be attended by calamitous results to their off-spring" (Bell, 1883, p. 11).

Bell argued, with breathtaking hubris, that to avoid this calamity, we must "commence our efforts on behalf of the deaf-mute by changing his social environment" (1883, p. 46). Residential schools, where most Deaf children acquired language, identity, and a life partner, should be closed and Deaf people educated in small day schools. Sign language should be banished; Deaf teachers fired. Bell's *Memoir* received wide newspaper coverage. Bell's actions led many to believe that there would be, or already were, laws prohibiting Deaf marriage. There was much consternation among Deaf people contemplating marriage. Some hearing parents of Deaf children chose to have their children sterilized (Mitchell, 1971).

A 1912 report from Bell's eugenics section of the Breeders' Association cites his census of blind and Deaf persons and lists "socially unfit" classes to "be eliminated from the human stock" (American Genetic Association, 1912, p. 3). The model eugenic law called for the sterilization of feebleminded, insane, criminalistic ("including the delinquent and the wayward"), epileptic, inebriate, diseased, blind, Deaf, deformed, and dependent people ("including orphans, ne'er-do-wells, the homeless, tramps, and paupers"). By the time of World War I, 16 states in the United States had sterilization laws in force. By 1940, 30 states had such laws (Haller, 1963). Physicians were actively involved in this eugenics movement (May & Hughes, 1987). . . .

Deaf Eugenics Today

Audiometric testing, labeling, special needs schooling, genetic research and counseling, surgery, and reproductive control all are means of currently or potentially exercising power over the Deaf body. In 1992, researchers at Boston University announced that they had identified the so-called genetic error responsible for a common type of inherited deafness. The director of the National Institute on Deafness and Other Communication Disorders [sic] called the finding a "major breakthrough that will improve diagnosis and genetic counseling and ultimately lead to substitution therapy or gene transfer therapy" ("BU Team," 1992, p. 6; "Deafness gene," 1992, p. 141). The goal of such efforts as gene transfer therapy is, of course, to reduce Deaf births, ultimately altogether. Thus, a new form of medical eugenics applied to Deaf people is envisioned, in this case by an agency of the U.S. government The primary characteristics of Deaf people with this particular genetic background to be eliminated are numerous Deaf relatives, sign language fluency, facial features such as widely spaced eyebrows, and coloring features such as white forelock and freckling (Fraser, 1976).

Imagine the uproar if medical scientists trumpeted a similar breakthrough for any other ethnic minority, promising a reduction in that ethnic group's children—promising fewer Navajos, fewer Jews, whatever the ethnic group. The Australian government indeed undertook a decades-long eugenic program to eliminate its aboriginal peoples by placing their children in white boarding houses in the city, where it was hoped they would marry white and have white children. In 1997, a government commission of inquiry classified these and other measures as genocide (National Inquiry, 1997). Under international law, an activity that has the foreseeable effect of diminishing or eradicating a minority group, even if it is undertaken for other reasons and is not highly effective, is guilty of genocide (National Inquiry, 1997; United Nations, 2003b). Why do governments fail to apply this moral principle and law to the Deaf? Americans fail to see the danger of pursuing a genocidal program in this instance because most Americans see Deaf people as having a disability arising from an impairment. And, the goal of eradicating a disability, although it may be in some circumstances unwise and unethical, is not seen as genocide.

If culturally Deaf people were understood to be an ethnic group, they would have the protections offered to such groups. It is widely held as an ethical principle that the preservation of minority cultures is a good. The variety of humankind and cultures enriches all cultures and contributes to the biological, social, and psychological well-being of humankind. Laws and covenants, such as the United Nations Declaration of the Rights of Persons Belonging to National or Ethnic, Religious and Linguistic Minorities (United Nations, 2003a), are founded on a belief in the value of protecting minority cultures. The declaration calls on states to foster their linguistic minorities and ensure that children and adults have adequate opportunities to learn the minority language. It further affirms the right of such minorities to enjoy their culture and language and participate in decisions on the national level that affect them. Programs that substantially diminish minority cultures are engaged in ethnocide and may constitute crimes against humanity. . . .

Wrong Solutions

Because they are an ethnic group whose language and mores were long disparaged, Deaf people commonly feel solidarity with other oppressed groups, the more so as the Deaf-World includes such groups as people with disabilities, seniors, women, blacks, and so on. Deaf people have special reasons for solidarity with hard-of-hearing and late-deafened people; their combined numbers have created services, commissions, and laws that the Deaf-World alone probably could not have achieved. Solidarity, yes, but when culturally Deaf people allow their ethnic identity to be subsumed under the construct of disability, they set themselves up for wrong solutions and bitter disappointments. After all, members of the Deaf-World differ from disabled people in their language and cultural experience, in their body of knowledge, in their system of rules and values, and in their models for selfhood.

If the Deaf-World were to embrace a disability identity, it would urge on Americans an understanding from which grow solutions that Deaf people oppose. Priorities of the disabilities rights movement include better medical care, rehabilitation services, and personal assistance services (Shapiro, 1993). Deaf people do not attach particular importance to any of these services and instead campaign for acceptance of their language and better and more interpreters. Whereas the disability rights movement seeks independence for people with disabilities, Deaf people cherish interdependence with other Deaf people. These differences in values and priorities far outweigh the areas, such as fighting job discrimination, in which Deaf goals are potentially advanced by joining ranks with disability groups. . . .

This article has presented a case that the sign language–using minority in the United States, the Deaf-World, is best viewed as an ethnic group, and it has cited reasons why it is inappropriate to view the Deaf-World as a disability group: Deaf people themselves do not believe they have a disability; the disability construction brings with it needless medical and surgical risks for the Deaf child; it also endangers the future of the Deaf-World. Finally, the disability construction brings bad solutions to real problems because it is predicated on a misunderstanding.

All of these objections to the disability construction of culturally Deaf people apply to the proposal that Deaf people be understood as both an ethnic group and a disability group at the same time. Taking up such a position would weaken the Deaf-World claim on ethnicity (is there any other ethnic group that is a disability group?) while inviting the risks and wrong solutions described here. The ethically troubling practices in which surgeons, scientists, and educators are engaged—operating on healthy Deaf children, seeking the means to diminish and ultimately eradicate the Deaf-World, opposing the Deaf child's right to full and fluent language—exist because this ethnic group is misunderstood as a disability group. They will not be avoided by affirming, contrary to the group's own judgment, that it is a disability group but also an ethnic group.

How we ultimately resolve these ethical issues goes well beyond Deaf people; it will say a great deal about what kind of society we are and the kind of society in which we wish to live. Difference and diversity not only have evolutionary significance but, I would argue, are a major part of what gives life its richness and meaning; ethnic diversity is a basic human good, and to choose to be with one's own kind is a fundamental right. There is reason for hope: Society *can* adopt a different understanding of a people. Native Americans were once seen as savages; black Americans as property; women as utterly dependent. The case for Deaf ethnicity built by the social sciences is powerful. Increasingly, linguists take account of ASL, sociologists of the social structure of the Deaf-World, historians of its history, educators of its culture, and so on. It remains to reform those other professions that have an outdated understanding or a representation that suits their agenda but not that of Deaf people. The challenge to the professions that seek to be of service to Deaf children and adults is to replace the normativness of medicine with the curiosity of ethnography.

DISCUSSION QUESTIONS

1. Is the ethnic group model of Deaf-World preferable to the disability model as Lane contends? What grounds should be used in making that calculation?
2. Why hasn't the ethnic group approach that Lane recommends so far taken hold in pubic policy or popular opinion?

REFERENCES

Abberley, P. (1987). The concept of oppression and the development of a social theory of disability. *Disability, Handicap and Society, 2,* 5–19.

Allen, T. E., Rawlings, B. W., & Remington, F. (1994). Demographic and audiologic profiles of deaf children in Texas with cochlear implants. *American Annals of the Deaf, 138,* 260–266.

American Genetic Association, Eugenics Section. (1912). *American sterilization laws. Preliminary report of the Committee of the Eugenics Section of the American Breeders Association to study and to report on she best practical means for cutting off the defective germ plasm in the human population.* London: Eugenics Educational Society.

Bahan, B. (2004, April). *The visual people.* Paper presented at the conference Deaf Studies Today, Utah Valley State College, Orem.

Balkany, T. J., Hodges, A. V., Eshraghi, A. A., Butts, S., Bricker, K., Lingvai, J., et al. (2002). Cochlear implants in children—a review. *Acta Otolaryngologica (Stockholm), 122,* 356–362.

Balkany, T., Hodges, A., & Goodman, K. (1999). Authors' reply [to Lane and Bahan]. *Otolaryngology—Head and Neck Surgery, 121,* 673–675.

Barth, F. (1969). *Ethnic groups and boundaries.* Boston: Little-Brown.

Baynton, D. (2000). Bodies and environments. In P. Blanet (Ed.), *Employment, disability and the Americans with Disabilities Act* (pp. 387–411). Evanston, IL: Northwestern University Press.

Baynton, D. (2002, July). *Deafness and disability.* Paper presented at the Deaf Studies Think Tank, Gallaudet University, Washington, DC.

Bell, A. G. (1883). *Memoir upon the formation of a deaf variety of the human race.* Washington, DC: Volta Bureau.

Binnie, C. (1994). The future of audiologic rehabilitation: Overview and forecast. In J. P. Gagné & N. Tye-Murray (Eds.), *Research in audiological rehabilitation* (pp. 13–24). Cedar Falls, IA: American Academy of Rehabilitative Audiology.

BU team finds genetic cause of Waardenburg syndrome. (1992, March). *Deaf Community News,* p. 6.

Bullard, D. (1986) *Islay.* Silver Spring, MD: TJ Publishers.

Center for Assessment and Demographic Studies, Gallaudet University. (1992). *Annual survey of hearing-impaired children and youth 1991–1992. Age at onset of deafness for students with profound hearing losses.* Washington, DC: Gallaudet University.

Christiansen, J. D., & Leigh, L. W. (2004). Children with cochlear implants: Changing parent and Deaf community perspectives. *Archives of Otolaryngology Head and Neck Surgery,* 130, 673–677.

Conrad, P., & Schneider, J. (1980). *Deviance and medicalization.* Columbus, OH: Merrill.

Daneshi, A., Farhadi, M., Emamjomeh, H., & Hasanzadeh, S. (2000). Management and the control of gusher during cochlear implant surgery. *Advances in Oto-Rino-Laryngology,* 57, 120–122.

Davis, L. (2002). *Postdeafness.* Paper presented at the Deaf Studies Think Thank, Gallaudet University, Washington, DC.

Deafness gene. (1992, February 18). *New York Times,* p. 141, B7, C 2.

Deshen, S. (1992). *Blind people.* Albany: State University of New York Press.

Downie, A. B., Mulligan, J., McCaughey, E. S., Stratford, R. J., Betts, P. R., & Voss, L. D. (1996). Psychological response to treatment in short normal children. *Archives of Disorders of Childhood,* 76, 92–95.

Dreger, A. (l998). *Hermaphrodites and the medical invention of sex.* Cambridge, MA: Harvard University Press.

Erting, C. (1978). Language policy and Deaf ethnicity in the United States. *Sign Language Studies,* 19, 139–152.

Erting, C. (1982). *Deafness, communication and social identity: An anthropological analysis of interaction among parents, teachers and deaf children in a preschool.* Unpublished doctoral dissertation, American University, Washington, DC.

Fine, H., & Fine, P. (Executive Producers). (1990, March). *Sixty Minutes.* New York, NY: Columbia Broadcasting System.

Finkelstein, V. (1981). Disability and the helper-helped relationship. In A. Brechin, P. Liddiard, & J. Swain (Eds.), *Handicap in, a social world,* (pp. 58–64). Sevenoaks, UK: Beckenham, Hodder, & Stoughton.

Finkelstein, V. (1991) "We" are not disabled, "you" are. In S. Gregory & G. M. Hartley (Eds.), *Constructing Deafness,* (pp. 265–271). London: Pinter.

Fishman, J. (1977). Language and ethnicity. In H. Giles (Ed.), *Language ethnicity, and intergroup relations* (pp. 15–57). New York: Academic Press.

Fishman, J. (1982). A critique of six papers on the socialization of the deaf child. In J. B. Christiansen (Ed.), *Conference highlights: National research conference on the social aspects of deafness* (pp. 6–20). Washington, DC: Gallaudet College.

Fishman, J. (1989). *Language and ethnicity in minority sociolinguistic perspective.* Philadelphia: Multilingual Matters.

Foucault, M. (1980). *Power/knowledge: Selected interviews and other writings, 1972–1977.* Brighton, UK: Harvester Press.

Fraser, G. R. (1976). *The causes of profound deafness in childhood.* Baltimore, MD: Johns Hopkins Press.

Gastman, B. R., Hirsch, B. E., Sando, I., Fukui, M. B., & Wargo M. L. (2002). The potential risk of carotid injury in cochlear implant surgery. *Laryngoscope,* 112, 262–266.

Geers, A. E., Nicholas, J. G., & Sedey, A. L. (2003). Language skills of children with early cochlear implantation. *Ear and Hearing,* 24(Suppl.), 46S–58S.

Gelb, S. A. (1987). Social deviance and the "discovery" of the moron. *Disability, Handicap and Society,* 2, 247–258.

Gonsoulin, T. P. (2001). Cochlear implant/Deaf-World dispute: Different bottom elephants. *Otolaryngology—Head and neck surgery,* 125, 552–556.

Gusfield, J. (1982). Deviance in the welfare state: The alcoholism profession and the entitlements of stigma. In M. Lewis (Ed.), *Research in social problems and public policy* (Vol. 2., pp. 1–20). Greenwich, CT: JAI Press.

Gusfield, J. (1984). On the side: Practical action and social constructivism in social problems theory. In J. Schneider & J. Kitsuse (Eds.), *Studies in the sociology of social problems* (pp. 31–51). Rutgers, NJ: Ablex.

Gusfield, J. (1989). Constructing the ownership of social problems: Fun and profit in the welfare state. *Social Problems,* 36, 431–441.

Haller, M. (1963). *Eugenics: Hereditarian attitudes in American thought.* New Brunswick, NJ: Rutgers University Press.

Humphries, T. (1993). Deaf culture and cultures. In K. M. Christensen & G. L. Delgado (Eds.), *Multicultural issues in deafness,* (pp. 3–15). White Plains, NY: Longman.

Huygen, P. L., Hinderink, J. B., van den Broek, P., van den Borne, S., Brokx, J. P., Mens, L. H., et al. (1995). The risk of vestibular function loss after intracochlear implantation. *Acta Otolaryngologica,* Pt. 2 (Suppl. 520), 270–272.

Jalbert, Y. (2003). Décès suite à un, implant cochléaire: Pas un type b. *Canadian Medical Association Journal,* 168, 256.

Johnson, R. E., & Erting, C. (1979, November). *Sign, solidarity, and socialization.* Paper presented at the meeting of the American Anthropological Association, Cincinnati, OH.

Johnson, R. E., & Erting, C. (1982). Linguistic socialization in the context of emergent deaf ethnicity. In C. Erting & R. Meisegeier (Eds.), *Working papers no. 1: Deaf children and the socialization process.* Washington, DC: Gallaudet College. (Unpaginated document).

Johnson, R. E., & Erting, C. (1984). Linguistic socialization in the context of emergent Deaf ethnicity. In K. Kernan (Ed.), *Wenner-Gren Foundation working papers in anthropology.* New York: Wenner-Gren.

Johnson, R. E., & Erting, C. (1989). Ethnicity and socialization in a classroom for Deaf children. In C. Lucas (Ed.), *The sociolinguistics of the Deaf community* (pp. 41–84). New York, NY: Academic Press.

Kelsall, D. C., Shallop, J. K., Brammeier, T. G., & Prenger, E. C. (1997). Facial nerve stimulation after Nucleus 22-channel cochlear implantation. *American Journal of Otology,* 18, 336–341.

Kennedy, D. (2003). *Little people.* New York: St. Martin's Press

Ladd, P. (2003). *Understanding deaf culture: In search of Deafhood.* London: Multilingual Matters.

Lane, H. (1984). *When the mind hears: A history of the Deaf.* New York: Random House.

Lane, H. (1995). Constructions of deafness. *Disability and Society,* 10, 171–89.

Lane, H. (2004a). *A Deaf artist in early America: The worlds of John Brewster Jr.* Boston: Beacon Press.

Lane, H., & Bahan, B. (1998). Effects of cochlear implantation in young children: A review and a reply from a Deaf-World perspective. *Otolaryngology: Head and Neck Surgery,* 119, 297–308.

Lane, H., Pillard, R., & French, M. (2000). Origins of the American Deaf-World: Assimilating and differentiating societies and their relation to genetic patterning. *Sign Language Studies,* 1, new series, 17–44.

Levesque, J. (1994). It's a Deaf Deaf Deaf-World. *DCARA News,* 15, 2.

Markowicz, H., & Woodward, J. (1978). Language and the maintenance of ethnic boundaries in the Deaf community. *Communication and Cognition,* 11, 29–37.

May, D., & Hughes, D. (1987). Organizing services for people with mental handicap: The Californian experience. *Disability, Handicap and Society,* 2, 213–230.

Mayberry, R., & Eichen, E. (1991). The long-lasting advantage of learning sign language in childhood: Another look at the critical period for language acquisition. *Journal of Memory and Language,* 30, 486–512.

Mills, M. (2002, April 9). Women: I am happy my child is Deaf. *The Guardian,* 8.

Mindess, A. (1999). *Reading between the signs: Intercultural communication for sign language interpreters.* Yarmouth, ME: Intercultural Press.

Mitchell, S. H. (1971). The haunting influence of Alexander Graham Bell. *American Annals of the Deaf.* 116, 349–356.

Nagel, J. (1994). Constructing ethnicity: Creating and recreating ethnic identity and culture. *Social problems,* 41, 152–176.

National Inquiry Into the Separation of Aboriginal and Torres Strait Islander Children From Their Families. (1997). *Bringing them home.* New South Wales, Australia: Sterling Press.

Newport, E. Maturational constraints on language learning. *Cognitive Science,* 14, 11–28.

Padden C., & Humphries, T. (1998). *Deaf in America: Voices from a culture.* Cambridge MA: Harvard University Press.

Padden, C., & Markowicz, H. (1976). Cultural conflicts between hearing and deaf communities. In F. B. Crammatte & A. B. Crammatte (Eds.), *Seventh World Congress of the World Federation of the Deaf* (pp. 407–411). Silver Spring, MD: National Association of the Deaf.

Padden, C., & Ramsey, C. (2000). American Sign Language and reading ability in Deaf children. In C. Chamberlain, J. Morford, & R. Mayberry (Eds.), *Language acquisition by eye* (pp. 165–189). Maway, NJ: LEA.

Petersen, W. (1980). Concepts of ethnicity. In S. Thernstrom (Ed.), *Harvard encyclopedia of American ethnic groups* (pp. 234–242). Cambridge, MA: Harvard University Press.

Petitto, L. (1993). On the ontogenetic requirements for early language acquisition. In E. de Boysson-Bardies, S. de Schonen, P. Jusczyk, & J. Morton (Eds.), *Developmental neurocognition: Speech and face processing in the first year of life* (pp. 365–383). New York: Kluwer Academic Press.

Ramsey, P. (1970). *The patient as person.* New Haven, CT: Yale University Press.

Reardon, W., Middleton-Price, H., Malcolm, S., Phelps, P., Bellman, S., Luxon, L., et al. (1992). Clinical and genetic heterogeneity in X-linked deafness. *British Journal of Audiology,* 26, 109–114.

Reefhuis, J., Honein, M. A., Whitney, C. G., Chamany, S., Mann, E. A., Biernath, K. R., et al. (2003). Risk of bacterial meningitis in children with cochlear implants. *New England Journal of Medicine,* 349, 435–445.

Reisenberg, D., & Glass, R. M. (1989). The medical outcomes study. *Journal of the American Medical Association,* 262, 943.

Saltus, R. (1989, July 10). Returning to the world of sound. *Boston Globe,* pp. 27, 29.

Schein J. D. (1989). *At home among strangers.* Washington, DC: Gallaudet University Press.

Schneider, D. M. (1969). Kinship, nationality and religion in American culture: Toward a definition of kinship. In R. F. Spencer (Ed.), *Forms of symbolic action* (pp. 116–125) Seattle, WA: University of Washington Press.

Schneider, D. M. (1972). What is kinship all about? In P. Reining (Ed.), *Kinship studies in the Morgan centennial year* (pp. 32–64). Washington, DC: Anthropological Society of Washington.

Shapiro, J. P. (1993). *No pity: People with disabilities forging a new civil rights movement.* New York: Times Books.

Smith, A. D. (1986). *The ethnic origin of nations.* Cambridge, UK: Blackwell.

Smith, S. (1995). Overview of genetic auditory syndromes. *Journal of the American Academy of Audiology,* 6, 1–14.

Smith, T. (1997). *Deaf people in context.* Unpublished doctoral dissertation, University of Washington, Seattle.

Sollors, W. (2001). Ethnic groups/ethnicity: Historical aspects. In N. J. Smelser & P. B. Baltes (Eds.), *International encyclopedia of the social sciences* (pp. 4813–4817). New York: Elsevier.

Strong, M., & Prinz, P. (1997). A study of the relationship between American Sign Language and English literacy. *Journal of Deaf Studies and Deaf Education,* 2, 37–46.

Svirsky, M., Teoh, S.-W., & Neuburger, H. (2004). Development of language and speech perception in congenitally, profoundly deaf children as a function of age at cochlear implantation. *Audiology, Neuro-Otology,* 9, 224–233.

Turnbull, C. M. (1962). *The forest people.* New York: Simon & Schuster.

Tye-Murray, N. (1992). *Cochlear implants and children: A handbook for parents, teachers and speech and hearing professionals.* Washington, DC: Alexander Graham Bell Association for the Deaf.

United Nations. (1948). *Convention on the Prevention and Punishment of the Crime of Genocide.* Resolution 96/I.

United Nations. (1992). *Declaration on the Rights of Persons Belonging to National or Ethnic, Religious and Linguistic Minorities.* Resolution 47/135.

United Nations (2003a). Declaration on the rights of persons belonging to national or ethnic, religious and linguistic minorities Resolution 47/135. In E. Osmanczyk & A. Mango (Eds.), *Encyclopedia of the United Nations and international agreements.* New York: Routledge.

United Nations (2003b). Genocide Convention, 1948 Resolution 96/1. In E. Osmanczyk & A. Mango (Eds.), *Encyclopedia of the United Nations and international agreements* (pp. 293–294). New York: Routledge.

Valenstein, E. (1986). *Great and desperate cures.* New York: Basic Books.

Van Cleve, J., & Crouch, B. (1989). *A place of their own: Creating the deaf community in America.* Washington, DC: Gallaudet University Press.

Werth, B. (1991, June 16). How short is too short? *New York Times Magazine,* Section 6, pp. 14–17, 28–29, 47.

Winzer, M. A. (1986). Deaf-Mutia: Responses to alienation by the deaf in the mid-19th century. *American Annals of the Deaf,* 131, 29–32.

Zola, I. K. (1993). Disability statistics, what we count and what it tells us. *Journal of Disability Policy Studies,* 4, 9–39.

EXPERIENCING DIFFERENCE

FRAMEWORK ESSAY

In the first framework essay, we considered the social construction of difference as master statuses were named, aggregated, dichotomized, and stigmatized. Now we turn to *experiencing* these statuses. A story from a friend provides an illustration of what we mean by this. Many years ago, she and her husband had wanted to see *Men in Black* when it opened in the theaters, but they had not been able to find a babysitter for their eight-year-old daughter. They had watched many movies as a family and thought their daughter had a good understanding of the difference between real and pretend, so they decided it would be all right to take her with them to the show. They were wrong.

> Our perception of the movie was that while there was plenty of action, it was definitely a comedy. The "alien monsters" were ridiculous to us, inspiring laughter or mild disgust like that of a yucky bug you find in your bathroom and flush down the toilet. Jenny, however, found the movie to be scary and gross. It was beyond her ability to laugh away as something that was "pretend." She hid her eyes through 90 percent of the movie and did not agree with us that it was funny. She talked for months about how scary it was and chastised us for letting her see it.

This story holds a small lesson about *experiencing* your social status. What we notice in the world depends in large part on the statuses we occupy; in this way we may be said to *experience* our social status. Jenny thought the movie was scary both because of the unique person she is and because of her age, a master status. Her parents did not see the movie that way for the same reasons. All experienced the movie through their unique personalities and as people of certain ages.

Although we do not specifically address age in this book, it operates in ways that are analogous to race, sex, class, sexuality, and disability. For example, being young affects the way a person is treated in innumerable ways: at a minimum, it restricts driving, employment, military enlistment, marriage, access to abortion, admission to movies, and alcohol and cigarette consumption; being young yields higher insurance rates and mandatory school attendance; youth also creates the category of "status offenses" (acts that are illegal only for minors). In addition, minors are excluded from voting and exercising other legal rights.

In these ways, those defined as "young" are treated differently from those who are not so defined. Because of that treatment, those who are younger see the world differently from those who are older and no longer operating within these constraints. The young notice things that older people need not notice, because they are not subject to the same rules. Our experiences are tied to the statuses we occupy.

A different example of experiencing one's status comes from the autobiography of one of the first black students in an exclusive white prep school. She recalls what it was like to hear white students say, "It doesn't matter to me if somebody's white or black or green or purple. I mean people are just people." While she appreciated the students' intentions, she also heard her own *real* experience being trivialized by comparison to the Muppets. Her status helps to explain what she noticed in these conversations.[1]

In all, you experience your social statuses; you live through them. They are the filters through which you see and make sense of the world, and in large measure they account for how you are treated and what you notice. In the sections that follow, we will focus on the experiences of both privilege and stigma associated with master statuses.

THE EXPERIENCE OF PRIVILEGE

Just as status helps to explain what we notice, it also explains what we *don't* notice. In the following classroom discussion between a black and a white student, the white student argues that because she and the black student are both female, they should be allies. The black woman responds,

> "When you wake up in the morning and look in the mirror, what do you see?"
>
> "I see a woman," replied the white woman.
>
> "That's precisely the issue," replied the black woman. "I see a black woman. For me, race is visible every day, because it is how I am *not* privileged in this culture. Race is invisible to you [because it is how you are privileged]."[2]

Thus, we are likely to be unaware of the statuses that *privilege* us, that is, provide us with advantage, and acutely aware of those that are the source of trouble—those that yield negative judgments and unfair treatment. Indeed, the mirror metaphor used by the black woman in this conversation emerges frequently among those who are stigmatized: "I looked in the mirror and saw a gay man." These moments of suddenly realizing your social position with all of its life-shaping ramifications are usually about recognizing how some statuses leave you stigmatized and underprivileged, but they are rarely about how you might be privileged or advantaged by other statuses.

Examples of Privilege

This use of the term *privilege* was first developed by Peggy McIntosh from her experience of teaching women's studies courses. Over time, McIntosh noticed that while many men were willing to grant that women were disadvantaged (or "underprivileged") because of sexism, it was far more difficult for them to acknowledge that they were themselves advantaged (or "overprivileged") because of it. Extending the analysis to race, McIntosh generated a list of the ways in which she, as a white woman, was overprivileged by virtue of racism. Her list of over forty white privileges included the following:

> I do not have to educate my children to be aware of systemic racism for their daily protection.
>
> I can arrange my activities so that I will never have to experience feelings of rejection owing to my race.
>
> I can be sure [that] if I need legal or medical help, my race will not work against me.
>
> I can take a job with an affirmative action employer without having my co-workers on the job suspect that I got it because of my race.
>
> I can worry about racism without being seen as self-interested or self-seeking.

As she talked to people about her list, McIntosh learned about other white privileges: "A black woman said she was glad to hear me 'working on my own people,' because if she said these things about white privilege, she would be seen as a militant." Someone else noted that one privilege of being white was being able to be oblivious of those privileges. "Those in privileged groups are educated [to be oblivious] about what it is like for others, especially for others who have to be in their presence."[3]

Privilege makes life easier: it is easier to get around, to get what one wants, and to be treated in an acceptable manner. For example, perhaps the privilege least noticed by nondisabled people is the simple ease of getting around—accessing buildings, restaurants, and movie theaters; easily reading store names, bus stops, and street signs; riding public transportation; being able to dependably find bathrooms one can use; in short, having fairly uncomplicated access to the world. By contrast, notice the rage and exhaustion that reporter John Hockenberry describes as he tries to hail a cab or use the Brooklyn subway (Reading 34). Or ponder the indignity detailed in *Tennessee v. Lane*, the 2004 Supreme Court case about county court houses that lacked elevators, which meant that paraplegic people had to crawl or be carried up the steps (Reading 37). Thus, one usually unnoticed privilege of not being disabled is the ability to get around. Life is just easier, because everything is designed for your use.

While privilege makes people's lives easier, it also makes their lives safer. For example, many black and Hispanic students describe being closely monitored by security guards for shoplifting when they are in department stores. Indeed, in one class discussion of this, an African American student mentioned that she had the habit of walking through stores with her hands held out, palms open in front of her, to prove that she was not stealing. Ironically, it is likely easier for white people to shoplift, since attention is focused on black and Latino customers.

This point was illustrated in a 2009 episode of ABC's *Primetime: What Would You Do?*, which was set in a public park in a predominantly white New Jersey suburb. Called "Teen Vandals," a hidden camera recorded the reaction of passersby to a group of white teenagers (who were actors) destroying a car. Almost no one called the police or attempted to stop them. As one of the white actors commented later, "I was actually shocked to see how many people would actually take a good look at what we were doing and just walk on by without even interfering at all." By contrast, people did call the police about the black teenagers who were sleeping in a nearby car waiting for their turn to act as vandals. Not surprisingly, when it was time for those actors to destroy the car, there were numerous calls to the police and attempts to stop them. Thus, one privilege of being white is the presumption that you are not really criminal, violent, or dangerous to others.

Although whites do not generally assume that other whites are a threat to them, they often assume that of blacks.[a] The percentage appears to be declining, but surveys indicate that about half of whites think blacks are aggressive or violent.[4] This is especially important because if one assumes that a person or group is dangerous, taking preemptive action against them to ward off violence is more likely to be seen as legitimate.

---

[a]Despite whites' fear of violence at the hands of African Americans, crime is predominately *intra*racial.

The 2013 Florida shooting death of unarmed, seventeen-year-old Trayvon Martin will unfortunately stand as the classic example of preemptive violence motivated by beliefs about which categories of people are dangerous. Martin, visiting his father in a gated community, was shot and killed by George Zimmerman, a neighborhood watch volunteer. Zimmerman was acquitted in part because he was protected by Florida's "Stand Your Ground" law, which allows the use of deadly force in self-defense. Such laws—now in effect in about half of U.S. states—can be expected to especially put African American men like Martin at risk, since they belong to the group most construed as potentially dangerous. As one editorialist commented afterward,

> One of the burdens of being a black male is carrying the heavy weight of other people's suspicions. . . . What this means is that black adolescents cannot afford to be normal American teenagers. They cannot experiment with pot. They cannot fight in any way ever, even if it means protecting themselves from a stranger. They cannot take sophomoric pictures with middle fingers, bare chests, or in silly gear. They cannot have improper conversations on social media. They can't wear anything society views as menacing. [All of these were raised as evidence against Martin at Zimmerman's trial.] And growing up, they can never make bad choices or mistakes—the types that teach life lessons, foster humility and build character.[5]

An example of the consequence of the belief that even black women are dangerous is provided by law professor and author Patricia J. Williams:

> My best friend from law school is a woman named C. For months now I have been sending her drafts of this book, filled with many shared experiences, and she sends me back comments and her own associations. Occasionally we speak by telephone. One day, after reading the beginning of this chapter, she calls me up and tells me her abiding recollection of law school. "Actually, it has nothing to do with law school," she says.
>
> "I'll be the judge of that," I respond.
>
> "Well," she continues, "It's about the time I was held at gunpoint by a SWAT team."
>
> It turns out that during one Christmas vacation C. drove to Florida with two friends. Just outside Miami they stopped at a roadside diner. C. ordered a hamburger and a glass of milk. The milk was sour, and C. asked for another. The waitress ignored her. C. asked twice more and was ignored each time. When the waitress finally brought the bill, C. had been charged for the milk and refused to pay for it. The waitress started to shout at her, and a highway patrolman walked over from where he had been sitting and asked what was going on. C. explained that the milk was sour and that she didn't want to pay for it. The highway patrolman ordered her to pay and get out. When C. said he was out of his jurisdiction, the patrolman pulled out his gun and pointed it at her.
>
> ("Don't you think," asks C. when I show her this much of my telling of her story, "that it would help your readers to know that the restaurant was all white and that I'm black?" "Oh, yeah," I say. "And six feet tall.")
>
> Now C. is not easily intimidated and, just to prove it, she put her hand on her hip and invited the police officer to go ahead and shoot her, but before he did so *he* should try to drink the damn glass of milk, and so forth and so on for a few more descriptive rounds. What cut her off was the realization that, suddenly and silently, she and her two friends had been surrounded by eight SWAT team officers, in full guerrilla gear, automatic weapons drawn. Into the pall of her ringed speechlessness, they sent a local black policeman, who offered her

twenty dollars and begged her to pay and be gone. C. describes how desperately he was perspiring as he begged and, when she didn't move, how angry he got—how he accused her of being an outside agitator, that she could come from the North and go back to the North, but that there were those of "us" who had to live here and would pay for her activism.

C. says she doesn't remember how she got out of there alive or why they finally let her go; but she supposes that the black man paid for her. But she does remember returning to the car with her two companions and the three of them crying, sobbing, all the way to Miami. "The damnedest thing about it," C. said, "was that no one was interested in whether or not I was telling the truth. The glass was sitting there in the middle of all this, with the curdle hanging on the side, but nobody would taste it because a black woman's lips had touched it."[6]

The privilege of not being considered criminal was highlighted in a nationwide review of the cases in which an undercover, plainclothes, or off-duty police officer had been fatally shot by fellow police officers.[7] For undercover and plainclothes officers, the review did not find any racial pattern in the shootings because training and prevention measures have long been in place,

> . . . but the reality is strikingly different for off-duty officers. As far as we can determine, 1982 was the last year in which an off-duty, white police officer was killed in a mistaken-identity, police-on-police shooting anywhere in the United States. Since then, nine off-duty officers of color have been killed in such shootings. . . .[8]

Thus, white off-duty officers who have to display their guns in a police action are safer than their black or Hispanic colleagues because other officers are less likely to assume they are criminal.

This assumption of white *non*-criminality is reinforced on a daily basis by television news reporting. In comparison with actual arrest rates, local news shows appear to underrepresent whites as perpetrators and overrepresent African Americans.[9] Because television is the primary news source for most Americans, the underrepresentation of whites as criminals yields a distorted view of the connection between race and crime.

> Even when suspects were clearly white, studies demonstrated that when white [television] viewers were asked to identify the suspect later, they consistently misidentified the suspect as African American, a disturbing finding that suggests that white viewers have been primed through years of viewing African Americans almost exclusively as criminals to see *all* criminals as African American.[10]

As English and journalism professor Carol Stabile concluded from her review of U.S. crime news since the 1830s, African Americans have been criminalized with a persistence unlike that experienced by any other group. While the threats presumably posed by Irish, Eastern European, and Chinese immigrants were framed in the same terms as those for African Americans, for those groups the stereotypes have faded over time. Not so for African Americans. Even methamphetamine users, who are predominately white, fare better in the media:

> Where crack addicts were cast as people disposed to escape reality and responsibility . . . white [methamphetamine] users were [cast as] rural, hardworking members of the working

class. Driven by circumstances to drug use, they found themselves hopeless captives to a powerful substance. The message was clear: white drug users were victims of their circumstances and therefore deserving of sympathy and rehabilitation; black drug addicts were social parasites, beyond redemption and worthy of nothing more than punishment.[11]

Indeed, the privilege of not being assumed to be a "real" criminal has consequences even in terms of the degree to which certain behaviors are criminalized. For example,

> In the late 1970s, crack first came on the scene in the form of cocaine freebasing. Many of its users were stockbrokers and investment bankers, rock stars, Hollywood types, and a few pro athletes. Some of them began to get into trouble with this form of cocaine use, showing up in hospital emergency rooms and police stations. Congress passed new laws to extend health insurance coverage to include drug treatment. The treatment industry expanded the number of beds available.
>
> In the mid-1980s, crack use spread into America's inner cities among impoverished African Americans and Latinos. Some of them began to get into trouble with this form of cocaine use, showing up in hospital emergency rooms and police stations. Congress passed new laws to extend the length of criminal sentences for crack offenses. The prison industry expanded the number of cells available.[12]

This comparison of crack cocaine and cocaine powder users is not frivolous. In the late 1980s, federal sentencing laws established a *mandatory* five-year sentence for *first-time* possession of *five grams* of crack cocaine. By contrast, it took *500 grams* (1.1 pounds) of cocaine powder to trigger the five-year sentence—an intentional 100:1 differential that was established based on the hyperbole that crack was somehow 100 times more powerful than cocaine. (Crack is cocaine powder "cooked" with baking soda and water.) The same ratio was applied to the ten-year mandatory sentence, which was trigged by 50 grams of crack cocaine but 5 kilograms (11 pounds) of cocaine powder.

In 2010, the Fair Sentencing Act raised the trigger weights and reduced the sentencing differential (the weight ratio is now 18:1 rather than 100:1). Nonetheless, the stage had been set for the differential imprisonment of black men.

> In the early 1970s, blacks were about twice as likely as whites to be arrested for a drug offense. The great growth in drug arrest rates through the 1980s had a large effect on African Americans. At the height of the drug war in 1989, arrest rates for blacks had climbed to 1,460 per hundred thousand compared to 365 for whites. Throughout the 1990s, drug arrest rates remained at these historically high levels.[13]

These differential arrest rates are in contrast to what we know about drug usage. National surveys have long shown that white high school students self-report more drug use than black students[14] and that black and white adults self-report similar levels of drug use.[15]

The War on Drugs that began in the 1980s produced a cascade of consequences that is still with us. The prison population has quadrupled since 1980,[16] with 2.2 million people now in prison or jail—a rate that exceeds the historic average in the United States by a factor of nearly five.[17] Although the incarceration rate started to decline slightly in 2007 (it declined by 0.3 percent in 2010), the

United States still has the highest incarceration rate in the world. Comparable developed nations incarcerate about 100 people per 100,000; the U.S. rate is 500 per 100,000.[18]

These rates vary significantly by race and ethnicity: "Incarceration rates are significantly higher for Blacks and Latinos than for Whites. In 2010, Black men were incarcerated at a rate of 3,074 per 100,000 residents; Latinos were incarcerated at 1,258 per 100,000; and White men were incarcerated at 459 per 100,000."[19] When added to the long prison terms mandated by drug sentencing, these differential incarceration rates have had a devastating effect on black communities. One in four African Americans has had a parent in prison; prisoners experience a significant reduction (by 40 percent) in annual earnings after they are released.[20]

Thus, as a category, whites experience the privileges of not being presumed criminal, not being depicted as criminal, not being at risk of preemptive violence, and able to pursue their "vices" with less chance of punishment. If they do not appear to be Middle Eastern, both whites and blacks are at little risk of being considered terrorists; if they do not look like immigrants, especially Hispanic immigrants, they are at little risk of being detained and deported. These privileges are the outcome of *racial profiling*.

Singling out members of a race or ethnic group for heightened police surveillance, that is *racial profiling,* is a way to act on the assumption that whole categories of people are dangerous. It became the subject of public debate following a 1996 Supreme Court decision that allowed the police to use routine traffic stops to investigate drug possession and other crimes. African Americans and Latinos argued that they were disproportionately pulled over—guilty of nothing more than "driving while black," or "driving while brown." Research by several social scientists confirmed the allegations, and national attention was focused by a 1998 shooting in which two New Jersey state troopers fired eleven shots into a van carrying black and Latino men from the Bronx to a basketball camp, wounding three of the passengers. At their sentencing, the troopers "said their supervisors had trained them to focus on black- and brown-skinned drivers because, they were told, they were more likely to be drug traffickers."[21] Thus, a national consensus against racial profiling—supported by public opinion, state legislation, and new federal policies barring racial profiling at the borders—began to emerge.

That consensus fractured with the September 11, 2001, terrorist attacks. Public opinion swung dramatically in favor of profiling Middle Eastern Americans as well as immigrants and visitors from the Middle East. Indeed, public debate about racial profiling only reemerged in 2013 with the shooting death of Trayvon Martin.

After the 9/11 attacks special national security measures were implemented—most notably the National Security Entry-Exit Registration System (NSEERS). When NSEERS was in place from 2002 until 2011, temporary visitors to the United States (that is, non-immigrant visa holders) who were male and from a

Middle Eastern or North African country were required to enter and exit the country at a designated port, present themselves for an in-person immigration office visit, and provide notice about any change of address, employment, or school.[22]

Middle Eastern Americans, unlike most other American minorities and white women, have not experienced an increase in the protection of their civil rights over time. Limitations on Arab immigration and access to permanent resident status, increased FBI surveillance, and restrictions on student visas followed not only the 9/11 attacks, but also the Gulf War of 1990–1991, the 1979 Iranian hostage crisis, and the terrorist attacks on the 1972 Olympic Games in Munich.[23] Indeed, only in 2014 did the New York City Police Department close the surveillance program it had run for eleven years monitoring Muslim neighborhoods by eavesdropping on conversations, infiltrating college-student groups, collecting information on the cars parked at mosques, and maintaining records of where people ate, prayed, and shopped. "After years of collecting information, however, the police acknowledged that it never generated a lead."[24]

As federal immigration laws have changed, not being subject to racial profiling has provided those who appear to be native-born, non-immigrants with the privilege of not being detained or deported. By contrast, two laws passed in 1996 (the Antiterrorism and Effective Death Penalty Act and the Illegal Immigration Reform and Immigrant Responsibility Act) made *lawful permanent residents* deportable for virtually any crime, from major offenses to shoplifting or drunk driving, depending on the wording of local statutes. (A *lawful permanent resident* is a visa status that allows the person to live and work in the United States, travel outside the country, and apply for U.S. citizenship after five years.)

The laws are retroactive, in that permanent residents can be deported for crimes that did not warrant deportation at the time they were committed or that they committed as minors. The laws are applied even to those who entered the country as children and have never actually resided in the country to which they are remanded.[25] If the home country refuses to accept the detainee once the U.S. prison time has been served, the detainee probably faces lifetime imprisonment in the United States. Nor can the outcome be changed by an immigration judge: "The legislation Congress passed in 1996 precluded immigration judges from considering whether deportation would be excessively harsh in light of the immigrants' family relationships, community ties, U.S. military service records, or the possibility of persecution if returned to their country of origin."[26]

While it is illegal to deport a U.S. citizen, there are increasing reports of that happening[27] as citizens are also sometimes swept up in immigration raids and imprisoned until they are able to convince authorities of their legal status. A 2010 survey of Latinos reported that 5 percent of both native-born and foreign-born Hispanic adults report being stopped by police or other authorities asking about their immigration status (down from about 9 percent in 2008).[28] Because detainees may be sent to any one of 300 detention centers and are likely to be poor, claims of citizenship are not easily resolved.

Whether the population profiled is Latino, African American, Middle Eastern, or immigrant, and whether the enforcing agency involves federal immigration, local police, or airport security, the efficacy of such profiling has long been questioned, specifically because race-based evaluations are much less useful than behavior-based ones. For example, in terms of using traffic stops to uncover drugs, guns, or criminals, "when stops and searches are not racialized, they are more productive."[29] "Profiling is a crude substitute for behavior-based enforcement and . . . invites screeners to take a less vigilant approach to individuals who don't fit the profile, even if they engage in conduct that should cause concern."[30] In all, those of us who do not look Middle Eastern, black, Hispanic, or foreign-born have the privilege of not being treated like criminals, illegal immigrants, or terrorists.

A quite different kind of privilege, likely to be invisible to those in single-race families, is the privilege of being recognized as a family. The following account by a mother illustrates how the failure to perceive a family is linked to the expectation of black criminality.

> When my son was home visiting from college, we met in town one day for lunch. . . . On the way to the car, one of us thought of a game we'd often played when he was younger.
>
> "Race you to the car!"
>
> I passed my large handbag to him, thinking to more equalize the race since he was a twenty-year-old athlete. We raced the few blocks, my heart singing with delight to be talking and playing with my beloved son. As we neared the car, two young white men yelled something at us. I couldn't make it out and paid it no mind. When we arrived at the car, both of us laughing, they walked by and mumbled "Sorry" as they quickly passed, heads down.
>
> I suddenly understood. They hadn't seen a family. They had seen a young Black man with a pocketbook, fleeing a pursuing middle-aged white woman. My heart trembled as I thought of what could have happened if we'd been running by someone with a gun.
>
> Later I mentioned the incident in a three-day diversity seminar I was conducting at a Boston corporation. A participant related it that evening to his son, a police officer, and asked the son what he would have done if he'd observed the scene.
>
> The answer: "Shot out his kneecaps."[31]

Turning now from privileges of race to *privileges of sexuality,* the most obvious privilege enjoyed by heterosexuals is that they are allowed to be open about their relationships—which is, after all, what heteronormativity is all about. From idle conversation and public displays of affection, to the legal and religious approval embodied in marriage, heterosexuals are able to declare that they love and are loved. That privilege has not been just *denied* to people in same-sex relationships; at least until very recently, they have been actively punished for such expressions by ostracism, physical assault, unemployment, and even loss of child custody and visitation—not so surprising given the still uncertain legal recognition of gay families.

Even the ability to display a picture of one's partner on a desk at work stands as an invisible privilege of heterosexuality.

> Consider, for example, an employee who keeps a photograph on her desk in which she and her husband smile for the camera and embrace affectionately. . . . [T]he photo implicitly

conveys information about her private sexual behavior. [But] most onlookers (if they even notice the photo) do not think of her partner primarily in sexual terms. . . .

[But] if the photograph instead shows the woman in the same pose with a same-sex partner, everyone is likely to notice. As with the first example, the photograph conveys the information that she is in a relationship. But the fact that the partner is a woman overwhelms all other information about her. The *sexual* component of the relationship is not mundane and implicit as with the heterosexual spouse.[32]

Because heterosexual public affection is so commonplace, it rarely conjures up images of sexual activity. But that is exactly what we may think of when we see a same-sex couple embrace or even hold hands. This is why gay and lesbian people are often accused of "flaunting" their sexuality: *any* display of affection between them is understood by many heterosexuals as virtually a display of the sex act.

Still, these attitudes appear to be changing dramatically. As we discuss in Reading 37, in 2013 the Supreme Court held (in *U.S. v. Windsor*) that the 1996 Defense of Marriage Act (DOMA), which limited "marriage" and "spouse" to a union of one man and one woman, was unconstitutional because it denied federal rights to couples in states where same-sex marriage is allowed. (Over a thousand federal laws, benefits, and programs apply to marital unions.) Though narrowly framed and by only a five to four vote, the Court's decision was consistent with significant change in American attitudes: in public opinion polls, support for the moral acceptability of gay and lesbian relations crossed the symbolic 50 percent threshold in 2010.[33] That change is almost entirely attributable to the increasing acceptance of same-sex relationships among men, especially those younger than fifty; indeed, the 2010 poll was the first in which men were more accepting of these relationships than women. Still, appreciating abstractly supportive poll data is not the same as feeling safe enough to express affection in public settings. For people in same-sex relationships, it is likely that will remain difficult for some time.

In the realm of *class privilege,* several readings in this book address the considerable differences in health, life span, educational access, and quality of life that accompany American class differences. But these are perhaps the more visible privileges of being middle and upper class. Less apparent is the privilege of being treated as a deserving and competent member of the community. Higher education institutions provide a number of examples of this. One of the boons of the legacy admission system, described by John Larew in Reading 32, is its invisibility. The students admitted to universities this way—who are predominately middle- and upper-class whites—don't have their qualifications questioned by faculty or other students, nor are they likely to agonize about whether they deserved to be admitted.

> Like many children of University of Virginia graduates, Mary Stuart Young of Atlanta, Georgia, wore Cavalier orange and blue long before she took an SAT or mailed an application.
>
> "Coming here just felt right," said Young, 21, who expects to graduate with a religious studies degree. . . . "This was where I should be."
>
> After all, with two generations of faithful alumni backing her, Young doubled her chances of getting into Thomas Jefferson's university.[34]

One of the privileges of being a legacy admission rather than an affirmative action admission is that you are treated as a deserving and competent member of the community.

The assumption that university students are middle or upper class is pervasive within higher education, so working-class students often find schools oblivious or even antagonistic to their needs. Students are presumed to understand how college works, because it is assumed that their parents are college graduates and can advise them: "In an article on working class students in higher education, one student was paraphrased as saying that college is a very unforgiving place. It is unforgiving not of those who don't know the rules, but rather of those who did not know the rules before arriving on campus."[35] Thus, one of the privileges of being a college student from the middle or upper classes is that you come to the university with a good deal of information about how it works.

Also, "[w]orking class students often have difficulty in their studies partially because colleges and universities—elite and nonelite—refuse to recognize that many students must work."[36] For example, schools that require unpaid internships, off-campus experiences, or study abroad trips may forget not only the costs associated with these requirements but also the fact that working-class students may have to quit their jobs to fulfill the requirement. The same is true of faculty office hours—set as if students could easily arrange their schedules to fit the professor's. If working-class students were seen as deserving and competent members of the community, their needs would be factored in automatically, not as a "special favor."

In all, one of the privileges of being middle or upper class is that higher education—which is absolutely critical to upward mobility—is in sync with one's experience. In college, middle-and upper-class students can expect to have their life experiences and perspectives treated as the norm. The institution will be organized around those experiences in ways large and small, from assuming that everyone should live on campus (and bear the expense of room and board) to assuming they will be able to cover the cost of texts or forgo employment. In these ways, students from the middle or upper classes have the privilege of feeling like they belong.

Overall, two privileges shape the experience of those in nonstigmatized statuses: *entitlement* and the privilege of being *unmarked*. Entitlement is the belief that one has the right to be respected, acknowledged, protected, and rewarded. This is so much taken for granted by those in nonstigmatized statuses that they are often shocked and angered when it is denied them.

> [After the lecture, whites in the audience] shot their hands up to express how excluded they felt because [the] lecture, while broad in scope, clearly was addressed first and foremost to the women of color in the room. . . . What a remarkable sense of entitlement must drive their willingness to assert their experience of exclusion! If I wanted to raise my hand every time I felt excluded, I would have to glue my wrist to the top of my head.[37]

Like entitlement, the privilege of occupying an unmarked status is shared by most of those in nonstigmatized categories. For example, *doctor* is an *unmarked* status; *woman* doctor is *marked.* Unmarked categories convey the usual and expected distribution of individuals in social statuses—the distribution that does not require any special comment. Thus, the unmarked category tells us what a society takes for granted.

Theoretically, the unmarked category might include anyone, but in truth it refers to white males. How do we know that? Because other occupants of that status are usually marked: woman doctor, black doctor, and so on. While the marking of a status signals infrequency—there are few female astronauts or male nurses—it may also imply inferiority. A "woman doctor" or a "black doctor" may be considered less qualified.

Thus, a final privilege of those who are not stigmatized is that their master statuses are not used to discount their accomplishments or imply that they serve only special interests. Someone described as "a politician" is presumed to operate from a universality that someone described as "a white male politician" is not. Because white male politicians are rarely described as such, their anchoring in the reality of their own master statuses is hidden. In this way, those in marked statuses appear to be operating from an "agenda," or "special interest" while those in unmarked statuses can appear to be agenda-free. Being white and male thus becomes invisible, because it is not regularly identified as important. For this reason, some recommend identifying *everyone's* race and sex as a way to recognize that we are all grounded in our master statuses.

In all, privilege is usually invisible to those who possess it; they may assume that everyone is treated as they are. When they learn about instances of discrimination, they may think that the incident was exceptional rather than routine, that the victim was overreacting or misinterpreting, or that the victim must have provoked the encounter. Such responses do not necessarily deny that the incident took place; rather, they deny that the event carries any negative or special meaning.

Through such dismissals, those operating from positions of privilege can deny the experience of those without privilege. For example, college-age students often describe university administrators as unresponsive until they have their parents call to complain. If the parents later said, "I don't know why *you* had such a problem with those people; they were very nice to *me.* Did you do something to antagonize them?" that would indicate that parents were oblivious to their privileged status in the university setting as well as unaware of their student's underprivileged status in it.

Dismissals like these treat the stigmatized person like a child inadequate to judge the world. Often such dismissals are framed in terms of the very stigma about which people are complaining. In this way, what stigmatized people say about their status is discounted precisely because they are stigmatized. The implication is that those who occupy a stigmatized status are somehow the ones *least* able to assess its consequence. The effect is to dismiss precisely those who have had the most experience with the problem.

This process, called *looping* or *rereading,* is described by many who have studied the lives of patients in psychiatric hospitals.[38] If a patient says, "The staff here are being unfair to me," and the staff respond, "Of course he would think that—he's crazy," they have reread, or looped, his words through his status. His words have been heard in view of his stigma and dismissed for exactly that reason.

These dismissals serve a function. Dismissing another's experience of status-based mistreatment masks the possibility that one has escaped such treatment precisely because of one's privilege. If we do not acknowledge that *their* status affects *their* treatment, we need not acknowledge that *our* status affects *our* treatment. Thus, we avoid the larger truth that those who are treated well, those who are treated poorly, and all the rest in between are always evaluated both as individuals and as occupants of particular esteemed and disesteemed categories.

THE EXPERIENCE OF STIGMA

We have so far considered the privileges conferred by some master statuses; now we examine the stigma conferred by other master statuses.

In his classic analysis of stigma, sociologist Erving Goffman (1963) distinguished between the *discredited,* whose stigma is immediately apparent to an observer (for example, race, sex, some disabilities), and the *discreditable,* whose stigma can be hidden (for example, sexuality, cognitive disabilities, social class, and sometimes race and ethnicity). Because stigma plays out differently in the lives of the discredited and the discreditable, each will be examined separately.

The Discreditable: "Passing"

The discreditable are those who are *passing,* that is, not publicly acknowledging the stigmatized statuses they occupy. (Were they to acknowledge that status, they would become discredited.) The term *passing* comes from "passing as white," which emerged as a phenomenon after 1875 when southern states reestablished racial segregation through hundreds of "Jim Crow"[b] laws. At that point, some African Americans passed as white as a way to get better-paying jobs.

> [S]ome who passed as white on the job lived as black at home. Some lived in the North as white part of the year and as black in the South the rest of the time. More men passed than women . . . the vast majority who could have passed permanently did not do so, owing to the pain of family separation, condemnation by most blacks, their fear of whites, and the loss of the security of the black community. . . . Passing as white probably reached an all-time peak between 1880 and 1925.[40]

"Passing as white" is now quite rare and strongly condemned by African Americans. We will use the term *passing* here to refer to those who have not made their stigmatized status evident. For example, in Reading 24, John Tehranian describes the ways Muslim Americans may sometimes mask their identity. "Passing" is similar to

---

[b]"Jim Crow" was "a blackface, singing-dancing-comedy characterization portraying black males as childlike, irresponsible, inefficient, lazy, ridiculous in speech, pleasure-seeking, and happy, [and was] a widespread stereotype of blacks during the last decades before emancipation. . . ."[39] Whites created segregation in the South after the Civil War by imposing what were called "Jim Crow" laws.

the phrase "being in the closet," which is usually applied to gays. "Passing" probably plays less of a role in the lives of gay and lesbian people now than it has in the past, but still it remains a significant concern and topic of discussion for both gays and straights.

One may engage in passing by chance as well as by choice. For example, the presumption that everyone is heterosexual can have the effect of putting gay people in the closet even when they had not intended to be. During a series of lectures on the family, one of our faculty colleagues realized that he had been making assignments, lecturing, and encouraging discussion under the assumption that all of the students in the class had, or wanted to have, heterosexual relationships. His actions forced gay and lesbian students to choose between announcing or remaining silent about their status. Had he assumed that students would be involved only with others of the same race, he would have created a similar situation for those in interracial relationships. Thus, assumptions about others' private lives—for example, by asking whether someone is married—may have the effect of making them choose between a lie or an announcement of something they may consider private.

Since most heterosexuals assume that everyone is heterosexual, many social encounters either put gay people in the closet or require that they announce their status. For example, in the first class session of one course, a student opened his remarks by saying, "Well, you all know I am a gay man, and as a gay man I think. . . ." The buzz of conversation stopped, other students stared at him, and one asked, "How would we know you were gay?" The student pointed to a pink triangle he had pinned to his book bag and explained that he thought they knew that someone wearing it would be gay. (Pink triangles were assigned to gay men during the Nazi era. Still, his logic was questionable: Anyone supportive of gay rights might wear the triangle.) This announcement—which moved the student from a discreditable to a discredited status—may have been intended to keep his classmates from making overtly antigay comments in his presence. His strategy was designed to counter the negative consequences of passing.

> Every encounter with a new classful of students, to say nothing of a new boss, social worker, loan officer, landlord, doctor, erects new closets [that] . . . exact from at least gay people new surveys, new calculations, new draughts and requisitions of secrecy or disclosure. Even an *out* gay person deals daily with interlocutors about whom she doesn't know whether they know or not [or whether they would care]. . . . The gay closet is not a feature only of the lives of gay people. But for many gay people it is still the fundamental feature of social life; there can be few gay people . . . in whose lives the closet is not a shaping presence.[41]

Inadvertent passing is also experienced by those whose racial status is not immediately apparent. An African American acquaintance of ours who looks white is often in settings in which others do not know that she is African American—or in which she does not know if they know. Thus, she must regularly decide how and when to convey that information. This is important to her as a way to discourage racist remarks, since whites sometimes assume it is acceptable to make racist remarks to one another (as men may assume it is acceptable to make sexist remarks to other men, or as straights presume it acceptable to make antigay remarks to those they think are also straight). It is also important to her that others know she is black so that they understand the meaning of her words—so that they will hear her words through her status as an African American woman. Those whose stigma is not apparent must go to some lengths to avoid being in the closet by virtue of others' assumptions.

Those with relatively invisible disabilities also face the tension of inadvertent passing. Beth Omansky, in Reading 36, describes the experiences of those who are legally, rather than totally, blind. Observers who assume the person is totally blind can react with disbelief or even anger when they learn otherwise; some may insist that the person behave as if they were totally blind, to avoid confusing observers. Either way, the person suffers the consequence of inadvertent passing.

Still, passing may be an intentional choice. For example, one of our students, who was in the process of deciding that he was gay, had worked for many years at a local library, where he became friends with several of his co-workers. Much of the banter at work, however, involved disparaging gay, or presumably gay, library patrons. As he grappled with a decision about his own sexual identity, his social environment reminded him that being gay is still a stigmatized status in American society. This student did not so much face prejudice personally (since he was not "out" to his work friends) as he faced an "unwilling acceptance of himself by individuals who are prejudiced against persons of the kind he can be revealed to be."[42] Thus, he was not the person his friends took him to be. While survey data indicate that those who personally know a gay man hold more positive feelings about gays in general,[43] the decision to publicly reveal a stigma that others have gone on record as opposing is not made lightly.

Revealing stigma changes one's interactions, even with those who are not particularly prejudiced. Such revelations are likely to alter important relationships. Parents sometimes disown gay children, just as they do children involved in interracial relationships. For the discreditable, "information management" is at the core of one's life. "To tell or not to tell; to let on or not to let on; to lie or not to lie; and in each case, to whom, how, when, and where."[44] Such choices are faced daily by those who are discreditable—not just by those who are gay and lesbian, but also by those who are poor, have been imprisoned, attempted suicide, terminated a pregnancy through abortion, are HIV-positive, are drug or alcohol dependent, or who have been the victims of incest or rape. By contrast, those who do not occupy stigmatized statuses don't have to invest emotional energy in monitoring information about themselves; they can choose to talk openly about their personal history.

Passing has both positive and negative aspects. On the positive side, passing lets the stigmatized person exert some power over the situation; the person controls the information, the flow of events, and their privacy. By withholding his or her true identity until choosing to reveal it, the person may create a situation in which others' prejudices are challenged. Passing also limits one's exposure to verbal and physical abuse, allows for the development of otherwise forbidden relationships, and improves employment security by minimizing one's exposure to discrimination.

On the negative side, passing consumes a good deal of time, energy, and emotion. It introduces deception and secrecy even into close relationships. Passing also denies others the opportunity to prove themselves unprejudiced, and it makes one vulnerable to blackmail by those who do know about one's stigma.

The Discredited: The Problems of Visibility

While the discreditable face problems of invisibility, *visibility* is the problem for those who are discredited. Those who are discredited suffer from undue attention and are subject to being stereotyped.

Being discredited means that one's stigma is immediately apparent to others. As essayist bell hooks describes, those who are discredited often have little patience for those who at least have the option of passing.

> Many of us have been in discussions where a non-white person—a black person—struggles to explain to white folks that while we can acknowledge that gay people of all colors are harassed and suffer exploitation and domination, we also recognize that there is a significant difference that arises because of the visibility of dark skin. . . . While it in no way lessens the severity of such suffering for gay people, or the fear that it causes, it does mean that in a given situation the apparatus of protection and survival may be simply not identifying as gay. In contrast, most people of color have no choice. No one can hide, change, or mask dark skin color. White people, gay and straight, could show greater understanding of the impact of racial oppression on people of color by not attempting to make these oppressions synonymous, but rather by showing the ways they are linked and yet differ.[45]

For the discredited, stigma is likely to always shape interaction even though its effect may not play out in ways one can easily determine. Florynce Kennedy, a black activist in the civil rights and women's movements, once commented that the problem with being black in America was that you never knew whether what happened to you, good or bad, was because of your talents or because you were black.[46] This situation was described in 1903 by sociologist W.E.B. Du Bois as the *double consciousness* of being black in America. The concept was key to Du Bois's classic, *The Souls of Black Folk,* for which he was rightfully judged "the father of serious black thought as we know it today."[47] Du Bois described double consciousness this way:

> [T]he Negro . . . [is] gifted with a second-sight in this American world—a world which yields him no true self-consciousness, but only lets him see himself through the revelation of the other world. It is a peculiar sensation, this double consciousness, this sense of always looking at one's self through the eyes of others, of measuring one's soul by the tape of a world that looks on in amused contempt and pity. One ever feels his twoness. . . .[48]

This is the sense of seeing oneself through the eyes of a harshly critical other, and it relates to our discussion of objectification in the first Framework Essay. When those who are stigmatized view themselves from the perspective of the nonstigmatized, they have reduced themselves to objects. This theme of double or "fractured" consciousness can also be found in contemporary analyses of women's experience.

The greatest effect of being visibly stigmatized is on one's life chances—literally, one's chances for living. Thus, the readings in this book detail differences in income, employment, health, life span, education, targeting for violence, and the likelihood of arrest and imprisonment. But the other end of the spectrum—affecting your life but not necessarily your chance of living—is also important. In 2013, Rosalind Wiseman wrote about the lives of preteen and adolescent boys. (Wiseman's earlier volume on girls was the basis of the 2004 movie, *Mean Girls*.) Her description of the prevalence of race and ethnic taunts in boys' lives, even among friends, is memorable:

> Here's what I hear most often in schools throughout the country:
>
> **Muslims and Sikhs** (whose religions are completely different) are constantly referred to as terrorists.
>
> **Jews** are confronted with boys throwing money at them and making jokes about ashes and ovens.
>
> **Asians** are said to have small penises, to not need calculators, and to have parents who drive them 24/7 and beat them if they don't become music or math prodigies.
>
> **Hispanics** are the butt of jokes about being deported, uneducated, and lazy. White kids in private schools commonly joke about their Hispanic friends having gotten into their school or getting a scholarship only because the school needed to increase its diversity.
>
> **Black guys** are greeted with forced, wannabe black slang or the use of the N-word.[49]

Taunts like these certainly affect the quality of young boys' lives. Similarly, it is worth considering the more mundane difficulties created by stigmatization, especially the sense of being "on stage." The discredited often have the feeling of being watched or on display when they are in settings dominated by nonstigmatized people. For example, when women walk through male-dominated settings, they often feel they are on display in terms of their physical appearance. Recently, the term *microaggression*[50] has been used to describe the verbal slights experienced by those in visibly stigmatized statuses. College students have been documenting these experiences in blogs, plays, and on Facebook pages. Examples of microaggressions—such as "Where are you from? Your English is perfect," to an Asian American student or "It's almost like you're not black" to an African American—reveal how much people who are visibly stigmatized are "on stage" in terms of their master status.[51] In such cases, the discredited are likely to feel that others are judging them in terms of their stigma.

As sociologist Rosabeth Moss Kanter[52] has shown, this impression is probably true. When Kanter studied corporate settings in which one person was visibly different from the others, that person was likely to get a disproportionate share of attention. In fact, people in the setting were likely to closely monitor what the minority person did, which meant his or her mistakes were more likely to be noticed—and the mistakes of those in the rest of the group were more likely to be overlooked because everyone was busy watching the minority person. Even in after-work socializing, the minority person was still subject to disproportionate attention.

Kanter also found that the minority person's behavior was likely to be interpreted in terms of the prevailing stereotypes about the members of that category. For example, when there were only a few men in a setting dominated by women, the men were subject to intense observation, and their behavior was filtered through the stereotypes about men. Perceptions were distorted to fit the preexisting beliefs.

Without the presence of a visibly different person, members of a setting are likely to see themselves as different from one another in various ways. Through contrast with the visibly different person, however, they notice their own similarities. In this way, majority group members may construct dichotomies—"us" and "them"—out of settings in which there are a few who are different. It is not surprising that those who are visibly different sometimes isolate themselves in response.

Still, none of this is inevitable. Kanter argued that once minority membership in a setting reaches 15 percent, these processes abate. Until that point, however, those who are in the minority (or visibly stigmatized) are the subject of a good deal of attention. As a consequence, they are often accused of flaunting their difference, of being "so" black, Latino, gay, and so on—of making a show of their status.

This is a charge that the nonstigmatized often level at those who are stigmatized. Although there are certainly occasions in which the discredited may deliberately make a show of their status, Kanter's work indicates that when their numbers are few, the discredited are likely to be charged with being too visible no matter what they do. When they are subjected to a disproportionate amount of attention and viewed through the lenses of stereotypes, almost anything the discredited do is likely to be noticed and attributed to the category to which they belong.

Those who are visibly stigmatized react to this excess of attention in various ways. Some are careful to behave in ways contrary to expectations. At other times, however, people may deliberately make reference to their stigmatized status. For example, in adolescence, light-skinned black men are often derided by their black and white peers as not "really" black, and so they may go to great lengths to counter that charge.

Overt displays of one's stigmatized status may also have an entertaining side. For example, many bilingual Latino students talk about how much they enjoy a loud display of Spanish when Anglos are present; some Asian American students have described their pleasure in pursuing extended no-English-used card games in public spaces on campus. Black and gay adolescents sometimes entertain themselves by loudly affecting stereotypical behavior and then watching the disapproving looks from observers. Those who do not occupy stigmatized statuses may better appreciate these displays by remembering their experience of deliberately acting like "obnoxious teenagers" in public settings. Thus, for some, flaunting their difference may also be fun.

In all, those who are visibly stigmatized—who cannot or will not hide their identity—generate a variety of mechanisms to try to neutralize that stigma and the undue attention that follows.

The Expectations of Those Who Share One's Stigma

The shame associated with stigma may keep people from affiliating with one another, or it might be the grounds for coming together in collective pride. For those stigmatized by color, sex, or social class, family members often provide the lessons about what to expect from those in and outside the category, as well as the "lessons" about how "people like us" are supposed to behave.[c] For those who are gay and lesbian, the lessons are usually provided later in life by members of the gay community.

Particularly for those with visible stigma, there are also frequent reminders that one will be seen as representative of *all* members of the category. Thus, many in stigmatized categories must factor in virtually everyone's opinion: What will others in my category think? What will those who are not stigmatized think? Indeed, they may even be criticized for failing to deal with themselves as stigmatized—"After all, who do you think you are?" In a sense, members of stigmatized categories may monitor one another much as they are policed by those outside the category, with the difference that those within their category can at least claim to be defending them.

This point is illustrated in a story by the late tennis champion Arthur Ashe. (Ashe was the first African American male to win tennis's Grand Slam singles title.) Ashe[53] described watching his daughter play with a gift she had just received—a white doll—as they sat in the audience of a televised match in his honor. When the cameras panned his section of seats, he realized that he needed to get the doll away from his daughter or risk the anger of some black viewers who would argue that by letting his child play with a white doll, he appeared to be a bad role model for the black community.

A different example is provided by a Mexican American acquaintance who worked in an office with only a few other Hispanics, most of whom felt that the routes to upward mobility were closed to them. Together they drafted a letter to the firm's president detailing their concerns and seeking some corrective action. Although he had qualms about signing the letter, our acquaintance felt there was no alternative. Because he worked for management, he was then called in to explain his behavior, which his supervisor saw as disloyal. Thus, he was put in the position of having to explain that, as a Chicano, he could not have refused to sign the letter.

Codes of conduct for those in stigmatized categories often require loyalty to the group. Indeed, the operating rule for many in stigmatized categories is to avoid public disagreement with one another or public airing of the group's "dirty laundry." Such codes are not trivial, because when the codes are violated, members of stigmatized categories risk ostracism from a critical support network. The reality of discrimination makes it foolhardy to reject those who share one's stigma. What would it have meant to Arthur Ashe to lose the support of other African Americans? To whom would our acquaintance have turned in that organization had he refused

---

[c]*People Like Us* (2001) is a well-known PBS documentary about social class in America. One message it describes is "don't get above your raising."

to sign the letter? When they are unaware of these pressures, those in privileged categories may make impossible demands of those who are stigmatized; if they are aware of these pressures, however, such requests are clear tests of loyalty.

Complexities in the Experience of Privilege and Stigma

Separating out the discussion of privileged and stigmatized statuses, as we have done here, has the benefit of allowing us to focus on these processes, but it carries multiple risks, especially that of making people's experience appear less complicated than it is. There are several of these complexities to consider.

First, stigma doesn't always produce disadvantage; it can sometimes yield a benefit, but not as frequently as the benefits that follow from privilege. For example, discrimination is sometimes measured through what are called "audit studies." In this case, researchers select, match, and train people (called testers) to play the part of an applicant for a job or apartment. "By presenting equally qualified individuals who differ only by race or ethnicity, researchers can assess the degree to which racial considerations affect access to opportunities."[54] While audit studies have found evidence of racial discrimination in a variety of arenas (for example, in housing rental and purchase and in call-backs on job résumés),[55] minority testers will still sometimes advance further than their white counterparts in a process. Thus, minority testers will sometimes experience preferential treatment, but they will not experience *as much* preferential treatment as their white counterparts.

Thus, concerns about "reverse discrimination" can often miss the mark. While blacks, Latinos, Asian Americans, or white women are sometimes favored—for example, in employment—they are not favored as *frequently* as white males. In her study of black and white graduates of a Baltimore technical school, Diedre Royster offers an example of how this complexity can be ignored. One of her white informants described being turned down for a job with the state police. He was standing with a group of other white applicants, when an officer approached them to say, "I'm sorry, fellas. Unfortunately, if you were black you would have had the job."

> For the whites involved in these sorts of interchanges, this is a win/win situation. The white applicant wins; he (or sometimes she) is reinforced in his (or her) belief that on merits he or she would have succeeded. . . . The white trooper (or other employing agency official dispensing bad advice) wins because he has found a way to deliver the news such that he and his agency will not encounter any hostility, despite the fact that they are rejecting applicants. [The trooper didn't say], "I'm sorry, fellas. We only had twenty-five places; two of them went to the sons of troopers, three went to cousins and neighbors, one went to a political connection, four were reserved for minority or female applicants (and frankly, those applicants had really strong records), and we had tons of great applicants for the remaining fifteen positions. In fact, we had three hundred applicants with scores higher than any of you."[56]

Thus, advantages may follow from stigma as well as privilege, though in different proportions and with different levels of visibility. This point is made by the dissenting justices in the Supreme Court's 2009 decision in *Ricci v. DeStefano* (Reading 37).

Second, analyzing stigma and privilege separately risks ignoring that those with privilege are nonetheless affected by stigma, even though they are not themselves stigmatized. For example, homophobia and sexism shape interaction between straight men and racism affects how white men and women interact, such as in the expectation that white men need to be the protectors of white women. Likewise, the stigma of disability affects the friends and relatives of those who are disabled and people's response to their own bodies. In all, privilege exists in interaction with stigma.

Third, as we mentioned in the first Framework Essay, although it may appear that people can be easily separated into two categories—stigmatized and privileged—every individual occupies several master statuses. The privilege or stigma that might be associated with one status emerges in the context of *all* of one's other statuses. For example, a middle-class, heterosexual, Mexican American male may be privileged in terms of class, sex, and sexual orientation, but stigmatized by virtue of being Hispanic. Given the invisibility of privilege, he is more likely to notice the ways in which his ethnic status stigmatizes him than to notice all the privileges that follow from his other statuses. Nevertheless, he is *simultaneously* all of his statuses; the privileges and disadvantages of each emerge in the context of all the others. Whereas an Anglo male and a Latino male may both be said to experience the privilege of sex, they do not experience the *same* privilege.

This gets us to the idea of *intersectionality*—also called the "matrix of domination" or "complex inequality"—which was articulated in the early 1990s by law professor Kimberlé Crenshaw as she sought to convey how the experience of black women in America was about the *interaction* of race and sex.[57] Crenshaw pointed to the inadequacy of thinking about black women's experiences as about *either* race or sex, or even about *both* race and sex additively. Rather—using the analogy of standing at the intersection of the streets of racism and sexism—she argued that the intersection was itself a unique place and process, not one in which forms of discrimination were just added together or even multiplied, but in which they interacted with one another.

In some ways, intersectionality can be compared to the idea of "interaction effect" in statistics. In statistics, a "main effect" is the effect of an independent variable on a dependent variable, for example, the effect of race on income, or the effect of sex on income. An "interaction effect," however, occurs when the effect of one variable *depends* on the level or presence of other variables, for example, when the effect of race on income *depends* on sex. In the analysis of multiple variables, theoretically one could find only direct (i.e., main) effects, only interaction effects, some mix of those, or no effects at all. In a statistical analysis, these outcomes would also be affected by which variable was loaded into the calculation *first,* that is, which status was given priority. A similar concern emerges in intersectional analyses in terms of whether some forms of inequality should be treated as taking priority over others.

Crenshaw was not the first to notice how the intersection of the "streets" of race and sex had been ignored. A well-known anthology released in the 1980s had been entitled *All the Women Are White, All the Blacks Are Men, but Some of*

Us Are Brave,[58] to convey that black women were both invisible as women in the women's movement and invisible as blacks in the civil rights movement. By virtue of standing at the intersection, black women were marginalized within both movements, even though they were doubly discriminated.

Since then, the study of intersectionality has stood as a unique contribution of feminist social science methodology. For example, Patricia Hill Collins—one of the preeminent sociological theorists of intersectionality—uses the concept to understand how gender, race, class, and nation are mutually constituted within and through the domain of "family." Similarly, in Reading 29, "Gendered Sexuality in Young Adulthood," Laura Hamilton and Elizabeth Armstrong examine the interaction of social class and gender on sexuality in college. Though scholars taking an intersectional approach have usually focused on the confluence of racism and sexism, the intersection of other dichotomies can also have important ramifications for people's lives, for example, being gay and a practicing Catholic would involve living at an "intersection" that encompasses a unique set of conflicts.

Responding to the experience of those at the intersection requires thinking differently about public policy, law, resource allocation, and political organization. For example, "Despite the commonsense notion that the more 'different' a worker is, the more likely she will encounter bias, empirical evidence shows that multiple claims—which may account for more than 50 percent of federal court discrimination actions—have even less chance of success than single claims. . . . [T]he more complex the claimant's identity, the wider must be cast the evidentiary net to find relevant comparative, statistical, and anecdotal evidence."[59]

Similarly, intersectional thinking would ask if women of different races would need different kinds of support in higher education or following domestic violence, or how black women voters would respond to a political contest between a white woman and a black man, as for example, in the 2007 primary contest between Hillary Clinton and Barack Obama. Were black women assumed to support Obama because they were black or to support Clinton because they were women? Would one status be treated as primary (the main effect), would black women's location be understood to be complicated and unique, or would both campaigns simply ignore them?

More prosaically, in its thirty-eight-year history *Saturday Night Live* has hired only four black female cast members, the latest in 2013 after a six-year hiatus. If they defended themselves by saying, "We have white women and black men on the show (not to mention black men who have *played* black women), so what's the problem?" that would be the equivalent of saying "Black women are 'sort of' black and 'sort of' women, and so we haven't worried about them very much over thirty-eight years!"

Still, intersectionality is a difficult concept and method. Understanding the complexity of lives at the intersection moves us away from the usual, and relatively easier, social science goal of finding generalizable knowledge, that is, knowledge that holds true for broad categories of people, for example "all" women or men. At the same time, intersectionality offers a thoroughgoing critique of essentialism, because it questions how much is really shared by those in a master status. After all, how much of our knowledge holds true for *both* black and white women? How much holds true for *both* black women and black men? Capturing that complexity requires a narrower research focus and more limited claims about knowledge—with the risk that the categories for analysis will endlessly proliferate—but the payoff is a better understanding of the real complexities of people's lives.

Fourth, while individuals may experience both privilege and stigma, some stigmas are so strong that they can cancel out the privileges other statuses might provide. This is often the case for people who are disabled. For example, the student quoted below describes how using a wheelchair "canceled out" expectations that she was intelligent.

> I find that people automatically assume your intelligence level is lower. They sort of talk maybe slower to you or in a patronizing way. . . . They don't speak right at you or act like you know anything. And they're always surprised to find out that I'm a college student. . . . They think "How could you go to U of M?" Sometimes they'll even say that.[60]

There is much evidence that the stigma of being black in America cancels privileges that might be expected to follow from being middle class. For example,

> A large body of published research reveals that racial and ethnic minorities experience a lower quality of health services and are less likely to receive even routine medical procedures than are white Americans. Relative to whites, African Americans—and in some cases, Hispanics—are less likely to receive hemodialysis and kidney transplantation, and are likely to receive a lower quality of basic clinical services such as intensive care, even when variations in such factors as insurance status, income, age, co-morbid conditions, and symptom expression are taken into account. . . . The majority of studies . . . find that racial and ethnic disparities remain even after adjustment for socioeconomic differences and other healthcare access-related factors.[61]

Fifth, separating out discussions of privilege and stigma can mistakenly connote that they are equivalent. For example, when Latino students in one class talked about their pleasure in speaking Spanish, their Anglo friend immediately described how excluded she felt on those occasions. While they understood her reaction, the Latino students made it clear that they were not willing to forgo the opportunity to speak Spanish: their friend would just have to understand it wasn't anything personal. The question that emerged for the students listening to this exchange was about equivalent "rights." Isn't the Latino exclusion of Anglos the same as the Anglo exclusion of Latinos?

As a way to approach this, consider the following two statements about gays and straights. In what ways are the statements similar, and in what ways different?

> A heterosexual says, "I can't stand gays. I don't want to be anywhere around them."
> A gay says, "I can't stand straights. I don't want to be anywhere around them."

Although the statements are almost identical, the speakers come from very different positions of power. A heterosexual could probably structure his or her life so as to rarely interact with anyone gay, or at least anyone self-identified as gay. Most important, however, at least until very recently the heterosexual's attitude has been consistent with major social, political, legal, and religious practices. Thus, the heterosexual in this example speaks from a position of some power, if only that derived from alignment with dominant cultural practices.

This is not the case for the gay person in this example, who is unlikely to be able to avoid contact with straights—and who would probably pay a considerable economic cost for self-segregation if that were attempted. There are no powerful institutional supports for hatred of heterosexuals. Similarly, whatever pleasure there might be in exclusiveness, it would exist against a backdrop of relative powerlessness, discrimination, and stigmatization. The same might be said of men's disparagement of women compared with women's disparagement of men. As a student once wrote,

> As a male I have at times been on the receiving end of comments like, "Oh, you're just like all men," or "Why can't men show more emotion?" but these comments or the sentiments behind them do not carry any power to affect my status. Even in the instance of a black who sees me as a representative of all whites, his vision of me does not change my privileged status.

Thus, when those in privileged statuses exclude others, that takes place in a context of relative powerfulness, a sense of entitlement, infrequent discrimination based on master status, and a general ability to avoid those who might be prejudiced against people like themselves. The forms of exclusion available to stigmatized people are unlikely to tangibly affect the lives of those in privileged statuses. Being able to exclude someone from a dance or a club is not as significant as being able to exclude that person from a job or residence. This is what is meant when it is said that members of stigmatized categories may be prejudiced but not discriminatory; they do not have access to the institutional power by which to significantly affect the lives of those in nonstigmatized groups.

Similarly, the term *racist* carries different connotations for blacks and whites. Among whites, being color conscious is often considered to be a sign of being racist. If, as the civil rights movement taught, color should not make a difference in the way people are treated, whites who make a point of *not* noticing race argue that they are being polite and not racist.

But given America's historical focus on race, it seems unrealistic for any of us to claim that we are oblivious to it. Although many consider it impolite to mention race, differential treatment does not disappear as a consequence. Further, a refusal to notice race conveys that being black, Asian, or Latino is a "defect" and that is indelicate (for whites) to mention. Thus, it can be argued that colorblindness is not really a strategy of politeness; rather, it is a strategy of power evasion. Because race, sex, sexual orientation, or disability clearly make a difference in people's lives, pretending not to see those statuses is a way to avoid noticing their effect. The alternative would be a strategy of awareness, that is, of paying systematic attention to the impact of these statuses on oneself and others.

Finally, the understanding of what it means to be stigmatized or privileged changes in the course of a person's identity development. A composite overview of the changes in race and ethnic identity development[62] helps make this point. These stages might also be applied to sex, class, and sexual orientation identities.

One important caution is necessary, however: Not everyone necessarily goes through each of these stages. For example, it is argued that African Americans are rarely found in the first of the stages we detail below.

For those in stigmatized statuses, the first stage of identity development involves an internalization of the culture's negative imagery. This stage may include the disparagement of others in one's group and a strong desire to be accepted by dominant group members. For women, this might mean being highly critical of other women. For people who are low income or gay, this stage might entail feelings of shame. For people of color, it might involve efforts to lighten one's skin, straighten one's hair, or have an eye tuck.

In the next stage, anger at the dominant culture emerges, usually as the result of specific encounters with discrimination. Philosopher Sandra Bartky,[63] focusing on women's discovery of the extent of sexism, describes this as a period in which sexism seems to be everywhere. Events and objects that previously had been neutral are discovered to be sexist; it becomes impossible to get through the day without becoming enraged—and the injustices one discovers are communicated to everyone within earshot. One's own behavior is also subject to increased scrutiny: "Am I being sexist to buy a doll for my niece?" Situations that used to be straightforward become moral tests.

This may be followed by what is sometimes called an immersion stage, because it involves deep involvement in one's own culture. In the previous stage, the individual is focused on evaluating and reacting to the dominant culture. In this stage, however, the focus shifts to one's own group. Dominant group members and the dominant group culture become less relevant to one's pursuits. This is often a period of participation in segregated activities and organizations as one seeks distance from dominant group members. Although anger is somewhat lessened here, the process of reevaluating one's old identity continues.

The final stage is described as a period of integration, as one's stigmatized status becomes integrated with the other aspects of one's life rather than taking precedence over them. Still, an opposition to prejudice and discrimination continues. At this point, one can distinguish between supportive and unsupportive dominant group members, and thus one is more likely to establish satisfying relations with them.

For those who do *not* occupy stigmatized statuses, the first stage of race or ethnic identity development is described as an unquestioning acceptance of dominant group values. This acceptance might take shape as being oblivious to discrimination or as espousing supremacist ideologies.

In the next stage, one becomes aware of others' stigmatization, often through an eye-opening encounter with discrimination. Such an experience may produce a commitment to social change or a sense of powerlessness. As is the case for those in stigmatized statuses, in this stage those in privileged statuses also find themselves overwhelmed by all the forms of discrimination they see, often accompanied by a sense of personal guilt. In an attempt to affiliate and offer assistance, they may seek alliances with those in stigmatized statuses. On college campuses, this timing may not be promising, since many of those in stigmatized statuses are at a high level of anger at those in privileged groups.

We have sometimes had white students of European ancestry describe a kind of envy that emerges at this point. As one said, black and Latino/a ethnic identity made him feel like "I just don't have anything." Even though his own ancestry was a mix of Russian Jew, Italian Catholic, and Scotch Irish Protestant, none of these seemed as compelling as the black, Asian, and Hispanic identities he saw around him.

This student's reaction reflects the transformed ethnic identity of the grand-children and great-grandchildren of people who arrived in the peak immigration period of 1880 to 1920. At that time, Hungarians, Bohemians, Slovaks, Czechs, Poles, Russians, and Italians differed culturally and linguistically from one another and from the Irish, German, Scandinavian, and English immigrants who preceded them. Over the generations—and through intermarriage—this ethnic distinctiveness has been replaced by a socioeconomic "convergence."[64] Among non-Hispanic whites, ethnic ancestry no longer shapes occupation, residence, or political interest, nor is it the basis of the creation of communities of interest.[d] Whereas many enjoy ethnic food and celebrations or have strong feelings attached to stories of immigration, the attachment is likely to be symbolic rather than meaningful. Ethnic identifications are also more likely to be situational and self-selected—for example, highlighting the Russian but ignoring the Irish and German sides of the family.

Eventually, however, those in privileged statuses focus less on trying to win the approval of those in stigmatized groups and instead explore the history of privileged and stigmatized statuses. Learning how privilege has affected one's own life is often a central question in this period.

The final stage involves integrating one's privileged statuses with all the other aspects of one's life, recognizing those in stigmatized categorizations as distinctive individuals rather than romanticizing them as a category ("just because oppressors are bad, doesn't mean that the oppressed are good"),[65] and understanding that many with privilege have worked effectively against discrimination.

Passage through the stages of ethnic or racial identity is positively related to self-esteem for all American race and ethnic groups, but the relationship is stronger for those who are Asian American, African American, and Latino than for those who are white.[66] Indeed, on various measures of self-esteem, African Americans score significantly higher than those in other race or ethnic groups.[67]

---

[d]An exception to the process of convergence among European-originated groups may be white, urban, Catholic ethnics. Throughout the nineteenth century, American Catholic churches were established as specifically ethnic churches (called "nationality churches"). These mostly urban churches were tailored to serve a particular ethnic group, which often included sending a priest from the home country who spoke the immigrants' native language. Thus, within a single urban area one might find separate Irish, Italian, and Polish Catholic churches, as well as effectively separate Catholic schools. The formation of ethnic churches meant that parishes also became ethnically segregated. On occasion, those parishes came to constitute stable, distinctive, working-class ethnic enclaves, for example, such as those found in Chicago. In these cases, ethnic identity continues as an active, viable reality.

CONCLUSION

In all, focusing on stigma and privilege uncovers social processes that might otherwise be invisible, but also risks understating the complexity of people's experiences. Indeed, building an analysis around stigma highlights victim status, as if the entire experience of a group could be characterized by stigma rather than coping and resistance. This point is illustrated in a classroom conversation we once observed, in which an African American student explained to his white classmates that he and his sister both self-identified as black, even though their mother was white. At that point a white student asked why he didn't call himself white since he looked white and that status would yield him more privilege. In response, he detailed all the qualities he prized in the black community and said he would never give up that status to be white. Much of what he said was new to the white students; many had never thought there was anything positive about being black in America.

This classroom discussion reflected the common assumption that those who are stigmatized wish they belonged to the privileged group. Yet the student who had asked the question was clear that she never wanted to be a male, which was equally surprising to the men in the class. Thus, many men presume there is nothing positive about being female, many straights assume there is nothing positive about being gay, many nondisabled people assume that disability ensures misery and loneliness, and many in the middle and upper classes assume there is nothing positive in life for those who are poor. But most people value and appreciate the statuses they occupy. We may wish those statuses weren't stigmatized or overprivileged, but that does not mean we would want to be other than who we are.

Our goal in this essay was to provide you with a framework by which to make sense of people's experience of privilege and stigma. Because there is a great deal of material that illustrates privilege and stigma, for this section's readings we have tried to select those with broad applicability.

KEY CONCEPTS

discredited and discreditable The discredited are those whose stigma is known or apparent to others. The discreditable are those whose stigma is unknown or invisible to others; they are not yet discredited. (page 206)

double consciousness A concept first offered by W.E.B. Du Bois to describe seeing oneself (or members of one's group) through the eyes of a critical, dominant group member. (page 209)

entitlement The belief that one has the right to respect, protection, reward, and other privileges. (page 204)

intersectionality A focus on the interaction of statuses, especially stigmatized statuses. (page 214)

looping or rereading Interpreting (and usually dismissing) someone's words or actions because of the status that the person occupies. (page 205)

marked and unmarked statuses A marked status is one identified as "special" in some way, for example, a *blind* musician or a *woman* doctor. Unmarked statuses, such as musician or doctor, do not have such qualifiers. (page 205)

microaggression Commonplace interpersonal behavior communicating negative race- or sex-based attitudes; subtle personal insults. (page 210)

passing Not revealing a stigmatized identity. (page 206)

privilege The advantages provided by some statuses. (page 195)

NOTES

1. Cary, 1991:83–84.
2. Kimmel and Messner, 1989:3; emphasis added.
3. McIntosh, 1989.
4. Smith, 2001.
5. Capehart, 2013
6. Williams, 1991:56–57.
7. New York State Task Force on Police-on-Police Shootings, 2010.
8. Ibid., iii.
9. Dixon and Linz, 2000; Entman and Rojeck, 2000; Entman, 1990, 1994.
10. Stabile, 2006:178.
11. Ibid., 172–3.
12. Reinarman and Levine, 2004:182.
13. Western, 2006:46.
14. Johnson et al., 2004.
15. Western, 2006.
16. Klein and Soltas, 2013.
17. Western, 2006:13.
18. Tsai and Scommegna, 2012.
19. Ibid.
20. Tierney, 2013.
21. Kocieniewski, 2002.
22. U.S. Immigration and Customs Enforcement, 2010; U.S. Department of Homeland Security, 2011.
23. Tehranian, 2009.
24. Apuzzo and Goldstein, 2014.
25. Atencia, 1999; Richards 2003.
26. Human Rights Watch, 2007.
27. Stevens, 2008; Amnesty International, 2009.
28. Lopez, Morin, and Taylor, 2010.
29. Harris, 2003:77.
30. Carter, 2002:12.
31. Lester, 1994:56–7.
32. Herek, 1992:95–6, emphasis added.
33. Gallup, 2010
34. Associated Press, 2003
35. Tokarczyk, 2004:163.
36. Ibid.
37. Ettinger, 1994:51.
38. For example, Rosenhan, 1973; Schur, 1984; Goffman, 1961, 1963.
39. Davis, 1991:51.
40. Davis, 1991:56–57.
41. Sedgwick, 1990:68.
42. Goffman, 1963:42.
43. Herek and Glunt, 1993.
44. Goffman, 1963:42.
45. hooks, 1989:125.
46. Kennedy, 1976.
47. Hare, 1982:xiii.
48. DuBois 1982:45.
49. Wiseman, 2013:215–216.
50. Sue, 2010.
51. Vega, 2014.
52. Kanter, 1980, 1993.
53. Ashe, 1993.
54. Pager and Shepherd, 2008:185.
55. Ibid.
56. Royster, 2003:170–71.
57. Crenshaw, 1991.
58. Hull, Scott, and Smith, 1982.
59. Kotkin, 2009: 1440.
60. McCune, 2001:7.
61. Institute of Medicine, 2003:1, 2.
62. Cross, 1971, 1978; Hazen, 1992, 1994; Helms, 1990; Morton and Atkinson, 1983; Thomas, 1970; Thomas and Thomas, 1971.
63. Bartkey, 1990.
64. Alba, 1990.
65. Spivak, 1994.
66. Hazen, 1994:55.
67. Hazen, 1992.

REFERENCES

Alba, Richard D. 1990. *Ethnic Identity: The Transformation of White America.* New Haven, CT: Yale University Press.

Amnesty International. 2009. Immigrants Languish in Detention in U.S. March 26. Retrieved June 25, 2010 (www.amnesty.org/en/news-and-updates/news/migrants-languish-detention-us-20090326).

Apuzzo, Matt, and Joseph Goldstein. 2014. New York Drops Unit That Spied on Muslims. *The New York Times,* April 15. Retrieved April 20, 2014.

www.nytimes.com/2014/04/16/nyregion/police-unit
-that-spied-on-muslims-is-disbanded
.html?hpw&rref=nyregion).

Ashe, Arthur. 1993. *Days of Grace.* New York:
Ballantine.

Associated Press. 2003. Are Legacy College Admissions Racist? March 5.

Atencia, Diana P. 1999. Deportation Defense Under
1996 Laws. Retrieved June 22, 2010 (http://library
.findlaw.com/1999/Nov/1/129798.html).

Bartky, Sandra. 1990. *Femininity and Domination:
Studies in the Phenomenology of Oppression.*
New York: Routledge.

Capehart, Jonathan. 2013. Trayvon Martin and the Stolen
Youth of Black Children. *Washington Post,* July 15.
Retrieved April 25, 2014 (www.washingtonpost.com
/blogs/post-partisan/wp/2013/07/15/trayvon-martin-and
-the-stolen-youth-of-black-children/).

Carter, Tom. 2002. Profiling Is "Flawed" Tool to Beat
Terror. *The Washington Times,* January 14, 12.

Cary, Lorene. 1991. *Black Ice.* New York: Knopf.

Crenshaw, Kimberlé Williams. 1991. Mapping the
Margins: Intersectionality, Identity Politics, and Violence against Women of Color. *Stanford Law Review*
43 (6):1241–99.

Cross, W. E., Jr. 1971. The Negro-to-Black Conversion
Experience: Toward a Psychology of Black Liberation. *Black World* 20 (9):13–17.

———. 1978. The Thomas and Cross Models of Psychological Nigrescence: A Review. *The Journal of
Black Psychology* 5 (1):13–31.

Davis, F. James. 1991. *Who Is Black? One Nation's
Definition.* University Park, PA: Pennsylvania
University Press.

Dixon, Travis L., and Daniel Linz. 2000. Overrepresentation and Underrepresentation of African
Americans and Latinos as Lawbreakers on Television
News. *Journal of Communication* 50:131–54.

Du Bois, W. E. B. 1982. *The Souls of Black Folk.*
New York: Penguin. (Originally published in 1903.)

Entman, Robert. 1990. Modern Racism and the Image
of Blacks in Local Television News. *Critical Studies
in Mass Communication* 7:332–45.

Entman, Robert. 1994. Representation and Reality in
the Portrayal of Blacks on Network Television News.
Journalism Quarterly 71:509–20.

Entman, Robert M., and Andrew Rojecki. 2000. *The
Black Image in the White Mind: Media and Race in
America.* Chicago: University of Chicago Press.

Ettinger, Maia. 1994. The Pocahontas Paradigm, or
Will the Subaltern Please Shut Up? *Tilting the
Tower,* edited by Linda Garber, 51–55. New York:
Routledge.

Gallup, Inc. 2010. Americans' Acceptance of Gay
Relations Crosses 50% Threshold. May 3–6.
Retrieved June 23, 2010 (www.gallup.com/poll
/135764/americans-acceptance-gay-relations-crosses
-threshold.aspx).

Goffman, Erving. 1961. *Asylums.* New York: Doubleday Anchor.

———. 1963. *Stigma: Notes on the Management of
Spoiled Identity.* Englewood Cliffs, NJ: Prentice Hall.

Hare, Nathan. 1982. W. E. Burghart Du Bois: An Appreciation, pp. xiii–xxvii in *The Souls of Black Folk.*
New York: Penguin. (Originally published in 1969.)

Harris, David. 2002. Flying While Arab: Lessons
from the Racial Profiling Controversy. *Civil Rights
Journal* 6 (1):8–14.

———. 2003. The Reality of Racial Disparity
in Criminal Justice: The Significance of Data
Collection. *Law and Contemporary Problems*
66 (3):71–95.

Hazen, Sharlie Hogue. 1992. *The Relationship
between Ethnic/Racial Identity Development and Ego
Identity Development.* Ph.D. proposal, Department of
Psychology, George Mason University.

———. 1994. *The Relationship between Ethnic/Racial
Identity Development and Ego Identity Development.*
Ph.D. dissertation, Department of Psychology,
George Mason University.

Helms, J. E. 1990. An Overview of Black Racial Identity Theory. *Black and White Racial Identity: Theory,
Research, and Practice,* edited by J. E. Helms, 9–33.
New York: Greenwood Press.

Herek, Gregory M. 1992. The Social Context of
Hate Crimes. *Hate Crimes: Confronting Violence
against Lesbians and Gay Men,* edited by Gregory
Herek and Kevin Berrill, 89–104. Newbury Park,
CA: Sage.

———, and Eric K. Glunt. 1993. Heterosexuals Who
Know Gays Personally Have More Favorable Attitudes. *The Journal of Sex Research* 30:239–44.

hooks, bell. 1989. *Talking Back: Thinking Feminist,
Thinking Black.* Boston: South End Press.

Hull, Gloria T., Patricia B. Scott, and Barbara Smith.
1982. *All the Women Are White, All the Blacks Are
Men, but Some of Us Are Brave.* New York: Feminist
Press.

Human Rights Watch. 2007. U.S.: Mandatory Deportation Law Harms American Families. July 17. Retrieved June 22, 2010 (www.hrw.org/en/news/2007/07/17/us-mandatory-deportation-laws-harm-american-families).

Institute of Medicine, Board on Health Sciences. 2003. *Unequal Treatment: Confronting Racial and Ethnic Disparities in Health Care.* Washington, DC: National Academy of Sciences.

Johnson, Lloyd D., Patrick M. O'Malley, Jerald G. Bachman, and John E. Schulenberg. 2004. *Monitoring the Future Survey Results on Drug Use, 1975–2003.* Bethesda, MD: National Institute on Drug Abuse.

Kanter, Rosabeth Moss. 1993. *Men and Women of the Corporation.* New York: Basic Books. (Originally published in 1976.)

———, with Barry A. Stein. 1980. *A Tale of 'O': On Being Different in an Organization.* New York: Harper and Row.

Kennedy, Florynce. 1976. *Color Me Flo: My Hard Life and Good Times.* Englewood Cliffs, NJ: Prentice Hall.

Kimmel, Michael S., and Michael A. Messner, eds. 1989. *Men's Lives.* New York: Macmillan.

Klein, Ezra, and Evan Soltas. 2013. Wonkbook: 11 Facts about America's Prison Population. *Washington Post,* August 13. Retrieved April 20, 2014 (www.washingtonpost.com/blogs/wonkblog/wp/2013/08/13/wonkbook-11-facts-about-americas-prison-population/).

Kocieniewski, David. 2002. New Jersey Troopers Avoid Jail in Case That Highlighted Profiling. *The New York Times,* January 15, A1.

Kotkin, M.J. 2009. Diversity and Discrimination: A Look at Complex Bias. *William and Mary Law Review* 50 (5):1439–1500.

Lester, Joan. 1994. *The Future of White Men and Other Diversity Dilemmas.* Berkeley, CA: Conari Press.

Lopez, Mark Hugo, Rich Morin, and Paul Taylor. 2010. Discrimination, Deportation, Detainment, and Satisfaction. Pew Hispanic Center, October 28. Retrieved April 21, 2014 (www.pewhispanic.org/2010/10/28/iii-discrimination-deportation-detainment-and-satisfaction/).

McCune, Pat. 2001. What Do Disabilities Have to Do with Diversity? *About Campus.* May/June, pp. 5–12.

McIntosh, Peggy. 1989. White Privilege: Unpacking the Invisible Knapsack. *Peace and Freedom.* July/August (no page numbers). Wellesley Centers for Women, Wellesley, MA.

Morton, G., and D. R. Atkinson. 1983. Minority Identity Development and Preference for Counselor Race. *Journal of Negro Education* 52 (2):156–61.

New York State Task Force on Police-on-Police Shootings. 2010. *Reducing Inherent Danger: Report of the Task Force on Police-on-Police Shootings.* Retrieved June 20, 2010 (www.ny.gov/governor/reports/pdf/Police_on_Police.pdf).

Pager, Devah, and Hana Shepherd. 2008. The Sociology of Discrimination: Racial Discrimination in Employment, Housing, Credit, and Consumer Markets. *Annual Review of Sociology* 34:181–209.

Primetime: What Would You Do? Teen Vandals. February 25, 2009 http://abcnews.go.com/video/playerIndex?id=6953414

Richards, Randall. 2003. Associated Press. *The Seattle Times.* Retrieved July 5, 2010 (www.thefreelibrary.com/The+deportation+of+crime+U.S.+policy+causing+problems+elsewhere.(ROP . . . -a0110245579).

Reinarman, Craig, and Harry G. Levine. 2004. Crack in the Rearview Mirror: Deconstructing Drug War Mythology. *Social Justice* 31(1–2):182–97.

Rosenhan, D. L. 1973. On Being Sane in Insane Places. *Science* 179:250–58.

Ross, Stephen, and John Yinger. 2002. *The Color of Credit: Mortgage Discrimination, Research Methodology, and Fair-Lending Enforcement.* Cambridge, MA: MIT Press.

Royster, Diedre A. 2003. *Race and the Invisible Hand: How White Networks Exclude Black Men from Blue Collar Jobs.* Berkeley: University of California Press.

Schur, Edwin. 1984. *Labeling Women Deviant: Gender, Stigma, and Social Control.* New York: Random House.

Sedgwick, Eve Kosofsky. 1990. *The Epistemology of the Closet.* Berkeley: University of California Press.

Smith, Tom W. 2001. *Intergroup Relations in a Diverse America: Data from the 2000 General Social Survey.* The American Jewish Committee. www.ajc.org.

Spivak, Gayatre. 1994. George Mason University Cultural Studies presentation.

Stabile, Carol. 2006. *White Victims, Black Villains: Gender, Race, and Crime News in U.S. Culture.* New York: Routledge.

Stevens, Jacqueline. 2008. Amid Anti-Immigrant Fervor, ICE Deporting More American Citizens.

Nation. June 10. Retrieved June 22, 2010 (www .alternet.org/immigration/87467/?page=entire).

Sue, Derald W. 2010. *Microaggressions in Everyday Life: Race, Gender, and Sexual Orientation.* Wiley: Hoboken, NJ.

Tehranian, John. 2009. *Whitewashed: America's Invisible Middle Eastern Minority.* New York: New York University Press.

Thomas, C. 1970. Different Strokes for Different Folks. *Psychology Today* 4 (4):48–53, 78–80.

———, and S. Thomas. 1971. Something Borrowed, Something Black. In *Boys No More: A Black Psychologist's View of Community,* edited by C. Thomas. Beverly Hills, CA: Glencoe Press.

Tierney, John. 2013. Prison and the Poverty Trap. *The New York Times.* February 18. Retrieved April 20, 2014 (www.nytimes.com/2013/02/19/science/long -prison-terms-eyed-as-contributing-to-poverty .html?pagewanted=all).

Tokarczyk, Michelle M. 2004. Promises to Keep: Working Class Students and Higher Education. *What's Class Got to Do with It? American Society in the Twenty-First Century,* edited by Michael Zweig, 161–167. Ithaca, NY: ILR Press.

Tsai, Tyjen, and Paola Scommegna. 2012, August. U.S. Has World's Highest Incarceration Rate. *Population Reference Bureau* (www.prb.org/Publications /Articles/2012/us-incarceration.aspx).

U.S. Department of Homeland Security. 2011, May. DHS Removes Designated Countries from NSEERS Registration. Retrieved April 21, 2014 (https://www .dhs.gov/dhs-removes-designated-countries-nseers -registration-may-2011).

U.S. Immigration and Customs Enforcement. 2010. Retrieved June 22, 2010 (www.ice.gov/pi /specialregistration/archive.htm#what).

Vega, Tanzina. 2014. Students See Many Slights as Racial "Microaggressions." *The New York Times.* March 24. Retrieved April 25, 2014 (www.nytimes .com/2014/03/22/us/as-diversity-increases-slights-get -subtler-but-still-sting.html).

Western, Bruce. 2006. *Punishment and Inequality in America.* New York: Russell Sage.

Williams, Patricia J. 1991. Teleology on the Rocks. *The Alchemy of Race and Rights.* Cambridge, MA: Harvard University Press.

Wiseman, Rosalind. 2013. *Masterminds and Wingmen: Helping Our Boys.* New York: Harmony Books.

RACE AND ETHNICITY

Formulating Identity in a Globalized World

Carola Suárez-Orozco

Increasing globalization has stimulated an unprecedented flow of immigrants worldwide. These newcomers—from many national origins and a wide range of cultural, religious, linguistic, racial, and ethnic backgrounds—challenge a nation's sense of unity. Globalization threatens both the identities of the original residents of the areas in which newcomers settle and those of the immigrants and their children. Integrating immigrants and the subsequent generations into the receiving society is a primary challenge of globalization; failing to do so, however, will have long-term social implications. The ability to formulate an identity that allows comfortable movement between worlds will be at the very heart of achieving a truly "global soul" (Iyer 2000).

At the beginning of the new millennium, there are over 175 million immigrants and refugees worldwide. In the United States alone, 32.5 million, or approximately 11.5 percent of the population, are immigrants (U.S. Bureau of the Census 2000). This is not simply a U.S. phenomenon, however. In 2000, 4.2 percent of the population in the United Kingdom and 5.6 percent of the population in France, was foreign-born. In other nations the percentage of foreign-born is greater than in the United States: 11.8 percent in Sweden, 17.4 percent in Canada, and 23.6 percent in Australia (Migration Information 2003). In almost all these countries, this trend has been steadily increasing. It is important to note that these figures reflect only the first generation. If one considers the children of these immigrants—the second generation—clearly,

many more individuals are involved in the task of negotiating a new identity that synthesizes elements of the culture of origin with those of the receiving culture.

The ever increasing flows of individuals from myriad backgrounds provide a number of aesthetic, cognitive, social, and marketplace opportunities. The ability to code-switch—to move fluidly between languages and cultures—has obvious social advantages. Bicultural and bilingual competence enables individuals to fluidly adapt themselves to evolving situations (Titone 1989). This skill has advantages for entering many professions in the business, diplomatic, and social service sectors. Sommer argues that bilingualism is essential for democracy as it "depends on constructing those miraculous and precarious points of contact from mismatches among codes and people" (Sommer 2004). Indeed, shortly after the last large wave of migration at the turn of the twentieth century, Stonequist argued that the marginality afforded to those individuals in between cultures could lead to individuals who play the essential role of cultural ambassadors adept at interpreting and bridging difference (Stonequist 1937). The cognitive flexibility that this multiple perspective taking requires is becoming an ever more essential trait for the global citizen (Gardner, this volume; Suárez-Orozco and Qin-Hilliard, this volume).

IMMIGRANT STRESS

Multiple pathways structure immigrants' journeys into their new homes. Immigrants and refugees are motivated by a variety of factors—relief from political, religious, or ethnic persecution (in the case of refugees); economic incentives; as well as the opportunity to be reunited with family members. Although for many immigrant families, migration results in substantial gains, it provides many challenges to the individuals involved. It removes individuals from many of their relationships and predictable contexts—extended families and friends, community ties, jobs,

Carola Suárez-Orozco is a professor of education at the University of California, Los Angeles.

living situations, customs, and often languages. Immigrants are stripped of many of their sustaining social relationships as well as the social roles that provide them with culturally scripted notions of how they fit into the world, resulting in acculturative stress (Berry 1997; C. Suárez-Orozco and M. Suárez-Orozco 2001).

Immigrant youth face particular challenges. They often immigrate not just to new homes but also to new family structures (C. Suárez-Orozco, Todorova, and Louie 2002). In our study of four hundred immigrant youth who came to the United States from a variety of origins, including Central America, China, the Dominican Republic, Mexico, and Haiti, we found that fully 85 percent of the youth in this project had been separated from one or both parents for periods of several months to several years (C. Suárez-Orozco et al. 2002). To compound this form of parental unavailability, many immigrant parents work long hours, rendering them relatively physically absent in the lives of their children. Further, depression and anger that may be associated with the migratory experience may make many immigrant parents psychologically unavailable to their children (Athey and Ahearn 1991). These forms of absence all too frequently leave immigrant children to their own devices long before it is developmentally ideal. Although in some cases it can lead to hyperresponsible children, in other cases it leads to depressed youth who are drawn to the lure of alternative family structures such as gangs—a particular risk for boys (Vigil 1988).

THE SECOND GENERATION

The challenges of the first generation are considerably different from those of the second generation. The first generation is largely concerned with surviving and adjusting to the new context. These immigrants may go through a variety of normative adverse reactions following the multiple losses of migration, including anxiety and depression. However, the first generation is protected from these psychological sequelae by several factors. The dual frame of reference by which immigrants can compare their current situation with that left behind often allows them to feel relatively advantaged in the new context (C. Suárez-Orozco and M. Suárez-Orozco 1995). Optimism is at the very heart of the immigrant experience: the possibility of a better tomorrow acts as both a tremendous motivator as well as a form of inoculation against encountered frustrations and barriers. Further, first-generation immigrants are often energized by the desire to support loved ones—by sending remittances home to those left behind, as well as by building the best possible life for their children. While not an easy road, it is one with a clear identity. Immigrants who arrive as adults maintain a sense of identity rooted deeply in their birthplaces. Many expatriates are, of course, quite comfortable in their new homeland. Nevertheless they tend to retain an outsider status as the cultural and linguistic hurdles are simply too high to be surmounted within one generation (C. Suárez-Orozco and M. Suárez-Orozco 2001).

The path for their children, the second generation, is less straightforward, offering a variety of pathways. For these youth, forging a sense of identity may be their single greatest challenge. Do they feel comfortable in their homeland? Do they feel accepted by the "native-born" of the host country? What relationship do they have with their parents' country of origin? Is their sense of identity rooted "here," "there," everywhere, or nowhere?

THE ARCHITECTURE OF CULTURAL IDENTITY

Stage versus Context

Erik Erikson (1968) argued that in the developmental stage of adolescence, identity is the critical maturational task. In forming an identity, youth attempt to create a self-identity that is consistent with how others view them. Identity is less challenging when there is continuity among the various social milieus youth encounter—home, school, neighborhood, and country. In the era of globalization, however, social spaces are more discontinuous and fractured than ever before.

A number of psychologists have claimed that identity goes through a variety of permutations during adolescence as the individual experiments with different identity strategies. Some argue that all youth move steadily from a stage of ethnic or "racial unawareness," to one of "exploration," to a final stage of an "achieved" sense of racial or ethnic identity (Marcia 1966). Others point out that the process of identity formation is, rather than being linear, more accurately described as "spiraling" back to revisit previous stages, each time from a different vantage point (Parham 1989).

Achieved and Ascribed Identities

Identity formation, I would argue, is not simply a process by which one passes through a variety of stages on the way to achieving a stable identity. Rather it is a process that is fluid and contextually driven. If raised in Beijing and immigrating as an adult, one may "discover" that one is "Asian" for the first time at age thirty. Prior to immigrating, that same individual in Beijing may never have considered her racial or ethnic identity (or if she did, it would be a neighborhood identity). In the Chinatown of the host society, the identity will be one of northern mainland Chinese origin (in contrast to Cantonese speakers from Hong Kong or Canton); but in the heartland of the host country the identity may become a more complex, "pan-Asian" construct. The social context is essential in predicting which identity is constructed (Suárez-Orozco 2000).

The tension between the dominant culture and minority newcomers lies at the heart of the ethnic and cultural identity formation drama of immigrants and their children (DeVos 1980). Youth are challenged to navigate between achieved identities and ascribed or imposed identities (C. Suárez-Orozco and M. Suárez-Orozco 2001). Achieved identity is the extent to which an individual achieves a sense of belonging—"I am a member of *this* group." An ascribed identity is imposed either by coethnics—"You are a member of *our* group"—or by members of the dominant culture—"You are a member of *that* group."

For some groups the imposed or ascribed identity is considerably stronger than for others. In the United States, for example, African identity is firmly ascribed, whereas Italian identity can be assumed at will. The degree to which ascribed origins are imposed may also evolve over time. At the turn of the twentieth century in Boston, having Irish origins had significant negative implications, whereas at the turn of the twenty-first century, being from Ireland merits little notice and can be articulated at will (for St. Patrick's Day events but not necessarily in a job interview).

Phenotypic racial features have considerable implications for the ease of assimilation. Historically, immigrants coming from Europe to the United States could more easily assimilate once they lost their accents and changed their names. The ability to join the mainstream unnoticed is more challenging when one is racially marked. Questions as to where one is "really from" or compliments made to Asian Americans who have been in the United States many generations on their English fluency lead to what law professor Frank H. Wu (2002) refers to as "perpetual foreigner syndrome." In this era of globalization, the fact that many immigrants of color originate in the developing world (Africa, Asia, the Caribbean, and Latin America) and enter postindustrial regions traditionally populated by Europeans (Europe, North America, Australia) makes "passing," or fully assimilating unnoticed, no longer possible for most new arrivals.

Contact with Cultures

Culture provides one with generally shared understandings and models for making meaning of one's experiences. Cultural beliefs present standards of behavior that are internalized over time, and cultural traditions offer a soothing sense of social safety. At the heart of these shared understandings are the interpersonal networks of relations in which one is embedded.

In order to maintain a sense of affinity with one's culture of origin, sustained contact is required. Regular visits back to the homeland—in what is described as a transnational existence—facilitates maintenance of the parent culture (Levitt 1996). Living in an ethnic enclave limits the opportunity for regular interaction with members of the mainstream culture. Ethnic communities, such as Chinatown in San Francisco, Mexican barrios in Los Angeles, the Dominican neighborhood in Washington Heights (in Manhattan), the Cuban enclave in Miami, and the like, nurture a sense of culture of origin without requiring return visits to the homeland. The strength of the effect of these ethnic neighborhoods and enclaves is determined by the density of the local ethnic population, the strength of the collective coethnic identity, the community's cohesiveness, and the availability of cultural role models.

If there is little contact with the culture of origin, however, then all of the "cultural lessons" fall upon the shoulders of the parents to teach. Parents are, no doubt, a critical source of information in the quest to form an identity. Immigration, however, undermines parents' ability to act as guides, by removing the "map of experience" necessary to successfully escort children in the new culture (Hoffman 1989). Without effortless proficiency in the new cultural expectations and practices, immigrant parents are less able to provide guidance in the ways of negotiating the currents of a complex society; in addition, they must rely on their children for cultural interpretations. As a seasoned immigrant comments to a prospective migrant in the novel *Accordion Crimes*, "the natural order of the world is reversed. The old learn from the children" (Proulx 1996).

The ease with which elements of the parent culture can be incorporated into the new culture will to some extent be affected by the "cultural distance" between the parent and new culture (Berry 1997). Youth growing up within dual contexts characterized by great degrees of dissimilarity between cultural beliefs and social practices are likely to suffer from greater identity confusion than those coming from more convergent cultural backgrounds (Arnett 2002). This would suggest that in the United States the children of rural Hmong in northern California (Fadiman 1998; Portes and Rumbaut 2001) or Yemeni immigrants in the Midwest would face more challenges than the children of Canadian immigrants in New England.

The fact that many immigrants enter highly segregated neighborhoods with large coethnic or minority populations complicates the potential for identification with mainstream culture. If there is little contact with the mainstream middle class in any form other than media representations encountered on television or in movies, identifying with the host culture becomes something of an abstraction.

Performing Identity

How does an individual demonstrate his ethnic affiliation? At the most basic level, the ethnic label an individual chooses signifies his identity (Maestes 2000; Waters 1996). Sociological research has used the self-selected label as a way of examining identity. Whether a second-generation person of Mexican origin calls herself Mexican or Mexican American, or Latina, or Chicana seems to be linked to quite different patterns of incorporation and engagement in schooling (Matute-Bianchi 1991; Portes and Rumbaut 2001; Waters 1996). Individuals who adopt a self-referential label that includes their parents' country of origin seem to do better in school than their counterparts who select a panethnicity (such as Hispanic or Latino) or who refer only to their country of residence (such as American). The same is true with self-selected labels adhered to by persons of Caribbean origin: Waters (1997) has demonstrated that Caribbean-origin youth who call themselves Jamaican American, for example, appear to have different perceptions of discrimination and opportunities than those who call themselves African American.

Feelings of belonging to rather than alienation from the various cultural groups an individual may be part of also has important implications (DeVos and Suárez-Orozco 1990). Whether or not one feels affiliation with and acceptance in the groups under consideration may be related to one's ability to incorporate elements of the culture into one's sense of self. Does the individual value his culture of origin? Does he feel accepted by other members of that culture? Is he drawn to the new culture (or cultures)? Does he feel welcome and incorporated into the new culture (or cultures)? Does he *wish* to be incorporated into the new culture, or does he find it alienating? These attitudes will have much to do with the fusion of culture that the individual internalizes (Maestes 2000).

Participation in a series of *ethnic activities,* as well as the *dominant culture's* activities and social practices, is one of the clearest ways in which cultural identity is performed (Maestes 2000). What language does the individual report feeling most comfortable using (Maestes 2000)? In what circumstances does she use the language of origin—spontaneously or under duress? What is the culture of the friends to whom she is drawn? Are these friends mostly persons of the individual's culture of origin, of the dominant culture, or of a range of origins? What religious practices are important, and to what degree? Do these practices occur on a daily basis, or are they more occasional, with a primarily social function? What foods does the individual most enjoy, particularly in social settings? What holidays does she celebrate? Are they largely those of the culture of origin, of the host society, or some combination? What entertainment choices does she make? Selections made in sports participation (baseball versus basketball versus soccer, for example), music (salsa versus rap versus pop), radio or television (ethnic versus mainstream), movies and videos (country of origin versus Hollywood versus an eclectic selection) can provide insight into relative comfort and affiliation with the points of cultural contact (Louie 2003).

The Ethos of Reception

The general social climate, or ethos of reception, plays a critical role in the adaptation of immigrants and their children (C. Suárez-Orozco and M. Suárez-Orozco 2001). Unfortunately, intolerance for newcomers is an all-too-common response all over the world. Discrimination against immigrants of color is particularly widespread and intense in many areas receiving large numbers of new immigrants, including Europe (Suárez-Orozco 1996), the United States (Espenshade and Belanger 1998), and Japan (Tsuda 2003). As today's immigrants are more diverse than ever before in ethnicity, skin color, and religion, they are particularly subject to the pervasive social trauma of prejudice and social exclusion (Tatum 1997).

The exclusion can take a structural form (when individuals are excluded from the opportunity structure) as well as an attitudinal form (in the form of disparagement and public hostility). These structural barriers and the social ethos of intolerance and racism encountered by many immigrants of color intensify the stresses of immigration. Although the structural exclusion suffered by immigrants and their children is tangibly detrimental to their ability to participate in the opportunity structure, prejudicial attitudes and psychological violence also play a toxic role. Philosopher Charles Taylor argues that "our identity is partly shaped by recognition or its absence, often by the misrecognition of others, and so a person or group of people can suffer real damage, real distortion, if the people or society around them mirrors back to them a confining or demeaning or contemptible picture of themselves" (Taylor 1994). How can youth of immigrant origin incorporate the notion that they are unwanted "aliens" who do not warrant the most basic rights of education and health care?

The Social Mirror

Child psychoanalyst D. W. Winicott suggests that a child's sense of self is profoundly shaped by the reflections mirrored back to him by significant others (Winicott 1971). Indeed, all human beings are dependent upon the reflection of themselves mirrored by others. "Others" include not just the mother (which was Winicott's principal concern) but also relatives, adult caretakers, siblings, teachers, peers, employers, people on the street, and even the media (C. Suárez-Orozco 2000). When the reflected image is generally positive, the individual (adult or child) is able to feel that she is worthwhile and competent. When the reflection is generally negative, it is extremely difficult to maintain an unblemished sense of self-worth.

These reflections can be accurate or inaccurate. When the reflection is a positive distortion, the response to the individual may be out of proportion to his actual contribution or achievement. In the most benign case, positive expectations can be an asset. In the classic "Pygmalion in the Classroom" study, teachers who believed that certain children were brighter than others (based on the experimenter randomly assigning some children that designation, unsubstantiated in fact) treated the children more positively and assigned them higher grades (Rosenthal and Feldman 1991). It is possible that some immigrant students, such as Asians, benefit somewhat from positive expectations of their competence as a result of being members of a "model minority"—though no doubt at a cost (Takaki 1993).

It is the negative distortions, however, that are most worrisome. What is the effect for children who receive mirroring from society that is predominantly negative and hostile? Such is the case with many immigrant and minority children (see Maira 2004). Commenting on the negative social mirroring toward Muslim students after September 11, Iraqi American Nuar Alsadir eloquently stated: "The world shouldn't be a funhouse in which we're forced to stand before the distorting mirror, begging for our lives" (Alsadir 2002). W. E. B. Du Bois famously articulated the challenge of what he termed "double-consciousness"—a "sense of always looking at one's self through the eyes of others, of measuring one's soul by the tape of a world that looks on in amused contempt and pity" (Du Bois 1903/1989). When the expectations are of sloth, irresponsibility, low intelligence, and even danger, the outcome can be toxic. When these reflections are received in a number of mirrors, including the media, classroom, and street, the outcome is devastating (Adams 1990).

Research from the Harvard Immigration Project, a study of youth immigrating to the United States from China, Central America, the Dominican Republic, Haiti, and Mexico, suggests that immigrant children are keenly aware of the prevailing ethos of hostility in the dominant culture (C. Suárez-Orozco 2000). A sample of four hundred children were asked to complete the sentence "Most Americans think that [Chinese, Dominicans, Central Americans, Haitians, Mexicans—depending on the child's country of origin] are_____." Disturbingly, fully 65 percent of the respondents provided a negative response to the sentence-completion task. The modal response was "bad"; others—even more disconcerting—included "stupid," "useless," "garbage," "gang members," "lazy," and "we don't exist" (C. Suárez-Orozco 2000).

What meanings do youth construct from and how do they respond to this negative social mirror? One possible pathway is for youth to become resigned to the negative reflections, leading to hopelessness and self-depreciation that may in turn result in low aspirations and self-defeating behaviors. The general affect associated with this pathway is depression and passivity. In this scenario, the child is likely to respond with self-doubt and shame, setting low aspirations in a kind of self-fulfilling prophecy: "They are probably right. I'll never be able to do anything." Other youth may mobilize to resist the mirrors and injustices they encounter. I differentiate between two types of resistance. The first is a project infused with hope, a sense of justice, and faith in a better tomorrow. The other form of resistance is eventually overcome by alienation leading to anomie, hopelessness, and a nihilistic view of the future. In this latter case, youth may actively resist the reflections they encounter but are unable to maintain hope for change or a better future. Without hope, the resulting anger and compensatory self-aggrandizement may lead to acting-out behaviors including the kinds of dystopic cultural practices typically associated with gang membership. For these youth, the response is "If you think I'm bad, let me show you just how bad I can be" (C. Suárez-Orozco and M. Suárez-Orozco 2001).

The social trajectories of youth are more promising for those who are able to actively maintain and cultivate a sense of hope for the future. Whether they are resigned, oblivious, or resistant to the reflections in the social mirror, those who are able to maintain hope are in fundamental ways partially inoculated to the toxicity they may encounter. These youth are better able to maintain pride and preserve their self-esteem. In these circumstances, their energies are mobilized in the service of day-to-day coping. Some may not only focus on their own advancement but also harness their energies in the service of their communities by volunteering to help others, acting as role models, or advocating and mobilizing for social change. In this scenario, youth respond to the negative social mirror as a goad toward "I'll show you I can make it in spite of what you think of me" (C. Suárez-Orozco and M. Suárez-Orozco 2001).

Social Disparagement and Academic Outcomes

Children of color are particularly subject to negative expectations that have profound implications for their academic performance (Weinstein 2002). Cross-cultural data from research focused on a variety of disparaged minorities in a number of contexts all over the world suggest that exposure to a negative social mirror adversely affects academic engagement. This research provides insight into a number of critical questions: In ethnically diverse and increasingly transnational societies, how does schooling relate to hierarchies of inequality (Freire 1995)? Does the educational system reproduce inequalities by replicating the existing social order? Or does schooling help to overcome social inequalities by emerging as an avenue for status mobility?

What is the experience of self in cultures where patterned inequality shapes social interactions? Anthropological cross-cultural evidence from a variety of regions suggests that the social context and ethos of reception plays an important role in immigrant adaptation. Ogbu (1978) has argued that minorities who were originally incorporated against their will through conquest and enslavement are more likely to give up on educational avenues as a route to social mobility than are those of immigrant origin who enter a new society voluntarily. DeVos and M. Suárez-Orozco (1990) have demonstrated that a cultural and symbolic ethos of reception

saturated with psychological disparagement and racist stereotypes has profound implications for the identity formation of minority and immigrant children, as well as for their schooling experiences.

In cases in which racial and ethnic inequalities are highly structured, such as for Algerians in France, Koreans in Japan, or Mexicans in California, "psychological disparagement" and "symbolic violence" may permeate the experience of many minority youth. Members of these groups not only are effectively locked out of the opportunity structure (through segregated and inferior schools and work opportunities in the least desirable sectors of the economy) but also commonly become the objects of cultural violence. The stereotypes of inferiority, sloth, and violence justify the sense that they are less deserving of full participation in the dominant society's opportunity structure. Facing such charged attitudes, which assault and undermine their sense of self, minority children may come to experience the institutions of the dominant society—especially its schools—as alien terrain reproducing an order of inequality (DeVos and M. Suárez-Orozco 1990). While all groups face structural obstacles, not all groups elicit and experience the same attitudes from the dominant culture. Some immigrant groups elicit more negative attitudes, encountering a more negative social mirror than others do. In U.S. public opinion polls, for example, Asians are seen more favorably than Latinos (Espenshade and Belanger 1998).

In past generations, assimilationist trajectories demonstrated a correlation between length of residence in the United States and better schooling, health, and income outcomes (Gordon 1964; M. Suárez-Orozco and Paez 2002). While assimilation was a goal and a possibility for immigrants of European origin, resulting in a generally upwardly mobile journey (Child 1943; Higham 1975), this alternative is more challenging for immigrants of color today. Further, increasing "segmentation" in the American economy and society is shaping new patterns of immigrant adaptation (Gans 1992; Portes and Rumbaut 2001; Rumbaut 1997; Waters 1999; Zhou 1997).

Certainly, a preponderance of evidence suggests that structural factors such as neighborhood segregation and poverty (see Massey and Denton 1993; Orfield and Yun 1999), as well as family-level factors (including parents' education and socioeconomic status), are significant predictors of long-term educational outcomes for children (Coleman et al. 1966). In a society powerfully structured by "the color line" (Du Bois 1903/1989), however, race and color are significant vectors for understanding the adaptations of immigrant youth of color.

Stanford University social psychologist Claude Steele has led new theoretical and empirical work on how "identity threats," based on group membership, can profoundly shape academic achievement. In a series of ingenious experimental studies, Steele and his colleagues have demonstrated that under the stress of a stereotype threat, performance goes down on a variety of academic tasks. For example, when high-achieving African American university students are told before taking an exam that the test has proven to differentiate between blacks and whites, in favor of whites, their performance was significantly worse than when they were not told that the test differentiated between groups (Steele 1997). Steele maintains that when negative stereotypes about one's group prevail, "members of these groups can fear being reduced to the stereotype" (Steele 1997, p. 614). He notes that in these situations, self-handicapping goes up. This "threat in the air" has not only an immediate effect on the specific situation that evokes the stereotype threat but also a cumulative erosive effect when events that evoke the threat continually occur. He argues that stereotype threat shapes both intellectual performance and intellectual identity.

How are identity and agency implicated in educational processes and outcomes? John Ogbu and his colleagues have done seminal work in the area of immigration, minority status, and schooling in plural societies (Matute-Bianchi 1991; Ogbu 1978, 1987). Inspired by George DeVos's comparative studies of social stratification and status inequality (DeVos 1973; DeVos and M. Suárez-Orozco 1990), Ogbu argued that parental and other socioeconomic factors

explain only part of the variance; when these factors are controlled for, differences become evident. On one hand, immigrants tend to develop cultural models and social practices that serve them well in terms of educational adaptations and outcomes. On the other hand, "involuntary minorities," after generations of living with structural inequities and symbolic violence, tend to develop social practices and cultural models that remove them from investing in schooling as the dominant strategy for status mobility.

A number of theorists of the new immigration have begun to examine how race and color complicate the process of immigrant adaptation. Waters (1999) claims that in this "race conscious society a person becomes defined racially and identity is imposed upon [him or her] by outsiders" (p. 6). She reports that her black West Indian immigrant informants are shocked by the level of racism against blacks in the United States. Though they arrive expecting structural obstacles (such as discrimination in housing and promotions), what they find most distressing is the level of both overt and covert prejudice and discrimination. Black immigrants tend to bring with them a number of characteristics that contribute to their relative success in the new setting. For their children, however, "over the course of one generation the structural realities of American race relations and the American economy undermine the cultures of the West Indian immigrants and create responses among the immigrants, and especially their children, that resemble the cultural responses of African Americans to long histories of exclusion and discrimination" (Waters 1999, p. 6). While cross-sectional data have been used to identify this transgenerational pattern, preliminary data from the Harvard Longitudinal Immigrant Student Adaptation study suggest that among many immigrant youth of color, this process unfolds at a rapid pace within a few years of migration.

In response to marginalization they encounter in their ethnic homeland, for example, Japanese Brazilians resist assimilationist cultural pressures by strengthening their Brazilian national identity. Similar trends found among Haitians in Miami (Stepick 1997), Dominicans in Providence, Rhode Island (Bailey 2001), and Caribbean American youth in New York (López 2002,) suggest that for many of today's new arrivals, the journey is a process of racial and ethnic self-discovery and self-authoring. New identities are crafted in the process of immigrant uprooting and resettlement through continuous feedback between the subjective sense of self and what is mirrored by the social milieu (Erikson 1968; C. Suárez-Orozco and M. Suárez-Orozco 2001).

Given that today nearly 80 percent of the new immigrants are of color, emigrating from the "developing world"—Latin America, the Caribbean, and Asia (Edmonston and Passel 1994; Fix and Passel 1994)—a pattern of racialization and adversarial identity formation within the school context is deeply concerning. In our increasingly globalized world, education becomes ever more crucial for functioning (Bloom, 2004; Suárez-Orozco and Qin-Hilliard, 2004). Formulating identities that allow individuals to move fluidly from context to context becomes critical to future functioning as global citizens.

IDENTITY PATHWAYS

Identities and styles of adaptation are highly context dependent and fluid. An immigrant youth might first gravitate toward one style of adaptation. Over time, as she matures and as her context changes, she may be drawn into new attitudes and social behaviors.

In some cases the identity that is forged is highly focused upon the culture of origin, with coethnics as the primary point of reference. In some of these cases, an identity that is adversarial to the dominant culture may emerge. In other cases youth of immigrant origin may embrace total assimilation and complete identification with mainstream American culture. In still other cases a new ethnic identity that incorporates selected aspects of *both* the culture of origin and mainstream American culture is forged. All of these identity styles have clear implications for adaptation to the new society, including the schooling experiences of immigrant youth. Within the same family, each child may adopt his or her own style, resulting in various siblings occupying very different sectors of the identity spectrum.

Coethnic Identities

Some immigrant-origin youth maintain a largely coethnic focus. Some may do so because they have limited opportunity to make meaningful contact with other groups in the host culture. Others may be responding to an understanding that a group with which they may have extensive contact is even more disparaged than they are as immigrants. Hence, Caribbean-origin individuals may distinguish themselves from African Americans in an attempt to ward off further disparagement (Waters 1999; Zéphir 2001).

Other youth of immigrant origin may develop an adversarial stance, constructing identities around rejecting—after having been rejected by—the institutions of the dominant culture. Princeton sociologist Alejandro Portes observes, "As second-generation youth find their aspirations for wealth and social status blocked, they may join native minorities in the inner city, adopting an adversarial stance toward middle-class white society, and adding to the present urban pathologies" (Portes 1993).

Immigrant children who find themselves structurally marginalized and culturally disparaged are more likely to respond to the challenges to their identities by developing an adversarial style of adaptation (Vigil 2002). These children of immigrants are responding in ways similar to those of other marginalized youth in the United States—such as many inner-city poor African Americans and Puerto Ricans (and elsewhere, such as Koreans in Japan or Algerians in France). Likewise, many of the disparaged and disenfranchised second-generation Italian American, Irish American, and Polish American adolescents of previous waves of immigration demonstrated a similar profile.

Today, some youth of immigrant origin respond to marginalization and the poisoned mirror by developing adversarial identities. Among children of immigrants who gravitate toward adversarial styles, embracing aspects of the culture of the dominant group is equated with giving up one's own ethnic identity (Fordham and Ogbu 1986). Like other disenfranchised youth, children of immigrants who develop adversarial identities tend to encounter problems in school and drop out, and consequently face unemployment in the formal economy. . . .

Ethnic Flight

The children of immigrants who shed their cultures structure their identities most strongly around the dominant mainstream culture (Berry 1997). Taking ethnic flight, these youth may feel most comfortable spending time with peers from the mainstream culture rather than with their less acculturated peers. For these youth, learning to speak standard English not only serves an instrumental function of communicating but also becomes an important symbolic act of identifying with the dominant culture. Among these youth, success in school may be seen not only as a route for individualistic self-advancement but also as a way to symbolically and psychologically move away from the world of the family and the ethnic group.

Often this identification with the mainstream culture results in a weakening of ties to members of one's own ethnic group. These young people all too frequently are alienated from their less acculturated peers, having little in common with them or even feeling superior to them. While they may gain access to privileged positions within mainstream culture, they must still deal with issues of marginalization and exclusion.

Even when immigrant-origin youth do not feel haughty toward their ethnic peers, they may find the peer group unforgiving of any behaviors that could be interpreted as "ethnic betrayal." It is not necessary for the child of an immigrant to consciously decide to distance himself from his culture. Among some ethnic groups, merely being a good student will result in peer sanctions. Accusations of "acting white" or being a "coconut," "banana," or "Oreo" (brown, yellow, or black on the outside and white on the inside) are frequent (Fordham and Ogbu 1986).

In an earlier era of scholarship, this style of adaptation was termed "passing" (DeVos 1992). While there were gains for the children of immigrants who "disappeared" into the mainstream culture, there were also hidden costs—primarily in terms of unresolved

shame, doubt, and self-hatred. While passing may have been a common style of adaptation among those who phenotypically looked like the mainstream, it is not easily available to today's immigrants of color, who visibly look like the "other." Further, while ethnic flight is a form of adaptation that can be adaptive in terms of "making it" by the mainstream society's standards, it frequently comes at a significant social and emotional cost.

Transcultural Identities

Between the coethnic and ethnic flight gravitational fields, we find the large majority of children of immigrants. The task of immigration for these children is crafting a transcultural identity. These youth must creatively fuse aspects of two or more cultures—the parental tradition and the new culture or cultures. In so doing, they synthesize an identity that does not require them to choose between cultures but rather allows them to incorporate traits of both cultures while fusing additive elements (Falicov 2002).

For Latinos, this state is what Ed Morales refers to as "living in Spanglish." He defines "the root of Spanglish [as] a very universal state of being. It is displacement from one place, home, to another place, home, in which one feels at home in both places, yet at home in neither place. . . . Spanglish is the state of belonging to at least two identities at the same time, and not being confused or hurt by it" (Morales 2002, pp. 7–8). Such is the identity challenge of youth of immigrant origin—their developmental task requires crafting new cultural formations out of two systems that are at once their own and foreign. These children achieve bicultural and bilingual competencies that become an integral part of their sense of self.

Among youth engaged in bicultural styles, the culturally constructed social strictures and patterns of social control of their immigrant parents and elders maintain a degree of legitimacy. Learning standard English and doing well in school are viewed as competencies that do not compromise their sense of who they are. These youth network, with similar ease, among members of their own ethnic group as well as with students, teachers, employers, colleagues, and friends of other backgrounds. A number of studies in the past two decades have demonstrated a link between racial and ethnic identity pathways and academic outcomes (Gibson 1988; Ogbu and Herbert 1998). These studies suggest that those who forge transcultural identities are more successful academically.

Many who successfully "make it" clearly perceive and appreciate the sacrifices loved ones have made to enable them to thrive in a new country. Rather than wishing to distance themselves from parents, these youth come to experience success as a way to "pay back" their parents for their sacrifices. At times, they experience a form of "survivor guilt" as a result of the deprivation their parents and other family members have suffered in order to move to the new land. Among many such adolescents, success in school serves not only the instrumental function of achieving self-advancement and independence but also, perhaps even more important, the expressive function of making the parental sacrifices worthwhile through the son or daughter's "becoming a somebody." For such youth, "making it" may involve restitution by "giving back" to parents, siblings, peers, and other less fortunate members of the community.

A transcultural identity is the most adaptive of the three styles. It blends the preservation of the affective ties of the home culture with the acquisition of instrumental competencies required to cope successfully in the mainstream culture. This identity style not only serves the individual well but also benefits the society at large. It is precisely such transcultural individuals whom Stonequist identified as being best suited to become the "creative agents" who might "contribute to the solution of the conflict of races and cultures" (Stonequist 1937, p. 15).

Transcultural identities are particularly adaptive in this era of globalism and multiculturalism. By acquiring competencies that enable them to operate within more than one cultural code, immigrant youth are at an advantage. The unilinear assimilationist model, which results in styles of adaptation I term ethnic flight, is no longer feasible. Today's immigrants are not unambivalently invited to join the mainstream society. The rapid abandonment of the home culture implied in ethnic flight almost always results in the collapse of the parental voice of authority. Furthermore, lack of group connectedness results in anomie and alienation. The key to a successful adaptation involves acquiring competencies that are relevant to the global economy while maintaining the social networks and connectedness essential to the human condition. Those who are at ease in multiple social and cultural contexts will be most successful and will be able to achieve higher levels of maturity and happiness.

Gendered Differences

An emerging body of literature reveals that boys from disparaged minority backgrounds seem to be particularly at risk of being marginalized, beginning in the educational system (Brandon 1991; Gibson 1988; J. Lee 2002; Portes and Rumbaut 2001; Qin-Hilliard 2003; Waters 1996). Consistent with this literature, data from the Harvard Immigration Project suggest that immigrant boys tend to demonstrate lower academic achievement (as measured by report card outcomes) and encounter more challenges in school than immigrant girls. Boys report feeling less support from teachers and staff and are more likely to perceive school as a negative, hostile, and racist environment (Qin-Hilliard 2003; Suárez-Orozco and Qin-Hilliard 2004). . . .

Several factors may contribute to this pattern. The negative social mirror that boys of color encounter appears to be significantly more distorting than that encountered by girls (López 2002). Boys of color are consistently viewed by members of the mainstream society they encounter as more threatening than are girls. Another factor that may help to explain boys' poorer school performance is peer pressure. Many researchers have noted that peer pressure to reject school is quite strong among boys (Gibson 1993; C. Suárez-Orozco and M. Suárez-Orozco 2001; Waters 1996). Furthermore, behaviors that gain boys respect with their peers often bring them into conflict with their teachers. Some researchers point out that immigrant boys are more pressured by their peers to reject school than immigrant girls from the same ethnic background (Gibson 1993; C. Suárez-Orozco and M. Suárez-Orozco 2001; Waters 1996). Gender differences in family responsibilities at home may also play a role in explaining differences in academic outcomes between girls and boys. Research findings consistently suggest that, compared with their brothers, immigrant girls have many more responsibilities at home (S. Lee 2001; Olsen 1997; Sarroub 2001; Smith 2002, Valenzuela 1999; Waters 1996). While these factors may account for this gendered pattern of academic engagement, more research is required to unpack the source of this trend.

EDUCATING THE GLOBAL CITIZEN

. . . Is there such a thing as a global identity? In recent decades, American youth culture has come to dominate the cultural scene among adolescents living in urban centers in Europe, Latin America, and Asia (C. Suárez-Orozco and M. Suárez-Orozco 2001). This pattern seems to be driven in large part by global media, including movies, television, music videos and recordings, and the Internet, as well as global marketing of such brands as Coca-Cola, McDonald's, and Nike (Arnett 2002). Whether this attraction to global brands translates into internalized cultural practices remains to be seen. . . .

Psychologist Jeffrey Jensen Arnett, however, argues that globalization has clear implications for identity development among youth. He maintains that "most people in the world now develop a bicultural identity," which incorporates elements of

PERSONAL ACCOUNT

Hair

I never hated my hair until I moved to America. My parents always told me that I was beautiful and that my full head of hair and thick curls were unique. I used to think so too, until we moved. In Egypt, other girls had curly hair, and it was commonplace for curly hair to be left wild and untamed. But in the States, words like "frizzy," "nappy," "poufy," and "interesting" were used to describe my hair. I have been approached many times by people wanting to touch my hair, and often it has been compared to dogs or carpet. This was hurtful, because I wanted so badly to be accepted as a beautiful person. I wanted to be acknowledged for characteristics like being intelligent and committed to my education, not my carpet-dog hair. School pictures were a nightmare; I am still taunted by boys from my elementary school about how my hair used to look, with threats that they will show my pictures to other people.

I began to think that beautiful hair was straight and shiny, like all the white girls had. That is when I began to straighten my hair. Enormous time and effort went into finding the latest "best way to make hair flat." Money was spent on hair products, hair irons, and blow dryers, all for the satisfaction of going to school the next day and finally being told that my hair looked pretty. When I went to the hair salon, I was charged extra for having curly hair and had to listen to unbearable comments from the stylists, not to mention their body language. Since my hair was curly, stylists knew no other way to straighten it than by blow-drying it into a "fro" and then using the hair iron afterwards. I was subject to many stares, grunts, and groans as the stylists expressed that my hair was not just a burden for me, but for them as well. All the while, I deceived myself into thinking that straight hair was more manageable and less of a burden than outrageously curly hair.

It has taken me more than ten years to realize that all this is wrong, and that I should go back to loving my hair for what it is and not wishing I had someone else's. Now, I am going through the slow process of growing it out and letting myself go back to my natural hair—wild, free, and untamed curliness.

My hair has played a huge part in establishing my feelings as a minority in the United States. Although the United States Census defines Egyptians as white, I certainly don't feel white. The words used to describe my hair are often used to describe black hair. I believe that my hair has caused much confusion for other people in terms of racial categorization. While my features and skin color might categorize me as white, my hair is black. Likewise, I'm not sure what race most people perceive me to be. I have been told I look Hispanic, Dominican, and half-black. This used to confuse me when I was younger. Am I one of the black, white, or Hispanic kids? Today, I don't describe myself as Arab or Middle Eastern. Rather, I'm Sarah, from Egypt, plain and simple.

Sarah Faragalla

the local culture with an awareness of a relation to the global culture (Arnett 2002, p. 777). As a result, he and others maintain that identity confusion may be increasing among youth (Nsamenang 2002). For many, however, the identity is less *bi*cultural than a "complex *hybrid*" (Arnett 2000, p. 778) or *trans*-cultural (C. Suárez-Orozco and M. Suárez-Orozco 2001). Indeed, ethnic identity options may involve more than simply two cultures. For those who remain in the land of birth with a legacy of colonization, the challenge is to reconcile local traditions with the imported practices *and* globalized culture (Nsamenang 2002). In the words of Henry Louis Gates Jr.: "Today the ideal of wholeness has largely been retired. And cultural multiplicity is no longer seen as the problem but as a solution—a solution to the confines of identity itself. Double consciousness, once a disorder, is now a cure. Indeed, the only complaint we moderns have is that Du Bois was too cautious in his accounting. He'd conjured 'two souls, two thoughts, two unreconciled strivings.' Just two, Dr. Du Bois? Keep counting" (Gates 2003, p. 31). . . .

DISCUSSION QUESTIONS

1. In what ways are the experiences of first and second-generation immigrants likely to differ?
2. What factors shape the identities of immigrant youth? To improve the outcome for immigrant youth, what would you recommend?

REFERENCES

Adams, P. L. (1990). Prejudice and exclusion as social trauma. In *Stressors and adjustment disorders.* J. D. Noshpitz and R. D. Coddington, eds. New York: John Wiley and Sons.

Alsadir, N. (2002). Invisible woman. *New York Times Magazine,* November 17, p. 98.

Arnett, J. J. (2002). The psychology of globalization. *American Psychologist* 57(10): 774–783.

Athey, J. L., and F. L. Ahearn (1991). *Refugee children: Theory, research, and services.* Baltimore, MD: Johns Hopkins University Press.

Bailey, B. H. (2001). Dominican-American ethnic/racial identities and United States social categories. *International Migration Review* 35(3): 677–708.

Berry, J. W. (1997). Immigration, Acculturation, and Adaptation. *International Journal of Applied Psychology* 46: 5–34.

Bloom, David E. (2004) Globalization and Education: An Economic Perspective. In *Globalization: Culture and education in the new millennium.* M. M. Suárez-Orozco and Desireé Baolian Qin-Hilliard, eds. Berkeley: University of California Press.

Brandon, P. (1991). Gender differences in young Asian Americans' educational attainment. *Sex Roles* 25(1–2): 45–61.

Child, I. L. (1943). *Italian or American? The second generation in conflict.* New Haven, CT: Yale University Press.

Coleman, J., et al. (1966). *Equality and educational opportunity.* Washington, DC: U.S. Government Printing Office.

DeVos, G. (1973). *Socialization for achievement: Essays on the cultural psychology of the Japanese.* Berkeley: University of California Press.

DeVos, G. (1980). Ethnic adaptation and minority status. *Journal of Cross-Cultural Psychology* 11(1): 101–125.

———— (1992). The passing of passing. In *Social cohesion and alienation: Minorities in the United States and Japan.* G. DeVos, ed. Boulder, CO: West-view Press.

DeVos, G., and M. Suárez-Orozco (1990). *Status inequality: The self in culture.* Newbury Park, CA: Sage Publications.

Du Bois, W. E. B. (1989). *The souls of black folks.* New York: Bantam. (Original work published 1903).

Edmonston, B., and J. Passel, eds. (1994). *Immigration and ethnicity: The integration of America's newest arrivals.* Washington, DC: Urban Institute.

Erikson, E. (1968). *Identity: Youth and crisis.* New York: W. W. Norton.

Espenshade, T., and M. Belanger (1998). Immigration and public opinion. In *Crossings: Mexican immigration in interdisciplinary perspective.* M. M. Suárez-Orozco, ed. Cambridge, MA: David Rockefeller Center for Latin American Studies.

Fadiman, A. (1998). *The spirit catches you and you fall down: A Hmong child, her American doctors, and the collision of two cultures.* New York: Farrar, Straus & Giroux.

Falicov, C. J. (2002). The family migration experience: Loss and resilience. In *Latinos: Remaking America.* M. M. Suarez-Orozco and M. M. Paez, eds. Berkeley: University of California Press.

Fix, M., and J. Passel (1994). *Immigration and immigrants: Setting the record straight.* Washington, DC: Urban Institute.

Fordham, S., and J. U. Ogbu (1986). Black students' school success: Coping with the burden of "acting white." *Urban Review* 18(3): 176–206.

Freire, P. (1995). *Pedagogy of the oppressed.* New York: Continuum.

Gans, H. (1992). Second-generation decline: Scenarios for the economic and ethnic futures of the post-1965 American immigrants. *Ethnic and Racial Studies* 15(April): 173–192.

Gardner, Howard. (2004). How education changes: Considerations of history, science, and values.

Gates, H. L., Jr. (2003) Both sides now. *New York Times Book Review,* April 4, p. 31.

Gibson, M. A. (1988). *Accommodation without assimilation: Sikh immigrants in an American high school.* Ithaca, NY: Cornell University Press.

_____ (1993). Variability in immigrant students' school performance: The U.S. case. Unpublished manuscript. Washington, DC.

Gordon, M. M. (1964). *Assimilation in American life: The role of race, religion, and national origins.* Oxford, UK: Oxford University Press.

Higham, J. (1975). *Send these to me: Jews and other immigrants in urban America.* New York: Atheneum.

Hoffman, E. (1989). *Lost in translation: A life in a new language.* New York: Penguin Books.

Iyer, P. (2000). *The global soul.* New York: Vintage Press.

Lee, J. (2002). Racial and ethnic achievement gap trends: Reversing the progress toward equity? *Educational Researcher* 31(1):3–12.

Lee, S. (2001). More than "model minorities" or "delinquents": A look at Hmong American high school students. *Harvard Educational Review,* 71(3): 505–528.

Levitt, P. (2001). *The transnational villagers.* Berkeley: University of California Press.

López, N. (2002). *Hopeful girls, troubled boys: Race and gender disparity in urban education.* New York: Routledge.

Louie, J. (2003). Media in the lives of immigrant youth. In *The Social worlds of immigrant youth: New directions for youth development.* C. Suárez-Orozco and I. Todorova, eds. New York: Jossey-Bass.

Maestes, M. (2000). *Acculturation and ethnic identity measures for Latinos and Asian Americans: Analyses of methodology and psychometrics.* Lincoln: University of Nebraska.

Maira, Sunaina. (2004). Imperial feelings: Youth culture, citizenship, and globalization.Marcia, J. (1966). Development and validation of ego-identity status. *Journal of Personality and Social Psychology* 3: 551–558.

Massey, D., and N. Denton (1993). *American apartheid.* Cambridge, MA: Harvard University Press.

Matute-Bianchi, M. E. (1991). Situational ethnicity and patterns of school performance among immigrant and non-immigrant Mexican descent students. In *Minority status and schooling: A comparative study of immigrant and involuntary minorities.* M. A. Gibson and J. Ogbu, eds. New York: Garland Publishing.

Migration Information (2003). *Global Data.* Retrieved January 3, 2003, from http://www.migrationinformation.org/GlobalData/countrydata/data.cfm.

Morales, E. (2002). *Living in Spanglish: The search for Latino identity in America.* New York: LA Weekly Books.

Nsamenang, B. (2002). Adolescence in sub-Saharan Africa: An image constructed from Africa's triple inheritance. In *The world's youth: Adolescence in eight regions of the globe.* B. B. Brown, R. Larson, and T. S. Saraswathi, eds. New York: Cambridge University Press.

Ogbu, J. U. (1978). *Minority education and caste: The American system in cross-cultural perspective.* New York: Academic Press.

_____ (1987). Variability in minority school performance: A problem in search of an explanation. *Anthropology and Education Quarterly* 18(4): 312–334.

Ogbu, J. U., and S. Herbert (1998). Voluntary and involuntary minorities: A cultural-ecological theory of school performance with some implications for education. *Anthropology and Education Quarterly* 29: 155–188.

Olsen, L. (1997). *Made in America: Immigrant students in our public schools.* New York: The New Press.

Orfield, G. (2002). Commentary. In *Latinos: Remaking America.* M. Suárez-Orozco and M. M. Paez, eds. Berkeley: University of California Press; Cambridge, MA: David Rockefeller Center for Latin American Studies.

Orfield, G., and J. T. Yun (1999). *Resegregation in American schools.* Cambridge, MA: The Civil Rights Project, Harvard University.

Parham, T. (1989). Cycles of psychological nigrescence. *Counseling Psychologist* 17(2): 187–226.

Portes, A. (1993). The "New Immigration." Press release, School of International Relations, Johns Hopkins University.

Portes, A., and R. G. Rumbaut (2001). *Legacies: The story of the second generation.* Berkeley: University of California Press.

Proulx, E. A. (1996). *Accordion crimes.* New York: Scribners.

Qin-Hilliard, D. B. (2003). Gendered expectations and gendered experiences: Immigrant students' adaptation in U.S. schools. In *The social worlds of immigrant youth: New directions for youth development.* C. Suárez-Orozco and I. Todorova, eds. New York: Jossey-Bass.

Rosenthal, D. A., and S. S. Feldman (1991). The influence of perceived family and personal factors on self-reported school performance of Chinese and Western high school students. *Journal of Research on Adolescents* 1: 135–154.

Rumbaut, R. (1997). *Passages to adulthood: The adaptation of children of immigrants in Southern California.* New York: Russell Sage Foundation.Sarroub, L. K. (2001). The sojourner experience of Yemeni American high school students: An ethnographic portrait. *Harvard Educational Review* 71(3): 390–415.

Smith, R. (2002). Gender, ethnicity, and race in school and work outcomes of second-generation Mexican Americans. In *Latinos: Remaking America.* M. M. Suarez-Orozco and M. M. Paez, eds. Berkeley: University of California Press.

Sommer, D. (2004). *Bilingual aesthetics: A new sentimental education.* Raleigh, NC: Duke University Press.

Steele, C. (1997). A threat in the air: How stereotypes shape intellectual identity and performance. *American Psychologist* 52(6): 613–629.

Stepick, A. (1997). *Pride against prejudice: Haitians in the United States.* Boston: Allyn & Bacon.

Stonequist, E. V. (1937). *The marginal man.* New York: Scribner and Sons.

Suárez-Orozco, C. (2000). Identities under siege: Immigration stress and social mirroring among the children of immigrants. In *Cultures under siege: Social violence and trauma.* A. Robben and M. Suárez-Orozco, eds. Cambridge, UK: Cambridge University Press.

Suárez-Orozco, C., and D. B. Qin-Hilliard (2004). The cultural psychology of academic engagement: Immigrant boys' experiences in U.S. schools. In *Adolescent boys in context.* N. Way and J. Chu, eds. New York: New York University Press.

Suárez-Orozco, C., and M. Suárez-Orozco (1995). *Transformations: Immigration, family life, and achievement motivation among Latino adolescents.* Stanford, CA: Stanford University Press.

Suárez-Orozco, C., and M. Suárez-Orozco (2001). *Children of immigration* (1st ed.). Cambridge, MA: Harvard University Press.

Suárez-Orozco, C., I. Todorova, and J. Louie (2002). Making up for lost time: The experience of separations and reunifications among immigrant families. *Family Process* 41(4): 625–643.

Suarez-Orozco, M., and Desirée Baolian Qin-Hilliard. (2004) Globalization: Culture and education in the new millennium.

Suárez-Orozco, M. M. (1996). Unwelcome mats. *Harvard Magazine* 98: 32–35.

Suárez-Orozco, M. M., and Paez, M. M. (2002). *Latinos: Remaking America.* Berkeley: University of California Press.

Takaki, R. (1993). *A different mirror: A history of multicultural America.* New York: Little, Brown.

Tatum, B. (1997). *"Why are all the black kids sitting together in the cafeteria?" and other conversations about race.* New York: Basic Books.

Taylor, C. (1994). *Multiculturalisim: Examining the politics of recognition.* Princeton: Princeton University Press.

Titone, R. (1989). The bilingual personality as a metasystem: The case of code switching. *Canadian Society for Italian Studies* 3: 55–64.

Tsuda, T. (2003). *Strangers in the ethnic homeland: Japanese Brazilian return migration in transnational perspective.* New York: Columbia University Press.

U.S. Bureau of the Census (2000). *Current population reports.* Washington, DC.

Valenzuela, A. (1999). Gender roles and settlement activities among children and their immigrant families. *American Behavioral Scientist* 42(4): 720–742.

Vigil, J. D. (1988). *Barrio gangs: Street life and identity in Southern California.* Austin: University of Texas Press.

Waters, M. (1996). The intersection of gender, race, and ethnicity in identity development of Caribbean American teens. In *Urban girls: Resisting stereotypes, creating identities.* B. J. R. Leadbeater and N. Way, eds. New York: New York University Press.

Waters, M. (1997). Ethnic and racial identities of second-generation black immigrants in New York City. *International Migration Review* 28(4): 795–820.

Waters, M. (1999). *Black identities: West Indian dreams and American realities.* Cambridge, MA: Harvard University Press.

Weinstein, R. (2002). *Reaching higher: The power of expectations in schooling.* Cambridge, MA: Harvard University Press.

Winicott, D. W. (1971). *Playing and reality.* Middlesex, UK: Penguin.

Wu, F. H. (2002). *Yellow: Race in America beyond black and white.* New York: Basic Books.

Zéphir, F. (2001). *Trends in ethnic identification among second-generation Haitian immigrants in New York City.* Westport, CT: Bergin & Garvey.

Zhou, M. (1997). Growing up American: The challenge confronting immigrant children and children of immigrants. *Annual Review* 23: 63–95.

PERSONAL ACCOUNT

The Americanization of a Reluctant Vietnamese-American

In life, I am certain of one thing: I am Vietnamese. My identity as a Vietnamese, to borrow President Obama's words, began "with the fact of my race." I was born in Vietnam—to Vietnamese parents—and lived in Vietnam for the first eight years of my life. As soon as I could speak, I learned Quốc Ngữ, the Vietnamese national language, and was inculcated to the Vietnamese culture.

My parents taught me to use chopsticks when I was two or three years old, when I started to sample Vietnamese fare such as Phở (Vietnamese noodle soup), Chả giò (egg rolls), and Bún Thịt Nướng (vermicelli with grilled pork and vegetables). As good Vietnamese parents, they instructed me on Vietnamese etiquette, such as bowing to my elders as a sign of respect. My parents impressed upon me the virtue of emotional restraint—to never raise my voice or speak with too many gestures. I learned early in life that my behavior is a reflection not only of myself but also of my family and lineage.

Born and raised in a country plagued by a civil war, I was taught to value freedom before I knew its meaning. Because death was a commonplace in my village, I understood the fragility of life at an early age. The civil war that began after the French withdrew in 1954 robbed my generation of our innocence—certainly we didn't grow up listening to "Twinkle Twinkle Little Star" or "If You're Happy and You Know It." Rather, we were exposed to songs about the despair of war and its horrendous consequences.

Under the remnant of French colonialism and amid the violence, cruelty, and betrayal of a nation at war with itself, I formed my Vietnamese identity—an identity that had been influenced and shaped by the Vietnam War. By the time my family and I escaped Vietnam in 1975, my identity as a Vietnamese had been firmly established and cemented. Or so I thought.

In America, we were sponsored by a Presbyterian Church from Victoria, Texas, and once we were settled in Victoria, my Vietnamese identity was immediately challenged in this new environment. Located 30 miles from the Gulf of Mexico on the coastal plains of Texas, Victoria had a population of 25,000 people in 1975. My family had been the only nonwhite members at the First Presbyterian Church; in fact, we had been the first Vietnamese family in Victoria. Our life in Victoria revolved around our church, and because our congregation was all white, I came to believe that Victoria was predominantly a white town. It was only years later that I learned that Victoria, even in 1975, had a sizable Hispanic population.

For the first two years in Victoria, I clung to my Vietnamese identity. As soon as I learned English, however, I was immediately struck by the differences in self-identities between my white and nonwhite peers. While my white peers identified themselves as "just Americans," my nonwhite peers used the hyphenated identity of African-American, Mexican-American, or Asian-American.

After a couple of years living in the United States, I, too, began using a hyphenated identity, that of Vietnamese-American. I no longer felt completely "Vietnamese," yet I didn't feel "American" either. The hyphenated identity allowed me to express the uniqueness of my Vietnamese identity within the American context. In a sense, the hyphenated identity represented my struggles between the Vietnamese and American cultures. I maintained this hyphenated identity until college, when I was exposed to other constructs of identity.

At 17 years of age, I left home to attend the University of Texas at Austin, a state university with one of the largest student enrollments in the United States. I had never lived away from home, so my first year at UT was both exciting and exhilarating. I encountered people from different walks of life, and as my world broadened and expanded, I began to question my hyphenated identity. What did it mean to be

"Vietnamese-American?" For that matter, what did it mean to be "just Vietnamese" or "just American?" When I chose my hyphenated identity in my early teens, it made sense; however, at the age of 18, I felt more restricted and confined by it. Eventually, I decided to embrace the humanitarian ideology and broadened my identity to be a "citizen of the world." With my newfound identity, I sought to incorporate multiple worldviews and perspectives in my life. My new identity impelled me to form friendships and relationships with people of different nationalities, religions, and socioeconomic backgrounds. As a "citizen of the world," I had no national identity and knew no national boundary. In short, I held no allegiance to any country.

After graduate school, I took a job as an assistant professor in the Department of Asian American Studies at San Francisco State University (SFSU). There, I experienced another shift in my self-identity. Given my profession, it's likely that I would have reclaimed my "blended bi-cultural identity" eventually.[1] But the racially charged environment at SFSU prompted me to question whether a "citizen of the world" identity, while an admirable goal, was attainable. We are the product of our family, culture, and society, and I didn't grow up as a "citizen of the world" but as a Vietnamese living in America. Toward the end of my first semester at SFSU, I assumed the identity of "Vietnamese American" or "Asian American." Unlike the previous hyphenated identity, I omitted the hyphen between "Vietnamese" and "American." Looking back, I am not sure if I knew precisely why I had omitted the hyphen from "Vietnamese American." Certainly, the difference between a hyphenated or nonhyphenated identity is nuanced and subtle. For me, the hyphenated identity signaled my struggles between the Vietnamese and American cultures, while the nonhyphenated identity indicated a more fluid and dynamic interaction between the two often conflicting cultures. The hyphen had called attention to my "Vietnameseness" set against the American context; the omission of the hyphen eliminated this distinction. Depending on the context, I could be more American or more Vietnamese, and while others may have perceived me to be more of one or the other, I made no such distinction for myself.

In 2004, my parents passed away, and this gave rise to another shift in my self-identity. Each year, on the anniversary of their passing, I hold a ceremony at a Buddhist temple in Houston, Texas, to commemorate them. As I sit cross-legged on the floor in the main part of the temple where service is held, the scene always seems unreal (especially to me as a Presbyterian). I sit facing the five-platform structure that is arranged in the shape of a pyramid and serves as an altar. The larger-than-life statue of Buddha sits in the center of the shrine on the uppermost platform while two smaller Buddha statues flank the main Buddha figure. The service begins, and I struggle to follow the chanting—although the chanting along with the beating of the drum sends me into an almost dreamlike state. After the metaphorical offering of food to my parents, I set off for the airport and fly home to Seattle.

This very act has confounded my relatives in both America and Vietnam. In their eyes, I am an "Americanized Vietnamese," so it befuddles them that I would embrace the Vietnamese tradition/ritual of ancestral worship. How could I be so "Vietnamese" yet so "American?" I didn't attempt to explain to my relatives on both sides of the pond that my Vietnamese parents believed in ancestral worship, and I chose to adhere to their belief system to honor them. Even if I could explain, would they accept that I have no vested interest in following the Vietnamese tradition or ritual for the sake of tradition? For me, it has been a means to an end.

In the years after my parents' passing, I began to travel extensively, and my travels took me to different places around the world and allowed me to explore my American identity. In some instances, I found myself rigorously asserting and defending it. No other place has made as significant and profound an impact on my American identity as Paris, where I spent the month of June in 2009. Instead of clinging to Vietnam and its legacy, especially with its history with France, I chose to cut my ties with it and embrace my American experience. When the French asked about my nationality, I just replied that "I'm American." I found that my American identity afforded me freedom from the history of oppression and domination that my people had endured under the French empire. In fact, by the time I landed at Newark Liberty International Airport on June 30, 2009, my identity had shifted from "Vietnamese American" to "just American." By chance, I had planned to spend the July 4th weekend in New York City before flying back to Seattle, and as I watched our nation celebrate our independence day that Saturday, I silently celebrated mine.

Since my return from France more than two years ago, I have assumed the identity of an American—an American of Vietnamese descent, but nevertheless an American. Unless asked, I haven't shared or volunteered this information. To be honest, I still would not if it weren't for the rise in vitriolic rhetoric in our national conversation about race/ethnicity and national identity.

When I am often asked by other Americans about my nationality, I often reply, with tongue in cheek, "I'm from Texas." Taken aback, they try to clarify. "No, I mean, where are you really from?" While I'm amused by their need to place me outside the American context because of my Asian features and skin color, in truth, I'm as American as they are (albeit a naturalized citizen of the United States). In fact, I could argue that I may even be more American because I have consciously chosen my national identity and allegiance to the United States of America.

Perhaps it was merely serendipitous that I woke up on August 15, 2011, to see Gary Locke, our new American ambassador to China, making headlines. The ruckus began when Tang Chaohui, a Chinese tech entrepreneur and blogger, snapped a photo of Ambassador Locke with a backpack, standing with his daughter at a Sea-Tac Starbucks, buying his own coffee. According to the blogger, Ambassador Locke even attempted to use a voucher. The post went viral, and the Chinese reacted with admiration, surprise, and confusion that Ambassador Locke "wore a backpack and bought his own coffee." In the meantime, we in America looked at the reaction of the Chinese and asked: "What's the big deal? We all have to buy our own coffee and carry our own backpack." Perhaps one Chinese commentator summed it up best when he wrote about Locke on iFeng.com: "In China, even a low-level official uses police to open up the road for them when they go out." Another further explained, "We are so used to Chinese officials' privileges that we're now not used to Gary Locke's normal behavior."

Given that I spent the weekend writing about the various shifts in my self-identity, I found the buzz around Ambassador Locke quite interesting. Certainly, I found it fascinating that both Chinese and Americans assigned the hyphenated identity of "Chinese-American" to Ambassador Locke even though he was born in the United States. Moreover, it was how Ambassador Locke identified himself that I found most interesting. In his statement, Ambassador Locke said: "I am both humbled and honored to stand here before you as a child of Chinese immigrants representing America, the land of my birth, and the American values my family holds dear. I can only imagine just how proud my dad, Jimmy, who passed away in January, would be for his son to be the first Chinese-American to represent the United States in the land of his and my mother's birth. My parents, my wife, our children—we all personally represent America and America's promise as a land of freedom, equality, and opportunity."[2]

Ambassador Locke, I couldn't agree with you more. I, too, may be ethnically Vietnamese; however, I'm all American (backpack, discount voucher, and buying my own coffee and all).

Hoai Huong Tran

---

[1] Citrin, Jack and David O. Sears. "Balancing National and Ethnic Identities: The Psychology of E Pluribus Unum." econfaculty.gmu.edu/bcaplan/citrin2.doc.

[2] Mong, Adrienne. August 15, 2011. "The 'ABCs' of Being Ambassador to China." http://behindthewall.msnbc.msn.com/_news/2011/08/15/7371518-the-abcs-of-being-ambassador-to-china.

READING 22

Latinos and the U.S. Race Structure

Clara E. Rodríguez

According to definitions common in the United States, I am a light-skinned Latina, with European features and hair texture. I was born and raised in New York City; my first language was Spanish, and I am today bilingual. I cannot remember when I first realized how the color of one's skin, the texture of one's hair, or the cast of one's features determined how one was treated in both my Spanish-language and English-language worlds. I do know that it was before I understood that accents, surnames, residence, class, and clothing also determined how one was treated.

Looking back on my childhood, I recall many instances when the lighter skin color and European features of some persons were admired and terms such as "pelo malo" (bad hair) were commonly used to refer to "tightly curled" hair. It was much later that I came to see that this Eurocentric bias, which favors European characteristics above all others, was part of our history and cultures. In both Americas and the Caribbean, we have inherited and continue to favor this Eurocentrism, which grew out of our history of indigenous conquest and slavery (Shohat and Stam 1994).

I also remember a richer, more complex sense of color than this simple color dichotomy of black and white would suggest, a genuine esthetic appreciation of people with some color and an equally genuine valuation of people as people, regardless of color. Also, people sometimes disagreed about an individual's color and "racial" classification, especially if the person in question was in the middle range, not just with regard to color, but also with regard to class or political position.[1]

As I grew older, I came to see that many of these cues or clues to status—skin color, physical features, accents, surnames, residence, and other class characteristics—changed according to place or situation. For example, a natural "tan" in my South Bronx neighborhood was attractive, whereas downtown, in the business area, it was "otherizing." I also recall that the same color was perceived differently in different areas. Even in Latino contexts, I saw some people as lighter or darker, depending on certain factors, such as their clothes, occupations, and families.[2] I suspect that others saw me similarly, so that in some contexts, I was very light, in others darker, and in still others about the same as everyone else. Even though my color stayed the same, the perception and sometimes its valuation changed.

I also realize now that some Latinos' experiences were different from mine and that our experiences affect the way we view the world. I know that not all Latinos have multiple or fluctuating identities. For a few, social context is irrelevant. Regardless of the context, they see themselves, and/or are seen, in only one way. They are what the Census Bureau refers to as *consistent;* that is, they consistently answer in the same way when asked about their "race." Often, but not always, they are at one or the other end of the color spectrum.

My everyday experiences as a Latina, supplemented by years of scholarly work, have taught me that certain dimensions of race are fundamental to Latino life in the United States and raise questions about the nature of "race" in this country. This does not mean that all Latinos have the same experiences, but that for most, these experiences are not surprising. For example, although some Latinos are consistently seen as having the same color or "race," many Latinos are assigned a multiplicity of "racial" classifications, sometimes in one day! I am reminded of the student who told me after class one day, "When people first meet me, they think I'm Italian, then when they find out my last name is Mendez, they think I'm Spanish, then when I tell them my mother is Puerto Rican, they think I'm nonwhite or Black." Although he had not changed

Clara E. Rodríguez is a professor of sociology at Fordham University's College at Lincoln Center.

his identity, the perception of it changed with each additional bit of information.

Latino students have also told me that non-Latinos sometimes assume they are African American. When they assert they are not "Black" but Latino, they are either reproved for denying their "race" or told they are out of touch with reality. Other Latinos, who see Whites as Other-than-me are told by non-Latinos, "But you're white." Although not all Latinos have such dramatic experiences, almost all know (and are often related to) others who have.

In addition to being reclassified by others (without their consent), some Latinos shift their own self-classifications during their lifetime. I have known Latinos, who became "black," then "white," then "human beings," and finally "Latino"—all in a relatively short time. I have also known Latinos for whom the sequence was quite different and the time period longer. Some Latinos who altered their identities came to be viewed by others as legitimate members of their new identity group. I also saw the simultaneously tricultural, sometimes trilingual, abilities of many Latinos who manifested or projected a different self as they acclimated themselves to a Latino, African American, or White context (Rodríguez 1989:77).

I have come to understand that this shifting, context-dependent experience is at the core of many Latinos' life in the United States. Even in the nuclear family, parents, children, and siblings often have a wide range of physical types. For many Latinos race is primarily cultural; multiple identities are a normal state of affairs; and "racial mixture" is subject to many different, sometimes fluctuating, definitions.

Some regard *racial mixture* as an unfortunate or embarrassing term, but others consider the affirmation of mixture to be empowering. Lugones (1994) subscribes to this latter view and affirms "mixture," *mestizaje,* as a way of resisting a world in which purity and separation are emphasized, and one's identities are controlled: "Mestizaje defies control through simultaneously asserting the impure, curdled multiple state and rejecting fragmentation into pure parts . . . [T]he mestiza . . . . has no pure parts

to be 'had,' controlled." (p. 460) Also prevalent in the upper classes is the hegemonic view that rejects or denies "mixture" and claims a "pure" European ancestry. This view also is common among middle- and upper-class Latinos, regardless of their skin color or place of origin. In some areas, people rarely claim a European ancestry, such as in indigenous sectors of Latin America, in parts of Brazil and in some coastal areas in Colombia, Venezuela, Honduras, and Panama (see, e.g., Arocha 1998; De la Fuente 1998). Recently, some Latinos have encouraged another view in which those historical components that were previously denied and denigrated, such as indigenous and African ancestry, were privileged (see, e.g., Moro; *La Revista de Nuestra Vida* [Bogota, Colombia, September 1998]; *La Voz del Pueblo Taino* [The Voice of the Taino People], official newsletter of the United Confederation of Taino People, U.S. regional chapter, New York, January 1998).

Many people, however—mostly non-Latinos—are not acquainted with these basic elements of Latino life. They do not think much about them; and when they do, they tend to see race as a "given," an ascribed characteristic that does not change for anyone, at any time. One is either white or not white. They also believe that "race" is based on genetic inheritance, a perspective that is just another construct of race.

Whereas many Latinos regard their "race" as primarily cultural, others, when asked about their race, offer standard U.S. race terms, saying that they are White, Black, or Indian. Still others see themselves as Latinos, Hispanics, or members of a particular national-origin group *and* as belonging to a particular race group.[3] For example, they may identify themselves as Afro-Latinos or white Hispanics. In some cases, these identities vary according to context, but in others they do not.

I have therefore come to see that the concept of "race" can be constructed in several ways and that the Latino experience in the United States provides many illustrations of this. My personal experiences have suggested to me that for many Latinos, "racial" classification is immediate, provisional, contextually dependent, and sometimes contested. But because these experiences apply to many non-Latinos as well, it is evident to me that the Latino construction of race and the racial reading of Latinos are not isolated phenomena. Rather, the government's recent deliberations on racial and ethnic classification standards reflect the experiences and complexities of many groups and individuals who are similarly involved in issues pertaining to how they see themselves and one another (U.S. Dept. of Commerce 1995; U.S. Office of Management and Budget 1995, 1997a, 1997b, 1999).

Throughout my life, I have considered racism to be evil and I oppose it with every fiber of my being. I study race to understand its influence on the lives of individuals and nations because I hope that honest, open, and well-meaning discussions of race and ethnicity and their social dynamics can help us appreciate diversity and value all people, not for their appearance, but for their character.

It was because of my personal experiences that I first began to write in this area and that I was particularly sensitive to Latinos' responses to the census' question about race. The U.S. Census Bureau's official position has been that race and ethnicity are two separate concepts. Thus, in 1980 and in 1990, the U.S. census asked people to indicate their "race"—white, black, Asian or Pacific Islander, American Indian or "other race"—and also whether or not they were Hispanic. Latinos responded to the 1990 census' question about race quite differently than did non-Latinos. Whereas less than 1% of the non-Hispanic population reported they were "other race," more than 40% of Hispanics chose this category. Latinos responded similarly in the previous decennial census (Denton and Massey 1989; Martin, DeMaio, and Campanelli 1990; Rodríguez 1989, 1990, 1991; Tienda and Ortiz 1986). Although the percentages of different Hispanic groups choosing this category varied, all chose it more than did non-Hispanics.

In addition, the many Hispanics who chose this category wrote—in the box explicitly asking for race—the name of their "home" Latino country or group, to "explain" their race—or "otherness."[4]

The fact that these Latino referents were usually cultural or national-origin terms, such as Dominican, Honduran, or Boricua (i.e., Puerto Rican) underscores the fact that many Latinos viewed the question of race as a question of culture, national origin, and socialization rather than simply biological or genetic ancestry or color. Indeed, recent studies have found that many Latinos understand "race" to mean national origin, nationality, ethnicity, culture (Kissam, Herrera, and Nakamoto 1993), or a combination of these and skin color (Bates et al. 1994:109; Rodríguez 1991, 1992, 1994; Rodríguez and Cordero-Guzmán 1992). For many Latinos, the term *race* or *raza* is a reflection of these understandings and not of those often associated with "race" in the United States, e.g., defined by hypodescent.[5] Studies have found that Latinos also tend to see race along a continuum and not as a dichotomous variable in which individuals are either white or black (Bracken and de Bango 1992; Rodríguez and Hagan 1991; Romero 1992).

This does not mean that there is one Latino view of race. Rather, there are different views of race within different countries, classes, and even families. Latinos' views of race are dependent on a complex array of factors, one of which is the racial formation process in their country of origin. Other variables also influence their views of race, for example, generational differences, phenotype, class, age, and education. But even though there is not just one paradigm of Latin American race, there are some basic differences between the way that Latinos view race and the way that race is viewed overall in the United States.

In the United States, rules of hypodescent and categories based on presumed genealogical-biological criteria have generally dominated thinking about race. Racial categories have been few, discrete, and mutually exclusive, with skin color a prominent element. Categories for mixtures—for example, mulatto—have been transitory. In contrast, in Latin America, racial constructions have tended to be more fluid and based on many variables, like social class and phenotype. There also have been many, often overlapping, categories, and mixtures have been consistently acknowledged and have had their own terminology. These general differences are what Latinos bring with them to the United States, and they influence how they view their own and others' "identity."

Although Latinos may use or approach "race" differently, this does not mean that "race" as understood by Latinos does not have overtones of racism or implications of power and privilege—in either Latin America or the United States. The depreciation and denial of African and Amerindian characteristics are widespread.[6] Everywhere in Latin America can be found ". . . a pyramidal class structure, cut variously by ethnic lines, but with a local, regional and nation-state elite characterized as 'white.' And white rules over color within the same class; those who are lighter have differential access to some dimensions of the market" (Torres and Whitten 1998:23).

Suffice it to say at this point that in my many years of research in this area, I have noticed in my and others' work that "race" is a recurring, sometimes amusing and benign, and sometimes conflictual issue.[7] For Latinos' responses to questions of race are seldom as simple and straightforward as they tend to be for most non-Hispanic Whites (Rodríguez et al. 1991).

In the past, new immigrants immediately underwent a racialization process, which conveyed an implicit hierarchy of color and power. The two elements of this racialization process were (1) the acceptance of and participation in discrimination against people of color (Bell 1992; Du Bois 1962:700 ff; Morrison 1993) and (2) negotiations regarding the group's placement in the U.S. racial-ethnic queue (Jacobson 1998; Rodríguez 1974; Smith 1997; Takaki 1994). Immigrants undergoing this racialization process discriminated implicitly or explicitly against others because of their color and status. Indeed, some immigrants realized that one way to become "White," or more acceptable to Whites, was to discriminate against others seen as "nonwhite" (Ignatiev 1995; Kim 1999; Loewen 1971). Kim (1999) reviewed the historical experience of Asian Americans being triangulated

with Blacks and Whites through a simultaneous process of valorization and ostracism. This racial triangulation continued to reinforce White racial power and insulate it from minority encroachment or challenge.

Some immigrants discriminated against Blacks and/or other depreciated minorities, by not living with "them," not hiring "them" in enclave economies, or articulating prejudices against "them." Institutionalized discrimination and normative behavior aided racialization so that, for example, it became difficult to rent or sell to members of certain groups because of exclusionary practices. Nearly all immigrant groups experienced this seldom-mentioned, but indisputable dimension of the Americanization process. Critical to the racialization process was the belief that there is always some "other" group to which one is superior. Indeed, this process has been an effective means of protecting the status quo because it made it difficult to understand and pursue areas of common interest and resulted in divide-and-conquer outcomes.

Latinos—and many other groups—come to the United States with different views on race and with their own racial hierarchies. The relation of these people's racialization to their hierarchies in the United States has not been widely studied. But it is clear that when they arrive, they too become part of a racialization process in which they are differentiated according to the official perception of their race, which may or may not be the same as their own perception. This racial reclassification immerses immigrants in a social education process in which they first learn—and then may ignore, resist, or accept—the state-defined categories and the popular conventions about race (particularly one's own) (Rodríguez 1994).

The racialization process also includes contradictory views of the way that Hispanics are generally regarded. At one extreme, Hispanics are a Spanish-speaking white ethnic group, who are simply the most recent in the continuum of immigrant groups and are expected to follow the traditional path of assimilation. Another view holds that the term *Hispanic*—which has generally not been unknown to new immigrants from Latin America—is subtly "colored" by negative and racial associations. For example, the stereotyped image (for both Hispanics and non-Hispanics) of a Hispanic is "tan." Within this perspective, Hispanics are often referred to as "light skinned," not as white. Yet, many Hispanics would be seen as White, Black, or Asian if it were not known that they were Hispanic. But seeing Hispanics/Latinos as "light" clearly restricts their "Whiteness" and thus makes them nonwhite by default, but not a member of other race groups. Thus, many Hispanics entering this country become generically "nonwhite" to themselves, or to others, regardless of their actual phenotype or ancestry.

The United States' racialization process affects all groups' sense of who they are, and how they are seen, in regard to color and race. There are few studies of this concerning Latinos, but some autobiographies suggest that the racialization process has had a significant impact (see, e.g., Rivera 1983; Rodríguez 1992; Santiago 1995; Thomas 1967). Whether this has been a dissonant impact and has affected Latinos' mobility and the quality of life has not yet been determined.

Some Latinos, influenced by movements such as the Black Power movement, Afrocentrism, pan-Africanism and African diaspora philosophies, and the celebration of negritude, have come to see themselves, and sometimes their group, as Black. Terms like *Afro-Latino, black Cuban,* and *black Panamanian* are now common, and some Latinos celebrate their African roots. Others focus on their Amerindian or indigenous component, while still others see themselves only as white or mixed or identify themselves only ethnically.

A Dominican student of mine told me that each of her and her husband's children claimed a different identity. So they had one Black child, one White child, and one Dominican child. Each of the children had different friends and tastes. Many variables contribute to and interact with the racialization process to determine how individuals decide on their group affiliation. Generation, phenotype, previous and current class position, and the size and accessibility of one's cultural or national-origin group, as well as the relative size of other groups, all affect how individual Latinos identify themselves.

My own life experiences have demonstrated the social constructedness of race, and subsequent research has shown that "race" is not fixed, is imperfectly measured, is at variance with scientific principles, is often conflated with the concept of "ethnicity," and is under increasing scientific criticism and popular interrogation. Nonetheless, race is still real; it still exists.[8] We may question its necessity, the right of anyone to establish such markers, and its validity as a scientific concept. We may see it as unjust and want to change it. But we must acknowledge its significance in our lives. It can be deconstructed, but it cannot be dismissed.

DISCUSSION QUESTIONS

1. What do you think Rodríguez means when she says that for Latinos, race is "cultural"?
2. What do you think is the impact of American racial constructions on immigrant Latino Americans?

NOTES

1. In her study of Spanish speaking Caribbeans, Dominguez states that "An individual may be identified as *indio, trigueno, blanco, prieto,* or whatever in different contexts by different people or even by the same person" (1986:275).
2. Except when specifically referring to women, I use the word *Latino* to refer to both women and men. At the descriptive level, my analyses of how Latinas and Latinos classify themselves racially have not revealed significant differences. But under more controlled conditions, some labor market differences by race and gender have been noted (Gómez n.d.; Rodríguez 1991).
3. I use both *Hispanic* and *Latino,* in part because both terms are used in the literature and I've tried to use those of the authors I cite when discussing their work. Works based on census material, for example, tend to use the term *Hispanic,* mainly because this is the category under which the data were collected. Other works refer to surveys employing the term *Latino.* See the following for different arguments concerning the preferred term: Gimenez 1989; Hayes-Bautista and Chapa 1987; Oboler 1995; Treviño 1987.

4. According to Jorge del Pinal, 42.7% of the Hispanics who chose the "other race" category in the 1990 census gave a Latino referent. However, 94.3% of "other race" persons who provided a write-in gave a Latino referent. (Personal communication, July 30, 1999.) In addition, two-thirds of all those who did not specify their race wrote in their Hispanic ethnicity (U.S. Office of Management and Budget 1995:44689).

5. *Hypodescent* is also referred to as the "one-drop rule," in which "one drop" of "nonwhite or Black blood" determines a person's "race."

6. The degree to which racism is perceived and experienced within the Latino framework may be related to phenotype. Consequently, those farthest from either the local mean or the ideal European model may be those most subject to, and therefore most aware of, racism and discrimination. In the dominant United States framework, those farthest from the stereotype "Latin look" may be those who are most acutely aware of, or in the best position to observe, discrimination.

7. See Davis et al. (1998a:III-22-23) for light and humorous discussions of skin color in cognitive interviews.

8. Marks (1994) maintains that folk concepts of race—flawed and scientifically deficient as they may be—are passed down from generation to generation, just as genetic material is inherited. This is part of what keeps the concept of "race" real.

REFERENCES

Arocha, Jaime. 1998. "Inclusion of Afro-Colombians: Unreachable National Goal?" *Latin American Perspectives* 25 (3) (May):70–89.

Bates, Nancy A., Manuel de la Puente, Theresa J. DeMaio, and Elizabeth A. Martin. 1994. "Research on Race and Ethnicity: Results from Questionnaire Design Tests." Paper presented at the U.S. Census Bureau's annual research conference, March 20–23, Rosslyn, VA.

Bell, Derrick. 1992. *Faces at the Bottom of the Well: The Permanence of Racism.* New York: Basic Books.

Bracken, Karen, and Guillermo de Bango. 1992. "Hispanics in a Racially and Ethnically Mixed Neighborhood in the Greater Metropolitan New Orleans Area." *Ethnographic Evaluation of the 1990 Decennial Census Report* 16. Prepared under Joint Statistical Agreement 89–45 with Hispanidad '87, Inc. Washington, DC: U.S. Bureau of the Census.

Davis, Diana K., Johnny Blair, Howard Fleischman, and Margaret S. Boone. 1998a. *Cognitive Interviews on the Race and Hispanic Origin Questions on the Census 2000 Dress Rehearsal Form.* Report prepared by Development Associates, Inc., Arlington, VA, under contract from the U.S. Census Bureau, Population Division, May 29.

De La Fuente, Alejandro. 1998. "Race, National Discourse, and Politics in Cuba: An Overview." *Latin American Perspectives* 25 (3) (May): 43–69. Issue 100 entitled "Race and National Identity in the Americas" and edited by Helen Safa.

Denton, N. A., and D. S. Massey. 1989. "Racial Identity among Caribbean Hispanics: The Effect of Double Minority Status on Residential Segregation." *American Sociological Review* 54:790–808.

Domínguez, Virginia R. 1986. *White by Definition: Social Classification in Creole Louisiana.* New Brunswick, NJ: Rutgers University Press.

Du Bois, W. E. B. 1962. *Black Reconstruction in America, 1860–1880.* Cleveland: World Publishing.

Gimenez, Martha. 1989. "Latino/'Hispanic'—Who Needs a Name? The Case against a Standardized Terminology." *International Journal of Health Services* 19 (3): 557–571.

Gómez, Christina. n.d. "The Continual Significance of Skin Color: An Exploratory Study of Latinos in the Northeast." *Hispanic Journal of Behavioral Sciences,* currently under review.

Hayes-Bautista, D. E., and J. Chapa. 1987. "Latino Terminology: Conceptual Basis for Standardized Terminology." *American Journal of Public Health* 77: 61–68.

Ignatiev, Noel. 1995. *How the Irish Became White.* New York: Routledge & Kegan Paul.

Jacobson, Mathew. 1998. *Becoming Caucasian: Whiteness and the Alchemy of the American Melting Pot.* Cambridge, MA: Harvard University Press.

Kim, Claire Jean. 1999. "The Racial Triangulation of Asian Americans." *Politics and Society* 27(1)(March): 105–138.

Kissam, Edward, Enrique Herrera, and Jorge M. Nakamoto. 1993. "Hispanic Response to Census Enumeration Forms and Procedures." Task order no. 46-YABC-2-0001, contract no. 50-YABC-2-66027, submitted by Aguirre International, 411 Borel Ave., Suite 402, San Mateo, CA 94402, to U.S. Bureau of the Census, Center for Survey Methods Research, March.

Lugones, María. 1994. "Purity, Impurity, and Separation." *Signs* 19 (2) (Winter): 459–479.

Marks, Jonathan. 1994. "Black, White, Other: Racial Categories Are Cultural Constructs Masquerading as Biology." *Natural History,* December, pp. 32–35.

Martin, E., T. J. DeMaio, and P. C. Campanelli. 1990. "Context Effects for Census Measures of Race and Hispanic Origin." *Public Opinion Quarterly* 54 (4): 551–566.

Morrison, Toni. 1993. "On the Backs of Blacks." *Time,* special issue (Fall), p. 57.

Oboler, Suzanne. 1995. *Ethnic Labels/Latino Lives: Identity and the Politics of (Re) Presentation in the United States.* Minneapolis: University of Minnesota Press.

Rivera, Edward. 1983. *Family Installments: Memories of Growing up Hispanic.* New York: Penguin Books.

Rodríguez, Clara. 1974. "Puerto Ricans: Between Black and White." *Journal of New York Affairs* 1 (4): 92–101.

———. 1989. *Puerto Ricans: Born in the USA.* Boston: Unwin Hyman.

———. 1990. "Racial Identification among Puerto Ricans in New York." *Hispanic Journal of Behavioral Sciences* 12 (4) (November): 366–79.

———. 1991. "The Effect of Race on Puerto Rican Wages." In *Hispanics in the Labor Force: Issues and Policies,* ed. Edwin Melíndez, Clara Rodríguez, and Janice Barry Figueroa. New York: Plenum Press.

———. 1992. "Race, Culture and Latino 'Otherness' in the 1980 Census." *Social Science Quarterly* 73 (4) (December): 930–937.

———. 1994. "Challenging Racial Hegemony. Puerto Ricans in the United States." In *Race,* ed. R. Sanjek and S. Gregory. New Brunswick, NJ: Rutgers University Press.

Rodríguez, Clara, Aida Castro, Oscar García, and Analisa Torres. 1991. "Latino Racial Identity: In the Eye of the Beholder?" *Latino Studies Journal* 2 (3) (December): 33–48.

Rodríguez, Clara, and Hector Cordero-Guzmán. 1992. "Placing Race in Context." *Ethnic and Racial Studies* 15 (4): 523–542.

Rodríguez, Nestor, and Jacqueline Hagan. 1991. *Investigating Census Coverage and Content among the Undocumented: An Ethnographic Study of Latino Immigrant Tenants in Houston. Ethnographic Evaluation of the 1990 Decennial Census Report* 3. Prepared under Joint Statistical Agreement 89-34 with the University of Houston, U.S. Bureau of the Census, Washington, DC.

Romero, Mary. 1992. *Ethnographic Evaluation of Behavioral Causes of Census Undercount of Undocumented Immigrants and Salvadorans in the Mission District of San Francisco, California. Ethnographic Evaluation of the 1990 Decennial Census Report* 18. Prepared under Joint Statistical Agreement 89-41 with the San Francisco State University Foundation, U.S. Bureau of the Census, Washington, DC.

Santiago, Roberto. 1995. "Black and Latino." In *Boricuas: Influential Puerto Rican Writings, an Anthology,* ed. Roberto Santiago. New York: Ballantine Books.

Shohat, Ella, and Robert Stam. 1994. *Unthinking Eurocentrism: Multiculturalism and the Media.* New York: Routledge & Kegan Paul.

Smith, Rogers M. 1997. *Civic Ideals: Conflicting Visions in U.S. History.* New Haven, CT: Yale University Press.

Takaki, Ronald. 1994. *From Different Shores: Perspectives on Race and Ethnicity in America.* 2d ed. New York: Oxford University Press.

Thomas, Piri. 1967. *Down These Mean Streets.* New York: Knopf.

Tienda, M., and V. Ortiz. 1986. "'Hispanicity' and the 1980 Census." *Social Science Quarterly* 67 (March): 3–20.

Torres, Arlene, and Norman E. Whitten Jr., eds. 1998. *Blackness in Latin America and the Caribbean.* Vol. 2. Bloomington: Indiana University Press.

Treviño, F. M. 1987. "Standardized Terminology for Standardized Populations." *American Journal of Public Health* 77: 69–72.

U.S. Department of Commerce. 1995. "1996 Race and Ethnic Targeted Test; Notice." *Federal Register,* 60:231: 62010-62014. December 1. Washington, DC: U.S. Government Printing Office.

U.S. Office of Management and Budget (OMB). 1995. "Standards for the Classification of Federal Data on Race and Ethnicity; Notice." *Federal Register,* part 6, vol. 60, no. 166, pp. 44674–44693, August 28.

———. 1997a. "Recommendations from the Interagency Committee for the Review of the Racial and Ethnic Standards to the Office of Management and Budget Concerning Changes to the Standards for the Classification of Federal Data on Race and Ethnicity; Notice." *Federal Register,* 62:131:36874–36946, July 9.

———. 1997b. "Revisions to the Standards for the Classification of Federal Data on Race and Ethnicity; Notices." *Federal Register,* 62:210:58782-58790, October 30.

———. 1999. "Provisional Guidance on the Implementation of the 1997 Standards for the Collection of Federal Data on Race and Ethnicity." Prepared by Tabulation Working Group, Interagency Committee for the Review of Standards for Data on Race and Ethnicity, Washington, DC, February 17.

READING 23

Everybody's Ethnic Enigma

Jelita McLeod

The forty-something black man I was sharing an elevator with looked at me for a while before he asked the question I had been expecting. He wanted to know my ethnicity.

"I'm mixed," I told him. "Half-Caucasian, half-Asian."

"Oh," he said, disappointed. "I thought you were one of us."

I knew what the question would be because people have been asking me the same thing as long

---

Jelita McLeod is an award-winning writer who works in education and public relations.

PERSONAL ACCOUNT

My Strategies

I speak differently around different people. When I am with white people I use my vocabulary, sharp wit, and smooth, concise statements. I try to keep my grammar in line and use acceptable slang and swearing. When I am in a formal setting, court, school, work, etc., I do the above, but I also change my inflection. I also use no slang or swearing. My white voice has gotten me loans, jobs, and makes my life easier. On the flip side when I am around black people, my speech is totally different. Black people, mostly, talk in a manner that is all inclusive. They don't want to talk down to anyone, or over anyone's head. Using a large vocabulary for no reason is considered rude and frowned upon. You are considered a snob. Black people worry about everyone understanding, seeing if you are on the level, and creating a relaxed environment. We are probably tired of talking in a fake manner all day, so the manner we choose has to be more relaxed.

White people size you up by the way you talk plus other things. If I were to use slang or talk in the manner I do around black people, I would be considered stupid and faking it. Yet when I talk with a high vocabulary and diction that is taken as the way I talk and assumed to be natural. Since it is the most comfortable for whites, and matches their own manner of speaking, they don't contest its authenticity. So when speaking I have to remember who I am talking to; context is, again, everything. I slip around my close friends often though, and they stare at me. "What it do Liz?" This will get no response beyond, ". . . what?" This isn't to say anything about all white people; these are general statements from my life. I know plenty of white people who have learned or always knew how to talk in the manner that black people do, but they are the exceptions. The same goes for black people. It stands to reason that if we can talk in a different manner, that white people can also learn.

There are other things I have to remember when moving between groups. Eye contact is a big one, because most black people don't like it, yet white people think you are distracted if you don't use it. I also don't like eye contact, but have learned to use it as needed. Handshakes are another issue, which factors in age, sex, race, etc. I won't go into the differences because it would be another paper. Needless to say, a lot of effort goes in to small tasks. I have to keep my ghetto pass and still not be thought silly and stupid.

Usually when someone figures out I am biracial, I'll have to pass some stupid test. It is usually a series of questions displaying their limited understanding. Here is a transcript:

Person A: I don't mean to be racist, but . . . (This means that they are going to say something very racist, always.)

Eric: Sigh, I am biracial. (To try and stop them before they offend me.)

Person A: No, you're not, really?

Eric: Father is a large black man.

Person A: NO WAY, laughter. You look so white.

Eric: Yep.

Person A: Is he like all the way black, or like really light?

Eric: Nope, *as black as you think black is.*

Person A: (Now apologizes for their racist comment that started this.) Yeah, but aren't you like still white, you look white? Do you have siblings? Which parent did you live with?

Eric: Happy to meet such a race expert. Yes, my older brother, Gene, and I have the same parents and he looks black. I lived with my mother, but saw my father whenever I wished.

Person A: But you look white, phhhh, look at you, you're white.

Eric: Thank you. I needed someone to tell me my race, thus saving all that time I would have spent already knowing.

Person A: Don't get mad or anything. I'm just saying, you look white, you act white.

Eric: *How is it that black people act?*

This could continue, but by now I usually end it by going to do something, or they start to get uncomfortable and change the subject. Things in italics are usually omitted if I have to work with the person at a job or in a class. No reason to be hostile if I am going to see them often. When I was very young I had to get used to people openly laughing at me. I still don't know why they laugh, but they always do. As if I said my father was a polar bear, thus making me half polar bear. That example is the only way I can try to make sense of it. I am so used to the tests that I can usually answer their questions before they ask.

Often the test is to prove you are black. My name is easy because Eric Michael Jackson is easy to pass as a black name. Most people will buy this right away. Then everything they knew about me gets converted to stigma mode, unless they are black, then it gets un-stigmatized. I also have to use stereotypes to prove who I am at times. I feel this is wrong, but it is better than punching someone in the face. Thus, all my actions for a limited time become black. I like chicken. This wasn't an issue when I was white, now it is. I can't say I know anyone, other than people who don't eat meat, who don't love chicken.

I enjoy seeing the looping and re-reading upon my newly discovered blackness. Before when I had an opinion on matters regarding race I was thought a tad extreme, but they could see my point. Now they either don't want to talk about it because any discussion of race outside one's own group is no longer "pc", or because they feel I'll get all black on them. As if I'll stand up and shout, "Free Mumia and H. Rap Brown!" then curse them for years of oppression. In reality they just disregard what I say because I am "biased." They are not biased because being white apparently gives you this supreme understanding of how things work. I remind them I am also white, something they like to remind me of as well, and then I get a "not really." So I am only white when it suits them, and then I am black the rest of the time. Where I am from, I was white enough to go in your home, but I won't be dating your daughter. I have often had people boast I was the first black man in their home. This usually makes me want to leave right away. Looking back on it, my entire life has been a sociological study and I just never knew it. I knew what ethnocentrism was when I was ten.

P. S. teachers hate it when you call them that, like twenty times a day.

Eric Jackson

as I can remember. I've found that curiosity easily overrides courtesy. I am asked in stores, on the bus, on the street, in line at McDonald's, even in public bathrooms. Almost always the inquirers are total strangers, as if not knowing me allows them to abandon social graces they might otherwise feel the need to display. Sometimes they will ask me straight out, but very often they use coded language, as in "What's your background?" Then there's "Where are you from?" which is really a two-part question, to be followed by "Where are you *really* from?"

Why is it that people feel they can approach me for this personal information? Would they ask total strangers their age or marital status? What do they need the information for? Are they census takers? Once, in a truly surreal episode, a casino dealer stopped in the middle of a hand of poker to ask me, as if he couldn't stand to wait a second longer. After I offered my usual answer, he shook his finger in my face and said he wasn't convinced, that I didn't look white enough. He was Asian.

I wonder why, after having been subjected to this treatment for years, I still respond. I can't remember a time when doing so has resulted in a pleasant encounter or a meaningful conversation. Yet I've never quite found the strength to meet such inquiries with "It's none of your business" or, better yet, silence. What's quite strange is that people often feel the need to comment, as if what I've told them is an opinion they can't quite agree with. Comedian Margaret Cho tells a story about a TV producer who asked her to act "a little more Chinese," to which she replied, "But I'm Korean." "Whatever," the producer said. I had a similar experience with a man in a bookstore, who crept out from behind a shelf of cookbooks to ask me where I was from. Before I had a chance to say anything, he guessed: "Japan?" I could have said Oregon, where my father is from, but I knew he wouldn't go for that, so I said, "Indonesia." "Ah," he said. "Close." It's not close. Not really. Not unless you consider London close to Djibouti. The distances are similar.

In the game of "Name that Ethnicity," I am the trick question. I have been mistaken for almost every Asian nationality, but also as Hispanic, Native American, Arab and, of course, African American. There's something in being a chameleon. It's human nature to look for unifying bonds. When people think that they have something in common with you, particularly something so personal as identity, they feel they know you and they imagine that you have an innate understanding of them, too. They will speak to you in a certain unguarded way. The idea that any person can be truly "colorblind" is a fallacy. As long as the human eye can detect differences in skin tone, eye shape, hair texture, these differences will play a role in how we interact with one another. Because of my ambiguous appearance, I have experienced from people the kind of familiarity they would normally reserve for one of their "own."

The unfortunate consequence of this ambiguity is the misunderstanding I frequently encounter from those who haven't gotten the full story. The Mexican immigration official who looks disgusted when I can't understand Spanish, as I surely should. The kindly Vietnamese waiter who helps me "remember" how to pronounce the names of dishes. This puts me in the slightly ridiculous position of being apologetic for not being what people expect me to be, however unreasonable.

When I think back to the man in the elevator, I feel disappointed, too. The way he said "I thought you were one of us" made me feel as if we might have bonded but now couldn't, as if I'd been refused entry into a club because I didn't have the right password. My immediate reaction was that I was missing out on something. But I see the artificiality of this classification mentality. If the opportunity for bonding existed before he knew my ethnic makeup, wasn't it still there after he found out? After all, I was still the same person.

When my parents were married, my grandfather was against the union. His objection was that the children of mixed marriages had no foothold in any one community but instead were doomed to a lifetime of identity crises and disorientation.

If my grandfather were still alive, I'd tell him that the crisis comes not from within, but from without.

I know who I am. It's everyone else that's having trouble.

DISCUSSION QUESTIONS

1. Does an ambiguous appearance lead to stereotypic assumptions?
2. If you don't identify with the questioner, what are the likely consequences?

READING 24

From Friendly Foreigner to Enemy Race

John Tehranian

The term *Middle East* likely emerged in the 1850s from Britain's India Office.[1] It did not enjoy widespread usage in policy circles, however, until the early twentieth century, when it was used in the work of famed American naval strategist Admiral Alfred Thayer Mahan. In an article first published in September 1902, Mahan used the term *Middle East* to refer to a region of growing strategic importance in the emerging conflict pitting Britain and the United States against Germany and Russia.[2] Mahan appeared to define that region as ranging, on a north-south axis, from Turkey to the Arabian Peninsula and, on an east-west axis, from Iran to Egypt. Thus, the designation was borne of geopolitical considerations and its construction wrought with semiotic meaning. . . .

The term *Middle East* therefore appears to eschew the typical hallmarks of regional definitions, which are often based on continental, linguistic, or perceived ethnic boundaries. Observes Sedat Laciner,

> This so-called region neighbors two oceans (Indian and Atlantic) and six seas (Mediterranean, Red Sea, Persian Gulf, Black Sea, Aegean Sea and the Caspian Sea). It extends to three continents (Africa, Asia and Europe). It consists of ten sub-regions (Southern and

John Tehranian is a professor of law at Chapman University School of Law.

Northern Caucasus, Northern Africa, Arabia, Greater Palestine and Syria, Mesopotamia, the Caspian Basin, Central Asia (Turkistan), and the Indian Peninsula). Three monotheistic religions (Islam, Christianity and Judaism), with their numerous sects and schools of thought, exist in this region. Thousands of religious and moral faiths, including atheism and paganism, are practiced in this wide geography and thus, it is one of the largest laboratories of the world. Although viewed by the West as all-Arab, the region consists of tens of different ethnic-linguistic communities, with Turks, Arabs and Persians as the main ones.[3]

At the same time, the term is riddled in ambiguity, sometimes encompassing the entire North African coast, from Morocco to Egypt, and other parts of Africa, including the Sudan and Somalia, the former Soviet, Caucasus Republics of Georgia, Azerbaijan, and Armenia, and occasionally Afghanistan, Pakistan, and Turkistan. The Middle East is therefore a malleable geopolitical construct of relatively recent vintage. . . .

A search of all reported federal and state court opinions reveals that there was not a single reference to the terms *Middle East* or *Middle Eastern* until 1946, when a New York court referred to a "European Middle Eastern Service Medal and Victory Medal" given to veterans.[4] Other than scattered references to similar medals, the next mention of the *Middle East* or *Middle Eastern* came in a 1955 IRS dispute involving the taxation of an oil worker who had taken employment in numerous countries, including Saudi Arabia, Lebanon, Syria, and Iraq. The court synoptically referred to the work as having resided in "Near or Middle Eastern countries."[5] The term was also used in a 1956 breach-of-contract suit in which the U.S. government failed to deliver certain airplane technology to "the Middle East" lest it be used in regional conflicts contrary to American foreign-policy interests.[6] Finally, several federal suits in 1957 linked the term to its most precious commodity, referring on numerous occasions to "Middle Eastern oil."[7] As these cases make clear, in the beginning, the Middle Eastern designation arose in a geopolitical and oil-related context.

In a time-honored process, the racialization of individuals from Turkey, Iran, and the Arab states as "Middle Eastern" came to serve broader economic and political needs. In their influential work on the formation of race, Michael Omi and Howard Winant highlight the "sociohistorical process by which racial categories are created, inhabited, transformed, and destroyed."[8] In prior eras, the racialization and stereotyping of various groups has taken on a distinctly utilitarian flavor.

Take the typecasting of African Americans through the course of history. . . . The demands of the plantation economy helped give rise to the Southern hierarchy and its black-white divide based on skin color (which supplanted the earlier hierarchy based on religious affiliation). As Richard Delgado reminds us, antiblack "prejudice sprang up with slavery. Previously, educated Europeans held generally positive attitudes toward Africans, recognizing the African civilization was highly advanced."[9] As slavery emerged, infantilization became commonplace in media portrayals, as blacks were stereotyped as buffoons unable to survive without the guidance of their masters. Blackface minstrelsy rose to popularity, in the guise of Sambo and other characters, conveying images of blacks as either "inept urban dandies or happy childlike slaves."[10] Following emancipation and the end of the Civil War, however, images became more ominous, with black men portrayed as rapists preying on white women and black women reduced to pliable domestic servants.[11] Stereotypes followed function, first legitimating slavery and later rationalizing lynching, segregation, imperialism, and Jim Crow.

Since "conquering nations generally demonize their subjects in order to rationalize exploiting them,"[12] Latino and Asian stereotypes have undergone a similar trajectory. As Delgado notes, "Anglo settlers in California and the Southwest began to circulate notions of Mexican inferiority only when the settlers came to covet Mexican lands and mining claims."[13] Similarly, early portraits of the Chinese and Japanese cast them as comical and hapless, though they were happily tolerated for their contribution to the American workforce. As economic and assimilatory fears related to these groups heightened, however, Charlie Chan–like stereotypes transformed and gave rise to the clichéd image of the wily, scheming, and menacing "Oriental" criminal mastermind.[14]

Quite simply, concludes Delgado, "Depictions vary depending on society's needs."[15] What then are we to make of the dramatic change in the status of Middle Easterners? It is hardly coincidence that it has occurred over the past generation—a time that has seen the Middle East rise to the forefront of global politics and economic importance due to its ample reserves of the great engine of industrialization: oil.

THE MIDDLE EASTERNER AS THE OTHER: THE SLIPPERY SLOPE FROM FRIENDLY FOREIGNER TO ENEMY ALIEN, ENEMY ALIEN TO ENEMY RACE

Inextricably intertwined with the rising tide of discrimination facing persons of Middle Eastern descent is the mythology surrounding racial construction and related religious and sociocultural perceptions. For prior generations, Middle Eastern Americans came closer to matching our constructed notions of whiteness. They were largely Christian; they came from an exotic but friendly, romantic, and halcyon foreign land imagined to contain magic lanterns, genies, flying carpets, and belly dancers; and they served as a chief vessel of the philosophical and cultural heritage of the West.[16] Thus, in previous generations, people of (what we now call) Middle Eastern descent were, more often than not, blended into the white category. . . .

[Now] in an era when we view the most immediate threat to our national security as emanating from the Middle East, it is not surprising that monolithic images of the Middle East and the Middle Easterner have leaped into existence. Middle Easterners have been irretrievably associated with Islam; they appear to hail from a decidedly

unfriendly foreign land imagined to contain nothing but terrorists, obstreperous mobs chanting "Death to America," unabashed misogynistic polygamists, and religious fundamentalists; and they seem to represent a wholly different civilization from our own—one with which the inevitable and apocalyptic clash of civilizations is unfolding.[17] Thus, they are the quintessential Other, and the Middle Easterner category, imposed on them by society at large, has become their appellation.

In popular perception, in which the notion of assimilability constitutes the sine qua non of the majority's acceptance of an immigrant group, it is not surprising that Middle Easterners have fared poorly. As Karen Engle has noted, the past century has witnessed a radical transformation in majority perceptions of Middle Eastern individuals: they are, in short, no longer thought capable of assimilation.[18] The changing religious composition of Middle Eastern immigrants to the United States has played a key role in this transformation. As the naturalization cases make clear, perceptions of race are frequently conflated with perceptions of religion. In 1924, about two hundred thousand Arabs resided in the United States. Of these, 80 percent were from Syria and Lebanon, of which group a startling 90 percent were Christian.[19] Many of these immigrants had fled oppression and persecution under the Ottoman Empire.[20] Indeed, an early study of the emerging Syrian and Lebanese community at the turn of the century in New York City found that only 2 of 2,482 residents were Muslim.[21] As the author of the study noted, "The Moslems, Druses and Metâwely are not found in sufficient numbers to warrant more than passing mention."[22]

Given the tendency to conflate race with religious affiliation, and Christianity with assimilability, it is not surprising that, at the beginning of the twentieth century, courts declared Armenians and even some Arabs white by law, thereby entitling them to the privileges of whiteness, including naturalization. However, the composition of the Middle Eastern American population has undergone a dramatic change in recent years, especially in the public imagination. Contrary to popular perceptions, only 23 percent of present-day Arab Americans are Muslim.[23] However, about 60 percent of Arab immigrants arriving in the United States since 1965 identify themselves as Muslim.[24] As it has grown less Christian, the Middle Eastern population in the United States is thought of as less assimilable and, consequently, less white.

As faith in their assimilatory capacity has diminished, Middle Easterners have come to represent enemy aliens, and even an enemy race, in the popular imagination. In the past, the paradigmatic noncitizen was the "Mexican illegal alien, or the inscrutable, clannish Asian."[25] Today, it is the Arab terrorist, and this vision has firmly taken hold of our immigration policies. As Victor Romero argues, "post-9/11, the age-old stereotype of the foreign, Arab terrorist has been rekindled, and placing our immigration functions under the auspices of an executive department charged with 'homeland security' reinforces the idea that immigrants are terrorists."[26] The recent wave of registration and deportation policies aimed at individuals of Middle Eastern descent also highlights this trend. Take, for example, the National Security Entry-Exit Registration System (NSEERS), which was formally announced by the attorney general on June 6, 2002, and then supplemented with a special "call-in" registration in November 2002. The NSEERS singles out a limited class of noncitizens—male, nonimmigrant visa holders over the age of sixteen who are from one of twenty-five Muslim and Middle Eastern countries—for special registration requirements.[27] . . .

THE NEGOTIATION OF MIDDLE EASTERN IDENTITY: SELECTIVE RACIALIZATION AND COVERING

The negotiation of the Middle Eastern identity is mediated by a two-fold process that moves both from the top down and from the bottom up. From the top down, society at large engages in a practice that can best be described as *selective racialization*. From the bottom up, Middle Easterners, both privileged and damned by their proximity to the white dividing line, engage in persistent (and frequently effective) covering of their ethnic background. These two social forces combine to create a pernicious stereotyping feedback loop that enervates the political strength of the Middle Eastern community, heightens its invisibility, and leaves little effective resistance to the growing assaults against its civil rights.

A Theory of Selective Racialization

. . . Specifically, in society at large, Middle Easterners are consistently subjected to a process of *selective racialization*. This largely undocumented and predominantly subconscious mechanism has profound ramifications. Systematically, famous individuals of Middle Eastern descent are usually perceived as white. Meanwhile, *infamous* individuals of Middle Eastern descent are usually categorized as Middle Eastern. When Middle Eastern actors conform to social norms and advance positive values and conduct, their racial identity as the Other recedes to the background as they merge into the great white abyss. By contrast, when Middle Eastern actors engage in transgressive behavior, their racial identity as the Other immediately becomes a central, defining characteristic of who they are. The result is an endless feedback loop that calcifies popular prejudices. Wholesome and socially redeeming activities, which might otherwise subvert public misperceptions of the community, do not get associated with Middle Eastern identity. By contrast, the image of transgression is continually correlated with the Middle Eastern racial category, serving only to reinforce negative connotations with the community.

Our country is filled with individuals of Middle Eastern descent who have contributed constructively to American society. Yet surprisingly few of these Americans are actually perceived as Middle Easterners. Instead, their ethnicity is frequently whitewashed.[28] On one hand, this fact highlights the assimilability of Middle Eastern immigrants in the United States. On the other hand, it creates a problematic signposting of Middle Eastern identity when it becomes associated with transgressive activities.

The long list of Middle Eastern Americans includes individuals from virtually every aspect of American life, including athletes such as tennis player Andre Agassi (Persian/Armenian), Indy 500 champion Bobby Rahal (Lebanese), and NFL quarterbacks Doug Flutie and Jeff George (both Lebanese); entertainers such as actresses Cher (Armenian), Kathy Najimi (Lebanese), Catherine Bell (half Persian), and Gabrielle Anwar (half Persian), actors Danny Thomas (Lebanese) and Tony Shalhoub (Lebanese), radio deejay Casy Kasem (Palestinian/Lebanese), and singer Paul Anka (Lebanese); prominent entrepreneurs such as hoteliers the Maloof family (Lebanese) and Apple CEO Steve Jobs (half Syrian); and politicians and activists such as former New Hampshire governor and White House chief of staff John Sununu (Lebanese), former senator George Mitchell (half Lebanese), and prominent consumer advocate and presidential candidate Ralph Nader (Lebanese/Egyptian). Even "good" Middle Easterners who are perceived as nonwhite are not racialized as Middle Eastern. For example, although they are both half Lebanese, neither Salma Hayek, a famous actress, nor Shakira, an internationally renowned singer, is identified as Middle Eastern. Instead, they are almost universally considered Latina.

Some observers might point to the whitewashing of Americans of Middle Eastern descent as evidence of our evolving colorblindness. But such an argument is belied by the systematic racialization of transgressive individuals. When individuals lie at the cusp of the white/nonwhite divide, we unconsciously categorize them as the Other when they engage in wrongdoing but blend them into the white when they behave within social norms. Andre Agassi is a (white) tennis player, and Ralph Nader is a (white) politician. But Osama bin Laden is labeled an Arab terrorist and the Ayatollah Khomeini was a Middle Eastern Islamic fundamentalist. The act of selective racialization is by no means limited to geopolitical struggles. It occurs on a far more pedestrian, but nevertheless important, level. Take the case of Dodi Al-Fayed, the wealthy businessman who was dating Princess Diana following her

divorce from Prince Charles. The escapades of the two, rumored to be engaged at the time of their deaths, were the subject of extensive media coverage. Throughout their relationship, Al-Fayed was repeatedly portrayed as an *Arab* businessman and *Middle Eastern* playboy—not merely an Englishman or a businessman without reference to his race. In other words, he was racialized. And the reason is clear: he was engaging in transgressive behavior, stealing away with the People's princess.

Other examples abound. Recently, Zenadine Zidane, a member of the French national soccer team, viciously headbutted Italian player Marco Materazzi in the finals of the 2006 World Cup. Zidane's violent outburst likely cost his team the championship and has gone down as one of the most infamous incidents in soccer history. While the incident sullied Zidane's previously untarnished reputation, it also did something else: it racialized Zidane in the United States. In the aftermath of the incident, Zidane went from simply being an otherwise ordinary native-born (white) Frenchman on the Gallican national soccer team to becoming an Arab. American media reports highlighted his Algerian roots. The racial subtext was all too clear—there was an implicit association of his apparent predilection for violence with his Arab background. He had brazenly violated social norms with his headbutt and, as such, had become a transgressor. Simultaneously, he went from being white to becoming the Other.

The process of selective racialization occurs with regularity in the mass media, serving to bolster and legitimize existing stereotypes. Although all the characters in the Middle Eastern-themed Disney film *Aladdin* share Arab descent, they are only selectively racialized. The chief wrongdoers—the greedy bazaar merchants, the thief Kazim, and the main antagonist, Jafar—all possess exaggerated stereotypical features. Both Kazim and Jafar sport thick Arab accents, facial hair, and prominent hooked noses. By contrast, the movie's sympathetic protagonists—Aladdin, Princess Jasmine, and the Sultan—possess few of the features traditionally associated with Arabs. Instead, their physiognomy is quintessentially European, and they speak with no trace of a Middle Eastern accent.[29] In other words, the transgressive characters are Arabized and the wholesome characters are Anglicized, thereby heightening negative stereotypes linked to Middle Easterners while concurrently reinforcing positive associations with whiteness. . . .

Negotiating Middle Eastern Racial Status in the New America: Covering and Its Implications

Drawing from the work of Erving Goffman,[30] who once observed "that persons who are ready to admit possession of a stigma . . . may nonetheless make a great effort to keep the stigma from looming large,"[31] Kenji Yoshino calls attention to a rampant, yet relatively unappreciated, consequence of our national impulse toward assimilation—the covering of disfavored identities. Based on pressures to conform to social norms enforced by the dominant culture, a rational distaste for ostracism and social opprobrium can lead individuals to engage in the purposeful act of toning down traits that identify them with a stigmatized group. . . .

Applying Yoshino's model in the Middle Eastern context is both revealing and instructive: what, after all, could be more coercively assimilationist than forcibly designating an entire population white de jure while simultaneously treating that population as nonwhite de facto? Not surprisingly, Middle Easterners have sought refuge in covering as a strategic response to the discrimination they face. . . .

Largely due to the existence of distinctive phenotypic characteristics, many African Americans cannot pretend to be anything but African American and many Asian Americans cannot pretend to be anything but Asian American.[32] Many Middle Easterners, however, can realistically opt out of their racial categorization. Middle Easterners are more prone to racial ambiguity because successive waves of diverse populations have passed through the Middle East, making it a veritable racial melting pot since antiquity. Since the stereotypical image of the Middle Easterner is much darker in skin, hair, and eye color than the average Middle Easterner, those who naturally possess lighter skin, hair, and eyes are particularly nimble in their covering. Either way, with the simple change of a revealing first or last name, many Middle Easterners can become Italian, French, Greek, Romanian, Indian, Mexican, Puerto Rican, or Argentine.[33]

The gravitation toward covering is often irresistible, especially through its seductive illusion of simplifying the lives of its purveyors. In the wake of 9/11, Middle Easterners throughout the United States felt under attack and responded with a series of rational covering responses just to survive the wave of hate surging throughout the country.[34] Lebanese and Persian restaurants conspicuously displayed "Proud to be American" signs over their entrances. Cab drivers from the Middle East and South Asia decorated their vehicles with large American flags.[35] A series of hate crimes prompted many Muslim women and Sikh men to remove their head coverings out of fear of being perceived as Middle Eastern.[36]

Four axes of covering—association, appearance, affiliation, and activism[37]—are prevalent in the Middle Eastern community. Consider the phenomenon of association. As one associates more with recognized whites, one better performs whiteness and is therefore perceived as more white. When I first moved to Newport Beach, California, the former hometown of John Wayne and an oceanside hamlet renowned as a bastion of wealth and white conservatism, a friend of mine joked, "Don't worry—I'll be your white sponsor." His wry comment had historical antecedents. A decade after Congress passed the Chinese Exclusion Act of 1882 prohibiting any new immigration from China, Chinese immigrants already residing in the United States had to prove the legality of their presence by providing the testimony of "one credible *white* witness."[38] Mingling with the white is a powerful form of obtaining white bona fides.

In an illuminating passage from her essay *I Grew Up Thinking I Was White*, Iranian American writer Gelareh Asayesh describes the associational covering that she undertakes to assimilate:

> My National Public Radio accent takes me further than my parents' voices, laden with inflections from a faraway land. The options may be limited when it comes to skin color, but it is possible to improve one's status in other ways. I think of it as race laundering: the right clothes, the right car, the right neighborhood can help compensate for that fundamental imperfection: nonwhiteness.[39]

Asayesh's reflections help to explain why Iranian Americans—like many others trying to earn their white stripes—are so often concerned with projecting images of success and wealth. Iranian Americans in Los Angeles are well-known for making their homes in Beverly Hills, driving only a BMW or Mercedes, and dressing in the most high-priced designer fashions. For example, 1995's Alicia Silverstone vehicle *Clueless,* set in Beverly Hills, had an incisive and comical reference to the city's Persian residents. At one point, the lead character points away from the camera and comments, "that's the Persian mafia. You can't hang with them unless you own a BMW."[40] The camera then turns to reveal a throng of Iranian American teenagers outfitted stylishly in black, driving their German imports.

Throughout the Middle Eastern community, the manipulation of appearance also emerges as a quintessential form of covering. Middle Eastern women frequently dye their hair blond or wear colored contact lenses to downplay their more "ethnic" features. Middle Eastern men will go by the name "Mike" for Mansour, "Mory" for Morteza, "Al" for Ali, and "Moe" for Mohammed. Such tactics may appear petty and even futile, but they can be surprisingly effective. I was recently told a story about an Iranian American attorney who went by the name "Moe" instead of his birth-name, Mohammed. One day, he was selected for extra screening at the airport. After showing his identification to the TSA workers and undergoing the additional security measures, he calmly protested, wondering out loud if he had been targeted on the basis of his ethnicity. The TSA guard looked puzzled "It's not like your name is Mohammed or

something," he guffawed. Absent the "Mohammed" stigma, Moe had become white. . . .

Many Iranians or Arabs of Jewish background cover by rationally exploiting mainstream (mis)-perceptions of "Jewishness" as both a religion and an ethnicity. For example, although the Jewish Iranian population is relatively large, especially in Los Angeles, the very existence of a Jewish Iranian population is a surprise to the many people who view Iran as an Islamic monolith. By identifying themselves to the world as Jewish, these Jewish Iranians tend to avoid any further questions about their ethnicity, as people assume their ethnicity is Jewish and that they therefore are white (i.e., Ashkenazi Jewish) and not Middle Eastern. A Jewish Iranian poet I once knew demonstrated her profound awareness of the way in which this popular misperception could be exploited for assimilatory purposes. Explaining the extent of her Persian pride, she pointed out that she had embraced her Iranian heritage despite the obvious covering tactics at her disposal "Since I'm Jewish, I don't have to be Iranian," she remarked. "Yet I choose to be."

Finally, with respect to activism, we have witnessed profound covering in the Middle Eastern community. As Kenji Yoshino argues, many minorities are reticent to become involved in the fight to protect their civil rights, lest they be associated with militant ethnics and become racialized. In the Middle Eastern American community, there is a profound wariness of political involvement, a fact revealed by the dearth of elected officials of Middle Eastern descent, even in areas with large concentrations. For example, it is believed that the highest ranking Iranian American public officeholder in the United States is Jimmy Delshad, the mayor of Beverly Hills.[41] Delshad was only elected to his post in 2007.[42] . . .

Beyond covering, Middle Eastern assimilation also crosses into the realm of passing and even conversion. As a matter of pride, many Middle Easterners (especially those from older generations, for which the importance of whiteness was perhaps more accentuated) insist on actually being considered white. In this regard, they are no different than prior immigrant groups. For example, in

PERSONAL ACCOUNT

Master Status: Pride and Danger

I consider myself to be privileged in many things in life, but my one master status that is a bit controversial is being Muslim. By controversial, I mean that to some it might be a privilege to be Muslim, whereas to others, well . . . not so much. Aside from dealing with those who are racist, ignorant, and cruel, I think being Muslim is a privilege for me. For example, people will assume because I look like I am a practicing Muslim, that I won't be dishonest or conniving. People assume that I will be honest. Take, for example, the time I forgot my campus parking permit. The ticketing officer was writing me a ticket, but when I pled with him that I had just forgotten my parking pass, he said, "Well, you seem like you are a practicing young Muslim lady. I don't think you would be lying to me, so I'll take that ticket back."

I have actually tested this out. I once asked a non-Muslim woman friend to wear the hijab (head scarf) for one day, so it would be assumed she was Muslim. She went to the bookstore to buy a used textbook. When she got there, however, there were no used books, so she had to buy a new one, but she didn't have enough money. She explained to the clerk that she really needed the book for class right away, and asked if she could come back later to pay the rest. This is actually against the school policy. But the lady working at the register said to her, "Muslims usually don't cheat people. I am going to take your word for it," and let her buy the book at a used price (but put a hold on her account until the rest was paid). My friend was amazed.

Even with these positive experiences, being Muslim today can be very dangerous. I was in the 5th grade, sitting in the library fixing the TV monitor to play a video, when 9/11 happened. The flashing red news alert caught my eye. I stopped and sat there watching the crazy scene they were broadcasting. People were on fire and flying out of windows. Women were screaming, blood was all over the streets, and police and firefighters were everywhere. It was like a horror movie to me. Soon the library staff and administrators came to see what was going on. They quickly rushed me out and put the school on a complete shutdown. Parents were coming in to pick up their kids and teachers were crying. School was dismissed.

When we came back two days later, everyone was upset. We had classmates and teachers whose loved ones had been killed or injured. However, school had to continue, so everyone tried to have a normal day. During recess, a boy from another classroom came up to me and said, "I know I don't know you, but I want to warn you. My friend wants to kill you." I thought it was a joke. I ignored him and asked him to stay away. But he came back to me three times, until I finally became so annoyed by him that I complained to my teacher, asking if she could ask him to stay away.

The teacher called the boy, and soon his friend, and to her surprise and mine, the boy was right. His friend was carrying a gun and told the teacher and me straight up, "I am coming to kill her. She is Osama's daughter, and we have to kill these Muslims." The kid had a real gun, with a bullet. I was in shock. The teacher tried to take it from him, but he ran away. The police found him a few hours later, hiding somewhere in the forest right behind our school. I really wanted to believe it was just a joke, maybe just a nightmare, and I would wake up soon and things would be totally fine. It could not be reality, I thought . . . but it was reality.

It soon became the reality that I live every day. I get threatened at school, made fun of in public, discriminated against during work, and humiliated in the comfort of my home. I am reminded over and over again how my people are the cause of all these wars, are violent terrorists, and that I have to pay the price. People judge and discriminate against me on the basis of the acts of a few followers of my religion. They seem to forget that Muslims are humans just like they are. They forget that Islam is not made up of ten terrorists, but 1.4 billion people striving to live a better life just like they are. But even with all of this, as strong believers, we behold with patience, and we keep our heads up high, ignoring the comments. We are cautious about what we do and say, and every day we pray that we come back home to our families safely.

Although today's society portrays Muslims negatively, I think I am still privileged to be a Muslim. It is my number one identity. Before people even judge my gender/sex, my social status, my educational status, or anything else, they see "Muslim" written on my forehead. I am proud of that identity and always will be.

Sumaya Al-Hajebi

all but one of the many reported racial-prerequisite naturalization cases,[43] the petitioners claimed to be white, despite the fact that it was much harder to establish white, rather than black, status. At the time, many states had laws on the books declaring any individual with a single quantum of black blood to be black by law.[44]

In the continental United States, . . . white privilege still reigns supreme, and, naturally, immigrant groups still seek white recognition.[45] This is certainly true for the Iranian American population. The United States has seen a huge wave of immigration from Iran since the 1979 revolution. In 1996, it was estimated that almost 1.5 million Iranians resided in the United States, a figure that had grown from just a few thousand in the 1970s.[46] However, despite changes to the 2000 census, which allowed Middle Eastern individuals such as Iranian Americans to identify themselves as something other than just "white," it appears that very few Iranian Americans took the opportunity to do so. In fact, only 338,266 individuals in the United States identified themselves as Iranian.[47] The majority of Iranians, it seems, chose conversion. Any visitor to Los Angeles (often referred to as Tehrangeles or Irangeles) can attest that there are probably 338,266 individuals of Iranian descent living in Southern California, let alone the rest of the country.

The reason for this statistical discrepancy is not too difficult to ascertain: having fled a severely repressive government in their homeland, many Iranians have a profound mistrust of government. As a result, it is hardly surprising that they would balk at the chance to single themselves out conveniently to the government for identification and tracking purposes. Additionally, there is a strong desire within the Iranian community to assimilate. Ask typical Iranian Americans if they are white, and they will say, "Of course." Then, inevitably, they will tell you that the word *Iran* comes from the Sanskrit word meaning "Land of the Aryans" and that they, not the Germans, are the original Aryans. . . .

DISCUSSION QUESTIONS

1. As oil has become more important, why has there been a change in the image of the Middle East?
2. Describe the process of selective racialization and its consequences.

NOTES

1. Clayton R. Koppes, *Captain Mahan, General Gordon, and the Origins of the Term "Middle East,"* 12 Middle Eastern Studies 95, 95–96 (1976).
2. Alfred T. Mahan, *The Persian Gulf and International Relations,* in Retrospect and Prospect 209, 237, 244–45 (1903).
3. Sedat Laciner, *Is There a Place Called "the Middle East"?* Journal of Turkish Weekly Opinion, June 2, 2006, available online at http://www.turkishweekly.net /comments.php?id=2117#.
4. *Fiore v. O'Connell,* 66 N.Y.S.2d 173, 175 (N.Y. Sup. Ct. 1946).
5. *Larsen v. Comm'r of Internal Revenue,* 23 T.C. 599, 601 (Tax Court 1955).
6. *Miller v. United States,* 140 F. Supp. 789, 790, 792 (Ct. Cl. 1956).
7. *Waldron v. British Petroleum Co.,* 149 F. Supp. 830, 836 (S.D.N.Y. 1957); United States v. Standard Oil Co. of California, 155 F. Supp. 121, 127 (S.D.N.Y. 1957).
8. Michael Omi and Howard Winant, Racial Formation in the United States 55 (1994).
9. Richard Delgado, *Two Ways to Think about Race: Reflections on the Id, the Ego, an Other Reformist Theories of Equal Protection* , 89 Geo. L.J. 2279, 2283 (2001) (footnote omitted).
10. Richard Delgado & Jean Stefancic, *Images of the Outsider in American Law and Culture: Can Free Expression Remedy Systemic Social Ills?* 77 cornell L. Rev. 1258, 1262–63 (1992).
11. *Id.*
12. Delgado, *supra,* at 2285.
13. *Id.* at 2283.
14. Delgado & Stefancic, *supra,* at 1271–72.
15. Delgado, *supra,* at 2285–86.
16. Of course, these romantic images have often served less than salutary ends, providing, as Edward Said has argued, implicit justification for colonial and imperial ambitions by the West toward the Middle East. *See* Edward Said, Orientalism (1978).
17. *See, e.g.,* Samuel P. Huntington, The Clash of Civilizations and The Remaking of World Order (1998).

18. *See* Karen Engle, *Constructing Good Aliens and Good Citizens; Legitimizing the War on Terror(ism),* 75 U Colo. L. Rev. 59, 75 (2004) (discussing the stereotyping of Middle Eastern individuals as religious extremists and terrorists incapable of assimilation in the United States).

19. Louise Cainkar, *The History of Arab Immigration to the U.S.: An Introduction for High School Students,* in Arab American Encyclopedia (2000), available online at http://www.adc.org/education/AAImmigration.htm (accessed Sept. 12, 2006).

20. Lucius Hopkins Miller, A Study of the Syrian Population of Greater New York 5 (1904).

21. *Id.* at 22.

22. *Id.* at 25.

23. Joyce Howard Price, *Census Counts 1.2 Million Arabs in U.S.: Most of Them Are Christian,* Washington Times, Dec. 4, 2003, at A1.

24. Engle, *supra,* at 74.

25. Victor Romero, *Race, Immigration and the Department of Homeland Security,* 19 ST. John's J. Legal Comment. 51, 55 (2004).

26. *Id.* at 52.

27. *See* Nancy Murray, *Profiled: Arabs, Muslims, and the Post-9/11 Hunt for the "Enemy Within,"* in Civil Rights In Peril: The Targeting of Arabs and Muslims 27, 44 (Elaine C. Hagopian ed., 2004).

28. Such a tack might be acceptable if we truly lived in a race-blind society in which racial perceptions were unimportant and all individuals were dissolved into a single catch-all "human" category. The "selective" aspect of the racialization process, however, belies the notion of race blindness.

29. Scott J. Simon, *Arabs in Hollywood: An Undeserved Image,* Latent Image (1996), available online at http://pages.emerson.edu/organizations/fas/latent_imageissues/1996-04/arabs.htm.

30. *See* Erving Goffman, Stigma: Notes on The Management of Spoiled Identity 12–13 (1963).

31. Kenji Yoshino, *Covering,* 111 Yale L. 169, 772–73.

32. There are certainly exceptions to this generalization, but I think it is fair to say that a determined individual of Middle Eastern descent would have a much easier time passing him- or herself off as a member of a different ethnic or racial group, or engaging in the act of covering, than an individual of African or East Asian descent. It should be noted that many Latinos, because of their inextricably mixed heritage, also "enjoy" the option of passing—for better or worse.

33. See, e.g., Lorraine Ali, *Laughter's New Profile,* Newsweek, Apr. 22, 2002, at 61 (quoting a line from a routine performed by an Iranian American comedian: "Since September 11, when people ask me about my ethnicity I look them straight in the eye and say, 'I'm Italian'. . . We're all named Tony now.").

34. Sunita Patel, *Performative Aspects of Race: "Arab, Muslim, and South Asian" Racial Formation after September 11,* 10 Asian Pac. Am. L.J. 61, 83-84 (2005) (describing many of the covering activities undertaken by individuals of Middle Eastern descent in the wake of 9/11).

35. *See, e.g.,* Muneer I. Ahmad, *A Rage Shared by Law: Post- September 11 Racial Violence as Crimes of Passion,* 92 Cal. L. Rev. 1259, 1278–79 (2004); New Yorker, Nov. 5, 2001 (depicting on the cover a Sikh taxi driver whose cab is covered with American flags).

36. Patel, *supra,* at 84.

37. Kenji Yoshino, Covering: The Hidden Assault on Our Civil Rights 125 (2006).

38. Geary Act of 1892, ch. 60, § 6, 27 Stat. 25 (1892) (repealed) (emphasis added).

39. Gelareh Asayesh, *I Grew Up Thinking I Was White,* in My Sister, Guard Your Veil; My Brother, Guard Your Eyes: Uncensored Iranian Voices 12, 17 (Lila Azam Zanganeh ed., 2006).

40. *Clueless* (Paramount Pictures 1995).

41. Prior to that, I would like to think that my uncle, Mansour Kia, was in the running for the title of highest ranking Iranian American elected official. He served as the mayor of the town of Stanton, Iowa (population: 714) at the turn of the century.

42. *In re* Cruz, 23 F. Supp. 774–75 (E.D.N.Y. 1938).

43. By the early 1900s, several Southern states had adopted this "one-drop" rule. *See* Luther Wright, Jr., *Who's Black, Who's White, and Who Cares? Reconceptualizing the United States's Definition of Race and Racial Classifications,* 48 Vand. L. Rev. 513, 524 (1995) (documenting the progression of states toward the one-drop rule); Peter Wallenstein, Tell The Court I Love My Wife 142 (2002) (nothing that Georgia, Virginia, Alabama, and Oklahoma all had laws defining as black anyone with any drop of African ancestry); *Plessy v. Ferguson,* 163 U.S. 537 (1896) (assuming that the petitioner, who possessed only one-eighth African blood, was black for the purposes of segregation laws). *But see In re* Cruz, 23 F. Supp. at 775 (finding one-quarter African blood insufficient to gain someone recognition of African descent for naturalization purposes).

44. This trend is, of course, not limited to recent immigrant groups but has a long history. See, for example, the history of Irish, Greek, Italian, and Slavic assimilation in the United States. *See* Noel Ignatiev, How The Irish Became White 2–3 (1995).

45. *See* Worldwide Persian Outreach, *The Persian Diaspora* Farsinet, http://www.farsinet.com/pwo/diaspora.html (accessed Nov. 21, 2006). Another, more conservative,

estimate suggests that the Iranian American population totaled approximately 540,000 by 2003. *See* Iranian Studies Group at MIT, *Factsheet on the*

Iranian-American Community (2003), http://isg-mit.org/projects-storage/census/Factsheet.pdf.
46. Iranian Studies Group at MIT, *supra*.

SEX AND GENDER

READING 25

The Privilege of Teaching About Privilege

Michael A. Messner

Arriving to my office at 7:30 a.m., I observe that the quiet halls are devoid of faculty, office staff, or students. I amble along the corridor and notice that the lights are on in our Sociology Center. From the hallway, I peek through the window and see one of the janitors who works in our building, standing in front of the chalkboard. A middle-aged mother of Mexican descent for whom English is a second language, she shows up for work five days a week at 5:00 a.m., cleans our hallways, offices, and restrooms. She empties our trashcans daily, and once or twice a year she can be seen on her hands and knees, scrubbing the black baseboards to a clean sheen, all the way down the long stretch of our hallways. She leaves the building by the early afternoon; faculty or students who are not "morning people" are unlikely to see her labor that keeps our workplace spanking clean. On this morning I view her through the Sociology Center window, and I pause to wave a friendly greeting. But she doesn't see me; she's standing perfectly still, her back to me, a long mop poised upright in her hand. She seems to be concentrating, reading the chalkboard, which is covered, side-to-side and top-to-bottom, with a professor's scrawlings from yesterday's

Michael Messner is a professor of sociology and gender studies at the University of Southern California.

theory lecture on Marx. Feudalism became capitalism; new social classes emerged; capitalists extracted surplus value and accumulated profits; an industrial labor class performed alienated labor. I proceed to my office, turn on my computer, and do a first sorting through today's e-mails. A few minutes later, I stroll to the restroom, and walking by the now-empty Sociology Center, I see that the chalkboard is now clean as a whistle, gleaming and ready for the next professor's lecture.

How do we, in our daily lives, make sense of moments like this? In particular, how do sociology professors square this sort of daily experience with our work—our research and our teaching—that so often focuses on social inequalities? For the moment, I want to leave these questions, and the image from this story, as something for the reader to ponder. I will return to them later. And I promise, I don't have a clean and tidy answer.

TELLING PRIVILEGE STORIES

Teaching is what first drew me to become a professor. When I attended my first Pacific Sociological Association meeting back in 1974 as a graduating senior at Chico State University, it was the organization's clear support for students and for the mission of teaching that I found most attractive. After a quarter-century of teaching there is plenty to ponder, but here I want to reflect on one challenge to which I have given a good deal of thought in recent years: how do I, as a white, male, tenured professor teach in a critical and self-reflexive way about privilege? . . .

I learned years ago as a new assistant professor, team-teaching courses on gender with women colleagues, that students tend to view and judge women professors differently, applying a double-standard that worked to the benefit of the male instructor. And I learned during six years of serving as a department chair, and reading many student evaluations of my colleagues' classes, that students often impute "bias" to faculty of color who are teaching courses on social inequality, especially race. White, heterosexual, male professors, I learned, are usually assumed to be "objective" when teaching about social inequalities (Messner 2000; 2003). How do we use this privilege in the classroom?

One starting point in thinking about this question is to familiarize our students with the burgeoning sociological research on inequalities and, in particular, the recent development of what Goode (1982) called a sociology of superordinates. There is of course a long tradition of research on the upper classes (e.g., Domhoff 1967; Marx 1867/1974; Mills 1956). By the late 1980s, the feminist creation of women's studies also germinated a critical study of masculinities and male privilege (e.g., Connell 1987; Kaufman 1987; Kimmel 1987). Sociologists of race and ethnicity have contributed to the more recent scholarship on white privilege (e.g., Lipsitz 1998; O'Brien and Feagin 2004), and to the burgeoning critical study of heterosexuality and heteronormativity (e.g., Ingraham 2004). And of course, sociologists have been in the forefront of developing analyses of intersectional (race, class, gender, sexual) privilege (e.g., Collins 1991; Ferber 1998; Kimmel and Ferber 2003).

How do we introduce this excellent research on privilege to our classrooms? Many teachers have utilized Peggy MacIntosh's "Invisible Knapsack of Privilege" as a point of entrée for classroom consciousness-raising exercises that illuminate the often-subtle interactional dynamics of privilege (MacIntosh 1989). After an engaging discussion of MacIntosh, a next logical question from students who have just "discovered" privilege is, "What do I do with my unearned privilege? Give it away? Relinquish it?" A sociological perspective, I tell my students, shows us that it is not likely that an individual can simply "give up" his or her privileges. Privilege is not merely an individual attribute, like a pair of shoes one can remove and discard; it is

also built into the fabric of institutions and organizations. And privilege operates interpersonally—as Cecilia Ridgeway (2009) has shown in her work, gender is "framed before we know it," serving as a kind of background substructure that shapes our reactions to and interactions with others. One way I convey this idea in the classroom is by telling stories from my own life, stories intended to illustrate the less-than-fully visible scaffolding underlying my own privilege. The following story about my summer job when I was a college student illustrates how a patriarchal dividend sometimes just "happens"—how men sometimes simply have to show up to reap its benefits:

During my junior year in 1973, I took a course at Chico State University on social stratification that focused mostly race and class inequality. There was scant research available as yet on gender, but my professor did include a short segment on the pay gap, illustrating that in the United States, women full-time workers earned about 59 cents to the male worker's dollar; even when doing the same jobs, women were routinely paid less. I was surprised by these data, and decided to write my term paper on this topic. I concluded the paper with an impassioned statement that, in America, everyone should be given equal opportunity and equal pay for equal work. I got an "A" on the paper. And I was proud of the position I'd taken; I was now a liberal.

That summer, I was back in my hometown, working my usual summer job for the Salinas Recreation and Park Department. Every summer, perhaps a dozen college students like me were hired to run programs for kids in the local parks. Most of my colleagues were young women, and they were routinely given assignments at the smaller parks that were only open 20–30 hours a week. Dave and I, the two men, were given 40 hour per week jobs at the larger parks. Frequently, at our weekly staff meetings, our supervisor would invite Dave and I to do extra work on a Saturday, so we'd routinely rack up 42–46 hours of work a week, which was great for saving money for September, when we'd head back to college. One day during a staff meeting, the supervisor said, "Mike, Dave, can you come down to the Center on Saturday morning?" Before I could say "yes," our colleague Susan interrupted and said, "I don't know why Dave and Mike always get the extra hours. We women can do those jobs as well as they can, and we need the extra hours and money as much as they do." A moment of uncomfortable silence settled on the room. And a defensive feeling, a sense that something was being taken away, crept up on me. I whispered to Dave—way too loudly, as it turned out—"Who does she think she is? Gloria Steinem?" Without missing a beat, Susan placed both arms on the table and said, "Mike, don't talk about something you don't know anything about." I thought to myself immediately, "Gee I do know a lot about this topic; I just wrote this great paper on it!" Fortunately I had the sense to keep my mouth shut and not say it.

I am happy to report that the blatantly unfair privilege informally bestowed upon men workers by the Salinas Recreation and Park Department in the summer of 1973 ceased immediately, once it was publicly named and confronted. But it was not I, or another male worker, who named or confronted it. And I learned an important lesson: it is one thing to take an academic position against the unfair treatment of women workers; it is yet another to align myself with feminist women in a situation where change might actually threaten to take an unearned privilege away from me.

The extra hours and more pay I received in this instance were unearned privileges from which I benefited, just for showing up to work as a male. Peggy Macintosh's "knapsack of privilege" exercise helps to illustrate how and why this sort of privilege often remains "invisible" to those who benefit from it. But my story also makes me wonder: How invisible really is privilege? Was I entirely unaware of my unearned privilege? Or was I simply turning a blind eye and a deaf ear to an unfair practice that benefitted me? Talking about privilege as "invisible" is a good strategic starting point for teaching about it, but perhaps also it is the flipside of viewing subordinates as dupes who suffer from false consciousness. After all, it is in the interests of the privileged to appear to be blind to the sources and consequences of our privilege: But maybe I *did* see the unfair treatment of my women colleagues. How, really, could I *not* have seen it, especially having so recently written that impassioned sociology paper on the topic? My sense of entitlement to unearned privilege allows me to look the other way—away in 1973 from my women colleagues who were not getting the same opportunities to earn money as I was; away today from the janitor who dusts and vacuums my office; and away too from the growing class of adjunct, part-time faculty who increasingly shoulder the teaching burden in our colleges and universities.

THE SINCERE FICTION OF INDIVIDUAL MERIT

What is it that allows us to look away from something that threatens our vested interests? Perhaps it's our sense of ourselves as good people—our belief in what O'Brien and Feagin (2004) call "sincere fictions"—the idea that *we* are fair-minded in our treatment of others, that *we* do not discriminate. But more broadly, sincere fictions are more than rosy self-deception. Their power and depth lies in their grounding in shared ideologies. Particularly important in this regard is the widely held commitment to the belief in individualism and meritocracy. Another personal story I convey to my students is intended to shine the light of intersectional analyses of inequality on my own immersion in an ideology of individualism and meritocracy.

I completed my master's degree in 1976, and dreamt of landing a job in a community college, at a time when few colleges were hiring. I was lucky to get an interview for a job as a full-time one-year replacement for a professor who was going on sabbatical from her job in a team-taught experimental college. I went to a daylong interview that included several one-on-one talks with faculty and a dean as well as a grueling two-hour interrogation from half a dozen faculty and students. When challenged about my inexperience, I thought I responded well in delivering an impromptu riff on how Paulo

Freire's theories could be put into play for libera-
tory pedagogy in the experimental college.

A couple of weeks later, I received a phone call
offering me the job. I was happy, but not shocked. I
really thought I'd wowed them at the interview. I
was perfect for the job. I ended up doing the year-
long gig, and then hung on for another year, teach-
ing sociology classes part-time, before getting laid
off in the wake of California's Proposition 13,
which eventually chased me back to graduate
school.

A few years later, I was having dinner with a
professor who had been among those who inter-
viewed me back in 1976 at the experimental col-
lege. He said, "Did I ever tell you how you got
hired?" "No," I said, "but I am curious." "Well,"
he said, "We interviewed two other people. One
was a black male, the other a white female, and
both had more experience than you. For a full day,
we debated which of those two we should hire; we
were split down the middle, and the split was threat-
ening to get ugly. So at one point, somebody said,
'Hey, how about this guy Messner?' We looked
around at each other, we were tired, and it seemed
nobody objected to you. So that's how it happened."

That's not the story I had expected to hear. I
thought he'd explain how I'd emerged as clearly the
most qualified candidate, or that maybe he'd gush
about how my mini-lecture on Friere had sealed the
deal with the search committee. I knew that I had
worked hard in college, and figured I'd fully earned
that job. Landing that job, I had thought, was a logical moment within my own developing narrative
of hard work, individual merit, and well-deserved
upward mobility. But with this added information a
few years later, I began retrospectively to re-read
my getting that first job as a moment where intersectional privilege had operated in my favor. I entered the academic labor force in the mid-1970s, a
contested moment of turbulent racial and gender
relations—in particular, a time during which tremendous tensions had built between an ascendant
feminist movement, led mostly by white, middle
class women, and a fragmenting black power and
civil rights movement, many of whose male leaders

held conservative views on gender. I don't know the
whole story, but it's reasonable to speculate that
this very tension, in local microcosm, produced me,
the white guy, as the compromise candidate least
likely to ignite an already-simmering race-gender
conflagration.

Getting that first job sparked future successes in
my academic career, including giving me two years
of teaching experience that helped me to build a
solid resume that got me admitted to the Ph.D. program at U.C. Berkeley. But like most "lucky
breaks," this one was not random; it was rooted in
the dynamics of the historical moment. Contextualized this way, my story hints at the shortcomings of
using individual stories in sociology classes, the
risk being that we can too easily lose the idea of *the
social,* an idea that is, I believe, our most radical
contribution in the face of beliefs in individualism
and meritocracy. . . .

CONTRADICTIONS OF TEACHING ABOUT PRIVILEGE

To this point, I have made a case for the importance
and utility of professors—especially those like me
who are members of privileged social groups—to
use our own stories to lay bare some of the underlying structural and interactional foundations of privilege. Having read this, some readers might very
well offer a skeptical rejoinder, suggesting that no
matter what I do in the classroom, I end up looking
good—that I reinforce my own white male heterosexual tenured professor privilege in the very act of
being so "open minded," of making myself so "personally vulnerable" in front of my students. This is
absolutely correct. And I would observe that this is
yet another way that privilege operates. A graduate
student I work with, Tal Peretz, coined a term for
this: when men openly support feminism, we benefit from what he calls "the pedestal effect" (Peretz
2010). The question for me then is, What do I do
with this? Part of the answer is to be reflexive not
only *about* my teaching . . . but also *in* my teaching,
for example, I tell my classes about how student
evaluations seem to hold women professors and

faculty of color to different standards, benefitting white male professors, and I present this to them as a problem to be discussed and analyzed. This invites students to look at their own gendered and raced assumptions about professors.

Ultimately, though, I come up against the limits of being the white heterosexual guy with a secure job, trying to teach about privilege. And here I want to return to the hallway outside my office, and to the question I raised at the outset: What do we do with moments when we experience so starkly our own privilege, as I did when I saw the USC janitor pausing to read about Marx, before cleaning the chalkboard that a professor had left for someone else to erase? In this same hallway last semester, I ran into a student who had taken my class the previous spring. We said hello, and I asked her what she was doing this term. She said that she was taking her research methods class from one of our new assistant professors, Veronica Terriquez. Curious, I asked her how the class was going. "Oh," she replied, "It's the most exciting class I've taken so far at USC."

This was the first time I had ever heard a student use the words "exciting" to describe a methods class. She went on to explain that Professor Terriquez had the class divided into small groups, doing community research projects. Her group was focusing on the USC janitors, with a particular focus on their educational aspirations for their children. The students surveyed the janitors, and the result was a research report, "Beyond the Mop," that garnered considerable attention across the USC community (Vargas-Johnson, Silverman, Marcus, Simmons, Gallardo, Gholani, and Juarez 2009). The report described the janitors' own educations and explored their aspirations for their children's educations. In the report, the students did their historical research too, pointing out that in 1995 the university had subcontracted the janitors. When the janitors lost their USC employee status, they also lost one of the most plum benefits of USC faculty and staff: free tuition for our children. In subcontracting the janitors, the University had in effect shifted the institutional context, creating new structural constraints within which the janitors and

their children exercise their educational aspirations and choices.

I sat down and interviewed four of the students from Veronica Terriquez's methods class. I explained that I was interested in learning from them how their project might have made visible the often invisible work of janitors, and also how the research might have led them to reflect on inequalities on campus, and their own privileged positions as students. One of the students punctured the assumption implicit in my question, that USC students all come from privileged backgrounds:

> I am from a low-income family, honestly because of that I've always been really social with everybody, like in high school I was always good friends with the janitors and the gardeners. So it's always been the same here at USC .. to me [the janitors] were never invisible, but I know for a lot of people they are, and it's evident when you see how people treat the campus, when it's littered with garbage or you see the classrooms and there's trash, like people just leave their cups and you know they don't care because they know someone's going to pick it up—they don't know who, but they know someone's going to pick it up.

Another student in the group who described himself as coming from a middle class family did experience the study as an eye-opener:

> I actually was blown away by some of the statistics we gathered. . . . The tuition remission, I didn't know anything about that. . . . Janitors may be living from paycheck to paycheck, or having trouble trying to pay their bills, but they don't get that incentive [of tuition remission for their children], and I thought wow, that surprised me. I was blown away by that. Some of the children of people who work here, they go to overcrowded schools. I saw the enormous amount of inequality.

Yet another member of the research group said that she experienced the study as an inspiration to change the goals and culture of the university, in order to shift the existing reality of unfairness and inequality toward a vision of social justice:

> [Doing the study] really made me question the whole culture of USC as a university, and what it means to

be a center for education. And I think for a lot of children of privilege who become students here, I feel that USC for them is not so much about the education, it's a necessary step in their path of career. . . . So to call USC an educational institution and have 250 workers, none of whom have college degrees, is like a clash between what should be and what is. I really gained a lot from doing the survey because it's like giving us a chance to use sociology as a way to make the dreams of the janitors—like getting their children into college—first of all, it puts that on the table: this is a goal. But in order to make that happen, things have to happen.

A fourth student in the research group had concrete ideas about what had to happen next, linking the research findings to her activism with the Student Coalition Against Labor Exploitation (SCALE), a longstanding student organization that supports laborers on campus:

> [We need to ask next about] the actual wages of the janitors, and why do they have to be subcontracted? Why can't they be USC employees? It'll be cool once the contract negotiations are happening that students can get involved. I'm involved in SCALE and we are getting more involved with the union these days . . . This [research] project laid a foundation and has opened a lot of doors to make change and make this better, and in a really productive way I think, because we have the findings to back up all of our initiatives, so it's definitely taught me the power of social research.

Few sociology professors, I would think, could read that last line—"it's definitely taught me the power of social research"—and not think about her teaching, "mission accomplished."

And here I believe I have brought us full circle in thinking about how to teach about privilege: To remain critical, a sociology of superordinates needs, still and always, to be grounded in the standpoints of subordinate groups of people. It is crucial continually to remind our students and ourselves that privilege is always a relational concept; the workings of privilege are illuminated when subordinate groups of people organize to improve their lives. It never

would have occurred to me during the 1970s to question male privilege, or to even think about the social construction of masculinity, if I had not first heard feminist women talking about gender oppression. I can't begin to understand the full range of privilege that is implied in the simple phrase that "Pierrette and I are married," without first having listened to sexually subordinated groups of people who still lack the legal right to marry. And I can't know the first thing about my own white privilege without first developing some empathy and understanding of the lives and experiences of racially subordinated peoples. There's a lot that I can't know, on my own, based simply on my own experience. And there's a good deal that, humbly, I must admit I am unable alone to teach to my students.

However, in the end, and at the very least, I can begin by erasing my own chalkboard.

DISCUSSION QUESTIONS

1. Can you give an example of intersectional privilege?
2. Why is privilege often so invisible?
3. What should you do with unearned privilege? Give it away or use it?

REFERENCES

Collins, Patricia Hill. 1991. *Black Feminist Thought.* Boston: Unwin Hyman.

Connell, Raewyn. 1987. *Gender and Power.* Stanford, CA: Stanford University Press.

Domhoff, G. William. 1967. *Who Rules America?* Englewood Cliffs, NJ: Prentice-Hall.

Ferber, Abby L. 1998. *White Man Falling: Race, Gender and White Supremacy.* Lanham, MD: Rowman and Littlefield.

Goode, William J. 1982. "Why Men Resist." Pp. 131–50 in *Rethinking the Family: Some Feminist Questions,* edited by B. Thorne and M. Yalom. New York: Longman.

Ingraham, Chrys. 2004. *Thinking Straight: The Power, Promise and Paradox of Heterosexuality.* New York: Routledge.

Kaufman, Michael, Ed. 1987. *Beyond Patriarchy: Essays by Men on Pleasure, Power and Change.* Toronto: Oxford University Press.

Kimmel, Michael S., Ed. 1987. *Changing Men: New Directions in Research on Men and Masculinity.* Newbury Park, CA: Sage.

———— and Abby L. Ferber, Eds. 2003. *Privilege.* Boulder, CO: Westview.

Lipsitz, George. 1998. *The Possessive Investment in Whiteness: How White People Profit from Identity Politics.* Philadelphia, PA: Temple University Press.

MacIntosh, Peggy. 1989. "White Privilege: Unpacking the Invisible Knapsack." *Peace and Freedom* July/August: l0–12.

Marx, Karl. 1867/1974. *Capital.* London: Lawrence & Wishart Publishers.

Messner, Michael A. 2000. "White Guy Habitus in the Classroom: Confronting the Reproduction of Privilege," *Men and Masculinities* 2(4):457–69.

————. 2003. "Men as Superordinates: Challenges for Gender Scholarship." Pp. 287–98 in *Privilege,* edited by in M. S. Kimmel and A. L. Ferber. Boulder, CO: Westview.

Mills, C. Wright. 1956. *The Power Elite.* London, Oxford, and New York: Oxford University Press.

O'Brien, Eileen and Joe R. Feagin. 2004. *White Men on Race: Power, Privilege, and the Shaping of Cultural Consciousness.* Boston: Beacon Press.

Peretz, Tal. 2010. "No More Mr. Goodguy? Stepping Off the Pedestal of Male Privilege." *VoiceMale: Changing Men in Changing Times* Winter:10–13.

Ridgeway, Cecilia. 2009. "Framed Before We Know It: How Gender Shapes Social Relations." *Gender & Society* 23(2):145–60.

Vargas-Johnson, Alejandra, Sabrina Silverman, Evan Marcus, Marcus Simmons, Mario Gallardo, Bernadette Gholani, and Angelica Juarez. 2009. "Beyond the Mop: The Untold Story of U.S.C. Janitors." Research report written for Sociology 313 (University of Southern California, Department of Sociology).

READING 26

Proving Manhood

Timothy Beneke

Instead of coming to ourselves . . . we grow all manner of deformities and enormities.

Saul Bellow

Timothy Beneke is a freelance writer and antirape activist.

. . . Why is it that successfully enduring distress is so central to proving manhood and proving superiority to women, not only in the United States, but in most of the cultures of the world? And why is it that manhood is something to be *proved*? And how do we confer manhood on men without also conferring upon them superiority to women? Or is the very business of conferring manhood inherently problematic? . . .

COMPULSIVE MASCULINITY

By compulsive masculinity I mean the compulsion or need to relate to, and at times create, stress or distress as a means of both proving manhood and conferring on boys and men superiority over women and other men. Failure to do so results in the social or private perception that one is less than a man. One must take distress "like a man" or run the risk of being perceived as feminine—a "sissy" or "mama's boy."

The content of the stress and distress can be usefully divided into three general categories:

1. That which would hurt anyone, e.g., physical pain, physical danger, large quantities of alcohol.
2. That which poses a psychological danger owing to the meaning it is given in relation to manhood, e.g., failing to win a sporting contest, losing physical strength and skill as one ages, and crying in public.
3. That which poses the greatest threat of all to manhood (a special case of category 2)—women. . . .

I will further divide compulsive masculinity into what I witness (and manifest) as an American man and what can be gleaned from other cultures through anthropological and other data. It is useful to keep in mind the distinction between activities performed as masculinity-proving in themselves (like many rites of passage), and activities like work where proving masculinity is not the primary goal, but rather a secondary gratification that influences how work is done.

COMPULSIVE MASCULINITY IN THE UNITED STATES

American culture is replete with examples of compulsive masculinity. Witness Norman Mailer writing about Muhammad Ali, who had recently lost an agonizing championship fight to Joe Frazier, in *Life* magazine in March of 1971: "For Ali had shown America what we all had hoped was secretly true. He was a man. He could endure moral and physical torture and he could stand."[1]

It wasn't enough that Ali had shown himself to be a great fighter; winning had been too easy for him. Ali had taken Frazier's punishment "like a man" and remained competent and whole: "he could stand." He did not give up or burst into tears or go soft. According to Mailer "we *all*" could only be sure he was a man if he suffered and endured. Otherwise he was too much of a woman and not a real man, or he was a boy and, implicitly, too soft and attached to his mother—too feminine. Mailer assumes that admirers of Ali tacitly subscribed to this manhood ideology and that readers of *Life* magazine already understood it. No explanation was required.

That one of America's most famous writers could write this about America's (then) most famous athlete in one of America's most popular magazines suggests the pervasiveness of this ideology. It was, and largely still is, central to American culture.

Tom Wolfe wrote about the "right stuff" that was required of men to be test pilots and astronauts. What was this right stuff? It was the ability to repeatedly endure severe physical and psychological distress—high g's; intense, physically induced anxiety; and rapid heartbeats—while remaining cool, competent, and able to make snap, life-or-death decisions. And this right stuff—possessed only by the few—Wolfe says, is nothing other than masculinity itself.[2]

Sociologist Michael Kimmel offers many examples in his essay on the cult of masculinity in the United States.[3] The National Commission on the Causes and Prevention of Violence stated that "proving masculinity may require frequent rehearsals of toughness, the exploitation of women, and quick aggressive responses" (237). To "rehearse toughness" is to repeatedly prove one's ability to withstand stress as a preparation for greater stress. Kimmel quotes General Homer Lea, writing in 1898: "the greatest danger that a long period of profound peace offers to a nation is that of creating effeminate tendencies in young men" (241). Without war to "masculinize" men, they are in danger of becoming like women. And the Boy Scout Manual of 1914 states:

> The wilderness is gone, the Buckskin Man is gone, the painted Indian has hit the trail over the Great Divide, the hardships and privations of pioneer life which did so much to develop sterling manhood are now but a legend of history, and we must depend upon the Boy Scout movement to produce the MEN of the future. (243)

Again, without stress or distress through which men could test their manhood, they risk becoming women or remaining boys.

It seems that virtually anything men experience as stressful can serve as an occasion to prove manhood, so long as it is also something experienced as stressful by women. It would appear unlikely that American men could prove masculinity doing something women find easy to do. Although, with the advent of a "mythopoetic men's movement," where men take pride and may even compete in displaying their feelings, it is possible that the ability to cry in public, something women do more easily than men, may become a means of proving manhood.

American men take pride in handling alcohol like a man—getting sick or drunk, becoming incompetent, too easily can threaten one's manhood. Boys and even men feel superior to women and other men through their greater capacity to handle "grossness": unpleasant sounds and smells, insects and rodents, dirt, and so on.

The whole domain of male sports constitutes an occasion for proving manhood. The ability to withstand physical pain and intense psychological pressure, as Ali had done, and remain competent, is a central part of this. Moments of physical danger, like facing a fast-moving baseball when at bat or on the field, or evading tacklers while carrying a football, are similar occasions. The sheer psychological pressure exerted by the importance of winning or performing well enables one to prove manhood.

Hypermasculine G. Gordon Liddy, of radio talk and Watergate fame, as a child toughened himself by placing his hand on a burning flame without flinching and eating a cooked rat.[4] And part of what makes some popular aftershave lotions like Old Spice manly is the stinging pain they cause when rubbed on the face.

What defines a sissy on the playground is regression in the face of stress: bursting into tears when hurt, growing soft and "choking" at a crucial moment in a sporting event, giving in to fear and refusing to accept dares or take risks.

Work is another realm where the ethos of the playground is often transferred and where competence has often been equated with masculinity. It is an open question to what extent the training one receives to become a doctor, lawyer, or other professional is motivated by compulsive masculinity—and to what extent the entrance of large numbers of women into the higher levels of these professions will change them.[5] Nor is it clear the degree to which proving manhood constitutes a source of creativity in work.

Clearly, the army claims to make a man out of its entrants.[6] A popular television commercial for the army presents a solider about to parachute from a plane. We hear a voice-over of him writing to his father, telling him that he would have been proud of him today. The solider remembers what his father told him: "Being a man means putting your fear aside and doing your job."

The degree to which work is motivated by ulterior, manhood-proving needs is an issue that demands exploration. And, as technology increasingly renders men's superior physical strength of less value, mastering technology itself increasingly becomes an important realm for proving manhood, as the popularity of the television sitcom, *Home Improvement,* ironically attests.

Another means of proving manhood requires resisting the impulse to "go soft" and empathize with or nurture those who are suffering or weaker—a skill strongly needed to remain cold-blooded when confronting suffering or horror. It would appear that at least some of the evils of the world, e.g., sexism, fascism, homophobia, and racism, are, in varying degrees, then, ways that men prove their manhood. Men engaging in a gang bang, committing political torture, bashing a gay man; white men deriding blacks and boys torturing a bug, are all in danger of being regarded as less manly by other men if they empathize with or try to help the rape or torture victim, the gay or black man, even the bug. They resist the impulse to empathize with victims in order to prove manhood. Though men aren't likely to explicitly regard these experiences as suffering "taken like a man," it is what's expected of them.

And, similarly, men mock and feel superior to women or men whose need to nurture is easily aroused at the sight of babies or cuddly animals. The capacity to experience other beings as "cute" is the capacity to have one's desire to nurture aroused. Many men find this threatening to their manhood. Men rather often, and women seldom, refer sarcastically to the actions of others as "cute." Typically, it is a way of saying that, in trying to be clever, another man has been incompetent; "cute" is, in this sense, a denigration of manhood. If a baseball pitcher throws an odd pitch or a basketball player shoots a wild and spectacular shot, they may be accused of "trying to be cute," that is, of not being a real man. "Getting cute" is perceived as the equivalent of seeking nurturance, being feminine, and is thus unacceptable.

Learning to swear is an interesting domain for proving manhood; saying what (supposedly) no "good" woman would say is a way of advertising one's toughness and separation from women; one learns to endure the implicit fear of one's parents, and maybe, God. A good swear is the opposite of a good cry; it hardens one in a self-image of toughness and attempts to inspire fear in one's real or imagined cohorts and adversaries.

Symbols of masculinity often contain and express a history of suffering successfully endured. Think of tattoos, sculpted muscles, and scars. Such symbols convey a willingness and capacity to suffer for a masculine identity, an achieved and visible toughness.

Threats to manhood need not be explicit, conscious, or labeled; they can be deeply internalized and can manifest themselves as shadowy anxiety, guilt, or defensiveness, among other things. Proving manhood need not be dramatic or overt, rather, typically, it becomes internalized and characterological. What makes the need to prove manhood compulsive is that it can never be satisfied; one is momentarily a man and then the doubts reassert themselves—you're only as masculine as your last demonstration of masculinity. Men internalize a draconian model of masculinity that is inherently masochistic.

Relating to stress together is a common way that men bond—the greater the stress the stronger the bond. The extraordinary connection men feel at war has often been observed.[7] Compulsive masculinity is inherently social, no matter how isolated the man or boy engaging in it.[8]

Women constitute the third major category of stress that threatens manhood. . . .

First, the presence of women when a man is encountering masculinity-threatening stress compounds the stress. Part of proving manhood includes being perceived by women as a "real man."

Second, in the realm of sex, manhood is proved through one's capacity to find sexual partners and to remain potent with them. Sex is often dominative for men, and sexual problems are typically seen more as problems of failed manhood than as sexual problems.[9] In American culture we seldom explicitly regard sex as an occasion to take distress "like a man." But we do regard it as a proving ground for masculinity, either in terms of success at finding sexual partners or performance in sex.

Third, men's competition with women in the workplace is increasingly a threat to masculinity; competence at work has been a defining feature of male identity and men's superiority to women. . . .

COMPULSIVE MASCULINITY AND SEXISM

Compulsive masculinity is inexorably tied to sexism—in proving manhood a man is proving his superiority to women by enduring distress that women supposedly cannot endure. The domination and degradation of women are a basic defense used to bolster men's vulnerable masculinity. Where men are compulsively masculine, they are also sexist.

What follows are some assumptions of sexist men, stated at their most extreme and stereotypical:[10]

> Men and women are inherently different.
> Real men are superior to women and superior to men who do not live up to models of masculinity.
> Activities normally associated with women are demeaning for men to engage in.
> Men should not feel or express vulnerable or sensitive emotions: the manly emotions are lust and anger.
> Toughness and the domination of others are central to men's identity.
> Sex is less about pleasure or relating and more about proving manhood and asserting power.
> Gay men are failed men.

Relatively few men may actively express such beliefs; far more men feel them than express them. But it is safe to say that all men in American society must—to some degree—negotiate their identities by way of such ideas. I am struck by the powerful psychic resonance such ideas have for me, even though I do not intellectually subscribe to them. They are far more alive in my emotions than I would like them to be. For instance, I react with anxiety to the thought of engaging in certain "women's activities" like sewing; I still have trouble acknowledging, much less expressing, vulnerable emotions; the element of performance as an end in itself is still more alive in my sex life than I want it to be. And it has been a struggle to acknowledge the liberatory potential that gay men offer straight men.

I find it impossible to imagine compulsive masculinity without sexism. The inability to empathize with women, to experience "vulnerable" emotions, to engage in egalitarian sex, or to empathize with gays is tied to the need to prove manhood by never regressing under stress.

DISCUSSION QUESTIONS

1. Is proving masculinity primarily about demonstrating superiority to women?
2. Do you think the need to prove manhood is as strong now as it was for your parents' generation?

PERSONAL ACCOUNT

Just Something You Did as a Man

In a class we had discussed the ways men stratify themselves in terms of masculinity. I decided I would put that discussion to the test at work.

As I sat at a table, one of my coworkers approached me with a copy of a popular men's magazine, which portrays nude women. He said, "Frank, there is this bitch in here with the most beautiful big tits I have ever seen in my life." I told him that I wasn't interested in looking at the magazine because I had decided I did not agree with the objectification of women. His reply was, "What's the matter, are you getting soft on us?" I joked that it was not a matter of getting soft, it was simply a decision I had made due to a "new and improved consciousness."

At my job, talk about homosexuals, the women who walk by, and graphic (verbal) depictions of sexual aggression toward women abound, but on this occasion I either rejected the conversation or said nothing at all. By the end of the day I was being called, sometimes jokingly and sometimes not, every derogatory homosexual slur in the English language. I was no longer "one of the boys."

I did not engage in the "manly" discourse of the day so therefore I was labeled (at best) a "sissy."

My coworkers assumed that I had had or was about to have a change of sexual orientation simply because I did not engage in their conversations about women and homosexuals. Since men decide how masculine another man is by how much he is willing to put down women and gays, I was no longer considered masculine.

This experience affected me as much as it did because it opened my eyes to a system of stratification in which I have been immersed but still had no idea existed. Demeaning women and homosexuals, to me, was just something you did as a man. But to tell you the truth, I don't think I could go back to talking like that. I am sure that my coworkers will get used to my new thinking, but even if they don't I believe that it is worth being rejected for a cause such as this. I had not thought about it, but I would not want men talking about my sisters and mother in such a demeaning way.

Francisco Hernandez

NOTES

1. Norman Mailer, *Existential Errands* (New York: Signet, 1974), 43.
2. Tom Wolfe, *The Right Stuff* (New York: Bantam, 1980), 22.
3. Michael Kimmel, "The Cult of Masculinity: American Social Character and the Legacy of the Cowboy," in *Beyond Patriarchy,* ed. Michael Kaufman (Oxford: Oxford University Press, 1983). Also see Kimmel's lucid and rich *Manhood in America* (New York: The Free Press, 1995), which promises to establish manhood-proving as an independent force in American history.
4. Gordon Liddy, *Will* (New York: St. Martin's Press, 1980), 24.
5. The issue of how work, indeed the Weberian rationalization of modern society, is informed and motivated by manhood-proving motivations is one that awaits demystification. For instance, will the massive entry of women into medical school alter the masochistic structure of medical training? The degree to which training for the professions is modeled on military training no doubt relates to the general militarization of society. The moral logic of the warrior still can be found throughout the world of work. Christine L. Williams has produced two thoughtful empirical studies about work and gender: *Still a Man's World: Men Who Do "Women's" Work* (Berkeley: University of California Press, 1995), and *Gender Differences at Work: Women and Men in Nontraditional Occupations* (Berkeley: University of California Press, 1989).
6. The likelihood that one will have to go to war some day is no doubt a major, underdiscussed factor among the objective social forces constructing masculinity and sexism. If a sense that someday they will have to fight and kill is drilled into men, if they have to be willing to risk death, to die as part of their gendered identity, then childhood becomes war preparedness and women become objects of protection and thus inferior.
7. See Glenn Gray, *The Warriors* (New York: Harper and Row, 1967).
8. This is as good a place as any to suggest a possible relation between compulsive masculinity and creativity. To wit, I am intrigued by a parallel between creating and conquering stress as a means of proving manhood, and creating and conquering stress as a part of the creative process in art. Sometimes in the creative process, an internalized dare is produced as one writes the first line of a poem (or puts the first daub of paint on canvas), and prepares for the second. Does compulsive masculinity

make such creative processes more psychically congenial to boys and men? There is considerable evidence that boys are more risk-taking in their cognitive styles than girls. And if creating and conquering distress separates men from mothers, does the same process in art gratify a need in men to emulate mothers by giving birth to something new? I owe this last observation to Jim Stockinger.

9. See Jeffrey Fracher and Michael Kimmel, "Hard Issues and Soft Spots: Counseling Men About Sexuality," in *Men's Lives,* eds. Michael Kimmel and Mike Messner (New York: Macmillan Publishing, 1989).

10. This summary is adopted from Harry Christian's useful *The Making of Anti-sexist Men* (London: Routledge and Kegan Paul, 1994), 10–11.

READING 27

"I'm Not a Feminist, But . . .": Popular Myths about Feminism

Penny A. Weiss

. . . As an undergraduate at the University of South Florida, I had to meet with my political science professor, who was, somewhat surprisingly for 1974, a woman. In the course of conversation, and for reasons now unknown to me, she asked whether I was a feminist. There I was, a first-generation college student, sitting in a small office with "A Professor." This was neither a familiar nor a particularly comfortable experience for me. What was I supposed to say? I fell back on the safest, most familiar response I could conjure up on the spur of the moment: "Well, I'm not a feminist, but I believe in equal pay."

In 1974, as I rattled off to my professor the things I believed in even though I was *not* a feminist, she said, "Oh, well, if you believe in that, then you *are* a feminist!" Hmmm, I thought, give me some time to think that over.

Since that time I have heard many say "I'm not a feminist, but . . . " with various endings to the sentence: "I'm not a feminist, but I believe in equal rights"; "I'm not a feminist, but I wouldn't tell my

Penny A. Weiss is a professor of political science and director of women's studies at St. Louis University.

wife she had to stay home and take care of the kids"; "I'm not a feminist, but I think women and men ought to be whatever they want to be"; "I'm not a feminist, but I don't think violence against women is right." Like my professor, I sometimes say, "Oh, well, if you think that, then you *are* a feminist." And I get back the same skeptical looks I'm quite certain I gave her.

After more than two decades of engagement in feminist politics, teaching, writing, speaking, and living, I find myself concerned to understand that reluctance and discomfort so many feel with saying, "Yes, I'm a feminist." After all, it seems unlikely that any significant percentage of those women . . . would say, "I don't eat meat, but I'm not a vegetarian," or "I'm not a Democrat, but I believe in the Democratic Party platform." What is at stake, then, in rejecting or adopting the label "feminist"?

One semester I asked my undergraduate "Women and the Law" class to help me out. On the first day of class this nonrandom sample[1] of Purdue students broke into small groups and came up with separate lists of the reasons people say, "I'm not a feminist, but . . ." My class divided themselves into fourteen groups of from two to five people. They wrote down what they came up with and turned the lists in anonymously. Grouping their responses, I found the following:

- Nine groups cited the fact that feminists are perceived as radical, which means, according to their notes, too radical, against tradition, too liberal, wanting to change everything, wanting too much.
- Seven groups cited concern with social rejection: society does not condone outspoken women; feminists will be outcasts in a male-dominated society; they will be rejected by men and/or society; they will offend, will end up arguing, will lose men's respect, will be perceived as pushy bitches, and might lose their jobs.
- Seven groups raised issues around sexuality, noting that feminists are identified as lesbians. One group, using *gay* rather than *lesbian,* perhaps acknowledged the possibility that men might be feminists, too, and those men too would be perceived as homosexual.

- Seven groups associated the reluctance to call ourselves feminists with social norms of masculinity and femininity, five saying feminists are unfeminine or downright masculine, two additional groups noting that feminist men were perceived as feminine or wimps.
- Four mentioned that feminists are seen as anti-male, man hating, or wanting to be dominant over men.
- Finally, four cited varied issues of style: feminists are associated, again according to their notes, with being outspoken, aggressive, macho, pushy, one-sided, narrow-minded, hard-line, cold, and harsh.

To what extent are the popular perceptions of feminism, as described by my students, accurate representations of feminist theory and practice? Why do certain myths and misconceptions exist—that is, how do they arise, and what functions do they serve?

The first noteworthy aspect of my students' responses was the degree of overlap in their lists. Without question, popular images of feminism and of feminists surround us. I think no one has managed to avoid them. A different semester I asked students to tell me what a feminist was like, and, to my surprise, they were able to come up with not only ideas about her political views but also stereotypes about everything from the shoes she wore and the haircut she sported to the food she ate, the pets she owned, and the books she read (vegetarian, cats, Alice Walker . . .)! The popular image is not only pervasive but also fairly detailed.

Most important, the popular image is largely a negative one, at least as judged by current social standards. Just how negatively and how costly feminism is seen to be is revealed by the number citing social rejection as part of their reluctance to endorse feminism. When are people most afraid of rejection? Perhaps it is when we care deeply about being accepted or when the consequences of rejection are dire. It is important to be clear here about who finds feminism unacceptable. What was most often mentioned by my students was that power structures, such as those in the world of paid labor, and people with power, namely men, would reject feminist women. Much of what is called fear of feminism is in fact fear of men, of what men might do or not do to women who somehow don't comply. The widespread existence of this fear is indicative of women's more vulnerable social and economic status, their dependence on males and male approval. This fear is all too real. The problem, however, is not the horror or the unacceptability of feminism itself but the horrible power of the status quo to punish what it deems unacceptable so that it may maintain itself. It is not so much that a woman thinks it horrible to challenge a boss who sexually harasses her, or to protest government cuts in Aid to Families with Dependent Children (AFDC), or to leave a husband who abuses her, or to question the ethos of domination that continually brings us to the brink of war. No, it is not feminism itself that is being called unacceptable. What is unacceptable, what is horrible, is that if she challenges her boss for sexual harassment, she will be fired, or be called delusional, or be told she asked for it, or be ostracized by her coworkers; if she protests the poverty of female-headed households, she will be treated as embodying or endorsing laziness and promiscuity; if she leaves her abusive husband, she'll be asked what she did to provoke him, or he will successfully pursue her and the police will say they cannot do anything; and if she challenges the military mentality, she will be called unpatriotic.

Feminism is unaccepted by too many with too much power, making feminists unacceptable and the costs of feminist identification and living real. That message has been heard, loud and clear. Much less visible to too many with both too much and too little power are the costs of antifeminism: rape, domestic violence, self-hatred, poverty, and lost potential, to name but a few. Equally as indistinct are the rewards of feminism. But how incredibly, wonderfully, powerfully real these gain are: relations of friendship between equals, true partnerships with our lovers, the restoration of our confidence in our own power, the reclaiming of our self-worth, the rejection of violence and exclusivity, and the integrity of the constant challenges presented by forsaking destructive sexist patterns. So, yes, there is some truth in the popular understanding that feminism is unacceptable, but a misperception persists that it is the tenets and practices of feminism itself that make it so, rather than those self-protective self-interested behaviors and structures of the status quo that reward conformity and punish resisters. Opportunities to evaluate and explore feminism openly are too few, so quickly and deeply has it been cast in a negative light by many well-respected individuals and institutions. Yet when we allow their judgment to become ours and shun identification with feminism, we leave the myths intact; we accept as valid the cat's version of the trouble-making mouse.

Antifeminism has had a larger part than has feminism in shaping popular perceptions of feminism. Judging by my students' comments, one of the most successful antifeminist themes has been that feminism is radical. The fact that feminism is understood as radical may be an unspoken acknowledgment that antifeminism is, very much, the status quo. If feminism wants to change antifeminism, and if feminism wants, as my students said, to change everything, then antifeminism must be pervasive. This acknowledgment is reminiscent of a court case in which a woman was being tried for the death of her extremely abusive husband. The judge said he was not going to give women licenses to kill their husbands. His fear was that if one woman got away with this, women everywhere would start killing their husbands. At some level he understood that huge numbers of women are being battered in their homes and that the criminal justice system is useless or counterproductive to them, which is why the prospect of battered women defending themselves so alarmed him.[2] The extent to which feminism seems and is radical is relative to the extent to which the norm is antifeminist. Or, as Pat Mainardi puts it in an article on sharing housework, "The measure of your oppression is his resistance."[3]

Calling something radical is often an indirect way of writing something off or challenging its legitimacy. Whether the group being labeled is war protesters, civil rights activists, animal rights advocates, union organizers, or feminists, calling them radical is a way of saying, "I don't have to think about what they're saying, do I? I don't have to change the way *I'm* doing things, do I? After all, they're so radical." This sort of dismissal through name-calling might reveal that the ideas being called radical are hitting something too close to home or something a little scary; something in which we have a vested interest, or something we have already declared decided. We thus desire to brush off this radical challenge as we do any intrusive or dangerous pest.

Etymologically, *radical* means "to the root." Feminist analysis that goes to the deep structural roots of gender identity and oppression inevitably forces us to rethink our ideas, restructure our institutions, review our daily practices, reconceive our relationships, reevaluate our mores, and revise our ideals. Systemic oppression based on sex, race, class, nationality, and sexuality will survive any less radical efforts. That is why we would rather brush feminism off as radical. It both seems like and is a lot of work. Furthermore, in our current framework of values, radical feminism is asking us to work for things we've been taught to understand as relatively unimportant. You know, feminists always make mountains out of molehills. What's the big deal, after all, about rape, when our culture teaches that women enjoy it? Why should we change the way we speak of women as objects when our culture teaches us to see this as flattery? Why should we care about job discrimination when our culture teaches us that women would really rather not be employed for pay anyway? Consequently, before we can convince people to change those things that contribute to the creation of dominant males and subordinant females, we first have to make the subordination of women something problematic. The highest authorities in every field have declared that women like their subordination: it's woman's nature; it's for their own good; it's all that can be expected; it's not really so bad. It is only against such a background and in such a context that feminism looks, and indeed is, radical. How radical feminism is stands as a measure of how patriarchal a society we confront. Feminism seems radical because, looking at the same event, feminists see subordination, injustice, and serious offense, while others will only reluctantly, if at all, see a misdemeanor of little consequence.

From another angle, there is nothing very radical about feminism. It is an expression of the time-honored, self-evident truth that we are all created equal (even if the authors of the Declaration of Independence forgot to use gender-inclusive language, the Constitution forgot to include women and minority men as full citizens, and it wasn't until 1971 that the Supreme Court first struck down a sex-based law as unconstitutional). Feminists want women and men to be treated with equal respect; to be given equal opportunity to express their potential and to be appreciated for their contribution; to have choices about the families they create, the jobs they hold, and the partnerships they form; and to have personal, social, economic, and political resources at work to eliminate exploitation, discrimination, oppression, abuse, and violence. This long and still incomplete list presents a very full conception of equality, a very inclusive and enabling conception. Not so easy to attain, perhaps, but clearly a worthy and admirable goal. Why, then, the ridicule of feminism, the titters about "those bra-burning libbers"?

To understand that we can look again at my students' responses. Seven groups cited issues of sexuality, and, related, seven mentioned norms of masculinity and femininity. I think we titter when we're nervous. And I think the reason we titter about feminism is because we're nervous about crossing those sacred boundaries that separate men from women everywhere but the private bedroom (where there is nervousness about the sexes *being* separated). Norms of masculinity, femininity, and heterosexuality are among the most powerful in our culture. Calling a man effeminate or a woman masculine or mannish is a serious accusation meant to provoke negative, disapproving, wary response. . . .

It is true that feminism challenges the sacred boundaries here, violating the clearly and pervasively

disseminated social requirement that there be two distinct, sharply polarized, and hierarchically arranged sexes. The male feminist wimp (among others), as my students noted, is someone who fails to fulfill this requirement in his life or in his politics. A wimp is a man who betrays men by refusing to be a bully to women. He's "henpecked," the only alternative to the exertion of masculine privilege our culture can manage to imagine. When they refuse to exert power over women, we call men wimps; we call them what is a dirty name in our society; we nab them for the crime of refusing to be real men. Real men dominate women. To be a man is to dominate women. And to be a real woman is to accept that domination, in at least some arenas on some levels, to live every day in quiet subjugation to men on the streets who harass us for their entertainment, to men on the job who underpay us for their profit, and to men at home who take advantage of us because it's become second nature. Systems of oppression justify this abuse, and those on top try to buy others off with worthless compensations in an attempt to mask and perpetuate the systemic privileges that work against us.

Maintaining the boundaries of masculinity and femininity, and of heterosexuality, are central tasks of education and public policy, of advertising and pornography, of fashion and storybooks. We are witnesses to the channeling of our economic, social, political, and psychic resources into maintaining male privilege. These boundaries define the sexes as different and men as better, making it absolutely essential to cross them and tear them down. In doing so we reject defining all human beings in terms, of their sex and all human relationships in terms of power. The power relationship between women and men obligates the members of one sex to harass, abuse, exploit, ignore, or ridicule the members of the other sex, who must acquiesce or at least limit their complaints to forms that are "appropriate" and therefore ultimately ineffective. It is made incumbent upon us to prove our manhood and womanhood repeatedly throughout our lives—every time we dress ourselves, get a flat tire, initiate a conversation, eat, or play games. In these and other situations, men prove their manhood by being taller, smarter, tougher, more competent, richer, cooler, more athletic, or more powerful than women, who prove their womanhood through subservience, nurturing, acquiescence, understanding, accommodation, incompetence, and weakness. To be a proper female, to be feminine, is to be disempowered.

And to be a female, to be feminine, is certainly also to be heterosexual, because to be a lesbian is to reject men and male rule, to question the myth that women need men, and to exist as a dangerous example, a challenge to patriarchy by being a woman yet *not* being subservient to a man, by refusing men access.[4]

When people say of feminists, "Oh, they're just a bunch of dykes," they are engaged in another variety of attempt at dismissal. The speaker of these words intends to write off all the claims of feminists by feeding on people's fears and prejudices about homosexuality. They hope to send shivers of horror up the spines of women who might be feminists, who might challenge the status quo, by warning them of the cost—the stigmatization that will follow. They hope, and often succeed, in scaring women into taking less radical stands and in making all alliances between women and for women's interests inherently suspect. Because the lesbian label is a powerful weapon wielded against feminists, challenging the norm of heterosexuality is a project critical to feminism. Our most popular model of sexuality demands male control over women, thus using sexuality to help keep women in their second-class seats.

When we hesitate to identify as feminists because we fear breaking sex-specific rules about what is masculine and feminine, about what is fitting for women and what is fitting for men, what we are leaving intact are those rules that actually create us as dominant males and subjugated females. And, yes, challenging the division of practically everything in the world—from colors and toys to names and professions—into masculine and feminine is frightening, because we are

challenging something very fundamental to our social system: its organization within and on a framework of sexual differentiation and inequality.

My students are right in another sense, this is to say, about the radicalness of feminism. Many feminists argue that sexual inequality affects much more than relations between the sexes: it bolsters, borrows from, provides a model for, and trains folks in other forms of domination, competition, and selfishness. Our ideology justifies or explains away wife abuse and, similarly, the abuse of natural resources. The system that denies the need for mandatory paid parental leave policies is well trained to ignore the needs of the homeless. The system that can make rape women's fault can make affirmative action reverse discrimination. A system of sexual differentiation that forces us to think of women and men as us and them prepares us well to create numerous divisions and hierarchies around the globe. . . .

By patriarchy's self-(pre)serving definitions of what is hateful and monstrous, feminists are indeed monsters: macho, pushy, narrow-minded man haters. Our feelings toward men, individually or as a group, positive or negative, have precious little to do with why we are portrayed as antimale. We live in a culture in which to be female and to do other than be subservient to men is said to be man hating. When women do something with their energy and their lives besides serve men, padding male egos and their paychecks, putting up with their remarks and their demands, then women are called man hating. When women stand up for themselves and demand a certain level of treatment, they are called man-hating. When a woman refuses to submit, she is said not to love men. Looking carefully at the actions and the attitudes that are labeled man hating shows that they have very little to do with hating men and a great deal to do with challenging male rule over and access to women. Only when to be loving is defined as to be self-sacrificing, long-suffering, uncomplaining, and acquiescent to men is feminism antimale. But it is not man hating to have strengths of one's own, ideas of one's own, work of one's own, and love for oneself. It is a lie that the only way to love men, or anyone, is to serve them, as a master, a god, a superior. It is a lie that we *should* love those who demand such tyrannical terms. How far man hating is from what we are about, and how little it captures of feminism, of the injustice of the status quo, of the imagination and passion of its resisters. . . .

DISCUSSION QUESTIONS

1. Weiss's article was written in 1998. Do you think women are still reluctant to call themselves feminists?

2. Is the image of feminists still the same as Weiss describes?

3. How do you explain the constancy or change you see in the meaning that the term *feminist* has for women and men?

NOTES

1. The sample might be thought to be more "liberal" than most given that it is composed of a majority of young, college-educated women. It might also be thought of as more "conservative" than other groups, since most of the class was white, midwestern, and middle-class. The lack of a random sample means what follows should not be seen as an exhaustive list of answers. But that the answers included are common is, I think, unquestionable. Also see Barbara Smith, "Some Home Truths on the Contemporary Black Feminist Movement," *The Black Scholar* (April 1995): 4–13. Smith discusses some of the same myths, some different ones.

2. Sharon Wyse, "She's Battered; Judged Guilty," *New Directions for Women* 17 (July/August 1988), 1.

3. Pat Mainardi, "The Politics of Housework," in *Sisterhood Is Powerful,* ed. Robin Morgan (New York: Vintage Books, 1970), 447–54.

4. See Marilyn Frye, "Some Reflections on Separatism and Power," in *The Politics of Reality: Essays in Feminist Theory* (Trumansburg, N.Y.: Crossing, 1983), 95–109.

SEXUALITY

READING 28

Dude, You're a Fag: Adolescent Male Homophobia

C. J. Pascoe

The sun shone bright and clear over River High's annual Creative and Performing Arts Happening, or CAPA. During CAPA the school's various art programs displayed students' work in a fairlike atmosphere. The front quad sported student-generated computer programs. Colorful and ornate chalk art covered the cement sidewalks. Tables lined with

C. J. Pascoe is a professor of sociology at the University of Oregon.

student-crafted pottery were set up on the grass. Tall displays of students' paintings divided the rear quad. To the left of the paintings a television blared student-directed music videos. At the rear of the back quad, a square, roped-off area of cement served as a makeshift stage for drama, choir, and dance performances. Teachers released students from class to wander around the quads, watch performances, and look at the art. This freedom from class time lent the day an air of excitement because students were rarely allowed to roam the campus without a hall pass, an office summons, or a parent/faculty escort. In honor of CAPA, the school district bussed in elementary school students from the surrounding grammar schools to participate in the day's festivities.

Running through the rear quad, Brian, a senior, yelled to a group of boys visiting from the elementary schools, "There's a faggot over there! There's a faggot over there! Come look!" Following Brian, the ten-year-olds dashed down a hallway. At the end of the hallway Brian's friend Dan pursed his lips and began sashaying toward the little boys. As he minced, he swung his hips exaggeratedly and wildly waved his arms. To the boys Brian yelled, "Look at the faggot! Watch out! He'll get you!" In response, the ten-year-olds raced back down the hallway screaming in terror. Brian and Dan repeated this drama throughout the following half hour, each time with a new group of young boys.

Making jokes like these about faggots was central to social life at River High. Indeed, boys learned long before adolescence that faggots were simultaneously predatory and passive and that they were, at all costs, to be avoided. Older boys repeatedly impressed upon younger ones through these types of homophobic rituals that whatever they did, whatever they became, however they talked, they had to avoid becoming a faggot.

Feminist scholars of masculinity have documented the centrality of homophobic insults and attitudes to masculinity (Kimmel 2001; Lehne 1998), especially in school settings (Burn 2000; Kimmel 2003; Messner 2005; Plummer 2001; G. Smith 1998; Wood 1984). They argue that homophobic teasing often characterizes masculinity in adolescence and early adulthood and that antigay slurs tend to be directed primarily at gay boys. This [discussion] both expands on and challenges these accounts of relationships between homophobia and masculinity. Homophobia is indeed a central mechanism in the making of contemporary American adolescent masculinity. A close analysis of the way boys at River High invoke the faggot as a disciplinary mechanism makes clear that something more than simple homophobia is at play in adolescent masculinity. The use of the word *fag* by boys at River High points to the limits of an argument that focuses centrally on homophobia. Fag is not only an identity linked to homosexual boys but an identity that can temporarily adhere to heterosexual boys as well. The fag trope is also a racialized disciplinary mechanism.

Homophobia is too facile a term with which to describe the deployment of *fag* as an epithet. By calling the use of the word *fag* homophobia—and letting the argument stop there—previous research has obscured the gendered nature of sexualized insults (Plummer 2001). Invoking homophobia to describe the ways boys aggressively tease each other overlooks the powerful relationship between masculinity and this sort of insult. Instead, it seems incidental, in this conventional line of argument, that girls do not harass each other and are not harassed in this same manner. This framing naturalizes the relationship between masculinity and homophobia, thus obscuring that such harassment is central to the formation of a gendered identity for boys in a way that it is not for girls.

Fag is not necessarily a static identity attached to a particular (homosexual) boy. Fag talk and fag imitations serve as a discourse with which boys discipline themselves and each other through joking relationships. Any boy can temporarily become a fag in a given social space or interaction. This does not mean that boys who identify as or are perceived to be homosexual aren't subject to intense harassment. Many are. But becoming a fag has as much to do with failing at the masculine tasks of competence, heterosexual prowess, and strength or in any way revealing weakness or femininity as it does with a sexual identity. This fluidity of the fag identity is what makes the specter of the fag such a powerful disciplinary mechanism. It is fluid enough that boys police their behaviors out of fear of having the fag identity permanently adhere and definitive enough so that boys recognize a fag behavior and strive to avoid it.

An analysis of the fag discourse also indicates ways in which gendered power works through racialized selves. The fag discourse is invoked differently by and in relation to white boys' bodies than it is by and in relation to African American boys' bodies. While certain behaviors put all boys at risk for becoming temporarily a fag, some behaviors can be enacted by African American boys without putting them at risk of receiving the label. The racialized meanings of the fag discourse suggest that something more than simple homophobia is involved in these sorts of interactions. It is not that gendered homophobia does not exist in African American communities. Indeed, making fun of "negro faggotry seems to be a rite of passage among contemporary black male rappers and filmmakers" (Riggs 1991, 253). However, the fact that "white women and men, gay and straight, have more or less colonized cultural debates about sexual representation" (Julien and Mercer 1991, 167) obscures varied systems of sexualized meanings among different racialized ethnic groups (Almaguer 1991). Thus far male homophobia has primarily been written about as a racially neutral phenomenon. However, as D. L. King's (2004) recent work on African American men and same-sex desire pointed out, homophobia is characterized by racial identities as well as sexual and gendered ones.

WHAT IS A FAG? GENDERED MEANINGS

"Since you were little boys you've been told, 'Hey, don't be a little faggot,'" explained Darnell, a football player of mixed African American and white heritage, as we sat on a bench next to the athletic field. Indeed, both the boys and girls I interviewed told me that *fag* was the worst epithet one guy could direct at another. Jeff, a slight white sophomore, explained to me that boys call each other fag because "gay people aren't really liked over here and stuff." Jeremy, a Latino junior, told me that this insult literally reduced a boy to nothing, "To call someone *gay* or *fag* is like the lowest thing you can call someone. Because that's like saying that you're nothing."

Most guys explained their or others' dislike of fags by claiming that homophobia was synonymous with being a guy. For instance, Keith, a white soccer-playing senior, explained, "I think guys are just homophobic." However, boys were not equal-opportunity homophobes. Several students told me that these homophobic insults applied only to boys and not to girls. For example, while Jake, a handsome white senior, told me that he didn't like gay people, he quickly added, "Lesbians, okay, that's *good.*" Similarly Cathy, a popular white cheerleader, told me, "Being a lesbian is accepted because guys think, 'Oh that's cool.' " Darnell, after telling me that boys were warned about becoming faggots, said, "They [guys] are fine with girls. I think it's the

guy part that they're like ewwww." In this sense it was not strictly homophobia but a gendered homophobia that constituted adolescent masculinity in the culture of River High. It is clear, according to these comments, that lesbians were "good" because of their place in heterosexual male fantasy, not necessarily because of some enlightened approach to same-sex relationships. A popular trope in heterosexual pornography depicts two women engaging in sexual acts for the purpose of male titillation. The boys at River High are not unique in making this distinction; adolescent boys in general dislike gay men more than they dislike lesbians (Baker and Fishbein 1998). The fetishizing of sex acts between women indicates that using only the term *homophobia* to describe boys' repeated use of the word *fag* might be a bit simplistic and misleading.

Girls at River High rarely deployed the word *fag* and were never called fags. I recorded girls uttering *fag* only three times during my research. In one instance, Angela, a Latina cheerleader, teased Jeremy, a well-liked white senior involved in student government, for not ditching school with her: "You wouldn't 'cause you're a faggot." However, girls did not use this word as part of their regular lexicon. The sort of gendered homophobia that constituted adolescent masculinity did not constitute adolescent femininity. Girls were not called dykes or lesbians in any sort of regular or systematic way. Students did tell me that *slut* was the worst thing a girl could be called. However, my field notes indicate that the word *slut* (or its synonym *ho*) appeared one time for every eight times the word *fag* appeared.

Highlighting the difference between the deployment of *gay* and *fag* as insults brings the gendered nature of this homophobia into focus. For boys and girls at River High *gay* was a fairly common synonym for "stupid." While this word shared the sexual origins of *fag,* it didn't *consistently* have the skew of gender-loaded meaning. Girls and boys often used *gay* as an adjective referring to inanimate objects and male or female people, whereas they used *fag* as a noun that denoted only unmasculine males. Students used *gay* to describe anything from someone's clothes to a new school rule that they didn't like. For instance, one day in auto shop, Arnie pulled out a large older version of a black laptop computer and placed it on his desk. Behind him Nick cried, "That's a gay laptop! It's five inches thick!" The rest of the boys in the class laughed at Arnie's outdated laptop. A laptop can be gay, a movie can be gay, or a group of people can be gay. Boys used *gay* and *fag* interchangeably when they referred to other boys, but *fag* didn't have the gender-neutral attributes that *gay* frequently invoked.

Surprisingly, some boys took pains to say that the term *fag* did not imply sexuality. Darnell told me, "It doesn't even have anything to do with being gay." Similarly, J. L., a white sophomore at Hillside High (River High's cross-town rival), asserted, "*Fag*, seriously, it has nothing to do with sexual preference at all. You could just be calling somebody an idiot, you know?" I asked Ben, a quiet, white sophomore who wore heavy-metal T-shirts to auto shop each day, "What kind of things do guys get called a fag for?" Ben answered, "Anything . . . literally, anything. Like you were trying to turn a wrench the wrong way, 'Dude, you're a fag.' Even if a piece of meat drops out of your sandwich, 'You fag!'" Each time Ben said, "You fag," his voice deepened as if he were imitating a more masculine boy. While Ben might rightly *feel* that a guy could be called a fag for "anything . . . literally, anything," there were actually specific behaviors that, when enacted by most boys, could render them more vulnerable to a *fag* epithet. In this instance Ben's comment highlights the use of *fag* as a generic insult for incompetence, which in the world of River High, was central to a masculine identity. A boy could get called a fag for exhibiting any sort of behavior defined as unmasculine (although not necessarily behaviors aligned with femininity): being stupid or incompetent, dancing, caring too much about clothing, being too emotional, or expressing interest (sexual or platonic) in other guys. However, given the extent of its deployment and the laundry list of behaviors that could get a boy in trouble, it is no wonder that Ben felt a boy could be called fag for "anything." These

nonsexual meanings didn't replace sexual meanings but rather existed alongside them.

One-third (thirteen) of the boys I interviewed told me that, while they might liberally insult each other with the term, they would not direct it at a homosexual peer. Jabes, a Filipino senior, told me, "I actually say it [*fag*] quite a lot, except for when I'm in the company of an actual homosexual person. Then I try not to say it at all. But when I'm just hanging out with my friends I'll be like, 'shut up, I don't want to hear you any more, you stupid fag.'" Similarly J. L. compared homosexuality to a disability, saying there was "no way" he'd call an actually gay guy a fag because "there's people who are the retarded people who nobody wants to associate with. I'll be so nice to those guys, and I hate it when people make fun of them. It's like, 'Bro do you realize that they can't help that?' And then there's gay people. They were born that way." According to this group of boys, gay was a legitimate, or at least biological, identity.

There was a possibility, however slight, that a boy could be gay and masculine (Connell 1995). David, a handsome white senior dressed smartly in khaki pants and a white button-down shirt, told me, "Being gay is just a lifestyle. It's someone you choose to sleep with. You can still throw around a football and be gay." It was as if David was justifying the use of the word *fag* by arguing that gay men could be men if they tried but that if they failed at it (i.e., if they couldn't throw a football) then they deserved to be called a fag. In other words, to be a fag was, by definition, the opposite of masculine, whether the word was deployed with sexualized or nonsexualized meanings. In explaining this to me, Jamaal, an African American junior, cited the explanation of the popular rap artist Eminem: "Although I don't like Eminem, he had a good definition of it. It's like taking away your title. In an interview they were like, 'You're always capping on gays, but then you sing with Elton John.' He was like 'I don't mean gay as in gay.'" This is what Riki Wilchins (2003) calls the "Eminem Exception. Eminem explains that he doesn't call people 'faggot' because of their sexual orientation but because they're weak and unmanly" (72). This is precisely the way boys at River High used the term *faggot*. While it was not necessarily acceptable to be gay, at least a man who was gay could do other things that would render him acceptably masculine. A fag, by the very definition of the word, could not be masculine.

This distinction between fag as an unmasculine and problematic identity and gay as a possibly masculine, although marginalized, sexual identity is not limited to a teenage lexicon; it is reflected in both psychological discourses and gay and lesbian activism. Eve Sedgwick (1995) argues that in contemporary psychological literature homosexuality is no longer a problem for men so long as the homosexual man is of the right age and gender orientation. In this literature a homosexual male must be an adult and must be masculine. Male homosexuality is not pathologized, but gay male *effeminacy* is. The lack of masculinity is the problem, not the sexual practice or orientation. Indeed, the edition of the *Diagnostic and Statistical Manual of Mental Disorders* (a key document in the mental health field) that erased homosexuality as a diagnosis in the 1970s added a new diagnosis in its wake: Gender Identity Disorder. According to Sedgwick, the criteria for diagnosis are different for girls and boys. A girl has to actually assert that she is a boy, indicating a psychotic disconnection with reality, whereas a boy need only display a preoccupation with female activities. The policing of boys' gender orientation and of a strict masculine identity for gay men is also reflected in gay culture itself. The war against fags as the specter of unmasculine manhood appears in gay male personal ads in which men look for "straight-appearing, straight-acting men." This concern with both straight and gay men's masculinity not only reflects teenage boys' obsession with hypermasculinity but also points to the conflict at the heart of the contemporary "crisis of masculinity" being played out in popular, scientific, and educational arenas.

BECOMING A FAG: FAG FLUIDITY

"The ubiquity of the word *faggot* speaks to the reach of its discrediting capacity" (Corbett 2001, 4). It's almost as if boys cannot help shouting it out on a regular basis—in the hallway, in class, or across campus as a greeting. In my fieldwork I was amazed by the way the word seemed to pop uncontrollably out of boys' mouths in all kinds of situations.[1] To quote just one of many instances from my field notes: two boys walked out of the PE locker room, and one yelled, "Fucking faggot!" at no one in particular. None of the other students paid them any mind, since this sort of thing happened so frequently. Similar spontaneous yelling of some variation of the word *fag,* seemingly apropos of nothing, happened repeatedly among boys throughout the school. This and repeated imitations of fags constitute what I refer to as a "fag discourse."

Fag discourse is central to boys' joking relationships. Joking cements relationships among boys (Kehily and Nayak 1997; Lyman 1998) and helps to manage anxiety and discomfort (Freud 1905). Boys both connect with one another and manage the anxiety around this sort of relationship through joking about fags. Boys invoked the specter of the fag in two ways: through humorous imitation and through lobbing the epithet at one another. Boys at River High imitated the fag by acting out an exaggerated "femininity" and/or by pretending to sexually desire other boys. As indicated by the introductory vignette in which an older boy imitated a predatory fag to threaten little boys, male students at River High linked these performative scenarios with a fag identity. They also lobbed the *fag* epithet at each other in a verbal game of hot potato, each careful to deflect the insult quickly by hurling it toward someone else. These games and imitations made up a fag discourse that highlighted the fag not as a static but rather as a fluid identity that boys constantly struggled to avoid.

In imitative performances the fag discourse functioned as a constant reiteration of the fag's existence, affirming that the fag was out there; boys reminded themselves and each other that at any moment they could become fags if they were not sufficiently masculine. At the same time these performances demonstrated that the boy who was invoking the fag was *not* a fag. Emir, a tall, thin African American boy, frequently imitated fags to draw laughs from other students in his introductory drama class. One day Mr. McNally, the drama teacher, disturbed by the noise outside the classroom, turned to the open door, saying, "We'll shut this unless anyone really wants to watch sweaty boys playing basketball." Emir lisped, "I wanna watch the boys play!" The rest of the class cracked up at his imitation. No one in the class actually thought Emir was gay, as he purposefully mocked both same-sex sexual desire (through pretending to admire the boys playing basketball) and an effeminate gender identity (through speaking with a lisp and in a high-pitched voice). Had he said this in all seriousness, the class most likely would have responded in stunned silence. Instead, Emir reminded them he was masculine by immediately dropping the fag act. After imitating a fag, boys assure others that they are not a fag by instantly becoming masculine again after the performance. They mock their own performed femininity and/or same-sex desire, assuring themselves and others that such an identity deserves derisive laughter. . . .

The constant threat of the fag regulated boys' attitudes toward their bodies in terms of clothing, dancing, and touching. Boys constantly engaged in repudiatory rituals to avoid permanently inhabiting the fag position. Boys' interactions were composed of competitive joking through which they interactionally created the constitutive outside and affirmed their positions as subjects.

EMBODYING THE FAG: RICKY'S STORY

Through verbal jockeying, most boys at River continually moved in and out of the fag position. For the one boy who permanently inhabited the fag position, life at River High was not easy. I heard about Ricky long before I met him. As soon as I talked to any student involved with drama, the choir, or the Gay/Straight Alliance, they told me I had to meet Ricky. Ricky, a lithe, white junior with a shy smile and downcast eyes, frequently sported multicolored hair extensions, mascara, and sometimes a skirt. An

extremely talented dancer, he often starred in the school's dance shows and choreographed assemblies. In fact, he was the male lead in "I've Had the Time of My Life," the final number in the dance show. Given how important other students thought it was that I speak to him, I was surprised that I had to wait for nearly a year before he granted me an interview. His friends had warned me that he was "heterophobic" and as a result was reluctant to talk to authority figures he perceived were heterosexual. After I heard his stories of past and present abuse at the hands of negligent adults, cruel teenagers, and indifferent school administrators, I understood why he would be leery of folks asking questions about his feelings, experiences, and opinions. While other boys at River High engaged in continual repudiatory rituals around the fag identity, Ricky embodied the fag because of his homosexuality and his less normative gender identification and self-presentation.

Ricky assumed (rightly so in this context) that other people immediately identified him with his sexuality. He told me that when he first met people, "they'll be like, 'Can I ask you a personal question?' And I'm like, 'sure.' And they say, 'Are you gay?' And I'm like, 'Yeeeaahh.' 'Okay, can I ask you another question?' And I'm like, 'Sure.' And they'll go, 'Does it hurt?' It always goes . . ." He rolled his eyes dismissively, telling me, "They go straight up to the most personal question! They skip everything else. They go straight to that. Sometimes I'll get the occasional 'Well, how did you know that you were [gay]?'" He answered with "For me it's just always been there. I knew from the time I could think for myself on. It was pretty obvious," he concluded gesturing to his thin frame and tight fitting tank top with a flourish. . . .

. . . Figuring out the social map of the school was central to Ricky's survival. Homophobic harassment at the hands of teachers and students characterized his educational experience. When he was beat up in a middle school PE class, the teacher didn't help but rather fostered this sort of treatment:

> They gave them a two-day suspension and they kind of kept an eye on me. That's all they could do. The PE

coach was very racist and very homophobic. He was just like "faggot this" and "faggot that." I did not feel comfortable in the locker room and I asked him if I could go somewhere else to change, and he said, "No, you can change here."

Sadly, by the time Ricky had reached River High he had become accustomed to the violence.

In a weird sense, in a weird way, I'm comfortable with it because it's just what I've known for as long as I can remember. I mean, in elementary school, I'm talking like sixth grade, I started being called a fag. Fifth grade I was called a fag. Third grade I was called a fag. I have the paperwork, 'cause my mom kept everything, I still have them, of kids harassing me, saying "Gaylord," at that time it was "Gaylord."

Contrary to the protestations of boys . . . that they would never call someone who was gay a fag, Ricky experienced this harassment on a regular basis, probably because he couldn't draw on identifiably masculine markers such as athletic ability or other forms of dominance to bolster some sort of claim on masculinity.

Hypermasculine environments such as sporting events continued to be venues of intense harassment at River High. "I've had water balloons thrown at me at a football game. Like, we [his friends Genevieve and Lacy] couldn't have stayed at the homecoming game. We had to go." The persecution began immediately at the biggest football game of the year. When he entered with his friend Lacy, "Two guys that started walking up to get tickets said, 'There's the fucking fag.' " When Ricky responded with "Excuse me?" the boy shot back, "Don't talk to me like you know me." The boy and his friends started to threaten Ricky. Ricky said, "He started getting into my face, and his friends started saying, 'Come on, man, come on, man' " as if they were about to hit Ricky. Ricky felt frustrated that "the ticket people are sitting there not doing a damn thing. This is right in front of them!" He found Ms. Chesney, the vice principal, after the boys finally left. While Ms. Chesney told him, "We'll take care of it," Ricky said he never heard about the incident again. Later at the game he and

Lacy had water bottles thrown at them by young boys yelling, "Oh look, it's a fag!" He said that this sentiment echoed as they tried to sit in the bleachers to watch the half-time show, which he had choreographed: "Left and right, 'What the fuck is that fag doing here?' 'That fag has no right to be here.' Blah blah blah. That's all I heard. I tried to ignore it. And after a while I couldn't take it and then we just went home." While many of the boys I interviewed said they would not actually harass a gay boy, that was not Ricky's experience. He was driven out of the event he had choreographed because of the intense homophobic harassment. . . .

Ricky developed different strategies to deal with the fag discourse, given that he was not just *a* fag but *the* fag. While other boys lobbed the epithet at one another with implied threats of violence (you are not a man and I am, so watch out), for Ricky that violence was more a reality than a threat. As a result, learning the unwritten rules of a particular school and mapping out its social and physical landscape was literally a matter of survival. He found River High to be one of the most homophobic schools he had attended: "It's the most violent school I think that I've seen so far. With all the schools the verbal part about, you know the slang, 'the fag,' the 'fuckin' freak,' 'fucking fag,' all that stuff is all the same. But this is the only school that throws water bottles, throws rocks, and throws food, ketchup, sandwiches, anything of that nature."[2]

While there is a law in California protecting students from discrimination based on sexual identity, when Ricky requested help from school authorities he was ignored, much as in his interaction with the vice principal at the homecoming game. Ricky responded to this sort of treatment with several evasion strategies. He walked with his eyes downcast to avoid meeting other guys' eyes, fearing that they would regard eye contact as a challenge or an invitation to a fight. Similarly he varied his route to and from school:

I had to change paths about three different times walking to school. The same people who drive the same route know, 'cause I guess they leave at the same time, *so* they're always checking something out. But I'm always prepared with a rock just in case. I have a rock in my hand so if anything happens I just chuck one back. I always walk with something like that.

Indeed, when I was driving him home from the interview that day, boys on the sidewalk glared at him and made comments I couldn't hear. He also, with the exception of the homecoming football game, avoided highly sexualized or masculinized school events where he might be subject to violence.[3]

RACIALIZING THE FAG

While all groups of boys, with the exception of the Mormon boys, used the word *fag* or fag imagery in their interactions, the fag discourse was not deployed consistently or identically across social groups at River High. Differences between white boys' and African American boys' meaning making, particularly around appearance and dancing, reveal ways the specter of the fag was racialized. The specter of the fag, these invocations reveal, was consistently white. Additionally, African American boys simply did not deploy it with the same frequency as white boys. For both groups of boys, the *fag* insult entailed meanings of emasculation, as evidenced by Darnell's earlier comment. However, African American boys were much more likely to tease one another for being white than for being a fag. Precisely because African American men are so hypersexualized in the United States, white men are, by default, feminized, so *white* was a stand-in for *fag* among many of the African American boys at River High. Two of the behaviors that put a white boy at risk for being labeled a fag didn't function in the same way for African American boys.

Perhaps because they are, by necessity, more invested in symbolic forms of power related to appearance (much like adolescent girls), a given African American boy's status is not lowered but enhanced by paying attention to clothing or dancing. Clean, oversized, carefully put-together clothing is central to a hip-hop identity for African American boys who identify with hip-hop culture.

Richard Majors (2001) calls this presentation of self a "cool pose" consisting of "unique, expressive and conspicuous styles of demeanor, speech, gesture, clothing, hairstyle, walk, stance and handshake," developed by African American men as a symbolic response to institutionalized racism (211). Pants are usually several sizes too big, hanging low on the hips, often revealing a pair of boxers beneath. Shirts and sweaters are similarly oversized, sometimes hanging down to a boy's knees. Tags are frequently left on baseball hats worn slightly askew and perched high on the head. Meticulously clean, unlaced athletic shoes with rolled-up socks under the tongue complete a typical hip-hop outfit. In fact, African American men can, without risking a fag identity, sport styles of self and interaction frequently associated with femininity for whites, such as wearing curlers (Kelley 2004). These symbols, at River High, constituted a "cool pose." . . .

Dancing was another arena that carried distinctly fag-associated meanings for white boys but masculine meanings for African American boys who participated in hip-hop culture. White boys often associated dancing with fags. However, dancing did not carry this sort of sexualized gender meaning for all boys at River High. For African American boys dancing demonstrates membership in a cultural community (Best 2000). At River, African American boys frequently danced together in single-sex groups, teaching each other the latest dance moves, showing off a particularly difficult move, or making each other laugh with humorous dance moves. In fact, while in drama class Liam and Jacob [who are white] hit each other and joked through the entire dancing exercise, Darnell and Maro [who are African American] seemed very comfortable touching one another. They stood close to one another, heel to toe, as they were supposed to. Their bodies touched, and they gently and gracefully moved the other's arms and head in a way that was tender, not at all like the flailing of the two white boys. . . .

None of this is to say that the sexuality of boys of color wasn't policed. In fact, because African American boys were regarded as so hypersexual, in the few instances I documented in which boys were punished for engaging in the fag discourse, African American boys were policed more stringently than white boys. It was as if when they engaged in the fag discourse the gendered insult took on actual combative overtones, unlike the harmless sparring associated with white boys' deployments. The intentionality attributed to African American boys in their sexual interactions with girls seemed to occur as well in their deployment of the fag discourse. One morning as I waited with the boys on the asphalt outside the weight room for Coach Ramirez to arrive, I chatted with Kevin and Darrell. The all-male, all-white wrestling team walked by, wearing gold and black singlets. Kevin, an African American sophomore, yelled out, "Why are you wearing those faggot outfits? Do you wear those tights with your balls hanging out?" The weight-lifting students stopped their fidgeting and turned to watch the scene unfold. The eight or so members of the wrestling team stopped at their SUV and turned to Kevin. A small redhead whipped around and yelled aggressively, "Who said that?!" Fingers from wrestling team members quickly pointed toward Kevin. Kevin, angrily jumping around, yelled back as he thrust his chest out, "Talk about jumping me, nigger?" He strutted over, advancing toward the small redhead. A large wrestler sporting a cowboy hat tried to block Kevin's approach. The redhead meanwhile began to jump up and down, as if warming up for a fight. Finally the boy in the cowboy hat pushed Kevin away from the team and they climbed in the truck, while Kevin strutted back to his classmates, muttering, "All they know how to do is pick somebody up. Talk about jumping me . . . weak-ass wrestling team. My little bro could wrestle better than any of those motherfuckers."

It would seem, based on the fag discourse scenarios I've described thus far, that this was, in a sense, a fairly routine deployment of the sexualized and gendered epithet. However, at no other time did I see this insult almost cause a fight. Members of the white wrestling team presumably took it so seriously that they reported the incident to school authorities. This in itself is stunning. Boys called

each other fag so frequently in everyday discussion that if it were always reported most boys in the school would be suspended or at least in detention on a regular basis. This was the only time I saw school authorities take action based on what they saw as a sexualized insult. As a result Mr. J. explained that somebody from the wrestling team told him that Kevin was "harassing" them. Mr. J. pulled Kevin out of weight-lifting class to discuss the incident. According to him, Kevin "kept mouthing off" and it wasn't the first time he had been in trouble, so they decided to expel him and send him to Hillside.

While Kevin apparently had multiple disciplinary problems and this interaction was part of a larger picture, it is important that this was the only time that I heard any boy (apart from Ricky) tattle on another boy for calling him gay or fag. Similarly it was the only time I saw punishment meted out by the administration. So it seems that . . . intentionality was more frequently attributed to African American boys. They weren't just engaging in the homophobic bantering to which teachers like Mr. Kellogg turned a blind eye or in which Mr. McNally participated. Rather, they were seen as engaging in actual struggles for dominance by attacking others. Because they were in a precarious economic and social position, the ramifications for African American boys for engaging in the fag discourse were more serious. Precisely because some of them were supposed to be attending, not River High, but the "bad" school, Chicago, in the neighboring school district, when they did encounter trouble their punishment was more severe.

REFRAMING HOMOPHOBIA

Homophobia is central to contemporary definitions of adolescent masculinity. Unpacking multilayered meanings that boys deploy through their uses of homophobic language and joking rituals makes clear that it is not just homophobia but a gendered and racialized homophobia. By attending to these meanings, I reframe the discussion as a fag discourse rather than simply labeling it as homophobia.

The fag is an "abject" (Butler 1993) position, a position outside masculinity that actually constitutes masculinity. Thus masculinity, in part, becomes the daily interactional work of repudiating the threatening specter of the fag. . . .

DISCUSSION QUESTIONS

1. What are the social uses and consequences of "fag discourse"?
2. Is that discourse racialized?

NOTES

1. In fact, two of my colleagues, both psychotherapists, suggested that the boys exhibited what we could think of as a sort of "Fag Tourette's Syndrome."
2. Though River was not a particularly violent school, it may have seemed like that to Ricky because sexuality-based harassment increases with grade level as gender differentiation becomes more intense. As youth move from childhood into adolescence there is less flexibility in terms of gender identity and self-presentation (Shakib 2003).
3. There were two other gay boys at the school. One, Corey, I learned about after a year of fieldwork. While he wasn't "closeted," he was not well known at the school and kept a low profile. The other out gay boy at the school was Brady. While he didn't engage in the masculinity rituals of the other boys at River High, he didn't cross-dress or engage in feminine-coded activities as did Ricky. As such, when boys talked about fags, they referenced Ricky, not Brady or Corey.

REFERENCES

Almaguer, Tomas. 1991. "Chicano Men: A Cartography of Homosexual Identity and Behavior." *Differences* 3, no. 2: 75–100.

Baker, Janet G., and Harold D. Fishbein. 1998. "The Development of Prejudice towards Gays and Lesbians by Adolescents," Journal of Homosexuality 36, no. 1:89–100.

Burn, Shawn Meghan. 2000. "Heterosexuals' Use of 'Fag' and 'Queer' to Deride One Another: A Contributor to Heterosexism and Stigma." *Journal of Homosexuality* 40, no. 2:1–11.

Butler, Judith. 1993. *Bodies That Matter: On the Discursive Limits of "Sex."* New York: Routledge.

Connell, R. W. 1995. *Masculinities.* Berkeley: University of California Press.

Corbett, Ken. 2001. "Faggot = Loser." *Studies in Gender and Sexuality* 2, no. 1:3–28.

Freud, Sigmund. 1905. *The Basic Writings of Sigmund Freud.* Translated by A. A Brill. New York: Modern Library.

Julien, Isaac, and Kobena Mercer. 1991. "True Confessions: A Discourse on Images of Black Male Sexuality." In *Brother to Brother: New Writings by Black Gay Men,* edited by Essex Hemphill, 167–73. Boston: Alyson Publications.

Kehily, Mary Jane, and Anoop Nayak. 1997. "'Lads and Laughter': Humour and the Production of Heterosexual Masculinities." *Gender and Education* 9, no.1:69–87.

Kelley, Robin D. G. 2004. "Confessions of a Nice Negro, or Why I Shaved My Head." In *Men's Lives,* edited by Michael Kimmel and Michael Messner, 335–41. Boston: Allyn and Bacon.

Kimmel, Michael S. 2001. "Masculinity as Homophobia: Fear, Shame, and Silence in the Construction of Gender Identity." In *The Masculinities Reader,* edited by Stephen Whitehead and Frank Barrett, 266–87. Cambridge: Polity Press.

———. 2003. "Adolescent Masculinity, Homophobia, and Violence Random School Shootings, 1982–2001." *American Behavioral Scientist* 46, no. 10:1439–58.

King, J. L. 2004. *On the Down Low: A Journey into the Lives of Straight Black Men Who Sleep with Men.* New York: Broadway Books.

Lehne, Gregory. 1998. "Homophobia among Men: Supporting and Defining the Male Role." In *Men's Lives,* edited by Michael Kimmel and Michael Messner 237–49 Boston: Allyn and Bacon.

Lyman, Peter. 1998. "The Fraternal Bond as a Joking Relationship: A Case Study of the Role of Sexist Jokes in Male Group Bonding." In *Men's Lives,* edited by Michael Kimmel and Michael Messner, 171–93. Boston: Allyn and Bacon.

Majors, Richard. 2001. "Cool Pose: Black Masculinity and Sports." In *The Masculinities Reader,* edited by Stephen Whitehead and Frank Barrett, 208–17. Cambridge-Polity Press.

Messner, Michael 2005. "Becoming 100% Straight." In *Gender through the Prism of Difference,* edited by Maxine Baca Zinn, Pierrette Hondagneu-Sotelo, and Michael Messner, 227–32. New York: Oxford University Press.

Plummer, David C. 2001, "The Quest for Modern Manhood: Masculine Stereotypes, Peer Culture and the Social Significance of Homophobia." *Journal of Adolescence* 24, no. 1:15–23.

Riggs, Marlon. 1991. "Black Macho Revisited: Reflections of a Snap! Queen." In *Brother to Brother: New Writings by Black Gay Men,* edited by Essex Hemphill 253–60. Boston: Alyson Publications.

Sedgwick, Eve Kosofsky. 1995. "'Gosh, Boy George, You Must Be Awfully Secure in Your Masculinity!'" In *Constructing Masculinity,* edited by Maurice Berger, Brian Wallis, and Simon Watson, 11–20. New York: Routledge.

Shakib, Sohaila. 2003. "Female Basketball Participation: Negotiating the Conflation of Peer Status and Gender Status from Childhood through Puberty." *American Behavioral Scientist* 46, no. 4:1405–22.

Smith, George W. 1998. "The Ideology of 'Fag': The School Experience of Gay Students." *Sociological Quarterly* 39, no. 2:309–35.

Wilchins, Riki. 2003. "Do You Believe in Fairies?" *Advocate,* February 4, 72.

Wood, Julian. 1984. "Groping Towards Sexism: Boy's Sex Talk." In *Gender and Generation,* edited by Angela McRobbie and Mica Nava, 54–84. London: Macmillan.

READING 29

Gendered Sexuality in Young Adulthood: Double Binds and Flawed Options

Laura Hamilton
Indiana University, Bloomington

Elizabeth A. Armstrong
University of Michigan

Paul, McManus, and Hayes (2000) and Glenn and Marquardt (2001) were the first to draw attention to the hookup as a distinct social form. As Glenn and Marquardt (2001, 13) explain, most students agree that "a hook up is anything 'ranging from kissing to having sex,' and that it takes place outside the context of commitment." Others have similarly found that *hooking up* refers to a broad range of sexual activity and that this ambiguity is part of the appeal of the term (Bogle 2008). Hookups differ from dates in that individuals typically do not plan to do something together prior to sexual activity. Rather, two people hanging out at a party, bar, or place of residence will begin talking, flirting, and/or dancing. Typically, they have been drinking. At some point, they move to a more private location, where sexual activity occurs (England, Shafer,

and Fogarty 2007). While strangers sometimes hook up, more often hookups occur among those who know each other at least slightly (Manning, Giordano, and Longmore 2006).

England has surveyed more than 14,000 students from 19 universities and colleges about their hookup, dating, and relationship experiences. Her Online College Social Life Survey (OCSLS) asks students to report on their recent hookups using "whatever definition of a hookup you and your friends use."[1] Seventy-two percent of both men and women participating in the OCSLS reported at least one hookup by their senior year in college.[2] Of these, roughly 40 percent engaged in three or fewer hookups, 40 percent between four and nine hookups, and 20 percent 10 or more hookups. Only about one-third engaged in intercourse in their most recent hookups, although—among the 80 percent of students who had intercourse by the end of college—67 percent had done so outside of a relationship.

Ongoing sexual relationships without commitment were common and were labeled "repeat," "regular," or "continuing" hookups and sometimes "friends with benefits" (Armstrong, England, and Fogarty 2009; Bogle 2008; Glenn and Marquardt 2001). Ongoing hookups sometimes became committed relationships and vice versa; generally, the distinction revolved around the level of exclusivity and a willingness to refer to each other as "girlfriend/boyfriend" (Armstrong, England, and Fogarty 2009). Thus, hooking up does not imply interest in a relationship, but it does not preclude such interest. Relationships are also common among students. By their senior year, 69 percent of heterosexual students had been in a college relationship of at least six months.

To date, however, scholars have paid more attention to women's experiences with hooking up than relationships and focused primarily on ways that hookups may be less enjoyable for women than for men. Glenn and Marquardt (2001, 20) indicate that "hooking up is an activity that women sometimes find rewarding but more often find confusing, hurtful, and awkward." Others similarly suggest that

Laura Hamilton is a professor of sociology at the University of California, Merced. Elizabeth A. Armstrong is a professor of sociology at the University of Michigan.

more women than men find hooking up to be a negative experience (Bogle 2008, 173; Owen et al. 2008) and focus on ways that hookups may be harmful to women (Eshbaugh and Gute 2008; Grello, Welsh, and Harper 2006).

This work assumes distinct and durable gender differences at the individual level. Authors draw, if implicitly, from evolutionary psychology, socialization, and psychoanalytic approaches to gender—depicting women as more relationally oriented and men as more sexually adventurous (see Wharton 2005 for a review). For example, despite only asking about hookup experiences, Bogle (2008, 173) describes a "battle of the sexes" in which women want hookups to "evolve into some semblance of a relationship," while men prefer to "hook up with no strings attached" (also see Glenn and Marquardt 2001; Stepp 2007).

The battle of the sexes view implies that if women could simply extract commitment from men rather than participating in hookups, gender inequalities in college sexuality would be alleviated. Yet this research—which often fails to examine relationships—ignores the possibility that women might be the losers in both hookups and relationships. Research suggests that young heterosexual women often suffer the most damage from those with whom they are most intimate: Physical battery, emotional abuse, sexual assault, and stalking occur at high rates in youthful heterosexual relationships (Campbell et al. 2007; Dunn 1999). This suggests that gender inequality in college sexuality is systemic, existing across social forms.

Current research also tends to see hooking up as solely about gender, without fully considering the significance of other dimensions of inequality. Some scholars highlight the importance of the college environment and traditional college students' position in the life course (Bogle 2008; Glenn and Marquardt 2001). However, college is treated primarily as a context for individual sexual behavior rather than as a key location for class reproduction. Analyzing the role of social class in sex and relationships may help to illuminate the appeal of hookups for both college women and men.

METHOD

The strength of our research strategy lies in its depth: We conducted a longitudinal ethnographic and interview study of a group of women who started college in 2004 at a university in the Midwest, collecting data about their entire sexual and romantic careers. . . .

A research team of nine, including the authors, occupied a room on an all-female floor in a mixed-gender dormitory. When data collection commenced, Laura was a graduate student in her early twenties and Elizabeth an assistant professor in her late thirties. The team also included a male graduate student, an undergraduate sorority member, and an undergraduate with working-class roots. Variation in age, approach, and self-presentation among team members allowed for different relationships with participants and brought multiple perspectives to data analysis—strengths of team ethnography (Erickson and Stull 1998).

Fifty-three 18- to 20-year-old unmarried women (51 freshmen, two sophomores) lived on the floor for at least part of the year. No one opted out of the ethnographic study. All but two identified as heterosexual.[3] All participants were white, a result of low racial diversity on campus overall and racial segregation in campus housing. Sixty-eight percent came from middle-, upper-middle-, or upper-class backgrounds; 32 percent came from working- or lower-middle-class backgrounds. Forty-five percent were from out of state; all of these women were from upper-middle-class or upper-class families. Thirty-six percent, mostly wealthier women, joined sororities in their first year.

Assessment of class background was based on parental education and occupation, student employment during the school year, and receipt of student loans. We refer to those from middle-, upper- middle-, or upper-class backgrounds as "more privileged" and those from working- or lower-middle-class backgrounds as "less privileged." There were distinct differences between women in these groups. Less privileged women did not have parents with college degrees and struggled to afford college. In contrast, more privileged women had at least one, and more often two, parents with degrees. They received a great deal of parental support, keeping their loans to a minimum and allowing most to avoid working during the year.

The residence hall in which they lived was identified by students and staff as one of several "party dorms." The term refers to the presumed social orientation of the modal resident, not to partying within the dorm itself. Students reported that they requested these dormitories if they were interested in drinking, hooking up, and joining the Greek system. This orientation places them in the thick of American youth culture. Few identified as feminist, and all presented a traditionally feminine appearance (e.g., not one woman had hair shorter than chin length). Most planned to marry and have children.

We observed throughout the academic year, interacting with participants as they did with each other—watching television, eating meals, helping them dress for parties, sitting in as they studied, and attending floor meetings. We let the women guide our conversations, which often turned to "boys," relationships, and hooking up. We also refrained from revealing our own predispositions, to the extent that women openly engaged in homophobic and racist behaviors in front of us. Our approach made it difficult for women to determine what we were studying, which behaviors might be interesting to us, and in which ways we might be judgmental. Consequently, we believe they were less likely to either underreport or exaggerate sexual behavior, minimizing the effects of social desirability. . . .

THE POWER OF GENDER BELIEFS

A battle of the sexes approach suggests that women have internalized a relational orientation but are unable to establish relationships because hooking up—which men prefer—has come to dominate college sexual culture. Rather that accepting stated individual-level preferences at face value we focus on the interactional contexts in which preferences are formed and expressed. We show that gender beliefs about what women should and should not do posed problems for our participants in both hookups and relationships.

The "Slut" Stigma

Women did not find hookups to be unproblematic. They complained about a pervasive sexual double standard. As one explained, "Guys can have sex with all the girls and *it makes them more of a man,* but if a girl does then all of a sudden she's a ho, and she's not as quality of a person" (10-1* emphasis added). Another complained, "Guys, they can go around and have sex with a number of girls and they're not called anything" (6-1). Women noted that it was "easy to get a reputation" (11-1) from "hooking up with a bunch of different guys" (8-1) or "being wild and drinking too much" (14-3). Their experiences of being judged were often painful; one woman told us about being called a "slut" two years after the incident because it was so humiliating (42-3).

Fear of stigma constrained women's sexual behavior and perhaps even shape their preferences. For example, several indicated that they probably would "make out with more guys" but did not because "I don't want to be a slut" (27-2). Others wanted to have intercourse on hookups but instead waited until they had boyfriends. A couple hid their sexual activity until the liaison was "official." One said, "I would not spend the night there [at the fraternity] because that does not look good, but now everyone knows we're boyfriend/girlfriend, so it's like my home now" (15-1). Another woman, who initially seemed to have a deep aversion to hooking up, explained, "I would rather be a virgin for as much as I can than go out and do God knows who." She later revealed a fear of social stigma, noting that when women engage in nonromantic sex, they "get a bad reputation. I know that I wouldn't want that reputation" (11-1). Her comments highlight the

---

*Number indicates participant and wave of the interview.

feedback between social judgment and internalized preference.

Gender beliefs were also at the root of women's other chief complaint about hookups—the disrespect of women in the hookup scene. The notion that hooking up is okay for men but not for women was embedded in the organization of the Greek system, where most parties occurred: Sorority rules prohibited hosting parties or overnight male visitors, reflecting notions about proper feminine behavior. In contrast, fraternities collected social fees to pay for alcohol and viewed hosting parties as a central activity. This disparity gave fraternity men almost complete control over the most desirable parties on campus—particularly for the underage crowd (Boswell and Spade 1996; Martin and Hummer 1989).

Women reported that fraternity men dictated party transportation, the admittance of guests, party themes such as "CEO and secretary ho," the flow of alcohol, and the movement of guests within the party (Armstrong, Hamilton, and Sweeney 2006). Women often indicated that they engaged in strategies such as "travel[ing] in hordes" (21-1) and not "tak[ing] a drink if I don't know where it came from" (15-1) to feel safer at fraternity parties. Even when open to hooking up, women were not comfortable doing so if they sensed that men were trying to undermine their control of sexual activity (e.g., by pushing them to drink too heavily, barring their exit from private rooms, or refusing them rides home). Women typically opted not to return to party venues they perceived as unsafe. As one noted, "I wouldn't go to [that house] because I heard they do bad things to girls" (14-1). Even those interested in the erotic competition of party scenes tired of it as they realized that the game was rigged. . . .

The Relationship Imperative

Women also encountered problematic gender beliefs about men's and women's different levels of interest in relationships. As one noted, women fight the "dumb girl idea"—the notion "that every girl wants a boy to sweep her off her feet and fall in love" (42-2). The expectation that women should want to be in relationships was so pervasive that many found it necessary to justify their single status to us. For example, when asked if she had a boyfriend, one woman with no shortage of admirers apologetically explained, "I know this sounds really pathetic and you probably think I am lying, but there are so many other things going on right now that it's really not something high up on my list. . . . I know that's such a lame-ass excuse, but it's true" (9-3). Another noted that already having a boyfriend was the only "actual, legitimate excuse" to reject men who expressed interest in a relationship (34-3).

Certainly, many women wanted relationships and sought them out. However, women's interest in relationships varied, and almost all experienced periods during which they wanted to be single. Nonetheless, women reported pressure to be in relationships all the time. We found that women, rather than struggling to get into relationships, had to work to avoid them.

The relational imperative was supported by the belief that women's relational opportunities were scarce and should not be wasted. Women described themselves as "lucky" to find a man willing to commit, as "there's not many guys like that, in college" (15-1). This belief persisted despite the fact that most women were in relationships most of the time. As one woman noted, "I don't think anyone really wants to be in a serious relationship, but most, well actually all of us, have boyfriends" (13-1). Belief in the myth of scarcity also led women to stay in relationships when they were no longer happy. A woman who was "sick of" her conflict-ridden relationship explained why she could not end it: "I feel like I have to meet somebody else. . . . I go out and they're all these asshole frat guys. . . . That's what stops me. . . . Boys are not datable right now because . . . all they're looking for is freshman girls to hook up with. . . . [So] I'm just stuck. I need to do something about it, but I don't know what" (30-3).

It took her another year to extract herself from this relationship. Despite her fears, when she decided she was ready for another relationship, she quickly found a boyfriend.

Women also confronted the belief that all women are relationally insatiable. They often told stories of men who acted entitled to relationships, expected their relational overtures to be accepted, and became angry when rebuffed—sometimes stalking the rejecting woman. As one explained about a friend, "Abby was having issues with this guy who likes her. He was like, 'You have to like me. . . . I'm not gonna take no for an answer. I'm gonna do whatever it takes to date you' " (24-3). Another noted that "last semester, this guy really wanted to date me, and I did not want to date him at all. He flipped out and was like, 'This is ridiculous, I don't deserve this'" (12-3). A third eventually gave in when a man continually rejected her refusals: "I was like, if I go [out with him]. . . maybe he'll stop. Because he wouldn't stop." She planned to act "extremely conservative" as a way to convince him that he did not want to be with her (39-4).

Gender beliefs may also limit women's control over the terms of interaction within relationships. If women are made to feel lucky to have boyfriends, men are placed in a position of power, as presumably women should be grateful when they commit. Women's reports suggest that men attempted to use this power to regulate their participation in college life. One noted, "When I got here my first semester freshman year, I wanted to go out to the parties . . . and he got pissed off about it. . . . He's like, 'Why do you need to do that? Why can't you just stay with me?' " (4-2). Boyfriends sometimes tried to limit the time women spent with their friends and the activities in which they participated. As a woman explained, "There are times when I feel like Steve can get . . . possessive. He'll be like . . . 'I feel like you're always with your friends over me.' He wanted to go out to lunch after our class, and I was like, 'No, I have to come have this interview.' And he got so upset about it" (42-3). Men's control even extended to women's attire. Another told us about

her boyfriend, "He is a very controlling person. . . . He's like, 'What are you wearing tonight?'. . . It's like a joke but serious at the same time" (32-4).

Women also became jealous; however, rather than trying to control their boyfriends, they often tried to change themselves. One noted that she would "do anything to make this relationship work." She elaborated, "I was so nervous being with Dan because I knew he had cheated on his [prior] girlfriend . . . [but] I'm getting over it. When I go [to visit him] now . . . I let him go to the bar, whatever. I stayed in his apartment because there was nothing else to do" (39-3). Other women changed the way they dressed, their friends, and where they went in the attempt to keep boyfriends.

When women attempted to end relationships, they often reported that men's efforts to control them escalated. We heard 10 accounts of men using abuse to keep women in relationships. One woman spent months dealing with a boyfriend who accused her of cheating on him. When she tried to break up, he cut his wrist in her apartment (9-2). Another tried to end a relationship but was forced to flee the state when her car windows were broken and her safety was threatened (6-4). Men often drew on romantic repertoires to coerce interaction after relationships had ended. One woman told us that her ex-boyfriend stalked her for months—even showing up at her workplace, showering her with flowers and gifts, and blocking her entry into work until the police arrived (25-2).

INTERSECTIONALITY: CONTRADICTIONS BETWEEN CLASS AND GENDER

Existing research about college sexuality focuses almost exclusively on its gendered nature. We contend that sexuality is shaped simultaneously by multiple intersecting structures. In this section, we examine the sexual and romantic implications of class beliefs about how ambitious young people should conduct themselves during college.

Although all of our participants contended with class beliefs that contradicted those of gender, experiences of this structural intersection varied by class location. More privileged women struggled to meet gender and class guidelines for sexual behavior, introducing a difficult set of double binds. Because these class beliefs reflected a privileged path to adulthood, less privileged women found them foreign to their own sexual and romantic logics.

More Privileged Women and the Experience of Double Binds

The Self-development Imperative and the Relational Double Bind

The four-year university is a classed structural location. One of the primary reasons to attend college is to preserve or enhance economic position. The university culture is thus characterized by the self-development imperative, or the notion that individual achievement and personal growth are paramount. There are also accompanying rules for sex and relationships: Students are expected to postpone marriage and parenthood until after completing an education and establishing a career.

For more privileged women, personal expectations and those of the university culture meshed. Even those who enjoyed relationships experienced phases in college where they preferred to remain single. Almost all privileged women (94 percent) told us at one point that they did not want a boyfriend. One noted, "All my friends here . . . they're like, 'I don't want to deal with [a boyfriend] right now. I want to be on my own'" (37-1). Another eloquently remarked, "I've always looked at college as the only time in your life when you should be a hundred percent selfish. . . . I have the rest of my life to devote to a husband or kids or my job . . . but right now, it's my time" (21-2).

The notion that independence is critical during college reflected class beliefs about the appropriate role for romance that opposed those of gender. During college, relational commitments were supposed to take a backseat to self-development. As an upper-middle-class woman noted, "College is the

only time that you don't have obligations to anyone but yourself. . . . I want to get settled down and figure out what I'm doing with my life before [I] dedicate myself to something or someone else" (14-4). Another emphasized the value of investment in human capital: "I've always been someone who wants to have my own money, have my own career so that, you know, 50 percent of marriages fail. . . . If I want to maintain the lifestyle that I've grown up with . . . I have to work. I just don't see myself being someone who marries young and lives off of some boy's money" (42-4). To become self-supporting, many privileged women indicated they needed to postpone marriage. One told us, "I don't want to think about that [marriage]. I want to get secure in a city and in a job. . . . I'm not in any hurry at all. As long as I'm married by 30, I'm good" (13-4). Even those who wanted to be supported by husbands did not expect to find them in college, instead setting their sights on the more accomplished men they expected to meet in urban centers after college.

More privileged women often found committed relationships to be greedy—demanding of time and energy. As one stated, "When it comes to a serious relationship, it's a lot for me to give into that. [What do you feel like you are giving up?] Like my everything. . . . There's just a lot involved in it" (35-3). These women feared that they would be devoured by relationships and sometimes struggled to keep their self-development projects going when they did get involved. As an upper-class woman told us, "It's hard to have a boyfriend and be really excited about it and still not let it consume you" (42-2). This situation was exacerbated by the gender beliefs discussed earlier, as women experienced pressure to fully devote themselves to relationships.

Privileged women reported that committed relationships detracted from what they saw as the main tasks of college. They complained, for example, that relationships made it difficult to meet people. As an upper-middle-class woman who had just ended a relationship described, "I'm happy that I'm able to go out and meet new people. . . . I feel like I'm doing what a college student should be doing.

I don't need to be tied down to my high school boy-friend for two years when this is the time to be meeting people" (14-3). A middle-class woman similarly noted that her relationship with her boy-friend made it impossible to make friends on the floor her first year. She explained, "We were to-gether every day. . . . It was the critical time of mak-ing friends and meeting people, [and] I wasn't there" (21-2).

Many also complained that committed rela-tionships competed with schoolwork (also see Holland and Eisenhart 1990). An upper-middle-class woman remarked, "[My boyfriend] doesn't understand why I can't pick up and go see him all the time. But I have school. . . . I just want to be a college kid" (18-3). Another told us that her major was not compatible with the demands of a boyfriend. She said, "I wouldn't mind having a boyfriend again, but it's a lot of work. Right now with [my major] and everything . . . I wouldn't have time even to see him" (30-4). She did not plan to consider a relationship until her workload lessened.

With marriage far in the future, more privi-leged women often worried about college rela-tionships getting too serious too fast. All planned to marry—ideally to men with greater earnings—but were clear about the importance of temporary independence. . . .

The Appeal of Hookups and the Sexual Double Bind   In contrast, hookups fit well with the self-development imperative of college. They allowed women to be sexual without the demands of relationships. For example, one upper-class woman described hooking up as "fun and non-threatening." She noted, "So many of us girls, we complain that these guys just want to hook up all the time. I'm going, these guys that I'm attracted to . . . get kind of serious." She saw her last hookup as ideal because "we were physical, and that was it. I never wanted it to go anywhere" (34-2). Many privileged women understood, if implicitly, that hooking up was a delay tactic, allowing sex without participation in serious relationships.

As a sexual solution for the demands of college, hooking up became incorporated into notions of what the college experience should be. When asked which kinds of people hook up the most, one woman noted, "All. . . . The people who came to college to have a good time and party" (14-1). With the help of media, alcohol, and spring break industries, hook-ing up was so institutionalized that many took it for granted. One upper-middle-class woman said, "It just happens. It's natural" (15-1). They told us that learning about sexuality was something they were supposed to be doing in college. Another described, "I'm glad that I've had my one-night stands and my being in love and having sex. . . . Now I know what it's supposed to feel like when I'm with someone that I want to be with. I feel bad for some of my friends. . . . They're still virgins" (29-1).

High rates of hooking up suggest genuine inter-est in the activity rather than simply accommoda-tion to men's interests. Particularly early in college, privileged women actively sought hookups. One noted, "You see a lot of people who are like, 'I just want to hook up with someone tonight.'. . . It's al-ways the girls that try to get the guys" (41-1). Data from the OCSLS also suggest that college women like hooking up almost as much as men and are not always searching for something more. Nearly as many women as men (85 percent and 89 percent, respectively) report enjoying the sexual activity of their last hookup "very much" or "somewhat," and less than half of women report interest in a relation-ship with their most recent hookup.

In private, several privileged women even used the classed logic of hooking up to challenge ste-reotyped portrayals of gender differences in sexu-ality. As one noted, "There are girls that want things as much as guys do. There are girls that want things more, and they're like, 'Oh it's been a while [since I had sex].' The girls are no more in-nocent than the guys. . . . People think girls are jealous of relationships, but they're like, 'What? I want to be single'" (34-1). When asked about the notion that guys want sex and girls want relation-ships another responded, "I think that is the abso-lute epitome of bullshit. I know so many girls who honestly go out on a Friday night and they're like, 'I hope I get some ass tonight.' They don't wanna have a boyfriend! They just wanna hook up with someone. And I know boys who want relationships. I think it goes both ways" (42-2). These women drew on gender-neutral understandings of sexuality characteristic of university culture to contradict the notion of women's sexuality as inevitably and naturally relational.

For more privileged women, enjoyment of hookups was tightly linked to the atmosphere in which they occurred. Most were initiated at college parties where alcohol, music, attractive people, sexy outfits, and flirting combined to generate a collective erotic energy. As one woman enthusiastically noted, "Everyone was so excited. It was a big fun party" (15-1). Privileged women often "loved" it when they had an "excuse to just let loose" and "grind" on the dance floor. They reported turning on their "make-out radar" (18-1), explaining that "it's fun to know that a guy's attracted to you and is willing to kiss you" (16-1). The party scene gave them a chance to play with adult sexualities and interact for purely sexual purposes—an experience that one middle-class woman claimed "empowered" her (17-1).

Hookups enabled more privileged women to conduct themselves in accordance with class expectations, but as we demonstrated earlier, the enforcement of gender beliefs placed them at risk of sanction. This conflict gets to the heart of a *sexual double bind:* While hookups protected privileged women from relationships that could derail their ambitions, the double standard gave men greater control over the terms of hooking up, justified the disrespectful treatment of women, supported sexual stigma, and produced feelings of shame.

Less Privileged Women and the Experience of Foreign Sexual Culture

Women's comfort with delaying commitment and participating in the hookup culture was shaped by class location. College culture reflects the beliefs of the more privileged classes. Less privileged women arrived at college with their own orientation to sex and romance, characterized by a faster transition into adulthood. They often attempted to build both relationships and career at the same time. As a result, the third of the participants from less privileged backgrounds often experienced the hookup culture as foreign in ways that made it difficult to persist at the university.

Less privileged women had less exposure to the notion that the college years should be set aside solely for educational and career development. Many did not see serious relationships as incompatible with college life. Four were married or engaged before graduating—a step that others would not take until later. One reminisced, "I thought I'd get married in college. . . . When I was still in high school, I figured by my senior year, I'd be engaged or married or something. . . . I wanted to have kids before I was 25" (25-4). Another spoke of her plans to marry her high school sweetheart: "I'll be 21 and I know he's the one I want to spend the rest of my life with. . . . Really, I don't want to date anybody else" (6-1).

Plans to move into adult roles relatively quickly made less privileged women outsiders among their more privileged peers. One working-class woman saw her friendships dissolve as she revealed her desire to marry and have children in the near future. As one of her former friends described,

> She would always talk about how she couldn't wait to get married and have babies. . . . It was just like, Whoa. I'm 18. . . . Slow down, you know? Then she just crazy dropped out of school and wouldn't contact any of us. . . . The way I see it is that she's from a really small town, and that's what everyone in her town does . . . get married and have babies. That's all she ever wanted to do maybe? . . . I don't know if she was homesick or didn't fit in. (24-4)

This account glosses over the extent to which the working-class woman was pushed out of the university—ostracized by her peers for not acclimating to the self-development imperative and, as noted below, to the campus sexual climate. In fact, 40 percent of less privileged women left the university, compared to 5 percent of more privileged women. In all cases, mismatch between the sexual culture of women's hometowns and that of college was a factor in the decision to leave.

Most of the less privileged women found the hookup culture to be not only foreign but hostile. As the working-class woman described above told us,

> I tried so hard to fit in with what everybody else was doing here. . . . I think one morning I just woke up and realized that this isn't me at all; I don't like the way I am right now. . . . I didn't feel like I was growing up. I felt like I was actually getting younger the way I was trying to act. Growing up to me isn't going out and getting smashed and sleeping around. . . . That to me is immature. (28-1)

She emphasized the value of "growing up" in college. Without the desire to postpone adulthood, less privileged women often could not understand the appeal of hooking up. As a lower-middle-class woman noted, "Who would be interested in just meeting somebody and then doing something that night? And then never talking to them again? . . . I'm supposed to do this; I'm supposed to get drunk every weekend. I'm supposed to go to parties every weekend . . . and I'm supposed to enjoy it like everyone else. But it just doesn't appeal to me" (5-1). She reveals the extent to which hooking up was a normalized part of college life: For those who were not interested in this, college life could be experienced as mystifying, uncomfortable, and alienating.

The self-development imperative was a resource women could use in resisting the gendered pull of relationships. Less privileged women did not have as much access to this resource and were invested in settling down. Thus, they found it hard to resist the pull back home of local boyfriends, who—unlike the college men they had met—seemed interested in marrying and having children soon. One woman noted after transferring to a branch campus, "I think if I hadn't been connected with [my fiancé], I think I would have been more strongly connected to [the college town], and I think I probably would have stayed" (2-4). Another described her hometown boyfriend: "He'll be like, 'I want to see you. Come home.' . . . The stress he was putting me under and me being here my first year. I could not take it" (7-2). The following year, she moved back home. A third explained about her husband, "He wants me at home. . . . He wants to have control over me and . . . to feel like he's the dominant one in the relationship. . . . The fact that I'm going to school and he knows I'm smart and he knows that I'm capable of doing anything that I want . . . it scares him" (6-4). While she eventually ended this relationship, it cost her an additional semester of school.

Women were also pulled back home by the slut stigma, as people there—perhaps out of frustration or jealousy—judged college women for any association with campus sexual culture. For instance, one woman became distraught when a virulent sexual rumor about her circulated around her hometown, especially when it reached her parents. Going home was a way of putting sexual rumors to rest and reaffirming ties that were strained by leaving.

Thus, less privileged women were often caught between two sexual cultures. Staying at the university meant abandoning a familiar logic and adopting a privileged one—investing in human capital while delaying the transition to adulthood. As one explained, attending college led her to revise her "whole plan": "Now I'm like, I don't even need to be getting married yet [or] have kids. . . . All of [my brother's] friends, 17- to 20-year-old girls, have their . . . babies, and I'm like, Oh my God. . . . Now I'll be able to do something else for a couple years before I settle down . . . before I worry about kids" (25-3). These changes in agendas required them to end relationships with men whose life plans diverged from theirs. For some, this also meant cutting ties with hometown friends. One resolute woman, whose friends back home had turned on her, noted, "I'm just sick of it. There's nothing there for me anymore. There's absolutely nothing there" (22-4).

DISCUSSION

Public gender beliefs are a key source of gender inequality in college heterosexual interaction. They undergird a sexual double standard and a relational imperative that justify the disrespect of women who hook up and the disempowerment of women in relationships—reinforcing male dominance across social forms. Most of the women we studied cycled back and forth between hookups and relationships, in part because they found both to be problematic. These findings indicate that an individualist, battle of the sexes explanation not only is inadequate but may contribute to gender inequality by naturalizing problematic notions of gender difference.

We are not, however, claiming that gender differences in stated preferences do not exist. Analysis of the OCSLS finds a small but significant difference between men and women in preferences for relationships as compared to hookups: After the most recent hookup, 47 percent of women compared to 37 percent of men expressed some interest in a relationship. These differences in preferences are consistent with a multilevel perspective that views the internalization of gender as an aspect of gender structure (Risman 2004). As we have shown, the pressure to internalize gender-appropriate preferences is considerable, and the line between personal preferences and the desire to avoid social stigma is fuzzy. However, we believe that widely shared beliefs about gender difference contribute more to gender inequality in college heterosexuality than the substantively small differences in actual preferences. . . .

DISCUSSION QUESTIONS

1. What are the ways that social class shapes sexuality for college men as well as for college women?
2. What problems and advantages follow from the self-development and relationship imperatives?

NOTES

1. Online College Social Life Survey data collection is ongoing. Thus, numbers vary slightly according to the version of the data set. This article references data prepared and distributed by Reuben J. Thomas on February 26, 2009.
2. This number is consistent with that reported by Paul, McManus, and Hayes (2000). Glenn and Marquardt (2001) found lower rates, perhaps because they include students attending religious and commuter colleges. Recently, Owen et al. (2008) found that white students, those who drink, and students with higher parental income are more likely to hook up.
3. The two women who identified as lesbian or bisexual are included as they also had sex with men. How the women on this floor responded to lesbianism is explored elsewhere (Hamilton 2007).

REFERENCES

Armstrong, Elizabeth A., Paula England, and Alison C. K. Fogarty. 2009. Orgasm in college hookups and relationships. In *Families as they really are,* edited by B. Risman. New York: Norton.

Bogle, Kathleen A. 2008. *Hooking up: Sex, dating, and relationships on campus.* New York: New York University Press.

Campbell, Jacquelyn C. Nancy Glass, Phyllis W. Sharps, Kathryn Laughon, and Tina Bloom. 2007. Intimate partner homicide. *Trauma, Violence, & Abuse* 8:246–69.

Dunn, Jennifer L. 1999. What love has to do with it: The cultural construction of emotion and sorority women's responses to forcible interaction. *Social Problems* 46: 440–59.

England, Paula, Emily Fitzgibbons Shafer, and Alison C.K. Fogarty. 2007. Hooking up and forming romantic relationships on today's college campuses. In *The gendered society reader,* edited by M. Kimmel. New York: Oxford University Press.

Glenn, Norval, and Elizabeth Marquardt. 2001. *Hooking up, hanging out, and hoping for Mr. Right: College women on mating and dating today.* New York: Institute for American Values.

Manning, Wendy D., Peggy C. Giordano, and Monica A. Longmore. 2006. Hooking up: The relationship contexts of "nonrelationship" sex. *Journal of Adolescent Research* 21:459–83.

Paul, Elizabeth L., Brian McManus, and Allison Hayes. 2000. "Hookups": Characteristics and correlates of college students' spontaneous and anonymous sexual experiences. *Journal of Sex Research* 37:76–88.

Risman, Barbara J. 2004. Gender as a social structure: Theory wrestling with activism. *Gender & Society* 18: 429–50.

PERSONAL ACCOUNT

Living Invisibly

For me, coming out is a Sisyphean task. Because of my invisible differences, I constantly have to reveal different parts of my identity. It's not an easy task, either. When I come out as a lesbian/queer woman, people are often surprised because I don't "look" queer. I can count on one hand the number of times I have been recognized by a stranger as part of the LGBT "family." Some people are also surprised to learn that I'm half Taiwanese. I am also half-white, and often assumed to be white, making my race another invisible identity. Because of this, there have been times when people have made racist jokes—either about Asians or other groups—because they thought I was white, and thus thought that these were "acceptable" jokes to tell in my presence.

Invisible identities work differently from other differences. I am lucky not to be harassed on the street because of my race, and since I don't appear queer to your average passerby, I don't usually get harassed for that. I benefit from the privilege of passing as a straight and white, but most days I wish that I could give up that privilege. It is extremely difficult to live your life where some of the most important things about you are hidden. For example, I never know when it is appropriate to come out as queer in class, and almost feel guilty if I never do, even though it may not always be necessary or appropriate. Because I am invisible, I bear the burden of disclosure. When someone assumes that I'm heterosexual, I have to correct her or him (my mother still doesn't believe that I'm queer). When someone assumes that I'm white, I do the same. Regardless, I come out all the time to new people in my life, and each time I do, I hope that they will be able to handle the information with care and respect.

Most people respond well when I come out to them, and I can breathe another sigh of relief when my peers accept me. College, especially, has been a (mostly) safe space for me to be out and proud about my race and sexuality. Living with my multiple invisible identities has taught me to be more assertive in all areas of my life, and I have learned to take risks. I know quite well how privilege works, and how that privilege can be taken away in an instant. I am also proud of all of my identities. The difficulty of coming out is well worth the satisfaction and pride I have of living my life the way that I have always wanted to.

Tara S. Ellison

READING 30

Sexual Orientation and Sex in Women's Lives: Conceptual and Methodological Issues

Esther D. Rothblum

In the novel *Never Say Never* (Hill, 1996), two coworkers, Leslie, who is a lesbian, and Sara, who is heterosexual, become close friends. Though it is obvious to the reader and to both women that they are sexually attracted to each other, the suspense builds as to whether or not Leslie and Sara will "consummate" their relationship—that is, become genitally sexual. Whether or not the women do "it" will affect the reader's perception as to whether the book had a happy ending (they became lovers) or an unhappy one (they remained "just friends"). It will also determine whether Sara "becomes" a lesbian.

What is sexual orientation? What does it mean to be a heterosexual, bisexual, or lesbian woman? Are these terms on a continuum or separate categories? Can all women categorize themselves in one of these three ways? This article will discuss conceptual issues of sexual orientation in women.

Esther D. Rothblum is a professor of women's studies at San Diego State University.

Closely related to sexual orientation is the concept of sexual behavior. Sexual orientation is usually defined in terms of the gender of one's sexual partner. This article will ask the question, what is "sex" for women? Finally, there has been so little research addressing these concepts that some methodological issues for future research will be presented.

CONCEPTUAL ISSUES IN SEXUAL ORIENTATION

Dichotomous Definitions

Fehr (1988) views categorical definitions as "classical" in the sense that they are defined by specific inclusion and exclusion criteria. She states:

> Category membership is therefore an all-or-none phenomenon; any instance that meets the criterion is a member; all others are non-members. Boundaries between concepts are thus clearly defined. Because each member must possess the particular set of attributes that is the criterion for category inclusion, all members have a full and equal degree of membership and therefore are equally representative of the category. (p. 558)

Similarly, Rosch (1978) has argued that categories in language can be structured into a model of best fits, followed by examples that resemble these best fits to some extent.

In a categorical definition of sexual orientation, all aspects of sexual orientation—desire, behavior, and identity—are presumed to be congruent. The terms "heterosexual" and "lesbian" are often used in ways that presume these are unidimensional. When a woman says that she is a "lesbian," we may take for granted that this identity includes homogeneity of sexual behavior, sexual fantasies, and participation in a lesbian community, for example. Consider the following quotation:

> I have been heterosexual as some homosexuals say they have been homosexual: forever. Already, at the age of 5, I was attracted (in some diffuse sense of "attract") to male movie stars in ways that were different from my fascination with female stars. Demands by lesbian separatists earlier in the Second Wave that

heterosexual feminists vacate their relationships with men seemed to me then and seem to me still both cruel and impossible. . . . The impossibility, for women like me, is akin to the impossibility I would feel if, in obedience to political fiat, I were asked to change my fingerprints. (Bartky, 1992, p. 426)

This quotation is noteworthy for highlighting several issues usually assumed about sexual orientation: that it forms at an early age, that it involves sexual attraction, and that it can't be changed. The quote is unusual in that heterosexual women are rarely asked to describe their own sexuality, since heterosexuality is the "default" sexual orientation in Western societies.

Let us assume that sexual orientation is categorical. This would imply that there is a distinct boundary between being a lesbian on the one hand and a heterosexual woman on the other. At one extreme, we could picture a woman who has felt sexual/affectional desire only toward females since she was a girl. Similarly, this woman has had sexual relations only with other females. She considers herself a lesbian and has integrated into the lesbian community.

In reality, few women fit this image. Young girls who are attracted to other girls and women quickly learn to hide these feelings from others and even from themselves. They may date boys and even get married in order to fit the dominant heterosexual lifestyles. Women who do have the courage to express sexual desire and relations with other women may avoid using the term "lesbian" to describe themselves because of its negative connotations.

At the other extreme, a woman may always have been attracted to males and had sexual relations only with men. Yet we know little about heterosexuality among women. Media images of women depict them as very sexual, but in passive, objectified roles (see Umiker-Sebeok, 1981, for a review of this literature). At the same time, there may be pressure by parents and schools for young women to remain celibate, and there are few approved roles for women to be heterosexually active outside of marriage (see Hyde and Jaffee, 2000). Consequently, even heterosexual women may know little about their own sexual desire and attraction.

Some of the earliest writings about sexual orientation focused on "stages" that gay men and lesbians go through in the process of coming out. Generally these stages described an initial sense of difference and identity confusion that eventually was replaced by identity acceptance and synthesis (see Cass, 1979; Coleman, 1981). In this way, lesbians were presumed to move from lack of congruence to congruence between identity and behavior.

How would a categorical definition of sexual orientation include bisexuality? Bisexuality may be viewed as a separate category for women who are attracted to and have sexual relationships with women and men. In the past, categorical definitions of sexual orientation would have excluded bisexuality, viewing bisexuals as women in transition to be lesbians, or as lesbians who wanted a less stigmatizing self-description (Rust, 2000b). Development of a strong bisexual movement and bisexual communities has demonstrated that bisexuality is not transient and in fact may be an even more stigmatized term than lesbianism.

In sum, a dichotomous definition of sexual orientation is bipolar, with heterosexual women and lesbians as opposite constructs. Bisexuality is seen as either nonexistent or as a transitional phase between being heterosexual and lesbian (this point is discussed in detail by Rust, 2000a). There is congruence between sexual identity, behavior, and desire. Thus, if a woman experiences any same-gender behavior or attraction, she is presumed to be a lesbian with a same-gender identity as well.

Continuous Definitions

On the other hand, sexual orientation can be conceptualized as multifaceted. Consider this quotation:

How does my heterosexuality contribute to my feminist politics? That is an impossible question for me to answer because, although I have lived monogamously with a man I love for over 26 years, I am not and never have been a "heterosexual." But neither have I ever been either a "lesbian" or a "bisexual." What I am—and have been for as long as I can remember—is someone whose gender and sexuality have just never seemed to mesh very well with the available cultural categories, and *that*—rather than my presumed heterosexuality—is what has most profoundly informed my feminist politics (Bem, 1992. p. 436)

This statement describes the experience of many women who have unsuccessfully tried to "fit" into categorical definitions. Even as new terminology has entered counterculture vocabularies (e.g., "queer" to describe people who do not have a mainstream sexual orientation), these individuals continue to feel marginalized and disenfranchised. . . .

In sum, from a continuous perspective, sexual orientation is a multidimensional concept that varies in degree and intensity. Sexual orientation is viewed as diverse, with each individual having a unique template of erotic and affectional identity, behavior, fantasies, relationships (including relationship status), and emotional attachments, all of which can change over time (Garnets & Kimmel, 1993). These components can be (and often are) incongruous, so there is no simple relationship among behavior, identity, and desire. For example, many more people engage in same-gender sexual behavior than those who identify as lesbian, gay, or bisexual.

RESEARCH ON SEXUAL ORIENTATION

Most research in this area has used categorical definitions of sexual orientation, such as asking participants to check off whether they are lesbian, bisexual, or heterosexual. Furthermore, a survey entitled "Lesbian Mental Health Survey" (Oetjen & Rothblum, 2000) is unlikely to obtain many respondents who identify as bisexual or heterosexual. Nor will it interest women who are sexually involved with women but who do not identify as lesbian. Such categorical methods introduce a level of artificiality that may not in fact correspond with the identity or experiences of women respondents. . . .

In a recent study, Jessica Morris and I (1999) examined the interrelationships among various dimensions of sexual orientation. The study examined the way in which over 2,000 women who answered a "Lesbian Wellness Survey" were distributed on five aspects of lesbian sexuality and the coming out process. The five aspects were sexual orientation on the "Kinsey Scale" (Kinsey, Pomeroy, & Martin, 1948; Kinsey, Pomeroy, Martin, & Gebhard, 1953); years out (length of time of self-identity as lesbian/gay/bisexual); outness/disclosure (amount of disclosure of sexual orientation to others); sexual experience (proportion of sexual relationships with women compared to men); and lesbian activities (extent of participation in lesbian community events). The intercorrelations among these dimensions were quite low, indicating that being lesbian is not a homogeneous experience.

Closer examination by the demographic characteristics of race/ethnicity and age revealed a diversity of experience. African American, Native American, and Latina respondents had moderate correlations among the aspects of the lesbian experience, whereas the intercorrelations of White and Asian American respondents tended to be mild or nonsignificant. The results indicate that researchers who are studying one aspect of the lesbian experience (e.g., outness to others) need to ensure that they are not assuming such behavior based on other dimensions (such as frequent participation in lesbian community activities or years of being out), especially among White and Asian American lesbians. Most studies of sexual orientation have focused on members of the visible gay and lesbian communities (there is still relatively little research on people who are bisexual). By recruiting participants at lesbian community events or using mailing lists of lesbian newsletters, for example, researchers are stratifying by lesbian *self-identity*. . . .

The limited research on dimensions of women's sexual orientation, whether conducted directly in lesbian/bisexual women's communities or via national surveys, indicates that identity as lesbian or bisexual, sexual activity with women, and sexual desire are separate and (somewhat) overlapping dimensions. This raises the question whether sexual orientation for women should be defined on the basis of sexual activity/attraction and, if so, what *does* sex mean for women?

CONCEPTUAL ISSUES IN FEMALE SEXUAL ACTIVITY

In the United States, the concept of "sex" is so closely linked with genital intercourse that most heterosexual women will not "count" experiences that didn't include this aspect of sexual activity. When asked when they first had "sex," women who have sex with men will often "count" the first time they had sexual intercourse with a man, even if this experience was not particularly sexual for them and even if they had prior sexual experiences that were quite arousing and even led to orgasm (see Rothblum, 1994, for a review). Loulan (1993) has described how female adolescents who have engaged in a variety of sexual activities but have not had intercourse will say that they have not "gone all the way." Thus, women's definition of what constitutes sexual activity with a male partner is often separate from their own sexual arousal and desire.

"Sex" when both partners are female is even more complex. On the one hand, lesbians and bisexual women will say that sex between women allows for a greater variety of sexual expression, exactly because it is not focused on intercourse (see Rothblum, 1999, for a review). On the other hand, sexual activity between women is socially constructed in the lesbian/bisexual communities to mean certain activities and not others. Two women who are "just" kissing and cuddling, for example, have not "gone all the way" (Rothblum, 1999). Interestingly, the current Vermont Youth Behavior Risk Survey (Vermont Department of Health, 1999) asks respondents whether they have had "intercourse" with males only, females only, both males and females, or neither. It is difficult to say how female adolescents will conceptualize "intercourse" between two females, but the wording of this item reflects the salience of the word "intercourse" to mean sexual activity in research.

Research on female sexuality has found lesbians to engage in sexual activity with relatively low frequency. A major survey of sexual activity among 12,000 people (Blumstein & Schwartz, 1983) indicated that lesbians are less likely to have genital sex than are married heterosexual, cohabiting heterosexual, or gay male couples. Loulan (1988) surveyed over 1,500 lesbians and found the majority (78%) to have been celibate for some period of time. Most had been celibate for less than 1 year, 35% had been celibate from 1 to 5 years, and 8% for 6 years or more. The national survey by Laumann et al. (1994) similarly found women to be lower than men on rates of sexual behavior.

The results of these surveys were interpreted as reflecting women's lack of socialization to initiate sexual encounters. Survey authors also indicated that lesbians, being women, placed more focus on love, affection, and romance than on genital sexual activity (e.g., Klinkenberg & Rose, 1994). Thus, heterosexual and bisexual women may have sex more often because men are more likely to want and initiate sexual activity.

It is difficult to obtain accurate data on sexual behavior. Sexual activity is private, and women in particular are not socialized to discuss details of sexual activity. This issue is confounded for lesbians and bisexual women, who may live in areas where same-gender sexual activity is against the law and who may lose their jobs or custody of their children if such knowledge became public. Most sex surveys have been criticized for being of questionable accuracy, as people may not respond honestly for a variety of reasons (see Laumann et al., 1994, for a discussion).

Certainly the low rates of sexual "activity" found in these surveys may in part be due to how sexual behavior is traditionally defined. What are the implications of lesbians engaging in genital sex less than heterosexual women or than men, yet at the same time using a genital-based definition to define "sex"? Is there a way that women of all sexual orientations should discuss the relative devaluation of alternatives to genital sex? Can we reclaim erotic, nongenital experiences as "real" sex?

CONCEPTUAL ISSUES IN FEMALE SEXUAL DESIRE

The lack of congruence between female sexual behavior and desire implies that sexual behavior per se may not be what is most important to women and may not define their sexual identity. On the one hand, women in Western societies live in a culture of sex (Rothblum, 1994) in which images of women being sexual are everywhere in the media and are used to promote a wide range of products in the economy. On the other hand, the overemphasis on sex ignores the reality that women have related passionately and emotionally to other women all their lives.

Some years ago, Kathy Brehony and I (Rothblum & Brehony, 1993) interviewed self-identified lesbians who considered themselves to be in a couple but who were not currently sexual with their partners (and may never have had sex with these partners). Here are some examples of the ways of relating that we found (all names are pseudonyms):

Laura became attracted to her heterosexual roommate, Violet. Violet seemed to encourage the relationship in multiple ways, such as having heart-shaped tattoos made with each other's names and telling Laura it was okay that people mistook them for lovers. When Laura suggested they become lovers, Violet said she couldn't do it. Laura was devastated.

Elizabeth and Marianne were briefly genitally sexual, then Marianne broke that off, saying that the age difference of 20 years was too great for her. Marianne, the younger of the two, became involved sexually with another woman, Eve, and Elizabeth decided to move out of state to get away. Elizabeth and Marianne continued their relationship over the telephone, and both agree that they are the most important people in each other's lives. Elizabeth says about Eve, Marianne's sexual partner, "she will never have access to the total person that I have."

Sarah and Hannah have a primary relationship, but without sex. They have an agreement that they can have other lovers, but only men. Sarah is confused because she is a lesbian, and now her friends only see her with male lovers. It has shaken her whole identity as a lesbian. Hannah is primarily heterosexual. They are both afraid that sex would make them even more intense, given their closeness already.

These examples bring up a number of themes related to sexual desire. When two members of a couple disagree on what constitutes sex and thus whether or not they are having sex, they may also differ on whether or not they are in a real relationship. Even when both members of the couple agree that their genitally asexual relationship makes them a real couple, society in general may not agree with this definition. The couple may hide their asexuality from their community in much the same way that women in past centuries hid their sexuality from the community at large. Societal validation is especially important for women who are not heterosexual, in light of the fact that many of these women felt invisible to society at large when growing up or while coming out. Furthermore, the examples above came from self-identified lesbians; others may exist among women who are passionate about women yet who are married to men, in celibate religious orders, or extremely closeted even to themselves.

METHODOLOGICAL ISSUES FOR FUTURE RESEARCH

. . . In conclusion, what can we say about female sexuality at the end of the millennium? Sexual behavior is still defined in genital ways that may not accurately reflect the totality of women's sexual experiences. Sexual behavior is only one dimension of women's sexuality, and not highly interrelated with sexual desire, attraction, sexual orientation, and so on. There is increasing knowledge that even the concept of gender itself is flexible, complex, and multidimensional, so that knowing who is a "woman" is not as clear-cut as once believed. Far fewer women may be heterosexual in the traditional sense, indicating that more research on women's sexuality is necessary to learn about women's ways

of being in sexual relationships. Even for women who *are* heterosexual, little is known about this "mainstream" group, such as how they came to be heterosexual, the ways that they might question their heterosexuality, and how their sexual desire and attraction differs from those of women who are bisexual or lesbian. Women's sexuality is an area in which we don't even know what most of the questions are, let alone the answers.

DISCUSSION QUESTIONS

1. What assumptions about women's sexuality does this article encourage us to question?
2. Should "sex" be defined as only genital intercourse?

REFERENCES

Bartky, S. L. (1992). Hypatia unbound: A confession. *Feminism & Psychology*, 2, 426–428.

Bem, S. L. (1992). On the inadequacy of our sexual categories: A personal perspective. *Feminism & Psychology*, 3, 436–437.

Blumstein, P., & Schwartz, P. (1983). *American couples.* New York: William Morrow.

Cass, V. C. (1979). Homosexual identity formation: A theoretical model. *Journal of Homosexuality, 4*, 219–235.

Coleman, E. (1981). Developmental stages of the coming out process. *Journal of Homosexuality, 4*, 31–43.

Fehr, B. (1988). Prototype analysis of the concepts of love and commitment. *Journal of Personality and Social Psychology, 55*(4), 557–579.

Garnets, L. D., & Kimmel, D. C. (1993). Introduction: Lesbian and gay male dimensions in the psychological study of human diversity. In L. D. Garnets & D. C. Kimmel (Eds.), *Psychological perspectives on lesbian and gay male experiences* (pp. 1–51). New York: Columbia University Press.

Hill, L. (1996). *Never say never.* Tallahassee, FL: Naiad Press.

Hyde, J. S., & Jaffee, S. R. (2000). Becoming a heterosexual adult: The experiences of young women. *Journal of Social Issues, 56*(2), 283–296.

Kinsey, A. C., Pomeroy, W., & Martin, C. (1948). *Sexual behavior in the human male.* Philadelphia: W. B. Saunders.

Kinsey, A. C., Pomeroy, W. B., Martin, C. F., & Gebhard, P. H. (1953). *Sexual behavior in the human female.* Philadelphia: Saunders.

Klinkenberg, D., & Rose, S. (1994). Dating scripts of lesbians and gay men. *Journal of Homosexuality, 26*, 23–35.

Laumann, E. O., Gagnon, J. H., Michael, R. T., & Michaels, S. (1994). *The social organization of sexuality: Sexual practices in the United States*. Chicago: University of Chicago Press.

Loulan. J. (1988). Research on the sex practices of 1566 lesbians and the clinical applications. *Women and Therapy, 7*, 221–234.

Loulan, J. (1993). Celibacy. In E. D. Rothblum & K. A. Brehony (Eds.), *Boston marriages: Romantic but asexual relationships among contemporary lesbians*. Amherst, MA: University of Massachusetts Press.

Morris, J. F., & Rothblum, E. D. (1999). Who fills out a "lesbian" questionnaire? The interrelationship of sexual orientation, years out, disclosure of sexual orientation, sexual experience with women, and participation in the lesbian community. *Psychology of Women Quarterly, 23*(3), 537–557.

Oetjen, H., & Rothblum, E. D. (2000). When lesbians aren't gay: Factors affecting depression among lesbians. *Journal of Homosexuality, 39*(1), 49–73.

Rosch, E. (1978). Principles of categorization. In E. Rosch & B. B. Lloyd (Eds.), *Cognition and categorization* (pp. 27–48). Hillsdale, NJ: Erlbaum.

Rothblum, E. D. (1994). I only read about myself on bathroom walls: The need for research on the mental health of lesbians and gay men. *Journal of Consulting and Clinical Psychology, 62*, 213–220.

Rothblum, E. D. (1999). Poly-friendships. *Journal of Lesbian Studies, 3*, 71–83.

Rothblum, E. D., & Brehony, K. A. (Eds.). (1993). *Boston marriages: Romantic but asexual relationships among contemporary lesbians*. Amherst, MA: University of Massachusetts.

Rust, P. C. (2000a). Bisexuality: A contemporary paradox for woman. *Journal of Social Issues, 56*(2), 205–221.

Rust, P. C. (2000b). *Bisexuality in the United States: A reader and guide to the literature*. New York: Columbia University Press.

Umiker-Sebeok, J. (1981). The seven ages of woman: A view from American magazine advertisements. In C. Mayo & N. M. Henley (Eds.), *Gender and nonverbal behavior* (pp. 209–252). New York: Springer-Verlag.

Vermont Department of Health. (1999). Vermont Youth Behavior Risk Survey. Unpublished survey currently in progress.

SOCIAL CLASS

READING 31

Cause of Death: Inequality

Alejandro Reuss

You won't see inequality on a medical chart or a coroner's report under "cause of death." You won't see it listed among the top killers in the United States each year. All too often, however, it is social inequality that lurks behind a more immediate cause of death, be it heart disease or diabetes, accidental injury or homicide. Few of the top causes of death are "equal opportunity killers." Instead, they tend to strike poor people more than rich people, the less educated more than the highly

educated, people lower on the occupational ladder more than those higher up, or people of color more than white people.

Statistics on mortality and life expectancy do not provide a perfect map of social inequality. For example, the life expectancy for women in the United States is about six years longer than the life expectancy for men, despite the many ways in which women are subordinated to men. Take most indicators of socioeconomic status, however, and most causes of death, and it's a strong bet that you'll find illness and injury (or "morbidity") and mortality increasing as status decreases.

Men with less than 12 years of education are more than twice as likely to die of chronic diseases (e.g., heart disease), more than three times as likely to die as a result of injury, and nearly twice as likely to die of communicable diseases, compared to those with 13 or more years of education. Women

---

Alejandro Reuss is co-editor of *Dollars & Sense* and an instructor at the Labor Relations and Research Center at the University of Massachusetts, Amherst.

with family incomes below $10,000 are more than three times as likely to die of heart disease and nearly three times as likely to die of diabetes, compared to those with family incomes above $25,000. African Americans are more likely than whites to die of heart disease; stroke; lung, colon, prostate, and breast cancer, as well as all cancers combined; liver disease; diabetes; AIDS; accidental injury; and homicide. In all, the lower you are in a social hierarchy, the worse your health and the shorter your life are likely to be.

THE WORSE OFF IN THE UNITED STATES ARE NOT WELL OFF BY WORLD STANDARDS

You often hear it said that even poor people in rich countries like the United States are rich compared to ordinary people in poor countries. While that may be true when it comes to consumer goods like televisions or telephones, which are widely available even to poor people in the United States, it's completely wrong when it comes to health.

In a 1996 study published in *The New England Journal of Medicine*, University of Michigan researchers found that African-American females living to age 15 in Harlem had a 65% chance of surviving to age 65, about the same as women in India. Meanwhile, Harlem's African-American males had only a 37% chance of surviving to age 65, about the same as men in Angola or the Democratic Republic of Congo. Among both African-American men and women, infectious diseases and diseases of the circulatory system were the prime causes of high mortality.

It takes more income to achieve a given life expectancy in a rich country like the United States than it does to achieve the same life expectancy in a less affluent country. So the higher money income of a low-income person in the United States, compared to a middle-income person in a poor country, does not necessarily translate into a longer life span. The average income per person in African-American families, for example, is more than five times the per capita income of El Salvador. The life expectancy for African-American men in the United States, however, is only about 67 years, the same as the average life expectancy for men in El Salvador.

HEALTH INEQUALITIES IN THE UNITED STATES ARE NOT JUST ABOUT ACCESS TO HEALTH CARE

Nearly one-sixth of the U.S. population lacks health insurance, including about 44% of poor people. A poor adult with a health problem is only half as likely to see a doctor as a high-income adult. Adults living in low-income areas are more than twice as likely to be hospitalized for a health problem that could have been effectively treated with timely outpatient care, compared with adults living in high-income areas. Obviously, lack of access to health care is a major health problem.

But so are environmental and occupational hazards; communicable diseases; homicide and firearm-related injuries; and smoking, alcohol consumption, lack of exercise, and other risk factors. These dangers all tend to affect lower-income people more than higher-income, less educated people more than more-educated, and people of color more than whites. African-American children are more than twice as likely as white children to be hospitalized for asthma, which is linked to air pollution. Poor men are nearly six times as likely as high-income men to have elevated blood-lead levels, which reflect both residential and workplace environmental hazards. African-American men are more than seven times as likely to fall victim to homicide as white men; African-American women, more than four times as likely as white women. The less education someone has, the more likely they are to smoke or to drink heavily. The lower someone's income, the less likely they are to get regular exercise.

Michael Marmot, a pioneer in the study of social inequality and health, notes that so-called diseases of affluence—disorders, like heart disease, associated with high calorie and high-fat diets, lack of physical activity, etc.—are most prevalent among the least affluent people in rich societies. While recognizing the role of such "behavioral" risk factors as smoking in producing poor health, he argues, "It is not sufficient . . . to ask what contribution smoking makes to generating the social gradient in ill health, but we must ask, why is there a social gradient in smoking?" What appear to be individual "lifestyle" decisions often reflect a broader social epidemiology.

GREATER INCOME INEQUALITY GOES HAND IN HAND WITH POORER HEALTH

Numerous studies suggest that the more unequal the income distribution in a country, state, or city, the lower the life expectancies for people at all income levels. One study published in the *American Journal of Public Health,* for example, shows that U.S. metropolitan areas with low per capita incomes and low levels of income inequality have lower mortality rates than areas with high median incomes and high levels of income inequality. Meanwhile, for a given per capita income range, mortality rates always decline as inequality declines.

R. G. Wilkinson, perhaps the researcher most responsible for relating health outcomes to overall levels of inequality (rather than individual income levels), argues that greater income inequality causes worse health outcomes independent of its effects on poverty. Wilkinson and his associates suggest several explanations for this relationship. First, the bigger the income gap between rich and poor, the less inclined the well off are to pay taxes for public services they either do not use or use in low proportion to the taxes they pay. Lower spending on public hospitals, schools, and other basic services does not affect wealthy people's life expectancies very much, but it affects poor people's life expectancies a great deal. Second, the bigger the income gap, the lower the overall level of social cohesion.

High levels of social cohesion are associated with good health outcomes for several reasons. For example, people in highly cohesive societies are more likely to be active in their communities, reducing social isolation, a known health risk factor. (See Thad Williamson, "Social Movements Are Good for Your Health")

Numerous researchers have criticized Wilkinson's conclusions, arguing that the real reason income inequality tends to be associated with worse health outcomes is that it is associated with higher rates of poverty. But even if they are right and income inequality causes worse health simply by bringing about greater poverty, that hardly makes for a defense of inequality. Poverty and inequality are like partners in crime. "[W]hether public policy focuses primarily on the elimination of poverty or on reduction in income disparity," argue Wilkinson critics Kevin Fiscella and Peter Franks, "neither goal is likely to be achieved in the absence of the other."

DIFFERENCES IN STATUS MAY BE JUST AS IMPORTANT AS INCOME LEVELS

Even after accounting for differences in income, education, and other factors, the life expectancy for African Americans is less than that for whites. U.S. researchers are beginning to explore the relationship between high blood pressure among African Americans and the racism of the surrounding society. African Americans tend to suffer from high blood pressure, a risk factor for circulatory disease, more often than whites. Moreover, studies have found that, when confronted with racism, African Americans suffer larger and longer-lasting increases in blood pressure than when faced with other stressful situations. Broader surveys relating blood pressure in African Americans to perceived instances of racial discrimination have yielded complex results, depending on social class, gender, and other factors.

Stresses cascade down social hierarchies and accumulate among the least empowered. Even researchers focusing on social inequality and health, however, have been surprised by the large effects on mortality. Over 30 years ago, Michael Marmot and his associates undertook a landmark study, known as Whitehall I, of health among British civil servants. Since the civil servants shared many characteristics regardless of job classification—an office work environment, a high degree of job security, etc.—the researchers expected to find only modest health differences among them. To their surprise, the study revealed a sharp increase in mortality with each step down the job hierarchy—even from the highest grade to the second highest. Over ten years, employees in the lowest grade were three times as likely to die as those in the highest grade. One factor was that people in lower grades showed a higher incidence of many "lifestyle" risk factors, like smoking, poor diet, and lack of exercise. Even when the researchers controlled for such factors, however, more than half the mortality gap remained.

Marmot noted that people in the lower job grades were less likely to describe themselves as having "control over their working lives" or being "satisfied with their work situation," compared to those higher up. While people in higher job grades were more likely to report "having to work at a fast pace," lower-level civil servants were more likely to report feelings of hostility, the main stress-related risk factor for heart disease. Marmot concluded that "psychosocial" factors—the psychological costs of being lower in the hierarchy—played an important role in the unexplained mortality gap. Many of us have probably said to ourselves, after a trying day on the job, "They're killing me." Turns out it's not just a figure of speech. Inequality kills—and it starts at the bottom.

DISCUSSION QUESTIONS

1. What explanation can you offer for why the rich are less likely to support public services in communities with a wide income gap between the rich and poor?
2. Why do you think there might be social class differences in smoking, drinking, or exercise?

REFERENCES

Lisa Berkman, "Social Inequalities and Health: Five Key Points for Policy-Makers to Know," February 5, 2001, Kennedy School of Government, Harvard University.

Kevin Fiscella and Peter Franks, "Poverty or income inequality as predictors of mortality: longitudinal cohort study," *British Medical Journal* 314: 1724–8, 1997.

Arline T. Geronimus, et al., "Excess Mortality among Blacks and Whites in the United States," *The New England Journal of Medicine* 335 (21), November 21, 1996.

Health, United States, 1998, with Socioeconomic Status and Health Chartbook, National Center for Health Statistics, www.cdc.gov/nchs.

Human Development Report 2000, UN Development Programme.

Ichiro Kawachi, Bruce P. Kennedy, and Richard G. Wilkinson, eds., *The Society and Population Health Reader, Volume I: Income Inequality and Health,* 1999.

Nancy Krieger, Ph.D., and Stephen Sidney, M.D., "Racial Discrimination and Blood Pressure: The CARDIA Study of Young Black and White Adults," *American Journal of Public Health* 86 (10), October 1996.

Michael Marmot, "Social Differences in Mortality: The Whitehall Studies," *Adult Mortality in Developed Countries: From Description to Explanation,* Alan D. Lopez, Graziella Caselli, and Tapani Valkonen, eds., 1995.

Michael Marmot, "The Social Pattern of Health and Disease," *Health and Social Organization: Towards a Health Policy for the Twenty First Century,* David Blane, Eric Brunner, and Richard Wilkinson, eds., 1996.

Thad Williamson, "Social Movements Are Good for Your Health," *Dollars and Sense,* May/June, 2001.

World Development Indicators 2000, World Bank.

READING 32

Why Are Droves of Unqualified, Unprepared Kids Getting into Our Top Colleges? Because Their Dads Are Alumni

John Larew

Growing up, she heard a hundred Harvard stories. In high school, she put the college squarely in her sights. But when judgment day came, the Harvard admissions guys were frankly unimpressed. Her academic record was solid—not special. Extracurriculars, interview, recommendations? Above average, but not by much. "Nothing really stands out" one admissions officer scribbled on her application folder. Wrote another, "Harvard not really the right place."

At the hyperselective Harvard, where high school valedictorians, National Merit Scholar finalists, musical prodigies—11,000 ambitious kids in all—are rejected annually, this young woman didn't seem to have much of a chance. Thanks to Harvard's largest affirmative action program, she got in anyway. No, she wasn't poor, black, disabled, Hispanic, native American, or even Aleutian. She got in because her mom went to Harvard.

Folk wisdom at Harvard holds that "Mother Harvard does not coddle her young." She sure treats her grandkids right, though. For more than 40 years, an astounding one-fifth of Harvard's students have received admissions preference because parents attended the school. Today, these overwhelmingly affluent, white children of alumni—"legacies"—are three times more likely to be accepted to Harvard than high school kids who lack that handsome lineage.

Yalies, don't feel smug: Offspring of the Old Blue are two-and-a-half times more likely to be accepted than their unconnected peers. Dartmouth this year admitted 57 percent of its legacy applicants, compared to 27 percent of nonlegacies.

At the University of Pennsylvania, 66 percent of legacies were admitted last year—thanks in part to an autonomous "office of alumni admissions" that actively lobbies for alumni children before the admissions committee. "One can argue that it's an accident, but it sure doesn't look like an accident," admits Yale Dean of Admissions Worth David.

If the legacies' big edge seems unfair to the tens of thousands who get turned away every year, Ivy League administrators have long defended the innocence of the legacy stat. Children of alumni are just smarter; they come from privileged backgrounds and tend to grow up in homes where parents encourage learning. That's what Harvard Dean of Admissions William Fitzsimmons told the campus newspaper, the *Harvard Crimson,* when it first reported on the legacy preference last year. Departing Harvard President Derek Bok patiently explained that the legacy preference worked only as a "tie-breaking factor" between otherwise equally qualified candidates.

Since Ivy League admissions data is a notoriously classified commodity, when Harvard officials said in previous years that alumni kids were just better, you had to take them at their word. But then federal investigators came along and pried open those top-secret files. The Harvard guys were lying.

This past fall, after two years of study, the U.S. Department of Education's Office for Civil Rights (OCR) found that, far from being more qualified or even equally qualified, the average admitted legacy at Harvard between 1981 and 1988 was significantly *less* qualified than the average admitted nonlegacy. Examining admissions office ratings on academics, extracurriculars, personal qualities, recommendations, and other categories, the OCR concluded that "with the exception of the athletic rating, [admitted] nonlegacies scored better than legacies in *all* areas of comparison."

Exceptionally high admission rates, lowered admission standards, preferential treatment . . . hmmm. These sound like the cries heard in the growing fury over affirmative action for racial minorities in America's elite universities. Only no one is outraged about legacies.

John Larew wrote this article when he was editor of Harvard's student newspaper, *The Harvard Crimson.*

- In his recent book, *Preferential Policies,* Thomas Sowell argues that doling out special treatment encourages lackluster performance by the favored and resentment from the spurned. His far-ranging study flits from Malaysia to South Africa to American college campuses. Legacies don't merit a word.

- Dinesh D'Souza, in his celebrated jeremiad *Illiberal Education,* blames affirmative action in college admissions for declining academic standards and increasing racial tensions. Lowered standards for minority applicants, he hints, may soon destroy the university as we know it. Lowered standards for legacies? The subject doesn't come up.

- For all his polysyllabic complaints against preferential admissions, William F. Buckley Jr. (Yale 50) has never bothered to note that son Chris (Yale 75) got the benefit of a policy that more than doubled his chance of admission.

With so much silence on the subject, you'd be excused for thinking that in these enlightened times hereditary preferences are few and far between. But you'd be wrong. At most elite universities during the eighties, the legacy was by far the biggest piece of the preferential pie. At Harvard, a legacy is about twice as likely to be admitted as a black or Hispanic student. As sociologists Jerome Karabel and David Karen point out, if alumni children were admitted to Harvard at the same rate as other applicants, their numbers in the class of 1992 would have been reduced by about 200. Instead, those 200 marginally qualified legacies outnumbered all black, Mexican-American, native American, and Puerto Rican enrollees put together. If a few marginally qualified minorities are undermining Harvard's academic standards as much as conservatives charge, think about the damage all those legacies must be doing.

Mind you, colleges have the right to give the occasional preference—to bend the rules for the brilliant oboist or the world-class curler or the guy whose remarkable decency can't be measured by the SAT. (I happened to benefit from a geographical edge: It's easier to get into Harvard from West Virginia than from New England.) And until standardized tests and grade point average perfectly reflect the character, judgment, and drive of a student, tips like these aren't just nice, they're fair. Unfortunately, the extent of the legacy privilege in elite American colleges suggests something more than the occasional tie-breaking tip. Forget meritocracy. When 20 percent of Harvard's student body gets a legacy preference, aristocracy is the word that comes to mind.

A CASTE OF THOUSANDS

If complaining about minority preferences is fashionable in the world of competitive colleges, bitching about legacies is just plain gauche, suggesting an unhealthy resentment of the privileged. But the effects of the legacy trickle down. For every legacy that wins, someone—usually someone less privileged—loses. And higher education is a high-stakes game.

High school graduates earn 59 percent of the income of four-year college graduates. Between high school graduates and alumni of prestigious colleges, the disparity is far greater. A *Fortune* study of American CEOs shows the usual suspects—graduates of Yale, Princeton, and Harvard—leading the list. A recent survey of the Harvard Class of 1940 found that 43 percent were worth more than $1 million. With some understatement, the report concludes, "A picture of highly advantageous circumstances emerges here, does it not, compared with American society as a whole?"

An Ivy League diploma doesn't necessarily mean a fine education. Nor does it guarantee future success. What it *does* represent is a big head start in the rat race—a fact Harvard will be the first to tell you. When I was a freshman, a counselor at the Office of Career Services instructed a group of us to make the Harvard name stand out on our résumés: "Underline it, boldface it, put it in capital letters."

Of course, the existence of the legacy preference in this fierce career competition isn't exactly news. According to historians, it was a direct result of the influx of Jews into the Ivy League during the twenties. Until then, Harvard, Princeton, and Yale had admitted anyone who could pass their entrance exams, but suddenly Jewish kids were outscoring the WASPs. So the schools began to use nonacademic criteria—"character," "solidity," and, eventually, lineage—to justify accepting low-scoring blue bloods over their peers. Yale implemented its legacy preference first, in 1925—spelling it out in a memo four years later: The school would admit "Yale sons of good character and reasonably good record . . . regardless of the number of applicants and the superiority of outside competitors." Harvard and Princeton followed shortly thereafter.

Despite its ignoble origins, the legacy preference has only sporadically come under fire, most notably in 1978's affirmative action decision, *University of California Board of Regents v. Bakke.* In his concurrence, Justice Harris Blackmun observed, "It is somewhat ironic to have us so deeply disturbed over a program where race is an element of consciousness, and yet to be aware of the fact, as we are, that institutions of higher learning . . . have given conceded preferences to the children of alumni."

If people are, in fact, aware of the legacy preference, why has it been spared the scrutiny given other preferential policies? One reason is public ignorance of the scope and scale of those preferences—an ignorance carefully cultivated by America's elite institutions. It's easy to maintain the fiction that your legacies get in strictly on merit as long as your admissions bureaucracy controls all access to student data. Information on Harvard's legacies became publicly available not because of any fit of disclosure by the university, but because a few civil rights types noted that the school had a suspiciously low rate of admission for Asian-Americans, who are statistically stronger than other racial groups in academics.

While the ensuing OCR inquiry found no evidence of illegal racial discrimination by Harvard, it did turn up some embarrassing information about how much weight the "legacy" label gives an otherwise flimsy file. Take these comments scrawled by admissions officers on applicant folders:

- "Double lineage who chose the right parents."
- "Dad's [deleted] connections signify lineage of more than usual weight. That counted into the

equation makes this a case which (assuming positive TRs [teacher recommendations] and Alum IV [alumnus interview]) is well worth doing."
- "Lineage is main thing."
- "Not quite strong enough to get the clean tip."
- "Classical case that would be hard to explain to dad."
- "Double lineage but lots of problems."
- "Not a great profile, but just strong enough #'s and grades to get the tip from lineage."
- "Without lineage, there would be little case. With it, we'll keep looking."

In every one of these cases, the applicant was admitted.

Of course, Harvard's not doing anything other schools aren't. The practice of playing favorites with alumni children is nearly universal among private colleges and isn't unheard of at public institutions, either. The rate of admission for Stanford's alumni children is "almost twice the general population," according to a spokesman for the admissions office. Notre Dame reserves 25 percent of each freshman class for legacies. At the University of Virginia, where native Virginians make up two-thirds of each class, alumni children are automatically treated as Virginians even if they live out of state—giving them a whopping competitive edge. The same is true of the University of California at Berkeley. At many schools, Harvard included, all legacy applications are guaranteed a read by the dean of admissions himself—a privilege nonlegacies don't get.

LITTLE WHITE ELIS

Like the Harvard deans, officials at other universities dismiss the statistical disparities by pointing to the superior environmental influences found in the homes of their alums. "I bet that, statistically, [legacy qualifications are] a little above average, but not by much," says Paul Killebrew, associate director of admissions at Dartmouth. "The admitted group [of legacies] would look exactly like the profile of the class."

James Wickenden, a former dean of admissions at Princeton who now runs a college consulting firm, suspects otherwise. Wickenden wrote of "one Ivy League university" where the average combined SAT score of the freshman class was 1,350 out of a possible 1,600, compared to 1,280 for legacies. "At most selective schools, [legacy status] doubles, even trebles the chances of admission," he says. Many colleges even place admitted legacies in a special "Not in Profile" file (along with recruited athletes and some minority students), so that when the school's SAT scores are published, alumni kids won't pull down the average.

How do those kids fare once they're enrolled? No one's telling. Harvard, for one, refuses to keep any records of how alumni children stack up academically against their nonlegacy classmates—perhaps because the last such study, in 1956, showed Harvard sons hogging the bottom of the grade curve.

If the test scores of admitted legacies are a mystery, the reason colleges accept so many is not. They're afraid the alumni parents of rejected children will stop giving to the colleges' unending fundraising campaigns. "Our survival as an institution depends on having support from alumni," says Richard Steele, director of undergraduate admissions at Duke University, "so according advantages to alumni kids is just a given."

In fact, the OCR exonerated Harvard's legacy preference precisely because legacies bring in money. (OCR cited a federal district court ruling that a state university could favor the children of out-of-state alumni because "defendants showed that the alumni provide monetary support for the university.") And there's no question that alumni provide significant support to Harvard: Last year, they raised $20 million for the scholarship fund alone.

In a letter to OCR defending his legacies, Harvard's Fitzsimmons painted a grim picture of a school where the preference did not exist—a place peeved alumni turned their backs on when their kids failed to make the cut. "Without the fundraising activities of alumni," Fitzsimmons warned darkly, "Harvard could not maintain many of its programs, including needs-blind admissions."

Ignoring, for the moment, the question of how "needs-blind" a system is that admits one-fifth of

each class on the assumption that, hey, their parents might give us money, Fitzsimmons's defense doesn't quite ring true. The "Save the Scholarship Fund" line is a variation on the principle of "Firemen First," whereby bureaucrats threatened with a budget cut insist that essential programs rather than executive perks and junkets will be the first to be slashed. Truth be told, there is just about nothing that Harvard, the richest university in the world, could do to jeopardize needs-blind admissions, provided that it placed a high enough priority on them.

But even more unclear is how closely alumni giving is related to the acceptance of alumni kids. "People whose children are denied admission are initially upset," says Wickenden, "and maybe for a year or two their interest in the university wanes. But typically they come back around when they see that what happened was best for the kids." Wickenden has put his money where his mouth is: He rejected two sons of a Princeton trustee involved in a $420 million fundraising project, not to mention the child of a board member who managed the school's $2 billion endowment, all with no apparent ill effect.

Most university administrators would be loath to take such a chance, despite a surprising lack of evidence of the legacy/largess connection. Fitzsimmons admits Harvard knows of no empirical research to support the claim that diminishing legacies would decrease alumni contributions, relying instead on "hundreds, perhaps thousands of conversations with alumni whose sons and daughters applied."

No doubt some of Fitzsimmons's anxiety is founded: It's only natural for alumni to want their kids to have the same privileges they did. But the historical record suggests that alumni are far more tolerant than administrators realize. Admit women and blacks? *Well, we would,* said administrators earlier this century—*but the alumni just won't have it.* Fortunately for American universities, the bulk of those alumni turned out to be less craven than administrators thought they'd be. As more blacks and women enrolled over the past two decades, the funds kept pouring in, reaching an all-time high in the eighties.

Another significant historical lesson can be drawn from the late fifties, when Harvard's selectiveness increased dramatically. As the number of applications soared, the rate of admission for legacies began declining from about 90 percent to its current 43 percent. Administration anxiety rose inversely, but Harvard's fundraising machine has somehow survived. That doesn't mean there's *no* correlation between alumni giving and the legacy preference, obviously; rather, it means that the people who would withhold their money at the loss of the legacy privilege were far outnumbered by other givers. "It takes time to get the message out," explains Fitzsimmons, "but eventually people start responding. We've had to make the case [for democratization] to alumni, and I think that they generally feel good about that."

HEIR CUT

When justice dictates that ordinary kids should have as fair a shot as the children of America's elite, couldn't Harvard and its sister institutions trouble themselves to "get the message out" again? Of course they could. But virtually no one—liberal or conservative—is pushing them to do so.

"There must be no goals or quotas for any special group or category of applicants," reads an advertisement in the right-wing *Dartmouth Review.* "Equal opportunity must be the guiding policy. Males, females, blacks, whites, Native Americans, Hispanics . . . can all be given equal chance to matriculate, survive, and prosper based solely on individual performance."

Noble sentiments from the Ernest Martin Hopkins Institute, an organization of conservative Dartmouth alumni. Reading on, though, we find these "concerned alumni" aren't sacrificing *their* young to the cause. "Alumni sons and daughters," notes the ad further down, "should receive some special consideration."

Similarly, Harvard's conservative *Salient* has twice in recent years decried the treatment of Asian-Americans in admissions, but it attributes their misfortune to favoritism for blacks and Hispanics. What about legacy university favoritism—a much bigger factor? *Salient* writers have twice endorsed it.

What's most surprising is the indifference of minority activists. With the notable exception of a few vocal Asian-Americans, most have made peace with the preference for well-off whites.

Mecca Nelson, the president of Harvard's Black Students Association, leads rallies for the hiring of more minority faculty. She participated in an illegal sit-in at an administration building in support of Afro-American studies. But when it comes to the policy that Asian-American activist Arthur Hu calls "a 20-percent-white quota," Nelson says, "I don't have any really strong opinions about it. I'm not very clear on the whole legacy issue at all."

Joshua Li, former co-chair of Harvard's Asian-American Association, explains his complacency differently: "We understand that in the future Asian-American students will receive these tips as well."

At America's elite universities, you'd expect a somewhat higher standard of fairness than that—especially when money is the driving force behind the concept. And many Ivy League types *do* advocate for more just and lofty ideals. One of them, as it happens, is Derek Bok. In one of Harvard's annual reports, he warned that the modern university is slowly turning from a truth-seeking enterprise into a money-grubbing corporation—at the expense of the loyalty of its alums. "Such an institution may still evoke pride and respect because of its intellectual achievements," he said rightly. "But the feelings it engenders will not be quite the same as those produced by an institution that is prepared to forgo income, if need be, to preserve values of a nobler kind."

Forgo income to preserve values of a nobler kind—it's an excellent idea. Embrace the preferences for the poor and disadvantaged. Wean alumni from the idea of the legacy edge. And above all, stop the hypocrisy that begrudges the great unwashed a place at Harvard while happily making room for the less qualified sons and daughters of alums.

After 70 years, it won't be easy to wrest the legacy preference away from the alums. But the long-term payoff is as much a matter of message as money. When the sons and daughters of today's college kids fill out *their* applications, the legacy preference should seem not a birthright, but a long-gone relic from the Ivy League's inequitable past.

DISCUSSION QUESTIONS

1. Do you think legacy preferences are unfair? Why or why not? How do you think they compare to minority preferences?

2. John Larew, then editor of the *Harvard Crimson,* was the first to bring the subject of legacy preference to national attention. Since then, these preferences have received a good deal of media attention. Do you think that legacy admissions are now stigmatized admissions like affirmative action admissions?

PERSONAL ACCOUNT

That Moment of Visibility

I never realized how much my working-class background and beliefs played a role in my education. My family, friends, and neighbors never placed much importance on college. Instead, we were strongly encouraged to find work immediately after high school so we could support ourselves financially. My sisters and I were encouraged to do secretarial work until we married. There was no particular positive status attached to obtaining a degree except maybe the chance of making a lot of money. In fact, friends who went to college were looked at somewhat suspiciously. Among my reference group, college was often seen as a way to get out of having to work.

No one in my family had ever gone to college. It was not financially feasible and a college environment was equal to the unknown. It really was scary terrain. When I decided to go to a local community college after having worked for five years in a secretarial position, family and friends could not understand my decision. Why would I choose college when I already had a job? I could pay bills, buy what I needed, and I had a savings account. So I started by taking a course a semester—and I barely got through the first course. Although I received a good grade, I felt incredibly isolated, like I was an impostor who did not belong in a classroom. I had no idea how someone in college was supposed to act. I stayed silent, scared, and consciously invisible most of the time. I was not even close to making a commitment to a college education when I signed up for a second course—but because my job paid for it (one of the benefits), I felt I had nothing to lose. I signed up for Introduction to Juvenile Delinquency and midway through, our class received an assignment to do a fifteen-page self-analysis applying some of the theories we were learning. The thought of

consciously revealing myself when I was trying so hard not to look, act, or be different was not something I was willing (or, I think, able at the time) to do. When I discussed the assignment with the people close to me, they agreed that the assignment was too personal and revealing. I decided not to do it and I also decided that college was probably not for me.

I went to see my professor (who was the only woman in her department) to let her know that I was refusing to do the assignment and would not complete the course. We had spoken two or three times outside of class and she knew a little about me. I knew that she was also from a working-class background and had returned to school after working some years. I felt the least I could do was tell her I was quitting the class. When I said that I was unwilling to do the assignment, she stared at me for some time, and then asked me what I would prefer to write about. I was stunned that I was noticed and was being asked what I would like to do. When I had no reply, she asked if I would write a paper on the importance of dissent. All I could think to say was yes. I completed the course successfully and found an ally in my department. I can't overstate the importance of that moment of acknowledgment. It was the first time I felt listened to. It was the moment when you feel safe enough to reveal who you are, the deep breath you can finally take when you figure out that the person you're talking to understands, appreciates, and may even share your identity.

I think of this experience as a turning point for me—when I realized that despite all my conscious efforts to be invisible and to "pass," it was that moment of visibility and acknowledgment that kept me in school.

Rose B. Pascarell

READING 33

The Myth of the "Culture of Poverty"

Paul Gorski

As the students file out of Janet's classroom, I sit in the back corner, scribbling a few final notes. Defeat in her eyes, Janet drops into a seat next to me with a sigh.

"I *love* these kids," she declares, as if trying to convince me. "I adore them. But my hope is fading."

"Why's that?" I ask, stuffing my notes into a folder.

"They're smart. I know they're smart, but . . ."

And then the deficit floodgates open: "They don't care about school. They're unmotivated. And their parents—I'm lucky if two or three of them show up for conferences. No wonder the kids are unprepared to learn."

At Janet's invitation, I spent dozens of hours in her classroom, meeting her students, observing her teaching, helping her navigate the complexities of an urban midwestern elementary classroom with a growing percentage of students in poverty. I observed powerful moments of teaching and learning, caring and support. And I witnessed moments of internal conflict in Janet, when what she wanted to believe about her students collided with her prejudices.

Like most educators, Janet is determined to create an environment in which each student reaches his or her full potential. And like many of us, despite overflowing with good intentions, Janet has bought into the most common and dangerous myths about poverty.

Chief among these is the "culture of poverty" myth—the idea that poor people share more or less monolithic and predictable beliefs, values, and behaviors. For educators like Janet to be the best

teachers they can be for all students, they need to challenge this myth and reach a deeper understanding of class and poverty.

ROOTS OF THE CULTURE OF POVERTY CONCEPT

Oscar Lewis coined the term *culture of poverty* in his 1961 book *The Children of Sanchez.* Lewis based his thesis on his ethnographic studies of small Mexican communities. His studies uncovered approximately 50 attributes shared within these communities: frequent violence, a lack of a sense of history, a neglect of planning for the future, and so on. Despite studying very small communities, Lewis extrapolated his findings to suggest a universal culture of poverty. More than 45 years later, the premise of the culture of poverty paradigm remains the same: that people in poverty share a consistent and observable "culture."

Lewis ignited a debate about the nature of poverty that continues today. But just as important—especially in the age of data-driven decision making—he inspired a flood of research. Researchers around the world tested the culture of poverty concept empirically (see Billings, 1974; Carman, 1985; Jones & Luo, 1999). Others analyzed the overall body of evidence regarding the culture of poverty paradigm (see Abell & Lyon, 1979; Ortiz & Briggs, 2003; Rodman, 1977).

These studies raise a variety of questions and come to a variety of conclusions about poverty. But on this they all agree: *There is no such thing as a culture of poverty.* Differences in values and behaviors among poor people are just as great as those between poor and wealthy people.

In actuality, the culture of poverty concept is constructed from a collection of smaller stereotypes which, however false, seem to have crept into mainstream thinking as unquestioned fact. Let's look at some examples.

- **MYTH:** Poor people are unmotivated and have weak work ethics.
- **The Reality:** Poor people do not have weaker work ethics or lower levels of motivation than

---

Paul Gorski is a professor of integrative studies at George Mason University.

wealthier people (Iversen & Farber, 1996; Wilson, 1997). Although poor people are often stereotyped as lazy, 83 percent of children from low-income families have at least one employed parent; close to 60 percent have at least one parent who works full-time and year-round (National Center for Children in Poverty, 2004). In fact, the severe shortage of living-wage jobs means that many poor adults must work two, three, or four jobs. According to the Economic Policy Institute (2002), poor working adults spend more hours working each week than their wealthier counterparts.

- **MYTH:** Poor parents are uninvolved in their children's learning, largely because they do not value education.
- **The Reality:** Low-income parents hold the same attitudes about education that wealthy parents do (Compton-Lilly, 2003; Lareau & Horvat, 1999; Leichter, 1978). Low-income parents are less likely to attend school functions or volunteer in their children's classrooms (National Center for Education Statistics, 2005)—not because they care less about education but because they have less *access* to school involvement than their wealthier peers. They are more likely to work multiple jobs, to work evenings, to have jobs without paid leave, and to be unable to afford child care and public transportation. It might be said more accurately that schools that fail to take these considerations into account do not value the involvement of poor families as much as they value the involvement of other families.
- **MYTH:** Poor people are linguistically deficient.
- **The Reality:** All people, regardless of the languages and language varieties they speak, use a full continuum of language registers (Bomer, Dworin, May, & Semingson, 2008). What's more, linguists have known for decades that all language varieties are highly structured with complex grammatical rules (Gee, 2004; Hess, 1974; Miller, Cho, & Bracey, 2005). What often are assumed to be *deficient* varieties of English—Appalachian varieties, perhaps, or what some

refer to as Black English Vernacular—are no less sophisticated than so-called "standard English."

- **MYTH:** Poor people tend to abuse drugs and alcohol.
- **The Reality:** Poor people are no more likely than their wealthier counterparts to abuse alcohol or drugs. Although drug sales are more visible in poor neighborhoods, drug use is equally distributed across poor, middle class, and wealthy communities (Saxe, Kadushin, Tighe, Rindskopf, & Beveridge, 2001). Chen, Sheth, Krejci, and Wallace (2003) found that alcohol consumption is *significantly higher* among upper middle class white high school students than among poor black high school students. Their finding supports a history of research showing that alcohol abuse is far more prevalent among wealthy people than among poor people (Diala, Muntaner, & Walrath, 2004; Galea, Ahern, Tracy, & Vlahov, 2007). In other words, considering alcohol and illicit drugs together, wealthy people are more likely than poor people to be substance abusers.

THE CULTURE OF CLASSISM

The myth of a "culture of poverty" distracts us from a dangerous culture that does exist—the culture of classism. This culture continues to harden in our schools today. It leads the most well intentioned of us, like my friend Janet, into low expectations for low-income students. It makes teachers fear their most powerless pupils. And, worst of all, it diverts attention from what people in poverty do have in common: inequitable access to basic human rights.

The most destructive tool of the culture of classism is deficit theory. In education, we often talk about the deficit perspective—defining students by their weaknesses rather than their strengths. Deficit theory takes this attitude a step further, suggesting that poor people are poor because of their own moral and intellectual deficiencies (Collins, 1988) Deficit theorists use two strategies for propagating this world view: (1) drawing on well-established stereotypes, and (2) ignoring systemic conditions, such as inequitable access to high-quality schooling, that support the cycle of poverty.

The implications of deficit theory reach far beyond individual bias. If we convince ourselves that poverty results not from gross inequities (in which we might be complicit) but from poor people's own deficiencies, we are much less likely to support authentic antipoverty policy and programs. Further, if we believe, however wrongly, that poor people don't value education, then we dodge any responsibility to redress the gross education inequities with which they contend. This application of deficit theory establishes the idea of what Gans (1995) calls the *undeserving poor*—a segment of our society that simply does not deserve a fair shake.

If the goal of deficit theory is to justify a system that privileges economically advantaged students at the expense of working-class and poor students, then it appears to be working marvelously. In our determination to "fix" the mythical culture of poor students, we ignore the ways in which our society cheats them out of opportunities that their wealthier peers take for granted. We ignore the fact that poor people suffer disproportionately the effects of nearly every major social ill. They lack access to health care, living-wage jobs, safe and affordable housing, clean air and water, and so on (Books, 2004)—conditions that limit their abilities to achieve to their full potential.

Perhaps most of us, as educators, feel powerless to address these bigger issues. But the question is this: Are we willing, at the very least, to tackle the classism in our own schools and classrooms?

This classism is plentiful and well documented (Kozol, 1992). For example, compared with their wealthier peers, poor students are more likely to attend schools that have less funding (Carey, 2005); lower teacher salaries (Karoly, 2001); more limited computer and Internet access (Gorski, 2003); larger class sizes; higher student-to-teacher ratios; a less-rigorous curriculum; and fewer experienced teachers (Barton, 2004). The National Commission on Teaching and America's Future (2004) also found that low-income schools were more likely to

suffer from cockroach or rat infestation, dirty or inoperative student bathrooms, large numbers of teacher vacancies and substitute teachers, more teachers who are not licensed in their subject areas, insufficient or outdated classroom materials, and inadequate or nonexistent learning facilities, such as science labs.

Here in Minnesota, several school districts offer universal half-day kindergarten but allow those families that can afford to do so to pay for full-day services. Our poor students scarcely make it out of early childhood without paying the price for our culture of classism. Deficit theory requires us to ignore these inequities—or worse, to see them as normal and justified.

What does this mean? Regardless of how much students in poverty value education, they must overcome tremendous inequities to learn. Perhaps the greatest myth of all is the one that dubs education the "great equalizer." Without considerable change, it cannot be anything of the sort.

WHAT CAN WE DO?

The socioeconomic opportunity gap can be eliminated only when we stop trying to "fix" poor students and start addressing the ways in which our schools perpetuate classism. This includes destroying the inequities listed above as well as abolishing such practices as tracking and ability grouping, segregational redistricting, and the privatization of public schools. We must demand the best possible education for all students—higher-order pedagogies, innovative learning materials, and holistic teaching and learning. But first, we must demand basic human rights for all people; adequate housing and health care, living-wage jobs, and so on.

Of course, we ought not tell students who suffer today that, if they can wait for this education revolution, everything will fall into place. So as we prepare ourselves for bigger changes, we must

- Educate ourselves about class and poverty.
- Reject deficit theory and help students and colleagues unlearn misperceptions about poverty.

- Make school involvement accessible to all families.
- Follow Janet's lead, inviting colleagues to observe our teaching for signs of class bias.
- Continue reaching out to low-income families even when they appear unresponsive (and without assuming, if they are unresponsive, that we know why).
- Respond when colleagues stereotype poor students or parents.
- Never assume that all students have equitable access to such learning resources as computers and the Internet, and never assign work requiring this access without providing in-school time to complete it.
- Ensure that learning materials do not stereotype poor people.
- Fight to keep low-income students from being assigned unjustly to special education or low academic tracks.
- Make curriculum relevant to poor students, drawing on and validating their experiences and intelligences.
- Teach about issues related to class and poverty—including consumer culture, the dissolution of labor unions, and environmental injustice—and about movements for class equity.
- Teach about the antipoverty work of Martin Luther King Jr., Helen Keller, the Black Panthers, César Chávez, and other U.S. icons—and about why this dimension of their legacies has been erased from our national consciousness.
- Fight to ensure that school meal programs offer healthy options.
- Examine proposed corporate-school partnerships, rejecting those that require the adoption of specific curriculums or pedagogies.

Most important, we must consider how our own class biases affect our interactions with and expectations of our students. And then we must ask ourselves, where, in reality, does the deficit lie? Does it lie in poor people, the most disenfranchised people among us? Does it lie in the education system itself—in, as Jonathan Kozol says, the savage inequalities of our schools? Or does it lie in us—educators with unquestionably good intentions who

too often fall to the temptation of the quick fix, the easily digestible framework that never requires us to consider how we comply with the culture of classism.

DISCUSSION QUESTIONS

1. Why do you think the culture of poverty myth has persisted despite research to the contrary?
2. Have you seen the operation of "deficit theory" in schools you have attended?
3. Would you agree that ability-tracking perpetuates the culture of classism?

REFERENCES

Abell, T., & Lyon, L. (1979). Do the differences make a difference? An empirical evaluation of the culture of poverty in the United States. *American Anthropologist, 6*(3), 602–621.

Barton, P. E. (2004). Why does the gap persist? *Educational Leadership, 62*(3), 8–13.

Billings, D. (1974). Culture and poverty in Appalachia: A theoretical discussion and empirical analysis. *Social Forces, 53*(2), 315–323.

Bomer, R., Dworin, J. E., May, L., & Semingson, P (2008). Miseducating teachers about the poor: A critical analysis of Ruby Payne's claims about poverty. *Teachers College Record,* 110(11). Available: www.tcrecord.org/Print Conteni.asp?ContentID=14591

Books, S. (2004). *Poverty and schooling in the U.S.: Contexts and consequences.* Mahway, NJ: Erlbaum.

Carey, K. (2005). *The funding gap 2004: Many states still shortchange low-income and minority students.* Washington, DC: Education Trust.

Carmon, N. (1985). Poverty and culture. *Sociological Perspectives, 28*(4), 403–418.

Chen, K., Sheth, A., Krejci, J., & Wallace, J. (2003, August). *Understanding differences in alcohol use among high school students in two different communities.* Paper presented at the annual meeting of the American Sociological Association, Atlanta, GA.

Collins, J. (1988). Language and class in minority education. *Anthropology and Education Quarterly, 19*(4), 299–326.

Compton-Lilly, C. (2003). *Reading families: The literate lives of urban children.* New York: Teachers College Press.

Diala, C. C., Muntaner, C., & Walrath, C. (2004). Gender, occupational, and socioeconomic correlates of alcohol and drug abuse among U.S. rural, metropolitan, and urban residents. *American Journal of Drug and Alcohol Abuse,* 30(2), 409–428.

Economic Policy Institute. (2002). *The state of working class America 2002–03.* Washington, DC: Author.

Galea, S., Ahem, J., Tracy. M., & Vlahov, D. (2007). Neighborhood income and income distribution and the use of cigarettes, alcohol, and marijuana. *American Journal of Preventive Medicine,* 32(6), 195–202.

Gans, H. J. (1995). *The war against the poor: The underclass and antipoverty policy.* New York: Basic Books.

Gee, J. P. (2004). *Situated language and learning: A critique of traditional schooling.* New York: Routledge.

Gorski, P. C. (2003). Privilege and repression in the digital era: Rethinking the sociopolitics of the digital divide. *Race, Gender and Class,* 10(4), 145–176.

Hess, K. M. (1974). The nonstandard speakers in our schools: What should be clone? *The Elementary School Journal,* 74(5), 280–290.

Iversen, R. R., & Farber, N. (1996). Transmission of family values, work, and welfare among poor urban black women. *Work and Occupations,* 23(4), 437–460.

Jones, R. K., & Luo, Y. (1999). The culture of poverty and African-American culture: An empirical assessment. *Sociological Perspectives,* 42(3), 439–458.

Karoly, L. A. (2001). Investing in the future: Reducing poverty through human capital investments. In S. Danzinger & R. Haveman (Eds.), *Understanding poverty* (pp. 314–356). New York: Russell Sage Foundation.

Kozol, J. (1992). *Savage inequalities: Children in America's schools.* New York: HarperCollins.

Lareau, A., & Horvat, E. (1999). Moments of social inclusion and exclusion: Race, class, and cultural capital in family-school relationships. *Sociology of Education,* 72, 37–53.

Leichter, H. J. (Ed.). (1978). *Families and communities as educators.* New York: Teachers College Press.

Lewis, O. (1961). *The children of Sanchez: Autobiography of a Mexican family.* New York: Random House.

Miller, P. J., Cho, G. E., & Bracey. J. R. (2005). Working-class children's experience through the prism of personal storytelling. *Human Development,* 48, 115–135.

National Center for Children in Poverty. (2004). *Parental employment in low-income families.* New York: Author.

National Center for Education Statistics. (2005). *Parent and family involvement in education;* 2002–03. Washington, DC: Author.

National Commission on Teaching and America's Future. (2004). *Fifty years after* Brown v. Board of Education: *A two-tiered education system.* Washington, DC: Author.

Ortiz, A. T., & Briggs, L. (2003). The culture of poverty, crack babies, and welfare cheats: The making of the "healthy white baby crisis." *Social Text,* 21(3), 39–57.

Rodman, R. (1977). Culture of poverty: The rise and fall of a concept. *Sociological Review,* 25(4), 867–876.

Saxe, L., Kadushin, C., Tighe, E., Rindskopf, D., & Beveridge, A. (2001). *National evaluation of the fighting back program: General population surveys, 1995–1999.* New York: City University of New York Graduate Center.

Wilson, W. J. (1997). *When work disappears.* New York: Random House.

DISABILITY

READING 34

Public Transit

John Hockenberry

New York was not like Iran.

It was a shock to return to the United States in 1990, where it routinely took an act of God to hail a taxi. There was nothing religious about New York City, even on Christmas Eve. I had taken a cab from midtown to Riverside Church on the west side of Manhattan only to find that my information about a Christmas Eve service there was mistaken. The church was padlocked, which I only discovered after getting out of the cab into the forty-mile-an-hour wind and the twenty-degree weather. I tried all of the doors of the church and found myself alone at close to midnight, without a taxi, on December 24 at 122d Street and Riverside Drive.

I was wearing a wool sports jacket and a heavy scarf, but no outer jacket. There were no cars on the street. Being wrong about the service and having come all the way uptown was more than a little frustrating. I suspected that I was not in the best

John Hockenberry is a journalist and author. He is the author of *Moving Violations: War Zones, Wheelchairs, and Declarations of Independence.*

psychological condition to watch the usual half-dozen or so New York cabs pass me by and pretend not to see me hailing them. I knew the most important thing was to try and not look like a panhandler. This was always hard. Many times in New York I had hailed a cab only to have the driver hand me a dollar. Once I was so shocked that I looked at the cabbie and said, as though I were correcting his spelling, "No, I give you the money."

"You want a ride?" he said. "Really?"

The worst were the taxis that stopped but had some idea that the wheelchair was going to put itself into the trunk. After you hopped into the backseat, these drivers would look at you as though you were trying to pull a fast one, tricking them into having to get out of their cabs and load something in the trunk that you had been cleverly hiding. Some cabbies would say that I should have brought someone with me to put the chair in, or that it was too heavy for them to lift. My favorite excuse was also the most frequent, "Look, buddy, I can't lift that chair. I have a bad back."

"I never heard of anyone who became paralyzed from lifting wheelchairs," I'd say. My favorite reply never helped. If the drivers would actually load the chair, you could hear them grumbling, throwing it around to get it to fit, and smashing the trunk lid down on it. When we would arrive at our destination, the driver would throw the chair at me like it was a chunk of nuclear waste and hop back behind the wheel. The only thing to do in these situations was to smile, try not to get into a fight, and hope the anger would subside quickly so you could make it wherever you were going without having a meltdown.

There were some drivers who wouldn't load the chair at all. For these people, at one time, I carried a Swiss army knife. The rule was, if I had to get back out of a cab because a driver wouldn't load my chair, then I would give the driver a reason to get out of his cab shortly after I was gone. I would use the small blade of the knife to puncture a rear tire before the cab drove away, then hail another one. A few blocks ahead, when the first driver had discovered his difficulties, he was generally looking in his trunk for the tire jack when I passed by, waving.

The trouble with this idea was that other people often did not have the same righteous attitude that I did about tire puncturing in Manhattan traffic, and using knives to get freelance revenge in New York City under any circumstances. Most of my friends put me in the same league with subway vigilante Bernard Goetz, and concluded that I needed serious help. So I had stopped using the Swiss army knife and was without it that Christmas Eve on 122nd and Riverside Drive.

The first cab drove toward me and slowed down; the driver stared, then quickly drove by. A second cab approached. I motioned emphatically. I smiled and tried to look as credible as I could. Out in this December wind, I was just another invisible particle of New York misery. The driver of the second cab shook his head as he passed with the lame, catch-all apologetic look New York cabbies use to say, "No way, Mac. Sorry, no way I can take you."

I had one advantage. At least I was white. Black males in New York City have to watch at least as many cabs go by as someone in a wheelchair does before getting a ride. Black male friends of mine say they consciously have to rely on their ritzy trench coats or conservative "Real Job" suits to counter skin color in catching a cab. If I could look more white than crippled, I might not freeze to death on Christmas Eve. I was a psychotic, twentieth-century hit man named Tiny Tim, imagining all sorts of gory ways to knock off a cabbie named Scrooge. The wind was blowing furiously off the Hudson, right up over Riverside Drive.

A third cab drove by. I wondered if I could force a cab to stop by blocking the road. I wished I had a baseball bat. For a period of a few minutes, there was no traffic. I turned and began to roll down Riverside. After a block, I turned around, and there was one more empty cab in the right lane coming toward me. I raised my hand. I was sitting directly under a streetlight. The cabbie clearly saw me, abruptly veered left into the turn lane, and sat there, signaling at the red light.

I rolled over to his cab and knocked on the window. "Can you take a fare?" The driver was pretending I had just landed there from space, but

I was freezing and needed a ride, so I tried not to look disgusted. He nodded with all of the enthusiasm of someone with an abscessed tooth. I opened the door and hopped onto the backseat. I folded the chair and asked him to open the trunk of his cab.

"Why you want me to do that?" he said.

"Put the chair in the trunk, please." I was half-sitting in the cab, my legs still outside. The door was open and the wheelchair was folded next to the cab. "No way, man," he said. "I'm not going to do that. It's too damn cold." I was supposed to understand that I would now simply thank him for his trouble, get back in my wheelchair, and wait for another cab. "Just put the chair in the trunk right now. It's Christmas Eve, pal. Why don't you just pretend to be Santa for five fucking minutes?" His smile vanished. I had crossed a line by being angry. But he also looked relieved, as though now he could refuse me in good conscience. It was all written clearly on his face. "You're crazy, man. I don't have to do nothing for you." I looked at him once more and said, "If you make me get back into this chair, you are going to be very sorry." It was a moment of visceral anger. There was no turning back now. "Go away, man. It's too cold."

I got back into the chair. I placed my backpack with my wallet in it on the back of my chair for safekeeping. I grabbed his door and, with all of my strength, pushed it back on its hinges until I heard a loud snap. It was now jammed open. I rolled over to his passenger window, and two insane jabs of my right fist shattered it. I rolled around to the front of the cab, and with my fist in my white handball glove took out first one, then the other headlight. The light I was bathed in from the front of the cab vanished. The face of the driver could now be seen clearly, illuminated by the dashboard's glow.

I could hear myself screaming at him in a voice that sounded far away. I knew the voice, but the person it belonged to was an intruder in this place. He had nothing to do with this particular cabbie and his stupid, callous insensitivity; rather, he was the overlord to all such incidents that had come before. Whenever the gauntlet was dropped, it was this interior soul, with that screaming voice and those hands, who felt no pain and who surfed down a wave of hatred to settle the score. This soul had done the arithmetic and chosen the weapons. I would have to live with the consequences.

I rolled over to the driver's seat and grabbed the window next to his face. I could see that he was absolutely terrified. It made me want to torture him. I hungered for his fear; I wanted to feel his presumptions of power and physical superiority in my hands as he sank up to his neck in my rage, my fists closed around his throat. I attacked his half-open window. It cracked, and as I hauled my arm back to finish it, I saw large drops of blood on the driver's face. I looked at him closely. He was paralyzed with fear and spattered with blood. There was blood on his window, as well. A voice inside me screamed, "I didn't touch you, motherfucker. You're not bleeding. Don't say that I made you bleed. You fucking bastard. Don't you dare bleed!"

I rolled back from the cab. It was my own blood shooting from my thumb. It gushed over the white leather of my glove: I had busted an artery at the base of my thumb, but I couldn't see it because it was inside the glove. Whatever had sliced my thumb had gone neatly through the leather first, and as I rolled down the street I could hear the cabbie saying behind me, "You're crazy, man, you're fucking crazy." I rolled underneath a street lamp to get a closer look. It was my left hand, and it had several lacerations in addition to the one at the base of my thumb. It must have been the headlight glass. The blood continued to gush. Wind blew it off my fingers in festive red droplets, which landed stiffly on the frozen pavement under the street lamp. Merry Christmas.

Up the street, a police squad car had stopped next to the cab, which still had its right rear door jammed open. I coasted farther down the street to see if I could roll the rest of the way home. With each push of my hand on the wheel rim of my chair, blood squirted out of my glove. I could feel it filled with blood inside. The cops pulled up behind me. "Would you like us to arrest that cabbie? Did he attack you?" All I could think of was the indignity of being attacked by him. I thought about screaming, "That piece of human garbage attacked me? No way. Maybe it was me who attacked him as a public service. Did you donut eaters ever think of that? I could have killed the bastard. I *was* trying to kill him, in fact. I insist that you arrest me for attempted murder right now, or I will sue the NYPD under the Americans with Disabilities Act." I thought better of this speech. Intense pain had returned my mind to practical matters. Spending the night in jail for assaulting a cabbie after bragging about it while bleeding to death seemed like a poor way to cap off an already less than stellar Christmas Eve.

"Everything's fine, officer. I'll just get another taxi." I continued to roll one-handed and dripping down Riverside Drive. The cops went back to talk to the cabbie, who was screaming now. I began to worry that he was going to have me arrested, but the cops drove back again. Once more, the officer asked if I wanted to file a complaint against the cabbie. As more blood dripped off my formerly white glove, the officers suggested that I go to the hospital. They had figured out what had happened. As I started to explain, they told me to get in the squad car. "Let's just say it was an unfortunate accident," one officer said. "I don't think he'll ever stop for someone in a wheelchair again. If we can get you to the emergency room in time, maybe you won't lose your thumb."

I got in the backseat while the cops put the chair in the trunk. Seven blocks away was the emergency room of St. Luke's Hospital. Christmas Eve services at St. Luke's included treatment of a young woman's mild overdose. An elderly man and his worried-looking wife were in a corner of the treatment room. His scared face looked out from beneath a green plastic oxygen mask. A number of men stood around watching CNN on the waiting-room television. A woman had been brought in with fairly suspicious-looking bruises on her face and arms. One arm was broken and being set in a cast. She sat quietly while two men talked about football in loud voices. The forlorn Christmas decorations added to the hopelessness of this little band of unfortunates in the emergency room.

When I arrived, everything stopped. Police officers are always an object of curiosity, signaling the arrival of a shooting victim or something more spectacular. For a Christmas Eve, the gushing artery at the base of my thumb was spectacular enough. The men sitting around the emergency room shook their heads. The overdose patient with the sunken cocaine eyes staggered over to inspect the evening's best carnage. "Where did you get that wheelchair?" She looked around as though she was familiar with all of the wheelchairs in this emergency room from previous visits. "It's my own," I replied. "That's a good idea," she said. "Why didn't I think of that?"

I got nine stitches from a doctor who suggested politely that whatever my complaint with the taxi driver, I was one person on the planet who could ill afford to lose a thumb. The deep laceration was just a few millimeters from the nerve and was just as close to the tendon. Severing either one would have added my thumb to an already ample chorus of numbness and paralysis. The thought of losing the use of my thumb was one thing, but what was really disturbing was the thought of its isolation on my hand, numb in the wrong zone. Trapped on a functional hand, a numb and paralyzed thumb would have no way of communicating with my numb and paralyzed feet. It would be not only paralyzed, it would be in exile: an invader behind enemy lines, stuck across the checkpoint on my chest.

Today, there is a one-inch scar that traces a half circle just to the left of my knuckle. The gloves were a total loss, but they no doubt saved my thumb. Nothing could save my pride, but pride is not always salvageable in New York City. I have taken thousands of cabs, and in each case the business of loading and unloading delivers some small verdict on human nature. Often it is a verdict I am in no mood to hear, as was the case on that Christmas Eve. At other times, the experience is eerie and sublime. At the very least, there is the possibility that I will make a connection with a person, not just stare at the back of an anonymous head.

In my life, cabbies distinguish themselves by being either very rude and unhelpful or sympathetic and righteous. Mahmoud Abu Holima was one of the latter. It was his freckles I remembered, along with his schoolboy nose and reddish-blond hair, which made his Islamic tirades more memorable. He was not swarthy like other Middle Eastern cabbies. He had a squeaky, raspy voice. He drove like a power tool carving Styrofoam. He used his horn a lot. He made constant references to the idiots he said were all around him.

He was like a lot of other New York cabbies. But out of a sea of midtown yellow, Mahmoud Abu Holima was the one who stopped one afternoon in 1990, and by stopping for me he wanted to make it clear to everyone that he was not stopping for anyone else, especially the people in expensive-looking suits waiting on the same street corner I was. His decision to pick me up was part of some protest Mahmoud delivered to America every day he drove the streets of Manhattan.

His cab seemed to have little to do with transporting people from place to place. It was more like an Islamic institute on wheels. A voice in Arabic blared from his cassette player. His front seat was piled with books in Arabic and more cassettes. Some of the books were dog-eared Korans. There were many uniformly bound blue and green books open, marked, and stacked in cross-referenced chaos, the arcane and passionate academic studies of a Muslim cabbie studying hard to get ahead and lose his day job, interrupting his studies in midsentence to pick up a man in a wheelchair.

I took two rides with him. The first time I was going somewhere uptown on Third Avenue. Four cabs had passed me by. He stopped. He put the chair in the trunk and, to make more space there, brought stacks of Arabic books from the trunk into the front seat. He wore a large, knit, dirty-white skullcap and was in constant motion. He seemed lost in the ideas he had been reading about before I got in. At traffic lights, he would read. As he drove, he continually turned away from the windshield to make eye contact with me. His voice careened from conversation to lecture, like his driving. He ignored what was going on around him on the street. He told me he thought my wheelchair was unusually

light. He said he knew many boys with no legs who could use such a chair. There were no good wheelchairs in Afghanistan.

"Afghanistan, you know about the war in Afghanistan?" he asked.

I said I knew about it. He said he wasn't talking about the Soviet invasion of Afghanistan and the American efforts to see that the Soviets were defeated. He said that the war was really a religious war. "It is the war for Islam." On a lark, in my broken, rudimentary Arabic, I asked him where he was from. He turned around abruptly and asked, "Where did you learn Arabic?" I told him that I had learned it from living in the Middle East. I apologized for speaking so poorly. He laughed and said that my accent was good, but that non-Muslims in America don't speak Arabic unless they are spies. "Only the Zionists really know how to speak," he said, his voice spitting with hatred.

I thanked him for picking me up. He removed my chair from his trunk, and as I hopped back into it I explained to him that it was difficult sometimes to get a cab in New York. He said that being in America was like being in a war where there are only weapons, no people. "In Islam," he said, "the people are the weapons."

"Why are you here?" I asked him.

"I have kids, family." He smiled once, and the freckles wrinkled on his nose and face, making him look like Tom Sawyer in a Muslim prayer cap. The scowl returned as he drove away. He turned up the cassette. The Arabic voice was still audible a block away.

The second time I saw him, I remembered him and he remembered me. He had no cassettes this time. There were no books in the car, and there was plenty of room in the trunk for my chair this time. Where were all of the books? He said he had finished studying. I asked him about peace in Afghanistan and the fact that Iran and Iraq were no longer at war. He said something about Saddam Hussein I didn't catch, and then he laughed. He seemed less nervous but still had the good-natured intensity I remembered from before. "Are you from Iran?" I asked him, and this time he answered.

He told me he was from Egypt. He asked me if I knew about the war in Egypt, and I told him I didn't.

Before he dropped me off, he said that he wanted me to know when we would lose the war against Islam. He said that we won't know when we have lost. "Americans never say anything that's important." He looked out the window. His face did not express hatred as much as disappointment. He shook his head. "It is quiet now."

He ran a red light and parked squarely in the middle of an intersection, stopping traffic to let me out. Cars honked and people yelled as I got into the wheelchair. He scowled at them and laughed. I laughed too. I think I said to him, "*Salaam,*" the Arabic word for peace and good-bye. He said something that sounded like "*Mish Salaam fi Amerika,*" no peace in America. Then he said, "*Sa'at.*" In Arabic, it means difficult. He got into his cab, smiled, and drove away. On February 26, 1993, cabbie, student of Islam, and family man Mahmoud Abu Holima, along with several others, planted a bomb that blew up in the World Trade Center. Today, he is serving a life sentence in a New York prison. . . .

When I returned to New York City from the Middle East in 1990, I lived in Brooklyn, just two blocks from the Carroll Street subway stop on the F train. It was not accessible, and as there appeared to be no plans to make it so, I didn't think much about the station. When I wanted to go into Manhattan, I would take a taxi, or I would roll up Court Street to the walkway entrance to the Brooklyn Bridge and fly into the city on a ribbon of oak planks suspended from the bridge's webs of cable that appeared from my wheelchair to be woven into the sky itself. Looking down, I could see the East River through my wheelchair's spokes. Looking up, I saw the clouds through the spokes of the bridge. It was always an uncommon moment of physical integrity with the city, which ended when I came to rest at the traffic light on Chambers Street, next to city hall.

It was while rolling across the bridge one day that I remembered my promise to Donna, my physical therapist, about how I would one day ride the rapid transit trains in Chicago. Pumping my arms up the incline of the bridge toward Manhattan and then coasting down the other side in 1990, I imagined that I would be able physically to accomplish everything I had theorized about the subway in Chicago in those first days of being a paraplegic back in 1976. In the Middle East, I had climbed many stairways and hauled myself and the chair across many filthy floors on my way to interviews, apartments, and news conferences. I had also lost my fear of humiliation from living and working there. I was even intrigued with the idea of taking the train during the peak of rush hour when the greatest number of people of all kinds would be underground with me.

I would do it just the way I had told Donna back in the rehab hospital. But this time, I would wire myself with a microphone and a miniature cassette machine to record everything that happened along the way. Testing my own theory might make a good commentary for an upcoming National Public Radio program about inaccessibility. Between the Carroll Street station and city hall, there were stairs leading in and out of the stations as well as to transfer from one line to another inside the larger stations. To get to Brooklyn Bridge/City Hall, I had to make two transfers, from the F to the A, then from the A to the 5, a total of nearly 150 stairs.

I rolled up to the Brooklyn Carroll Street stop on the F train carrying a rope and a backpack and wired for sound. Like most of the other people on the train that morning I was on my way to work. Taking the subway was how most people crossed the East River, but it would have been hard to come up with a less practical way, short of swimming, for a paraplegic to cover the same distance. Fortunately, I had the entire morning to kill. I was confident that I had the strength for it, and unless I ended up on the tracks, I felt sure that I could get out of any predicament I found myself in, but I was prepared for things to be more complicated. As usual, trouble would make the story more interesting.

The Carroll Street subway station has two staircases. One leads to the token booth, where the fare is paid by the turnstiles at the track entrance, the other one goes directly down to the tracks. Near the entrance is a newsstand. As I rolled to the top of the stairs, the man behind the counter watched me closely and the people standing around the newsstand stopped talking. I quickly climbed out of my chair and down onto the top step.

I folded my chair and tied the length of rope around it, attaching the end to my wrist. I moved down to the second step and began to lower the folded chair down the steps to the bottom. It took just a moment. Then, one at a time, I descended the first flight of stairs with my backpack and seat cushion in my lap until I reached a foul-smelling landing below street level. I was on my way. I looked up. The people at the newsstand who had been peering sheepishly down at me looked away. All around me, crowds of commuters with briefcases and headphones walked by, stepping around me without breaking stride. If I had worried about anything associated with this venture, it was that I would just be in the way. I was invisible.

I slid across the floor to the next flight of stairs, and the commuters arriving at the station now came upon me suddenly from around a corner. Still, they expressed no surprise and neatly moved over to form an orderly lane on the side of the landing opposite me as I lowered my chair once again to the bottom of the stairs where the token booth was.

With an elastic cord around my legs to keep them together and more easily moved (an innovation I hadn't thought of back in rehab), I continued down the stairs, two steps at a time, and finally reached the chair at the bottom of the steps. I stood it up, unfolded it, and did a two-armed, from-the-floor lift back onto the seat. My head rose out of the sea of commuter legs, and I took my place in the subway token line.

"You know, you get half price," the tinny voice through the bulletproof glass told me, as though this were compensation for the slight inconvenience of having no ramp or elevator. There, next to his piles of tokens, the operator had a stack of official half-price certificates for disabled users. He seemed thrilled to have a chance to use them. "No, thanks, the tokens are fine." I bought two and rolled through the rickety gate next to the turnstiles and to the head of the next set of stairs. I could hear the trains rumbling below.

I got down on the floor again, and began lowering the chair. I realized that getting the chair back up again was not going to be as simple as this lowering maneuver. Most of my old theory about riding the trains in Chicago had pertained to getting up to the tracks, because the Chicago trains are elevated. Down was going well, as I expected, but up might be more difficult.

Around me walked the stream of oblivious commuters. Underneath their feet, the paper cups and straws and various other bits of refuse they dropped were too soiled by black subway filth to be recognizable as having any connection at all to their world above. Down on the subway floor, they seemed evil, straws that could only have hung from diseased lips, plastic spoons that could never have carried anything edible. Horrid puddles of liquid were swirled with chemical colors, sinister black mirrors in which the bottoms of briefcases sailed safely overhead like rectangular airships. I was freshly showered, with clean white gloves and black jeans, but in the reflection of one of these puddles, I too looked as foul and discarded as the soda straws and crack vials. I looked up at the people walking by, stepping around me, or watching me with their peripheral vision. By virtue of the fact that my body and clothes were in contact with places they feared to touch, they saw and feared me much as they might fear sudden assault by a mugger. I was just like the refuse, irretrievable, present only as a creature dwelling on the rusty edge of a dark drain. By stepping around me as I slid, two steps at a time, down toward the tracks, they created a quarantined space, just for me, where even the air seemed depraved.

I rolled to the platform to wait for the train with the other commuters. I could make eye contact again. Some of the faces betrayed that they had seen me on the stairs by showing relief that I had not been stuck there, or worse, living there. The details they were too afraid to glean back there by pausing to investigate, they were happy to take as a happy ending which got them off the hook. They were curious as long as they didn't have to act on what they had learned. As long as they didn't have to act, they could stare.

I had a speech all prepared for the moment anyone asked if I needed help. I felt a twinge of satisfaction over having made it to the tracks without having to give it. My old theory, concocted while on painkillers in an intensive care unit in Pennsylvania, had predicted that I would make it. I was happy to do it all by myself. Yet I hadn't counted on being completely ignored. New York is such a far cry from the streets of Jerusalem, where Israelis would come right up to ask how much you wanted for your wheelchair, and Arabs would insist on carrying you up a flight of stairs whether you wanted to go or not. . . .

I rolled to the stairs and descended into a corridor crowded with people coming and going. "Are you all right?" A black woman stopped next to my chair. She was pushing a stroller with two seats, one occupied by a little girl, the other empty, presumably for the little boy with her, who was standing next to a larger boy. They all beamed at me, waiting for further orders from Mom.

"I'm going down to the A train," I said. "I think I'll be all right, if I don't get lost."

"You sure you want to go down there?" She sounded as if she was warning me about something. "I know all the elevators from having these kids," she said. "They ain't no elevator on the A train, young man." Her kids looked down at me as if to say, *What can you say to that?* I told her that I knew there was no elevator and that I was just seeing how many stairs there were between Carroll Street and city hall. "I can tell you, they's lots of stairs." As she said good-bye, her oldest boy looked down at me as if he understood exactly what I was doing, and why. "Elevators smell nasty," he said.

Once on the A train, I discovered at the next stop that I had chosen the wrong side of the platform and was going away from Manhattan. If my physical therapist, Donna, could look in on me at this point in my trip, she might be more doubtful about my theory than I was. By taking the wrong train, I had probably doubled the number of stairs I would have to climb.

I wondered if I could find a station not too far out where the platform was between the tracks, so that all I had to do was roll to the other side and catch the inbound train. The subway maps gave no indication of this, and the commuters I attempted to query on the subject simply ignored me or seemed not to understand what I was asking. Another black woman with a large shopping bag and a brown polka-dotted dress was sitting in a seat across the car and volunteered that Franklin Avenue was the station I wanted. "No stairs there," she said.

At this point, every white person I had encountered had ignored me or pretended that I didn't exist, while every black person who had come upon me had offered to help without being asked. I looked at the tape recorder in my jacket to see if it was running. It was awfully noisy in the subway, but if any voices at all were recorded, this radio program was going to be more about race than it was going to be about wheelchair accessibility. It was the first moment that I suspected the two were deeply related in ways I have had many occasions to think about since.

At Franklin Avenue I crossed the tracks and changed direction, feeling for the first time that I was a part of the vast wave of migration in and out of the Manhattan that produced the subway, all the famous bridges, and a major broadcast industry in traffic reporting complete with network rivals and local personalities, who have added words like *rubbernecking* to the language. I rolled across the platform like any other citizen and onto the train with ease. As we pulled away from the station, I thought how much it would truly change my life if there were a way around the stairs, if I could actually board the subway anywhere without having to be Sir Edmund Hillary.

DISCUSSION QUESTIONS

1. As Hockenberry notes, black men and disabled people share the inability to get cabs to pick them up. Why does that experience make them so angry?

2. Why do people shun interaction with the disabled?

READING 35

"Can You See the Rainbow?" The Roots of Denial

Sally French

Some of my earliest memories are of anxious relatives trying to get me to see things. I did not understand why it was so important that I should do so, but was acutely aware of their intense anxiety if I could not. It was aesthetic things like rainbows that bothered them most. They would position me with great precision, tilting my head to precisely the right angle, and then point to the sky saying "Look, there it is; look, there, there . . . THERE!" As far as I was concerned there was nothing there, but if I said as much their anxiety grew even more intense; they would rearrange my position and the whole scenario would be repeated.

In the end, despite a near total lack of color vision and a complete indifference to the rainbow's whereabouts, I would say I could see it. In that way I was able to release the mounting tension and escape to pursue more interesting tasks. It did not take long to learn that in order to avert episodes such as these and to protect the feelings of the people around me, I had to deny my disability.

The adults would also get very perturbed if ever I looked "abnormal." Being told to open my eyes and straighten my face, when all I was doing was trying to see, made me feel ugly and separate. Having adults pretend that I could see more than I could, and having to acquiesce in the pretence, was a theme throughout my childhood.

Adults who were not emotionally involved with the issue of whether or not I could see also led me along the path of denial. This was achieved by their tendency to disbelieve me and interpret my behavior as "playing up" when I told them I could

not see. Basically they were confused and unable to cope with the ambiguities of partial sight and were not prepared to take instruction on the matter from a mere child. One example of this occurred in the tiny country primary school that I attended. On warm, sunny days we had our lessons outdoors where, because of the strong sunlight, I could not see to read, write or draw. It was only when the two teachers realized I was having similar difficulties eating my dinner that they began to doubt their interpretation that I was a malingerer. On several occasions I was told off by opticians when I failed to discriminate between the different lenses they placed before my eyes. I am not sure whether they really disbelieved me or whether their professional pride was hurt when nothing they could offer seemed to help; whatever it was I rapidly learned to say "better" or "worse," even though all the lenses looked the same.

It was also very difficult to tell the adults, when they had scraped together the money and found the time to take me to the pantomime or wherever, that it was a frustrating and boring experience. I had a strong sense of spoiling other people's fun, just as a sober person among a group of drunken friends may have. As a child, explaining my situation without appearing disagreeable, sullen and rude was so problematic that I usually denied my disability and suffered in silence. All of this taught me from a very early age that, while the adults were working themselves up about whether or not I could see rainbows, my own anxieties must never be shared.

These anxieties were numerous and centered on getting lost, being slow, not managing and, above all, looking stupid and displaying fear. I tried very hard to be "normal," to be anonymous and to merge with the crowd. Beaches were a nightmare; finding my way back from the sea to specific people in the absence of landmarks was almost impossible, yet giving in to panic was too shameful to contemplate. Anticipation of difficulties could cause even greater anguish than the difficulties themselves and was sufficient to ruin whole days. The prospect of outings with lots of sighted children to unfamiliar

Sally French is a lecturer at the Open University in the United Kingdom.

places was enough to make me physically ill, and with a bewildering mix of remorse and relief, I would stay at home.

Brownie meetings were worrying if any degree of independent movement was allowed; in the summer when we left the confines and safety of our hut to play on the nearby common, the other children would immediately disperse, leaving me alone among the trees, feeling stupid and frightened and wondering what to do next. The adults were always adamant that I should join in, that I should not miss out on the fun, but how much they or the other children noticed my difficulties I do not know; I was never teased or blamed for them, they were simply never discussed, at least not with me. This lack of communication gave me a powerful unspoken message that my disability must be denied.

By denying the reality of my disability I protected myself from the anxiety, disapproval, frustration and disappointment of the adults in my life. Like most children I wanted their acceptance, approval and warmth, and quickly learned that this could best be gained by colluding with their perceptions of my situation. I denied my disability in response to their denial, which was often motivated by a benign attempt to integrate me in a world which they perceived as fixed. My denial of disability was thus not a psychopathological reaction, but a sensible and rational response to the peculiar situation I was in.

Special School

Attending special school at the age of nine was, in many ways, a great relief. Despite the crocodile walks,[1] the bells, the long separations from home, the regimentation and the physical punishment, it was an enormous joy to be with other partially sighted children and to be in an environment where limited sight was simply not an issue. I discovered that many other children shared my world and, despite the harshness of institutional life, I felt relaxed, made lots of friends, became more confident and thrived socially. For the first time in my life I was a standard product and it felt very good.

The sighted adults who looked after us were few in number with purely custodial roles, and although they seemed to be in a permanent state of anger, provided we stayed out of trouble we were basically ignored. We lived peer-orientated, confined and unchallenging lives where lack of sight rarely as much as entered our heads.

Although the reality of our disabilities was not openly denied in this situation, the only thing guaranteed to really enthuse the staff was the slightest glimmer of hope that our sight could be improved. Contact lenses were an innovation at this time, and children who had previously been virtually ignored were nurtured, encouraged and congratulated, as they learned to cope with them, and were told how good they looked without their glasses on. After I had been at the school for about a year, I was selected as one of the guinea pigs for the experimental "telescopic lenses" which were designed, at least in part, to preserve our postures (with which there was obsessive concern) by enabling us to read and write from a greater distance. For most of us they did not work.

I remember being photographed wearing the lenses by an American man whom I perceived to be very important. First of all he made me knit while wearing them, with the knitting held right down on my lap. This was easy as I could in any case knit without looking. He was unduly excited and enthusiastic and told me how much the lenses were helping. I knew he was wrong. Then he asked me to read, but this changed his mood completely; he became tense, and before taking the photograph he pushed the book, which was a couple of inches from my face, quite roughly to my knees. Although I knew he had cheated and that what he had done was wrong, I still felt culpable for his displeasure and aware that I had failed an important test.

We were forced to use equipment like the telescopic lenses even though it did not help, and sometimes actually made things worse; the behavior of the adults clearly conveyed the message, "You are not acceptable as you are." If we dared to reject the equipment we were reminded of the cost, and asked to reflect on the clever and dedicated people who were tirelessly working for the benefit of ungrateful creatures like ourselves. No heed was ever taken of our own suggestions; my requests to try tinted lenses were always ignored and it was not until I left school that I discovered how helpful they would be.

The only other times that lack of sight became an issue for us at the school were during the rare and clumsy attempts to integrate us with able-bodied children. The worst possible activity, net-ball,[2] was usually chosen for this. These occasions were invariably embarrassing and humiliating for all concerned and could lead to desperate maneuvers on the part of the adults to deny the reality of our situation—namely that we had insufficient sight to compete. I am reminded of one netball match, with the score around 20/nil, during which we overheard the games mistress[3] of the opposing team anxiously insisting that they let us get some goals. It was a mortifying experience to see the ball fall through the net while they stood idly by. Very occasionally local Brownies would join us for activities in our extensive grounds. We would be paired off with them for a treasure hunt through the woods, searching for milk-bottle tops—the speed at which they found them was really quite amazing. They seemed to know about us, though, and would be very kind and point the "treasure" out, and even let us pick it up ourselves sometimes, but relying on their bounty spoiled the fun and we wished we could just talk to them or play a different game.

Whether the choice of these highly visual activities was a deliberate denial of our disabilities or simply a lack of imagination on the part of the adults, I do not know. Certainly we played such games successfully among ourselves, and as we were never seen in any other context, perhaps it was the latter. It was only on rare occasions such as these that our lack of sight (which had all but been forgotten) and the artificiality of our world became apparent.

As well as denying the reality of their disabilities, disabled children are frequently forced to deny painful feelings associated with their experiences because their parents and other adults simply cannot cope with them. I am reminded of a friend who, at the age of six or seven, was repeatedly promised expensive toys and new dresses provided she did not cry when taken back to school; we knew exactly how we must behave. Protecting the feelings of the adults we cared about became an arduous responsibility which we exercised with care.

Bravery and stoicism were demanded by the institution too; any outward expression of sadness was not merely ridiculed and scorned, it was simply not allowed. Any hint of dejection led to stern reminders that, unlike most children, we were highly privileged to be living in such a splendid house with such fantastic grounds—an honor which was clearly not our due. There was no one to turn to for comfort or support, and any tears which were shed were, of necessity, silent and private. In contrast to this, the institution, normally so indifferent to life outside its gates, was peculiarly concerned about our parents' states of mind. Our letters were meticulously censored to remove any trace of despondency and the initial letter of each term had a compulsory first sentence: "I have settled down at school and am well and happy." Not only were we compelled to deny our disabilities, but also the painful feelings associated with the lifestyles forced upon us because we were disabled.

Such was our isolation at this school that issues of how to behave in the "normal" world were rarely addressed, but at the next special school I attended, which offered a grammar school education and had an entirely different ethos, much attention was paid to this. The headmaster, a strong, resolute pioneer in the education of partially sighted children, appeared to have a genuine belief not only that we were as good as everyone else, but that we were almost certainly better, and he spent his life tirelessly battling with people who did not share his view.

He liked us to regard ourselves as sighted and steered us away from any connection with blindness; for example, although we were free to go out by ourselves to the nearby town and beyond, the use of white canes was never suggested although many of us use them now. He delighted in people who broke new, visually challenging ground, like acceptance at art school or reading degrees in mathematics, and "blind" occupations, like physiotherapy, were rarely encouraged. In many ways his attitudes and behavior were refreshing, yet he placed the onus to achieve and succeed entirely on ourselves; there was never any suggestion that the world could adapt, or that our needs could or should be accommodated. The underlying message was always the same: "Be superhuman and deny your disability."

ADULTHOOD

In adulthood, most of these pressures to deny disability persist, though they become more subtle and harder to perceive. If disabled adults manage to gain control of their lives, which for many is very difficult, these pressures may be easier to resist. This is because situations which pose difficulties, create anxieties or cause boredom can be avoided, or alternatively adequate assistance can be sought; many of the situations I was placed in as a child I now avoid. As adults we are less vulnerable and less dependent on other people, we can more easily comprehend our situation, and our adult status makes the open expression of other people's disapproval, frustration and disbelief less likely. In addition, disabled adults arouse less emotion and misplaced optimism than disabled children, which serves to dilute the insatiable drive of many professionals to cure or "improve" us. Having said this, many of the problems experienced by disabled adults are similar to those experienced by disabled children.

Disabled adults frequently provoke anxiety and embarrassment in others simply by their presence. Although they become very skillful at dealing with this, it is often achieved at great cost to themselves by denying their disabilities and needs. It is not unusual for disabled people to endure boredom or distress to safeguard the feelings of others. They may, for example, sit through lectures without hearing or seeing rather than embarrass the lecturer, or endure being carried rather than demanding an accessible venue. In situations such as these reassuring phrases such as "I'm all right" or "Don't worry about me" become almost automatic.

One of the reasons we react in this way, rather than being assertive about our disabilities, is to avoid the disapproval, rejection and adverse labeling of others, just as we did when we were children. Our reactions are viewed as resulting from our impairments rather than from the ways we have been treated. Thus being "up front" about disability and the needs which emanate from it can easily lead us to be labeled "awkward," "selfish" or "warped." Such labeling is very difficult to endure without becoming guilty, anxious and depressed; it eats away at our confidence, undermining our courage and leading us to deny our disabilities.

Disbelief remains a common response of able-bodied people when we attempt to convey the reality of our disabilities. If, for example, I try to explain my difficulty in coping with new environments, the usual response is, "Don't worry we all get lost" or "It looks as if you're doing fine to me." Or when I try to convey the feelings of isolation associated with not recognizing people or not knowing what is going on around me, the usual response is "You will in time" or "It took me ages too." This type of response renders disabled people "just like everyone else." For those of us disabled from birth or early childhood, where there is no experience of "normality" with which to compare our situation, knowing how different we really are is problematic and it is easy to become confused and to have our confidence undermined when others insist we are just the same.

An example of denial through disbelief occurred when I was studying a statistics component as part of a course in psychology. I could see absolutely nothing of what was going on in the lectures and yet my frequent and articulate requests for help were met with the response that all students panic about statistics and that everything would work out fine in the end. As it happens it did, but only after spending many hours with a private tutor. As people are generally not too concerned about how we "got there," our successes serve to reinforce the erroneous assumption that we really are "just like everyone else." When I finally passed the examination, the lecturer concerned informed me, in a jocular and patronizing way, that my worries had clearly been unfounded! When people deny our disabilities they deny who we really are.

This tendency to disbelieve is exacerbated by the ambiguous nature of impairments such as partial sight. It is very hard for people to grasp that although I appear to manage "normally" in many situations, I need considerable help in others. The knowledge of other people's perceptions of me is sufficiently powerful to alter my behavior in ways which are detrimental to myself; for example, the knowledge that fellow passengers have seen me use a white cane to cross the road, can be enough to deter me from reading a book on the train. A more common strategy among people with limited sight is to manage roads unaided, thereby risking life and limb to avoid being labeled as frauds.

A further reaction, often associated with the belief that we are really no different, is that because our problems are no greater than anyone else's we do not deserve any special treatment or consideration. People who react in this way view us as whining and ungrateful complainers whenever we assert ourselves, explain our disabilities, ask that our needs be met or demand our rights. My most recent and overt experience of this reaction occurred during a visit to Whitehall to discuss the lack of transport for disabled people. Every time I mentioned a problem which disabled people encounter, such as not being able to use the underground system or the buses, I was told in no uncertain terms that many other people have transport problems too; what about old people, poor people, people who live in remote areas? What was so special about disabled people, and was not a lot being done for them anyway? I was the only disabled person present in this meeting and my confidence was undermined sufficiently to affect the quality of my argument. Reactions such as this can easily give rise to feelings of insecurity and doubt; it is, of course, the case that many people do have problems, but disabled people are among them and cannot afford to remain passive or to be passed by.

College

At the age of 19, after working for two years, I started my physiotherapy training at a special segregated college for blind and partially sighted students. For the first time in my life my disability was, at least in part, defined as blindness. Although about half the students were partially sighted, one of the criteria for entry to the college was the ability to read and write braille (which I had never used before) and to type proficiently, as, regardless of the clarity of their handwriting, the partially sighted students were not permitted to write their essays or examinations by hand, and the blind students were not permitted to write theirs in braille. No visual teaching methods were used in the college and, for those of us with sight, it was no easy matter learning subjects like anatomy, physiology and biomechanics without the use of diagrams.

The institution seemed unable to accept or respond to the fact that our impairments varied in severity and gave rise to different types of disability. We were taught to use special equipment which we did not need and were encouraged to "feel" rather than "peer" because feeling, it was thought, was aesthetically more pleasing, especially when dealing with the poor, unsuspecting public. There was great concern about the way we looked in our professional roles; white canes were not allowed inside the hospitals where we practiced clinically, even by totally blind students, and guide dogs were completely banned. It appeared that the blind students were expected to be superhuman whereas the partially sighted students were expected to be blind. Any attempt to defy or challenge these rules was very firmly quashed so, in the interests of "getting through," we outwardly denied the reality of our disabilities and complied.

Employment

Deciding whether or not to deny disability probably comes most clearly to the fore in adult life when we attempt to gain employment. Until very recently it was not uncommon to be told very bluntly that, in order to be accepted, the job must be done in exactly the same way as everyone else. In many ways this was easier to deal with than the situation now, where "equal opportunity" policies have simultaneously raised expectations and pushed negative attitudes underground, and where, in reality, little has changed. Although I have no way of proving it, I am convinced that the denial of my disability has been absolutely fundamental to my success in gaining the type of employment I have had. I have never completely denied it (it is not hidden enough for that) but rather, in response to the interviewers' skeptical and probing questions, I have minimized the difficulties I face and portrayed myself in a way which would swell my headmaster's pride.

Curiously, once in the job, people have sometimes decided that certain tasks, which I can perform quite adequately, are beyond me, while at the same time refusing to relieve me of those I cannot do. At one college where I worked it was considered impossible for me to cope with taking the minutes of meetings, but my request to be relieved of invigilating large numbers of students, on the grounds that I could not see them, was not acceded to; once again the nature of my disability was being defined by other people. On the rare occasions I have been given "special" equipment or consideration at work it has been regarded as a charitable act or donation for which I should be grateful and beholden. This behavior signals two distinct messages: first that I have failed to be "normal" (and have therefore failed), and second that I must ask for nothing more.

In these more enlightened days of "equal opportunities," we are frequently asked and expected to educate others at work about our disabilities. "We know nothing about it, you must teach us" is the frequent cry. In some ways this is a positive development but, on the other hand, it puts great pressure on us because few formal structures have been developed in which this educative process can take place. In the absence of proactive equal opportunity policies, we are rarely taken seriously and what we say is usually forgotten or ignored. Educating others in this way can also mean that we talk of little

else but disability, which, as well as becoming boring to ourselves, can lead us to be labeled adversely or viewed solely in terms of problems. Challenging disabling attitudes and structures, especially as a lone disabled person, can become frustrating and exhausting, and in reality it is often easier and (dare I say) more functional, in the short term at least, to cope with inadequate conditions rather than fight to improve them. We must beware of tokenistic gestures which do little but put pressure on us.

CONCLUSION

The reasons I have denied the reality of my disability can be summarized as follows:

1. To avoid other people's anxiety and distress.
2. To avoid other people's disappointment and frustration.
3. To avoid other people's disbelief.
4. To avoid other people's disapproval.
5. To live up to other people's ideas of "normality."
6. To avoid spoiling other people's fun.
7. To collude with other people's pretences.

I believe that from earliest childhood denial of disability is totally rational given the situations we find ourselves in, and that to regard it as a psychopathological reaction is a serious mistake. We deny our disabilities for social, economic and emotional survival and we do so at considerable cost to our sense of self and our identities; it is not something we do because of flaws in our individual psyches. For those of us disabled from birth or early childhood, denial of disability has deeply penetrating and entangled roots; we need support and encouragement to make our needs known, but this will only be achieved within the context of genuine structural and attitudinal change.

In this paper I have drawn upon my life experiences and personal reactions to elucidate the pressures placed upon disabled people to deny the reality of their experience of disability. This approach is limited inasmuch as personal experiences and responses can never be divorced from the personality and biography of the person they concern. In addition these pressures will vary according to the individual's impairment. But with these limitations in mind, I am confident that most disabled people will identify with what I have described and that only the examples are, strictly speaking, mine.

DISCUSSION QUESTIONS

1. What are all the ways that French and those around her conspire to deny that she is disabled?
2. Would those in other stigmatized statuses have experiences similar to French's?

NOTES

1. Walking two-by-two in a long file.
2. Girls' basketball.
3. Physical education teacher.

READING 36

Not Blind Enough: Living in the Borderland Called Legal Blindness

Beth Omansky

. . . Human beings are uncomfortable with uncertainty. For instance, when waiting for medical test results or news about a missing loved one, how often we hear people say, "It's the not knowing that's so hard." The human mind, including sight and vision, seeks to make order out of chaos—to organise and categorise, and to find comfort in closure, which relieves the anxieties of uncertainty. Moreover, in an ocularcentric world, the predominant method of making sense of the surrounding environment is sight (Elkins 1996). After all, social culture informs us that "seeing is believing." Because legal blindness is abundantly ambiguous, the

Beth Omansky is a sociologist, author, disability studies scholar, and community activist.

sighted might fail to apprehend how borderland blind people make sense of the physical world; what is more, they feel tentative about how to treat borderland blind people or even to trust that those who claim the identity of legal blindness are, in fact, blind.

Unlike totally blind people, borderland blind people are often accused of fraud because they act too sighted. John Hull (1990, pp. 67–69) describes this social phenomenon in a journal entry titled, "You Bastard! You're Not Blind." Hull tells of a passerby repeatedly yelling at him, insisting that he was not *really* blind; Hull's orientation and mobility skills failed to replicate societal stereotypes of how blindness presents itself in everyday life.

Borderland blind people are subjected to pressures that totally blind people do not endure; they are pushed and pulled back and forth across the border between sightedness and blindness, resulting in disallowance of citizenship in both lands, which leaves them in a state of what Black American pacifist civil rights leader, Bayard Rustin, aptly called "social dislocation" (D'Emilio 2004).

Totally blind people fall into a discrete stereotyped classification of blindness as darkness (Monbeck 1973), which in many ways is comforting to sighted people because they do not have to guess what the blind person can or cannot see. In an effort to relieve their own dubiety, sighted people might try to force borderland blind people to choose one side or the other—usually pushing them into the socially preferred land of the sighted—a land in which they experience egregious inequality. Borderland blind people are vulnerable to attempted regulation by disquieted but well-meaning acquaintances, friends and family, who yearn for their loved one to be "normal"; in reaction, borderland blind people might internally regulate their own behaviour or else succumb to external pressures as they try to "pass" even during times when they clearly reside on the blind side of the pale. The dynamics of such interactions press everyone concerned into denial (French 1993). Participants in this study reported experiences which echo these phenomena.

PATROLLING THE BORDER

. . . This subtheme is consistent with Sally French's personal account, "Can You See the Rainbow?" [Reading 35], which receives the most reprint permission requests of her entire body of work (personal communication, September 2003). . . .

Two of [one of my informant's] anecdotes are consistent with French's reminiscences. Uncomfortable with the contradictions of "border" behaviour, a companion requested that Larry refrain from reading the newspaper in restaurants while his guide dog lay at his side because it would "confuse" sighted restaurant-goers and give them false impressions of what blindness is. Perhaps she was afraid observers would disbelieve Larry's claim of blindness, and by association, might just reflect on her own character. She also urged him to call colours by the names most commonly used by sighted people despite the fact that he saw them as another colour. For example, if he sees a building as brown even though he knows it's red, he calls it brown, but she thinks he should call it red because that's what it is to sighted people and also, to how he used to see it. She is more comfortable with him pretending to see as sighted people do, and as he used to even though she did not know him before he went blind. Colours are important to Larry's profession as an artist and photographer; so now he encounters a conundrum common to legal blindness. Which is more valid? An accurate description of what the borderland blind person sees, or is the sighted population's naming and interpretation of things *more* valid because it is the majority opinion? And if the latter is accepted as "truth," does this place borderland blind people in the position of having to lie about their own experience to satisfy sighted people's perception of "reality"—of truth? . . .

I, too, have often experienced people placing me on the sighted ("normal") side of the border despite my own choice to stake my claim on the blindness side. On two separate occasions, sighted people grabbed my white cane away from me when my picture was about to be taken. As I posed in front of a statue of George Mason on the campus where we had just attended my master's degree graduation ceremony, one of my relatives walked up and took my cane from my hand. I understood and appreciated his good intentions, but I didn't like it. I didn't say anything because I didn't want to cause tension between us or hurt his feelings. Another time I was getting my picture taken at the Molly Malone statue in Dublin, Ireland. The man in charge of the statue looked through his camera to set the pose, and then reached up in an attempt to remove my cane from my hand. I was not as surprised as I was at graduation, so this time I refused to hand it over and got my picture taken as I am. I guess they both thought the cane was unsightly, which, come to think of it, is a pretty telling word.

Stephen Kuusisto's (1998, p. 13) family left him with a mixed message that placed him on the fence of the border, ill-equipped to fit in on either side; first, that he was blind, and next, that he "was taught to disavow it." He explains the emotional consequences thus, "I grew bent over like the dry tinder grass. I couldn't stand up proudly, nor could I retreat" (Kuusisto 1998, p. 13).

Sighted people do not always attempt to place blind people on the sighted side: a critical factor is acceptance of their loved one's blindness. For example, Larry's daughter accepted his blindness from the outset, and she understands the limitations of an ocularcentric built environment. Every year, she sends him a new bright yellow parka because she wants him to be easily seen by motorists. Soon after Larry told his family that he had become blind, one of his sons offered to act as driver on a trip across the country—a role Larry traditionally assumed. His son told him that he would drive, and Larry still could take photographs of the Southwest desertscape, just as he had always done on previous trips.

RESISTANCE AND CHALLENGE IN EVERYDAY LIFE

Larry, Catherine, J. R. and I have been subjected to social treatment based on common myths about blind people, and we each found various ways to

READING 36: Not Blind Enough

challenge these stereotypes. We all used humour as a strategy to resist and challenge societal misperceptions about blindness. J. R. believes that those who use humour are the ones who "survive" blindness.

For instance, when Larry shook hands with someone to whom he was introduced, he made a "lucky guess" that the person was a piano player. The person making the introduction cried out in amazement, "Oh, my God! How did you get that?" Larry then spun a yarn about how his blindness gave him special hypersensitivity to touch. Larry laughed as he told me, "So you know I am definitely just perpetrating a hoax."

One of J. R.'s anecdotes speaks directly to the stereotype that blindness means darkness (Monbeck, 1973), and it also highlights what it is like to be both observer and observed. When J. R. goes to the optician's office he observes that people notice that he wears tinted (not dark) glasses, yet he carries a white cane. He jokes, "They think, 'Oh you have glasses you're not blind.'" But then, there is the presence of the white cane. J. R. suspects the observers wonder about the optician's abilities, thinking, "This is the best they can do?" His anecdote illustrates the cognitive dissonance sighted people experience when they witness the alterity of legal blindness. But J. R.'s social commentary was not as funny to me once I connected the dots back to when I was fired from my much-needed receptionist job at the optician's office because, "It looked bad" for the optical company.

J. R. told about when he was using his white cane during an outing, and a child asked her mother, "Why is that man using that white stick?" The mother explained that he used the cane because he is blind. As J. R. passed them, he said to the mother, "Don't tell her about the 25 bonus points," which refers to the old joke about drivers earning "bonus points" for running over a blind person. He made his point that he is well aware of "blind" jokes.

None of the participants reported engaging in self-demeaning humour; instead, they turned the joke onto society in the form of social observation, and they all used humour to resist internalised oppression—a strategy used by many authors (e.g., Hull 1990; Knipfel 1999; Kudlick 2005; Kuusisto 1998; Michalko 1998, 1999).

Blind People as Public Property

Frequently, acting blind (i.e., using low vision aids and other blindness skills) elicits invasive, infantilising questions from strangers such as, "Oh my, what happened to you?" or, "How do you cross the street by yourself?" or, "Aren't you afraid?" Sometimes this line of questioning is followed with something along the lines of, "Oh, you're just so brave," or, "You're such an inspiration." Strangers seem to have no compunction about prying into private medical and even financial matters as if they have a right to know; and if the blind person refuses to answer, the strangers either redouble their efforts or turn away as if they were the ones insulted. Larry manages blindness questions in different ways depending upon whether they come from strangers, acquaintances or family. He said:

> It's like they wonder what it is that you see . . . if it's like my niece . . . I'll take more care in analogies and stuff like that whereas if it's my brother or my sister-in-law or one of the guys I'm with, um, I would just give them a couple of different things.

Larry reports, however, that as for the general public, he doesn't "give a shit what they think." Be that as it may, he remains aware of how people might perceive him.

Borderland blind people report that they make decisions about whether they should disclose their visual impairment from moment to moment and situation to situation. Act sighted or flaunt blindness? Or should they just do what they need to do to get around without feeling the need to explain themselves to anyone? Self-disclosure decisions are aroused by the needs of embodied consequences of blindness; by awareness of societal attitudes and predictable consequences of presenting oneself as blind; and by issues around identity. All these factors influence how blind (and other disabled) people negotiate a world "from the vantage point of the atypical" (Linton 1998, p. 6).

As illustration, fast-food restaurants almost always hang their menus high up on walls several feet behind the service counter. Blind people cannot read the sign for two reasons; first, their impairment limits their sensory ability to read print from a distance; and second, the location, position and font size of the menu is rendered inaccessible because the restaurant designers falsely assumed their customers are all sighted. Faced with the barrier of an inaccessible menu, borderland blind customers must decide whether to "ask for help" (request access), knowing through past experience their request might evoke pity, disdain, or that they will be outright shunned. One alternative I adopted in the past is to memorize what I wish to order and just order the same thing every time I go to that restaurant. Blind people often choose this option to avoid making themselves vulnerable to stigmatization, rudeness, public embarrassment or pity, but the downside is that they surrender gastronomic variety (Gordon 1996; Linton 1998).

Restaurants can be particularly troublesome for borderland blind people because the ocularcentric environment and the embodied experience bump up against the pressure of social graces. The fancier the restaurant, the dimmer the lighting most likely is. People sit across from each other, so the table width breaches any possibility of eye contact; add flickering candles, an undercurrent of simultaneously humming conversations punctuated with loud laughter, and now the setting becomes a recipe for social *faux pas* and other mishaps. Catherine said:

> [t]hey just think you're absolutely stupid. And it's just like you can't get away from that. That's your embarrassment . . . And then it's all over. It's all over. [Laughs] And then you go to the bathroom and cry . . . breathe . . . panic attack. It's like, Christ! Why can't anything go right? Why couldn't the mashed potatoes be over here? Why couldn't the butter be . . . ?

Finding the bathroom in a dark restaurant is like running an obstacle course—wending one's way through tables, booths, wait staff carrying head-level trays, feet and handbags in aisles, coats on chair backs, swinging kitchen doors with wait staff moving quickly in all directions, and the dark hallway that inevitably houses the rest rooms, which are more than likely not clearly marked because the signs are hung high above eye level, written in fancy script, or marked with artistically gender-specific designs with no print as clues:

> I cannot count on both hands how many times I've walked into the men's room in restaurants because no one was around to whom I could ask direction. When I see a urinal on the wall, I turn around and head off into the restroom next door, hoping no one saw me enter or leave.

ASKING FOR HELP

When borderland blind people ask for impairment-related assistance, they must identify themselves as blind. It is very difficult to pass as sighted and ask for help reading a street sign six feet above where you are standing. Identity is a two-way social process; people identify themselves and people are identified by others (Rosenblum & Travis 1996). Since borderland blind people may not use typical blindness artifacts (e.g., white cane, dark glasses) the sighted public may respond to requests for assistance in demeaning, curt or other unhelpful ways. Sighted people might be more ready to offer help to someone who is obviously blind; yet they may feel intruded upon by an unidentifiable borderland blind person. Catherine said:

> Yeh, you have to ask everyone, and it's like people, they can be really—brush you off mean. You have to be really cordial and demure as a blind person.

Larry's reluctance to ask for help is bound up in his desire for self-sufficiency. He said:

> . . . to find out that yeah you know damn it I need help reading this label because I don't know if it's apple juice or apple vinegar . . . So um, there was a time when I wouldn't have bought it. That's, that's the thing that can eat at you. You know?

POLICING ONE'S SELF

The traditional medical establishment, indeed, all of society, teaches disabled people to act like everyone else if they hope to lead successful lives—they have to act "normal," which requires them to "overcome" their impairments. But as Linton (1998), Michalko (2002), and others note, people do not "overcome" as that is impossible; people live with their impairments. As Linton (1998) observes:

> "overcoming" disability [sic] assumes that there is something inferior about their group membership, and the responsibility is left on the individual to work harder to be successful and to triumph over what otherwise would be a tragic life (p. 17).

Another message in the concept of "overcoming" is that the person has gone beyond societal expectations of what people with impairments can achieve; the person has overcome the "social stigma of having a disability" (Linton 1998, p. 17).

I Can See Clearly Now: Passing as Sighted

"Passing" is an interactional social tool employed by all people, in one way or another, as they produce personal identities within (and influenced by) the cultural contexts in which they live. Some blind people employ premeditated strategies as they attempt to pass as sighted and/or to engage in social interaction in ways that are understood and unquestioned by sighted people. Michalko (1999) and Hull (1990) describe intricate ways they negotiate meeting and greeting oncoming people beyond their field of vision. Michalko (1998) uses eye contact with sighted people. He stays aware not only of his seeing, but of how and where he directs his eyes so that sighted people assume he is making direct eye contact. If he gazes where he needs to in order to see them, he appears as though he is not looking at the other person at all. I have central vision loss, so when I look at a person's face, they often think I am looking behind them or looking at their hair instead of into their eyes:

> Depending on where I am and who I'm with, I might try to appear as if I'm making eye contact. Sometimes I will tell people that even though it appears I'm not looking at them, I really am, but I have to feel emotionally ready for an onslaught of nosy questions before I do that.

Catherine said she has problems with relationships just because of her vision. She can't pick up signals such as body language or a "certain look" to know, for example, if someone is "getting pissed off." In concert with Michalko (1999) and Hull (1990), Catherine can't identify people approaching her. She has to learn the sound of their walk. She said, "I have to know them because you can feel people's energy in a way." But, when borderland blind people use familiar clues to identify people or things, sighted people disbelieve their blindness, and then they have to re-assert that, yes, they really are blind, which is another social pitfall distinctive to the borderland. The struggle to be believed can be emotionally draining because such disbelief assaults their integrity and essential as well as social identity. Catherine said:

> . . . it's like you're always having to confirm "I'm blind but I'm not too blind." It's like back and forth, and you're just like constantly pulling at them and you don't realize that; and they don't realize that you feel like you're manipulating the crap out of them and that they're invalidating you. And they're invalidating your blindness. You're just like, either way I go they hate me. [Laughs] It's like you just feel like you're hated even though you know yes, no it's not about you.

Borderland blind people might attempt to pass or, at the very least, to remain unnoticed, which keeps things simpler in social situations. Explaining one's blindness several times a day to several different strangers gets tiresome, distracting and boring. Catherine believes sighted people act like "little anthropologists" trying to figure out blindness culture, and ". . . in the process they're destroying the living hell out of it and objectifying your blindness, and objectifying you, and, oh. This is *huge*."

Sometimes borderland blind people deny themselves use of access equipment such as white canes or low vision glasses; or they might take unnecessary risks such as not asking a passerby what colour the traffic light is at an idle intersection—all to avoid the attention that a "spoiled identity" attracts (Goffman 1986). *Passing* is *acting*, that is, to practice in a creative, methodical way, how to perform as something they are not—sighted. Larry said that his need for perfectionism drives how he presents himself in public:

> Yeah, the challenge is greater; therefore the perfection has to be greater . . . See, if people come up to you and say, "Gee I didn't know you were blind." I say I hit a home run.

Catherine hesitates to use her blindness as an excuse even when it is a quite legitimate reason for a particular behaviour, explaining, "You don't want to blame it on you being blind though, that's the problem." She describes her reticence to be judged by sighted people:

> . . . when a lot of things are caused by not seeing you don't want to keep saying it over and over again because people get kind of like, okay, you're going to blame everything on that, you know . . . You have to be really self-sufficient sounding, even if you're kind of leaving out bits of the reason. . . .

I understand Catherine's reasoning. I think long and hard before invoking blindness as a reason for something I did or did not do because I am concerned that people will think I'm using my blindness—as Sally French (1993) writes, "playing up"; they might think I'm a complainer or not "adjusted." Multiple identities further confound the dilemma. For example:

> I think people might misconstrue my holding money close up to my face to read the denominations on bills, or feel the edges of coins to tell quarters with their ridged edges apart from smooth-edged pennies and nickels. I'm concerned that people will think I'm doing all this because I am Jewish; that is, inviting them to invoke stereotypes about Jews having an extreme attachment to money. I guess I'd rather be thought of as a pitiful blind person than a money-hungry Jew. So, I try to be inconspicuous.

Personal Costs of Passing or Coming Out

A lot of thought, creativity, time and energy gets spent carrying out strategies for passing as sighted, and the personal costs can be high. Catherine said that when she self-discloses her blindness, she feels vulnerable, and she does her best to resist falling prey to the negative societal stereotypes that blind people are "fools" (Monbeck 1973). She said:

> [Y]ou don't see it. And so you're constantly dealing with these things that come at you and you don't know what it is . . . Um, ah, and you know it's like having to explain to people. It's like yeah I might not see but . . . you *cannot* pull one over on me.

Sometimes people choose not to disclose their blindness, which results in exclusion from activities not because of sighted people leaving them out, but because they have left themselves out. On the other hand, they might disclose their impairments and ask for what they need despite feeling awkward and running the risk of being treated as different. Either way, there is a trade-off. . . .

Just because someone asks for what he or she needs does not guarantee they will get it. J. R. talked about people who think they know what blind people are going through, and say something like, "Oh gee, my brother knew a friend who was, had a friend who was blind, or something like that," and then proceed to give unwanted or the wrong kind of assistance. Blind people tell stories about sighted people grabbing them by the arm at street corners, and then tugging them across the street even though they had not asked for assistance or even wanted to go across the street in the first place. One evening, a woman grabbed me as I made my way through a theatre aisle and literally pulled me to where she thought I wanted to go without ever asking if I needed assistance (Omansky Gordon 2003, p. 224). Apparently, my white cane drafted her into do-gooder duty. Rod Michalko (1998) relates a story about someone pressing a dollar in his hand as he and his dog guide stood at a traffic light together. He told the man he did not need it, and asked him to take it back. The man insisted Rod take it. So, he did, and then gave it to a panhandler. . . .

PERSONAL ACCOUNT

A Time I Didn't Feel Normal

I was tested for Learning Disabilities (LD) when I was in third grade and diagnosed with being ADD and LD because of short-term memory loss and mild dyslexia. I thought nothing of it because I didn't really understand what it meant. All I knew was it got me out of class to go work with a woman on my schoolwork. However, the next year I moved from Ohio to Virginia and discovered that I was different from most of my peers. It got worse when I got to fifth grade because I still had to leave class twice a week to go work with the disabilities counselor with two other kids in my class. I soon realized that people would actually talk down to me in my class because I wasn't really "one of them," that I wasn't as smart. The stereotype, even at such a young age, about being LD was not a good one. The other two kids that were in my LD class were not exactly popular and a little weird. So because I was with them, I became one of them. I would get made fun of and stopped really trying in class because if I messed up people would look at me as though it was expected that I would do things wrong. It got so bad that I told my mom I didn't want to go back to school. I asked her to home school me so that I wouldn't have to deal with the other kids in my class judging me and making me feel like I was stupid. My mom refused to do it, so I did the only other thing I could think of: I forced my way out of the LD program at my school. I don't know how I got

them to let me out but I felt that it was the only way for me to be "normal." I continued to struggle throughout my school career but I wasn't treated as differently, I was more socially accepted.

Today, I don't have a problem with telling people about my "disabilities," but back then I would never have admitted it. I have grown to the point where my "disabilities" don't really affect me all that much. I've learned to cope with them and still do well in school. So, I don't feel like an idiot, or stupid, or a lesser student because of my LD anymore. However, back then I would cry because I thought I wasn't as smart as everyone else and that there was something wrong with me that made me different from everyone else. I felt isolated at times and envied my friends who were "normal." My parents did what they could to help me with my homework and in overcoming my difficulties, but no one really stuck up for me at school or seemed to care how I felt, or even notice how upset I was. I am a better person today because of this though; I realize how hard it is for people to be treated as though there is something wrong with them even though there really isn't. Judging people for their "disabilities" is wrong and cruel and people really need to step back and think about how their actions affect others.

Heather Callender

DISCUSSION QUESTIONS

1. Why would people who are legally blind be reluctant to ask for help?
2. What are the costs and benefits of passing as sighted?

REFERENCES

D'Emilio, John, 2004. *Lost Prophet: The Life and Times of Bayard Rustin*. Chicago: University of Chicago Press.

Elkins, James, 1996. *The Object Stares Back*. New York: Simon & Schuster.

French, Sally, 1993. Can You See the Rainbow? The Roots of Denial. In John Swain, Vic Finkelstein, Sally French & Michael Oliver (eds.), *Disabling Barriers, Enabling Environments*. London: Open University Press.

Goffman, Erving, 1986. *Stigma: Notes on the Management of a Spoiled Identity*. Englewood Cliffs, NJ: Prentice-Hall.

Gordon, Beth. 1996. I am Legally Blind. In Rosenblum, Karen E. & Toni-Michele C. Travis (eds). *The Meaning of Difference: American Constructions of Race, Sex and Gender, Social Class, and Sexual Orientation*. New York: McGraw-Hill.

Hull, John, 1990. *Touching the Rock: An Experience of Blindness*. New York: Pantheon Books.

Knipfel, Jim, 1999. *Slack Jaw*. New York: Penguin Putnam.

Kudlick, Catherine J., 2005. The Blind Man's Harley: White Canes and Gender Identity in America. In *Signs: Journal of Women and Culture in Society,* vol. 30, no. 2, pp. 1589–1606.

Kuusisto, Stephen, 1998. *Planet of the Blind: A Memoir.* New York: G. K. Hall.

Linton, Simi, 1998. *Claiming Disability: Knowledge and Identity.* New York: New York University Press.

Michalko, Rod, 1998. *Mystery of the Eye and the Shadow of Blindness.* Toronto: University of Toronto Press.

———, 1999. *The Two in One: Walking with Smokie, Walking with Blindness.* Philadelphia: Temple University Press.

———, 2002. *The Difference That Disability Makes.* Philadelphia: Temple University Press.

Monbeck, Michael, 1973. *The Meaning of Blindness: Attitudes Toward Blindness and Blind People.* Bloomington: Indiana University Press.

Omansky Gordon, Beth, 2003. I am Legally Blind. In Rosenblum, Karen E. & Toni-Michelle C. Travis (eds.), *The Meaning of Difference: American Constructions of Race, Sex and Gender, Social Class, and Sexual Orientation.* New York: McGraw-Hill.

Rosenblum, Karen E. & Toni-Michelle C. Travis, 1996, (eds.). *The Meaning of Difference: American Constructions of Race, Sex and Gender, Social Class, and Sexual Orientation.* New York: McGraw-Hill.

THE MEANING OF DIFFERENCE

FRAMEWORK ESSAY

In the first framework essay we considered how contemporary American master statuses are named, dichotomized, and stigmatized. In the second essay, we focused on the experience of privilege and stigma that accompanies those master statuses. In this third section, we will look at the meaning that is conferred on difference. In effect, what difference does difference make?

The readings in this section highlight social institutions that have some of the strongest effects on what difference ultimately means—the economy, education, public policy, law, popular culture. The concept of *ideology* gets special attention here because it both shapes and is shaped by the operation of these social institutions.

In looking at the interaction of ideology and social institutions, our approach parallels the metaphor of the "birdcage" developed by philosopher Marilyn Frye in her now classic discussion of the concept of oppression.[1] Frye suggests that if we are to understand how categories of people are "pressed" by social forces, we must attend to the *systematic* and *systemic* nature of this "press." Using the metaphor of a birdcage, she argues that oppression cannot be understood by looking at only one obstacle or "wire"; one must consider the *set of wires* that together form the cage. Ideology, economy, education, policy, law, and popular culture *together and in interaction* form the "cage" that people confront. Above and beyond the construction and experience of difference, these social forces give *difference* tangible meaning; they make difference matter.

Ideology

The concept of *ideology* was first elaborated by Marx and Engels, particularly in *The German Ideology* (1846). It is now a concept used throughout the social sciences and humanities. In general, an ideology can be defined as a widely shared belief or idea that has been constructed and disseminated by the powerful, primarily reflects their experiences, and functions for their benefit.

Ideologies are anchored in the experiences of their creators; thus, they offer only a partial view of the world. "Ideologies are not simply false, they can be 'partly true,' and yet also incomplete [or] distorted. . . . [They are not] consciously crafted by the ruling class and then injected into the minds of the majority; [they are] instead *produced* by specifiable, complex, social conditions."[2] Because those who control the means of disseminating ideas have a better chance of having their ideas prevail, Marx and Engels concluded that "the ideas of the ruling class are in every epoch the ruling ideas." Ideologies have the power to supplant, distort, or silence the experiences of those outside their production.

The idea that people are rewarded on the basis of their merit is an example of an ideology. It is an idea promoted by those with power—for example, teachers and supervisors—and many opportunities are created for the expression of the belief. Report cards, award banquets, and merit raises are all occasions for the expression of the belief that people are rewarded on the basis of their merit.

But certainly, most of us recognize this idea is not really true: as Stephen McNamee and Robert Miller illustrate in Reading 13, people are not rewarded only, or even primarily, on the basis of their individual merit. The idea that merit is rewarded is only partly true and reflects only *some* people's experiences. The frequent repetition of the idea, however, has the potential to overwhelm contrary experience. Even those who have not generally experienced people being rewarded on merit are likely to subscribe to this philosophy, because they hear it so often. In any event, there are few safe opportunities to describe beliefs to the contrary or have those beliefs widely disseminated.

Thus, the idea that people are rewarded on the basis of merit is an ideology. It is a belief that reflects primarily the experiences of those with power, but it is presented as universally valid. The idea overwhelms and silences the voices of those who are outside its production. In effect, ideologies ask us to discount our own experience.

This conflict between one's own experience and the ideas conveyed by an ideology is implied in W. E. B. Du Bois's description of the "double conscious-ness" experienced by African Americans discussed in Framework Essay II. It is also what many feminists refer to as the double or fractured consciousness experienced by women. In both cases, the dominant ideas fail to reflect the real-life experiences of people in these categories. For example, the *actual* expe-rience of poverty, discrimination, teen motherhood, disability, sexual assault, or life in a black neighborhood or in a gay relationship rarely coincide with the public discussion of these topics. Because those in stigmatized categories do not control the production or distribution of the prevailing ideas, *their* experi-ence is not likely to be reflected in them. The ideology not only silences their experience; it may invalidate it even in their own minds: "I must be the one who's crazy!" In this way, the dominant discourse can invade and overwhelm our own experience.[3]

An ideology that so dominates a culture that it becomes the prevailing and unquestioned belief was described in the 1920s by Italian political theorist Antonio Gramsci as the *hegemonic,* or ruling, ideology. Gramsci argued that social control was primarily accomplished by the control of ideas and that whatever was con-sidered to be "common sense" was especially effective as a mechanism of social control. We are all encouraged to adhere to common sense even when that requires discounting our own experience. The discussion of natural-law language that fol-lows highlights that process.

Conveying Ideologies: Natural-Law Language and Stereotypes

Hegemonic, or ruling, ideologies often take the form of *natural-law language* and *stereotypes.*

Natural-Law Language   When people use the word *natural,* they usually mean that something is inevitable, predetermined, or outside human control.[4] *Human nature* and *instinct* are often used in the same way. For example, "It's only natural to care about what others think," "It's human nature to want to get ahead," or "It's just instinctive to be afraid of someone different" all convey the sense that something is inevitable, automatic, and independent of one's will.

Thus, it is not surprising when, in discussions about discrimination, someone says, "It's only natural for people to be prejudiced," or "It's human nature to want to be with your own kind." Each of these commonsense ideas conveys a belief in the inevitability of discrimination and prejudice, as if such processes emerged independently of anyone's will.

Even when describing something we oppose, the word *natural* can convey a sense of inevitability. For example, "I am against racism, but it's only natural," puts nature on the side of prejudice. Arguing that something is natural because it happens frequently has the same consequence. "All societies have discriminated against women," implies that something that happens frequently is therefore inevitable. But in truth, something that happens frequently more likely indicates that there is an extensive set of social controls ensuring the outcome.

At least three consequences follow from natural-law language. First, it ends discussion, as if having described something as natural makes any further exploration of the topic unnecessary. This makes sense, given that the word *natural* is equated with inevitability: If something is inevitable, there is little sense in questioning it.

Second, because natural-law language treats behavior as predetermined, it overlooks the actual cultural and historical variation of human societies. If something is natural, logically it should always happen. Yet virtually no human behavior emerges everywhere and always; all social life is susceptible to change. Thus, natural-law language ignores the variability of social life.

Third, if it is "natural" to dislike those who are different, then there is really nothing we can do about that feeling. It is no one's responsibility; it is just natural. If there is nothing I can do about my own behavior, I can expect to do little about the behavior of others. Human nature thus is depicted as a limitation beyond which people cannot expect to move.[5] Describing certain behavior as "only natural" implies that personal and social change are impossible.

In all these ways—by closing off discussion, masking variation and change, and treating humans as passive—natural-law language tells us not to question the world that surrounds us. Natural-law language has this effect whatever its specific content: "It's only natural to discriminate." "It's only natural to want to have children." "It's only natural to marry and settle down." "Inequality is only natural; the poor will always be with us." "Aggression and war are just human nature." "Greed is instinctive." Indeed, in several of the early Supreme Court decisions described in Reading 37—for example, *Dred Scott v. Sanford, Minor v. Happersett, Plessy v. Ferguson, Elk v. Wilkins*—being a slave, black, Native American, and/or female is treated as a "natural class," a limited and fixed "condition" that is unaffected by individual differences or societal change.

Perhaps more important than any of these, however, is the fact that natural-law language often carries a hidden recommendation about what you *ought* to do. If something is "just natural," you cannot prevent others from doing it, and you are well advised to do it yourself. Thus, natural-law language serves as a forceful mechanism of social control.

In all, natural-law language is used to reinforce hegemonic ideologies. It reduces the complexity and historic variability of the social world to a claim for universal processes, offering a partial and distorted truth that silences those with contrary experience. Natural-law language can make discrimination appear to be natural, normal, and inevitable. It tells us simply to accept the world around us and not seek to improve it. Thus, natural-law language itself creates and maintains ideas about difference.

An Example of Natural-Law Language: "People just want to be with their own kind" As we have said, describing something as "natural" helps us to ignore how *social* forces—for example, those of economy, policy, education, and law—have created the conditions that we attribute to "nature."

For example, the idea that blacks and whites naturally live in separate neighborhoods because they "like living with their own kind" makes it seem as if these groups have *always* been segregated and indeed choose that segregation. But as Richard Rothstein in Reading 42 describes, the hypersegregation experienced by African Americans is of fairly recent origin. It is the product of specific discriminatory policies initiated and enforced by the federal government, as well as the failure of federal policies to correct that damage. The policies that have reduced discrimination in employment and education and generated a broad social consensus that these are valuable outcomes—have not materialized regarding residential segregation. The persistence of this residential form of segregation deeply limits groups' access to resources for an improved life: education, jobs, transportation, safety, recreation, nutrition, and health care are all closely connected to where one lives.

A variety of factors contribute to ongoing residential segregation—from the local "tipping point" at which the nonwhite population in a neighborhood becomes large enough to prompt white flight; to an individual's willingness to live in a neighborhood in which there are few others from their race or ethnic group; to deliberate discrimination on the part of landlords, real estate agents, and mortgage lenders. Indeed, overt discrimination, continues to be found in housing audits. For example, black, Hispanic, and Asian renters are told about fewer available units than equally qualified whites; as potential home buyers, blacks and Asian Americans learn about and are shown fewer homes than equally qualified whites.[6]

In all, the residential segregation that appears "just natural" is constituted not simply by individual acts of discrimination, but by the social structural forces of economy, policy, law, and ideology. Though its levels have "modestly declined" since 1980,[7] residential segregation continues even though "surveys consistently show that whites and blacks alike prefer integrated neighborhoods by wide margins."[8]

Similarly, despite the Supreme Court's 1967 rejection of state laws banning interracial marriage (in *Loving v. Virginia*), those historic prohibitions still contributed to our current ideas that people "just naturally" love and marry others of the same race. Although law no longer bars such marriages, the persistence of these beliefs about what is "natural" may help explain the low rate of black-white intermarriage compared to the rates of intermarriage involving Asians and Latinos,[9] as well as the preferences that emerge in online dating sites. As the authors of a 2009 study of Yahoo! Personals found, "Race is one of the main selection criteria for white Internet daters—whites express racial preferences even more commonly than religious or educational preferences."[10]

This is the case despite surveys now showing historically high acceptance of black-white marriages among whites: As of 2013, 96 percent of blacks and 84 percent of whites report that they approve of black-white marriage (the smallest gap of opinion between blacks and whites since Gallup started asking this question in 1968, when the gap was about 40 percentage points).[11] Like the contrast between actual residential segregation and survey results that affirm the desire to live in an integrated neighborhood, here the contrast is between a modestly increasing but still low rate of actual interracial dating and marriage, and surveys that show historically high levels of their acceptance.

Why is residential segregation reproduced even when people say they do not want to live in segregated environments? Why do interracial marriage and dating remain infrequent despite attitudes that are increasingly tolerant? Although there are many factors at work, the gap between attitudes and behavior highlights one of the paradoxes of our time, that "it is possible to reproduce racial categories [and hierarchies] even while ostensibly repudiating them."[12] Unfortunately, all of this real complexity is masked by a claim that "it's only natural for people to want to stay with their own kind."

Stereotypes   A *stereotype* is a "prediction that members of a group will behave in certain ways"—for example, that black men will have athletic ability or that Asian American students will excel in the sciences.

Stereotypes assume that all the individuals in a category possess the same characteristics. Stereotypes persist despite evidence to the contrary because they are not formulated in a way that is testable or falsifiable.[13] In this way, stereotypes differ from descriptions. Description offers no prediction; it can be tested for accuracy and rejected when wrong. Description also encourages explanation and a consideration of historical variability.

For example, "Most great American athletes are African American" is a description. First, there is no prediction that a particular African American can be expected to be a good athlete, or that someone who is white will be a poor one. Second, the claim is verifiable; that is, it can be tested for accuracy and proven wrong (e.g., by asking what proportion of the last two decades' American Olympic medal winners were African American). Third, the statement turns our attention to explanation and historical variation: Why might this be the case? Has this always been the case?

In contrast, "African Americans are good athletes" is a stereotype. It attempts to characterize a whole population, thus denying the inevitable differences among the people in the category. It predicts that members of a group will behave in a particular way. Further, the stereotype denies the reality of historical and cultural variation by suggesting that this has always been the case. Thus, stereotypes essentialize: They assume that if you know something about the physical package someone comes in, you can predict that person's behavior.

Both stereotypes and natural-law language offer broad-based predictions about behavior. Stereotypes predict that members of a particular category will possess particular attributes; natural-law language predicts that certain behavior is inevitable. Neither stereotypes nor natural-law language is anchored in any social or historical context, and for that reason, both are frequently wrong. Basketball great Bill Russell's reaction when asked if he thought African Americans were "natural" athletes makes clear the similarity of natural-law language and stereotyping. As Russell said, this was a stereotypic image of African American athletes that deprecated the skill and effort he brought to his craft—as if he was great because he was black rather than because of the talent he cultivated in hours of practice.

An Example of Stereotypes: The Model Minority   As we have said, stereotypes explain life outcomes by attributing some essential, shared quality to all those in a particular category. The current depiction of Asian Americans as a "model minority" is a good example of this. Apart even from differences between individuals, this stereotype masks the considerable economic, educational, and occupational heterogeneity among Asian Americans. For example, the proportion of those holding college degrees varies considerably among Asian American groups, at rates of 64 percent for Asian Indians, 46 percent for Chinese, 42 percent for Filipinos, 40 percent for Japanese, 44 percent for Koreans, 26 percent for Vietnamese, 14 percent for Cambodians and Hmong, and 12 percent for Laotians.[14]

These groups differ for many reasons, but one important factor is that some have arrived as immigrants and others have arrived as refugees. As David Haines describes in Reading 39, from the horrors that they have been subjected to or witnessed, to their levels of education and knowledge of the English language, refugees differ significantly from other immigrants. Whereas it can be said that immigrants have chosen America and in that sense have been oriented toward it for some time, refugees more often suddenly find themselves in the country. Thus, refugees are more different from Americans than other immigrants. Still, they are often subject to the model minority stereotype.

Finally, it is good to remember that the model minority stereotype is itself a fairly recent invention. Among those now called "model minority" are groups who were previously categorized as undesirable immigrants, denied citizenship through naturalization, and placed in internment camps as potential traitors.

In American culture, stereotypes are often driven by the necessity to explain why some categories of people succeed more than others. Thus, the model-minority stereotype is often used to claim that if racism has not been an impediment to Asian Americans' success, it could not have hurt African Americans' likelihood of success.

The myth of the Asian-American "model minority" has been challenged, yet it continues to be widely believed. One reason for this is its instructional value. For whom are Asian

Americans supposed to be a "model"? Shortly after the Civil War, southern planters recruited Chinese immigrants in order to pit them against the newly freed blacks as "examples" of laborers willing to work hard for low wages. Today, Asian Americans are again being used to discipline blacks. . . . Our society needs an Asian-American "model minority" in an era anxious about a growing black underclass.[15]

A brief review of U.S. immigration policy explains the misguided nature of the comparison between African and Asian Americans. Until 1965, U.S. immigration was restricted by quotas that set limits on the number of immigrants from each nation based on the percentage of people from that country residing in the United States at the time of the 1920 census. This had the obvious and intended effect of severely restricting immigration from Asia, as well as that from Southern and Eastern Europe and Africa. The civil rights movement of the 1960s raised national embarrassment about this quota system[16] such that in 1965, Congress replaced national-origin quotas with an annual 20,000-person limit for every nation regardless of its size. Within that quota, preference went first to those who were relatives of U.S. citizens and then to those with occupational skills needed in America.

The result was a total increase in immigration and a change in its composition. Because few individuals from non-European countries could immigrate on the grounds of having family in America—previous restrictions would have made that almost impossible—the quotas were filled with people meeting designated *occupational* needs. Thus, those immigrating to the United States since 1965 have had high educational and occupational profiles. The middle- and upper-class professionals and entrepreneurs who have immigrated to the United States did not suddenly become successful here; rather, they continued their home-country success here. These high occupational and educational profiles have characterized immigrants from African as well as Asian countries.

Interestingly, the contemporary comparison—if Asian Americans can make it, why can't African Americans?—echoes an earlier question: If European immigrants can make it, why can't African Americans? The answer to that question is summarized as follows:

Conditions within the cities to which they had migrated [beginning in the 1920s], not slavery, strained blacks' ability to retain two-parent families. Within those cities, blacks faced circumstances that differed fundamentally from those found earlier by European immigrants. They entered cities in large numbers as unskilled and semiskilled manufacturing jobs were leaving, not growing. The discrimination they encountered kept them out of the manufacturing jobs into which earlier immigrants had been recruited. One important goal of public schools had been the assimilation and "Americanization" of immigrant children; by contrast, they excluded and segregated blacks. Racism enforced housing segregation, and residential concentration among blacks increased at the same time it lessened among immigrants and their children. Political machines had embraced earlier immigrants and incorporated them into the system of "city trenches" by which American cities were governed; they excluded blacks from effective political power until cities had been so abandoned by industry and deserted by whites that resistance to black political participation no longer mattered. All the processes that had opened opportunities for immigrants and their children broke down for blacks.[17]

An Example of Stereotypes: Whites' Racial Attitudes The relationship between stereotypes, prejudice, and discrimination has long been the subject of research in the field of social psychology. Like the paradox we noted earlier between the simultaneous reproduction and repudiation of racial hierarchies, here we see the simultaneous persistence and disavowal of bias.

> Since the inception of research on stereotyping and prejudice, social psychologists have documented two seemingly contradictory observations: the pervasiveness of these phenomena and the presence of culturally valued norms that repudiate them. A plethora of research demonstrates that stereotyping and prejudice abound, so much so that they seem to be part of the cultural fabric. Despite initial assertions that these stereotypes were becoming less consensual,[18] closer examination indicates wide agreement on the content of ethnic stereotypes even now.[19] Recent research paints a similar picture, with a Web-based measure that captures individuals' less conscious (i.e., implicit) ethnic attitudes. Data gathered from several thousand people show that 68% of respondents had more generally negative associations toward black than toward white people.[20]

Thus, in terms of a willingness to endorse principles of integration and job equality, surveys show a dramatic and sustained improvement in whites' attitudes.[21] Yet, alongside support for these principles, the research points to pervasive and persistent negative stereotypes held by whites about blacks.[22]

As they have grappled with this inconsistency, some theorists have argued that the old-fashioned, explicit forms of racism have been replaced by new, more subtle manifestations. Because these new forms are so unlike the old ways that prejudice was displayed, dominant group members may not recognize their own bias. For example, in the readings included here, author Malcolm Gladwell takes the Implicit Association Test and describes his shock at the levels of unconscious stereotyping the test reveals (Reading 38).

The obliviousness to prejudice—especially one's own—is an aspect of what social psychologists Samuel Gaertner and John Dovidio have described as *aversive racism*. Unlike those who are overtly prejudiced, white aversive racists are unaware of their negative attitudes, instead considering themselves unprejudiced and even supportive of racial equality. Despite endorsing the principles of fair treatment, they feel personally so uneasy with blacks that they tend to avoid interracial interaction.

> When interracial interaction is unavoidable, aversive racists experience anxiety and discomfort, and consequently they try to disengage from the interaction as quickly as possible. In addition, because part of the discomfort that aversive racists experience is due to a concern about acting inappropriately and appearing prejudiced, aversive racists are motivated primarily by avoiding wrongdoing in interracial interactions.[23]

Out of their discomfort and desire to minimize interaction—especially in the absence of situational norms that compel engagement—aversive racists are likely to discriminate against blacks but in ways they are unaware of, for example, by failing to help blacks in emergencies to the same extent that they would help whites. As Gaertner and Dovidio summarize the research literature, "Taken together, the results from a substantial number of studies drawing on a range of different paradigms demonstrate the systematic operation of aversive racism producing in Whites a failure to help, to hire or admit, and to treat Blacks fairly under the law."[24]

In the context of an overall change from "old-fashioned" to "modern" racism, whites are more likely to attribute discrimination to isolated events or individuals, or to the failings of minorities themselves. For example,

> [T]o Whites, the [New York City police] officers who tortured Abner Louima constitute a few bad apples. To Blacks, these officers represent only the tip of the iceberg. [Haitian immigrant Abner Louima was beaten and sexually assaulted by police after he was arrested outside a Brooklyn nightclub in 1997.]
>
> To Whites, the Texaco tapes are shocking. To Blacks, the tapes merely reflect that in this one instance the guilty were caught. [In 1996, a Texaco executive turned over audiotapes of Texaco executives making racist remarks and plotting to purge the documents in a discrimination case. Ultimately, Texaco paid more than $115 million for having failed to hire, promote, and treat its Black staff with general decency.]
>
> But differences in perception cut deeper than this. . . . Although many Whites recognize that discrimination plays some part in higher rates of unemployment, poverty, and a range of hardships in life that minorities often face, the central cause is usually understood to be the level of effort and cultural patterns of the minority group members themselves.[25] For minorities, especially Blacks, it is understood that the persistence of race problems has something to do with how our institutions operate. For many Whites, larger patterns of inequality are understood as mainly something about minorities themselves. . . . [T]he most popular view holds that Blacks should "try harder," should get ahead "without special favors," and fall behind because they "lack motivation."[26]

Social Institutions and the Support of Ideologies

The specific messages carried by natural-law language and stereotypes are often echoed by social institutions. The term *social institution* refers to the established mechanisms by which societies meet their predictable needs. For example, the need to socialize new members of the society is met by the institutions of the family and education. In addition to these, social institutions include science, law, religion, politics, the economy, military, medicine, mass media, and popular culture. Ideologies—in our case ideologies about the meaning of difference—naturally play a significant role in the operation of social institutions. In the discussion that follows, we will consider how late 19th- and early 20th-century science and popular culture constructed the meaning of race, class, sex, disability, and sexual orientation differences. Just as Roger Lancaster (Reading 16), Riki Wilchins (Reading 10), and Sally French (Reading 35) describe for our contemporary era, in this historic material there is also a troubling congruence among scientific pronouncements, popular culture messages, and the prejudices of the day.

Science The need to explain the meaning of human difference forcefully emerged when 15th-century Europeans encountered previously unknown regions and peoples. "Three centuries of exploration brought home as never before the tremendous diversity of human behavior and life patterns within environments and under circumstances dramatically different from those of Europe. . . . Out of that large laboratory of human experience was born the [idea of the] conflict between nature and nurture."[27]

The "nature-nurture" conflict offered two ways to explain human variation. Explanations from the nature side stressed that the diversity of human societies, and the ability of some to conquer and dominate others, argued for significant biological differences among populations. Explanations from the nurture side argued that human diversity resulted from historical, environmental, and cultural difference. From the nature side, humans were understood to act out biologically driven behaviors. From the nurture side, humans were something of a *tabula rasa,* a blank slate, on which particular cultural expectations were inscribed.

Whether nature or nurture was understood to dominate, however, the discussion of the meaning of human difference always assumed that people could be ranked as to their worth. Thus, the real question was whether the rankings reflected in social hierarchies were the result of nature, and thus inevitable and fixed, or whether they could be affected by human action and were thus subject to change.

The question was not merely theoretical. The 1800s in America witnessed appropriation of Native American territories and the forced relocation of vast numbers of people under the Indian Removal Act of 1830. The 1848 signing of the Treaty of Guadalupe Hidalgo ended the Mexican-American War and ceded what is now Texas, New Mexico, California, Utah, Nevada, Colorado, and Arizona to the United States with 75,000 Mexican nationals residing in those territories becoming U.S. citizens. The 19th century also included passage of the 1892 Chinese Exclusion Act; a prolonged national debate about slavery and women's suffrage; and the arrival of an unprecedented number of poor and working-class immigrants from Southern and Eastern Europe. The century closed with the internationally publicized trial of Irish playwright Oscar Wilde, who was sentenced to two years' hard labor for "gross indecency," which in that case meant homosexuality.

Thus, a profound question was whether social hierarchy reflected natural, permanent, and inherent differences in capability (the nature side) or was the product of specific social and historical circumstances and therefore susceptible to change. Because Africans were held by whites in slavery, did that mean Africans were by their nature inferior to whites? Were Native Americans literally "savages" occupying some middle ground between animals and civilized humans, and did they therefore benefit from domination by those who supposedly were more advanced? Did the dissimilarity of Chinese immigrants from American whites mean they were not "human" in the way whites were? If homosexuality was congenital as was the thinking in the 1800s, did that mean homosexuals were profoundly different from heterosexuals? Were women closer to plants and animals than to civilized men? Were the deaf also "dumb"? Were the poor and working classes composed of those who not only lacked the talents by which to rise in society but also passed their defects on to their children? In all, were individuals and categories of people located in the statuses for which they were best suited? This was the question driving public debate. If one believed that the social order simply reflected immutable biological differences, the answer to that question would probably be "Yes." That would not have been the case, however, for those who believed these differences were the outcome of specific social and historical processes overlaying a shared humanity. In all, the question behind the nature-nurture debate was about the *meaning* of what appeared to be *natural* difference. The answer to that question was shaped by the hegemonic ideologies of the time— especially those informed by science.

Charles Darwin's publication of *The Origin of the Species* (1859) and *The Descent of Man* (1871) shifted the weight of popular and scholarly opinion. In particular, his conclusions challenged the two central beliefs of the time. First, his idea of evolutionary change challenged "traditional, Christian belief in a single episode of creation of a static, perfect, and unchanging world." The significance of evolutionary change was clear: "If the world were not created perfect, then there was no implicit justification for the way things were. . . ."[28]

Second, Darwin's work implied that all humans share a common ancestry. If differences among birds were the result of their adaptation to distinctive environments, then *their differences existed within an overall framework of similarity and common ancestry.* By analogy, the differences within human populations might also be understood as "variability within overall similarity"[29]—a shocking possibility at the time even for Darwin. "It was the age of imperialism and most non-Europeans were regarded, even by Darwin, as 'barbarians'; he was astonished and taken aback by their wildness and animality. The differences among humans seemed so extreme that the humanity . . . of some living groups was scarcely credible."[30]

Darwin's idea that change in the physical environment resulted in the perpetuation of some species and demise of others (the idea of natural selection), however, also bolstered a preexistent concept of "survival of the fittest." This phrase had been coined by English sociologist Herbert Spencer, who had been considering the evolutionary principles of human societies several years before Darwin published *The Origin of the Species.*

Spencer's position, eventually called *social Darwinism,* was extremely popular in the United States. Spencer strongly believed that modern societies are inevitably improvements over earlier forms of social organization and that progress would necessarily follow from unimpeded competition for social resources. In all, social Darwinism argued that those who are more advanced will naturally rise to the top of any stratification ladder.

Through social Darwinism, the prevailing hierarchies—slave owner over people held in slavery, white over Mexican and Native American, native born over immigrant, upper class over poor, male over female—could be attributed to natural processes and justified as a reflection of inherent differences among categories of people. As one sociologist at the turn of the century framed it, "under the tutelage of Darwinism the world returns again to the idea that *might* as evidence of fitness has something to do with *right.*"[31] Thus, the ideology of social Darwinism was used to justify slavery, colonialism, immigration restrictions, the criminalization of homosexuality, the forced relocation of Native Americans, and the legal subordination of women. Because social Darwinism affirmed that difference meant defect, it was also compatible with the historical oppression of disabled people.

The social Darwinist position was used by those opposed to providing equal education for women. Just when American institutions of higher education were opening to women—Vassar College was founded in 1865, Smith and Wellesley colleges ten years later, and by 1870 many state universities had become coeducational—biologist Edward Clarke published *Sex in Education* (1873), which argued that the physical energy education required would endanger women's reproductive abilities (an idea first put forward by Spencer). Clarke's case was based on meager and questionable empirical evidence: seven clinical cases, only one of which actually supported his position.[32] His work was a response to *social* rather than scientific developments, since it was prompted by no new discoveries in biology. Nonetheless, the book was an immediate and enduring success. For the next thirty years, it was used in the argument against equal education despite the accumulation of evidence refuting its claims. While Clarke's research should have been suspect, it instead became influential in policymaking. In part, "the reason why Clarke's argument seemed so serviceable to those opposed to women's higher education was that it was couched in biological terms and thus appeared to offer a legitimate scientific basis for conservative opposition to equal education."[33]

In a similar fashion, science shaped ideas about the meaning of same-sex relationships. In Europe, by the turn of the century, a gay rights movement had arisen in Germany and gay themes had emerged in French literature. At the same time, however, an international move to criminalize sexual relations between men gathered momentum. A revision of the German criminal code increased the penalties for male homosexuality; the British imprisoned Oscar Wilde; and Europe and the United States experienced a social reform movement directed against prostitution and male homosexuality. The possibility of sexual relations between women was not considered until later.

The move to criminalize homosexuality was countered by physicians arguing, from a social Darwinist position, that homosexuality is the product of "hereditary weakness" and is thus beyond individual control. Though their hope was for increased tolerance, those who took this position offered the idea of "homosexuality as a medical entity and the homosexual as a distinctive kind of person."[34] Thus, they contributed to the idea that heterosexual and homosexual people were biologically different from each other.

Science also supported the argument that people of different skin colors were different in significant, immutable ways. Certainly Spencer's idea of the survival of the fittest was understood to support the ideology that whites were superior to all people of color. Thus, "the most prevalent form of social Darwinism at the turn of the century was actually racism, that is, the idea that one people might be superior to another because of differences in their biological nature."[35]

The use of questionable research to support prevailing beliefs was also evident in the development of intelligence testing. In 1904, Alfred Binet, director of the psychology lab at the Sorbonne, was commissioned by the French minister of public education to develop a test to identify children whose poor performance in school might indicate a need for special education. Binet developed a test with a series of tasks that children of "normal" intelligence were expected to have mastered. Binet's own claims for the test were fairly limited. He did not equate intelligence with the score produced by his test, arguing that intelligence was too complex a factor to be reduced to a simple number. Nor did he construe his test as measuring inborn, permanent, or inherited limitations.

Binet's hesitations regarding the significance of the test, however, were ignored by the emerging field of American psychology, which used intelligence as a way to explain social hierarchies. "The people who are doing the drudgery are, as a rule, in their proper places," wrote H. H. Goddard, who introduced the Binet test to America. Stanford psychologist Lewis M. Terman (author of the Stanford-Binet IQ test) argued that "the children of successful and cultured parents test higher than children from wretched and ignorant homes for the simple reason that their heredity is better."[36] Indeed, "Terman believed that class boundaries had been set by innate intelligence."[37]

Such conclusions were used to shape decisions about the distribution of social resources. For example, intelligence was described as a capacity like the capacity of a jug to hold a certain amount of milk. A pint jug could not be expected to hold a quart of milk; similarly, it was pointless to waste "too much" education on someone whose capacity was supposedly limited. Intelligence Quotient (IQ) tests were used to assess mental deficiency, including the newly developed categories of idiots, imbeciles, and morons. Morons were judged the highest of the "mental defectives," with the potential to be trained to function in society. Nonetheless, Goddard recommended that they be "institutionalized, carefully regulated, made happy by catering to their limits, . . . prevented from breeding"[38] and not allowed into the country as immigrants. Toward that end, intelligence tests were used to identify the "mental defectives" as they landed at Ellis Island:

> [C]onsider a group of frightened men and women who speak no English and who have just endured an oceanic voyage in steerage. Most are poor and have never gone to school; many have never held a pencil or pen in their hand. They march off the boat; one of Goddard's . . . [inspectors] takes them aside shortly thereafter, sits them down, hands them a pencil, and asks them to reproduce on paper a figure shown to them a moment ago, but now withdrawn from their sight. Could their failure be a result of testing conditions, of weakness, fear, or confusion, rather than of innate stupidity? Goddard considered the possibility, but rejected it.[39]

In the early decades of the 20th century, the eugenics movement, a form of social Darwinism, spearheaded the use of forced sterilization to limit the growth of "defective" populations. Eugenicists lobbied for state laws endorsing the sterilization of the "feebleminded, insane, criminalistic, epileptic, inebriate, diseased, blind, deaf, deformed, and dependent."[40] The practice was approved by the Supreme Court in *Buck v. Bell* in 1927, with Justice Oliver Wendell Holmes, Jr., writing the majority opinion:

> It is better for all the world, if instead of waiting to execute degenerate offspring for crime or to let them starve for their imbecility, society can prevent those who are manifestly unfit from continuing their kind. . . . Three generations of imbeciles are enough.

Only in 1942, in *Skinner v. Oklahoma*, did the Supreme Court back away from its position, but by that point thirteen states had laws allowing the sterilization of criminals. Thus,

> sterilization of people in institutions for the mentally ill and mentally retarded continued through the mid-1970's. At one time or another, 33 states had statutes under which more than 60,000 Americans endured involuntary sterilization. The *Buck v. Bell* precedent allowing sterilization of the so-called "feebleminded" has never been overturned.[41]

The findings of intelligence testers were also used to advocate particular social policies such as restrictions on immigration. While it is not clear that the work of intelligence testers directly affected the Immigration Restriction Act of 1924, the ultimate shape of the legislation limited immigration from Southern and Eastern Europe, which was consistent with intelligence testers' claims about the relative intelligence of the "races" in Europe. These quotas barred the admission of European Jews fleeing the impending holocaust.

Still, by 1930, a considerable body of research showed that social environment more than biology accounted for differing IQ scores and that the tests themselves measured not innate intelligence but familiarity with the culture of those who wrote the tests. In the end, the psychologists who had promoted intelligence testing were forced to repudiate the idea that intelligence is inherited or that it can be separated from cultural knowledge.[a]

Whether measuring cranial capacity, developing paper-and-pencil intelligence tests, worrying about the effect of education on women, or arguing for hereditary weakness as an explanation of homosexuality, the work of these scientists supported the prevailing ideologies about the merit and appropriate social position of people of different sexes, races, ethnic groups, sexual orientations, and social classes. Most of these scientists were not overtly motivated by ideology; indeed they were sometimes troubled by their own findings. Still, their research was riddled with technical errors and questionable findings. Their research proved "the surprising malleability of 'objective,' quantitative data in the interest of a preconceived idea."[43] Precisely because their research confirmed prevailing beliefs, it was more likely to be celebrated than scrutinized.

Why were these findings eventually repudiated? Since they offered a defense of the status quo and confirmed the prevailing ideology, who would have criticized them? First, the scientific defense of immutable hierarchy was eroded by the steady accumulation of evidence about the "intellectual equality and therefore the

---

[a]"There is also a lot of evidence for the whole American population, for American ethnic groups, and for populations wherever tests are given that IQ is changing in ways that can't possibly be genetic because they happen too fast. It is widely recognized that average IQs are increasing fairly rapidly. These changes in IQ clearly must have more to say about relationships between testing and real performance, or about social patterns of learning, than about biologically rooted 'intelligence.' The genes of a large population don't change that fast unless there is a very dramatic episode of natural selection such as an epidemic."[42]

equal cultural capacity of all peoples."[44] A good deal of the research that made that point was produced by the many "prominent or soon to be prominent" scholars of African American, Chinese, and European immigrant ancestry who, after finally being admitted to institutions of higher education, were pursuing scientific research. African American scholars such as W. E. B. Du Bois and E. Franklin Frazier, and scholars of recent European immigrant ancestry such as anthropologists Franz Boas, Alfred Kroeber, and Edward Sapir, trenchantly criticized the social science of the day and by their very presence challenged the prevailing expectations about the "inherent inferiority" of people like themselves.

The presumptions about the meaning of race were also challenged by increased interracial contact. The 1920s began the Great Migration, in which hundreds of thousands of African Americans from the rural South moved to northern cities. This movement continued through two world wars as black, Latino, Asian, and Native American men joined the armed forces and women followed wartime employment opportunities. The 1920s also brought the Harlem Renaissance, an outpouring of creativity from black writers, scholars, and artists in celebration of African and African American culture. Overall, white social scientists "gained an unprecedented opportunity to observe blacks in a fresh and often transforming way."[45] Their attitudes and expectations changed as a result of this increased contact.

In sum, the scientific argument for the inherent inferiority of some groups of people was advanced by upper-class, native-born, white male faculty members of prestigious universities. Few others would have had the means with which to disseminate their ideas or the prestige to make those ideas influential. These theories of essential difference were not written by Native Americans, Mexicans, women, gays, African Americans, or immigrants from Asia or Southern and Eastern Europe. Most of these people lacked access to the public forums to present their experiences until the rise of the antislavery, suffrage, labor, and gay rights movements. Insofar as the people in these categories could be silenced, it was easier to depict them as essentially and profoundly different.

Popular Culture   Like the sciences, popular culture (the forms of entertainment available for mass consumption such as popular music, theater, film, literature, and television) may convey ideologies about difference and social stratification. At virtually the same time that social Darwinism gained popularity in America, America's first minstrel show was organized. Like social Darwinism, minstrel shows offered a defense of slavery.

Minstrel shows, which became an enormously popular form of entertainment, were musical variety shows in which white males in "blackface" ridiculed blacks, abolitionism, and women's suffrage. Their impact can be seen in the movies and cartoons of the 1930s and 1940s and in current American stereotypes. As the shows traveled the country, their images were impressed on whites who often had no direct contact with blacks and thus no information to contradict the minstrel images.

The three primary characters of the minstrel show were the happy slave, Zip Coon, and the mammy.[46] The image of the happy slave—singing and dancing, naive and childlike, taken care of through old age by the white master as a virtual member of the family—asserted that blacks held in slavery were both content and cared for. Zip Coon was a northern, free black man characterized by an improper use of language and laughable attempts to emulate whites; the caricature was used to show that blacks lacked the intelligence to handle freedom. The mammy was depicted as a large and presumably unattractive black woman fully devoted to the white family she served. Like the happy slave, the mammy was unthreatening and content—no sexual competition to the white mistress of the house, no children of her own needing attention, committed to and fulfilled by her work with her white family. Thus, the characters of the minstrel show hid the reality of slavery. The happy slave and mammy denied the brutality of the slave system. Zip Coon denied the reality of blacks' organization of the underground railroad, their production of slave narratives in books and lectures, and their undertaking of slave rebellions and escapes.

In all, minstrel shows offered an ideology about slavery constructed by and in the interests of those with power. They ridiculed antislavery activists and legitimatized the status quo. Minstrel shows asserted that blacks did not mind being held as slaves and that they did not suffer loss and pain in the same way whites did. The minstrel show was not the only source of this ideology, but as a form of popular entertainment, it was a very effective means of disseminating such beliefs. The shows traveled to all parts of the country, with a hostile racial message masked as mere entertainment.

But within popular culture, an effective counter to the ideology of the minstrel show emerged through the speakers of the antislavery lecture circuit and the publication of numerous slave narratives. Appearing as early as 1760, these narratives achieved an enormous and enduring popularity among northern white readers. Frederick Douglass, former slave and a renowned antislavery activist, was the most famous public lecturer on the circuit and wrote a best-selling slave narrative. Whether as book or lecture, slave narratives provided an image of blacks as human beings. Access to these life histories provided the first opportunity for most whites to see a shared humanity between themselves and those held in slavery.[47] Thus, slave narratives directly countered the images of the minstrel show. Although popular culture may offer a variety of messages, all parties do not meet equally on its terrain. Those with power have better access and more legitimacy, but popular culture cannot be so tightly controlled as to entirely exclude the voice of the less powerful.

Conclusion

As we have seen, ideologies confer meaning on difference; they both shape and are shaped by social institutions. Their content is not fixed, nor need it be internally consistent. Most important in terms of the subject matter of this text, ideologies can simultaneously reproduce and repudiate, maintain and disavow social hierarchies.

KEY CONCEPTS

aversive racism Unrecognized prejudices that affect behavior. (page 347)

hegemonic Dominating or ruling. A *hegemonic ideology* is a belief that is pervasive in a culture. (page 349)

ideology A widely shared belief that primarily reflects the experiences of those with power, but is presented as universally valid. (page 341)

natural-law language Language that treats human behavior as bound by natural law. (page 341)

social Darwinism The belief that those who dominate a society are necessarily the fittest. (page 350)

social institution Established system for meeting societal needs; for example, the family. (page 348)

stereotype A characterization of a category of people as all alike, as possessing the same set of characteristics and likely to behave in the same ways. (page 341)

NOTES

1. Frye, 1983.
2. Brantlinger, 1990:80.
3. D. Smith, 1978, 1990.
4. Pierce, 1971.
5. Gould, 1981.
6. U.S. Department of Housing and Urban Development, 2013.
7. Pager and Shepherd, 2008:188.
8. Ford, 2008:287–8.
9. Lee, Jennifer and Frank D. Bean, 2004.
10. Feliciano, et al., 2009:49–50.
11. Newport, 2013.
12. Winant, 2004:47.
13. Andre, 1988:259
14. Le, 2007; Reuters, 2012.
15. Takaki, 1993:416
16. Skrentny, 2002,
17. Katz, 1989:51.
18. Gilbert, 1951; Karlins, Coffman, and Walters, 1969.
19. Devine and Elliott, 1995; Maden, Guyll, and Aboufadel, 2001.
20. Sinclair and Lun, 2010:214–215.
21. Ibid
22. Bobo, 2001.
23. Gaertner and Dovidio, 2005:619.

24. Gaertner and Dovidio, 2005:623.
25. Schuman, 1971; Apostle et al., 1983; Kluegel and Smith, 1986; Schuman, et al., 1997.
26. Bobo, 2001:281–282.
27. Degler, 1991:4–5.
28. Shipman, 1994:18.
29. Shipman, 1994:22
30. Shipman, 1994:19.
31. Degler, 1991:13.
32. Sayers, 1982:14.
33. Sayers, 1982:11.
34. Conrad and Schneider, 1980:184.
35. Degler, 1991:15.
36. Degler, 1991:50.
37. Gould, 1981:183.
38. Gould, 1981:160,
39. Gould, 1981:166.
40. Lombardo, n.d..
41. Lombardo, n.d.
42. Cohen, 1998:210.
43. Gould, 1981:147.
44. Degler, 1991:61.
45. Degler, 1991:197.
46. Riggs, 1987.
47. Bodziock, 1990.

REFERENCES

Andre, Judith. 1988. Stereotypes: Conceptual and Normative Considerations. *Racism and Sexism: An Integrated Study,* edited by Paula S. Rothenberg, 257–62. New York: St. Martin's Press.

Apostle, Richard, Charles Glock, Thom Piazza, and Marijean Suelzle. 1983. *The Anatomy of Racial Attitudes.* Berkeley, CA: University of California Press.

Bobo, Lawrence D. 2001. Racial Attitudes and Relations at the Close of the Twentieth Century. *America Becoming: Racial Trends and Their Consequences,* edited by Neil J. Smelser, William Julius Wilson, and Faith Mitchell, 264–301. Washington, DC: National Academy Press.

Bodziock, Joseph. 1990. The Weight of Sambo's Woes. *Perspectives on Black Popular Culture,* edited by Harry B. Shaw, 166–79. Bowling Green, OH: Bowling Green State University Popular Press.

Brantlinger, Patrick. 1990. *Crusoe's Footprints: Cultural Studies in Britain and America.* New York: Routledge.

Cohen, Mark Nathan. 1998. *Culture of Intolerance: Chauvinism, Class, and Race in the United States.* New Haven, CT: Yale University Press.

Conrad, Peter, and Joseph W. Schneider. 1980. *Deviance and Medicalization.* Philadelphia: Temple University Press.

Degler, Carl N. 1991. *In Search of Human Nature: The Decline and Revival of Darwinism in American Social Thought.* New York: Oxford University Press.

Devine, Patricia G., and Andrew J. Elliott. 1995. Are Racial Stereotypes Really Fading?: The Princeton Trilogy Revisited. *Personality and Social Psychology Bulletin* 21: 1139–50.

Feliciano, Cynthia, Belinda Robnett, and Golnaz Komaie. 2009. Gendered Racial Exclusion among White Internet Daters. *Social Science Research* 38(1): 39–54.

Ford, Richmond Thompson. 2008. *The Race Card: How Bluffing about Bias Makes Race Relations Worse.* New York: Farrar, Straus and Giroux.

Frye, Marilyn. 1983. *The Politics of Reality: Essays in Feminist Theory.* Freedom, CA: The Crossing Press.

Gaertner, Samuel L., and John F. Dovidio. 2005. Understanding and Addressing Contemporary Racism: From Aversive Racism to the Common Ingroup Identity Model. *Journal of Social Issues* 61: 615–39.

Gilbert, G M. 1951. Stereotype Persistence and Change among College Students. *Journal of Abnormal and Social Psychology* 46: 245–54.

Gould, Stephen Jay. 1981. *The Mismeasure of Man.* New York: W. W. Norton.

Katz, Michael B. 1989. *The Undeserving Poor.* New York: Pantheon Books.

Karlins, Marvin, Coffman, Thomas L., and Walters, Gary. 1969. On the Fading of Social Stereotypes: Studies in Three Generations of College Students. *Journal of Personality and Social Psychology* 13: 1–16.

Kluegel, James, and Eliot Smith. 1986. *Beliefs about Inequality: Americans' Views of What Is and What Ought to Be.* New York: Aldine de Gruyter.

Le, C. N. 2007. Socioeconomic Statistics and Demographics. *Asian-Nation: The Landscape of Asian America.* www.asian-nation.org/model-minority.shtml. Retrieved May 2007.

Lee, Jennifer, and Frank D. Bean. 2004. America's Changing Color Lines: Race/Ethnicity, Immigration, and Multi-racial Identification. *Annual Review of Sociology* 30: 221–42.

Lombardo, P. n.d. Eugenic Sterilization Laws. *The Eugenics Archive.* Dolan DNA Learning Center, Cold Spring Harbor Laboratory. www.eugenicsarchive.org/eugenics/list3.pl. Retrieved June 2005.

Maden, Stephanie, Max Guyll, Kathy Aboufadel, Eulices Montiel, Alison Smith, Polly Palumbo, and Lee Jussim. 2001. Ethnic and National Stereotypes: The Princeton Trilogy Revisited and Revised. *Personality and Social Psychology Bulletin,* 27: 966–1010.

Newport, Frank. 2013. In U.S. 87% Approve of Black-White Marriage, vs. 4% in 1958. *Gallup Politics.* July 25. www.gallup.com/poll/163697/approve-marriage-blacks-whites.aspx. Retrieved May 16, 2014.

Pager, Devah, and Hana Shepherd. 2008. The Sociology of Discrimination: Racial Discrimination in Employment, Housing, Credit, and Consumer Markets. *Annual Review of Sociology* 34: 181–209.

Pierce, Christine. 1971. Natural Law Language and Women. *Woman in Sexist Society,* edited by Vivian Gornick and Barbara K. Moran, 242–58. New York: New American Library.

Reuters. 2012. Asians Lead U.S. in College Degrees: Census. May 12. http://www.reuters.com/article/2012/05/24/us-usa-census-education-id USBRE84N05120120524. Accessed on May 20, 2014.

Riggs, Marlon. 1987. *Ethnic Notions.* California Newsreel (video).

St. John, C., and T. Heald-Moore. 1995. Fear of Black Strangers. *Social Science Research* 24: 262–80.

Sayers, Janet. 1982. *Biological Politics: Feminist and Antifeminist Perspectives.* London: Tavistock Publications.

Schuman, Howard. 1971. Free Will and Determinism in Beliefs about Race. *Majority and Minority: The Dynamics of Racial and Ethnic Relations,* edited by N. Yetman and C. Steeh, 375–80. Boston: Allyn & Bacon.

————, Charlotte Steeh, Lawrence Bobo, and Maria Krysan. 1997. *Racial Attitudes in America: Trends and Interpretations.* Rev. ed. Cambridge: Harvard University Press.

Shipman, Pat. 1994. *The Evolution of Racism: Human Differences and the Use and Abuse of Science.* New York: Simon and Schuster.

Sinclair, Stacey, and Janetta Lun. 2010. Social Tuning of Ethnic Attitudes. *The Mind in Context,* edited by Batja Mesquita, Lisa Feldman Barrett, and Elliot R. Smith, 214–32. New York: Guilford Press.

Skrentny, John D. 2002. *The Minority Rights Revolution.* Cambridge, MA: Harvard University Press.

Smith, Dorothy. 1978. A Peculiar Eclipsing: Women's Exclusion from Men's Culture. *Women's Studies International Quarterly* 1: 281–95.

————. 1990. *The Conceptual Practices of Power: A Feminist Sociology of Knowledge.* Boston: Northeastern University Press.

Takaki, Ronald. June 1993. *A Different Mirror: A History of Multicultural America.* Boston: Little, Brown.

U.S. Department of Housing and Urban Development. 2013. Executive Summary. *Housing Discrimination Against Racial and Ethnic Minorities 2012 June.*

Winant, Howard. 2004. *The New Politics of Race: Globalism, Difference, Justice.* Minneapolis, MN: University of Minnesota Press.

RACE AND ETHNICITY

READING 37

Fourteen Key Supreme Court Cases and the Civil War Amendments

Individuals' lives are affected not only by social practices but also by law as interpreted in the courts. Under U.S. federalism, Congress makes laws, the president swears to uphold the law, and the Supreme Court interprets the law. When state laws appear to be in conflict with the United States Constitution or when the terminology of the Constitution is vague, the Supreme Court interprets such laws. We will focus here on Supreme Court rulings that have defined the roles individuals are allowed to assume in American society.

As the supreme law above laws enacted by Congress, the U.S. Constitution determines individual and group status. A brief document, the Constitution describes the division of power between the federal and state governments, as well as the rights of individuals. Only 16 amendments to the Constitution have been added since the ratification of the Bill of Rights (the first 10 amendments). Although the Constitution appears to be sweeping in scope—relying on the principle that all men are created equal—in reality it is an exclusionary document. It omitted women, Native Americans, and African Americans except for the purpose of determining a population count. In instances where the Constitution was vague on the rights of each of these groups, clarification was later sought through court cases.

Federalism provides four primary methods by which citizens may influence the political process. First, the Constitution grants citizens the right to petition the government, that is, the right to lobby. Second, as a civic duty, citizens are expected to vote and seek office. Once in office, citizens can change conditions by writing new legislation, known as *statutory law*. Third, changes can be achieved through the lengthy procedure of passing constitutional amendments, which affect all citizens. Controversial amendments have often become law after social movement activists advocated passage for several years or after a major national upheaval, such as the Civil War.

Last, the Constitution provides that citizens can sue to settle disputes. Through this method, sweeping social changes can take place when Supreme Court decisions affect all the individuals in a class. Thus, the assertion of individual rights has become a key tool of those who were not privileged by the Constitution to clarify their status in American society.

An examination of landmark cases reveals the continuous difficulties some groups have had in securing their rights through legal remedy. The Court has often taken a narrow perspective on which classes of people were to receive equal protection of the law or were covered under the privileges and immunities clause.[1] Each group had to bring suit in every area where barriers existed. For example, white women who were citizens had to sue to establish that they had the right to inherit property, to serve on juries, to enter various professions, and in general to be treated as a class apart from their husband and family. Blacks sued to attend southern state universities and law schools, to participate in the all-white Democratic Party primary election,[2] to attend public schools that had been ordered to desegregate by the Supreme Court, and to vote without having to pay a poll tax. When these landmark cases were decided, they were perceived to herald sweeping changes in policy. Yet they proved to be only a guide to determining the rights of individuals.

I. *DRED SCOTT V. SANFORD* (1857)

Before the Civil War, the Constitution was not precise on whether one was simultaneously a citizen of a given state and of the entire United States. Slavery further complicated the matter because the status of slaves and free persons of color was not specified in the Constitution, nor were members of either group considered citizens. Each state had the option of determining the status and rights of these nonwhites.

A federal form of government permitted flexibility by allowing states to differ on matters such as rights for its citizens. Yet as it was a newly invented form of government, a number of issues that were clear under British law were not settled until the Thirteenth, Fourteenth, and Fifteenth Amendments were added to the United States Constitution. Federalism raised questions about rights and privileges because a citizen was simultaneously living under the laws of a state and of the United States. Who had rights and privileges guaranteed by the Constitution? Did all citizens have all rights and privileges?

For example, what was the status of women? The Constitution provided for citizenship, but it did not specify which rights and privileges were granted to female citizens. State laws considered white men and white women citizens, yet white women were often not allowed to own property, sue in court, or vote. Under federalism, each state enacted laws determining the rights and status of free blacks, slaves, white men, and white women so long as the laws did not conflict with the United States Constitution.

The *Dred Scott* case of 1846 considered the issues of slavery, property, citizenship, and the supremacy of the United States over individual states when a slave was taken to a free territory. The Court's holding primarily affected blacks, now called African Americans,[3] who sought the benefits of citizenship. Broadly, the case addressed American citizenship, a matter not clearly defined until passage of the Fourteenth Amendment in 1868.

Dred Scott was an enslaved man owned by Dr. John Emerson, a U.S. Army surgeon stationed in Missouri. When Emerson was transferred to Rock Island, Illinois, where slavery was forbidden, he took Dred Scott with him. Emerson was subsequently transferred to Fort Snelling, a territory (now Minnesota) where slavery was forbidden by the Missouri Compromise of 1820. In 1838, he returned to Missouri with Dred Scott.

In 1846, Scott brought suit in a Missouri circuit court to obtain his freedom on the grounds he had resided in free territory for periods of time. Scott won the case and his freedom. However, the judgment was reversed by the Missouri Supreme Court. Later, when Emerson's brother-in-law, John Sanford—who was a

citizen of New York—arranged for the sale of Scott, the grounds were established for Scott to take his case to the federal circuit court in Missouri. The federal court ruled that Scott and his family were slaves and therefore the "lawful property" of Sanford. With the financial assistance of abolitionists, Scott appealed his case to the Supreme Court.

The Court's decision addressed these key questions:

1. Are blacks citizens?
2. Are blacks entitled to sue in court?
3. Can one have all the privileges and immunities of citizenship in a state, but not the United States?
4. Can one be a citizen of the United States and not be qualified to vote or hold office?

Excerpts from the Supreme Court Decision in *Dred Scott v. Sanford*[4]

Mr. Chief Justice Taney delivered the opinion of the Court:

. . . The question is simply this: Can a Negro, whose ancestors were imported into this country and sold as slaves, become a member of the political community formed and brought into existence by the Constitution of the United States, and as such become entitled to all the rights, and privileges and immunities, guaranteed by that instrument to the citizen? One of which rights is the privilege of suing in a court of the United States. . . .

The question before us is whether the class of persons described are constituent members of this sovereignty? We think they are not, and that they are not included, and were not intended to be included, under the word "citizens" in the Constitution, and can therefore claim none of the rights and privileges which that instrument provides for and secures to citizens of the United States.

In discussing this question, we must not confound the rights of citizenship which a State may confer within its own limits and the rights of citizenship as a member of the Union. It does not by any means follow, because he has all the rights and privileges of a citizen of a State, that he must be a citizen of the United States. He may have all of the rights and privileges of a citizen of a State, and yet not be entitled to the rights and privileges of a citizen in any other State. . . .

Undoubtedly a person may be a citizen . . . although he exercises no share of the political power, and is incapacitated from holding particular office. Those who have not the necessary qualifications cannot vote or hold the office, yet they are citizens.

The court is of the opinion, that . . . Dred Scott was not a citizen of Missouri within the meaning of the Constitution of the United States, and not entitled as such to sue in its courts: and, consequently, that the Circuit Court had no jurisdiction. . . .

II. THE CIVIL WAR AMENDMENTS

The Civil War (1861–1865) was fought over slavery, as well as the issue of supremacy of the national government over the individual states.

After the Civil War, members of Congress known as the Radical Republicans sought to protect the freedom of the former slaves by passing the Thirteenth, Fourteenth, and Fifteenth Amendments. These amendments, especially the Fourteenth, have provided the foundation for African Americans—as well as women, gays, Native Americans, immigrants, and those who are disabled—to bring suit for equal treatment under the law.

Amendment XIII, 1865

(Slavery)

This amendment prohibited slavery and involuntary servitude in the United States. The entire amendment follows:

Section 1. Neither slavery nor involuntary servitude, except as a punishment whereof the party shall have been duly convicted, shall exist within the United States, or any place subject to their jurisdiction.

Section 2. Congress shall have power to enforce this article by appropriate legislation.

Amendment XIV, 1868

(Citizenship, Due Process, and Equal Protection of the Laws)

This amendment defined citizenship; prohibited the states from making or enforcing laws that abridged the privileges or immunities of citizenship; forbade

states to deprive persons of life, liberty, or property without due process of law; and forbade states to deny equal protection of the law to any person. Over time, the Fourteenth Amendment became the most important of the Reconstruction amendments. Key phrases such as "privileges and immunities," "deprive any person of life, liberty, or the pursuit of justice," and "deny to any person within its jurisdiction equal protection of the law" have caused this amendment to be the subject of more Supreme Court cases than any other provision of the Constitution. The entire amendment follows:

Section 1. All persons born or naturalized in the United States, and subject to the jurisdiction thereof, are citizens of the United States and of the State wherein they reside. No State shall make or enforce any law which shall abridge the privileges or immunities of citizens of the United States; nor shall any State deprive any person of life, liberty, or property, without due process of law; nor deny to any person within its jurisdiction the equal protection of the laws.

Section 2. Representatives shall be apportioned among the several States according to their respective numbers, counting the whole number of persons in each State, excluding Indians not taxed. But when the right to vote at any election for the choice of electors for President and Vice President of the United States, Representatives in Congress, the Executive and Judicial officers of a State, or the members of the Legislature thereof, is denied to any of the male inhabitants of such State, being twenty-one years of age, and citizens of the United States, or in any way abridged, except for participation in rebellion, or other crime, the basis of representation therein shall be reduced in proportion which the number of such male citizens shall bear to the whole number of male citizens twenty-one years of age in such State.

Section 3. No person shall be a Senator or Representative in Congress, or elector or President and Vice President, or hold any office, civil or military, under the United States, or under any State, who, having previously taken an oath, as a member of Congress, or as an officer of the United States, or as a member of any State legislature, or as an executive or judicial officer of any State, to support the Constitution of the United States, shall have engaged in insurrection or rebellion against the same, or given aid or comfort to the enemies thereof. But Congress may by a vote of two-thirds of each House, remove such disability.

Section 4. The validity of the public debt of the United States, authorized by law, including debts incurred for payments of pensions and bounties for services in suppressing insurrection or rebellion, shall not be questioned. But neither the United States nor any State shall assume or pay any debt or obligation incurred in aid of insurrection or rebellion against the United States, or any claim for the loss or emancipation of any slave, but all such debts, obligations and claims shall be held illegal and void.

Section 5. The Congress shall have power to enforce, by appropriate legislation, the provisions of this article.

Amendment XV, 1870
(The Right to Vote)

The entire amendment follows:

Section 1. The right of citizens of the United States to vote shall not be denied or abridged by the United States or by any State on account of race, color, or previous condition of servitude.

Section 2. The Congress shall have power to enforce this article by appropriate legislation.

As we have seen, the Thirteenth, Fourteenth, and Fifteenth Amendments were added to the Constitution expressly with former slaves in mind. In Section 1 of the Fourteenth Amendment, the definition of *citizenship* was clarified and granted to blacks. In the Fifteenth Amendment, black males, former slaves, were granted the right to vote. For women, however, the situation was different.

During the 19th century, there was no doubt that white females were U.S. citizens, but their rights as citizens were unclear. For example, although they were citizens, women were not automatically enfranchised. Depending on state laws, they were barred from owning property, holding office, or voting. The 1872 case of *Bradwell v. The State of Illinois* specifically tested whether women as United States citizens had the right to become members of the bar. More generally, it addressed whether the rights of female citizens included the right to pursue any employment.

III. *MINOR V. HAPPERSETT* (1875)

The Fifteenth Amendment was not viewed as a triumph for women because it specifically denied them the vote. Section 2 of the Fourteenth Amendment for the first time made reference to males as citizens. Since black men were included but women of all races were omitted, women were left to continue to seek changes through the courts. This was a difficult route, because in subsequent cases, judges often held a narrow view that the legislators wrote the amendment only with black males in mind. Thus, a pattern was soon established in which white women followed black men and women in asserting their rights as citizens, as seen in the 1875 case of *Minor v. Happersett.* In *Dred Scott,* the question was whether Scott was a citizen; in *Minor,* the question was whether *Minor* as a citizen had the right to vote. In both cases, the Supreme Court said no.

Virginia Minor, a native-born, free, white citizen of the United States and the state of Missouri, and over the age of 21 wished to vote for president, vice president, and members of Congress in the election of November 1872. She applied to the registrar of voters but was not allowed to vote because she was not a "male citizen of the United States." As a citizen of the United States, Minor sued under the privileges and immunities clause of the Fourteenth Amendment.

The Court's decision addressed these key questions:

1. Who is covered under the term *citizen?*
2. Is suffrage one of the privileges and immunities of citizenship?
3. Did the Constitution, as originally written, make all citizens voters?
4. Did the Fifteenth Amendment make all citizens voters?
5. Can a state confine voting to only male citizens without violating the Constitution?

Although women were citizens of the United States and of the state where they resided, they did not automatically possess all the privileges granted to male citizens, such as suffrage. This landmark case was not overturned until the passage of the Nineteenth Amendment, which enfranchised women, in 1920.[5]

Excerpts from the Supreme Court Decision in *Minor v. Happersett*[6]

Mr. Chief Justice Waite delivered the opinion of the Court:

. . . It is contended [by Minor's counsel] that the provisions of the Constitution and laws of the State of Missouri which confine the right of suffrage and registration therefore to men, are in violation of the Constitution of the United States, and therefore void. The argument is, that as a woman, born or naturalized in the United States and subject to the jurisdiction thereof as a citizen of the United States and of the State in which she resides, she has the right of suffrage as one of the privileges and immunities of her citizenship, which the State cannot by its laws or Constitution abridge.

There is no doubt that women may be citizens. . . .

. . . From this it is apparent that from the commencement of the legislation upon this subject alien women and alien minors could be made citizens by naturalization, and we think it will not be contended that . . . native women and native minors were already citizens by birth.

. . . More cannot be necessary to establish the fact that sex has never been made one of the elements of citizenship in the United States. In this respect men have never had an advantage over women. The same laws precisely apply to both. The Fourteenth Amendment did not affect the citizenship of women any more than it did of men . . . therefore, the rights of Mrs. Minor do not depend upon the amendment. She has always been a citizen from her birth, and entitled to all the privileges and immunities of citizenship. The amendment prohibited the State, of which she is a citizen, from abridging any of her privileges and immunities as a citizen of the United States. . . .

. . . The direct question is, therefore, presented whether all citizens are necessarily voters.

The Constitution does not define the privileges and immunities of citizens. For that definition we must look elsewhere.

. . . The [Fourteenth] amendment did not add to the privileges and immunities of a citizen. It simply furnished an additional guaranty for the protection of such as he already had. No new voters were necessarily made by it.

. . . No new State has ever been admitted to the Union which has conferred the right of suffrage upon women, and this has never been considered a valid objection to her admission. . . .

. . . Certainly, if the courts can consider any question settled, this is one. For nearly ninety years the people have acted upon the idea that the Constitution, when it conferred citizenship, did not necessarily confer the right of suffrage. . . . Our province is to decide what the law is, not to declare what it should be.

The *Dred Scott, Bradwell,* and *Minor* cases point to the similarity in the status of black men and women of all races in 19th-century America. As one judicial scholar noted, race and sex were comparable classes, distinct from all others. Historically, these "natural classes" were considered permanent and unchangeable.[7] Thus, both slavery and the subjugation of women have been described as a caste system where one's status is fixed from birth and not alterable based on wealth or talent.[8]

Indeed, the connection between the enslavement of black people and the legal and social standing of women was often traced to the Old Testament. Historically, slavery was justified on the grounds that one should look to Abraham; the Bible refers to Abraham's wives, children, men servants, maid servants, camels, and cattle as his property. A man's wife and children were considered his slaves. By the logic of the 19th century, if women were slaves, why shouldn't blacks be also?

Thus, the concepts of race and sex have been historically linked. Since "the doctrines were developed by the same people for the same purpose it is not surprising to find anti-feminism to be an echo of racism, and vice versa."[9]

Additional constitutional amendments were necessary if women and African Americans were to exercise the privileges of citizenship that were automatically granted to white males. Nonetheless, even after amendments were enacted, African Americans still had to fight for enforcement of the law.

IV. *PLESSY V. FERGUSON* (1896)

After the Civil War, the northern victors imposed military rule on the South.[10] White landowners and former slaveholders often found themselves with unproductive farmland and no free laborers. Aside from the economic loss of power, white males were in a totally new political environment: Black men had been elevated to citizens; former slaves were now eligible to vote, run for office, and hold seats in the state or national legislature. To ensure the rights of former slaves, the U.S. Congress passed the Civil War Amendments and provided federal troops to oversee federal elections.

However, when federal troops were withdrawn from the southern states in 1877, enfranchised black men became vulnerable to former masters who immediately seized political control of the state legislatures. In order to solidify political power, whites rewrote state constitutions to disenfranchise black men. To ensure that all blacks were restricted to a subordinate status, southern states systematically enacted "Jim Crow" laws, rigidly segregating society into black and white communities. These laws barred blacks from using the same public facilities as whites, including schools, hospitals, restaurants, hotels, and recreation areas. With the cooperation of southern elected officials, the Ku Klux Klan, a white supremacist, terrorist organization, grew in membership. The return of political power to whites without any federal presence to protect the black community set the stage for "separate but equal" legislation to become a constitutionally valid racial doctrine.

Under slavery, interracial sexual contact was forbidden, but white masters nonetheless had the power to sexually exploit the black women who worked for them. The children of these relationships, especially if they looked white, posed potential inheritance problems because whites feared that such children might seek to exercise the privileges accorded to their white fathers. In order to keep all children of such relationships subordinate in the two-tiered racial system, descent was based on the race of the mother. Consequently, regardless of color, all the children of black women were defined as black.

This resulted in a rigid biracial structure where all persons with "one drop" of black blood were labeled black. Consequently, the "black" community consisted of a wide range of skin color based on this one-drop rule. Therefore, at times individuals with known black ancestry might look phenotypically white. This situation created a group of African Americans who had one-eighth or less African ancestry.

Louisiana was one of the few states to modify the one-drop rule of racial categorization because it considered mulattoes a valid racial category. A term derived from Spanish, *mulatto* refers to the offspring of a "pure African Negro" and a "pure white." Over time, *mulatto* came to encompass children of whites and "mixed Negroes."

These were the social conditions in 1896, when Homer Adolph Plessy, a mulatto, sought to test Louisiana laws that imposed racial segregation. Plessy and other mulattoes decided to test the applicability of the law requiring racial separation on railroad cars traveling in interstate transportation.

In 1890, Louisiana had followed other southern states in enacting Jim Crow laws that were written in compliance with the Equal Protection Clause of Section 1 of the Fourteenth Amendment. These laws required separate accommodations for white and black railroad passengers. In this case, Plessy, a U.S. citizen and a resident of Louisiana who was one-eighth black, paid for a first-class ticket on the East Louisiana Railway traveling from New Orleans to Covington, Louisiana. When he entered the passenger train, Plessy took a vacant seat in a coach designated for white passengers. He claimed that he was entitled to every "recognition, right, privilege, and immunity" granted to white citizens of the United States by the Constitution. Under Louisiana law, the conductor, who knew Plessy, was required to ask him to sit in a coach specifically assigned to nonwhite persons. By law, passengers who sat in the inappropriate coach were fined or imprisoned. When Plessy refused to comply with the order, he was removed from the train and imprisoned.

The decision in *Plessey v. Ferguson* established that separation of the races was legal under the U.S.

constitution, it solidified the power of whites over blacks in southern states. Through state laws, and with the additional federal weight in the *Plessy* decision, whites began to enforce rigid separation of the races in every aspect of life.

In *Plessy,* Justice John Marshall Harlan wrote the only dissenting opinion. Usually in Supreme Court cases, attention is focused on the majority, rather than the dissenting opinion. However, in this case Justice Harlan's dissent is noteworthy because his views on race and citizenship pointed out a line of reasoning that eventually broke down segregation and second-class citizenship for blacks.

Justice Harlan's background as a Kentucky slaveholder who later joined the Union side during the Civil War is cited as an explanation of his views. Some scholars speculate that his shift from slaveholder to a defender of the rights of blacks was caused by his observation of beatings, lynchings, and the use of intimidation tactics against blacks in Kentucky after the Civil War. In a quirk of history, when *Plessy v. Ferguson* was overturned in 1954 by a unanimous opinion in *Brown v. Board of Education,* Justice Harlan's grandson was a member of the Supreme Court.

The Court's decision addressed these key questions:

1. How is a black person defined?
2. Who determines when an individual is black or white?
3. Does providing separate but equal facilities violate the Thirteenth Amendment?
4. Does providing separate but equal facilities violate the Fourteenth Amendment?
5. Does a separate but equal doctrine imply inferiority of either race?
6. Can state laws require the separation of the two races in schools, theaters, and railway cars?
7. Does the separation of the races when applied to commerce within the state of Louisiana abridge the privileges and immunities of the "colored man,"[11] deprive him of equal protection of the law, or deprive him of his property without due process of law under the Fourteenth Amendment?

Excerpts from the Supreme Court Decision in *Plessy v. Ferguson*[12]

Mr. Justice Brown delivered the opinion of the Court:

. . . An [1890] act of the General Assembly of the State of Louisiana, provid[ed] for separate railway carriages for the white and colored races.

. . . No person or persons, shall be admitted to occupy seats in coaches, other than the ones assigned to them on account of the race they belong to.

. . . The constitutionality of this act is attacked upon the ground that it conflicts both with the Thirteenth Amendment of the Constitution, abolishing slavery, and the Fourteenth Amendment, which prohibits certain restrictive legislation.

. . . A statute which implied merely a legal distinction between the white and colored races . . . has no tendency to destroy the legal equality of the two races, or reestablish a state of servitude.

. . . The object of the amendment [the Fourteenth Amendment] was undoubtedly to enforce the absolute equality of the two races before the law, but in the nature of things it could not have been intended to abolish distinctions based upon color, or a commingling of the two races upon terms unsatisfactory to either.

Laws permitting and even requiring their separation in places where they are liable to be brought into contact do not necessarily imply the inferiority of either race to the other, and have been generally, if not universally recognized as within the competency of the state legislatures in the exercise of their police power. The most common instance of this is connected with the establishment of separate schools for white and colored children, which has been held to be a valid exercise of the legislative power even by courts of States where the political rights of the colored race have been longest and most earnestly enforced. One of the earliest of these cases is that of *Roberts v. City of Boston,* 5 Cush. 198, in which the Supreme Judicial Court of Massachusetts held that the general school committee of Boston had power to make provision for the instruction of colored children in separate schools established exclusively for them, and to prohibit their attendance upon the other schools.

. . . We are not prepared to say that the conductor, in assigning passengers to the coaches according to their race, does not act at his peril. . . . The power to assign to a particular coach obviously implies the power to determine to which race the passenger belongs, as well as the power to determine who, under the laws of the particular State, is to be deemed a white, and who is a colored person.

. . . We consider the underlying fallacy of the plaintiff's argument to consist in the assumption that the enforced separation of the two races stamps the colored race with a badge of inferiority. If this be so, it is not by reason of anything found in the act, but solely because the colored race chooses to put that construction upon it. . . . The argument also assumes that social prejudices may be overcome by legislation, and that equal rights cannot be secured to the negro except by an enforced commingling of the two races. We cannot accept this proposition. If the two races are to meet upon terms of social equality, it must be the result of natural affinities, a mutual appreciation of each other's merits and a voluntary consent of individuals.

. . . If the civil and political rights of both races be equal one cannot be inferior to the other civilly or politically. If one race be inferior to the other socially, the Constitution of the United States cannot put them upon the same plane.

It is true that the question for the proportion of colored blood necessary to constitute a colored person, as distinguished from a white person, is one upon which there is a difference of opinion in the different States, some holding that any visible admixture of black blood stamps the persons as belonging to the colored races, others that it depends upon the preponderance of blood . . . still others that the predominance of white blood must only be in the proportion of three fourths. . . . But these are questions to be determined under the laws of each State. . . .

Mr. Justice Harlan in the dissenting opinion:

. . . It was said in argument that the statute of Louisiana does not discriminate against either race, but prescribes a rule applicable alike to white and colored citizens. . . . [But] everyone knows that the statute in question had its origin in the purpose, not so much to exclude white persons from railroad cars occupied by blacks, as to exclude colored people from coaches occupied by or assigned to white persons.

. . . It is one thing for railroad carriers to furnish, or to be required by law to furnish, equal accommodations for all whom they are under a legal duty to carry. It is quite another thing for government to forbid citizens of the white and black races from traveling in the same public conveyance, and to punish officers of railroad companies for permitting persons of the two races to occupy the same passenger coach. If a State can prescribe, as a rule of civil conduct, that whites and blacks shall not travel as passengers in the same railroad coach, why may it not so regulate the use of the streets of its cities and towns as to compel white citizens to keep on one side of a street and black citizens to keep on the other? Why may it not, upon like grounds, punish whites and blacks who ride together in street cars or in open vehicles on a public road or street? Why may it not require sheriffs to assign whites to one side of a court-room and blacks to the other? And why may it not also prohibit the commingling of the two races in the galleries of legislative halls or in public assemblages convened for the consideration of the political questions of the day? Further, if this statute of Louisiana is consistent with the personal liberty of citizens, why may not the State require the separation in railroad coaches of native and naturalized citizens of the United States, or of Protestants and Roman Catholics?

. . . In my opinion, the judgment this day rendered will, in time, prove to be quite pernicious as the decision made by this tribunal in the Dred Scott case.

. . . The thin disguise of "equal" accommodations for passengers in railroad coaches will not mislead anyone, nor atone for the wrong this day done.

Thus, the *Plessy v. Ferguson* decision firmly established the separate but equal doctrine in the South until the National Association for the Advancement of Colored Persons (NAACP) began to systematically attack Jim Crow laws. It is ironic that in *Plessy* the systematic social, political, and economic suppression of blacks in the South through Jim Crow laws was justified in terms of a case decided in the northern city of Boston, where the segregation of schools occurred in practice (*de facto*), but not by force of law (*de jure*). In that 1849 case (*Roberts v. City of Boston*, 5 Cush. 198), a parent had unsuccessfully sued on behalf of his daughter to attend a public school. Thus, educational access became both the first and last chapter—in the 1954 case of *Brown v. Board of Education*—of the doctrine of separate but equal.

V. *YICK WO V. HOPKINS* (1886)

In the 1880s, the questions of citizenship and the rights of citizens were raised again by Native Americans and Asian immigrants. While the status of citizenship for African Americans was settled by the Thirteenth and Fourteenth Amendments, the extent of the privileges and immunities clause still needed clarification. Yick Wo, a Chinese immigrant living in San Francisco, brought suit under the Fourteenth Amendment to see if it covered all persons in the territorial United States regardless of race, color, or nationality.

The Chinese were different from European immigrants because they came to the United States under contract to work as laborers building the transcontinental railroad. When Chinese workers remained, primarily in California, after the completion of the railroad in 1869, Congress became anxious about this "foreign element" that was non-Christian and non-European. Chinese immigrants were seen as an economic threat because they would work for less than white males. To address the issue of economic competition, the Chinese Exclusion Act was passed in 1882 to prohibit further immigration to the United States. This gave the Chinese the unique status among immigrants of being the only group barred from entry into the United States and barred from becoming naturalized U.S. citizens.

Yick Wo, a subject of the Emperor of China, went to San Francisco in 1861, where he operated a laundry at the same premise for 22 years with consent from the Board of Fire Wardens. When the consent decree expired on October 1, 1885, Yick Wo routinely reapplied to continue to operate a laundry. He was, however, denied a license. Of the over 300 laundries in the city and county of San Francisco, about 240 were owned by Chinese immigrants. Most of these laundries were wooden, the most common construction material used at that time, although it posed a fire hazard. Yick Wo and more than 150 of his countrymen were arrested and charged with carrying on business without having special consent, while those who were not subjects of China and were operating some 80 laundries under similar conditions, were allowed to conduct business.

Yick Wo stated that he and 200 of his countrymen with similar situations petitioned the Board of Supervisors for permission to continue to conduct business in the same buildings they had occupied for more than 20 years. The petitions of all the Chinese were denied, while all petitions of those who were not Chinese were granted (with one exception).

Did this prohibition of the occupation and destruction of the business and property of the Chinese laundrymen in San Francisco constitute the proper regulation of business, or was it discrimination and a violation of important rights secured by the Fourteenth Amendment?

The Court's decision addressed these key questions:

1. Does this municipal ordinance regulating public laundries within the municipality of San Francisco violate the United States Constitution?
2. Does carrying out this municipal ordinance violate the Fourteenth Amendment?
3. Does the guarantee of protection of the Fourteenth Amendment extend to all persons within the territorial jurisdiction of the United States regardless of race, color, or nationality?
4. Are the subjects of the Emperor of China who, temporarily or permanently, reside in the United States entitled to enjoy the protection guaranteed by the Fourteenth Amendment?

Excerpts from the Supreme Court Decision in *Yick Wo v. Hopkins*[13]

Mr. Justice Matthews delivered the opinion of the Court:

> . . . In both of these cases [*Yick Wo v. Hopkins* and *Wo Lee v. Hopkins*] the ordinance involved was simply a prohibition to carry on the washing and ironing of clothes in public laundries and washhouses, within the city and county of San Francisco, from ten o'clock p.m. until six o'clock a.m. of the following day. This provision was held to be purely a police regulation, within the competency of any municipality.
>
> . . . The rights of the petitioners are not less because they are aliens and subjects of the Emperor of China.

The Fourteenth Amendment to the Constitution is not confined to the protection of citizens. It says: "Nor shall any State deprive any person of life, liberty, or property without due process of law; nor deny to any person within its jurisdiction the equal protection of the laws." These provisions are universal in their application, to all persons within the territorial jurisdiction, without regard to any differences of race, or color, or of nationality; and the equal protection from the laws is a pledge of the protection of equal laws. . . .

Though the law itself be fair on its face and impartial in appearance, yet, it is applied and administered by public authority with an evil eye and unequal hand, so as practically to make unjust and illegal discriminations between persons in similar circumstances. . . .

. . . No reason whatever, except the will of the supervisors, is assigned why they should not be permitted to carry on, in the accustomed manner, their harmless and useful occupation, on which they depend for a livelihood. And while this consent of the supervisors is withheld from them and from two hundred others who have also petitioned, all of whom happened to be Chinese subjects, eighty others, not Chinese subjects, are permitted to carry on similar business under similar conditions. The fact of this discrimination is admitted. No reason for it is shown, . . . no reason for it exists except hostility to the race and nationality to which the petitioners belong, and which in the eye of the law is not justified. The discrimination is, therefore, illegal, and the public administration which enforces it is a denial of the equal protection of the laws and a violation of the Fourteenth Amendment of the Constitution. The imprisonment of the petitioners is, therefore illegal, and they must be discharged.

The decision in *Yick Wo* demonstrated the Court's perspective that the Fourteenth Amendment applied to all persons, citizens and noncitizens.

VI. *ELK V. WILKINS* (1884)

In the late 19th century, Native Americans constituted a problematic class when the Supreme Court considered citizenship. Although Native Americans were the original inhabitants of the territory that became the United States, they were considered outside the concept of citizenship. They were viewed as a separate nation, and described as uncivilized, alien people who were not worthy of citizenship in the political community. As Native Americans were driven from their homeland and pushed farther west, the United States government developed a policy of containment by establishing reservations. Native Americans who lived with their tribes on such reservations were presumed to be members of "not strictly speaking, foreign states, but alien nations." The Constitution made no provisions for naturalizing Native Americans or defining the status of those who chose to live in the territorial United States rather than be assigned to reservations. It was presumed that Native Americans would remain on the reservations. The framers of the Constitution had not given any thought as to when or how a Native American might become a U.S. citizen. When the Naturalization Law of 1790 was written, only Europeans were anticipated as future citizens. The citizenship of Native Americans was not settled until 1924, when a statutory law, not a constitutional amendment, granted citizenship.

Elk v. Wilkins raised the question of citizenship and voting behavior as a privilege of citizenship. In 1857, the Court had easily dismissed Dred Scott's suit on the grounds that he was not a citizen. Since he did not hold citizenship, he could not sue. *Minor v. Happersett* in 1872 considered the citizenship and voting issue with a female plaintiff. In that case, citizenship was not in doubt but the court stated that citizenship did not automatically confer the right to suffrage. In *Elk,* a Native American claimed citizenship and the right to vote. Before considering the right to vote, the Court first examined whether Elk was a citizen and the process by which one becomes a citizen.

As midwestern cities emerged from westward expansion in the 1880s, a few Native Americans left their reservations to live and work in those cities. John Elk left his tribe and moved to Omaha, Nebraska, under the jurisdiction of the United States. In April 1880, he attempted to vote for members of the city council. Elk met the residency requirements in Nebraska and Douglas County for voting. Claiming that he complied with all of the statutory provisions, Elk asserted that under the Fourteenth and Fifteenth Amendments, he was a citizen of the United States who was entitled to exercise the franchise, regardless of race or color. He further claimed that Wilkins, the voter registrar, "designedly, corruptly, willfully, and maliciously" refused to register him for the sole reason that he was a Native American.

The Court's decision addressed these key questions:

1. Is a Native American still a member of an Indian tribe when he voluntarily separates himself from his tribe and seeks residence among the white citizens of the state?
2. What was the intent of the Fourteenth Amendment regarding who could become a citizen?
3. Can Native Americans become naturalized citizens?
4. Can Native Americans become citizens of the United States without the consent of the U.S. government?
5. Must Native Americans adopt the habits of a "civilized" life before they become U.S. citizens?
6. Is a Native American who is taxed a citizen?

Excerpts from the Supreme Court Decision in *Elk v. Wilkins*[14]

Mr. Justice Gray delivered the opinion of the Court.

. . . The plaintiff . . . relies on the first clause of the first section of the Fourteenth Amendment of the Constitution of the United States, by which "all persons born or naturalized in the United States, and subject to the jurisdiction thereof, are citizens of the United States and of the State wherein they reside"; and on the Fifteenth Amendment, which provides that "the right of citizens of the United States to vote shall not be denied or abridged by the United States or by any State on account of race, color, or previous condition of servitude."

. . . The question then is, whether an Indian, born a member of the Indian tribes within the United States, is, merely by reason of his birth within the United States, and of his afterwards voluntarily separating himself from his tribe and taking up his residence among white citizens, a citizen of the United States, within the meaning of the first section of the Fourteenth Amendment of the Constitution.

. . . The Indian tribes, being within the territorial limits of the United States, were not, strictly speaking, foreign States; but they were alien nations, distinct political communities, with whom the United States might and habitually did deal, as they thought fit, either through treaties made by the President and Senate, or through acts of Congress in the ordinary forms of legislation. The members of those tribes owed immediate allegiance to their several tribes, and were not a part of the United States. They were in a dependent condition, a state of pupilage, resembling that of a ward to his guardian.

. . . They were never deemed citizens of the United States, except under explicit provisions of treaty or statute to that effect, either declaring a certain tribe, or such members of it as chose to remain behind on the removal of the tribe westward, to be citizens, or authorizing individuals of particular tribes to become citizens. . . .

This [opening] section of the Fourteenth Amendment contemplates two sources of citizenship, and two sources only: birth and naturalization.

. . . Slavery having been abolished, and the persons formerly held as slaves made citizens. . . . But Indians not taxed are still excluded from the count [U.S. Census count for apportioning seats in the U.S. House of Representatives],[15] for the reason that they are not citizens. Their absolute exclusion from the basis of representation, in which all other persons are now included, is wholly inconsistent with their being considered citizens.

. . . Such Indians, then, not being citizens by birth, can only become so in the second way mentioned in the Fourteenth Amendment, by being "naturalized in the United States," by or under some treaty or statute.

. . . The treaty of 1867 with the Kansas Indians strikingly illustrates the principle that no one can become a citizen of a nation without its consent, and directly contradicts the supposition that a member of an Indian tribe can at will be alternately a citizen of the United States and a member of the tribe.

. . . But the question whether any Indian tribes, or any members thereof, have become so far advanced in civilization, that they should be let out of the state of pupilage, and admitted to the privileges and responsibilities of citizenship, is a question to be decided by the nation whose wards they are and whose citizens they seek to become, and not by each Indian for himself.

. . . And in a later case [Judge Deady in the District Court of the United States for the District of Oregon] said: "But an Indian cannot make himself a citizen of the United States without the consent and co-operation of the government. The fact that he has abandoned his nomadic life or tribal relations, and adopted the habits and manners of civilized people, may be a good reason why he should be made a citizen of the United States, but does not of itself make him one. To be a citizen of the United States is a political privilege which no one, not born to, can assume without its consent in some form.

Mr. Justice Harlan in the dissenting opinion:

. . . We submit that the petition does sufficiently show that the plaintiff is taxed, that is, belongs to the class which, by the laws of Nebraska, are subject to taxation.

. . . The plaintiff is a citizen and *bona fide* resident of Nebraska. . . . He is subject to taxation, and is taxed, in that State. Further: The plaintiff has become so far incorporated with the mass of the people of Nebraska that . . . he constitutes a part of her militia.

By the act of April 9, 1866, entitled "An Act to protect all persons in the United States in their civil rights, and furnish means for their vindication" (14 Stat. 27), it is provided that "all persons born in the United States and not subject to any foreign power, excluding Indians not taxed, are hereby declared to be citizens of the United States." . . . Beyond question, by that act, national citizenship was conferred directly upon all persons in this country, of whatever race (excluding only "Indians not taxed"), who were born within the territorial limits of the United States, and were not subject to any foreign power. Surely everyone must admit that an Indian, residing in one of the States, and subject to taxation there, became by force alone of the act of 1866, a citizen of the United States, although he may have been, when born, a member of a tribe.

. . . If he did not acquire national citizenship on abandoning his tribe [moving from the reservation] and . . . by residence in one of the States, subject to the complete jurisdiction of the United States, then the Fourteenth Amendment has wholly failed to accomplish, in respect of the Indian race, what, we think, was intended by it, and there is still in this country a despised and rejected class of persons, with no nationality; who born in our territory, owing no allegiance to foreign power, and subject, as residents of the States, to all the burdens of government, are yet not members of any political community nor entitled to any of the rights, privileges, or immunities of citizens of the United States.

In all, the Court never addressed Elk's right to vote because the primary question involved Elk's citizenship. By excluding him from citizenship because he had not been naturalized and because there was no provision for naturalization, John Elk was left outside of the political community as was Dred Scott.

VII. *BROWN V. BOARD OF EDUCATION* (1954)

Unlike many of the earlier cases brought by individual women, blacks, or Native Americans, *Brown v. Board of Education* was the result of a concerted campaign against racial segregation led by Howard University School of Law graduates and the NAACP. In the 1930s, the NAACP Legal Defense Fund began to systematically fight for fair employment, fair housing, and desegregation of public education. Key lawyers in the campaign against segregation were Charles Houston, Thurgood Marshall, James Nabrit, and William Hastie. Marshall later became a Supreme Court justice, Nabrit became president of Howard University, and Hastie became a federal judge.

By using the Fourteenth Amendment, *Brown* became the key case in an attempt to topple the 1896 separate but equal doctrine. Legal strategists knew that educational opportunity and better housing conditions were essential if black Americans were to achieve upward mobility. While one group of lawyers focused on restrictive covenant cases,[16] which prevented blacks from buying housing in white neighborhoods, another spearheaded the drive for blacks to enter state-run professional schools.

In 1954, suits were brought in Kansas, South Carolina, Virginia, and Delaware on behalf of black Americans seeking to attend nonsegregated public schools. However, the case is commonly referred to as *Brown v. Board of Education.* The plaintiffs in the suit contended that segregation in the public schools denied them equal protection of the laws under the Fourteenth Amendment. The contention was that since segregated public schools were not and could not be made equal, black American children were deprived of equal protection of the laws.

The Court's unanimous decision addressed these key questions:

1. Are public schools segregated by race detrimental to black children?
2. Does segregation result in an inferior education for black children?
3. Does the maintenance of segregated public schools violate the Equal Protection Clause of the Fourteenth Amendment?
4. Is the maintenance of segregated public school facilities *inherently* unequal?
5. What was the intent of the framers of the Fourteenth Amendment regarding distinctions between whites and blacks?
6. Is the holding in *Plessy v. Ferguson* applicable to public education?
7. Does segregation of children in public schools *solely on the basis of race,* even though the physical facilities and other "tangible" factors may be equal, deprive the children of the minority group of equal educational opportunities?

Excerpts from the Supreme Court Decision in *Brown v. Board of Education*[17]

Mr. Chief Justice Warren delivered the opinion of the Court:

. . . In each of these cases [NAACP suits in Kansas, South Carolina, Virginia, and Delaware] minors of the Negro race, through their legal representatives, seek the aid of the courts in obtaining admission to the public schools of their community on a nonsegregated basis. . . . This segregation was alleged to deprive the plaintiffs of the equal protection of the laws under the Fourteenth Amendment. In each of the cases other than the Delaware case, a three-judge federal district court denied relief to the plaintiffs on the so-called "separate but equal" doctrine announced by this Court in *Plessy v. Ferguson,* 163 U.S. 537. Under that doctrine, equality of treatment is accorded when the races are provided substantially equal facilities, even though these facilities be separated. . . .

The plaintiffs contend that segregated schools are not "equal" and cannot be made "equal," and that hence they are deprived of the equal protection of the laws.

. . . The most avid proponents of the post–[Civil] War amendments undoubtedly intended them to remove all legal distinctions among "all persons born or naturalized in the United States."

In the first cases in this Court construing the Fourteenth Amendment, decided shortly after its adoption, the Court interpreted it as proscribing all state imposed discriminations against the Negro race. The doctrine of "separate but equal" did not make its appearance in this Court until 1896 in the *Plessy v. Ferguson, supra,* involving not education but transportation.

In these days, it is doubtful that any child may reasonably be expected to succeed in life if he is denied the opportunity of an education. Such an opportunity where the state has undertaken to provide it, is a right which must be made available to all on equal terms.

We come then to the question presented: Does segregation of children in public schools solely on the basis of race, even though the physical facilities and other "tangible" factors may be equal, deprive the children of the minority group of equal educational opportunities? We believe that it does.

To separate them [the children] from others of similar age and qualifications solely because of their race generates a feeling of inferiority as to their status in the community that may affect their hearts and minds in a way unlikely ever to be undone.

We conclude that in the field of public education the doctrine of "separate but equal" has no place. Separate educational facilities are inherently unequal. Therefore, we hold that the plaintiffs and others similarly situated for whom the actions have been brought are, by reason of the segregation complained of, deprived of the equal protection of the laws guaranteed by the Fourteenth Amendment.

. . . We have now announced that such segregation is a denial of the equal protection of the laws.

VIII. *LAU V. NICHOLS* (1974)

In the 19th century, Native Americans and Asian immigrants sought to exercise rights under the Fourteenth Amendment although it had been designed explicitly to protect blacks. In the 20th century, issues first raised by African Americans, such as equality in public education, again presented other minority groups with an opportunity to test their rights under the Constitution.

Brown v. Board of Education forced the Court to consider the narrow question of the distribution of resources between black and white school systems. The *Brown* decision addressed only education. It did not extend to the other areas of segregation in American society, such as the segregation of public transportation (e.g., buses) or public accommodations (e.g., restaurants and hotels). Indeed, *Brown* had not even specified how the integration of the school system was to take place. All of these questions were taken up by the Civil Rights movement that followed the *Brown* decision.

Once the separate but equal doctrine was nullified in education, immigrants raised other issues of equality. In the 1970s, suits were brought on behalf of the children of illegal immigrants, non-English-speaking children of Chinese ancestry, and children of low-income parents.

In *Lau v. Nichols,* a non-English-speaking minority group questioned equality in public education. The case was similar to *Brown* because it concerned public education, the Equal Protection Clause of the Fourteenth Amendment, and the suit was brought on behalf of minors; but the two cases also differed in many respects. The 1954 decision in *Brown* was part of a series of court cases attacking segregated facilities primarily in southern states. It addressed only the issues of black-white interaction.

In *Lau v. Nichols,* a suit was brought on behalf of children of Chinese ancestry who attended public schools in San Francisco. Although the children did not speak English, their classes in school were taught entirely in that language. (Some of the children received special instruction in the English language; others did not.) The suit did not specifically ask for bilingual education, nor did the Court require it, but *Lau* led to the development of such programs. In bilingual education, the curriculum is taught in children's native language, but they are also given separate instruction in the English language, and over time they are moved into English throughout their courses.

The *Lau* decision hinged in part on Department of Health, Education, and Welfare guidelines that prohibited discrimination in federally assisted programs. The decision was narrow because it instructed only the lower court to provide appropriate relief. The Court's ruling did not guarantee minority language rights, nor did it require bilingual education.

The Court's decision addressed these key questions:

1. Does a public school system that provides for instruction only in English violate the equal protection clause of the Fourteenth Amendment?
2. Does a public school system that provides for instruction only in English violate Section 601 of the Civil Rights Act of 1964?
3. Do Chinese-speaking students who are in the minority receive fewer benefits from the school system than the English-speaking majority?
4. Must a school system that has a minority of students who do not speak English provide bilingual instruction?

Excerpts from the Supreme Court Decision in *Lau v. Nichols*[18]

Mr. Justice Douglas delivered the opinion of the Court:

The San Francisco, California, school system was integrated in 1971 as a result of a federal court decree.

The District Court found that there are 2,856 students of Chinese ancestry in the school system who do not speak English. Of those who have that language deficiency, about 1,000 are given supplemental courses in the English language. About 1,800 however, do not receive that instruction.

This class suit brought by non-English-speaking Chinese students against officials responsible for the operation of the San Francisco Unified School District seeks relief against the unequal educational opportunities, which are alleged to violate, *inter alia,* the Fourteenth Amendment. No specific remedy is urged upon us. . . .

The Court of Appeals [holding that there was no violation of the Equal Protection Clause of the Fourteenth Amendment or of Section 601 of the Civil Rights Act of 1964] reasoned that "[e]very student brings to the starting line of his educational career different advantages and disadvantages caused in part by social, economic and cultural background, created and continued completely apart from any contribution by the school system." . . . Section 71 of the California Education Code states that "English shall be the basic language of instruction in all schools." That Section permits a school district to determine "when and under what circumstances instruction may be given bilingually." . . .

Under these state-imposed standards there is no equality of treatment merely by providing students with the same facilities, textbooks, teachers, and curriculum; for students who do not understand English are effectively foreclosed from any meaningful education.

. . . We know that those who do not understand English are certain to find their classroom experiences wholly incomprehensible and in no way meaningful.

We do not reach the Equal Protection Clause argument which has been advanced but rely solely on Section 601 of the Civil Rights Act of 1964, 42 U.S.C. section 2000d. to reverse the Court of Appeals.

That section bans discrimination based "on the ground of race, color, or national origin, in any program or activity receiving Federal financial assistance." The school district involved in this litigation receives large amounts of federal financial assistance. The Department of Health, Education, and Welfare (HEW), which has authority to promulgate regulations prohibiting discrimination in federally assisted school systems, in 1968 issued one guideline that "[s]chool systems are responsible for assuring that students of a particular race, color, or national origin are not denied the opportunity to obtain the education generally obtained by other students in the system." In 1970 HEW made the guidelines more specific, requiring school districts that were federally funded "to rectify the language deficiency in order to open" the instruction to students who had "linguistic deficiencies." . . .

It seems obvious that the Chinese-speaking minority receive fewer benefits than the English-speaking majority from respondents' school system which denies them a meaningful opportunity to participate in the educational program—all earmarks of the discrimination banned by the regulations. . . .

Lau differed from *Brown* because it was decided not on the basis of the Fourteenth Amendment but on the Civil Rights Act of 1964. In reference to *Brown,* the justices noted that equality of treatment was not achieved by providing students with the same facilities, textbooks, teachers, or curriculum. *Lau* underscores the idea that equality may not be achieved by treating different categories of people in the same way.

IX. *SAN ANTONIO SCHOOL DISTRICT V. RODRIGUEZ* (1973)

The 1973 case of *San Antonio School District v. Rodriguez* raised the question of equality in public education from another perspective. As was the case in *Brown* and *Lau,* the Fourteenth Amendment required interpretation. However, unlike the earlier cases, the issue was the financing of local public schools.

Education is not a right specified in the Constitution. Under a federal system, education is a local matter in each state. This allows for the possibility of vast differences among states and even within states on the quality of instruction, methods of financing, and treatment of nonwhite students. Whereas the *Brown* decision examined inequality between races, *San Antonio* considered inequality based on financial resources through local property taxes. *San Antonio* raised the question of the consequence of the unequal distribution of wealth among Texas school districts. As with

Brown and *Lau,* minors were involved; however, the issue was not race or language instruction but social class. Did the Texas school system discriminate against the poor?

Traditionally, the states have financed schools based on property tax assessments. Since wealth is not evenly distributed, some communities are able to spend more on education and provide greater resources to children. This is the basis of the *San Antonio* case, where the charge was that children in less affluent communities necessarily received an inferior education because those communities had fewer resources to draw on. The Rodriguez family contended that the Texas school system of financing public schools through local property taxes denied them equal protection of the laws in violation of the Fourteenth Amendment.

Financing public schools in Texas entailed state and local contributions. About half of the revenues were derived from a state-funded program that provided a minimal educational base; each district then supplemented state aid with a property tax. The Rodriguez family brought a class action suit on behalf of school children who claimed to be members of poor families who resided in school districts with a low property tax base. The contention was that the Texas system's reliance on local property taxation favored the more affluent and violated equal protection requirements because of disparities between districts in per-pupil expenditures.

The Court's decision addressed these key questions:

1. Does Texas's system of financing public school education by use of a property tax violate the Equal Protection Clause (Section 1) of the Fourteenth Amendment?
2. Does the Equal Protection Clause apply to wealth?
3. Is education a fundamental right?
4. Does this state law impinge on a fundamental right?
5. Is a state system for financing public education by a property tax that results in interdistrict disparities in per-pupil expenditures unconstitutionally arbitrary under the Equal Protection Clause?

Excerpts from the Supreme Court Decision in *San Antonio School District v. Rodriguez*[19]

Mr. Justice Powell delivered the opinion of the Court:

. . . The District Court held that the Texas system [of financing public education] discriminates on the basis of wealth in the manner in which education is provided for its people. Finding that wealth is a "suspect" classification and that education is a "fundamental" interest, the District Court held that the Texas system could be sustained only if the State could show that it was premised upon some compelling state interest.

. . . We must decide, first, whether the Texas system of financing public education operates to the disadvantage of some suspect class or impinges upon a fundamental right explicitly or implicitly protected by the Constitution, thereby requiring strict judicial scrutiny. If so, the Texas scheme must still be examined to determine whether it rationally furthers some legitimate, articulated state purpose and therefore does not constitute an invidious discrimination in violation of the Equal Protection Clause of the Fourteenth Amendment.

. . . In concluding that strict judicial scrutiny was required, the [District] court relied on decisions dealing with the rights of indigents to equal treatment in the criminal trial and appellate processes, and on cases disapproving wealth restrictions on the right to vote. Those cases, the District Court concluded, established wealth as a suspect classification. Finding that a local property tax system discriminated on the basis of wealth, it regarded those precedents as controlling. It then reasoned, based on decisions of this Court affirming the undeniable importance of education, that there is a fundamental right to education and that, absent some compelling state justification, the Texas system could not stand.

We are unable to agree that this case, which in significant aspects is *sui generis,* may be so neatly fitted under the Equal Protection Clause. Indeed, we find neither the suspect-classification nor the fundamental-interest analysis persuasive.

The wealth discrimination discovered by the District Court in this case, and by several other courts that have recently struck down school financing in other States, is quite unlike any of the forms of wealth discrimination heretofore reviewed by this Court.

. . . First, in support of their charge that the system discriminates against the "poor," appellees have made no effort to demonstrate that it operates to the peculiar disadvantage of any class fairly definable as indigent, or as composed of persons whose incomes are beneath any designated poverty level. Indeed, there is reason to believe that the poorest families are not necessarily clustered in the poorest property districts. . . .

Second, neither appellees nor the District Court addressed the fact that . . . lack of personal resources has not occasioned an absolute deprivation of the desired benefit. The argument here is not that the children in districts having relatively low assessable property values are receiving no public education; rather, it is that they are receiving a poorer quality education than that available to children in districts having more assessable wealth. Apart from the unsettled and disputed question whether the quality of education may be determined by the amount of money expended for it, a sufficient answer to appellee's argument is that, at least where wealth is involved, the Equal Protection Clause does not require absolute equality or precisely equal advantages. . . .

For these two reasons . . . the disadvantaged class is not susceptible of identification in traditional terms. . . .

. . . [I]t is clear that appellee's suit asks this Court to extend its most exacting scrutiny to review a system that allegedly discriminates against a large, diverse, and amorphous class, unified only by the common factor of residence in districts that happen to have less taxable wealth than other districts. The system of alleged discrimination and the class it defines have none of the traditional indicia of suspectness: the class is not saddled with such disabilities, or subjected to such a history of purposeful unequal treatment, or relegated to such a position of political powerlessness as to command extraordinary protection from the majoritarian political process.

We thus conclude that the Texas system does not operate to the peculiar disadvantage of any suspect class. . . .

Education, of course, is not among the rights afforded explicit protection under our Federal Constitution. Nor do we find any basis for saying it is implicitly so protected. . . .

In sum, to the extent that the Texas system of school financing results in unequal expenditures between children who happen to reside in different districts, we cannot say that such disparities are the product of a system that is so irrational as to be invidiously discriminatory. . . .

Mr. Justice White, with whom Mr. Justice Douglas and Mr. Justice Brennan join, dissenting:

. . . In my view, the parents and children in Edgewood, and in like districts, suffer from an invidious discrimination violative of the Equal Protection Clause. . . .

There is no difficulty in identifying the class that is subject to the alleged discrimination and that is entitled to the benefits of the Equal Protection Clause. I need go no further than the parents and children in the Edgewood district, who are plaintiffs here and who assert that they are entitled to the same choice as Alamo Heights to augment local expenditures for schools but are denied that choice by state law. This group constitutes a class sufficiently definite to invoke the protection of the Constitution. . . .

In *San Antonio v. Rodriguez,* the Court did not find that the differences between school districts constituted invidious discrimination. A majority of the justices felt that Texas satisfied constitutional standards under the Equal Protection Clause. On the other hand, four justices in dissenting opinions saw a class (the poor) that was subject to discrimination and that lacked the protection of the Constitution.

X. *REGENTS OF THE UNIVERSITY OF CALIFORNIA V. BAKKE* (1978)

The Supreme Court has reviewed several cases concerning equitable treatment in public education. Key cases include racially separate public schools (*Brown v. Board of Education,* 1954); the practice of English-only instruction for Chinese students in public schools (*Lau v. Nichols,* 1974); and the practice of operating public schools based solely on revenue from local property taxes (*San Antonio School District v. Rodriguez,* 1973).

African Americans not only had to fight for equity in public schools but also had to sue to gain admission to law and medical schools in state universities. See *Sipuel v. Oklahoma,* 1948; *Missouri ex rel Gaines,* 1938; and *Sweatt v. Painter,* 1950.

In 1978, race-based admissions became an issue again when a *white* person sued for admission to the medical school at the University of California at Davis. The case of *The Regents of the University of California v. Bakke,* however, must be seen in light of the policy of affirmative action, which sought to redress historic injustices against racial minorities and other specified groups by providing educational and employment opportunities to members of these groups.

In 1968, the University of California at Davis opened a medical school with a track admission policy for a 100-seat class. In 1974, applicants who identified themselves as economically and/or educationally disadvantaged or a member of a minority group (blacks, Chicanos, Asians, American Indians) were reviewed by a special committee. They could also compete for the remaining 84 seats. However, no disadvantaged white was ever admitted to the school through the special admissions program, although some applied. Bakke, a white male, applied to the medical school in 1973 and 1974 under the general admissions program. He was rejected both times because he did not meet the requisite cutoff score. In both years, special applicants with significantly lower scores than Bakke were admitted. After his second rejection, Bakke sued for admission to the medical school, alleging that the special admissions program excluded him on the basis of his race in violation of the Equal Protection Clause of the Fourteenth Amendment, a provision of the California Constitution, and Section 601 of Title VI of the Civil Rights Act of 1964, which provides that no person shall, on the ground of race or color, be excluded from participating in any program receiving federal financial assistance. The California Supreme Court applied a strict-scrutiny standard. It concluded that the special admissions program was not the least intrusive means of achieving the goals of the admittedly compelling state interests of integrating the medical profession and increasing the number of doctors willing to serve minority patients. The California court held that UC Davis's special admissions program violated the Equal Protection Clause of the

U.S. Constitution. The Davis School of Medicine was ordered to admit Bakke.

The Court's divided opinion addressed these key questions:

1. Does the University of California Davis School of Medicine admission policy violate the Fourteenth Amendment?
2. Does giving preference to a group of nonwhite applicants constitute discrimination?
3. Does the University of California Davis School of Medicine School use a racial classification that is suspect?
4. Was Bakke denied admission to the University of California Davis School of Medicine on the basis of race?
5. Can race be used as a criterion for admission to a university?

Excerpts from the Supreme Court Decision in *The Regents of the University of California v. Bakke*[20]

Mr. Justice Powell delivered the opinion of the Court:

The guarantees of the Fourteenth Amendment extend to all persons. Its language is explicit: "No State shall . . . deny to any person within its jurisdiction the equal protection of the laws." . . . The guarantee of equal protection cannot mean one thing when applied to one individual and something else when applied to a person of another color. . . .

. . . the [Fourteenth] Amendment itself was framed in universal terms, without reference to color, ethnic origin, or condition of prior servitude.

Petitioner [University of California, Davis] urges us to adopt for the first time a more restrictive view of the Equal Protection Clause and hold that discrimination against members of the white "majority" cannot be suspect if its purpose can be characterized as "benign."

. . . Moreover, there are serious problems of justice connected with the idea of preference itself. First, it may not always be clear that a so-called preference is in fact benign. . . . Second, preferential programs may only reinforce common stereotypes holding that certain groups are unable to achieve success without special protection based on a factor having no relationship to individual worth. Third, there is a measure of inequity in forcing innocent persons in respondent's position to bear the burdens of redressing grievances not of their making.

. . . When a classification denies an individual opportunities or benefits enjoyed by others solely because of his race or ethnic background, it must be regarded as suspect.

If petitioner's purpose is to assure within its student body some specified percentage of a particular group merely because of its race or ethnic origin, such a preferential purpose must be rejected. . . . Preferring members of any one group for no reason other than race or ethnic origin is discrimination for its own sake. This the Constitution forbids.

. . . [A] goal asserted by petitioner is the attainment of a diverse student body. This clearly is a constitutionally permissible goal for an institution of higher education. Academic freedom, though not a specifically enumerated constitutional right, long has been viewed as a special concern of the First Amendment. . . .

Ethnic diversity, however, is only one element in a range of factors a university properly may consider in attaining the goal of a heterogeneous student body.

It may be assumed that the reservation of a specified number of seats in each class for individuals from the preferred ethnic groups would contribute to the attainment of considerable ethnic diversity in the student body. But petitioner's argument that this is the only effective means of serving the interest of diversity is seriously flawed. . . . Petitioner's special admissions program, focused solely on ethnic diversity, would hinder rather than further attainment of genuine diversity.

. . . In summary, it is evident that the Davis special admissions program involves the use of an explicit racial classification never before countenanced by this Court. It tells applicants who are not Negro, Asian, or Chicano that they are totally excluded from a specific percentage of the seats in the class.

The fatal flaw in petitioner's preferential program is its disregard of individual rights as guaranteed by the Fourteenth Amendment. Such rights are not absolute.

Mr. Justice Brennan, Mr. Justice White, Mr. Justice Marshall, and Mr. Justice Blackmun, concurring in part and dissenting in part:

We conclude . . . that racial classifications are not *per se* invalid under the Fourteenth Amendment.

Unquestionably we have held that a government practice or statute which restricts "fundamental rights" or which contains "suspect classifications" is to be subjected to "strict scrutiny" and can be justified only if it furthers a compelling government purpose. . . . But no fundamental right is involved here. Nor do whites as a class have any of the "traditional indicia of suspectness; the class is not saddled with such disabilities, or subjected to such a history of purposeful unequal treatment, or relegated to such a history of purposeful unequal treatment, or relegated to such position of political powerlessness as to command extraordinary protection from the majoritarian political process." . . .

Certainly . . . Davis had a sound basis for believing that the problem of under-representation of minorities was substantial and chronic. . . . Until at least 1973, the practice of medicine in this country was, in fact, if not in law, largely the prerogative of whites. In 1950, for example, while Negroes constituted 10% of the total population, Negro physicians constituted only 2.2% of the total number of physicians. The overwhelming majority of these . . . were educated in two predominantly Negro medical schools, Howard and Meharry. By 1970, the gap between the proportion of Negroes in medicine and their proportion in the population had widened: The number of Negroes employed in medicine remained frozen at 2.2% while the Negro population had increased to 11.1%. The number of Negro admittees to predominantly white medical schools, moreover, had declined in absolute numbers during the years 1955 to 1964.

Moreover, Davis had very good reason to believe that the national pattern of under-representation of minorities in medicine would be perpetuated if it retained a single admissions standard. . . .

Davis clearly could conclude that the serious and persistent under-representation of minorities in medicine depicted by these statistics is the result of handicaps under which minority applicants labor as a consequence of . . . deliberate, purposeful discrimination against minorities in education and in society generally, as well as in the medical profession. . . .

It is not even claimed that Davis' program in any way operates to stigmatize or single out any discrete . . . or even any identifiable, nonminority group. Nor will harm comparable to that imposed upon racial minorities by exclusion or separation on grounds of race be the likely result of the program. . . .

Nor was Bakke in any sense stamped as inferior by the Medical School's rejection of him. Indeed, it is conceded by all that he satisfied those criteria regarded by the school as generally relevant to academic performance better than most of the minority members who were admitted. Moreover, there is absolutely no basis for concluding that Bakke's rejection that was a result of Davis' use of racial preference will affect him throughout his life in the same way as the segregation of the Negro schoolchildren in *Brown I* would have affected them. Unlike discrimination against racial minorities, the use of racial preferences for remedial purposes does not inflict a pervasive injury upon individual whites in the sense that wherever they go or whatever they do there is a significant likelihood that they will be treated as second-class citizens because of their color. . . .

In addition, there is simply no evidence that the Davis program discriminated intentionally or unintentionally against any minority group which it purports to benefit. The program does not establish a quota in the invidious sense of a ceiling on the number of minority applicants to be admitted. . . .

Finally, Davis' special admissions program cannot be said to violate the Constitution. . . .

. . . we would reverse the judgment of the Supreme Court of California holding the Medical School's special admissions program unconstitutional and directing respondent's admission.

Justices Stevens and Stewart, along with Chief Justice Rehnquist, concurred and dissented in part. They found that the university's special admissions program violated Title VI of the Civil Rights Act of 1964, which prohibits discrimination under any program or activity receiving federal funding assistance. This dissent found that Bakke was not admitted to the Davis Medical School because of his race.

Race-based admissions were again considered in *Hopwood v. Texas,* a 1994 case in the Western District of Texas. The suit, brought by four white Texas residents, claimed that the affirmative action admissions program of the University of Texas School of Law violated the Equal Protection Clause of the Fourteenth Amendment and Title VI of the Civil Rights Act of 1964. The district court agreed that the plaintiffs' equal protection rights had been violated,

but refused to direct the school to cease making admission decisions based on race. The case was subsequently appealed in the Court of Appeals for the Fifth Circuit, which held that the University of Texas School of Law could not use race as an admissions factor in order to achieve a diverse student body. The holding of the circuit court stands because the Supreme Court refused to hear the case.

This decision in effect overruled Justice Powell's opinion in *Bakke,* which held that universities can take account of an applicant's race in some circumstances. He asserted that the goal of achieving a diverse student body was permissible under the Constitution.

XI. *TENNESSEE V. LANE* (2004)

Historically, disabled people have been thought of as possessed or wicked. Often they were scorned and shut off from society in mental institutions. Today, however, the medical model is the dominant perspective that "those with disabilities have some kind of physical, mental, or emotional defect that not surprisingly limits their performance." Essentially, we don't expect those who are "flawed" to function as well as other people.[21]

Disabled people constantly face discrimination resulting in exclusion from housing, public buildings, and public transportation. This has prevented them from attending school, visiting museums, shopping, or living without assistance.

The 1990 Americans with Disabilities Act forbids discrimination against persons with disabilities in three key areas of public life. Title I covers employment; Title II encompasses public services, programs, and activities; and Title III covers public accommodations. In 2001 Casey Martin sued the PGA Tour,[22] under the public accommodations provisions of Title III to allow him to play golf on the tour while riding a golf cart because he suffers from Klippel-Trenaunay-Weber syndrome, a degenerative circulatory disorder that causes severe pain in his lower leg. Martin won his case when the Court held that the PGA walking rule was not compromised by allowing him to use a cart.

The provisions of Title II, which include access to the services, programs, or activities of a public entity such as a courthouse are questioned in *Tennessee v. Lane.* In this case, residents of the state who are paraplegics sued Tennessee under Title II of the Americans with Disabilities Act (ADA) because they were denied access to a courthouse. Because this case involves a suit by an individual against a state, the Supreme Court has to consider the provisions of the Eleventh Amendment,[23] which provides state immunity against suits by citizens seeking equity and the enforcement clause, Section 5 of the Fourteenth Amendment.[24] After Tennessee was unsuccessful in getting the case dismissed because the plaintiffs sought damages, the case went to the Supreme Court. This issue then became an interpretation of Congress's power to enforce by appropriate legislation (Section 5) the guarantee that "no State shall make or enforce any law which shall abridge the privileges or immunities of citizens of the United States; nor shall any State deprive any person of life, liberty, or property, without due process of law; nor deny to any person within its jurisdiction the equal protection of the laws."

In 1998 George Lane and Beverly Jones, both paraplegics who use wheelchairs, filed suit against the state of Tennessee and a number of counties under Title II of the ADA, which states that no qualified individual with a disability shall, because of the disability be excluded from participation or denied the benefits of the services, programs, or activities of a public entity. Both parties claimed that they were denied access to the state court system because of their disability. Lane alleged that he was forced to appear to answer criminal charges on the second floor of a county courthouse. The courthouse had no elevator. In his first court appearance Lane crawled up two flights to reach the courtroom. When Lane had to return for a second time, he refused to crawl or to be carried to the courtroom. He was arrested and sent to jail for failure to appear for his hearing. Jones, a certified court reporter, claimed that she had not been able to obtain work because she could not gain access to several county courthouses.

The court's decision addressed these key questions:

1. Is Title II a valid exercise of Congress's Section 5 enforcement powers under the Fourteenth Amendment?
2. Does Title II enforce a variety of basic constitutional guarantees such as the right of access to the courts?
3. Does Title II validly enforce these constitutional rights?
4. Is Title II an appropriate response to this history of discrimination and pattern of unequal treatment?

Excerpts from the Supreme Court Decision in *Tennessee v. George Lane et al.*[25]

Mr. Justice Stevens delivered the opinion of the Court:

> The ADA was passed by large majorities in both Houses of Congress after decades of deliberation and investigation into the need for comprehensive legislation to address discrimination against persons with disabilities.
>
> . . . Title II, Sections 12131–12134, prohibits any public entity from discrimination against "qualified" persons with disabilities in the provision or operation of public services, programs, or activities. The Act defines the term "public entity" to include state and local governments. . . .
>
> Title II, like Title I, seeks to enforce this prohibition on irrational disability discrimination. But it also seeks to enforce a variety of other basic constitutional guarantees, infringements of which are subject to more searching judicial review. . . . These rights include some, like the right of access to the courts at issue in this case, that are protected by the Due Process Clause of the Fourteenth Amendment. The Due Process Clause [as] applied to the States via the Fourteenth Amendment both guarantee to a criminal defendant such as respondent Lane the "right to be present at all stages of the trial where his absence might frustrate the fairness of the proceedings." . . . The Due Process Clause also requires the States to afford certain civil litigants a "meaningful opportunity to be heard" by removing

obstacles to their full participation in judicial proceedings. . . . And, finally, we have recognized that members of the public have a right of access to criminal proceedings secured by the First Amendment.

. . . It is not difficult to perceive the harm that Title II is designed to address. Congress enacted Title II against a backdrop of pervasive unequal treatment in the administration of state services and programs, including systematic deprivations of fundamental rights.

. . . With respect to the particular services at issue in this case, Congress learned that many individuals, in many States across the country, were being excluded from courthouses and court proceedings by reason of their disabilities. A report before Congress showed that some 76% of public services and programs housed in state-owned buildings were inaccessible to and unusable by persons with disabilities. . . .

The conclusion that Congress drew from this body of evidence is set forth in the text of the ADA itself: "Discrimination against individuals with disabilities persists in such critical areas as . . . education, transportation, communication, recreation, institutionalization, health services, voting, and access to public services. . . ." This finding, together with the extensive record of disability discrimination that underlies it, makes clear beyond peradventure that inadequate provision of public services and access to public facilities was an appropriate subject for prophylactic legislation.

. . . Whatever might be said about Title II's other applications, the question presented in this case is not whether Congress can validly subject the States to private suits for money damages for failing to provide reasonable access to hockey rinks, or even to voting booths, but whether Congress had the power under Section 5 to enforce the constitutional right of access to the courts. Because we find that Title II unquestionably is valid Section 5 legislation as it applies to the class of cases implicating the accessibility of judicial services, we need go no further.

. . . Title II's affirmative obligation to accommodate persons with disabilities in the administration of justice cannot be said to be "so out of proportion to a supposed remedial or preventive object that it cannot be understood as responsive to, or designed to prevent, unconstitutional behavior. . . . It is, rather, a reasonable prophylactic measure, reasonably targeted to a legitimate end.

For these reasons, we conclude that Title III, as it applies to the class of cases implicating the fundamental right of access to the courts, constitutes a valid exercise of Congress's Section 5 authority to enforce the guarantees of the Fourteenth Amendment.

XII. THE MICHIGAN CASES

Gratz v. Bollinger et al. (2003) and *Grutter v. Bollinger et al.* (2003) considered admission standards for the University of Michigan's undergraduate program and its Law School. This marked the first time in the 25 years since the *Bakke* decision that the Supreme Court had considered the legal status of race-conscious admissions. In *Bakke,* Justice Powell held that race could be taken into consideration if it served a compelling government interest. He then held that the goal of achieving a diverse student body was a circumstance where race could be considered. However, the *Bakke* decision generated six separate opinions, but no majority opinion.[26]

The University of Michigan cases question whether Justice Powell's opinion set a precedent for considering diversity a constitutional justification for race-conscious admissions.

Gratz v. Bollinger et al. (2003)

Jennifer Gratz and Patrick Hamacher were both white residents of Michigan who applied for admission to the University of Michigan's College of Literature, Science, and the Arts (LSA). Both were considered qualified for admission. However, both were denied early admission, and upon further review neither was admitted to the university. The university's Undergraduate Admissions Office uses a written guideline system that includes such factors as high school grades, standardized test scores, the quality of the high school, curriculum strength, geography, alumni relationships, leadership, and race. Although the guidelines have changed since 1995, the university consistently considered African Americans, Hispanics, and Native Americans as "underrepresented minorities." The guidelines provided that all applicants from an underrepresented racial or ethnic minority group were automatically given 20 points out of the 100 needed for admission. The university never disputed the claim that practically every qualified applicant from these groups was admitted.

In 1997, Gratz and Hamacher filed a class-action suit alleging violation of their rights under the Fourteenth Amendment and the Civil Rights Act of 1964. The Equal Protection Clause of the Fourteenth Amendment provides that a state cannot act unfairly or arbitrarily toward or discriminate against a person within its jurisdiction because the individual has "the equal protection of the laws." Title VI of the Civil Rights Act prohibits discrimination on the grounds of race, color, or national origin against anyone participating in a program or activity which receives federal financial assistance.

The Court's decision addressed these key questions:

1. Under strict scrutiny, does the university's use of race in its current admission policy constitute narrowly tailored measures that further compelling government interests?
2. Does the undergraduate admission policy violate the Equal Protection Clause of the Fourteenth Amendment?
3. Does the undergraduate admission policy violate Title VI of the Civil Rights Act of 1964?

Excerpts from the Supreme Court Decision in *Gratz v. Bollinger et al.* (2003)[27]

Chief Justice Rehnquist delivered the opinion of the Court:

> . . . Because the University's use of race in its current freshman admission policy is not narrowly tailored to achieve respondents' asserted interest in diversity, the policy violates the Equal Protection Clause. For the reasons set forth in *Grutter v. Bollinger* . . . the Court has today rejected petitioners' argument that diversity cannot constitute a compelling state interest. However, the Court finds that the University's current policy, which automatically distributes 20 points, or one-fifth of the points needed to guarantee admission, to every single "underrepresented minority" applicant solely because of race, is not narrowly tailored to achieve educational diversity. In *Bakke,* Justice Powell

> explained his view that it would be permissible for a university to employ an admissions program in which "race or ethnic background may be deemed a 'plus' in a particular applicant's file" . . . he emphasized, however, the importance of considering each particular applicant as an individual, assessing all of the qualities that individual possesses, and in turn, evaluating that individual's ability to contribute to the unique setting of higher education. The admissions program Justice Powell described did not contemplate that any single characteristic automatically ensured a specific and identifiable contribution to a university's diversity. . . . The current LSA policy does not provide the individualized consideration Justice Powell contemplated. The only consideration that accompanies the 20-point automatic distribution to all applicants from underrepresented minorities is a factual review to determine whether an individual is a member of one of these minority groups. Moreover, unlike Justice Powell's example, where the race of a "particular black applicant" could be "considered without being decisive" . . . the LSA's 20-point distribution has the effect of making "the factor of race . . . decisive" for virtually every minimally qualified underrepresented minority applicant. The fact that the LSA has created the possibility of an applicant's file being flagged for individualized consideration only emphasizes the flaws of the University's system as a whole when compared to that described by Justice Powell. The record does not reveal precisely how many applications are flagged, but it is undisputed that consideration is the exception and not the rule in the LSA's program. Also, this individualized review is only provided *after* admissions counselors automatically distribute the University's version of a "plus" that makes race a decisive factor for virtually every minimally qualified underrepresented minority applicant. . . .

> Nothing in Justice Powell's *Bakke* opinion signaled that a university may employ whatever means it desires to achieve diversity without regard to the limits imposed by strict scrutiny. Because the University's use of race in its current freshman admission policy violates the Equal Protection Clause, it also violates Title VI.

Grutter v. Bollinger et al. (2003)

Barbara Grutter, a white Michigan resident, applied to the University of Michigan Law School in 1996. She was originally placed on a waiting list but was ultimately not admitted. She alleged that her application was rejected because the Law School used race as a "predominant" factor, which gave applicants from certain minority groups "a significantly greater chance of admission than students with similar credentials from disfavored racial groups." The Law School asserted that it had a compelling interest in obtaining the educational benefits derived from a diverse student body. Law School officials contended that the admissions staff was not directed to admit a specific percentage or number of minority students, but rather to consider race among several factors. The goal was to obtain a "critical mass" of underrepresented minority students in order to realize the educational benefits of a diverse student body. The critical mass concept was never stated in terms of a fixed number, or percentage, or even a range of numbers or percentages. Admission officers acknowledged that minority group membership was a strong factor in the acceptance decisions and that applicants from minority groups were given large allowance for admission compared to applicants from nonfavored groups. However, it was asserted that race was not considered the predominant factor in the Law School's admission formula.

The Court's decision addressed these key questions:

1. Was race a predominant or a plus factor when reviewing the files of Law School applicants?
2. Did the Law School have a compelling interest in creating a diverse study body?
3. Does seeking a critical mass of minority students equal a quota?
4. Does the Law School admissions policy violate the Fourteenth Amendment and Title VI of the Civil Rights Act of 1964?

Excerpts from the Supreme Court Decision in *Grutter v. Bollinger et al.*[28]

Justice O'Connor delivered the opinion of the Court:

We last addressed the use of race in public higher education over 25 years ago. In the landmark *Bakke* case, we reviewed a racial set-aside program that reserved

16 out of 100 seats in a medical school class for members of certain minority groups. . . . The decision produced six separate opinions, none of which commanded a majority of the Court. . . . The only holding for the court in *Bakke* was that a "State has a substantial interest that legitimately may be served by a properly devised admissions program involving the competitive consideration of race and ethnic origin."

. . . Public and private universities across the nation have modeled their own admissions programs on Justice Powell's views on permissible race-conscious policies.

. . . Justice Powell approved the university's use of race to further only one interest: "the attainment of a diverse student body" . . . Justice Powell grounded his analysis in the academic freedom that long has been viewed as a special concern of the First Amendment. Justice Powell emphasized that nothing less than the "'nation's future depends upon leaders trained through wide exposure' to the ideas and mores of students as diverse as this Nation of many peoples." . . .

Both "tradition and experience lend support to the view that the contribution of diversity is substantial."

Justice Powell was, however, careful to emphasize that in his view race "is only one element in a range of factors a university properly may consider in attaining the goal of a heterogeneous student body." . . .

For Justice Powell "[i]t is not an interest in simple ethnic diversity, in which a specified percentage of the student body is in effect guaranteed to be members of selected ethnic groups," that can justify the use of race. . . . Rather, "[t]he diversity that furthers a compelling state interest encompasses a far broader array of qualifications and characteristics of which racial or ethnic origin is but a single though important element."

. . . We have held that all racial classifications imposed by government "must be analyzed by a reviewing court under strict scrutiny." . . . This means that such classifications are constitutional only if they are narrowly tailored to further compelling governmental interests.

. . . The Law School asks us to recognize, in the context of higher education, a compelling state interest in student body diversity.

. . . Today, we hold that the Law School has a compelling interest in attaining a diverse student body.

. . . Our conclusion that the Law School has a compelling interest in a diverse student body is informed by our view that attaining a diverse student body is at the heart of the Law School's proper institutional mission, and that "good faith" on the part of a university is "presumed" absent "a showing to the contrary."

. . . The Law School's concept of critical mass is defined by reference to the educational benefits that diversity is designed to produce.

These benefits are substantial. As the District Court emphasized, the Law School's admissions policy promotes "cross-racial understanding," helps to break down racial stereotypes, and "enables [students] to better understand persons of different races."

. . . The Law School has determined, based on its experience and expertise, that a "critical mass" of underrepresented minorities is necessary to further its compelling interest in securing the educational benefits of a diverse student body.

. . . To be narrowly tailored, a race-conscious admissions program cannot use a quota system—it cannot "insulat[e] each category of applicants with certain desired qualifications from competition with all other applicants" (opinion of Justice Powell). Instead, a university may consider race or ethnicity only as a "'plus' in a particular applicant's file," without "insulat[ing] the individual from comparison with all other candidates for the available seats."

. . . We find that the Law School's admissions program bears the hallmarks of a narrowly tailored plan. As Justice Powell made clear in *Bakke,* truly individualized consideration demands that race be used in a flexible, nonmechanical way.

. . . We are satisfied that the Law School's admissions program . . . does not operate as a quota. Properly understood, a "quota" is a program in which a certain fixed number or proportion of opportunities are "reserved exclusively for certain minority groups."

. . . The Law School's goal of attaining a critical mass of underrepresented minority students does not transform its program into a quota. . . . "[S]ome attention to numbers," without more, does not transform a flexible admissions system into a rigid quota.

. . . The Law School affords this individualized consideration to applicants of all races. There is no policy, either *de jure* or *de facto,* of automatic acceptance or rejection based on any single "soft" variable. Unlike the program at issue in *Gratz v. Bollinger,* the Law School awards no mechanical, predetermined diversity "bonuses" based on race or ethnicity.

. . . What is more, the Law School actually gives substantial weight to diversity factors besides race.

The Law School frequently accepts nonminority applicants with grades and test scores lower than underrepresented minority applicants (and other nonminority applicants) who are rejected.

. . . We agree that, in the context of its individualized inquiry into the possible diversity contributions of all applicants, the Law School's race-conscious admissions program does not unduly harm nonminority applicants.

. . . the Equal Protection Clause does not prohibit the Law School's narrowly tailored use of race in admissions decisions to further a compelling interest in obtaining the educational benefits that flow from a diverse student body.

XIII. *RICCI V. DESTEFANO* (2009)

Racial equity has been an issue in hiring and the promotion of municipal workers such as teachers, police officers, and firefighters since the Civil Rights legislation of 1964. In this case in New Haven, Connecticut, when firefighters sought promotion, questions were raised about racially biased tests and the history of discrimination in the firefighting profession, as well as disparate treatment and impact.

In 2003, the city of New Haven used written and oral examinations to identify which firefighters would be promoted to the rank of lieutenant or captain. Under the "Rule of Three," the City was required to fill vacancies by selecting a candidate from the top three scorers on the list. Application of this rule excluded all black firefighters from promotion because they did not score high enough on the examination. The test results were reviewed by an independent review board because the results created a racial disparity, which could mean that the test was racially biased. The review board split evenly on whether to certify the examination results. The City then decided that no one would be promoted on the basis of the test results. When the city decided not to certify the test results, white and Hispanic firefighters who had passed the exam but were denied promotion, sued the City, alleging that by discarding the test results they had been discriminated against under Title VII of the 1964 Civil Rights Act.

The Court's divided opinion addressed these questions:

1. Can New Haven justify discrimination because it fears a lawsuit?
2. Did the City's action of discarding the test results violate Title VII of the Civil Rights Act?

Excerpts from the Supreme Court Decision in *Ricci v. DeStefano* (2009)[29]

Justice Kennedy delivered the opinion of the Court:

In 2003, 118 New Haven firefighters took examinations to qualify for promotion to the rank of lieutenant or captain. Promotion examinations in New Haven (or City) were infrequent, so the stakes were high. . . .

Certain white and Hispanic firefighters who likely would have been promoted based on their good test performance sued the City . . . the suit alleges that, by discarding the test results, the City . . . discriminated against the plaintiffs based on their race, in violation of . . . Title VII of the Civil Rights Act of 1964. . . .

. . . Title VII of the Civil Rights Act of 1964 . . . as amended, prohibits employment discrimination on the basis of race, color, religion, sex, or national origin. Title VII prohibits both intentional discrimination (known as "disparate treatment") as well as, in some cases, practices that are not intended to discriminate but in fact have a disproportionately adverse effect on minorities (known as "disparate impact").

As enacted in 1964, Title VII's principal nondiscrimination provision held employers liable only for disparate treatment. . . .

Our analysis begins with this premise: The City's actions would violate the disparate-treatment prohibition of Title VII absent some valid defense. All the evidence demonstrates that the City chose not to certify the examination results because of the statistical disparity based on race—i.e., how minority candidates had performed when compared to white candidates. As the District Court put it, the City rejected the test results because "too many whites and not enough minorities would be promoted were the lists to be certified."

The City argues that, even under the strong-basis-in evidence standard, its decision to discard the examination results were permissible under Title VII. . . .

We conclude there is no-strong-basis-in-evidence to establish that the test was deficient. . . .

. . . Fear of litigation alone cannot justify an employer's reliance on race to the detriment of individuals who passed the examinations and qualified for promotions. The City's discarding the test results was impermissible under Title VII. . . .

. . . [T]he City was not entitled to disregard the test based solely on the racial disparity in the results.

Justice Ginsburg, with whom Justice Stevens, Justice Souter, and Justice Breyer join, dissenting:

In assessing claims of race discrimination, [c]ontext matters . . . Congress extended Title VII of the Civil Rights Act of 1964 to cover public employment. At that time, municipal fire departments across the county, including New Haven's pervasively discriminated against minorities . . . . The white firefighters who scored high on New Haven's promotion exams understandably attract this Court's sympathy. But they had no vested right to promotion. Nor have other persons received promotions in preference to them.

. . . The Court's recitation of the facts leaves out important parts of the story. Firefighting is a profession in which the legacy of racial discrimination casts an especially long shadow. In extending Title VII to state and local government employers in 1972, Congress took note of a U.S. Commission on Civil Rights (USCCR) report finding racial discrimination in municipal employment even "more pervasive than in the private sector." . . . According to the report, overt racism was partly to blame but so too was a failure on the part of municipal employers to apply merit-based employment principles. In making hiring and promotion decisions, public employers often "rel[ied] on criteria unrelated to job performance," including nepotism or political patronage. . . . Such flawed selection methods served to entrench preexisting racial hierarchies. The USCCR report singled out police and fire departments for having "[b]arriers to equal employment . . . greater . . . than in any other area of State or local government," with African Americans "hold[ing] almost no position in the officer ranks." . . . (Racial minorities are underrepresented in the fire departments in nearly every community in which they live.")

The city of New Haven (City) was no exception. In the early 1970s, African Americans and Hispanics composed 30 percent of the New Haven's population, but only 3.6 percent of the City's 502 firefighters. The racial disparity in the officer ranks was even more pronounced. . . .

. . . It is against this backdrop of entrenched inequality that the promotion process at issue in this litigation should be assessed. . . .

. . . The (test) results showed significant racial disparities. . . .

These stark disparities, the Court acknowledges, sufficed to state *prima facie* case under Title VII disparate-impact provision. . . . New Haven thus had cause for concern about the prospect of Title VII litigation and liability. . . .

. . . Between January and March 2004, the Civil Service Board (CSB) held five public meetings to consider the proper course. . . .

At its fourth meeting, the CSB solicited the views of three individuals with testing-related expertise. . . . Dr. Christopher Hornick, an industrial/organizational psychology consultant with 25 years' experience with police and firefighter test, described the exam results as having "relatively high adverse impact." . . .

Specifically, Hornick questioned New Haven's union-prompted 60/40 written/oral examination structure, noting the availability of "different types of testing procedures that are much more valid in terms of identifying the best potential supervisors in [the] fire department."

Respondents were no doubt conscious of race during their decision making process, the court acknowledged, but this did not mean they had engaged in racially disparate treatment. The conclusion they had reached and the action thereupon taken were race-neutral in this sense: "[A]ll the test results were discarded. . . . .

. . . Title VII . . . aims to eliminate all forms of employment discrimination, unintentional as well as deliberate. Until today . . . . this Court has never questioned the constitutionality of the disparate-impact component of Title VII. . . .

. . . This Court has repeatedly emphasized that the statute "should not be read to thwart" efforts at voluntary compliance . . . (Title VII permits employers and unions voluntarily to make use of reasonable race-conscious affirmative action") . . .

Applying what I view as the proper standard to the record thus far made, I would hold that New Haven had ample cause to believe its selection process was flawed and not justified by business necessity. Judged by that standard, petitioners have not shown that New Haven's failure to certify the exam results violated Title VII's disparate-treatment provision. . . .

Chief among the City's problems was the very nature of the tests for promotion. In choosing to use written and oral exams with a 60/40 weighting, the City simply adhered to the union's preference and apparently gave no consideration to whether the weighting was likely to identify the most qualified fire-officer candidates. There is strong reason to think it was not.

Relying heavily on written tests to select fire officers is a questionable practice . . . successful fire officers, the City's description of the position make clear, must have the "[a]bility to lead personnel effectively, maintain discipline, promote harmony, exercise sound judgment, and cooperate with other officials." . . . these qualities are not well measured by written tests. . . .

It is indeed regrettable that the City's noncertification decision would have required all candidates to go through another selection process. But it would have been more regrettable to rely on flawed exams to shut out candidates who may well have the command presence and other qualities needed to excel as fire officers. . . .

XIV. *U.S. V. WINDSOR* (2013)

The *Windsor* case is the most recent in a line of cases that consider the rights of same-sex couples. Previous cases had pertained to conduct, rather than rights. For example, in 2004, *Lawrence and Gartner v. Texas* questioned the legality of Texas's "homosexual conduct" law, which had criminalized sexual relations for same-sex couples, but not for heterosexual couples engaging in the same behavior. The Supreme Court held that the Texas statute violated the Constitution's Due Process Clause. The decision found that as adults, Lawrence and Garner were free to express their rights to engage in private sexual intimacy.

The fight for the rights of gays had been growing since the 1990s. In 1993, Hawaii was poised to legalize same-sex marriage. Congress responded quickly by passing legislation to prevent claims of federal recognition by other states following Hawaii. The result was the 1996 Defense of Marriage Act (DOMA).

The *Windsor* case challenged the provisions of the Defense of Marriage Act, which defined marriage as "a legal union between one man and one woman as husband and wife, and the word 'spouse' to a person of the opposite sex who is a husband or a wife." Section 3 of the Act codified that the federal government would not recognize same-sex marriages. This prohibited same-sex couples from receiving insurance benefits for government employees, Social Security survivors' benefits, as well as filing joint tax returns.

Edith Windsor and Thea Spyer were residents of New York, lawfully married in 2007 in Ontario, Canada. They then returned to their home in New York City. When Spyer died in 2009 she left her estate to Windsor. Windsor then tried to claim the estate tax exemption for surviving spouses, but was barred by the Defense of Marriage Act, a federal law. This act "excluded a same-sex partner from the definition of 'spouse' as that term is used in federal statutes." Windsor paid the taxes, but also filed suit to test the constitutionality of this provision.

The Court's decision addressed these key questions:

1. Can the federal government set aside its tradition of deference to the states on issues pertaining to marriage?
2. Does DOMA seek to injure a class?
3. Does Section 3 of DOMA violate the Fifth Amendment which guarantees equal protection to persons who are legally married under the laws of their state?
4. Did the Windsor decision effectively kill DOMA?
5. Will Windsor get a refund from the federal government?

Excerpts from the Supreme Court Decision in *U.S. v. Windsor*[30]

Justice Kennedy delivered the opinion of the court:

Section 3 of DOMA provides as follows: . . . [T]he word "marriage" means only a legal union between one man and one woman as husband and wife, and the word "spouse" refers only to a person of the opposite sex who is a husband or a wife. 1 U.S.C. Section 7.

The provision does not by its terms forbid States from enacting laws permitting same-sex marriages or civil unions or providing state benefits to residents in that status. The enactment's comprehensive definition of marriage for purposes of all federal statutes control[s] over 1,000 federal laws in which marital or spousal status is addressed as a matter of federal law.

. . . The state of New York deems their Ontario marriage to be a valid one.

. . . Windsor paid $363,053 in estate taxes and sought a refund. The Internal Revenue Service denied the refund, concluding that, under DOMA Windsor was not a "surviving spouse." . . . [Windsor] contended that DOMA violates the guarantee of equal protection, as applied to the Federal Government through the Fifth Amendment.

. . . The District Court ruled against the United States. It held that Section 3 of DOMA is unconstitutional and ordered the Treasury to refund the tax with interest. . . . Windsor has not received her refund, and the Executive Branch continues to enforce Section 3 of DOMA.

. . . [H]er injury (failure to obtain a refund allegedly required by law) was concrete, persisting, and unredressed.

. . . [S]ome States concluded that same-sex marriage ought to be given recognition and validity in the law for those same-sex couples who wish to define themselves by their commitment to each other. The limitation of lawful marriage to heterosexual couples, which for centuries had been deemed both necessary and fundamental, came to be seen in New York and certain other States as an unjust exclusion.

. . . By history and tradition the definition and regulation of marriage . . . has been treated as being within the authority and realm of the separate States. Yet it is further established that Congress, in enacting discrete statutes, can make determinations that bear on marital rights and privileges. Just this Term the Court upheld the authority of the Congress to preempt state laws. . . .

. . . DOMA . . . enacts a directive applicable to over 1,000 federal statutes and the whole realm of federal regulations. And its operation is directed to a class of persons that the laws of New York, and 11 other States, have sought to protect.

. . . The significance of state responsibilities for the definition and regulation of marriage dates to the Nation's beginning; for "when the Constitution was adopted the common understanding was that the domestic relations of husband and wife and parent and child were matters reserved to the States". . . Here the State's decision to give this class of persons the right to marry conferred upon them a dignity and status of immense import.

. . . What the State of New York treats as alike the federal law deems unlike by a law designed to injure the same class the State seeks to protect.

. . . Private, consensual sexual intimacy between two adult persons of the same sex may not be punished by the State, and it can form "but one element in a personal bond that is more enduring" (*Lawrence v. Texas,* 539 U.S. 558, 567 [2003]). By its recognition of the validity of same-sex marriages performed in other jurisdictions and then by authorizing same-sex unions and same-sex marriages, New York sought to give further protection and dignity to that bond. For same-sex couples who wished to be married, the State acted to give their lawful conduct a lawful status.

. . . DOMA seeks to injure the very class New York seeks to protect. By doing so it violates basic due process and equal protection principles applicable to the Federal Government. As the title and dynamics of the bill indicate, its purpose is to discourage enactment of state same-sex marriage laws and to restrict the freedom and choice of couples married under those laws if they are enacted. The congressional goal was "to put a thumb on the scales and influence a state's decision as to how to shape its own marriage laws." . . .

DOMA's principal effect is to identify a subset of state-sanctioned marriages and make them unequal. . . .

This requires the Court to hold, as it now does, that DOMA is unconstitutional as a deprivation of the liberty of the person protected by the fifth Amendment of the Constitution.

Justice Alito and Justice Thomas joined in a dissent to parts II and III. Chief Justice Roberts also wrote a separate dissent.

XV. SCHUETTE V. COALITION TO DEFEND AFFIRMATIVE ACTION, INTEGRATION AND IMMIGRATION RIGHTS AND FIGHT FOR EQUALITY BY ANY MEANS NECESSARY (BAMN) (2013)

This case presents another perspective on the affirmative action debate. Although previous cases have focused on admissions policies, this case questions whether an amendment to the Michigan state constitution violated the Equal Protection Clause of the Fourteenth Amendment by banning race and sex-based discrimination in public university admissions.

The University of Michigan had been the focus of previous Supreme Court affirmative action cases. *Gratz v. Bollinger* in 2003 held that it was unconstitutional to award extra points to minorities in undergraduate admissions. *Grutter v. Bollinger* in 2003 held that the University of Michigan law school had "a compelling interest in attaining a diverse student body." It further stated that race could be one of the factors in the admissions process because it did "not unduly harm nonminority applicants."

In 2006, Michigan voters amended the state constitution "to ban affirmative action in public employment, education or contracting, except where it was necessary to comply with federal law."

The Court's decision addressed these key questions:

1. Does Michigan's constitutional amendment, which was approved by the voters, violate the Equal Protection clause of the Fourteenth Amendment?
2. Can voters prohibit consideration of racial preferences by passing a constitutional amendment?
3. Should a policy of granting race-based preferences be continued?

Excerpts from the Supreme Court Decision in *Schuette v. BAMN*[31]

Mr. Justice Kennedy delivered the opinion of the Court:

> The court in this case must determine whether an amendment to the Constitution of the State of Michigan, approved and enacted by its voters, is invalid under the Equal Protection Clause of the Fourteenth Amendment to the Constitution of the United States. . . .
>
> . . . Under the terms of the amendment, race-based preferences cannot be part of the admissions process for state universities. . . .

As noted, the amendment is in broad terms. Section 26 states, in relevant part, as follows:

1. The University of Michigan, Michigan State University, Wayne State University, and any other public college or university, community college, or school district shall not discriminate against, or grant preferential treatment to, any individual or group on the basis of race, sex, color, ethnicity, or national origin in the operation of public employment, public education, or public contracting.
2. The state shall not discriminate against, or grant preferential treatment to, any individual or group on the basis of race, sex, color, ethnicity, or national origin in the operation of public employment, public education, or public contracting.

. . . [T]he question here concerns not the permissibility of race-conscious admissions policies under the Constitution but whether, and in what manner, voters in the States may choose to prohibit the consideration of racial preferences in governmental decisions, in particular with respect to school admissions.

. . . That question is not how to address or prevent injury caused on account of race but whether voters may determine whether a policy of race-based preferences should be continued.

By approving proposal 2 and thereby adding Section 26 to their State Constitution, the Michigan voters exercised their privilege to enact laws as a basic exercise of their democratic power.

. . . What is at stake here is not whether injury will be inflicted but whether government can be instructed not to follow a course that entails, first, the definition of racial categories and, second, the grant of favored status to persons in some racial categories and not others. . . .

This case is not about how the debate about racial preferences should be resolved. It is about who may resolve it. . . . Democracy does not presume that some subjects are either too divisive or too profound for public debate.

The judgment of the Court of Appeals for the Sixth Circuit is reversed.

Justices Sotomayor and Justice Ginsburg dissented.

. . . Michigan does not assert that Section 26 satisfies a compelling state interest. That should settle the matter. . . .

. . . Race-sensitive admissions policies are now a thing of the past in Michigan after Section 26, even though—as experts agree and as research shows—those policies were making a difference in achieving educational diversity. . . .

Section 26 has already led to decreased minority enrollment at Michigan's public colleges and universities.

. . . This Court has recognized that diversity in education is paramount. With good reason. Diversity ensures that the next generation moves beyond the stereotypes. . . .

. . . But I cannot ignore the unfortunate outcome of today's decision: Short of amending the State Constitution, a Herculean task, racial minorities in Michigan are deprived of even an opportunity to convince Michigan's public colleges and universities to consider race in their admissions plans when other attempts to achieve racial diversity have proved unworkable, and those institutions are unnecessarily hobbled in their pursuit of a diverse student body.

. . . Today's decision eviscerates an important strand of our equal protection jurisprudence. For members of historically marginalized groups, which rely on the federal courts to protect their constitutional rights, the decision can hardly bolster hope for a vision of democracy that preserves for all the right to participate meaningfully and equally in self-government.

NOTES

1. *Privileges and immunities* refer to the ability of one state to discriminate against the citizens of another state. A resident of one state cannot be denied legal protection, access to the courts, or property rights in another state.
2. In *Smith v. Allwright,* 321 U.S. 649 (1944), the Supreme Court held that a 1927 Texas law that authorized political parties to establish criteria for membership in the state Democratic party violated the Fifteenth Amendment. In effect, the criteria excluded nonwhites from the Democratic party. Since only party members could vote in the primary election, the result was a whites-only primary. The Democratic party so dominated politics in the southern states after the Civil War that winning the primary was equivalent to winning the general election.
3. Americans of African descent have been called *blacks, Negroes, colored,* or *African Americans,* depending on the historical period.
4. 19 Howard 393 (1857).
5. The Nineteenth Amendment that was ratified on August 18, 1920, stated, "The right of citizens of the United States to vote shall not be denied or abridged by the United States or by any state on account of sex. Congress shall have the power to enforce this article by appropriate legislation."
6. 21 Wallace 162 (1875).
7. Crozier, "Constitutionality of Discrimination Based on Sex," 15 *B.U.L. Review,* 723, 727–28 (1935) as quoted in William Hodes, "Women and the Constitution: Some Legal History and a New Approach to the Nineteenth Amendment," *Rutgers Law Review,* Vol. 25, 1970, p. 27.
8. Hodes, p. 45.
9. Gunnar Myrdal, *An American Dilemma: The Negro Problem and Modern Democracy.* New York: Harper and Row (2nd ed. 1962 [1944]), pp. 1073–74, as quoted in Hodes, p. 29. This same biblical ground has yielded the idea that a woman is an extension of her husband and his status.
10. The states under military rule were Virginia, North Carolina, South Carolina, Georgia, Florida, Tennessee, Alabama, Mississippi, Texas, Louisiana, and Arkansas.
11. The term *colored* was used in Louisiana to describe persons of mixed race who had some African ancestry.
12. 163 U.S. 537 (1896).
13. 118 U.S. 356 (1886).
14. 112 U.S. 94 (1884).
15. Native Americans and slaves posed a problem when taking the census count, which was the basis for apportioning seats in the U.S. House of Representatives. Some states stood to lose representation if some of their slave or Native American population was not counted. Blacks were counted as three-fifths of a white man, and only those Native Americans who were taxed were counted.
16. Restrictive covenants were written in deeds restricting the use of the land. Covenants could prohibit the sale of land to nonwhites or non-Christians.
17. 347 U.S. 483 (1954).
18. 414 U.S. 563 (1974).
19. 411 U.S. 1 (1973).
20. 438 U.S. 265 (1978).
21. Paul C. Higgins, *Making Disability.* Springfield, IL: Charles C. Thomas (1992), pp. 26–27.
22. *PGA Tour, Inc. v. Casey Martin,* 532 U.S. 661.
23. The Eleventh Amendment pertains to suits against the states. The interpretation is that a state cannot be sued by U.S. citizens of that state or another state nor by a foreign country.
24. Section 5 of the Fourteenth Amendment grants Congress the power to enforce the provisions of this amendment by appropriate legislation.
25. 124 S. Ct. 1978 (2004).
26. Four justices supported the University of California's admissions program against all objections on the ground that the government could use race "to remedy disadvantages cast on minorities by past racial prejudice." Four other justices did not interpret *Bakke* on constitutional grounds, but instead struck down the program on statutory grounds. Justice Powell's position was against the set-aside admissions policy, but was also for "reversing the state court's injunction against any use of race whatsoever." The holding in *Bakke* was that a "State has a substantial interest that legitimately may be served by a properly devised admissions program involving the competitive consideration of race and ethnic origin."
27. 539 U.S. 244 (2003).
28. 539 U.S. 982 (2003).
29. 129 S. Ct. 2658.
30. *U.S. v. Windsor* 570 U.S. ___(2013).
31. *Schuette v. BAMN,* 527 U.S. ___(2014).

READING 38

Blink in Black and White

Malcolm Gladwell

Over the past few years, a number of psychologists have begun to look more closely at the role unconscious—or, as they like to call them, implicit—associations play in our beliefs and behavior, and much of their work has focused on a very fascinating tool called the Implicit Association Test (IAT). The IAT was devised by Anthony G. Greenwald, Mahzarin Banaji, and Brian Nosek, and it is based on a seemingly obvious—but none-theless quite profound—observation. We make connections much more quickly between pairs of ideas that are already related in our minds than we do between pairs of ideas that are unfamiliar to us. What does that mean? Let me give you an example. Below is a list of words. Take a pencil or pen and assign each name to the category to which it belongs by putting a check mark either to the left or to the right of the word. You can also do it by tapping your finger in the appropriate column. Do it as quickly as you can. Don't skip over words. And don't worry if you make any mistakes.

Male	Female
.... John ....
.... Bob ....
.... Amy ....
.... Holly ....
.... Joan ....
.... Derek ....
.... Peggy ....
.... Jason ....
.... Lisa ....
.... Matt ....
.... Sarah ....

Malcolm Gladwell is an author and staff writer for *The New Yorker.*

That was easy, right? And the reason that was easy is that when we read or hear the name "John" or "Bob" or "Holly," we don't even have to think about whether it's a masculine or a feminine name. We all have a strong prior association between a first name like John and the male gender, or a name like Lisa and things female.

That was a warm-up. Now let's complete an actual IAT. It works like the warm-up, except that now I'm going to mix two entirely separate categories together. Once again, put a check mark to either the right or the left of each word, in the category to which it belongs.

Male or Career	Female or Family
.... Lisa ....
.... Matt ....
.... Laundry ....
.... Entrepreneur ....
.... John ....
.... Merchant ....
.... Bob ....
.... Capitalist ....
.... Holly ....
.... Joan ....
.... Home ....
.... Corporation ....
.... Siblings ....
.... Peggy ....
.... Jason ....
.... Kitchen ....
.... Housework ....
.... Parents ....
.... Sarah ....
.... Derek ....

My guess is that most of you found that a lit-tle harder, but that you were still pretty fast at putting the words into the right categories. Now try this:

Male or Family	Female or Career
.... Babies	....
.... Sarah	....
.... Derek	....
.... Merchant	....
.... Employment	....
.... John	....
.... Bob	....
.... Holly	....
.... Domestic	....
.... Entrepreneur	....
.... Office	....
.... Joan	....
.... Peggy	....
.... Cousins	....
.... Grandparents	....
.... Jason	....
.... Home	....
.... Lisa	....
.... Corporation	....
.... Matt	....

Did you notice the difference? This test was quite a bit harder than the one before it, wasn't it? If you are like most people, it took you a little longer to put the word "Entrepreneur" into the "Career" category when "Career" was paired with "Female" than when "Career" was paired with "Male." That's because most of us have much stronger mental associations between maleness and career-oriented concepts than we do between femaleness and ideas related to careers. "Male" and "Capitalist" go together in our minds a lot like "John" and "Male" did. But when the category is "Male or Family," we have to stop and think—even if it's only for a few hundred milliseconds—before we decide what to do with a word like "Merchant."

When psychologists administer the IAT, they usually don't use paper and pencil tests like the ones I've just given you. Most of the time, they do it on a computer. The words are flashed on the screen one at a time, and if a given word belongs in the left-hand column, you hit the letter *e,* and if the word belongs in the right-hand column, you hit the letter *i.* The advantage of doing the IAT on a computer is that the responses are measurable down to the millisecond, and those measurements are used in assigning the test taker's score. So, for example, if it took you a little bit longer to complete part two of the Work/Family IAT than it did part one, we would say that you have a moderate association between men and the workforce. If it took you a lot longer to complete part two, we'd say that when it comes to the workforce, you have a strong automatic male association.

One of the reasons that the IAT has become so popular in recent years as a research tool is that the effects it is measuring are not subtle; as those of you who felt yourself slowing down on the second half of the Work/Family IAT above can attest, the IAT is the kind of tool that hits you over the head with its conclusions. "When there's a strong prior association, people answer in between four hundred and six hundred milliseconds," says Greenwald. "When there isn't, they might take two hundred to three hundred milliseconds longer than that—which in the realm of these kinds of effects is huge. One of my cognitive psychologist colleagues described this as an effect you can measure with a sundial."

If you'd like to try a computerized IAT, you can go to www.implicit.harvard.edu. There you'll find several tests, including the most famous of all the IATs, the Race IAT. I've taken the Race IAT on many occasions, and the result always leaves me feeling a bit creepy. At the beginning of the test, you are asked what your attitudes toward blacks and whites are. I answered, as I am sure most of you would, that I think of the races as equal. Then comes the test. You're encouraged to complete it quickly. First comes the warm-up. A series of pictures of faces flash on the screen. When you see a black face, you press *e* and put it in the left-hand category. When you see a white face, you press *i* and put it in the right-hand category. It's *blink, blink, blink:* I didn't have to think at all. Then comes part one.

European American or Bad	African American or Good
.... Hurt ....
.... Evil ....
.... Glorious ....

.... Wonderful ....

And so on. Immediately, something strange happened to me. The task of putting the words and faces in the right categories suddenly became more difficult. I found myself slowing down. I had to think. Sometimes I assigned something to one category when I really meant to assign it to the other category. I was trying as hard as I could, and in the back of my mind was a growing sense of mortification. Why was I having such trouble when I had to put a word like "Glorious" or "Wonderful" into the "Good" category when "Good" was paired with "African American" or when I had to put the word "Evil" into the "Bad" category when "Bad" was paired with "European American"? Then came part two. This time the categories were reversed.

European American or Good	African American or Bad
.... Hurt ....
.... Evil ....
.... Glorious ....

.... Wonderful ....

And so on. Now my mortification grew still further. Now I was having no trouble at all.

Evil? *African American or Bad.*
Hurt? *African American or Bad.*
Wonderful? *European American or Good.*

I took the test a second time, and then a third time, and then a fourth time, hoping that the awful feeling of bias would go away. It made no difference.

It turns out that more than 80 percent of all those who have ever taken the test end up having pro-white associations, meaning that it takes them measurably longer to complete answers when they are required to put good words into the "Black" category than when they are required to link bad things with black people. I didn't do quite so badly. On the Race IAT, I was rated as having a "moderate automatic preference for whites." But then again, I'm half black. (My mother is Jamaican.)

So what does this mean? Does this mean I'm a racist, a self-hating black person? Not exactly. What it means is that our attitudes toward things like race or gender operate on two levels. First of all, we have our conscious attitudes. This is what we choose to believe. These are our stated values, which we use to direct our behavior deliberately. The apartheid policies of South Africa or the laws in the American South that made it difficult for African Americans to vote are manifestations of conscious discrimination, and when we talk about racism or the fight for civil rights, this is the kind of discrimination that we usually refer to. But the IAT measures something else. It measures our second level of attitude, our racial attitude on an *unconscious* level—the immediate, automatic associations that tumble out before we've even had time to think. We don't deliberately choose our unconscious attitudes. And . . . we may not even be aware of them. The giant computer that is our unconscious silently crunches all the data it can from the experiences we've had, the people we've met, the lessons we've learned, the books we've read, the movies we've seen, and so on, and it forms an opinion. That's what is coming out in the IAT.

The disturbing thing about the test is that it shows that our unconscious attitudes may be utterly incompatible with our stated conscious values. As it turns out, for example, of the fifty thousand African Americans who have taken the Race IAT so far, about half of them, like me, have stronger associations with whites than with blacks. How could we not? We live in North America, where we are surrounded every day by cultural messages linking white with good. "You don't choose to make positive associations with the dominant group," says Mahzarin Banaji, who teaches psychology at Harvard University and is one of the leaders in IAT research. "But you are required to. All around you, that group is being paired with good things. You open the newspaper and you turn on the television, and you can't escape it."

The IAT is more than just an abstract measure of attitudes. It's also a powerful predictor of how we act in certain kinds of spontaneous situations. If you have a strongly pro-white pattern of associations, for example, there is evidence that that will affect the way you behave in the presence of a black person. It's not going to affect what you'll choose to say or feel or do. In all likelihood, you won't be aware that you're behaving any differently than you would around a white person. But chances are you'll lean forward a little less, turn away slightly from him or her, close your body a bit, be a bit less expressive, maintain less eye contact, stand a little farther away, smile a lot less, hesitate and stumble over your words a bit more, laugh at jokes a bit less. Does that matter? Of course it does. Suppose the conversation is a job interview. And suppose the applicant is a black man. He's going to pick up on that uncertainty and distance, and that may well make him a little less certain of himself, a little less confident, and a little less friendly. And what will you think then? You may well get a gut feeling that the applicant doesn't really have what it takes, or maybe that he is a bit standoffish, or maybe that he doesn't really want the job. What this unconscious first impression will do, in other words, is throw the interview hopelessly off course.

Or what if the person you are interviewing is tall? I'm sure that on a conscious level we don't think that we treat tall people any differently from how we treat short people. But there's plenty of evidence to suggest that height—particularly in men—does trigger a certain set of very positive unconscious associations. I polled about half of the companies on the Fortune 500 list—the list of the largest corporations in the United States—asking each company questions about its CEO. Overwhelmingly, the heads of big companies are, as I'm sure comes as no surprise to anyone, white men, which undoubtedly reflects some kind of implicit bias. But they are also almost all tall: in my sample, I found that on average, male CEOs were just a shade under six feet tall. Given that the average American male is five foot nine, that means that CEOs as a group have about three inches on the rest of their sex. But this statistic actually understates the matter. In the U.S. population, about 14.5 percent of all men are six feet or taller. Among CEOs of Fortune 500 companies, that number is 58 percent. Even more striking, in the general American population, 3.9 percent of adult men are six foot two or taller. Among my CEO sample, almost a third were six foot two or taller.

The lack of women or minorities among the top executive ranks at least has a plausible explanation. For years, for a number of reasons having to do with discrimination and cultural patterns, there simply weren't a lot of women and minorities entering the management ranks of American corporations. So, today, when boards of directors look for people with the necessary experience to be candidates for top positions, they can argue somewhat plausibly that there aren't a lot of women and minorities in the executive pipeline. But this is not true of short people. It is possible to staff a large company entirely with white males, but it is not possible to staff a large company without short people. There simply aren't enough tall people to go around. Yet few of those short people ever make it into the executive suite. Of the tens of millions of American men below five foot six, a grand total of ten in my sample have reached the level of CEO, which says that being short is probably as much of a handicap to corporate success as being a woman or an African American. (The grand exception to all of these trends is American Express CEO Kenneth Chenault, who is both on the short side—five foot nine—and black . . .).

Is this a deliberate prejudice? Of course not. No one ever says dismissively of a potential CEO candidate that he's too short. This is quite clearly the kind of unconscious bias that the IAT picks up on. Most of us, in ways that we are not entirely aware of, automatically associate leadership ability with imposing physical stature. We have a sense of

what a leader is supposed to look like, and that stereotype is so powerful that when someone fits it, we simply become blind to other considerations. And this isn't confined to the executive suite. Not long ago, researchers who analyzed the data from four large research studies that had followed thousands of people from birth to adulthood calculated that when corrected for such variables as age and gender and weight, an inch of height is worth $789 a year in salary. That means that a person who is six feet tall but otherwise identical to someone who is five foot five will make on average $5,525 more per year. As Timothy Judge, one of the authors of the height-salary study, points out: "If you take this over the course of a 30-year career and compound it, we're talking about a tall person enjoying literally hundreds of thousands of dollars of earnings advantage." Have you ever wondered why so many mediocre people find their way into positions of authority in companies and organizations? It's because when it comes to even the most important positions, our selection decisions are a good deal less rational than we think. We see a tall person and we swoon. . . .

DISCUSSION QUESTIONS

1. Do you think some of your unconscious attitudes may be different from your stated conscious values? Why?

2. What are some examples of two words that are not usually thought of together?

NOTES

For more on the IAT, see Anthony G. Greenwald, Debbie E. McGhee, and Jordan L. K. Schwartz, "Measuring Individual Differences in Implicit Cognition: The Implicit Association Test," *Journal of Personality and Social Psychology* 74, no. 6 (1998): 1464–1480.

For an excellent treatment of the height issue, see Nancy Etcoff, *Survival of the Prettiest: The Science of Beauty* (New York: Random House, 1999), 172.

The height-salary study can be found in Timothy A. Judge and Daniel M. Cable, "The Effect of Physical Height on Workplace Success and Income: Preliminary Test of a Theoretical Model," *Journal of Applied Psychology* 89, no. 3 (June 2004): 428–441.

PERSONAL ACCOUNT

Just Like My Mama Said

I remember when I was just a little boy, my mother used to tell me, "Anthony you have to work twice as hard in life as everyone else, because being black means that you already have one strike against you." When I was growing up in a predominately black area, I did not know what she meant by this. Then we moved to an area that was filled with white people. I found myself constantly lagging behind, and I couldn't figure out why.

When I was 19 years old, I hit rock bottom and had nothing. I then remembered what my mama had said, and I began to work twice as hard as everyone else. I managed to afford my own apartment and eventually get married.

My wife is white, but her parents dislike me because of my color. They told her all the stereotypes about "the black male" and swore to her that I would follow suit. Soon after we moved in together, I was laid off from my job. I began to worry that she would think her parents were correct, so I tried to teach her about the black experience. I began to worry that her parents would negatively influence her and I would lose her. I was ready to give in and let her parents win, when I remembered something that my mama had said: "Sometimes you can't teach people; they have to learn on their own." Little did I know an appropriate lesson would soon follow.

As I was going through the want ads, I saw an advertisement for a job delivering pianos. The job paid more money than I had ever earned. I set up an interview for that evening. When my then-fiancée arrived home, I put on a shirt and a tie, grabbed my résumé, and headed for the interview. When I asked her if she thought I would get the job, she said, "I don't see why not. You work hard, you have good references, and you are enrolled in school." Needless to say I felt pretty good about my chances. I interviewed with a middle-aged white lady. The interview went very well. She nearly assured me that I had the job, but said that she just needed to run it by the store owner. She left and returned with the owner minutes later. He was a middle-aged man of apparently white and Asian descent. He looked at me for a few seconds, and our eyes met. Then he shook his head and said, "No this is not who I want for the job" and walked out. The lady and I dejectedly looked at each other. She attempted to make an excuse for him, but I told her, "Don't worry, it's not your fault." I walked out and told my fiancée what had happened. We rode home in silence. She had just gotten her first taste of what it is like to be black in America.

Anthony McNeill

READING 39

Safe Haven in America? Thirty Years after the Refugee Act of 1980

David W. Haines

As Senator Edward Kennedy began hearings on the bill that would become the Refugee Act of 1980, he commented for the record that "I believe our national policy of welcome to the homeless has served our country and our traditions well. But

---

David Haines is a professor of anthropology at George Mason University.

we are here this morning to explore how we can do this job better." The result of those hearings, the Refugee Act of 1980, formalized a system of refugee admissions and post-arrival assistance separate from the other immigration programs that are now largely in the Department of Homeland Security. The program is based on an allocation of roles among several federal agencies (especially the Departments of State and Health and Human Services), state and local governments, and a wide range of voluntary agencies. There is a system of annual consultations with the Congress on refugee admissions, and those admissions provide broad global representation in the origins of refugees and general adherence to international standards in the definition of who refugees are. This U.S. refugee program remains absolutely central to the international efforts at refugee resettlement, accounting for the great majority of formal refugee resettlement cases designated by the United Nations High Commissioner for Human Rights.

Despite its merits, however, this refugee program accounts for only a very small fraction of the number of immigrants legally admitted to the United States, roughly five percent over the last decade. There are many reasons for that small size, but one reason is that refugees are, by and large, different from Americans and often far more different from Americans than are other immigrants. Refugees are . . . a relatively unknown set of newcomers. The unknown represents potential uncertainty, and thus possible danger. There is no security in uncertainty. That is why, for example, the refugee program was shut down for four months after September 11, 2001, and why admissions for the next two years were more than cut in half (from 68,000 before 9/11 to 27,000 in 2002 and 28,000 in 2003). Only in 2009 did the number of annual admissions match that at the beginning of the decade.

The reasons why refugees are different are multiple. One reason is that refugees are often already different in their home countries: whether because of religion, race or ethnicity, social background, or political opinions. Refugees are rarely typical representatives of the countries from which they come. That is why they have to leave. Consider some recent examples. The most recent set of refugees from Somalia are hardly Somali in an ethnic sense; rather they are Bantu people trafficked north into Somalia as labor. The refugees coming from Myanmar (Burma) are not ethnic Burmese; rather they are hill tribes who have fled from a government dominated by ethnic Burmese who differ from them in culture, language, politics, and often religion. The Bhutanese refugees coming from Nepal are actually Nepalese in origin but, having migrated to Bhutan during colonial times, were not readily accepted when they fled back to Nepal after the outbreak of ethnic turmoil in Bhutan in 1990. These examples illustrate the complexity of refugee situations, but also suggest why Americans might feel uncertain about these new arrivals. After all, the Burmese refugees aren't ethnically Burman,

the Somalian refugees aren't ethnically Somali, and the Bhutanese refugees aren't Bhutanese.

Many other differences come from the disrupted nature of refugee lives, much less the frequent horrors of which they have been victims and witnesses. One consequence is that, unlike other immigrants, most refugees have limited opportunity for planning their migration. They must seize opportunities to flee on quick notice, must navigate complex geographical and political mazes, and must usually make such a sharp break with their home country that they cannot return. They thus tend to lack the social resources of kin and community on which most immigrants can rely, either by having those resources with them in the United States or at least being able to utilize them at a distance through visits and easy communication.

There are also economic consequences. Refugees, for example, often lack the three factors that a vast body of research indicates are crucial for finding work in America: English competence (and refugees sometimes lack literacy in any language); education (often limited and almost certainly interrupted for most refugees); and occupational skills (particularly a problem for refugees coming from agricultural backgrounds). So refugees are different not simply in a general cultural sense but also by often being rather poorly prepared to be new immigrants to America.

Refugees in America were not always so different. America was, after all, founded at least in part by refugees. So it would seem the idea of refuge—perhaps especially for freedom of religion—lies at the core of American consciousness. In that sense, the willingness of the contemporary U.S. refugee program to accept refugees of many different religions is quite encouragingly traditional—whether Buddhists from Southeast Asia, Muslims from Bosnia, Baha'is from Iran, or Hindus coming from camps in Nepal after fleeing from Bhutan. However, much of the early American attitude toward refugees was not so expansive. When the Acadians were expelled from Nova Scotia in the mid-1700s, for example, they found little refuge in the American colonies. They were, after all, both French and Catholic. In more recent times, there was little support for displaced persons after the Second World War until it was established how many of them were Christian rather than Jewish.

It was always easier when refugees were not so very different, whether the issues were linguistic and religious, or simple socioeconomic characteristics. When the U.S. accepted some 37,000 Hungarian refugees in 1956 and 1957, for example, a classified CIA memo would note the "happy" fact that these refugees were young, well-educated, and with non-agricultural occupations. They were, of course, "freedom fighters" so they were acceptable on political grounds. But they also looked like very good regular immigrants as well. They were not so different after all.

The more broadly inclusive U.S. refugee program that emerged from those hearings chaired by Kennedy three decades ago was, in retrospect, a rather significant change in the relationship between America and refugees, above all in the willingness to accept people who would not necessarily be such "happy" cases of young, educated people well positioned to survive and prosper in the United States. Many refugees, of course, continue to do very well in the United States but that is, in the context of the 1980 revisions, not the purpose of their admission. Indeed if the U.S. refugee program produced wonderful statistics about only cases of successful adaptation and refugee prosperity, it might well raise some suspicions about whether the program was truly responding to those in most need.

Overall, then, there are two key points to be made about the U.S. refugee program: first, it has some very meritorious features and, second, it is very small considering the overall size of U.S. immigration. With immigration reform once again coming into view, it is an opportune time to reconsider the relative importance and scale of refugee admissions in that larger immigration framework.

Since 2000, the number of refugee admissions has averaged about 50,000 per year. During that same period, overall legal immigration has averaged slightly over 1,000,000 per year. So refugee admissions have indeed been a very small part of overall immigration during this past decade. Three other numbers help put that general figure into clearer perspective. The first of those other numbers involves immigrants who are admitted because they have family connections in the United States. Since 2000, the number of family-related immigrants has averaged about 650,000 per year. That figure is high enough to permit the generalization that new Americans are largely people who are already connected to other Americans. That implies a certainty security. What else, after all, could provide such a certainty of new immigrants' commitment to America? What else could provide such a certainty of knowing they will be able to survive and prosper in the United States? Unlike refugees from new places and uncertain backgrounds, these immigrants are already family.

The second crucial number involves the undocumented. The Department of Homeland Security estimates that since 2000 the annual net entry of undocumented immigrants has been about 390,000 per year—although the effects of the recession on the undocumented population are still in dispute. These non-legal migrants must be savvy enough to cross the U.S. border undetected and to navigate through America without legal status, learning to work, live, and often raise children. They too are often already family: of other undocumented people, of legally resident foreigners, or of U.S. citizens. The generalization here is that America seems to want to fill its immediate labor needs without extending legal status. That makes for a simpler business deal that can be revoked as needed—for example, when there is a recession.

The third crucial number involves asylees. During that same period since 2000, the number of new asylees has averaged nearly 30,000 per year (compared to the roughly 50,000 refugee admissions per year). These asylees are, in legal terms, people who had already arrived in the United States and were then ruled to have met the same fear of persecution standard that applies to refugees. The difference might seem a simple one: whether someone is approved as a refugee and then comes to America, or whether someone comes to America first and is then recognized as meeting the refugee standard. However, that simple difference implies a rather different journey to America. Asylum applicants have to travel clandestinely and often along transit routes that pose danger, require money, and often take very long periods of time. That puts a preference on people who have the personal and financial resources to make such a journey and, because of the dangers, tends to select for the young, the single, and the disproportionately male.

Those requirements for asylum seekers are, of course, almost exactly the same as for other parts of the undocumented population with which they intermingle. Asylum seekers must have the skills and resources to reach U.S. borders, to cross them without documentation, and then live in the shadows at least long enough to find people who can help them develop a viable legal claim for asylum. They thus provide some measure of familiarity: they are already here and they know how America works. In many ways, that is a good thing. However, the increasing number of asylees compared to refugees raises the question of whether, in the humanitarian aspects of immigration policy, America is choosing to passively let people enter the country who can already pass this kind of competency test, rather than proactively reaching out beyond its borders for those most in need, whether or not they have the economic, social, and cultural resources to reach America on their own.

Back to the Refugee Act of 1980. After Senator Kennedy opened the initial hearings with an evocation of refugees as "one of the oldest and most important themes in our Nation's history," Senator Strom Thurmond proposed a different standard that also "has served us well." We should, he cautioned "weigh the cultural and demographic impact of the refugee problem" and "be guided by enlightened interest tempered with compassion." Thirty years later, we seem to have something of each of these two positions: following Kennedy: a refugee program that reaches out to all; following Thurmond, a refugee program small enough that it is but a "tempering" of the self-interest that guides most American immigration policy, whether it is the economic self-interest of having cheap labor, the social and cultural self-interest of emphasizing family ties, or the cognitive self-interest of avoiding the uncertainties of refugees with their unknown (and often unknowable) experiences, and their unpredictable futures.

DISCUSSION QUESTIONS

1. Why do you think the refugee program is so small compared to immigration? Why do you think refugee programs have not been expanded?
2. Why is the distinction between asylee and refugee an important one in understanding American immigration policy?
3. What unique difficulties and benefits would arise from the fact that refugees are more different from Americans than are other immigrants?

READING 40

Hispanics Are Forgotten in Civil Rights History

Nicholas Dauphine

Whenever civil rights has been covered in history class, or when I've seen a documentary or read an article concerning such, I have always been very aware of what is missing, and it is something that I am interested in and looking for. As an American of Hispanic descent, I never see any information related to my ethnicity's cause for civil rights. Where is the plight of Hispanics represented in the civil rights discussion and history of the United States?

In my household, I have heard the stories from older relatives about the treatment of Mexican-Americans in Texas in the 1900s. From what has been relayed to me, it was not much different from how black Americans were treated in Mississippi. Through my parents, I have heard of schools for Mexican children, separate drinking fountains, having to sit in the "black" balconies at movies, and not being able to go to restaurants and other establishments that were designated as "whites only."

But the public record of what the conditions were for the people of my background is severely

---

Nicholas D. Dauphine was a high school senior in San Antonio, Texas, when his essay won first prize in the LBJ Library "Civil Rights Today" essay contest. He is now a student at St. Mary's University in San Antonio, Texas.

lacking. It is as if we did not exist in this country between the Alamo in 1836 and the introduction of Freddie Prinze to the world in *Chico and the Man* in 1974.

When discussing civil rights milestones, where are the discussions about *Mendez, et al. v. Westminster School District of Orange County, et al.?* This 1946 case challenged the racial segregation that was occurring in Orange County, Calif., schools against Mexicans and Mexican-Americans. This landmark litigation was instrumental in repealing many of the segregationist provisions in California law, but it is not presented at all in the canon of civil rights milestones. In fact, even as a Hispanic, I had not heard of this case until President Barack Obama awarded the Presidential Medal of Freedom to Sylvia Mendez, the daughter of the lead plaintiff of the lawsuit, in February 2011, and I searched for who she was and why she was being honored.

When discussing civil rights milestones, where are the discussions about *Hernandez v. Texas?* This 1954 case established that the protection granted by the 14th Amendment of the U.S. Constitution was not only for white and black Americans, but that all racial groups required equal protection. This case questioned the use of Jim Crow laws against other classes of Americans, and determined that Americans of Hispanic, Asian, Middle Eastern, Inuit, Native American, and other nonwhite or black descent should also be treated equally.

Along with the discussions of the Freedom Riders and freedom marches, where are the discussions of the 1938 pecan shellers' strike and the wrongful arrest and imprisonment of over 700 Mexican-Americans peacefully protesting a cut in wages and walking off the job in San Antonio? This action was seen as impacting the creation of the Fair Labor Standards Act of 1938, which defines many of the occupational rules that govern workers' rights. Should the name of the Mexican-American labor leader Emma Tenayuca be, at least, presented alongside other civil and women's rights activists when the conditions that led to the Civil Rights Act of 1964 are presented?

Considering that people of Hispanic descent make up more than 16 percent of the total population of the United States today, efforts should be made to shine a light on the history, conditions, people, and effects of Latino activists and legislation. It's time to give a large portion of the population its due, so that maybe when educational resources are developed into lesson plans, Hispanics have an element of pride and purpose in knowing that our predecessors also played a role in shaping the world and civil rights that we enjoy today.

DISCUSSION QUESTIONS

1. Did you know about the contribution of Mexican Americans to the American civil rights movement or about the segregation they experienced? If you did, where did you learn about that?
2. Why do you think there is so little attention to the role and experience of Mexican Americans in this historic era?

READING 41

Balancing Identities: Undocumented Immigrant Asian American Students and the Model Minority Myth

Tracy Poon Tambascia, Jonathan Wang, Breanne Tcheng, and Viet T. Bui

If I weren't an illegal immigrant, I think my life would be vastly different. Undocumented Asian American students are a largely invisible population. Their experiences are unique in part because of the pressures of the model minority myth. . . .

Tracy Poon Tambascia is a professor of education at the University of Southern California.
Jonathan Wang is assistant director of Asian Pacific American Student Services at the University of Southern California.
Breanne Tcheng is an admissions counselor in the Sol Price School of Public Policy at the University of Southern California.
Viet T. Bui is a graduate assistant in the office of Asian Pacific American Student Services at the University of Southern California.

The estimated number of undocumented immigrants in the United States is 11.5 million (Hoefer, Rytina, & Baker, 2012) with California supporting the largest population of undocumented immigrants—2.8 million. While the majority of this population is from Mexico (59%), the total from Asian countries makes up approximately 10%.

Research has examined the experiences of undocumented Latino students and the challenges they face in completing their college degrees (Gildersleeve & Ranero, 2010). However, a dearth of literature exists regarding the experiences of undocumented Asian American students. Although Asian American students are well-represented on college and university campuses, the broad term Asian American hides the fact that not all ethnic groups in this category are accessing education and well-paying jobs (Ho, 2003; Ng, Lee, & Pak, 2007). These groups can become further marginalized if their needs for resources, advocacy, and services are not met (Libby, Nguyen, & Teranishi, 2013). The prevalence of the model minority myth may compound pressures on undocumented Asian American students. This myth of universal success creates unrealistic expectations for academic achievement, financial success, and other markers of success (Suzuki, 2002).

This study seeks to increase the awareness and visibility of a population that exists in the shadows of a larger societal debate about immigration reform. The following analysis encompasses several interviews with current college students who identified as undocumented Asian Americans at some point in their college career. Several themes have initially emerged.

SOCIAL ISOLATION

Loneliness is a common experience of these participants. One participant said, "I'm a very outgoing person. . . . It's hard to open up to new people and even if good people try to approach, you might kind of push them away." Another student revealed her undocumented immigrant status to a friend in high school with negative consequences:

"We got in an argument and she threatened me that she's going to report my family." Many students do not learn about their status until they start planning for college. One participant felt isolated after discovering her undocumented immigrant status. She sought support from other undocumented immigrant students at her high school but generally felt she had to "manage things on [her] own." She described her relationships with friends as being short-term and temporary. Another student's parents limited relationships outside of the family. Thus, the family may also contribute to social isolation. Undocumented status may have other effects as well. Some students have chosen to marry, sometimes at a young age, so they can establish legal residency. These students feel pressured to make decisions about a lifetime commitment just to resolve the issue of their citizenship status.

THE ROLE OF FAMILY

Participants were asked about the role of family and whether parents or siblings influenced their college attendance. The responses were mixed. One student said she received little familial support and struggled because her parents were underemployed and concerned about finances: "When I got accepted to [omitted] University, the only question they asked me was how much it would cost." In contrast, another student had strong support from her parents, who not only encouraged her to attend college but also paid the expenses. Although her undocumented immigrant status was an obstacle, this student cited her parents' journey and the risks they took to remain in the United States as motivations to earn her degree.

MODEL MINORITY STEREOTYPE

All participants had experienced the impact of the model minority myth. Some described overemphasis on academic outcomes, comparison with peers, and self-perceptions of not meeting expectations.

Other students noted their frustration at being generalized as high achieving and perceived as overly independent. But some participants said that high expectations were part of their upbringing and that such stereotypes did not have a negative effect on their experiences.

CONCLUSION

Frustration and loneliness seem to permeate the experiences of students who are forced to learn and work on the margins of society. Limited dialogue about these issues in the Asian American and immigrant communities perpetuates these students' feelings of isolation and invisibility. Conversations and sharing of resources occur only with confidantes and close relatives. Higher education needs to name and recognize Asian American students who are undocumented immigrants. . . .

DISCUSSION QUESTIONS

1. Is it true that Americans do not usually expect Asian American students to be undocumented immigrants?
2. How would the experience of being an undocumented immigrant be different for Hispanic, European, or Asian American students?

REFERENCES

Gildersleeve, R. E., & Ranero, J. J. (2010). Precollege contexts of undocumented students: Implications for student affairs professionals. In J. Price (Ed.), *Understanding and supporting undocumented students* (*New directions for student services,* No. 131, pp. 19–33). San Francisco, CA: Jossey-Bass.

Ho, P. (2003). Performing the "Oriental": Professionals and the Asian model minority myth. *Journal of Asian American Studies,* 6(2), 149–175.

Hoefer, M., Rytina, N., & Baker, B. (2012). Estimates of the unauthorized immigrant population residing in the United States: January 2011. Retrieved from www.dhs.gov/estimatesunauthorized-immigrant-population-residing-united-statesjanuary-2011.

Libby, L., Nguyen B. M., & Teranishi, R. (2013). iCount: A data quality movement for Asian Americans and Pacific Islanders in higher education. Retrieved from www.nyu.edu/projects/care/docs/2013_iCount_Report.pdf.

Liang, H. (Ed.), *Working with Asian American college students* (*New directions for student services,* No. 97, pp. 21–32). San Francisco, CA: Jossey-Bass.

Ng, J. C., Lee, S. S.,& Pak, Y. K. (2007). Contesting the model minority and perpetual foreigner stereotypes: A critical review of literature on Asian Americans in education. *Review of Higher Education,* 31, 95–130.

Suzuki, B. H. (2002). Revisiting the model minority stereotype: Implications for student affairs practice and higher education. In M. K. McEwen, C. M. Kodama, A. N. Alvarez, S. Lee, & & C.T.H. Liang, (Eds.), *Working with Asian American college students* (*New directions for student services,* No. 97, pp. 21–32). San Francisco, Jossey-Bass.

PERSONAL ACCOUNT

Let Me Work for It!

I remember once in a sociology of education class that I was asked to describe my educational experience. At first, I was quick to say that it was very positive. Although racial remarks and jokes were passed around school, teachers and administrators paid little or no attention to them. I always felt uneasy with such remarks, but because the teachers and administrators would play ignorant to what was being said, I felt that maybe I was being too sensitive. Therefore, I learned to suck it up and was taught to view such comments as harmless.

Still, at a very young age I was very aware of racism and sexism. Both of my Vietnamese parents came to the United States when they were 20 years old. They arrived right before the Vietnam War ended, which explains the stigmatization they experienced. "VC" was a common epithet addressed to my dad along with "Gook" and "Charlie." My mom, on the other hand, struggled with gender/racial stereotypes such as being labeled mindless, dependent, and subservient. I can recall many times watching people mentally battering my parents. Numerous looks of disgust and intolerance of my parents' accent or confusion with the English language were some unpleasant cases that I experienced. Yet the snide remarks and mistreatment thrown at my parents remain the most hurtful. Many times my parents were told that their lack of proficiency in English would doom them from success and from any self-worth. They were also ostracized for holding on to their Vietnamese culture and were persuaded to assimilate to the American culture. The accumulation of these events reinforced the idea that being different, in this case Vietnamese, was negative. As far as I was concerned, my family was my only community. It was only within my family that I felt the sense of security, love, support, and, most importantly, connection. After all, I was just a "Gook" like my parents.

Yet I experienced support and love at school. I can trace this feeling all the way back to third grade. I remember how I was constantly praised for being so bright, even before turning in my first assignment. This did not send alarms to my brain. As a student, I felt great. I felt validated. But looking back on it now, there are alarms going off for me. Why? Because now I wonder if I was being labeled as a model student, a positive stereotype. Many Americans have held positive stereotypes about Asians and their work/study ethic, and making these stereotypes prior to a person's performance can create the possibility of drowning in the pressure of high expectations. Teachers have always had unreasonably high expectations for me. Although I did not experience this as pressure, I do feel that I have been robbed of the equal chance to prove myself, to see my mistakes and grow. I feel that I have so much to give, but my audience is content with what they "know" of me (which is usually built upon assumptions). I was never given the chance to work for the standing ovation; nor was I given the privilege of criticism.

At the personal level, the model minority stereotype has denied me human dignity, individuality, and the acknowledgment of my own strengths and weaknesses. I feel that I have been prejudged in this fictitious view of Asian Americans. These positive portrayals depict Asians as so flawless that they are robbed of any humanity. Some may feel indifferent to my story or ask if I really reject the positive stereotype. My only reply is this: positive and negative stereotyping are different sides of the same coin. Both invalidate individuals as human beings and lead to negative consequences.

Isabelle Nguyen

READING 42

Segregated Housing, Segregated Schools

Richard Rothstein

School reform alone cannot substantially raise performance of the poorest African-American students unless we also improve the conditions that leave too many children unprepared to take advantage of what schools have to offer.

Social and economic disadvantage depresses student performance; concentrating disadvantaged students in racially and economically homogeneous schools depresses it further.

Schools that most disadvantaged black children attend today are located in segregated neighborhoods far distant from middle-class suburbs. Our ability to desegregate is hobbled by historical ignorance. We've persuaded ourselves that residential isolation of low-income black children is only *de facto*—the accident of economic circumstance, personal preference, and private discrimination. Unless we relearn how residential segregation is *de jure*—racially motivated public policy—we can't remedy school segregation that flows from neighborhood isolation.

When a school's proportion of students at risk of failure grows, the consequences of disadvantage are exacerbated. In schools with high proportions of disadvantaged children, remediation becomes the norm; with high student mobility, teachers spend more time repeating lessons for newcomers. When classrooms fill with students less ready to learn, teachers discipline more and instruct less. Children surrounded by neighborhood violence suffer greater stress that depresses learning. When few parents have strong educations themselves, schools cannot benefit from parental pressure for stronger curriculum; children have few college-educated role

Richard Rothstein is a research associate of the Economic Policy Institute and a senior fellow of the Chief Justice Earl Warren Institute on Law and Social Policy at the University of California (Berkeley) School of Law.

models to emulate, and few classroom peers whose own families raise academic expectations.

Nationwide, low-income black children's isolation has increased. It's a problem not only of poverty but of race. Roughly 40 percent of black students attend schools that are more than 90 percent minority, up from 34 percent 20 years ago. Then, black students typically attended schools where 40 percent were low-income; it's now 60 percent.

Even sophisticated policymakers now generally assert that black students' residential isolation is *de facto,* but the proposition is dubious.

The federal government led in establishing metropolitan residential segregation. From its New Deal inception, federally funded public housing was explicitly segregated by government. Nationwide (not only in the South), projects were officially designated either for whites or blacks. Once white families left the projects for the suburbs, most public housing was purposely placed only in black neighborhoods.

In the mid-20th century, the federal government subsidized relocation of whites to suburbs and prohibited similar relocation of blacks. The Federal Housing Administration and the Veterans Administration recruited builders to construct giant developments in the East like the Levittowns, most famously in New York's Long Island, but also in Delaware, New Jersey, and Pennsylvania; in the West like Lakeview, Panorama City, and Westlake (Daly City) in California; and in numerous metropolises in between. These builders received federal loan guarantees on explicit condition that no sales or resales be made to blacks.

Federal and state bank regulators approved and encouraged "redlining" policies, banning loans to black families in white suburbs and even, in most cases, to black families in black neighborhoods, leading to those neighborhoods' deterioration and ghettoization.

The Internal Revenue Service unconstitutionally extended tax favoritism to universities, churches, and other nonprofits that enforced racial segregation. For example, Robert Maynard Hutchins, known for promoting the liberal arts, headed the University of Chicago from 1929 to 1951. His office organized homeowners' associations to establish racial restrictions in surrounding neighborhoods, and employed university lawyers to evict black families who moved nearby, all while the university enjoyed tax-deductible and tax-exempt status.

Urban renewal programs of the mid-20th century often had undisguised purposes of forcing low-income black residents away from universities, hospital complexes, or business districts and into new ghettos. Real estate is highly regulated, but state authorities never punished brokers for racial discrimination, and rarely do so even today when discriminatory practices remain. Public police and prosecutorial power enforced racial boundaries: North, South, East, and West, in thousands of incidents police stood by as mobs firebombed and stoned homes purchased by blacks in white neighborhoods, while prosecutors refused to charge easily identifiable arsonists. These and other forms of racially explicit state action to segregate the urban landscape violated the Fifth, 13th, and 14th Amendments. Yet the term "*de facto* segregation," describing a never-existent reality, persists among otherwise well-informed advocates and scholars.

Private prejudice certainly played a large role, but the federal government helped create and sustain private prejudice. White homeowners' resistance to black neighbors was fed by fears that African-Americans who moved into their neighborhoods would bring slum conditions with them. Yet slum conditions were created by overcrowding caused almost entirely by government refusal to permit African-Americans to expand their housing supply and by municipalities' discriminatory denial of public services. In the ghetto, garbage was collected less frequently, and neighborhoods were often rezoned for industrial or even toxic use. White homeowners came to see these conditions as characteristics of black residents themselves, not the result of racially motivated government policy.

Even those today who understand this dramatic history may think that because these policies are mostly those of the past, segregation persists mostly because few blacks can afford to live in middle-class neighborhoods.

Yet the federal government also contributed to this unaffordability with discriminatory labor-market policy. At the behest of Southern congressmen, New Deal labor standards, like minimum wages and the right to unionize, excluded from coverage, for undisguised racial purposes, occupations in which black workers predominated.

The federal government granted exclusive collective bargaining rights to segregated private-sector unions, including some that entirely excluded African-Americans from their trades, into the 1970s. Government thus depressed income levels of African-American workers below levels of comparable white workers, contributing to black families' inability to accumulate the wealth needed to move to equity-appreciating white suburbs.

Reacquaintance with this history should lead us to conclude that racially segregated metropolitan areas have a constitutional obligation to integrate, with inclusionary zoning laws, scattered public and private housing for low- and moderate-income families (including in the wealthiest suburbs), and even the removal of tax subsidies for property in communities that fail to take aggressive steps to integrate.

Yet we fail to tell young people this story so, as adults, they will be unlikely to understand our constitutional obligation to integrate. School curricula typically ignore, or worse, misstate historical truth. For example, in over 1,200 pages of McDougal Littell's widely used high school textbook *The Americans,* a single paragraph is devoted to 20th-century "Discrimination in the North." It devotes one passive-voice sentence to residential segregation, stating that "African-Americans found themselves forced into segregated neighborhoods," with no explanation of how government did the forcing.

Another widely used textbook, Prentice Hall's *United States History,* attributes segregation to mysterious forces: "In the North, too, African-Americans faced segregation and discrimination. Even where there were no explicit laws, *de facto* segregation, or segregation by unwritten custom or tradition, was a fact of life. African-Americans in the North were denied housing in many neighborhoods."

History Alive!, a popular textbook published by the Teachers Curriculum Institute, teaches that segregation was mostly a Southern problem: "Even New Deal agencies practiced racial segregation, especially in the South," making no reference to liberal Democrats' embrace of Northern residential segregation in return for Southern support for progressive economic policies.

We have a national concern with the racial achievement gap, but school reform cannot succeed without housing reform. We're unlikely to accomplish either if we suppress knowledge of how they came to be connected.

DISCUSSION QUESTIONS

1. Were you surprised to learn about the role of the federal government in the creation and maintenance of residential segregation?
2. Rothstein concludes his essay with the observation that secondary school textbooks ignore the history of residential segregation, especially outside the South. How would you explain that?
3. What are the practical consequences of our failure to educate students about the history of residential segregation?

SEX AND GENDER

READING 43

Many Faces of Gender Inequality

Amartya Sen

It was more than a century ago, in 1870, that Queen Victoria wrote to Sir Theodore Martin complaining about "this mad, wicked folly of 'Woman's Rights'." The formidable empress certainly did not herself need any protection that the acknowledgment of women's rights might offer. Even at the age of eighty, in 1899, she could write to A.J. Balfour, "We are not interested in the possibilities of defeat; they do not exist." That, however, is not the way most people's lives go—reduced and defeated as they frequently are by adversities. And within each community, nationality and class, the burden of hardship often falls disproportionately on women.

The afflicted world in which we live is characterised by deeply unequal sharing of the burden of adversities between women and men. Gender inequality exists in most parts of the world, from Japan to Morocco, from Uzbekistan to the United States of America. However, inequality between women and men can take very many different forms. Indeed, gender inequality is not one homogeneous phenomenon, but a collection of disparate and interlinked problems. Let me illustrate with examples of different kinds of disparity.

(1) Mortality inequality: In some regions in the world, inequality between women and men directly involves matters of life and death, and takes the brutal form of unusually high mortality rates of women and a consequent preponderance of men in the total population, as opposed to the preponderance of women found in societies with little or no gender bias in health care and nutrition. Mortality inequality has been observed extensively in North Africa and in Asia, including China and South Asia.

(2) Natality inequality: Given a preference for boys over girls that many male-dominated societies have, gender inequality can manifest itself in the form of the parents wanting the newborn to be a boy rather than a girl. There was a time when this could be no more than a wish (a daydream or a nightmare, depending on one's perspective), but with the availability of modern techniques to determine the gender of the foetus, sex-selective abortion has become common in many countries. It is particularly prevalent in East Asia, in China and South Korea in particular, but also in Singapore and

Amartya Sen is Thomas W. Lamont University Professor and Professor of Economics and Philosophy at Harvard University. He was awarded the *Nobel Memorial Prize in Economic Sciences* in 1998 for his work in welfare economics.

Taiwan, and it is beginning to emerge as a statistically significant phenomenon in India and South Asia as well. This is high-tech sexism.

(3) Basic facility inequality: Even when demographic characteristics do not show much or any anti-female bias, there are other ways in which women can have less than a square deal. Afghanistan may be the only country in the world the government of which is keen on actively excluding girls from schooling (it combines this with other features of massive gender inequality), but there are many countries in Asia and Africa, and also in Latin America, where girls have far less opportunity of schooling than boys do. There are other deficiencies in basic facilities available to women, varying from encouragement to cultivate one's natural talents to fair participation in rewarding social functions of the community.

(4) Special opportunity inequality: Even when there is relatively little difference in basic facilities including schooling, the opportunities of higher education may be far fewer for young women than for young men. Indeed, gender bias in higher education and professional training can be observed even in some of the richest countries in the world, in Europe and North America.

Sometimes this type of division has been based on the superficially innocuous idea that the respective "provinces" of men and women are just different. This thesis has been championed in different forms over the centuries, and has had much implicit as well as explicit following. It was presented with particular directness more than a hundred years before Queen Victoria's complaint about "woman's rights" by the Reverend James Fordyce in his *Sermons to Young Women* (1766), a book which, as Mary Wollstonecraft noted in her *A Vindication of the Rights of Women* (1792), had been "long made a part of woman's library." Fordyce warned the young women, to whom his sermons were addressed, against "those masculine women that would plead for your sharing any part of their province with us," identifying the province of men as including not only "war," but also "commerce, politics, exercises of strength and dexterity, abstract philosophy and all the abstruser sciences."[1] Even

though such clear-cut beliefs about the provinces of men and women are now rather rare, nevertheless the presence of extensive gender asymmetry can be seen in many areas of education, training and professional work even in Europe and North America.

(5) Professional inequality: In terms of employment as well as promotion in work and occupation, women often face greater handicap than men. A country like Japan may be quite egalitarian in matters of demography or basic facilities, and even, to a great extent, in higher education, and yet progress to elevated levels of employment and occupation seems to be much more problematic for women than for men.

In the English television series called *Yes, Minister,* there is an episode where the Minister, full of reforming zeal, is trying to find out from the immovable permanent secretary, Sir Humphrey, how many women are in really senior positions in the British civil service. Sir Humphrey says that it is very difficult to give an exact number; it would require a lot of investigation. The Minister is still insistent, and wants to know approximately how many women are there in these senior positions. To which Sir Humphrey finally replies, "Approximately, none."

(6) Ownership inequality: In many societies the ownership of property can also be very unequal. Even basic assets such as homes and land may be very asymmetrically shared. The absence of claims to property can not only reduce the voice of women, but also make it harder for women to enter and flourish in commercial, economic and even some social activities.[2] This type of inequality has existed in most parts of the world, though there are also local variations. For example, even though traditional property rights have favoured men in the bulk of India, in what is now the State of Kerala, there has been, for a long time, matrilineal inheritance for an influential part of the community, namely the Nairs.

(7) Household inequality: There are, often enough, basic inequalities in gender relations within the family or the household, which can take many different forms. Even in cases in which there are no overt signs of anti-female bias in, say, survival or son-preference or education, or even in promotion to higher executive positions, the family arrangements can be quite unequal in terms of sharing the burden of housework and child care. It is, for example, quite common in many societies to take it for granted that while men will naturally work outside the home, women could do it if and only if they could combine it with various inescapable and unequally shared household duties. This is sometimes called "division of labour," though women could be forgiven for seeing it as "accumulation of labour." The reach of this inequality includes not only unequal relations within the family, but also derivative inequalities in employment and recognition in the outside world. Also, the established fixity of this type of "division" or "accumulation" of labour can also have far-reaching effects on the knowledge and understanding of different types of work in professional circles. When I first started working on gender inequality, in the 1970s, I remember being struck by the fact that the *Handbook of Human Nutrition Requirement* of the World Health Organisation (WHO), in presenting "calorie requirements" for different categories of people, chose to classify household work as "sedentary activity," requiring very little deployment of energy.[3] I was, however, not able to determine precisely how this remarkable bit of information had been collected by the patrician leaders of society.

It is important to take note of the variety of forms that gender inequality can take. First, inequality between women and men cannot be confronted and overcome by any one set of all-purpose remedy. Second, over time the same country can move from one type of gender inequality to harbouring other forms of that inequity. . . . Third, the different forms of gender inequality can impose diverse adversities on the lives of men and boys, in addition to those of women and girls. In understanding the different aspects of the evil of gender inequality, we have to look beyond the predicament of women and examine the problems created for men as well by the asymmetric treatment of women. These causal connections, which (as I shall presently illustrate) can be very significant, can vary with the form of gender inequality. Finally, inequalities of different kinds can also, frequently enough, feed each other, and we have to be aware of their interlinkages.

Even though part of the object of this paper is to discuss the variety of different types of gender inequality, a substantial part of my empirical focus will, in fact, be on two of the most elementary kinds of gender inequality, namely, mortality inequality and natality inequality. I shall be concerned, in particular, with gender inequality in South Asia, or the Indian subcontinent. While I shall separate out the subcontinent for special attention, I must also warn against the smugness of thinking that the United States or Western Europe is free from gender bias simply because some of the empirical generalisations that can be made about the subcontinent would not hold in the West. Given the many faces of gender inequality, much would depend on which face we look at. . . .

In the bulk of the subcontinent, with only a few exceptions (such as Sri Lanka and the State of Kerala in India), female mortality rates are very significantly higher than what could be expected given the mortality patterns of men (in the respective age groups). This type of gender inequality need not entail any conscious homicide, and it would be a mistake to try to explain this large phenomenon by invoking the occasional cases of female infanticide that are reported from China or India; these are truly dreadful events when they occur, but they are relatively rare. Rather, the mortality disadvantage of women works mainly through a widespread neglect of health, nutrition and other interests of women that influence survival.

It is sometimes presumed that there are more women than men in the world, since that is well-known to be the case in Europe and North America, which have a female to male ratio of 1.05 or so, on the average (that is, about 105 women per 100 men). But women do not outnumber men in the world as a whole; indeed there are only about 98 women per 100 men on the globe. This "shortfall" of women is most acute in Asia and North Africa. For example, the number of females per 100 males in the total population is 97 in Egypt and Iran, 95 in Bangladesh and Turkey, 94 in China, 93 in India and Pakistan, and 84 in

Saudi Arabia (though the last ratio is considerably reduced by the presence of male migrant workers from elsewhere who come to Saudi Arabia).

It has been widely observed that given similar health care and nutrition, women tend typically to have lower age-specific mortality rates than men do. Indeed, even female foetuses tend to have a lower probability of miscarriage than male foetuses have. Everywhere in the world, more male babies are born than female babies (and an even higher proportion of male foetuses are conceived compared with female foetuses), but throughout their respective lives the proportion of males goes on falling as we move to higher and higher age groups, due to typically greater male mortality rates. The excess of females over males in the population of Europe and North America comes about as a result of this greater survival chance of females in different age groups.

However, in many parts of the world, women receive less attention and health care than men do, and particularly girls often receive very much less support than boys. As a result of this gender bias, the mortality rates of females often exceed those of males in these countries. The concept of "missing women" was devised to give some idea of the enormity of the phenomenon of women's adversity in mortality by focussing on the women who are simply not there, due to unusually high mortality compared with male mortality rates. The basic idea is to find some rough and ready way to understand the quantitative difference between (1) the actual number of women in these countries, and (2) the number we could expect to see if the gender pattern of mortality were similar in these countries as in other regions of the world that do not have a significant bias against women in terms of health care and other attentions relevant for survival.

For example, if we take the ratio of women to men in sub-Saharan Africa as the standard (there is relatively little bias against women in terms of health care, social status and mortality rates in sub-Saharan Africa, even though the absolute numbers are quite dreadful for both men and women), then its female-male ratio of 1.022 can be used to calculate the number of missing women in women-short

countries.[4] For example, with India's female–male ratio of 0.93, there is a total difference of 9 percent (of the male population) between that ratio and the standard used for comparison, namely, the sub-Saharan African ratio of 1.022. This yielded a figure of 37 million missing women already in 1986 (when I first did the estimation). Using the same sub-Saharan standard, China had 44 million missing women, and it was evident that for the world as a whole the magnitude of shortfall easily exceeded 100 million.[5] Other standards and different procedures can also be used, as has been done by Ansley Coale and Stephan Klasen, getting somewhat different numbers, but invariably very large ones (Klasen's total number is about 80 million missing women).[6] Gender bias in mortality does take an astonishingly heavy toll.

How can this be reversed? . . . Women's gainful employment, especially in more rewarding occupations, clearly does play a role in improving the deal that women and girls get. And so does women's literacy, and other factors that can be seen as adding to the status, standing and voice of women in family decisions.[7] . . .

However, there is [also] clear evidence that traditional routes of changing gender inequality, through using public policy to influence female education and female economic participation, may not serve as a path to the removal of natality inequality. A sharp pointer in that direction comes from countries in East Asia, which all have high levels of female education and economic participation. Despite these achievements, compared with the biologically common ratio across the world of 95 girls being born per hundred boys, Singapore and Taiwan have 92 girls, South Korea only 88, and China a mere 86. In fact, South Korea's overall female-male ratio for children is also a meagre 88 girls for 100 boys and China's 85 girls for 100 boys. In comparison, the Indian ratio of 92.7 girls for 100 boys (though lower than its previous figure of 94.5) still looks far less unfavourable.[8] . . .

I may end by trying briefly to identify some of the principal issues I have tried to discuss. First,

I have argued for the need to take a plural view of gender inequality, which can have many different faces. The prominent faces of gender injustice can vary from one region to another, and also from one period to the next.

Second, the effects of gender inequality, which can impoverish the lives of men as well as women, can be more fully understood by taking detailed empirical note of specific forms of inequality that can be found in particular regions. . . .

To have an adequate appreciation of the far-reaching effects of disparities between women and men, we have to recognise the basic fact that gender inequality is not one affliction, but many, with varying reach on the lives of women and men, and of girls and boys. There is also the need to reexamine and closely scrutinise some lessons that we have tended to draw from past empirical works. There are no good reasons to abandon the understanding that the impact of women's empowerment in enhancing the voice and influence of women does help to reduce gender inequality of many different kinds, and can also reduce the indirect penalties that men suffer from the subjugation of women. However, the growing phenomenon of natality inequality raises questions that are basically much more complex. When women in some regions themselves strongly prefer having boys to girls, the remedying of the consequent natality inequality calls at least for broader demands on women's agency, in addition to examining other possible influences.

Indeed, in dealing with the new—"high tech"—face of gender disparity, in the form of natality inequality, there is a need to go beyond just the agency of women, but to look also for more critical assessment of received values. When anti-female bias in action (such as sex-specific abortion) reflects the hold of traditional masculinist values from which mothers themselves may not be immune, what is needed is not just freedom of action but also freedom of thought—in women's ability and willingness to question received values. Informed and critical agency is important in combating inequality of every kind. Gender inequality, including its many faces, is no exception.

DISCUSSION QUESTIONS

1. What social consequences—local and global— would follow from the size of the "missing women" population?
2. Sen argues that gender inequality is damaging to boys and men, as well as to girls and women. What are some examples of the damage to boys and men?
3. Sen focuses much of his attention on gender differences in morbidity and natality in India and East Asia. Would the United States be immune to such problems? If not, where and when might they appear?

NOTES

1. See William St. Clair, *The Godwins and the Shelleys* (New York: Norton, 1989), pp. 504–8.
2. Bina Agarwal, among others, has investigated the far-reaching effects of landlessness of women in many agricultural economies; see particularly her *A Field of One's Own* (Cambridge: Cambridge University Press, 1994).
3. World Health Organisation, *Handbook of Human Nutrition Requirement* (Geneva: WHO, 1974); this was based on the report of a high-level expert committee jointly appointed by the WHO and FAO—the Food and Agriculture Organisation.
4. Presented in my "More Than a Hundred Million Women Are Missing," *The New York Review of Books,* Christmas Number, December 20, 1990, and in "Missing Women," *British Medical Journal,* 304 (March 1992).
5. The fact that I had used the sub-Saharan African ratio as the standard, rather than the European or North American ratio, was missed by some of my critics, who assumed (wrongly as it happens) that I was comparing the developing countries with advanced Western ones; see for example Ansley Coale, "Excess Female Mortality and the Balances of the Sexes in the Population: An Estimate of the Number of 'Missing Females'," *Population and Development Review,* 17 (1991). In fact, the estimation of "missing women" was based on the contrasts within the so-called third world, in particular between sub-Saharan Africa, on the one hand, and Asia and North Africa, on the other. The exact methods used were more elaborately discussed in my "Africa and India: What Do We Have to Learn from Each Other?," in Kenneth J. Arrow, ed., *The Balance between Industry and Agriculture in Economic Development* (London: Macmillan, 1988); and (with Jean Drze), *Hunger and Public Action* (Oxford: Clarendon Press, 1989).

6. Stephan Klasen, "'Missing Women' Reconsidered," *World Development*, 22 (1994).

7. On this see my "Women and Cooperative Conflict," in Irene Tinker, *Persistent Inequalities* (New York: Oxford University Press, 1990). See also J. C. Caldwell, "Routes to Low Mortality in Poor Countries," *Population and Development Review*, 12 (1986); Jere Behrman and B. L. Wolfe, "How Does Mother's Schooling Affect Family Health, Nutrition, Medical Care Usage and Household Sanitation," *Journal of Econometrics*, 36 (1987); Jean Dreze and Amartya Sen, *Hunger and Public Action* (Oxford: Clarendon Press, 1989).

8. Note, however, that the Chinese and Korean figures cover children between 0 and 4, whereas the Indian figures relate to children between 0 and 6. However, even with appropriate age adjustment, the general comparison of female–male ratios holds in much the same way.

PERSONAL ACCOUNT

He Hit Her

I was raised in Charleston, South Carolina, a city where racial and class lines are both evident and defined by street address. I had been taught all my life that black people were different than "us" and were to be feared, particularly in groups.

One summer afternoon when I was 18 or 19, I was sitting in my car at a traffic light at the corner of Cannon and King streets, an area on the edge of the white part of the peninsular city, but progressively being inhabited by more and more blacks. It was hot, had been for weeks, and the sticky heat of South Carolina can be enraging by itself.

As I waited at the light, a young black couple turned the corner on the sidewalk and began to walk towards where I was sitting. The man was yelling and screaming and waving his arms about his head. The woman, a girl really, looked scared and was walking and trying to ignore his tirade. Perhaps it was her seeming indifference that finally did it, perhaps the heat, I don't know. As they drew right up next to my car though, he hit her. He hit her on the side of her head, open palmed, and her head bounced off the brick wall of the house on the corner and she sprawled to the ground, dazed and crying. The man stood over her, shaking his fist and yelling.

I looked around at the other people in cars around me, mostly whites, and at the other people on the sidewalks, mostly blacks, and I realized as everyone gaped that no one was going to do anything, no one was going to help, and neither was I. I don't think it was fear of the man involved that stopped me; rather, I think it was fear generated by what I had been told about the man that stopped me. Physically I was bigger than he was and I knew how to handle myself in a fight: I worked as a bouncer in a nightclub. What I was afraid of was what I had been told about blacks: that *en masse,* they hated whites, and that given the opportunity they would harm me. I was afraid getting out of the car in that neighborhood would make me the focus of the fight and in a matter of time I would be pummeled by an angry black crowd. Also in my mind were thoughts of things I had heard voiced as a child: "They are different. Violence is a part of life for them. They beat, stab, and shoot each other all the time, and the women are just as bad as the men." So I sat and did nothing. The light changed and I pulled away.

The incident has haunted me over the last almost 15 years. I have often thought about it and felt angry when I did. I believe that as I examined it over time the woman who had been hit, the victim, became less and less prominent, and the black man and myself more prominent. Then I had an epiphany about it.

What bothered me about the incident was not that a man had hit a woman and I had done nothing to intervene, not even to blow my horn, but that a man had hit a woman and I had done nothing to intervene and that this reflected on me as a man. "Men don't hit women, and other men don't let men hit women," was also part of my masculinity training as a boy. There was a whole list of things that "real" men did and things that "real" men didn't do, and somewhere on there was this idea that men didn't let other men hit women. I realized that the incident haunted me not because a man had hit a woman, but because my lack of response was an indictment of *my* masculinity. The horror had become that I was somehow less of a man because of my inaction. Part of the dichotomy that this set up was the notion that the black man had done something to *me,* not to the woman he hit, and it was here that my anger lay. I wonder how this influenced my perception of black men I encountered in the future.

Tim Norton

READING 44

The Not-So-Pink Ivory Tower

Ann Mullen

Since 1982, women in the United States have been graduating from college at higher rates than men; they currently earn 57 percent of all bachelor's degrees. Some view this trend as a triumphant indicator of gender egalitarianism, while others sound the alarm about the supposed "male crisis" in higher education and the problem of increasingly "feminized" universities.

Recently, the *New York Times* reported that when it comes to college, "women are leaving men in the dust," the Minneapolis *Star Tribune* announced that women's "takeover is complete," and the *Weekly Standard* described colleges as "where the boys aren't." Some have even predicted that sorority sisters will face increasing difficulty finding dates for formals, or eligible men to marry. Thomas Mortenson, a senior scholar at the Pell Institute for the Study of Opportunity in Higher Education, warned that if current trends continue, "the graduation line in 2068 will be all female."

But is higher education really feminizing? Have women's advances come at the cost of men? In 50 years, when they look around their classrooms, will undergraduate students be hard-pressed to see a male face? In other words, has the trend towards gender equality in higher education gone too far? To answer these questions, we need to look beyond the single statistic of the gender distribution of bachelor's degrees, and take a broader approach to understanding the contours of gender in higher education.

WHO'S GETTING DEGREES

During the past 40 years, the gender distribution of bachelor's degrees reversed. In 1970, men earned 57 percent of all degrees; today, women do. This

trend leads some to conclude that women are squeezing men out of higher education, and that women's success has led to men's decline. In fact, this zero-sum scenario is incorrect: the college-going rates for both men and women have increased substantially. Both genders are far more likely to graduate from college now than at any previous point in time. Women's increasing graduation rate isn't due to a decrease in the number of graduating male students, but to the fact that women's increases occurred faster than men's. Particularly between 1970 and 1990, as employment opportunities for women expanded, their college graduation rates grew more rapidly than did those of men.

The rates of growth for men and women have now equalized. Over the past decade [since 2002], the number of degrees earned by both men and women actually increased by the identical rate of 38 percent. The U.S. Department of Education predicts that over the course of the next decade women's share of bachelor's degrees will rise by only one percentage point, to 58 percent of all degrees. In looking at these figures over time, we see that women's successes did not come at the expense of men, and that the gender gap is not growing uncontrollably. It has in fact stabilized, and has held steady for more than 10 years.

To fully assess the gender distribution of bachelor's degrees, we also need to look at what kinds of men and women graduate from college, and whether men and women of different racial, ethnic and class backgrounds have the same chances of graduating. Among 25- to 29-year-olds, across all racial and ethnic groups, more women than men hold bachelor's degrees. The gap is just over 7 percent among whites and Hispanics, 6 percent among blacks, and about 10 percent for Asians.

But in terms of race and ethnicity, the gaps in college completion far exceed that of gender: 56 percent of Asians between 25 and 29 years old hold bachelor's degrees, compared to only 39 percent of whites, 20 percent of blacks, and nearly 13 percent of Hispanics. Both white and Asian men are far more likely than black or Hispanic students of either gender to earn a bachelor's degree. These racial gaps are actually larger now than they were in

---

Ann Mullen is a professor of sociology at the University of Toronto.

the 1960s: while students from all backgrounds are now more likely to graduate from college, the rates have increased more quickly for whites and Asians.

Social class continues to be the strongest predictor of who will attend and graduate from college—one that far outweighs the effects of either gender, or race and ethnicity. Surveys by the U.S. Department of Education show that 70 percent of high school students from wealthy families will enter four-year colleges, compared to only 21 percent of their peers from low-income families. Gender differences also vary by social class background. According to education policy analyst Jackie King, for the wealthiest students, the gender gap actually favors men. (For families in the highest income quartile, men comprise 52 percent of college students, compared to 44 percent in the lowest income quartile, and 47 percent in the middle two quartiles.) Age also plays a role: among adults 25 years and older, women are far more likely than men to return to college for a bachelor's degree. But among those 24 and under, women make up only 55 percent of all students, and the gender difference among enrollment rates for recent high school graduates is small (41 percent of men and 44 percent of women).

In other words, women's overall advantage in earning college degrees is not shared equally among all women. White women, Asian women, and wealthy women outpace women from other backgrounds. Gender differences are largest among students 25 years and up, Asians, and low-income students. But differences in relation to class, race and ethnicity greatly overshadow gender gaps in degree attainment.

NOT AT CALTECH

In assessing gender equity in higher education, it's also necessary to take into account where men and women earn their degrees. While more women than men tend to graduate from college, women are disproportionately represented in less competitive institutions. Sociologist Jayne Baker and I found that women earned more than 60 percent of degrees in the least selective institutions, but only slightly more than half in the most selective institutions. Women's gains have been greatest at institutions with lower standardized test scores and higher acceptance rates, while men and women are roughly on par with each other at elite institutions. Women are also underrepresented at the top science and engineering institutions, like Caltech and MIT. So, while women may be in the majority overall, their integration into higher education has been uneven, and they are more likely to attend lower status institutions.

Perhaps the most striking disparities are in the choice of college majors. In spite of their overall minority status, men still earn 83 percent of all degrees in engineering, 82 percent in computer and information sciences, 70 percent in philosophy, and 69 percent in economics. Women, on the other hand, continue to earn the lion's share of degrees in traditionally female-dominated fields: 77 percent in psychology, 80 percent in education, and 85 percent in nursing and other health professions. About a third of all men (or women) would have to change majors in order to achieve gender parity across majors today. This hasn't changed much in the last 25 years. (Through the 1970s and early 1980s, fields moved steadily toward becoming more integrated, but in the mid-1980s, this trend slowed and then stalled, shifting very little since then.)

Sociologists Paula England and Su Li found that most of the decrease in segregation came from the growth of gender-integrated fields, like business, and from the flow of women into previously male-dominated fields. Men are much less likely to move into female-dominated fields. They also found that women's entrance into predominantly male fields discourages later cohorts of men from choosing those fields. Women gain status and pay by entering predominantly male fields, while men lose out when they enter devalued, predominantly female fields of study.

Women and men are ostensibly free to select any field they wish, and they no longer face the blatant kinds of barriers to entry that have historically existed. But, other factors influence students' choices subtly, but powerfully. Sociologist Shelly Correll has done innovative experiments with undergraduate students that demonstrate how cultural beliefs about gender shape individuals' career aspirations. When exposed to the idea that men are better at certain tasks, male participants in the study rated their own abilities higher than the women, even though they were all given the same scores. These subjective assessments of their own competencies then influenced students' interest in related careers. Correll argues that widely shared cultural beliefs about gender and different kinds of competencies (like math and science) bias men's and women's perceptions of their own abilities, and their interest in pursuing these fields. She finds that men assess their own capabilities in math more generously than do women, which then encourages them to go into math and science fields.

Education researcher Maria Ong has studied the challenges young women of color majoring in physics face. Because their bodies do not conform to prevalent images of "ordinary" white, male scientists, their belonging and competence are questioned. To persevere in physics, these women confront the necessity of developing strategies for managing their physical appearance. In my own work, I found that students at an elite liberal arts institution choose majors in order to both carve out intellectual identities and settle on a career path. Students identify with the qualities of knowledge of different fields of study, which they often interpret in gendered ways. Men tend to reject female-dominated fields because of their perceived lack of rigor and objectivity.

Men and women also experience college differently. Education scholar Linda Sax uses 40 years of data about college freshmen, along with research from the 1990s that tracked individual students over time. She found some gender differences that have persisted over the past four decades, such as women's lower levels of academic self-confidence. Among first-year college students, according to Sax, women rate themselves lower than men on three out of four indicators of confidence, in spite of their significantly higher high school grades. In terms of overall intellectual self-confidence, only about half of women consider themselves above average or in the highest 10 percent compared to over two-thirds of men. This gender gap widens even further during the college years.

Because more women than men come from low-income families, women also come to college with greater concerns about financing their education. Women study harder than men during college, spend more time talking with their professors, and get better grades, while men are more likely to miss classes and not complete homework. By focusing only on the relative numbers of men and women at college, we overlook the ways their college experiences diverge, and the different obstacles and challenges they encounter along the way.

AFTER COLLEGE

Paradoxically, women's success in closing the gender gap in higher education has not closed the gender gaps in the labor market. Men and women still generally work in different kinds of jobs, and women still earn considerably less than men (even with the same levels of education). Occupational segregation remains high and the trend toward narrowing the gender gap in pay has slowed. Currently, young, college-educated, full time working women can expect to earn only 80 percent of the salaries of men ($40,000 annually compared to $49,800), a ratio identical to that of 1995. In fact, women with bachelor's degrees earn the same as men with associate degrees. Some of this pay gap can be attributed to students' undergraduate fields of study. Engineering graduates, for example, earn about $55,000 annually in their first year after graduation, while education majors bring home only $30,500. However, even after taking into account fields of study, women still earn less than men.

These pay disparities suggest an economic rationale for women's vigorous pursuit of higher education. Not only do women need to acquire more education in order to earn the same salaries as men, they also receive higher returns on their educational investments. Education scholar Laura Perna has found that even though women's salaries are lower than men's, women enjoy a greater pay-off in graduating from college than men do. In the early years after graduating, a woman with a college degree will earn 55 percent more than a woman with a high school degree. For men, that difference is only 17 percent. What's more, men with only a high school education earn a third more than women do, and are more likely to find work in traditionally male blue-collar jobs that offer health care and other benefits—which are not available in the sales and service jobs typically held by women.

Though men with high school educations enjoy higher salaries and better benefits than do women, they are also more vulnerable to unemployment. In general, the rates of unemployment are twice as high for high school graduates as they are for college graduates. They are also slightly higher for men than for women at all educational levels below the bachelor's degree. According to data from a 2010 U.S. Census survey, the unemployment rate for high school graduates was 11.3 percent for men versus 9 percent for women (compared to 4.8 percent and 4.7 percent, respectively, for those with at least a bachelor's degree), due in part to the effects of the recent recession on the manufacturing sector.

In addition to offering access to better jobs, higher salaries, and less risk of unemployment, going to college offers a host of other advantages. College graduates live longer, healthier lives. They are less likely to smoke, drink too much, or suffer from anxiety, depression, obesity, and a variety of illnesses. They are more likely to vote, to volunteer, and to be civically engaged. Because of this broad array of social and economic benefits, we should be concerned about patterns of underrepresentation for any group.

INCOMPLETE INTEGRATION

To some, the fact that women earn 57 percent of all degrees to men's 43 percent suggests the gender pendulum has swung too far. They claim that if the ratio still favored men, there would be widespread protest. But such claims fail to see the full picture: though women earn more degrees than men, the gender integration of higher education is far from complete. Men and women still diverge in the fields of study they choose, their experiences during college, and the kinds of jobs they get after graduating.

In the early 1970s, when men earned 57 percent of college degrees, women faced exclusion and discrimination in the labor market and earned less than two-thirds of what men earned. Many professions, and most positions of power and authority, were almost completely closed to women. While the ratio of college graduates now favors women, women are not benefiting from more education in ways that men did 40 years ago. In terms of the economic rewards of completing college, women are far from matching men, let alone outpacing them.

By paying exclusive attention to the gender ratio, we tend to overlook much more serious and enduring disparities of social class, race and ethnicity. This lessens our ability to understand how gender advantages vary across groups. If there is a crisis of access to higher education, it is not so much a gender crisis, as one of race and class. Young black and Hispanic men and men from low-income families are among the most disadvantaged, but women from these groups also lag behind their white, Asian and middle-class counterparts. Addressing the formidable racial and economic gaps in college access will improve low-income and minority men's chances far more than closing the gender gap would.

The higher proportion of degrees earned by women does not mean that higher education is feminizing, or that men are getting crowded out. It seems that if women hold an advantage in any area, even a relatively slim one, we jump to the conclusion that it indicates a catastrophe for men. In the case of access to college degrees, that's simply not true.

DISCUSSION QUESTIONS

1. Why do you think the popular discussion about gender differences in higher education has been so misinformed?

2. In your own words, explain why it is erroneous to describe higher education as increasingly feminized.

3. How would you explain women's lack of academic self-confidence and men's excess of it?

READING 45

The Gender Revolution: Uneven and Stalled

Paula England

We sometimes call the sweeping changes in the gender system since the 1960s a "revolution." Women's employment increased dramatically (Cotter, Hermsen, and England 2008); birth control became widely available (Bailey 2006); women caught up with and surpassed men in rates of college graduation (Cotter, Hermsen, and Vanneman 2004, 23); undergraduate college majors desegregated substantially (England and Li 2006); more women than ever got doctorates as well as professional degrees in law, medicine, and business (Cotter, Hermsen, and Vanneman 2004, 22–23; England et al. 2007); many kinds of gender discrimination in employment and education became illegal (Burstein 1989; Hirsh 2009); women entered many previously male-dominated occupations (Cotter, Hermsen, and Vanneman 2004, 10–14); and more women were elected to political office (Cotter, Hermsen, and Vanneman 2004, 25). As sweeping as these changes have been, change in the gender system has been uneven—affecting some groups more than others and some arenas of life more than others, and change has recently stalled. My goal in this article is not to argue over whether we should view the proverbial cup as half empty or half full (arguments I have always found uninteresting) but, rather, to stretch toward an understanding of why some things change so much more than others. To show the uneven nature of gender change, I will review trends on a number of indicators. While

Paula England is a professor of sociology at New York University.

the shape of most of the trends is not in dispute among scholars, the explanations I offer for the uneven and halting nature of change have the status of hypotheses rather than well-documented conclusions.

I will argue that there has been little cultural or institutional change in the devaluation of traditionally female activities and jobs, and as a result, women have had more incentive than men to move into gender-nontraditional activities and positions. This led to asymmetric change; women's lives have changed much more than men's. Yet in some subgroups and arenas, there is less clear incentive for change even among women; examples are the relatively low employment rates of less educated women and the persistence of traditionally gendered patterns in heterosexual romantic, sexual, and marital relationships.

I also argue, drawing on work by Charles and Bradley, that the type of gender egalitarianism that did take hold was the type most compatible with American individualism and its cultural and institutional logics, which include rights of access to jobs and education and the desideratum of upward mobility and of expressing one's "true self" (Charles 2011; Charles and Bradley 2002, 2009). One form this gender egalitarianism has taken has been the reduction of discrimination in hiring. This has made much of the gender revolution that has occurred possible; women can now enter formerly "male" spheres. But co-occurring with this gender egalitarianism, and discouraging such integration is a strong (if often tacit) belief in gender essentialism—the notion that men and women are innately and fundamentally different in interests and skills (Charles forthcoming; Charles and Bradley 2002, 2009; Ridgeway 2009). A result of these co-occurring logics is that women are most likely to challenge gender boundaries when there is no path of upward mobility without doing so, but otherwise gender blinders guide the paths of both men and women.

Devaluation of "Female" Activities and Asymmetric Incentives for Women and Men to Change

Most of the changes in the gender system heralded as "revolutionary" involve women moving into positions and activities previously limited to men, with few changes in the opposite direction. The source of this asymmetry is an aspect of society's valuation and reward system that has not changed much—the tendency to devalue and badly reward activities and jobs traditionally done by women.

Women's Increased Employment

One form the devaluation of traditionally female activities takes is the failure to treat child rearing as a public good and support those who do it with state payments. In the United States, welfare reform took away much of what little such support had been present. Without this, women doing child rearing

are reliant on the employment of male partners (if present) or their own employment. Thus, women have had a strong incentive to seek paid employment, and more so as wage levels rose across the decades (Bergmann 2005). As Figure 1 shows, women's employment has increased dramatically. But change has not been continuous, as the trend line flattened after 1990 and turned down slightly after 2000 before turning up again. This turndown was hardly an "opt-out revolution," to use the popular-press term, as the decline was tiny relative to the dramatic increase across 40 years (Kuperberg and Stone 2008; Percheski 2008). But the stall after 1990 is clear, if unexplained.

Figure 1 also shows the asymmetry in change between men's and women's employment; women's employment has increased much more than men's has declined. There was nowhere near one man leaving the labor force to become a full-time homemaker for every woman who entered, nor did men pick up household work to the extent women

FIGURE 1
Percentage of U.S. men and women employed, 1962–2007
Source: Cotter, Hermsen, and Vanneman (2009).
Note: Persons are considered employed if they worked for pay anytime during the year. Refers to adults aged 25 to 54.

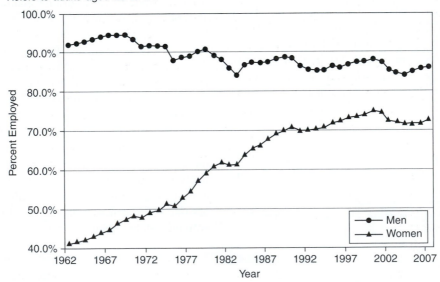

added hours of employment (Bianchi, Robinson, and Milkie 2006). Men had little incentive to leave employment.

Among women, incentives for employment vary. Class-based[1] resources, such as education, affect these incentives. At first glance, we might expect less educated women to have higher employment rates than their better-educated peers because they are less likely to be married to a high-earning man. Most marriages are between two people at a similar education level (Mare 1991), so the less educated woman, if she is married, typically has a husband earning less than the husband of the college graduate. Her family would seem to need the money from her employment more than the family headed by two college graduates. Let us call this the "need for income" effect. But the countervailing "opportunity cost" factor is that well-educated women have more economic incentive for employment because they can earn more (England, Garcia-Beaulieu, and Ross 2004). Put another way, the opportunity cost of staying at home is greater for the woman who can earn more. Indeed, the woman who did not graduate from high school may have potential earnings so low that she could not even cover child care costs with what she could earn. Thus, in typical cases, for the married college graduate, her own education encourages her employment, while her husband's high earnings discourage it. The less educated woman typically has a poor husband (if any), which encourages her employment, while her own low earning power discourages her employment.[2] It is an empirical question whether the "need for income" or "opportunity cost" effect predominates.

Recent research shows that the opportunity-cost effect predominates in the United States and other affluent nations. England, Gornick, and Shafer (2008) use data from 16 affluent countries circa 2000 and show that, in all of them, among women partnered with men (married or cohabiting), those with more education are more likely to be employed. Moreover, there is no monotonic relationship between partner's earnings and a woman's employment; at top levels of his income, her employment is deterred. But women whose male partners are at middle income levels are more likely to be employed than women whose partners have very low or no earnings, the opposite of what the "need for income" principle suggests. . . .

Women Moving into "Male" Jobs and Fields of Study

The devaluation of and underpayment of predominantly female occupations is an important institutional reality that provides incentives for both men and women to choose "male" over "female" occupations and the fields of study that lead to them. Research has shown that predominantly female occupations pay less, on average, than jobs with a higher proportion of men. At least some of the gap is attributable to sex composition because it persists in statistical models controlling for occupations' educational requirements, amount of skill required, unionization, and so forth. I have argued that this is a form of gender discrimination—employers see the worth of predominantly female jobs through biased lenses and, as a result, set pay levels for both men and women in predominantly female jobs lower than they would be if the jobs had a more heavily male sex composition (England 1992; Kilbourne et al. 1994; England and Folbre 2005). While the overall sex gap in pay has diminished because more women have moved into "male" fields (England and Folbre 2005), there is no evidence that the devaluation of occupations because they are filled with women has diminished (Levanon, England, and Allison 2009). Indeed, as U.S. courts have interpreted the law, this type of between-job discrimination is not even illegal (England 1992, 225–51; Steinberg 2001), whereas it is illegal to pay women less than men in the same job, unless based on factors such as seniority, qualifications, or performance. Given this, both men and women continue to have a pecuniary incentive to choose male-dominated occupations. Thus, we should not be surprised that desegregation of occupations has largely taken the form of women moving into male-dominated fields, rather than men moving into female-dominated fields.

Consistent with the incentives embedded in the ongoing devaluation of female fields, desegregation of fields of college study came from more women going into fields that were predominantly male, not from more men entering "female" fields. Since 1970, women increasingly majored in previously male-dominated, business-related fields, such as business, marketing, and accounting; while fewer chose traditionally female majors like English, education, and sociology; and there was little increase of men's choice of these latter majors (England and Li 2006, 667–69). . . .

Women have also recently increased their representation in formerly male-dominated professional degrees, getting MDs, MBAs, and law degrees in large numbers. Women were 6 percent of those getting MDs in 1960, 23 percent in 1980, 43 percent in 2000, and 49 percent in 2007; the analogous numbers for law degrees (JDs) were 3, 30, 46, and 47 percent, and for MBAs (and other management first-professional degrees), 4, 22, 39, and 44 percent (National Center for Education Statistics 2004–2008). There was no marked increase in the proportion of men in female-dominated graduate professional programs such as library science, social work, or nursing (National Center for Education Statistics 2009).

As women have increasingly trained for previously male-dominated fields, they have also integrated previously male-dominated occupations in management and the professions in large numbers (Cotter, Hermsen, and Vanneman 2004, 10–13). Women may face discrimination and coworker resistance when they attempt to integrate these fields, but they have a strong pecuniary incentive to do so. Men lose money and suffer cultural disapproval when they choose traditionally female-dominated fields; they have little incentive to transgress gender boundaries. While some men have entered female-intensive retail service jobs after losing manufacturing jobs, there is little incentive for voluntary movement in this direction, making desegregation a largely one-way street.

What about employers' incentives? There is some debate about whether, absent equal employment legislation, employers have an incentive to engage in hiring and placement discrimination or are better off simply hiring gender-blind (for debate, see Jackson 1998; England 1992, 54–68). Whichever is true, legal enforcement of antidiscrimination laws has imposed some costs for hiring discrimination (Hirsh 2009), and this has probably reduced discrimination in hiring, contributing to desegregation of jobs.

The "Personal" Realm

"The personal is political" was a rallying cry of 1960s feminists, urging women to demand equality in private as well as public life. Yet conventions embodying male dominance have changed much less in "the personal" than in the job world. Where they have changed, the asymmetry described above for the job world prevails. For example, parents are more likely to give girls "boy" toys such as Legos than they are to give dolls to their sons. Girls have increased their participation in sports more than boys have taken up cheerleading or ballet. Women now commonly wear pants, while men wearing skirts remains rare. A few women started keeping their birth-given surname upon marriage (Goldin and Shim 2004), with little adoption by men of women's last names. Here, as with jobs, the asymmetry follows incentives, albeit nonmaterial ones. These social incentives themselves flow from a largely unchanged devaluation of things culturally defined as feminine. When boys and men take on "female" activities, they often suffer disrespect, but under some circumstances, girls and women gain respect for taking on "male" activities.

What is more striking than the asymmetry of gender change in the personal realm is how little gendering has changed at all in this realm, especially in dyadic heterosexual relationships. It is still men who usually ask women on dates, and sexual behavior is generally initiated by men (England, Shafer, and Fogarty 2008). Sexual permissiveness has increased, making it more acceptable for both heterosexual men and women to have sex outside committed relationships. But the gendered part of this—the double standard—persists stubbornly; women are judged much more harshly than men for casual sex (Hamilton and Armstrong 2009; England, Shafer, and Fogarty 2008). The ubiquity of asking about height in Internet dating Web sites suggests that the convention that men should be taller than their female partner has not budged. The double standard of aging prevails, making women's chances of marriage decrease with age much more than men's (England and McClintock 2009). Men are still expected to propose marriage (Sassler and Miller 2007). Upon marriage, the vast majority of women take their husband's surname. The number of women keeping their own name increased in the 1970s and 1980s but little thereafter, never exceeding about 25 percent even for college graduates (who have higher rates than other women) (Goldin and Shim 2004). Children are usually given their father's surname; a recent survey found that even in cases where the mother is not married to the father, 92 percent of babies are given the father's last name (McLanahan forthcoming). While we do not have trend data on all these personal matters, my sense is that they have changed much less than gendered features of the world of paid work.

The limited change seen in the heterosexual personal realm may be because women's incentive to change these things is less clear than their incentive to move into paid work and into higher-paying "male" jobs. The incentives that do exist are largely noneconomic. For example, women may find it meaningful to keep their birth-given surnames and give them to their children, and they probably enjoy sexual freedom and initiation, especially if they are not judged adversely for it. But these noneconomic benefits may be neutralized by the noneconomic penalties from transgressing gender norms and by the fact that some have internalized the norms. When women transgress gender barriers to enter "male" jobs, they too may be socially penalized for violating norms, but for many this is offset by the economic gain.

Co-Occurring Logics of Women's Rights to Upward Mobility and Gender Essentialism

I have stressed that important change in the gender system has taken the form of women integrating traditionally male occupations and fields of study. But even here change is uneven. The main generalization is shown by Figure 2, which divides all occupations by a crude measure of class, calling professional, management, and nonretail sales occupations

FIGURE 2

Sex segregation of middle-class and working-class occupations in the United States, 1950–2000
Source: Cotter, Hermsen, and Vanneman (2004, 14).
Note: Middle-class occupations include professional, management, and nonretail sales. All others are classified as working-class occupations.

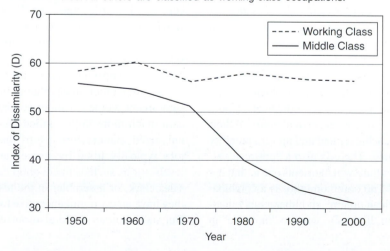

"middle class," and all others "working class" (including retail sales, assembly work in manufacturing, blue-collar trades, and other nonprofessional service work). Using the index of dissimilarity to measure segregation, Figure 2 shows that desegregation has proceeded much farther in middle-class than working-class jobs. Middle-class jobs showed dramatic desegregation, although the trend lessened its pace after 1990. By contrast, working-class jobs are almost as segregated as they were in 1950! Women have integrated the previously male strongholds of management, law, medicine, and academia in large numbers. But women have hardly gained a foothold in blue-collar, male-dominated jobs such as plumbing, construction, truck driving, welding, and assembly in durable manufacturing industries such as auto and steel (Cotter, Hermsen, and Vanneman 2004, 12–14). This is roughly the situation in other affluent nations as well (Charles and Grusky 2004). This same class difference in trend can be seen if we compare the degree of segregation among those who have various levels of education; in the United States, sex segregation declined much more dramatically since 1970 for college graduates than any other group (Cotter, Hermsen, and Vanneman 2009, 2004, 13–14).

Why has desegregation been limited to high-level jobs? The question has two parts: why women did not integrate blue-collar male jobs in significant numbers, and why women did integrate professional and managerial jobs in droves. Why one and not the other? Many factors were undoubtedly at work,[3] but I will focus on one account, which borrows from Charles and Bradley (Charles forthcoming; Charles and Bradley 2002, 2009). In the United States and many Western societies today, a certain kind of gender egalitarianism has taken hold ideologically and institutionally. The logic is that individuals should have equal rights to education and jobs of their choice. Moreover, achievement and upward mobility are generally valued. There is also a "postmaterialist" aspect to the culture which orients one to find her or his "true self." The common ethos is a combination of "the American dream" and liberal individualism. Many women, like men, want to "move up" in

earnings and/or status, or at least avoid moving down. But up or down relative to what reference group? I suggest that the implicit reference group is typically those in the previous generation (or previous birth cohorts) of one's own social class background and one's own sex. For example, women might see their mothers or aunts as a reference, or women who graduated with their level of education 10 years ago. Persons of the same-sex category are the implicit reference group because of strong beliefs in gender essentialism, that notion that men and women are innately and fundamentally different (Charles forthcoming; Ridgeway 2009). While liberal individualism encourages a commitment to "free choice" gender egalitarianism (such as legal equality of opportunity), ironically, orienting toward gender-typical paths has probably been encouraged by the emerging form of individualism that stresses finding and expressing one's "true self." Notions of self will in fact be largely socially constructed, pulling from socially salient identities. Because of the omnipresent nature of gender in the culture (Ridgeway 2009; West and Zimmerman 1987), gender often becomes the most available material from which to construct aspirations and may be used even more when a job choice is seen as a deep statement about self (Charles and Bradley 2009).

Given all this, I hypothesize that if women can move "up" in status or income relative to their reference group while still staying in a job typically filled by women, then because of gender beliefs and gendered identities, they are likely to do so. If they cannot move up without integrating a male field, and demand is present and discrimination not too strong, they are more likely to cross the gender boundary. Applying this hypothesis, why would women not enter male blue-collar fields? To be sure, many women without college degrees would earn much more in the skilled blue-collar crafts or unionized manufacturing jobs than in the service jobs typically filled by women at their education levels—jobs such as maid, child care worker, retail sales clerk, or assembler in the textile industry. So they have an economic incentive to enter these jobs. But such women could also move "up" to clerical work or teaching, higher status and better paying but still traditionally female jobs. Many take this path, often getting more education.

In contrast, consider women who assumed they would go to college and whose mothers were in female-dominated jobs requiring a college degree like teacher, nurse, librarian, or social worker. For these women, to move up in status or earnings from their reference group options requires them to enter traditionally male jobs; there are virtually no heavily female jobs with higher status than these female professions. These are just the women, usually of middle-class origins, who have been integrating management, law, medicine, and academia in recent decades. For them, upward mobility was not possible within traditional boundaries, so they were more likely to integrate male fields.

In sum, my argument is that one reason that women integrated male professions and management much more than blue-collar jobs is that the women for whom the blue-collar male jobs would have constituted "progress" also had the option to move up by entering higher-ranking female jobs via more education. They thus had options for upward mobility without transgressing gender boundaries not present for their middle-class sisters. . . .

CONCLUSION

Change in the gender system has been uneven, changing the lives of some groups of people more than others and changing lives in some arenas more than others. Although many factors are at play, I have offered two broad explanations for the uneven nature of change.

First, I argued that, because of the cultural and institutional devaluation of characteristics and activities associated with women, men had little incentive to move into badly rewarded, traditionally female activities such as homemaking or female-dominated occupations. By contrast, women had powerful economic incentives to move into the traditionally male domains of paid employment and male-typical occupations; and when hiring discrimination declined, many did. These incentives varied

by class, however; the incentive to go to work for pay is much stronger for women who can earn more; thus employment levels have been higher for well-educated women. I also noted a lack of change in the gendering of the personal realm, especially of heterosexual romantic and sexual relationships.

Second, I explored the consequences of the co-occurrence of two Western cultural and institutional logics. Individualism, encompassing a belief in rights to equal opportunity in access to jobs and education in order to express one's "true self," promotes a certain kind of gender egalitarianism. It does not challenge the devaluation of traditionally female spheres, but it encourages the rights of women to upward mobility through equal access to education and jobs. To be sure, this ideal has been imperfectly realized, but this type of gender egalitarianism has taken hold strongly. But co-occurring with it, somewhat paradoxically, are strong (if tacit) beliefs in gender essentialism—that men and women are innately and fundamentally different in interests and skills (Charles 2011; Charles and Bradley 2002, 2009; Ridgeway 2009). Almost no men and precious few women, even those who believe in "equal opportunity," have an explicit commitment to undoing gender differentiation for its own sake. Gender essentialism encourages traditional choices and leads women to see previous cohorts of women of their social class as the reference point from which they seek upward mobility. I concluded that the co-occurrence of these two logics—equal opportunity individualism and gender essentialism—make it most likely for women to move into nontraditional fields of study or work when there is no possible female field that constitutes upward mobility from the socially constructed reference point. This helps explain why women integrated male-dominated professional and managerial jobs more than blue-collar jobs. Women from working-class backgrounds, whose mothers were maids or assemblers in nondurable manufacturing, could move up financially by entering blue-collar "male" trades but often decide instead to get more education and move up into a female job such as secretary or teacher. It is women with middle-class backgrounds, whose mothers were teachers or nurses, who cannot move up without entering a male-dominated career, and it is just such women who have integrated management, law, medicine, and academia. Yet even while integrating large fields such as academia, women often gravitate toward the more female-typical fields of study.

As sociologists, we emphasize links between parts of a social system. For example, we trace how gender inequality in jobs affects gender inequality in the family, and vice versa (England and Farkas 1986). Moreover, links between parts of the system are recognized in today's prevailing view in which gender is itself a multilevel system, with causal arrows going both ways from macro to micro (Risman 2004). All these links undoubtedly exist, but the unevenness of gender-related change highlights how loosely coupled parts of the social system are and how much stronger some causal forces for change are than others. For example, because it resonated with liberal individualism well, the part of the feminist message that urged giving women equal access to jobs and education made considerable headway and led to much of what we call the gender revolution. But even as women integrated employment and "male" professional and managerial jobs, the part of feminism challenging the devaluation of traditionally female activities and jobs made little headway. The result is persistently low rewards for women who remain focused on mothering or in traditionally female jobs and little incentive for men to make the gender revolution a two-way street.

While discussing the uneven character of gender change, I also noted that the type of gender change with the most momentum—middle-class women entering traditionally male spheres—has recently stalled (Cotter, Hermsen, and Vanneman 2004, 2009). Women's employment rates stabilized, desegregation of occupations slowed down, and desegregation of fields of college study stopped. Erosion of the sex gap in pay slowed as well (Cotter, Hermsen, and Vanneman 2009). While the reason for the stalling is unclear, like the unevenness of change, the stalling of change reminds us how contingent and path-dependent gender egalitarian change is, with no inexorable equal endpoint.

Change has been as much unintended consequence of larger institutional and cultural forces as realization of the efforts of feminist organizing, although the latter has surely helped.[4] Indeed, given the recent stalling of change, future feminist organizing may be necessary to revitalize change.

DISCUSSION QUESTIONS

1. What is gender egalitarianism?
2. What stereotypes and double standards still remain for women?

NOTES

1. In this article, I use the term *class* to cover both categoric notions of class and gradational notions of socioeconomic position. Often I use education or occupation as imperfect but readily available indicators of class.
2. A complementary hypothesis about why employment rates are lower for less educated women is that, compared to women with more education, they place a higher value on motherhood and find less intrinsic meaning in the jobs they can get. In this vein, Edin and Kefalas (2005) argue that low-income women place a higher value on motherhood because they have so few alternative sources of meaning. However, Ferree (1976) found that working-class women were happier if employed; they worked for the money but also gained a sense of competence, connectedness, and self-determination from their jobs. McQuillan et al. (2008) find that neither education nor careerism is associated with the value placed on motherhood. Overall, there is no clear conclusion on class differences in how women value motherhood and jobs.
3. One important additional factor is that blue-collar male jobs have been contracting (Morris and Western 1999), so integrating them would have been more difficult even if women had wanted to do so. Moreover, male coworkers may fight harder to harass and keep women out of blue-collar than professional and managerial jobs; lacking class privilege, blue-collar men may feel a stronger need than more privileged men to defend their gender privilege. Finally, it is possible that the Equal Employment Opportunity Commission had an institutional bias toward bringing cases challenging discrimination in high-level managerial and professional positions, particularly when they became concerned with the "glass ceiling." This could explain why Burstein (1989) found more discrimination cases in high-level jobs.
4. Risman (2009) reminds us that our own teaching has probably had an effect on keeping feminism alive, as today's young feminists often say that the college classroom is where they began to identify as feminists.

REFERENCES

Bailey, Martha J. 2006. More power to the pill: The impact of contraceptive freedom on women's life cycle labor supply. *Quarterly Journal of Economics* 121:289–320.

Bergmann, Barbara. 2005. *The economic emergence of women.* 2nd ed. New York: Basic Books.

Bianchi, Suzanne, John P. Robinson, and Melissa A. Milkie. 2006. *Changing rhythms of American family life.* New York: Russell Sage Foundation.

Burstein, Paul. 1989. Attacking sex discrimination in the labor market: A study in law and politics. *Social Forces* 67:641–65.

Charles, Maria. 2011. A world of difference: International trends in women's economic status. *Annual Review of Sociology.*

Charles, Maria, and Karen Bradley. 2002. Equal but separate: A cross-national study of sex segregation in higher education. *American Sociological Review* 67:573–99.

Charles, Maria, and David B. Grusky. 2004. *Occupational ghettos: The worldwide segregation of women and men.* Stanford, CA: Stanford University Press.

Charles, Maria, and Karen Bradley. 2009. Indulging our gendered selves: Sex segregation by field of study in 44 countries. *American Journal of Sociology* 114:924–76.

Cotter, David A., Joan M. Hermsen, and Paula England. 2008. Moms and jobs: Trends in mothers' employment and which mothers stay home. In *American families: A multicultural reader,* 2nd ed., edited by Stephanie Coontz, with Maya Parson and Gabrielle Raley, 379–86. New York: Routledge.

Cotter, David A., Joan M. Hermsen, and Reeve Vanneman. 2004. *Gender inequality at work.* New York: Russell Sage Foundation.

Cotter, David A., Joan M. Hermsen, and Reeve Vanneman. 2009. End of the gender revolution website, www.bsos .umd.edu/socy/vanneman/endofgr/default.html (accessed December 14, 2009).

Edin, Kathryn, and Maria Kefalas. 2005. *Promises I can keep: Why poor women put motherhood before marriage.* Berkeley: University of California Press.

England, Paula 1992. *Comparable worth: Theories and evidence.* New York: Aldine.

England, Paula, and George Farkas. 1986. *Households, employment, and gender: A social, economic, and demographic view.* New York: Aldine.

England, Paula, and Nancy Folbre. 2005. Gender and economic sociology. In *The handbook of economic sociology,* edited by N. J. Smelser and R. Swedberg, 627–49. New York: Russell Sage Foundation.

England, Paula, Carmen Garcia-Beaulieu, and Mary Ross. 2004. Women's employment among Blacks, whites, and three groups of Latinas: Do more privileged women have higher employment? *Gender & Society* 18 (4):494–509.

England, Paula, and Elizabeth Aura McClintock. 2009. The gendered double standard of aging in U.S. marriage markets. *Population and Development Review* 35:797–816.

England, Paula, Emily Fitzgibbons Shafer, and Alison C. K. Fogarty. 2008. Hooking up and forming romantic relationships on today's college campuses. In *The gendered society reader,* 3rd ed., edited by Michael Kimmel and Amy Aronson, 531–46. New York: Oxford University Press.

England, Paula, Janet C. Gornick, and Emily Fitzgibbons Shafer. 2008. Is it better at the top? How women's employment and the gender earnings gap vary by education in sixteen countries. Paper presented at the 2008 annual meeting of the American Sociological Association.

England, Paula, Paul Allison, Su Li, Noah Mark, Jennifer Thompson, Michelle Budig, and Han Sun. 2007. Why are some academic fields tipping toward female? The sex composition of U.S. fields of doctoral degree receipt, 1971–2002. *Sociology of Education* 80:23–42.

England, Paula, and Su Li. 2006. Desegregation stalled: The changing gender composition of college majors, 1971–2002. *Gender & Society* 20:657–77.

Ferree, Myra Marx. 1976. Working-class jobs: Paid work and housework as sources of satisfaction. *Social Problems* 23 (4):431–41.

Goldin, Claudia, and Maria Shim. 2004. Making a name: Women's surnames at marriage and beyond. *Journal of Economic Perspectives* 18:143–60.

Hamilton, Laura, and Elizabeth A. Armstrong. 2009. Gendered sexuality in young adulthood: Double binds and flawed options. *Gender & Society* 23:589–616.

Hirsh, C. Elizabeth. 2009. The strength of weak enforcement: The impact of discrimination charges on sex and race segregation in the workplace. *American Sociological Review* 74 (2):245–71.

Jackson, Robert Max. 1998. *Destined for equality: The inevitable rise of women's status.* Cambridge, MA: Harvard University Press.

Kilbourne, Barbara Stanek, Paula England, George Farkas, Kurt Beron, and Dorothea Weir. 1994. Returns to skills, compensating differentials, and gender bias: Effects of occupational characteristics on the wages of white women and men. *American Journal of Sociology* 100:689–719.

Kuperberg, Arielle, and Pamela Stone. 2008. The media depiction of women who opt out. *Gender & Society* 2:497–517.

Levanon, Asaf, Paula England, and Paul Allison. 2009. Occupational feminization and pay: Assessing causal dynamics using 1950-2000 census data. *Social Forces* 88:865–92.

Mare, Robert D. 1991. Five decades of educational assortative mating. *American Sociological Review* 56:15–32.

McLanahan, Sara. Forthcoming. Children in fragile families. In *Families in an unequal society,* edited by Marcia Carlson and Paula England. Stanford, CA: Stanford University Press.

McQuillan, Julia, Arthur L. Greil, Karina M. Shreffler, and Veronica Tichenor. 2008. The importance of motherhood among women in the contemporary United States. *Gender & Society* 22:477–96.

Morris, Martina, and Bruce Western. 1999. Inequality in earnings at the close of the twentieth century. *Annual Review of Sociology* 25:623–57.

National Center for Education Statistics. 1971–2003. *Digest of education statistics.* Washington, DC: Government Printing Office.

National Center for Education Statistics. 2004–2007. Table numbers by year: 2004: 253, 2005: 252, 2006: 58, 2007: 264, 2008: 279. http://nces.ed.gov/programs/digest (accessed December 14, 2009).

Percheski, Christine. 2008. Opting out? Cohort differences in professional women's employment rates from 1960 to 2000. *American Sociological Review* 73:497–517.

Ridgeway, Cecilia L. 2009. Framed before we know it: How gender shapes social relations. *Gender & Society* 23:145–60.

Risman, Barbara J. 2004. Gender as a social structure: Theory wrestling with activism. *Gender & Society* 18:429–50.

Risman, Barbara J. 2009. From doing to undoing: Gender as we know it. *Gender & Society* 23:81–84.

Sassler, Sharon, and Amanda Miller. 2007. Waiting to be asked: Gender, power and relationship progression among cohabiting couples. Presented at the annual meeting of the American Sociological Association, New York, August.

Steinberg, Ronnie J. 2001. Comparable worth in gender studies. In *International encyclopedia of the social and behavioral sciences,* vol. 4, edited by Neil J. Smelser and Paul B, Baltes. Cambridge: Cambridge University Press.

West, Candace, and Donald H. Zimmerman. 1987. Doing gender. *Gender & Society* 1:125–51.

SEXUALITY

READING 46

Sex Education and the Promotion of Heteronormativity

Tanya McNeill

What can I do if I am attracted to someone of the same sex?

You probably have many friends that are of the same sex as yourself. Some teenagers today are confused about the differences between friendship and homosexuality. This confusion comes from how television and movies present sex. Too often, homosexuality is shown as a legitimate lifestyle equal to a heterosexual lifestyle. These same sex "unions" cannot provide an adequate means of achieving a genuine physical relationship with another human being because this type of "union" is contrary to the laws of nature. There can be no real union because same sex bodies do not even physically fit together. If you or someone you know is struggling with same sex attraction, you can find help and obtain more information at these websites: narth.com; peoplecan-change.com; and couragerc.net. (Kelly and Houck, 2006).

Nearly two decades ago, Lisa Duggan proposed that queer theorists and scholars organize under a campaign of "No Promo Hetero" (1994: 9). She argued that such a project should "outline the ways in which heterosexuality is endorsed through state activity (education, tax law, marriage, family life and so on), specifying the unfair preferences that operate in each area" (1994: 9). This remains an imperative political and scholarly project, particularly within the context of the state's increasingly explicit promotion and regulation of heterosexuality.[1] The quotation with which I open this article is from a pamphlet distributed to students at a public Alabama middle-school in May 2006 as part of a school sponsored sexuality education program (Associated Press, 2006). One of the students who received this pamphlet was a 12-year-old whose mother is a lesbian. Like many school children in the USA, this young girl was informed, at her public school, that her family is unacceptable. Such curricula are common, particularly in schools that provide abstinence-only and abstinence-until-marriage sexuality education to students.

Tanya McNeill is a sociologist and independent scholar researching cultural and political representations of gender-creative children.

In this article, I take up Duggan's call and analyze how sexuality education policy and curricula promote heterosexuality, or more precisely, heteronormativity. I engage in a discourse analysis of federal- and state-level sexuality education laws and policies. . . . I find that these policies and documents promote a specific normative form of monogamous, marital, middle-class, normatively gendered, and in many implicit and explicit ways, white, heterosexuality—that is best described as heteronormative. In other words, they promote a specific family form—a nuclear family made up of married heterosexual parents with children who are biologically theirs. . . .

"Heteronormativity promotes the norm of social life as not only heterosexual but also married, monogamous, white, and upper middle class" (Brandzel, 2005: 190). Heteronormativity is not equivalent to heterosexuality; it posits a very specific normative form of heterosexuality, one that also regulates heterosexuals (see e.g., Cohen, 1997). . . . The promotion of heteronormativity occurs within a larger cultural and social context that simultaneously reproduces heterosexuality as an affectively sacred, special and sparkly space (e.g., in children's movies, see Martin and Kazyak, 2009) and simultaneously as "mundane," everyday practice (Myers and Raymond, 2010).

Schools, as sites of the production of citizens, exert a powerfully disciplining force on heterosexual and LGBTQ non-heteronormative family forms (Pallotta-Chiarolli, 2010). Within schools, sexuality education is perhaps one of the most explicit sites of the regulation of gender and sexuality. As Mayo argues, sexuality education curricula and policies include "clear and specific messages about properly gendered behavior and proper sexual behavior" (2004: 65). Sexuality education policy can also be read as an explicit form of bio-politics, which entails political or governmental regulation and disciplining of all aspects of life at the level of the body, and at the level of population (Foucault, 1990: 139). . . .

Pathologizing Homosexuality

It is not uncommon for public schools to pathologize homosexuality. State laws in Alabama, Arizona, Mississippi, Oklahoma, South Carolina, and Utah require that sexuality education present homosexuality in a negative light (see the Sexuality Information and Education Council of the United States publication SIECUS, 2011b). For example, Alabama State Code (Section 16-40A-2) requires "an emphasis, in a factual manner and from a public health perspective, that homosexuality is not a life style acceptable to the general public and that homosexual conduct is a criminal offense under the laws of the state."[2] Not only does the state here specifically articulate lesbian, gay and bisexual sexualities as "unacceptable," but this statute references anti-sodomy laws, which are still on the books in South Carolina, despite the Supreme Court's 2003 *Lawrence vs. Texas* decision,[3] which declared such laws unconstitutional. Arizona state code prohibits schools from "promoting homosexuality" in its sexuality education curriculum. "No district shall include in its course of study instruction which: (1) Promotes a homosexual lifestyle. (2) Portrays homosexuality as a positive alternative life-style. (3) Suggests that some methods of sex are safe methods of homosexual sex" (Arizona State Legislature, n.d.). Louisiana prohibits the use of "any sexually explicit materials depicting male or homosexual activity" (Louisiana State Legislature, n.d.). Mississippi mandates that schools teach that "a mutually faithful, monogamous relationship in the context of marriage is the only appropriate setting for sexual intercourse."[4] Oklahoma requires schools to provide AIDS education and mandates that such education "specifically teach students that (1) engaging in homosexual activity, promiscuous sexual activity, intravenous drug use or contact with contaminated blood products is now known to be primarily responsible for contact with the AIDS virus" (Oklahoma State Department of Education, n.d). In addition to pathologizing "homosexuality," these policies are medically inaccurate; sex between two females, for example, is a relatively low-risk sexual activity (Center for Disease Control and Prevention, 2006).[5] Such state laws also pathologize any sexual activity that occurs outside of heterosexual marriage. The articulation of heterosexuality as normative and homosexuality as diseased is made explicit in South Carolina's state code on health education, which prohibits any "discussion of alternate sexual lifestyles from heterosexual relationships including, but not limited to, homosexual relationships except in the context of instruction concerning sexually transmitted diseases."[6]

Although these six states may seem extreme in their explicit pathologization of gay, lesbian, and bisexual sexualities, an additional 22 states require public schools to "stress" or "cover" abstinence if they offer sexuality education (Guttmacher Institute, 2011). The abstinence-until-marriage education mandated by many federal and state policies is inherently heteronormative and frequently ignores and/or denigrates the existence of gay, lesbian, bisexual, transgender and intersex youth (Irvine, 2006; Lipkin, 1999; Mayo, 2004). The emphasis on "sex" as heterosexual penetrative intercourse is one aspect of this heteronormativity (Jackson, 1995: 21 cited in Weeks et al., 2001). This limited definition of "sex" precludes other forms of sexual behavior in which students (whether or not they are heterosexual) may engage. The emphasis on "marriage," which is central to many sexuality education curricula is another aspect of the heteronormativity of much sexuality education. . . .

The federal government's emphasis on abstinence-only sexuality education has been a key aspect of its regulation of poor women's sexuality for over 30 years. Welfare policy has always been a racial project (Omi and Winant, 1994) that regulates sexuality, race, and gender and imposes heteronormative (white, marital, monogamous, heterosexual, and middle-class) familial standards on poor women (Mink, 1995; see also Collins' discussion of the "normative yardstick" 1990: 46). The 1996 Personal Responsibility Act, which draws on language eerily similar to the Moynihan report,[7] pathologizes single mothers (who were racialized as black and Latina during the welfare reform debates of the late 20th century) and disproportionately regulates the reproductive and familial lives of women of color, created a new funding source for abstinence-only-until-marriage programs through Title V, Section 510(b) of the Social Security Act. Title V sexuality education is described in the law as

an educational or motivational program which . . .

(A) has as its exclusive purpose, teaching the social, psychological, and health gains to be realized by abstaining from sexual activity;

(B) teaches abstinence from sexual activity outside marriage as the expected standard for all school age children;

(C) teaches that abstinence from sexual activity is the only certain way to avoid out-of-wedlock pregnancy, sexually transmitted diseases, and other associated health problems;

(D) teaches that a mutually faithful monogamous relationship in context of marriage is the expected standard of human sexual activity;

(E) teaches that sexual activity outside of the context of marriage is likely to have harmful psychological and physical effects;

(F) teaches that bearing children out-of-wedlock is likely to have harmful consequences for the child, the child's parents, and society;

(G) teaches young people how to reject sexual advances and how alcohol and drug use increases vulnerability to sexual advances; and

(H) teaches the importance of attaining self-sufficiency before engaging in sexual activity (Section 510 of Title V of the Social Security Act).

While there has been some variation in how strictly states have been required to meet these standards,[8] Title V may be the federal government's most explicit articulation and promotion of heteronormativity. It lays out a set of sexual standards for U.S. citizens and emphasizes the importance of teaching these sexual standards in schools.

While I focus here on Title V sexuality education funds, there are at least three other programs through which the federal government funds abstinence-only education. In 1981, the federal government passed the Adolescent Family Life Act (AFLA), which funds abstinence-only education in an effort to prevent teen pregnancy (Perrin and DeJoy, 2003). Additional abstinence-only funds are available to state and community organizations through Community Based Abstinence Education grants, established by the federal government in 2001. In 2010, Congress created the Personal Responsibility Education Program, which funds comprehensive sexuality education. The range of federal funding streams for sexuality education are emblematic of the ambivalence of federal policy and of sexuality education as a flexible and varied form of regulation. For example, even as Title V policies require sexuality education to follow heteronormative guidelines, the call for proposals for Personal Responsibility Education Program (PREP) grants suggests that states should take into account the needs of LGBTQ youth and to strive to be "inclusive . . . and non-stigmatizing." While this is a clear move away from the explicit heteronormativity of Title V and AFLA sexuality education funds, the fact that states can apply for both Title V and PREP funds means that sexuality education curricula can be contradictory within a given state. This demonstrates a peculiar kind of ambivalence on the part of federal and state policy around the regulation of sexuality.

Curricula that promote abstinence—particularly abstinence until marriage—assume that full belonging as an adult and a citizen in the community, family, and nation requires heteronormative family relations. This co-exists with a national imagery of an American character of fairness, equality, and tolerance, which creates a contradiction emblematic of the state's attitude towards gender nonconformity and non-heteronormative sexualities (heterosexual and LGBTQ). As Cohen (1997) points out, the promotion of heteronormativity not only pathologizes LGBTQ families and individuals, but relies on the stigmatization of single mothers, particularly poor women of color. The state engages in the affective production and regulation of the family when it upholds heteronormative families and sexuality and gender normativity as desirable by the community and the nation. Even in states where same-sex marriage is permitted (which does not actually change the regulatory logic of heteronormativity), abstinence-only curricula pathologize and marginalize all individuals (and families) who do not

conform to the marriage mandate, who choose to have non-monogamous relationships, or who otherwise deviate from heteronormativity. In some cases this is achieved through the articulation of the superiority of heteronormative nuclear families in curricula and policy.

THE HETERONORMATIVE FAMILY AS SUPERIOR

Only 12 states and Washington DC require that schools include what SIECUS and the Guttmacher Institute describe as "positive" information about LGBTQ issues.[9] California, for example, is required to provide sexuality education curricula "appropriate for use with pupils of all races, genders, sexual orientations, ethnic and cultural backgrounds, and pupils with disabilities" (Official California Legislative Information, n.d.a). Moreover, the California Education Code prohibits discrimination on the basis of "disability, gender, nationality, race or ethnicity, religion, [or] sexual orientation" (Official California Legislative Information (n.d.b). Despite the state's anti-discrimination mandate, the state policy document *Health Framework for California Public Schools: Kindergarten Through Grade Twelve* articulates the superiority of heteronormative families. It does so in two brief paragraphs that describe such families in an affectively dense manner. This description demonstrates the ambivalence of the state towards non-heteronormative or "nontraditional" individuals and families.

A functional family unit is vital to the well-being of children. Children usually develop best when they live in a stable environment with their mother and father and receive from their parents consistent love, support, and direction. However, children from nontraditional families can also develop successfully. Given the variety of nontraditional families in contemporary society, it is important that children not reared in two-parent families be convinced that their situation can also be conducive to growth and development.

Further, it is important that children not be denigrated because of their living arrangement or the composition of their family. All students, regardless of their current living arrangement, can benefit from classroom instruction and discussion on family living. They can learn how they can contribute to making the family unit harmonious and successful now as well as in the future—when they will likely become parents (California Department of Education, 2003: 63).

Heteronormative families are characterized as "functional," "stable," and "consistent," which links normative and affective concepts. The description links these normative families as sites of "love, support, and direction." Positive affects and affective states are linked with normative family forms. The juxtaposition of the description of two-parent heterosexual, married families with a discussion of "non-traditional" families (and the use of the word "however") implies that non-heteronormative families are not "functional," "stable," or "consistent" and that they are unlikely to offer the same level of "love, support, and direction" as "traditional" families can. This logic pathologizes unmarried heterosexual parents as well as LGBTQ parents. Moreover the state articulates the norm of parenthood, and family as central to adulthood and citizenship by positing that these students "will likely become parents."

The Prince William County School District (in Virginia) articulates a similar message in its eighth-grade curriculum objectives.

> Teachers will teach that, although it is desirable for a family to include both a mother and a father, due to circumstances beyond the control of a child, this does not always occur. As many children in a classroom will not have a traditional family, the teacher should reinforce that these children should not feel "less worthy" because their family does not resemble the family of other students (Prince William County Public Schools, 2009: 4; emphasis in original).

The assertion of the superiority of a particular family form raises affective and pedagogical problems in the classroom. According to these state policies, teachers in California[10] and in Prince William County must simultaneously teach their students that the heteropatriarchal family is most "desirable" *and* manage (or discipline) the negative

feelings that might emerge for students whose families look "different."[11] Although these statements seem to be articulating the importance of respecting all students and all families, they produce the very ideas about "non-traditional families" that they then attempt to counter. The discussion of the superiority of heteronormative families produces inequality and itself is a form of "denigration" of children from gay and lesbian families, single-parent families, foster families, grandparent or legal guardian headed families, polyamorous families, or any number of other non-heteronormative family formations. These assumptions about both normative and "non-traditional" families permeate U.S. public policy and demonstrate the limitations of diversity discourses. Discussions of family "difference" in sexuality education policy and curricula reveal a deep ambivalence towards diversity; these texts create a hierarchy of family forms within schools, and within society at large. Certain families are more valuable to the state than others.[12]

Teaching that the heteronormative family is preferable to all other family forms generates tensions around how to manage students' feelings of "worth" and belonging. This illustrates the affective nature of heteropatriarchy as a social structure. It is also a moment of ambivalence in public school policy; it pits conflicting pedagogical goals against each other. How are students to be taught self-esteem and feelings of competence and worth (all included in Virginia's standards), when they are simultaneously taught that their families do not fit the desired norm? These moments of ambivalence and contradiction are frequent in curricular documents dealing with sexuality and family. . . .

Conclusion

In 1991, Eve Sedgwick wrote, "it's always open season on gay kids," (1991: 18). Moreover, she continued a few pages later, ". . . the scope of institutions whose programmatic undertaking is to prevent the development of gay people is unimaginably large. There is no major institutionalized discourse that offers a firm resistance to that undertaking . . ." (1991: 24).

While the cultural and legal terrain has shifted significantly in the past 20 years, Sedgwick's indictment is still all too relevant. Schools do not "offer resistance" to the "prevention of development of gay people." In fact, educational policies and school curricula often actively pathologize and stigmatize LGBTQ youth. As I have demonstrated throughout this article, the state actively regulates sexuality and promotes a normative form of heterosexuality through sexuality education policy and curricula. The promotion of normative heterosexuality and the structuring force of heteronormativity offer a framework of legitimacy that produces the symbolic and material exclusion of non-heteronormative families of all kinds from full participation in the nation and in their communities. . . .

Discourses about school bullying and school safety for LGTBQ youth locate homophobic, transphobic, and misogynistic harassment as *external* to the standards, goals, and daily practices of schools. Yet, as I have demonstrated here, the pathologization of homosexuality, and the valorization of heterosexuality, are actually central to much sexuality education policy and curricula. And these are only the most visible and explicit of these forms of heteronormativity. The institutions and the larger socio-cultural-legal structures that surround the debates around school bullying elide the extent to which heteronormativity structures school standards, curricula and state education policies. In other words, while we frequently hear critiques (and fears) over the "promotion of homosexuality" in schools when policies and curricula are inclusive and accepting of LGBTQ individuals and families, the range of explicit and implicit educational policies and curricula that promote heteronormativity are rarely central to public debates about the safety of LGBTQ students. The fact that in some schools students are explicitly told that their sexual desires are immoral, unhealthy or socially unacceptable is not central to debates about homophobic bullying. The findings of the Gay, Lesbian and Straight Education Network's (GLSEN) 2011 School Climate Survey suggests that further research and advocacy are needed on this. "A greater percentage of LGBT students regularly experienced verbal harassment because of their sexual orientation or gender identity in schools with abstinence-only curricula" (GLSEN, 2012: 50). In schools with abstinence-only sexuality education, 65.9% of students reported harassment due to sexual orientation and 48% due to gender identity, compared with 55.5% and 41.2% in schools with "other sexual health education" (GLSEN, 2012: 50). Moreover GLSEN found "inclusive curriculum," defined as "curriculum that includes positive representations of LGBT people, history and events" (2012: xvi), correlated with lower rates of absenteeism, "a greater sense of connectedness," less homophobic language prevalent in schools, and greater reported acceptance. GLSEN reports that "less than half (43.4%) of students in schools with an inclusive curriculum felt unsafe because of their sexual orientation, compared to almost two thirds (67.5%) of other students" (2012: xvi). This evidence suggests that the state's policies and curriculum may indeed legitimate homophobic, transphobic, sexist, and racist bullying in schools. . . .

DISCUSSION QUESTIONS

1. Would changing state laws prevent situations where "it's always open season on gay kids"?
2. What effect do you think the increased acceptance of gay marriage will have on sex education programs?

NOTES

1. For example, the federal government explicitly promotes marriage, through the Healthy Marriage Initiative, through marriage incentives in welfare policy and through abstinence-only sexuality education. Most states regulate marriage through state-level Defense of Marriage Acts and/or state constitutional amendments that ban same-sex marriage.
2. Section 16-40A-2 of the Alabama State Code (Code of Alabama, 1975).
3. *Lawrence vs. Texas* itself needs to be understood within the racialized regulation of sexuality (Puar, 2007).
4. See Mississippi Code of 1972 Miss. Code Ann. § 37-13-171 (LexisNexis Custom Solution, 2011).

5. Because some men might not be male (e.g., female to male transsexuals), and some women not female (e.g., male to female transsexuals), I use the terms "female" and "male" here in an attempt to gesture towards the difference between gender and sex and the possibility of disjuncture between them (i.e., male ≠ man). It is also important to point out that "sex" is no more natural a category than "gender" (see e.g., Butler, 1990; Kessler, 1990).

6. See South Carolina Legislature Online (n.d.) S.C. Code Ann. § 59-32-30(A)(5).

7. See Gans 2011 for a discussion of the Moynihan Report.

8. In some years, grantees for Title V funds have been permitted to use grants for programs that met some of the requirements, but were not required to meet all requirements. The 2007 call for applications for Title V funds had very strict guidelines. *All* of the requirements (A–H) needed to be "meaningfully represented" in state curricula funded by Title V monies. As a result, a number of states decided not to apply for Title V funds for the 2007 fiscal year. In many cases, state legislation regarding AIDS prevention in sexuality education prohibited states from meeting the stricter requirements. In 2010, curricula funded by using Title V funds were simply forbidden from contradicting requirements A–H (SIECUS, 2011a).

9. These states are: California, Delaware, Iowa, Maryland, Massachusetts, New Hampshire, New Jersey, New Mexico, Oregon, Rhode Island, Washington, and Wisconsin (see Guttmacher, 2011; SIECUS, 2011b).

10. It is possible that California's 2011 *Fair, Accurate, Inclusive and Respectful (FAIR) Education Act,* which mandates the inclusion of LGBTQ individuals' contributions to California and U.S. history, and prohibits materials that discriminate against LGBTQ individuals will supersede the language discussed in this section.

11. I cannot make a claim, of course, about what happens in the classroom. The point here is that these documents create particular mandates and whether or not they are always followed, the epistemological and psychic effects are worthy of interrogation. Again, the ethnographic research conducted by Jessica Fields (2008) and Lorena Garcia (2009) demonstrates that in-class sexuality education experiences in public schools tend to reinforce heteronormative, sexist, and racist social messages about sexuality.

12. This is, of course, not a new message. The state has always valued some families over others, as even a cursory glance at U.S. history demonstrates. See for example, eugenics policy and forced sterilization (Davis, 1983), the enslavement of Black adults and children (Collins, 1990), the removal of Native American children from their homes and communities (Smith, 2005), the internment of Japanese Americans during the Second World War and immigration policies (Luibhéid, 2002). These are all examples of the state's regulation of the family—and its preference for a specific (white, middle-class, heteronormative) family form.

REFERENCES

Arizona State Legislature (n.d.) Available at: www.azleg.gov/ars/15/00716.htm (accessed 21 June 2011).

Associated Press (2006) Lesbian mom objects to sex education pamphlet at Dothan School. Available at: http://legacy.decaturdaily.com/decaturdaily/news/060503/sex.shtm (accessed 20 June 2011).

Brandzel A (2005) Queering citizenship? Same-sex marriage and the state. *GLQ: A Journal of Lesbian and Gay Studies* 11(2): 171–204.

California Department of Education (2003) *Health Frameworks for California Public Schools.* Available at: www.cde.ca.gov/ci/he/cf/ (accessed 7 March 2011).

Center for Disease Control and Prevention (2006) *HIV/AIDS among Women Who Have Sex with Women: CDC HIV/AIDS Fact Sheet.* Available at: www.cdc.gov/hiv/topics/women/resources/factsheets/wsw.htm (accessed 29 May 2012).

Code of Alabama (1975) Available at: http://alisondb.legislature.state.al.us/acas/ACASLoginFire.asp (accessed 21 June 2011).

Cohen C (1997) Punks, bulldaggers, and welfare queens: The radical potential of queer politics? *GLQ* 3(4): 437–465.

Collins PH (1990) *Black Feminist Thought.* New York: Routledge.

Davis A (1983) Racism, birth control, and reproductive rights. In: Davis A (ed.) *Women, Race and Class.* New York: Vintage Books, pp. 202–221.

Duggan L (1994) Queering the state. *Social Text* 39 (Summer): 1–14.

Duggan L (2003) *The Twilight of Equality: Neoliberalism, Cultural Politics, and the Attack on Democracy.* Boston, MA: Beacon Press.

Fields J (2008) *Risky Lessons: Sex Education and Social Inequality.* New Brunswick, NJ: Rutgers University Press.

Foucault M (1990) *The History of Sexuality: An Introduction.* New York: Vintage Books.

Gans H (2011) "The Moynihan Report and its aftermath": A critical analysis. *Du Bois Review* 8(2): 315–327.

Garcia L (2009) "Now why do you want to know about that?": Heteronormativity, sexism, and racism in the sexual (mis)education of Latina youth. *Gender & Society* 23(4): 520–541.

GLSEN – Gay, Lesbian & Straight Education Network (2010) *2009 National School Climate Survey.* Available at: www.glsen.org/cgi-bin/iowa/all/news/record/2624 .html (accessed 7 March 2011).

GLSEN – Gay, Lesbian & Straight Education Network (2012) *2011 National School Climate Survey,* Available at: www .glsen.org/cgi-bin/iowa/all/library/record/2897.html?state =rcsearch&type=rescarch (accessed 18 October 2012).

Guttmacher Institute (2011) State policies in brief as of August 5, 2011: Sex and HIV education. Available at: www.guttmacher.org/stateccnter/spibs/index.html (accessed 9 August 2011).

Irvine J (2006) A conservative in liberal's clothing. *Women's Review of Books* 23(6): 10–12.

Jackson S (1995) Gender and heterosexuality: A materialist feminist analysis. In: Maynard M and Purvis J (eds) *(Hetero)sexual Politics.* London: Taylor and Francis, pp. 11–27.

Kelly M and Houck M (2006) *The Top Ten Questions Teenagers Ask about Sex.* Snowflake, AZ: Heritage House '76. Available at: www.abortionfacts.com/literature/literature _9435tt.asp (accessed 21 June 2011).

Kessler S (1990) The medical construction of gender: Case management of intersex infants. *Signs: Journal of Women in Culture and Society* 16(1): 3–26.

LexisNexis Custom Solution (2011) Mississippi Code of 1972. LexisNexis Custom Solution: Mississippi Code Research Tool. Available from: www.lexisnexis.com /hottopics/mscode/ (accessed 8 August 2011).

Lipkin A (1999) *Understanding Homosexuality, Changing Schools: A Text for Teachers. Counselors, and Administrators.* Boulder. CO: Westview Press.

Louisiana State Legislature (n.d.) Available at: www.legis .state.la.us/lss/lss.asp?doc=80423 (accessed 21 June 2011).

Luibhéid E (2002) *Entry Denied: Controlling Sexuality at the Border.* Minneapolis, MN: University of Minnesota Press.

Martin K and Kazyak E (2009) Hetero-romantic love and heterosexiness in children's G-rated films. *Gender & Society* 23(3): 215–336.

Mayo C (2004) *Disputing the Subject of Sex: Sexuality and Public School Controversies.* New York: Rowman & Littlefield Publishers.

Mink G (1995) *The Wages of Motherhood: Inequality in the Welfare State.* Ithaca, NY: Cornell University Press.

Myers K and Raymond L (2010) Elementary school girls and heteronormativity: The girl project. *Gender & Society* 24(2): 167–288.

Official California Legislative Information (n.d.a) Available at: www.leginfo.ca.gov/cgi-bin/displaycode?section =edc&group=51001-52000&file=51933 (accessed 23 June 2011).

Official California Legislative Information (n.d.b) CA Codes (edc:220-221.1). Available at: www.leginfo.ca.gov/cgi -bin/displaycode?section=edc&group=00001- 01000&file=220–221.1 (accessed 23 June 2011).

Oklahoma State Department of Education (n.d.) Title 210-State Department of Education—Oklahoma State Department of Education. Available at: www.ok.gov/sde /title-210-state-department-education-38 (accessed 14 September 2013).

Omi M and Winant H (1994) *Racial Formation in the United States: From the 1960s to the 1990s.* New York: Routledge.

Perrin K and De Joy (2003) Abstinence-only education: How we got here and where we're going. *Journal of Public Health Policy* 24(3–4): 445–459.

Prince William County Public Schools (2009) *Family Life Education Grade 8 Health: Curriculum Objectives for Use in Mapping Family Life Education Instruction August 2009.* Available at: http://english.pwcs.science .schoolfusion.us/modules/locker/files/group_riles.pht ml?parent=5499258&gid=1179544&sessionid=f6536d 90d2dbcc8217472138053c7cl0 (accessed 14 June 2011).

Puar J (2007) *Terrorist Assemblages: Homonationalism in Queer Times.* Durham, NC: Duke University Press.

Sedgwick E (1991) How to bring your kids up gay. *Social Text* 29: 18–27.

SIECUS (2011a) *State by State Decisions: The Personal Responsibility Education Program and Title V Abstinence-Only Program.* Available at: http://siecus.org/index.cfm? *fuscaction=Featurc.showFeaturc&FeaturcID=l934* (accessed 11 August *2011).*

SIECUS (2011b) *Sexuality Education Policies-Select Topics.* Available at: www.siecus.org/index.cfm?fuseaction=page .viewPage&pageID=l163&nodeID=l (accessed 8 August 2011).

Smith A (2002) *Conquest: Sexual Violence and American Indian Genocide.* Cambridge, MA: South End Press.

Weeks J, Heaphy B and Donovan C (2001) *Same Sex Intimacies: Families of Choice and Other Life Experiments.* New York: Routledge.

PERSONAL ACCOUNT

Learning My Own Privilege

My social class has afforded me the privilege to go about my daily life and education with relative ease and comfort, despite the fact that as a mixed-race, learning disabled woman I belong to many socially devalued groups. I grew up in a safe yet diverse area where my ethnicity and status as the daughter of an immigrant, on the one hand, and a gay man on the other, had few negative social consequences. My father, an American diplomat, met my mother and got married while stationed in the Philippines. We moved around a lot, which caused a great deal of familial stress. Despite the fact that their marriage was falling apart, my mom and dad provided a very happy home and a good education for both their children. They divorced in the late 1990s; my mother remarried, and while I was in high school, my father came out.

Likely because my father came out later in life, and he and my mother divorced relatively amicably, the legal custody he had over my sister and me was never contested. I also never directly encountered anti-immigrant resentment or the threat of my mother being deported. My parents did such a good job insulating me from the prejudice they encountered, that I did not realize what kind of investments and sacrifices they made until I was in college.

Growing up, I often thought about how my learning disability disadvantaged me. I felt ashamed of being pulled out of my regular class during English. I also resented not being able to take electives because I had to spend that extra time catching up with everyone else in my grade. I remember the summer between third and fourth grade, when I realized that most of my friends were going to the school for "gifted" children. I didn't understand why I couldn't go with them. My father explained that I needed a little bit more help than everyone else, and that I'd be spending a lot more time outside my normal class in the coming years working with "special" teachers. I came to hate the word "special." I wanted to be "special" in the same way the "gifted" kids were—no one cared how great I was at social studies or how fast I could run. I felt like the only thing that made me "special" was the fact I couldn't read well.

I didn't realize how incredibly fortunate I was to be able to attend quality schools that had the resources to detect my disability early and give me the extra attention I desperately needed. The reason I got that kind of help was because my parents could afford to buy a house in a nationally ranked school district. They also had the resources to send me to specialists, as well as the leisure time to help me at home. So, whereas the story of my "overcoming" my disability, eventually taking Advanced Placement classes in high school, and going on to college can be told as a great personal triumph, it can be more fully understood as the most likely outcome for a very upper middle-class girl who was always expected to go to college.

Mireille M. Cecil

READING 47

Gaga Relations: The End of Marriage

J. Jack Halberstam

Without getting too academic about this, it's important to understand the activist emphasis on marriage within a much longer history of homo/sexuality.

J. Jack Halberstam is a professor of American studies and ethnicity, gender studies, and comparative literature at the University of Southern California.

Gay marriage as an activist target seems to complete a long process of human classification that began in the late nineteenth century and is ongoing today. This process that began by making fundamental assumptions about human difference by distinguishing between people with homo and people with hetero desires comes full circle when homo people ask to be recognized just like hetero people.

One theorist, Michel Foucault, someone who has greatly influenced the ways that academics write and think about sex, linked the emergence of the category of "homosexual" (1869) to the onset of industrialization, the rise of a culture of expertise (a medical culture then but nowadays more of a talk show culture—think Dr. Phil and self-help literature), the increasing intrusion of medical terms into everyday modes of identifying oneself, and the fragmentation of society/groups/families into people/individuals/subjects: these developments, many people agree, are the hallmarks of the modern world.

Foucault did not stop there, however; he also proposed that a transition occurs between seeing people as part of a group or class and as engaged in actions or practices to seeing folks as defined by hardwired identities and as separate selves. This process begins in the medical lab or the therapist's office but it is only confirmed when the very people whom the doctors are busily classifying actually begin to think of themselves in those terms: while doctors and psychologists might have agreed upon definitions of "normal" and "perverse," those definitions do not take on a sense of permanence and inevitability until someone actually identifies with the terms.

So, while in the 1910s an effeminate man in New York City who has sex with other men may think of himself as a "fairy" may not have ruled out the possibility of marrying a woman, and may consider himself as harboring a vice or as sinning against God, some twenty or thirty years later, a similar kind of man may think of himself as incurably homosexual, as doomed to a life of loneliness and stigma and as someone whom society has marginalized and cast as a pedophile. He will certainly think of himself as having a homosexual identity and may be seeking psychiatric help. Evidence for this framework can be found in the many films of the 1930s to 1960s that depict male homosexuality in precisely these terms—as sad, compulsive, pathological, and antisocial. Such films—like Alfred Hitchcock's *Rope* (1948), Richard Brooks's *Cat on a Hot Tin Roof* (1958), Basil Dearden's *Victim* (1961), and John Huston's *Reflections in a Golden Eye* (1967)—never had to name the sin they depicted (they literally could not name it, because the Hays Code, enforced to control media influence, forbade the depiction of homosexuality); they merely had to indicate that there was something "unmentionable" about the pathology from which the main character suffers.

And by the 1970s, a similar man will think of himself as gay, out, proud; he may be super invested in his masculinity and may resist the categories of "fairy" or "homosexual" altogether and think of his identification with the term "gay" as liberatory! So how, you might ask, did we begin with a diagnosis, move through social marginalization, and arrive at gay pride and gay marriage? But even if you don't ask, you might want to ask, because the struggles that people endured before us have often afforded us our sense of "liberation." And what is more, other political trajectories would have led to other kinds of goals for liberation.

Indeed, the desire for marriage completes a long process by which LGBT people, having been separated out from normative society and called pathological, now are embraced and in turn embrace the very cultures that previously rejected them. In fact, I would take this point further: the participation of LGBT couples in state-sanctioned marriages lends credibility to the very institution that has acquired meaning precisely through excluding gays and lesbians, among others, from marriage in the first place. In other words, marriage has been an exclusionary system rather than an inclusionary one; it has functioned precisely by drawing lines between those who can and those who cannot legally marry. In the twentieth century, people who have been prohibited from marrying include gays, lesbians, trans people, and mixed-race couples. An institution that has been defined through such exclusions and that has been enforced as a system of class alliance, of racial purity, of religious sanction, should surely be dismantled rather than expanded!

Just as new classifications (medical and psychological) of personhood at the end of the nineteenth century created "homosexual" people and "heterosexual" people, they also, through a kind of conceptual sleight of hand, forced people to speak about homo- and heterosexuals, men and women, as if they belonged to different species and as if the differences between each group was distinct, clear, and, above all, natural. One legacy of this division of sexualities and genders into "separate species," has been a lasting inability to see connections when we might want to make more general statements about shifts and changes in gender and sexuality across the culture. And so we speak of gay and lesbian history as if there is one single narrative for all lesbians and all gay men and as if that narrative has coherence and unfolds in terms of exclusion and marginalization followed by protests and revolts and then resolves in terms of accommodation and assimilation. But of course, history unfolds along very different lines for people in different classes, people in different racial groups, and people of different genders. Gay male history does not line up nicely with lesbian history; black histories of sexuality look very different from white ones; histories involving queer people who emigrate from one region to another look massively different from histories of people who spend their whole lives in one area, one city, one neighborhood, even.

Scholars have grappled for years with the challenge of mapping these very disparate differences, and so, too often, one history, a history of white gay men, has come to represent all of gay, lesbian, and transgender history. Why? Because there are paper trails for gay male history that are missing for other histories—gay men have been legally prosecuted, tried, convicted, and sentenced to prison (Oscar Wilde's famous trial, for example, in the late nineteenth century); gay male history has intersected with the histories of dominant culture, but lesbian and trans histories tend to leave less archival material and less traces. For this reason, conventional histories of sexual minorities often take the form of focusing on one event (Stonewall) and then turning it into a representative moment. And so while the history of early twenty-first century LGBT politics will inevitably get told later as a story of the struggle for gay marriage, gay marriage is merely a part of the much more diverse and radical fabric of queer activism, and it may not even be the most popular cause for gays and lesbians and trans people. It has become the most visible, however, because its goals mesh well with the status quo and they seem to confirm the rightness of the social values in which heterosexuals have chosen to invest.

And gay marriage may have very different meaning for different queer communities: as even the Williams Institute studies make clear, gay marriage will do little for queer people currently living in poverty, while it has definite tax benefits for the middle class and the very rich. The hallmark of post–World War II LGBT social movements has tended to be the attempt to change society, to model a different way of relating, of cohabiting, of desiring. So how did we arrive at this historical juncture where an assimilationist politics of marriage now stands in for all queer political aspiration? Many queers today still believe in social movements far less focused on marriage equality and far more interested in changing the structures of intimate modes of relating, belonging, and cohabiting altogether. Many activists outside of the mainstream LGBT marriage-equality movement try to make connections between homophobia and other forms of social and political exclusion. Not content to slip smoothly into already existing corrupt and bankrupt institutions, radical queers still hold on to the idea that something lies "beyond marriage" (as one group calls itself), and, moreover, that human difference should flourish not in the rounding out of existing structures but in the creative invention of new ones.

THE CASE AGAINST GAY MARRIAGE

Let's discuss a more imaginative kind of activism, one that is less tied to a politics of respectability, one that is more committed to change and transformation, and one that is less invested in maintaining U.S. social institutions as they have been formulated in relation to racist and homophobic commitments. I want to summarize quickly the opposition to gay marriage as formulated by progressive or left-leaning groups such as Beyond Gay Marriage, think about the question posed in a number of conversations as to whether "gay marriage is racist" or even specifically "anti-black," and then end with some speculations on activism less focused on changing laws and more intent upon the transformation of social, psychic, and political worlds. At stake here are questions about what counts as political in any given context, oppositions between pragmatism and utopianism, and more questions about how to argue for change, how to recognize change when it actually occurs, and how to think about political pasts, presents, and futures in ways that do not simply produce a sense of political inevitability.

As I have said, not all queer people are advocates of gay marriage; indeed, according to some activist groups, for most queer people this is not their main political priority. In mainstream political circles, however, gay marriage has become the cause célèbre and has come to stand in for gay and lesbian politics as a whole. Any heterosexual celebrity who wants to be seen as an ally to LGBT communities will stick the gay-marriage feather in his or her cap as a sign of solidarity. Indeed, Lady Gaga has dedicated public appearances to giving speeches calling for marriage equality, as she did for the repeal of Don't Ask, Don't Tell. While this only adds to her appeal to white gay men in particular, it reminds us that we should not confuse the representational mayhem that Lady Gaga has been able to wreak in her videos with her actual politics. I am not saying that Lady Gaga should stop talking about gay causes, but I am saying that what makes her interesting, what makes her gaga, has very little to do with the clichéd political positions she takes. In other words, while it is brave to stand up and speak on behalf of sexual minorities, and while it is important, especially to young people, for fans to see their idols support meaningful causes, it is still the case that actions and words are two very different things. And while Lady Gaga's words in political speeches are ordinary, her performances, her costumes, her gestures, the worlds she creates and peoples are extraordinary. For this reason, I build gaga feminism on the bedrock of the outrageous performance archive that Lady Gaga has created and not in relation to her speeches on behalf of marriage equality or gays in the military, positions that offer no critique of marriage on the one hand or the military on the other.

So, for Lady Gaga and others who wonder why some queer people actually oppose gay marriage, consider the following points.

Reactive Politics Are Weak Politics

Gay marriage has become a central issue partly because right-wing Christian groups mount such a furious opposition to it. In other words, "we" have made it into a big issue because "they" have made it into a big issue—the politics around gay marriage, then, in part is reactive rather than proactive.

Reactive politics are weak and defensive, are defined by the opposition, and tend to retreat into justifications instead of moving forward through provocations. Furthermore, marriage-equality movements have the unfortunate tendency to bolster other conservative marriage movements, often Christian, by lending credibility to a failing arrangement in its hour of need.

Inclusion Maintains the Status Quo

Gay marriage is being formulated by legal-reform groups as a "stand-alone" issue, it tends not to be linked to other social justice projects, and it borrows heavily from a civil rights-era "rights" discourse around inclusion and extension of the status quo. Making marriage into a stand-alone issue actually makes nonsense of the comparison to civil rights struggles. While the civil rights struggles against institutionalized racism sought to transform the whole society, the marriage-equality activists seek to maintain the status quo while demanding a bigger slice of the pie. When gay people get married, keep in mind, they may well extend the institution of marriage, but they do not change it. What is more, while many marriage activists make the analogy to civil rights struggles, much of the white gay-marriage leadership make no connections between race and sexuality and few overtures to communities of color harboring misgivings about gay marriage. . . .

In some popular media, gay marriage is depicted as a black-and-white issue, with white gays wanting to get married and black Christians opposing them. The opposition to gay marriage is all too often read monolithically as part and parcel of right-wing moral outrage and a "values" agenda when in fact people from different backgrounds may have different reasons for opposing not simply gay marriage but what it represents in terms of the landscape of political action in the United States. For black families that have long been represented as dysfunctional, and that have been destabilized by prison expansion and welfare reform, many of the so-called rights attached to marriage have not necessarily benefited them. As feminist and queer scholar Priya Kandaswamy put it in an interview published in

2004: "While many of its advocates argue that gay marriage would secure parental rights for gay and lesbian couples, I think this actually depends on a lot more than marital status. In the U.S., race is the strongest determinant of whether or not the state chooses to recognize your parental ties. Black families are the most likely of any racial group to be disrupted by Child Protection authorities and 42% of all children in foster care in the U.S. are black. If being married does not protect straight black families from having their children taken away, it's unlikely it will protect queer black families."[1]

Black communities are also sometimes angered by simple comparisons between gay-marital-equality struggles and black civil rights battles—gay mainstream groups catering to white people have used this language of comparison without any accompanying attention to racism within white gay and lesbian communities or to poverty issues or health care issues for people of color, and the mainstream groups pushing for marriage almost never link their struggle to other social justice issues like prison reform. And marriage is not the only arena where white gays and lesbians seem to be locked in a struggle for political credibility with communities of color.

For example, one film, *Flag Wars*, a documentary from 2003 by Linda Goode Bryant and Laura Poitras, has documented the ways in which black communities get pitted against gay and lesbian white home-owners, with the gay and lesbian realtors and buyers trying to access property and gentrify, while the local black communities face housing discrimination and redlining. The film tells a rather unwelcome story about the impact of gentrification, portraying white gays and lesbians as part of the system that economically oppresses people of color rather than as people who share in the experience of marginalization. The film depicts a warts-and-all confrontation between house-proud gentrifiers and long-term residents, renters, in the neighborhood. The white home-buyers, though never overtly racist, fail to appreciate, whether deliberately or not, the impact that they are having on a historically black neighborhood. And they never link their own experience with oppression to the

economic disenfranchisement that they see all around them.

. . . And of course, I am not at all suggesting here that gays and lesbians are white and communities of color are straight, I am rather trying to unpack the complex racial politics at work in these struggles that get represented as streamlined and simple. The main problem with a politics of inclusion, where a group of people seek to be folded into existing institutions like marriage, ultimately lies with the economic divisions that marriage politics ignore. Marriage remains an issue that appeals to affluent white gays and lesbians who will benefit from it. It has far less appeal to queers living in poverty or queers actively working on social justice issues that stretch beyond securing individual benefits or tax breaks.

Rights Should Not Be Marriage-Dependent

. . . As Nancy D. Polikoff comments in her astute book *Beyond (Straight and Gay) Marriage,* the problem for many couples seeking to secure health benefits, . . . cannot be resolved through either marriage or domestic partnership. Only universal health coverage would really allow everyone access to the benefits that some people seek through marriage and civil unions. Polikoff provides a quick historical sketch of how the United States came to bundle health insurance into employment pay packages rather than structuring it as a universally accessible system. She reminds us that concepts like the "family wage," which emerged in the nineteenth century, assumed that men earned the money and then shared their resources with their wives and children in ways that made women and children structurally dependent upon men. Polikoff writes: "Consistent with the concept of the family wage, when benefits became a part of employee compensation, employers took into account a worker's responsibility to support his wife and children. Women presumed not to have such needs, did not receive equal benefits."[2]

Arguing that as family forms have changed—more women have entered the workplace, more marriages have ended in divorce, more elderly people have moved in with their middle-aged children, and so on—so too should the system that assigns benefits and access to health care. Polikoff is succinct in her evaluation of the present state of health benefits, and she proposes adjusting "eligibility to reflect today's families," adding, as she explains why employers should cover all the diverse forms that families take now, that "marriage should not be required." There is no better way to say it—marriage and domestic partnerships should not be required in the first place in order for partners and children and dependents to access adequate health care.

Alternative Intimacies Are Not Served by the Marriage Model

There are many ways of creating family, kinship, intimacy, and community that exceed the marriage model. Some of these may include: shared parenting arrangements, split families, communities living together without children, and, last but certainly not least, threesomes. (A Los Angeles group called the Toxic Titties developed a fabulous performance piece where they sought to be married as three people.) The privileging of long-term, permanent arrangements between couples, especially those that include childrearing, grants priority to forms of relation that can be tracked and documented over forms of relation that are ephemeral and temporary. Given that there can easily be more intimacy in an occasional relationship with spark and passion than in an inert domestic partnership that has long outlived its original intensity, why value one over the other when it comes to social stability, or happiness, or the benefit of children?

One of the most compelling reasons given to push for gay marriage, as mentioned above, has been the access to health and other benefits that marriage would confer upon gay as well as straight couples. But again, as I note above, this issue can be approached and resolved in other ways, and in its privileging of marriage, it calls attention to the way we value some forms of social connection over

other equally valid ones. Polikoff s work, again, is very useful here, as she gives the legal perspective on why marriage equality is not the solution for working toward the recognition of diverse households. Polikoff comments:

> . . . Given the vast increase in couples living together without marrying, in the context of a legal system that has made getting married and staying married more optional, there is no basis for requiring marriage or its same-sex analogue for someone to count as a family member.[3]

For example, one could argue that everyone should have the option to extend their benefits packages to others, to a "plus one" instead of verifiable relatives. If the guy in the office next to me has five kids with three different women and can add any of these kids to his medical insurance, why can't I sign up the old lady who lives next door and who watches my apartment for me when I am gone? Or the man down the street who is between jobs but does odd jobs around the neighborhood? Why not have a system where anyone can pay for up to six others as a "family"? Why not value forged connection as much as blood in terms of ways we think about belonging? We could argue that these "alternative intimacies" would make society much stronger and in much more elaborate ways than marriage does. Marriage pits the family and the couple against everyone else; alternative intimacies stretch connections between people and across neighborhoods like invisible webs, and they bind us to one another in ways that foster communication, responsibility, and generosity. If we are really committed to making life better for as many people as possible, then we should consider replacing marriage with wider units of connection and relation.

And in fact, new family arrangements involving gender-variant partners in queer relationships are changing the sex/gender styles and beliefs of a whole new generation, and it is quite possible that within our lifetimes, gays and lesbians and LGBT families will become as ubiquitous and as accepted as divorced households and that divorced households will lose their stigma and simply be seen as a practical way of raising children outside of nuclearity. The goal here, then, should be to recognize the variety within which households can come—the diversity of domestic relations, the inventiveness of human connection, and not the singling out of one form of relation (coupledom, marriage) over all others.

Marriage Is an Oppressive Ideology

In terms of principled opposition to gay marriage, some queer scholars have tried to expose the ways in which young people are led to believe that marriage and babies represent the only possible future within which they can live out their adult desires. And so, we lead young girls in particular to believe that they will be swept naturally along from one life-defining event to another—that love leads to marriage, marriage to babies, babies to family contentment, and that once in the shelter of the family, life will be sweet, simple, and fulfilling. And for some people, fairy tales really do come true. But for most of us, the arc along which our lives will play out will be considerably more complicated than this normal timeline implies. There will be stops and starts, ups and downs, and the family, rather than a sanctuary, may for many be a kind of prison that we assiduously avoid.

I read a story in a magazine a few years ago about a guy, a young man, handsome and on his way to a successful career, who was missing one thing in his life: a wife. His parents were deeply disappointed in him, dismayed that he could go forward in life without a (female) partner. The young man started dating; became serious about a young woman; proposed to her; and walked out on her the day before their wedding. His therapist diagnosed him as suffering from a fear of intimacy, and his parents were hurt and bewildered. The guy eventually left the United States altogether and went to live in Germany, alone; he never married and was totally happy without a partner. While the magazine story used this man to think through intimacy disorders, it is quite possible that there is no disorder here at all—only a perfectly reasonable desire to be alone, to live alone, to avoid intimacy where intimacy is so tethered to a one-size-fits-all format of cohabitation and marriage.

Marriage, the supposedly "big" event in the life of a young person, is, as so many feminists have pointed out, as much of an ending as a beginning (as Jane Eyre states quietly at the end of the famed eponymous novel about looking for love in all the wrong places: "Reader, I married him."). And for too many people, especially young women, alternative life paths are shut down, by themselves and society, almost before they have even been considered. While feminists of a certain stripe have spent years opposing marriage and trying to unseat marriage from its central place in the gendered imaginary, it is ironic to see marriage as an unquestioned good and a worthy goal in a gay imaginary. And it is not as if the opposition to marriage is a new thing and has gone unexpressed until now. Indeed, some of the earliest opposition to marriage came in the form of feminist critiques of what was then called "patriarchy." Feminists like Mary Wollstonecraft in the late eighteenth century in her *A Vindication of the Rights of Woman* described marriage as "legal prostitution." John Stuart Mill, some seventy years later, argued against marriage on the grounds that it coerced women to legally submit to unequal relations with men. Simone de Beauvoir, one hundred years later, reiterated Mill's point that marriage can never be freely chosen by women as long as it is based upon unequal relations between men and women, and she depicted marriage in *The Second Sex* as a trap for both sexes: however, while men can escape the confines of marriage through prostitution and the indulging of their "sexual caprices," women can only find a way out by cheating. Indeed, she writes: "Adultery becomes a natural part of marriage."[4] And it is this argument, that marriage necessitates adultery, that finds its way into contemporary feminist critiques of marriage by Laura Kipnis and others.

Laura Kipnis, in a hilarious and razor-sharp polemic, *Against Love*,[5] reveals how love lures young and unsuspecting idealists into marriage and then traps them there through a series of social set pieces that establish couples as each others' jailors (she gives the example of how couples have to tell each other everything they are doing, report back on where they are going and with whom, and check in periodically throughout the day or evening—recall the Lady Gaga video *Telephone* and the recurrent lyric "stop calling, stop calling"). Eventually one or both of the members of this "domestic gulag" rebels and escapes through an adulterous affair that offers a brief glimpse of freedom before it becomes love . . . and then marriage . . . and then the cycle begins again. In Kipnis's polemic, the social structure within which love occurs is the real problem, but because it is hard to change structural conditions, we instead blame each other for the dysfunction of love and marriage and agree to "work on it," going to therapy to do so. Kipnis's polemic is all the more effective for the way it nails some of the most familiar routines of married or even just coupled life, and so lets no one off the hook. The clichés of the wedding and romantic love, as she shows, quickly harden into the formulaic routines of married life; and so we tame, domesticate, and manage the explosive intimacies between lovers and turn them into the humdrum schedule of the everyday, leaving all the fantasy, the action, and the Utopian possibility behind and dreaming of it only when we go to see the latest lame romantic comedy. . . .

So, to summarize: marriage is an agenda forced upon LGBT groups by the widespread opposition to gay marriage, and while some gays and lesbians choose to marry, it's not a cause that lies at the heart of queer community. Marriage flattens out the varied terrain of queer social life and reduces the differences that make queers, well, queer, to legal distinctions that can be ironed out by the strong hand of the law. Why not work on other forms of legal recognition than marriage, forms that allow for conventional and unusual household arrangements? Why invest only in long-term, permanent attachments? Why not think beyond marriage, especially at this moment when marriage is a floundering institution even for heterosexuals? In other words, how in the world did we end up with a gay agenda that seeks marriage equality when the world is going to hell in a handbag and what we really need is complete and utter social transformation? . . .

DISCUSSION QUESTIONS

1. Should marriage equality be the prime goal of gay activists? What other goals might be more important?
2. Why do you think the marriage equality movement has been so successful?

REFERENCES

1. "Is Gay Marriage Racist? A Conversation with Marlon M. Bailey, Priya Kandaswamy, and Mattie Udora Richardson," in *That's Revolting! Queer Strategies for Resisting Assimilation,* ed. Mattilda Bernstein Sycamore (Brooklyn, NY: Soft Skull Press, 2008), 89.
2. Nancy Polikoff, *Beyond (Straight and Gay) Marriage: Valuing All Families Under the Law* (Boston: Beacon Press, 2008), 147.
3. Ibid., 151.
4. Simone De Beauvoir, *The Second Sex,* trans. Constance Borde and Sheila Malovany-Chevallier, introduced by Judith Thurman (orig. 1949; New York: Knopf, 2009), 63.
5. Laura Kipnis, *Against Love: A Polemic* (New York: Pantheon Books, 2003).

READING 48

Queers without Money: They Are Everywhere. But We Refuse to See Them

Amber Hollibaugh

I mean, homosexuals have high incomes, they have high levels of education; they're owners of major credit cards. There was a survey done. So you're not talking about poor people, homeless people living under a bridge.—Reverend Lou Sheldon, a conservative Christian leader

I lived the first year of my life in a converted chicken coop in back of my grandmother's trailer. The coop was hardly tall enough for my 6'4" father and 5'8" mother to stand up in. My dad, a carpenter, tore out the chickens' egg-laying ledges and

---

Amber Hollibaugh is a writer, filmmaker, and political activist.

rebuilt the tiny inside space to fit a bed, a table, two chairs, a basin they used as a sink (there was no running water), a shelf with a hot plate for cooking, and a small dresser. They used the hose outside to wash with, and ran extension cords in from my grandmother's trailer for light and heat. My bed, a dresser drawer, sat on top of the table during the day. At night it was placed next to where they slept.

I was sick the entire first year of my life. So was my mother, recovering from a nasty C-section and a series of ensuing medical crises. By the time she and I were discharged, three months later, whatever money my parents had managed to save was used up, and they were deeply in debt. They had been poor before my birth, and poor all of their lives growing up, but this was the sinker.

After my first year, we moved from the chicken coop into a trailer. My father worked three jobs simultaneously, rarely sleeping. My mother took whatever work she could find: mending, washing, and ironing other people's clothes. But we never really recovered. We were impoverished. Growing up, I was always poor. I am also a lesbian.

This, then, is my queer identity: I am a high-femme, mixed-race, white-trash lesbian. And even after all these years of living in a middle-class gay community, I often feel left outside when people speak about their backgrounds, their families. And if you listen to the current telling of "our" queer tale, people like me would seem an anomaly. Because, we are told—and we tell ourselves—queerness can't be poor.

Yet this seeming anomaly is the tip of the proverbial iceberg. It represents hundreds of thousands of us who come from poor backgrounds, or are living them still—and are very, very queer.

That would seem obvious when you combine the proportion of the population reputed to be queer (between 4 and 10 percent) with the 37 million poor people in America. Yet the early surveys done on gay and lesbian economic status in this country told a different tale: that queers had more disposable income than straights, lived more luxurious lives, and were all DINKs (Dual Income No Kids). "My book begins as a critique of those early

surveys, which were done largely to serve the interests of gay and lesbian publications and a few marketing companies," says economist M. V. Lee Badgett in her book, *Money, Myths, and Change: The Economic Lives of Lesbians and Gay Men.* "Those surveys are deeply flawed."

Badgett notes that "opposition to gay people is often based on the perception that queers are better off than everybody else; that we're really asking for 'special rights'—and that breeds resentment." Badgett's research shows something else. It constitutes the first true picture of queer economic reality. Among other things, Badgett found that:

Gays, lesbians, and bisexuals do *not* earn more than heterosexuals, or live in more affluent households.

Gay men earn 13 to 32 percent less than similarly qualified straight men (depending on the study).

Though lesbians and bisexual women have incomes comparable to straight women—earning 21 percent less than men—lesbian couples earn significantly less than heterosexual ones.

But . . . try finding representations of poor or working-class gay people on *Will & Grace.* See how hard you have to search for media images of queers who are part of the vast working poor in this country. Find the homeless transgendered folks. Find stories of gay immigrants, lesbian moms working three jobs, bisexual truckers falling asleep from too many hours on the road, gay men in the unemployment line. Try finding an image of queer people who are balancing on the edge—or have fallen off.

The myth of our wealth goes deep, so deep that even other gay people seem to believe it. We have tried to protect ourselves from the hard truths of our economic diversity by perpetuating the illusion of material wealth, within the confines of male/female whiteness. This is a critical aspect of how we present ourselves in this country at this point in time. We treat the poverty that exists among us—as well as the differences of class—as a dirty secret to be hidden, denied, repelled. We treat economic struggle as something that functions outside the pull of queer desires, removed from our queerly lived lives.

As Badgett notes, by celebrating the myth of queer affluence, we have "drawn attention to exactly the kind of picture that Lou Sheldon is drawing of gay and lesbian people." There is a richer—and ultimately more sympathetic—queer reality: "We are everywhere—but we're all different."

Why is it so hard to acknowledge this? Why is poverty treated as a queer secret? And why does it produce a particular kind of homosexual shame? Bear with me. Imagine what you've never allowed yourself to see before.

When I directed the Lesbian AIDS Project at Gay Mens' Health Crisis, stories of the hundreds of HIV-positive lesbians who were a part of that project literally came roaring out of those women's mouths. These were lesbians who had almost never participated in queer politics or visited any of New York City's queer institutions. On those rare occasions when they had tried, they quickly departed, unseen and unwelcomed.

Anorew Spieldenner, a young gay organizer of color who has worked for years with men who have sex with men, has a name for this phenomenon. He calls it "a queer and invisible body count." It is made up of poor lesbians and gay men, queer people of color, the transgendered, people with HIV and AIDS and—always and in large numbers—the queer young and the queer elderly.

The Metropolitan Community Church, a largely gay denomination, reports that the demand for food at its New York pantry has doubled since the beginning of welfare reform in 1996. The Lesbian & Gay Community Services Center says that homeless people in their addiction programs have tripled since then. The Hetrick-Martin Institute, which serves "gay and questioning youth," estimates that 50 percent of homeless kids in New York City are queer.

"We are entering a time when the economy is going into a slump," says Joseph De Filippis, who coordinates the Queer Economic Justice Network. "This isn't going to be like the '90s, when it was easy for employers to give things like domestic-partner benefits. There are going to be more and more of us who are affected by joblessness and economic crisis. . . ."

Ingrid Rivera, director of the Racial & Economic Justice Initiative of the National Gay and Lesbian Task Force, has lived this issue. "I was on welfare, I was homeless, I thought I'd be lucky if I finished high school. I am a woman of color, I am a mother, and I am queer. I've worked and lived in a poor world and I've worked in queer organizations that are primarily white. I've seen it from both perspectives, and there's a kind of disconnect. In the gay, mostly white world, race and economic justice isn't talked about as a queer issue. And because of that split, queerness becomes a white thing."

Poverty and outright destitution can happen to anyone—and the queerer you are, the fewer safety nets exist to hold you up or bounce you back from the abyss. Queerness intensifies poverty and compounds the difficulty of dealing with the social service system. The nightmares . . . include:

Being separated from your partner if you go into the shelter system. Straight couples can remain together by qualifying for the family system.

Being mandated into homophobic treatment programs for drug or drinking problems and having the program decide to treat your queerness instead of your addiction. If you leave the program, you lose any right to benefits—including Medicaid.

Being unable to apply as a family for public housing.

Ending up a queer couple in the only old-age home you can afford and being separated when you try to share a room.

Barbara Cassis came from a wealthy Long Island family. But when he began to understand and acknowledge his transgendered nature, his parents kicked him out. He was homeless, young, and broke. "Thank God for drag queens," she says, looking back. "A drag queen found me crying in Times Square and took me home. She talked to me about what I was going through, let me stay with her in her apartment, taught me how to support myself, how to get clients as a prostitute or in the gay bars where I could work as I transitioned. But then she died of AIDS and I was homeless again."

The homeless shelters were the worst experience of all for Barbara as a trans woman. Often, it felt easier to just stay on the streets. If you're homeless, and you haven't transitioned—which costs a fortune—you're forced to go to a shelter based on birth gender. The risk of violence and danger is always high for everyone; the shelters are crowded, short of staff, and the staff that is there has no training in how to deal with trans or gay issues. So if you are a trans person, just taking a shower means that you're taking your life in your hands.

"It took me years to get on my feet," says Cassis, now an administrative assistant at the Positive Health Project, "to start dealing with being HIV-positive, and get the training and education I needed to find a decent job. It has also taken years for me to reconcile with my family, which I have. If it hadn't been for the kind of people the gay community often discounts and despises, I wouldn't be here today."

Like my mother said, the only difference between a poor drunk and a rich one is which drunk can hide it. The shame of being poor is an acutely public shame, difficult to hide. And *queer* homosexuality—the kind of queerness that makes gender differences and radical sexual desires crystal clear—this queerness triggers similar ruinous social perils.

We punish people in this country for being poor and we punish homosexuality. When both are combined, it does more than double the effect: It twists and deepens it, gives it sharper edges, and heightens our inability to duck and cover or slide through to a safer place. It forces you to live more permanently outside than either condition dictates.

The problem intensifies when you realize what queers are in the mind of America. We stand for the culture's obsession with the erotic. It is we who are portrayed as always doing it or trying to, we who quickly become the sexual criminals at the heart of any story. We are the ones who are dangerous; our sexuality is more explosive, more explicit, more demanding, more predatory.

And so it goes for poor people: part stereotype (read trailer trash or welfare queen), part object of blame for being too stupid not to have done better. The underlying assumption is that the only appropriate desires are those that rest comfortably atop plenty of money. The desires and needs afforded by wealth—and plenty of it, earned or not—are appropriate, acceptable, good. But messy desires? Desires that combine with class and color? Desires and needs that ricochet around the erotic? These needs are not acceptable. They are condemned.

No wonder the gay movement can't see the poverty in its midst. The one thing this culture longs for and seems to value in queer life is the image of wealth. It appears to be the only thing we do right. And it is the only piece of our queerness that we can use when our citizenship is at stake. We learned this at the beginning of the AIDS crisis, when we activated that wealth to do what the government wouldn't: We built institutions to care and protect and serve our own. It is a riveting example of how we have claimed our own and valued what the mainstream culture despised about our lives. We could do the same with queer poverty.

"If the community got involved in the issues of being queer and poor," says Jay Toole, a lesbian in the LGBT caucus of the Coalition for the Homeless, "it would be like the community saying, 'I'm here, and here's my hand. You can go further, I'm here.'"

Toole is finishing school now. She plans to work as a substance abuse counselor, to go back into the shelters and bring gay people into the community, "so that they don't have to be so alone as I was. Because when Ann Dugan [from the Coalition] brought me back down to the Lesbian & Gay Center from the shelter, it was finally like coming home."

DISCUSSION QUESTIONS

1. Why do poor gays and lesbians seem to be invisible if they are everywhere?
2. Why do we punish people for being poor?

SOCIAL CLASS

READING 49

Rethinking American Poverty

Mark R. Rank

It's a fundamental paradox: in America, the wealthiest country on earth, one also finds the highest rates of poverty in the developed world. Whether we examine children's rates of poverty, poverty among working age adults, poverty within single parent families, or overall rates of poverty, the story is much the same—the United States has exceedingly high levels of impoverishment.

As a result, half of U.S. children will reside in a household that uses food stamps at some point during childhood. Life expectancy in Harlem is shorter than in Bangladesh. The bottom 60 percent of the American population currently holds less than 1 percent of the financial wealth in the country. And two thirds of the counties that black children are growing up in are considered high poverty with respect to impoverished neighborhoods.

Although there are several possible explanations for why these conditions exist, the argument developed here is that a major reason has to do with how we as a society have tended to conceptualize the issue of poverty and, based upon this thinking, how we have acted (or better put, failed to act) toward the issue.

The traditional manner of thinking about poverty in the U.S. has viewed impoverishment as largely the result of individual inadequacies and failings. These shortcomings include not working hard enough, failure to acquire sufficient skills, or just making bad decisions. Consequently, the problem of poverty is often seen through a lens of individual pathology. Since individuals are perceived as having brought poverty onto themselves, our

collective and societal obligations are seen as limited. The age-old distinction between the deserving versus the undeserving poor reflects this perspective—unless the working-age poor have very good grounds for their poverty, they're deemed largely undeserving of help. Poverty is therefore understood as primarily affecting those who choose not to play by the rules of the game. Ultimately, this perspective reflects and reinforces the myths and ideals of American society: there are economic opportunities for all, individualism and self-reliance are paramount, and hard work is rewarded.

This overall mindset has long influenced both the general public's attitudes toward the poor and much of the policy and academic work analyzing poverty. Nevertheless, it seriously misconstrues the true nature of poverty and fosters a lack of political and social will to address the problem itself. Three major changes are essential for realistically and proactively reframing American impoverishment.

A first fundamental shift in thinking is the recognition that poverty affects us all. All too often we view poverty as someone else's problem, or think that poverty is confined to certain areas and neighborhoods (such as inner cities or remote rural areas), and that by avoiding such areas we can simply ignore the issue. The notion is "out of sight, out of mind."

Clearly, this perspective is incorrect and intellectually lazy. In one way or another, poverty affects us all. There are at least two ways of thinking about this. The first is that whether we realize it or not, we pay a steep price for our high rates of poverty. As mentioned earlier, the extent and depth of poverty and economic inequality in the U.S. are far greater than in any other Western industrialized country.

As a result, we spend considerably more money than needed on social problems associated with poverty. These include greater health problems, family problems, a less able work force, and so on down a long list. When we speak about homeland security, these are the issues that undermine us and our

---

Mark Rank is a professor of social welfare at the University of Wisconsin.

security as a nation. We wind up paying a tremendous price for quietly allowing so many of our citizens and communities to remain mired in poverty.

As an example, a study by the economist Harry Holzer and colleagues attempted to quantify the annual monetary cost of childhood poverty in the U.S. They calculated the economic costs that growing up in poverty had for future earnings, risk of engaging in crime, and health quality in later life. Their estimate was that the overall cost of childhood poverty was an eye opening $500 billion per year—nearly 4 percent of this country's GDP.

The result is that we end up spending much of our tax dollars and resources on the by-products of poverty, assuredly a more expensive approach over the long term than preventing poverty in the first place. In short, each of us pays dearly in a number of ways for letting poverty exist at such levels, but we too often fail to see this connection.

However, there is also a second way of thinking about poverty as affecting us all. And that comes in considering the chances that an average American will directly encounter poverty at some point during his or her lifetime. As it turns out, the number of Americans who are touched by poverty during adulthood is exceedingly high. My co-author, sociologist Thomas Hirschl, and I have estimated that between the ages of 20 and 75, nearly 60 percent of Americans will experience at least one year below the poverty line and three quarters will experience a year either in or near poverty. Perhaps more surprising is the fact that two thirds of Americans between the ages of 20 and 65 will wind up using a social welfare program such as Food Stamps or Medicaid; 40 percent will use such a program in at least five years scattered throughout their working age adulthood.

Consequently, although those in poverty and welfare recipients are routinely vilified and portrayed as members of "marginalized groups" on the fringes of society, most of us will find ourselves below the poverty line and using a social safety net program at some point. After all, during the course of a lifetime, any number of unexpected, detrimental things can happen—job loss, family break ups, or the development of a major health problem. In addition, recent research has shown that this life course risk of poverty and economic instability has been rising since the 1990s. More and more families, including middle class ones, are experiencing greater income volatility, greater instability in the labor market, and a lack of benefits such as health and unemployment insurance. Jobs are no longer as stable as they once were, health care benefits are harder to get, and the safety net has weakened over time.

A first shift in thinking therefore asks the question, "Who is at risk of poverty and its consequences?" The answer is: virtually all of us. As a result, each of us has a vested interest in and an imperative for reducing poverty in the U.S.

A second critical change in thinking is a recognition that American poverty is largely the result of failings at the economic and political levels, rather than at the individual level. In the past, we've emphasized individual inadequacies as the major reason for poverty; that is, people aren't motivated enough, aren't working hard enough, have failed to acquire enough skills and education, or have just made bad decisions. These behaviors and attributes are seen as leading people into poverty and keeping them there. And in fact, we tend to confront most social problems in this country as individual pathologies.

In contrast to this perspective, the basic problem lies in a shortage of viable opportunities for all Americans. Certainly, particular individual shortcomings, such as the lack of education or skills, help explain who is more likely to be left out in the competition to locate and secure good opportunities, but they cannot explain why there's a shortage of such opportunities in the first place. In order to answer that question, we must turn to the inability of the economic and political structures to provide the supports and opportunities necessary to lift all of us out of poverty.

The most obvious example is in the mismatch between the number of decent paying jobs and the pool of labor in search of those jobs. Over the past 30 years, the U.S. economy has been producing more and more low-paying jobs, part-time jobs, and jobs without benefits (it's estimated that approximately one third of all jobs are low-paying—less than $11.50 an hour). And of course, beyond those in low-paying jobs, there are millions of unemployed Americans at any point in time. During the recent economic downturn, six to seven people have been competing for every single job opening. Coupled with the country's lack of universal coverage for child care, health care, and affordable housing, this situation leaves an increasing number of families economically vulnerable.

In class, I often use the analogy of musical chairs to help students recognize this disconnect. Picture a game with ten players, but only eight chairs. When the music stops, who's most likely to be left standing? It will be those who are at a disadvantage in terms of competing for the available chairs (less agility, reduced speed, a bad position when the music stops, and so on). However, given that the game is structured in a way such that two players are *bound* to lose, these individual attributes only explain who loses, not why there are losers in the first place. Ultimately, there are simply not enough chairs for those playing the game.

The critical mistake that's been made in the past is that we've equated the question of who loses at the game with the question of why the game inevitably produces losers. They are, in fact, distinct and separate questions. So while characteristics such as deficiencies in skills or education or being in a single parent family help to explain who's at a heightened risk of encountering poverty, the fact that poverty exists in the first place results not from these characteristics, but from a failure of the economic and political structures to provide enough decent opportunities and supports for the whole of society.

By focusing solely upon individual characteristics, we can shuffle people up or down in terms of their likelihood to land a job with good earnings, but when there aren't enough of these jobs to go around, somebody will still end up in poverty. We're playing a large-scale version of musical chairs.

The recognition of this dynamic represents a fundamental shift in thinking from the past. It helps explain why the social policies of the last three decades have been largely ineffective in reducing poverty rates. We've spent our attention and resources on altering players' incentives and disincentives through various welfare reform measures, or, in a very limited way, upgrading their skills and ability to compete with various job training programs, but we've left the structure of the game untouched.

Overall rates of poverty do go up and down, but primarily as a result of changes on the structural level (that is, increases or decreases in the number of available opportunities—the "chairs"). In particular, the performance of the economy has been historically important, since, when the economy is expanding, more opportunities are available for the competing pool of labor and their families. The reverse occurs when the economy slows down, as we saw in the 2000s and the economic collapse that began in 2008. To attribute the rise of poverty over the past ten years to individual inadequacies or lowered motivation is absurd. Rather, the increase in poverty has everything to do with deteriorating economic conditions, particularly in the last few years.

Likewise, changes in various social supports and the social safety net affect how well families are able to avoid poverty. When such supports were increased by the War on Poverty initiatives of the 1960s and buoyed by a strong economy, poverty rates declined significantly. Likewise, when Social Security benefits were expanded during the 1960s and 1970s, poverty rates among the elderly dropped sharply. Conversely, when social supports have been eroded, as in the case of children's programs over the past 30 years, rates of poverty among those relying on such services have gone up.

The recognition of poverty as a structural failing also makes it clear why the U.S. has such high rates of poverty when compared to other Western countries. It's not that Americans are less motivated or less skilled than those in other countries, but that our economy has been producing millions of low-wage jobs and our social policies have done relatively little to economically support families compared to other industrialized countries.

From this perspective, one key to addressing poverty is to increase the labor market opportunities and social supports available to American households. We must shift our thinking to recognize the fundamental distinction between who loses at the game and why the game produces losers in the first place.

Let's turn to the third shift in thinking that's needed to create a more realistic and proactive approach toward poverty. And that is the moral ground on which we view poverty in America must change. In the past, our moral perspective has been rooted in the ethos of individual blame, with a resulting general acceptance of the status quo. In other words, since people bring it upon themselves, poverty's their problem, not mine.

But poverty is a moral problem. It represents an injustice of a substantial magnitude. Severe deprivation and hardship have been documented in countless studies—not to mention millions of human lives. And, as argued earlier, a large portion of this poverty is the result of failings at the structural rather than the individual level, which places much of the responsibility for poverty beyond the poor.

However, what makes this injustice particularly grievous is the stark contrast between the wealth, abundance, and resources of America and its levels of destitution. Something is seriously wrong when we find that, in a country with the most abundant resources in the world, there are children without enough to eat, families who cannot afford health care, and people sleeping on the streets for lack of shelter.

It should also be noted that the gap between extreme prosperity and vulnerability has never been wider. The venerable economist Paul Samuelson, writing in the first edition of his introductory economics textbook in 1948, observed that if we were to make an income pyramid out of a child's play blocks, with each layer representing $1,000 of income, the peak would be somewhat higher than the Eiffel Tower, but almost all of us would be within several yards of the ground. By the time of Samuelson's 2001 edition of the textbook, most of us would still be within several yards of the ground, but the Eiffel Tower would now have to be replaced with Mount Everest to represent those at the top.

Or consider the distance between the average worker's salary and the average CEO's salary. In 1980, the average CEO of a major corporation earned around 42 times the pay of the average worker. Today, it is well over 400 times. Adding insult to injury, during the past 30 years, an increasing number of companies have demanded concessions from their workers, including pay cuts and the elimination of health benefits in order to keep their labor costs down, while those at the top have prospered beyond any sense of decency.

Patterns of wealth accumulation have become even more skewed. The top one percent of the U.S. population currently owns 42 percent of the country's entire financial wealth, while the bottom 60 percent of Americans are in possession of less than 1 percent. And while all of these trends have been emerging, our social policies have continued to give more to the well-to-do and less to the economically vulnerable, with the argument that these policies help all Americans through "trickle-down economics."

A new way of thinking recognizes this as a moral outrage. Injustice, rather than blame, becomes the moral compass with which to view poverty amidst abundance. The magnitude of such injustice constitutes a strong impetus for change. It signals that a wrong is being committed and cries out for a remedy. A shift in thinking is premised upon the idea that social change is essential for addressing the injustices of poverty.

This is in sharp contrast with the old way of thinking, in which the moral focus is upon individual blame. Such thinking simply reinforces the status quo by letting us do little while poverty rates climb. The perspective of injustice exhorts us to actively engage and confront poverty, rather than comfortably settling for widespread impoverishment.

In his last book, *Where Do We Go from Here: Chaos or Community?,* the Rev. Dr. Martin Luther King, Jr. wrote, "A true revolution of value will soon cause us to question the fairness and justice of many of our past and present policies. We are called to play the Good Samaritan on life's roadside; but that will be only an initial act. One day the whole Jericho road must be transformed so that men and women will not be beaten and robbed as they make their journey through life. True compassion is more than flinging a coin to a beggar; it understands that an edifice that produces beggars needs restructuring. A true revolution of values will soon look uneasily on the glaring contrast of poverty and wealth." This revolution of values must begin with a fundamental shift in how American society understands, and ultimately acts toward, the poverty in which so many of our citizens live. These are the building blocks on which to challenge and confront the paradox of poverty amidst plenty.

DISCUSSION QUESTIONS

1. What are some of the consequences of childhood poverty?
2. What should be the government's role in preventing poverty?
3. What would change if the United States recognized poverty as a structural failing?

READING 50

Tearing Down the Gates
Confronting the Class Divide in American Education

Peter Sacks

When we Americans talk about access to a college education, we tend to narrow the acceptable boundaries of the conversation. We ask why the cost of college has gotten so out of control compared to the costs of other goods and services, and we sometimes talk about the closely related subject of financial aid. But very rarely do we discuss the dramatic changes to the financial aid system that have made college increasingly unaffordable to the very students who need financial aid most. In researching my book *Tearing Down the Gates,* I came to the conclusion that, despite the oft-repeated rhetoric to

Peter Sacks is an author, economist, essayist, and social critic.

the contrary, the American education system actually helps perpetuate inequality of opportunity.

INCREASING CLASS STRATIFICATION

Colleges and universities have been vigorous advocates of diversity, but on the whole they have not been as vigorous as advocates for addressing inequality of educational opportunity. Although affirmative action programs in admissions and financial aid became the primary tools for achieving diversity, it would be a mistake to conclude that the affirmative action movement was fueled by higher education's drive for social justice or its desire to remedy inequality. After the civil rights battles, affirmative action morphed from a social justice remedy to an educational rationale, based on the notion that diversity of cultures, races, and points of view all contribute to the educational mission of the university. As a result, institutions of higher education have seen diversity primarily through the lens of race, ethnicity, and gender—a limitation that, regrettably, has hampered the drive for a deeper and perhaps more meaningful kind of diversity. Because the diversity movement has narrowly focused on race, and not necessarily justice, the movement has left intact the very mechanisms in admissions and financial aid that institutions have long employed systematically to sort potential students by class.

In terms of enrollments at America's most selective colleges and universities, the class divide in higher education had become quite extreme by the end of the twentieth century. When Anthony Carnevale and Stephen Rose (2003) examined the socioeconomic distribution of freshmen enrollments at the most selective 146 colleges and universities in the United States, they discovered that more than 90 percent of the freshmen came from families in the top half of the socioeconomic distribution. Just 10 percent came from families at the bottom half of the socioeconomic distribution. Even as race-based affirmative action policies have been expanded over the years, class has become a more formidable barrier to access than even race. Carnevale and Rose found that 22 percent of the freshmen at the most selective colleges and universities were from underrepresented minority groups, compared to just 3 percent from low-income families.

Notwithstanding these disparities, some observers will contend that anybody who really wants to go to college can still gain admission to some college or university in America. But just how true is this contention? It seems hard to fathom, given our persistent belief that, in America, educational opportunity is widespread, but the chance of getting a bachelor's degree by age twenty-four has improved only for those from families in the upper half of the nation's income distribution. In 1970, just 6 percent of high school graduates from families in the bottom income quartile attained a bachelor's degree by age twenty-four. This statistic essentially flatlined in subsequent decades, and remained at 6 percent in 2002. The number of students from lower-middle-class families—those in the second-lowest income quartile—who attained a bachelor's degree also stagnated during this period, remaining at 10–15 percent. In contrast, students from upper-middle-income families—those in the third income quartile—saw their prospects nearly double, from 15 percent to 28 percent. And for students from the highest income families, the prospect of attaining a bachelor's degree by age twenty-four improved significantly—from 40 percent to more than 70 percent (Mortensen 2008).

Over the past twenty or thirty years, the American higher education system has become deeply stratified along class lines. Whether a high school graduate goes to college, and where he or she goes to college, powerfully depends on his or her class status at birth and during childhood. That is, one's prospects for post-secondary education depend significantly on whether one's parents went to college, on the family's annual income, and on financial wealth. What is more, the correlations between class status and prospects for success in higher education have become even more pronounced in recent decades.

One glaring aspect of class stratification in American higher education is the growing concentration of poor and working-class students at the bottom of the educational pyramid, in community colleges. Four-year colleges and universities have become more exclusive domains for America's upper-middle class and above. In the early 1970s, public four-year institutions enrolled 40 percent of all Pell Grant recipients; by 2001, this figure had dropped to just 31 percent. Private four-year institutions enrolled 22 percent of Pell Grant recipients in the early 1970s, but only about 13 percent a quarter of a century later (Snyder, Tan, and Hoffman 2004). Where did these lower-income students end up? If they went to college at all, they increasingly wound up going to public community colleges.

Community colleges represent a conundrum in terms of creating meaningful educational opportunity for students of modest means. Admirably, two-year colleges have, by definition, greatly expanded access to college, and those students who attain associate's degrees or who transfer to four-year institutions to attain a bachelor's degrees are better off than they would be without community colleges. What remains a controversial question, however, is whether community colleges have made a sufficient difference for a sufficient number of people.

The vast majority of community college students—some 63 percent—would like to earn at least a bachelor's degree, but relatively few actually do so. In fact, of students who start at a community college and expect eventually to transfer to a four-year institution, just one in five will have earned a bachelor's degree six years later (Hoachlander, Sikora, and Horn 2003). Thus, when we talk about the kind of equal educational opportunity, what we're really saying is that anybody has a shot at college because of the large number of relatively inexpensive, open-admission community colleges. We have, in a sense, created a system of educational reservations by separating the low-class masses from the higher-class elites who matriculate at four-year colleges and universities and, thus, obtain the credentials necessary for coveted leadership positions in our society.

THE SAT AND COLLEGE RANKINGS

Higher education appears to be reaching a critical historical juncture: the end of the SAT era may be at hand. Only by understanding how this particular version of meritocracy came to be, and why it is no longer suitable for American society, can we go forward in creating new, more broadly defined systems of merit that select individuals less by class, race, and ethnic origins and more by their real-world talents, motivations, accomplishments, and achievements.

The story begins with a series of historical accidents, starting with the invention of IQ testing in Europe. Next came the importation and subsequent commercialization of mental aptitude testing in the United States. The uses of IQ testing technology were pushed to extremes in Europe and the United States, shaped in part by a eugenics ideology holding that certain individuals with deficient bloodlines—variously including Poles, Italians, Jews, Africans, and so on, depending on the historical period—were cognitively doomed to an intellectual inferiority that no amount of schooling could remedy.

The SAT is a direct descendent of this ideology. So, too, are the countless IQ and other aptitude tests still used by scores of elite private and public schools to identify the supposed best and brightest students for admission. As a norm-referenced test, the SAT has never been about solving meaningful problems using math or science, but rather about how many multiple-choice questions one could answer in a given period of time compared to other test takers. In other words, the SAT is primarily a sorting device, not an educational tool. Using the IQ test as a sorting mechanism was emphatically not what Alfred Binet intended for the early IQ scale he developed for French schoolchildren. Yet that's exactly how we Americans commercialized Binet's invention.

The founders of the SAT believed that scientific testing would legitimately reward the best and brightest with coveted spots at the best universities. Thus, the cocktail of American meritocracy: take the American fixation with mental testing of the standardized variety, add the commercial interests behind standardized testing, and then mix in a bit of an unspoken elitist superiority. The result is a powerful brew of pseudo-meritocracy. The SAT has long been a tool for the intentional exclusion of unwanted classes and races—a point not widely enough understood. Early mental testers clearly recognized the close correlation between the economic and social class of a student's family and his or her performance on the early IQ tests. In his writings about the development of his IQ scale, Alfred Binet himself remarked on how the children who did best on his test were the sons and daughters of physicians, professors, and lawyers.

The conflict between the elitist tendencies of American education and the egalitarian spirit of our democracy has also been evident throughout the history of the SAT. Because the SAT was born from the IQ testing movement, its backers have had to battle for its legitimacy over the years in the face of changing public sentiments about the compatibility of IQ testing and education in a democratic society. One adaptation, for instance, was to change the name of the test from the Scholastic Aptitude Test to simply the SAT, an attempt to sever the test—if just in name only—from its IQ testing bloodlines.

Despite occasional flare-ups that challenge the hegemony and the utility of the SAT and similar admissions tests, the SAT—and, increasingly, the ACT—has remained the linchpin of selective admissions systems in American education. We came to believe that how a student performs on the SAT is synonymous with how smart he or she is and how well he or she will do in college. Over the years, a pseudoscientific legitimacy has flowered around the SAT enterprise, creating its own self-perpetuating and self-serving ideology of merit.

What, alas, did the SAT sort for? The entrance exam's amazingly successful run as a commercial enterprise has had little relationship to any meaningful definition of merit. We've known for many years that, compared to other assessments of learning, the

SAT is a relatively weak predictor of academic success in college. The SAT adds little value to what admissions officers can glean from high school grades, writing samples, and other assessment tools that predict performance in the real world, including the classroom. So if the SAT is not a particularly useful correlate to academic performance, then what explains its longevity for selective college admissions? The early adopters of the SAT saw it as a useful tool for excluding certain kinds of people based on race, religion, and socioeconomic background—and for doing so under the legitimating guise of meritocracy. Today, that rationale has been superseded by a less intentional but no less flawed and damaging means of exclusion.

Despite the rhetoric extolling colleges and universities as democratic enterprises dedicated to servicing the public good and rooted in egalitarian values, these institutions are businesses that operate within a competitive marketplace. They are strange businesses, to be sure, but they're money-maximizing enterprises nonetheless. Colleges and universities don't maximize profits, but they are very much in the business of maximizing institutional prestige and endowments. Endowment building and prestige are reliant on the higher education marketplace's determination of relative "quality." This determination is almost entirely based on selectivity in admissions, which, in turn, is wholly a function of the average SAT score of entering freshmen.

Thus did the dominant paradigm of individual merit and college quality evolve from historical accident, commercial ambition, and political ideology. And from this paradigm was born a modern-day prophet, who trumpets the notion that colleges can be ranked based on this particular prophet's determination of academic quality. Because the essential ideology of the SAT was already in place and widely accepted, this prophet—in the form of a weekly newsmagazine we all know as *U.S. News & World Report*—had simply to collect the data and rank the colleges.

If you think that a lot more goes into the determination of America's "Best Colleges" than SAT scores, then you need only to consult the research showing that a college's average SAT or ACT score correlates almost perfectly to its *U.S. News & World Report* ranking. One such study concluded that "once the average SAT/ACT score is taken into account, the other so-called 'quality' indices have little additional influence on where an institution falls on the list" (Kuh and Pascarella 2004, 53). Hence, the college rankings game, refereed by *U.S. News & World Report,* further entrenches the dominance of SAT (or ACT) scores as the primary measure of college quality. Instead of measuring what colleges actually do for students, in an educational sense, once they arrive on campus, the current rankings paradigm says that a good college is one that admits students with high SAT scores and that turns away those with modest SAT scores.

We are left with a system that is dominated by privilege, elitism, and money. More often than not, a marginally bright rich kid can get into a top college because of a well-trained SAT performance. And more often than not, the creative genius from an impoverished family is lucky to attend a community college—or even to go to college at all.

To be sure, some colleges and universities are devising new kinds of admissions tests, some of which seek to measure so-called "noncognitive" characteristics that are not captured by tests such as the SAT. And we're finding that these new tests actually do a pretty good job of predicting college success. Recently, too, the National Association of College Admissions Counseling (2008) released a landmark report calling on colleges and universities to rethink their reliance on admissions tests like the SAT. There are also efforts underway to create better indicators for consumers about college quality than traditional rankings from the likes of *U.S. News & World Report.*

Yet despite these efforts, the old paradigm remains the dominant paradigm. It is highly resistant to change because, so far, there has been little incentive for the educational establishment to change. This brings us to the subject of financial aid, and particularly those aspects of the financial aid system that rarely receive public attention.

TRENDS IN FINANCIAL AID

All selective colleges want certain students as their customers. These students primarily include the sons and daughters of affluent professionals. They attend excellent schools, live in safe and attractive neighborhoods, and—most important—score reasonably well on the SAT. Colleges covet such students not because they believe the SAT is the final word on the potential for success in college, but rather because these students and their SAT scores enhance the prestige of the institution. Colleges want these students so badly that they're even willing to pay for them. Under the guise of "merit," colleges have drastically increased the amount of scholarship money they offer high-scoring students. Indeed, the most-coveted students rarely pay full tuition—the "sticker price" that colleges advertise.

The tuition hikes we all hear about are borne in dramatically different ways by students from different economic classes. Mounting evidence shows that the lion's share of the merit awards and steep tuition discounts have been directed to wealthier students—those who would go to college even without the merit aid—at the expense of need-based scholarships to lower-income students. Unfortunately, need-based financial aid from other federal, state, or private sources has not made up for the dramatic shrinkage in institutional aid for lower-income students. In fact, many states have created their own merit scholarship programs, and most of the funds are also going to wealthier students.

As a result of these perverse trends in financial aid, the dream of a college education has become increasingly unattainable for students from families earning low and modest incomes. As evidence, consider the class disparities in net college costs as a percentage of family income. To send a child to a four-year public university in 1999, a family in the lowest income bracket faced a net cost equivalent to 39 percent of the total family income. By 2008, the net cost had risen to the equivalent of 55 percent of family income. By contrast, in 1999, a family in the top income bracket faced a net cost equivalent to just 7 percent of the total family income; by 2008, that burden had increased to 9 percent (National Center for Public Policy and Higher Education 2008).

The interrelated trends in affordability, financial aid, and college admissions practices have created an American higher education system that is increasingly hostile to lower-income students and families. Moreover, these students and families often lack the social, cultural, and economic capital on which colleges and universities place such high value in their admissions and financial aid systems. What do I mean by "cultural capital"? Consider the tenth grader who doesn't have a computer at home, whose parents don't read magazines or newspapers and don't expose the child to a world beyond his or her neighborhood. Or consider the family that doesn't know what the FAFSA is or even what the SAT is.

Instead of being a great democratic force for rectifying economic inequality, colleges and universities have played an important, if unwitting, role in worsening inequality. Despite our belief that education is a great equalizer, our education system tends to be a procyclical rather than countercyclical force for addressing inequality. We have created institutional rules of the game that reinforce huge disparities in educational opportunity. The vicious cycle is rarely broken.

Following the prevailing business model, the most ambitious colleges and universities have sought to improve their position in national rankings by tightening admissions standards and reallocating financial aid to students from relatively affluent backgrounds. Yet ongoing demographic and economic trends have made this business model increasing unsustainable tor individual institutions. By 2013, for example, fully half of all high school graduates will come from families earning $50,000 a year or less. Just 15 percent of high school graduates will come from families earning $100,000 or more—the sort of families traditionally targeted by selective colleges (Western Interstate Commission for Higher Education 2008). In order to avoid steep and possibly fatal declines in enrollments, colleges and universities that rely mostly on tuition revenue will have to reform their admissions and financial aid policies to make them less hostile to lower-income students. Yet an era of severe retrenchment in taxpayer support has only served to fan the fires of elitism at our best public universities. To the grave detriment of first-generation and low-income students, these so-called "public" universities have cut enrollments and raised admissions standards.

The macroeconomic implications of these trends are not pleasant. We are fostering an increasingly class-bound education system in which only a small segment of the population can realistically hope to earn postsecondary degrees. If we continue along this path, the United States will become a second- or even third-tier economic power. Indeed, this decline has already begun. In terms of educational attainment, we are entering a period of stagnation. Unlike recent cohorts of college-age people in many European and Asian countries, who are earning postsecondary degrees at far higher rates than previous generations, recent cohorts of Americans are no better educated than previous generations (National Center for Public Policy and Higher Education 2008). This is just one of many educational and economic indicators that demonstrate the urgent need to shed the last vestiges the old paradigm. We must tear down the gates and make higher education more inclusive, rather than more exclusive.

DISCUSSION QUESTIONS

1. According to Peter Sacks, why haven't universities been advocates for reducing economic inequalities?
2. Sacks's article was first published in 2009. Do you think things have changed since then?
3. Would you be in favor of eliminating the SAT requirement for college admission? Do you think it will ever be eliminated?

REFERENCES

Carnevale, A. P., and S. J. Ruse. 2003. *Socioeconomic status, race/ethnicity, and selective college admissions.* New York: The Century Foundation.

Hoachlander, G., A. Sikora, and L. Horn. 2003. *Community college students: Goals, academic preparation, and outcomes.*

U.S. Department of Education. Washington, DC: National Center for Education Statistics.

Kuh, G. D., and E. T. Pascarella. 2004. What does institutional selectivity tell us about academic quality? *Change* 36 (5): 53–58.

Mortensen, T. 2008. Family income and educational attainment, 1970 to 2007. *Postsecondary Education Opportunity* 143.

National Association of College Admissions Counseling. 2008. *Report of the Commission on the Use of Standardized Tests in Undergraduate Admission.* Arlington, VA: National Association of College Admissions Counseling.

National Center for Public Policy and Higher Education. 2008. *Measuring up 2008: The national report card on higher education.* San Jose, CA: National Center for Public Policy and Higher Education.

Snyder, T. D., A. G. Tan, and C. M. Hoffman. 2004. *Digest of education statistics 2003.* U.S. Department of Education. Washington, DC: National Center for Education Statistics.

Western Interstate Commission for Higher Education. 2008. *Knocking at the college door: Projections of high school graduates by state and race/ethnicity 1992–2022.* Boulder, CO: Western Interstate Commission for Higher Education.

READING 51

Wealth Stripping: Why It Costs So Much to Be Poor

James H. Carr

Within the public policy arena, the contemporary use of the term wealth stripping has generally referred to financial products and services like payday lenders, rent-to-own stores, and the like that exploit the lack of financial sophistication among economically

James H. Carr is a housing finance, banking, and urban policy consultant. He is also a senior fellow with the Center for American Progress and Distinguished Scholar with the Opportunity Agenda.

disadvantaged populations. Awareness of the problem among policy-makers and advocates arguably originated with Michael Sherraden's 1991 book, *Assets and the Poor.* Sherraden's landmark work spawned a virtual avalanche of research, proposals, and innovative initiatives on asset building. Out of that body of research grew significant attention toward wealth stripping. John Caskey's seminal 1996 book, *Fringe Banking: Check-Cashing Outlets, Pawnshops, and the Poor,* was the subject's foundational text, highlighting how the high cost of alternative or fringe lenders strips away the financial resources of the poor. Many other scholars have since followed with different perspectives on both saving opportunities and the wealth-stripping challenges confronting the poor.

Even today, writings on the subject of wealth stripping tend to focus principally on the high cost of alternative financial services. But the Great Recession—driven by the foreclosures that hit minority communities especially hard—demands a broader examination of the issue to include ways in which the failure to impose or enforce consumer protection and anti-discrimination laws can lead to even greater harms. This broader perspective is essential if we are to understand and address the unique hurdles faced by low- and moderate-income households and people of color, who are disproportionately affected by these problems.

Wealth stripping has only increased during the economic crisis. Since the onset of the Great Recession, Americans have lost $7 trillion in equity in their homes. The Federal Reserve estimates the median American family has lost nearly two decades of wealth, or almost 40 percent of their assets. In a separate report, the Pew Research Center estimates that Latinos, Asians, and African Americans have experienced wealth losses of 66 percent, 54 percent, and 53 percent respectively, compared to 13 percent for whites. These losses are largely due to home foreclosures and lost equity.

In the wake of the crisis, it is imperative that we understand wealth stripping to include both predatory financial services and the huge loss in wealth that resulted from foreclosures that stemmed from subprime lending. Millions of households that neither accessed a predatory loan product nor were foreclosed upon have nevertheless experienced exceptional wealth loss due to the concentration of foreclosures in their neighborhoods. Millions of borrowers also now hold mortgages that are valued at more than the price of their homes. While the recently established Consumer Financial Protection Bureau (CFPB) should help in eradicating much of the predatory lending that occurred prior to the Great Recession, the CFPB is not empowered to address the fallout from the financial crisis. Dealing with that aftermath is essential to avoid further substantial wealth stripping as we climb out of the recession's rubble.

According to the Federal Deposit Insurance Corporation, roughly nine million households are unbanked. Adults in these homes do not have a savings or checking account from a mainstream bank or credit union. An additional 21 million households are underbanked, meaning they have a checking or savings account but rely instead on alternative financial services provided by check cashers, payday lenders, pawn shops, and automobile-title lenders. This translates into roughly 60 million adults who operate outside of the financial-services mainstream. More than half of all African Americans and nearly 45 percent of Latinos and American Indian/Alaskans fall into this category.

The alternative financial-services industry is big business, with an estimated 340 million transactions each year costing customers $13 billion annually. Janneke Ratcliffe, executive director of the Center for Community Capital, points out that check-cashing and payday-lending storefronts outnumber all McDonald's, Burger King, Target, Sears, J.C. Penney, and Wal-Mart stores and branches combined (33,000 versus 29,000 respectively). The fees these alternative (also known as fringe) lenders charge are steep. Nonbank check-cashing costs on average $40 per payroll check. Although expensive, relatively speaking, that's a bargain compared, say, to rent-to-own stores, where a computer that retails for $851 can end up costing $4,459 ($49 per week for 21 months or 91 payments). Ratcliffe further finds that a subprime credit card with a $300 limit can come with fees totaling $250.

Initial high-cost fees are not the only or even greatest financial harm that can result from using an alternative financial-services provider. Relying on an auto-title lender, for example, can result in the loss of one's automobile since the borrower's car title is pledged as collateral for the loan. The typical auto-title loan is generally only 30 to 50 percent of the value of the vehicle used as collateral, but if the borrower fails to make the full repayment on time, he or she stands to lose the entire value of car, not just the outstanding loan amount. (And if that car is needed for work, then the loss of it can mean the loss of a job.)

Payday loans are widely known for being financially ruinous to their customers. Such loans are generally 14-day cash advances that cost between $15 and $30 per $100 borrowed, and range in size from $100 to $1,000 with the median loan size about $350. In addition to interest rates that typically exceed 400 percent annually, payday loans can trap consumers into rolling over the same debt multiple times, incurring excessive expenses on relatively small initial loan amounts. The Center for Responsible Lending estimates that more than 75 percent of all payday loans are the rollovers of previous unaffordable debt.

In their defense, these lenders claim they serve communities that banks do not. To some extent, they have a point. There are far fewer banks in minority neighborhoods than in white ones. But physical proximity is not the only barrier to greater bank usage cited by lower-income and minority consumers. Many alternative financial-services customers do not trust banks, do not feel welcome at them, do not understand the products they offer, and cannot afford the steep fees they charge. For debit cards, the typical overdraft fee of $34 is triggered by transactions that average just $17. And bank fees have been rising since the onset of the current economic crisis. According to a report by the Pew Charitable Trust, the median extended overdraft penalty fee at the nation's 12 largest banks has increased 32 percent since 2010.

Disappointingly, there are substantial and growing connections between mainstream banks and alternative lenders. One study found that more than 40 percent of the payday-loan industry is financed by the nation's largest banks.

Moreover, some recent bank products mirror those of the most predatory alternative storefront lenders. Many traditional banks have entered the payday-loan arena, for example, with a product called a "checking account advance" loan. Those loans typically are for a ten-day period and carry an annualized interest rate of 365 percent. It's worth noting that the nation's largest banks are able to borrow at a practically 0 percent interest rate due to the Federal Reserve's monetary policy.

Of course, the most damaging and predatory loan product of all was the subprime mortgage that triggered the ongoing foreclosure crisis. The loss of wealth from foreclosures has been unnecessarily compounded by our inability to respond adequately to the crisis and the continued failures of the federal foreclosure-prevention programs.

The higher numbers of foreclosures among minority households related to predatory loan products has been extensively documented. Prince George's County in Maryland is the highest-income majority African-American county in the nation and, ironically, also the foreclosure capital of that state. In a recent study on foreclosures in that community, high-income borrowers in African-American neighborhoods were 42 percent more likely to go into foreclosure than typical borrowers in white neighborhoods. High-income borrowers in Latino communities fared worse: They were about 160 percent more likely to experience a foreclosure.

The reasons for the differences in foreclosure rates between residents in minority and nonminority communities are not known; they are not explained by differences in basic money management or loan or product type, since these variables are controlled for. Some possible causes could be a failure to apply for or receive similar treatment with respect to loan modifications, fewer savings to cushion financial shocks, higher levels of unemployment or underemployment, and higher levels of negative equity for minority households. Gaining a full understanding of these causes is critical.

In addition to this direct loss of wealth, neighboring residents in the communities in which foreclosures have been concentrated have also suffered. Distressed home sales drag down adjacent home prices, and improperly maintained vacant and abandoned properties can cause home prices in a community to collapse. (Not all neighborhoods are treated the same by the mortgage servicers who are responsible for the maintenance of their foreclosed properties: A recent investigation by the National Fair Housing Alliance found that foreclosed properties in communities of color were more than 80 percent more likely than those in white areas to have broken or boarded-up windows and other visible maintenance deficiencies.) Failing to prevent foreclosures and maintain vacant and abandoned properties has contributed to wealth stripping, particularly in minority communities. Research by the Woodstock Institute found that African-American and Latino communities in the Chicago area are likely to experience twice the amount of negative home equity (that is, when the value of a mortgage exceeds the value of a home) as non-Hispanic white communities.

Foreclosures have other harmful impacts on community. One consequence is a decrease in property tax revenue as a result of falling property values, which can harm local schools and other essential social services. Large numbers of foreclosures can also cause a loss in community cohesion and stability as families that have lost their homes relocate out of the neighborhood. And large numbers of foreclosures can lead to increasing crime that accompanies vacant and abandoned properties.

Going forward, there are some changes that must at a minimum be made. First, people should be able to access bankruptcy protection in order to maintain their homes. Right now, the family home is the only asset that cannot be restructured in bankruptcy proceedings—though the outstanding debt on a luxury yacht, vacation home, or investment property can be modified. This serves no legitimate public purpose and disproportionately harms those families and communities most affected by the current foreclosure crisis. It has been estimated that bankruptcy protection could have prevented thousands of foreclosures, and at no cost to the American taxpayer.

Second, credit reports should distinguish whether poor credit repayment behavior is the result of a mainstream or predatory financial product. Such a distinction would permit many subprime mortgage borrowers—whose default was due to deceptive loan products, not their unwillingness to pay—to obtain credit cards or other consumer credit, as well as to secure employment opportunities.

Third, policy-makers and regulators should remain aware that access to a full continuum of affordable and reliable financial products and services is essential, and that vulnerable consumers need to be protected. They need to exercise their authority with both urgency and care—urgency in purging the excessive and exploitative costs of fringe financial products and services, care in maintaining the customer-friendly marketing and operations that alternative-lending customers value. This includes affordable homeownership financial products that will be essential to jump-start the housing market and begin the process of rebuilding the enormous wealth loss resulting from the pre-crisis proliferation of reckless and unsustainable subprime mortgages.

The recently established CFPB goes a long way toward addressing the concerns I've laid out here. The agency has broad authority over predatory lending in the mortgage markets as well as retail consumer financial services. The worst of the subprime lending practices that were virulent prior to 2008 have already been eliminated and the CFPB has the authority to ensure they do not return. And, for the first time, the federal government, through the CFPB, has direct authority over the financial-services practices of alternative or fringe lenders. But the CFPB is not a panacea. For example, it is not authorized to address the challenges presented by vacant and abandoned properties resulting from foreclosures.

While much progress has been made, a great deal of work still needs to be done. The failure of private institutions to serve all families and communities equally has been an important impediment to disadvantaged families. Getting our leaders to begin caring about such families is essential to creating greater economic equality and a financially stronger America.

DISCUSSION QUESTIONS

1. Considering the risks and costs of alternative lenders, why do you think people use them?
2. How do foreclosed houses affect the surrounding community?

DISABILITY

READING 52

Disability Trouble

Bradley A. Areheart

Disability has long been understood as a simple consequence of biology. Because this perspective encourages "biological determinism"[1] and ignores the role of culture in disabling people, disability advocates developed the social model of disability ("social model") as a response. The social model has been called the "the big idea" of the disability movement.[2] It reframed disability as being in part a social construct by distinguishing social disablement from physiological impairment.[3] Disablement—in contrast to impairment—was "all the things that impose restrictions on disabled people; ranging from individual prejudice to institutional discrimination, from inaccessible public buildings to unusable transport systems, from segregated education to excluding work arrangements, and so on."[4]

Separating disability into its biological and social components has thus been the linchpin for a social model of disability.[5] Indeed, Michael Oliver, who is widely credited with formalizing and establishing the social model in Western academia,[6] emphasized disability's social nature precisely by distinguishing disablement from impairment.[7] He explained that disablement has "nothing to do with

the body."[8] Impairment, however, is "nothing less than a description of the physical body."[9] Oliver thus used the disability binary to emphasize the constructed nature of disability. The disability binary has since been considered key to the social model.[10]

The social model's constructionist account offers several benefits for disability advocates: (1) It dispels uncritical assumptions that a disadvantage resulting from disability is natural or necessary;[11] (2) it explains how social conditions contribute to disability disadvantage (which implies that such disadvantage can be changed through political struggle);[12] and (3) it liberates disabled persons by shifting the attention from an individual's physical or mental deficits to the ways in which society includes or excludes them.[13] The social model has been discussed widely both as it pertains to the meaning of disability and as a justification for certain policy and legal prescriptions, and it has become a fixture in legal disability scholarship.[14]

One major drawback of the social model is that it has not been substantially developed, revised, or rethought since the 1970s.[15] Other social movement ideologies such as feminism have developed and transformed substantially over time—responding to criticism and changing circumstances.[16] But social disability theory has clung to a strict reading of its founding assumptions.[17]

One possible explanation for this lack of criticality is that disability has been theorized largely by advocates.[18] The social model, for example, was forged by disability rights advocates with policy preferences already in mind.[19] It provided

---

Bradley A. Areheart is a professor of law at Baylor University.

intellectual justification for the predetermined goals of the disability rights movement.[20] Later, as leaders of the disability rights movement became academics, "the social model became an intellectual export. It moved from interest group device to scholar's tool."[21] . . .

While the social model has provided a useful vocabulary for theorizing disability, its terms merit greater scrutiny. The social model—by relying on a binary division between social disablement and physiological impairment—unwittingly underscores the notion that disability has a biological essence. In other words, although the social model was formulated to indicate disability's constructed nature, it inadvertently reifies the idea that disability is built in part upon non-social, biological, and essential facts. . . .[22]

In this article, I argue that impairment is actually substantially socially constructed and thereby make "disability trouble." I have coined this phrase as an allusion to Judith Butler's *Gender Trouble*,[23] a seminal contribution to feminist scholarship that challenged the gender/sex binary.[24] The gender/sex binary states that sex is physiological, while gender is socially constructed.[25] One of Butler's concerns was that the gender/sex binary, by effectively designating sex as non-social, left room for biological determinism.[26] I am similarly concerned that the disability binary, by designating impairment as non-social, has left room for biological essentialism. Accordingly, I seek to make disability trouble by suggesting that (1) the meaning of disability is not fixed and has a way of transcending the disablement/impairment binary; and (2) disability is more social and less biologically laden than previously theorized.[27]

I am not invoking Butler's popular theory that gender is performative by, for example, building a case that disablement is merely a stylized repetition of acts that, over time, produce the appearance of substance.[28] My argument instead focuses on appropriating Butler's claim that biological sex is just as culturally constructed as social gender, and applying it to the disability context.[29] Just as gender trouble became a rallying cry for scholars seeking to rethink sex and gender, it is my hope that

disability trouble evokes and invites new ideas about the meaning of disability.

Before proceeding, it bears noting that while many social model theorists use the term "disability" instead of "disablement" to refer to disability that is socially constructed, I have used "disablement" for two reasons. First, this is the term used most often by Michael Oliver, who formalized and popularized the disability binary within disability studies. Second, there is an analytic benefit to using "disablement" to denote disability that is constructed socially: Doing so preserves "disability" as a holistic term that encompasses both impairment and disablement. In other words, using "disablement" to refer to the socially constructed component of the disability binary avoids confusion over whether "disability" is being discussed generally or as part of a dichotomy. Here, I have endeavored to use "disability" exclusively as a non-dichotomous, holistic term. However, it is important to note that many of my sources equivocally use "disability" as both a holistic term and as the dichotomous counterpart to "impairment" within the disability binary.[30] . . .

. . . Is impairment solely biological? Put another way, is impairment devoid of social input? Oliver and other social modelists like him would seem to answer this question in the affirmative. As Oliver stated, impairment is "nothing less than a description of the [disabled person's] physical body."[31] Contemporary disability scholars have consistently recognized that this biology-centered definition of impairment is fundamental to the social model.[32] Such a definition of impairment raises the critical question of who is disabled in the first place. What or who determines whether someone is disabled?

IMPAIRMENT AS DIAGNOSIS

In answering the question of how a person comes to be considered disabled, the issue of diagnosis immediately emerges since the disabled person's body is described as impaired principally through medical diagnoses. Diagnosis is a core element for structuring and understanding disability. Indeed, without diagnoses, many disabilities would not be understood as such by either the person diagnosed or by others. Moreover, most disabled persons interface with medical professionals who diagnose them throughout their lives. . . . And medical diagnoses are often difficult to escape, given that medical (and especially psychiatric) records seem to have unusually long shelf lives.[33] In short, impairments, understood as the physical traits associated with disabilities, seem to be little more than diagnosis. Thus, in answering the question of how a person comes to be considered disabled, we may pose a second, closely related question: Is the diagnosis of impairments based solely on biology?

My argument in this part is that diagnosis involves more than non-social biology. Rather, diagnosis is a social concept in at least two tangible ways. First, acceptable categories of diagnoses are created by a variety of non-medical factors and take form as interested parties interact. The very existence of many impairments is thus largely contingent upon political and social factors. Second, the actual process of diagnosing an individual includes various social inputs that assist the medical professional in concluding that a person has a particular impairment. Examining the creation of diagnoses and the acts of diagnosis through the lens of specific impairments illuminates the constructed and contested nature of impairment. . . .

THE CREATION OF DIAGNOSES

It may be tempting to assume that diagnoses are divined from nature, that they are a "self-evident reflection of biological and epidemiological facts."[34] Indeed, this seems to be the default, unreflective view. Yet, in a very real sense, an impairment does not exist until we agree that it does—until it is created.[35] For example, a child who 100 years ago might have been described as a "bad student" might today be described as having dyscalculia (a learning disorder associated with comprehending mathematics) or dysgraphia (a deficiency in the ability to write). Similarly, a person who at one time might have been seen as a "glutton" might now be understood as having bulimia nervosa. Such diagnoses

thus exist as a confluence of both biological and cultural factors. Despite the modern tendency to see new diagnoses as the natural result of cumulative scientific progress, this section will show that the creation of diagnoses is often a multi-factored process spurred along by political negotiation, financial incentives, and/or social judgments and norms.

1. Mental Illness

Mental illness is a keen example of how diagnoses can be constructed when key interests among medical scientists, doctors, patients, and businesses align. For example, the creation of Chronic Fatigue Syndrome—despite its nonspecific pathology—was beneficial for a variety of social groups. Medical scientists received credit for discovering a new condition, clinicians found a diagnostic solution to idiosyncratic suffering, patients received relief from uncertainty and the promise of effective therapy, and businesses (especially insurance and pharmaceutical companies) saw the prospect of additional revenue.[36] The "discovery" of Chronic Fatigue Syndrome can thus be seen as resulting from a confluence of key social factors and interests.[37]

The *Diagnostic and Statistical Manual of Mental Disorders (DSM),* the authoritative manual of the American Psychiatric Association (APA), provides a window into how the creation of diagnoses is both politically and economically driven. The *DSM* plays a critical gatekeeping role in determining which mental illnesses are valid for insurance and clinical purposes. Each time a new edition of the *DSM* is forthcoming, expert panels are established to meet and deliberate about which diagnoses should be included and excluded.[38]

[The 2012 iteration of the *DSM* involved heated battles between] various political and legal interests. For example, many transgendered persons [fought] diagnostic categories of Gender Identity Disorder and Transvestite Fetishism.[39] Binge Eating,[40] Internet Addiction,[41] and Parental Alienation Syndrome[42] are also tentative diagnostic categories [that] engender great controversy.

Such battles over whether a diagnostic category ought to exist in the first place are legion. Past examples include the exclusion of homosexuality,[43] the inclusion of Post-Traumatic Stress Disorders,[44] and the proposal and rejection of the gender-biased Self-Defeating Personality Disorder.[45] Each of these aforementioned decisions had deep cultural implications and was ultimately effected by pressure from political constituencies—demonstrating that far more was at work than just raw biology and objective science.[46]

The creation of mental illnesses is also driven by financial incentives in the form of pharmaceutical money. While the role of pharmaceutical companies in the development of diagnoses has historically been less publicized than many of the political interests noted above, the connection between these companies and the *DSM* is starting to receive more press. Pharmaceutical companies have a general financial interest in expanding the number of diagnostic categories (and concomitantly, the total number of persons who can be diagnosed),[47] and the individual companies also have particular financial interests in medical practitioners prescribing their specific medications.[48] Pharmaceutical companies also provide substantial funding to the APA.[49] However, even more direct evidence of financial connections between pharmaceutical companies and the *DSM* has surfaced within the last five years.

In 2006, researchers at the University of Massachusetts and Tufts University published a study entitled *Financial Ties Between DSM-IV Panel Members and the Pharmaceutical Industry.*[50] This study provided empirical support for what many had suspected all along: Pharmaceutical money was connected to the creation of the *DSM*'s diagnostic categories. In particular, the study found that the majority of *DSM* panel members for the most recently published edition of the *DSM* had substantial financial ties to one or more pharmaceutical companies.[51]

Even the APA's President later acknowledged publicly that such ties exist and could not be fully eliminated.[52] Indeed, in 2008, the Center for Science in the Public Interest found that more than half of the twenty-eight members of the forthcoming *DSM-V* task force have ties to the drug industry.[53]

2. Sensory Impairments

Sensory impairments provide an example of how even diagnoses with seemingly unassailable biological foundations are constructed in significant respects.

Who is blind? We certainly do not live in a world with only two types of people: the blind and the sighted. Similarly, a diagnosis of blindness is not a dividing line between those without sight and those with perfect sight. Indeed, eighty percent of people who are legally blind have some amount of vision.[54] Rather, the diagnosis of blindness represents a dividing line on a continuum that ranges from perfect sight to total lack of sight. And drawing the line requires judgment about who ought to count as blind (and just how much inability to see the label "blind" entails). Accordingly, a diagnosis of blindness is not just an issue of the body; it is also a social judgment by the medical community about who ought to be considered "blind."[55] Deafness may be understood in much the same way.

3. Eating Disorders

One way of examining whether diagnosis is a social creation is to ask whether diagnoses are new or transient, i.e., whether they exist or have existed only at certain times and in certain places (and are thus context-dependent).[56]

Although identified in the 1870s, anorexia nervosa was a rare disorder for nearly a century.[57] However, in the 1970s and 1980s, the nature of anorexia's symptomatology began to change and its incidence increased dramatically in America.[58] Two new (but now common) symptoms emerged: compulsive physical activity and bulimia (bingeing and purging).[59] The reasons given for the symptom of not eating also began to shift from somatic (for example, "I cannot eat because it hurts") to psychosomatic (for example, "I don't need to eat; I am too fat").[60] What exactly happened?

Any attempt to explain changes in anorexia's incidence and symptomatology from a purely biological perspective fails.[61] It is only when one adds in heightened cultural pressure to exercise and be thin, women's personal freedom, desocialized eating environments, a lack of adolescent supervision, and the ubiquity of food for purchase, that one begins to understand how the cultural climate in America helped make anorexia a common condition with new symptomatology.[62] Anorexia may thus be seen as a transient mental illness that has flourished at specific times in specific places—namely contemporary ones that extol a particular version of beauty.[63] In this respect, "eating disorders appear ultimately to be cultural productions, no matter what biological mechanisms they provoke."[64]

4. Intellectual Impairments

Mental retardation is another example of a diagnosis constituted by social norms. With ever-changing criteria and tests, one might reasonably see mental retardation as "a historically contingent way of talking about people who appear to be in need of assistance and who are not very good at IQ tests."[65] Mental retardation is, in this way, a relative concept and a social judgment of sorts.[66] None of this indicates that retardation is imaginary or not a real disability. However, the diagnosis is also not a simple reflection of self-evident, physiological facts; it requires an implicit cultural judgment about how much competence is normal, and when deviation from that normality is substantial enough to be considered an impairment.

Or consider learning disabilities (LDs). Much like the diagnoses discussed above under the *DSM,* the dozen or so conditions lumped together under the umbrella term "LD"[67] have been legitimated largely by economic and political interests.[68] The term "learning disabilities" was itself invented in 1963 by a psychologist attempting to expand the circle of students who could be diagnosed as "disabled" and thus entitled to federal protections and funding.[69] By the 1980s, LD diagnoses were soaring and the numbers continue to grow today.[70] The

scope of what constitutes an LD has continued to widen since the term's inception, thereby subsuming an increasing number of Americans.[71]

The salient question might be "why?" While some media outlets have loosely attributed the growth of LD diagnoses to factors such as diet, exposure to chemicals, and sedentary lifestyles,[72] most scholars examining the issue have concluded that the growth is due to distinct political and financial interests.[73] Carl Elliott, a professor at the Center for Bioethics at the University of Minnesota, has argued that the ballooning of such diagnoses is not because people have suddenly detected conditions that were hidden for hundreds of years.[74] Rather, he notes it is because "all mental disabilities, even those with biological roots, have a social component."[75] Just like the *DSM* diagnoses discussed above, many interests drive this trend, including those of LD educators (who obtain federal aid for each student diagnosed as having an LD); psychologists (who charge thousands of dollars to diagnose students); LD researchers (who are incentivized by the lure of federal grants); attorneys (who can win judgments in ADA cases); and pharmaceutical companies (who have pocketed billions of dollars from medicines that target learning disabilities).[76]

5. Age-Related Impairments

A slightly different case for seeing impairment as socially constructed is where the predicate physical conditions have always existed, but have not always been considered problematic and diagnosed. For example, hip fractures, spinal deformities and loss of height were all once thought of as normal byproducts of aging.[77] They were not considered impairments or diagnosed in any meaningful way.[78] However, since 1994, the World Health Organization has classified osteoporosis (a major factor in each of the aforementioned symptoms) as a disease that can be diagnosed, prevented, and treated.[79] Such institutional shifts have significant consequences because they affect medical norms, which in turn affect the process of diagnosis.[80] The development of age-related impairments shows that normality and disease do not issue from an unmediated form of biology; instead, biological data are interpreted through existing knowledge of the body and in accordance with cultural standards.[81]

THE ACTS OF DIAGNOSIS

A related way of challenging the assumption that impairment is only biological is by examining the acts of diagnosis. To the extent that diagnosing an individual requires interaction with the patient or interpretation of patient-reported data, social norms become embedded into the ultimate diagnosis.

1. Mental Illness

Mental illness is one area of medicine that relies heavily on patient reporting. For example, in cases of depression, the medical practitioner's diagnosis often relies on the patient's psychological self-assessment, which will almost necessarily be informed by social meanings. A depressed person, to be classified and diagnosed as such, must be able to communicate.[82] Instead of listing off symptoms, the depressed subject must often produce a narrative of her depression.[83] In producing such a narrative, the person's preconceptions relating to depression and its symptoms will likely be incorporated. The very formation of depression as an impairment thus depends upon patients' internalization of their distress and later articulation to a medical professional.[84] In this sense, the diagnosis of depression involves an aggregation of social norms, a person's view of her own symptoms, and a narrative dispensed to the medical professional. Any effort to isolate the part of depression that is biological impairment (as opposed to social disablement) would seem artificial at best.

Other diagnoses can similarly be seen as controlled more by the patient than the physician.[85] For example, the criteria for Chronic Fatigue Syndrome are patient-centered, permitting the patient to effectively define the disease based on her particular symptomatology.[86] There has been a steady rise in diagnoses that depend upon patient-reported symptoms—the result of a trend toward "functional" diagnoses, or solutions to "the problem of idiosyncratic suffering not readily explainable by specific pathology."[87]

Another reason that impairment is less objective and more social than previously theorized is that diagnoses for mental illness involve considerable subjectivity and interpretation on the part of medical practitioners. Psychiatry is not like cardiology or nephrology, where the basic diseases are well understood and identifiable by non-subjective criteria:[88] "No blood tests exist for the disorders in the *DSM*."[89] Rather, patients rely on judgments from practitioners, who in turn rely on subjective phenomena and the manual.[90] Yet once subjective phenomena (such as finding difficulty in practical life tasks or not doing well on IQ tests) are re-described as symptoms, a cultural condition is transformed into a medically identifiable pathology.[91] There have even been published studies in which psychiatrists, trained in using the *DSM,* cannot even agree on which class of diagnoses (such as "personality disorder") a disability falls into, much less reach agreement on a specific diagnosis within that class.[92] Some disagreement as to application is, of course, natural; still, disagreement illuminates the fact that diagnosis is a process that is not immune from social influences.[93]

2. Intellectual Impairments

Another example of the constructed nature of diagnosis can be found in considering the use of diagnostic assessments to determine diagnoses. Mark Rapley, a professor of psychology at the University of East London, has explored how intellectual disabilities are constructed through the psychological assessments intended to diagnose them.[94] He notes that this occurs in part because of an "acquiescence bias," in which respondents to surveys have a tendency to indicate a positive answer to questions, or simply agree.[95] This dynamic is amplified in the realm of intellectual disabilities because medical professionals often assume that their patients are incapable of reporting on their own conditions.[96] One result of this bias for assessments is that an interviewee may be shepherded into apparently inconsistent answers by a range of interactional phenomena: the interviewee's perceived need to reformulate responses to questions;[97] the interviewer's pursuit of "correct" answers (based on his or her expectations);[98] and the interviewer's desire to obtain an answer in the official vocabulary of the interview schedule.[99] While it is difficult to provide concise examples of these phenomena, Rapley's conclusions are supported through extensive use of case studies and examples.[100] In such cases, inconsistencies are produced by the logic of the interviewer's demands.[101] Raley concludes that such methods of diagnosis necessarily shift intellectual disability from the realm of an individual, biological problem to an interactional social product.[102]

IMPAIRMENT EXISTS ON A CONTINUUM

The creation of diagnoses and acts of diagnosis reveal how impairment exists as part of a continuum, rebutting the tempting inference that impairment is itself a binary concept (with a world full of impaired and non-impaired people). For example, mental illness diagnoses implicate a wide array of socialized behaviors, including the way in which one responds to stress, how much anxiety or sadness one should feel, and when and how one should sleep, eat, and express oneself sexually.[103] All of these behaviors exist on a continuum and are not binary concepts. This means that in order to make particular diagnoses, a line must be drawn somewhere to mark the point at which normal behavior has crossed into pathology.

Blindness, deafness, disordered eating, and intellectual impairments all represent a range of qualities and/or abilities regarding certain aspects of the body. Who is blind, deaf, bulimic, or mentally retarded is thus a question of degree based on graduated differences. At some point on each continuum, a line must be drawn to effectuate the diagnosis.

The same principle applies to the process of diagnosis; there, lines must be drawn to determine whether particular people's behavior or sensory abilities fall within the realm of predetermined disabilities. This line-drawing is complicated and made inconsistent by the interactional phenomena associated with physician and patient. Accordingly, where we draw lines for diagnoses may change over time (creation of diagnoses), or may change depending on the patient and/or physician (acts of diagnosis). The result is that impairment is most aptly understood as a non-binary, spectrum concept. This observation underscores my thesis that impairment, understood as diagnosis, is socially constructed.

PERHAPS IMPAIRMENT WAS ALWAYS ALREADY DISABLEMENT

Having explained how biological impairment is often constructed, one might question whether impairment (and ultimately disability) is entirely constructed. After building the case that sex was constructed, Butler similarly questioned whether sex "was always already gender, with the consequence that the distinction between sex and gender turns out to be no distinction at all."[104] Within the disability framework, given my argument that impairment is thoroughly constructed, we might question whether impairment is always already disablement, with the result that the division between impairment and disablement turns out to be inconsequential. And if the distinction is no distinction at all, what then is left of biology?

This latter question has often consumed the attention of Butler's critics, who argue that she has lost sight of "the concrete, historical body that loves, suffers, and dies."[105] Butler acknowledges that there is indeed something necessary and inescapable about such "primary and irrefutable experiences."[106] She does not claim that there is no material body, just that we can only apprehend that material body through discourse.[107] This means that while the body is not reducible to language,[108] it is only accessible through language.[109] In other words, there is no reference to a pure body which is not at the same time a further formation of that body."[110] Her ultimate concern is to interrogate constructions of sex that have come to be seen as essential and natural.[111]

Here, I simultaneously converge with and depart from Butler's project. Like Butler, I am not denying that biology exists, but endeavoring to show how the version of biology with which medical professionals interact is contested and refracted by social interests. I am unconcerned with demarcating culture from nature or social inputs from biology; in many ways, the question of what is left of biology reintroduces that which was problematically an assumption of the gender/sex and disability binaries from the start: the presence of a raw biological core that may be neatly extricated from the concept of woman or disability. I am interested in showing *how* impairment is constructed and the interests that are served by its construction, not in drawing lines to show the boundaries of biology.

Unlike Butler, I am less focused on discourse and more focused on attempting to provide an account of the impaired body that provides political and historical context. Social constructionism has, in recent years, become a trendy and often obtuse way to discuss a subject.[112] Here, I have labored to employ social constructionism usefully by providing concrete examples of how impaired bodies are produced.

One final point that bears reiteration is that my argument, as applied to particular disabilities, does not imply that those disabilities are not real or valid. Social constructionism (here, my claim that biological impairment is socially constructed) is often caricatured as asserting that a particular thing is a "mere" construct and thus arbitrary or illegitimate.[113] I am not denying that biology exists; instead, I am challenging the idea that biological accounts of the body (that is to say, diagnoses) are asocial, or merely descriptive. My general point is that we need to think more carefully about disabled identity, not that socially constructed diagnoses are illegitimate.

DISCUSSION QUESTIONS

1. Are there points at which you find yourself objecting to Areheart's analysis? Which points and why?
2. What are the practical implications of Areheart's analysis for the social model of disability?

NOTES

1. My use of the term "biological determinism" is intended to denote the idea that our genetic makeup determines and makes inevitable our development as people with certain traits and opportunities.
2. SHAKESPEARE, *supra* note 3, at 29.
3. A key moment in the social model's intellectual and political history occurred in 1976, when the Union of the Physically Impaired Against Segregation (UPIAS) published its *Fundamental Principles of Disability*. UPIAS's differentiation between impairment and disability would later form the basis of what Michael Oliver coined "The Social Model of Disability." Union of the Physically Impaired Against Segregation (UPIAS), Fundamental Principles of Disability (1976); *see* Oliver, *Understanding Disability, supra* note 3, at 1–2 ("I should say at this point that the original simple idea underpinning my work was not my original idea but was an idea that I came across in encountering *Fundamental Principles of Disability* for the first time." (citation omitted)); *id.* at 28 (affirming the impairment/disability distinction in *Fundamental Principles of Disability* as being "valid to this day"); *see also* Tom Shakespeare, "The Social Model of Disability," in *The Disability Studies Reader, supra* note 6 at 197, 197 ("While the problems of disabled people have been explained historically in terms of divine punishment, karma or moral failing, and post-Enlightenment in terms of biological deficit, the disability movement has focused attention onto social oppression, cultural discourse, and environmental barriers."); *id.* at 198–99 (explaining that the "redefinition of disability itself" is what sets the social model apart from other socio-political approaches to disability).
4. Oliver, *Understanding Disability, supra* note 3, at 33. One of the most common illustrations for understanding disability as a social construct are the architectural barriers faced by wheelchair users. Adam Samaha has stated: "It is one thing to be unable to walk. It is quite another matter to be unable to enter a building unassisted because the architect preferred stairs to ramps." Adam Samaha, What Good Is the Social Model of Disability?, 74 U. *Chi. L. Rev.* 1251, 1258–59 (2007). In such a situation, a person is disabled—or made to feel

disabled—at least in part by factors outside of the person's own body. Such factors may, under the social model, include physical, institutional, and attitudinal barriers. Areheart, *supra* note 2, at 188.

Tom Shakespeare has explained that one key to understanding the social model is viewing it as a series of dichotomies: impairment is distinguished from disability (or what I call "disablement," see *infra* note 41) thereby creating the disability binary; the social model is distinguished from the medical model of disability; and disabled people are distinguished from non-disabled people. Shakespeare, *supra* note 10, at 198–99. Furthermore, under the disability binary, impairment is individual and private, while disablement is structural and public. *Id.* at 198. In this way, impairment might be seen as a remnant of the medical model of disability, a paradigm that historically has focused on the impact of an individual's own physical or mental impairments rather than on factors that reside outside of the person's body.

5. Colin Barnes and Geof Mercer, *Disability* 65 (2003); Mark Rapley, *The Social Construction of Intellectual Disability* 62 (2004) (noting that the "fractioning of a monolithic 'disability' into notions of a (physical or mental) *impairment,* with concomitant *disability* caused by social barriers" is "central" to the social model).

6. Samaha, *supra* note 11, at 1251–52 (noting that although the social model's causation story has been around since the 1970s, it was Michael Oliver who launched the social model in Western academia in 1990); *see also* Rapley, *supra* note 12, at 62 ("[T]he social model as a formal statement of social scientific theory is usually held to originate in the work of Mike Oliver . . .").

7. *See supra* note 3.

8. Oliver, *Understanding Disability: From Theory to Practice* (1996), at 35.

9. *Id.*

10. *Id.* (noting that the disability binary "remains valid to this day"); Rapley, *supra* note 12, at 62; Samaha, *supra* note 11, at 1257 ("Key to the social model is a distinction between personal impairments and disability.").

11. Samaha, *supra* note 11, at 1253.

12. *Id.* at 1255; *see also* Shakespeare, *supra* note 3, at 30.

13. Shakespeare, *supra* note 3, at 29–30.

14. Samaha, *supra* note 11, at 1268 (noting that Mary Crossley "helped import the social model into legal scholarship"); *see* Mary Crossley, The Disability Kaleidoscope, 74 *Notre Dame L. Rev.* 621, 653–59 (1999) [hereinafter Crossley, Disability Kaleidoscope]; *see also* Carlos A. Ball, Looking for Theory in All the Rights Places: Feminist and Communitarian Elements of Disability Discrimination Law, 66 *Ohio St. L. J.* 105, 130–31 (2005) (noting that the social model defines disability as a social construct and that this viewpoint has become

"quite pervasive in the legal academic literature"); Mary Crossley, Reasonable Accommodation as Part and Parcel of the Antidiscrimination Project, 35 *Rutgers L. J.* 861, 875–77 (2004) [hereinafter Crossley, Reasonable Accommodation] (noting that work on the social model "has gained the attention of the legal academy").

15. Shakespeare, *supra* note 3, at 33–34; *see also* Mairian Corker and Tom Shakespeare, Mapping the Terrain, in *Disability/Postmodernity, supra* note 6, at 1 (noting that disability studies have "suffered from a theoretical deficit"); Shakespeare, *supra* note 10, at 199 ("Many leading advocates of the social model approach maintain that the essential insights developed by UPIAS in the 1970S still remain accurate and valid three decades later."); *id.* at 202 ("While acknowledging the benefits of the social model in launching the disability movement, promoting a positive disability identity, and mandating civil rights legislation and barrier removal, it is my belief that the social model has now become a barrier to further progress.").

16. Shakespeare, *supra* note 3, at 33–34.

17. *Id.* at 34.

18. *See infra* notes 26–28.

19. Samaha, *supra* note 11, at 1254 (noting that disability rights advocates forged the social model "alongside a political platform"); *id.* at 1255 ("[T]he social model was generated within a disability rights movement with policy objectives."); *id.* at 1280–82 ("Similar notions were percolating elsewhere, but a social model of disability was driven to the forefront by a movement of disabled people dissatisfied with existing institutions and policies. Participants sought to define disability, and thus the movement, in accord with their experience and objectives . . . Given this history, it is not surprising that original proponents of the social model supported social reconstruction to ameliorate disadvantage. This goal was the inspiration for the model in the first place." (footnote omitted)).

20. *Id.* at 1282 (noting that the social model was "an accoutrement" to the disability rights movement); *id.* at 1269 (noting that the regular connection between the social model and policy "might follow from affiliation with the disability rights movement").

21. *Id.* at 1283 (footnote omitted).

22. Rapley, *supra* note 12, at 66 (noting that impairment and disablement, under the social model, are paradoxically "reified as structurally given things"). In this way, impairment might be seen as a remnant of the medical model of disability, which posits biology as an essential characteristic of the disabled individual. *Id.*

23. *See supra* note 7.

24. Toril Moi notes that Butler's scholarship, including *Gender Trouble,* was "by far the most important work on

sex and gender in the 1990s." Toril Moi, What Is a Woman?, in *What Is A Woman? and Other Essays* 3, 45 (2001); *see also* Alison Stone, *An Introduction to Feminist Philosophy* 61 (2007) ("[Butler's] *Gender Trouble* . . . is one of the most important and influential books in contemporary feminist philosophy.").

25. Stone, *supra* note 35, at 30–34.

26. Butler, *Gender Trouble*, *supra* note 7, at 9 ("The presumption of a binary gender system implicitly retains the belief in a mimetic relation of gender to sex whereby gender mirrors sex or is otherwise restricted by it.").

27. This use of "disability trouble" parallels Judith Butler's use of the phrase "gender trouble." Butler, Undoing Gender, *supra* note 7, at 42–43 ("[When] one refers to 'gender trouble'. . . one is . . . suggesting that gender has a way of moving beyond [the] naturalized [gender/sex] binary.").

28. Butler, *Gender Trouble*, *supra* note 7, at 45.

29. *Id.* at 9–10.

30. It is thus imperative to discern how such scholars are using the term "disability" in order to avoid confusion.

31. Oliver, *Understanding Disability, supra* note 3, at 35.

32. Areheart, *supra*, note 2 at 188 (identifying the impairment/disablement distinction as foundational to the social model); Crossley, Disability Kaleidoscope, *supra* note 21, at 657 (contrasting "bodily impairments" with "disability" under the social model); Shakespeare, *supra* note 10, at 197 (noting the dichotomy between biological impairment and social disability as key to the social model).

33. In *Madness, Distress, and Postmodernity,* Anne Wilson and Peter Beresford document their status as "psychiatric system survivors" and demonstrate how medical and psychiatric records may restrict future life opportunities, understandings, and rights. Anne Wilson and Peter Beresford, Madness, Distress and Postmodernity: Putting the Record Straight, in *Disability/Postmodernity, supra* note 6, at 143.

34. ARONOWITZ, *supra* note 78, at 58. Professor Aronowitz argues that such an approach is flawed. He points to the creation of Lyme disease as an example of a diagnosis built "implicitly and incrementally from a number of interacting factors," and not as a necessary result of analyzing objective biological facts. *Id.*

35. Rosenberg, *supra* note 76, at xiii.

36. *See* Aronowitz, *supra* note 78, at 36.

37. *Id.* at 179.

38. *See generally* Lisa Cosgrove et al., Financial Ties Between *DSM-IV* Panel Members and the Pharmaceutical Industry, 75 *Psychotherapy & Psychosomatics* 154 (2006) (noting the role expert panels play in determining which particular diagnoses are included in the *DSM*).

39. Benedict Carey, Psychiatry's Struggle to Revise the Book of Human Troubles, N.Y. *Time,* Dec 18, 2008, at

A1 (noting that the *DSM*-related debate over gender identity "is already burning hot among transgender people"); Arline Kaplan, *DSM-V* Controversies, *Psychiatric Times,* Jan 1, 2009, www.psychiatrictimes.com/display /article/10168/1364926.

40. Carey, *supra* note 88, at A1.

41. Kaplan, *supra* note 88.

42. Karen Franklin, Psychiatric Bible to Add New Diagnoses: *DSM* Makeover Process Shrouded in Secrecy, *Am. Chron.,* Oct 15, 2008, www.americanchronicle.com /articles/view/77790.

43. *See* Herb Kutchins and Stuart A. Kirk, Making Us Crazy, *DSM: The Psychiatric Bible and the Creation of Mental Disorders* 18, 55–99 (1997) (explaining how protests by gay activists led to the elimination of homosexuality from the *DSM-II* in 1974).

44. *See id.* at 18, 100–25 (explaining how Vietnam veterans fought for and achieved inclusion of Post-Traumatic Stress Disorder in the *DSM* despite the opposition of many leading psychiatric experts).

45. *See id.* at 19, 126–75 (explaining how feminism fought against the inclusion of Masochistic Personality Disorder in the *DSM,* which was later relabeled and rejected as Self-Defeating Personality Disorder).

46. *See id.* at 24 ("[L]ike a large and popular mutual fund, *DSM*'s holdings are constantly changing as the managers' estimates and beliefs about the value of those holdings change.").

47. *See id.* at 13. One forensic psychologist cynically writes: It's a tried-and-true formula: Do a quick-and-dirty study or two. Find a huge, perhaps escalating, problem that has heretofore been overlooked. Create a product label (aka diagnosis). And, voila! The drug companies will take it from there. A diagnosis that was once just a twinkle in the eye of a creative researcher becomes reified as a concrete entity. Franklin, *supra* note 91. Since the first edition of the *DSM,* the number of disorders has tripled—an increase paralleled by an increase in sales of drugs. Ron Grossman, Psychiatry Manual's Secrecy Criticized, *L.A. Times,* Dec 29, 2008, at A19.

48. *See* Benedict Carey and Gardiner Harris, Psychiatric Association Faces Senate Scrutiny over Drug Industry Ties, *N.Y. Times,* July 12, 2008, at A13 (noting that, on average, psychiatrists who received at least $5,000 from newer-generation antipsychotic drugs wrote three times as many prescriptions to children for said drugs than psychiatrists who received less money or none).

49. Kutchins & Kirk, *supra* note 92, at 13; Cosgrove et al., *supra* note 87, at 155 ("Pharmaceutical companies provide substantial funding for conventions, journals, and research related to what is included in the *DSM,* because

what is considered diagnosable directly impacts the sale of their drugs."); *see also* Carey and Harris, *supra* note 97 (noting that in 2006, the latest year for which data was available, the drug industry accounted for thirty percent of the APA's $62.5 million in financing).

50. Cosgrove et al., *supra* note 87.

51. *Id.* at 156. Revisions of the *DSM* are organized around working groups or panels. Of the 170 *DSM* panel members, ninety-five of them, or fifty-six percent, had one or more financial ties to a company in the pharmaceutical industry. *Id.* However, even this statistic is understated since *DSM* panels for diagnostic categories in which pharmacological interventions are standard treatment had much higher percentages of financial ties to the pharmaceutical industry. *Id.* at 156, 159. For example, one hundred percent of the panel members for the "Mood Disorders Work Group" (8 out of 8) and the "Schizophrenia and Other Psychotic Disorders Work Group" (7 out of 7) had financial ties to the pharmaceutical industry. *Id.* at 156–57. In contrast, the authors note that the panel for "Substance-Related Disorders"—an area in which psychopharmacological treatment is much less likely—had a much lower concentration (1 out of 6). *Id.*

The authors conclude that while receiving financial support from a pharmaceutical company should not disqualify a person from serving on a *DSM* panel, "the public and mental health professionals have a right to know about these financial ties, because pharmaceutical companies have a vested interest in what mental disorders are included in the *DSM*." Cosgrove et al., *supra* note 87, at 159.

52. Kaplan, *supra* note 88 ("We have anticipated and addressed questions about conflicts of interest in the *DSM* process. The abolition of conflict is a myth. . . . [W]hat we can do is to be very clear about what those interests are." (quoting Nada Stotland, APA President)).

53. Psych Working Group Again Rife with Conflicts of Interests, Integrity in Science Watch: Week of May 5, 2008, http://cspinet.org/integrity/watch/200805051 .html#4 (last visited April 3, 2011). Conflict-of-interest concerns were substantial enough to prompt Congress to launch an investigation into the APA's funding and doctors' financial arrangements with drug makers in 2008. *See* Carey and Harris, *supra* note 87.

54. Shelley Kinash, *Seeing Beyond Blindness* 5 (2006).

55. *See generally* Tanya Titchkosky, Cultural Maps: Which Way to Disability?, in *Disability/Postmodernity, supra* note 6, at 101, 101–11 (exploring the ways in which blindness is socially constructed).

56. In his book on social constructionism, Ian Hacking notes that some mental illnesses are transient in that "they show up only at some times and some places, for reasons which we can only suppose are connected with the culture of those times and places." Hacking, *supra* note 79, at 100.

57. Joan Jacobs Brumberg, From Psychiatric Syndrome to "Communicable" Disease: The Case of Anorexia Nervosa, in *Framing Disease, supra* note 76, at 134, 135.

58. *Id.* at 138–39.

59. *Id.* at 138.

60. *Id.* at 137.

61. *Id.*

62. *Id.*

63. Hacking, *supra* note 79, at 2, 100–01.

64. Brumberg, *supra* note 106, at 149.

65. Rapley, *supra* note 42, at 42.

66. *Id.* at 41, 42, 202–03.

67. Craig S. Lerner, "Accommodations" for the Learning Disabled: A Level Playing Field or Affirmative Action for Elites?, 57 *Vand. L. Rev.* 1043, 1064–65 (2004) (noting that LD is a broad term encompassing dyslexia, dysgraphia, dyspraxia, dyscalculia, dysrationalia, Attention-Deficit/Hyperactivity Disorder (ADD/ADHD), "language-based disability," and "auditory processing disability").

68. Kenneth A. Kavale & Steven R. Forness, The Politics of Learning Disabilities, 21 *Learning Disability* Q. 245, 245 (1998); Lerner, *supra* note 116, at 1058, 1076; *see also* Kathleen Ross-Kidder, Interventions with Comorbid Emotional/Behavioral Disordered Children, in *Contemporary Interdisciplinary Interventions for Children with Emotional/Behavioral Disorders* 559, 560 (David A. Sabatino and Benjamin L. Brooks eds., 1998) (examining the quandary faced by parents of seemingly intelligent children who had "unmet educational needs," and the perceived need for those children to receive some type of educational intervention).

69. Lerner, *supra* note 116, at 1058.

70. *Id.* at 1071–73.

71. *Id.* at 1044–45.

72. *Id.* at 1074.

73. *See supra* note 117.

74. Carl Elliott, Costing an Arm and a Leg, *Slate,* July 10, 2003, http://slate.msn.com/id/2085402.

75. *Id.*

76. Lerner, *supra* note 116, at 1077.

77. Jackie Leach Scully, A Postmodern Disorder: Moral Encounters with Molecular Models of Disability, in *Disability/Postmodernity, supra* note 6, at 48.

78. *Id.*

79. *Id.*

80. *See id.* (noting that there are significant consequences for such classification).

81. *Id.*

82. Anna Mollow, "When Black Women Start Going on Prozac . . .": The Politics of Race, Gender, arid Emotional Distress in Meri Nana-Ama Danquah's *Willow Weep for Me,* in *The Disability Studies Reader, supra* note 6, at 283, 290.

83. *Id.* at 290.

84. *Id.* at 290 n.30 (noting that "the formation of depression as an impairment category has depended in large part upon patients' verbal articulations of their distress").

85. Aronowitz, *supra* note 78, at 31.

86. *Id.* at 31.

87. *Id.* at 16.

88. Carey, *supra* note 88, at A1 ("This is not cardiology or nephrology, where the basic diseases are well known" (quoting Edward Shorter, History Professor, University of Toronto)).

89. Dan Vergano, Study: Medical Manual's Authors Often Tied to Drugmakers, *USA Today,* April 20, 2006, at A6 (quoting Lisa Cosgrove, psychology professor, University of Massachusetts Boston).

90. *Id.*

91. Rapley, *supra* note 12, at 43–44.

92. Kutchins and Kirk, *supra* note 92, at 52–53; *see also* Lars Noah, Pigeonholing Illness: Medical Diagnosis as a Legal Construct, 50 *Hastings L.J.* 241, 248 (1999) ("[M]ental health professionals often express greater disagreements about an appropriate diagnosis for a particular patient because the relevant symptoms tend to be non-specific, which means that any number of mental illnesses could account for the particular complaint.").

93. *See* Kutchins and Kirk, *supra* note 92, at 53 ("Serious confusion about distinguishing mental disorders from nondisordered conditions and the inability of clinicians to use the manual reliably make the development and use of *DSM* vulnerable to a host of nonscientific pressures."). Even medicine's technical aspects, which are seemingly unrelated to cultural influences, are "shaped in part by the shared intellectual worlds and institutional structures of particular communities and subcommunities of scientists and physicians." Rosenberg, *supra,* note 76 at xiv.

94. See, e.g., Rapley, *supra* note 12; Goodley and Rapley, *supra* note 66.

95. Rapley, *supra* note 12, at 80–84.

96. *See id.* at 28–29 (noting that, given the tests employed, it is unsurprising that medical professionals view people with intellectual disabilities as unreliable reporters on their own lives).

97. Because the normal question-and-answer means of verbal exchange is suspended, the imbalance may produce pseudo-acquiescence. *Id.* at 93.

98. Interviewers often do not accept a respondent's first answer and push the interviewees into self-contradictory responses. *Id.* at 95. However, these contradictions are a logical consequence of the (often convoluted) path of questioning. *See id.* at 94–96.

99. *Id.* at 96–101. Interviewers may suggest improvements to answers to "shepherd[] the respondent's answer into more acceptably official shape." *Id.* at 205.

100. *See id.* at 78–110 (providing detailed analyses of conversations between medical professionals and people with intellectual disabilities).

101. *Id.* at 89–90.

102. *See id.* at 202 ("[Intellectual] competence is *very much* a relative concept and moreover one which is, in actual social practices, actively negotiated."); *id.* at 208 ("I think that it is reasonable to suggest that what we have become used to thinking [of] as an essentialised condition afflicting persons is . . . nothing but a social construct and cultural artifact. . . . Intellectual disability is, then, not a thing-in-the-world awaiting discovery, but rather is a disreputable moral status socially constructed, by psy, as a speakable truth about [people considered intellectually disabled]." (citation and quotation marks omitted)).

103. Kutchins and Kirk, *supra* note 92, at 15.

104. Butler, *Gender Trouble, supra* note 7, at 9–10.

105. Moi, *supra,* note 35 at 49. *See generally* Martha C. Nussbaum, The Professor of Parody: The Hip, Defeatist Feminism of Judith Butler, *New Republic,* Feb 22, 1999, at 37 (criticizing Butler's radical social constructionism).

106. Butler, *supra,* note 69 at xi, 66–67; *see also* Moya Lloyd, *Judith Butler: From Norms to Politics* 70–71 (2007).

107. *See* Judith Butler, Sex and Gender in Simone de Beauvoir's *Second Sex,* in 72 *Yale French Studies: Simone de Beauvoir: Witness to a Century* 35, 45 (Hélène v. Wenzel ed., 1986) ("As a locus of cultural interpretations, the body is a material reality which has already been located and defined within a social context. The body is also the situation of having to take up and interpret that set of received interpretations."); *see also* Sara Salih, Judith Butler 74–75 (2002) (arguing that Butler acknowledges the material body, but noting that she also emphasizes discourse as the only way to apprehend that body).

108. Butler, *supra* note 69, at 6.

109. *Id.* at 10.

110. *Id.*

111. *Id.* at xi.

112. *See, e.g.,* Hacking, *supra* note 79, at vii–viii, 1–3 (explaining that the language of social constructionism is trendy, overused, and often not very meaningful).

113. Aronowitz, *supra* note 78, at 14.

READING 53

Learning Disabilities: The Social Construction of a Special Education Category

Christine E. Sleeter

Learning disabilities were officially founded with the birth of the Association for Children with Learning Disabilities (ACLD) in 1963. Learning disabled children suffer chiefly from an inability to achieve certain standards for literacy. These standards have changed historically as requirements of the American economy and the race for international supremacy have changed. Let us examine how the raising of reading standards, coupled with social expectations that schools help America's cold war effort and also sort students for future work roles in a stratified economy, led to the creation of learning disabilities.

Before the twentieth century, most information could be exchanged face to face and records were relatively simple. At that time, children with reading difficulties did not present a great social problem because most Americans did not need to be able to acquire new information through reading. Industrial expansion escalated literacy standards, requiring more and more people who could keep and understand increasingly complex records, pursue advanced professional training, and follow written directions in the workplace. As literacy standards in society escalated, schools responded by emphasizing reading more and by expecting students to attain increasingly higher levels of literacy (Chall, 1983; Resnick & Resnick, 1977).

Before the 1980s, the most recent major escalation of reading standards followed the Soviet Union's launching of Sputnik in 1957. Americans reacted to Sputnik by charging schools with failing to produce scientists and technicians needed for the U.S. to remain ahead internationally in technological development. This charge was widely publicized in numerous popular magazines (e.g., *Good Housekeeping, Time*). American schools were compared with Russian schools and found deficient. The chief problem, critics believed, was lax standards. For example, in March of 1958, *Life* magazine compared the schooling of two boys; one in Moscow and one in Chicago. It reported that in the Soviet Union, "The laggards are forced out [of school] by tough periodic examinations and shunted to less demanding trade schools and apprenticeships. Only a third—1.4 million in 1957—survive all 10 years and finish the course" ("School Boys," p. 27). In contrast, American students lounge in classrooms that are "relaxed and enlivened by banter," and in which the "intellectual application expected of [students] is moderate" (p. 33).

Recommendations for reforming American education included (a) toughening elementary reading instruction (Trace, 1961); (b) introducing uniform standards for promotion and graduation and testing students' mastery of those standards through a regular, nation-wide examination system ("Back to the 3 R's?," 1957; Bestor, 1958); (c) grouping students by ability so the bright students can move more quickly through school and then go on to college and professional careers, while the slower students move into unskilled or semiskilled labor ("Famous Educator's Plan," 1958; "Harder Work for Students," 1961; Woodring, 1957); and (d) assigning the most intellectually capable teachers to the top group of students (Rickover, 1957). To some extent, all these reforms were implemented in the late 1950s and early 1960s.

In reading, elementary textbooks were toughened and some tests were renormed. Chall (1977) analyzed the readability levels of widely used textbooks published between 1930 and 1973. She found elementary readers to offer progressively less challenge from 1944 until 1962; in 1962 first grade readers appearing on the market were more difficult, a trend that continued into the 1970s. There is also evidence that some widely used achievement tests

---

Christine E. Sleeter is a Professor Emerita in the College of Professional Studies at California State University Monterey Bay.

were renormed shortly after Sputnik to reflect escalated standards for literacy. The 1958 version of the Metropolitan Achievement Tests were renormed in 1964; the new norms reflected average reading levels 2 to 13 months higher for students in grades 2 through 9 (no gain was found for first grade) (Special Report No. 7, 1971). Similarly, the 1957 version of the Iowa Tests of Basic Skills was renormed in 1964. Hieronymus and Lindquist (1974) reported that the average gain in reading was 1.9 months at the 90th percentile, 2.6 months at the 50th, and 1.0 months at the 10th.

Many children were unable to keep up, but few blamed the raising of standards. Instead, students who scored low on reading achievement tests were personally blamed for their failure. By the early 1960s, children who failed in reading were divided into five categories, differentiated by whether the cause of the problem was presumed to be organic, emotional, or environmental, and whether the child was deemed intellectually normal or subnormal. They were called slow learners, mentally retarded, emotionally disturbed, culturally deprived, and learning disabled.

Slow learners and the mentally retarded were distinguished mainly on the basis of IQ: Those scoring between 75 and 90 were considered slow learners, and those scoring below were considered retarded. Both categories included disproportionate numbers of low-income children and children of color. As adults, slow learners were expected to occupy semiskilled and unskilled occupations, and retarded individuals were expected to occupy unskilled occupations or work in sheltered workshops (Goldstein, 1962). The emotionally disturbed also included large numbers from low-income backgrounds (Dunn, 1963). A subcategory was the "socially maladjusted," who were concentrated in Black, Puerto Rican, and immigrant neighborhoods (Shaw & McKay, 1942). A fourth category, which overlapped considerably with the previous three, was referred to as the culturally deprived. The National Conference on Education and Cultural Deprivation held in 1964 identified them as Puerto Ricans, Mexicans, southern Blacks and whites who moved to urban areas, and the poor already living in inner cities and rural areas (Bloom, Davis, & Hess, 1965). They were believed severely handicapped by home environments that lacked environmental stimuli; systematic ordering of stimuli sequences; language training; and training in the value of intellectual work, delayed gratification, individuality, and the belief that hard work brings success (e.g., Deutsch, 1963; Riessman, 1962).

A fifth category came to be known as the learning disabled. Of the five categories, this is the only one for which descriptions of the kinds of neighborhoods most likely to produce them were virtually absent from literature. The closest statement one finds is that they are essentially "normal" or come from "normal family stock" (Strauss & Lehtinen, 1963, p. 112), whatever that means (Strauss and Lehtinen), reknown pioneers in learning disabilities research, reported 12 case studies that give some indication of what "normal family stock" meant to them. Of the eight whose race was specified, all were white, and of the four whose race was not specified, two were of "above average" social standing or home environment. (No data were given for the other two.)

The cause of LD reading retardation was believed to be organic. Hypothesized causes included minimal brain damage (e.g., Strauss & Kephart, 1955), a maturational lag in general neurological development (e.g., Bender, 1957; Rabinovitch, 1962), a failure of the brain to establish cerebral dominance (Orton, 1937), or a failure to achieve certain stages of neurological development (Delcato, 1959)....

WHO WAS CLASSIFIED AS LEARNING DISABLED?

... The learning disabilities category probably was not consciously established just for white middle class children, even though it was populated mainly by them. It was established for children who, given the prevailing categories used to describe failing children, did not seem to fit any other category. Since most educators explained the failures of children of color and lower socioeconomic backgrounds with reference to the other four categories, such children tended not to have been placed in LD classes. White middle class parents and educators who saw their failing children as different from poor or minority children pressed for the creation and use of this category. By defining the category in terms of organic causality and IQ score, the white middle class preserved for itself some benefits.

First, the use of IQ to help distinguish LD students from other categories of failing children suggested its members "really" belonged in the middle or upper tracks or ability groups. As proponents of tracking during the late 1950s clearly pointed out, students were to be sorted for differentiated education based on ability, and members of each track were destined to hold different kinds of jobs in the labor market (e.g., Woodring, 1957). White children tend to score about 15 points higher on IQ tests than children of color, ensuring a greater likelihood that they would be seen as intellectually "normal" and thus potentially able to fill higher status positions. The intent of defining the category partly on the basis of IQ score was probably not to disadvantage the "disadvantaged" further, but to provide failing children whom educators saw as intellectually normal their best chance for moving ahead as rapidly and as far as possible.

Second, distinguishing between environmental and organic causes of failure helped legitimate the "superiority" of white middle class culture. The literature during the early 1960s contains much about the failings of low-income homes, and especially those of people of color. For example, readers of *Saturday Review* in 1962 were told that "slow learners appear most frequently in groups whose home environment affords restricted opportunity for intellectual development" ("Slow Learners," p. 53), and that "culturally deprived children" learn "ways of living [that] are not attuned to the spirit and practice of modern life" ("Education and the Disadvantaged American," p. 58). One does not find similar condemnations of the average white middle class home. If one were to accept such homes as normal, organic explanations for failure would seem plausible. One must view this as peculiar, since the main proponents of raising school standards to help America retain economic and political international supremacy were members of the white middle class. Yet rather than questioning the culture that viewed children as raw material for international competition, most educators questioned the organic integrity of members of that culture who could not meet the higher demands.

Third, some viewed minimal brain dysfunction as an organ deficiency that could potentially be cured in the same way diseases can be cured. The cure was hypothesized as involving the training of healthy brain cells to take over functions of damaged cells (e.g., Cruickshank et al., 1961; Frostig & Horne, 1964; Strauss & Lehtinen, 1963), the promoting of overall neurological development (e.g., Doman, Delcato, & Doman, 1964), the training of the brain to assume greater hemispheric dominance (Orton, 1937), or the altering of chemical balances through diet or drugs (e.g., Feingold, 1975; Sroufe & Stewart, 1973). Professionals may have cautioned against overoptimism, but the popular press did not. For example, in 1959, *Newsweek* readers were told about "Johnnies" with "very high IQ's" who can't read due to inherited neurological conditions. These "Johnnies" were described as educationally treatable using the Gillingham reading method; "Of the 79 Parker students taught under the method so far, 96 percent have become average or above average readers" ("Learning to Read," p. 110). In 1964, *Reader's Digest* provided case descriptions of children who were brain-injured at birth and experienced difficulty learning language, physical movements, and reading. A new program for motor development by Delcato and the Doman brothers was reported to "activate the millions of surviving [brain] cells to take over the functions of the dead ones" (Maisel, 1964, p. 137). Prognosis was reported excellent, and readers were told that it even helped affected children learn to read.

Probably due to these optimistic perceptions, students in LD classes seem to have suffered lesser negative teacher attitudes than other categories of failing students. Research studies have found that regular teachers see the LD student as less different from the "norm" than the emotionally disturbed or educable mentally retarded student, and as demanding less of their time and patience (Moore & Fine, 1978; Shotel, Iano, & McGettigan, 1972; Williams & Algozzine, 1979), even when they observe behavior that contradicts their expectations for the label (Foster & Ysseldyke, 1976; Salvia, Clark, & Ysseldyke, 1973; Ysseldyke & Foster, 1978). Studies have not compared teacher attitudes toward LD and "culturally deprived" students, but there is evidence that teachers have more negative attitudes toward and lower expectation of children of color and lower class children than white or middle class children (e.g., Anyon, 1981; Jackson & Cosca, 1974; Rist, 1970).

Whether teacher attitudes toward various categories of exceptionality actually affected how students were taught in school has not been reported in the literature. However, there is evidence from outside special education that teacher attitudes toward children based on social class or presumed intellectual ability do affect the quality and amount of instruction they give (e.g., Brookover et al., 1979; Rosenthal & Jacobson, 1968; Rist, 1970). Thus, it is reasonable to assume that teachers gave more and better instruction to low-achieving students labeled as learning disabled than to low-achieving students bearing other labels, even if actual behavioral differences among such students would not in itself warrant differential treatment.

LEARNING DISABILITIES IN THE 1970s

Since the early 1970s, there has been a shift in who has been classified as learning disabled and how the category has been used politically. That shift was propelled by a decline in the late 1960s in school standards for achievement, the civil rights movement and subsequent school responses, and a redefinition of mental retardation.

Although standards for school achievement were raised immediately after Sputnik, student test scores have caused many to believe standards were not maintained, for a variety of reasons (Goodlad, 1984). Declines in SAT scores, beginning in about 1966, have been widely publicized, and some state achievement tests also have shown declines (Boyer, 1983). One would think that if standards for achievement dropped during the late 1960s, fewer students would have been seen as failures and interest in classifying students as learning disabled would have waned. What happened was the reverse, due to other social developments.

During the late 1960s and early 1970s, minority groups pressured schools to discard the notion of cultural deprivation and stop classifying disproportionate numbers of minority children as mentally retarded. In 1973, the category of mental retardation (MR) was redefined, lowering the maximum IQ score from one standard deviation below the mean to two (Grossman, 1973), which dissolved the category of slow learner. The intent of these moves was to pressure schools to teach a wider diversity of students more effectively. Instead, many students who previously were or would have been classified as retarded, slow, or culturally deprived were now classified as learning disabled.

For example, based on a study of the racial composition of LD and MR classes in over 50 school districts between 1970 and 1977, Tucker (1980) found Black students overrepresented in MR classes but underrepresented in LD classes until 1972. After 1972, the proportion of the total school population in MR classes declined and Blacks lost some overrepresentation in that category, but they rapidly gained representation in LD classes, where they were overrepresented by 1974. Thus, even though pressure may have subsided during the late 1960s and early 1970s to provide a protected placement for failing white middle class children, learning disabilities has been used increasingly as a more palatable substitute for other categories to "explain" the failure of lower class children and children of color. . . .

DISCUSSION QUESTIONS

1. What is the current effect of a learning-disability diagnosis on a student's secondary education?

2. In examining the history of the learning disabilities category, is Sleeter implying that learning disabilities are not "real"?

REFERENCES

Anyon, J. (1981). Elementary schooling and distinctions of social class. *Interchange, 12,* 118–132.

Apple, M. W. (Ed.). (1981). *Cultural and economic reproduction in education.* Boston: Routledge and Kegan Paul.

Back to the 3 R's? (1957, March 15). *U.S. News and World Report,* pp. 38–44.

Bender, L. (1957). Specific reading disability as a maturational lag. *Bulletin of the Orton Society, 7,* 9–18.

Bloom, B. S., Davis, A., & Hess, R. (1965). *Compensatory education for the culturally deprived.* New York: Holt, Rinehart, and Winston.

Boyer, E. L. (1983). *High school.* New York: Harper and Row.

Brookover, W. B., Beady, C., Flood, P., Schweitzer, J., & Wisenbaker, J. (1979). *School social systems and student achievement: Schools can make a difference.* New York: Praeger.

Chall, J. S. (1977). *An analysis of textbooks in relation to declining SAT scores.* Princeton, NJ: College Entrance Examination Board.

Chall, J. S. (1983). *Stages of reading development.* New York: McGraw-Hill.

Cruickshank, W. M., Bentzen, F. A., Ratzeburg, F. H., & Tannhauser, M. T. (1961). *A teaching method for brain-injured and hyperactive children.* Syracuse, NY: Syracuse University Press.

Delcato, C. H. (1959). *The treatment and prevention of reading problems.* Springfield, IL: Charles C. Thomas.

Deutsch, M. (1963). The disadvantaged child and the learning process. In A. H. Passow (Ed.), *Education in depressed areas,* (pp. 163–179). New York: Teachers College Press.

Doman, G., Delcato, C., & Doman, R. (1964). *The Doman-Delcato developmental profile.* Philadelphia: Institutes for the Achievement of Human Potential.

Dunn, L. M. (1963). *Exceptional children in the schools.* New York: Holt, Rinehart, and Winston.

Education and the disadvantaged American. (1962, May 19). *Saturday Review,* p. 58.

Famous educator's plan for a school that will advance students according to ability. (1958, April 14). *Life* pp. 120–121.

Feingold, B. F. (1975). *Why your child is hyperactive.* New York: Random House.

Foster, G., & Ysseldyke, J. (1976). Expectancy and halo effects as a result of artificially induced teacher bias. *Contemporary Education Psychology, 1,* 37–45.

Frostig, M., & Horne, D. (1964). *The Frostig program for the development of visual perception.* Chicago: Follett.

Goldstein, H. (1962). *The educable mentally retarded child in the elementary school.* Washington, DC: National Education Association.

Goodlad, J. I. (1984). *A place called school.* New York: McGraw-Hill.

Grossman, H., Ed. (1973). *Manual on terminology and classification in mental retardation* (rev. ed.). Washington, DC: American Association on Mental Deficiency.

Harder work for students. (1961, Sept. 4). *U.S. News and World Report,* p. 45.

Hieronymus, A. N. & Lindquist, E. G. (1974). *Manual for administrators, supervisors, and counselors, Forms 5&6, Iowa tests of basic skills.* Boston: Houghton Mifflin.

Jackson, G., & Cosca, C. (1974). The inequality of educational opportunity in the Southwest: An observational study of ethnically mixed classrooms. *American Educational Research Journal, 11,* 219–229.

Learning to Read. (1959). *Newsweek,* p. 110.

Maisel, A. Q. (1964). Hope for brain-injured children. *The Reader's Digest, 11,* 219–229.

Moore, J., & Fine, M. J. (1978). Regular and special class teachers' perceptions of normal and exceptional children and their attitudes toward mainstreaming. *Psychology in the Schools, 15,* 253–259.

Orton, S. T. (1937). *Reading, writing, and speech problems in children.* New York: W. W. Norton.

Persell, C. A. (1977). *Education and inequality.* New York: The Free Press.

Rabinovitch, R. D. (1962). Dyslexia: Psychiatric considerations. In J. Money (Ed.), *Reading disability: Progress and research needs in dyslexia.* Baltimore: Johns Hopkins Press.

Resnick, D. P., & Resnick, L. B. (1977). The nature of literacy: An historical exploration. *Harvard Educational Review, 47,* 370–385.

Riessman, F. (1962). *The culturally deprived child.* New York: Harper and Row.

Rist, R. C. (1970). Student social class and teacher expectations in ghetto education. *Harvard Educational Review, 40,* 411–451.

Rosenthal, R., & Jacobson, L. (1968). *Pygmalion in the classroom.* NYC: Holt, Rinehart, & Winston.

Salvia, J., Clark, G., & Ysseldyke, J. (1973). Teacher retention of stereotypes of exceptionality. *Exceptional Children, 39,* 651–652.

Shaw, C. R., & Mckay, H. D. (1942). *Juvenile delinquency and urban areas.* Chicago: University of Chicago Press.

Shotel, J. R., Iano, R. P. & McGettigan, J. F. (1972). Teacher attitudes associated with the integration of handicapped children. *Exceptional Children, 38,* 677–683.

Special Report No. 7.(1971). Guidelines for standardization sampling *Metropolitan achievement tests special report*. New York: Harcourt Brace Jovanovich.

Sroufe, L. A., & Stewart, M. A. (1973). Treating problem children with stimulant drugs. *New England Journal of Medicine, 289,* 407–413.

Strauss, A. A., & Kephart, N. C. (1955). *Psychopathology and education of the brain-injured child.* New York: Grune and Stratton.

Strauss, A. A., & Lehtinen, L. E. (1963). *Psychology and education of the brain-injured child.* New York: Grune and Stratton.

Trace, A. S., Jr. (1961, May 27). Can Ivan read better than Johnny? *Saturday Evening Post,* pp. 30+.

Williams, R. J., & Algozzine, B. (1979). Teachers' attitudes toward mainstreaming. *Elementary School Journal, 80,* 63–67.

Woodring, P. (1957, *Sept.* 2). Reform plan for schools. *Life,* pp. 123–136.

Ysseldyke, J. E., Algozzine, B., Shinn, M. R., & McGue, M. (1982). Similarities and differences between low achievers and students classified as learning disabled. *Journal of Special Education, 16,* 73–85.

The following LD textbooks were reviewed in preparing this article: Adelman, H. S. and Taylor, L. (1983) *Learning Disabilities in Perspective* (Dallas, TX: Scott Foresman); DeRuiter, J. A. and Wansart, W. L. (1982) *Psychology of Learning Disabilities* (Rockville, MD: Aspen); Gearheart, B. R. (1981) *Learning Disabilities: Educational Strategies* (St. Louis, MO: Mosby); Hallahan, D. P. Kauffman, J. M. and Lloyd, J. W. (1985) *Introduction to Learning Disabilities* (Englewood Cliffs, NJ: Prentice Hall); Johnson, S. W. and Morasky, R. L. (1980) *Learning Disabilities,* 2nd ed. (Boston, MA: Allyn and Bacon); Kirk, S. A. and Chalfant, J. C. (1984) *Academic and Developmental Learning Disabilities* (Denver, CO: Love Pub. Co.); Lerner, J. (1981) *Learning Disabilities* 3rd ed. (Boston, MA: Houghton Mifflin); Mercer, C. D. (1983) *Students with Learning Disabilities,* 2nd ed. (Columbus, OH: Charles E. Merrill); Reid, D. K., and Hresko, W. P. (1981) *A Cognitive Approach to Learning Disabilities* (New York: McGraw-Hill); Sabatino, D. A., Miller, T. L., and Schmidt, C. (1981) *Learning Disabilities* (Rockville, MD: Aspen); Siegel. E. and Gold, R. (1982) *Educating the Learning Disabled* (New York: Macmillian); Sloan, H. A. (1982) *The Treatment and Management of Children with Learning Disabilities* (Springfield, IL: Charles C. Thomas); Smith, C. R. (1983) *Learning Disabilities* (Boston, MA: Little, Brown, and Co.); Smith, D. D. (1981) *Teaching the Learning Disabled* (Englewood Cliffs, NJ: Prentice Hall); Woodward, D. M. and Peters, D. J. (1983) *The Learning Disabled Adolescents* (Rockville, MD: Aspen).

READING 54

(Re)Creating a World in Seven Days: Place, Disability and Salvation in *Extreme Makeover: Home Edition*

Emily Askew

The world is sick. A readjustment has become necessary. Readjustment? No, that is too tame. It is the possibility of a great adventure that lies before mankind: the building of a whole new world . . . because there is no time to be lost.—Le Corbusier 1967[1]

We live within and among a series of overlapping places: nation, city, neighborhood, home, and body, whose meanings are formed and reformed at the intersection of ideology, practices, and the built environment. As an example of this complex interplay, libraries are interpreted to be quiet places, thus we build the structure with sound absorbing carpeting and acoustic emendations for sound, but we build them as quiet places as well when we "shush" a person in a neighboring carrel, we glare at those breeching the quiet contract, or finally we see that the unrepentant transgressor is ejected from the place itself, and perhaps forbidden return. Generation after generation, ideologies, practices, and the built environment construct and reconstruct libraries as quiet places.[2] In like manner are bodies interpreted as "disabled." Average bodies, in need of reassurance as to their sufficiency, construct buildings to keep some people out or severely inconvenienced; we construct bodies as "disabled" when we patronize, infantilize, or sanctify people with particular bodies, perpetuating and ultimately sedimenting their "otherness" to our "sameness."

Emily Askew is a professor of systematic theology at the Lexington Theological Seminary in Lexington, Kentucky.

Generation after generation, the almost seamless interplay between ideology, practices, and the built environment constructs and reconstructs the identities we inhabit, from nation to body. We reinforce these dominant interpretations of places until the interpretations themselves recede to make room for "the way things are." The insight from place theorists—geographers, philosophers, postcolonial theorists, and cultural theorists, among others—that places are never "naturally" endowed with meaning parallels the insight from contemporary disability theorists that there are no "natural" bodies: "The body can be explained as the object of the actions and interests of others."[3] Thus the "natural" body is a euphemism for agreed upon notions of, for example, male/female, straight/gay, young/old, white/black, healthy/ill, and able/unable/disabled.[4] Place theorists recognize that definitions of place are dialectically related to persons in (or out of) that place. Popular visual media contributes a great deal to the illusion of "the way things are."

It is within this semiotic matrix, defined by place theorists and postmodern theories of disability, that the ABC TV "reality" program *Extreme Makeover: Home Edition (EMHE)* functions to interpret the image of people with disabilities. The architectural salvation epic that is *EMHE* exemplifies the insight that the relationships between persons and place are mutually reinforcing until a dominant interpretation is secured. For *EMHE,* this reflexive reinterpretation is exemplified in the heart of the show when the condition of one's home describes the condition of one's body and the quality of one's life. In what follows, I consider the ways that *EMHE* constructs the human body as disabled through the medium of architecture, borne along by the narrative movements most often associated with classical theories of sacrificial atonement.

GEOGRAPHY IS IDENTITY[5]

States of Disrepair

At its most superficial rhetorical level, *EMHE* equates the condition of the family home with the condition of the bodies inside the home. Consider these examples: James is the youngest of four children of a single mother. Having spent time in a homeless shelter with his mother and siblings, James now lives with his family of five in a tenement. Unable to walk, talk, or care for himself, James is carried from place to place by his mother and siblings, including upstairs to the bathroom and in and out of the bathtub. The house is a shambles, James is growing larger and harder to carry, and his mother is getting less and less able to care for him alone.[6] Shelby Pope is a 12-year-old girl who is deathly allergic to the sun, a rare condition called Polymorphous Light Eruption (PMLE). She cannot be near the windows in her present home; she cannot play in her yard or ride in a car during the day without stringent precautions. She does not go to school because of PLME but is home schooled. Her house, it is determined, is keeping her imprisoned. If her home is "fixed" her life will be more "normal."[7] . . .

You Get What You Deserve

Thank you for your interest in applying for "Extreme Makeover: Home Edition." When casting our show we look for families that are inspirational and deserving.—from the online application[8]

Not everyone with needs is eligible for architectural salvation; only those who are both "inspirational and deserving" are desirable. To be inspirational and deserving seems to mean that not only do the families/individuals suffer bravely, but they also minimize their own needs by caring for the "less fortunate" in the community. To be inspirational and deserving of a house in which one can move freely and accomplish the tasks of life means surrendering the normal human emotions that accompany the limits imposed by architecture and society: no anger or frustration here, no active depression, no withdrawing from the world. Rather, the "deserving family" must exhibit only "grit" and gratitude. Nancy Eiseland and many others have documented the cultural trope of the brave sufferer. The brave sufferer is the woman or man who does not complain but rather accepts her/his "fate" with gratitude and equanimity. Clearly, *EMHE* reinforces the illusion that the virtuous sufferer is more "inspirational and deserving" than someone madder than hell that American culture has made life so difficult. Expressions of anger are described in the past tense, during a period before grit and gratitude overcame them:[9] "Martha Walswick has nine children but she lost her husband to cancer. The family has struggled to cope with their loss but are [sic] determined to face the future with a positive disposition."[10]

Over the seven seasons of its existence, *EMHE* has apparently ratcheted up the criteria for "inspirational and deserving." Whereas in the first season (2004) a single illness, disability, natural disaster, or heroic deed qualified a family for a makeover,[11] now a "deserving" family needs multiple catastrophes to qualify. For instance, the Vardon family is considered deserving in the 2005 season. Here, a 15-year-old boy cares for two parents who are deaf, along with his blind/deaf, autistic little brother who frequently escapes the house.[12] Also deserving is the Hassall family from the 2006 season. In this family, Brian, a police officer shot in the head while on duty, now suffers incapacitating migraine headaches when exposed to natural light. Thus, he lives in the unfinished basement of the home, protected from the sun. His wife Michelle, who has cancer, lives on the main floor with their two adopted children, one African American and one Chinese with a cleft palate.[13]

Without a doubt, the selected families have extraordinary needs, but what kind of message does showcasing families with Jobian level suffering send about the challenges of living in the world with "only" a single issue? Equating "deserving" only with confluences of multiple social and physical problems suggests that unless the challenges are Herculean and the emotional responses to the challenges equally heroic, one is not deserving of an accessible home and/or relief from poverty, or even homelessness. "Deserving" also means those individuals with a primary, "visible" disability and those whose family structures are heterosexual (even for single parents). Invisible disabilities and gay families make for less acceptable television because invisible disabilities *can* be faked and being a gay family *cannot* be.[14]

WE CAN SAVE YOU

As the plastic surgery version did before it, the architectural extreme makeover functions according to a time-honored formula embodied in most Western stories of salvation, from Sleeping Beauty to Jesus Christ. Because *EMHE* relies so heavily on religious language and imagery, I trace this formula through the language of Christian sacrificial atonement. The theological story of God's sacrifice for humans' redemption goes something like this: "God made a perfect world, but Adam and Eve sinned. Their crime was passed down to all of us in the form of 'original sin,' and now all human beings are sinners, and deserve God's condemnation. . . . We had no way to escape that punishment, or ever to make ourselves acceptable to God—until Jesus came. Jesus died for us. . . . If we believe that . . . then we are saved. By saved that means we are now acceptable to God . . . and will go to heaven."[15] The movements in this story consist of the following sequence: (a) fall from a perfect world, resulting in (b) radical, perpetual human brokenness, and (c) the inability to save ourselves from this state, requiring (d) the sacrifice of a supernatural savior for our sakes, resulting in (e) the end of our brokenness and estrangement from the perfect world.

"God Made a Perfect World . . ."

In the traditional Christian interpretation of the story of Adam, Eve, and the serpent, in Genesis 3, the Garden of Eden is described as the perfect world: no strife, no lust, no pain, no suffering, no evil. Through the actions of Eve, this perfection was destroyed for human beings for all time, with the result that we must live lives of pain, suffering, and labor. Historically, human beings have attempted to determine the signs of our "fall"; we have labeled aspects of human embodiment as markers of our sinful, fallen state. At one time or another, being black, being female, being gay, and/or being disabled have functioned as markers of sin. (And if one is all four. . .?) As DeVries points out, the theological interpretation of an originally perfect creation to which we should return is perilous for people with disabilities. Such an interpretation results in constructing people with disabilities as damaged by virtue of sin—either their own or someone else's.[16] Pairing diseased bodies with a diseased spiritual state functions as a theological rationale for the random dispersal of pain and suffering. Thus the disabled, black, female person bears these "limitations" as punishment from God for her own sins or the sins of her ancestors. Diversity of embodiment becomes a function of the imperfect realm outside of Eden, whereas conformity in appearance reiterates the perfection of Eden.

In the *EMHE* discourse, the perfect world-theory is at work in statements like these from Carlton Marshall, a Dallas police officer paralyzed by a gunshot in the neck who subsequently suffered a stroke and was made deaf from meningitis. He grieves that he cannot do what a husband/father/breadwinner should do.[17] Parents cannot tuck children in at night, children cannot play outside, heterosexual, married, parents cannot sleep in the same bed (and we assume be intimate), children must be parents and parents feel like children. Clearly these are inversions of the perfect order in which men, women and children all function according to dominant, American gender- and age-appropriate roles.[18]

EMHE attempts to minimize the implication of personal failure as the root cause of the pain for "deserving" families. However, two elements in the narrative arc of the show mitigate against completely dismissing the connection between fallenness and human (in)action: (1) the very construction of "deserving" simultaneously defines its opposite. Something about the actions, attitudes, scope of disability, or other aspects of their human natures, keeps most families who apply from being considered "deserving" of a home that functions for them. They have or have not done or said or embodied something that would garner the favor of the producers. (2) To underscore the heroic sacrifices borne by the team, the "brokenness" of the family has to be emphasized, complete with their admission that they cannot save themselves.

". . . But Adam and Eve Sinned"

The prerequisite for theological, and now architectural, supernatural assistance is human brokenness. In the classical theory of atonement, brokenness is the fault of humans, more specifically the fault of Eve, the first woman, who blew it for all humanity with the apple (Gen. 2:4b–3). Archetypal brokenness, the result of Eve's act, is named "original sin." Traditionally, original sin has been considered a constitutional state from which no one escapes and which, if left un-atoned for, dooms one to an eternal life in hell. Theologically, original sin is the human-caused condition that results in our estrangement from God. Repairing the rift requires a sacrifice greater than that which mere mortals can accomplish, thus God, in God's love, sacrifices Godself for us through the God-man Jesus. Human brokenness and estrangement, which would result in eternal damnation, are thus foundational conditions for the larger *EMHE* narrative of redemption.

In *EMHE,* human brokenness and the hell that results are laid out first in the application video, then reinforced by a tour of the dilapidated home, and finally summed up in interviews with family members. Known as the "before" setting, in makeover parlance, the images and comments from the application videos and the tour of the "before" house serve to describe just how dire the conditions are for the deserving families. Emotional breakdown is critical to the inscription of brokenness. In the section of the online application for *EMHE* entitled "How to Make a Family Casting Video," the family is encouraged to "Sit down and talk to camera like an interview and tell us your story. Explain your situation, why you think you deserve a makeover? *During this portion you want to be emotional, open up and ask for help*"[19] [Italics mine]. The "before" discourse describes dreams dashed, intimate relationships fractured, parental responsibilities abdicated to children, financial resources run dry, and hope teetering on the edge of some abyss. The visual representation of these social and existential conditions is the family home—burned or flooded, mold-infested or leaking, toxic and dangerous to the family in all manner of ways: a physical hell. They have run out of their own financial and physical but never spiritual resources.

"We Had No Way to Escape That Punishment, or Ever to Make Ourselves Acceptable to God."

The *EMHE* narrative formula must include the confession that the family can no longer help themselves (though they have tried repeatedly). By abandoning agency, the *EMHE* family is rewarded with a week's vacation and a new house. The family's abjection is the necessary relief against which the supernatural efforts of the *EMHE* crew will be cast.[20] The *EMHE* families must fit themselves into what Garland-Thomson, citing Susan Bordo, calls "a life-enhancing fiction" to deserve a made-over life.[21] By positioning themselves within the dominant discursive construction of disability, the *EMHE* families become eligible for the benefits of the show and more widely become acceptable to a larger audience, who insists on reliable tropes of disability over/against which to assess their own adequacy. But what are the liabilities of adopting this or any essentialism? Moreover, what are effects on persons called "disabled" when agency is in question in this way?[22] . . .

". . . Until Jesus Came."

The interpretation of the adjective "extreme" in ABC's makeover genre applies to three elements of *Home Edition*. First, the transformation of the house is so extensive (and expensive) that it qualifies as "extreme." Second, the condition of the family is so dire, due to the interplay of illness, impairment, and natural and societal disaster, that the family is narratively marked as an "extreme" example of human suffering. Finally, "extreme" applies to the sacrifices of the cast and crew in accomplishing the transformation of the home/family in seven days.

In the penultimate movement in the Christian, theological, salvation narrative, a supernatural savior, who is yet human, is sacrificed to restore broken (sinful) humanity to a wholeness we cannot accomplish for ourselves. This extreme gesture of God, sacrificing Godself to death on our behalf, is the mark of God's extreme love for humankind. God loves us so much (even in our brokenness) that God is willing to die for us. Further, the extraordinary nature of this sacrifice is marked by its obliteration of the limits of space/time. After three days in the tomb, Jesus' body is gone—resurrected—defying the bounds of physical death. We remember, as well, that the God of self-sacrifice and the empty tomb is also the God of cosmic creation. In the first Genesis story, Gen. 1–2:4, God forms the entirety of the earth in six days, with the seventh off for rest. In humble contrast, Ty and crew require the entire seven days of work to (re)create human lives.

The manipulation of time is a central hook of *EMHE* and, in fact, all "extreme" reality shows: "It's a race against time on a project that would normally span several months, involving a team of designers, contractors and hundreds of workers who all have just seven days to totally rebuild an entire house!"[23] Sacrificing sleep, defying the elements, keeping up construction through illness, accidents, and irritations, Ty Pennington seems to have given himself completely for the benefit of the "deserving" family.[24] Recipient families describe the crew as angels, sing hallelujah, and fall to their knees to thank God that their prayers have been answered when the crew pulls up into their yard—many "deserving" families believe that Ty has been sent by God to help relieve them of the pain they could not ease themselves.

". . . Then We Are Saved . . . and Will Go to Heaven."

At the end of seven days' building, tense to the very end, the deserving family returns from their vacation to their new life in a new world, the ideal, American, architectural world: "You'll see dingy kitchens get completely tricked out, spa-inspired bathrooms built where icky ones once were, and olympic-sized [sic] swimming pools installed in what were once shabby overgrown yards. . . . And

Ty and his crew do it from the ground up, adding five-star luxuries and the occasional theme park attraction . . . a house pimped out to the extreme"[25] Not only does this new house meet the physical needs of the family, it also meets the criteria for "pimped out." The new life can begin.

The interpersonal results of the external glory are articulated as the ability of parents and children to fulfill their proper roles in the family and in society. Accessible bathrooms and hallways let disabled adults function independently, no longer requiring child-like care. Fathers can return to "bread-winning" when car repair shops, woodworking sheds, and the like are built on their new properties.[26] The myth of American individualism, with its tyrannical insistence on radical independence, heteronormativity, and capitalist "productivity," has its flag planted on the front lawns of these McMansions.[27]

ENFREAKMENT AS ENLIGHTENMENT AS ENFREAKMENT

In a memo purportedly from the casting director of *EMHE* during its fourth season, "The Smoking Gun" reports that instead of selecting families for *EMHE* from application videos sent in voluntarily, *EMHE* may solicit specific "disabilities" for its show. The producer seeks children with "[c]ongenital insensitivity to pain with anhidrosis, referred to as CIPA by the few people who know about it. (There are 17 known cases in the US—let me know if one is in your town!) This is where kids cannot feel any physical pain." Also desirable is a "family who has multiple children w/Down Syndrome (either adopted or biological)," and a family that suffered a home invasion—one that has had a lasting, damaging effect: "kids fear safety in their home now."[28] If there weren't enough markers prior to this solicitation, we can now ask about the ambiguous relationship between enlightenment and enfreakment in *EMHE*. Does this architectural spiritual epic, which appears to educate its viewership about "orphan"

illnesses, function by "enfreaking" individuals, and if so, what are the possible long term social consequences of this for persons with disabilities?

As used by David Hevey in *The Creatures That Time Forgot: Photography and Disability Imagery,* enfreakment reinforces limiting stereotypes under the rubric of compassion and enlightenment.[29] Garland-Thomson suggests that "freaks are created when certain bodies serve as the raw material for the ideological and practical ends of both the mediators and the audiences . . . the sideshow freak was made to exceed wildly the common, familiar expectations set by the spectator's own ordinary body."[30] Consider the O'Connoll family. They received a home makeover because five of their six children have some form of autism spectrum disorder ranging from moderate to severe. In addition, the home is hours away from being foreclosed on. This family is identified as the family with the greatest number of biological children with ASD in the United States. The *EMHE* rhetoric showcases the family to increase compassion for ASD and to inspire courage in its viewership. But it does so by inscribing the normalcy of the viewer, because at base, enfreakment is really about reassurance that, for now, we are not them. We are reassured of our sufficiency corporally, architecturally, and theologically (i.e., our normalcy is a blessing from God).[31]

In the most optimistic interpretation of *EMHE,* we might apply this insight from Tanya Titchkosky: "The hope of such encounter is that, upon interrogation, it can lead to understanding, where understanding means neither acquiescing nor accepting, but rather discerning how our culture already lives through us and how we might better live through it. I am suggesting that various and even conflicting textual renderings of disability as hope, burden, charity, promise, etc. are occasions to question how we make bodies mean and to evaluate the sorts of relations people can and do establish with the meaning of disability."[32] Cynically, we can argue that the show enshrines the "normal" by enfreaking families and individuals as a means of educating the masses. Moreover, *EMHE* re-inscribes the Christian salvation narrative, in which confessing debasement is the precondition for new, restored life, a life made possible by the "extreme" sacrifices of the god-man who, not accidentally, is a carpenter who embodies the "American ideal self": young, male, white, educated, wealthy, heterosexual and able-bodied.

DISCUSSION QUESTIONS

1. What is the experience of watching *Extreme Makeover: Home Edition?* What would an able-bodied audience find appealing in the shows?
2. Askew notes that, over the years, *EMHE* has "ratcheted up its criteria for 'inspiration and deserving'." Why would that have happened?
3. What stereotypes are reinforced by shows such as *EMHE?*

REFERENCES

Cresswell, Tim. *In Place/Out of Place: Geography, Ideology and Transgression.* Minneapolis: University of Minnesota Press, 1996.

Cullinan, Colleen Carpenter. *Redeeming the Story: Women, Suffering and Redemption.* New York: Continuum, 2004.

DeVries, Dawn. "Creation, Handicappism and the Community of Difference." In *Christian Theology: An Introduction to Its Traditions and Tasks.* Eds. Peter Hodgson and Robert King. Philadelphia: Fortress Press, 1985.

Dick, Kirby, Director. *Sick: The Life and Death of Bob Flanagan, Supermasochist* (DVD). (1997).

Douglas, Mary. *Natural Symbols: Explorations in Cosmology.* London: Routledge, 1996.

Eiseland, Nancy. *The Disabled God: Toward a Liberatory Theology of Disability.* Nashville: Abingdon Press, 1994.

Garland-Thomson, Rosemary. *Extraordinary Bodies: Figuring Physical Disability in American Culture and Literature.* New York: Columbia University Press, 1997.

Hevey, David. *The Creatures Time Forgot: Photography and Disability Imagery, 1840–1940.* London: Routledge, 1992.

Imrie, Rob. *Disability and the City: International Perspectives.* New York: St. Martin's Press, 1996.

Jones, Serene. *Feminist Theory and Christian Theology: Cartographies of Grace.* Minneapolis: Augsburg Fortress, 2000.

Koosed, Jennifer and Darla Schumm, "Out of the Darkness: Examining the Rhetoric of Blindness in the Gospel of John." *Disability Studies Quarterly,* Vol. 25, No. 1. http://www.dsq-sds.org/article/view/528/705

Titchkosky, Tanya. "Acting Blind: A Revelation of Culture's Eye." In *Bodies in Commotion: Disability and Performance.*

Eds. Philip Auslander and Carrie Sandhal. Ann Arbor: Univ. of Michigan Press, 2005.

Titchkosky, Tanya. *Disability, Self, and Society.* Toronto: University of Toronto Press, 2003.

Tischkosky, Tanya. *Reading and Writing Disability Differently: The Textured Life of Embodiment.* Toronto: University of Toronto Press, 2007.

Weber, Brenda, "Beauty, Desire and Anxiety: The Economy of Sameness in ABC's Extreme Makeover," *Genders,* Issue 41, Spring 2005. http://www.genders.org/.

Electronic Resources

Extreme Makeover Home Edition, Application, http://a.abc.com/media/primetime/xtremehome/apply/EMHE ApplicationS7.pdf.

Extreme Makeover Home Edition, Episode Guide, http://abc.go.com/shows/extreme-makeover-home-edition/episodes-list.

The Smoking Gun, www.thesmokinggun.com/archive/0327062extreme1.html.

Ted Kazynski's Cabin, www.umt.edu/journalism/student_work/unabomber/cabin.htm.

The X-Files, "Arcadia Falls." http://x-files.wikia.com/wiki/Arcadia.

NOTES

1. Rob Imrie, *Disability and the City: International Perspectives* (St. Martin's Press: New York, 1996), 35.
2. Tim Cresswell, *In Place/Out of Place: Geography, Ideology, and Transgression* (Minneapolis: University of Minnesota Press, 1996), 16.
3. Tanya Titchkosky, "Acting Blind: A Revelation of Culture's Eye." In *Bodies in Commotion: Disability and Performance,* Ed. Philip Auslander and Carrie Sandhal (Ann Arbor: Univ. of Michigan Press, 2005), 204.
4. Mary Douglas, *Natural Symbols: Explorations in Cosmology* (London: Routledge, 1996), Introduction xxxvi.
5. Cresswell, *In Place/Out of Place,* 8–9
6. The Latif Family, Season 5, Episode 22. http://abc.go.com/shows/extreme-makeover-home-edition/episodes-list. Accessed January 2010.
7. The Pope Family, Season 2, Episode 3. "A young girl with a sun poisoning condition gets a new lease on life," October 10, 2004. http://abc.go.com/shows/extreme-makeover-home-edition/episodes-list.
8. http://a.abc.com/media/primetime/xtremehome/apply/EMHEApplicationS7.pdf. Accessed July 27, 2009.
9. Titchkosky, 2005, 211, citing Robillard (1999): "The most powerful and common ideology that surrounds disability is 'strength of the human spirit.'" If one should suffer virtuously in order to gain spiritual merit, virtuous suffering in the *EMHE* narrative gains one physical

merit. On virtuous suffering see Nancy Eiseland, *The Disabled God: Toward a Theology of Disability* (Nashville: Abingdon Press, 1994), 70–75.

10. http://www.ultimatedisney.com/extrememakeover homeedition-season1.html. Accessed Jan 2010.

11. For instance, in the first season of *EMHE,* the Powers family has one child with leukemia, the Cox family is poor and the father was a youth pastor, the Mendoza family is comprised of a single mother with foster sons. Gradually the stakes get raised: the hugely memorable "Sweet Alice" Harris feeds the homeless, contributes to the lives of poor children in the community, *and* has lost everything in a flood. Season 1, Episodes 1, 3, and 5. http://abc.go.com/shows/extreme-makeover-home-edition/episodes-list. Accessed November 2009.

12. The Vardon Family; Season 2 Episode 7. http://abc.go.com/shows/extreme-makeover-home-edition/episodes-list. Accessed November 2009.

13. The Hassell Family, Season 3, Episode 28. http://abc.go.com/shows/extreme-makeover-home-edition/episodes-list. Accessed November 2009.

14. "Invisible" disabilities include problems like chronic pain, as with fibromyalgia, dyslexia, and other learning disabilities, mental illnesses, birth defects, and other challenges that do not manifest in the need for a wheelchair or appear otherwise "visible" to the general public. According to Garland-Thomson (*EB,* 14), "An invisible disability, much like a homosexual identity, always presents the dilemma of whether or when to come out or pass."

Tanya Titchkosky notes the 'problem of "invisible disabilities"—they are often seen as made up when a student needs accommodation in the classroom. *Disability, Self, and Society* (Toronto: University of Toronto Press, 2003), 166.

15. Colleen Carpenter Cullinan, *Redeeming the Story: Women, Suffering and Redemption* (New York: Continuum, 2004), 10–11. This interpretation draws primarily on the work of the Anselm, Church Father, from his work *Cur Deus Homo,* and John Calvin in the *Institutes.*

16. Dawn DeVries, "Creation, Handicappism and the Community of Difference," in Peter Hodgson and Robert King, eds. *Christian Theology: An Introduction to its Traditions and Tasks* (Philadelphia: Fortress Press, 1985).

17. The Marshall Family, Season 7, Episode 6. http://abc.go.com/shows/extreme-makeover-home-edition/episodes-list. Accessed Dec 2009.

18. Garland-Thomson, *Extraordinary Bodies,* 64. Garland-Thomson describes the American ideal self as "an autonomous producer—self-governing and self-made—a generic individual capable of creating his own perfected self." Anything less than this kind of agency is considered unfortunately limited and deserving of pity. This cultural interpretation of agency is possible only for a small minority of Americans: male, white, young, upper-middle class, educated, heterosexual, and able-bodied. Yet, this ideal of agency has been inscribed in the American psyche as a transcendent good, yea a right, of everyone, though the system is set for only a few to achieve this end, and then only temporarily.

19. *EMHE* application, http://a.abc.com/media/primetime/xtremehome/apply/EMHEApplicationS7.pdf. Accessed July 27, 2009.

20. ". . . . the Cowans are against the wall and are pleading for help." Cowan family, Season 7, Episode 14. http://abc.go.com/shows/extreme-makeover-home-edition/episode-guide/cowan-family/364606. Accessed January 2010.

21. Garland-Thomson, *Extraordinary Bodies,* 23.

22. Titchkosky, *Disability, Self, and Society,* 166. The issue is agency—disabled people are considered lacking in agency because they cannot control their bodies.

23. http://abc.go.com/shows/extreme-makeover-home-edition/about-the-show. Accessed November 2009. For an analysis of the manipulation of time in aesthetic plastic surgery "reality" television, see Brenda Weber, "Beauty, Desire and Anxiety: The Economy of Sameness in ABC's Extreme Makeover," *Genders,* Issue 41, Spring 2005. http://www.genders.org/.

24. In his book analyzing photographic images of people with impairments in charity advertising, David Hevey writes, "Disabled people appear in advertising to demonstrate the successes of their administrators." *The Creatures Time Forgot: Photography and Disability Imagery,* 1840–1940 (London: Routledge, 1992), 54.

25. Ibid.

26. The Nutsch Family, Season 3, Episode 12. http://abc.go.com/shows/extreme-makeover-home-edition/episode-guide/nutsch-family/55255. Accessed January 2010.

27. Eiseland, *The Disabled God.*

28. "The Smoking Gun." http://www.thesmokinggun.com/archive/0327062extreme1.html. Accessed Jan 2010.

29. For the genesis of this fine concept see Hevey, *The Creatures Time Forgot.*

30. Garland-Thomson, *Extraordinary Bodies,* 60.

31. Never mind the implication here that others remain "unblessed" (cursed, perhaps?) by God because they do not share our "normal" lives.

32. Titchkosky, *Reading and Writing Disability Differently,* 16.

BRIDGING DIFFERENCES

FRAMEWORK ESSAY

A book such as *The Meaning of Difference* runs the risk of leaving students with the feeling that there is little they can do to challenge the constructions of difference. Having recognized the power of master statuses and the significance of our conceptions of difference in everything from personal identity to world events, it is easy to feel powerless in the face of what appear to be overwhelming social forces.

But we did not write this book because we felt powerless or wanted you to feel that way. For us, the idea of looking at race, sex, social class, sexuality, and disability *all together* opened up new possibilities for understanding and creating alliances. When we first started to talk about this book, comparing our teaching experiences in a highly diverse university and our personal experiences of stigma and privilege, we were amazed by the connections we saw. That impression grew as we talked with students and friends who were members of other groups. Over time, we learned that understanding the similarities *across* groups opened up new ways of thinking: experiences could be accumulated toward a big picture, rather than being suffered in relative isolation; people could be different but still have had the same experience; people who never had the experience might still have ways to understand it. We believe the world is more interesting and hopeful with the realization that the experience of being in "the closet" is generally the same irrespective of which status brought you there, or that a variety of race and ethnic groups are subject to racial profiling, or that white women often experience the double consciousness that W. E. B. Du Bois described for blacks. When we realized how readily people could generalize from their own experience of stigma and privilege to what others might experience, we were energized.

That energy led to this book. But what should you do with your energy and insight? Or if you are feeling beaten down and depressed, rather than energized, what can you do about that?

Let us start with the worst-case scenario—that is, the possibility that you feel powerless to bring about social change and hopelessly insignificant in the face of overwhelming social forces. Unfortunately, this is not an uncommon outcome in higher education, nor is it distinctive to this subject matter. The emphasis in higher education is more on "understanding" than "doing." Most university coursework stresses detached, value-neutral reasoning, not passionate advocacy for social change.

> In the natural sciences, it is taken for granted that the aim is to explain an external order of nature. In literature, the text is an object to be interpreted. In politics, government is a phenomenon to be analyzed. Everywhere, it is intimated that the stance of the educated person should be that of the spectator. . . . In the contemporary university, one quickly learns that certain questions are out of order. One does not ask persistently about what ought to be done, for normative questions entail what are called value judgments, and these are said to be beyond the scope of scientific analysis.[1]

Paradoxically, however, education is also the source of much social change. We all know this almost instinctively. Educational institutions teach us our rights and our history, sharpen our thinking and decision-making, and open us to others'

lived experience. Learning *changes* us, and higher education is explicit in its intention to produce that effect. The university is, after all, "an *educational* institution. As such, it is expected to have an impact on the society of which it is a part. . . . [T]he task of the university is not only to explore, systematically, the nature of the world, but also to scrutinize the practices of everyday life to see if they can be improved."[2]

Recognizing the paradoxical nature of higher education, that it can both empower and disempower, means, in truth, that an element of choice—your choice—is involved in whether you are discouraged or inspired at the end of a course.

There is, however, another reason you might leave this material feeling powerless. This has more to do with the nature of society than with the nature of education, but it again involves paradox and personal choice. Eminent sociologist Peter Berger called this the "Janus-faced" nature of human society. The Roman god Janus, for whom January was named, symbolized beginnings and endings, past and future, change and transition, and was depicted as having two faces looking in opposite directions. Berger used that image to convey that just as individuals are rarely wholly powerful, neither are they wholly powerless. In this analogy, Berger found a visual image for the truth that we are *both* the authors and victims—architects and prisoners—of social life. We *both* make society and are made by it. (And in our own spirit of powerfulness, we have edited out the sexism in Berger's prose below.)

> No social structure, however massive it may appear in the present, existed in this massivity from the dawn of time. Somewhere along the line each one of its salient features was concocted by human beings, whether they were charismatic visionaries, clever crooks, conquering heroes or just individuals in positions of power who hit on what seemed to them a better way of running the show. Since all social systems were created by [humans], it follows that [humans] can also change them.
>
> Every [person] who says "I have no choice" in referring to what his [or her] social role demands of him [or her] is engaged in "bad faith." . . . [People] are responsible for their actions. They are in "bad faith" when they attribute to iron necessity what they themselves are choosing to do.[3]

While you do not have the power to change everything, you certainly have the power to change some things. Gandhi's paradox, discussed by Allan Johnson in Reading 56, captures this point: "Gandhi once said that nothing we do as individuals matters, but that it's vitally important to do it anyway."

So we urge you to move beyond your sense of being powerless and get on with the work of social change. We offer some suggestions here for that process, much of it drawn from work we have found both inspirational and practical.

We Make the Road by Walking

"We make the road by walking" was Spanish poet Antonio Machado's (1875–1939) adaptation of a proverb: "*se hace camino al andar,*" or "you make the way as you go." It is also the title of a published dialogue between two famous educator-activists, Myles Horton and Paulo Freire.[4]

Myles Horton founded the Highlander Folk School in Tennessee in 1932, when American racial segregation was still firmly in place. A unique school, Highlander offered racially integrated adult education—especially in history, government, and leadership—to the rural poor and working-class residents of the Cumberland Mountain communities. Horton's aim was to "use education as one of the instruments for bringing about a new social order."[5] While many southern labor union leaders studied at Highlander, the school is probably best known for its contribution to the civil rights movement. Highlander taught the methods of nonviolence and started "Citizenship Schools," which taught southern blacks to read and write, so that they could pass the tests required to vote. (Literacy tests have been used in many countries to keep poor people from voting. In the United States, they were used in southern states to keep African Americans from voting, until passage of the 1965 Voting Rights Act.) Probably the most famous Highlander student was Rosa Parks, whose refusal to move to the back of the bus sparked the Montgomery, Alabama, bus boycott and the civil rights movement.

The second member of the dialogue, Paulo Freire, was author of the classic book, *Pedagogy of the Oppressed.* Freire was in charge of a Brazilian national literacy program in the 1960s, before the government was overthrown by a military coup. Like American blacks before 1965, Brazil's poor were also denied the right to vote with the excuse that they were illiterate. After the military coup, Freire was forced to flee from Brazil, but he went on to write and develop literacy programs elsewhere. His work was distinguished by its emphasis on teaching literacy through real community issues. His belief that education must operate as a dialogue, rooted in values and committed to transforming the world, made him one of the most influential thinkers of the last century.

Apart from the example that Myles Horton's and Paulo Freire's lives provide for the power of education to produce social change, we turn to them here for some basic lessons about transforming learning into action. First, we hope the phrase "we make the road by walking" helps you remember that *you* are the best person to know which "social interventions" will work for you. There is probably nothing more fundamental to social change than learning who you are; finding and honoring that authentic self; recognizing that it is multifaceted, complex, and *evolving*—and then making sure that the social change methods you use are consistent with that self. If you are going to pursue something as important as social change, it might as well be *you* who is doing it, not your impersonation of someone else.

"We make the road by walking" also conveys that the road has not already been built. Although there are many helpful resources, you will not find a recipe book designed for all the situations you will face, nor would that necessarily be a good idea. One of Myles Horton's experiences with a union strike committee illustrates this point:

> [Members of the committee] were getting desperate. They said: "Well, now you've had more experience than we have. You've got to tell us what to do. You're the expert." I said: "No, let's talk about it a little bit more. In the first place I don't know what to do, and if I did know what to do I wouldn't tell you, because if I had to tell you today then I'd have to tell

you tomorrow, and when I'm gone you'd have to get somebody else to tell you." One guy reached in his pocket and pulled out a pistol and says, "Goddamn you, if you don't tell us I'm going to kill you." I was tempted then to become an instant expert, right on the spot! But I knew that if I did that, all would be lost and then all the rest of them would start asking me what to do. So I said: "No. Go ahead and shoot if you want to, but I'm not going to tell you." And the others calmed him down.[6]

So it is important to recognize that, to some extent, you will need to be your *own* resource, *and* you will never have all the answers you need. Horton described two approaches to this inevitable incompleteness. First, "What I finally decided, after three or four years of reading and studying and trying to figure this thing out, was that *the way to do something was to start doing it and learn from it.*"[7] And second, "*People learn from each other.* You don't need to know the answer."[8]

President Barack Obama's route to becoming a community organizer in Chicago has some parallels. Without knowing what the job entailed or anyone who made a living that way, he decided that was what he wanted to do when he finished college. Obama goes on to say, "And so, in the months leading up to graduation, I wrote to every civil rights organization I could think of, to any black elected official in the country with a progressive agenda, to neighborhood councils and tenant rights groups."[9] No one wrote back. Several months, jobs, and periods of unemployment later, a Jewish community organizer funded by local churches, who was trying to create a coalition of urban blacks and suburban whites to save manufacturing jobs in Chicago, hired him as a trainee. "He needed someone to work with him, he said. Somebody black."[10] Things did not go especially well: community members, who had already been at this for several years, were discouraged and ready to quit; the black Chicago political establishment was not supportive; it was difficult to find the issues that could bind and motivate people; and people were skeptical about the involvement of a college student with no apparent religious motivation. Only after many long months did a clear and compelling community issue emerge—the fact that there were no Mayor's Employment and Training (MET) programs in the parts of Chicago where the neediest African Americans lived.

Two weeks of preparation and yet, the night of the meeting, my stomach was tied up in knots. At six forty-five only three people had shown up: a young woman with a baby who was drooling onto her tiny jumper, an older woman who carefully folded a stack of cookies into a napkin that she then stuffed into her purse, and a drunken man who immediately slouched into a light slumber in a back-row seat. As the minutes ticked away, I imagined once again the empty chairs, the official's change of mind at the last minute, the look of disappointment on the leadership's faces—the deathly smell of failure.

Then, at two minutes before seven, people began to trickle in. Will and Mary brought a group from West Pullman; then Shirley's children and grandchildren walked in, filling up an entire row of seats; then other Altgeld residents who owed Angela or Shirley or Mona a favor. There were close to a hundred people in the room by the time Ms. Alvarez [representing MET] showed up—a large imperious, Mexican American woman with two young white men in suits trailing behind her. . . .

The leadership acquitted themselves well that night. Angela laid out the issue for the crowd and explained to Ms. Alvarez what we expected from her. When Ms. Alvarez avoided giving a definite response, Mona jumped in and pushed for a yes-or-no answer. And when Ms. Alvarez finally promised to have a MET intake center in the area within six months, the crowd broke into hearty applause. . . .[11]

Thus, Obama's experience demonstrates that "we make the road by walking."

Work on Yourself First

Challenging social constructions of difference by working on yourself first may not seem earth shattering, but it is the unavoidable first step on the road. We think there are four main lessons on which to concentrate:

1. Increase your tolerance for making mistakes.   In his dialogue with Miles Horton, Paulo Freire remarked, "I am always in the beginning, as you"—and at that point Freire was 66 years old and Horton 82. Realizing how little you know about other people's life experience is a way to prepare for the absolute inevitability that, in trying to build connections across difference, *you will make mistakes.* You must increase your tolerance of your mistakes or risk giving up altogether, and you must try to focus on learning from all these attempts—good, bad, or ugly. As one of our colleagues often tells her students, when you are worried that you'll say the wrong thing, you wind up holding back, not extending yourself—and missing an opportunity for connection. Our advice is to just get used to making mistakes. There is no way around them.

2. Appreciate the statuses you occupy.   "Appreciating" your statuses— *stigmatized and privileged*—may sound odd, but it is the foundation that allows you to respond with more clarity to others' experiences of their statuses. By appreciating your own statuses, we mean honoring, valuing, and having some reasonable level of comfort about being white, black, Asian, or Latino; male or female; wealthy, middle class, or poor; disabled or nondisabled; straight, bisexual, or gay. Appreciating your status means not being ashamed of who you are.

> Is there a part of your identity of which you are not proud? Is there a part of who you are that you tend to hide from people? *One of the most profound blows to oppression is claiming legitimate delight in who we are. . . .* Notice where you struggle in claiming pride in who you are. This is the preliminary work that must be done to work against all forms of oppression.
>
> Reclaiming pride in our identities entails knowing our histories, becoming familiar not only with the side of history that causes us shame but also with the side that offers us hope. Ever mindful not to distort historical realities, it is nonetheless possible, even in the midst of the worst acts of oppression, to claim as our ancestors the few people who resisted the oppression. For example, in the present, it is useful for many people of German heritage to remember that there were heroic Germans who resisted Nazi anti-Semitism. . . . [A]long with the unfathomable devastation of the Holocaust, this minority tradition of resistance is also part of the history of the German people.[12]

Ironically, at this juncture in American society, some level of shame seems to adhere to both stigmatized *and* privileged statuses. We don't want to mislead you into thinking that getting over that shame is an easy task, but recognizing the existence of shame and its dysfunction is an important first step. As Brown and Mazza suggest in the previous quote, learning the *full* history of "your people"—good deeds and bad—will help you find heroes, as well as avoid false pride.

3. Learn to "sit in the fire." For those in privileged statuses, guilt seems to be the most common reaction to discussions of prejudice and discrimination. For those in stigmatized statuses, anger probably ranks at the top. Those who occupy both privileged and stigmatized statuses are "privileged" to experience both ends of this emotional continuum! Insofar as race, sex, social class, disability, and sexuality are *all* on the table, *everyone* will probably have the opportunity for an intense emotional experience. That's a lot of emotion, not to mention that people have varying abilities to talk about—or even experience—those feelings. Either way, bridging differences sometimes means we must be willing to "sit in the fire"[13] of conflict and intense emotion.

Regarding guilt, our advice is not to succumb to it. It is both immobilizing and distracting. Focusing on how badly *you* feel means that *you* are the subject of attention, not the people whose experience you are trying to understand.

About anger, our advice is more complicated. When it's someone else's anger, listen carefully so that you can understand it. Don't stop listening because you don't like the message or the way it is packaged. Don't take an expression of anger personally unless you are told it actually is about you. Try not to let someone else's anger trigger your own, because that will distract you from listening. Recognize that you can withstand someone's anger.

When you are the one who is angry, try not to let it overwhelm you. Try to distinguish between a setting in which you are under attack and one populated by friends, or potential friends, who are trying to learn about your experience. Try to distinguish people who are malevolent from those who are misguided, or simply awkward in their efforts to help. Try to avoid self-righteousness. Your having been injured doesn't mean that you have not also inflicted injury. Remember that "every person is important, even those who belong to majority groups that have historically oppressed other groups."[14]

As you experience sitting in the fire, remember that *the benefits of diversity derive from engagement, not passive observation. Interaction about difference will inevitably entail periods of disagreement and conflict.* Parker Palmer is a sociologist and nationally renowned expert on higher education. We quote him at length below, because he offers such a clear picture of what both frightens and draws us to engagement across difference.

We collaborate with the structures of separation because they promise to protect us against one of the deepest fears at the heart of being human—the fear of having a live encounter with alien "otherness," whether the other is a student, a colleague, a subject, or a self-dissenting voice within. *We fear encounters in which the other is free to be itself, to speak its own truth, to tell us what we may not wish to hear. We want those encounters on our own terms, so that we can control their outcomes, so that they will not threaten our view of world and self. . . .*

This fear of the live encounter is actually a sequence of fears that begins in the fear of diversity. As long as we inhabit a university made homogeneous by our refusal to admit otherness, we can maintain the illusion that we possess the truth about ourselves and the world—after all, there is no "other" to challenge us! But as soon as we admit pluralism, we are forced to admit that ours is not the only standpoint, the only experience, the only way, and the truths we have built our lives on begin to feel fragile. . . .

Otherness, taken seriously, always invites transformation, calling us not only to new facts and theories and values but also to new ways of living our lives—and that is the most daunting threat of all.[15]

But what if there appears to be no diversity in the setting in which you find yourself? The odds are that is just how things look. No matter how homogeneous a group may seem, there will be layers of significant difference beneath the appearances. "Taking the time to examine [those less visible differences] can be invaluable, not only for creating a climate that welcomes the differences already present in the group, but also for laying the groundwork for becoming more inclusive of other differences."[16]

4. Be an ally. Appreciate your allies.   We conclude this list with what we think is the most important of the lessons. Be an ally; find allies; appreciate your allies. There is nothing complicated about the concept of an ally: an ally is simply someone committed to eliminating stigma and the ill-treatment of those in stigmatized statuses. If you remember a time when you were treated unfairly because of a status you occupy and think about what you *wish* someone had done or said on your behalf, you will then understand the critical role an ally can play, and you will have a good sense of what the role calls for. Beyond that, you can learn about being an ally by asking people what would be helpful and by educating yourself about the history and experience of those in stigmatized groups.

Many of the personal accounts in this book are about having or wishing for an ally. John Larew's article on legacy admissions (Reading 32) is an example of being an ally. The article—written while he was editor of Harvard's *Crimson Tide*—sparked an extended national discussion on legacy admissions. Larew can take considerable credit for the attention now being paid to the underrepresentation of low-income students in colleges and universities.

While Larew's article grew out of his daily experience and the media access he had as editor of the *Crimson Tide,* other ways of being an ally are available to virtually anyone, anytime—even, for example, at lunch. We single out this meal, because it is generally a public one, in which members of stigmatized categories are likely to find themselves with limited options: eat with other members of the category, eat alone, or hide. So an ally (or potential ally) might extend an invitation to share a sandwich.

Being an ally, however, is not only about what you can do on your own. It is also about joining with others in collective action. The social movements that have historically transformed the status of stigmatized groups in America, such as the women's movement or the civil rights movement, included some people from privileged statuses, just as privileged allies have joined with members of stigmatized groups in innumerable more localized ways: university chapters of Men against Sexism, community groups like Parents and Friends of Lesbians and Gays, elected officials who sponsor antidiscrimination legislation, the 1960s college students who risked their lives to register black voters in the South, the Muslims in Rwanda who helped Tutsis escape from the 1994 genocide. You might consider how you could become an ally who makes a difference.

Still, *getting* allies sometimes requires *asking for help* and even telling people what you specifically want or don't want them to do. People who are disabled do this in a powerful video on YouTube called "A Credo for Support," telling their potential allies:

> Do not see my disability as the problem. Recognize that my disability is an attribute.
> Do not try to fix me, because I am not broken. Support me. I can make my contribution to the community in my way.
> Do not see me as your client. I am your fellow citizen. See me as your neighbor. Remember, none of us can be self-sufficient.
> Do not try to change me. You have no right. Help me learn what I want to know.
> Do not try to be my friend. I deserve more than that. Get to know me. We may become friends.
> Do not help me, even if it does make you feel good. Ask me if I need your help.
> Do not admire me. A desire to live a full life does not warrant adoration. Respect me, for respect presumes equality.
> Do not tell, correct, and lead. Listen, support, and follow.
> Do not work on me. Work with me.[17]

While you might wish for allies who could read your mind and step in and out at exactly the right moment, it is unlikely you will find people like that. The people you do find, however, will probably be more easily recruited to become allies with appreciation than with guilt.

> We rarely increase our effectiveness by dwelling on all of the things we still need to get right. This principle is especially important for those of us who are seeking allies. Pointing out only how the people around us have failed usually only increases their discouragement. Remembering the successes can lead to increased confidence and a greater ability to be an effective ally.[18]

White men who are straight and nondisabled can often be powerful allies. When such a person speaks on behalf of those in stigmatized statuses, he stands a good chance of being heard, if only because he appears not to be acting out of vested interest. His intervention can change the dynamic, provide a role model for others, and give those in stigmatized statuses a break from always being the ones to raise the contentious points. Once, on a panel about gender, we saw one of the men flag issues of sexism that the women panelists would otherwise have had to note. It seemed to us that they appreciated his intervention.

Being an ally is also sometimes called for among one's friends and loved ones, in those more private settings where people feel freer to air and cultivate their prejudices. Like Paul Kivel, who suggests in Reading 58, some ways to respond in these situations, we would also urge you to be an "ally with a heart" in these settings.

> Condemning people, shaming them, and making them feel guilty are all unproductive strategies: They all increase defensiveness rather than creating an opening for change. . . . Condemning people rarely helps them to change their behavior. Instead, think about what you honestly appreciate about the person. Also consider the ways that person has made any progress, even if it's only slight, on the issue that is of concern to you. Practice telling that person the things she is doing right. Appreciation leads to action; condemnation leads to paralysis.
>
> People are often afraid to appreciate someone whose behavior they disapprove of, for fear that the appreciation will keep the oppressive behavior unchallenged. However, only by seeing what is human in the person who acts oppressively can we hope to bring about change. All of us are more receptive to suggestions to change when we know we are liked.[19]

A Concluding Note

We opened this essay worried that our readers felt powerless and insignificant. We close with the hope that you now understand that challenging the constructions of difference is well within *all* of our capabilities.

KEY CONCEPTS

ally Someone from a privileged status committed to eliminating stigma and the ill-treatment of those in stigmatized statuses. (page 488)

Gandhi's paradox Although nothing we do as individuals matters, it is important to take action anyway. (page 483)

Janus-faced nature of society That people are neither wholly powerful nor wholly powerless; they are both the architects and prisoners of social life. (page 483)

ENDNOTES

1. Anderson, 1993:34–35, 36.
2. Ibid., 59.
3. Berger, 1963:128, 143–44.
4. Bell, Gaventa, and Peters, 1990.
5. Ibid., 1990: xxiii.
6. Ibid., 1990:126.
7. Ibid., 1990:40; emphasis added.
8. Ibid., 1990:55; emphasis added.
9. Obama, 2004:135.
10. Ibid., 141.
11. Ibid., 184-85.
12. Brown and Mazza, 1997:5–6; emphasis added.
13. Mindell, 1995.
14. Brown and Mazza, 1997:5.
15. Palmer, 1998: 36–38; emphasis added.
16. Brown and Mazza, 1997:13.
17. Kunc and Van der Klift, 2007.
18. Brown and Mazza, 1997:49.
19. Ibid., 3.

REFERENCES

Anderson, Charles W. 1993. *Prescribing the Life of the Mind: An Essay on the Purpose of the University, the Aims of Liberal Education, the Competence of Citizens, and the Cultivation of Practical Reason.* Madison: University of Wisconsin Press.

Bell, Brenda, John Gaventa, and John Peters. 1990. *We Make the Road by Walking: Conversations on Education and Social Change.* Philadelphia: Temple University Press.

Berger, Peter L. 1963. *Invitation to Sociology: A Humanistic Perspective.* New York: Anchor Books.

Brown, Cherie R., and George J. Mazza. 1997. *Healing into Action: A Leadership Guide for Creating Diverse Communities.* Washington, DC: National Coalition Building Institute.

Kunc, Norman, and Emma Van der Klift. 2007. A Credo for Support (People First Version). People First of San Luis Obispo. www.youtube.com/watch?v=wunHDfZFxXw (accessed May 2007).

Mindell, Arnold. 1995. *Sitting in the Fire: Large Group Transformation Using Conflict and Diversity.* Portland, OR: Lao Tse Press.

Obama, Barack. 2004. *Dreams from My Father: A Story of Race and Inheritance.* New York: Three Rivers Press.

Palmer, Parker J. 1998. *The Courage to Teach: Exploring the Inner Landscape of a Teacher's Life.* San Francisco: Jossey-Bass.

READING 55

ADOLESCENT MASCULINITY IN AN AGE OF DECREASED HOMOHYSTERIA

Eric Anderson

September 17, 2012, my (same-sex) husband and I touched-down in London Heathrow Airport with our two new baby boys: created through an egg donor and a surrogate in Southern California. We returned to our middle-class neighborhood outside of Southampton, and were immediately barraged with social support: offers of babysitting, Facebook messages of congratulations, and requests to meet the babies. One of these invitations came from "the group" who wished to meet on "the hill" to hold a celebratory reception.

The group is comprised of 20 heterosexual, adolescent boys and five girls, one of whom is bisexual. I met them while walking my dog in a local park. I sat and talked with them, and was henceforth invited to join them, on a semi-regular basis, to their social events. The gesture of love and acceptance of someone who was not only gay, but three times their age, was overwhelming for me; but normal for them. In fact, this type of gay-inclusivity is the norm for adolescent boys in today's culture.

Exemplifying this, the night before my family left Southern California, I was emotionally impacted by another group of adolescents: 45 fifteen- to seventeen-year-old males (of which two were openly gay) who ran for a local high school that I spent the summer coaching. The team (comprised of White, Hispanic and Asian youth) was as supportive and inclusive as "the group" back in England. In fact, at a going away party they organized for me, one of the seventeen-year-old boys presented me with baby clothes featuring a rainbow-colored heart and the inscription, "Two dads is better than one."

Eric Anderson is a professor of sociology, masculinities, and sexuality at the University of Winchester in England.

This social inclusion is heart-warming, yes; but it should not be surprising. I have spent the last eight years conducting dozens of ethnographic studies into adolescent and undergraduate heterosexual masculinities: on athletic teams (Adams, Anderson & McCormack, 2010; Anderson, 2005, 2008a, 2008b, 2009, 2011a, 2011b; Anderson, McCormack & Lee, 2012; Anderson & McGuire, 2010), within P.E. classes (Anderson 2012a), high schools (McCormack & Anderson, 2010a), fraternities (Anderson, 2008c), and multiple other groups of youths across the United States and the United Kingdom (Anderson, 2011c; Anderson, Adams & Rivers, 2012). Collectively, this research finds that young men today have redefined what it means to be masculine.

I support my ethnographic findings with survey data across the United States, the United Kingdom, and Australia (Bush, Anderson & Carr, 2012; Southall et al., 2011). Collectively, colleagues and I show a strong relationship between decreasing cultural homophobia and a softening of heterosexual masculinities in Western cultures.

Almost all of the youth that I study distance themselves from the type of conservative forms of muscularity, hyper-heterosexuality, aggression, and stoicism that Connell (1987), Messner (1992), Pollack (1999), and others (Plummer, 1999) have described males of the previous generation exhibiting as adolescents. Data from my studies of heterosexual men, in both feminized and masculinized spaces, highlights that the literature drawn on heterosexual men in the 1980s and 1990s—and even some of which was impactful in the early 2000s (Pascoe, 2005)—is no longer accurate. This is something affirmed by a growing body of scholars examining the impact of declining homophobia on young men's masculinities (Cavalier, 2011; Cashmore & Cleland, 2011, 2012; Dashper, 2012; Flood, 2008, 2009; Gottzén & Kremer-Sadlik, 2012; Lyng, 2009; McCormack, 2011a, 2011b, 2012; Peterson, 2011; Roberts, 2012; Swain, 2006; Thorpe, 2010; Way, 2011).

My findings, unable to be accounted for through hegemonic masculinity theory (Connell, 1987) led me to a new way of theorizing modern masculinities (Anderson, 2009) and of understanding how the relationship between homophobia and the awareness of homosexuality operates in society (Anderson, 2011c). Principally speaking, my theory—inclusive masculinity theory—with its embedded concept of *homohysteria,* explains how there is no longer a hierarchical stratification of masculinities. Instead, decreasing cultural homophobia and the diminishment of homohysteria permits various forms of adolescent masculinities to exist without hegemonic dominance of any one type. The reduction of homophobia has permitted youth to be accepting and inclusive (Savin-Williams, 2005)—including advocating for homosexuality. Additionally, the reduction of homohysteria has made more feminized appearances and homosocial tactility normal—something exemplified by the homosocial contact between members of the popular boy band *One Direction.*

In this article, I first provide a snap-shot of what it is like to be a heterosexual 16-year-old in contemporary British culture. I then summarize my body of work among youth, showing what they do to be different, important, and positive in comparison to how young men constructed masculinity two decades earlier. I provide a conceptual explanation for these events with my notion of homohysteria, placing it within inclusive masculinity theory more broadly.

ON BEING 16 TODAY

Jake is a sixteen-year-old, heterosexual male. He is just one of many I studied among a group of lower-class, non-educationally aspiring youths in Bristol, England. Jake lives in something of an impoverished neighborhood with his mother and sister on a street which is renowned for the wide availability of drugs. Jake, however, feels safe here. He has a rich network of various types of friends: both male and female, gay and straight, criminally hardened and higher educated. Most of all, Jake expresses his love for his best mate, Tom. He does so both in person and on his Facebook page. Here, Jake expresses as

much love for Tom as he does his girlfriend. In fact, he speaks of him in similar terms; freely identifying his friendship to me as "love." This intimacy, oftentimes described as a bromance, simulates ancient notions of Greek and Roman brotherhood; a time in which men's homosocial bonds were culturally prized (Spencer, 1995).

Illustrating this, Jake told me that he was preparing to go on a thirteen-day holiday to Spain with Tom. When I inquired as to whether he feared that he might fight with Tom, being in close company for such duration, he answered, "No mate. We're too close for that." I responded, "Fair enough." Before asking what his girlfriend thought of the fact that he was taking Tom and not her, Jake answered, "She knows how close we are. She's gotta share me."

Although Jake still lives in a heterosexist culture (Ripley et al., 2012), it is one that permits him to have the same level of emotional and physical intimacy with his best male friend as it does his female partner. For example, Jake tells me that he has a busy weekend coming up. He's spending Friday night with his girlfriend, including sex and cuddling. He will then be spending Saturday night with Tom, doing the same activities with the exception of sex. He informs me that he and Tom sleep in the same bed and cuddle two or three nights a week. This is not unusual; bed sharing is a common practice for adolescent males in England (Anderson, 2009). In fact, Jake spends as many nights in bed with Tom as he does with his girlfriend.

While fishing on an unusually warm spring day, Jake tells me to "Look at this message Tom sent me yesterday." He hands me his mobile phone and I read the message aloud, "Jake I love you, this week has made me realise how weak I can be without you. And I don't like not being with you :/x." "Oh, your girlfriend is sweet," I tell him. "No, that's from Tom," he states matter-of-factly.

What is interesting about Jake's story is that he is not alone in expressing this type of homosocial intimacy among adolescents in the UK. Jake is therefore not selected here because he is an exception, but because his behaviors are normal in the UK; something McCormack (2012) also documents.

The type of emotional and physical intimacy I describe among British youth also extends to kissing. In other research on 16-year-old boys in the UK (Anderson, Adams & Rivers, 2012), colleagues and I show that 40% of the heterosexual youths studied have kissed another male friend on the lips. In survey research conducted at a British university, we showed this number to be 89 per cent (Anderson, Adams & Rivers, 2012). Replicated (yet to be published) studies conducted internationally show that 30 per cent of Australian undergraduate men have kissed on the lips, and ten percent of American undergraduates.

Regardless of how one theorizes these findings, the data is compelling: not only do boys bond over talk of cars, girls, sports, and video games; but they now also bond over disclosing secrets to one another and supporting each other emotionally (Anderson, 2011c); shopping together and dressing in softer more metrosexual ways (Pompper, 2010); accepting sexual minorities (Keleher & Smith, 2012); shunning violence (McCormack, 2012); and being physically closer than boys have ever been permitted to be without fear of being thought gay (Anderson, 2011c). In this matter, adolescent boys today bond over intimacy in the same way that men once used to over a century ago (Ibson, 2002), before homosexuality was widely understood to exist as an immutable, sizeable, and stigmatized portion of men. And this should tell us something important about masculinity theory.

HOMOHYSTERIA

. . . [I]t is not just homophobia that is important for the distribution of masculinities in the 1980s . . . but the awareness that homosexuality exists in real and consistent numbers within the population (Kinsey, Pomeroy, Martin & Gebhard, 1948). I suggested it was this combination of elements that limited same-sex physical and emotional intimacy among heterosexual men. . . . This I explicate through my notion of *homohysteria* (Anderson, 2009, 2011).

A homohysteric culture necessitates three factors: 1) widespread awareness that homosexuality exists as a static sexual orientation within a given culture; 2) cultural disapproval towards homosexuality (i.e., homonegativity); and 3) disapproval of men's femininity due to association with homosexuality. Importantly, all three conditions must be maintained for homohysteria to persist.

Illustrating how a homohysteric culture is differentiated from a country that is simply homophobic, I highlight that men in many Arabic cultures are socially permitted to hold hands with another male in public without fear of being labeled as gay. This is because, although there is an extant degree of homophobia in most of the Arabic world (Frank, Camp & Boutcher, 2010), there also exists a belief that gay men do not exist as a sizeable portion of the population (Zuhur, 2005). Thus, in comparison to American and Western European nations, most Arabic cultures are homophobic but not homohysteric (Anderson, 2011). Men are capable of engaging in physical tactility without the specter of being thought gay.

Ibson (2002) poignantly highlights, through utilizing photos of American men's friendships before the turn of the 20th century, that not only do levels of homohysteria vary between cultures, but that they are temporally variable within. His photos of men lying in bed together, wearing feminine-coded clothing and expressing all manner of homosocial physical tactility, suggests that any given culture can oscillate on homohysteria—dependent upon varying levels of the awareness of homosexuality and the dominant social attitude toward it. I suggest that, in the Western world, homophobia preceded homohysteria in that we had a notion of what homosexuality was, even if vague. This is to say there is an era of pre-homohysteria.

The era of homohysteria in the West slowly grew as the 20th century progressed. This was because there was an increasing cultural awareness that homosexuality existed as a stable and sizeable percent of the population (Kimmel, 1996), much of which came through the works of Sigmund Freud (1905) and Alfred Kinsey et al. (1948).

In the 1980s homohysteria reached full fruition. This was a product of HIV/AIDS, which forced homosexuals into the public's view (Peterson & Anderson, 2012). As Loftus (2001, p. 765) wrote, "From the 1970s through the mid-1980s, Americans held increasingly traditional religious beliefs, with more people supporting prayer in school, and believing the Bible was the literal word of God." In this homohysteric culture, gay men were pathologized as feminine, perverted, and dangerous; they were therefore politically vilified (Peterson & Anderson, 2012a). Taking into consideration that homosexuality is not as readily socially visible as other categories of stigmatized people, heterosexual men pushed their hyper-masculine and heterosexualizing behaviors to the extreme in order to disassociate themselves from anything related to homosexuality. It was here, in replicating Rambo or Terminator, that heterosexual men desired to be stoic, aggressive, and vehemently homophobic. For it was only in this predisposition that one could hope to escape the specter of the fag.

DECREASING HOMOHYSTERIA

I argue that homohysteria peaked in the mid-1980s (Anderson, 2009) along with the apex of AIDS. However, AIDS also brought a more unified and fervent campaign for the legal and social equality of sexual minorities. By the time the mid-1990s got underway, we began to see a more balanced cultural dialogue about homosexuality (Frank, Camp & Boutcher, 2010; Loftus, 2001). Furthermore as evidence of HIV/AIDS in the heterosexual community grew, the stigma it had previously brought exclusively to gay men waned. This is not to say that the disease was not (and is still not) associated predominately with homosexuality, but that lay people came to understand that HIV/AIDS is not *caused* by homosexuality. A generation of youth grew up knowing AIDS not as a gay disease, but simply a sexually transmitted disease. As this knowledge took hold, social attitudes toward homosexuality began to change.

Changing laws and social norms have begun to erode cultural homonegativity at an accelerated rate. Today, attitudes about homosexuality are markedly better than they were during the 1990s, or even the early years of the new millennium (Andersen & Fetner, 2008; Keleher & Smith, 2012; Kozloski, 2011; McCormack, 2010). This is particularly true of youth, who are emerging into a new zeitgeist.

The reasons for this are complex, but likely reside along other changing mores of sexuality (Anderson, 2012b). Over the last two decades there have been wholesale changes to our sexual and gendered society. Changes that add to the massive overhaul of our attitudes toward sex and our sexual practices since Kinsey et al. (1948) conducted their study of male sexuality. These changes have come from many social influences, including decreasing religiosity of Western cultures, women's liberation, and gay liberation.

Additional influence has come from the advancement of technologies of culture. Particularly, the introduction of social media—which has permitted widespread exposure to alternative identities—and the increased accessibility to internet pornography—which has ushered in a democratization of sexual desire (Attwood, 2010; McNair, 2002). For example, whereas teenage boys once traded baseball cards, today they trade digital pornography clips obtained freely from websites. The internet provides anyone the ability to instantly access a display of sexual variety. Here a whole range of bodies fuck in all combinations, styles, mixtures, manners, and video quality. And, relating to decreased homophobia, today's Porntube.com generation see, early and often, video clips of gays, lesbians, and other identities once stigmatized through a Victorian demand for heterosexual missionary sex. Often a heterosexual cannot find his preferred images of heterosexual intercourse without filtering through the images of the acts once highly socially tabooed. Curiosity of the other, or perhaps a desire to simply see what others enjoy, tempts today's heterosexual adolescents into clicking on the link and watching what their heterosexual fathers despised so much. In viewing gay sex, they grow desensitized to it. Thus, the internet, I propose, has been instrumental in exposing the forbidden fruit of homosexual sex, commoditizing and normalizing it in the process.

The internet has also provided sexual and gendered minorities a forum to organize for political action; forums to share life narratives; and forums for heterosexuals to ask sexual minorities "anything" about their sexual lives. Clearly, the internet has been beneficial in making visible the lives of sexual and gender minorities to the "normal" heterosexual world. It has taken away our social taboo against asking one's sexual orientation, too. For example, MySpace was the first popular social media site to ask for one's sexual orientation; Facebook, asks whether one is interested in men, women, or both. This has severely reduced the notion that homosexuality (particularly) is a "private" affair. Thus it has helped reduce heterosexism and explicit homonegativity among adolescent males (Keleher & Smith, 2012; Kozloski, 2011). This may allow them to establish homosocial peer relationships characterized by emotional intimacy and physical tactility (McCormack, 2012) the way the members of *One Direction* do.

The reduction of homophobia has meant that today's youth all know that gay men exist, and they likely believe that they exist in higher percentages than they actually do. But significantly, they increasingly do not care. Importantly, as heterosexuals cease to care about whether one is gay or not, it frees them up to associate with things that used to be coded as feminine, and therefore gay. Accordingly, as a cultural level of homohysteria changes, the range of acceptable behaviors for adolescent boys also changes. . . .

INCLUSIVE MASCULINITIES

In studying young men in both the United States and the United Kingdom, I show that adolescents are eschewing the homophobic orthodox masculinity of the 1980s. Instead, men are establishing homosocial relationships based on a number of traits including: 1) increased emotional intimacy (Adams, 2011, McCormack, 2011a); 2) increased physical tactility (McCormack, 2011b); 3) eschewing violence

(Anderson, 2011b); and 4) the social inclusion of gay male peers (Anderson & Adams, 2011; Bush, Anderson & Carr, 2012; McCormack, 2012b).

I argue that these improving cultural conditions have been the result of decreasing homophobia among adolescent males, which results in further softening of masculinity—something McCormack (2012, p. 63) calls a "virtuous circle of decreasing homophobia and expanded gendered behaviours." Collectively, I call the various forms of masculinities embodied by these boys, "inclusive masculinities."

Increased Emotional Intimacy

The above section, explicating the life of Jake, captures the type of emotionality common among young men in my various studies. Whether it be running with high school boys in California, fishing with sixteen-year-olds in Bristol, or hanging out with "the group" in Southampton, one characteristic remains constant: support. In each of these ethnographies emotionally supporting one another is fundamental to their friendships. Uniquely, this support does not permit a "suck it up" mentality. Boys are generally interested in hearing the feelings of their friends, even when those feelings are an admission of fear or weakness.

For example, when Tim announced on Facebook status that his parents decided to divorce, his wall was loaded with messages of support. His friends wrote that they cared about him and were worried for him. And when Ben entered a singing competition, he received dozens of messages of support on his FB wall. McCormack's (2011a) study of a British sixth form, where boys are esteemed for providing emotional support, provides detailed analysis of this.

Increased Physical Tactility

The emotional support that young men show for each other extends into acts of physical tactility, too. In addition to finding a great deal of hugging, caressing, and cuddling (McCormack, 2012; McCormack & Anderson, 2010a), my colleagues and I (Anderson, Adams & Rivers, 2012) show that eighty-nine per cent (of those randomly or strategically selected for interview) have, at least once, kissed another heterosexual male friend on the lips. The men understand these kisses as being free of sexual connotation and instead understand them as an expression of homosociality.

The fear of homosexualization that deterred my high school teammates from sleeping in the same bed, even if fully clothed, without a great deal of homophobic posturing (Flowers & Buston, 2001) does not exist for adolescents today. Not only do boys sleep together, but they oftentimes do so in their underwear. Nudity is also important to adolescent male bonding, particularly in sport (McCormack, 2012). It is common and easy to find shirtless photos of adolescent males embracing their male friends. Some youths post photos of themselves showering with their friends (usually when on holiday).

Eschewing Violence

In ethnographic work with 22 heterosexual players from a small, Catholic, university soccer team in the American Midwest, I show (Anderson, 2011b) that violence among these players was less than one might expect for contact-sport athletes: only three reported having fought in high school (all occurred on the soccer field), and only one player has been in a fight since coming to university (again on the soccer field). Conversely, most of the men had never been in a fight.

When we asked Tom about his fighting history, he said, "No. I have never been in a fight. Why would I?" John said, "Fighting is just stupid. It accomplishes nothing. It's not like after two guys fight one goes, 'Oh, I see things your way now.'" However, I was particularly struck by Clint's attitude toward fighting. While spitting tobacco into a cup, and with his baseball cap twisted backward, he told me "No. I've never been in a fight. There's just no reason to fight."

Similarly, McCormack (2012) found among the 16–18-year-old boys he studied in the United Kingdom, at a high school he investigated for a one-year period, there was not a single fight. An examination of school records indicate that there had not been a fight at the school in the previous three years.

The Inclusion of Gay Male Peers

In ethnographic work at "Standard High," McCormack and I (2010) found that teenage boys stood firmly against homophobia. When we raised the issue of homophobia in interviews, all informants positioned themselves against it. Although this is not in-and-of-itself proof of a homophobia-free culture, it is nonetheless noteworthy that no male student expressed homophobia in an interview. Instead, homophobia was regarded as a sign of immaturity. Matt said that if someone was homophobic he would be policed by his peers. "He wouldn't keep at it for long," he said, "It's just childish." Justin added, "When I was in middle school, some kids would say 'that's gay' around the playground, but they wouldn't get away with it anymore. We'd tell them it's not on." The youths studied agreed that homophobia, in any form, was not acceptable. Sam said, "You might find that [homophobia] before [sixth form], but not here. It's just not acceptable anymore."

Supporting these statements, participant observation highlighted that the word *gay* is not used to describe dissatisfaction by these young men. In fact, neither researcher heard any homophobic epithet in any social setting we investigated. Terms such as *queer* and *poof* were not used, while *fag* was only used when referring to a cigarette. *Gay* was only used in sensible discussions about gay identity and sexuality.

McCormack (2012b) has provided further evidence of the inclusion of sexual minority students in an ethnography of a religious sixth form. He showcases the stories of one lesbian, one gay, one bisexual, and one transgendered student, drawing out the differences in their experiences, but nonetheless showing positive changes in their school experiences compared with research from previous decades (see also Ripley et al., 2011).

THEORIZING MASCULINITIES FOR A NEW GENERATION

The type of masculinity exhibited by the youth that my colleagues and I have studied is starkly different than what the dominant paradigm suggests about young men, which maintains that they are homophobic, sexist, violent, emotionally repressed, and afraid of physical contact with other males. The most important theoretical tool for understanding masculinities and the social stratification of men since sex role theory has come through Connell's (1987) concept of hegemonic masculinity, which has also embedded in it this "man as jerk" archetype (Carrigan, Connell & Lee, 1985).

Developed from a social constructionist perspective in the mid-1980s, hegemonic masculinity theory has articulated two social processes. The first concerns how all men benefit from patriarchy; however, it is the second social process that has been heavily adopted by the masculinities literature. Here, Connell's theoretical contribution has been particularly adopted for its conceptualization of the mechanisms by which an intra-masculine hierarchy is created and legitimized. It is solely this aspect of her theory that I address here.

In conceptualizing intra-masculine domination, Connell argues that one hegemonic archetype of masculinity is esteemed above all other masculinity types, so that boys and men who most closely embody this one standard are accorded the most social capital, relative to other boys and men. Some of the characteristics of hegemonic masculinity concern variables which are earned, like attitudinal dispositions (including the disposition of homophobia) while other variables concern static traits (i.e., whiteness, heterosexuality, and youth). Connell argued, however, that regardless of body mass, age, or even sporting accomplishments, gay men are at the bottom of this hierarchy. Furthermore, Connell maintained that straight men who behaved in ways that conflict with the dominant form of masculinity are also marginalized. It was for these reasons that I have argued homophobia has traditionally been an effective weapon to stratify men in deference to a hegemonic mode of heteromasculine dominance (Anderson, 2005a; Kimmel, 1994).

Connell theorized (1987) that the power of a hegemonic form of masculinity was that those subjugated by it nonetheless believed in the right of those with power to rule. So instead of disputing their marginalized position, they revered those at the top. Hegemonic masculinity theory was precise in its ability to predict masculine configurations in the 1980s, and it likely continued to be useful throughout the 1990s. The high level of homophobia and hypermasculinity of the mid-1980s—something measured through General Social Survey data in the States alongside the *British Survey of Social Attitudes* in the United Kingdom—has serious implications for not only attitudes toward gay men, but also on how straight men performed their gender (Peterson & Anderson, 2012). Thus, hegemonic masculinity theory is historically contextualized within its own temporal moment—specifically, and although Connell did not understand it this way, it existed in a homohysteric culture (Anderson, 2009).

The collection of these findings, and the development of my heuristic concept of homohysteria, led me to the development of a new gendered theory of masculinity studies.

Inclusive masculinity theory captures the social dynamics of men in non-homohysteric settings. The theory is simple: it maintains that as homohysteria decreases, men no longer need to position themselves as hypermasculine in order to be thought heterosexual. As homohysteria decreases the vertical stratification that Connell describes is no longer accurate, as culture shifts to permit multiple types of masculinity without hierarchy or hegemony. Should cultural matters change, and homohysteria were to again rise, the ordering of men would likely return to the way Connell conceptualized.

Inclusive masculinity supersedes hegemonic masculinity theory because it is a more dynamic theory. It can be used to explain men's masculinities within multiple settings, and within a culture of any level of homohysteria. When Connell devised hegemonic masculinity theory in the mid-1980s, there was no such thing as a Western culture low in homohysteria. But the significant change that had occurred since makes Connell's theory unuseful in today's culture.

Multiple other scholars have recognized this, and used my theory (Adams, 2011; Cavalier, 2011; Daspher, 2012; Cleland & Cashmore, 2011, 2012; McCormack, 2011a, 2011b, 2011c, 2012; Peterson, 2011; Roberts, 2012). While it is not yet possible to tell whether inclusive masculinity theory will replace hegemonic masculinity theory, its adoption by other scholars is evidence of the erosion of the dominance of hegemonic masculinity theory.

Finally, I make inclusive masculinity theory very simplistic, intentionally. It was my desire to avoid inaccessible, and oftentimes vague, theorizing by elitist and intellectually marginalizing academics. To me a social theory should be simple, and have the ability to make a prediction. I shun academic elitism. Thus, I have made an open invitation to other scholars to examine my theory and add to it (hoping they do so in accessible and practical ways).

McCormack (2011a, 2011b, 2011c, 2012) is one scholar who has met this challenge. He recently contributed to inclusive masculinity theory by explicating how popularity is achieved in cultures where bullying and marginalization are not present. McCormack (2012) shows that what makes boys popular is not regulating others, but instead being inclusive, being emotionally open, having charisma, and holding social fluidity. Thus, hegemony, he argues, is replaced by heterogeneity.

DISCUSSION

In this overview of the research I have been conducting on gay and straight male youths over the previous decade, I have argued that inclusive masculinity theory (Anderson, 2009) supersedes hegemonic masculinity theory (Connell, 1987) as it explains the diminishment of a stratification of men during times of lower homohysteria. The theory was constructed to explain settings in which young heterosexual men are no longer afraid to act or otherwise associate with symbols of homosexuality.

Here, heterosexual boys are permitted to engage in an increasing range of behaviors that once led to homosexual suspicion, all without threat to their publicly perceived heterosexual identities. This is why the boy band *One Direction* can be so tactile with each other compared to all previous boy-bands. This is not a marketing strategy but a reflection of the masculine culture they emerged in.

Supporting this, in my various ethnographies I have found that fraternity members (Anderson, 2008b), rugby players (Anderson & McGuire, 2010), school boys (McCormack & Anderson, 2010a), heterosexual cheerleaders (Anderson, 2008c), and even the men of a Catholic college soccer team in the Midwest (Anderson, 2011b) have all been shown to maintain close physical and emotional relationships with each other. Collectively, these studies (and many more) highlight that as cultural homohysteria diminishes it frees heterosexual men to act in more feminine ways without threat to their heterosexual identity. I suggest that in the United States, United Kingdom, Canada, and Australia (and likely in other Western cultures) we have dropped out of homohysteria. Whereas homophobia used to be the chief policing mechanism of a hegemonic form of masculinity (Kimmel, 1994, 1996), there no longer remains a strident cultural force to regulate a singular type of homophobic masculinity.

I do not, however, claim that inclusive masculinities are completely free of oppression and subordination. A diminished state of homohysteria is not to be mistaken as a gender Utopia. Men categorized as belonging to one archetype of a set of inclusive masculinities might still reproduce heteronormativity (Ripley et al., 2012); they might still sexually objectify women (Anderson, 2008a); they might still value excessive risk taking (Adams, Anderson & McCormack, 2010); they might even use homophobic discourse without intent to wound (McCormack, 2011c). My data do however indicate that in the process of proliferating inclusive masculinities, gender itself, as a constructed binary of opposites, may be somewhat eroding. I argue that the efforts of the first, second, and now third, waves of feminism—combined with advancements in technology, the gay liberationists efforts of the past four decades, and the erosion of other sexual mores, are slowly erasing the gender binary (Anderson, 2009). Increasingly, gender is a business of decreasing polarization between not only women and men, but between heterosexual and gay men as well.

DISCUSSION QUESTIONS

1. Would you agree that for adolescent boys, the era of "homohysteria" is coming to a close? What evidence and experience would you look to in making that assessment?

2. What is Eric Anderson's explanation for the historic variations of "homohysteria"?

3. For Anderson, how is "homohysteria" different from homophobia?

REFERENCES

Adams, A. (2011). "Josh wears pink cleats": Inclusive masculinity on the soccer field. *Journal of Homosexuality, 58* (5), 579–596.

Adams, A., & Anderson, E. (2012). Homosexuality and sport: Exploring the influence of coming out to the teammates of a small, Midwestern Catholic college soccer team. *Sport, Education and Society, 17*(3), 347–363.

Adams, A., Anderson, E., & McCormack, M. (2010). Establishing and challenging masculinity: The influence of gendered discourses in organized sport. *Journal of Language and Social Psychology, 29*(3), 278–300.

Andersen, R., & Fetner, T. (2008). Cohort differences in tolerance of homosexuality: Attitudinal change in Canada and the United States, 1981–2000. *Public Opinion Quarterly, 72*, 311–330.

Anderson, E. (2005). Orthodox and inclusive masculinity: Competing masculinities among heterosexual men in a feminized terrain. *Sociological Perspectives, 48*(3), 337–355.

Anderson, E. (2008a). "I used to think women were weak:" Orthodox masculinity, gender-segregation and sport. *Sociological Forum, 23*(2), 257–280.

Anderson, E. (2008b). "Being masculine is not about who you sleep with . . . ": Heterosexual athletes contesting masculinity and the one-time rule of homosexuality. *Sex Roles: A Journal of Research, 58*(1–2), 104–115.

Anderson, E. (2008c). Inclusive masculinity in a fraternal setting. *Men and Masculinities, 10*(5), 604–620.

Anderson, E. (2009). *Inclusive masculinity: The changing nature of masculinities.* New York, NY: Routledge.

Anderson, E. (2011a). Updating the outcome: Gay athletes, straight teams, and coming out at the end of the decade. *Gender & Society, 25*(2), 250–268.

Anderson, E. (2011b). Inclusive masculinities of university soccer players in the American Midwest. *Gender and Education, 23*(6), 729–744.

Anderson, E. (2011c). The rise and fall of western homohysteria. *Journal of Feminist Scholarship, 1*(1), 80–94.

Anderson, E. (2012a). Inclusive masculinity in a physical education setting. *Thymos: Journal of Boyhood Studies, 6*(2), 151–165.

Anderson, E. (2012b). *The monogamy gap: Men, love and the reality of cheating.* New York, NY: Oxford University Press.

Anderson, E., & Adams, A. (2011). "Aren't we all a little bisexual?": The recognition of bisexuality in an unlikely place. *Journal of Bisexuality, 11*(1), 3–22.

Anderson, E., & Kian, T. (2012). Contesting violence, masculinity, and head trauma in the National Football League. *Men and Masculinities, 15*(2), 152–173.

Anderson, E., & McGuire, R. (2010). Inclusive masculinity and the gendered politics of men's rugby. *The Journal of Gender Studies, 19*(3), 249–261.

Anderson, E., Adams, A., & Rivers, I. (2012). "I kiss them because I love them": The emergence of heterosexual men kissing in British institutes of education. *Archives of Sexual Behavior, 41*(2), 421–430.

Anderson, E., McCormack, M., & Lee, H. (2012). Male team sport hazing initiations in a culture of decreasing homohysteria. *Journal of Adolescent Research, 27*(4), 427–448.

Attwood, F. (2010). *Porn.com: Making sense of online pornography.* New York, NY: Peter Lang.

Bush, A., Anderson, E., & Carr, S. (2012). The declining existence of men's homophobia in British sport. *Journal for the Study of Sports and Athletes in Education, 6*(1), 107–121.

Carrigan, T., Connell, R. W., & Lee, J. (1985). Toward a new sociology of masculinity. *Theory and Society, 14*, 551–604.

Cashmore, E., & Cleland, J. (2011). Glasswing butterflies: Gay professional football players and their culture. *Journal of Sport and Social Issues, 35*(4), 420–436.

Cashmore, E., & Cleland, J. (2012). Fans, homophobia and masculinities in association football: Evidence of a more inclusive environment. *British Journal of Sociology, 63*(2), 370–387.

Cavalier, E. S. (2011). Men at sport: Gay men's experiences in the sport workplace. *Journal of Homosexuality, 58*(5), 626–646.

Connell, R. W. (1987). *Gender and power.* Stanford, CA: Stanford University Press.

Dashper, K. (2012). Dressage is full of Queens: Masculinity, sexuality and equestrian sport. *Sociology, 46*(6), 1109–1124.

Flood, M. (2008). Men, sex and homosociality. *Men and Masculinities, 10*(3), 339–359.

Flood, M. (2009). Bent straights. In H. Oleksy (Ed.), *Intimate citizenships: Gender, sexualities, politics* (pp. 95–107). London: Routledge.

Flowers, P., & Buston, K. (2001). "I was terrified of being different": Exploring gay men's accounts of growing up in a heterosexist society. *Journal of Adolescence, 24*, 51–65.

Frank, D. J., Camp, B., & Boutcher, S. (2010). Worldwide trends in the criminal regulation of sex, 1945 to 2005. *American Sociological Review, 75*, 867–893.

Freud, S. (1905).Three essays on the theory of sexuality. In *Complete psychological works* (Vol. 7). London: Hogarth.

Gottzén, L., & Kremer-Sadlik, T. (2012). Fatherhood and youth sports: A balancing act between care and expectations. *Gender & Society, 26*(4), 639–664.

Ibson, J. (2002). *A century of male relationships in everyday American photography.* Washington, DC: Smithsonian Books.

Keleher, A., & Smith, E. (2012). Growing support for gay and lesbian equality since 1990. *Journal of Homosexuality, 59*, 1307–1326.

Kimmel, M. (1994). Homophobia as masculinity: Fear, shame and silence in the construction of gender identity. In H. Brod & M. Kaufman (Eds.), *Theorizing masculinities* (pp. 223–242). Thousand Oaks, CA: Sage.

Kimmel, M. (1996). *Manhood in America: A cultural history.* New York, NY: The Free Press.

Kinsey, A., Pomeroy, W., Martin, C., & Gebhard, P. (1948/1998). *Sexual behavior in the human male.* Philadelphia, PA: W. B. Saunders/Bloomington, IN: Indiana University Press.

Kozloski, M. (2011). Homosexual moral acceptance and social tolerance: Are the effects of education changing? *Journal of Homosexuality, 57*, 1370–1383

Loftus, J. (2001). America's liberalization in attitudes toward homosexuality, 1973 to 1998. *American Sociological Review, 66*, 762–782.

Lyng, S. T. (2009). Is there more to "antischoolishness" than masculinity? On multiple student styles, gender, and educational self-exclusion in secondary school. *Men and Masculinities, 11*(4), 462–487.

McCormack, M. (2011a). Hierarchy without hegemony: Locating boys in an inclusive school setting. *Sociological Perspectives, 54*(1), 83–101.

McCormack, M. (2011b). The declining significance of homohysteria for male students in three sixth forms in the south of England. *British Educational Research Journal, 37*(2), 337–353.

McCormack, M. (2011c). Mapping the terrain of homosexually-themed language. *Journal of Homosexuality, 58*(5), 664–679.

McCormack, M. (2012). *The declining significance of homophobia: How teenage boys are redefining masculinity and heterosexuality.* New York, NY: Oxford University Press.

McCormack, M., & Anderson, E. (2010). "It's just not acceptable any more": The erosion of homophobia and the softening of masculinity in an English state school. *Sociology, 44*(5), 843–859.

McNair, B. (2002). *Striptease culture: The democratization of desire.* London: Routledge.

Messner, M. (1992). *Power at play: Sports and the problem of masculinity.* Boston, MA: Beacon Press.

Pascoe, C. J. (2005). "Dude, you're a fag": Adolescent masculinity and the fag discourse. *Sexualities, 8*, 329–346.

Peterson, G. (2011). Clubbing masculinities: Gender shifts in gay men's dance floor choreographies. *Journal of Homosexuality, 58*(5), 608–625.

Peterson, G., & Anderson, E. (2012). The performance of softer masculinities on the university dance floor. *Journal of Men's Studies, 20*(1), 3–15.

Plummer, D. (1999). *One of the boys.* New York, NY: Harrington Park Press.

Pollack, W. (1999). *Real boys: Rescuing our sons from the myth of boyhood.* New York, NY: Henry Holt and Company.

Pompper, D. (2010). Masculinities, the metrosexual, and media images: Across dimensions of age and ethnicity. *Sex Roles, 63*(9–10), 682–696.

Ripley, M., Anderson, E., McCormack, M., & Rockett, B. (2012). Heteronormativity in the university classroom: Novelty attachment and content substitution among gay friendly students. *Sociology of Education, 85*(2), 121–130.

Ripley, M., Anderson, E., McCormack, M., Adams, A., & Pitts, R. (2011). The decreasing significance of stigma in the lives of bisexual men. *Journal of Bisexuality, 11*(2–3), 195–206.

Roberts, S. (2012). "I just got on with it": The educational experiences of ordinary, yet overlooked, boys. *British Journal of Sociology of Education, 33*(2), 203–221.

Savin-Williams, R. (2005). *The new gay teenager.* London: Harvard University Press.

Southall, R., Anderson, E., Southall, C., Nagel, M., & Polite, F. (2011). An investigation of ethnicity as a variable related to US male college athletes' sexual-orientation behaviors and attitudes. *Ethnic and Racial Studies, 34*(2), 293–313.

Swain, J. (2006). Reflections on patterns of masculinity in school settings. *Men and Masculinities, 8*(3), 331–349.

Thorpe, H. (2010). Bourdieu, gender reflexivity, and physical culture: A case of masculinities in the snowboarding field. *Journal of Sport and Social Issues, 34*(2), 176–214.

Way, N. (2011). *Deep secrets: Boys' friendships and the crisis of connection.* Cambridge, MA: Harvard University Press.

Zuhur, S. (2005). Gender, sexuality and the criminal laws in the Middle East and North Africa: A comparative study. *Women for Women's Human Rights, 1*–76.

READING 56

What Can We Do? Becoming Part of the Solution

Allan G. Johnson

The challenge we face is to change patterns of exclusion, rejection, privilege, harassment, discrimination, and violence that are everywhere in this society and have existed for hundreds (or, in the case of gender, thousands) of years. We have to begin by thinking about the trouble and the challenge in new and more productive ways. . . .

Large numbers of people have sat on the sidelines and seen themselves as neither part of the problem nor the solution. Beyond this shared trait, however, they are far from homogeneous. Everyone is aware of the whites, heterosexuals, and men who intentionally act out in oppressive ways. But there is less attention to the millions of people who know inequities exist and want to be part of the solution. Their silence and invisibility allow the trouble to continue. Removing what silences them and stands in their way can tap an enormous potential of energy for change. . . .

MYTH 1: "IT'S ALWAYS BEEN THIS WAY, AND IT ALWAYS WILL"

If you don't make a point of studying history, it's easy to slide into the belief that things have always been the way we've known them to be. But if you look back a bit further, you find racial oppression has been a feature of human life for only a matter of centuries, and there is abundant evidence that male dominance has been around for only seven thousand years or so, which isn't very long when you

consider that human beings have been on the earth for hundreds of thousands of years.[1] So when it comes to human social life, the smart money should be on the idea that *nothing* has always been this way or any other.

This idea should suggest that nothing *will* always be this way or any other, contrary to the notion that privilege and oppression are here to stay. If the only thing we can count on is change, then it's hard to see why we should believe for a minute that *any* kind of social system is permanent. Reality is always in motion. Things may appear to stand still, but that's only because humans have a short attention span, dictated perhaps by the shortness of our lives. If we take the long view—the *really* long view—we can see that everything is in process all the time.

Some would argue that everything *is* process, the space between one point and another, the movement from one thing toward another. What we may see as permanent end points—world capitalism, Western civilization, advanced technology, and so on—are actually temporary states on the way to other temporary states. Even ecologists, who used to talk about ecological balance, now speak of ecosystems as inherently unstable. Instead of always returning to some steady state after a period of disruption, ecosystems are, by nature, a continuing process of change from one arrangement to another. They never go back to just where they were.

Social systems are also fluid. A society isn't some hulking *thing* that sits there forever as it is. Because a system happens only as people participate in it, it can't help being a dynamic process of creation and re-creation from one moment to the next. In something as simple as a man following the path of least resistance toward controlling conversations (and a woman letting him do it), the reality of male privilege in that moment comes into being. This is how we *do* male privilege, bit by bit, moment by moment. This is also how individuals can contribute to change: by choosing paths of *greater* resistance, as when men don't take control and women refuse their own subordination.

Allan G. Johnson is a sociologist, writer, and public speaker who has worked on issues of privilege, oppression, and social unequality.

Since people can always choose paths of greater resistance or create new ones entirely, systems can only be as stable as the flow of human choice and creativity, which certainly isn't a recipe for permanence. In the short run, systems of privilege may look unchangeable. But the relentless process of social life never produces the exact same result twice in a row, because it's impossible for everyone to participate in any system in an unvarying and uniform way. Added to this are the dynamic interactions that go on among systems—between capitalism and the state, for example, or between families and the economy—that also produce powerful and unavoidable tensions, contradictions, and other currents of change. Ultimately, systems can't help changing.

Oppressive systems often *seem* stable because they limit people's lives and imaginations so much that they can't see beyond them. But this masks a fundamental long-term instability caused by the dynamics of oppression itself. Any system organized around one group's efforts to control and exploit another is a losing proposition, because it contradicts the essentially uncontrollable nature of reality and does violence to basic human needs and values. For example, as the last two centuries of feminist thought and action have begun to challenge the violence and break down the denial, patriarchy has become increasingly vulnerable. This is one reason male resistance, backlash, and defensiveness are now so intense. Many men complain about their lot, especially their inability to realize ideals of control in relation to their own lives,[2] women, and other men. Fear of and resentment toward women are pervasive, from worrying about being accused of sexual harassment to railing against affirmative action.

No social system lasts forever, but this is especially true of oppressive systems of privilege. We can't know what will replace them, but we can be confident that they will go, that they *are* going at every moment. It's only a matter of how quickly, by what means, and toward what alternatives, and whether each of us will do our part to make it happen sooner rather than later and with less rather than more human suffering in the process.

MYTH 2: GANDHI'S PARADOX AND THE MYTH OF NO EFFECT

Whether we help change oppressive systems depends on how we handle the belief that nothing we do can make a difference, that the system is too big and powerful for us to affect it. The complaint is valid if we look at society as a whole: it's true that we aren't going to change it in our lifetime. But if changing the entire system through our own efforts is the standard against which we measure the ability to do something, then we've set ourselves up to feel powerless. It's not unreasonable to want to make a difference, but if we have to *see* the final result of what we do, then we can't be part of change that's too gradual and long term to allow that. We also can't be part of change that's so complex that we can't sort out our contribution from countless others that combine in ways we can never grasp. The problem of privilege and oppression requires complex and long-term change coupled with short-term work to soften some of its worst consequences. This means that if we're going to be part of the solution, we have to let go of the idea that change doesn't happen unless we're around to see it happen.

To shake off the paralyzing myth that we cannot, individually, be effective, we have to alter how we see ourselves in relation to a long-term, complex process of change. This begins by altering how we relate to time. Many changes can come about quickly enough for us to see them happen. When I was in college, for example, there was little talk about gender inequality as a social problem, whereas now there are more than five hundred women's studies programs in the United States. But a goal like ending oppression takes more than this and far more time than our short lives can encompass. If we're going to see ourselves as part of that kind of change, we can't use the human life span as a significant standard against which to measure progress.

To see our choices in relation to long-term change, we have to develop what might be called "time constancy," analogous to what psychologists call "object constancy." If you hold a cookie in front of very young children and then put it behind your back while they watch, they can't find the cookie because they apparently can't hold on to the image of it and where it went. They lack object constancy. In other words, if they can't see it, it might as well not even exist. After a while, children develop the mental ability to know that objects or people exist even when they're out of sight. In thinking about change and our relation to it, we need to develop a similar ability in relation to time that enables us to carry within us the knowledge, the faith, that significant change happens even though we aren't around to see it.

Along with time constancy, we need to clarify for ourselves how our choices matter and how they don't. Gandhi once said nothing we do as individuals matters, but that it's vitally important to do it anyway. This touches on a powerful paradox in the relationship between society and individuals. Imagine, for example, that social systems are trees and we are the leaves. No individual leaf on the tree matters; whether it lives or dies has no effect on much of anything. But collectively, the leaves are essential to the whole tree because they photosynthesize the sugar that feeds it. Without leaves, the tree dies.

So leaves matter and they don't, just as we matter and we don't. What each of us does may not seem like much, because in important ways, it *isn't* much. But when many people do this work together, they can form a critical mass that is anything but insignificant, especially in the long run. If we're going to be part of a larger change process, we have to learn to live with this sometimes uncomfortable paradox.

A related paradox is that we have to be willing to travel without knowing where we're going. We need faith to do what seems right without necessarily being sure of the effect that will have. We have to think like pioneers who may know the direction they want to move in or what they would like to find, without knowing where they will wind up. Because they are going where they've never been before, they can't know whether they will ever arrive at anything they might consider a destination, much less the kind of place they had in mind when they first set out. If pioneers had to know their destination

from the beginning, they would never go anywhere or discover anything.

In similar ways, to seek out alternatives to systems of privilege it has to be enough to move away from social life organized around privilege and oppression and to move toward the certainty that alternatives are possible, even though we may not have a clear idea of what those are or ever experience them ourselves. It has to be enough to question how we see ourselves as people of a certain race, gender, class, and sexual orientation, for example, or examine how we see capitalism and the scarcity and competition it produces in relation to our personal striving to better our own lives, or how oppression works and how we participate in it. Then we can open ourselves to experience what happens next.

When we dare ask core questions about who we are and how the world works, things happen that we can't foresee; they don't happen unless we *move,* if only in our minds. As pioneers, we discover what's possible only by first putting ourselves in motion, because we have to move in order to change our position—and hence put perspective—on where we are, where we've been, and where we might go. This is how alternatives begin to appear.

The myth of no effect obscures the role we can play in the long-term transformation of society. But the myth also blinds us to our own power in relation to other people. We may cling to the belief that there is nothing we can do precisely because we subconsciously know how much power we *do* have and are afraid to use it because people may not like it. If we deny our power to affect people, then we don't have to worry about taking responsibility for how we use it or, more significant, how we don't.

This reluctance to acknowledge and use power comes up in the simplest everyday situations, as when a group of friends starts laughing at a racist, sexist, or homophobic joke and we have to decide whether to go along. It's just a moment among countless such moments that constitute the fabric of all kinds of oppressive systems. But it's a crucial moment, because the group's seamless response to the joke affirms the normalcy and unproblematic nature of it in a system of privilege. It takes only one person to tear the fabric of collusion and apparent consensus. On some level, we each know we have this potential, and this knowledge can empower us or scare us into silence. We can change the course of the moment with something as simple as visibly not joining in the laughter, or saying "I don't think that's funny." We know how uncomfortable this can make the group feel and how they may ward off their discomfort by dismissing, excluding, or even attacking us as bearers of bad news. Our silence, then, isn't because nothing we do will matter, our silence is our not *daring* to matter.

Our power to affect other people isn't simply the power to make them feel uncomfortable. Systems shape the choices people make primarily by providing paths of least resistance. Whenever we openly choose a different path, however, we make it possible for others to see both the path of least resistance they're following and the possibility of choosing something else.

If we choose different paths, we usually won't know if we're affecting other people, but it's safe to assume that we are. When people know that alternatives exist and witness other people choosing them, things become possible that weren't before. When we openly pass up a path of least resistance, we increase resistance for other people around that path, because now they must reconcile their choice with what they've seen us do, something they didn't have to deal with before. There's no way to predict how this will play out in the long run, but there's certainly no good reason to think it won't make a difference.

The simple fact is that we affect one another all the time without knowing it. When my family moved to our house in the woods of northwestern Connecticut, one of my first pleasures was blazing walking trails through the woods. Some time later I noticed deer scat and hoofprints along the trails, and it pleased me to think they had adopted the trail I'd laid down. But then I wondered if perhaps I had followed a trail laid down by others when I cleared "my" trail. I realized that there is no way to know that anything begins or ends with me and the choices I make. It's more likely that the paths others have chosen influence the paths I choose.

This suggests that the simplest way to help others make different choices is to make them myself, and to do it openly. As I shift the patterns of my own participation in systems of privilege, I make it easier for others to do so as well, and harder for them not to. Simply by setting an example—rather than trying to change them—I create the possibility of their participating in change in their own time and in their own way. In this way I can widen the circle of change without provoking the kind of defensiveness that perpetuates paths of least resistance and the oppressive systems they serve.

It's important to see that in doing this kind of work, we don't have to go after people to change their minds. In fact, changing people's minds may play a relatively small part in changing societies. We won't succeed in turning diehard misogynists into practicing feminists, for example, or racists into civil rights activists. At most, we can shift the odds in favor of new paths that contradict the core values that systems of privilege depend on. We can introduce so many exceptions to the paths that support privilege that the children or grandchildren of diehard racists and misogynists will start to change their perception of which paths offer the least resistance. Research on men's changing attitudes toward the male provider role, for example, shows that most of the shift occurs *between* generations, not within them.[3] This suggests that rather than trying to change people, the most important thing we can do is contribute to the slow evolution of entire cultures so that forms and values which support privilege begin to lose their "obvious" legitimacy and normalcy and new forms emerge to challenge their privileged place in social life.

In science, this is how one paradigm replaces another.[4] For hundreds of years, for example, Europeans believed that the stars, planets, and sun revolved around Earth. But scientists such as Copernicus and Galileo found that too many of their astronomical observations were anomalies that didn't fit the prevailing paradigm: if the sun and planets revolved around the Earth, then they wouldn't move as they did. As such observations accumulated, they made it increasingly difficult to hang on to an Earth-centered paradigm. Eventually the anomalies became so numerous that Copernicus offered a new paradigm, which he declined to publish for fear of persecution as a heretic, a fate that eventually befell Galileo when he took up the cause a century later. Eventually, however, the evidence was so overwhelming that a new paradigm replaced the old one.

In similar ways, we can see how systems of privilege are based on paradigms that shape how we think about difference and how we organize social life in relation to it. We can openly challenge those paradigms with evidence that they don't work and produce unacceptable consequences for everyone. We can help weaken them by openly choosing alternative paths in our everyday lives and thereby provide living anomalies that don't fit the prevailing paradigm. By our example, we can contradict basic assumptions and their legitimacy over and over again. We can add our choices and our lives to tip the scales toward new paradigms that don't revolve around privilege and oppression. We can't tip the scales overnight or by ourselves, and in that sense we don't amount to much. But on the other side of Gandhi's paradox, it is crucial where we choose to place what poet Bonaro Overstreet called "the stubborn ounces of my weight":

STUBBORN OUNCES

(To One Who Doubts the Worth of Doing Anything If You Can't Do Everything)

You say the little efforts that I make
will do no good; they will never prevail to tip
   the hovering scale
where Justice hangs in balance.
           I don't think
I ever thought they would.
But I am prejudiced beyond debate
In favor of my right to choose which side
shall feel the stubborn ounces of my weight.[5]

PERSONAL ACCOUNT

Parents' Underestimated Love

"Coming out of the closet" to my parents has been the most liberating thing that I have done in my life because having my homosexuality discovered by my parents was my biggest fear. Although I didn't grow up in a particularly homophobic environment, innately I knew that homosexuality was different and wasn't accepted because of rigid social norms and religious doctrines. I lived in anguish of being exposed and of the consequences that would come with being the queer one.

Keeping the secret from my traditional Salvadoran parents created a wedge that made it difficult for me to bond with my parents and have them participate fully in my life. I became a recluse and avoided much parental interaction to avoid questions about girlfriends. During my teenage years, girlfriends were expected from a "good and healthy" boy such as myself. I felt that my lack of interest in girls would have led to probes from my parents, and plus, I wasn't the typical macho boy who was into sports, cars, etc. . . . I was the "sensitive type." To avoid any suspicion, I limited my interaction with my parents. I felt that if I opened up to them, my sexuality would be questioned and questions like "Are you gay?" would follow. Being an academic overachiever in high school made things easier for me. Whenever the question was asked of why I didn't have a girlfriend, I had the perfect excuse, "I'm too busy with school to focus on girls . . . do you want a playboy or an honor student?"

During my sophomore year in college I took a bold step and moved out of my parents' house. My move facilitated my "coming out" to my parents because the possibility of being kicked out of the house when I told them I was gay wouldn't loom over me. I didn't know if my parents would kick me out, but I couldn't run the risk of finding out. One year after moving out, I "came out." Ironically it didn't come as a surprise to my parents, and frankly it wasn't a big deal! After years of living in fear of rejection and shame, my parents accepted and reaffirmed their love and support. I underestimated the power of my parents' love.

Octavio N. Espinal

It is in such small and humble choices that oppression and the movement toward something better actually happen.

DISCUSSION QUESTIONS

1. In a sense, Allan Johnson's discussion highlights the paradoxes inherent in the efforts to create social change. What are those paradoxes, and how does Johnson resolve them?
2. What would Johnson's advice be to someone who wants to make a difference in society? Can it be summarized in a sentence or two?

NOTES

1. See Elizabeth Fisher, *Woman's Creation: Sexual Evolution and the Shaping of Society* (New York: McGraw-Hill, 1979); Gerda Lerner, *The Creation of Patriarchy* (New York: Oxford University Press, 1986).
2. This is what Warren Farrell means when he describes male power as mythical. In this case, he's right. See *The Myth of Male Power* (New York: Berkley Books, 1993).
3. J. R. Wilkie, "Changes in U.S. Men's Attitudes towards the Family Provider Role, 1972–1989," *Gender and Society* 7, no. 2 (1993): 261–79.
4. The classic statement of how this happens is by Thomas S. Kuhn, *The Structure of Scientific Revolutions* (Chicago: University of Chicago Press, 1970).
5. Bonaro W. Overstreet, *Hands Laid Upon the Wind* (New York: Norton, 1955), p. 15.

READING 57

In Defense of Rich Kids

William Upski Wimsatt

My family never talked much about money, except to say that we were "middle-class . . . well maybe upper-middle-class." A few years ago, it became clear that both my parents and my grandmother had a lot more money than I realized. As an only child, I stood to inherit a nice chunk of it. I didn't know how much and I didn't know when. They did not want me to become spoiled or think I didn't have to work.

A lot of people will use this information to write me off. Oh, he's a rich kid. No wonder he could publish a book, probably with his parents' money. And why's he going around bragging about it? What is he, stupid? Some of us have to work for a living, etc.

You can hate me if you want to. I am the beneficiary of a very unfair system. The system gives me tons of free money for doing nothing, yet it forces you to work two and three jobs just to get out of debt.

On top of that, I have the nerve to sit up here and talk about it and—for some it will seem—to rub it in. Most rich people are considerate enough to shut their mouths and pretend they're struggling too. To get on TV talking about, "I got this on sale."

I didn't really have anyone to talk about it with. I knew a lot of the kids I had gone to school with were in a similar situation but we never discussed our family money, except in really strange ways like how broke we were and how those other rich people were so spoiled/lucky. Our judgments of them betrayed our own underlying shame.

And let's talk right now about motives. As soon as you bring up philanthropy, people want to talk about motives. "Is he doing this for the right reasons or is he just doing this to make himself feel good?" Well, let me tell you, I am definitely doing this to make myself feel good and—call me crazy—I believe doing what you feel good about is one of the right reasons.

Yes, I have the luxury to give my money away because I know I'm going to inherit more later in life. But don't come to me with this bullshit, "Oh, it's easy for you to give away your money because you're gonna inherit more later." If it's so easy, how come more rich people aren't doing it? How come Americans only give 2% to charity across the board, whether they are rich, poor, or middle-class? I usually give away 20–30% of my income every year. But I just got my first steady job, so this year, if you throw in the book, I'll probably be giving away more like 50%.

William Upski Wimsatt is a social entrepreneur, political activist, and author of *Bomb the Suburbs* and *No More Prisons*. He has also written for the *Chicago Tribune* and *Vibe*.

Hell no, I'm not some kind of saint who has taken a vow of poverty and is now sitting in judgment of you or anyone else's money decisions. But be aware, it's easy to criticize my actions when you don't have much money. If you were in my situation, who's to say you'd be any different from 99% of other rich people who keep it all for themselves. Or if they do give it away, it's to big colleges, big arts, big religion, or big service, supporting bureaucratic institutions that maintain systemic problems by treating symptoms and obscuring root causes.

Which brings me to the next very selfish reason for my philanthropy. I have a political agenda and my philanthropic "generosity" plus my sense of strategy gives me more philanthropic power to change the world than people with 50 times my income.

The deeper reason why I give away my money is because I love the world. Because I'm grateful to be alive at all. Because I'm scared about where we're headed. Because we owe it to our great-grandchildren. Because we owe it to the millions of years of evolution it took to get us here. And to everyone before us who fought to change history and make things as good as they are now. Because I know how to change history and I know it takes money. Because I get more joy out of making things better for everyone than I get out of making things materially better for myself. Because I know how to make and spend money on myself. It's boring. There's no challenge in it. And no love in it. I love helping good things happen, and supporting people I believe in. Especially people and organizations that have NO money put into them by traditional foundations and charities. I'm not talking about your everyday charities like diabetes or your college(s) that already have multi-million dollar budgets set up to fight for them.

They're new.

They don't exist yet.

They're like diabetes in 1921, the year before they extracted insulin.

They're like your college the year before it was founded.

Don't get me wrong. My father has juvenile diabetes. And I love my college too. But the money supporting the Juvenile Diabetes Foundation, and my college is already so big, their fundraising operations so effective, that giving my money to them is a drop in the bucket.

For the organizing efforts I want to support, every dollar is like a seed, helping not only to create a new kind of organization, but an organization that will be copied and that decades from now will establish new fields of work. It is the most strategic way possible to change the course of history, and the most unpopular because it's so high-risk. . . .

THE MOST EFFECTIVE THING YOU EVER DO

. . . What if we could double the number of cool rich people who are funding social change from say five hundred to a thousand? Then we could double the number of organizers on the street, lawyers in the court rooms, lobbyists in Congress. Double the number of investigative reporters. There are so many people who want to do progressive work who can't because there aren't enough activist jobs. People come out of law school to become environmental lawyers and they end up having to defend corporations because they have to pay off their student loans. Environmental groups can't afford to hire them. The same goes for radical artists and journalists, forced to get jobs in advertising and public relations.

Five hundred more cool rich people could change all that.

Five hundred cool rich people could change the political landscape of this country.

Now don't get me wrong. I'm not saying philanthropy will solve all our problems, especially not the way 99% of it is done now. I'm not saying cool rich people are any more important or worthy than any other people. Poor people are made to feel like they aren't worth anything and that's wrong. I don't want to feed into that by focusing on rich people for a while. We need billions of people from billions of backgrounds trying billions of strategies to save this planet. It's just that every serious effort to change things takes people with money who understand how to support a movement. All these naive college or punk or hip-hop revolutionaries talking about, "Fuck that. I don't know any rich people and if I do they're assholes and anyway, I don't need their money." I only have one thing to say. Wait until your community center gets shut down. Wait until your broke grassroots genius friends start burning out because they have to do menial shit all day because they don't have the time or capital to make their dreams come true.

Consider these statistics. There are about five million millionaire households in the U.S. That's approximately one out of every 50 people. So, if you are a social person (not a hermit) and you are not currently serving a life sentence in prison, then chances are you will have the opportunity at some point in your life to get to know a number of people who are, at the very least, millionaires. Most of the time you will not know they are millionaires. Half of the time, millionaires don't even realize they are millionaires. My parents didn't realize they were. People usually have their assets tied up in many different forms such as houses, trusts, mutual funds, stocks, bonds and retirement accounts.

Less than 1% of all charitable giving ends up in the hands of people who are working to change the system. As Teresa Odendahl has pointed out in her ironically titled book *Charity Begins at Home,* contrary to popular belief, most charity money does not go to help poor children help themselves. The vast majority of money goes to big churches, big colleges, big hospitals, big arts and social service organizations which either directly cater to privileged people, or which treat the symptoms of social ills without ever addressing the root causes. . . .

Over the next 50 years, the upper-classes of my generation stand to inherit or earn the greatest personal fortune in history, while the lower classes both here and internationally will continue slipping deeper into poverty and debt.

That's where the Cool Rich Kids Movement comes in. Actually there isn't much of a "Cool Rich Kids Movement." That's just what I call the loose-knit network of maybe 100 of us young people with wealth who are in conversation with each other, and who support each other in taking small but significant

actions. We are asking our parents to teach us about money. We are helping our families make responsible decisions about investments. Some of us are getting on the boards of family foundations or helping our families to start them. We introduce each other to amazing grassroots people to break the isolation of wealth. We are just in the process of getting organized. We had our first conference last spring, sponsored by the Third Wave Foundation in New York. More are planned.

My goal is to get more young people with wealth in on the conversation. With five million millionaires in the U.S., even if we only spoke to the coolest 1% of all millionaire kids, that's still 50,000 people!

One half of the money I give away every year goes directly to grassroots youth activist organizations that I have a relationship with. (No, I don't make them kiss up to me. I just give it to them, thank them for their hard work and if they feel funny about it, I remind them that the only reason I have the money in the first place is because I've been so privileged and so many people have helped me. So it wasn't really "my" money to begin with. Oftentimes I have to *insist* that people take my money. We've all had so many bad experiences.)

The other half of my money I donate to organizing people with wealth.

That may seem strange at first.

Why give money to people who already have wealth?

From all my experience with grassroots organizations, I believe that organizing people with wealth is the most powerful work I do. And paradoxically, it is some of the hardest work to fundraise for because everybody including rich people thinks, "Why give rich people more money?" And that's why only a few dozen people in America have the job of helping rich people figure out how to come to terms with and do cool things with their money.

I think we need more of those people in the world.

So recently, I've changed my focus in a big way.

I joined the board of More Than Money. I am helping to start the Active Element Foundation, which is the first foundation that will specifically work with young donors on funding grassroots youth activism. And I'm also helping to start the Self-Education Foundation, which will tap successful people who either didn't like school or who dropped out to fund self-education resource centers which will support poor kids to take learning into their own hands. I am helping to organize a series of conferences around the country for young people with wealth, put on by The Third Wave Foundation and the Comfort Zone. . . .

I believe the most effective thing I do for the world every year is to buy gift subscriptions of *More Than Money Journal* for my privileged friends and to keep a ready supply of *Money Talks. So Can We.* for every cool young person I meet who has money. This is the most effective action I do. Any other possible action I could do, one cool rich person could hire ten more people to take my place.

But there's very little room in our culture to talk about having money and funding renegade work. Most rich people be like, "See you later." And most grassroots people be like, "It's easy for you because you're rich." There's resentment either way. People who aren't rich can play a huge role supporting us. So many of my friends who aren't wealthy act like, "Ha ha ha, going to your rich kids conference." That's not going to make me want to talk to you. If you are truly down to change the world, don't try to score points by alienating your rich friends with snide remarks. If you take the time to truly understand us and support us as people, more than likely, we will do the same for you. Rich people don't choose to be born rich any more than poor people choose to be born poor. The sickness of our society damages us each in different and complicated ways, and we sometimes forget that rich people get damaged too. Not just in a mocking way, like, "Oh, they're so spoiled." But in a real way. One of the most common ways privileged people get damaged is that we are taught not to talk about money. We put a wall around ourselves, and then it is hard for us to be honest with people who aren't rich. This makes us cold and creates a vicious cycle of not trusting and not sharing ourselves or our money.

There are only a few of us out here doing this work, which is why I have been thrust into the spotlight. It's a little ridiculous actually that I am speaking for rich kids when I haven't even inherited my money yet. But there was a deafening silence and someone needed to come out here and give us a bold public voice. Do you have any cool rich friends who may be looking for people in similar situations to talk to?

Hint: You do.

Please please please pass this along to them.

It just might be the most effective thing you ever do.

DISCUSSION QUESTIONS

1. Would you rather have money or a large number of supporters if you were seeking to create social change?
2. How much money would you want to have before you considered giving away some of it to create social change?

PERSONAL ACCOUNT

Where Are You From?

As a freshman at a predominantly white private college, I was confronted with a number of unusual situations. I was extremely young for a college freshman (I was sixteen), I was African American, and I was placed in upper-division courses, because of my academic background. So being accepted and fitting in were crucial to me.

I was enrolled in a course, political thought, with approximately thirty other students, mostly juniors and seniors who had taken courses with this professor before. I was the only African American in the class. During introductions for the first class, he never got around to letting me speak, even though he went alphabetically on the list (my last name begins with a "C"). Later, I began to be aware of his exclusion of me from class discussion. By

the third class, I guess he felt there was no longer any way he could avoid speaking to me. He asked me a few questions about myself—where I was from, what high school had I attended, and what was my major. His questions began to seem like a personal attack, and then finally he asked, "Why are you here?" "Where are you from?" I was quite taken aback by his line of questioning, when one of the upperclassmen (a white man) responded for me. "She's a freshman, Dr. B. Any more questions?" That guy became one of my closest friends. We have maintained contact ever since college. His response to Dr. B. totally changed the professor's way of treating me.

C.C.

READING 58

Uprooting Racism: How White People Can Work for Racial Justice

Paul Kivel

A person of color who is angry about discrimination or harassment is doing us a service. That person is pointing out something wrong, something that contradicts the ideals of equality set forth in our Declaration of Independence and Bill of Rights. That person is bringing our attention to a problem that needs solving, a wrong that needs righting. We could convey our appreciation by saying, "Thank you, your anger has helped me see what's not right here." What keeps us from responding in this way?

Anger is a scary emotion in our society. In mainstream white culture we are taught to be polite, never to raise our voices, to be reasonable and to keep calm. People who are demonstrative of their

feelings are discounted and ridiculed. We are told by parents just to obey "because I said so." We are told by bosses, religious leaders and professional authorities not to challenge what they say, "or else" (or else you'll be fired, go to hell, be treated as "crazy"). When we do get angry we learn to stuff it, mutter under our breath and go away. We are taught to turn our anger inward in self-destructive behaviors. If we are men we are taught to take out our frustrations on someone weaker and smaller than we are.

When we have seen someone expressing anger, it has often been a person with power who was abusing us or someone else physically, verbally or emotionally. We were hurt, scared or possibly confused. Most of us can remember a time from our youth when a parent, teacher, coach, boss or other adult was yelling at us abusively. It made us afraid when those around us became angry. It made us afraid of our own anger.

A similar response is triggered when a person of color gets angry at us about racism. We become scared, guilty, embarrassed, confused and we fear everything is falling apart and we might get hurt. If the angry person would just calm down, or go away, we could get back to the big, happy family feeling.

Paul Kivel is a social justice educator, activist, writer, trainer, and speaker on men's issues.

Relationships between people of color and whites often begin as friendly and polite. We may be pleased that we know and like a person from another cultural group. We may be pleased that they like us. We are encouraged because despite our fears, it seems that it may be possible for people from different cultures to get along together. The friendships may confirm our feelings that we are different from other white people.

But then the person of color gets angry. Perhaps they are angry about something we do or say. Perhaps they are angry about a comment or action by someone else, or about racism in general. We may back off in response, fearing that the relationship is falling apart. We aren't liked anymore. We've been found out to be racist. For a person of color, this may be a time of hope that the relationship can become more intimate and honest. The anger may be an attempt to test the depths and possibilities of the friendship. They may be open about their feelings, to see how safe we are, hoping that we will not desert them. Or the anger may be a more assertive attempt to break through our complacency to address some core assumptions, beliefs or actions.

Many white people have been taught to see anger and conflict as a sign of failure. They may instead be signs that we're becoming more honest, dealing with the real differences and problems in our lives. If it is not safe enough to argue, disagree, express anger and struggle with each other what kind of relationship can it be?

We could say, "Thank you for pointing out the racism because I want to know whenever it is occurring." Or, "I appreciate your honesty. Let's see what we can do about this situation." More likely we get scared and disappear, or become defensive and counterattack. In any case, we don't focus on the root of the problem, and the racism goes unattended.

When people of color are angry about racism it is legitimate anger. It is not their oversensitivity, but our lack of sensitivity, that causes this communication gap. They are vulnerable to the abuse of racism every day. They are experts on it. White society, and most of us individually, rarely notice racism.

It is the anger and actions of people of color that call our attention to the injustice of racism. Sometimes that anger is from an individual person of color who is talking to us. At other times it is the rage of an entire community protesting, bringing legal action or burning down buildings. Such anger and action is almost always a last resort, a desperate attempt to get our attention when all else fails.

It is tremendously draining, costly and personally devastating for people of color to have to rage about racism. They often end up losing their friends, their livelihoods, even their lives. Rather than attacking them for their anger, we need to ask ourselves how many layers of complacency, ignorance, collusion, privilege and misinformation have we put into place for it to take so much outrage to get our attention?

The 1965 riots in Watts, as never before, brought our attention to the ravages of racism on the African-American population living there. In 1968 a national report by the Kerner Commission warned us of the dangers of not addressing racial problems. Yet in 1992, when there were new uprisings in Los Angeles, we focused again on the anger of African Americans, on containing that anger, protecting property and controlling the community, rather than on solving the problems that cause poverty, unemployment, crime and high drop-out rates. As soon as the anger was contained, we turned our attention elsewhere and left the underlying problems unaddressed. The only way to break this cycle of rage is for us to seriously address the sources of the anger, the causes of the problems. And in order to do that, we need to talk about racism directly with each other.

BEING A STRONG WHITE ALLY

What kind of active support does a strong white ally provide? People of color that I have talked with over the years have been remarkably consistent in describing the kinds of support they need from white allies. The following list is compiled from their statements at workshops I have facilitated.

The focus here is on personal qualities and interpersonal relationships. More active interventions are discussed in the next part of [this discussion].

What people of color want from white allies:

"Respect"

"Find out about us"

"Don't take over"

"Provide information"

"Resources"

"Money"

"Take risks"

"Don't take it personally"

"Understanding"

"Teach your children about racism"

"Speak up"

"Don't be scared by my anger"

"Support"

"Listen"

"Don't make assumptions"

"Stand by my side"

"Don't assume you know what's best for me"

"Your body on the line"

"Make mistakes"

"Honesty"

"Talk to other white people"

"Interrupt jokes and comments"

"Don't ask me to speak for my people"

BASIC TACTICS

Every situation is different and calls for critical thinking about how to make a difference. Taking the statements above into account, I have compiled some general guidelines.

1. *Assume racism is everywhere, every day.* Just as economics influences everything we do, just as our gender and gender politics influence everything we do, assume that racism is affecting whatever is going on. We assume this because it's true, and because one of the privileges of being white is not having to see or deal with racism all the time. We have to learn to see the effect that racism has. Notice who speaks, what is said, how things are done and described. Notice who isn't present. Notice code words for race, and the implications of the policies, patterns and comments that are being expressed. You already notice the skin color of everyone you meet and interact with—now notice what difference it makes.

2. *Notice who is the center of attention and who is the center of power.* Racism works by directing violence and blame toward people of color and consolidating power and privilege for white people.

3. *Notice how racism is denied, minimized and justified.*

4. *Understand and learn from the history of whiteness and racism.* Notice how racism has changed over time and how it has subverted or resisted challenges. Study the tactics that have worked effectively against it.

5. *Understand the connections between racism, economic issues, sexism and other forms of injustice.*

6. *Take a stand against injustice.* Take risks. It is scary, difficult, risky and may bring up many feelings, but ultimately it is the only healthy and moral human thing to do. Intervene in situations where racism is being passed on.

7. *Be strategic.* Decide what is important to challenge and what's not. Think about strategy in particular situations. Attack the source of power.

8. *Don't confuse a battle with the war.* Behind particular incidents and interactions are larger patterns. Racism is flexible and adaptable. There will be gains and losses in the struggle for justice and equality.

9. *Don't call names or be personally abusive.* Since power is often defined as power over others—the ability to abuse or control people—it is easy to become abusive ourselves. However, we usually end up abusing people who have less power than we do because it is less dangerous. Attacking people doesn't address the systemic nature of racism and inequality.

10. *Support the leadership of people of color.* Do this consistently, but not uncritically.

11. *Don't do it alone.* You will not end racism by yourself. We can do it if we work together. Build support, establish networks, work with already established groups.

12. *Talk with your children and other young people about racism.*

IT'S NOT JUST A JOKE

"Let me tell you about the Chinaman who . . ." What do you do when someone starts to tell a joke which you think is likely to be a racial putdown? What do you do if the racial nature of the joke is only apparent at the punchline? How do you respond to a comment which contains a racial stereotype?

Interrupting racist comments can be scary because we risk turning the attack or anger toward us. We are sometimes accused of dampening the mood, being too serious or too sensitive. We may be ridiculed for being friends of the _____. People may think we're arrogant or trying to be politically correct. They may try to get back at us for embarrassing them. If you're in an environment where any of this could happen, then you know that it is not only not safe for you, it's even more unsafe for people of color.

People tell jokes and make comments sometimes out of ignorance, but usually knowing at some level that the comment puts down someone else and creates a collusion between the speaker and the listener. The joketeller is claiming that we're normal, intelligent and sane, and others are not. The effect is to exclude someone or some group of people from the group, to make it a little (or a lot) more unsafe for them to be there. Furthermore, by objectifying someone, it makes it that much easier for the next person to tell a joke, make a comment or take stronger action against any member of the objectified group.

The reverse is also true. Interrupting such behavior makes it less safe to harass or discriminate, and more safe for the intended targets of the abuse. Doing nothing is tacit approval and collusion with the abuse. There is no neutral stance. If someone is being attacked, even by a joke or teasing, there are no innocent bystanders.

As a white person you can play a powerful role in such a situation. When a person of color protests against being put down in an atmosphere where they are already disrespected, they are often discounted as well. You, as a white person interrupting verbal abuse, may be listened to and heeded because it breaks the collusion from other white people that was expected by the abuser. If a person of color speaks up first then you can support them by stating why you think it is right to challenge the comments. In either case, your intervention as a white person challenging racist comments is important and often effective.

What can you actually say in the presence of derogatory comments? There are no right or wrong answers. The more you do it the better you get. Even if it doesn't come off as you intended, you will influence others to be more sensitive and you will model the courage and integrity to interrupt verbal abuse. Following are suggestions for where to start.

If you can tell at the beginning that a joke is likely to be offensive or involves stereotypes and putdowns, you can say something like, "I don't want to hear a joke or story that reinforces stereotypes or puts down a group of people." Or, "Please stop right there. It sounds like your story is going to make fun of a group of people and I don't want to hear about it." Or, "I don't like humor that makes it unsafe for people here." Or, "I don't want to hear a joke that asks us to laugh at someone else's expense." There are many ways to say something appropriate without attacking or being offensive yourself.

Using "I" statements should be an important part of your strategy. Rather than attacking someone, it is stronger to state how you feel, what you want. Other people may still become defensive, but there is more opportunity for them to hear what you have to say if you word it as an "I" statement.

Often you don't know the story is offensive until the punchline. Or you just are not sure what you're hearing, but it makes you uncomfortable. It is appropriate to say afterwards that the joke was inappropriate because . . . , or the story was offensive because . . . , or it made you feel uncomfortable because . . . Trust your feelings about it!

In any of these interactions you may need to explain further why stories based on stereotypes reinforce abuse, and why jokes and comments that put people down are offensive. Rather than calling someone racist, or writing someone off, interrupting abuse is a way to do public education. It is a way to put what you know about racial stereotypes and abuse into action to stop them.

Often a person telling a racial joke is defensive about being called on the racism and may argue or defend themselves. You don't have to prove anything, although a good discussion of the issues is a great way to do more education. It's now up to the other person to think about your comments and to decide what to do. Everyone nearby will have heard you make a clear, direct statement challenging verbal abuse. Calling people's attention to something they assumed was innocent makes them more sensitive in the future and encourages them to stop and think about what they say about others.

Some of the other kinds of reactions you can expect are:

"It's only a joke." "It may 'only' be a joke but it is at someone's expense. It creates an environment that is less safe for the person or group being joked about. Abuse is not a joke."

"I didn't mean any harm." "I'm sure you didn't. But you should understand the harm that results even if you didn't mean it, and change what you say."

"Is this some kind of thought patrol?" "No, people can think whatever they want to. But we are responsible for what we say in public. A verbal attack is like any other kind of attack, it hurts the person attacked. Unless you intentionally want to hurt someone, you should not tell jokes or stories like this."

"This joke was told to me by a member of that group." "It really makes no difference who tells it. If it is offensive then it shouldn't be told. It is sad but true that some of us put down our own racial or ethnic group. That doesn't make it okay or less hurtful."

Sometimes the speaker will try to isolate you by saying that everyone else likes the story, everyone else laughed at the joke. At that point you might want to turn to the others and ask them if they like hearing jokes that are derogatory, do they like stories that attack people?

Sometimes the joke or derogatory comment will be made by a member of the racial group the comment is about. They may believe negative stereotypes about their racial group, they may want to separate themselves from others like themselves, or they may have accepted the racial norms of white peers in order to be accepted. In this situation it is more appropriate, and probably more effective, to talk to that person separately and express your concerns about how comments reinforce stereotypes and make the environment unsafe.

Speaking out makes a difference. Even a defensive speaker will think about what you said and probably speak more carefully in the future. I have found that when I respond to jokes or comments, other people come up to me afterwards and say they are glad I said something because the comments bothered them too but they didn't know what to say. Many of us stand around, uneasy but hesitant to intervene. By speaking out we model effective intervention and encourage other people to do the same. We set a tone for being active rather than passive, challenging racism rather than colluding with it.

The response to your intervention also lets you know whether the abusive comments are intentional or unintentional, malicious or not. It will give you information about whether the speaker is willing to take responsibility for the effects words have on others. We all have a lot to learn about how racism hurts people. We need to move on from our mistakes, wiser from the process. No one should be trashed.

If the speaker persists in making racially abusive jokes or comments, then further challenge will only result in arguments and fights. People around them need to take the steps necessary to protect themselves from abuse. You may need to think of other tactics to create a safe and respectful environment, including talking with peers to develop a plan for dealing with this person, or talking with a supervisor.

If you are in a climate where people are being put down, teased or made the butt of jokes based on their race, gender, sexual orientation, age or any other factor, you should investigate whether other forms of abuse such as sexual harassment or racial discrimination are occurring as well. Jokes and verbal abuse are obviously not the most important forms that racism takes. However, we all have the right to live, work and socialize in environments free from verbal and emotional harassment. In order to create contexts where white people and people of color can work together to challenge more fundamental forms of racism, we need to be able to talk to each other about the ways that we talk to each other.

DISCUSSION QUESTIONS

1.   When is anger about racism appropriate?
2.   What are some of the contradictions between the American ideals of equality and reality?

CREDITS

Eric Anderson, "Adolescent Masculinity in an Age of Decreased Homohysteria" from *Thymos: Journal of Boyhood Studies* 7, no. 1 (Spring 2013): 79. Reprinted with the permission of The Mens Studies Press, LLC.

Bradley A. Areheart, "Disability Trouble" from *Yale Law & Policy Review* 29 (2011): 347. Reprinted by permission.

Emily Askew, "(Re)creating a world in 7 days: Place, Disability and Salvation in *Extreme Makeover: Home Edition*" from *Disability Studies Quarterly* 31, no. 2 (2011). Reprinted with the permission of the author.

Timothy Beneke, "Proving Manhood" from *Proving Manhood: Reflections on Men and Sexism* (Berkeley: University of California Press, 1997), pp. 35–48. Reprinted with the permission of the author.

James H. Carr and Nandinee K. Kutty, "Wealth Stripping: Why It Costs So Much to Be Poor" from *Democracy: A Journal of Ideas* (Fall 2012) no. 26. Reprinted by permission.

Nicholas Dauphine, "Hispanics Are Forgotten in Civil Rights History" from *Education Week* (May 2014). Reprinted with the permission of the author.

F. James Davis, "Who Is Black? One Nation's Definition" (originally titled "The Nation's Rule") from *Who Is Black? One Nation's Definition*. Copyright © 1991 by The Pennsylvania State University. Reprinted with the permission of The Pennsylvania State University Press.

Lisa Diamond, excerpt from *Sexual Fluidity: Understanding Women's Love and Desire*. Copyright © 2008 by the President and Fellows of Harvard College. Reprinted by permission of Harvard University Press.

Alice Dreger, "The Olympic Struggle for Sex" from *The Atlantic Monthly* (July 2, 2013). Copyright © 2013 by Alice Dreger. Reprinted with the permission of the author.

Paula England, excerpts from "The Gendered Revolution: Stalled and Uneven" from *Gender & Society* 24, no. 2 (April 2010). Copyright © 2010 by Sociologists for Women in Society. Reprinted by permission of Sage Publications, Inc.

Cordelia Fine, "Gender Detectives" from *Delusions of Gender: How Our Minds, Society, and Neurosexism Create Difference*. Copyright © 2012 by Cordelia Fine. Used by permission of W.W. Norton & Company, Inc.

Ruth Frankenberg, "Whiteness as an 'Unmarked' Cultural Category" from *White Women, Race Matters*. Copyright © 1993 by the Regents of the University of Minnesota. Reprinted with the permission of the author and the University of Minnesota Press.

Sally French, "'Can You See the Rainbow?' The Roots of Denial" from John Swain, Vic Finkelstein, Sally French, and Mike Oliver (eds.), *Disabling Barriers—Enabling Environments*. Copyright © 1993 by The Open University. Reprinted by permission of Sage Publications, Ltd.

Eva Marie Garroutte, excerpt from *Real Indians: Identity and the Survival of Native America*. Copyright © 2003 by The Regents of the University of California. Reprinted with the permission of the University of California Press.

Malcolm Gladwell, excerpt from Chapter Three: "The Warren Harding Error: Why We Fall for Tall, Dark, and Handsome" from *Blink: The Power of Thinking Without Thinking*. Copyright © 2005 by Malcolm Gladwell. Reprinted by permission of Little, Brown and Company. All rights reserved.

Tanya Golash-Boza and William Darity Jr., excerpt from "Latino Racial Choices: The Effects of Skin Colour and Discrimination on Latinos' and Latinas' Racial Self-identifications" from *Ethnic and Racial Studies* 31.5 (July 2008): 899–934. Copyright © 2008 by Taylor & Francis. Reprinted with the permission of Taylor & Francis, Inc.

Paul Gorski, "The Myth of the 'Culture of Poverty'" from *Educational Leadership* 65, no. 7 (April 2008): 32–36. Copyright © 2008 by the Association for Supervision & Curriculum Development.

David Haines, "Safe Haven in America?" from *Global Studies Review* 6, no. 1 (Spring 2010). Reprinted with the permission of *Global Studies Review*, Center for Global Studies, George Mason University.

The following Personal Accounts have been reprinted with the permission of the authors:

Sumaya M. Al-Hajebi, "Master Status: Pride and Danger"

Andrea M. Busch, "Basketball"

C.C., "Where Are You From?"

Heather Callender, "A Time I Didn't Feel Normal"

Mireille M. Cecil, "Learning My Own Privilege"

Tara S. Ellison, "Living Invisibly"

Octavio N. Espinal, "Parents' Underestimated Love"

Sarah Faragalla, "Hair"

Ruth C. Feldsberg, "What's in a Name?"

Niah Grimes, "A Loaded Vacation"

Francisco Hernandez, "Just Something You Did as a Man"

Eric Jackson, "My Strategies"

Anthony McNeill, "Just Like My Mama Said"

Julia Morgenstern, "The Price of Nonconformity"

Isabelle Nguyen, "Let Me Work for It!"

Tim Norton, "He Hit Her"

Rose B. Pascarell, "That Moment of Visibility"

Sherri H. Pereira, "I Thought My Race Was Invisible"

Heather L. Shaw, "Invisibly Disabled"

Hoorie I. Siddique, "I Am a Pakistani Woman"

Hoai Huong Tran, "The Americanization of a Reluctant Vietnamese-American: Third of a Series"

Photo Credits

Section 1
Page 1: © John A. Rizzo/Getty Images RF

Section 2
Page 193: © Realistic Reflections RF

Section 3
Page 339: © Hisham F. Ibrahim/Getty Images RF; p. 392 (centre left): © Tomas Rodriguez/Fancy Collection/SuperStock RF; p. 392 (centre Left): © Purestock/Superstock RF; p. 392 (centre Right): © Tomas Rodriguez/Fancy Collection/SuperStock RF; p. 392 (centre Right): © Purestock/Superstock RF

Section 4
Page 481: © Evan Cantwell/Creative Services/George Mason University

INDEX

A page number followed by *fig* indicates an illustrated figure; one followed by *fn* indicates a footnote; one followed by *t* indicates a table.

ableism, 6, 43

abstinence education, 426–427

Adolescent Family Life Act
    of 1981, 426

"Adolescent Masculinity in an
    Age of Decreased Homohysteria," 492–501

adolescent boys
    heterosexual masculinities
        and, 492–501
    homohysteria and, 492–501
    homophobia and, 277–287
    immigrant identity development among girls
        and, 226–237
    new intimacies for, 49
    race and ethnic taunts among, 210

adversarial identities, 233

affirmative action
    college admissions and, 447
    legacy admissions and, 307–312
    Regents of the University of California and,
        375–378
    *Schutte v. Coalition to Defend Affirmative
        Action, Integration, and Immigration Rights
        and Fight for Equality by Any Means
        Necessary* (2013), 387–389
    whites' perceptions of black competence
        and, 38

African American exceptionalism, 22–23,
    111, 112

African Americans
    aggregate category of, 18
    changes in categorical names of, 9

arrest for drug offenses and, 199

athletic stereotypes about, 344–345

characteristics attributed to
    women, 40*fn*

construction of whiteness and, 111

Dred Scott v. Sanford (1857) and, 359–361

European immigrants
    compared to, 346

gay marriage and, 435–436

health and, 27, 216, 305

multiracial identification of, 21, 57

one drop rule and, 61–69

Plessy v. Ferguson (1896) and,
    364–367

residential segregation of, 403–405

self-esteem of, 219

stereotype threat and, 232

whites' perceptions of, 38, 196

African Diaspora, 59

Afrocentrism, 56–57

Afro-Latino, 246

Agassi, Andre, 255

age, master status of, 194

age-related impairments, 460–461

aggregate category, 15–20, 18, 43

AIDs-related deaths, 148

Aladdin (movie), 255

Alexander the Great, 52

Al-Fayed, Dodi, 255

Al-Hajebi, Sumaya, 258

Ali, Muhammad, 268

Alien Land Law of 1920, 17*fn*

"All Together Now: Intersex Infants And IGM," 117–123

Allen, Theodore, 55, 59

ally
definition of, 490
how to get and be an, 488–489
white and, 512–516

alternative financial services industry, 452

American Anthropological Association 1998 Statement on Race, 25

American as white, 22

American Breeders Association, 186

American Community Survey, 13, 16

American exceptionalism
construction of "defective black" and, 165
disability and, 165–166
income inequality and, 139

American Psychological Association, 11

American Sign Language, 176

American Sociological Association Statement on Importance of Collecting Data, 25

American/non-American, 22

"The Americanization of a Reluctant Vietnamese American," 239–241

Americans with Disabilities Act, 18, 165

Amherst College T-shirt, 39

anatomist perspective, 115–116

ancient world
ethnicity in, 51
kinship in, 51
racialized world view in, 51–54
slavery in, 52

Anderson, Eric, 492–501

androcentrism, 19, 43

Androgen Insensitivity Syndrome, 116

androgens, 116

anger, 511–512

Anglo, 9

Anglo-Saxonism, 55

Anka, Paul, 255

Anti-discrimination laws, 14–15

antifeminism, 274

anti-miscegenation statutes, 65

Anti-Terrorism and Effective Death Penalty Act, 201

Anwar, Gabrielle, 255

Arab/Middle Easterners
assimilability and, 253–254
Census category and, 14, 23
covering, 256–259
religion and, 253–254
selective racialization and, 254–256

Areheart, Bradley A., 456–467

Ashe, Arthur, 212

Asian American Movement, 83–84

Asian American panethnicity, 80, 83

Asian Americans
aggregate category of, 16–17
"almost white" as, 110–111
diversity of, 22*fn*, 82
English language and, 85
model minority myth and, 42, 86, 345–347
national-origin categories of, 17*fn*
"perpetual foreigners" and, 22
San Francisco Bay Area and, 80–89
undocumented immigrants and, 399–401

Asian Indians, 17*fn*

Asian Pacific Americans, *see* Asian Americans

Askew, Emily, 473–480

assimilation, 90, 93, 94

Association of Children with Learning Disabilities, 468

asylum seekers, 397–398

attractiveness, 38

audit studies, 213

auto-title lenders, 452

aversive racism, 347, 348, 356

Ayatolla Khomeini, 255

Bacon's Rebellion, 55

Badget, M.V. Lee, 440–441

Bailey, Michael, 147, 149–150

Bakke, University of California Board of Regents v. (1978), 309, 375–378

"Balancing Identities: Undocumented Immigrant Asian American Students and the Model Minority Myth," 399–401

Baldwin, James, 67

Bartkey, Sandra, 218
"Basketball," 115
Basow, Susan, 35
Bean, Frank D., 22, 107–114
The Bell Curve, 58
bell hooks, 209
Bell, Alexander Graham, 186
Bell, Catherine, 255
Beneke, Timothy, 267–272
Beyond Gay and Straight Marriage, 436–437
"bi erasure," 29
BiDil, 27
bilingual education, 372–373
bilingualism, 225
bin Laden, Osama, 255
Binet, Alfred, 351–352
"The Biology of the Homosexual," 147–157
"biphobia," 29
birdcage metaphor, 340
bisexuality, 29, 30, 142–147, 299
Black American ethnic groups, 23
Black Cubans, 246
Black Panamanians, 246
Black Power movement, 9, 246
"black"
   history of changing terminology,
     9, 63
   Latin American definitions of, 66
black/non black divide, 110–111
black/non-black dichotomy, 22
blackface, 354–355
Blackmun, Harry A., 309
blindness
   asking for help and, 334
   borderline, 331–338
   employment and, 329–330
   expectations about, 325–326
   legal blindness and, 331–338
   passing as sighted and, 208, 335–337
   pressures to deny, 325–331
   stereotypes about, 332–333
"Blink in Black and White," 390–394
blood quantum
   "card-carrying Indian" and, 72
   definitions of, 71, 72, 74

Native American authenticity
   and, 73
   one drop rule vs., 75
   Shania Twain and, 72–73
   tribal citizenship and, 71–79
Boas, Franz, 354
boomerang children, 134
"brown paper bag test," 75
Brown v. Board of Education (1954), 370–372
Buck v. Bell (1927), 352
Buckley, William F. Jr, 308
bullying, 429
Busch, Andrea M., 115

C.C., 511
California prison riots, 94
Callendar, Heather, 337
"'Can You See the Rainbow?': The Roots of
   Denial," 325–331
Cantril, Hadley, 3
capitalist class, 128–129
"card-carrying Indian," 72
Carr, James H., 452–456
Cash Assistance Program, 42
categorical distinctions, 298
categorical inequalities, 20–21
categories of people, creating, 11–15
"Cause of death: Inequality," 303–306
Cecil, Mireille M., 432
-centric and -centrism, 43
Charles, Suzette, 62
Chase, Cheryl, 118–120
Chasing Amy (movie), 142
Cher, 255
Chicago ex-gang members, 163–176
Chicano and Chicanismo, 9
child rearing, and devaluation of women, 416
childhood poverty, 444
The Children of Sanchez, 313
children's clothing, 123–124
Chinese Exclusion Act, 349
Chinese immigrants in
   Mississippi, 111
Cho, Margaret, 250

Citizenship Schools, 483
Civil Rights Act of 1964, 12, 107
Civil Rights movement
    Hispanics and, 398–399
    U.S, immigration policy and, 346
Civil War Amendments, 361–361
Civil War, 21, 56
Clarke, Edward, 351
Clausen, Jan, 142
Clinton, Bill, 42
Clinton, Hillary, 215
closet, 207
Clueless (movie), 257
cochlear implants, 176, 184, 185
code-switching, 225
coethnic identities, 233–234
"collective Black," 109
college, *see* higher education
Collins, Patricia Hill, 215
color blindness, 217
color line, 108
"colored," 64
Commission on Civil Rights, 12
compulsive masculinity, 267–270
    Boy Scout Manual of 1914 and, 268
    definition of, 267
    sexism and, 270
    stress of, 267–272
Congenital Adrenal Hyperplasia, 116
Connell, R.J., 498–499
Constitution, U.S., 275
constructionist and essentialist perspectives,
        3–7
    definition of, 43
    race and, 27
    sexuality terminology and, 4
    social movements and, 4
    social sciences and, 4
    tale of three umpires and, 3
Cool Rich Kids Movement, 509–510
covering
    four axes of, 256
    Middle Easterners and, 256–259
crack vs. cocaine powder, 199
Crash (movie), 23

"A Credo for Support," 489
Crenshaw, Kimberlé, 214
"crip," 165
cultural capital, 133
culture of poverty
    classism and, 314–315
    history of idea of, 313
    myths vs. reality of, 313–314
    research on, 313
culture, 227
    disability and, 456–467
Cypher, Julie, 142

Darity, William Jr., 16, 89–100
Darwin, Charles, 350
Dauphine, Nicholas, 398–399
Davis, F. James, 21, 61–69
Dawes Act, 74
Deaf World, 176–191
    boundaries between hearing world and,
        179–180
    definition of, 176
    ethnic group and, 176–191
    eugenics and, 186–187
    kinship and, 178–179
    language and, 177–178, 181–182
    sense of community and, 177
    socialization into, 178
deafness
    debate about disability of, 181
    hereditary proportion of,
        179, 186, 187
    professional associations and, 182–183
    rejection of disability status of, 183–188
    sexuality/race/gender comparison with,
        181–182
Declaration of Independence, 275
Defense of Marriage Act (DOMA), 203, 385–387
deficit perspective, 314–315
DeGeneres, Ellen, 142
"Delusions of Gender: How Our Minds, Society,
        and Neuroscience Create Difference,"
        123–127
deportation, 201

The Descent of Man (1871), 350
description vs. stereotype, 344
Diamond, Lisa M., 29, 142–147
"dichotomania," 21*fn*
dichotomization, 20–35
  definition of, 44
  disability and, 34
  race and, 21–23
  sex/gender and, 30–32
  sexuality and, 28–30, 298–299
  social class and 32–34
differential arrest rates, 199
differential undercount, 44
"Disability Definitions: The Politics of Meaning,"
  159–162
"Disability Trouble," 456–467
disability
  aggregate category of, 17–18
  ally for, 489
  blindness as, 325–338
  "brave sufferer" and, 474–475
  built environment and, 473–480
  Christianity and, 476–477
  definition of, 5, 11, 34, 159–160, 456–457
  denying, 325–331
  "deserving" and 464–475
  employment and, 159, 329–330
  "enfreakment" and 478–479
  gunshot wounds and, 164
  home makeover and, 474–475
  learning disabilities as, 6
  panethnic groups and, 17–18
  "personal failure" and, 475–476
  race and, 164–165
  sensory impairments and, 459
  social and medical models of, 165–166
  social class and, 164–165
  social construction of, 5
  stigma and, 38–41
  story telling and, 169
  Tennessee v. Lane (2004) and, 378–380
  transportation and, 317–324
  U.N. Convention on the Rights of Persons with
    Disabilities, and, 6
disabled ex-gang members

illness narratives of, 169
  medical model of disability and, 169
  story telling by, 169
  war veterans and, 166–167
disablement vs. impairment,
  456–457
disaggregate, 16, 44
discreditable stigma, 206–209, 220
discredited stigma, 209–212, 220
discrimination
  prejudice vs., 217
  role of unconscious and, 390–394
diseases of affluence, 304–305
"diversity," 2
Dominican immigrants, 92–93
Dorris, Michael, 77
double consciousness, 209, 220, 230, 341
Douglass, Frederick, 64, 355
Dovidio, John, 347
Dred Scott v. Sanford (1857), 359–361
Dreger, Alice, 31, 115–117
"driving while black," 200
"driving while brown," 200
D'Souza, Denish, 308
Dubois, W.E.B., 9, 108, 209, 341, 354
"Dude, You're a Fag: Adolescent Male
  Homophobia," 277–287
Duggan, Lisa, 424
durability of inequality, 21

eating disorders, 459–460
Edelin, Ramona H., 9
education
  negative presentation of homosexuality and,
    425–427
  perpetuation of inequality and, 447–452
  racial segregation of, 370–372
  San Antonio School District v. Rodriguez
    (1973), 373–375
  Sputnik satellite and, 468–469
effeminacy, 37
Elizabeth Armstrong, 287–297
Elk v. Wilkins (1884), 368–370
Ellis Island, 352

Ellison, Tara S., 297
employment discrimination,
    legal/illegal forms of, 417
    Ricci v. DeStefano (2009) and, 383–385
    women and, 405–423
Engels, Friedrich, 340
England, Paula, 415–424
entitlement, 204–205, 220
Erikson, Erik, 226
Espinal, Octavio N., 506
Espiritu, Yen Le, 80–81
essential identity
    definition of, 29–30, 44
    sexuality and, 30
essentialism
    and stereotypes, 345
    definition of, 44
essentialist and constructionist perspectives, *see*
        constructionist and essentialist perspectives
estate tax, 133
Etheridge, Melissa, 142
ethnic enclave, 228
ethnic flight, 234
ethnic identity
    ancient world and, 51–60
    ethnic activities and, 228–229
    grandchildren of European immigrants
        and, 219
ethnicity, 23, 44, 177*t*
    ethnie, 178
    Statistical Directive No. 15, Office of
        Management and Budget and, 12
    U.S. Census categories and, 11–15, 70
"Ethnicity, Ethics, and the Deaf World,"
        176–191
ethos of reception, 229
eugenics, 186–187, 352–353
Eurocentric, 19, 43
Europe, 18*fn*
European immigrants vs. African
        Americans, 346
Europeans
    "people in the boat" as, 19
    aggregate category as, 18*fn*
"Everybody's Ethnic Enigma," 248, 251

execution rates, 42
ex-gang members, 163–176
experiencing social status, 194
Extreme Makeover: Home Edition, 473–480

Facebook, 31
"fag,"
    discourse and, 281
    trope and, 37
    adolescents and, 277–283
Fair Deal, 33
Fair Labor Standards Act of 1938, 399
Fair Sentencing Act of 2010, 199
family wage, 436
Faragalla, Sarah, 236
Fausto-Sterling, Anne, 118
federalism, 359
female hyperandrogenism, 116
feminism, 272–276
    avoidance of term, 272–273
    gender norms and, 275–276
    patriarchy and, 276
    power and, 273
    sexuality and, 276
    unacceptability of, 273–274
    stereotypes about, 273
"feminization" of higher education, 411–414
Fifteenth Amendment (1870), 362
"finding blacks, losing Indians," 75
Fine, Cordelia, 123–127
First Americans in the Arts, 73
Flag Wars (movie), 436
"flaunting" sexuality, 203
Flutie, Doug, 255
Forbes, Jack, 75
forced sterilizations, 352–53
foreclosures, 452
"Formulating Identity in a Globalized World,"
        225–238
Foucault, Michel, 118, 432, 433
Fourteenth Amendment (1868), 361–362
Frankenberg, Ruth, 101–106
Frazier, E. Franklin, 354
Frazier, Joe, 268

Freedom Riders, 399
Freire, Paolo, 483–485
French, Sally, 325–331
"From Friendly Foreigner to Enemy Race,"
    251–261
Frye, Marilyn, 340

Gaertner, Samuel, 347
"Gaga Relations: The End of Marriage," 432–439
Gallup Polls,
    interracial marriage attitudes and, 344
    sexuality attitudes and, 4–5
Gandhi's paradox, 490, 503, 507
gangs, 163–176
    family and, 170
    internal Other and, 166
    relations of debt/obligation and, 164
    vengeance and, 171
Gans, Herbert, 111
Garroutte, Eva Marie, 71–79
"gay brain," 147–149
"gay gene," 150–156
gay marriage, 432–439
    case against, 434–439
    civil rights and, 436
    race and, 435
    reactive politics of, 435
    social class and, 434
    Supreme Court and, 385–387
Gay Pride marches, 42
gay twins studies, 149–150
"gay," 9 fn
gay/lesbian
    aggregate category of, 18–19
    changing attitudes toward, 203
    myth of affluence of, 440–441
    poverty and, 440–441
gender detectives, 125
Gender Identity Disorder, 120
"Gender Revolution: Uneven and Stalled,"
    415–424
gender (see also sex)
    American cultural values and, 40, 415
    asymmetric change in, 415–424

career aspirations and, 412–413
changing conceptions of, 31, 415
characteristics attributed to, 39–40
children's clothing and, 123–124
college and, 411–413
definition of, 31, 44
employment and, 413, 416–420
essentialism and, 415
essentialism vs. individualism and,
    421–422
facility inequality and, 405–406
female-valued characteristics and, 39–40
feminism and, 275–276
immigrant youth adaptation and, 234
left/right handedness analogy to, 124–125
life expectancy and, 303–304
mortality inequality and, 405
mortality rates and, 407–408
natality inequality and, 405–406
occupational reference group and, 420
ownership inequality and, 406
pay gap and, 413–414, 417
professional inequality and, 406
relationship imperative and, 290–291
slut stigma and, 289–290
special opportunity inequality and, 406
transgender and, 30
"Gendered Sexuality in Young Adulthood: Double
    Binds and Flawed Options," 287–297
General Allotment (Dawes) Act of 1887, 74
George, Jeff, 255
The German Ideology (1846), 340
Gini Index, 138
Gini, Corrado, 138
girl/woman boy/man, word choice of, 10
Gladwell, Malcolm, 347, 390–394
Goddard, Robert H., 352,
Goffman, Erving, 40, 206, 256,
Golash-Boza, Tanya, 16, 89–100
Gorski, Paul, 40, 313–317
Gramsci, Antonio, 341
Grant, Madison, 67
Gratz v. Bollinger et al (2003), 380–381,
    382–383
Great Chain of Being, 55

Great Depression, 139

"The Great Divergence: America's Growing Inequality Crisis and What We Can Do about It," 137–142

Great Migration of 1920s, 354

Grimes, Niah, 71,

gunshot wounds, 164

Haines, David W., 345, 393, 398

"Hair," 236

Halberstam, J. Jack, 432–439

Hamer, Dean, 147, 150–156

Hamilton, Laura, 287–297

"handicapped," 11

"happy slave" image, 355

Harlan, John Marshall, 365

Harlem Renaissance, 354

Hart-Celler Act, 107

"has-bian," 142

hate crimes, 39

Hayek, Salma, 255

"He Hit Her," 410

health/illness
    access to health care and, 304
    race/gender/social class and, 303–304
    health-wealth connection and, 134–136

health-wealth gradient, 136

hearing impaired, vs. Deaf World, 176

Heche, Anne, 142

hegemonic ideology, 341, 356

hegemonic masculinity theory, 498–499

height, 393–394

Herek, Gregory, 20

heritability
    homosexuality and, 155–156
    scienific understanding of, 154–155

"herm," 118

hermaphrodite, 118

Hermaphrodites with Attitude, 118

Hernandez v. Texas (1954), 399

Hernandez, Francisco, 271

Herodotus, 54

heterocentric, 43

heteroflexibility, 142

heteronormativity
    definition of, 19–20, 44, 425
    depictions of superiority of, 427–428
    examples of, 202–203
    inclusive masculinity and, 499–500
    state and federal educational policy and, 424–425

heterosexism, 20

"The Heterosexual Questionnaire," 28, 158

hierarchy, 349–350

higher education
    admissions to, 387–389
    affirmative action and, 387–389
    class privileges and, 204
    financial aid and, 451–452
    gender graduation rates and, 411–412
    race/ethnicity graduation rates and, 345, 411–412
    social change vs. powerlessness and, 203–204, 411–412, 482–483
    social class vs. race and, 447–448

Highlander Folk School, 483–485

"Hispanics Are Forgotten in Civil Rights History," 398–399

Hispanics, federal use of term, 7

Hispanics, *see* Latinos/Hispanics

HIV/AIDS, 495

Hockenberry, John, 6, 317–324

Holima, Mahmoud Abu, 321

Hollibaugh, Amber, 439–442

Holmes, Oliver Wendell, 352

home foreclosures, 455

Home Improvement (TV show), 269

homohysteria
    decrease in since 1980s, 495–496
    era of, 494–495
    inclusive masculinity theory and, 492
    situations of low, 498–499

homophobia
    adolescent males and, 277–285
    adolescent opposition to, 497–498
    gendered, 278–281
    origin and meaning of term, 19–20

"homosexual," 9

homosexuality
  media on causes of, 154
  public schools and pathologization of, 425–427
  biological cause of, 150–156
  social Darwinism and, 351
"honorary whites," 109
"hook ups," 293–294
Horne, Lena, 62–63
Horton, Myles, 483–485
Human Genome Project, 26
hyperandrogenism, 116
hypersegregation, 343
hypodescent, 63, 244, 225
hypothalamus, 147–149

"I Am a Pakistani Woman, 135
"I Grew Up Thinking I Was White," 256–257
"I Thought My Race Was Invisible," 89
identification-assimilation hypothesis, 94
identity
  ancient world and, 51–54
  self-selected label and, 228,
ideology, 33, 340–341, 356
  built environment and, 473–480
  individual merit and, 341
  popular culture and, 354–355
"If he gets a nosebleed, he'll turn into a white," 72
Illegal Immigration Reform and Immigrant Responsibility Act, 201
illness narratives, 169
"'I'm Not a Feminist But …':
  Popular Myths about Feminism," 272–277
immersion stage of identity development, 219
immigrant youth, 225–242
  adversarial stance and, 233
  assimilation of, 231–232
  coethnic identity among, 233–224
  ethnic flight and, 234
  ethos of reception and, 231
  family and, 226, 228
  gender and, 234
  identity performance and, 228–229
  transcultural identities and, 234–235

immigrants
  first vs. second generation experiences of, 226
  racialization and, 245
  refugees vs., 225, 345
  stressors of, 225–226
  whiteness and, 22
Immigration Act of 1917, 17fn
Immigration and Nationality Act, 82
Immigration Restriction Act of 1924, 353
immigration
  family-based admissions and, 397
  IQ testing and, 353–354
  U.S. policy since 1965, 346
impairment
  continuum of, 462
  cultural production of, 161–162
  definition of, 5, 11, 44
  disablement and, 456–457
  medical diagnosis and, 457–458
  social class and, 161–162
  social construction of, 457–467
Implicit Association Test (IAT), 347, 390–394
"In Defense of Rich Kids," 507–510
incarceration rates, 199–200
inclusive fitness-maximizing theory of selection, 132
inclusive masculinities, 492–502
  heteronormativity of, 499–500
  increased emotional intimacy and, 496
  physical touching and, 496–497
  violence and, 497
  theory of, 492–492, 498–499
income inequality
  heritability of, 140fig
  1948 compared to 2001, 446
  global, 138
  ill health and, 305
  increase in, 33, 139
  U.S. levels of, 137–139
inconvenient bodies, 118
index of dissimilarity, 420
Indian Removal Act of 1830, 349
Indians, *see* Native Americans
individualism vs. gender essentialism, 421–422
inherited advantages, 132–137

intellectual impairments, 462–463
intelligence testing, 352–354
inter vivos transfers, 133–134
interaction effect, 214
intergenerational race to get ahead, 131*fig*
interlocking panethnicity, 81–82
"An Interlocking Panethnicity: The Negotiation of
    Multiple Identitites among Asian American
    Social Movement Leaders," 80–88
interracial marriage
    acceptance of, 343–344
    rates of, 344
intersectionality, 214–216, 263–264
    definition of, 4, 44, 81, 220
    interaction effect and, 214
    sexuality and, 291–293
Intersex Society of North America, 118
intersex
    definition of, 118
    estimates of the rates of, 118
    genital mutilation (IGM) and, 119–123
    hermaphrodism and, 118
intra-racial murder rates, 42
invention of the white race, 55
"invisible black ancestry," 36
"Invisibly Disabled," 163
IQ testing
    immigrants and, 352
    immigration restrictions and, 353–354
    learning disability and, 468–471
Iranians
    Jews as, 257
    Arabs distinguished from, 23
    Iranian-Americans, 256, 259
Irish immigrants and whiteness, 21–22, 110

Jackson, Eric, 249–250
Jane Doe v. State of Louisiana (1983), 65
Janus-faced nature of society, 483, 490,
Japanese Americans, 111
Jews
    intelligence stereotypes about, 42
    Ivy League universities exclusion of, 308–309
    women, 40*fn*

Jim Crow laws, 206, 206*fn*, 364–365
Johnson, Allan G., 502–507
jokes, 514–516
judicial notice, 64
Judith Butler, 457
"Just Something You Did as a Man," 271

Kanter, Rosabeth Moss, 210
Kasem, Casy, 255
Kennedy, Edward, 395
Kennedy, Florynce, 209
Kimmel, Michael, 10, 268
King, Martin Luther, 446–447
Kissing Jessica Stein (movie), 142
Kivel, Paul, 511–516
Kroeber, Alfred, 354
Kwan, Michelle, 22

Lady Gaga, 435
Lancaster, Roger, 5, 147–157
Lane, Harlan, 23, 176, 191
Lapinsky, Tara, 22
Larew, John, 307–312, 488
Latin Americanization thesis, 110
Latino National Political Survey, 93, 96–97
"Latino Racial Choices: The Effects of Skin
    Colour and Discrimination on Latinos'
    and Latinas' Racial Self-Identification,"
    89–100
Latinos/Hispanics
    2050 population estimates for, 89
    aggregate category of, 16
    assimilation and, 94
    characteristics attributed to females, 40*fn*
    civil rights movement and, 398–399
    health services for, 216
    naming preferences of, 8, 16
    police stops of, 201
    racial and ethnic identifications of,
        16, 89–100, 242–248
    racialized ethnic label of, 90
    racism and, 245
    social class and, 243
Lau v. Nichols (1974), 372–373

lawful permanent resident
    defined, 201
    grounds for deportation, 201
learning disabilities, 468–473
    1960s history of, 468–469
    history of, 6
    teacher attitudes and, 471
    1970s diagnoses, 471
    organic vs. environmental causes, 470–471
"Learning My Own Privilege," 432
Lee, Jennifer, 22, 107–114
left/right handedness analogy to gender, 124–125
legacy admissions, 203–204, 307–312
legal blindness, 332
lesbians
    sexual activity and, 301–302
    sexual identity defined, 145
    sexuality research about, 299–300
"Let Me Work for It," 402
LeVay, Simon, 147–149
Lewis, Oscar, 313
LGBTQ, 10
Liddy, G. Gordon, 269
life chances, 210
life expectancy
    global comparisons of, 304
    inheritance and, 134–135
    sex/gender and, 303–304
Lincoln, Robert, 62
lineal tribal citizenship, 71
literacy, 468, 483
"Living Invisibly," 297
"A Loaded Vacation," 71
looping and rereading, 205–206, 220
Louima, Abner, 348
Loving v. Virginia (1967), 343–344

Madonna, 142
Mailer, Norman, 268
Mainardi, Pat, 274
male-valued characteristics, 39–40
mammy image, 355
"man as jerk' archetype, 498
"The Many Faces of Gender Inequality," 405–410

marked and unmarked statuses, 38, 204–205, 220
marriage (*see also* gay marriage)
    alternative intimacies and, 436–437
    exclusionary institution of, 433
    oppressive ideology of, 438–439
Marmot, Michael, 304, 306
Marshall, Thurgood, 59
Martin, Trayvon, 197
Marx, Karl, 340
masculinity
    behaviors that must be avoided and, 37
    effeminacy and, 37
    rejection of hypermasculinity and, 493–494
mass media
    selective racialization in, 255–256
    under-reporting of white criminality in, 198–199
master status
    age as, 194
    definition of, 2, 44
"Master Status: Pride and Danger," 258
McIntosh, Peggy, 195–196, 262–263
McLeod, Jelita, 4, 248–251
McNamee, Stephen J., 131–137, 341
McNeill, Anthony, 395
McNeill, Tanya, 424–431
Mean Girls (movie), 210
medical diagnoses, 458–462
medical model of disability, 7, 169, 174 (*see also* social and medical models of disability)
Men in Black (movie), 194
men
    characteristics attributed to, 39–40
    femininity and, 37
    women's fields and, 421
Mencia, Carlos, 8
Mendez, et al, v. Westminster School (1946), 399
mental illness, 458–461
merit scholarships, 451
meritocracy, 134, 139, 263–264, 307–312
Messner, Michael A., 261–267
mestizaje, 242
mestizo, 91
methamphetamine users, 198–199

Mexican Americans
  race and, 21
  treatment prior to civil rights movement,
    398–399
  triracial hierarchy and, 110
Mexican-American War, 349
Michigan state constitution, 387–389
microaggression, 210, 220
middle class, 129–130
Middle East, regional identification of, 17
Middle Eastern Americans, 251–261
  aggregate category of, 17
  avoidance of activism/politics, 257
  covering and, 256–259
  enemy aliens and, 254
  Other as, 253–254
  selective racialization of, 254–256
  surveillance of, 201
  use of term, 251–252
  "white" and, 253, 257–258
Miller, Robert K. Jr., 131–137
Minor v. Happersett (1875), 362–363
minority group
  analogy to blacks and, 109
  benefits of status of, 107
  disability and, 159
  history of term, 12
minstrel shows, 252, 354–355
mirage of health, 34
mirror metaphor, 195
Miss America Pageant, 62
"missing women," 408
Mitchell, George, 255
model minority myth, 86, 345–347
  Asian American undocumented students and,
    400–401
  recent invention of, 345
  transformation from "yellow horde" to, 111
  African Americans and, 345–346
morbidity, 303
Morgan, Edmund, 56
Morgenstern, Julia, 114
Morrison, Toni, 22
mortality, 405, 407–408
mulatto, 70*fig*, 55, 63, 64, 91

Mullen, Ann, 411–414
multiracial
  identification, 107–114
  families' experience of, 202
  Native Americans as, 73
  problematic identity of, 57
  U.S. Census designation of, 14
Muppets, 194
"My Strategies," 249–250
myth of "no effect," 503–504
"The Myth of the 'Culture of Poverty'," 313–317
mythopoetic men's movement, 268

Nader, Ralph, 255
Najimi, Kathy, 255
Nakano, Dana Y., 80–88
names/naming, 7–11
natality inequality, 405–406
National Commission on Teaching and America's
    Future, 315
National Commission on the Causes and
    Prevention of Violence, 268
national origins quotas, 67
National Security Entry-Exit Registration System
    (NSEERS), 200–201, 254
National Survey of Latinos, 92
nationality churches, 219*fn*
Native Americans,
  aggregate category, 18
  appearance and ceremonial roles of, 76–77
  blood quantum measure of, 71, 72, 74, 71–79
  "card-carrying Indians" and, 72
  characteristics attributed to women, 40*fn*
  Constitutional definition of, 72
  discrimination against, 75–76
  expropriation of territories of, 349
  forced relocation of, 349
  full vs. mixed bloods and, 73–74
  "person outside the boat" as, 18
  tribal citizenship, rights and benefits, 71–73
Nativism, 56
natural law language, 341–344, 356
natural selection, 350
"natural," 341–342

Naturalization Act of 1906, 108–109
nature/nurture debate
    Charles Darwin and, 350
    human variation and, 349
    implicit rankings and, 349
Near, Holly, 142
negative social mirror, 230–231
Negritude, 56
"Negro," 9, 64
neoliberalism, 34
Never Say Never, 297
New Deal, 33, 404
New World, 56
Nguyen, Isabelle, 402
Nixon, Cynthia, 142
no promo hetero, 424
"no race" position, 25
Noah, Timothy, 33, 137–142
non-profit organizations, 87
Norton, Tim, 410
"Not Blind Enough: Living in the Borderland
    Called Legal Blindness," 331–338
"The Not-So-Pink Ivory Tower," 411–414
NSEERS, 200–201, 254

Obama, Barack, 21, 215, 485–486
objectification, 38, 44
occupation, ancient world role of, 51
occupational health hazards, 136
occupations, sex segregation of 419*fig*
Occupy Wall Street movement, 33
octoroon, 64, 70*fig*
Office of Management and Budget, 12
O'Leary, Hazel, 59
Oliver, Michael, 7, 11, 159–162
Olympic Committee
    anatomists and identifiers, 115–116
    Stockholm Consensus and, 116
    transsexual athletes and, 116
    women athletes and, 115–116
"The Olympic Struggle over Sex," 115–117
Omansky, Beth, 208, 331–338
On Our Backs, 142
one drop rule, 21, 63–67

anti-miscegenation and, 65, 67
applied to other American racial groups, 68
assimilation and, 68
blood quantum vs., 75
ethnicity and, 67
Native Americans and, 65
Passing of the Great Race and, 67
Plessy v. Ferguson (1896) and, 364–365
South Africa and, 21
one black ancestor rule, 63
opportunity costs, 416–417
oppositional racial consciousness, 18
oppression, 340
    instability of, 503
    interlocking systems of, 81
    interview questions and, 160–161
    resisting, 502–507
    scientific method and, 160–161
Organization for Economic Cooperation and
    Development, 138
Origin of the Species (1859), 350
Oscar Wilde, 349
other sex, vs. opposite sex, 144
Other
    constructing the, 35–37, 44
    gang members as, 166
    Middle Eastern Americans as, 253–254
    risks of associating with, 36–37
    sanctions against those who associate with the,
        36–37
    social control mechanism of, 37
other-sex sexuality, 144
overlapping normal curves, 35
ownership inequality, 406
owning a social problem, 182

panethnic/panethnicity, 80–89
    definition of, 17, 44, 80
    disability as, 17–18
    interlocking, 81–82
    nationality self-identification vs., 228
    protest chants as example of, 80
    recognizing ethnic groups within, 84
    social movements and, 17

panethnic/panethnicity (*Continued*)
  theories about, 80
  utility and stability of, 17
paraplegic and quadriplegic, 168
parental desire to secure children's future, 132
parental rescue, 134
"Parents' Underestimated Love," 506
Parks, Rosa, 483
Pascarell, Rose, 312
Pascoe, C.J., 37, 277–287
passing
  as white, 36, 67–68, 206–207
  as black, 67–68
  being in the closet as, 207
  blindness and, 208, 333–334
  definition of, 220
  discreditable stigma and,
    206–209
  immigration and, 227
  Middle Eastern Americans and, 257
  positive and negative aspects of, 208–209
  sexuality and, 207
  unwitting acceptance by others and, 208
The Passing of the Great Race (1916), 67
pastoralism, 104
paternalism, 41
Patino, Maria, 116
patriarchy, 276
payday loans, 452
pecan shellers' strike of 1938, 399
"pedigree study," 150
"people first" language, 11
"people just want to be with their own kind,"
    343–344
People Like Us (movie), 212*fn*
"people of color," 109
People v. Hall, (1854), 21
perceptions of discrimination, 41–42
perceptions of whiteness, 101–106
Pereira, Sherri, 89
performing identity, 228–229
"perpetual foreigner" syndrome, 227
"personal is political," 418
Personal Responsibility Act, 426
Personal Responsibility Education Program, 427

pharmaceutical industries, 459
philanthropy, 507–510
Phipps, Susie Guillory, 65–66
physicalist, 19
Pillard, Richard, 147, 149–150
pink triangle, 207
Plessy v. Ferguson (1896), 21, 64, 342,
    364–365
Plus ça Change …? Multiraciality and the
    Dynamics of Race Relations in the
    United States," 107–114
"plus-one" model, 437
Polikoff, Nancy D., 436–437
Poon Tambascia, Tracy, and Jonathan Wang,
    Breanne Tcheng, and Viet T Bui, 399–401
poor whites, 55–56
pornography, 495–496
poverty
  community college enrollments and, 448
  community effects of, 443–444
  economic recession of 2008 and, 445
  moral problem for society and, 446
  musical chairs analogy and, 445
  rising life-course risk of, 444
  social opportunities and, 444–445
  structural failing and, 445–446
Powell, Adam Clayton, 62
power evasion, 217
power, 127–130, 216–217
powerlessness, 482–483
Pratt, Minnie Bruce, 145
preemptive violence, 196–197
prejudice
  aversive racism and, 347–348
  discrimination vs., 217
  new forms of, 347–48
"The Price of Nonconformity," 114
Primetime: What Would You Do? (TV show), 196
Princess Diana, 255
prison population, 199–200
"The Privilege of Teaching about Privilege,"
    261–267
privilege
  ability to exclude as, 216–217
  daily experience of, 261–267

definition of, 220
experience of, 194–206
invisibility of, 195, 205
not being seen as criminal and, 197–200
preemptive violence and, 196–197
race/ethnicity and, 201, 102, 195–202
resisting, 502–507
sexuality and, 202–203, 292–293
social class and, 203–204
stigma compared to, 216–217
teaching about, 264–266
prostate cancer, 27
"Proving Manhood," 267–272
"Public Transit," 317–324
Puerto Rican racial identity, 93

quadroon, 64, 70 *fig*
Queen Victoria, 405
Queer Eye (TV show), 10
Queer Nation, 9
"Queers Without Money," 439–442
quotas, 346

race differences
    college graduation rates and, 411–412
    crime/arrest/incarceration rates and, 42,
        199–200
    health/illness and, 216, 303, 306
    higher education and, 380–383
    immigrant youth identity development
        and, 227
    Implicit Association Test and,
        390–394
    internet daters and, 344
    learning problems diagnoses and, 469–471
    mass media and, 198–199
    perceptions of discrimination and, 41–42
    preemptive violence and, 196–197
    privilege and, 195–202
    wealth loss and, 452–455
race
    ancient world and, 51–61
    Asian Indians and, 17 *fn*

birth certificates and, 66
contemporary folk story of, 27–28
defining, 23–28, 44
Human Genome Project and, 26
Latino/Hispanic classifications of, 89–99,
    242–248
multiraciality and, 107–114
"no race position" and, 25
one drop rule of, 61–69
social concept of, 27
stages of identity development and, 217–219
Statistical Directive No. 15, Office of
    Management and Budget and, 12
U.S. Census categories and, 11–15, 70
racial profiling, 200–202
racialization, 252–259
racialized social structure, 24
racism
    color blind, 217
    high blood pressure among Blacks, 305
    jokes/taunts and, 210, 504–505, 514–516
    new forms of, 347–348
radical feminism, 274
Ralph, Laurence, 7, 163–176
Rank, Mark R., 443–447
Raza, 244
"Real Indians: Identity and the Survival of Native
    America," 71–79
recession of 2007–2009, 33, 138–139, 452, 445
"(Re)creating a World in Seven Days: Place,
    Disability, and Salvation in *Extreme
    Makeover: Home Edition*," 473–480
redlining, 403
Reeves, Christopher, 169
refugees, 395–398
    distinctiveness to, 396–397
    education and, 396
    English language competence of, 396
    immigrants, comparison to, 396–397
    numbers of, 397
Regents of the University of California v. Bakke
    (1978), 375–378
relational double bind, 292–294
rereading, 205–206
residential segregation, 403–405

"Rethinking American Poverty," 443–447
Reuss, Alejandro, 303–306
reverse discrimination, 213
reverse inheritance, 132
Ricci v. DeStefano (2009), 213, 383–385
Ridgeway, Cecilia, 44
Right to Vote, 362
Rist, Darryl, 5
Roberts, Dorothy, 26
Rochlin, Martin, 28, 158
Rodriguez, Clara E., 242–248
Rothblum, Esther D., 28, 297–303
Rothstein, Richard, 343, 403–405
Royster, Diedre, 213
Russell, Bill, 345

Sacks, Peters, 447–452
"Safe Haven in America? Thirty Years after the
    Refugee Act of 1980," 395–398
Salazar, Ruben, 9
San Antonio School District v. Rodriguez (1973),
    373–375
San Francisco Bay area, 80–89
Sapir, Edward, 354
SAT exam, 449–450
Saturday Night Live (TV show), 215
school segregation, 403–405
Schuette v. Coalition, 387–389
Schur, Edwin, 38–39
science
    explanations of human variation and, 348–355
    herm bodies and, 120
    ideologies of racial difference and, 348–355
"Segregated Housing, Segregated Schools,"
    403–405
selective racialization, 254–256
self-development imperative, 292–293
self-esteem, 21
self-fulfilling prophecy, 38
self-objectification, 39
Sen, Amartya, 405–410
Separate But Equal doctrine, 64, 364–365
sex determination of athletes, 115–117
sex differences
    all-or-none categorizing of, 35–36, 36*fig*
    perception of discrimination and, 41–42
"Sex Education and the Promotion of
    Heteronormativity," 424–431
sex ratio, 407–408
sex
    assignment of, 31
    definition of, 30–31, 44
"Sexual Fluidity: Understanding Women's Love
    and Desire," 142–147
sexual fluidity, 29, 142–147
sexual identity, 4*fn*, 28 (*see also* sexuality)
    definition of, 144
    "Sexual Orientation and Sex in Women's Lives:
        Conceptual and Methodological Issues,"
        297–303
sexual orientation, *see* sexuality
sexual preference, *see* sexuality
sexuality
    assumptions about, 298–299
    brain studies and, 147–149
    college and, 287–297
    constructionist/essentialist terminology
        and, 4
    definition of, 143–144
    dichotomous definitions of, 297–299
    education about, 424–431
    false-negative judgments of, 37
    feminism and, 276
    gene research and, 150–156
    hook ups and, 293–294
    intersectionality and, 291–293
    privileges of, 202–203
    relational double bind and, 292–293
    self-development imperative and, 292–293
    sexual fluidity and, 29, 142–147
    women and, 297–303
Shakira, 255
Shalhoub, Tony, 255
shame, 212, 442
Shaw, Heather L., 163
Siddique, Hoorie I., 135
"The Silver Spoon: Inheritance and the Staggered
    Start," 131–137
"sitting in the fire," 487–488

Skinner v. Oklahoma (1942), 353
Slav, 53–54
slave narratives, 355
slave rebellions, 56
slavery, 52–53, 55
Sleeter, Christine E., 468–473
slums, 404
slut stigma, 289–290
Smedley, Audrey, 24, 51–60
Smith College, 351
Snowden, Frank, 53
social and medical models of disability, 5–7,
    164–166, 456–457
social capital, 133
social change
    becoming an ally, 488–89
    engagement and, 487–488
    paradigm change and, 505–506
    philanthropy and, 507–510
    "sitting in the fire," 487–488
    working on yourself and, 486–487
social class
    childhood quality of life and, 132–133
    "culture of poverty" and, 313–317
    definition of, 127–131
    dichotomization of, 32–34
    education and, 313–317, 351, 411–412, 447–452
    growing inequality of, 137–141
    health/illness and, 134–136, 303–306
    heritability of, 131–141
    learning problems and, 469–471
    low paying jobs and, 444–445
    power and, 127–130
    privileges of, 203–204
    social mobility and, 33–34, 134, 139–141
    stigmatization and, 40
    tabooed topic of, 32
    wealth accumulation, 446
    wealth stripping and, 452–456
    wealth-health gradient, 136
    women's incentive for employment and,
        415–424
    working class and, 128–129
social Darwinism, 350–351
social gradient of health, 305

social institution, 340, 348, 356
social mirror, 229–233
social whitening hypothesis, 94
socioeconomic convergence, 219
socioeconomic status, *see* social class
The Souls of Black Folk, 209
Sowell, Thomas, 308
Spanglish, 234
Spears, Britney, 142
spinal cord injuries, 168–169
Sputnik, 468–469
Stabile, Carol, 198
Stand Your Ground laws, 197
Standards for Federal Reporting of Race and
    Ethnic Categories, 12
Stanford-Binet IQ test, 352
Statistical Directive No. 15, 12
status, 2, 44
statutory law, 359
Steele, Claude, 232
stereotypes
    definition of, 344
    natural law language and, 344–345
    stigmatized people and, 41–43
    threat of, 232
stigma, 38–44
    ability to exclude and, 216–217
    benefits from, 213
    codes of conduct and, 212
    discredited and discreditable and, 206–209
    experience of, 206–213
    privileged affected by, 214,
    visible, 209–212
Stockholm Consensus, 116
Stonewall riot, 43
structural mobility, 134
"Stubborn Ounces," 506
Suarez-Orozco, Carola, 225–238
sub-prime lending, 452
Sundahl, Deborah, 142
Sununu, John, 255
Superman, 169
Supreme Court decisions, 359–389
Survey of Disabled Adults, 161*t*
"survival of the fittest," 350

Takao Ozawa v. United States (1922), 108
tale of three umpires, 3
tax favoritism, 403
"Tearing Down the Gates: Confronting the Class
    Divide," 447–452
Teen Vandals (TV show), 196
teenagers, 42
Tehranian, John, 17, 251–261
Tenayuca, Emma, 399
Tennessee v. Lane (2004), 196, 378–380
Terman, Lewis M., 352
Texaco tapes, 348
"That Moment of Visibility," 312
Third World Liberation Front, 82
Thirteenth Amendment (1865), 361
Thomas, Danny, 255
Thomas, W.I., 159
Thurmond, Strom, 398
time constancy, 503–504
"A Time I Didn't Feel Normal," 337
Title V of the Social Security Act, 426
traceable amount rule, 65
Tran, Hoia Huong, 239–241
transcultural identities, 234–235
transgender/transgendered, 31, 44
Treaty of Guadalupe Hidalgo (1848), 21, 349
tribal citizenship, 71
triracial hierarchy, 109–110
T-shirt objectifying women, 39
Twain, Shania, 72–73

U.N. Convention on the Rights of Persons with
    Disabilities, 6
U.S. Census Bureau
    Arab, Middle Eastern categories in, 14, 23
    Asian-origin categories in, 17*fn*
    Asian Indian categories in, 17*fn*
    Hispanic Advisory Committee and, 12
    Latino/Hispanic categories in, 15, 242
    Latino/Hispanic responses to, 16, 244
    multiracial identification and, 14
    race and ethnicity questions in, 11–15, 70*fig*,
        66, 90
    unmarried partner category in, 14

U.S. Constitution, 359
U.S. v. Bhaghat Thind (1923), 17*fn*, 108–109
U.S. v. Takao Ozawa (1922), 108
U.S. v. Windsor (2013), 385–387
U.S., number of immigrants and refugees to, 225
undercount, 12, 14
undercover off-duty police, 198
"undeserving poor," 315
undocumented Asian American students, 399–401
Union of Physically Impaired Against Segregation
    (UPIAS), 6
unions
    membership in, 129
    segregation of, 404
    working class and, 129
*University of California Board of Regents v.
    Bakke* (1978), 309, 375–378
University of Michigan, 380–383
unmarked and marked statuses, 38, 220,
    204–205
"unmarried partner," 14
"Uprooting Racism: How White People Can
    Work for Racial Justice," 511–516
urban renewal policies, 404
urban violence, 164
US News and World Report, 450

Vassar College, 351
Virginia Racial Integrity Law of 1924, 108
visible stigma, 209–212
Voting Rights Act of 1965, 483

War on Drugs, 199–200
Warner, Michael, 20
Washington, Booker T., 64
Watergate, 269
"we make the road by walking," 483–486
wealth stripping, 452–453
"Wealth Stripping: Why It Costs So Much to Be
    Poor," 452–456
wealth, 132–137, 446
wealth-health gradient, 136
Weinberg, George, 19–20
Weiss, Penny A., 10, 272–277

Wellesley College, 351
"What Wounds Enable: The Politics of Disability and Violence in Chicago," 163–176
"What's Class Got to Do with It?," 127–131
white ethnics, Catholic church and, 219*fn*
white flight, 343
White, Jane, 63
White, Walter, 63
white/non-white divide, 21–22, 108–109
Whitehall I Study, 306
whiteness
   colonial discourse, 101–106
   de jure vs. de facto and, 256
   unmarked racial category of, 101–106
whites
   allies and, 512–514
   characteristics attributed to women and, 40*fn*
   colorblindness and, 217
   Census category of, 14
   culture of, 19, 101–106
   emergence of racial category of, 56
   Middle Easterners as, 253
   "people in the boat" as, 19
   racial attitudes of, 347–348
"Who is Black? One's Nation's Definition," 61–69
"Why Are Droves of Unqualified, Unprepared Kids Getting into Our Top Colleges? Because Their Dads Are Alumni," 307–312?
Wilchins, Riki, 31, 117–123
Wilde, Oscar, 434
Wilkinson, R.G, 305
Williams Institute, 29

Williams, Patricia J., 197
Williams, Vanessa, 62
Wimsatt, William Upski, 507–510
Winicott, D.W., 229
Wiseman, Rosalind, 210
within vs. between group difference, 35
Wolfe, Thomas, 268
woman vs. girl, choice of term, 10
women
   double consciousness of, 341
   employment and, 411–424
   missing, 405–411
   occupational reference group of, 420–421
   self-objectification and, 39
   sexuality of, 142–147, 287–302
   Social Darwinism and, 351
   stigma and, 38–41
   suffrage, 349, 362–363
worker vs. CEO salary, 446
Wu, Frank H., 227

Yahoo! Personals, 344
"yellow horde," 111
Yick Wo. V. Hopkins (1886), 367–368
Yoshino, Kenji, 256

zambo, 91–92
Zimmerman, George, 19
Zip Coon, 354
Zola, Irving, 34
Zweig, Michael, 32–33, 127–130